The Excursion

The Cornell Wordsworth

General Editor: Stephen Parrish
Associate Editor: Mark L. Reed
Associate Editor: James A. Butler

Coordinating Editor: Jared Curtis

Advisory Editors: M. H. Abrams, Geoffrey Hartman, Jonathan Wordsworth

---

Early Poems and Fragments, 1785–1797, edited by Carol Landon and Jared Curtis
An Evening Walk, edited by James Averill
Descriptive Sketches, edited by Eric Birdsall
The Salisbury Plain Poems, edited by Stephen Gill
The Borderers, edited by Robert Osborn
The Ruined Cottage and *The Pedlar*, edited by James Butler
Lyrical Ballads, and Other Poems, 1797–1800, edited by James Butler and Karen Green
Peter Bell, edited by John Jordan
The Prelude, 1798–1799, edited by Stephen Parrish
Home at Grasmere, edited by Beth Darlington
The Thirteen-Book *Prelude*, edited by Mark L. Reed
Poems, in Two Volumes, and Other Poems, 1800–1807, edited by Jared Curtis
Benjamin the Waggoner, edited by Paul F. Betz
The Tuft of Primroses, with Other Late Poems for *The Recluse*, edited by Joseph Kishel
The White Doe of Rylstone, edited by Kristine Dugas
Shorter Poems, 1807–1820, edited by Carl Ketcham
The Excursion, edited by Sally Bushell, James A. Butler, and Michael C. Jaye
Translations of Chaucer and Virgil, edited by Bruce E. Graver
The Fourteen-Book *Prelude*, edited by W. J. B. Owen
Sonnet Series and Itinerary Poems, 1820–1845, edited by Geoffrey Jackson
Last Poems, 1821–1850, edited by Jared Curtis

Modern Language Association MLA
An Approved Edition
Committee on Scholarly Editions

The Excursion

by William Wordsworth

Edited by

Sally Bushell, James A. Butler, and Michael C. Jaye

with the assistance of David García

CORNELL UNIVERSITY PRESS

ITHACA AND LONDON

PUBLICATION OF THIS BOOK WAS ASSISTED BY GRANTS FROM THE PROVOST'S OFFICE, LA SALLE UNIVERSITY, FROM THE HULL MEMORIAL PUBLICATION FUND OF CORNELL UNIVERSITY, AND FROM THE PROGRAM FOR EDITIONS OF THE NATIONAL ENDOWMENT FOR THE HUMANITIES, AN INDEPENDENT FEDERAL AGENCY.

First published 2007 by Cornell University Press

Printed in the United States of America

Cornell University Press strives to use environmentally responsible suppliers and materials to the fullest extent possible in the publishing of its books. Such materials include vegetable-based, low-VOC inks and acid-free papers that are recycled, totally chlorine-free, or partly composed of nonwood fibers. For further information, visit our website at www.cornellpress.cornell.edu.

Library of Congress Cataloging-in-Publication Data

Wordsworth, William, 1770–1850.
The Excursion / by William Wordsworth ; edited by Sally Bushell, James A. Butler, and Michael C. Jaye ; with the assistance of David García.
p. cm. – (The Cornell Wordsworth)
Includes bibliographical references.
ISBN 978-0-8014-4653-5 (cloth : alk. paper)
I. Bushell, Sally. II. Butler, James, 1945- III. Jaye, Michael C., 1941- IV. Title. V. Series: Wordsworth, William, 1770–1850. Selections. 1975.

PR5858.A2B87 2007
821'.7–dc22

2007029242

The Cornell Wordsworth

The individual volumes of the Cornell Wordsworth series, some devoted to long poems, some to collections of shorter poems, have had two common aims. The first has been to bring the early Wordsworth into view. Wordsworth's practice of leaving his poems unpublished for years after their completion and his lifelong habit of revision—Ernest de Selincourt called it "obsessive"—have obscured the original, often thought the best, versions of his work. These original versions are normally presented in the form of clean, continuous "reading texts" from which all layers of later revision have been stripped away. In volumes that cover the work of Wordsworth's middle and later years, bringing the "early Wordsworth" into view means simply presenting as "reading texts," wherever possible, the earliest finished versions of the poems, not the latest revised versions.

The second aim of the series is to provide, for the first time, a complete and accurate record of variant readings, from Wordsworth's earliest drafts down to the final lifetime (or first posthumous) publication. The most important manuscripts are shown in full transcription; for the most complex and interesting transcriptions, photographs of the manuscript pages are also provided. Besides the transcriptions and the photographs, on which draft revisions may be seen, and an *apparatus criticus* in which printed variants are collected, a third device for the study of revisions is adopted: when two versions of a work match sufficiently well, they are arrayed so that the steps by which one was converted into the other become visible.

Volumes in the series are unnumbered, but upon publication their titles are inserted into the list of volumes in print in the order in which the works were written. A more detailed introduction to the series may be found in the first volume published, *The Salisbury Plain Poems*, edited by Stephen Gill.

S. M. Parrish

Ithaca, New York

For Stephen Maxfield Parrish

Allor si mosse, e io li tenni dietro.
Dante, *Inferno,* I, 136

Contents

Preface

This volume presents the first scholarly edition of William Wordsworth's *The Excursion* to be published since the appearance of Ernest de Selincourt and Helen Darbishire's fifth volume of the *Poetical Works* (Oxford, 1949). De Selincourt and Darbishire based their edition on the text of 1850, the many-times revised version that issued from the press in the year of the poet's death. We provide as our reading text the poem as first published in 1814, together with cross-references enabling easy comparison of this text with the one edited by de Selincourt and Darbishire. Because *The Excursion* has not appeared in a scholarly edition for so long—and because no annotated edition of the 1814 text has been published before this one—we include extensive editors' notes. Wordsworth's own notes to the poem are located, as they are in 1814, after the reading text (cross-references are given on the relevant pages of the poem itself). The notes that Wordsworth dictated to his friend Isabella Fenwick in 1843 are in Appendix III.

The complex manuscripts of *The Excursion* are reduced to an *apparatus* by de Selincourt and Darbishire, resulting in the loss of many readings and the obscuring of the process of composition. In our volume, we show below the reading text all post-publication verbal variants in manuscripts and printed editions, but we also separately and completely transcribe all *Excursion* manuscripts that were produced under the author's supervision between c. 1806 and the poem's publication in 1814. Several manuscripts unknown to de Selincourt and Darbishire are included among these transcriptions. Sample photographs of especially complex or interesting manuscript pages supplement the transcriptions; a Key to Manuscript Transcriptions in Appendix I makes it possible to find all manuscript versions of a particular passage. Cross-references in this volume to earlier Cornell Wordsworth volumes—particularly *Home at Grasmere, "The Ruined Cottage" and "The Pedlar," Shorter Poems: 1807–1820, The Thirteen-Book "Prelude,"* and *"The Tuft of Primroses" with Other Late Poems for "The Recluse"*—help the reader to see how Wordsworth used this material in *The Excursion.*

Additional states of parts of *The Excursion* are here identified by the inclusion of right-margin italic numbers within the transcriptions. For example, an early stage of *Excursion*, I–III, 330, written before the deaths of two of the Wordsworths' children in 1812 resulted in major alterations to the poem, can be followed in the transcriptions of Dove Cottage Manuscripts 47, 69, 70, and 71. Similarly, a long account of rural life (much of that narrative excised from the published poem) is given its own italic numbering in transcriptions of Dove Cottage Manuscript 74. Appendix II contains reading texts of *The Peasant's Life* (in a shortened version that Wordsworth seems to have considered publishing, perhaps in 1815), as well as of two passages removed from *The Excursion* before publication: *The Shepherd of Bield Crag* and "As when upon the smooth pacific deep."

The convoluted manuscript history of *The Excursion* is traced in a number of ways in this edition: (1) a Manuscript Census (pp. xix–xxix), describing the contents and dates of usage for the thirty-five manuscripts that we have consulted; (2) a brief, general account included as an Introduction to the poem (pp. 3–24); (3) a table showing Eight Stages of *Excursion* Composition (pp. 426–428); (4) a lengthy, detailed analysis of The Manuscript History of *The Excursion* (pp. 429–477), supplemented by headnotes and notes to the various transcriptions.

By means of the material provided in this edition, it is now possible, for the first time, to follow the complete compositional history of Wordsworth's epic, *The Excursion.*

Preparation of this volume, as of all volumes in the series, was made possible by the Trustees of the Wordsworth Trust, Grasmere, who generously gave access to manuscripts and books in the Wordsworth Library at Grasmere and authorized the publication of manuscript material. We are grateful as well for the access and able assistance provided to us by the keepers of Wordsworth manuscripts in other libraries. We have been granted permission to cite from and in some instances to reproduce selected portions of manuscripts by the governing bodies of the following libraries and institutions (specific manuscripts and their locations are listed in the Manuscript Census): The Henry W. and Albert A. Berg Collection of English and American Literature, New York Public Library, Astor, Lenox, and Tilden Foundations; Houghton Library, Harvard University, Cambridge, Massachusetts; Huntington Library, San Marino, California; Division of Rare Books and Manuscript Collections, Carl A. Kroch Library, Cornell University, Ithaca, New York; Lilly Library, Indiana University, Bloomington, Indiana; Pierpont Morgan Library, New York; The Provost, Fellows, and Scholars of the Queen's College, Oxford; Special Collections, Wellesley College, Wellesley, Massachusetts; The Royal Collection Trust, The Royal Library, Windsor Castle.

In addition, the staffs of the following libraries have been unfailingly helpful to us in aiding our research: British Library, London; Bodleian Library, Oxford; Cambridge University Library; Connelly Library, La Salle University, Philadelphia; University of Lancaster Library; McCabe Library, Swarthmore College, Swarthmore, Pennsylvania; John Rylands University Library of Manchester; Van Pelt Library, University of Pennsylvania, Philadelphia.

Jared Curtis and Mark Reed worked so much (and so well) on this volume that their names should be on the title page. David García cheerfully and expertly negotiated the minefield of working with three editors to prepare the manuscript for publication. Over the years many other people have assisted us, and we particularly wish to acknowledge the following: Paul Betz, Stephen Breedlove, Claire Busse, David Chandler, Jeff Cowton, Brother Gabriel Fagan, F.S.C., Robert Thomas Fallon, Stephen Gill, Bruce Graver, Keith Hanley, Kevin Harty, Stephen Hebron, Natalie Karelis, Carol Landon, the late Peter Laver,

Antonia Losano, Francine Lottier, Georgina Murphy, Richard Nigro, James Shiel, the late Sally Woodhead, the late Jonathan Wordsworth, the late Robert Woof, and Arleen Zimmerle. Sally Bushell's work was supported by the British Academy and by Lancaster University; James Butler had several grants from La Salle University; Michael Jaye held a fellowship from the National Endowment for the Humanities. Peter Manning vetted this edition for the Modern Language Association Committee on Scholarly Editions, and we are grateful for his thorough and helpful report.

This volume is the final edition in the Cornell Wordsworth series, a project that began four decades ago. Three of the Cornell Wordsworth editors did not live to see the completion of the series, and we here remember John Jordan, Carl Ketcham, and W. J. B. Owen. The first volume (1975) began with a dedication of the series to the memory of John Alban Finch and George Harris Healey. We would like to dedicate our volume to the General Editor of the Cornell Wordsworth series. Stephen Parrish, mentor and friend, no words can ever thank sufficiently: his vision of this edition and this series sustained us all.

Sally Bushell, James A. Butler, Michael C. Jaye

Lancaster, England
Philadelphia, Pennsylvania
London, England

Abbreviations

At the end of the Editorial Procedure the reader will find short forms of citation used in transcriptions, as well as those employed to record textual variants and lifetime editions in the *apparatus criticus* and notes. The Manuscript Census lists short forms of citation for manuscripts.

Abrams	M. H. Abrams, *Natural Supernaturalism: Tradition and Revolution in Romantic Literature* (New York, 1971).
Beer	John Beer, "Coleridge's Annotations to a Copy of Wordsworth's *Excursion*," *Notes and Queries*, 49, no. 4 (2002): 460–463.
BF	Barron Field, or his *Memoirs* (quoted from *Memoirs of Wordsworth*, ed. Geoffrey Little [Sydney, 1975]).
Borderers	*The Borderers* (the play), cited from *"The Borderers" by William Wordsworth*, ed. Robert Osborn (Ithaca, 1982).
Bushell	Sally Bushell, *Re-reading "The Excursion": Narrative, Response, and the Wordsworthian Dramatic Voice* (Aldershot, England, 2002).
CC	*Characteristics of a Child three Years old* (the poem), by William Wordsworth, cited from the transcriptions in this volume.
Chronology: EY	Mark L. Reed, *Wordsworth: The Chronology of the Early Years, 1770–1799* (Cambridge, Mass., 1967).
Chronology: MY	Mark L. Reed, *Wordsworth: The Chronology of the Middle Years, 1800–1815* (Cambridge, Mass., 1975).
CL	Charles Lamb.
CLL	*The Letters of Charles and Mary Lamb*, ed. Edwin W. Marrs (Ithaca 1975–).
Connell	Philip Connell, *Romanticism, Economics and the Question of "Culture"* (Oxford, 2001).
DC, DC MS.	Dove Cottage, Dove Cottage Manuscript (Wordsworth Library, Grasmere).
DW	Dorothy Wordsworth.
Early Poems, 1785–1797	*Early Poems and Fragments, 1785–1797, by William Wordsworth*, ed. Carol Landon and Jared Curtis (Ithaca, 1997).
EdeS	Ernest de Selincourt, or his note(s).
EQ	Edward Quillinan, husband of Wordsworth's daughter, Dora.
EW	*"An Evening Walk" by William Wordsworth*, ed. James Averill (Ithaca, 1984).
Exc	*The Excursion* (the poem).

EY	*The Letters of William and Dorothy Wordsworth: The Early Years, 1787–1805,* ed. Ernest de Selincourt (2d ed., rev. Chester L. Shaver; Oxford, 1967).
Hartman	Geoffrey Hartman, *Wordsworth's Poetry, 1787–1814* (New Haven, 1964).
H at G	*"Home at Grasmere, Part First, Book First, of The Recluse," by William Wordsworth,* ed. Beth Darlington (Ithaca, 1977; corr. 1989).
Hazlitt	William Hazlitt, "Character of Mr. Wordsworth's New Poem, *The Excursion,*" *The Examiner,* August 21, 1814, 541–542; August 28, 1814, 555–558; October 2, 1814, 636–638.
Healey	George Harris Healey, *The Cornell Wordsworth Collection* (Ithaca, 1957).
Hickey	Alison Hickey, *Impure Conceits: Rhetoric and Ideology in Wordsworth's Excursion* (Stanford, 1997).
Hill, *Ariel*	Alan G. Hill, "New Light on 'The Excursion,'" *Ariel* 2 (1974): 37–47.
Hill, *Proceedings*	Alan G. Hill, "Wordsworth's 'Grand Design,'" *Proceedings of the British Academy* 72 (1986): 188–204.
IF	Isabella Fenwick, or note(s) dictated to her by Wordsworth in 1843 (quoted from *The Fenwick Notes of William Wordsworth,* ed. Jared Curtis [London, 1993]). Curtis's notes are designated "(Curtis)."
JC	John Carter, Wordsworth's secretary at Rydal Mount.
Jeffrey	Francis Jeffrey, "*The Excursion,* being a portion of the Recluse, A Poem. By William Wordsworth," *Edinburgh Review* 24 (November 1814): 1–30.
Journals	Dorothy Wordsworth, *The Grasmere Journals,* ed. Pamela Woof (Oxford, 1991).
Johnston	Kenneth R. Johnston, *Wordsworth and The Recluse* (New Haven, 1984).
Lamb	Charles Lamb, "*The Excursion;* A Poem, By William Wordsworth," *Quarterly Review* 12 (October 1814, issue appeared January 14, 1815): 100–111.
Lyon	Judson Stanley Lyon, *The Excursion: A Study* (New Haven, 1950).
LB, 1797–1800	*"Lyrical Ballads," and Other Poems, 1797–1800, by William Wordsworth,* ed. James Butler and Karen Green (Ithaca, 1992).
LJK	*The Letters of John Keats,* ed. Hyder Edward Rollins (2 vols; Cambridge, Mass., 1958).
LY, I, II, III, IV	*The Letters of William and Dorothy Wordsworth: The Later Years, 1821–1853,* ed. Ernest de Selincourt (4 vols.; 2d ed., rev., arranged, and ed. Alan G. Hill; Oxford, 1978, 1979, 1982, 1988). Roman numerals refer to parts.
MG	*Maternal Grief* (the poem), by William Wordsworth, cited from the transcriptions in this volume.
M of H	Jonathan Wordsworth, *The Music of Humanity: A Critical Study of Wordsworth's "Ruined Cottage"* (London, 1969).
Montgomery	James Montgomery, "Wordsworth's Excursion," *Eclectic Review,* n.s., 3 (January 1815): 13–39.
MW	Mary Wordsworth.
MY, I, II	*The Letters of William and Dorothy Wordsworth: The Middle Years, 1806–1820,* ed. Ernest de Selincourt (2 vols.; 2d ed.; Part

	I, 1806–1811, rev. Mary Moorman, Oxford, 1969; Part II, 1812–1820, rev. Mary Moorman and Alan G. Hill, Oxford, 1970). Roman numerals refer to parts.
OED	*Oxford English Dictionary.*
Owen	W. J. B. Owen, "Letters of Longmans & Co. to Wordsworth, 1814–36," *The Library* 9 (1954): 25–34.
PL	*Paradise Lost,* quoted from *Complete Poems and Major Prose of John Milton,* ed. Merritt Y. Hughes (New York, 1957).
Poems, 1785–1797	*Early Poems and Fragments, 1785–1797, by William Wordsworth,* ed. Carol Landon and Jared Curtis (Ithaca, 1997).
Poems, 1800–1807	*"Poems, in Two Volumes," and Other Poems, 1800–1807,* ed. Jared Curtis (Ithaca, 1983; corr. 1990).
Poems, 1807–1820	*Shorter Poems, 1807–1820, by William Wordsworth,* ed. Carl H. Ketcham (Ithaca, 1989).
Poems, 1821–1850	*Last Poems, 1821–1850, by William Wordsworth,* ed. Jared Curtis (Ithaca, 1999).
Prelude	The poem, cited from the AB-stage text in *The Thirteen-Book "Prelude," by William Wordsworth,* ed. Mark L. Reed (2 vols.; Ithaca, 1991).
Prose	*The Prose Works of William Wordsworth,* ed. W. J. B. Owen and Jane Smyser (3 vols.; Oxford, 1974).
PW	*The Poetical Works of William Wordsworth,* ed. Ernest de Selincourt and Helen Darbishire (5 vols.; Oxford, 1940–1949; rev. 1952–1959).
PW, 18—	The edition of Wordsworth's *Poetical Works* published in the year given.
PW Dowden	*The Poetical Works of William Wordsworth,* ed. Edward Dowden (7 vols.; London, 1893).
PW Knight	*The Poetical Works of William Wordsworth,* ed. William Knight (8 vols.; London and New York, 1896).
PW Smith	*The Poems of William Wordsworth,* ed. Nowell Charles Smith (3 vols; London, 1908).
RC	*The Ruined Cottage* (the poem), by William Wordsworth.
RC & Pedlar	*"The Ruined Cottage" and "The Pedlar" by William Wordsworth,* ed. James Butler (Ithaca, 1979; corr. 1989).
RS	Robert Southey.
SBC	*The Shepherd of Bield Crag* (the poetic fragment) by William Wordsworth, cited from the transcriptions in this volume.
SH	Sara Hutchinson.
SHL	*The Letters of Sara Hutchinson from 1800 to 1835,* ed. Kathleen Coburn (Toronto, 1954).
Sonnet Series	*Sonnet Series and Itinerary Poems, 1820–1845, by William Wordsworth,* ed. Geoffrey Jackson (Ithaca, 2003).
SPP	*The Salisbury Plain Poems of William Wordsworth,* ed. Stephen Gill (Ithaca, 1975; corr. 1991).
STC	Samuel Taylor Coleridge.
STCBL	Samuel Taylor Coleridge, *Biographia Literaria,* ed. James Engell and W. Jackson Bate (2 vols.; Princeton, 1983).
STCF	*The Friend,* ed. Barbara E. Rooke, in *The Collected Works of Samuel Taylor Coleridge* (2 vols., London and Princeton, 1969).
STCL	*Collected Letters of Samuel Taylor Coleridge,* ed. Earl Leslie Griggs (6 vols.; Oxford, 1956–1971).

STCNB	*The Notebooks of Samuel Taylor Coleridge,* ed. Kathleen Coburn, vol. 4 co-ed. with M. Christensen, vol. 5 co-ed. with Anthony John Harding (5 vols.; London and Princeton, 1957–2002).
STCPW	*The Collected Works of Samuel Taylor Coleridge*: vol. 16, *Poetical Works: I. Poems (Reading Text), II. Poems (Variorum Text),* ed. J. C. C. Mays (Princeton, 2001).
13-Bk Prelude	*The Thirteen-Book "Prelude" by William Wordsworth,* ed. Mark L. Reed (2 vols; Ithaca, 1991).
TPL	*The Peasant's Life* (the poetic fragment) by William Wordsworth, cited from the transcriptions in this volume.
Tuft	*"The Tuft of Primroses" with Other Late Poems for "The Recluse" by William Wordsworth,* ed. Joseph F. Kishel (Ithaca, 1986).
Wilson	John Wilson, "On Sacred Poetry," *Blackwood's Edinburgh Magazine,* December 24, 1828, 917–938.
Wu, *Reading I*	Duncan Wu, *Wordsworth's Reading, 1770–1799* (Cambridge, 1993).
Wu, *Reading II*	Duncan Wu, *Wordsworth's Reading, 1800–1815* (Cambridge, 1995). Includes an appendix to *Wordsworth's Reading, 1770–1799.*
WW	William Wordsworth.

Manuscript Census

Short forms of citation for the manuscripts that bear directly on the texts in this edition are listed below in three categories: (1) pre-*Excursion* manuscripts contributing to the poem; (2) pre-publication *Excursion* manuscripts; (3) post-publication *Excursion* manuscripts. Arrangement within each section is alphabetical.

Manuscripts in the first category are treated briefly, since they are all fully described in other volumes in this series; cross-references provide information about where those descriptions and those lines contributing to specific *Excursion* passages may be found. The intent in this first category is not to give a full manuscript history of the *Ruined Cottage/Pedlar* manuscripts that became Book I of *The Excursion* (for that history, *see RC & Pedlar*). Rather, we wish to indicate which particular manuscripts Wordsworth seemed to turn to when he incorporated earlier material into *The Excursion.*

Descriptions are usually fuller for manuscripts in the second category, since they are the ones transcribed in this volume; each entry is followed by an indication of the type and size of paper (the horizontal measurement followed by the vertical) and any watermarks or other distinguishing features; by the current location, where appropriate; and by the names of the users or transcribers and the occasions and stages of use.

Finally, the most important manuscripts in the third category are printed editions of Wordsworth's poetry that were used to revise *The Excursion* in preparation for subsequent editions. (An early version of one gathering in MS. 1814/27 includes printed text and handwritten changes that precede the state of *The Excursion* as published in 1814.) The third category also includes post-1814 manuscripts in which Wordsworth wrote out quotations from *The Excursion* for friends and autograph seekers; those manuscripts are described using the conventions presented in the preceding paragraph.

References provided to the various stages of *Excursion* composition refer to the table on pp. 426–428, below. Most abbreviations will be found in the list on pp. xv–xviii, above. Short forms of citation for Wordsworth's lifetime editions and other publications are listed in the Editorial Procedure (see pp. 26–28, below). *Excursion* line references are to the 1814 reading text in this volume.

(1) Pre-*Excursion* Manuscripts Contributing to the Poem

DC MS. 14 (Alfoxden Notebook) Described in *RC & Pedlar*, pp. 105–109, and in *LB, 1797–1800*, pp. 713–716. This notebook was in use in 1798 and (for a fragment of *The Pedlar*, see *RC & Pedlar*, pp. 126–129) in 1802. A passage in the notebook contributes at the seventh stage of composition to *Exc*, IX, 89–93 (16^r; see *RC & Pedlar*, pp. 114–115).

DC MS. 15 (*Christabel* Notebook) Described in *RC & Pedlar*, pp. 96–97, and in *LB, 1797–1800*, pp. 716–725. A passage on 26^r ("Dull, to the joy of its own motions dead") contributes at the sixth stage of composition to *Exc*, VIII, 327–334; see *LB, 1797–1800*, pp. 307–308, 718–719. A passage on 63^r ("There is an active principle alive in all things") contributes at the seventh stage of composition to *Exc*, IX, 129–138; see *LB, 1797–1800*, pp. 309–310, 721.

DC MS. 16 (*Ruined Cottage* MS. D) Described in *RC & Pedlar*, pp. 282–283, and in *LB, 1797–1800*, pp. 725–729. This manuscript—dating from February to November 1799, with revisions between December 21, 1801, and July 8, 1802—contains, among other materials, much of what became Book I of *Exc*; the story of Margaret is here copied under the title *The Ruined Cottage* and the history of the Pedlar is copied as an overflow passage (see *RC & Pedlar*, pp. 284–375). DC MS. 16 directly contributes at the second stage of composition to *Exc*, I, 1–61; at the third stage to *Exc*, IV, 1201–1260 ("Not useless do I deem," 67^v–69^r; see *RC & Pedlar*, pp. 372–374); at the sixth stage to *Exc*, VIII, 289–294, 304–308, 317–334 ("There is a law severe of penury," 79^r–80^r; see *LB, 1797–1800*, pp. 307–308, 728); and at the seventh stage to *Exc*, IX, 1–26, 129–138, 142–153 ("There is an active principle alive in all things," 77^v–78^v; see *LB, 1797–1800*, pp. 309–310, 728).

DC MS. 17 (*Ruined Cottage* MS. B) Described in *RC & Pedlar*, pp. 130–131, and fully transcribed there on pp. 132–281. This *Ruined Cottage* manuscript, dating from 1798, contains much of what became Book I of *Exc*.

DC MS. 28 (*Home at Grasmere* MS. R) Described in *H at G*, pp. 139–141. This notebook—in use for *Home at Grasmere* work in 1800 and/or 1806 and in 1831–32—contributes at the third stage of composition to *Exc*, IV, 335–353, 357–371 ("Happy is He"; $148/149i^r$–$150/151i^r$; see *H at G*, pp. 187–189, and at the sixth stage of composition to *Exc*, VI, 1100–1232 (132–$138/141i^v$; see *H at G*, 144–165). These drafts, once part of *Home at Grasmere* but contributing to *Exc*, probably date from 1806 or perhaps from 1800.

DC MS. 37 (*Ruined Cottage/Pedlar* MSS. E and E²) Described in *RC & Pedlar*, pp. 32–33, 378–379, with readings fully recorded there on pp. 382–448. The main MS. E section—dating from late November 1803 to about March 6, 1804—contains a complete copy of what would eventually become *Exc*, I. MS. E², which was originally the first gathering of DC MS. 44 (see below), dates from about March 6, 1804, and contains a copy of what became *Exc,* I, 1–386. MS. E contributes at the second stage of composition to *Exc,* I, 1–61 (1^{v}; see *RC & Pedlar,* p. 453); MS. E^{2} contributes to the same lines (1^{r}–2^{r}; see *RC & Pedlar,* pp. 383, 385–387).

DC MS. 44 (*Ruined Cottage/Pedlar* MS. M) Described in *RC & Pedlar,* pp. 378–379. What became Book I of *Exc* is present (except for an initial missing leaf, containing about sixty-one lines) on 7^{r}–22^{v}; see the full transcription in *RC & Pedlar,* pp. 387–449. This manuscript—dating from between March 6 and 18, 1804—contributes to *Exc,* I, 62–end; as the last manuscript of *Ruined Cottage/ Pedlar* as a separate work, DC MS. 44 was used as part of the process of producing *Exc,* I, during the second stage of composition.

DC MS. 48 (*Prelude* MS. Y) Described in *13-Bk Prelude,* I, 42–51. This manuscript—dating from late spring and autumn of 1804—contains five passages that contribute to *Exc*: (1) II, 2–28 (lines about minstrel, 15^{v}; see *13-Bk Prelude,* II, 374–375); (2) IV, 404–414 (lines about lamb in solitude, 36^{r}–36^{v}, 50^{v}; see *13-Bk Prelude,* II, 402–403, 420); (3) IV, 526–531 ("As at a first creation and in haste," 55^{v}; see *13-Bk Prelude,* II, 427); (4) IV, 760–762 ("We live by admiration, hope, and love," 4^{v}, 18^{r}; see *13-Bk Prelude,* II, 359, 378); (5) IX, 440–451 (lines about ram reflected in water, 34^{r}–34^{v}, 36^{v}–37^{r}; see *13-Bk Prelude,* II, 399–400, 403). The first passage, above, was probably added to *Exc* at the first stage of composition; the second, third, and fourth passages were probably added at the third stage; the fifth passage was probably added at the seventh stage.

DC MS. 59 (*Home at Grasmere* MS. B) Described in *H at G,* pp. 270–271. This notebook—in use for its initial fair copy by MW in 1806—contains as part of *Home at Grasmere* a passage later revised to become *Exc,* VI, 1101–1128 (tales of Wilfred Armathwaite and of the widowed Father with Six Daughters; 21^{v}–27^{r}; see *H at G,* pp. 322–343). WW's revisions of this passage in DC MS. 59 date from the sixth stage of composition of *Exc.* DC MS. 59 also contains as part of *Home at Grasmere* a passage later used as the *Prospectus* to the *Exc* (see *H at G,* pp. 394–403, and for earlier work in other manuscripts pp. 255–267).

DC MS. 65 (*Tuft of Primroses*) Described in *Tuft,* p. 151. Work on *The Tuft of Primroses* in this manuscript dates from 1808. Two passages once part of that poem were revised to become part of *Exc*: (1) III, 374–410 (lines about the Hermit in his Cell; 43^{v}–45^{r}; see *Tuft,* pp. 244–249); (2) VII, 261–309 (tale of the Patriarch of the Vale; 36^{r}–38^{v}; see *Tuft,* pp. 214–225). WW's revisions of these passages in DC MS. 65 date from the third stage of composition of *Exc* for what was eventually used in Book III and from the sixth stage for the lines used in Book VII.

(2) Pre-publication *Excursion* Manuscripts

Berg MS. A single sheet of paper similar to what is in DC MS. 74A and to the flimsier of the two kinds of paper that comprise DC MS. 75. Like its DC MSS. 74A and 75 counterparts, the Berg MS. dates from the sixth stage of *Exc* composition. WW's drafts for *Exc*, VIII, 463–486, on the recto of the Berg MS. precede the text on 25^r–25^v in DC MS. 74 (there is no parallel passage in DC MS. 74 to WW's verso draft of VIII, 496–523, in the Berg MS.). The Berg MS. is enclosed by a paper frame—the paper of the frame is watermarked 1822—on which is written, in an unidentified hand, "A leaf from Wordsworth's 'Excursion'—." Henry W. and Albert A. Berg Collection of English and American Literature, New York Public Library, Astor, Lenox and Tilden Foundations.

Commonplace Book This folio notebook, once owned by Lord and Lady Beaumont, is described in *Poems, 1800–1807*. On the pages hand numbered 136–139 is a copy—in an unidentified hand—of *Exc*, VII, 412–498, titled, "From a Poem in M.S. by William Wordsworth." The text in the Commonplace Book is closely related to what is in DC MS. 67—the account of the deaf dalesman—and is probably based on a version (not known to survive) of the passage that the Wordsworths apparently sent to the Beaumonts shortly after February 28, 1810 (see *Chronology: MY*, p. 307, n. 42). Thus, like DC MS. 67, the Commonplace Book falls into the second stage of *Exc* composition. MA 1581, Beaumont Collection, Pierpont Morgan Library, New York.

DC MS. 47 Also known as *Prelude* MS. X, this notebook—similar to DC MS. 70 (see below)—is described in *13-Bk Prelude* (I, 21–22, 42; II, 314, 315; see also *Poems, 1800–1807*, pp. xxi–xxii, and *Chronology: MY*, p. 645). Originally 64 leaves (the first and last leaves pasted to the covers) in a single gathering, this notebook now contains 41 whole leaves and 11 stubs, excluding the pasted-down endpapers. The leaves measure 9.9 by 15.3 cm. and are of laid paper watermarked with the letters FD or F. WW originally used DC MS. 47, probably in 1804, for work on *Prelude*, VI, VII, and VIII. Subsequently, WW employed the notebook early in 1806 for a page of draft for *Benjamin the Waggoner* and in 1806 or 1809–10 (the first stage of composition) for extensive work on what became *Exc*, II. The foliation of this manuscript in *13-Bk Prelude* includes in its count the pasted-down front endpaper, but we do not; leaf numbers of DC MS. 47 in this volume are thus one lower than in *13-Bk Prelude*.

DC MS. 67 Described (under its former designation as MS. Prose 6) in *Prose*, II, 48. On 6^r and 6^v at the end of the gathering containing *Essay upon Epitaphs, III*, SH copied (as part of the *Essay*) *Exc*, VII, 412–498 (the account of the deaf dalesman). The *Essay* was probably composed between c. December 1809 and February 28, 1810 (see *Chronology: MY*, pp. 49, 443); the *Exc* passage was therefore also complete by the end of February, thus falling into the second stage of *Exc* composition.

DC MS. 69 A notebook, lacking its covers, consisting of eleven gatherings (ten gatherings of 24 leaves and a final gathering now comprised of eight stubs). There may have been a twelfth gathering, as the spine to which the gatherings are sewn appears to allow space for it. The leaves measure 12.5 by 22 cm. and are made of laid paper with chain lines 2.5 cm. apart. The paper has a trefoil watermark over the date 1802. Many of the leaves have been removed, presumably to facilitate revision and copying, leaving only stubs, whose contents can sometimes be conjectured with reasonable certainty from initial or terminal letters or words. Eight leaves (sixteen sides) of the eleventh gathering appear to be missing; they may have contained some version of Book V, 1–c. 299, leading up to stub 248^{v} with its copy beginning with V, c. 300.

Work, in the hands of WW and MW, proceeds from both ends of the notebook and covers several stages of *Exc* composition. Book III material, entered in the front and earliest part of the notebook, dates from the first stage of composition; Book I work, following, dates from the second stage. At the opposite end, inverted and working toward the middle of the notebook, Book V copy belongs to the fourth stage of composition; Book IV material, following, dates from the fifth stage.

Also found in this notebook are prose drafts entitled "Borrowdale" (8^{r}–21^{v}) and "From Ambleside to Keswick" (inverted, 218^{v}–216^{r}), related to WW's work on expanding the letterpress to his *Select Views* into a commercially viable Lake District guide, sometime between 1810 and 1813, possibly c. November 1813. See *Prose*, II, 148 (where this MS. is listed under its former number of MSS. Verse 57), 340 (n. to l. 1591/1592), 340–348, and *Chronology: MY*, pp. 517, 670–673, 678. Also present in DC MS. 69 are the lines beginning, "As when, upon the smooth pacific deep" (198^{r}), provided as a reading text in Appendix II, below.

DC MS. 70 Like DC MS. 47 (see above), DC MS. 70 is one of a series of small notebooks with blue-green cardboard covers and a flap for closure; other such notebooks of similar type—and perhaps origin—include DC MSS. 38, 45, and 48. For a description of paper and construction of those five notebooks, see *13-Bk Prelude*, I, 22–23. DC MS. 70 is one gathering of sixty-four leaves in thirty-two bifolia, with the first and last leaves pasted down on the inside covers; one leaf (5) has been removed. All contents (other than an opening Latin quotation in the hand of DW) relate to *Exc*: II, 160–340; III, 374–385; IV, 261–262, 335–821, 847–843, 941–1046, 1055–96. The writers are WW, DW, and MW. Some of this material is a reworking of passages from earlier notebooks: "We live by admiration, hope, and love" (DC MS. 48); "Happy is He" (DC MS. 28); lines about a lamb in solitude (DC MS. 48); the Hermit in his Cell (DC MS. 65). At the second stage of composition, MW and DW reworked from DC MS. 47 the material in DC MS. 70 (58^{v}–back endpaper) in preparation for leaves inserted at Book II in DC MS. 71. Work in DC MS. 70 for Books III, IV, and V dates from the third stage of composition.

DC MS. 71 Described in *Poems, 1807–1820*, p. xxv: "A hand-sewn notebook, 116 leaves, bound in boards (white front, blue-gray back) with brown cloth spine. First two leaves and last leaf pasted to covers. . . . The sheets, folded, measure approximately 10 by 16 cm. Contains a number of sewn-in inserts (see *Chronology: MY*, p. 676); the foliations given here refer to the notebook as now constituted.

Chiefly *Excursion* materials with one earlier passage: the first three lines and part of the fourth line of 'Say, what is Honour?' in WW's hand, on 113^{v}, inverted. Also contains, as part of *Excursion, Characteristics of a Child three Years old,* with verbs in past tense (93^{v}–94^{r}), and the materials from which *Maternal Grief* was derived (91^{v}–93, 94^{v}–95)." The notebook is composed mainly of laid paper (chain lines are at intervals of 2.7 cm), watermarked with a crowned medallion bearing a seated Britannia and countermarked 1803. Five sets of inserts on other kinds of paper (see below) were added to the original notebook. See also the description in *Chronology: MY*, pp. 676–677.

In DC MS. 71, DW, MW, and WW entered the whole of *Exc*, Books I and II (in continuous fair copy with inserts) and of Book III (ll. 1–330 in fair copy, with revisions; ll. 301–998 in draft). In MW's original fair copy of Book II, her text continued on from what is now l. 96 on 35^{v} directly to a new verse paragraph at l. 350 on 46^{v}, which was originally the following leaf. Later, in order to reposition the Wanderer's initial account of the Solitary, Insert A was added (now stubs 42–43, leaves 44–45: two bifolia, the first cut out, the second on laid paper showing a "1798" countermark). At a still later date, six leaves—Insert B, now leaves 36–41—of laid paper watermarked with a cursive "P" and countermarked 1810 were sewn in to replace the first of the two bifolia of Insert A. There are also three inserts, all composed of the same kind of paper as Insert B, sewn into the Book III section: Insert C (leaves 75–76, drawing on *Tuft of Primroses*); Insert D (leaves 87–90, drawing on WW to Lord Lonsdale), Insert E (leaves 102–105, a fair copy of messy revision on the surrounding original leaves, two of which are now stubs 106 and 107). On this complex series of inserts, see pp. 435, 439–440, 453–454, below, as well as the notes to the relevant leaves of transcriptions of DC MS. 71. Books I, II, III (up to l. 330), and Insert A date from the second stage of composition on *Exc;* Book III (ll. 331–998) and Inserts B–E date from the fifth stage—after the deaths of two of WW's children in 1812.

DC MS. 73 Described in *Chronology: MY*, p. 679. This homemade notebook was assembled from the same kind of paper in the same format as DC MS. 69 (see above) but with fewer than half the original number of leaves in DC MS. 69. WW used DC MS. 73 for *Exc* drafting at several different stages of the poem's composition: (1) at the third stage, after running out of space in DC MS. 70, he continued work on 2^{v}–7^{v} for Book IV (ll. 1111–1284 and 79–81); (2) also at the third stage, he next drafted on 8^{r}–9^{r} a passage for Book III (ll. 976–995); (3) at the seventh stage of composition, after running out of space in DC MS. 74, the poet continued work on Book IX, using 9^{r}–9^{v}, 14^{v}–46^{r} (ll. 678–end, then another copy from ll. 292–end); (4) finally, at the eighth stage of composition, WW used 46^{v}–65^{v} for the last half of Book VI. A draft for IX, 400–410, is at the back of the notebook on 95^{v}, inverted.

DC MS. 74 Described in *Poems, 1800–1807* as a "bound notebook of 125 leaves of laid paper measuring 12.5 by 20.2 cm., watermarked with a fleur-de-lys and countermarked 1802" (p. xxiii; see also *Chronology: MY*, p. 679, where DC MS. 74 is described as appearing "to have been a twin of MS. 73"). A gap between the front cover and 1^{r} suggests the possibility of lost leaves, perhaps as many as about two dozen. Two sets of loose leaves were at one time stored in a folder with DC MS. 74 but have recently been restored to their proper locations within the notebook: leaves 43–46 (*SBC* and, on 46^{v}, *Exc*, IX, 38–54, which continues on 47^{r}); leaves 68–71 (*Exc*, VI, 1046–1188, the story—together with surrounding material—of Wilfred Armathwaite). (Included in a folder with DC MS. 74 is a bifolium containing work unrelated to *Exc*: geometry exercises, *Prelude*, X, 445–466, 568–574 [see *13-Bk Prelude*, II, 469–470], and "There Was a Spot" [see *LB, 1797–1800*, pp. 286–287].)

WW, DW, and MW made entries in DC MS. 74 at several stages of *Exc* composition: (1) at the fourth stage, Book V, which at this point included work on *SBC* and extensive work on *TPL*; (2) at the sixth stage, Book VII and the second half of Book VI, as well as part of Book VIII; (3) at the seventh stage, the first half of Book IX; (4) at the eighth stage, cancellation of large sections of *TPL* as part of recopying Book V into a manuscript not now extant and then into DC MS. 74A. On 123^{v} and 124^{r} of DC MS. 74 is a draft of *Yew-Trees*, which Jared Curtis indicates "was probably transcribed by WW between June 1811 and late March 1814" (*Poems, 1800–1807*, p. xxiii). On 37^{v} and 125^{r} is work related to *Essay Upon Epitaphs*, I, which was included by WW in his note to *Exc*, V, 984; that work probably dates from the time WW was preparing the final text of *Exc* for the printer.

DC MS. 74A This manuscript consists of an unbound group of loose leaves sewn together at their center folds to form four gatherings (leaves 1–30) and a loose bifolium with a fair copy revision of 1^{r}–2^{r}. The manuscript contains a complete copy of Book V, primarily fair copy in MW's hand, corrected and revised by WW; it dates from the eighth stage of composition of *Exc*. The leaves of DC MS. 74A measure 13.3 by 21.8 to 22 cm. and are laid paper watermarked with a cursive "P" over the date 1806. Chain lines vary between 2.5 cm. and 2.75 cm. As Mark Reed notes, the paper is similar to that of DC MS. 75 (see *Chronology: MY*, p. 682).

The first gathering of DC MS. 74A consists of eight conjugate leaves (1–8). Since leaves 3–4 and 5–6 are conjugate, it is probable that leaf 4 (now a stub but once containing lines related to V, 257–286, probably leading directly into 8^{r}) originally followed what is now leaf 6 (but once was leaf 5) to form a uniform gathering with original leaves 3 and 6 as conjugate. During the immediate sequence of composition, probably before composition proceeded on 7^{r}, leaf 4 was revised and removed and that expanded revision copied on 7^{r}–7^{v}. The remaining stub of leaf 4 was later sewn with its conjugate leaf out of its original sequence. MW's page and line numbering do not include this stub and its contents, reinforcing the supposition that the revision and removal of leaf 4 was made during the initial process of copying. The second gathering consists of eight conjugate leaves (9–16), and the third gathering consists of four conjugate leaves (17–20). The fourth gathering (21–30) originally consisted of eight conjugate leaves, with leaves now designated 26–27 (unnumbered by MW) replacing leaf 25, which remains as a stub, at a later date, and with leaf 30 left blank. MW's page and first line count (28^{r}, l. 960) assume leaf 25 and its contents running directly into leaf 28^{r} and leaf 25 containing forty lines (see notes to the transcription of DC MS. 74A).

The loose bifolium provides a fair copy of V, 1–65, based on revisions to 1^{r}–2^{r}; two sewing holes at the top and some thread ends indicate that the loose bifoilum was once loosely attached to the front of the four gatherings, and we have so placed it in our transcriptions.

DC MS. 75 Described in *Chronology: MY*, p. 682: "MS. 75 is a set of seven octavo double sheets similar to those of MS. 74A. These sheets like those appear to have been made by dividing folio sheets. The paper of two of the double sheets, however, is distinctly heavier than that of the others, and resembles the paper of MS. 74A rather than the other sheets in this MS." These seven loose bifolia have been assigned the letters "A" through "E" (the ones composed of the flimsier paper mentioned above) and "F" and "G" (the heavier paper). The text on those bifolia composed of the flimsier paper (including the related Berg MS.; see above) precedes the text in DC MS. 74; the entries are all by WW, with the exception of bifolia "E," which has fair copy by MW as well as redrafting by WW. On the heavier paper is MW's fair copy, revised by WW; those entries are later than the text in DC MS. 74. The text on these seven bifolia dates from the sixth stage of *Exc* composition and contributes to the following passages: ("A") Story of Oswald: VII, 804–878; ("B") Stories of Ellen, Patriarch (brief mention, later omitted), and Woodsman: VI, 805–839, and VII, 608–648; ("C") Entry of two boys, Wanderer's Speech: VIII, 552–581, and IX, 57–94; ("D") Wanderer's Speech: IX, 106–183; ("E") Pastor's summing up: V, 929–947, and VII, 536–547; ("F") Description of churchyard/Patriarch's Tale: VII, 30–59, 202–237; ("G") Description of churchyard/Patriarch's Tale: VII, 271–304.

DC MS. 80 Described in *Poems, 1800–1807*, p. xxiii. WW's principal use for DC MS. 80 was to assemble drafts and copies of poems as part of the preparation for publishing *PW*, 1815; this use of the notebook dates from September and October, 1814. On 32^{v}–35^{r} WW copied a shortened version of *TPL* (a much longer version was once part of *Exc*, V, in DC MS. 74). Below *TPL* on 35^{r}—and almost certainly copied later—is *Extract from the Conclusion of a Poem, composed upon leaving School*; that *Extract* was probably entered into DC MS. 80 before October 15, 1814 (see *Poems, 1807–1820*, pp. 141–142). Revision on 32^{v} of the main text of *TPL* seems to be later than a passage on the same page for *Artegal and Elidure*, which dates from late 1814–early 1815 (see *Poems, 1807–1820*, pp. 155, 386–387, 531). Drafting on the inside front cover and on 1^{r}–2^{r} of DC MS. 80 may be further work for *TPL*, perhaps toward a concluding passage; this material is further developed on the verso of the Morgan MS. Copying of *TPL* into DC MS. 80 during the eighth stage of *Exc* composition suggests that *TPL* may have been considered for inclusion in *PW*, 1815, but it was not published by WW. See our reading text of *TPL*, in its DC MS. 80 state, in Appendix II, below.

Houghton MS. A single sheet once folded as a cover to enclose a letter (no text for the letter itself is present) addressed in an unknown hand to "Capt. Luff / &^{c}.–&^{c}.–&^{c}.– / Patterdale / Penrith." The sheet, of laid paper with chain lines at intervals of 2.2 cm., measures 32.3 by 19.8 cm. and is watermarked with a fleur-de-lys above MOLINEUX JOHNSTON / S A LIEF. The address panel is stamped "CARLISLE / 298," but there is no date. During the sixth stage of *Exc* composition, WW used both sides of this sheet for drafts of *Exc*, VII, 554–603, 648–654. bMS Eng 327(1), Houghton Library, Harvard University.

Morgan MS. This single sheet of cream wove paper, measuring 15.8 by 18.8 cm., contains on one side WW's copy of *TPL*, ll. 378–390, probably revising what is on DC MS. 80, 32^{v}–34^{r}, 34^{r}. At this stage, *TPL* had been detached from the *Exc*; the revisions to *TPL* in the Morgan MS. were probably entered in 1814 or later (the eighth stage of *Exc* composition), perhaps as part of an aborted plan to include a shortened version of *TPL* in *PW*, 1815. The verso of the Morgan MS. contains a twenty-line passage (developing material drafted in DC MS. 80, inside front cover and 1^{r}–2^{r}) possibly related to *TPL*. MA 101, Pierpont Morgan Library, New York.

WW to Lord Lonsdale, January 8, 1813. At the fifth stage of composition of *Exc*, WW reused a draft copy of this letter (for the final version, see *MY*, II, 66–67) to compose *Exc*, III, 592–607. The passage appears on 2^{v} of a bifolium of laid paper measuring 19.8 by 23.6 cm. with chain lines at intervals of 2.6 cm.; the sheet is watermarked with the top half of a crowned horn-in-shield. WL.

(3) Post-publication *Excursion* Manuscripts

Cornell MS. 1 WW's copies of *Exc*, IV, 1059a–1074, and of V, 269b–288a, written into a commonplace book inscribed on the first page by Dora Wordsworth to Emma Ayling, July 7, 1824 (see the description in *Poems, 1821–1850*, p. xxx). Both of the *Exc* passages are signed by WW; the passage from Book IV is also dated "Rydal Mount / 22nd Oct^{b} , 1826." Healey, 2558; Kroch Library, Cornell University.

Cornell MS. 2 WW's copy of *Exc*, IV, 1059a–1074 on a single sheet of wove paper measuring 18.8 by 23 cm., signed and dated "Wm Wordsworth / Rydal Mount / April 23 1832." Healey, 2284; Kroch Library, Cornell University.

Huntington MS. WW's copy of *Exc*, III, 236–237a, on a single sheet of wove paper measuring 18.1 by 11.1 cm., signed and dated "Wm Wordsworth / Rydal / March 31st –42." MS. HM12310, Huntington Library.

Lilly MS. According to a handwritten entry on a single undated sheet in an unknown hand, WW wrote *Exc*, III, 1018–1022, into "a copy of his poems belonging to Dr. Gough & now in the possession of Mr. H. Arnold—Solicitor, Kendal." The unknown writer indicates that the lines copied into the book were

"Published in the Westmoreland Gazette" and quotes WW's passage from the newspaper. The passage contains no verbal differences from what is in *1814*; the nonverbal variants (twice removed in the Lilly MS. from WW's entry and thus of no authority) are not reported in this edition. Lilly Library, Indiana University, Bloomington, Indiana.

MS. 1814/27 Revisions and drafts in a copy of *Exc*, 1814, principally entered in preparation for the edition of *Exc* published in 1820 (these revisions are mostly nonverbal, in pencil, and in a hand not identifiable) and for the edition of 1827 (most of the verbal revisions are in the hands of WW and MW, often in pencil or in MW's ink over WW's pencil). One gathering in MS. 1814/27 also contains a few proof corrections and additions that precede the 1814 text as issued. Gathering Y (pp. 161–168) in MS. 1814/27 preserves a unique state, earlier than in any other copies, that includes IV, 481–482, omits IV, 505–507, and has as IV, 538–539, a reading that appears in no other printed copy. Drafts for the 1814 text—as issued—of IV, 505–507, 538–539, are entered in MS. 1814/27; in the subsequent resetting required, IV, 481–482 seem to have been inadvertently omitted. When *Exc* was then published in 1814, its first state had this error of the omitted ll. 481–482. In the second, corrected state of the 1814 edition, Leaf Y1 was canceled and replaced to include IV, 481–482.

Two leaves from the *Exc* edition of 1820 (beginning with VI, 1236, through the conclusion of the book, VI, 1308) are inserted in MS. 1814/27 between its correspondent pages (*Exc*, 1814, pp. 304 and 305), closing with VI, 1235, and opening with VI, 1236; the pagination of *1820E* is identical to that of MS. 1814/27 (i.e., *1814*). Lines on these inserted leaves from *1820E* are deleted in pencil with large crosses, and the passage was omitted in the edition of 1827. The presence of these inserted leaves suggests the possibility that WW used a copy of *1820E* in revising MS. 1814/27 for *1827* and/or in preparing printer's copy for *1827*.

On the verso of the half title in MS. 1814/27, MW copied a poem by R. P. Gillies, *To the Author of The Excursion* (beginning "Though feebly in my harassed mind the light"). WW entered on the verso of the Dedication page his poem *Written, November 13, 1814, on a blank leaf in . . . The Excursion* (here titled *Occasioned by a Recent Death in the Town of Kendal*; see *Poems, 1807–1820*, pp. xxxiii, 154). MW copied on p. [2] a poem from Fulke Greville's *A Treatie of Humane Learning* (no. 143, beginning "The chief use then in man of that he knows"). According to the donor's note on the half title, MS. 1814/27 was once owned by John Wordsworth, son of the poet, and was in 1902 given by his son (also named John) to The Queen's College, Oxford University.

MS. 1827/32C Described in *Poems, 1821–1850*, p. lxix. An annotated set of *PW*, 1827, in which WW, in pencil, and MW, in ink, entered alternate readings and revisions that were in part adopted in *PW*, 1832. Kroch Library, Cornell University.

MS. 1832/36 Described in *Poems, 1821–1850*, p. lxix. Revisions and drafts in various hands in the copy of *PW,* 1832, used in the preparation of the 1836 one-volume edition of *The Excursion* (*1836E*) and of the six-volume *PW,* 1836. (The sixth volume—dated 1837—of *PW,* 1836, contains *The Excursion*; that sixth volume and *1836E* were printed from the same plates, with minor variations.) A large part of the corrected leaves of MS. 1832/36 served as printer's copy. See Jared Curtis, "The Wellesley Copy of Wordsworth's *Poetical Works,* 1832," *Harvard Library Bulletin* 28 (January 1980): 5–15. The English Poetry Collection, Wellesley College Library.

MS. 1836/45 Described in *Poems, 1821–1850,* p. lxx, and in *Some Variants in Wordsworth's Texts in the Volumes of 1836–7 in the King's Library,* ed. Helen Darbishire (Oxford, 1949). WW's revisions in the copy of *PW,* 1836, which he used when preparing the editions of 1840 and 1845. Almost all the revisions for *PW,* 1840, are in the hand of WW's secretary at Rydal Mount, John Carter; those for *PW,* 1845, were dictated to MW or Dora Wordsworth, or written out by WW himself. Evidence indicates that this copy, or part of it, was probably made up of unused sheets from an early, uncorrected state of the 1836 edition. The Royal Collection, the Royal Library, Windsor Castle.

MS. 1849 WW's copy, measuring 18.9 by 11.6 cm., of *Exc,* V, 1018–1022 (there are no verbal variants), signed and dated "Wm Wordsworth / Rydal Mount / 1st August 1849." The manuscript has not been located, and the description draws on a bookseller's catalog; a photocopy is at the British Library, R.P. 1457, Box 27, 942A.

WW to Mrs. J. M. Müleen, February 28, 1838. WW's letter (on a blue-tinted wove sheet 18 by 17.6 cm., with the poet's signature cut away) contains a copy of *Exc,* IV, 187–189. MA 101, Pierpont Morgan Library, New York.

The Excursion

Introduction

I

I am convinced that there are three things to rejoice at in this Age—The Excursion Your Pictures, and Hazlitt's depth of Taste. (John Keats to Benjamin Robert Haydon, *LJK*, I, 203)

I have been reading Wordsworth's "Excursion," with many tears and prayers too. To me he is not only poet, but preacher and prophet of God's new and divine philosophy—a man raised up as a light in a dark time. (Charles Kingsley)[1]

The Excursion was Wordsworth's second long poem, his public attempt at a "Great Poem,"[2] and his only work of any length to be read by most of his contemporaries. As John Keats's words suggest, the poem had a positive influence over younger Romantic writers, mainly through its handling of classical mythology and natural religion in Book IV. On the whole, however, Romantic response was less enthusiastic than that of Keats, and *The Excursion* had to wait for its most appreciative audience until later in the nineteenth century when a Victorian public largely overlooked the posthumous publication of *The Prelude* (1850) in favor of Wordsworth's already published long poem. It has been suggested that Wordsworth "gave his Victorian epic to the Romantics; his Romantic one, to the Victorians" (Johnston, p. 291), and a response such as Kingsley's (above) typifies this position, as he reads back Victorian values and needs onto the earlier poem. For the most part, it would seem that the Victorians were content to respond to *The Excursion* as Wordsworth's most influential work—a source of spiritual strength in an uncertain world—until Matthew Arnold's arguments in favor of selections from Wordsworth's poetry in 1879 began to place the emphasis elsewhere.

Response to *The Excursion* upon its publication in 1814 was far less enthusiastic. The most famous critic of the poem was Francis Jeffrey, editor of *The Edinburgh Review*, who attacked this poem (as he attacked all of Wordsworth's writing) primarily in terms of class. Jeffrey famously began his review with the statement "This will never do!" and went on to ask, "Why should Mr Wordsworth have made his hero

[1] *Charles Kingsley: His Letters and Memories of His Life* (2 vols; London, 1877), I, 120.

[2] John Wilson, in an article of 1831, asks, "But has he—even he—ever written a Great Poem? If he has—it is not the Excursion" ("An Hour's Talk about Poetry," *Blackwood's Magazine* 30 [1831]: 477).

a superannuated Pedlar?" (Jeffrey, pp. 1, 29–30). A second common criticism concerned dramatic voice and the question of whether Wordsworth could speak convincingly in a voice other than his own. William Hazlitt, in his review of the poem, commented, "The recluse, the pastor, and the pedlar, are three persons in one poet" (Hazlitt, p. 542). Finally, concerns about the poem's wordiness were voiced by many, not least by Byron in *Don Juan* ("I think the quarto holds five hundred pages" ["Dedication," l. 26]) and of course Jeffrey, again: "What Mr. Wordsworth's ideas of length are, we have no means of accurately judging; but we cannot help suspecting that they are liberal, to a degree that will alarm the weakness of most modern readers" (Jeffrey, p. 1).

As Jeffrey was well aware (since Wordsworth's "Preface" made it explicit), *The Excursion* was only one part of the great whole—*The Recluse*—that Wordsworth and Coleridge had projected in 1798. What exactly they outlined together in the early years is not clear, but it led Coleridge to describe his friend as "The Giant Wordsworth" (*STCL*, I, 391) and to declare a few years later, in January 1804, "I prophesy immortality to his *Recluse*, as the first & finest philosophical Poem" (*STCL*, II, 1034).

The project emerged from a specific historical context, based on the optimistic belief that a great philosophical work in poetry could counteract the negative effects of the French Revolution. For both Coleridge and Wordsworth, *The Recluse* had a strong moral and social aim, bearing upon immediate events. By the time *The Excursion*, the only part of this project published in Wordsworth's lifetime, finally appeared in 1814 (a year before the battle of Waterloo), the poem necessarily offered a longer, less urgent, perspective back over the wars and their psychological effects. In 1798 Wordsworth was fired up to begin work on the project immediately, as letters of the time plainly indicate, but the only full explanation of the original proposal that has survived is the retrospective one of 1815, given by Coleridge in a letter of criticism to Wordsworth after the publication of *The Excursion*:

> I supposed you first to have meditated the faculties of Man in the abstract, in their correspondence with his Sphere of action, and first, in the Feeling, Touch, and Taste, then in the Eye, & last in the Ear, to have laid a solid and immoveable foundation for the Edifice by removing the sandy Sophisms of Locke, and the Mechanic Dogmatists, and demonstrating that the Senses were living growths and developements of the Mind & Spirit. . . . Next, I understood that you would take the Human Race in the concrete . . . Fallen men contemplated in different ages of the World . . . to point out however a manifest Scheme of Redemption from this Slavery, of Reconciliation from this Enmity with Nature . . . and to conclude by a grand didactic swell on the necessary identity of a true Philosophy with true Religion. . . . In short, Facts elevated into Theory—Theory into Laws—& Laws into living & intelligent Powers—true Idealism necessarily perfecting itself in Realism, & Realism refining itself into Idealism.—Such or something like this was the Plan, I had supposed that you were engaged on. . . . (*STCL*, IV, 574–575)

The final remark here is perhaps the most telling, since it reminds us of Coleridge's distance from Wordsworth by 1815 and stands in contrast to the detailed engagement and cooperative involvement of earlier years, which the first part of the letter so strongly suggests. Above all, according to Coleridge, the poem was to have been antimechanistic, replacing empiricism with a more spiritual and transcendental model of response to the natural world, emphasizing man's analytic, synthetic, discursive, and intuitive powers.[3] The poem was also to have represented man as spiritually fallen with various illustrations of "the sore evils, under which the whole Creation groans" (p. 575) before offering a strongly Christian way forward. For Coleridge the core aim was "a general revolution in the modes of developing & disciplining the human mind by the substitution of Life, and Intelligence . . . for the philosophy of mechanism" (p. 575). Although there are ways in which we can see *The Excursion* trying to do some of these things (as in the accounts of different natural religions in Book IV, or in the poem's emphasis on ways of seeing and understanding developed through dialogue), on the whole Coleridge's plan sounds too abstract, and too firmly rooted in philosophy, for the kind of poet Wordsworth was and the kind of poetry he would have been capable of producing. Coleridge's outline seems more suited to his own personal ambitions than to Wordsworth's talents.[4]

In his "Preface" to *The Excursion* Wordsworth famously gives an organic model of his whole poetic œuvre as "a gothic Church" in which *The Prelude* is "the Anti-chapel." At the same time as Wordsworth unites the whole, he also clearly distinguishes parts within the major project: "the first and third parts of the Recluse will consist chiefly of meditations in the Author's own Person; and that in the intermediate part (The Excursion) the intervention of Characters speaking is employed, and something of a dramatic form adopted" (see p. 39, below). Coleridge too, in the letter of 1815, combines an organic model of relation between the parts with a clear definition of their distinctiveness when he recalls the original plan:

> In order therefore to explain the *disappointment* I must recall to your mind what my *expectations* were: and as these again were founded on the supposition, that (in whatever order it might be published) the Poem on the growth of your own mind [*The Prelude*] was as the ground-plat and the Roots, out of which the Recluse was to have sprung up as the Tree—as far as the same Sap in both, I expected them doubtless to have formed one compleat Whole, but in matter, form, and product to be different, each not only a distinct but a different Work. (*STCL*, IV, 573)

Each part, then, was to have its distinct place within the whole project of *The Recluse,* but the nature of that place and the success of the voice adopted remain uncertain. For Coleridge, the model of creative growth had failed to bring forth the fruits he had anticipated.

---

[3]STC touches upon the difference between discursive and intuitive powers, "the former chiefly useful as perfecting the latter" (p. 575), in a way which could be seen to bear upon the use of conversation and dialogue in *Exc.*

[4]Kenneth Johnston suggests that STC reclaims the model of *The Recluse* for *Biographia Literaria* (1817): "*The Recluse* came home to rest in the mind of its progenitor, reappropriated by Coleridge to help define his own account of mental growth" (Johnston, p. 333).

II

As a dramatic poem, *The Excursion* advances largely through debate among the four main speakers: the Poet, the Wanderer, the Solitary, and the Pastor. The contents of the work can be simply summarized. In Book I ("The Wanderer"), the Poet and the Wanderer meet beside the ruin of a house, and the Wanderer tells the Poet the tale of the family and of Margaret, who once lived there. In Book II ("The Solitary"), the Poet and the Wanderer, after further traveling, ascend a steep hill up to the Solitary's hidden valley, the Wanderer giving a brief account of the Solitary's life on the way. They hear a funeral service and mistakenly fear that he is dead. After their encounter with the Solitary, he then takes them to his home and relates the story of the Old Pensioner (whose funeral it was), concluding with an account of his own visionary experience on the mountainside. Immediately afterward (in Book III: "Despondency"), they journey to a nearby waterfall, where, after some debate, the Solitary tells his life story in detail, explaining how personal and political tragedies have broken his spirit and his faith. In Book IV ("Despondency Corrected"), the Wanderer responds to this narrative discursively, trying to address all of the Solitary's difficulties. This book ends optimistically with the Solitary apparently open to the Wanderer's teachings.

However, the next morning (in Book V: "The Pastor") the Solitary has returned to his previous state of mind. The travelers decide to walk on to the churchyard further down the valley, and they persuade the Solitary to join them. They wander into the church and then out among the graves, where the Pastor meets them. The Wanderer summarizes the debate so far and asks the Pastor to "Epitomize the life; pronounce, You can, / Authentic epitaphs" (V, 652–653). Books VI and VII, both entitled "The Churchyard Among The Mountains," then develop as a series of epitaphic tales, relating to the largely unmarked graves around them. There is a brief debate on the effects of poverty and the need to help the rural peasant. At the end of the debate, the characters wander down to the Pastor's house, where they are greeted by his daughter and wife and then interrupted by the joyful entry of his son and his son's friend, who have been fishing (Book VIII: "The Parsonage"). At the start of Book IX ("Discourse of the Wanderer and An Evening Visit to the Lake"), the Wanderer gives his long speech, ending with a call for National Education for the poor and praising the wonders of industrialization that will make England a great nation. The characters then walk down to the lake and row across it, first to an island and then to the other side, where the Pastor utters a prayer upon the hillside as the sun goes down. They return, and the Solitary (who has been showing increasing signs of disquiet) leaves them there, promising that he will meet with them again.

The action of the poem seems to take place over five days (although only three days are directly represented in the poem). The tale of Margaret is told on the first day (Book I), but the Poet and the Wanderer travel together for three further days (summarized at the start of Book II) before setting out on the last of these (i.e., on the fourth day) for the Solitary's valley. On that day they meet and debate with him (Books II–IV), then stay the night, and on the fifth day they all walk together to the churchyard and parsonage (V–IX).

Possible sources for *The Excursion* are clearly outlined by the critic Judson Stanley Lyon: "There are really four principal streams of eighteenth-century literature which meet in the structure of *The Excursion.* These are the long blank-verse didactic poem; the philosophical dialogue; the short verse narrative of humble life . . . and the funeral elegy" (Lyon, p. 31). As Lyon illustrates, comparison can be made to a range of works: James Thomson's *The Seasons*; William Cowper's *The Task*; David Mallet's blank verse poem *The Excursion*; George Berkeley's *Alciphron,* to name but a few. Geoffrey Hartman also notes that Wordsworth's poem "certainly has roots in the topographical and contemplative poetry of the eighteenth century" (Hartman, p. 296). He goes on to comment further on another key element, the importance of tale telling within the poem—"it is not an ideal but a storied landscape" (p. 299)—while also comparing the work to Milton's poetry and to Dante's. Wordsworth's ambitions in relation to Milton are strongly felt in the *Prospectus* (published at the start of *The Excursion* but originally written for *Home at Grasmere*), which claims for the Wordsworthian humanist agenda a value equal to that of the Christian epic.[5]

It is clear that *The Excursion* draws upon and moves among a number of different generic forms. There is, though, one particular source that offered Wordsworth the kind of multigeneric structural journey with which he underpinned the poem: *The Peripatetic* (1793) by his acquaintance John Thelwall. The full title of Thelwall's work is *The Peripatetic; or Sketches of the Heart, of Nature and Society; in a Series of Politico-sentimental Journals, in Verse and Prose, of the Eccentric Excursions of Sylvanus Theophrastus,* a fact that is quite telling when we consider that Wordsworth's first projected subtitle for *The Recluse* was "*views of Nature, Man, and Society*" (*EY,* p. 214). In Thelwall's poem his good-hearted hero, Sylvanus Theophrastus, travels in a coach and on foot, declaiming poetry and philosophical thoughts along the way. The poem finds its focus in the disaffected figure of Belmour, who is made to journey with Sylvanus and his companions from time to time and who is offered consolation by them in a manner reminiscent of *The Excursion.*[6] The loose generic nature of the work, combined with the structure of the journey and the value of walking and talking together, suggests that *The Peripatetic* may have provided a useful model for Wordsworth. Henry Crabb Robinson, who describes Thelwall's admiration for *The Excursion* in his diaries, also remarks that "Wordsworth borrows without acknowledgement from Thelwall himself" (see Wu, *Reading I,* pp. 135–136).

Such critics as Lyon and Hartman both address troubling questions concerning the role of the misanthropic Solitary and where the center of *The Excursion* really lies. According to Hartman, "At the dramatic center of the poem stands the Solitary: Can his mind be restored to health? Wordsworth is honest enough

[5]The *Prospectus* was probably written between spring 1800 and 1802, earlier than most of the writing for *Exc.* It directly echoes Milton as well as addressing Urania as the heavenly muse, as Milton does in *PL.* Other Miltonic echoes (linguistic and syntactical) are found throughout the poem and are provided in our Editors' Notes on pp. 373–422, below.

[6]WW first met Thelwall briefly in 1797 while he was living at Alfoxden and saw him again a number of times afterward. Thelwall was a prominent member of the Jacobin Corresponding Society; as a well-known radical, he was arrested and charged with sedition in the Treason Trials of 1794. His work thus has a much stronger political strain in it than does *Exc.*

not to resolve the question" (p. 300). Lyon for his part concludes: "There is no single message in *The Excursion.* There are many problems raised and many solutions provided" (p. 120). Certainly, the figure of the Solitary as one whose life, faith, and philosophy have been destroyed by historical events is central to the poem, and this aspect of his character recalls the early ambitions for *The Recluse* as expressed in a letter from Coleridge of September 10, 1799: "I wish you would write a poem, in blank verse, addressed to those, who, in consequence of the complete failure of the French Revolution, have thrown up all hopes of the amelioration of mankind, and are sinking into an almost epicurean selfishness . . . " (*STCL,* I, 527). The Solitary is representative of his generation and of those who were caught up in the Revolution in their youth and thrown into despair by its failure to live up to the expectations it had generated. In *The Prelude* Wordsworth had charted his own personal despair and then salvation through poetry. In *The Excursion* similar ideas are now dealt with dramatically, and through dialogue, as the other characters try to argue and persuade the Solitary to view the world differently. However, his case is less easily solved. The fact that the Solitary returns home alone (and unconverted) at the end of the poem is one of the work's most interesting features, although this outcome disturbed Wordsworth's more religious readership.[7] The poem's open-endedness returns us to Lyon's point that "There is no single message" (p. 120) and also, perhaps, to Hartman's description of the poem as "a storied landscape" (p. 299). An excursion may be not so much about where you journey to as about what occurs along the way.

III

Before we turn to the complexities of the manuscripts themselves, tracing the composition of *The Excursion* through evidence provided in the letters will help to build up a sense of the way in which the poem develops. However, any attempt to analyze those letters is immediately confronted with a difficulty: it is almost impossible to untangle the early stages of writing the poem from work on other related material (particularly that done for *Home at Grasmere*) because of Wordsworth's use of the term "Recluse." On March 11, 1798, Wordsworth wrote to James Losh, "I have written 1300 lines of a poem which I hope to make of considerable utility; its title will be *The Recluse or views of Nature, Man, and Society*" (*EY,* p. 214). From this point onward Wordsworth typically uses "Recluse" when discussing any work that might form part of the whole project, including *The Ruined Cottage, The Pedlar, Home at Grasmere, The Tuft of Primroses,* and other fragments. Until the poem is published, *The Excursion* is also referred to as part of the grander project of *The Recluse* rather than as a distinctive work. Thus the modern reader is often unsure which one of a number of related texts is being referred to; in particular, it is difficult to define the clear starting point of new work (beyond Book I) for *The Excursion.* At the same time, however, use of the

---

[7]For more detail on this aspect of the poem, see the Editors' Notes to the Reading Text for the end of Book IX (p. 422, below).

generic title *Recluse* does serve to remind us that during early composition, and possibly until quite late in the process, Wordsworth did not feel himself to be working on one poem entitled *Home at Grasmere*, another *The Tuft of Primroses*, and a third *The Excursion*. Rather, he had before him a considerable body of work that could be adapted, merged, or separated at any point up to the final preparations for publication of *The Excursion*.

References in the letters to work for *The Recluse* occur from 1798 onward, but until 1806 they relate fairly unambiguously to either *Ruined Cottage* material or *Home at Grasmere*.[8] In some of the 1806 letters, however, there is an element of uncertainty as to which material is being referred to, with significant implications for dating *The Excursion*. Although it has been generally agreed that these 1806 references apply to *Home at Grasmere*, there is at least a possibility that work for *The Excursion* began at this time. In a letter to Catherine Clarkson of July 23, 1806, Dorothy states that "William goes on rapidly with the Recluse" (*MY*, I, 61). Then, on August 1, 1806, Wordsworth himself provides a progress report for Sir George Beaumont: "Within this last month I have returned to the Recluse, and have written 700 additional lines. Should Coleridge return, so that I might have some conversation with him upon the subject, I should go on swimmingly."[9] Beth Darlington argues that Wordsworth's comment refers to *Home at Grasmere* (see *H at G*, pp. 16–18). Certainly, evidence suggests that Wordsworth in the summer of 1806 was working on that text (material that included the tales of Wilfred Armathwaite and of the Man with Six Daughters, both later incorporated into Book VI of *The Excursion*). However, as Beth Darlington acknowledges, Mark Reed points out another possibility: "It seems entirely possible that a large number of verses were composed c. Sept. 1806 that are now unidentified. . . . Much further speculation about the identity of such lines would seem profitless. Some portion of *Exc* II may be, however, a remote possibility" (*Chronology: MY*, p. 661). Reed goes on to consider this "possibility," stating that one part of Book II (the vision of the Solitary) could not have been composed before September 5, 1807 (since the fantastic cloud formation upon which it was based occurred on that date), but other parts of Book II could have been written from November 1805 onward.

The earliest surviving manuscript for this Book II material is DC MS. 47, which runs more or less continuously from line 1 to line 789 of the final poem, with two gaps of 53 and 75 lines. In total, then, this material amounts to a little under 700 lines. It could possibly be the "700 additional lines" that Wordsworth referred to in his letter to Beaumont of August 1, 1806. In the same letter Wordsworth goes on to describe himself writing in his "Moss hut" in the garden of Dove Cottage and tells us: "I cannot however refrain from smiling at the situation in which I sometimes find myself here; as, for instance, the other morning when I was calling some lofty notes out of my harp, chaunting of Shepherds,

[8]See Beth Darlington's introduction (*H at G*, pp. 13–16) for a detailed discussion of these early references.

[9](*MY*, I, 64). EdeS and Moorman have as a note to this reference that "The '700 additional lines' were probably part of Book IV of *The Excursion*. . . . Soon afterwards he wrote most of the second book and part of the third" (*MY*, I, 64). The MSS. suggest that WW began with Book II, not Book IV, so the first claim of that note seems unlikely. However, the second claim is a distinct possibility, as argued below.

and solitude, etc., I heard a voice . . . crying out from the road below . . . " (*MY*, I, 64). Reed, on the whole, sides in favor of the 700 lines referring to *Home at Grasmere*, stating of the supporting description given in Wordsworth's letter that it is "obviously if loosely suggestive of the content" of that poem (*Chronology: MY*, p. 658). However, the description could equally well refer to the contents of Book II of *The Excursion* in which the Poet and Wanderer travel up the Langdale Valley, staying with local people before climbing to the bleaker, lonelier valley of the Solitary.

On September 8, 1806, Wordsworth again wrote to Sir George Beaumont: "You will be glad to hear that I have been busily employed lately; I wrote one book of the Recluse nearly 1000 lines, then had a rest, last week began again and have written 300 more; I hope all tolerably well, and certainly with good views" (*MY*, I, 79). Darlington (after John Finch) offers a detailed argument relating this line count to *Home at Grasmere*, although she concludes, "To be sure Wordsworth's line counts in the letters do not match those in the manuscripts very closely" (*H at G*, p. 18). An argument that this line count matches work on *The Excursion* would have to suggest that the 1,000 lines might be a rather over-generous estimate of the approximately 700 lines of Book II material already mentioned, together with the possible addition of the tale of the Old Pensioner (but without the Solitary's vision). This tale is not in DC MS. 47; if it had been written up elsewhere, it would add approximately 150 lines to Book II.[10] The "300 more" lines mentioned in Wordsworth's letter *could* then refer to the material for Book III in DC MS. 69. Although the surviving material in that notebook is on stubs and only occasional pages, there is strong evidence to suggest that lines 1–330 of Book III were entered in the notebook and that they were the first entry here.

There is a tendency to construct an argument wholly in favor of *Home at Grasmere* or wholly in favor of *The Excursion* for the *Recluse* material of these two letters, but it is also possible that one reference might be to *Home at Grasmere* and another to *The Excursion*. There is, unfortunately, no way of knowing for sure. On the whole it seems reasonable to argue for early work on *The Excursion* as a definite possibility in 1806. Material in Book II (and to a lesser extent the first part of Book III) has a distinctive identity within the poem. It seems to be more closely allied with the earlier work on *The Ruined Cottage* and has a much stronger topographical sense than the later books.

These 1806 letters indicate to us an initial block of work, either on *The Excursion* itself or on other *Recluse* materials (some of which would later be used in the published poem) that took place over the summer of 1806, with Wordsworth sounding engaged and enthusiastic. However, following this period of activity, there is a complete absence of any reference to *The Recluse* (and therefore to *The Excursion*) until February 1810, which may indicate a forty-month break from the work. One possible reason for this loss of momentum might be Wordsworth's relationship with Coleridge. In August 1806, Wordsworth's letters show that he was anticipating close intellectual engagement with his ideas on his friend's return. Coleridge did finally return to the Lakes in October 1806, but Dorothy's

[10]The total, however, would still only amount to about 850 and not 1,000 lines.

description of the long-anticipated encounter vividly communicates the disappointment of it:

[H]is misery has made him so weak, and he has been so dismally irresolute in all things since his return to England, that I have more of fear than hope. He is utterly changed; and yet sometimes, when he was animated in conversation concerning things removed from him, I saw something of his former self. But never when we were alone with him. (*MY*, I, 86)

If Wordsworth had been working eagerly on the new poem, motivated by the desire to share it with Coleridge on his return, then the change in his friend must have been a severe blow to him—not only personally but also in terms of the role he expected Coleridge to play in the development of the larger *Recluse* structure.

Knowing of Coleridge's marital difficulties, Wordsworth wrote to him in November 1806, inviting his friend to come to Grasmere to live with the Wordsworths:

I write . . . to recommend your coming hither where you may sit down at leisure and look about you before you decide. You might bring Hartley with you and live here as long as you liked free of all expense but washing, you would be altogether uninterrupted and might proceed as rapidly as you liked with your Book of Travels, which would be certain of a great sale. Other things might be planned when we are together. (*MY*, I, 90)

Coleridge took up the invitation. From September 1808 to October 1810, he spent some time with his family in Keswick but also lived for long periods with the Wordsworths in their larger house, Allan Bank, into which they had moved from Dove Cottage. However, Coleridge's marital problems, his obsession with Sara Hutchinson, and his attempt to give his own life focus by working intensively on *The Friend* seem to have occupied most of his time, at the expense of "Other things [that] might be planned" when the two poets were together. One entry in Coleridge's notebooks for July–September 1809 shows some loose engagement with the projected *Recluse*: "A fine subject to be introduced in William's great poem is the Savage Boy of Aveyron in Itard's account—viz—his restless joy & blind conjunction of his Being with natural Scenery" (*STCNB*, III, entry 3538).[11] But, apart from that passing reference, there is no evidence of Wordsworth's discussing *The Excursion* with Coleridge in any depth or of the poem's advancing in any distinctive way. On Wordsworth's part it looks as though he initially put the *Recluse* aside and worked instead on other projects: writing of prose; the publication of *Poems, in Two Volumes* in 1807; and composition of *The White Doe of Rylstone*. In 1808 he returned to *The Recluse* (though not directly to *The Excursion*) in working on *The Tuft of Primroses* and *To The Clouds*, and this material is probably what is referred to in the letter to Samuel Rogers of September 29, 1808, when Wordsworth tells

[11]This description could be related to WW's work on *TPL* in which the young boy "In pure activity of rustic childhood" sends a large stone crashing down the mountainside (see transcriptions of MS. 74, 94^r and 95^r, below).

him that "I have written since I saw you about 500 lines of my long Poem" (*MY*, I, 269). Some of that material was later to be incorporated into *The Excursion.*

The earliest phase of work toward *The Excursion,* then, from 1806 to 1809, represents a stage in which other poems are written, parts of which will be used within the final text, as well as, possibly, a large part of Book II and the first part of Book III (Book I, in its base form as *The Ruined Cottage,* was already complete by 1804). Wordsworth seems to have been hopeful and expectant as he looked forward to sharing the material and the planning of the poem with Coleridge. When this model of future development failed to materialize, with the realization that Coleridge would not provide the major stimulus for the poem's development as he had (even by his absence) for *The Prelude,* Wordsworth seems to have temporarily lost direction.

The Excursion as a clearly distinct poem comes into being only from about 1810 onward, as Mark Reed suggests: "[A] great amount of continuous or methodical composition toward a poem similar to the present *Exc* cannot have taken place before late 1809 or early 1810" (*Chronology: MY*, p. 666). The point at which Wordsworth begins in earnest to develop the poem, and one reason for the return to it, can perhaps be located in Dorothy's letter of February 19, 1810, to Jane Marshall, commenting on Coleridge's journal, *The Friend*: "The concluding part of the 17th Number, and the 20th Number were by my Brother, and the Essay of this week, upon Epitaphs, is by him. . . . The Translations also of Epitaphs from Chiabrera are by my Brother" (*MY*, I, 388). About the same time, work on *The Excursion* appears to recommence, with the strong likelihood that Wordsworth's prose writing on epitaphs stimulates his poetic work for the long poem.[12] In a letter of February 28, 1810, to Lady Beaumont, Dorothy excuses her slowness in replying on domestic grounds:

> These circumstances will partly account to you for my having been more than usually engaged in domestic employments. To which I may add another reason, that my Sister, though in good health, is not able to go through much fatigue, and also that her chief employment of late has been transcribing for William. (*MY*, I, 390)

Just preceding the above-quoted remarks in the letter, Dorothy speaks of the return of Sara Hutchinson to her brother's farm in Wales, stating that "Coleridge most of all will miss her, as she has transcribed almost every Paper of the Friend for the press" (p. 390). Then, immediately below the account of Mary's transcribing the poem for Wordsworth, Dorothy returns to Coleridge, telling us that his "spirits have been irregular of late" (p. 390). It is telling that this first reference to serious poetic work for *The Excursion,* after a lengthy break from it, should be framed by references to Coleridge's physical health and state of mind. It is as though this ending of a key phase in Coleridge's life (which the loss of his beloved

[12]At the end of the third *Essay on Epitaphs* in MS. 67, SH copied (as part of the *Essay*) *Exc*, VII, 412–498. This *Essay* was probably composed between c. December 1809 and February 28, 1810 (see *Chronology: MY*, pp. 49, 443); the *Exc* passage was therefore also complete by the end of February 1810.

Sara, or "Asra," represented) marks a new beginning for Wordsworth. Indeed, the sense of the two poets' relative positions is encapsulated in this letter, and so too is the imminent breach between them. Dorothy touches on her brother's reluctance to publish the first *Essay upon Epitaphs* in *The Friend* ("He did not intend it to be published now; but Coleridge was in such bad spirits that when the time came he was utterly unprovided" [p. 391]) and voices a combined rebuke by brother and sister against Coleridge: "[H]ere I must observe that we have often cautioned Coleridge against making promises, which even if performed are of no service, and if broken must be of great disservice" (p. 391). Some months later, on October 18, 1810, when Coleridge traveled down to London with the indiscreet Basil Montagu, these petty disagreements erupted into a rift between Wordsworth and Coleridge that was never overcome.

Finally, in the same letter, Dorothy goes on to mention new work by Wordsworth on *The Recluse*: "He is deeply engaged in composition. Before he turns to any other labour, I hope he will have finished 3 books of the Recluse. He seldom writes less than 50 lines every day" (*MY*, I, 391–392). Again, we cannot be certain about what material Dorothy is describing. When she talks of Wordsworth's finishing three books, is she referring back to the transcribed material (perhaps Books I–III in DC MS. 71) or to fresh work? And if the latter, then what was it? De Selincourt and Moorman annotate Dorothy's letter by stating that "Mary was transcribing *The Excursion*, which Wordsworth now resumed, writing the fifth, sixth and seventh Books between Feb. and May 1810" (*MY*, I, 390), but Reed is less sure: "One may hardly feel certain . . . that the three books which DW was hoping on 28 Feb 1810 that W. would finish . . . were definitely 'The Pastor' and the two books following" (*Chronology: MY*, pp. 684–685). We can conclude only that a large amount of work, probably toward the epitaphic Books VI and VII, must have been undertaken at this time. The notebook (or notebooks) in which this material was written appears to have been lost.

The next letter by Dorothy that mentions work on the poem, to Catherine Clarkson in May 1811, comes again amidst a stream of anxieties about Coleridge's state of mind and how to put things right between Coleridge and Wordsworth after the quarrel:

> Poor creature! unhappy as he makes others how much more unhappy is he himself! Do not mention this subject I entreat you to Mr Clarkson or any other person (of course when I exclude him)—William has begun to work at his great poem. I wish you could hear him read it. (*MY*, I, 490)

In this stage of composition on *The Excursion*, it would appear that Coleridge's absence and final removal from his friend's life releases Wordsworth and allows him to return to the work and to develop it now in his own way, as an independent piece not reliant upon Coleridgean input. The poem, however, does not develop continuously and fluently. In August 1811, Dorothy stated, "William's poem has been at a stand ever since he made a visit to Water-Millock. It is very unfortunate that any interruption stops him" (*MY*, I, 502). By December things seem to be better, as Dorothy tells us: "William is at work with his great poem and is arranging anew his published ones" (p. 527).[13] But Sara Hutchinson's letters suggest only partial application by the poet when she states on March 29, 1812, that "William has been busy with the *Recluse* but the smoke puts him off" (*SHL*, pp. 46–47). There is a sense, in this slow progress toward composition, that the very existence of the all-encompassing *Recluse* project had become stifling to creativity.[14]

On June 4, 1812, Wordsworth's youngest daughter, Catharine, aged four, died unexpectedly of a seizure. Both Mary and William were away from home at the time—William in London, Mary in Wales—and it was a terrible blow, even though the child had always been weak. Then in December 1812, just as the family was beginning to recover from the loss of Catharine, a second child, Thomas (aged six), died of pneumonia following measles. These domestic tragedies seem not to have acted, as one might expect, as a major interruption to the writing of *The Excursion* but as a spur that led toward its completion. Soon after the second death, in January 1813, Dorothy tells Catherine Clarkson that Wordsworth has returned to the poem:

> William has begun to look into his poem the Recluse within the two last days and I hope he will be the better for it—he looks better and his stomach has been less deranged. It would have pitied the hardest heart to witness what he has gone through—he went for Mr Scambler to the child without fear of danger, he returned and found him dying—That miserable night. . . . (*MY*, II, 64)

Dorothy makes an explicit link among recent events, Wordsworth's physical and mental state, and the act of writing poetry. As she suggests, and as the manuscripts for this section of the poem strongly illustrate, Wordsworth turns to poetry as a means of working through his sense of loss. It is at this point that he adds to the Solitary's life story a tale of personal loss, and on August 27, 1813, Sara Hutchinson tells us that Wordsworth is "over head & ears in his verses" (*SHL*, 64). The final major burst of work upon the poem thus takes place between early 1813 and mid-1814.

Further comment in the family letters about *The Excursion* does not come until the poem is in press, even though between 1812 and 1814 he must have been writing, rewriting, transcribing, and pulling the whole text together. As Mark Reed says, "[C]omposition of *Exc* from about the beginning of 1810 was proceeding under conceptions of principal characters and main themes similar to those of the poem as published, but the final organization of the poem was fixed during the period of intense work commencing 3 Jan. 1813" (*Chronology: MY*, p. 675). The next reference we have to the poem, toward the end of the process, comes on April 24, 1814, in Dorothy's expression of anxiety at being away from home at a crucial point:

---

[13] EdeS and Moorman note: "i.e. *The Excursion*, completed this winter" (*MY*, I, 527). This note is inaccurate. It seems unlikely that the poem was completed until shortly before publication in July 1814.

[14] Kenneth Johnston outlines a structure of advance and retreat for *The Recluse* as a whole, arguing that "Wordsworth first made starts upon *The Recluse* that ended in fragmented failure; that he recoiled, second, in direct reaction to his perceived failure . . . and that these recoils evidently restored him" (Johnston, p. xiv).

> Besides *now* above all other time I should have wished to be at home, for William is actually printing 9 books of his long poem. It has been copied in my absence, and great alterations have been made some of which indeed I had an opportunity of seeing during my week's visit. But the printing has since been going on briskly, and not one proof-sheet has yet met my eyes. We are all most thankful that William has brought his mind to consent to printing so much of this work; for the MSS. were in such a state that, if it had pleased Heaven to take him from this world, they would have been almost useless. I do not think the book will be *published* before next winter. . . . (*MY*, II, 139–140)

Dorothy's comment on the unpublished text contains some intriguing information. First she tells us "it has been copied in my absence, and great alterations have been made." Dorothy had stayed in Keswick from January 1814 to this date, April 24 (when she was due to return home but was delayed by bad weather), with only a brief return visit for a week in mid-March. We therefore know that William and Mary must have been working together intensively on the poem during this four-month period. We cannot be certain what the "great alterations" might be that are referred to here, but one possibility would certainly be the removal of *The Peasant's Life* from Book V and the clean transcription of that book in Mary Wordsworth's hand (with *The Peasant's Life* material removed) in DC MS. 74A. A second interesting comment is Dorothy's remark that "William has brought his mind to consent to printing so much of this work." Her expression here is powerfully indirect. It suggests both that her brother previously could not bring himself to publish it and also that considerable effort was involved in even making the decision to do so. Such comments anticipate Dorothy's final point that "the MSS. were in such a state," which implies that the decision to publish brought with it a final stage of preparation that was not one of simply reorganizing and transcribing but still involved creative decisions. It suggests that the poem only achieved its final organized form immediately preceding publication. A letter from the publisher, Longman, to Wordsworth, dated May 20, 1814, contains the postscript "If we had all the Ms. of the Excursion, we could very soon get the volumes published" (Owen, p. 26). Again, such remarks suggest that immediately before publication Wordsworth was still working through the manuscript in stages to produce a final clean copy for the printers. Several notebooks must have contained these materials revised for final publication, but this final stage of work is not represented in the surviving manuscripts.

Wordsworth's own comments on the final stages of preparation make clear the effort that the poem has demanded from him. On April 26, 1814, he writes to Francis Wrangham: "I am busy with the Printers' Devils. A Portion of a long Poem from me will see the light ere long. I hope it will give you pleasure. It is serious, and has been written with great labour" (*MY*, II, 144). On April 28, 1814, the poet tells Thomas Poole, "My poetical Labours have often suffered long interruptions; but I have at last resolved to send to the Press a portion of a Poem which, if I live to finish it, I hope future times will 'not willingly let die'" (*MY*, II, 146). In both letters, Wordsworth still emphatically views *The Excursion* not as a distinct work but as part of *The Recluse*, and this attitude may also explain the reason for Dorothy's distancing syntax to explain her brother's reluctance in publishing "so much of this work."

By publishing the material at this stage, and by putting it together into this one poem, Wordsworth may well have feared that he was dooming *The Recluse* to incompletion. As long as large blocks of material from many different stages of writing existed in manuscript form, the whole poetic project still had the potential to be created. However, when much of the material had been "used up" as a distinct and published part of that whole, the ambition became much harder to fulfill. Once *The Excursion* has been published, clear lines and boundaries are drawn: the very act of publishing the poem creates those boundaries. In a letter to Sir George Beaumont on Christmas Day, 1804, Wordsworth gives one of the fullest descriptions of the *Recluse* project: "Of this Poem, that of 'the Pedlar' which Coleridge read you is part and I may have written of it altogether about 2,000 lines. It will consist, I hope, of about 10 or 12 thousand" (*EY*, p. 518). Yet *The Excursion* alone comes to a total of 9,068 lines. It is as though Wordsworth's fear of failure leads him constantly to deny that he is actually writing the major work. Beth Darlington comments on such fears in relation to *The Prelude* when she states, "[T]he enlargement of *The Prelude* enabled him to compose poetry associated with *The Recluse* but to avoid direct confrontation with his sense of inadequacy to proceed with it" (*H at G*, p. 14). Something similar seems to be at work with *The Excursion*, as Coleridge's 1815 letter of criticism also strongly suggests. Coleridge refers first to the poem later published as *The Prelude* and then to *The Excursion*:

> *This* I considered as 'the EXCURSION'; and the second as 'THE RECLUSE' I had (from what I had at different times gathered from your conversation on the Plan) anticipated as commencing with you set down and settled in an abiding Home, and that with the Description of that Home you were to begin a *Philosophical Poem*, the result and fruits of a Spirit so fram'd & so disciplin'd, as had been told in the former. (*STCL*, IV, 574)

Coleridge's point seems to be that Wordsworth is endlessly delaying and deviating from the core intention; in writing *The Prelude* and then *The Excursion*, Wordsworth has effectively strayed from his task twice over. Coleridge thus directly anticipates Helen Darbishire's remark that all we have of *The Recluse* is "a Prelude to the main theme, and an Excursion from it."[15]

IV

So often for *The Excursion*, it seems as though Wordsworth needs some kind of external stimulus in order to keep writing. For *The Prelude* he had the anticipated presence of Coleridge as a key motivating force, but with *The Excursion* there was no longer any likelihood that Coleridge would provide such support. Instead there is a sense in which Wordsworth creates the necessary support structure out of other material in prose and poetry that he is working on. In turning to the manuscripts of *The Excursion*, we can see this model of development implicit

[15] *The Poet Wordsworth: The Clark Lectures, Trinity College, Cambridge* (Oxford, 1950), p. 90.

throughout. While the poem develops in a loosely chronological order (earlier manuscripts generally contain material for earlier books), the stimulus for taking the poem forward does not always seem to come out of the text already generated. Instead, *The Excursion* often seems to draw upon, or be interwoven with, Wordsworth's other writings: *Home at Grasmere* (1806) and *The Tuft of Primroses* (1808); the *Essays on Epitaphs* of 1810; his *Guide to the Lakes* (the first version of which appeared without Wordsworth's name in the Rev. Joseph Wilkinson's serially published *Select Views in Cumberland, Westmoreland and Lancashire,* 1810);[16] the biographical sketch of Robert Walker that was later published in the notes to *The River Duddon* (1820). These works overlap with *The Excursion* in various ways: (1) passages of poetry in *The Tuft of Primroses* and *Home at Grasmere* are reworked and then incorporated into the later poem; (2) the first *Essay* is given as an extended footnote to Book V, and work related to it is found in DC MS. 74 alongside epitaphic poetry; the poetic description of the deaf dalesman in Book VII of *The Excursion* is included at the end of the third *Essay;* (3) DC MS. 69 contains passages of prose written toward Wordsworth's later *Guide* alongside *Excursion* material; (4) *The Excursion,* Book VII, contains a poetic account of Walker that anticipates the later note in *The River Duddon.* Thus, all these other texts feed into the poem's development, and if we can chart such direct evidence of textual overlap we can surely also assume the *unseen* importance of related material and ideas.[17] As a result the text could be said to develop almost "concentrically" or "contextually" as much as sequentially.

For those readers who wish a detailed compositional history of *The Excursion,* we provide an extended treatment (see pp. 429–477, below) as prefatory to the manuscript transcriptions. At this point, however, it may be useful to present a brief account of the stages of the poem's complex manuscript history. The exact dates for any of the stages of the poem's development are difficult to ascertain. Nonetheless, we know that the poem takes as its starting point material for *Ruined Cottage/Pedlar* (completed in March 1804), which eventually became Book I of *The Excursion.* Book II was probably written at an early date, possibly in 1806, with the first 330 lines of Book III also perhaps being composed at this time (it is possible that these two sections may not have been written until December 1809). This early work, appearing in DC MSS. 47 and 69, constitutes the first stage of the poem's development.

The second stage can be dated to 1809–1812, when Wordsworth copied the *Ruined Cottage/Pedlar* material out twice over, the first time in a single block in DC MS. 69 and the second time as part of a longer fair copy text of Books I–III (up to l. 330), a fair copy that assembled material written up to this point into a single manuscript, DC MS. 71. This fair copy ends just before the Solitary's tale in Book III, and early revision to his tale, later inserted into the fair copy text,

[16] On the dating of the various parts of the *Guide* (and of WW's composition of them), see *Prose,* II, 124–135, and *Chronology: MY,* pp. 671–674.

[17] In their introduction to the *Essays Upon Epitaphs,* Owen and Smyser explicitly address the question of overlap, stating, "In appending Essay I to *The Excursion,* Wordsworth drew attention to affinities between the Essay and Books V, VI, and VII of the poem. . . . It is difficult to find precise verbal parallels, but parallels of mood and thought are obvious" *(Prose,* II, 46).

likely occurred at this time. At this stage and in a manuscript no longer extant, Wordsworth probably also wrote material toward the epitaphic books (VI, VII, and VIII). Surviving Book VI material (ll. 412–498) in DC MS. 67 supports this dating, and the poet must have been engaging closely with the subject in writing his *Essays on Epitaphs,* one of which was published in Coleridge's *Friend* in 1810.

The third and fourth stages of writing involve the philosophical debate of Book IV (work from l. 335 onward in DC MSS. 70 and 73) and Book V. The development of Book V in DC MSS. 69, 70, and 74 is complicated by the existence of other material—most notably *The Peasant's Life* (less problematically, *The Shepherd of Bield Crag*)—that was originally part of drafting for Books V and VI but was not included in the published *Excursion.* The concluding image of Book III (the account of life as a river) was also written at this time as a discrete piece in DC MS. 73.

In 1812 the deaths of two of Wordsworth's children returned the poet to Book III; at this fifth stage, then, he wrote up the Solitary's life in full, giving it a tragic, familial dimension. Once this highly personal work—and also the rest of Book III—had been completed in DC MS. 71, Wordsworth was able to turn to Book IV and write into DC MS. 69 the opening block of work that connected it to Book III. He must have also realized that the new Book III material had implications for the first telling of the Solitary's tale in Book II and so revisited this material and added inserted pages to the fair copy in DC MS. 71 to have Book II take into account the changes made in Book III.

The sixth and seventh stages of development concern the latter sections of the poem: Books VI, VII, VIII, and IX. Wordsworth principally worked with DC MSS. 73, 74, and 75 in composing this material; there are a few other manuscript scraps for this stage, and additional draft work—now no longer extant—probably once existed. Earlier material from *Home at Grasmere* and *The Tuft of Primroses* was also incorporated into *The Excursion* at this point. These two stages of composition reached completion with the writing of the conclusion of Book IX (and of the poem) into DC MS. 73.

There was still more work to be done, however. Wordsworth now had to turn back to Book V and make decisions about which material should be kept for the final poem. At this point—or possibly earlier (before writing Book IX)—he decided to remove *The Shepherd of Bield Crag* and *The Peasant's Life* from the poem. A fair copy version of Book V without *The Shepherd of Bield Crag* or *The Peasant's Life* was therefore copied into DC MS. 74A, and a discrete version of the now-excluded *Peasant's Life* was also written into DC MS. 80. The only section of the poem still unfinished was the first half of Book VI—which had been waiting for decisions to be made about Book V and could now be written up. Material for this first half of Book VI appears in DC MS. 73 along with the concluding sections of Book IX.

The final form of the poem now existed across a range of materials, but much of the text was in a fairly rough and discontinuous state (particularly for Books IV, VI, and VII). The manuscripts as they now survive are certainly not complete or comprehensive enough to have been used to set type; for some passages, no manuscript material whatsoever exists. The Wordsworths must thus at this point have copied some, if not all, of *The Excursion* into a series of notebooks in order to create a final fair copy text for the printer. Because this printer's manuscript of *The Excursion* is not extant, this edition takes as its reading text the first edition published by early August 1814.[18]

V

Five hundred copies of *The Excursion* were produced in an expensive quarto edition, with the result that it sold slowly, causing Dorothy much anxiety:

> It is the great price of the work that keeps it on hand there is no doubt: for many who cannot spare 2 guineas are waiting—and unfortunately the fashionable will not buy till Wm becomes one of their fraternity. . . . Alas alas—but this I care not for,—I only want the Edition to be sold. (*MY,* II, 222)

The second edition of 1820, a smaller and cheaper octavo edition, contained only minor revisions. The *Excursion* volume in most of the multivolume British collected editions published between 1827 and the poet's death in 1850 could also be purchased separately, and the poem appeared in the final position—emphasizing the poem's importance to its author—in the one-volume collected editions of 1845, 1847, and 1849.[19] Minor changes were made to the poem upon each republication, but two editions in particular are worth more detailed attention in terms of Wordsworth's revisions: the 1827 edition (when the poem was first incorporated into *Poetical Works*) and the 1845 single-volume edition.

In his letters Wordsworth makes it clear that he has taken some trouble over the 1827 changes. He tells Henry Crabb Robinson in January 1827 that "I have revised the poems carefully particularly the Excursion—and I trust with considerable improvement" (*LY,* I, 511). Writing to Alexander Dyce in April 1830, he describes *The Excursion* as being "diligently revized" (*LY,* II, 235) and in a later letter advises him, "When you read the Excursion do not read the Quarto—it is improved in the 8vo Ed" (*LY,* II, 373).[20] These revisions mainly concerned the removal of material, sometimes passages of some length. In Book I, for example, Wordsworth excised some lines describing the Wanderer's childhood (I, 115–127), a revision that seems likely to have been a direct response to Coleridge's criticism of them in *Biographia Literaria.* In that work, under the heading "Defects of Wordsworth's Poetry," Coleridge had referred to these lines as an example of Wordsworth's excessive attention to "minute matters of fact" (*STCBL,* II, 134).

---

[18]There is some uncertainty over the exact date of the poem's publication. WW dated the introductory sonnet "29th July," but this date is possibly an error for "29th June"; another possibility is that WW may have instructed Longman to append the date on which the poem was published (see *Chronology: MY,* p. 554). The poem was certainly printed by August 4 when Longman sent copies of it to the author (see *Chronology: MY,* p. 562; Owen, pp. 25–34). Advertisements in the *Monthly Literary Advertiser* and *The Times* occur on August 10.

[19]For details of the poem's British publishing history, see pp. 23–24, below.

[20]This remark can be presumed to refer to the 1827 octavo edition rather than the 1820 one. In the previous letter to Dyce, WW had referred explicitly to the "edition of 27" (*LY,* II, 235).

Most of the other major changes in the 1827 edition occur toward the end of Book VI in lines originally written for *Home at Grasmere* and *The Tuft of Primroses*, revisions that perhaps suggest some dissatisfaction with the integration of passages not written explicitly for *The Excursion*. The most extensive removal is that of the final narrative in Book VI, of the widower who remarries. One editor of the poem, Nowell Charles Smith, suggests that this change was due to Wordsworth's increasing distaste for second marriages, reminding us that material removed from Book I also includes a description of the Wanderer's mother taking a "second Mate."[21] On the other hand, the reason for cutting some of Book VI could simply be one of structural balance; Book VI is the second longest one in the poem, and its stories perhaps do become repetitive. Wordsworth also shortened the tale of Wilfred Armathwaite in Book VI (removing ll. 1106–1133) and reduced material for the narrative of the "Patriarch of the Vale" in Book VII (removing ll. 243–260).

For this 1827 edition Wordsworth also altered one of his end-of-volume "Notes," the one that originally referred to the positive representation of the wandering life as given in Robert Heron's *Observations Made in a Journey Through the Western Counties of Scotland* (1793). In the 1814 and 1820 editions, Wordsworth had paraphrased the relevant sections of Heron's text, but in the 1827 edition he quoted from Heron at some length. That expanded note was preceded by Wordsworth's indirect response to the negative critical reception of *The Excursion* (and of the Pedlar/Wanderer as its spokesperson) in terms of class: "At the risk of giving a shock to the prejudices of artificial society, I have ever been ready to pay homage to the Aristocracy of Nature; under a conviction that vigorous human-heartedness is the constituent principle of true taste" (*PW*, 1827, V, 393). In this edition also the "Summary of Arguments" for each book, previously printed with all the others at the start of the poem, was now placed to precede the book to which it referred, and this change to the layout was then followed in all subsequent editions.

Wordsworth's last significant attempt to revise his poetry occurred with the 1845 single volume edition of *Poetical Works* published partly as a response to his appointment as Poet Laureate. In this same year as his appointment (1843), and in preparation for revision, Wordsworth dictated notes to his friend Isabella Fenwick as he looked over the 1841 edition of *Poetical Works* and the one-volume 1842 collection *Poems, Chiefly of Early and Late Years*. In these Fenwick Notes, Wordsworth discusses the sources and origins of many of his poems in some detail. The notes were used by Christopher Wordsworth in his *Memoirs of William Wordsworth* (1851) and then as headnotes to poems in the collected edition of 1857; they were published in their entirety in Alexander Grosart's edition of Wordsworth's *Prose* (1876).[22]

---

[21] See *Exc*, I, 120, and *PW*Smith, III, 561. According to Smith, "Wordsworth, whether from his own thoughts or from external influences, came to regard second marriages with disfavour." However, there does not appear to be any firm evidence for this position as early as 1827. WW's unhappiness over Dora's marrying the widower Edward Quillinan (on a number of grounds as well as that of second marriages) occurs from 1838 onward.

[22] For a fuller account see Jared Curtis, *The Fenwick Notes of William Wordsworth* (Bristol, 1993). The Fenwick Notes relevant to *Exc* are reproduced in Appendix III, below.

The 1845 volume was intended to be a relatively cheap edition, as is shown by its double-column format.[23] The letters attest to Wordsworth's efforts for this volume and to what Mary Wordsworth calls his "too long-continued labour in the attempt to correct what he deems to be faults (*chiefly in the versification*) of the Excursion" (*LY*, IV, 542). The significance of these changes largely relates to the expression of religious belief in Wordsworth's poetry. Without doubt, the 1845 revisions show Wordsworth attempting to add explicit Christian expression to the poem at key points within it. By the 1840s Wordsworth (now in his seventies) had become a much more devout Christian and was more willing to be viewed, in part at least, as a "Christian" poet.[24] Although there were local and personal influences informing these changes to the poem (especially in the persons of Isabella Fenwick and Frederick William Faber), Wordsworth may also have been responding to John Wilson's article "On Sacred Poetry," originally published in *Blackwood's Edinburgh Magazine* in December 1828.[25] Wordsworth had commented very negatively upon this article in 1829 when, in an exchange with Henry Crabb Robinson about Wilson, he dismissed "what passes with him for poetical Christianity—more mawkish stuff I never encountered" (*LY*, II, 17). Despite this statement, however, Wordsworth's revisions for the 1845 edition do strongly suggest a response to Wilson's essay, which had been recently republished in *The Recreations of Christopher North* (1842).

In his article, Wilson turned to *The Excursion* as a poem that ought to have alluded directly to revealed religion but failed to do so. Two points in particular seem to bear upon the nature of Wordsworth's revisions. The first of these is Wilson's general comment:

> The hopes that lie beyond the grave—and the many holy and awful feelings in which on earth these hopes are enshrined and fed, are rarely if ever part of the character of any of the persons—male or female—old or young—that are brought before us in his beautiful Pastorals. (Wilson, p. 925)

The main criticism here—the need for a human and individualized expression of Christianity—is possibly felt within *The Excursion* in changes made by Wordsworth that allow minor characters to exhibit some reliance on Christianity. So, for example, in Book V the old woman of the Solitary Couple now declares at the end of her speech to the Wanderer:

> "But, above all, my thoughts are my support,
> My comfort:—would that they were oftener fixed
> On what, for guidance in the way that leads
> To heaven, I know, by my Redeemer taught."
> (*PW*, V, 179: *Exc*, V, 823–826)

---

[23]WW had originally intended this layout for *Exc* in the 1841 volume and discusses the idea in the letters with the hope that "it may circulate as cheaply as can be afforded" (*LY*, IV, 153).

[24]See Stephen Gill, *William Wordsworth: A Life* (Oxford, 1989), pp. 415–419. Gill points out that WW had become "devout enough to have a cedar cross nailed above his bedroom window in 1842, so that his eye could rest on it as soon as he awoke" (p. 417); see also Appendix IV, below.

[25]*PW*, V, 415, suggests this connection in a note to *Exc*, I, 934–955.

In this revision Wordsworth inserts a direct expression of faith from the mouth of a minor character (more commonly such assertions of belief are stated indirectly by either the Wanderer or the Pastor).

Wilson's second key point concerned the question of Margaret's belief:

> Was Margaret a Christian?—Let the answer be yes. . . . If she was,—then the picture painted of her and her agonies, is a libel not only on her character, but on the character of all other poor Christian women in this Christian land. (Wilson, p. 927)

Again, it seems likely that the lines that Wordsworth added to the end of Book I in the 1845 revisions are a response to Wilson's criticism here and to his assertion that "her soul surely must have turned sometimes—aye, often, and often, and often, . . . towards her Lord and Saviour" (p. 927). Wordsworth depicts Margaret in just such a way in the lines he adds at the end of Book I, replacing the early pantheism of *The Ruined Cottage* by direct Christian consolation:

> Nor more would she have craved as due to One
> Who, in her worst distress, had ofttimes felt
> The unbounded might of prayer; and learned, with soul
> Fixed on the Cross, that consolation springs,
> From sources deeper far than deepest pain,
> For the meek Sufferer. Why then should we read
> The forms of things with an unworthy eye?
> (*PW*, V, 39: *Exc*, I, 934–940)

Other changes made throughout the poem are largely concerned with placing explicit emphasis upon man's hope of immortality.[26] So, for example, the Wanderer's speech in Book IX, which values human Reason and Imagination, now also praises

> immortality conceived
> By all,—a blissful immortality,
> To them whose holiness on earth shall make
> The Spirit capable of heaven, assured.
> (*PW*, V, 293: *Exc*, IX, 225–228)

Such changes accorded well with Victorian tastes and with the desire to respond to spiritual elements in Wordsworth's poetry in orthodox Christian terms. Those revisions, however, have done the poem few favors in more recent times.

Before concluding this summary of the lifetime editions of the poem, it is worth noting that the 1836–37 edition contains an interesting detail concerning Wordsworth's poetic ambitions. In this volume for the first time the title page reads simply "*The Excursion*" without reference to it as "Being A Portion of *The Recluse*," the wording of all previous editions. This alteration strongly suggests that by this

---

[26]These changes are all referred to in the Editors' Notes to the Reading Text, below.

date Wordsworth had given up on his ambition to complete *The Recluse.* Negative reception of the poem by the critics, as well as by Coleridge, may have contributed to this decision, although no clear statement that he is abandoning the project is ever explicitly made by Wordsworth. In February 1815, completing the poem had still seemed a distinct possibility to William—and to Dorothy, who wrote, "as he intends completely to plan the first part of the Recluse before he begins the composition, he must read many Books before he will fairly set to labour again" (*MY,* II, 200). This comment, however, was made before Wordsworth received the letter of criticism from Coleridge, and a long silence about *The Recluse* follows that letter. The next mention of intended work upon the project does not occur until fourteen years later, in November 1829, when Dorothy states, "He does intend to fall to the 'Recluse' being seriously impressed with the faith that very soon it must be too late" (*LY,* II, 169). Finally, in January 1830, we are told that "he shrinks from his great work" (*LY,* II, 191).[27]

Even though *The Excursion* in its entirety continued to be published within Wordsworth's *Poetical Works* (and in some separate editions) during the second half of the nineteenth century, there was a clear shift toward publishing parts of the poem separately. The first of these smaller volumes, published in 1859, is an elaborate and beautifully illustrated edition of Books I and II published together under the title *The Deserted Cottage.*[28] The preface to this book makes it explicit that it is a direct response to Coleridge's expressed wish that the "two first books of the Excursion should have been published alone under the name of the 'Deserted Cottage,' and they would have formed, what indeed they are, one of the most beautiful poems of the language."[29] However, this luxury edition did not set a trend and was rapidly replaced by more functional paper-covered school pamphlets costing two or three pence that reflected the increasing educational value placed upon Wordsworth's poetry. Book I was by far the most frequent text of choice, with occasional publications of Book III and Book IX.[30]

The falling away of interest in these separate book publications toward the end of the nineteenth century is almost certainly related to the increasing popularity of *The Prelude,* which has dominated study of Wordsworth's longer poetry ever

---

[27]Elsewhere in the letters there is discussion of *The Recluse* but only in terms of WW's inability to proceed with it (see *LY,* I, 50, 126, 292, 500, 582). Fuller details on late references to *The Recluse* by Dora, as well as in the diaries of Benjamin Robert Haydon and Henry Crabb Robinson, are given in *H at G* (pp. 26, 28, 30–31). George Ticknor records a conversation with WW about his not finishing *The Recluse*: "On my asking him why he does not finish it, he turned to me very decidedly, and said, 'Why did not Gray finish the long poem he began on a similar subject? Because he found he had undertaken something beyond his powers to accomplish. And that is my case'" (*The Life, Letters, and Journals of George Ticknor* [2 vols.; Boston, 1876], II, 167).

[28]Described on the title page as "Illustrated with Twenty-one Designs by Birket Foster, J. Wolf, and John Gilbert, engraved by the Brothers Dalziel" (London and New York, 1859) and published the same year as *Passages from 'The Excursion,'* described on its title page as "Illustrated with Etchings on Steel by Agnes Fraser" (London, 1859).

[29]Samuel Taylor Coleridge, *Table Talk,* ed. Carl Woodring (2 vols.; London and Princeton, 1990), I, 306.

[30]The educational nature of these publications can be seen from titles such as: *The Wanderer: Edited with Notes to Aid in Grammatical Analysis and In Paraphrasing* by H. O. Robinson (London, 1863) and *The Wanderer With Life, Introduction, and Notes* by H. H. Turner (London, 1874) for English School Classics. The latter was clearly a popular text since it was reprinted a number of times.

since. *The Excursion*, however, has had its recent champions, even if their rhetoric of praise has not reached the pitch of John Keats and Charles Kingsley (with whom this Introduction began) or of Charles Lamb, who joyfully declared that the work was "the noblest conversational poem I ever read. A day in heaven."[31]

[31] *CLL*, III, 95. For some of those champions, see Bushell; William H. Galperin, *Revision and Authority in Wordsworth* (Philadelphia, 1989); Hickey; Hill, *Ariel*; Hill, *Proceedings*; Russell Noyes, "Why Read *The Excursion*?" *The Wordsworth Circle* 4 (1973): 139–151; and the *Exc* special issue of *The Wordsworth Circle* 9, no. 2 (Spring 1978). For an account of criticism before 1991, see Dan Kenneth Crosby, "Wordsworth's *Excursion*: An Annotated Bibliography of Criticism," *Bulletin of Bibliography* 48 (1991): 33–49.

Editorial Procedure

The aim of this edition is to present, in conjunction with other volumes in this series, a complete historical record of *The Excursion.* The primary reading text is that of the corrected second issue of the first edition of 1814. The edition also presents complete transcriptions of all *Excursion* manuscripts written between c. 1806 (when Wordsworth may have begun work on what became Book II) and the poem's publication in 1814. Cross-references direct the reader to other volumes in this series that have material that bears on the historical development of the poem, most notably *Home at Grasmere, The Ruined Cottage and the Pedlar, Shorter Poems, 1807–1820, The Thirteen-Book Prelude,* and *The Tuft of Primroses with Other Late Poems for "The Recluse."* For example, manuscripts related to the *Prospectus* to *The Recluse,* quoted by Wordsworth in his "Preface" to *The Excursion,* have already been provided in the Cornell edition of *Home at Grasmere*; and those for *The Ruined Cottage* and *The Pedlar,* which later formed the basis of Book I of *The Excursion,* have been provided in the Cornell edition. Inevitably, however, repetition is occasionally required in order to show the development of *The Excursion* as a poem in its own right.

Three subsidiary reading texts are included and discussed in Appendix II: "As when, upon the smooth pacific deep," *The Peasant's Life,* and *The Shepherd of Bield Crag.* Other subsidiary texts are embedded in the manuscript transcriptions: the early text of Books I–III, c. 330, *Characteristics of a Child three Years old, Maternal Grief,* and a version of *The Peasant's Life* longer than that of the reading text in Appendix II. These embedded texts are numbered in italic type in the right margins, supplemented by roman-type line references (at the top of the transcriptions or in the left-hand margins) to the 1814 reading text of *The Excursion.* The early text of Books I–III, c. 330, is found in DC MSS. 47, 69, 70, and 71, and the italic numbering there enables the reader to follow this early version as it appeared before Wordsworth revised and rewrote substantial portions of Books II and III after the deaths of two of his children in 1812.

Manuscripts of *The Excursion* are listed and described in the Manuscripts Census at the beginning of this volume. Fuller discussion of the role of each manuscript in the process of composition appears in The Manuscript History of *The Excursion,* which precedes the transcriptions. A Key to Manuscript Transcriptions, provided in Appendix I, allows the reader to find all manuscript passages that contribute to a specific passage in the published *Excursion*.

Historical collations of verbal and nonverbal variants report textual changes found in lifetime editions and in post-1814 authorially influenced manuscripts, including printed copies of the poems annotated in processes of revision (MS. 1814/27, MS. 1827/32C, MS. 1832/36, MS. 1836/45). Verbal variants are reported beneath the reading text. Nonverbal variants, with the exception of those embedded in verbal variants, are normally reported separately in a list following the reading text. These variants include changes in punctuation, spelling, capitalization, and paragraphing. We have not usually reported changes in layout, running heads, page numbers in contents and notes, and the styling of book numbers (e.g., Book the First, Book First, Book I).

In the reports of variants in lifetime printings, the following short forms of citation are used. Short-form entries in the first column indicate editions in the main series of collected works—which from 1827 included *The Excursion*—while those in the second indicate selections or individual works:

	Friend	S. T. Coleridge, *The Friend: A Literary, Moral, and Political Weekly Paper* (Penrith, 1809–1810). Passages from *The Excursion* first published here: Book I, lines 531b–533a, in issue no. 21 of January 15, 1810 (see *STCF*, II, 292); Book I, lines 657–666a, in issue no. 13 of November 16, 1809 (see *STCF*, II, 172).
	1814	*The Excursion, Being a Portion of The Recluse, A Poem* (London, 1814).
	1820E	*The Excursion, Being a Portion of The Recluse, A Poem* (London, 1820).
1827		*The Poetical Works of William Wordsworth* (5 vols.; London, 1827).
	1827E	*The Excursion, Being a Portion of The Recluse, A Poem* (London, 1827). From the same setting as volume 5 of *1827*.
	1831	*Selections from the Poems of William Wordsworth, Esq.*, ed. Joseph Hine (London, 1831). Passages from *The Excursion*: all of Book I; Book IV, lines 1055–1279a; Book VI, lines 794–1100a; Book VII, lines 913–1079.
1832		*The Poetical Works of William Wordsworth* (4 vols.; London, 1832).
	1832E	*The Excursion, Being a Portion of The Recluse, A Poem* (London, 1832). From the same setting as volume 4 of *1832*.
	1834	*Selections from the Poems of William Wordsworth*, Esq., ed. Joseph Hine (London, 1834). Second edition, entirely reset, of *1831*; *Excursion* selections are the same as in the first edition.
	Guide 1835	*A Guide through the District of the Lakes* (Kendal and London, 1835). Reprints *Excursion*, II, 347b–368.
	1836E	*The Excursion; A Poem* (London, 1836). From the same printing as volume 6 of *1836*.
1836		*The Poetical Works of William Wordsworth* (6 vols.; London, 1836–1837). Volume 6 (*The Excursion*) from the same printing as *1836E* but with title page dated 1837. Reissued from stereotype, with various alterations, 1840, 1841, 1843, 1846, and 1849.

1840 — *The Poetical Works of William Wordsworth* (6 vols.; London, 1840). The revised stereotype reissue of *1836*.

1841 — The revised stereotype reissue of *1840*.

1841E — *The Excursion. A Poem* (London, 1841). From the same stereotype printing as volume 6 of *1841*.

Guide 1842 — *A Complete Guide to the Lakes . . . with Mr. Wordsworth's Description of the Scenery of the Country* (Kendal and London, 1842). Reprints same *Excursion* passage as *Guide 1835*.

Guide 1843 — *A Complete Guide to the Lakes . . . with Mr. Wordsworth's Description of the Scenery of the Country*, 2d ed. (Kendal, 1843). Reprints same *Excursion* passage as *Guide 1835*.

1843 — The revised stereotype reissue of *1841*.

1844E — *The Excursion. A Poem* (London, 1844). Stereotype reissue of volume 6 of *1843*.

1845 — *The Poems of William Wordsworth* (London, 1845). Reissued in stereotype, with a few alterations, 1847 and 1849.

1846 — *The Poetical Works of William Wordsworth* (7 vols.; London, 1846). Another stereotype reissue of the six volumes of *1836*, incorporating further alterations, with an additional volume incorporating *Poems, Chiefly of Early and Late Years*, 1842; reissued, again with a few alterations, 1849.

Guide 1846 — *A Complete Guide to the Lakes . . . with Mr. Wordsworth's Description of the Scenery of the Country*, 3d ed. (Kendal and London, 1846). Reprints same *Excursion* passage as *Guide 1835*.

1847 — The revised stereotype reissue of *1845*.

1847E — *The Excursion. A Poem* (London, 1847). Stereotype reissue of volume 7 of *1846*.

1849 — The revised stereotype reissue of *1846*.

1849P — The revised stereotype reissue of *1847*.

1850 — *The Poetical Works of William Wordsworth* (6 vols.; London, 1849–1850).

For the reprinting of seven passages from *The Excursion* in "Contributions of Wm. Wordsworth to the Revival of Catholic Truths" in *The Christian's Miscellany* (October 1842), see Appendix IV, below.

In the *apparatus criticus*, a citation of the following volumes in the list above implies successive texts, unless otherwise noted, as follows:

1827 implies *1827E, 1831, 1834*
1831 implies *1834*
1832 implies *1832E, Guide 1835*
Guide 1835 implies *Guide 1842, Guide 1843, Guide 1846*
Guide 1842 implies *Guide 1843, Guide 1846*

A citation of any of the stereotype editions implies related edition(s), unless otherwise noted, as follows:

1836 implies *1836E*
1840 implies *1841, 1841E*
1841 implies *1841E, 1843, 1844E*
1843 implies *1844E*

1845 implies *1847, 1849P*
1846 implies *1847E, 1849*
1847 implies *1849P*

In the reports of verbal and nonverbal manuscript variants in the four printed copies of the poems annotated in processes of revision (MS. 1814/27, MS. 1827/32C, MS. 1832/36, MS. 1836/45), alterations are assumed to be the author's, in his own hand or made at his direction. All entries may be assumed to be in ink unless the use of pencil is specified. In reporting manuscript variants in printed texts, boldface type is used to represent the printed text. These annotated copies are described in the Manuscript Census, above; additional information about the reporting of variants in them is provided below:

MS. 1814/27 (at Queen's College, Oxford) appears to be the author's proof copy of the 1814 volume, and its printed text in a few particulars is unique. MS. 1814/27 was used in at least three separate stages of correction and revision. First, it was used for correction and revision for the first edition (see Book IV, lines 481–482, 505–507, 508 [nonverbals], 538–539). Second, it was used for revision toward the second edition (1820) of *The Excursion*. Most of these revisions toward 1820 are nonverbal and entered in pencil by an unidentified hand. The verbal revisions from this second period of use are in the hand of Wordsworth and Mary, often in pencil or Mary Wordsworth's ink over Wordsworth's pencil. Manuscript revisions in MS. 1814/27 that are adopted in the *Excursion* edition of 1820 specify that edition: *MS. 1814/27, 1820E–*. If the revision is adopted solely in the edition of 1820, it is cited as *MS. 1814/27, 1820E.* Third, MS. 1814/27 was extensively used for or toward revisions that are adopted in the collected edition of 1827. When handwritten entries are adopted in all editions following 1827, revisions are cited as *MS. 1814/27–*; inclusion just in the edition of 1827 is cited as *MS. 1814/27, 1827.*

MS. 1827/32C (at Cornell University) appears to have been used for revisions and corrections toward the 1832 edition. Because few of these revisions were subsequently included in later editions, most of the variants are listed simply as *MS. 1827/32C.* If the variant does continue into the collected edition of 1832, it is cited as *MS. 1827/32C, 1832*; continuation beyond the edition of 1832 is cited as *MS. 1827/32C–*.

MS. 1832/36 (at Wellesley College) was used for revisions and corrections toward the 1836 edition, probably in 1836, and was also used as printer's copy. Revisions are primarily in the hands of Wordsworth, Mary, and Dora, in both ink and pencil. When a handwritten revision is adopted only in the edition of 1836, the citation will appear as *MS. 1832/36, 1836*; if it is also included in editions following that of 1836, it is cited as *MS. 1832/36–*.

MS. 1836/45 (at The Royal Library, Windsor Castle) contains revisions that are often more complex, more extensive, and richer than any of the other printed texts used for manuscript revision. Revisions are primarily in the hands of Wordsworth, Mary, Dora, and Wordsworth's secretary, John Carter. MS. 1836/45 was used for at least two different stages of correction and revision toward the collective editions of 1840 and 1845. The majority of the revisions toward the edition of 1840 are nonverbal variants, essentially corrections of the 1836 edition, and in the hand of Wordsworth's secretary, John Carter; the revisions toward the text of 1845 are more substantive. When a manuscript revision is adopted, the edition is always cited; e.g., *MS. 1836/45, 1840–* or *MS. 1836/45, 1845–*.

In this volume's full transcriptions of all pre-publication *Excursion* manuscripts over which Wordsworth exercised some control, the aim is to show with reasonable typographic accuracy everything in the manuscript that can be helpful to a study of the poem's development. Even false starts and corrected letters can sometimes indicate the writer's intentions, and they are recorded; simple reinforcement of letters, however, is not. Punctuation and underlining in all manuscripts are treated (both in transcriptions and in the *apparatus*) as original or "base text" punctuation except in obvious cases of addition, particularly where different punctuation marks are clearly distinguishable, or where one mark has clearly been converted to another, or where punctuation has been added together with verbal revision. Passages in Wordsworth's hand are in roman type, those in other hands in italic, though identification of hands must sometimes be conjectural, especially for scattered words or parts of words. Doubled-back lines are shown approximately as they appear in the manuscript. Revisions appear in reduced type—single words or parts of lines positioned as nearly as possible as they appear in the manuscript, entire lines of revision emphasized by indentation. Material written over erasure and enclosed by a screen is not, however, reduced, since the screen itself signals a revision. Words of irrelevant material on the same page as the poem being reproduced are omitted but noted. Unless otherwise noted, the numbering of leaves counts stubs but not pasted-down endpapers; numbers assigned to stubs and leaves thus include both in the consecutive count (i.e., stub 35, leaf 36, stub 37). Editorial line numbers in the left-hand margins or at the top of the transcriptions are keyed to the 1814 reading text of *The Excursion*; italic line numbering in the right-hand margins of transcriptions is used for numbering subsidiary and embedded texts. Line numbers in square brackets indicate successive states of line revision. Selected photographs, bundled together after all of the transcriptions, are provided for manuscript leaves of particular interest or complexity. To avoid unnecessary elaboration in the Introduction, The Manuscript History of *The Excursion*, the *apparatus*, and the notes, quotations from transcriptions normally appear in roman type.

The following abbreviations are used in the transcription notes and in the *apparatus criticus*:

alt	Alternate reading; original not deleted.
apos	Apostrophe.
cap, caps	Capital, capitals.
corr	Corrected; corrected to.
del	Reading deleted; deletion.
eras	Erased, erasure.
exclam	Exclamation point.
illeg	Illegible.

ital	Italics.
MS., MSS.	Manuscript, manuscripts. Followed by a number (not a date or number-letter combination), a shortened reference to a Dove Cottage manuscript or manuscripts.
om	Reading omitted; omission.
orig	First reading, originally.
para	Indentation, usually beginning a prose or verse paragraph; or a marking indicating indentation.
paren, parens	Parenthesis, parentheses.
punct	Punctuation (excluding apostrophes and hyphens).
quot, quots	Quotation mark, quotation marks.
rev	Revised; revision; revise; revised by (with initials). (The original may be canceled in any of various ways, including deletion, erasure, overwriting, or blotting, but will be given if legible.)

The following symbols are used in transcriptions and the *apparatus criticus*; the first two also appear in reading texts:

[ ]	Blank, defacement, tear, or trimmed-off word in the manuscript.
[?last]	Conjectural reading, or missing word supplied editorially in a reading text.
[?love/?live]	Alternate readings seem equally possible.
[? ?]	Illegible words; each question mark represents one word.
[~~? ?~~]	Deleted and illegible word or words.
$\text{ha}\left\{\begin{matrix}\text{d}\\ \text{ve}\end{matrix}\right.$	An overwriting: original reading, "have," converted to "had" by the writing of "d" on top of "ve."
s}	A short addition, sometimes only a mark of punctuation.
that more	Words written over a totally illegible erasure.
$\left\{\begin{matrix}\text{that more}\\ \text{wh wa}\end{matrix}\right.$	Words written over a legible or partly legible erasure.

The Excursion

Reading Text of 1814 Edition

Establishing the Text of *The Excursion*, 1814
Reading Text, with Historical Collations of Verbal Variants
Historical Collations of Nonverbal Variants
Editors' Notes

Establishing the Text of *The Excursion*, 1814

The reading text here presented is that of the corrected second issue of *The Excursion* as first published, with profound effect on later Romantic poets and literary history, in 1814.[1] It includes all of Wordsworth's prefatory matter and notes. Editorial line numbering is added in the right margins of the text and notes and, in square brackets, in the left margins of the text. Left-margin numbers key lines to corresponding lines of the 1850 text, the last authorized lifetime edition of *The Excursion*, and enable easy comparison with the text as edited by Ernest de Selincourt and Helen Darbishire (see *PW*, V).

The *apparatus* below the reading text records verbal variants in authorized lifetime editions and post-1814 authorially influenced manuscripts. Nonverbal variants other than those embedded in verbal variants are normally recorded separately following the reading text. Short forms of citation of lifetime printings provided in reports of variants are listed in the Editorial Procedure, where may also be found detailed discussion of methods of presentation of pre-publication manuscripts.

All readings on the errata sheet in the 1814 volume have been incorporated into the reading text. Those changes appear at II, 904; III, 192, 193, 382; IV, 186, 330, 1207; V, 308, 316, 357; VI, 407; and VII, 800. A very few editorial emendations have been made of errors accidental or typographical, such as misspellings, omitted apostrophes or quotation marks, and missing terminal punctuation (see I, 923; II, 389; VI, 279, 999; VIII, 6; Note to V, 984: *Essay on Epitaphs*, l. 271). The heading to Book I (originally "BOOK FIRST") has been emended to "BOOK THE FIRST" to make it consistent with the style the publisher used for the following eight books, and—also for consistency—an announcement of the "END OF THE SEVENTH BOOK" has been editorially added. The hyphen in "CHURCH-YARD" in the heading to Book VII has been editorially supplied to make the reading consistent with the heading of Book VI and with all other occurrences of the word in *The Excursion* (1814).

For the convenience of the reader, the accounts of variants related to the printing of the 1814 edition have been included in the *apparatus* below the reading text, whether the variants are verbal or nonverbal.

[1] For further information about the corrected second issue, see the entry for MS. 1814/27 in the Manuscript Census, p. xxviii, and the account in Healey, p. 13.

Reading Text, with Historical Collations of Verbal Variants

THE EXCURSION;

BEING A PORTION OF

THE RECLUSE,

A POEM.

BY

WILLIAM WORDSWORTH.

title THE EXCURSION; . . . POEM.] THE EXCURSION, BEING A PORTION OF THE RECLUSE. *1827 (but 1827E as 1814), 1832* THE EXCURSION. *1836– but* THE EXCURSION; A Poem. *1836E and* THE EXCURSION. A Poem *1841E, 1844E, 1847E*

TO
THE RIGHT HONORABLE
WILLIAM, EARL OF LONSDALE, K. G. &C. &C.

OFT, through thy fair domains, illustrious Peer!
In youth I roamed, on youthful pleasures bent;
And mused in rocky cell or sylvan tent,
Beside swift-flowing Lowther's current clear.
—Now by thy care befriended, I appear
Before thee, LONSDALE, and this Work present,
A token (may it prove a monument!)
Of high respect and gratitude sincere.
Gladly would I have waited till my task
Had reached its close; but Life is insecure,
And Hope full oft fallacious as a dream:
Therefore, for what is here produced I ask
Thy favour; trusting that thou wilt not deem
The Offering, though imperfect, premature.

WILLIAM WORDSWORTH.

Rydal Mount, Westmorland,
July 29, 1814.

PREFACE.

THE Title-page announces that this is only a Portion of a Poem; and the Reader must be here apprized that it belongs to the second part of a long and laborious Work, which is to consist of three parts.—The Author will candidly acknowledge that, if the first of these had been completed, and in such a manner as to satisfy his own mind, he should have preferred the natural order of publication, and have given that to the World first; but, as the second division of the Work was designed to refer more to passing events, and to an existing state of things, than the others were meant to do, more continuous exertion was naturally bestowed upon it, and greater progress made here than in the rest of the Poem; and as this part does not depend upon the preceding, to a degree which will materially injure its own peculiar interest, the Author, complying with the earnest entreaties of some valued Friends, presents the following Pages to the Public.

It may be proper to state whence the Poem, of which The Excursion is a part, derives its Title of THE RECLUSE.—Several years ago, when the Author retired to his native Mountains, with the hope of being enabled to construct a literary Work that might live, it was a reasonable thing that he should take a review of his own Mind, and examine how far Nature and Education had qualified him for such employment. As subsidiary to this preparation, he undertook to record, in Verse, the origin and progress of his own powers, as far as he was acquainted with them. That Work, addressed to a dear Friend, most distinguished for his knowledge and genius, and to whom the Author's Intellect is deeply indebted, has been long finished; and the result of the investigation which gave rise to it was a determination to compose a philosophical Poem, containing views of Man, Nature, and Society; and to be entitled, The Recluse; as having for its principal subject the sensations and opinions of a Poet living in retirement.—The preparatory Poem is biographical, and conducts the history of the Author's mind to the point when he was emboldened to hope that his faculties were sufficiently matured for entering upon the arduous labour which he had proposed to himself; and the two Works have the same kind of relation to each other, if he may so express himself, as the Anti-chapel has to the body of a gothic Church. Continuing this allusion, he may be permitted to add, that his minor Pieces, which have been long before the Public, when they shall be properly arranged, will be found by the attentive Reader to have such connection with the main Work as may give them claim to be likened to the little Cells, Oratories, and sepulchral Recesses, ordinarily included in those Edifices.

The Author would not have deemed himself justified in saying, upon this occasion, so much of performances either unfinished, or unpublished,

title PREFACE.] PREFACE, To the Edition of 1814. *MS. 1836/45 (pencil)* PREFACE TO THE EDITION OF 1814. *1840–*

if he had not thought that the labour bestowed by him upon what he has heretofore and now laid before the Public, entitled him to candid attention for such a statement as he thinks necessary to throw light upon his endeavours to please, and he would hope, to benefit his countrymen. —Nothing further need be added, than that the first and third parts of the Recluse will consist chiefly of meditations in the Author's own Person; and that in the intermediate part (The Excursion) the intervention of Characters speaking is employed, and something of a dramatic form adopted.

It is not the Author's intention formally to announce a system: it was more animating to him to proceed in a different course; and if he shall succeed in conveying to the mind clear thoughts, lively images, and strong feelings, the Reader will have no difficulty in extracting the system for himself. And in the mean time the following passage, taken from the conclusion of the first Book of the Recluse, may be acceptable as a kind of *Prospectus* of the design and scope of the whole Poem.

"On Man, on Nature, and on Human Life
Musing in Solitude, I oft perceive
Fair trains of imagery before me rise,
Accompanied by feelings of delight
Pure, or with no unpleasing sadness mixed;
And I am conscious of affecting thoughts
And dear remembrances, whose presence soothes
Or elevates the Mind, intent to weigh
The good and evil of our mortal state.
—To these emotions, whencesoe'er they come,
Whether from breath of outward circumstance,
Or from the Soul—an impulse to herself,
I would give utterance in numerous Verse.
—Of Truth, of Grandeur, Beauty, Love, and Hope—
And melancholy Fear subdued by Faith;
Of blessed consolations in distress;
Of moral strength, and intellectual power;
Of joy in widest commonalty spread;
Of the individual Mind that keeps her own
Inviolate retirement, subject there
To Conscience only, and the law supreme
Of that Intelligence which governs all;
I sing: —"fit audience let me find though few!"

So prayed, more gaining than he asked, the Bard,
Holiest of Men.—Urania, I shall need
Thy guidance, or a greater Muse, if such
Descend to earth or dwell in highest heaven!
For I must tread on shadowy ground, must sink
Deep—and, aloft ascending, breathe in worlds

25 *Holiest of Men.—*] *In holiest mood. 1845–*

To which the heaven of heavens is but a veil.
All strength—all terror, single or in bands,
That ever was put forth in personal form;
Jehovah—with his thunder, and the choir
Of shouting Angels, and the empyreal thrones,
I pass them, unalarmed. Not Chaos, not
The darkest pit of lowest Erebus,
Nor aught of blinder vacancy—scooped out
By help of dreams, can breed such fear and awe
As fall upon us often when we look
Into our Minds, into the Mind of Man,
My haunt, and the main region of my Song.
—Beauty—a living Presence of the earth,
Surpassing the most fair ideal Forms
Which craft of delicate Spirits hath composed
From earth's materials—waits upon my steps;
Pitches her tents before me as I move,
An hourly neighbour. Paradise, and groves
Elysian, Fortunate Fields—like those of old
Sought in the Atlantic Main, why should they be
A history only of departed things,
Or a mere fiction of what never was?
For the discerning intellect of Man,
When wedded to this goodly universe
In love and holy passion, shall find these
A simple produce of the common day.
—I, long before the blissful hour arrives,
Would chaunt, in lonely peace, the spousal verse
Of this great consummation:—and, by words
Which speak of nothing more than what we are,
Would I arouse the sensual from their sleep
Of Death, and win the vacant and the vain
To noble raptures; while my voice proclaims
How exquisitely the individual Mind
(And the progressive powers perhaps no less
Of the whole species) to the external World
Is fitted:—and how exquisitely, too,
Theme this but little heard of among Men,
The external World is fitted to the Mind;
And the creation (by no lower name
Can it be called) which they with blended might
Accomplish:—this is our high argument.
—Such grateful haunts foregoing, if I oft
Must turn elsewhere—to travel near the tribes
And fellowships of men, and see ill sights
Of madding passions mutually inflamed;
Must hear Humanity in fields and groves
Pipe solitary anguish; or must hang

Brooding above the fierce confederate storm
Of sorrow, barricadoed evermore
Within the walls of Cities; may these sounds
Have their authentic comment,—that, even these
Hearing, I be not downcast or forlorn!
—Come thou prophetic Spirit, that inspir'st
The human Soul of universal earth,
Dreaming on things to come; and dost possess
A metropolitan Temple in the hearts
Of mighty Poets; upon me bestow
A gift of genuine insight; that my Song
With star-like virtue in its place may shine;
Shedding benignant influence,—and secure,
Itself, from all malevolent effect
Of those mutations that extend their sway
Throughout the nether sphere!—And if with this
I mix more lowly matter; with the thing
Contemplated, describe the Mind and Man
Contemplating; and who, and what he was,
The transitory Being that beheld
This Vision,—when and where, and how he lived;—
Be not this labour useless. If such theme
May sort with highest objects, then, dread Power,
Whose gracious favour is the primal source
Of all illumination, may my Life
Express the image of a better time,
More wise desires, and simpler manners;—nurse
My Heart in genuine freedom:—all pure thoughts
Be with me;—so shall thy unfailing love
Guide, and support, and cheer me to the end!"

83 *"Come thou*] *"Descend, MS. 1814/27–1836* *'Descend, MS. 1836/45, 1840–*
95 *and*] *of 1820E, 1827*

83–84 For WW's end-of-volume note, see p. 298, below.

SUMMARY OF CONTENTS.

BOOK FIRST.

THE WANDERER.

A summer forenoon—The Author reaches a ruined Cottage upon a Common, and there meets with a revered Friend, the Wanderer, of whom he gives an account—The Wanderer while resting under the shade of the Trees that surround the Cottage relates the History of its last Inhabitant.

BOOK SECOND.

THE SOLITARY.

The Author describes his travels with the Wanderer, whose character is further illustrated—Morning scene, and view of a Village Wake—Wanderer's account of a Friend whom he purposes to visit—View, from an eminence, of the Valley which his Friend had chosen for his retreat—feelings of the Author at the sight of it—Sound of singing from below—a funeral procession—Descent into the Valley—Observations drawn from the Wanderer at sight of a Book accidentally discovered in a recess in the Valley—Meeting with the Wanderer's friend, the Solitary—Wanderer's description of the mode of burial in this mountainous district—Solitary contrasts with this, that of the Individual carried a few minutes before from the Cottage—Brief conversation—The Cottage entered—description of the Solitary's apartment—repast there—View from the Window of two mountain summits—and the Solitary's description of the Companionship they afford him—account of the departed Inmate of the Cottage—description of a grand spectacle upon the mountains, with its effect upon the Solitary's mind—Quit the House.

BOOK THIRD.

DESPONDENCY.

Images in the Valley—Another Recess in it entered and described—Wanderer's sensations—Solitary's excited by the same objects—Contrast between these—Despondency of the Solitary gently reproved—Conver-

---

3 whom] whose education and course of life *MS. 1832/36–*

---

5 feelings of the Author at the sight of it— *del MS. 1832/36, om 1836–*
11–12 Brief conversation— *del MS. 1832/36, om 1836–*
17 Quit] Leave *MS. 1832/36–*

---

no verbal changes

sation exhibiting the Solitary's past and present opinions and feelings, till he enters upon his own History at length—His domestic felicity—afflictions—dejection—roused by the French Revolution—Disappointment and disgust—Voyage to America—disappointment and disgust pursue him—his return—His languor and depression of mind, from want of faith in the great truths of Religion, and want of confidence in the virtue of Mankind.

BOOK FOURTH.

DESPONDENCY CORRECTED.

State of feeling produced by the foregoing Narrative—A belief in a superintending Providence the only adequate support under affliction—Wanderer's ejaculation to the supreme Being—Account of his own devotional feelings in youth involved in it—Implores that he may retain in age the power to find repose among enduring and eternal things—What these latter are—Acknowledges the difficulty of a lively faith—Hence immoderate sorrow—but doubt or despondence not therefore to be inferred—And proceeds to administer consolation to the Solitary—Exhortations—How these are received—Wanderer resumes—and applies his discourse to that other cause of dejection in the Solitary's mind—the disappointment of his expectations from the French Revolution—States the rational grounds of hope—and insists on the necessity of patience and fortitude with respect to the course of the great revolutions of the world—Knowledge the source of tranquility—Rural life and Solitude particularly favourable to a knowledge of the inferior Creatures—Study of their habits and ways recommended for its influence on the affections and the imagination—Exhortation to bodily exertion and an active Communion with Nature—Morbid Solitude a pitiable thing—If the elevated imagination cannot be exerted—try the humbler fancy—Superstition better than

---

1 A *del MS. 1814/27*

3 to the supreme Being *om 1827–*

3–4 Account of his own devotional feelings in youth involved in it— *om 1836–*

4 involved in it—] involved— *1827, 1832*

4–6 Implores that he may retain in age the power to find repose among enduring and eternal things—What these latter are— *om 1827– ; so MS. 1814/27 but also cancels two additional words* Acknowledges the *in l. 6 and substitutes for entire del* What he wishes for in age—

7–9 but doubt] doubt *1827, 1832* And proceeds to administer] *del MS. 1814/27, om 1827, 1832* consolation to] consolation administered to *MS. 1814/27* Consolation to *1827, 1832* *1832 reading in ll. 7–9* doubt or despondence not therefore to be inferred—Consolation to the Solitary *del MS. 1832/36, om 1836–*

9 How these are] How *1827–*

10 resumes—and *del MS. 1814/27, om 1827–*

11 the disappointment] disappointment *MS. 1814/27–* of his expectations *del MS. 1814/27, om 1827–*

12 States the rational] States *1827–* and insists] insists *1827, 1832*

14 the great] great *MS. 1814/27–* of the world *del MS. 1814/27, om 1827–*

15 life and . . . particularly *del MS. 1814/27, om 1827–* a *om 1827–*

17–18 for its influence on the affections and the imagination *om 1827–*

18 an active *om 1827–*

19 a pitiable thing—] pitiable— *MS. 1814/27– but* pitiable.— *1850*

19–20 If the elevated imagination cannot be exerted—try the humbler fancy *om 1827–*

apathy—Apathy and destitution unknown in the infancy of society—The various modes of Religion prevented it—this illustrated in the Jewish, Persian, Babylonian, Chaldean and Grecian modes of belief—Solitary interposes—Wanderer, in answer, points out the influence of religious and imaginative feeling on the mind in the humble ranks of society, in rural life especially—This illustrated from present and past times—Observation that these principles tend to recal exploded superstitions and popery—Wanderer rebuts this charge, and contrasts the dignities of the Imagination with the presumptive littleness of certain modern Philosophers, whom the Solitary appears to esteem—Recommends to him other lights and guides—Asserts the power of the Soul to regenerate herself—Solitary agitated, and asks how—Reply—Personal appeal—Happy for us that the imagination and affections in our own despite mitigate the evils of that state of intellectual Slavery which the calculating understanding is so apt to produce—Exhortation to activity of Body renewed—How Nature is to be communed with—Wanderer concludes with a prospect of a legitimate union of the imagination, the affections, the understanding, and the reason—Effect of the Wanderer's discourse—Evening—Return to the Cottage.

BOOK FIFTH.

THE PASTOR.

Farewell to the Valley—Reflections—Sight of a large and populous Vale—Solitary consents to go forward—Vale described—The Pastor's Dwelling, and some account of him—The Church-yard—Church and Monu-

---

22 this *om 1827–*
24 Wanderer, in answer,] Wanderer *1827–*
25 on the mind *om 1827–*
25–26 in rural life especially— *om 1827–*
26 This illustrated] Illustrated *1827, 1832* illustrated *1836–*
26–27 Observation that these] These *1827–*
29 presumptive] Argument 4th Book Query Presumptuous *pencil on recto of second free front endpaper MS. 1836/45* Query presumptuous? *pencil MS. 1836/45 in margin of "Argument" for Book IV* presumptuous *adopted 1845, 1850*
30 whom the Solitary appears to esteem *del MS. 1814/27, om 1827–*
31 to him *om 1827–* him] the Solitary *MS. 1814/27*
32 agitated, and *om 1827–*
33–35 Happy for us that the imagination and affections in our own despite mitigate the evils of that state of intellectual Slavery which the calculating understanding is so apt to produce—] Happy that the imagination and the affections mitigate the evils of that intellectual Slavery which the calculating understanding is apt to produce— *1827, 1832; om 1836– ; MS. 1814/27 as 1827 but* that the imagination] that imagination
36 How Nature is to be communed with—] How to commune with Nature— *1827– but* Nature.— *1850*
37 a prospect of *om 1827–*
38 the affections . . . the understanding . . . the reason] affections . . . understanding . . . reason— *1827– but* reason.— *1850*
38–39 the Wanderer's] his MS. *1814/27–*

1–2 Sight of a large and populous Vale—Solitary consents to go forward—Vale described] A large and populous Vale described *MS. 1832/36–*
3 The Church-yard— *del MS. 1832/36, om 1836–*

ments—The Solitary musing, and where—Roused—In the Church-yard the Solitary communicates the thoughts which had recently passed through his mind—Lofty tone of the Wanderer's discourse of yesterday adverted to—Rite of Baptism, and the professions accompanying it, contrasted with the real state of human life—Inconsistency of the best men—Acknowledgement that practice falls far below the injunctions of duty as existing in the mind—General complaint of a falling-off in the value of life after the time of youth—Outward appearances of content and happiness in degree illusive—Pastor approaches—Appeal made to him—His answer—Wanderer in sympathy with him—Suggestion that the least ambitious Inquirers may be most free from error—The Pastor is desired to give some Portraits of the living or dead from his own observation of life among these Mountains—and for what purpose—Pastor consents—Mountain cottage—Excellent qualities of its Inhabitants—Solitary expresses his pleasure; but denies the praise of virtue to worth of this kind—Feelings of the Priest before he enters upon his account of Persons interred in the Church-yard—Graves of unbaptized Infants—What sensations they excite—Funereal and sepulchral Observances—Whence—Ecclesiastical Establishments—Whence derived—Profession of Belief in the doctrine of Immortality.

BOOK SIXTH.

THE CHURCH-YARD AMONG THE MOUNTAINS.

Poet's Address to the State and Church of England—The Pastor not inferior to the ancient Worthies of the Church—He begins his Narratives with an Instance of unrequited love—Anguish of mind subdued—and how—The lonely Miner, an Instance of Perseverance, which leads by contrast to an Example of abused talents, irresolution, and weakness—Solitary, applying this covertly to his own case, asks for an Instance of some Stranger, whose dispositions may have led him to end his days here—Pastor, in answer, gives an account of the harmonizing influence of Solitude upon two Men of opposite principles, who had encountered agitations in public life—The Rule by which Peace may be obtained expressed—and where—Solitary hints at an overpowering Fatality—Answer of the Pastor—What subjects he will exclude from his Narratives—Conversation upon this—Instance of an unamiable Character, a Female—and why given—Contrasted with this, a meek Sufferer, from unguarded and betrayed Love—Instance of heavier guilt—and its consequences to the Offender—With this Instance of a Marriage Contract broken is contrasted one of a Widower, evidencing his faithful affection towards his deceased Wife by

8 human life—Inconsistency] human life—Apology for the Rite—Inconsistency *MS. 1832/36– but* life.— *1850*
21 What sensations they excite— *del MS. 1832/36–*, *om 1836–*

3–4 —Anguish of Mind subdued—and how *del MS. 1832/36*
14 Female] Woman *MS. 1836/45*

his care of their female Children—Second Marriage of a Widower prudential and happy.

BOOK SEVENTH.

THE CHURCH-YARD AMONG THE MOUNTAINS,
CONTINUED.

Impression of these Narratives upon the Author's mind—Pastor invited to give account of certain Graves that lie apart—Clergyman and his Family—Fortunate influence of change of situation—Activity in extreme old age—Another Clergyman, a character of resolute Virtue—Lamentations over misdirected applause—Instance of less exalted excellence in a deaf Man—Elevated character of a blind Man—Reflection upon Blindness—Interrupted by a Peasant who passes—his animal cheerfulness and careless vivacity—He occasions a digression on the fall of beautiful and interesting Trees—A female Infant's Grave—Joy at her Birth—Sorrow at her Departure—A youthful Peasant—his patriotic enthusiasm—distinguished qualities—and untimely Death—Exultation of the Wanderer, as a patriot, in this Picture—Solitary how affected—Monument of a Knight—Traditions concerning him—Peroration of Wanderer on the transitoriness of things and the revolutions of society—Hints at his own past Calling—Thanks the Pastor.

BOOK EIGHTH.

THE PARSONAGE.

Pastor's apprehensions that he might have detained his Auditors too long—Invitation to his House—Solitary disinclined to comply—rallies the Wanderer; and somewhat playfully draws a comparison between his itinerant profession and that of the Knight-errant—which leads to Wanderer's giving an account of changes in the Country from the manufacturing spirit—Favourable effects—The other side of the picture, and chiefly as it has affected the humbler classes—Wanderer asserts the hollowness of all national grandeur if unsupported by moral worth—gives Instances—Physical science unable to support itself—Lamentations over an excess of manufacturing industry among the humbler Classes of Society—Picture of a Child employed in a Cotton-mill—Ignorance and degradation of Children among the agri-

---

19–20 —Second Marriage of a Widower prudential and happy. *om 1827–*

---

11 enthusiasm— . . . and] enthusiasm and . . . his *MS. 1832/36–*
14 Wanderer] the Wanderer *1827–*

---

1 apprehensions] apology and apprehensions *MS. 1832/36–*
2 long—Invitation to his House] long with the Pastors invitation to his house *MS. 1832/36–but* long, . . . Pastor's *1836–*
3 somewhat *del MS. 1832/36–, om 1836–*
9 gives Instances— *del MS. 1832/36, om 1836–*

cultural Population reviewed—Conversation broken off by a renewed Invitation from the Pastor—Path leading to his House—Its appearance described—His Daughter—His Wife—His Son (a Boy) enters with his Companion—Their happy appearance—The Wanderer how affected by the sight of them.

BOOK NINTH.

DISCOURSE OF THE WANDERER, &c.

Wanderer asserts that an active principle pervades the Universe—Its noblest seat the human soul—How lively this principle is in Childhood—Hence the delight in old age of looking back upon childhood—The dignity, powers, and privileges of Age asserted—These not to be looked for generally but under a just government—Right of a human Creature to be exempt from being considered as a mere Instrument—Vicious inclinations are best kept under by giving good ones an opportunity to shew themselves—The condition of multitudes deplored from want of due respect to this truth on the part of their superiors in society—Former conversation recurred to, and the Wanderer's opinions set in a clearer light—Genuine principles of equality—Truth placed within reach of the humblest—Happy state of the two Boys again adverted to—Earnest wish expressed for a System of National Education established universally by Government—Glorious effects of this foretold—Wanderer breaks off—Walk to the Lake—embark—Description of scenery and amusements—Grand spectacle from the side of a hill—Address of Priest to the Supreme Being—in the Course of which he contrasts with ancient Barbarism the present appearance of the scene before him—The change ascribed to Christianity—Apostrophe to his Flock, living and dead—Gratitude to the Almighty—Return over the Lake—Parting with the Solitary—Under what circumstances.

6–8 Vicious inclinations are best kept under by giving good ones an opportunity to shew themselves— *del MS. 1832/36, om 1836–*

8–9 from want of due respect to this truth on the part of their superiors in society *del MS. 1832/36, om 1836–*

11 Genuine principles of equality— *del MS. 1832/36, om 1836–*

12 humblest—] humblest—equality *MS. 1832/36* humblest—Equality— *1836– but* humblest.—Equality.— *1850*

14–15 Wanderer breaks off— *del MS. 1832/36, om 1836–*

15 embark—Description of scenery and amusements— *del MS. 1832/36, om 1836–*

BOOK THE FIRST.

THE WANDERER.

'Twas summer, and the sun had mounted high:
Southward, the landscape indistinctly glared
Through a pale steam; but all the northern downs,
In clearest air ascending, shew'd far off
A surface dappled o'er with shadows, flung
From many a brooding cloud; far as the sight
Could reach, those many shadows lay in spots
Determined and unmoved, with steady beams
Of bright and pleasant sunshine interposed.
Pleasant to him who on the soft cool moss
Extends his careless limbs along the front
Of some huge cave, whose rocky ceiling casts
A twilight of its own, an ample shade,
Where the wren warbles; while the dreaming Man,
Half conscious of the soothing melody,
With side-long eye looks out upon the scene,
By that impending covert made more soft,
More low and distant! Other lot was mine;

BOOK THE FIRST] *emended to match styling of all other book headings in first edition* BOOK FIRST *1814*

6–7 From brooding clouds; shadows that lay in spots *MS. 1814/27–*

10 Pleasant to him] To him most pleasant *MS. 1836/45* the *del MS. 1836/45* To him most pleasant who on soft cool moss *1845–*

17–18 By power of that impending covert thrown / To finer distance. *1827–1843 (for later readings see verbal variants to I, 17–20, below); MS. 1814/27 as 1827 but* distance!

17–20 By power of that impending covert, thrown,
To finer distance. Mine was at that hour
Far other lot, yet with good hope that soon
Under a shade as grateful I should find
Rest, and be welcomed there to livelier joy. *1845– ; MS. 1836/45 has draft for ll.* [3]–[5], *above: but* Yet [*rev from* Though] with good hope, to chear the su[l]try hour / That under shade as grateful I should find / Rest and be welcom'd there to livelier joy *for other MS. 1836/45 drafts, see verbal variants to I, 18–28, below*

18–28 *MS. 1836/45 drafts:*
A toilsome lot, yet with good hope that soon
Under a shade as grateful I should find
Rest, and be welcomed there to livelier joy
A} C}
[?Wh]}cross a bare wide c}ommon I was travelling
each
Where oft ~~my~~ footsteps by the slippery turf
{as
W{ere baffled, nor could my weak ~~arm~~
arm disperse
The host of insects gathered round my face
And ever with me as I paced along,
Now with eyes turnd towards the far-distant hills
a
Now toward a grove that from the wide spread Moor
Rose up, the port to which my course was bound.
Thither I came—

[18] Yet with good hope that soon I should obtain
[19/20] As grateful resting-place, and livelier joy.
Across a bare wide Common I was toiling
With languid feet, which by the slippery ground
Were baffled; nor could my weak arm disperse
The host of insects gathering round my face,
[25] And ever with me as I paced along.

Upon that open level stood a Grove,
The wished-for Port to which my steps were bound.
Thither I came, and there—amid the gloom
Spread by a brotherhood of lofty elms—
[30] Appeared a roofless Hut; four naked walls
That stared upon each other! I looked round,
And to my wish and to my hope espied
Him whom I sought; a Man of reverend age,
But stout and hale, for travel unimpaired.
[35] There was he seen upon the Cottage bench,
Recumbent in the shade, as if asleep;
An iron-pointed staff lay at his side.

[38] Him had I marked the day before—alone
And in the middle of the public way
Stationed, as if to rest himself, with face
[40] Turned tow'rds the sun then setting, while that staff
Afforded to his Figure, as he stood,
Detained for contemplation or repose,
Graceful support; the countenance of the Man
Was hidden from my view, and he himself
[45] Unrecognized; but, stricken by the sight,
With slacken'd footsteps I advanced, and soon

---

22 feet, which] steps that *MS. 1814/27–* ground] turf *1845–*
26 That open level, till I reached a grove *MS. 1836/45* level] moorland *1845–*
27 steps were] course was *MS. 1814/27–*
33 Him whom] The Friend *MS. 1836/45, 1845–*
35 There I beheld him on the Cottage bench *pencil alt MS. 1836/45*
38–41 *MS. 1836/45 has a series of rev, the first group interlined:* marked *del to* chanced to see *over illeg eras and del in pencil to* chanced to see the *in pencil with* see *del in pencil;* stet *and bracket in pencil in left margin of ll. 38–40 indicate rejection of the interlined rev and of the two pencil drafts below:*

Him had I chanc d to see, the day before
Standing alone in the open public-way
Erect as a statue, motionless
Westwar *top of page*
Him had I chanced to mark the day before,
Alone, and stationed in the publick way;
Westward he looked as if his eyes were fixed
Upon the sun then setting while that staff *page foot*

39–40 And station'd in the public way, with face *MS. 1814/27– but* stationed *1832–*
42 Afforded to the Figure of the Man *1827– but* figure . . . man *1836–; MS. 1814/27 as 1827 but* Figure,
44 the countenance of the Man] his countenance meanwhile *MS. 1814/27–* meanwhile] as he stood *pencil MS. 1836/45, 1845–*
45 himself] remained *MS. 1814/27– but* remain'd *1827*

A glad congratulation we exchanged
At such unthought-of meeting.—For the night
We parted, nothing willingly; and now
[50] He by appointment waited for me here,
Beneath the shelter of these clustering elms.

We were tried Friends: I from my Childhood up
Had known him.—In a little Town obscure,
[53] A market-village, seated in a tract
Of mountains, where my school-day time was pass'd,
One room he owned, the fifth part of a house,
[55] A place to which he drew, from time to time,
And found a kind of home or harbour there.

He loved me; from a swarm of rosy Boys
Singled out me, as he in sport would say,
For my grave looks—too thoughtful for my years.
[60] As I grew up it was my best delight
To be his chosen Comrade. Many a time,
[62] On holidays, we wandered through the woods,
A pair of random travellers; we sate—
[63] We walked; he pleas'd me with his sweet discourse
Of things which he had seen; and often touch'd
[65] Abstrusest matter, reasonings of the mind
Turned inward; or at my request he sang
Old songs—the product of his native hills;
A skilful distribution of sweet sounds,
Feeding the soul, and eagerly imbibed
[70] As cool refreshing Water, by the care
Of the industrious husbandman, diffused
Through a parched meadow-ground, in time of drought.
Still deeper welcome found his pure discourse:
How precious when in riper days I learn'd
[75] To weigh with care his words, and to rejoice
In the plain presence of his dignity!

Oh! many are the Poets that are sown
By Nature; Men endowed with highest gifts,

---

52 Beneath the shelter] Under the covert *ink following pencil MS. 1836/45, 1845–*

53–58 We were tried Friends: amid a pleasant vale,
In the antique market village where were pass'd
My school-days, an apartment he had own'd,
To which at intervals the Wanderer drew, *1827– but* market-village *1836–* where were] where was *1845–* passed . . . owned, *1832–* school-days,] school-time, *1845–*; *MS. 1814/27 as 1827 but* Vale, . . . market-village . . . school-days an . . . owned, *rev from* owened,

65 wandered] rambled *MS. 1814/27–*

66–67 We sate—we walked; he pleas'd [*rev from* entertain'd] me with report *MS. 1814/27, adopted (as rev) 1827– but* walk'd; *1827 and* pleased *1827–*

70 he sang] would sing *1827–*

71 the product of] brought with him from *ink over illeg pencil MS. 1836/45*

The vision and the faculty divine,
Yet wanting the accomplishment of Verse,
(Which in the docile season of their youth
It was denied them to acquire, through lack
Of culture and the inspiring aid of books,
Or haply by a temper too severe,
Or a nice backwardness afraid of shame),
Nor having e'er, as life advanced, been led
By circumstance to take unto the height
The measure of themselves, these favored Beings,
All but a scattered few, live out their time,
Husbanding that which they possess within,
And go to the grave, unthought of. Strongest minds
Are often those of whom the noisy world
Hears least; else surely this Man had not left
His graces unrevealed and unproclaimed.
But, as the mind was filled with inward light,
So not without distinction had he lived,
Beloved and honoured—far as he was known.
And some small portion of his eloquent speech,
And something that may serve to set in view
The feeling pleasures of his loneliness,
The doings, observations, which his mind
Had dealt with—I will here record in verse;
Which, if with truth it correspond, and sink
Or rise, as venerable Nature leads,
The high and tender Muses shall accept
With gracious smile, deliberately pleased,
And listening Time reward with sacred praise.

Among the hills of Athol he was born:
There, on a small hereditary Farm,
An unproductive slip of rugged ground,
His Father dwelt; and died in poverty;
While He, whose lowly fortune I retrace,
The youngest of three sons, was yet a babe,
A little One—unconscious of their loss.
But ere he had outgrown his infant days
His widowed Mother, for a second Mate,
Espoused the Teacher of the Village School;
Who on her offspring zealously bestowed

83–84 yet *pencil in right margin between the two lines MS. 1836/45*
105 His habits, observations, & the thoughts *MS. 1814/27* His observations, and the thoughts his mind *1827–*
106 Had dealt with] He cherished— *MS. 1814/27*
112 Athol] Perth-shire *pencil alt MS. 1836/45*
113 There,] Where, *MS. 1814/27–*
115–127 *reduced to* His Parents, with their numerous Offspring, dwelt; *1827– but* offspring, *1836–; MS. 1814/27 as 1827 but no commas, and* dwelt. *with period in pencil*

Needful instruction; not alone in arts
Which to his humble duties appertained,
But in the lore of right and wrong, the rule
Of human kindness, in the peaceful ways
Of honesty, and holiness severe.
A virtuous Household though exceeding poor!
Pure Livers were they all, austere and grave,
And fearing God; the very Children taught
Stern self-respect, a reverence for God's word,
And an habitual piety, maintained
With strictness scarcely known on English ground.

From his sixth year, the Boy of whom I speak,
In summer, tended cattle on the Hills;
But, through the inclement and the perilous days
Of long-continuing winter, he repaired
To his Step-father's School, that stood alone,
Sole Building on a mountain's dreary edge,
Far from the sight of City spire, or sound
Of Minster clock! From that bleak Tenement
He, many an evening to his distant home
In solitude returning, saw the Hills
Grow larger in the darkness, all alone
Beheld the stars come out above his head,
And travelled through the wood, with no one near
To whom he might confess the things he saw.
So the foundations of his mind were laid.
In such communion, not from terror free,
While yet a Child, and long before his time,
He had perceived the presence and the power
Of greatness; and deep feelings had impress'd
Great objects on his mind, with portraiture

---

138 Equipp'd with satchel, to a School, that stood *1827– but* Equipp'd] Equipped *1832–* School] school *MS. 1832/36–*; *MS. 1814/27 as 1827 but* satchel to *and possible comma in pencil after* stood
140 Far from the sight] Remote from view *MS. 1814/27–*
151 He had] Had he *MS. 1832/36–*
153–156 So vividly great objects that they lay
Upon his mind like substances, whose presence
Perplexed the bodily sense. *1845–; MS. 1836/45 has interlined rev:*
Upon great objects so distinct
~~Great objects on~~ his mind, ~~with portraiture~~
In portraiture in colouring so vivid
And colour so distinct, that on his mind
^ That on his mind
They lay like substances, ~~and almost seemed~~
With things of
~~To haunt the~~ bodily sense.
MS. 1836/45 also has pencil drafts: with portraiture / so lovely & with colour so dist *page foot* And indistinguishably seemd to mix / With things of bodily sense *top of page*
Upon his mind, great object[?s], so distinct
In portraiture, with colouring so vivid
That on his mind they lay like substances *left margin; entry continues, below*

And colour so distinct, that on his mind
They lay like substances, and almost seemed
To haunt the bodily sense. He had received
(Vigorous in native genius as he was)
A precious gift; for, as he grew in years,
With these impressions would he still compare
All his remembrances, thoughts, shapes, and forms;
And, being still unsatisfied with aught
Of dimmer character, he thence attained
An active power to fasten images
Upon his brain; and on their pictured lines
Intensely brooded, even till they acquired
The liveliness of dreams. Nor did he fail,
While yet a Child, with a Child's eagerness
Incessantly to turn his ear and eye
On all things which the moving seasons brought
To feed such appetite: nor this alone
Appeased his yearning:—in the after day
Of Boyhood, many an hour in caves forlorn,
And 'mid the hollow depths of naked crags
He sate, and even in their fix'd lineaments,
Or from the power of a peculiar eye,
Or by creative feeling overborne,
Or by predominance of thought oppress'd,
Even in their fix'd and steady lineaments
He traced an ebbing and a flowing mind,
Expression ever varying!
Thus informed,
He had small need of books; for many a Tale
Traditionary, round the mountains hung,
And many a Legend, peopling the dark woods,
Nourished Imagination in her growth,
And gave the Mind that apprehensive power
By which she is made quick to recognize
The moral properties and scope of things.
But eagerly he read, and read again,
Whate'er the Minister's old Shelf supplied;

153–156 *further pencil drafts in MS. 1836/45:*
almost mix d [?mix]
And indistinguishably, ~~seem'd to [?flow]~~
with things of bodily sense *right margin*
Great objects, so disinct in portrai
his
And colour that upon [?the] mind
[?And/As] substance, whose presence seemed to [?] *top of facing page*
whose presence
Upon his mind great objects so distinct
In lineament, in colouring so distin
In lineament in colouring so *right margin of facing page*
157 *del MS. 1814/27, om 1827–*
158 A precious gift] Precious the gift *pencil alt bottom of facing page MS. 1836/45*

The life and death of Martyrs, who sustained,
With will inflexible, those fearful pangs
Triumphantly displayed in records left
[175] Of Persecution, and the Covenant—Times
Whose echo rings through Scotland to this hour!
And there by lucky hap had been preserved
A straggling volume, torn and incomplete,
That left half-told the preternatural tale,
[180] Romance of Giants, chronicle of Fiends
Profuse in garniture of wooden cuts
Strange and uncouth; dire faces, figures dire,
Sharp-knee'd, sharp-elbowed, and lean-ankled too,
With long and ghostly shanks—forms which once seen
Could never be forgotten!
[185] In his heart
Where Fear sate thus, a cherished visitant,
Was wanting yet the pure delight of love
By sound diffused, or by the breathing air,
Or by the silent looks of happy things,
[190] Or flowing from the universal face
Of earth and sky. But he had felt the power
Of Nature, and already was prepared,
By his intense conceptions, to receive
Deeply the lesson deep of love which he,
[195] Whom Nature, by whatever means, has taught
[196] To feel intensely, cannot but receive.

From early childhood, even, as hath been said,
From his sixth year, he had been sent abroad
In summer to tend herds: such was his task
Thenceforward 'till the later day of youth.
[198] O then what soul was his, when, on the tops
Of the high mountains, he beheld the sun
[200] Rise up, and bathe the world in light! He looked—
Ocean and earth, the solid frame of earth
And ocean's liquid mass, beneath him lay
In gladness and deep joy. The clouds were touch'd,
And in their silent faces did he read
[205] Unutterable love. Sound needed none,
Nor any voice of joy; his spirit drank

---

212 he,] one, *then* he, *restored MS. 1814/27*

215–220 Such was the Boy—but for the growing Youth
What soul was his, when, from the naked top
Of some bold headland, he beheld the sun *with para at* Such *1827–; so MS. 1814/27 but* —Such was the Boy but . . . his when from . . . headland he . . . sun

223–224 And ocean's liquid mass, in gladness lay / Beneath him:—Far and wide the clouds were touched, *1845–; so MS. 1836/45 but* beneath him lay *rev to* in gladness lay *and* In gladness and deep joy *del to* Beneath him. Far & wide the clouds were touched *ink over pencil*

225 did] could *MS. 1832/36–*

The spectacle; sensation, soul, and form
All melted into him; they swallowed up
His animal being; in them did he live,
And by them did he live; they were his life.
In such access of mind, in such high hour
Of visitation from the living God,
Thought was not; in enjoyment it expired.
No thanks he breathed, he proffered no request;
Rapt into still communion that transcends
The imperfect offices of prayer and praise,
His mind was a thanksgiving to the power
That made him; it was blessedness and love!

A Herdsman on the lonely mountain tops,
Such intercourse was his, and in this sort
Was his existence oftentimes *possessed.*
Oh then how beautiful, how bright appeared
The written Promise! He had early learned
To reverence the Volume which displays
The mystery, the life which cannot die:
But in the mountains did he feel his faith;
There did he see the writing;—all things there
Breathed immortality, revolving life
And greatness still revolving; infinite;
There littleness was not; the least of things
Seemed infinite; and there his spirit shaped
Her prospects, nor did he believe,—he saw.
What wonder if his being thus became
Sublime and comprehensive! Low desires,
Low thoughts had there no place; yet was his heart
Lowly; for he was meek in gratitude,
Oft as he called those extacies to mind,
And whence they flowed; and from them he acquired
Wisdom, which works through patience; thence he learned
In many a calmer hour of sober thought
To look on Nature with a humble heart,
Self-questioned where it did not understand,
And with a superstitious eye of love.

So passed the time; yet to a neighbouring town
He duly went with what small overplus

---

244 He had early] Early had he *MS. 1814/27–*
245 which] that *MS. 1814/27–*
248 There did he see the writing;—] Responsive to the writing, *1827; so MS. 1814/27 but* writing;— All things, responsive to the Writing, there *1832– but* writing, *1836–*
260 which] that *pencil MS. 1836/45*
261 many a calmer hour] oft-recurring hours *MS. 1814/27–*
265 a neighbouring] the nearest *MS. 1814/27–*

His earnings might supply, and brought away
The Book which most had tempted his desires
While at the Stall he read. Among the hills
He gazed upon that mighty Orb of Song
[250] The divine Milton. Lore of different kind,
The annual savings of a toilsome life,
His Step-father supplied; books that explain
The purer elements of truth involved
In lines and numbers, and, by charm severe,
[255] (Especially perceived where nature droops
And feeling is suppressed,) preserve the mind
Busy in solitude and poverty.
These occupations oftentimes deceived
The listless hours, while in the hollow vale,
[260] Hollow and green, he lay on the green turf
In pensive idleness. What could he do
With blind endeavours, in that lonesome life,
Thus thirsting daily? Yet still uppermost
Nature was at his heart as if he felt,
[265] Though yet he knew not how, a wasting power
In all things which from her sweet influence
Might tend to wean him. Therefore with her hues,
Her forms, and with the spirit of her forms,
He clothed the nakedness of austere truth.
[270] While yet he lingered in the rudiments
Of science, and among her simplest laws,
His triangles—they were the stars of heaven,
The silent stars! Oft did he take delight
To measure th' altitude of some tall crag
[275] Which is the eagle's birth-place, or some peak
Familiar with forgotten years, that shews
[277] Inscribed, as with the silence of the thought,
Upon it's bleak and visionary sides,
The history of many a winter storm,—
Or obscure records of the path of fire.

[280] And thus, before his eighteenth year was told,
Accumulated feelings pressed his heart

---

268 which] that *MS. 1814/27–*
273 Step-father] Schoolmaster *MS. 1814/27* School-master *1827–*
283–284 Thus daily thirsting, in that lonesome life, / With blind endeavours? . . . *MS. 1814/27–*
287 which] that *1827–*
296 Which] That *MS. 1814/27–*
298–299 *l. 298 del and rev in pencil at page foot* Inscribed, for intercourse with speechless thought *MS. 1836/45* Inscribed upon its visionary sides, *1845–*
300–301 *MS. 1836/45 pencil drafts:*
The history of wide-spread ruin, wrought
By torrent, tempest, or departing frost
Or obscure *top of page*
[?] of long departed frost *and* sweeping storm *right margin*

With an increasing weight; he was o'erpower'd
By Nature, by the turbulence subdued
Of his own mind; by mystery and hope,
[285] And the first virgin passion of a soul
Communing with the glorious Universe.
Full often wished he that the winds might rage
When they were silent; far more fondly now
Than in his earlier season did he love
[290] Tempestuous nights—the conflict and the sounds
That live in darkness:—from his intellect
And from the stillness of abstracted thought
[293] He asked repose; and I have heard him say
That often, failing at this time to gain
[294] The peace required, he scanned the laws of light
[295] Amid the roar of torrents, where they send
From hollow clefts up to the clearer air
[297] A cloud of mist, which in the sunshine frames
A lasting tablet—for the observer's eye
[298] Varying it's rainbow hues. But vainly thus,
And vainly by all other means, he strove
[300] To mitigate the fever of his heart.

In dreams, in study, and in ardent thought,
[302] Thus, even from Childhood upward, was he reared;
For intellectual progress wanting much,
[303] Doubtless, of needful help—yet gaining more;
And every moral feeling of his soul
[305] Strengthened and braced, by breathing in content
The keen, the wholesome air of poverty,
And drinking from the well of homely life.
—But, from past liberty, and tried restraints,
He now was summoned to select the course
[310] Of humble industry which promised best
To yield him no unworthy maintenance.
[312] The Mother strove to make her Son perceive
With what advantage he might teach a School
In the adjoining Village; but the Youth,
Who of this service made a short essay,

---

304 an] still— *MS. 1814/27* still *1827–*
315–316 He asked repose; and failing oft to ~~gain~~ win *MS. 1814/27* He ask'd repose; and, failing oft to win *1827– but* asked *1832–* *MS. 1827/32C drafts at page foot:* and oftimes failing [?thence] / To win the peace required he [?] *with last word trimmed away*
320–322 A cloud of mist, that smitten by the sun / Varies *MS. 1814/27–* it's] its *1827–*
326–328 Thus was he rear'd; much wanting to assist / The growth of intellect, yet gaining more, *1827– but* reared *1832– ; MS. 1814/27 as 1827 but* reared; . . . intellect—yet . . . more;
335 which] that *MS. 1814/27–*
337–342 Urged by his Mother, he essay'd to teach
A Village-school—but wandering thoughts were then
A misery to him; and the Youth resign'd *1827– but* essayed *1832–* village-school— *1836–* resigned *1832– ; MS. 1814/27 as 1827 but* Mother he essayed . . . village School, but . . . him; & . . . resigned *rev to* resigns

[313] Found that the wanderings of his thought were then
A misery to him; that he must resign
[315] A task he was unable to perform.

That stern yet kindly spirit, Who constrains
The Savoyard to quit his naked rocks,
The free-born Swiss to leave his narrow vales,
(Spirit attached to regions mountainous
[320] Like their own stedfast clouds)—did now impel
His restless Mind to look abroad with hope.
—An irksome drudgery seems it to plod on,
Through dusty ways, in storm, from door to door,
[324] A vagrant Merchant bent beneath his load!
[326] Yet do such Travellers find their own delight;
And their hard service, deemed debasing now,
Gained merited respect in simpler times;
When Squire, and Priest, and they who round them dwelt
[330] In rustic sequestration, all, dependant
Upon the PEDLAR's toil—supplied their wants,
Or pleased their fancies, with the wares he brought.
Not ignorant was the Youth that still no few
Of his adventurous Countrymen were led
[335] By perseverance in this Track of life
To competence and ease;—for him it bore
[337] Attractions manifold;—and this he chose.
He asked his Mother's blessing; and, with tears
Thanking his second Father, asked from him
[338] Paternal blessings. The good Pair bestowed
Their farewell benediction, but with hearts
[340] Foreboding evil. From his native hills
He wandered far; much did he see of Men,
Their manners, their enjoyments, and pursuits,
Their passions, and their feelings; chiefly those
Essential and eternal in the heart,
[345] Which, mid the simpler forms of rural life,
Exist more simple in their elements,
And speak a plainer language. In the woods,
A lone Enthusiast, and among the fields,
Itinerant in this labour, he had passed
[350] The better portion of his time; and there

---

351 Through hot and dusty ways, or pelting storm, *1827– ; so MS. 1814/27– but* and] &
352 A vagrant Merchant under a heavy load / Bent as he moves, and needing frequent rest; *1836– ; MS. 1832/36 draft:* under a heavy load / Bent; yet such Traveller
363 —for him it bore] —to him it offered *1845– ; so MS. 1836/45 in pencil then ink*
365–367 His Parents on the enterprise bestow'd *1827– but* bestow'd] bestowed *1832–* His *para MS. 1832/36* —His *1836–; MS. 1814/27 as 1827 but* His *overwrites* The *and* enterprize bestowed
374 Which] That *MS. 1814/27–*

---

370 For WW's end-of-volume note, see pp. 298–299, below.

Spontaneously had his affections thriven
Upon the bounties of the year, and felt
The liberty of Nature; there he kept
In solitude and solitary thought
[355] His mind in a just equipoise of love.
Serene it was, unclouded by the cares
Of ordinary life; unvexed, unwarped
By partial bondage. In his steady course
No piteous revolutions had he felt,
[360] No wild varieties of joy and grief.
Unoccupied by sorrow of it's own
His heart lay open; and, by Nature tuned
And constant disposition of his thoughts
To sympathy with Man, he was alive
[365] To all that was enjoyed where'er he went;
And all that was endured; for in himself
Happy, and quiet in his chearfulness,
He had no painful pressure from without
That made him turn aside from wretchedness
[370] With coward fears. He could *afford* to suffer
With those whom he saw suffer. Hence it came
That in our best experience he was rich,
And in the wisdom of our daily life.
For hence, minutely, in his various rounds,
[375] He had observed the progress and decay
Of many minds, of minds and bodies too;
The History of many Families;
How they had prospered; how they were o'erthrown
By passion or mischance; or such misrule
[380] Among the unthinking masters of the earth
[381] As makes the nations groan.—This active course,
Chosen in youth, through manhood he pursued,
[382] Till due provision for his modest wants
Had been obtained;—and, thereupon, resolved
To pass the remnant of his days—untasked
[385] With needless services,—from hardship free.
His Calling laid aside, he lived at ease:
But still he loved to pace the public roads
And the wild paths; and, when the summer's warmth
Invited him, would often leave his home
[390] And journey far, revisiting those scenes

381 Upon . . . and felt] Amid . . . the peace, *1827– but* peace *1832–*
382 The] And *1827–*
410 makes] make *1820E*
411–413 He follow'd till provision for his wants / Had been obtain'd;—the Wanderer then resolved *1827– but* followed . . . obtained;— *1832– ; MS. 1814/27 as 1827 but* followed, till . . . obtained;—
418 when] by *MS. 1814/27–*
419 Invited, often would he leave his home *MS. 1814/27–*
420 those] the *MS. 1814/27–*

Which to his memory were most endeared.
—Vigorous in health, of hopeful spirits, untouched
By worldly-mindedness or anxious care;
Observant, studious, thoughtful, and refreshed
[395] By knowledge gathered up from day to day;—
Thus had he lived a long and innocent life.

The Scottish Church, both on himself and those
With whom from childhood he grew up, had held
The strong hand of her purity; and still
[400] Had watched him with an unrelenting eye.
This he remembered in his riper age
With gratitude, and reverential thoughts.
But by the native vigour of his mind,
By his habitual wanderings out of doors,
[405] By loneliness, and goodness, and kind works,
Whate'er in docile childhood or in youth
He had imbibed of fear or darker thought
Was melted all away: so true was this
That sometimes his religion seemed to me
[410] Self-taught, as of a dreamer in the woods;
Who to the model of his own pure heart
Framed his belief, as grace divine inspired,
Or human reason dictated with awe.
—And surely never did there live on earth
[415] A Man of kindlier nature. The rough sports
[416] And teazing ways of Children vexed not him,
Nor could he bid them from his presence, tired
With questions and importunate demands:
[417] Indulgent listener was he to the tongue
Of garrulous age; nor did the sick man's tale,
To his fraternal sympathy addressed,
Obtain reluctant hearing.
[420]   Plain his garb
Such as might suit a rustic sire, prepared
For sabbath duties; yet he was a Man
Whom no one could have passed without remark.
Active and nervous was his gait; his limbs
[425] And his whole figure breathed intelligence.
Time had compressed the freshness of his cheek
Into a narrower circle of deep red
But had not tamed his eye; that under brows

---

421 Which] That *MS. 1814/27–*
422 untouched] undamp'd *MS. 1814/27, 1827* undamped *1832–*
442 Framed] Shaped *MS. 1814/27–*
443 Or] And *1836–*
447–448 *del MS. 1814/27, om 1827–*

Shaggy and grey had meanings which it brought
From years of youth; which, like a Being made
Of many Beings, he had wondrous skill
To blend with knowledge of the years to come,
Human, or such as lie beyond the grave.

So was He framed; and such his course of life
Who now, with no Appendage but a Staff,
The prized memorial of relinquish'd toils,
Upon that Cottage bench reposed his limbs,
Screened from the sun. Supine the Wanderer lay,
His eyes as if in drowsiness half shut,
The shadows of the breezy elms above
Dappling his face. He had not heard my steps
As I approached; and near him did I stand
Unnotic'd in the shade, some minutes' space.
At length I hailed him, seeing that his hat
Was moist with water-drops, as if the brim
Had newly scooped a running stream. He rose,
And ere the pleasant greeting that ensued
Was ended, "'Tis," said I, "a burning day;
My lips are parched with thirst, but you, I guess,
Have somewhere found relief." He, at the word,
Pointing towards a sweet-briar, bade me climb
The fence hard by, where that aspiring shrub
Looked out upon the road. It was a plot
Of garden-ground run wild, it's matted weeds
Marked with the steps of those, whom, as they pass'd,

473–475 He had not heard the sound
Of my approaching steps, and in the shade
Unnoticed did I stand, some minutes' space. *1827– but* stand some *1845–; MS. 1814/27 as 1827 but* steps & . . . Unnotic'd *MS. 1836/45 pencil line transposes third line above to* some minutes' space. Unnoticed did I stand

479–480 And ere our lively greeting into ~~calm~~ peace / Had settled, *MS. 1814/27, adopted (as rev) 1827–*

481 I guess,] it seems, *MS. 1814/27–*

482–483 at the word, / Pointing towards] raised his hand / And Pointing to *ink over pencil MS. 1836/45, which also has a series of pencil drafts:* To a [?last] sweet briar pointin *interlined and* And to a sweet-briar pointing bade me climb *interlined* With ready finger / He pointing toward a sweet br *pencil at top of facing page* wall *pencil in right margin of l. 484, possible alt for* fence

To a To an {[?last] / [?] / [?arch'd]} sweet point *pencil in right margin*

He, to a sweet briar,
Pointing with ready finger, bade [?me] climb
The garden wall *pencil on verso of first free endpaper*

484–485 The fence where that aspiring shrub look'd out / Upon the public way. It was a plot *1827– but* look'd] looked *1832–; MS. 1814/27 as 1827 but* fence, *and* way *rev to* Way

The gooseberry trees that shot in long lank slips,
Or currants hanging from their leafless stems
In scanty strings, had tempted to o'erleap
The broken wall. I looked around, and there,
Where two tall hedge-rows of thick alder boughs
Joined in a cold damp nook, espied a Well
Shrouded with willow-flowers and plumy fern.
My thirst I slaked, and from the chearless spot
Withdrawing, straightway to the shade returned
Where sate the Old Man on the Cottage bench;
And, while, beside him, with uncovered head,
I yet was standing, freely to respire,
And cool my temples in the fanning air,
Thus did he speak. "I see around me here
Things which you cannot see: we die, my Friend,
Nor we alone, but that which each man loved
And prized in his peculiar nook of earth
Dies with him, or is changed; and very soon
Even of the good is no memorial left.
—The Poets, in their elegies and songs
Lamenting the departed, call the groves,
They call upon the hills and streams to mourn,
And senseless rocks; nor idly; for they speak,
In these their invocations, with a voice
Obedient to the strong creative power
Of human passion. Sympathies there are
More tranquil, yet perhaps of kindred birth,
That steal upon the meditative mind,
And grow with thought. Beside yon Spring I stood,
And eyed its waters till we seemed to feel
One sadness, they and I. For them a bond
Of brotherhood is broken: time has been
When, every day, the touch of human hand
Dislodged the natural sleep that binds them up
In mortal stillness; and they minister'd

488–490 *MS. 1836/45 has interlined rev:*
shewed their dwindled fruit
The gooseberry trees that shot in long lank slips,
Hanging in long lank slips
~~Or currants, hanging from their~~ leafless stems, strings
Or currants might have
~~In scanty strings, had~~ tempted to o'erleap
MS. 1836/45 has pencil draft in left margin of facing page:
The gooseberry trees that showed their dwindled fruit
Hanging in long lank slips or scanty [?~~crown~~] strings
Of currants, might have tempted to oerleap

491 *MS. 1836/45 pencil drafts:* The broken [?barrier]. I *page foot* The rude wall's shattered [?barrier]. I looked round / As [?] *top of page* The wall, a broken [?barrier]; I looked round *left margin*

509 hills and streams *transposed by pencil line to* streams and hills *MS. 1836/45*

To human comfort. As I stooped to drink,
Upon the slimy foot-stone I espied
The useless fragment of a wooden bowl,
[494] Green with the moss of years; a pensive sight
That moved my heart!—recalling former days
[498] When I could never pass that road but She
Who lived within these walls, at my approach,
[499] A Daughter's welcome gave me; and I loved her
[500] As my own child. O Sir! the good die first,
And they whose hearts are dry as summer dust
Burn to the socket. Many a Passenger
Hath blessed poor Margaret for her gentle looks,
When she upheld the cool refreshment drawn
[505] From that forsaken Spring; and no one came

---

523 As I stooped] Stooping down *MS. 1814/27–*
524 near[?by] *pencil alt above* Upon the *MS. 1836/45*
526–529 Green with the moss of years, and subject only
To the soft handling of the Elements:
There let the relic lie—fond thought—vain words!
Forgive them—never did my steps approach
This humble door but she who dwelt within *1827– but* [*2*] elements: *1836–* [*3*] There let it lie—fond, foolish thought—vain words! *MS. 1832/36* There let it lie—how foolish are such thoughts! *1836–* [*4–5*] Forgive them;—never—never did my steps / Approach this door but . . . *1832–; entry continues, below*

526–529 *MS. 1814/27 drafts:*
Green with the moss of years; & subject only
To the soft handling of the elements
There let the relic lie—fond thoughts—vain words
Forgive
~~Pardon~~ ^ ~~Forgive~~ them for the sake of her who dwells
Within these walls, who here so oft hath giv'n
To me a Daughter's greeting; *with* Pardon *del in pencil* Forgive *added in pencil; caret in left margin is possibly also intended to signal pencil rev at page foot:*
Forgive them—never did { my steps appro / [?I pass this way } ach
{ This humble door but she who dwelt within
But she [?who dwelt] within [?mouldering walls]
A Daughters welcome gave me
MS. 1836/45 has a series of pencil rev, the first interlined:
a forlorn relick
Green with the moss of years, and subject only
To the soft handling of the elements:
in memory of days
There let it lie—how foolish are such thoughts!
~~Departed—for~~
Forgive them;—never—never did my steps
Unmoved, never never did step of mine *this line at top of facing page*
Green with the moss of years. Upon the relique
As there it lay I could not look unmoved
Forgive this weakness. Never did step of mine
Approach that door *right margin*
Upon the simple sight I could not look
Unmoved—never—never did step of mine *page foot*
a forlorn relique
~~upon~~ the relique
On which as there it lay
~~As there~~ it lay I had not heart to look
Unmoved—never never did *bottom of facing page*
532 they] those *Friend*

But he was welcome; no one went away
But that it seemed she loved him. She is dead,
The light extinguished of her lonely Hut,
The Hut itself abandoned to decay,
And She forgotten in the quiet grave!

"I speak," continued he, "of One whose stock
Of virtues bloom'd beneath this lowly roof.
She was a Woman of a steady mind,
Tender and deep in her excess of love,
Not speaking much, pleased rather with the joy
Of her own thoughts: by some especial care
Her temper had been framed, as if to make
A Being—who by adding love to peace
Might live on earth a life of happiness.
Her wedded Partner lacked not on his side
The humble worth that satisfied her heart:
Frugal, affectionate, sober, and withal
Keenly industrious. She with pride would tell
That he was often seated at his loom,
In summer, ere the Mower was abroad
Among the dewy grass,—in early spring,
Ere the last Star had vanished.—They who passed
At evening, from behind the garden fence
Might hear his busy spade, which he would ply,
After his daily work, until the light
Had failed, and every leaf and flower were lost
In the dark hedges. So their days were spent
In peace and comfort; and a pretty Boy
Was their best hope,—next to the God in Heaven.

Not twenty years ago, but you I think
Can scarcely bear it now in mind, there came
Two blighting seasons when the fields were left
With half a harvest. It pleased heaven to add
A worse affliction in the plague of war;
This happy Land was stricken to the heart!
A Wanderer then among the Cottages
I, with my freight of winter raiment, saw
The hardships of that season; many rich
Sank down, as in a dream, among the poor;
And of the poor did many cease to be
And their place knew them not. Meanwhile abridg'd
Of daily comforts, gladly reconciled
To numerous self-denials, Margaret
Went struggling on through those calamitous years

561 work, until the] labour till *MS. 1827/32C*

[550] With chearful hope: but ere the second autumm
Her life's true Help-mate on a sick-bed lay,
Smitten with perilous fever. In disease
He lingered long; and when his strength return'd,
He found the little he had stored, to meet
[555] The hour of accident or crippling age,
[556] Was all consumed. Two children had they now,
One newly born. As I have said, it was
[557/559] A time of trouble; shoals of Artisans
[560] Were from their daily labour turn'd adrift
To seek their bread from public charity,
They, and their wives and children—happier far
Could they have lived as do the little birds
That peck along the hedges, or the Kite
[565] That makes his dwelling on the mountain Rocks!

A sad reverse it was for Him who long
Had filled with plenty, and possess'd in peace,
This lonely Cottage. At his door he stood,
And whistled many a snatch of merry tunes
[570] That had no mirth in them; or with his knife
Carved uncouth figures on the heads of sticks—
Then, not less idly, sought, through every nook
In house or garden, any casual work
Of use or ornament; and with a strange,
[575] Amusing, yet uneasy novelty,
He blended, where he might, the various tasks
Of summer, autumn, winter, and of spring.
But this endured not; his good humour soon
Became a weight in which no pleasure was:
[580] And poverty brought on a petted mood
And a sore temper: day by day he drooped,
And he would leave his work—and to the Town,
Without an errand, would direct his steps,

---

581 but ere] until *MS. 1814/27–*
582 Her life's true Help-mate] When Her life's Help-mate *MS. 1814/27– but* her . . . Helpmate *1827–*
587–591 Was all consumed. A second Infant now
Was added to the troubles of a time
Laden, for them and all of their degree,
With care and sorrow; shoals of Artisans
From ill requited labour turn'd adrift
Sought daily bread . . . *1827– but* Artisans, . . . adrift, *MS. 1827/32C* turned *1832–* artisans . . . ill-requited *MS. 1832/36–* infant . . . sorrow: *1836–; MS. 1827 as 1827 but* Laden for . . . them & . . . degree . . . care & . . . ill-requited
594 hedges,] hedgerows, *MS. 1814/27* hedge-rows, *1827–*
595 his] her *MS. 1814/27–*
598 his] the *1836–*
606 blended] mingled *1836–*
613 direct] he turn *MS. 1832/36* Would turn, without an errand, his slack steps; *1836– but* turn,] turn *pencil MS. 1836/45, 1840– and* errand,] errand *1840–*

Or wander here and there among the fields.
One while he would speak lightly of his Babes,
And with a cruel tongue: at other times
He toss'd them with a false unnatural joy:
And 'twas a rueful thing to see the looks
Of the poor innocent children. "Every smile,"
Said Margaret to me, here beneath these trees,
"Made my heart bleed."
At this the Wanderer paused;
And, looking up to those enormous Elms,
He said, "'Tis now the hour of deepest noon.—
At this still season of repose and peace,
This hour, when all things which are not at rest
Are chearful; while this multitude of flies
Is filling all the air with melody;
Why should a tear be in an Old Man's eye?
Why should we thus, with an untoward mind,
And in the weakness of humanity,
From natural wisdom turn our hearts away,
To natural comfort shut our eyes and ears,
And, feeding on disquiet, thus disturb
The calm of nature with our restless thoughts?"

He spake with somewhat of a solemn tone:
But, when he ended, there was in his face
Such easy chearfulness, a look so mild,
That for a little time it stole away
All recollection, and that simple Tale
Passed from my mind like a forgotten sound.
A while on trivial things we held discourse,
To me soon tasteless. In my own despite
I thought of that poor Woman as of one
Whom I had known and loved. He had rehearsed
Her homely Tale with such familiar power,
With such an active countenance, an eye
So busy, that the things of which he spake
Seemed present; and, attention now relax'd,

---

627 With tuneful hum is filling all the air; *1845–; so MS. 1836/45 (ink over pencil) following preliminary drafts in pencil:* was [is *alt*] . . . air With [?] / Fills the [?] with [?their] *page foot* With ceaseless [*alt* tuneful] hum is filling all the air *left margin*

628 in . . . eye?] on . . . cheek? *1845–*

There was a heart-felt chillness in my veins.—
[620] I rose; and, turning from the breezy shade,
Went forth into the open air, and stood
[621] To drink the comfort of the warmer sun.
Long time I had not staid, ere, looking round
Upon that tranquil Ruin, I return'd,
And begged of the Old Man that, for my sake,
[625] He would resume his story.—
He replied,
"It were a wantonness, and would demand
Severe reproof, if we were Men whose hearts
Could hold vain dalliance with the misery
Even of the dead; contented thence to draw
[630] A momentary pleasure, never marked
By reason, barren of all future good.
But we have known that there is often found
In mournful thoughts, and always might be found,
A power to virtue friendly; were't not so,
[635] I am a Dreamer among men, indeed
An idle Dreamer! 'Tis a common Tale,
An ordinary sorrow of Man's life,
A tale of silent suffering, hardly clothed
In bodily form.—But, without further bidding,
[640] I will proceed.—
While thus it fared with them,
To whom this Cottage, till those hapless years,
Had been a blessed home, it was my chance
[643] To travel in a Country far remote.
And glad I was, when, halting by yon gate
That leads from the green lane, once more I saw
[644] These lofty elm-trees. Long I did not rest:
[645] With many pleasant thoughts I chear'd my way
O'er the flat Common.—Having reached the door
[648] I knock'd,—and, when I entered with the hope
Of usual greeting, Margaret looked at me

649–653 A heart-felt chillness crept along my veins.
I rose; and, having left the breezy shade,
Stood drinking comfort from the warmer sun,
That had not cheer'd me long—ere, looking round *1827– but* cheered *1832– ; MS. 1814/27 as 1827 but*

along
~~crept~~ A crept [?]
~~There was~~ ^a heart-felt chillness ~~in~~ my veins.—
~~passing~~ having left
I rose; and, ~~turning from~~ the breezy shade, *and* sun / That . . . long, ere,

675–681 And when these lofty Elms once more appear'd,
What pleasant expectations lured me on
O'er the flat Common!—With quick step I reach'd
The threshold, lifted with light hand the latch;
But, when I entered, Margaret look'd at me *1827– but* elms *MS. 1832/36* appeared, *1832, 1836* appeared *1840–* reached . . . looked *1832– ; MS. 1814/27 as 1827 but* elms . . . appear'd . . . Common.— . . . threshold lifted . . . latch / But when

A little while; then turn'd her head away
Speechless,—and sitting down upon a chair
Wept bitterly. I wist not what to do,
Or how to speak to her. Poor Wretch! at last
She rose from off her seat, and then,—O Sir!
I cannot *tell* how she pronounced my name.—
With fervent love, and with a face of grief
Unutterably helpless, and a look
That seemed to cling upon me, she enquired
If I had seen her Husband. As she spake
A strange surprize and fear came to my heart,
Nor had I power to answer ere she told
That he had disappear'd—not two months gone.
He left his House: two wretched days had pass'd,
And on the third, as wistfully she rais'd
Her head from off her pillow, to look forth,
Like one in trouble, for returning light,
Within her chamber-casement she espied
A folded paper, lying as if placed
To meet her waking eyes. This tremblingly
She open'd—found no writing, but therein
Pieces of money carefully enclosed,
Silver and gold.—"I shuddered at the sight,"
Said Margaret, "for I knew it was his hand
Which placed it there: and ere that day was ended,
That long and anxious day! I learned from One
Sent hither by my Husband to impart
The heavy news,—that he had joined a Troop
Of Soldiers, going to a distant Land.
—He left me thus—he could not gather heart
To take a farewell of me; for he fear'd
That I should follow with my Babes, and sink
Beneath the misery of that wandering Life."

This Tale did Margaret tell with many tears:
And when she ended I had little power
To give her comfort, and was glad to take
Such words of hope from her own mouth as served
To chear us both:—but long we had not talked
Ere we built up a pile of better thoughts,

---

685 Or] Nor *1832–*

689–690 *MS. 1836/45 pencil drafts:* Unutterable, and a helpless look that seemed / To cling upon me, faltering she in *top of page* faintly she inqui *right margin* With feint voice she [?aske] / To cling upon me, faintly she inquir *page foot*

702 therein] beheld *MS. 1814/27–*

706–709 That must have placed it there; and ere that day
Was ended, that long anxious day, I learned
From one who by my husband had been sent
With the sad news, that he had joined a troop *1836– but* learned, *pencil rev MS. 1836/45, 1840– ; MS. 1832/36 as 1836 but* been] be *and* there, . . . news that

And with a brighter eye she look'd around
As if she had been shedding tears of joy.
We parted.—'Twas the time of early spring;
I left her busy with her garden tools;
And well remember, o'er that fence she looked,
And, while I paced along the foot-way path,
Called out, and sent a blessing after me,
With tender chearfulness; and with a voice
That seem'd the very sound of happy thoughts.

I roved o'er many a hill and many a dale,
With my accustomed load; in heat and cold,
Through many a wood, and many an open ground,
In sunshine and in shade, in wet and fair,
Drooping, or blithe of heart, as might befal;
My best companions now the driving winds,
And now the "trotting brooks" and whispering trees,
And now the music of my own sad steps,
With many a short-lived thought that pass'd between,
And disappeared.—I journey'd back this way
Towards the wane of Summer; when the wheat
Was yellow; and the soft and bladed grass
Springing afresh had o'er the hay-field spread
Its tender verdure. At the door arrived,
I found that she was absent. In the shade,
Where now we sit, I waited her return.
Her Cottage, then a chearful Object, wore
Its customary look,—only, I thought,
The honeysuckle, crowding round the porch,
Hung down in heavier tufts: and that bright weed,
The yellow stone-crop, suffered to take root
Along the window's edge, profusely grew,
Blinding the lower panes. I turned aside,
And strolled into her garden. It appeared
To lag behind the season, and had lost
[722/723] Its pride of neatness. From the border lines
Composed of daisy and resplendent thrift,
[723] Flowers straggling forth had on those paths encroached
Which they were used to deck:—Carnations, once

729/730 first *del to* first visit *pencil note right margin MS. 1836/45; cf. verbal variants to I, 739, 848, 887*

739 second visit *pencil note right margin MS. 1836/45; cf. verbal variants to I, 729, 848, 887*

740 When, in the warmth of Midsummer, the wheat *1827– but* mid-summer; *MS. 1832/36* midsummer, *1836–; MS. 1814/27 as 1827 but* When in . . . mid-Summer;

747 I thought,] it seemed, *MS. 1814/27– but* seem'd, *1827*

755–758 Its pride of neatness. Daisy-flow'rs and thrift
Had broken their trim lines, and straggled o'er
The paths they used to deck:—Carnations, once *1827– but* Daisy-flowers *1832–* trim lines, and straggled o'er / The paths] trim border lines, and straggled / O'er paths *MS. 1836/45, 1845– but* border-lines, *1845–* deck: *1836–* carnations, *MS. 1832/36–; MS. 1814/27 as 1827 but* Daisy flowers & . . . lines &

[725] Prized for surpassing beauty, and no less
For the peculiar pains they had required,
Declined their languid heads—without support.
The cumbrous bind-weed, with its wreaths and bells,
Had twined about her two small rows of pease,
[730] And dragged them to the earth.—Ere this an hour
[731] Was wasted.—Back I turned my restless steps,
And, as I walked before the door, it chanced
[732] A Stranger passed; and, guessing whom I sought,
He said that she was used to ramble far.—
The sun was sinking in the west; and now
[735] I sate with sad impatience. From within
Her solitary Infant cried aloud;
Then, like a blast that dies away self-stilled,
The voice was silent. From the bench I rose;
But neither could divert nor soothe my thoughts.
[740] The spot, though fair, was very desolate—
The longer I remained more desolate.
And, looking round, I saw the corner stones,
Till then unnotic'd, on either side the door
With dull red stains discolour'd, and stuck o'er
[745] With tufts and hairs of wool, as if the Sheep,
That fed upon the Common, thither came
Familiarly; and found a couching-place
Even at her threshold. Deeper shadows fell
From these tall elms;—the Cottage-clock struck eight;—
[750] I turned, and saw her distant a few steps.
Her face was pale and thin, her figure too
Was changed. As she unlocked the door, she said,
"It grieves me you have waited here so long,
But, in good truth, I've wandered much of late,
[755] And, sometimes,—to my shame I speak, have need
Of my best prayers to bring me back again."
While on the board she spread our evening meal
She told me,—interrupting not the work
Which gave employment to her listless hands,
[760] That she had parted with her elder Child;
To a kind Master on a distant farm
Now happily apprenticed—"I perceive
You look at me, and you have cause; to-day
I have been travelling far; and many days
[765] About the fields I wander, knowing this
Only, that what I seek I cannot find.

761 without] wanting *1832–*
766 *del MS. 1814/27, om 1827–*
777–778 And, looking round me, now I first observed / The corner stones, on either side the porch, *1827–; so MS. 1814/27 but* porch

And so I waste my time: for I am changed;
And to myself, said she, have done much wrong
And to this helpless Infant. I have slept
Weeping, and weeping I have waked; my tears
Have flowed as if my body were not such
As others are; and I could never die.
But I am now in mind and in my heart
More easy; and I hope," said she, "that heaven
Will give me patience to endure the things
Which I behold at home." It would have grieved
Your very soul to see her; Sir, I feel
The story linger in my heart: I fear
'Tis long and tedious; but my spirit clings
To that poor Woman:—so familiarly
Do I perceive her manner, and her look,
And presence, and so deeply do I feel
Her goodness, that, not seldom, in my walks
A momentary trance comes over me;
And to myself I seem to muse on One
By sorrow laid asleep;—or borne away,
A human being destined to awake
To human life, or something very near
To human life, when he shall come again
For whom she suffered. Yes, it would have grieved
Your very soul to see her: evermore
Her eyelids drooped, her eyes were downward cast;
And, when she at her table gave me food,
She did not look at me. Her voice was low,
Her body was subdued. In every act
Pertaining to her house affairs, appeared
The careless stillness of a thinking mind
Self-occupied; to which all outward things
Are like an idle matter. Still she sighed,
But yet no motion of the breast was seen,
No heaving of the heart. While by the fire
We sate together, sighs came on my ear,
I knew not how, and hardly whence they came.

Ere my departure to her care I gave,
For her Son's use, some tokens of regard,
Which with a look of welcome She received;
And I exhorted her to have her trust
In God's good love, and seek his help by prayer.
I took my staff, and when I kissed her babe

805 I have] have I *MS. 1814/27–*
809 heaven] God *1831, 1832–*
827 were downward] downward were *MS. 1836/45, 1845–*
842 have] place *MS. 1814/27–*

The tears stood in her eyes. I left her then
With the best hope and comfort I could give;
She thanked me for my wish;—but for my hope
Methought she did not thank me.
I returned,
And took my rounds along this road again
Ere on its sunny bank the primrose flower
Peeped forth, to give an earnest of the Spring.
I found her sad and drooping; she had learned
No tidings of her Husband; if he lived
She knew not that he lived; if he were dead
She knew not he was dead. She seem'd the same
In person and appearance; but her House
Bespake a sleepy hand of negligence.
The floor was neither dry nor neat, the hearth
Was comfortless, and her small lot of books,
Which, in the Cottage window, heretofore
Had been piled up against the corner panes
In seemly order, now, with straggling leaves
Lay scattered here and there, open or shut,
As they had chanced to fall. Her Infant Babe
Had from its Mother caught the trick of grief,
And sighed among its playthings. Once again
I turned towards the garden gate, and saw,
More plainly still, that poverty and grief
Were now come nearer to her: weeds defaced
The harden'd soil, and knots of wither'd grass;
No ridges there appeared of clear black mold,
No winter greenness; of her herbs and flowers,
It seemed the better part were gnawed away

---

848 Methought] It seemed *MS. 1832/36–* 3[d] visit *pencil note right margin MS. 1836/45; cf. verbal variants to I, 729, 739, 887*

850 Ere on] When from *ink over pencil MS. 1836/45* When on *1845–*

852–853 *MS. 1836/45 has a series of rev:*
Time had brough
~~she had learned~~
which might lead her anxious min
~~No tidings of her husband; if he lived,~~
To a source of quiet; if her Husband lived *ink over pencil, following pencil rev:*
Time had brought
~~She had learned~~
No tidings that might lead her anxious mind
To a source of quiet: If her husband livd *left margin*
No tidings none—if her [?lost] husband livd *page foot*

866–867 . . . playthings. I withdrew, / And once again entering the garden saw, *1845–but* withdrew,] withdrew *1846; so MS. 1836/45, ink over pencil, but* saw,] saw *MS. 1836/45 also has pencil drafts:* And once again entering the garden ~~gate~~ saw *interlined, over eras* I withdrew / But not alone & entering once again / The [?garden I] could not, but [?perceive] *right margin of facing page* I withdrew *del left margin of facing page* I withdrew / Entering the garden there I [?turned] *page foot* There / I withdrew / Entering the garden / And turning towards the garden [?did] *top of page* once again / I [?plod] the garden [?did] *top of facing page*

Or trampled into earth; a chain of straw,
Which had been twined about the slender stem
Of a young apple-tree, lay at its root;
The bark was nibbled round by truant Sheep.
—Margaret stood near, her Infant in her arms,
And, noting that my eye was on the tree,
She said, "I fear it will be dead and gone
Ere Robert come again." Towards the House
Together we returned; and she enquired
If I had any hope:—but for her Babe
And for her little orphan Boy, she said,
She had no wish to live, that she must die
Of sorrow. Yet I saw the idle loom
Still in its place; his Sunday garments hung
Upon the self-same nail; his very staff
Stood undisturbed behind the door. And when,
In bleak December, I retraced this way,
She told me that her little Babe was dead,
And she was left alone. She now, released
From her maternal cares, had taken up
The employment common through these Wilds, and gain'd
By spinning hemp a pittance for herself;
And for this end had hired a neighbour's Boy
To give her needful help. That very time
Most willingly she put her work aside,
And walked with me along the miry road
Heedless how far; and, in such piteous sort
That any heart had ached to hear her, begged
That, wheresoe'er I went, I still would ask
For him whom she had lost. We parted then,
Our final parting; for from that time forth
Did many seasons pass ere I return'd
Into this tract again.
Nine tedious years;
From their first separation, nine long years,
She lingered in unquiet widowhood;
A Wife and Widow. Needs must it have been
A sore heart-wasting! I have heard, my Friend,
That in yon arbour oftentimes she sate

881–882 Ere Robert come again.' Towards the house
We turned together—silent till she asked *MS. 1836/45*
Ere Robert come again.' When to the House
We had returned together, she enquired *1845–; pencil draft on DC MS. 107 (B),* 1^{v}*, may be related to this rev (see Poems, 1821-1850, pp. xxxiv-xxxvi, 698-699):*
We sought the House
To shun the garden and as we approach'd
The silent door the afflicted [afflicted *rev from* wretched] One replied
If I had any [?hope]

887 4th visit *pencil note in right margin MS. 1836/45; cf. verbal vaiants to I, 848, 739, 729*

Alone, through half the vacant Sabbath-day,
And if a dog passed by she still would quit
The shade, and look abroad. On this old Bench
For hours she sate; and evermore her eye
Was busy in the distance, shaping things
That made her heart beat quick. You see that path,
Now faint,—the grass has crept o'er its grey line;
There, to and fro, she paced through many a day
Of the warm summer, from a belt of hemp
That girt her waist, spinning the long drawn thread
With backward steps. Yet ever as there pass'd
A man whose garments shewed the Soldier's red,
Or crippled Mendicant in Sailor's garb,
The little Child who sate to turn the wheel
Ceas'd from his task; and she with faultering voice
Made many a fond enquiry; and when they,
Whose presence gave no comfort, were gone by,
Her heart was still more sad. And by yon gate,
That bars the Traveller's road, she often stood,
And when a stranger Horseman came the latch
Would lift, and in his face look wistfully;
Most happy, if, from aught discovered there
Of tender feeling, she might dare repeat
The same sad question. Meanwhile her poor Hut
Sank to decay: for he was gone—whose hand,
At the first nipping of October frost,
Closed up each chink, and with fresh bands of straw
Chequered the green-grown thatch. And so she lived
Through the long winter, reckless and alone;
Until her House by frost, and thaw, and rain,
Was sapped; and while she slept the nightly damps
Did chill her breast; and in the stormy day
Her tattered clothes were ruffled by the wind;
Even at the side of her own fire. Yet still
She loved this wretched spot, nor would for worlds
Have parted hence; and still that length of road,
And this rude bench, one torturing hope endeared,
Fast rooted at her heart: and here, my Friend,
In sickness she remained; and here she died,
Last human Tenant of these ruined Walls."

The Old Man ceased: he saw that I was moved;
From that low Bench, rising instinctively
I turn'd aside in weakness, nor had power
To thank him for the Tale which he had told.

---

923 Soldier's] *so 1820E, 1827* Soldiers *1814* soldier's *1832–*
949 in sickness *added, then del (both in pencil) above* Friend *MS. 1836/45*
949–950 To smooth the way where thankfully she ~~pas~~ sank / Into the *pencil MS. 1836/45*

I stood, and leaning o'er the Garden wall,
Reviewed that Woman's sufferings; and it seemed
To comfort me while with a Brother's love
I bless'd her—in the impotence of grief.
[925] At length towards the Cottage I returned
Fondly,—and traced, with interest more mild,
That secret spirit of humanity
Which, mid the calm oblivious tendencies
Of Nature, mid her plants, and weeds, and flowers,
[930] And silent overgrowings, still survived.
The Old Man, noting this, resumed, and said,
"My Friend! enough to sorrow you have given,
[933] The purposes of wisdom ask no more;
[939] Be wise and chearful; and no longer read
[940] The forms of things with an unworthy eye.
She sleeps in the calm earth, and peace is here.
I well remember that those very plumes,
Those weeds, and the high spear-grass on that wall,
By mist and silent rain-drops silver'd o'er,
[945] As once I passed, did to my heart convey
So still an image of tranquillity,
So calm and still, and looked so beautiful
Amid the uneasy thoughts which filled my mind,
That what we feel of sorrow and despair
[950] From ruin and from change, and all the grief

960–961 Then towards the cottage I returned; and traced / Fondly, though with an interest more mild, *1836–*

965 And *del in pencil to* Those *pencil left margin* These *pencil alt interlined MS. 1836/45*

969–970 Nor more would she have craved as due to One
Who, in her worst distress, had ofttimes felt
The unbounded might of prayer; and learned, with soul
Fixed on the Cross, that consolation springs,
From sources deeper far than deepest pain,
For the meek Sufferer. Why then should we read
The forms of things with an unworthy eye? *1845–*

MS. 1836/45 has extensive rev: Be . . . longer *del in l. 969* dejected *pencil alt to* unworthy *and question mark added* eye? *in l. 970* *partly legible pencil draft overwrites an illeg pencil draft, eras:*

[?christian faith]
[?Think not that consolation] [—?—]
[?to wait]
[?Is gaind by] [? ?] [?the spirit] *page foot*
Doubt not that oftimes in her soul she felt
The unbounded might of prayer—(Upon her knees
Was taught that heavenly consolation springs
From sources deeper far than deepest pain[?s]
the
To ~~all~~ meek Sufferers [—?——?——?—]
Why then should we read
The forms of things with a dejected eye *right margin; another draft in ink at top of page as immediately above but prefaced by* ask no more *and* prayer—upon . . . pain *and concludes* For the meek Sufferer: Why then should we read *another pencil draft on the fly title for Book II as indented text immediately above but begins* ask no more / Doubt not that oftimes in her soul she felt / The unbounded might . . . *and concludes* The forms of things with a dejected eye. / She sleeps in the calm earth &c

975 As once I passed, into my heart conveyed *MS. 1832/36–*

The passing shews of Being leave behind,
[952] Appeared an idle dream, that could not live
[954/955] Where meditation was. I turned away
And walked along my road in happiness."

He ceased. Ere long the sun declining shot
A slant and mellow radiance, which began
To fall upon us, while beneath the trees
[960] We sate on that low Bench: and now we felt,
Admonished thus, the sweet hour coming on.
A linnet warbled from those lofty elms,
A thrush sang loud, and other melodies,
At distance heard, peopled the milder air.
[965] The Old Man rose, and, with a sprightly mien
Of hopeful preparation, grasped his Staff:
Together casting then a farewell look
Upon those silent walls, we left the Shade;
And, ere the Stars were visible, had reached
[970] A Village Inn,—our Evening resting-place.

END OF THE FIRST BOOK.

981 The] That *1845–* passing] transient *pencil MS. 1836/45*
982–984 Appeared an idle dream, that could maintain,
Nowhere, dominion o'er the enlightened spirit
Whose meditative sympathies repose
Upon the breast of Faith. I turned away,
And walked along my road in happiness." *1845– ; so MS. 1836/45 but* that . . . was *del in pencil and* not live *del in ink and interlined rev through l. 984:* maintain / No where . . . oer . . . Spirit . . . away . . . happiness *also entered on fly title of Book II in MS. 1836/45 as 1845 but* dream that . . . oer . . . enlighten'd Spirit . . . away,] away
995 casting then] then casting *MS. 1832/36*

THE SOLITARY.

In days of yore how fortunately fared
The Minstrel! wandering on from Hall to Hall,
Baronial Court or Royal; cheered with gifts
Munificent, and love, and Ladies' praise;
[5] Now meeting on his road an armed Knight,
Now resting with a Pilgrim by the side
Of a clear brook;—beneath an Abbey's roof
One evening sumptuously lodged; the next
Humbly, in a religious Hospital;
[10] Or with some merry Outlaws of the wood;
Or haply shrouded in a Hermit's cell.
Him, sleeping or awake, the Robber spared;
He walked—protected from the sword of war
By virtue of that sacred Instrument
[15] His Harp, suspended at the Traveller's side;
His dear Companion wheresoe'er he went
Opening from Land to Land an easy way
By melody, and by the charm of verse.
Yet not the noblest of that honoured Race
[20] Drew happier, loftier, more empassioned thoughts
From his long journeyings and eventful life,
[22] Than this obscure Itinerant (an obscure,
But a high-souled and tender-hearted Man)
[22/23] Had skill to draw from many a ramble, far
[23] And wide protracted, through the tamer ground
Of these our unimaginative days;
[25] Both while he trod the earth in humblest guise
Accoutred with his burthen and his staff;
And now, when free to move with lighter pace.

What wonder, then, if I, whose favourite School
[29] Hath been the fields, the roads, and rural lanes,
And pathways winding on from farm to farm,
[30] Looked on this Guide with reverential love?
Each with the other pleased, we now pursued
Our journey—beneath favourable skies.
Turn wheresoe'er we would, he was a light
Unfailing: not a Hamlet could we pass,

22–25 Than this obscure Itinerant had skill / To gather, ranging through the tamer ground *1827–; so MS. 1814/27 but* (had skill / To gather ranging
32 *del MS. 1814/27, om 1827–*
35 beneath] under *MS. 1832/36–*

Rarely a House, which did not yield to him
Remembrances; or from his tongue call forth
Some way-beguiling tale. Nor less regard
Accompanied those strains of apt discourse,
Which Nature's various objects might supply:
And in the silence of his face I read
His overflowing spirit. Birds and beasts,
And the mute fish that glances in the stream,
And harmless reptile coiling in the sun,
And gorgeous insect hovering in the air,
The fowl domestic, and the household dog,
In his capacious mind—he loved them all:
Their rights acknowledging he felt for all.
Oft was occasion given me to perceive
How the calm pleasures of the pasturing Herd
To happy contemplation soothed his walk
Along the field, and in the shady grove;
How the poor Brute's condition, forced to run
Its course of suffering in the public road,
Sad contrast! all too often smote his heart
With unavailing pity. Rich in love
And sweet humanity, he was, himself,
To the degree that he desired, beloved.
—Greetings and smiles we met with all day long
From faces that he knew; we took our seats
By many a cottage hearth, where he received
The welcome of an Inmate come from far.
—Nor was he loth to enter ragged Huts,
Wherein his charity was blessed; his voice
Heard as the voice of an experienced Friend.
And, sometimes, where the Poor Man held dispute
With his own mind, unable to subdue
Impatience, through inaptness to perceive

---

38 which] that *MS. 1814/27–*

42 supply:] inspire: with *possibly an attempt, eras, to change colon into period MS. 1814/27* inspire; *1827–*

51 perceive] observe *pencil alt MS. 1836/45*

54 *del MS. 1814/27, om 1827–*

61–62 Smiles of good-will from faces that he knew / Greeted us all day long; we took our seats *1845–; so MS. 1836/45 from* Smiles *through* long *interlined without punct or hyphen; pencil, partially eras, in left margin without punct;* Smiles of good-will we met with *pencil, eras, at page foot; continuous copy of ll. 61–64 in pencil at bottom of facing page without punct; additional draft in pencil in right margin:*

Smiles of good will
{G
{~~greetings and smiles~~ from faces that he knew
greeted us
We met with all day long we took our seats

64 come from far.] from afar, *1845–*

64/65 And I at once forgot, I was a Stranger. *1845–; so MS. 1836/45 interlined ink over pencil, eras, without comma; line but with* Stranger.] stranger *in pencil at page foot; line in pencil but no punct in right margin of facing page; pencil in left margin of facing page:* And I who, as his youthful Friend, had entered / Not loth, forgot at once I was a Stranger. *then del*

66 Huts where his charity was blest; his voice *1827–; so MS. 1814/27 but* Where

General distress in his particular lot;
Or cherishing resentment, or in vain
Struggling against it, with a soul perplexed,
And finding in itself no steady power
To draw the line of comfort that divides
Calamity, the chastisement of heaven,
From the injustice of our brother men;
To Him appeal was made as to a judge;
Who, with an understanding heart, allayed
The perturbation; listened to the plea;
Resolved the dubious point; and sentence gave
So grounded, so applied, that it was heard
With softened spirit,—even when it condemned.

Such intercourse I witnessed, while we roved
Now as his choice directed, now as mine;
Or both, with equal readiness of will,
Our course submitting to the changeful breeze
Of accident. But when the rising sun
Had three times called us to renew our walk,
My Fellow Traveller said with earnest voice,
As if the thought were but a moment old,
That I must yield myself without reserve
To his disposal. Glad was I of this:
We started—and he led towards the hills;
Up through an ample vale, with higher hills
Before us, mountains stern and desolate;
But in the majesty of distance now
Set off, and to our ken appearing fair
Of aspect, with aerial softness clad,
And beautified with morning's purple beams.

The Wealthy, the Luxurious, by the stress
Of business roused, or pleasure, ere their time,
May roll in chariots, or provoke the hoofs
Of the fleet coursers they bestride, to raise
From earth the dust of morning, slow to rise;
And They, if blessed with health and hearts at ease,
Shall lack not their enjoyment:—but how faint
Compared with our's! who, pacing side by side,
Could with an eye of leisure look on all
That we beheld; and lend the listening sense
To every grateful sound of earth and air,

---

74 itself] herself *MS. 1814/27–*
90 said with] claim'd with *MS. 1814/27, 1827* with *1832–*
92–93 An absolute dominion for the day. *1827– but* An] Claimed *1832– ; MS. 1814/27 as 1827 but* day:
94 led towards] led me toward *1836–*

Pausing at will; our spirits braced, our thoughts
Pleasant as roses in the thickets blown,
[110] And pure as dew bathing their crimson leaves.

Mount slowly Sun! and may our journey lie
[112] Awhile within the shadow of this hill,
This friendly hill, a shelter from thy beams!
[113] Such is the summer Pilgrim's frequent wish;
And as that wish, with prevalence of thanks
For present good o'er fear of future ill,
[114] Stole in among the morning's blither thoughts,
[115] 'Twas chased away: for, tow'rds the western side
Of the broad Vale, casting a casual glance,
We saw a throng of People;—wherefore met?
Blithe notes of music, suddenly let loose
On the thrilled ear, did to the question yield
[120] Prompt answer: they proclaim the annual Wake,
Which the bright season favours.—Tabor and Pipe
In purpose join to hasten and reprove
The laggard Rustic; and repay with boons
Of merriment a party-coloured Knot,
[125] Already formed upon the Village green.
—Beyond the limits of the shadow cast
By the broad hill, glistened upon our sight
That gay Assemblage. Round them and above,
Glitter, with dark recesses interposed,
[130] Casement, and cottage-roof, and stems of trees
Half-veiled in vapoury cloud, the silver steam
Of dews fast melting on their leafy boughs
By the strong sun-beams smitten. Like a mast
Of gold, the Maypole shines; as if the rays
[135] Of morning, aided by exhaling dew,
With gladsome influence could reanimate
The faded garlands dangling from its sides.

Said I, "the music and the sprightly scene
Invite us; shall we quit our road and join
[140] These festive matins?"—He replied, "Not loth
Here would I linger, and with you partake,
Not one hour merely, but till evening's close,
The simple pastimes of the day and place.
By the fleet Racers, ere the Sun be set,

115–117 Mount slowly, Sun! that we may journey long, / By this dark hill protected from thy beams! *1827– but* sun! *1836–; MS. 1814/27 as 1827 but* slowly Sun that . . . long *MS. 1832/36 at page foot in ink, del by pencil:* Their brightness seeing, by their heat untou *and beneath* untou *is* untouch *in pencil*

119–121 But quickly from among our morning thoughts, *MS. 1814/27–*

126 did the question yield] and flags uprising, yield *1827–; so MS. 1814/27 but* uprising

129 and] or *MS. 1832/36–*

148 To linger I would here with you partake, *1845–; so MS. 1836/45, in ink over illeg pencil, but* linger, . . . partake

[145] The turf of yon large pasture will be skimmed:
There, too, the lusty Wrestlers will contend:—
But know we not that he, who intermits
The appointed task and duties of the day,
Untunes full oft the pleasures of the day;
[150] Checking the finer spirits that refuse
To flow, when purposes are lightly changed?
We must proceed—a length of journey yet
Remains untraced." Then, pointing with his staff
Towards those craggy summits, his intent
[155] He thus imparted.
"In a spot that lies
Among yon mountain fastnesses concealed,
You will receive, before the hour of noon,
Good recompence, I hope, for this day's toil—
From sight of One who lives secluded there,
[160] Lonesome and lost: of whom, and whose past life,
(Not to forestal such knowledge as may be
More faithfully collected from himself,)
This brief communication shall suffice.

Though now sojourning there, he, like myself,
[165] Sprang from a stock of lowly parentage
Among the wilds of Scotland; in a tract
Where many a sheltered and well-tended plant,
[168] Upon the humblest ground of social life,
Doth at this day, I trust, the blossoms bear
[169] Of piety and simple innocence.
[170] Such grateful promises his youth displayed:
[171] And, as he shewed in study forward zeal,
All helps were sought, all measures strained, that He,
By due scholastic discipline prepared,
[172] Might to the Ministry be called: which done,
Partly through lack of better hopes—and part

---

153 will] shall *MS. 1814/27–*
159–160 A length of journey yet remains untraced: / Let us proceed." Then, pointing with his staff *1845– ; so MS. 1836/45 interlined through* proceed *but* untrace *and no quots or punct; interlined words repeated in pencil at page foot but* untrac'd . . . proceed.
161 Towards] Raised toward *1832–*
174 plant,] plan *1850*
175–177 Bears, on the humblest ground of social life, / Blossoms of piety and innocence. *1827– ; MS. 1814/27 draft:* Bears ~~at this day I trust~~ on the humblest ground of rural life / Blossoms [*inserted*] Of piety and innocence.
179–185 And, having shown in study forward zeal,
He to the Ministry was duly call'd;
And straight incited by a curious mind
Fill'd with vague hopes, he undertook the charge *1827– but* called; . . . Filled
1832– straight, *MS. 1832/36–*; *MS. 1814/27 as 1827 but* shewn . . . called: . . . mind, . . . hopes
he *drafts in MS. 1814/27:* course of *pencil, eras, in left margin; above l. 181:*
[? ? ?]
[?By course of due] [? ? ?]
[? ?] to the ministry was call'd
[?And when by due scholastic discip] *pencil, eras, at page foot*

[173] Perhaps incited by a curious mind,
In early life he undertook the charge
[175] Of Chaplain to a Military Troop
Cheered by the Highland Bagpipe, as they marched
In plaided vest,—his Fellow-countrymen.
This Office filling, and, by native power
And force of native inclination, made
[180] An intellectual Ruler in the haunts
Of social vanity—he walked the World,
Gay, and affecting graceful gaiety;
Lax, buoyant—less a Pastor with his Flock
Than a Soldier among Soldiers—lived and roamed
[185] Where Fortune led:—and Fortune, who oft proves
The careless wanderer's Friend, to him made known
A blooming Lady—a conspicuous Flower,
Admired for beauty, for her sweetness praised;
Whom he had sensibility to love,
[190] Ambition to attempt, and skill to win.

For this fair Bride, most rich in gifts of mind,
Nor sparingly endowed with worldly wealth,
His Office he relinquished; and retired
From the world's notice to a rural Home.
[195] Youth's season yet with him was scarcely past,
[196/197] And she was in youth's prime. How full their joy,
[196] How free their love! nor did their love decay;
[197] Nor joy abate, till, pitiable doom!
In the short course of one undreaded year
Death blasted all.—Death suddenly o'erthrew
[200] Two lovely Children—all that they possessed!
The Mother followed:—miserably bare
The one Survivor stood; he wept, he prayed
For his dismissal; day and night, compelled
By pain to turn his thoughts towards the grave,
[205] And face the regions of Eternity.

---

188 vest] garb *pencil MS. 1836/45*
189 and,] yet, *MS. 1814/27* yet *1827–*
208 their] that *MS. 1814/27–1843, see ll. 207–209, below*
207–209 And she was in youth's prime. How free their love, / How full their joy! 'Till, pitiable doom! *1845– ; MS. 1836/45 has a series of drafts:* nor . . . abate *in printed text del to* All in one [?woeful] year *pencil in right margin*

How free their love till all was blasted
In one undreaded year Death swept away *pencil at top of page*
~~How free their love, till, in~~ the [?year] of one
~~Undreaded~~ *pencil at top of facing page*
Till all by death [?was] blasted
In one undread year Death swept [?awa] *pencil in right margin of facing page*

216–217 To hold communion with the grave, and face / With pain the regions of eternity. *1845– ; MS. 1836/45 drafts:* To commune with the grave, soul sick, & face/ With pain *interlined*

soul-sick
To commune with the grave, soul-sick and face
With pain the regions of eternity *pencil at page foot*

An uncomplaining apathy displaced
This anguish; and, indifferent to delight,
To aim and purpose, he consumed his days,
To private interest dead, and public care.
[210] So lived he; so he might have died.
But now,
To the wide world's astonishment, appeared
The glorious opening, the unlooked-for dawn,
[213] That promised everlasting joy to France!
That sudden light had power to pierce the gloom
In which his Spirit, friendless upon earth,
In separation dwelt, and solitude.
[214] The voice of social transport reached even him!
[215] He broke from his contracted bounds, repaired
To the great City, an Emporium then
Of golden expectations, and receiving
Freights every day from a new world of hope.
Thither his popular talents he transferred;
[220] And from the Pulpit zealously maintained
The cause of Christ and civil liberty,
As one; and moving to one glorious end.
Intoxicating service! I might say
A happy service; for he was sincere
[225] As vanity and fondness for applause,
And new and shapeless wishes, would allow.

That righteous Cause of freedom did, we know,
Combine, for one hostility, as friends,
Etherial Natures and the worst of Slaves;
[230] Was served by rival Advocates that came
From regions opposite as heaven and hell.
One courage seemed to animate them all:
And, from the dazzling conquests daily gained
By their united efforts, there arose
[235] A proud and most presumptuous confidence
In the transcendent wisdom of the age,
And its discernment; not alone in rights,
And in the origin and bounds of power,
Social and temporal; but in laws divine,
[240] Deduced by reason, or to faith revealed.
An overweening trust was raised; and fear
Cast out,—alike of person and of thing.

---

224 The] A *MS. 1814/27–*
226–228 *del MS. 1814/27, om 1827–*
229 The] Her *MS. 1814/27–*
242–243 That righteous Cause (such power hath Freedom) bound, / For one hostility, in friendly league *1827– but* cause . . . freedom) *MS. 1832/36–* league, *1845–* ; *MS. 1814/27 as 1827 but* Cause, such . . . freedom, bound
252 its] her *MS. 1814/27–*

Plague from this union spread, whose subtle bane
The strongest did not easily escape;
And He, what wonder! took a mortal taint.
How shall I trace the change, how bear to tell
That he broke faith with those whom he had laid
In earth's dark chambers, with a Christian's hope!
An infidel contempt of holy writ
Stole by degrees upon his mind; and hence
Life, like that Roman Janus, double-faced;
Vilest hypocrisy, the laughing, gay
Hypocrisy, not leagued with fear, but pride.
Smooth words he had to wheedle simple souls;
But, for disciples of the inner school,
Old freedom was old servitude, and they
The wisest, whose opinions stooped the least
To known restraints: and who most boldly drew
Hopeful prognostications from a creed,
Which, in the light of false philosophy,
Spread like a halo round a misty moon,
Widening its circle as the storms advance.

His sacred function was at length renounced;
And every day and every place enjoyed
The unshackled Layman's natural liberty;
Speech, manners, morals, all without disguise.
I do not wish to wrong him;—though the course
Of private life licentiously displayed
Unhallowed actions—planted like a crown
Upon the insolent aspiring brow
Of spurious notions—worn as open signs
Of prejudice subdued—he still retained,
'Mid such abasement, what he had received
From nature—an intense and glowing mind.
Wherefore, when humbled Liberty grew weak
And mortal sickness on her face appeared,
He coloured objects to his own desire
As with a Lover's passion. Yet his moods
Of pain were keen as those of better men,
Nay keener—as his fortitude was less.
And he continued, when worse days were come,
To deal about his sparkling eloquence,
Struggling against the strange reverse with zeal
That showed like happiness; but, in despite

---

262 those] them *MS. 1814/27–*
275 Which] That *MS. 1814/27–*
287 he still] still he *MS. 1832/36–*
288 such] much *1836–*

[285] Of all this outside bravery, within,
He neither felt encouragement nor hope.
For moral dignity, and strength of mind,
Were wanting; and simplicity of Life;
And reverence for himself; and, last and best,
[290] Confiding thoughts, and love and fear of Him
Before whose sight the troubles of this world
Are vain as billows in a tossing sea.

The glory of the times fading away,
The splendor, which had given a festal air
[295] To self-importance, hallowed it, and veiled
From his own sight,—this gone, therewith he lost
All joy in human nature; was consumed,
And vexed, and chased, by levity and scorn,
And fruitless indignation; galled by pride;
[300] Made desperate by contempt of Men who throve
Before his sight in power or fame, and won,
Without desert, what he desired; weak men,
[303] Too weak even for his envy or his hate!
—And thus beset, and finding in himself
Nor pleasure nor tranquillity, at last,
[304] After a wandering course of discontent
[305] In foreign Lands, and inwardly oppressed
With malady—in part, I fear, provoked
By weariness of life, he fixed his Home,
Or, rather say, sate down by very chance,
Among these rugged hills; where now he dwells,
[310] And wastes the sad remainder of his hours
In self-indulging spleen, that doth not want
Its own voluptuousness;—on this resolved,
With this content, that he will live and die
Forgotten,—at safe distance from a "world
[315] Not moving to his mind."
These serious words
Closed the preparatory notices

---

305 and] through *MS. 1814/27–*
311 therewith he lost] he forfeited *MS. 1814/27–*
313 chased] chafed *pencil MS. 1814/27, 1820E–*
319–322 Tormented thus, after a wandering course / Of discontent, and inwardly oppress'd *1827–; so MS. 1814/27 but* oppressed *MS. 1814/27 first adds* Tormented thus *pencil in left margin and an illeg pencil draft, probably of ll. 319–322, at page foot and then eras*
328 Steeped in a self-indulging spleen, that wants not *1845–; so MS. 1836/45 but* Steep'd . . . not *interlined, then* Steep'd in a self-indulging spleen that wants *pencil at page foot*

---

313 Early alteration of the 1814 reading "chased" to "chafed" (in pencil in MS. 1814/27, adopted in 1820E and subsequent editions) raises the possibility that "chased" is a mistake. In the two surviving MSS that contain this line (MS. 71, 45^{r}, and MS. 70, 62^{v}), MW wrote "chased," and we have thus kept that word in the reading text. It is conceivable, however, that MW's "chased" is the result of mishearing "chafed" in taking dictation.

With which my Fellow-traveller had beguiled
The way, while we advanced up that wide Vale.
Now, suddenly diverging, he began
To climb upon its western side a Ridge
Pathless and smooth, a long and steep ascent;
As if the object of his quest had been
Some secret of the Mountains, Cavern, Fall
Of water—or some boastful Eminence,
Renowned for splendid prospect far and wide.
We clomb without a track to guide our steps;
And, on the summit, reached a heathy plain,
With a tumultuous waste of huge hill tops
Before us; savage region! and I walked
In weariness: when, all at once, behold!
Beneath our feet, a little lowly Vale,
A lowly Vale, and yet uplifted high
Among the mountains; even as if the spot
Had been, from eldest time by wish of theirs,
So placed,—to be shut out from all the world!
Urn-like it was in shape, deep as an Urn;
With rocks encompassed, save that to the South
Was one small opening, where a heath-clad ridge
Supplied a boundary less abrupt and close.
A quiet treeless nook, with two green fields,
A liquid pool that glittered in the sun,
And one bare Dwelling; one Abode, no more!
It seemed the home of poverty and toil
Though not of want: the little fields, made green
By husbandry of many thrifty years,
Paid cheerful tribute to the moorland House.
—There crows the Cock, single in his domain:
The small birds find in spring no thicket there
To shroud them; only from the neighbouring Vales
The Cuckoo straggling up to the hill tops
Shouteth faint tidings of some gladder place.

---

334 That served my Fellow-traveller to beguile *1827–; so MS. 1814/27 in pencil but* that served *eras*

336–339 Diverging now (as if his quest had been *1827–; so MS. 1814/27 but* now, as e*arlier rev in MS. 1814/27: in l. 337* climb] scale *pencil, eras; in l. 338* smooth] steep *pencil, eras*

341 some boastful] conspicuous *alt MS. 1836/45* boastful] lofty *pencil MS. 1836/45, 1845–*

343 clomb . . . guide] scaled, . . . ease *1827–; so MS. 1814/27 but* scaled,] scaled

344 A steep ascent; and reach'd a dreary plain, *1827– but* reached *1832–*; *MS. 1814/27 as 1827 but* ascent, . . . reached at length a dreary plain,

346 and I walked] which I paced *MS. 1814/27–*

347 In weariness:] Dispirited: *MS. 1814/27–*

357 nook,] nook,* *with note* No longer strictly applicable, on account of recent plantations. *Guide 1835*

Ah! what a sweet Recess, thought I, is here!
Instantly throwing down my limbs at ease
Upon a bed of heath;—full many a spot
Of hidden beauty have I chanced to espy
Among the mountains; never one like this;
So lonesome, and so perfectly secure:
Not melancholy—no, for it is green,
And bright, and fertile, furnished in itself
With the few needful things which life requires.
—In rugged arms how soft it seems to lie,
How tenderly protected! Far and near
We have an image of the pristine earth,
The planet in its nakedness; were this
Man's only dwelling, sole appointed seat,
First, last, and single in the breathing world,
It could not be more quiet: peace is here
Or no where; days unruffled by the gale
Of public news or private; years that pass
Forgetfully; uncalled upon to pay
The common penalties of mortal life,
Sickness, or accident, or grief, or pain.

On these and other kindred thoughts intent,
In silence by my Comrade's side I lay,
He also silent: when from out the heart
Of that profound Abyss a solemn Voice,
Or several Voices in one solemn sound,
Was heard—ascending: mournful, deep, and slow
The cadence, as of Psalms—a funeral dirge!
We listened, looking down towards the Hut,
But seeing no One: meanwhile from below
The strain continued, spiritual as before;
And now distinctly could I recognize
These words;—*"Shall in the Grave thy love be known,*
In Death thy faithfulness?"—"God rest his Soul,"
The Wanderer cried, abruptly breaking silence,
"He is departed, and finds peace at last!"

---

377 which] that *MS. 1814/27–*
378 —In rugged arms how softly does it lie, *1836–*
389 pain.] *so 1820E–* pain *1814*
390–391 On these and kindred thoughts intent I lay / In silence musing by my Comrade's side, *MS. 1814/27– but* lay, *1827* musing In silence *word order altered by transposition mark MS. 1836/45*
397 towards] upon *1827–*
403 Said the old man, abruptly breaking silence,— *1845– but* Man, *1846; MS. 1836/45 drafts:*

~~Belike~~ ~~Perhaps~~ those words
Said my companion sighing as he spake
Were chosen by himself—God rest his soul. *page foot*
Said my Companion sighing as he spake *interlined*
Thus by the Wanderer was our silence broken *pencil interlined*

[385] This scarcely spoken, and those holy strains
Not ceasing, forth appeared in view a band
Of rustic Persons, from behind the hut
Bearing a Coffin in the midst, with which
They shaped their course along the sloping side
[390] Of that small Valley; singing as they moved;
A sober company and few, the Men
Bare-headed, and all decently attired!
Some steps when they had thus advanced, the dirge
Ended; and, from the stillness that ensued
[395] Recovering, to my Friend I said, "You spake,
Methought, with apprehension that these rites
Are paid to Him upon whose shy retreat
This day we purposed to intrude."—"I did so.
But let us hence, that we may learn the truth:
[400] Perhaps it is not he but some One else
For whom this pious service is performed;
Some other Tenant of the Solitude."

So, to a steep and difficult descent
Trusting ourselves, we wound from crag to crag,
[405] Where passage could be won; and, as the last
Of the mute train, upon the heathy top
Of that off-sloping Outlet, disappeared,
I, more impatient in the course I took,
Had landed upon easy ground; and there
[410] Stood waiting for my Comrade. When behold
An object that enticed my steps aside!
[412] It was an Entry, narrow as a door;
A passage whose brief windings opened out
[413] Into a platform; that lay, sheepfold-wise,
Enclosed between a single mass of rock
[415] And one old moss-grown wall;—a cool Recess,
And fanciful! For, where the rock and wall
[417] Met in an angle, hung a tiny roof,
Or penthouse, which most quaintly had been framed
[418] By thrusting two rude sticks into the wall
And overlaying them with mountain sods;

---

405 spoken] uttered *ink over pencil, interlined, and pencil in right margin, alt MS. 1836/45*
420 He is it not perhaps *interlined in pencil, eras;* It is not he perhaps *and* He it is not, perhaps, but some one else *in pencil at page foot MS. 1836/45*
422 Some other Tenant] [?For] another ten *pencil MS. 1836/45*
426 upon] behind *1836–*
428 I, more impatient in my downward course, *MS. 1814/27–*
432–433 A narrow, winding Entry opened out *1827– but* winding, *pencil MS. 1836/45, 1845– and* entry *1836–*; *MS. 1814/27 as 1827 but* narrow winding
435 a single] an upright *MS. 1814/27–*
438–439 Met in an angle, hung a penthouse, framed *1827– ; so MS. 1814/27 but* penthouse framed
440 sticks] staves *MS. 1814/27–*

[420] To weather-fend a little turf-built seat
Whereon a full-grown man might rest, nor dread
The burning sunshine, or a transient shower;
But the whole plainly wrought by Children's hands!
[424] Whose simple skill had thronged the grassy floor
With work of frame less solid, a proud show
[425] Of baby-houses, curiously arranged;
Nor wanting ornament of walks between,
With mimic trees inserted in the turf,
And gardens interposed. Pleased with the sight
I could not choose but beckon to my Guide,
[430] Who, having entered, carelessly looked round,
And now would have passed on; when I exclaimed,
"Lo! what is here?" and, stooping down, drew forth
A Book, that, in the midst of stones and moss
And wreck of party-coloured earthen-ware,
[435] Aptly disposed, had lent its help to raise
One of those petty structures. "Gracious Heaven!"
The Wanderer cried, "it cannot but be his,
And he is gone!" The Book, which in my hand
Had opened of itself, (for it was swoln
[440] With searching damp, and seemingly had lain
To the injurious elements exposed
From week to week,) I found to be a work

446–447 Whose skill had throng'd the floor with a proud show *1827– but* thronged *1832– and* a proud show *rev to* proud display *pencil alt MS. 1836/45; MS. 1814/27 as 1827 but* throng'd . . . shew

449 ornament] ornaments *1832* ornament *MS. 1832/36–*

451 sight] show *pencil alt MS. 1836/45; see verbal variants to II, 446–447, above*

453–454 Who, entering, round him threw a careless glance, / Impatient to pass on, when . . . *1827–; so MS. 1814/27 but* Who entering, . . . glance / Impatient . . . on; when . . . when *del in pencil MS. 1836/45, which has illeg pencil rev in right margin MS. 1827/32C interlinear rev:*

{E he [?thr] ~~he threw~~ around
~~Who,~~ ^ {**entering, round him threw a careless glance,**
Entering he threw around [?a]

459–460 One of those petty structures. "His it must be!" / Exclaimed the Wanderer, "cannot but be his, *1845–; MS. 1836/45 drafts:*

~~A sad tale~~
{Verily}
{Merciful Heavens}
~~"Gracious Heaven!"~~
It cannot said the Wanderer but be his
This [?tells] the Wanderer cried it must be his
~~The Wanderer cried, "it cannot but be his,~~
At the sight
[?~~less surprized~~]
[?Than grieved] the wanderer said—this must be his *pencil at top of page*
In a voice
Of wonder
~~Of pity~~ not unmixd with wonder *pencil in right margin*
verily
~~At the sight~~
It cannot, said the Wanderer, but be his
And he is gone!— *pencil at page foot*
He exclaimed / The Wanderer sigh *pencil top of facing page* with a look / And in a *pencil at bottom of facing page*

In the French Tongue, a Novel of Voltaire,
His famous Optimist. "Unhappy Man!"
[445] Exclaimed my Friend; "here then has been to him
Retreat within retreat, a sheltering-place
Within how deep a shelter! He had fits,
Even to the last, of genuine tenderness,
And loved the haunts of Children; here no doubt
[450] He sometimes played with them; and here hath sate
Far oftener by himself. This Book, I guess,
[452] Hath been forgotten in his careless way;
Left here when he was occupied in mind;
[453] And by the Cottage Children has been found.
Heaven bless them, and their inconsiderate work;
[455] To what odd purpose have the Darlings turned
This sad memorial of their hapless Friend!"

"Me, said I, most doth it surprize, to find
Such Book in such a place!" "A Book it is,"
He answered, "to the Person suited well,
[460] Though little suited to surrounding things;
Nor, with the knowledge which my mind possessed,
[461] Could I behold it undisturbed: 'tis strange,
[461/462] I grant, and stranger still had been to see
The Man, who was its Owner, dwelling here,

473–477 Pleasing and pleased, he shared their simple sports,
Or sate companionless; and here the Book,
Left and forgotten in his careless way,
Must by the Cottage Children have been found: *1827– but* book, *MS. 1832/36–* cottage children *MS. 1832/36–1843* cottage-children *1845–; so MS. 1814/27 as 1827 but* & pleas'd he shar'd . . . companionless, & . . . Left, & . . . found.
MS. 1814/27 drafts:

here ,} {no doubt / ~~**no doubt**~~}
~~shared their simple sport~~
{h ~~oftener sat~~
~~Doubtless~~ {**He** ~~**sometimes**~~ ~~**played with them; and here hath sate**~~
~~With no companion but a busy mind~~
~~Hath sate~~ ~~**Far oftener by himself. This Book, I guess,**~~
~~This Book,~~ ~~**Hath been forgotten in his careless way;**~~ ~~[?that] here~~
~~**Left here when he was occupied in mind;**~~
Must have been
~~**And**~~ **by the Cottage Children** ~~**has been**~~ **found.** *with* [?that here] *in right margin, eras, and* [?With no companion but a busy mind] *in pencil, eras, at page foot; thus two early stages of rev seem possible:*

[*1*] here no doubt
He sometimes shared their simple sport and here
Hath sate far oftener by himself.
[*2*] here, [?]
Doubtless he played with them, and oftener sate
With no companion but a busy mind
This Book, forgotten in his careless way
Must by the Cottage Children have been found.

485–486 *del MS. 1814/27, om 1827–*

487–488 'Tis strange, I grant; and stranger still had been / To see the Man who own'd it, dwelling here, *1827– but* owned *1832–; so MS. 1814/27 as 1827 but* grant, . . . Man,

With one poor Shepherd, far from all the world!
Now, if our errand hath been thrown away
As from these intimations I forebode,
Grieved shall I be—less for my sake than your's;
And least of all for Him who is no more."

By this the Book was in the Old Man's hand;
And he continued, glancing on the leaves
An eye of scorn. "The Lover," said he, "doomed
To love when hope hath failed him—whom no depth
Of privacy is deep enough to hide,
Hath yet his bracelet or his lock of hair,
And that is joy to him. When change of times
Hath summoned Kings to scaffolds, do but give
The faithful Servant, who must hide his head
Henceforth in whatsoever nook he may,
A kerchief sprinkled with his Master's blood,
And he too hath his comforter. How poor,
Beyond all poverty how destitute,
Must that Man have been left, who, hither driven,
Flying or seeking, could yet bring with him
No dearer relique, and no better stay,
Than this dull product of a Scoffer's pen,
Impure conceits discharging from a heart
Hardened by impious pride!—I did not fear
To tax you with this journey;"—mildly said
My venerable Friend, as forth we stepped
Into the presence of the cheerful light—
"For I have knowledge that you do not shrink
From moving spectacles;—but let us on."
So speaking, on he went, and at the word
I followed, till he made a sudden stand:
For full in view, approaching through the gate
That opened from the enclosure of green fields
Into the rough uncultivated ground,
Behold the Man whom he had fancied dead!
I knew, from the appearance and the dress,
That it could be no other; a pale face,
A tall and meagre person, in a garb
Not rustic, dull and faded like himself!
He saw us not, though distant but few steps;
For he was busy, dealing, from a store
Which on a leaf he carried in his hand,

---

510 dull] vile *pencil alt MS. 1836/45*
520 the] a *1827–*
524 I knew, from his deportment, mien, and dress, *MS. 1814/27– but* knew *1836–*
526 A meagre person, tall, and in a garb *1845– ; so MS. 1836/45 but* tall &
530 in] on *1820E, see verbal variants to II, 530–531, below*
530–531 Upon a broad leaf carried, choicest strings / Of red ripe currants; . . . *MS. 1814/27–*

[505] Strings of ripe currants; gift by which he strove,
With intermixture of endearing words,
To soothe a Child, who walked beside him, weeping
As if disconsolate.—"They to the Grave
Are bearing him, my little One," he said,
[510] "To the dark pit; but he will feel no pain;
[511] His body is at rest, his soul in Heaven."

Glad was my Comrade now, though he at first,
I doubt not, had been more surprized than glad.
But now, recovered from the shock and calm,
He soberly advanced; and to the Man
[514] Gave cheerful greeting.—Vivid was the light
[515] Which flashed at this from out the Other's eyes;
He was all fire: the sickness from his face
Passed like a fancy that is swept away;
Hands joined he with his Visitant,—a grasp,
An eager grasp; and, many moments' space,
[520] When the first glow of pleasure was no more,
[522] And much of what had vanished was returned,
An amicable smile retained the life
Which it had unexpectedly received,
[525] Upon his hollow cheek. "How kind," he said,

538–543 More might have follow'd—but my honour'd Friend
Broke in upon the Speaker with a frank
And cordial greeting.—Vivid was the light
That flash'd and sparkled from the Other's eyes; *1827– but* followed—but my honoured . . . flashed *1832–* other's *1836–; MS. 1814/27 as 1827 but* followed but . . . honoured . . . speaker . . . flashed

544–545 He was all fire: no shadow on his brow / Remained, nor sign of sickness on his face. *1845–; MS. 1836/45 drafts:* Passed . . . that is *del in l. 545 of printed text, then two or three words of illeg pencil and* no shadow on his brow / No sign of sickness left upon his face;

549 And, of the sad appearance which at once / Had vanished, much was come and coming back— *1840–; MS. 1836/45 has a series of rev related to ll. 547–549: in l. 548* pleasure *del to* tran *(pencil, eras) and in l. 549* was returned *del to* [?much] *(pencil, eras); then printed ll. 548–549 del*

~~When~~ of the sad appearance which at once
Had vanished, much was come & coming back *interlined*
moments space
When the first glow of {pleasure / transport} was no more
the
And ~~when~~ of sad appearance which at once
Had vanished, much was come [?or] coming back *pencil at page foot*
from [?his]
~~And while, of what had vanished~~ both in [?mien]
And
In cariage, much was come
{and / or ~~come com back~~}
~~came again~~ *pencil at top of facing page (continuing from previous page foot)*
~~sad appearance~~
~~And while, of what had vanished on his mien~~
~~which at once~~
[?or]
~~Had vanished, much was come & coming back~~
~~And carriage, much was come or comin back~~ *pencil at top of facing page*

"Nor could your coming have been better timed;
For this, you see, is in our little world
A day of sorrow. I have here a charge"—
And, speaking thus, he patted tenderly
The sun-burnt forehead of the weeping Child—
"A little Mourner whom it is my task
To comfort;—but how came Ye?—if yon track
(Which doth at once befriend us and betray)
Conducted hither your most welcome feet
Ye could not miss the Funeral Train—they yet
Have scarcely disappeared." "This blooming Child,"
Said the Old Man, "is of an age to weep
At any grave or solemn spectacle,
Inly distressed, or overpowered with awe,
He knows not why;—but he, perchance, this day,
Is shedding Orphan's tears; and you yourself
Must have sustained a loss."—"The hand of Death,"
He answered, "has been here; but could not well
Have fallen more lightly, if it had not fallen
Upon myself."—The Other left these words
Unnoticed, thus continuing.—
"From yon Crag,
Down whose steep sides we dropped into the Vale,
We heard the hymn they sang—a solemn sound
Heard anywhere, but in a place like this
'Tis more than human! Many precious rites
And customs of our rural ancestry
Are gone, or stealing from us; this, I hope,

---

554 little] narrow *MS. 1814/27–*
567–568 He knows not wherefore;—but the boy to-day, / Perhaps is shedding orphan's tears; you also *1845– ; MS. 1836/45 has a series of rev related to these lines:*

He knows not ~~why—but he, perchance, this day,~~
wherefore; but the Boy today
i}
Perhaps **I}s shedding orphan's tears; and you ~~yourself~~** also *with rev over two lines of previous interlining:*
[?] [?he is now ~~perchance~~]
Shedding a [?new made] orphan's tears, and you *pencil, eras*
[?] perchance, today
The Boy is shedding Orphan's tears you also *pencil at page foot*
but perhance is shedding
you also
This day, a new made Orphans tears, and yo *pencil in left margin*
But he perchance is now
new-made
new}
Shedding a [?]} made orphans tears—you also
Must have sustained a loss
not} The Boy today
He ~~knows~~ [?wher]} wherefore but ~~perchance~~ today
The Boy} O}
Perchance} is shedding o}rphans tears— *pencil in right margin*

Will last for ever. Often have I stopped
When on my way, I could not chuse but stop,
So much I felt the awfulness of Life,
In that one moment when the Corse is lifted
In silence, with a hush of decency,
Then from the threshold moves with song of peace,
And confidential yearnings, to its home,
Its final home in earth. What Traveller—who—
(How far soe'er a Stranger) does not own
The bond of brotherhood, when he sees them go,
A mute Procession, on the houseless road,
Or passing by some single tenement
Or clustered dwellings, where again they raise
The monitory voice? But most of all
It touches, it confirms, and elevates,
Then, when the Body, soon to be consigned
Ashes to ashes, dust bequeathed to dust,
Is raised from the church-aisle, and forward borne
Upon the shoulders of the next in love,
The nearest in affection or in blood;
Yea by the very Mourners who had knelt
Beside the Coffin, resting on its lid
In silent grief their unuplifted heads,
And heard meanwhile the Psalmist's mournful plaint,
And that most awful scripture which declares
We shall not sleep, but we shall all be changed!
—Have I not seen?—Ye likewise may have seen
Son, Husband, Brothers—Brothers side by side,
And Son and Father also side by side,
Rise from that posture:—and in concert move,
On the green turf following the vested Priest,
Four dear Supporters of one senseless Weight,
From which they do not shrink, and under which
They faint not, but advance towards the grave
Step after step—together, with their firm
Unhidden faces; he that suffers most
He outwardly, and inwardly perhaps,
The most serene, with most undaunted eye!

---

580 Often have I stopped] Oft, on my way have I *MS. 1832/36– but* Oft,] Oft *1836–; see following entry*

581 *del MS. 1814/27, om 1827, 1832* Stood still, though but a casual Passenger, *MS. 1832/36– but* passenger, *1836–* *interleaved in MS. 1832/36 is a letter in WW's hand, the envelope addressed to "Moxon Dover St" with instructions to the printer for the changes here for II, 580–581, and below for II, 919–920:* Mr Evans, dear Sir ~~Be~~ so good as to alter two passages ~~towards~~ in the ~~close of~~ 2nd Book of the Excursion as below— W—

586 to] towards *MS. 1836/45* tow'rds *1845–*

587 in] on *1836–*

613 the] the open *1836–*

Oh! blest are they who live and die like these,
Loved with such love, and with such sorrow mourned!"

"That poor Man taken hence to day," replied
The Solitary, with a faint sarcastic smile
Which did not please me, "must be deemed, I fear,
Of the unblest; for he will surely sink
Into his mother earth without such pomp
Of grief, depart without occasion given
By him for such array of fortitude.
Full seventy winters hath he lived, and mark!
This simple Child will mourn his one short hour,
And I shall miss him; scanty tribute! yet,
This wanting, he would leave the sight of men,
If love were his sole claim upon their care,
Like a ripe date which in the desart falls
Without a hand to gather it." At this
I interposed, though loth to speak, and said,
"Can it be thus among so small a band
As ye must needs be here? in such a place
I would not willingly, methinks, lose sight
Of a departing cloud."—"'Twas not for love"—
Answered the sick man with a careless voice—
"That I came hither; neither have I found
Among Associates who have power of speech,
Nor in such other converse as is here,
Temptation so prevailing as to change
That mood, or undermine my first resolve."—
Then, speaking in like careless sort, he said
To my benign Companion,—"Pity 'tis
That fortune did not guide you to this house
A few days earlier; then would you have seen
What stuff the Dwellers in this Solitude,
(That seems by Nature framed to be the seat
And very bosom of pure innocence)
Are made of; an ungracious matter this!
Which for truth's sake, yet in remembrance too
Of past discussions with this zealous Friend
And Advocate of humble life, I now
Will force upon his notice; undeterred
By the example of his own pure course,
And that respect and deference which a soul
May fairly claim, by niggard age enriched

---

628 his] for *pencil MS. 1836/45*
649 this] a *1827–*
650–651 That seems by Nature hollow'd out to be / The seat and bosom of pure innocence, *1827–but* hollowed *1832–; MS. 1814/27 as 1827 but* come & . . . hollowed

In what it values most—the love of God
And his frail creature Man;—but ye shall hear.
[635] I talk—and ye are standing in the sun
[636/638] Without refreshment!"
Saying this he led
[638] Towards the Cottage;—homely was the spot;
And, to my feeling, ere we reached the door,
[640] Had almost a forbidding nakedness;
Less fair, I grant, even painfully less fair,
Than it appeared when from the Valley's brink
We had looked down upon it. All within,
As left by that departed company,
[645] Was silent; and the solitary clock
Ticked, as I thought, with melancholy sound.—
Following our Guide we clomb the cottage stairs
And reached a small apartment dark and low,
Which was no sooner entered than our Host
[650] Said gaily, "This is my domain, my cell,
My hermitage, my cabin, what you will.—
I love it better than a snail his house.
But now Ye shall be feasted with our best."
So, with more ardour than an unripe girl
[655] Left one day mistress of her mother's stores,
He went about his hospitable task.
My eyes were busy, and my thoughts no less,
And pleased I looked upon my grey-haired Friend
As if to thank him; he returned that look,
[660] Cheered plainly, and yet serious. What a wreck

---

660 it] she *MS. 1814/27–* In what she most doth value, love of God *1845–* *MS. 1836/45 has a series of drafts related to II, 659–661:* In . . . the *del to* And more as years are multiplied / With what he most delighted in, *interlined*

With what
In what he most delighted
With what he most delighted in, love of
And his frail creat *pencil at page foot*
niggardly age enriched,
Even
~~And~~ more & more as years are multiplied,
With what he most delighted in, love of God
And his frail Creature Man,— *pencil in right margin*
by niggard age enrich d,
even more & more as years are multiplied
With what he most delights in, love of god
And his frail creature *pencil on verso of half title*

663–664 Without refreshment!" Quickly had he spoken,
And with light steps still quicker than his words,
Led tow'rds the Cottage;— . . . *1836– but para at* Quickly *MS. 1836/45, 1845–* And, . . . Cottage. *1845–* tow'rds] toward *MS. 1836/45, 1840–*

668 Valley's brink] beetling rock *MS. 1814/27–*

670 that] the *MS. 1814/27–*

671 and] save *MS. 1836/45, 1845–*

672 That on mine ear ticked with a mournful sound.— *MS. 1836/45, 1845–* *MS. 1836/45 also has right-margin pencil draft as 1845 but* mine] my *and* sound.—] sound

We had around us! scattered was the floor,
And, in like sort, chair, window-seat, and shelf,
With books, maps, fossils, withered plants and flowers,
And tufts of mountain moss; and here and there
[665] Lay, intermixed with these, mechanic tools,
[665] And scraps of paper,—some I could perceive
[666] Scribbled with verse: a broken angling-rod
And shattered telescope, together linked
By cobwebs, stood within a dusty nook;
And instruments of music, some half-made,
[670] Some in disgrace, hung dangling from the walls.
—But speedily the promise was fulfilled,
A feast before us, and a courteous Host
Inviting us in glee to sit and eat.
A napkin, white as foam of that rough brook
[675] By which it had been bleached, o'erspread the board;
And was itself half-covered with a load
Of dainties,—oaten bread, curds, cheese, and cream,
And cakes of butter curiously embossed,
[679/680] Butter that had imbibed a golden tinge,
[680] A hue like that of yellow meadow flowers
Reflected faintly in a silent pool.
Nor lacked, for more delight on that warm day,
Our Table, small parade of garden fruits,
And whortle-berries from the mountain-sides.
[685] The Child, who long ere this had stilled his sobs,
Was now a help to his late Comforter,
And moved a willing Page, as he was bid,
Ministering to our need.
In genial mood
While at our pastoral banquet thus we sate
[690] Fronting the window of that little Cell,
I could not ever and anon forbear
To glance an upward look on two huge Peaks,
That from some other Vale peered into this.
"Those lusty Twins on which your eyes are cast,"

687 We had around us!] Had we around us! *MS. 1814/27–1843* Had we about us! *ink over pencil MS. 1836/45, 1845–*
690–692 And tufts of mountain moss; mechanic tools / Lay intermix'd with scraps of paper,—some *1827– but* moss: *1832* moss. Mechanic . . . paper, some *MS. 1832/36–* intermixed *1832–; MS. 1814/27 as 1827 but* Lay, intermixed . . . paper some
699 a] the *MS. 1814/27*
703 load] store *pencil and ink MS. 1836/45, 1845–*
704 curds] curd *MS. 1814/27–*
706 a golden tinge] from meadow-flowers *1832–*
707–708 From meadow flowers, hue delicate as theirs / Faintly reflected in a lingering stream; *1827; so MS. 1814/27 but* flowers hue . . . Faintly Reflected . . . stream. A golden hue, delicate as their own, / Faintly reflected in a lingering stream; *1832– but* own / Faintly . . . stream. *MS. 1832/36–*
711 mountain-sides] mountain-side *1827, 1832* mountain side *1836–*
713 Was now] Became *MS. 1814/27*

Exclaimed our Host, "if here you dwelt, would be
Your prized Companions.—Many are the notes
Which in his tuneful course the wind draws forth
From rocks, woods, caverns, heaths, and dashing shores;
And well those lofty Brethren bear their part
In the wild concert—chiefly when the storm
Rides high; then all the upper air they fill
With roaring sound, that ceases not to flow,
Like smoke, along the level of the blast
In mighty current; theirs, too, is the song
Of stream and headlong flood that seldom fails;
And, in the grim and breathless hour of noon,
Methinks that I have heard them echo back
The thunder's greeting:—nor have Nature's laws
Left them ungifted with a power to yield
Music of finer frame; a harmony,
So do I call it, though it be the hand
Of silence, though there be no voice;—the clouds,
The mist, the shadows, light of golden suns,
Motions of moonlight, all come thither—touch,
And have an answer—thither come, and shape
A language not unwelcome to sick hearts
And idle spirits:—there the sun himself
At the calm close of summer's longest day
Rests his substantial Orb;—between those heights
And on the top of either pinnacle,
More keenly than elsewhere in night's blue vault,
Sparkle the Stars as of their station proud.
Thoughts are not busier in the mind of man
Than the mute Agents stirring there:—alone
Here do I sit and watch.—"
                                        With brightening face
The Wanderer heard him speaking thus, and said,

721–722 "Those lusty Twins," exclaim'd our host, "if here / It were your lot to dwell, would soon become *1827– but* twins *1836–* exclaimed *1832–*; *MS. 1814/27 as 1827 but* Twins" exclaimed our Host "if . . . dwell would

737 frame] tone *MS. 1814/27–*

752–759 Here do I sit and watch.—"
                                        A fall of voice,
Regretted like the Nightingale's last note,
Had scarcely closed this high-wrought Rhapsody,
Ere with inviting smile the Wanderer said,
"Now for the Tale with which you threaten'd us!"
"In truth the threat escaped me unawares;
Should the tale tire you, let this challenge stand
For my excuse. Dissever'd from mankind,
As to your eyes and thoughts we must have seem'd *1827– but* Nightingale's] nightingale's *MS. 1832/36–* Rhapsody,] rhapsody, *MS. 1832/36–1843* rhapsody,] strain of rapture *1845– but MS. 1836/45 has rev:* this strain of gratitude *pencil in right margin, and* strain of thankful rapture *interlined, and* & closed this strain of thankful rapture *pencil at page foot* said,] said: *1836–* Dissever'd] Dissevered *1832–* seem'd] seemed *1832– but* seemed *rev to* seemed, *MS. 1836/45; entry continues, below*

"Now for the Tale with which you threatened us!"
[730] "In truth the threat escaped me unawares
And was forgotten. Let this challenge stand
[732] For my excuse, if what I shall relate
Tire your attention.—Outcast and cut off
[733] As we seem here, and must have seemed to you
When ye looked down upon us from the crag,
[735] Islanders of a stormy Mountain sea,
We are not so;—perpetually we touch
Upon the vulgar ordinance of the world,
And he, whom this our Cottage hath to-day
Relinquished, was dependant for his bread
[740] Upon the laws of public charity.
The Housewife, tempted by such slender gains
As might from that occasion be distilled,
Opened, as she before had done for me,
Her doors to admit this homeless Pensioner;
[745] The portion gave of coarse but wholesome fare
Which appetite required—a blind dull nook
Such as she had—the *kennel* of his rest!
This, in itself not ill, would yet have been
Ill borne in earlier life; but his was now
[750] The still contentedness of seventy years.
Calm did he sit beneath the wide-spread tree
Of his old age; and yet less calm and meek,
Winningly meek or venerably calm,

752–759 *MS. 1814/27 has two rev:*
[*1*] A fall of voice
~~**With brightening face**~~
Regretted like the Nightingale's last note
~~**The Wanderer heard him speaking thus, and said,**~~
~~Closing this rapsody~~
~~**"Now for the Tale with which you threatened us!"**~~
"In truth the threat escaped me unawares
Should the tale tire you let
~~**And was forgotten**~~**. Let this challenge stand**
For my excuse, if what I shall relate
Dissevered from mankind
~~**Tire your attention.—Outcast and cut off**~~
As to your eyes & thoughts we must have seem'd
As we seem here, and must have seemed to you *interlined*
[*2*] ~~A fall~~ A fall of voice
Regretted like the Nightingale's last note
ug
Had scarcely closed this high-wrote rapsody
Ere with inviting voice the Wanderer said
~~In truth~~
Now for the Tale with which you threatened us!
"In truth *page foot with first* A fall *in initial line del by eras*
761 of] mid *pencil and ink MS. 1836/45, 1845–*
763 ordinance] ordinances *MS. 1832/36–*
765 was] lived *MS. 1814/27–*
777 beneath] under *MS. 1832/36–*
779 Winningly] Willingly *1832* Winningly *MS. 1832/36–*

Than slow and torpid; paying in this wise
A penalty, if penalty it were,
For spendthrift feats, excesses of his prime.
I loved the Old Man, for I pitied him!
A task it was, I own, to hold discourse
With One so slow in gathering up his thoughts,
But he was a cheap pleasure to my eyes;
Mild, inoffensive, ready in *his* way,
And useful to his utmost power: and there
Our Housewife knew full well what she possess'd!
He was her Vassal of all labour, tilled
Her garden, from the pasture fetched her Kine;
And, one among the orderly array
Of Hay-makers, beneath the burning sun
Maintained his place; or heedfully pursued
His course, on errands bound, to other vales,
Leading sometimes an inexperienced Child
Too young for any profitable task.
So moved he like a Shadow that performed
Substantial service. Mark me now, and learn
For what reward! The Moon her monthly round
Hath not completed since our Dame, the Queen
Of this one cottage and this lonely dale,
Into my little sanctuary rushed,
Voice to a rueful treble humanized,
And features in deplorable dismay.—
I treat the matter lightly, but alas!
It is most serious: from mid-noon the rain
Had fallen in torrents; all the mountain tops
Were hidden, and black vapours coursed their sides;
This had I seen and saw; but, till she spake,
Was wholly ignorant that my ancient Friend,
Who at her bidding, early and alone,
Had clomb aloft to delve the mountain turf
For winter fuel, to his noontide meal
Came not, and now perchance upon the Heights
Lay at the mercy of this raging storm.

---

788 useful] helpful *MS. 1814/27–*
788–797 *del MS. 1827/32C*
795 course] track *pencil interlined* way *left margin MS. 1836/45*
798 And moving like *interlined* And moving like a Shadow *page foot MS. 1827/32C*
806 alas] in truth *pencil in right margin, alt* sooth *partially eras MS. 1836/45*
807 It is most serious: persevering rain *MS. 1814/27–*
809 vapours *del to* mists scu *interlined in pencil* Were hiden in a blak mists / scudding along their sides *pencil in right margin MS. 1836/45*
811 [?Had] *pencil, eras, in left margin* [?with pain] [?] *pencil, eras, in right margin MS. 1814/27*
813 mountain] moorland *MS. 1814/27–*
815 Return'd not, and now, haply, on the Heights *1827– but* Returned *1832–* heights *MS. 1832/36–; MS. 1814/27 as 1827 but* Returned . . . now haply on

"Inhuman!"—said I, "was an Old Man's life
Not worth the trouble of a thought?—alas!
This notice comes too late." With joy I saw
Her Husband enter—from a distant Vale.
[795] We sallied forth together; found the tools
Which the neglected Veteran had dropped,
But through all quarters looked for him in vain.
We shouted—but no answer! Darkness fell
Without remission of the blast or shower,
[800] And fears for our own safety drove us home.
I, who weep little, did, I will confess,
The moment I was seated here alone,
Honour my little Cell with some few tears
Which anger or resentment could not dry.
[805] All night the storm endured; and, soon as help
Had been collected from the neighbouring Vale,
With morning we renewed our quest: the wind
Was fallen, the rain abated, but the hills
Lay shrouded in impenetrable mist;
[810] And long and hopelessly we sought in vain.
Till, chancing by yon lofty ridge to pass
A heap of ruin, almost without walls
And wholly without roof (in ancient time
It was a Chapel, a small Edifice
[815] In which the Peasants of these lonely Dells
[816] For worship met upon that central height)—
Chancing to pass this wreck of stones, we there
[817] Espied at last the Object of our search,
Couched in a nook, and seemingly alive.
It would have moved you, had you seen the guise
In which he occupied his chosen bed,
[818] Lying full three parts buried among tufts
Of heath-plant, under and above him strewn,
[820] To baffle, as he might, the watery storm:
And there we found him breathing peaceably,
Snug as a Child that hides itself in sport
Mid a green hay-cock in a sunny field.
We spake—he made reply, but would not stir

---

830 or] and *MS. 1814/27–*
831 and] [?but] *pencil, then del MS. 1836/45*
835 mist] vapour *pencil, then del MS. 1836/45*
837 by yon] on that *MS. 1814/27–*
839–844 And wholly without roof, (the bleach'd remains
Of a small Chapel, where, in ancient time,
The Peasants of these lonely valleys used
To meet for worship on that central height)—
We there espied the Object of our search, *1827– but* roof (the *MS. 1832/36–* bleached *1832–* chapel, *1836–* peasants *MS. 1832/36–* object *1836–; MS. 1814/27 as 1827 but* roof (the bleached . . . where in ancient time / The . . . Vallies . . . Height)— . . . Espied
845–847 *del MS. 1814/27, om 1827–*

At our entreaty; less from want of power
Than apprehension and bewildering thoughts.
So was he lifted gently from the ground,
And with their freight the Shepherds homeward moved
Through the dull mist, I following—when a step,
A single step, that freed me from the skirts
Of the blind vapour, opened to my view
Glory beyond all glory ever seen
By waking sense or by the dreaming soul!
—Though I am conscious that no power of words
Can body forth, no hues of speech can paint
That gorgeous spectacle—too bright and fair
Even for remembrance; yet the attempt may give
Collateral interest to this homely Tale.
The Appearance, instantaneously disclosed,
Was of a mighty City—boldly say
A wilderness of building, sinking far
And self-withdrawn into a wondrous depth,
Far sinking into splendor—without end!
Fabric it seemed of diamond and of gold,
With alabaster domes, and silver spires;
And blazing terrace upon terrace high
Uplifted; here, serene pavilions bright,
In avenues disposed; there, towers begirt
With battlements that on their restless fronts
Bore stars—illumination of all gems!
By earthly nature had the effect been wrought
Upon the dark materials of the storm
Now pacified; on them, and on the coves
And mountain-steeps and summits, whereunto
The vapours had receded, taking there
Their station under a cerulean sky.
O, 'twas an unimaginable sight!
Clouds, mists, streams, watery rocks and emerald turf,
Clouds of all tincture, rocks and sapphire sky,
Confused, commingled, mutually inflamed,
Molten together, and composing thus,
Each lost in each, that marvellous array
Of temple, palace, citadel, and huge
Fantastic pomp of structure without name,
In fleecy folds voluminous, enwrapp'd.
Right in the midst, where interspace appeared
Of open court, an object like a throne
Beneath a shining canopy of state

---

858 And with their freight homeward the Shepherds moved *MS. 1832/36– but* shepherds *1836–*
864–868 *del MS. 1814/27, om 1827–*
872 wondrous] boundless *1845–*
898 Beneath] Under *MS. 1832/36–*

Stood fixed; and fixed resemblances were seen
To implements of ordinary use,
But vast in size, in substance glorified;
Such as by Hebrew Prophets were beheld
In vision—forms uncouth of mightiest power,
For admiration and mysterious awe.
Below me was the earth; this little Vale
Lay low beneath my feet; 'twas visible—
I saw not, but I felt that it was there.
That which I *saw* was the revealed abode
Of Spirits in beatitude: my heart
Swelled in my breast.—"I have been dead," I cried,
"And now I live! Oh! wherefore do I live?"
And with that pang I prayed to be no more!—
—But I forget our Charge, as utterly
I then forgot him:—there I stood and gazed;
The apparition faded not away,
And I descended.—Having reached the House
I found its rescued Inmate safely lodged,
And in serene possession of himself,
Beside a genial fire; that seemed to spread
A gleam of comfort o'er his pallid face.
Great shew of joy the Housewife made, and truly
Was glad to find her conscience set at ease;
And not less glad, for sake of her good name,
That the poor Sufferer had escaped with life.
But, though he seemed at first to have received
No harm, and uncomplaining as before
Went through his usual tasks, a silent change
Soon shewed itself; he lingered three short weeks;
And from the Cottage hath been borne to-day.

So ends my dolorous Tale, and glad I am
That it is ended." At these words he turned—

---

904 awe.] awe *1814* awe. *errata 1814*
905 A dwelling-place for man—this little vale *MS. 1836/45* This little Vale, a dwelling-place of Man, *1845–*
919–920 *MS. 1814/27 has a series of pencil drafts:*
ly
~~Beside a new kinded fire [?d] that~~ warmed
~~His limbs, and in a~~
Beside a newly kindl[?ed]-fire with gleams
Of comfort spread *page foot of facing verso*
Beside a [?ruddy] with limbs
[?Reviving] in its genial warmth, & gleams
Of comfort spread *page foot of facing recto*
in l. 920 of MS. 1832/36 o'er] over *and then ll. 919–920 rev to*
Beside a fire whose genial warmth seemed met
By a faint shining from the heart, a gleam
Of comfort spread over his pallid face. *WW's letter (see verbal variants to II, 581, above) interleaved in MS. 1832/36, adopted 1836– but* comfort, *MS. 1836/45, 1840–*

And, with blithe air of open fellowship,
Brought from the Cupboard wine and stouter cheer,
Like one who would be merry. Seeing this
My grey-haired Friend said courteously—"Nay, nay,
You have regaled us as a Hermit ought;
Now let us forth into the sun!"—Our Host
Rose, though reluctantly, and forth we went.

END OF THE SECOND BOOK.

BOOK THE THIRD.

DESPONDENCY.

A humming Bee—a little tinkling Rill—
A pair of Falcons, wheeling on the wing,
In clamorous agitation, round the crest
Of a tall rock, their airy Citadel—
By each and all of these the pensive ear
Was greeted, in the silence that ensued,
When through the Cottage-threshold we had passed,
And, deep within that lonesome Valley, stood
Once more, beneath the concave of the blue
And cloudless sky.—Anon! exclaimed our Host,
Triumphantly dispersing with the taunt
The shade of discontent which on his brow
Had gathered,—"Ye have left my Cell,—but see
How Nature hems you in with friendly arms!
And by her help ye are my Prisoners still.
But which way shall I lead you?—how contrive,
In Spot so parsimoniously endowed,
That the brief hours, which yet remain, may reap
Some recompence of knowledge or delight?"
So saying, round he looked, as if perplexed;
And, to remove those doubts, my grey-haired Friend
Said—"Shall we take this pathway for our guide?—
Upwards it winds, as if, in summer heats,
Its line had first been fashioned by the flock
A place of refuge seeking at the root
Of yon black yew-tree; whose protruded boughs
Darken the silver bosom of the crag,
From which it draws its meagre sustenance.
There in commodious shelter may we rest.
Or let us trace this Streamlet to its source;
Feebly it tinkles with an earthy sound,
And a few steps may bring us to the spot
Where, haply, crowned with flowerets and green herbs,
The mountain Infant to the sun comes forth,
Like human Life from darkness."—At the word
We followed where he led:—a sudden turn
Through a strait passage of encumbered ground,

---

9 the] a *1827–*
25 A place of refuge seeking] Seeking a place of refuge *pencil MS. 1832/36–*
28 it . . . its] she . . . her *MS. 1814/27–*
30 its] his *1832–1843*
35 —At the word] —A quick turn *MS. 1814/27–*
36 *del 1814/27, om 1827–*

Proved that such hope was vain:—for now we stood
Shut out from prospect of the open Vale,
And saw the water, that composed this Rill,
Descending, disembodied, and diffused
O'er the smooth surface of an ample Crag,
Lofty, and steep, and naked as a Tower.
All further progress here was barred;—And who,
Thought I, if master of a vacant hour,
Here would not linger, willingly detained?
Whether to such wild objects he were led
When copious rains have magnified the stream
Into a loud and white-robed Waterfall,
Or introduced at this more quiet time.

Upon a semicirque of turf-clad ground,
The hidden nook discovered to our view
A Mass of rock, resembling, as it lay
Right at the foot of that moist precipice,
A stranded Ship, with keel upturned,—that rests
Fearless of winds and waves. Three several Stones
Stood near, of smaller size, and not unlike
To monumental pillars: and, from these
Some little space disjoined, a pair were seen,
That, with united shoulders bore aloft
A Fragment, like an Altar, flat and smooth.
Barren the tablet, yet thereon appeared,
Conspicuously stationed, one fair Plant,
A tall and shining Holly, which had found
A hospitable chink, and stood upright,
As if inserted by some human hand,
In mockery, to wither in the sun,
Or lay its beauty flat before a breeze,
The first that entered. But no breeze did now
Find entrance;—high, or low, appeared no trace
Of motion, save the Water that descended,
Diffused adown that Barrier of steep rock,
And softly creeping, like a breath of air,
Such as is sometimes seen, and hardly seen,
To brush the still breast of a chrystal Lake.

"Behold a Cabinet for Sages built,
Which Kings might envy!"—Praise to this effect
Broke from the happy Old Man's reverend lip;
Who to the Solitary turned, and said,
"In sooth, with love's familiar privilege,

---

63 *del MS. 1814/27, om 1827–*
64 which] that *MS. 1814/27–*

[79] You have decried, in no unseemly terms
Of modesty, that wealth which is your own.
[80] Among these Rocks and Stones, methinks, I see
More than the heedless impress that belongs
To lonely Nature's casual work: they bear
A semblance strange of power intelligent,
And of design not wholly worn away.
[85] Boldest of plants that ever faced the wind,
How gracefully that slender Shrub looks forth
From its fantastic birth-place! And I own,
[88] Some shadowy intimations haunt me here,
I cannot but incline to a belief
[89] That in these shows a chronicle survives
[90] Of purposes akin to those of Man,
But wrought with mightier arm than now prevails.
—Voiceless the Stream descends into the gulph
With timid lapse;—and lo! while in this Strait
I stand—the chasm of sky above my head
[95] Is heaven's profoundest azure; no domain
For fickle, short-lived clouds to occupy,
Or to pass through, but rather an Abyss
In which the everlasting Stars abide;
And whose soft gloom, and boundless depth, might tempt
[100] The curious eye to look for them by day.
—Hail Contemplation! from the stately towers,
Reared by the industrious hand of human Art
To lift thee high above the misty air,
And turbulence, of murmuring cities vast;
[105] From academic groves, that have for thee
Been planted, hither come and find a Lodge
To which thou mayest resort for holier peace,—
From whose calm centre Thou, through height or depth,
Mayest penetrate, wherever Truth shall lead;
[110] Measuring through all degrees, until the scale
Of time and conscious Nature disappear,
Lost in unsearchable Eternity!"

A pause ensued; and with minuter care
We scanned the various features of the scene:
[115] And soon the Tenant of that lonely Vale

81–82 You have decried the wealth which is your own. *1827– ; so MS. 1814/27 but* decried, . . . own

92 *del MS. 1814/27, om 1827–*

117–120 *MS. 1814/27 has interlined draft, eras:*
A pause ensued; but [?soon with courteous voice]
While with minuter care we scann'd the spot
The Solitary spake—
related illeg draft in pencil, eras, at page foot and stet *entered in left margin*

---

116 For WW's end-of-volume note, see pp. 299–300, below.

With courteous voice thus spake—
                                        "I should have grieved
Hereafter, should perhaps have blamed myself,
If from my poor Retirement ye had gone
Leaving this Nook unvisited: but, in sooth,
Your unexpected presence had so roused
My spirits, that they were bent on enterprize;
And, like an ardent Hunter, I forgot,
Or, shall I say?—disdained, the game that lurked
At my own door. The shapes before our eyes,
And their arrangement, doubtless must be deemed
The sport of Nature, aided by blind Chance
Rudely to mock the works of toiling Man.
And hence, this upright Shaft of unhewn stone,
From Fancy, willing to set off her stores
By sounding Titles, hath acquired the name
Of Pompey's Pillar; that I gravely style
My Theban Obelisk; and, there, behold
A Druid Cromlech!—thus I entertain
The antiquarian humour, and am pleased
To skim along the surfaces of things,
Beguiling harmlessly the listless hours.
But, if the spirit be oppressed by sense
Of instability, revolt, decay,
And change, and emptiness, these freaks of Nature
And her blind helper Chance, do *then* suffice
To quicken, and to aggravate, to feed
Pity and scorn, and melancholy pride,
Not less than that huge Pile (from some abyss
Of mortal power unquestionably sprung)
Whose hoary Diadem of pendant rocks
Confines the shrill-voiced whirlwind, round and round
Eddying within its vast circumference,
On Sarum's naked plain;—than Pyramid
Of Egypt, unsubverted, undissolved;
Or Syria's marble Ruins towering high
Above the sandy Desart, in the light
Of sun or moon.—Forgive me, if I say
That an appearance, which hath raised your minds
To an exalted pitch, (the self-same cause
Different effect producing) is for me
Fraught rather with depression than delight,
Though shame it were, could I not look around me,
By the reflection of your pleasure, pleased.
Yet happier, in my judgment, even than you,

---

121 Hereafter, not escaping self-reproach, *1827–; so MS. 1814/27 but* self reproach,
123 Leaving] And left *then eras MS. 1814/27*
127 lurked] lurks *1827–*
161 around me,] around, *MS. 1814/27–*

[160] With your bright transports, fairly may be deemed,
Is He (if such have ever entered here)
The wandering Herbalist,—who, clear alike
From vain, and, that worse evil, vexing thoughts,
Casts on these uncouth Forms a slight regard
[165] Of transitory interest, and peeps round
For some rare Floweret of the hills, or Plant
Of craggy fountain; what he hopes for wins,
Or learns, at least, that 'tis not to be won:
Then, keen and eager, as a fine-nosed Hound
[170] By soul-engrossing instinct driven along
Through wood or open field, the harmless Man
Departs, intent upon his onward quest!
Nor is that Fellow-wanderer, so deem I,
Less to be envied (you may trace him oft
[175] By scars which his activity has left
Beside our roads and pathways, though, thank heaven!
This covert nook reports not of his hand)
He, who with pocket hammer smites the edge
[179] Of every luckless rock or stone that stands
Before his sight, by weather-stains disguised,
[180] Or crusted o'er with vegetation thin,
Nature's first growth, detaching by the stroke
A chip, or splinter,—to resolve his doubts;
And, with that ready answer satisfied,
Doth to the substance give some barbarous name,
[185] Then hurries on; or from the fragments picks
His specimen, if haply interveined
With sparkling mineral, or should chrystal cube
Lurk in its cells—and thinks himself enriched,
Wealthier, and doubtless wiser, than before!
[190] Entrusted safely—each to his pursuit,
This earnest Pair may range from hill to hill,
And, if it please them, speed from clime to clime;
The mind is full—no pain is in their sport."

---

165 *del MS. 1814/27, om 1827–*
168 Casts if he ever chance to enter here *MS. 1814/27*
Casts, if he ever chance to enter here,
Upon these uncouth Forms a slight regard *1827– but* forms *MS. 1832/36*
183–186 Of luckless rock or prominent stone, disguised
In weather-stains, or crusted o'er by Nature
With her first growths— . . . *1827– but* weather-stains *1832–* growths, *MS. 1832/36–; MS. 1814/27 as 1827 but* stone disguised, / In weather stains . . . oer by nature . . . growths, . . .
189 Doth to the substance give] The substance classes by *MS. 1814/27–*
190 Then] And *MS. 1814/27–*
191 if haply] if but haply *1845–*
192 cube] tube *1814* cube *errata 1814*
193 Lurk in its cells—] Be lodged therein— *1814* Lurk in its cells— *errata 1814*
196–197 Earnest alike, let both from hill to hill / Range; if . . . *MS. 1814/27– but alt* Let these [?] *overwritten illeg eras MS. 1814/27*
198 no pain is in their sport."] their pastime free from pain. *MS. 1836/45* and free from pain their pastime." *1845–*

"Then," said I, interposing, "One is near
Who cannot but possess in your esteem
Place worthier still of envy. May I name,
Without offence, that fair-faced Cottage-boy?
Dame Nature's Pupil of the lowest Form,
Youngest Apprentice in the School of Art!
Him, as we entered from the open Glen,
You might have noticed, busily engaged,
Heart, soul, and hands,—in mending the defects
Left in the fabric of a leaky dam,
Framed for enabling this penurious stream
To turn a slender mill (that new-made plaything)
For his delight—the happiest he of all!"

"Far happiest," answered the desponding Man,
"If, such as now he is, he might remain!
Ah! what avails Imagination high
Or Question deep? what profits all that Earth,
Or Heaven's blue Vault, is suffered to put forth
Of impulse or allurement, for the Soul
To quit the beaten track of life, and soar
Far as she finds a yielding element
In past or future; far as she can go
Through time or space; if neither in the one
Nor in the other region, nor in aught
That Fancy, dreaming o'er the map of things,
Hath placed beyond these penetrable bounds,
Words of assurance can be heard; if no where
A habitation, for consummate good,
Or for progressive virtue, by the search
Can be attained, a better sanctuary
From doubt and sorrow, than the senseless grave?"

"Is this," the grey-haired Wanderer mildly said,
"The voice, which we so lately overheard,
To that same Child, addressing tenderly
The Consolations of a hopeful mind?
'His body is at rest, his soul in heaven.'
These were your words; and, verily, methinks
Wisdom is oft-times nearer when we stoop
Than when we soar."—
The Other, not displeased,
Promptly replied—"My notion is the same.
And I, without reluctance, could decline
All act of inquisition whence we rise,
And what, when breath hath ceased, we may become.

---

209 Framed] Raised *MS. 1814/27–*
227 Or] Nor *MS. 1814/27–1843*

Here are we, in a bright and breathing World!
Our origin, what matters it? In lack
Of worthier explanation, say at once
With the American (a thought which suits
The place where now we stand) that certain Men
Leapt out together from a rocky Cave;
And these were the first Parents of Mankind!
Or, if a different image be recalled
By the warm sunshine, and the jocund voice
Of insects—chirping out their careless lives
On these soft beds of thyme-besprinkled turf,
Chuse, with the gay Athenian, a conceit
As sound; with that blithe race who wore ere-while
Their golden Grasshoppers, in sign that they
Had sprung from out the soil whereon they dwelt.
But stop!—these theoretic fancies jar
On serious minds; for doubtless, in one sense,
The theme *is* serious; then, as Hindoos draw
Their holy Ganges from a skiey fount,
Even so deduce the Stream of human Life
From seats of Power divine; and hope, or trust,
That our Existence winds its stately course
Beneath the Sun, like Ganges, to make part
Of a living Ocean: or, if such may seem
Its tendency, to be engulphed and lost
Like Niger, in impenetrable sands
And utter darkness: thought which may be faced,
Though comfortless!—Not of myself I speak;
Such acquiescence neither doth imply,
In me, a meekly-bending spirit—soothed
By natural piety; nor a lofty mind,
By philosophic discipline prepared
For calm subjection to acknowledged law;
Pleased to have been, contented not to be.
Such palms I boast not:—no! to me, who find,
Reviewing my past way, much to condemn,
Little to praise, and nothing to regret
(Save some remembrances of dream-like joys
That scarcely seem to have belonged to me)

254–255 As sound—blithe race! whose mantles were bedecked / With golden Grasshoppers, . . . *1827– but* grasshoppers, *MS. 1832/36– ; MS. 1814/27 as 1827 but* sound; blithe race whose . . . bedeck'd

256 Had sprung, like those bright creatures, from the soil / Whereon their endless generations dwelt. *1827– ; so MS. 1814/27 but* sprung like those bright Creatures from *illeg pencil draft, eras at page foot, probably related to l. 254;* [?They dwelt] *pencil, eras, in left margin of l. 257*

258–259 On serious minds; then, as the Hindoos draw *MS. 1814/27– but* minds: *pencil MS. 1836/45, 1840–*

263 its] her *MS. 1814/27–*

265–266 Of a living Ocean; or, to sink engulfed *1827– but* ocean; *MS. 1832/36–* engulfed, *1832– ; MS. 1814/27 as 1827 but* Ocean: or, . . . engulphed

If I must take my choice between the pair
That rule alternately the weary hours,
Night is than day more acceptable;—sleep
Doth, in my estimate of good, appear
A better state than waking; death than sleep:
Feelingly sweet is stillness after storm,
Though under covert of the wormy ground!

Yet be it said, in justice to myself,
That in more genial times, when I was free
To explore the destiny of human kind;
Not as an intellectual game pursued
With curious subtilty, thereby to cheat
Irksome sensations; but by love of truth
Urged on, or haply by intense delight
In feeding thought, wherever thought could feed;
I did not rank with those (too dull or nice,
For to my judgment such they then appeared,
Or too aspiring, thankless at the best)
Who, in this frame of human life, perceive
An object whereunto their souls are tied
In discontented wedlock; nor did e'er,
From me, those dark, impervious shades, that hang
Upon the region whither we are bound,
Exclude a power to enjoy the vital beams
Of present sunshine.—Deities that float
On wings, angelic Spirits, I could muse
O'er what from eldest time we have been told
Of your bright forms and glorious faculties,
And with the imagination be content,
Not wishing more; repining not to tread
The little sinuous path of earthly care,
By flowers embellished, and by springs refreshed.
—"Blow winds of Autumn!—let your chilling breath
"Take the live herbage from the mead, and strip
"The shady forest of its green attire,—
"And let the bursting Clouds to fury rouse
"The gentle Brooks!—Your desolating sway,"
Thus I exclaimed, "no sadness sheds on me,
"And no disorder in your rage I find.
"What dignity, what beauty, in this change
"From mild to angry, and from sad to gay,
"Alternate and revolving! How benign,

---

292 thereby] from wish *MS. 1814/27–*

309 be] rest *MS. 1836/45, 1845–*

312 *MS. 1836/45 has several rev in pencil: comma del and* and by springs refreshed. *del to* sweet— *and then del* Embellished by sweet-flowers by spring refresh *page foot* The sinuous path of earthly care, by flow *top of facing page*

318 'Sheds,' I exclaimed, 'no sadness upon me, *1836–*

"How rich in animation and delight,
"How bountiful these elements—compared
"With aught, as more desirable and fair,
"Devised by Fancy for the Golden Age;
"Or the perpetual warbling that prevails
"In Arcady, beneath unaltered skies,
"Through the long year in constant quiet bound,
"Night hush'd as night, and day serene as day!"
—But why this tedious record?—Age we know
Is garrulous; and solitude is apt
To anticipate the privilege of Age.
From far ye come; and surely with a hope
Of better entertainment—let us hence!"

Loth to forsake the spot, and still more loth
To be diverted from our present theme,
I said, "My thoughts, agreeing, Sir, with yours,
Would push this censure farther;—for, if smiles
Of scornful pity be the just reward
Of Poesy, thus courteously employed
In framing models to improve the scheme
Of Man's existence, and recast the world,
Why should not grave Philosophy be stiled,
Herself, a Dreamer of a kindred stock,
A Dreamer yet more spiritless and dull?
Yes," said I, "shall the immunities to which
She doth lay claim, the precepts she bestows,
Establish sounder titles of esteem
For Her, who (all too timid and reserved
For onset, for resistance too inert,
Too weak for suffering, and for hope too tame)
Did place, in flowery Gardens curtained round
With world-excluding groves, the Brotherhood
Of soft Epicureans, taught—if they
The ends of being would secure, and win
The crown of wisdom—to yield up their souls
To a voluptuous unconcern, preferring
Tranquillity to all things. Or is She,"
I cried, "more worthy of regard, the Power,
Who, for the sake of sterner quiet, closed
The Stoic's heart against the vain approach
Of admiration, and all sense of joy?"

---

347 Yes, shall the fine immunities she boasts *MS. 1814/27–*
348 *del MS. 1814/27, om 1827–*
353 Did place, in flowery Gardens] Placed among flowery gardens, *1827– but* Placed, . . . gardens *MS. 1832/36–; MS. 1814/27 as 1827 but* Plac'd . . . Gardens

His Countenance gave notice that my zeal
Accorded little with his present mind;
I ceased, and he resumed.—"Ah! gentle Sir,
Slight, if you will, the *means*; but spare to slight
The *end* of those, who did, by system, rank,
As the prime object of a wise Man's aim,
Security from shock of accident,
Release from fear; and cherished peaceful days
For their own sakes, as mortal life's chief good,
And only reasonable felicity.
What motive drew, what impulse, I would ask,
Through a long course of later ages, drove
The Hermit to his Cell in forest wide;
Or what detained him, till his closing eyes
Took their last farewell of the sun and stars,
Fast anchored in the desart?—Not alone
Dread of the persecuting sword—remorse,
Wrongs unredressed, or insults unavenged
And unavengeable, defeated pride,
Prosperity subverted, maddening want,
Friendship betrayed, affection unreturned,
Love with despair, or grief in agony:—
Not always from intolerable pangs
He fled; but, compassed round by pleasure, sighed
For independent happiness; craving peace,
The central feeling of all happiness,
Not as a refuge from distress or pain,
A breathing-time, vacation, or a truce,
But for its absolute self; a life of peace,
Stability without regret or fear;
That hath been, is, and shall be evermore!
Such the reward he sought; and wore out Life,
There, where on few external things his heart
Was set, and those his own; or, if not his,
Subsisting under Nature's steadfast law.

What other yearning was the master tie
Of the monastic Brotherhood; upon Rock
Aerial, or in green secluded Vale,
One after one, collected from afar,
An undissolving Fellowship?—What but this,
The universal instinct of repose,
The longing for confirmed tranquillity,
Inward and outward; humble, yet sublime:—
The life where hope and memory are as one;

382 unavengeable] unavengable *1814* unavengeable *errata 1814, MS. 1814/27*

[401/403] Earth quiet and unchanged; the human Soul
[404] Consistent in self-rule; and heaven revealed
[405] To meditation, in that quietness!
[406] Such was their scheme:—thrice happy he who gained
The end proposed! And,—though the same were missed
[407] By multitudes, perhaps obtained by none,—
They, for the attempt, and for the pains employed,
Do, in my present censure, stand redeemed
[410] From the unqualified disdain, that once
Would have been cast upon them, by my Voice
Delivering its decisions from the seat
Of forward Youth:—that scruples not to solve
Doubts, and determine questions, by the rules
[415] Of inexperienced judgment, ever prone
To overweening faith; and is inflamed,
By courage, to demand from real life
The test of act and suffering—to provoke
Hostility, how dreadful when it comes,
[420] Whether affliction be the foe, or guilt!

408–409 Where earth is quiet and her face unchanged
Save by the simplest toil of human hands
Or seasons' difference; the immortal Soul *1845–; MS. 1836/45 has extensive drafting:*
Where present time is [?noise]less as the past
Or as a thing unborn, the face of earth
Save by the simplest toil of human hands
Or seasons difference unchanged—the souls *pencil in left margin of facing page*
the face of earth
Save by the simplest toil of human hands
Or season's difference unchanged—the Sou *right margin of facing page*
Where earth is quiet, and her face unchanged
toil
Save by the simplest of human [?] hands
[?]
Or ~~by the~~ seasons differences—the soul
Consistent in self rule *bottom of facing page*
Where earth is quiet and her face unchange
toil
Save by the simplest of human hands
welcome ~~and the~~
Or seasons difference the ~~human~~ soul
Consistent in self rule, & heaven reveal'd *top of page*
Where, hands
~~Save~~ ~~save by simplest toil of human~~ *(del in pencil except save del in ink)*
~~Or seasons difference the face of earth~~
~~Is undisfigured and un~~
W
The|here present time is [?noise]less as the past
Or as a thing unborn the face of earth *right margin*
Where Earth is quiet & her face unchanged
Save by the simplest toil of hum-
Save by the season's difference—The Sou
soul *page foot*
Where earth [?is] *between printed ll. 408 and 409*

411–414 Such was their scheme: and though the wished for end
By multitudes was missed, perhaps attained
By none, they for the attempt, and pains employed, *MS. 1836/45, 1845–*

418 its] her *1832–*

A Child of earth, I rested, in that stage
Of my past course to which these thoughts advert,
Upon earth's native energies; forgetting
That mine was a condition which required
[425] Nor energy, nor fortitude—a calm
Without vicissitude; which, if the like
Had been presented to my view elsewhere,
I might have even been tempted to despise.
But that which was serene was also bright;
[430] Enlivened happiness with joy o'erflowing,
With joy, and—oh! that memory should survive
To speak the word—with rapture! Nature's boon,
Life's genuine inspiration, happiness
Above what rules can teach, or fancy feign;
[435] Abused, as all possessions are abused
That are not prized according to their worth.
And yet, what worth? what good is given to Men,
More solid than the gilded clouds of heaven,
What joy more lasting than a vernal flower?
[440] None! 'tis the general plaint of human kind
In solitude, and mutually addressed
From each to all, for wisdom's sake:—This truth
The Priest announces from his holy seat;
And, crowned with garlands in the summer grove,
[445] The Poet fits it to his pensive Lyre.
Yet, ere that final resting-place be gained,
[447] Sharp contradictions hourly shall arise
To cross the way; and we, perchance, by doom
[448] Of this same life, shall be compelled to grieve
That the prosperities of love and joy
[450] Should be permitted, oft-times, to endure
So long, and be at once cast down for ever.
Oh! tremble Ye to whom hath been assigned
A course of days composing happy months,
And they as happy years; the present still
[455] So like the past, and both, so firm a pledge
Of a congenial future, that the wheels
Of pleasure move without the aid of hope.
For Mutability is Nature's bane;
And slighted Hope will be avenged; and, when
[460] Ye need her favours, Ye shall find her not;
But, in her stead—fear—doubt—and agony!"

---

435 But no—for the serene was also bright; *1836–*

453–455 Sharp contradictions may arise by doom / Of this same life, compelling us to grieve *MS. 1814/27– but* arise, *MS. 1836/45, 1840–*

467 her *underlined MS. 1836/45; in right margin:* [?their] *rev to* [?them] *both del, entry of* them *then del*

468 their *added and del below* her *MS. 1836/45*

This was the bitter language of the heart;
But, while he spake, look, gesture, tone of voice,
Though discomposed and vehement, were such
[465] As skill and graceful Nature might suggest
To a Proficient of the tragic scene,
Standing before the multitude, beset
[468] With sorrowful events; and we, who heard
And saw, were moved. Desirous to divert,
[469] Or stem, the current of the Speaker's thoughts,
[470] We signified a wish to leave that Place
Of stillness and close privacy, which seemed
A nook for self-examination framed,
Or, for confession, in the sinner's need,
Hidden from all Men's view. To our attempt
[475] He yielded not; but, pointing to a slope
Of mossy turf, defended from the sun;
And, on that couch inviting us to rest,
Towards that tender-hearted Man he turned
A serious eye, and thus his speech renewed.

[480] "You never saw, your eyes did never look
On the bright Form of Her whom once I loved.—
Her silver voice was heard upon the earth,
A sound unknown to you; else, honored Friend,
Your heart had borne a pitiable share
[485] Of what I suffered, when I wept that loss,
And suffer now, not seldom, from the thought
That I remember, and can weep no more.—
Stripped as I am of all the golden fruit
Of self-esteem; and by the cutting blasts
[490] Of self-reproach familiarly assailed;
I would not yet be of such wintry bareness,

---

471 Though sometimes discomposed & ~~vehemen~~ vehement / Beyond control, yet in the main were such *alt, del in pencil MS. 1836/45*

474 Tears of compassion [?] for a life beset *inserted after* multitude *then del MS. 1836/45*

475–476 With dark events. Desirous to divert *1827–; so MS. 1814/27– but* divert, *MS. 1836/45 has several rev:* With dark events *del in pencil*

~~in grief~~
And [?he]
~~With trouble pangs whose outward~~ signs [?] [?sooth]
[?smooths]
Far *page foot*
beset
By
~~With~~ trouble conflict that he seeks & shirks
With the same breath—Desirous to divert *pencil in left margin, then del*

479–480 Of stillness and close privacy, a nook / That seemed for self-examination made, *MS. 1814/27– but* made; *1836–*

486 Towards] Full on *MS. 1814/27–*

487 thus his speech] his speech thus *pencil MS. 1832/36–*

499 Yet would I not be . . . *1836–*

But that some leaf of your regard should hang
Upon my naked branches:—lively thoughts
Give birth, full often, to unguarded words;
I grieve that, in your presence, from my tongue
Too much of frailty hath already dropped;
But that too much demands still more.
                                                            You know,
Revered Compatriot;—and to you, kind Sir
(Not to be deemed a Stranger as you come
Following the guidance of these welcome feet
To our secluded Vale) it may be told,
That my demerits did not sue in vain
To One, on whose mild radiance many gazed
With hope, and all, with pleasure. This fair Bride—
In the devotedness of youthful Love
Preferring me to Parents, and the choir
Of gay companions, to the natal roof,
And all known places and familiar sights,
(Resigned with sadness gently weighing down
Her trembling expectations, but no more
Than did to her due honour, and to me
Yielded, that day, a confidence sublime
In what I had to build upon)—this Bride,
Young, modest, meek, and beautiful, I led
To a low Cottage in a sunny Bay,
Where the salt sea innocuously breaks,
And the sea breeze as innocently breathes,
On Devon's leafy shores;—a sheltered Hold,
In a soft clime encouraging the soil
To a luxuriant bounty!—As our steps
Approach the embowered Abode, our chosen Seat,
See, rooted in the earth, its kindly bed,
The unendangered Myrtle, decked with flowers,
Before the threshold stands to welcome us!
While, in the flowering Myrtle's neighbourhood,
Not overlooked but courting no regard
Those native plants, the Holly and the Yew,
Gave modest intimation to the mind
Of willingness with which they would unite
With the green Myrtle, to endear the hours
Of winter, and protect that pleasant place.
—Wild were the walks upon those lonely Downs,
Track leading into track, how marked, how worn
Into bright verdure, among fern and gorse

---

530 its] her *MS. 1814/27–*
537 How willingly their aid they would unite *MS. 1814/27–*
542 among] between *MS. 1814/27–*

Winding away its never-ending line,
On their smooth surface, evidence was none:
But, there, lay open to our daily haunt,
A range of unappropriated earth,
Where youth's ambitious feet might move at large;
Whence, unmolested Wanderers, we beheld
The shining Giver of the Day diffuse
His brightness, o'er a tract of sea and land
Gay as our spirits, free as our desires,
As our enjoyments boundless.—From these Heights
We dropped, at pleasure, into sylvan Combs;
Where arbours of impenetrable shade,
And mossy seats detained us side by side,
With hearts at ease, and knowledge in our hearts
"That all the grove and all the day was ours."

But in due season Nature interfered,
And called my Partner to resign her share
In the pure freedom of that wedded life,
Enjoyed by us in common.—To my hope,
To my heart's wish, my tender Mate became
The thankful captive of maternal bonds;
And those wild paths were left to me alone.
There, could I meditate on follies past;
And, like a weary Voyager escaped
From risk and hardship, inwardly retrace
A course of vain delights and thoughtless guilt,
And self-indulgence—without shame pursued.
There, undisturbed, could think of, and could thank
Her—whose submissive spirit was to me
Rule and restraint, my Guardian;—shall I say
That earthly Providence, whose guiding love
Within a port of rest had lodged me safe;
Safe from temptation, and from danger far?
Strains followed of acknowledgment addressed
To an Authority enthroned above
The reach of sight; from whom, as from their source,
Proceed all visible ministers of good
That walk the earth—Father of heaven and earth,
Father and king, and judge, adored and feared!
These acts of mind, and memory, and heart,
And spirit,—interrupted and relieved
By observations—transient as the glance

---

552 these] those *MS. 1814/27–*
557/558 O happy time! still happier was at hand; *para 1845–*
558–560 But Nature called my Partner to resign / Her share in the pure freedom of that life, *MS. 1814/27– but* But] "But *1832* For *1845– ; rev to no para in MS. 1836/45, no para 1845– (see verbal variant to III, 557/558, above)*

Of flying sunbeams, or to the outward form
Cleaving with power inherent and intense,
As the mute insect fixed upon the plant
[580] On whose soft leaves it hangs, and from whose cup
Draws imperceptibly its nourishment,—
Endeared my wanderings; and the Mother's kiss,
And Infant's smile, awaited my return.

In privacy we dwelt—a wedded pair
[585] Companions daily, often all day long;
Not placed by fortune within easy reach
Of various intercourse, nor wishing aught
Beyond the allowance of our own fire-side,
The Twain within our happy cottage born,
[590] Inmates, and heirs of our united love;
[591] Graced mutually by difference of sex,
By the endearing names of nature bound,
[592] And with no wider interval of time
Between their several births than served for One
To establish something of a leader's sway;
[595] Yet left them joined by sympathy in age;
Equals in pleasure, fellows in pursuit.
On these two pillars rested as in air
Our solitude.
It soothes me to perceive,
Your courtesy withholds not from my words
[600] Attentive audience. But oh! gentle Friends,
As times of quiet and unbroken peace
Though for a Nation times of blessedness,
Give back faint echoes from the Historian's page;
So, in the imperfect sounds of this discourse,
[605] Depressed I hear, how faithless is the voice
Which those most blissful days reverberate.
What special record can, or need be given
To rules and habits, whereby much was done
But all within the sphere of little things?
[610] Of humble, though, to us, important cares,
And precious interests! Smoothly did our life
Advance, not swerving from the path prescribed;
Her annual, her diurnal round alike
Maintained with faithful care. And you divine
[615] The worst effects which our condition saw
If you imagine changes slowly wrought,
And in their progress imperceptible,

---

589 It draws its nourishment imperceptibly— *1845–*
600 out *in left margin indicates del of line MS. 1836/45, line om 1845–*
621 not swerving] swerving not *MS. 1832/36– but pencil transposition line MS. 1836/45*
624 which] that *MS. 1814/27–*
626 imperceptible;] unperceivable; *1845–*

Not wished for, sometimes noticed with a sigh,
(Whate'er of good or lovely they might bring)
Sighs of regret, for the familiar good,
And loveliness endeared—which they removed.

Seven years of occupation undisturbed
Established seemingly a right to hold
That happiness; and use and habit gave
To what an alien spirit had acquired
A patrimonial sanctity. And thus,
With thoughts and wishes bounded to this world,
I lived and breathed; most grateful, if to enjoy
Without repining or desire for more,
For different lot, or change to higher sphere,
(Only except some impulses of pride
With no determined object, though upheld
By theories with suitable support)
Most grateful, if in such wise to enjoy
Be proof of gratitude for what we have;
Else, I allow, most thankless.—But at once
From some dark seat of fatal Power was urged
A claim that shattered all.—Our blooming Girl,
Caught in the gripe of Death, with such brief time
To struggle in as scarcely would allow
Her cheek to change its colour, was conveyed
From us, to regions inaccessible;
Where height, or depth, admits not the approach
Of living Man, though longing to pursue.
—With even as brief a warning—and how soon
With what short interval of time between
I tremble yet to think of—our last prop,
Our happy life's only remaining stay—
The Brother followed; and was seen no more!

Calm as a frozen Lake when ruthless Winds
Blow fiercely, agitating earth and sky,
The Mother now remained; as if in her,
Who, to the lowest region of the soul,
Had been erewhile unsettled and disturbed,
This second visitation had no power
To shake; but only to bind up and seal;
And to establish thankfulness of heart
In Heaven's determinations, ever just.
The eminence on which her spirit stood,
Mine was unable to attain. Immense
The space that severed us! But, as the sight

---

651 From us to inaccessible worlds, to regions *1845–*
668 on which] whereon *ink and pencil MS. 1836/45, 1845–*

Communicates with heaven's etherial orbs
Incalculably distant; so, I felt
That consolation may descend from far;
(And that is intercourse, and union, too,)
While, overcome with speechless gratitude,
And with a holier love inspired, I looked
On her—at once superior to my woes
And Partner of my loss.—O heavy change!
Dimness o'er this clear Luminary crept
Insensibly;—the immortal and divine
Yielded to mortal reflux; her pure Glory,
As from the pinnacle of worldly state
Wretched Ambition drops astounded, fell
Into a gulph obscure of silent grief,
And keen heart-anguish—of itself ashamed,
Yet obstinately cherishing itself:
And, so consumed, She melted from my arms;
And left me, on this earth, disconsolate.

What followed cannot be reviewed in thought;
Much less, retraced in words. If She, of life
Blameless; so intimate with love and joy,
And all the tender motions of the Soul,
Had been supplanted, could I hope to stand?
Infirm, dependant, and now destitute!
I called on dreams and visions, to disclose
That which is veiled from waking thought; conjured
Eternity, as men constrain a Ghost
To appear and answer; to the Grave I spake
Imploringly;—looked up, and asked the Heavens
If Angels traversed their cerulean floors,
If fixed or wandering Star could tidings yield
Of the departed Spirit—what Abode
It occupies—what consciousness retains
Of former loves and interests. Then my Soul
Turned inward,—to examine of what stuff
Time's fetters are composed; and Life was put
To inquisition, long and profitless!
By pain of heart—now checked—and now impelled—
The intellectual Power, through words and things,
Went sounding on, a dim and perilous way!
And from those transports, and these toils abstruse,
Some trace am I enabled to retain
Of time, else lost;—existing unto me
Only by records in myself not found.

From that abstraction I was rouzed,—and how?
Even as a thoughtful Shepherd by a flash

Of lightening startled in a gloomy cave
Of these wild hills. For, lo! the dread Bastile,
With all the chambers in its horrid Towers,
Fell to the ground:—by violence o'erthrown
Of indignation; and with shouts that drowned
The crash it made in falling! From the wreck
A golden Palace rose, or seemed to rise,
The appointed Seat of equitable Law
And mild paternal Sway. The potent shock
I felt; the transformation I perceived,
As marvellously seized as in that moment
When, from the blind mist issuing, I beheld
Glory—beyond all glory ever seen,
Confusion infinite of heaven and earth,
Dazzling the soul! Meanwhile, prophetic harps
In every grove were ringing, "War shall cease;
"Did ye not hear that conquest is abjured?
"Bring garlands, bring forth choicest flowers, to deck
"The Tree of Liberty."—My heart rebounded;
My melancholy Voice the chorus joined;
—"Be joyful all ye Nations, in all Lands,
"Ye that are capable of joy be glad!
"Henceforth, whate'er is wanting to yourselves
"In others ye shall promptly find;—and all
"Be rich by mutual and reflected wealth."

Thus was I reconverted to the world;
Society became my glittering Bride,
And airy hopes my Children.—From the depths
Of natural passion, seemingly escaped,
My soul diffused itself in wide embrace
Of institutions, and the forms of things;
As they exist, in mutable array,
Upon life's surface. What, though in my veins
There flowed no Gallic blood, nor had I breathed
The air of France, not less than Gallic zeal
Kindled and burnt among the sapless twigs
Of my exhausted heart. If busy Men
In sober conclave met, to weave a web
Of amity, whose living threads should stretch
Beyond the seas, and to the farthest pole,
There did I sit, assisting. If, with noise
And acclamation, crowds in open air

---

741 "Be rich] 'Enriched *1832–*
741/742 'Shall with one heart honour their common kind.' *1832–*
746 itself] herself *MS. 1814/27–*
752 burnt] burned *pencil MS. 1836/45*

Expressed the tumult of their minds, my voice
There mingled, heard or not. The powers of song
I left not uninvoked; and, in still groves,
Where mild Enthusiasts tuned a pensive lay
Of thanks and expectation, in accord
With their belief, I sang Saturnian Rule
Returned,—a progeny of golden years
Permitted to descend, and bless mankind.
—With promises the Hebrew Scriptures teem:
I felt the invitation; and resumed
A long-suspended office in the House
Of public worship, where, the glowing phrase
Of ancient Inspiration serving me,
I promised also,—with undaunted trust
Foretold; and added prayer to prophecy;
The admiration winning of the crowd,
The help desiring of the pure devout.

Scorn and contempt forbid me to proceed!
But History, Time's slavish Scribe, will tell
How rapidly the Zealots of the cause
Disbanded—or in hostile ranks appeared;
Some, tired of honest service; these, outdone,
Disgusted, therefore, or appalled, by aims
Of fiercer Zealots—so Confusion reigned,
And the more faithful were compelled to exclaim,
As Brutus did to Virtue, "Liberty,
"I worshipped Thee, and find thee but a Shade!"

Such recantation had for me no charm,
Nor would I bend to it; who should have grieved
At aught, however fair, which bore the mien
Of a conclusion, or catastrophe.
Why then conceal, that, when the simple good
In timid selfishness withdrew, I sought
Other support, not scrupulous whence it came,
And by what compromise it stood, not nice?
Enough if notions seemed to be high-pitched,
And qualities determined.—Ruling such,
And with such herding, I maintained a strife
Hopeless, and still more hopeless every hour;
But, in the process, I began to feel
That, if the emancipation of the world

768 the] that *del to* their *pencil MS. 1836/45* their *1840–*
788 which] that *MS. 1814/27–*
790 simple] simply *MS. 1814/27–*
795–796 And qualities determined.—Among men / So charactered did I maintain a strife *1827–; so MS. 1814/27 but* charactered,

Were missed, I should at least secure my own,
And be in part compensated. For rights,
Widely—inveterately usurped upon,
I spake with vehemence; and promptly seized
Whate'er Abstraction furnished for my needs
Or purposes; nor scrupled to proclaim,
And propagate, by liberty of life,
Those new persuasions. Not that I rejoiced,
Or even found pleasure, in such vagrant course,
For its own sake; but farthest from the walk
Which I had trod in happiness and peace,
Was most inviting to a troubled mind;
That, in a struggling and distempered world,
Beheld a cherished image of itself.
Yet, mark the contradictions of which Man
Is still the sport! Here Nature was my guide,
The Nature of the dissolute; but Thee,
O fostering Nature! I rejected, smiled
At others' tears in pity; and in scorn
At those, which thy soft influence sometimes drew
From my unguarded heart.—The tranquil shores
Of Britain circumscribed me; else, perhaps,
I might have been entangled among deeds,
Which, now, as infamous, I should abhor—
Despise, as senseless: for I strangely relished
The exasperated spirit of that Land,
Which turned an angry beak against the down
Of its own breast; as if it hoped, thereby,
To disencumber its impatient wings.
—But all was quieted by iron bonds
Of military sway. The shifting aims,
The moral interests, the creative might,
The varied functions and high attributes
Of civil Action, yielded to a Power
Formal, and odious, and contemptible.
—In Britain, ruled a panic dread of change;
The weak were praised, rewarded, and advanced;
And, from the impulse of a just disdain,
Once more did I retire into myself.
There feeling no contentment, I resolved
To fly, for safeguard, to some foreign shore,

804 All that Abstraction furnished . . . *1836–*

813 Saw a seductive image of herself. *1827– ; so MS. 1814/27 but* Saw] Beheld *as 1814*

824–825 Despise, as senseless: for my spirit relished / Strangely the exasperation of that Land, *MS. 1814/27–*

827–828 Of her own breast; confounded into hope / Of disencumbering thus her fretful wings. *MS. 1814/27– ; MS. 1814/27 drafts:* To disencumber thus her [?] wings *pencil, eras, at page foot* [?Impatient] *pencil at l. 828, then del by eras*

Remote from Europe; from her blasted hopes;
Her fields of carnage, and polluted air.

Fresh blew the wind, when o'er the Atlantic Main
The Ship went gliding with her thoughtless crew:
And who among them but an Exile, freed
From discontent, indifferent, pleased to sit
Among the busily-employed, not more
With obligation charged, with service taxed,
Than the loose pendant—to the idle wind
Upon the tall mast, streaming! But, ye Powers
Of soul and sense—mysteriously allied,
O, never let the Wretched, if a choice
Be left him, trust the freight of his distress
To a long voyage on the silent deep!
For, like a Plague, will Memory break out,
And, in the blank and solitude of things,
Upon his Spirit, with a fever's strength,
Will Conscience prey.—Feebly must They have felt
Who, in old time, attired with snakes and whips
The vengeful Furies. *Beautiful* regards
Were turned on me—the face of her I loved;
The Wife and Mother, pitifully fixing
Tender reproaches, insupportable!
Where now that boasted liberty? No welcome
From unknown Objects I received; and those,
Known and familiar, which the vaulted sky
Did, in the placid clearness of the night,
Disclose, had accusations to prefer
Against my peace. Within the cabin stood
That Volume—as a compass for the soul—
Revered among the Nations. I implored
Its guidance; but the infallible support
Of faith was wanting. Tell me, why refused
To One by storms annoyed and adverse winds,
Perplexed with currents, of his weakness sick,
Of vain endeavours tired, and by his own,
And by his Nature's ignorance, dismayed.

Long-wished-for sight, the Western World appeared;
And, when the Ship was moored, I leapt ashore
Indignantly—resolved to be a Man,
Who, having o'er the past no power, would live
No longer in subjection to the past,
With abject mind—from a tyrannic Lord
Inviting penance, fruitlessly endured.
So like a Fugitive, whose feet have cleared
Some boundary, which his Followers may not cross

In prosecution of their deadly chace,
Respiring I looked round.—How bright the Sun,
How promising the Breeze! Can aught produced
In the old World compare, thought I, for power
And majesty with this gigantic Stream,
Sprung from the Desart? And behold, a City
Fresh, youthful, and aspiring! What are these
To me, or I to them? As much at least
As He desires that they should be, whom winds
And waves have wafted to this distant shore,
In the condition of a damaged seed,
Whose fibres cannot, if they would, take root.
Here may I roam at large;—my business is,
Roaming at large, to observe, and not to feel;
And, therefore, not to act—convinced that all
Which bears the name of action, howsoe'er
Beginning, ends in servitude—still painful,
And mostly profitless. And, sooth to say,
On nearer view, a motley spectacle
Appeared, of high pretensions—unreproved
But by the obstreperous voice of higher still;
Big Passions strutting on a petty stage;
Which a detached Spectator may regard
Not unamused.—But ridicule demands
Quick change of objects; and, to laugh alone,
In woods and wilds, or any lonely place,
At a composing distance from the haunts
Of strife and folly,—though it be a treat
As choice as musing Leisure can bestow;
Yet, in the very centre of the crowd
To keep the secret of a poignant scorn,
May suit an airy Demon; but, of all
Unsocial courses, 'tis the one least fit
For the gross spirit of Mankind,—the one
That soonest fails to please, and quickliest turns
Into vexation.—Let us, then, I said,
Leave this unknit Republic to the scourge
Of its own passions; and to Regions haste,
Whose shades have never felt the encroaching axe,
Or soil endured a transfer in the mart

---

889 The breeze how soft! Can any thing produced *1845– ; MS. 1836/45 has several drafts:* How promising the breeze *del in pencil to* The air how soft! *followed by* any thing *alt to* Can aught produced The air how soft! *pencil in left margin* The air how soft can anything produc d *entered vertically in pencil in right margin on facing page* how bright the sun *del at page foot*

912 *del MS. 1814/27, om 1827–*

918–919 Howe'er to airy Demons suitable, / Of all unsocial courses, is least fit *1827–; so MS. 1814/27 but* Howeer . . . suitable / Unsocial courses, is least fit *with* Of all *in left margin*

924 its] her *MS. 1814/27–*

Of dire rapacity. There, Man abides,
Primeval Nature's Child. A Creature weak
In combination (wherefore else driven back
So far, and of his old inheritance
So easily deprived?) but, for that cause,
More dignified, and stronger in himself,
Whether to act, judge, suffer, or enjoy.
True, the Intelligence of social Art
Hath overpowered his Forefathers, and soon
Will sweep the remnant of his line away;
But contemplations, worthier, nobler far
Than her destructive energies, attend
His Independence, when along the side
Of Mississippi, or that Northern Stream
Which spreads into successive seas, he walks;
Pleased to perceive his own unshackled life,
And his innate capacities of soul,
There imaged: or, when having gained the top
Of some commanding Eminence, which yet
Intruder ne'er beheld, he thence surveys
Regions of wood and wide Savannah, vast
Expanse of unappropriated earth,
With mind that sheds a light on what he sees;
Free as the Sun, and lonely as the Sun,
Pouring above his head its radiance down
Upon a living, and rejoicing World!

So, westward, tow'rd the unviolated Woods
I bent my way; and, roaming far and wide,
Failed not to greet the merry Mocking-bird;
And while the melancholy Muccawiss
(The sportive Bird's companion in the Grove)
Repeated, o'er and o'er, his plaintive cry,
I sympathized at leisure with the sound;
But that pure Archetype of human greatness,
I found him not. There, in his stead, appeared
A Creature, squalid, vengeful, and impure;
Remorseless, and submissive to no law
But superstitious fear, and abject sloth.
—Enough is told! Here am I—Ye have heard
What evidence I seek, and vainly seek;
What from my Fellow-beings I require,

---

941 Which] That *MS. 1814/27–*
953 westward] westering *then del and* stet *entered in margin MS. 1836/45*
965 learned *pencil in right margin, alt to* heard *MS. 1836/45*

---

940 For WW's end-of-volume note, see p. 300, below.

[960/961] And cannot find; what I myself have lost,
[962] Nor can regain; how languidly I look
Upon this visible fabric of the World,
May be divined—perhaps it hath been said:—
[965] But spare your pity, if there be in me
Aught that deserves respect: for I exist—
Within myself—not comfortless.—The tenor
Which my life holds, he readily may conceive
Whoe'er hath stood to watch a mountain Brook
[970] In some still passage of its course, and seen,
Within the depths of its capacious breast,
Inverted trees, and rocks, and azure sky;
And, on its glassy surface, specks of foam,
And conglobated bubbles undissolved,
[975] Numerous as stars; that, by their onward lapse,
Betray to sight the motion of the stream,
Else imperceptible; meanwhile, is heard
Perchance, a roar or murmur; and the sound
Though soothing, and the little floating isles
[980] Though beautiful, are both by Nature charged
With the same pensive office; and make known
Through what perplexing labyrinths, abrupt
Precipitations, and untoward straits,

965–970 *MS. 1836/45 has rev on verso of first free front endpaper:*
~~enough as~~ ye have learned
What evidence I seek as [?I] vainly [?]
m|
What form I|y fellow beings I require
And either they have not to give or I
Lack virtue to receive, what of [? ?]
Too oft, perhaps, less useful forfeiture
—|
Have lost nor can recover, | th[?is] ye have heard
t|
With pa |ient ears. How languidly I look
Upon the visible
968 And either they have not to give, or I
Lack virtue to receive; what I myself,
Too oft by wilful forfeiture, have lost *1845– ; MS. 1836/45 has a series of drafts: l. 968 del, ink over pencil, to* ([?Belike] too oft by wilful forfeiture) *cross in left margin signals pencil rev* I fear / Often by wilful for *interlined*
And either they have not to give or
I
Lack virtue to receive, what I myself
have lost nor can recover, this
ye have [?heard]
with patient care *pencil at top of page*
And either they have not to give, or I
~~Want skill to [?save]~~
Lack virtue to receive, what I myself
To oft by wilful forfeiture, have lost
Nor can regain. How languidly I look *ink over illeg pencil at page foot*
979 Inverted trees, rocks, clouds, . . . *1836–*
984–985 meanwhile, a roar / Is heard or soften'd murmur; *MS. 1814/27*
985 Perchance, a roar or murmur] A softened roar, a murmur; *1827– but* a] or *MS. 1832/36–*

The earth-born wanderer hath passed; and quickly,
That respite o'er, like traverses and toils
Must be again encountered.—Such a stream
Is human Life; and so the Spirit fares
In the best quiet to its course allow'd:
And such is mine,—save only for a hope
That my particular current soon will reach
The unfathomable gulph, where all is still!"

END OF THE THIRD BOOK.

---

993 Must be again encountered] Must he again encounter *1845–*
995 its] her *MS. 1832/36–*

BOOK THE FOURTH.

DESPONDENCY CORRECTED.

HERE closed the Tenant of that lonely Vale
His mournful Narrative—commenced in pain,
In pain commenced, and ended without peace:
Yet tempered, not unfrequently, with strains
Of native feeling, grateful to our minds;
And doubtless yielding some relief to his,
While we sate listening with compassion due.
Such pity yet surviving, with firm voice,
That did not falter though the heart was moved,
The Wanderer said—
"One adequate support
For the calamities of mortal life
Exists, one only;—an assured belief
That the procession of our fate, howe'er
Sad or disturbed, is ordered by a Being
Of infinite benevolence and power,
Whose everlasting purposes embrace
All accidents, converting them to Good.
—The darts of anguish *fix* not where the seat
Of suffering hath been thoroughly fortified
By acquiescence in the Will Supreme

6–7 And doubtless yielding] And yielding surely *1845–; MS. 1836/45:* And such as yielded *in ink following pencil drafts:*

in sympathy
[?&] which, no doubt, while we with due compassion
Sate listening, yielding some relief *top of facing page*
while with symp
And doubtless while with due
moved
[?List] *bottom of facing page*
[?the] while we
And which, ~~no doubt~~ while with [?compassion] due
Sate listening
And [?by which] we
Sate listening yielded some relief to his
And which no doubt, while with compassion due *top of page*
Sate listening, yielded some relief to him *eras, top of page*

8–9 firm] clear *1836–1843* *for l. 8* A pause of silence followed; then, with voice *1845–; so MS. 1836/45 but* followed then with *and an earlier draft:*

And
A pause of silence followed, then with voice
That did not falter though the heart was mov[?ed] *pencil, eras, in right margin; see verbal variants to l. 9, below*

9 That falter'd not, albeit the . . . *with* faltered *rev to* falter'd *MS. 1832/36, adopted (as rev) 1836–1843* That did not falter though the heart was moved, *1845–; MS. 1836/45 as 1845 (for earlier draft, see verbal variants to ll. 8–9, above)*

10 *MS. 1836/45 has a mostly illeg pencil draft, eras, below this line:* Of thoughts [? ? ?]

For Time and for Eternity; by faith,
Faith absolute in God, including hope,
And the defence that lies in boundless love
Of his perfections; with habitual dread
Of aught unworthily conceived, endured
Impatiently; ill-done, or left undone,
To the dishonour of his holy Name.
Soul of our souls, and safeguard of the world!
Sustain, Thou only canst, the sick of heart;
Restore their languid spirits, and recal
Their lost affections unto Thee, and thine!"

Then, as we issued from that covert Nook,
He thus continued—lifting up his eyes
To Heaven.—"How beautiful this dome of sky,
And the vast hills, in fluctuation fixed
At thy command, how awful! Shall the Soul,
Human and rational, report of Thee
Even less than these?—Be mute who will, who can,
Yet I will praise thee with empassioned voice:
My lips, that may forget thee in the crowd,
Cannot forget thee here; where Thou hast built,
For thy own glory, in the wilderness!
Me didst thou constitute a Priest of thine,
In such a Temple as we now behold
Reared for thy presence: therefore, am I bound
To worship, here, and everywhere—as One
Not doomed to ignorance, though forced to tread,
From childhood up, the ways of poverty;
From unreflecting ignorance preserved,
And from debasement rescued.—By thy grace
The particle divine remained unquenched;
And, mid the wild weeds of a rugged soil,
Thy bounty caused to flourish deathless flowers,
From Paradise transplanted. Wintry age
Impends; the frost will gather round my heart;
And, if they wither, I am worse than dead!
—Come Labour, when the worn-out frame requires
Perpetual sabbath; come disease and want;
And sad exclusion through decay of sense;
But leave me unabated trust in Thee—
And let thy favour, to the end of life,
Inspire me with ability to seek
Repose and hope among eternal things—
Father of heaven and earth! and I am rich,
And will possess my portion in content!

---

56 And if they wither,] If the flowers wither, *1836–*

And what are things Eternal?—Powers depart,"
The grey-haired Wanderer steadfastly replied,
Answering the question which himself had asked,
"Possessions vanish, and Opinions change,
And Passions hold a fluctuating seat:
But, by the storms of circumstance unshaken,
And subject neither to eclipse or wane,
Duty exists;—immutably survive,
For our support, the measures and the forms,
Which an abstract Intelligence supplies;
Whose kingdom is, where Time and Space are not:
Of other converse, which mind, soul, and heart,
Do, with united urgency, require,
What more, that may not perish? Thou, dread Source,
Prime, self-existing Cause and End of all,
That, in the scale of Being, fill their place,
Above our human region, or below,
Set and sustained;—Thou—who didst wrap the cloud
Of Infancy around us, that Thyself,
Therein, with our simplicity awhile
Might'st hold, on earth, communion undisturbed—
Who from the anarchy of dreaming sleep,
Or from its death-like void, with punctual care,
And touch as gentle as the morning light,
Restor'st us, daily, to the powers of sense,
And reason's steadfast rule—thou, thou alone
Art everlasting, and the blessed Spirits,
Which thou includest, as the Sea her Waves:
For adoration thou endurest; endure
For consciousness the motions of thy will;
For apprehension those transcendent truths
Of the pure Intellect, that stand as laws,
(Submission constituting strength and power)
Even to thy Being's infinite majesty!
This Universe shall pass away—a frame
Glorious! because the shadow of thy might,
A step, or link, for intercourse with Thee.
Ah! if the time must come, in which my feet
No more shall stray where Meditation leads,
By flowing stream, through wood, or craggy wild,
Loved haunts like these, the unimprisoned Mind
May yet have scope to range among her own,
Her thoughts, her images, her high desires.
If the dear faculty of sight should fail,
Still, it may be allowed me to remember

---

72 or] nor *1827–*
100 frame] work *MS. 1814/27–*

What visionary powers of eye and soul
In youth were mine; when, stationed on the top
Of some huge hill—expectant, I beheld
The Sun rise up, from distant climes returned
Darkness to chase, and sleep, and bring the day
His bounteous gift! or saw him, tow'rds the Deep
Sink—with a retinue of flaming Clouds
Attended; then, my Spirit was entranced
With joy exalted to beatitude;
The measure of my soul was filled with bliss,
And holiest love; as earth, sea, air, with light,
With pomp, with glory, with magnificence!

Those fervent raptures are for ever flown;
And, since their date, my Soul hath undergone
Change manifold, for better, or for worse:
Yet cease I not to struggle, and to aspire
Heavenward; and chide the part of me that flags,
Through sinful choice; or dread necessity,
On human Nature, from above, imposed.
'Tis, by comparison, an easy task
Earth to despise; but to converse with Heaven,
This is not easy:—to relinquish all
We have, or hope, of happiness and joy,—
And stand in freedom loosened from this world;
I deem not arduous:—but must needs confess
That 'tis a thing impossible to frame
Conceptions equal to the Soul's desires;
And the most difficult of tasks to *keep*
Heights which the Soul is competent to gain.
—Man is of dust: etherial Hopes are his,
Which, when they should sustain themselves aloft,
Want due consistence; like a Pillar of smoke,
That with majestic energy from earth
Rises; but, having reached the thinner air,
Melts, and dissolves, and is no longer seen.
From this infirmity of mortal kind
Sorrow proceeds, which else were not;—at least,
If Grief be something hallowed and ordained,
If, in proportion, it be just and meet,

---

126 to aspire] aspire *MS. 1814/27–*

136 frame] form *MS. 1836/45*

147 Sorrow & griefs proceed, which else were not; *MS. 1836/45; see verbal variants to l. 150, below*

148 *MS. 1836/45 drafts:* And, they be ordained & hallowed Powers *del* be *added above* and & Hallowed Power[?s] *added*

149/150 O pitiable weakness of man's heart, *del MS. 1836/45*

130–131 For WW's end-of-volume note, see p. 300, below.

[150/151] Through this, 'tis able to maintain its hold,
In that excess which Conscience disapproves.
For who could sink and settle to that point
[154] Of selfishness; so senseless who could be
In framing estimates of loss and gain,
[155] As long and perseveringly to mourn
For any Object of his love, removed
From this unstable world, if he could fix
A satisfying view upon that state
Of pure, imperishable blessedness,
[160] Which Reason promises, and holy Writ
Ensures to all Believers?—Yet mistrust
Is of such incapacity, methinks,
[163] No natural branch; despondency far less.
[165] —And, if there be whose tender frames have drooped
Even to the dust; apparently, through weight
Of anguish unrelieved, and lack of power
An agonizing sorrow to transmute,
Infer not hence a hope from those withheld
[170] When wanted most; a confidence impaired
So pitiably, that, having ceased to see
With bodily eyes, they are borne down by love
Of what is lost, and perish through regret.
Oh! no, full oft the innocent Sufferer sees
[175] Too clearly; feels too vividly; and longs
To realize the Vision with intense
And overconstant yearning—there—there lies
The excess, by which the balance is destroyed.
Too, too contracted are these walls of flesh,
[180] This vital warmth too cold, these visual orbs,
Though inconceivably endowed, too dim
For any passion of the soul that leads
To extacy; and, all the crooked paths
Of time and change disdaining, takes its course
[185] Along the line of limitless desires.
I, speaking now from such disorder free,
Nor rapt, nor craving, but in settled peace,

---

150 Yet, through this weakness of the general heart, / Is it enabled to maintain its hold *1836–; so MS. 1832/36 but* through *over illeg eras* Is it *rev from* It is *and* heart / Is . . . hold, *MS. 1836/45 drafts:* their *added above* its Are they enabled to maintain their hold *then ll. 147–150 del and*

else were not
Or would exist only to sanctify ~~th~~
The spirit and invigorate the mind

Beauty then [?rules] controlled while they {[?whose] / [—?—]} [?chastity] *page foot; see verbal variants to l. 147 through l. 150, above*

154 framing *del to* making *before entire line del in pencil MS. 1814/27, line om 1827–*

163/164 And, least of all, is absolute despair. *MS. 1832/36–*

168 Deem not that proof is here of hope withheld *MS. 1832/36–*

173 Oh! no, the innocent Sufferer often sees *MS. 1832/36–*

186 rapt] sleep *1814* rapt *errata 1814, MS. 1814/27; see note to IV, 186, on p. 395, below*

I cannot doubt that They whom you deplore
Are glorified; or, if they sleep, shall wake
[190] From sleep, and dwell with God in endless love.
Hope,—below this, consists not with belief
In mercy carried infinite degrees
Beyond the tenderness of human hearts:
Hope,—below this, consists not with belief
[195] In perfect Wisdom, guiding mightiest Power,
That finds no limits but its own pure Will.

[197] Here then we rest: not fearing to be left
In undisturbed possession of our creed
[198] For aught that human reasoning can achieve,
To unsettle or perplex us: yet with pain
[200] Acknowledging, and grievous self-reproach,
That, though immoveably convinced, we want
Zeal, and the virtue to exist by faith
As Soldiers live by courage; as, by strength
Of heart, the Sailor fights with roaring seas.
[205] Alas! the endowment of immortal Power
Is matched unequally with custom, time,
And domineering faculties of sense
In *all*; in most with superadded foes,
[209] Idle temptations—open vanities
Of dissipation; countless, still-renewed,
[210] Ephemeral offspring of the unblushing world;
And, in the private regions of the mind,
Ill-governed passions, ranklings of despite,
Immoderate wishes, pining discontent,
Distress and care. What then remains?—To seek
[215] Those helps, for his occasions ever near,
Who lacks not will to use them; vows, renewed
On the first motion of a holy thought;
Vigils of contemplation; praise; and prayer,
A Stream, which, from the fountain of the heart,
[220] Issuing however feebly, no where flows
Without access of unexpected strength.
But, above all, the victory is most sure
For Him, who, seeking faith by virtue, strives
To yield entire submission to the law
[225] Of Conscience; Conscience reverenced and obeyed,
As God's most intimate Presence in the soul,

---

195 its] her *1827–*
196–198 Here then we rest: not fearing for our creed / The worst that human reasoning can achieve, *MS. 1814/27– but* "Here *1832* not fearing] fearing not *MS. 1832/36*
199 us] it *MS. 1814/27–*
210 *del MS. 1814/27, om 1827–*

205–206 For WW's end-of-volume note, see pp. 300–301, below.

And his most perfect Image in the world.
—Endeavour thus to live; these rules regard,
These helps solicit; and a steadfast seat
Shall then be yours among the happy few
Who dwell on earth yet breathe empyreal air,
Sons of the morning. For your nobler Part,
Ere disencumbered of her mortal chains,
Doubt shall be quelled and trouble chased away;
With only such degree of sadness left
As may support longings of pure desire;
And strengthen love, rejoicing secretly
In the sublime attractions of the Grave."

While, in this strain, the venerable Sage
Poured forth his aspirations, and announced
His judgments, near that lonely House we paced
A plot of green-sward, seemingly preserved
By Nature's care from wreck of scattered stones,
And from the encroachment of encircling heath:
Small space! but for reiterated steps
Smooth and commodious; as a stately deck
Which to and fro the Mariner is used
To tread for pastime; talking with his Mates,
Or haply thinking of far-distant Friends,
While the Ship glides before a steady breeze.
Stillness prevailed around us: and the Voice,
That spake, was capable to lift the soul
Tow'rds regions yet more tranquil. But, methought,
That He, whose fixed despondency had given
Impulse and motive to that strong discourse,
Was less upraised in spirit than abashed;
Shrinking from admonition, like a man
Who feels, that to exhort, is to reproach.
Yet not to be diverted from his aim,
The Sage continued.—"For that other loss,
The loss of confidence in social Man,
By the unexpected transports of our Age
Carried so high, that every thought—which looked
Beyond the temporal destiny of the Kind—
To many seemed superfluous; as, no cause
For such exalted confidence could e'er
Exist; so, none is now for such despair:

---

245 the encroachment] encroachment *MS. 1814/27–*
266–267 *MS. 1836/45 drafts:* no cause / No pleas could justify / That *pencil at top of page*
no cause
No plea could the[?re on] [? ?]
Su
Whi|ch confidence, [? ? ?] *pencil, partly eras, in right margin*
267 Could e'er for such exalted confidence *1845–*
268 such] fixed *MS. 1814/27–*

The two extremes are equally remote
[269] From Truth and Reason;—do not, then, confound
One with the other, but reject them both;
[271] And choose the middle point, whereon to build
Sound expectations. This doth he advise
Who shared at first the illusion; but was soon
Cast from the pedestal of pride by shocks
[275] Which Nature gently gave, in woods and fields;
Nor unreproved by Providence, thus speaking
To the inattentive Children of the World,
"Vain-glorious Generation! what new powers
"On you have been conferred? what gifts, withheld
[280] "From your Progenitors, have Ye received,
"Fit recompence of new desert? what claim
"Are ye prepared to urge, that my decrees
"For you should undergo a sudden change;
"And the weak functions of one busy day,
[285] "Reclaiming and extirpating, perform
"What all the slowly-moving Years of Time,
"With their united force, have left undone?
"By Nature's gradual processes be taught,
"By Story be confounded. Ye aspire
[290] "Rashly, to fall once more; and that false fruit,
"Which, to your over-weening spirits, yields
"Hope of a flight celestial, will produce
"Misery and shame. But Wisdom of her sons
"Shall not the less, though late, be justified."

269–272 The two extremes are equally disowned
By reason; if, with sharp recoil, from one
You have been driven far as its opposite,
Between them seek the point whereon to build *1827– but* reason: *1836–*
MS. 1814/27 has extensive rev:
The transcient sadness were as natural
As that a cloud albeit silver bright
Should fling yon dark spot on the mountain side.
Forced by sharp recoil from one extreme
You have been driven far as its opposite
Between them seek the point whereon to build *interlined ink over pencil, eras*
{The two extremes are equally disown'd
{Alternatives there are [?alike disdained]}
{By reason; if, with sharp recoil, from one
{[? ? ? ? ?]}
{You have been driven far as its opposite,
{[? ? ? ? ?]}
{Between them seek the point whereon to build
{[? ? ? ? ? ?]}
{Sound expectations. So doth he advise
{[? ? ? ?] [?to build]}
{Who shared
{[?Sound expectations &c} *page foot; underwriting in pencil, eras and mostly illeg*

273 This] So *1827–*

292 yields] feeds *MS. 1836/45*

293 *MS. 1836/45 drafts:* flight celestial will produce *del to* [?God—] light flight (*possibly* light *intended for "like") with pencil, eras, below l. 295:* Of a celestial flight

[295] Such timely warning," said the Wanderer, "gave
That visionary Voice; and, at this day,
When a Tartarian darkness overspreads
The groaning nations; when the Impious rule,
By will or by established ordinance,
[300] Their own dire agents, and constrain the Good
To acts which they abhor; though I bewail
This triumph, yet the pity of my heart
Prevents me not from owning, that the law,
By which Mankind now suffers, is most just.
[305] For by superior energies; more strict
Affiance in each other; faith more firm
In their unhallowed principles; the Bad
Have fairly earned a victory o'er the weak,
The vacillating, inconsistent Good.
[310] Therefore, not unconsoled, I wait—in hope
To see the moment, when the righteous Cause
Shall gain Defenders zealous and devout
As They who have opposed her; in which Virtue
Will to her efforts tolerate no bounds
[315] That are not lofty as her rights; aspiring
By impulse of her own etherial zeal.
That Spirit only can redeem Mankind;
And when that sacred Spirit shall appear
Then shall *our* triumph be complete as their's.
[320] Yet, should this confidence prove vain, the Wise
Have still the keeping of their proper peace;
Are guardians of their own tranquillity.
[323] They act, or they recede, observe, and feel;
"Knowing"—(to adopt the energetic words
Which a time-hallowed Poet hath employed)
[324] "Knowing the heart of Man is set to be
[325] The centre of this World, about the which
Those revolutions of disturbances
Still roll; where all the aspècts of misery
Predominate; whose strong effects are such
As he must bear, being powerless to redress;
[330] *And that unless above himself he can*
Erect himself, how poor a thing is Man!"*

Happy is He who lives to understand!
Not human Nature only, but explores

*Daniel

325–326 *del MS. 1814/27, om 1827–*
330 aspècts] aspects *1814* aspècts *errata 1814, MS. 1814/27* aspécts *1820E–1832* aspects *1836– but* aspècts *pencil MS. 1836/45, 1845, 1850*

---

325 For WW's end-of-volume note, see pp. 301–302, below.

All Natures,—to the end that he may find
The law that governs each; and where begins
The union, the partition where, that makes
Kind and degree, among all visible Beings;
The constitutions, powers, and faculties,
Which they inherit,—cannot step beyond,—
And cannot fall beneath; that do assign
To every Class its station and its office,
Through all the mighty Commonwealth of things;
Up from the creeping plant to sovereign Man.
Such Converse, if directed by a meek,
Sincere, and humble Spirit, teaches love;
For knowledge is delight; and such delight
Breeds love; yet, suited as it rather is
To thought and to the climbing intellect,
It teaches less to love, than to adore;
If that be not indeed the highest Love!"

"Yet," said I, tempted here to interpose,
"The dignity of Life is not impaired
By aught that innocently satisfies
The humbler cravings of the heart; and He
Is a still happier Man, who, for those heights
Of speculation not unfit, descends;
And such benign affections cultivates
Among the inferior Kinds; not merely those
That he may call his own, and which depend,
As individual objects of regard,
Upon his care,—from whom he also looks
For signs and tokens of a mutual bond,—
But others, far beyond this narrow sphere,
Whom, for the very sake of love, he loves.
Nor is it a mean praise of rural life
And solitude, that they do favour most,
Most frequently call forth, and best sustain
These pure sensations; that can penetrate
The obstreperous City; on the barren Seas
Are not unfelt,—and much might recommend,
How much they might inspirit and endear,
The loneliness of this sublime Retreat!"

"Yes," said the Sage, resuming the discourse
Again directed to his downcast Friend,
"If, with the froward will and groveling soul
Of Man offended, liberty is here,
And invitation every hour renewed,

---

371 that] which *pencil MS. 1836/45*
374 they might] might they *pencil transposition mark MS. 1836/45*

To mark *their* placid state, who never heard
Of a command which they have power to break,
[380] Or rule which they are tempted to transgress;
These, with a soothed or elevated heart,
May we behold, their knowledge register,
Observe their ways; and, free from envy, find
Complacence there:—but wherefore this to You?
[385] I guess that, welcome to your lonely hearth,
[386/387] The Redbreast feeds in winter from your hand;
A box perchance is from your casement hung
For the small Wren to build in;—not in vain,
[390] The barriers disregarding that surround
This deep Abiding-place, before your sight
Mounts on the breeze the Butterfly—and soars,
Small Creature as she is, from earth's bright flowers
Into the dewy clouds. Ambition reigns
[395] In the waste wilderness: the Soul ascends
Towards her native firmament of heaven,
When the fresh Eagle, in the month of May,
Upborne, at evening, on replenished wing,
This shady valley leaves,—and leaves the dark
[400] Empurpled hills,—conspicuously renewing
A proud communication with the sun
Low sunk beneath the horizon!—List!—I heard,
[403] From yon huge breast of rock, a solemn bleat;
Sent forth as if it were the Mountain's voice,
[404] As if the visible Mountain made the cry.
[405] Again!"—The effect upon the soul was such
As he expressed; for, from the mountain's heart
The solemn bleat appeared to come; there was
No other—and the region all around

389 The redbreast, ruffled up by winter's cold / Into a 'feathery bunch,' feeds at your hand: *1836–; so MS. 1832/36 but* winters cold, *and* "feathery bunch" feeds
398 Towards] Drawn towards *MS. 1832/36–*
401 shady] shaded *1820E–*
405–406 From yon huge breast of rock, a voice sent forth *MS. 1836/45, 1845–*
406 voice] Self *pencil MS. 1836/45*
405–408 breast of rock a voce sent forth
[?As if] the visible mountain [?spoke] the cry
Again! In the surrounding vaccancy
The effect upon the soul was [?verily] such *right margin of facing page MS. 1836/45*
408 in the surrounding vacancy *del above line MS. 1836/45* such] [?verily] such *right margin then del MS. 1836/45*
409–411 As he expressed; from out the mountain's heart
The solemn bleat appeared to issue, startling
The blank air—for the region . . . *1827– but* bleat] voice *1845–; MS. 1814/27 as 1827 but* issue; startling,
MS. 1814/27 at page foot has a pencil draft of ll. 409–413:
As he described;—the region all around
Stood silent
And from the mountains stony heart the voice
Appeared to come tho' but the unanswered bleat
Of a poor lamb*; entry continues, below*

Stood silent, empty of all shape of life.
—It was a Lamb—left somewhere to itself,
The plaintive Spirit of the Solitude!—
He paused, as if unwilling to proceed,
Through consciousness that silence in such place
Was best,—the most affecting eloquence.
But soon his thoughts returned upon themselves,
And, in soft tone of speech, he thus resumed.

"Ah! if the heart, too confidently raised,
Perchance too lightly occupied, or lulled
Too easily, despise or overlook
The vassalage that binds her to the earth,
Her sad dependance upon time, and all
The trepidations of mortality,
What place so destitute and void—but there
The little Flower her vanity shall check;
The trailing Worm reprove her thoughtless pride?

These craggy regions, these chaotic wilds,
Does that benignity pervade, that warms
The Mole contented with her darksome walk
In the cold ground; and to the Emmet gives
Her foresight; and the intelligence that makes
The tiny Creatures strong by social league;
Supports the generations, multiplies
Their tribes, till we behold a spacious plain
Or grassy bottom, all, with little hills—
Their labour—covered, as a Lake with waves;
Thousands of Cities, in the desart place
Built up of life, and food, and means of life!
Nor wanting here, to entertain the thought,
Creatures, that in communities exist,
Less, as might seem, for general guardianship
Or through dependance upon mutual aid,

409–411 *MS. 1836/45 has several drafts:*
Appeared to come that voice, the unanswered bleat *page foot*
Appeared to come [?that solemn]
[?So] the bleat *pencil at page foot*
As he expressed for from the mountains self
~~The [?v]~~ Appear d to come that Voice the [?solemn] bleat *left margin of facing page*
As he described:—the region all around
Stood silent, empty of all shape of life;
And from the mountains strong heart the voice
Appeared to come, though but the unanswered bleat *right margin*

412–413 Yet was the cry only the unanswered bleat / Of a poor lamb *MS. 1836/45; for additional drafts, see verbal variants to IV, 409–411, above*
Stood empty of all shape of life, and silent
Save for that single cry, the unanswer'd bleat
Of a poor lamb—left somewhere to itself, *1845–*

419 he thus] thus he *MS. 1832/36–*

433 the intelligence] intelligence *MS. 1814/27–*

Than by participation of delight
And a strict love of fellowship, combined.
[445] What other spirit can it be, that prompts
The gilded summer Flies to mix and weave
Their sports together in the solar beam,
Or in the gloom of twilight hum their joy?
More obviously, the self-same influence rules
[450] The feathered kinds; the Fieldfare's pensive flocks,
The cawing Rooks, and Sea-mews from afar,
Hovering above these inland Solitudes,
[453] Unscattered by the wind, at whose loud call
[455] Their voyage was begun: nor is its power
Unfelt among the sedentary Fowl
That seek yon Pool, and there prolong their stay
In silent congress; or together rouzed
Take flight; while with their clang the air resounds.
[460] And, over all, in that etherial arch
Is the mute company of changeful clouds;
—Bright apparition suddenly put forth
The Rainbow, smiling on the faded storm;
The mild assemblage of the starry heavens;
[465] And the great Sun, earth's universal Lord!

How bountiful is Nature! he shall find
Who seeks not; and to him, who hath not asked,
Large measure shall be dealt. Three sabbath-days
Are scarcely told, since, on a service bent
[470] Of mere humanity, You clomb those Heights;
And what a marvellous and heavenly Shew
Was to your sight revealed! the Swains moved on,
[473] And heeded not; you lingered, and perceived.
[475] There is a luxury in self-dispraise;
And inward self-disparagement affords
To meditative Spleen a grateful feast.
Trust me, pronouncing on your own desert,
You judge unthankfully; distempered nerves
[480] Infect the thoughts; the languor of the Frame
Depresses the Soul's vigour. Quit your Couch—
Cleave not so fondly to your moody Cell;

---

452 flocks] flock *MS. 1814/27–*
455 By the ~~fierce~~ rough wind unscattered, at whose call *MS. 1814/27, adopted (as rev) 1827–*
455/456 Up through the trenches of the long-drawn vales *1836– ; so MS. 1832/36 but* vale
456 was begun] they began *pencil in right margin, ink over pencil above line, MS. 1836/45*
461 arch,] vault, *1832–*
473 to your sight] suddenly *MS. 1832/36–*
474 and] you *MS. 1832/36–*
474/475 And felt, deeply as living man could feel. *MS. 1832/36–*
481–482 *om in printed text of first issue of 1814 (see entry for MS. 1814/27 in Manuscript Census, p. xxviii, above)*

Nor let the hallowed Powers, that shed from heaven
Stillness and rest, with disapproving eye
Look down upon your taper, through a watch
Of midnight hours, unseasonably twinkling
In this deep Hollow; like a sullen star
Dimly reflected in a lonely pool.
Take courage, and withdraw yourself from ways
That run not parallel to Nature's course.
Rise with the Lark! your Matins shall obtain
Grace, be their composition what it may,
If but with her's performed; climb once again,
Climb every day, those ramparts; meet the breeze
Upon their tops,—adventurous as a Bee
That from your garden thither soars, to feed
On new-blown heath; let yon commanding rock
Be your frequented Watch-tower; roll the stone
In thunder down the mountains: with all your might
Chase the wild Goat; and, if the bold red Deer
Fly to these harbours, driven by hound and horn
Loud echoing, add your speed to the pursuit:
So, wearied to your Hut shall you return,
And sink at evening into sound repose."

The Solitary lifted towards the hills
An animated eye; and thoughts were mine
Which this ejaculation clothed in words—
"Oh! what a joy it were, in vigorous health,
To have a Body (this our vital Frame
With shrinking sensibility endued,
And all the nice regards of flesh and blood)
And to the elements surrender it
As if it were a Spirit!—How divine,
The liberty, for frail, for mortal man
To roam at large among unpeopled glens
And mountainous retirements, only trod
By devious footsteps; regions consecrate
To oldest time! and, reckless of the storm

---

501 these] those *1836–*

505–507 *om in printed text of MS. 1814/27 (see entry for MS. 1814/27 in Manuscript Census, p. xxviii, above) but drafted there at bottom of p. 163:*

The Solitary lifted toward the hills
~~An animated eye; and thoughts were mine~~
~~Which this ejaculation clothed in words~~
A kindling eye—poetic feelings rush'd [?~~into my bosom~~]
Into my bo
And these som—whence these words broke forth *first three lines are adopted in 1814; rev of ll. 506–507 (by deleting lines two and three and adding the last two lines in an ink differing from the first three lines) is adopted in 1827:*

A kindling eye;—poetic feelings rushed
Into my bosom, whence these words broke forth: *1827– but* eye: *1836–* poetic] accordant *pencil in margin, ink over pencil interlined MS. 1836/45,* accordant *adopted 1845–*

That keeps the raven quiet in her nest,
Be as a Presence or a Motion—one
Among the many there; and, while the Mists
Flying, and rainy Vapours, call out Shapes
And Phantoms from the crags and solid earth
As fast as a Musician scatters sounds
Out of an instrument; and, while the Streams—
(As at a first creation and in haste
To exercise their untried faculties)
Descending from the region of the clouds
And starting from the hollows of the earth
More multitudinous every moment—rend
Their way before them, what a joy to roam
An Equal among mightiest Energies;
And haply sometimes with articulate voice,
Amid the deafening tumult, scarcely heard
By him that utters it, exclaim aloud
Be this continued so from day to day,
Nor let it have an end from month to month!"

"Yes," said the Wanderer, taking from my lips
The strain of transport, "whosoe'er in youth

536–537 *l. 537 rev in MS. 1814/27:*
Nor let the fierce commotion have an end
Ruinous tho' it be from month to month!" *so 1827–1843 but* end, . . . though . . . be, *ll. 536–537 rev in MS. 1835/45 and adopted 1845–*:
'Rage on ye elements! let moon and stars
Their aspects lend, and mingle in their turn
With this commotion (ruinous though it be)
From day to night, from night to day, prolonged!'"
MS. 1836/45 also has drafts: Re[?turn not] [?] & [?wake to your best heaven] / Nor let this fierce [?commotion] *pencil at top of page, overwritten in ink:*
May this wild uproar last from day to day
Nor let from month to month the fierce commotion
Ruinous though it be abate its rage *followed by:*
Rage on ye elements
~~May this continue~~—Let sun moon and stars
[?]
Their aspects lend and with their powers take part
In the commotion (ruinous though it be)
From day to night from night to day, prolonged. *in right margin, all del by cross, with pencil overwriting* to mingle in their [?t]
[? ?]
Ye winds [?and water]
[?Be this fierce] [?] [?through] & day continue
~~Nor let~~ Their aspects lend & mingle in their [?turn] *in pencil in left margin*
538–539
"Yes," said the Wanderer "{taking from my lips / [?whosoeer in youth]}
~~**Whoe'er hath known such transports, who in youth**~~
The strain of transport, "whosoe'er in youth
Ha{s / th}, through ambition of his soul, given way *adopted 1814– (as rev) but* "Yes,"] Yes," *1836* "Yes," *pencil MS. 1836/45, 1840– and* Wanderer, taking *1814–* *the bold-face lines* Whoe'er . . . way *begin a para with* Whoe'er *and are printed text apparently present only in MS. 1814/27 (see entry for MS. 1814/27 in Manuscript Census, p. xxviii, above); the rev, a pre-publication one, is a variant of the text in MS. 70, 23*[v]

Has, through ambition of his soul, given way
To such desires, and grasped at such delight,
Shall feel the stirrings of them late and long;
[545] In spite of all the weakness that life brings,
Its cares and sorrows; he, though taught to own
The tranquillizing power of time, shall wake,
Wake sometimes to a noble restlessness—
Loving the spots which once he gloried in.

[550] Compatriot, Friend, remote are Garry's Hills,
The Streams far distant of your native Glen;
[552] Yet is their form and Image here express'd
As by a duplicate, at least set forth
[553] With brotherly resemblance. Turn your steps
Wherever fancy leads, by day by night
[555] Are various engines working, not the same
As those by which your soul in youth was moved,
But by the great Artificer endued
With no inferior power. You dwell alone;
You walk, you live, you speculate alone;
[560] Yet doth Remembrance, like a sovereign Prince,
For you a stately gallery maintain
Of gay or tragic pictures. You have seen,
Have acted, suffered, travelled far, observed
With no incurious eye; and books are your's,
[565] Within whose silent chambers treasure lies
Preserved from age to age; more precious far
Than that accumulated store of gold
And orient gems, which for a day of need
The Sultan hides within ancestral tombs.
[570] These hoards of truth you can unlock at will:
And music waits upon your skilful touch,—
Sounds which the wandering Shepherd from these Heights
Hears, and forgets his purpose;—furnished thus
How can you droop, if willing to be raised?

[575] A piteous lot it were to flee from Man—
Yet not rejoice in Nature. He—whose hours
Are by domestic Pleasures uncaressed

---

541 desires] delight *then restored to* desires *MS. 1814/27*
542 the stirrings of them] congenial stirrings *MS. 1814/27–*
546 *MS. 1836/45 drafts:* Wake sometimes] not seldom *pencil, del, in left margin; illeg word in pencil, eras, in right margin;* [?Thy] / [?–] [?Maker] let thy [? ? ?] *in pencil at page foot*
547 spots] sports *1827–*
551 *del MS. 1814/27, om 1827–*
555 by] with *MS. 1832/36–*
556 endued] endowed *1836–*
568 within] deep in *MS. 1832/36–*
573 raised] upraised *MS. 1832/36–*

And unenlivened; who exists whole years
Apart from benefits received or done
[580] 'Mid the transactions of the bustling crowd;
Who neither hears, nor feels a wish to hear,
Of the world's interests—such a One hath need
Of a quick fancy and an active heart,
That for the day's consumption books may yield
[585] A not unwholesome food, and earth and air
[586] Supply his morbid humour with delight.
[588] —Truth has her pleasure-grounds, her haunts of ease
And easy contemplation,—gay parterres,
[590] And labyrinthine walks, her sunny glades
[591/592] And shady groves, for recreation framed:
These may he range, if willing to partake
Their soft indulgences, and in due time
[595] May issue thence, recruited for the tasks
And course of service Truth requires from those
Who tend her Altars, wait upon her Throne,
And guard her Fortresses. Who thinks, and feels,
And recognises ever and anon
[600] The breeze of Nature stirring in his soul,
Why need such man go desperately astray,
And nurse "the dreadful appetite of death?"
If tired with Systems—each in its degree
Substantial—and all crumbling in their turn,
[605] Let him build Systems of his own, and smile
At the fond work—demolished with a touch;
If unreligious, let him be at once,
Among ten thousand Innocents, enrolled
A Pupil in the many-chambered school,
[610] Where Superstition weaves her airy dreams.

Life's Autumn past, I stand on Winter's verge,
And daily lose what I desire to keep:
Yet rather would I instantly decline
To the traditionary sympathies
[615] Of a most rustic ignorance, and take

584–585 Food not unwholesome; earth and air correct / His morbid humour, with delight supplied. *MS. 1832/36– but* [?For] delight [?or] *pencil, eras, in right margin MS. 1836/45*
585/586 Or solace, varying as the seasons change. *MS. 1836/45, 1845–* *MS. 1836/45 has scattered pencil drafts:*

for delight
as ~~with~~
Or solace, vary~~ing as~~ the seasons *top of page*
Or silence, varying as the seasons change *page foot*
[?runs]
Or ~~And~~ solace varying as the year goes round
In ample measure [?to] the year *entered vertically left margin*

589 And shady groves in studied contrast—each, / For recreation, leading into each: *1836–; so MS. 1832/36 but* contrast, each:

A fearful apprehension from the owl
Or death-watch,—and as readily rejoice,
If two auspicious magpies crossed my way;
This rather would I do than see and hear
[620] The repetitions wearisome of sense,
Where soul is dead, and feeling hath no place;
Where knowledge, ill begun in cold remark
On outward things, with formal inference ends:
[624/625] Or if the Mind turn inward 'tis perplexed,
Lost in a gloom of uninspired research;
Meanwhile, the Heart within the Heart, the seat
Where Peace and happy Consciousness should dwell,
On its own axis restlessly revolves,
[630] Yet nowhere finds the cheering light of truth.

Upon the breast of new-created Earth
Man walked; and when and wheresoe'er he moved,
Alone or mated, Solitude was not.
He heard, upon the wind, the articulate Voice
[635] Of God; and Angels to his sight appeared,
Crowning the glorious hills of Paradise;
Or through the groves gliding like morning mist
Enkindled by the sun. He sate—and talked
With winged Messengers; who daily brought
[640] To his small Island in the etherial deep
Tidings of joy and love.—From these pure Heights
(Whether of actual vision, sensible
To sight and feeling, or that in this sort
Have condescendingly been shadowed forth
[645] Communications spiritually maintained,
And Intuitions moral and divine)
Fell Human-kind—to banishment condemned
That flowing years repealed not: and distress
And grief spread wide; but Man escaped the doom

---

616 This rather would I do] To this would rather bend *MS. 1814/27–*
621 Or, if the mind turn inward, she recoils / At once—or, not recoiling, is perplexed— *1836–*
625 revolves,] revolving, *pencil MS. 1836/45, 1845–*
625–626 *MS. 1836/45 drafts:*
Rest not, but on its axis [?on ever more]
On }
[?Rest]} its own axis restless ever more
Revolving, no where finds the light of [?tru] *pencil in right margin*
Restless on its own axis evermore / Revolving *in pencil in right margin of facing page*
626 Seeks yet can nowhere find Truths cheering light *pencil MS. 1836/45* Seeks, yet can nowhere find, the light of truth. *1845–*
630 upon] born on *MS. 1832/36* borne on *1836–*
637 these] those *1836–*

---

620 The colon after "ends" dropped away in the course of the printing of revised gathering Y of the first edition and is missing from many copies.

Of destitution;—Solitude was not.
—Jehovah—shapeless Power above all Powers,
Single and one, the omnipresent God,
By vocal utterance, or blaze of light,
Or cloud of darkness, localized in heaven,
On earth, enshrined within the wandering ark;
Or, out of Sion, thundering from his throne
Between the Cherubim—on the chosen Race
Showered miracles, and ceased not to dispense
Judgments, that filled the Land from age to age
With hope, and love, and gratitude, and fear;
And with amazement smote;—thereby to assert
His scorned, or unacknowledged Sovereignty.
And when the One, ineffable of name,
In nature indivisible, withdrew
From mortal adoration or regard,
Not then was Deity engulphed, nor Man,
The rational Creature, left, to feel the weight
Of his own reason, without sense or thought
Of higher reason and a purer will,
To benefit and bless, through mightier power:
—Whether the Persian—zealous to reject
Altar and Image and the inclusive walls
And roofs of Temples built by human hands,
The loftiest heights ascending, from their tops,
With myrtle-wreathed Tiara on his brows—
Presented sacrifice to Moon and Stars,
And to the winds and Mother Elements,
And the whole Circle of the Heavens, for him
A sensitive Existence, and a God,
With lifted hands invoked, and songs of praise:
Or, less reluctantly to bonds of Sense
Yielding his Soul, the Babylonian framed
For influence undefined a personal Shape;
And, from the Plain, with toil immense, upreared
Tower eight times planted on the top of Tower;
That Belus, nightly to his splendid Couch
Descending, there might rest; and, from that Height
Pure and serene, the Godhead overlook
Winding Euphrates, and the City vast
Of his devoted Worshippers, far-stretched;
With grove, and field, and garden, interspersed;
Their Town, and foodful Region for support

---

660 In] Of *MS. 1814/27–*
670 The] To *MS. 1814/27–*
671 brows—] brow— *MS. 1814/27* brows, *1820E* brow, *1827–*
683 and, from] upon *MS. 1814/27–*
684 the Godhead overlook] diffused—to overlook *1827–; so MS. 1814/27 but* diffus'd

Against the pressure of beleaguring war.

Chaldean Shepherds, ranging trackless fields,
Beneath the concave of unclouded skies
Spread like a sea, in boundless solitude,
Looked on the Polar Star, as on a Guide
And Guardian of their course, that never closed
His steadfast eye. The Planetary Five
With a submissive reverence they beheld;
Watched, from the centre of their sleeping flocks,
Those radiant Mercuries, that seemed to move
Carrying through Ether, in perpetual round,
Decrees and resolutions of the Gods;
And, by their aspects, signifying works
Of dim futurity, to Man revealed.
—The Imaginative Faculty was Lord
Of observations natural; and, thus
Led on, those Shepherds made report of Stars
In set rotation passing to and fro,
Between the orbs of our apparent sphere
And its invisible counterpart, adorned
With answering Constellations, under earth
Removed from all approach of living sight,
But present to the Dead; who, so they deemed,
Like those celestial Messengers, beheld
All accidents, and Judges were of all.

The lively Grecian, in a Land of hills,
Rivers, and fertile plains, and sounding shores,
Under a cope of variegated sky,
Could find commodious place for every God,
Promptly received, as prodigally brought,
From the surrounding Countries—at the choice
Of all Adventurers. With unrivalled skill,
As nicest observation furnished hints
For studious fancy, did his hand bestow
On fluent Operations a fixed Shape;
Metal or Stone, idolatrously served.
And yet—triumphant o'er this pompous show
Of Art, this palpable array of Sense,
On every side encountered; in despite
Of the gross fictions, chaunted in the streets
By wandering Rhapsodists; and in contempt

715/716 He, born to breathe, under a cope of sky / More variegated, air more changeable, *MS. 1832/36*
716 variegated sky,] sky more variable, *1836–*
722 did his hand bestow] his quick hand bestowed *1836–*

Of doubt and bold denials hourly urged
[735] Amid the wrangling Schools—a SPIRIT hung,
Beautiful Region! o'er thy Towns and Farms,
Statues and Temples, and memorial Tombs;
And emanations were perceived; and acts
Of immortality, in Nature's course,
[740] Exemplified by mysteries, that were felt
As bonds, on grave Philosopher imposed
And armed Warrior; and in every grove
A gay or pensive tenderness prevailed
When piety more awful had relaxed.
[745] —"Take, running River, take these Locks of mine"—
Thus would the Votary say—"this severed hair,
"My Vow fulfilling, do I here present,
"Thankful for my beloved Child's return.
"Thy banks, Cephisus, he again hath trod,
[750] "Thy murmurs heard; and drunk the chrystal lymph
"With which thou dost refresh the thirsty lip,
"And moisten all day long these flowery fields."
And doubtless, sometimes, when the hair was shed
Upon the flowing stream, a thought arose
[755] Of Life continuous, Being unimpaired;
That hath been, is, and where it was and is
[757] There shall be,—seen, and heard, and felt, and known,
And recognized,—existence unexposed
[758] To the blind walk of mortal accident;
From diminution safe and weakening age;
[760] While Man grows old, and dwindles, and decays;
And countless generations of Mankind
Depart; and leave no vestige where they trod.

We live by admiration, hope, and love;
And even as these are well and wisely fixed,
[765] In dignity of being we ascend.
But what is error?—"Answer he who can!"
The Sceptic somewhat haughtily exclaimed,
"Love, Hope, and Admiration—are they not
Mad Fancy's favourite Vassals? Does not Life
[770] Use them, full oft, as Pioneers to ruin,
Guides to destruction? Is it well to trust
Imagination's light when Reason's fails,
The unguarded taper where the guarded faints?
—Stoop from those heights, and soberly declare
[775] What error is; and, of our errors, which

730 denials] denial *1832–*
748 'And, all day long, moisten these flowery fields!' *1845–*
753–754 There shall endure,—existence unexposed *MS. 1814/27–*

Doth most debase the mind; the genuine seats
Of power, where are they? Who shall regulate,
With truth, the scale of intellectual rank?"

"Methinks," persuasively the Sage replied,
"That for this arduous office You possess
Some rare advantages. Your early days
A grateful recollection must supply
Of much exalted good that may attend
Upon the very humblest state.—Your voice
Hath in my hearing often testified
That poor Men's Children, they, and they alone,
By their condition taught, can understand
The wisdom of the prayer that daily asks
For daily bread. A consciousness is your's
How feelingly religion may be learned
In smoky Cabins, from a Mother's tongue—
Heard while the Dwelling vibrates to the din
Of the contiguous Torrent, gathering strength
At every moment—and, with strength, increase
Of fury; or while Snow is at the door,
Assaulting and defending, and the Wind,
A sightless Labourer, whistles at his work—
Fearful, but resignation tempers fear,
And piety is sweet to Infant minds.
—The Shepherd Lad, who in the sunshine carves,
On the green turf, a dial—to divide
The silent hours; and who to that report
Can portion out his pleasures, and adapt
His round of pastoral duties, is not left
With less intelligence for *moral* things
Of gravest import. Early he perceives,
Within himself, a measure and a rule,
Which to the Sun of Truth he can apply,
That shines for him, and shines for all Mankind.
Experience, daily fixing his regards
On Nature's wants, he knows how few they are,
And where they lie, how answered and appeased.
This knowledge ample recompence affords
For manifold privations; he refers
His notions to this standard; on this rock
Rests his desires; and hence, in after life,

780–781 Of much exalted good by Heaven vouchsafed / To dignify the humblest state.— . . . *1827–; so MS. 1814/27 interlined over illeg eras but* heaven vouchsaf'd *MS. 1814/27 also has a pencil draft, eras, at page foot:* Of much exalted good by Heav'n vouchsafed / To [?recompense the] humblest state

792 besets the door *pencil in right margin MS. 1836/45*

797 who] that *MS. 1832/36–*

800/801 Throughout a long and lonely summer's day, *1836– but* day,] day *1840–*

Soul-strengthening patience, and sublime content.
Imagination—not permitted here
To waste her powers, as in the Worldling's mind,
On fickle pleasures, and superfluous cares,
And trivial ostentation—is left free
And puissant to range the solemn walks
Of time and nature, girded by a zone
That, while it binds, invigorates and supports.
Acknowledge, then, that whether by the side
Of his poor hut, or on the mountain top,
Or in the cultured field, a Man like this
(Take from him what you will upon the score
Of ignorance or illusion) lives and breathes
For noble purposes of mind: his heart
Beats to the heroic song of ancient days;
His eye distinguishes, his soul creates.
And those Illusions, which excite the scorn
Or move the pity of unthinking minds,
Are they not mainly outward Ministers
Of inward Conscience? with whose service charged
They come and go, appear and disappear;
Diverting evil purposes, remorse
Awakening, chastening an intemperate grief,
Or pride of heart abating: and, whene'er
For less important ends those Phantoms move,
Who would forbid them, if their presence serve,
Among wild mountains and unpeopled heaths,
Filling a space else vacant, to exalt
The forms of Nature, and enlarge her powers?

Once more to distant Ages of the world
Let us revert, and place before our thoughts
The face which rural Solitude might wear
To the unenlightened Swains of pagan Greece.
—In that fair Clime, the lonely Herdsman, stretched
On the soft grass through half a summer's day,
With music lulled his indolent repose:
And, in some fit of weariness, if he,
When his own breath was silent, chanced to hear
A distant strain, far sweeter than the sounds

---

824 like this] so bred *MS. 1814/27–*

834 They came and go, appeared and disappear, *1827– ; so MS. 1814/27 but* and go *del and* appear'd

840 mountains and unpeopled heaths.] hills & thinly peopled shores *pencil MS. 1836/45* On thinly-peopled mountains and wild heaths, *1845–*

844 place before our thoughts] contemplate the face *pencil MS. 1836/45*

845 which] that *pencil MS. 1836/45* Which Nature in her Solitudes might wear *pencil alt page foot MS. 1836/45*

846 Swains] sons *pencil alt MS. 1836/45*

Which his poor skill could make, his Fancy fetched,
Even from the blazing Chariot of the Sun,
A beardless Youth, who touched a golden lute,
And filled the illumined groves with ravishment.
The nightly Hunter, lifting up his eyes
Towards the crescent Moon, with grateful heart
Called on the lovely wanderer who bestowed
That timely light, to share his joyous sport:
And hence, a beaming Goddess with her Nymphs,
Across the lawn and through the darksome grove,
(Not unaccompanied with tuneful notes
By echo multiplied from rock or cave)
Swept in the storm of chase, as Moon and Stars
Glance rapidly along the clouded heavens,
When winds are blowing strong. The Traveller slaked
His thirst from Rill or gushing Fount, and thanked
The Naiad.—Sunbeams, upon distant Hills
Gliding apace, with Shadows in their train,
Might, with small help from fancy, be transformed
Into fleet Oreads sporting visibly.
The Zephyrs, fanning as they passed, their wings,
Lacked not, for love, fair Objects, whom they wooed
With gentle whisper. Withered Boughs grotesque,
Stripped of their leaves and twigs by hoary age,
From depth of shaggy covert peeping forth
In the low vale, or on steep mountain side;

855–869 *MS. 1836/45 pencil drafts related to IV, 855–869, and marked for insertion at l. 866:*
~~The youthful~~ Maid
~~Or rather [?say] the Lover at her side~~
Looking with earnest eye into the depths
Of a still lake amid the glimmering [?growt]
Of plants that there were nourished [?and create]
Helped by reflection of her own fair face
Some beautiful inhabitant who there ~~might~~
~~Might dwell~~ in calm security unknown
~~To mortal Creatures. Hence the~~ gree *alt at page foot, continued at bottom of facing page, with final four lines above del by vertical slash*
her own fair face
Help d by reflection of ~~a human~~ face
Or if not she the Lover at her side
Some beautiful Inhabitant who there
Might dwell in calm security unknown
To mortal creatures: Hence the green [?haired] brood
Nym [?readily induced]
Of Waters [?naids] phs. And tempted to [?behave]
[?To]
In like belief the Traveller when he slakes
His thirst from rill or gushing fount woul thank *right margin of facing page and then del in pencil*

857 up his eyes] a bright eye *1836–*
858 Towards] Up towards *1836–*
866 heavens] heaven *MS. 1814/27–*
869 distant] far off *alt MS. 1836/45*
870 with *possible alt to* and *MS. 1836/45*

And, sometimes, intermixed with stirring horns
Of the live Deer, or Goat's depending beard;
These were the lurking Satyrs, a wild brood
Of gamesome Deities! or Pan himself,
The simple Shepherd's awe-inspiring God."

No apter Strain could have been chosen: I marked
Its kindly influence, on the yielding brow
Of our Companion, gradually diffused;
While, listening, he had paced the noiseless turf,
Like one whose untired ear a murmuring stream
Detains; but tempted now to interpose
He with a smile exclaimed—
"'Tis well you speak
At a safe distance from our native Land,
And from the Mansions where our youth was taught.
The true Descendants of those godly Men
Who swept from Scotland, in a flame of zeal,
Shrine, Altar, Image, and the massy Piles
That harboured them,—the Souls retaining yet
The churlish features of that after Race
Who fled to caves, and woods, and naked rocks,
In deadly scorn of superstitious rites,
Or what their scruples construed to be such,
How, think you, would they tolerate this scheme
Of fine propensities? that tends, if urged
Far as it might be urged, to sow afresh
The weeds of Romish Phantasy, in vain
Uprooted; would re-consecrate our Wells
To good Saint Fillan and to fair Saint Anne;
And from long banishment recal Saint Giles,
To watch again with tutelary love
O'er stately Edinborough throned on crags.
A blessed restoration to behold
The Patron, on the shoulders of his Priests,
Once more parading through her crowded streets;
Now simply guarded by the sober Powers
Of Science, and Philosophy, and Sense!"

This answer followed.—"You have turned my thoughts
Upon our brave Progenitors, who rose
Against Idolatry with warlike mind,
And shrunk from vain observances to lurk

---

884 As this apt strain proceeded I could mark *MS. 1814/27–1843 but* proceeded, *1827–1843* The strain was aptly chosen; and I could mark *1845–*
885 on] o'er *MS. 1814/27–*
898 Who fled to woods, caverns, and jutting rocks, *1836–*

In caves, and woods, and under dismal rocks,
Deprived of shelter, covering, fire, and food;
Why?—for this very reason that they felt,
And did acknowledge, wheresoe'er they moved
A spiritual Presence, oft-times misconceived;
But still a high dependance, a divine
Bounty and government, that filled their hearts
With joy, and gratitude, and fear, and love;
And from their fervent lips drew hymns of praise
With which the desarts rang. Though favoured less,
Far less, than these, yet such, in their degree,
Were those bewildered Pagans of old time.
Beyond their own poor Natures and above
They looked; were humbly thankful for the good
Which the warm Sun solicited—and Earth
Bestowed; were gladsome,—and their moral sense
They fortified with reverence for the Gods;
And they had hopes that overstepped the Grave.

Now, shall our great Discoverers," he exclaimed,
Raising his voice triumphantly, "obtain
From Sense and Reason less than These obtained,
Though far misled? Shall Men for whom our Age
Unbaffled powers of vision hath prepared,
To explore the world without and world within,
Be joyless as the blind? Ambitious Souls—
Whom Earth, at this late season, hath produced
To regulate the moving spheres, and weigh
The planets in the hollow of their hand;
And They who rather dive than soar, whose pains
Have solved the elements, or analysed
The thinking principle—shall They in fact
Prove a degraded Race? and what avails
Renown, if their presumption make them such?
Oh! there is laughter at their work in Heaven!
Enquire of ancient Wisdom; go, demand
Of mighty Nature, if 'twas ever meant
That we should pry far off yet be unraised;
That we should pore, and dwindle as we pore,

919–920 In woods, and dwell beneath impending rocks / Ill-sheltered, and oft wanting fire and food; *1836– but* beneath] under *1845–*

928 With which the desarts] And through the desart *MS. 1814/27* That through the desert *1827–*

937ff. *MS. 1836/45 pencil drafts:* or our bodily life / Trace[?s] to its fountain *top of page* delive to the [?very fountain] / Of [?our] *top of facing page*

943 Souls—] spirits— *1836–*

947 rather dive] dive rather *MS. 1832/36*

949–950 *MS. 1836/45 pencil drafts:* shall [?prove] in fact / Only *page foot* And The [?other] element whereby / We *right margin*

Viewing all objects unremittingly
In disconnection dead and spiritless;
And still dividing, and dividing still,
Break down all grandeur, still unsatisfied
With the perverse attempt, while littleness
May yet become more little; waging thus
An impious warfare with the very life
Of our own Souls!—And if indeed there be
An all-pervading Spirit, upon whom
Our dark foundations rest, could He design,
Or will his rites and services permit,
That this magnificent effect of Power,
The Earth we tread, the Sky which we behold
By day, and all the pomp which night reveals,
That these—and that superior Mystery
Our vital Frame, so fearfully devised,
And the dread Soul within it—should exist
Only to be examined, pondered, searched,
Probed, vexed, and criticised?—Accuse me not
Of arrogance, unknown Wanderer as I am,
If, having walked with Nature threescore years,
And offered, far as frailty would allow,
My heart a daily sacrifice to Truth,
I now affirm of Nature and of Truth,
Whom I have served, that their DIVINITY
Revolts, offended at the ways of Men
Swayed by such motives, to such end employed;
Philosophers, who, when the human Soul
Is of a thousand faculties composed,
And twice ten thousand interests, do yet prize
This Soul, and the transcendent Universe,
No more than as a Mirror that reflects
To proud Self-love her own intelligence;
That one, poor, finite Object, in the Abyss
Of infinite Being, twinkling restlessly!

Nor higher place can be assigned to Him
And his Compeers—the laughing Sage of France.—
Crowned was He, if my Memory doth not err,
With laurel planted upon hoary hairs,
In sign of conquest by his Wit atchieved,
And benefits his Wisdom had conferred.

---

967 *del MS. 1814/27, om 1827–*
969 which] that *MS. 1814/27–*
984 when] though *MS. 1814/27–*
985 Is] Be *MS. 1814/27–*
994 doth] do *1827–*

His tottering Body was oppressed with flowers;
Far less becoming ornaments than those
With which Spring often decks a mouldering Tree!
Yet so it pleased a fond, a vain Old Man,
And a most frivolous People. Him I mean
Who framed, to ridicule confiding Faith,
This sorry Legend; which by chance we found
Piled in a nook, through malice, as might seem,
Among more innocent rubbish."—Speaking thus,
With a brief notice when, and how, and where,
We had espied the Book, he drew it forth;
And courteously, as if the act removed,
At once, all traces from the good Man's heart
Of unbenign aversion or contempt
Restored it to its owner. "Gentle Friend,"
Herewith he grasped the Solitary's hand,
"You have known better Lights and Guides than these—
Ah! let not aught amiss within dispose
A noble Mind to practise on herself,
And tempt Opinion to support the wrongs
Of Passion: whatsoe'er is felt or feared,
From higher judgment-seats make no appeal
To lower: can you question that the Soul
Inherits an allegiance, not by choice
To be cast off, upon an oath proposed
By each new upstart Notion? In the ports
Of levity no refuge can be found,
No shelter, for a spirit in distress.
He, who by wilful disesteem of life
And proud insensibility to hope
Affronts the eye of Solitude, shall learn
That her mild nature can be terrible;
That neither she nor Silence lack the power
To avenge their own insulted Majesty.
—O blest seclusion! when the Mind admits
The law of duty; and thereby can live,
Through each vicissitude of loss and gain,
Linked in entire complacence with her choice;
When Youth's presumptuousness is mellowed down,

---

998 His tottering Body was with wreaths of flowers *1827–1836 but* body *MS. 1832/36, 1836; MS. 1814/27 as 1827 but* flowers; His stooping body tottered with wreaths of flowers *pencil MS. 1836/45, 1840– ; MS. 1836/45 also has earlier rev of 1836 text:* was] stooped

999–1000 Oppress, far less becoming ornaments / Than Spring oft twines about a mouldering Tree; *1827– but* tree; *MS. 1832/36– ; MS. 1814/27 as 1827 but* Oppressed far . . . Tree!

1003 framed,] penn'd, *MS. 1814/27, 1827* penned, *1832–*

1014 better Lights and Guides] lights and guides better *1845–*

1018 is] be *MS. 1814/27–*

1033 thereby can live,] can therefore move *MS. 1814/27–*

And Manhood's vain anxiety dismissed;
When Wisdom shews her seasonable fruit,
Upon the boughs of sheltering leisure hung
In sober plenty; when the spirit stoops
To drink with gratitude the chrystal stream
Of unreproved enjoyment; and is pleased
To muse,—and be saluted by the air
Of meek repentance, wafting wall-flower scents
From out the crumbling ruins of fallen Pride
And chambers of Transgression, now forlorn.
O, calm contented days, and peaceful nights!
Who, when such good can be obtained, would strive
To reconcile his Manhood to a couch,
Soft as may seem; but, under that disguise,
Stuffed with the thorny substance of the past,
For fixed annoyance; and full oft beset
With floating dreams, disconsolate and black,
The vapoury phantoms of futurity?

Within the soul a Faculty abides,
That with interpositions, which would hide
And darken, so can deal, that they become
Contingences of pomp; and serve to exalt
Her native brightness. As the ample Moon,
In the deep stillness of a summer even
Rising behind a thick and lofty Grove,
Burns like an unconsuming fire of light,
In the green trees; and, kindling on all sides
Their leafy umbrage, turns the dusky veil
Into a substance glorious as her own,
Yea with her own incorporated, by power
Capacious and serene. Like power abides
In Man's celestial Spirit; Virtue thus
Sets forth and magnifies herself; thus feeds
A calm, a beautiful, and silent fire,
From the incumbrances of mortal life,
From error, disappointment,—nay from guilt;
And sometimes, so relenting Justice wills,
From palpable oppressions of Despair."

The Solitary by these words was touched
With manifest emotion, and exclaimed,
"But how begin? and whence?—The Mind is free,
Resolve—the haughty Moralist would say,
This single act is all that we demand.

1053 disconsolate and black,] black and disconsolate, *MS. 1832/36–*
1064 Their] The *Cornell MS. 1*

Alas! such wisdom bids a Creature fly
Whose very sorrow is, that time hath shorn
His natural wings!—To Friendship let him turn
For succour; but perhaps he sits alone
On stormy waters, in a little Boat
That holds but him, and can contain no more!
Religion tells of amity sublime
Which no condition can preclude; of One
Who sees all suffering, comprehends all wants,
All weakness fathoms, can supply all needs;
But is that bounty absolute?—His gifts,
Are they not still, in some degree, rewards
For acts of service? Can his Love extend
To hearts that own not Him? Will showers of grace,
When in the sky no promise may be seen,
Fall to refresh a parched and withered land?
Or shall the groaning Spirit cast her load
At the Redeemer's feet?"
                                        In rueful tone
With some impatience in his mien he spake;
And this reply was given.—
                                        "As Men from Men
Do in the constitution of their Souls
Differ, by mystery not to be explained;
And as we fall by various ways, and sink
One deeper than another, self-condemned,
Through manifold degrees of guilt and shame,
So, manifold and various are the ways
Of restoration, fashioned to the steps
Of all infirmity, and tending all
To the same point,—attainable by all;
Peace in ourselves, and union with our God.
—For Him, to whom I speak, an easy road
Lies open: we have heard from You a voice
At every moment softened in its course
By tenderness of heart; have seen your Eye,
Even like an Altar lit by fire from Heaven,

1084 in] tossed in *MS. 1832/36–*

1095 parched and withered land?] land withered & parched *pencil at page foot MS. 1832/36 and interlined in ink but* &] and

1098/1099 Back to my mind rushed all that had been urged
To calm the Sufferer when his story closed;
I looked for counsel as unbending now;
But a discriminating sympathy . . . *1827– ; so MS. 1814/27 but* rush'd . . . urg'd . . . clos'd / I look'd . . . now / But . . . sympathy

1099 And this reply was given.—] Stooped to this ~~prompt~~ apt reply *MS. 1814/27* Stooped to this apt reply,— *1827– but* reply:— *1836–*

1110 *del MS. 1814/27 to* Then do not droop a hopeful road for you *MS. 1814/27* For you, assuredly, a hopeful road *1827–*

1111 Lies open *del to* Despair not *then* Lies open *restored MS. 1814/27*

Kindle before us.—Your discourse this day,
That, like the fabled Lethe, wished to flow
In creeping sadness, through oblivious shades
[1125] Of death and night, has caught at every turn
The colours of the Sun. Access for you
Is yet preserved to principles of truth,
Which the Imaginative Will upholds
In seats of wisdom, not to be approached
[1130] By the inferior Faculty that moulds,
With her minute and speculative pains,
Opinion, ever changing!—I have seen
A curious Child, who dwelt upon a tract
Of inland ground, applying to his ear
[1135] The convolutions of a smooth-lipped Shell;
To which, in silence hushed, his very soul
Listened intensely; and his countenance soon
[1138] Brightened with joy; for murmurings from within
Were heard,—sonorous cadences! whereby,
[1139] To his belief, the Monitor expressed
[1140] Mysterious union with its native Sea.
Even such a Shell the Universe itself
Is to the ear of Faith; and there are times,
I doubt not, when to You it doth impart
Authentic tidings of invisible things;
[1145] Of ebb and flow, and ever-during power;
And central peace, subsisting at the heart
Of endless agitation. Here you stand,
Adore, and worship, when you know it not;
Pious beyond the intention of your thought;
[1150] Devout above the meaning of your will.
—Yes, you have felt, and may not cease to feel.
The estate of Man would be indeed forlorn
If false conclusions of the reasoning Power
Made the Eye blind, and closed the passages
[1155] Through which the Ear converses with the heart.
Has not the Soul, the Being of your Life
Received a shock of awful consciousness,
In some calm season, when these lofty Rocks
At night's approach bring down the unclouded Sky,

1129 To which] And while *MS. 1836/45*
1131–1133 Brightened with joy; for from within were heard / Murmurings, whereby the monitor expressed *1845–*
1132–1133 Were heard, by which the monitor expressed *MS. 1836/45, which also has a series of pencil drafts:* were *right margin of l. 1131* sonorous . . . belief, in *ll. 1132–1133 del to* by which
Murmurs by which as they [?might rise] or fall
The [?monitor] to his belief, expressed *top of page*
[?rising]
Sonorous interactions rise or fall
Were [?hear] by what the monitor [?] express *page foot*

To rest upon their circumambient walls;
A Temple framing of dimensions vast,
And yet not too enormous for the sound
Of human anthems,—choral song, or burst
Sublime of instrumental harmony,
To glorify the Eternal! What if these
Did never break the stillness that prevails
Here, if the solemn Nightingale be mute
And the soft Woodlark here did never chaunt
Her vespers, Nature fails not to provide
Impulse and utterance. The whispering Air
Sends inspiration from the shadowy heights,
And blind recesses of the caverned rocks;
The little Rills, and Waters numberless,
Inaudible by day-light, blend their notes
With the loud Streams: and often, at the hour
When issue forth the first pale Stars, is heard,
Within the circuit of this Fabric huge,
One Voice—the solitary Raven, flying
Athwart the concave of the dark-blue dome,
Unseen, perchance above the power of sight—
An iron knell! with echoes from afar,
Faint—and still fainter—as the cry, with which
The wanderer accompanies her flight
Through the calm region, fades upon the ear,
Diminishing by distance till it seemed
To expire, yet from the Abyss is caught again,
And yet again recovered!

But descending
From these Imaginative Heights, that yield
Far-stretching views into Eternity,
Acknowledge that to Nature's humbler power
Your cherished sullenness is forced to bend
Even here, where her amenities are sown
With sparing hand. Then trust yourself abroad
To range her blooming bowers, and spacious fields,
Where on the labours of the happy Throng
She smiles, including in her wide embrace
City, and Town, and Tower,—and Sea with Ships
Sprinkled,—be our Companion while we track
Her rivers populous with gliding life;
While, free as air, o'er printless sands we march,
And pierce the gloom of her majestic woods;
Roaming, or resting under grateful shade
In peace and meditative chearfulness;

1174 the] all *MS. 1814/27–*
1179 seemed] seems *1820E* seem'd *1827* seemed *1832–*
1195 And] Or *MS. 1814/27–*

Where living Things, and Things inanimate,
Do speak, at Heaven's command, to eye and ear,
And speak to social Reason's inner sense,
With inarticulate language.
—For the Man,
Who, in this spirit, communes with the Forms
Of Nature, who with understanding heart,
Doth know and love, such Objects as excite
No morbid passions, no disquietude,
No vengeance, and no hatred, needs must feel
The joy of that pure principle of love
So deeply, that, unsatisfied with aught
Less pure and exquisite, he cannot choose
But seek for objects of a kindred love
In Fellow-natures, and a kindred joy.
Accordingly, he by degrees perceives
His feelings of aversion softened down;
A holy tenderness pervade his frame.
His sanity of reason not impaired,
Say rather, all his thoughts now flowing clear,
From a clear Fountain flowing, he looks round
And seeks for good; and finds the good he seeks:
Until abhorrence and contempt are things
He only knows by name; and, if he hear
From other mouths, the language which they speak,
He is compassionate; and has no thought,
No feeling, which can overcome his love.

And further; by contemplating these Forms
In the relations which they bear to Man,
He shall discern, how, through the various means
Which silently they yield, are multiplied
The spiritual Presences of absent Things,
Convoked by knowledge; and for his delight
Still ready to obey the gentle call.
Trust me, that for the Instructed time will come
When they shall meet no object but may teach
Some acceptable lesson to their minds
Of human suffering, or of human joy.
For them shall all things speak of Man, they read
Their duties in all forms; and general laws,

1204 Doth know and love] Both knows and loves *1836–*

1207 The joy of that pure principle of love *added in errata 1814, MS. 1814/27, adopted 1820E– but* Love *1820E–1832* love *MS. 1832/36–*

1229–1230 *del MS. 1814/27, om 1827–*

1235 So shall they ~~read~~ learn while all things speak of Man, *MS. 1814/27, adopted (as rev) 1827– but* learn, *1827– and* man, *MS. 1832/36–*

1236 in] from *MS. 1814/27–*

And local accidents, shall tend alike
To rouze, to urge; and with the will confer
The ability to spread the blessings wide
Of true philanthropy. The light of love
Not failing, perseverance from their steps
Departing not, they shall at length obtain
The glorious habit by which Sense is made
Subservient still to moral purposes,
Auxiliar to divine. That change shall clothe
The naked Spirit, ceasing to deplore
The burthen of existence. Science then
Shall be a precious Visitant; and then,
And only then, be worthy of her name.
For then her Heart shall kindle; her dull Eye,
Dull and inanimate, no more shall hang
Chained to its object in brute slavery;
But taught with patient interest to watch
The processes of things, and serve the cause
Of order and distinctness, not for this
Shall it forget that its most noble use,
Its most illustrious province, must be found
In furnishing clear guidance, a support
Not treacherous, to the Mind's *excursive* Power.
—So build we up the Being that we are;
Thus deeply drinking-in the Soul of Things
We shall be wise perforce; and while inspired
By choice, and conscious that the Will is free,
Unswerving shall we move, as if impelled
By strict necessity, along the path
Of order and of good. Whate'er we see,
Whate'er we feel, by agency direct
Or indirect shall tend to feed and nurse

1242 Departing not, for them shall be confirmed *1827– ; so MS. 1814/27 but* confirm'd
1264 Shall move unswerving, even as if impelled *MS. 1832/36–*
1265–1266 Along the path of order & of good / By strict necessity . . . *MS. 1836/45*
1267–1268 Or feel, shall tend to quicken or refine / The humblest functions corporeal sense *pencil at page foot MS. 1814/27* Whate'er we feel, shall tend to feed and nurse, / By agency direct or indirect, *MS. 1832/36–1843, see verbal variants to IV, 1267–1270, below*
1267–1270 Or feel, shall tend to quicken and refine;
Shall fix, in calmer seats of moral strength,
Earthly desires; and raise, to loftier heights *1845– ; MS. 1836/45 drafts:* feed and nurse *in l. 1268 del to* quicken & refine *right margin, then del* Of moral strength *in l. 1270 del to* Earthly desires *ll. 1267–1269 and half of l. 1270 del to*
Or feel shall tend to quicken & refine
The humblest functions of corporeal sense
Shall fix in calmer seats of moral strength
Earthly desires, . . .
an earlier draft at page foot is del:
sense
The humblest functions of corporeal ~~streng~~
Shall fix in calmer seats of moral streng
Earthly desires, & raise

Our faculties, shall fix in calmer seats
Of moral strength, and raise to loftier heights
[1275] Of love divine, our intellectual Soul."

Here closed the Sage that eloquent harangue,
Poured forth with fervour in continuous stream;
Such as, remote 'mid savage wilderness,
An Indian Chief discharges from his breast
[1280] Into the hearing of the assembled Tribes,
In open circle seated round, and hushed
As the unbreathing air, when not a leaf
Stirs in the mighty woods.—So did he speak:
[1284] The words he uttered shall not pass away;
[1287] For they sank into me—the bounteous gift
Of One whom time and nature had made wise,
Gracing his language with authority
[1290] Which hostile spirits silently allow;
Of One accustomed to desires that feed
On fruitage gathered from the Tree of Life,
To hopes on knowledge and experience built;
Of One in whom persuasion and belief
[1295] Had ripened into faith, and faith become
A passionate intuition; whence the Soul,
Though bound to Earth by ties of pity and love,
From all injurious servitude was free.

The Sun, before his place of rest were reached,
[1300] Had yet to travel far, but unto us,
To us who stood low in that hollow Dell
He had become invisible,—a pomp
Leaving behind of yellow radiance spread
Upon the mountain sides, in contrast bold
[1305] With ample shadows, seemingly no less
Than those resplendent lights his rich bequest,
A dispensation of his evening power.
—Adown the path which from the Glen had led

1269–1271 *MS. 1814/27 has interlined pencil rev:*
Shall fix in calmer seats of moral strength
Earthly desire, and raise to loftier heights
Of love divine our intellectual Soul."
1271 love divine] divine love *MS. 1832/36–*
1276 the assembled] assembled *MS. 1814/27–*
1280/1281, 1281 Dispersed, like music that the wind takes up
By snatches, and lets fall—{,} to be forgotten;
No—they sank into me—{,} the bounteous gift *MS. 1832/36, adopted (as rev) 1836–*
1283 language] doctrine *MS. 1832/36–*
1298 Upon] Over *MS. 1832/36–*
1302 which] that *1827–*

The funeral Train, the Shepherd and his Mate
Were seen descending;—forth in transport ran
Our little Page; the rustic Pair approach;
And in the Matron's aspect may be read
A plain assurance that the words which told
How that neglected Pensioner was sent,
Before his time, into a quiet grave,
Had done to her humanity no wrong.
But we are kindly welcomed; promptly served
With ostentatious zeal.—Along the floor
Of the small Cottage in the lonely Dell
A grateful Couch was spread for our repose;
Where, in the guise of Mountaineers, we slept,
Stretched upon fragrant heath, and lulled by sound
Of far-off Torrents charming the still night,
And to tired limbs and over-busy thoughts
Inviting sleep and soft forgetfulness.

END OF THE FOURTH BOOK.

1304 in transport] to greet them *MS. 1814/27–* Were seen descending;—forth to greet them ran *1827–* *but* descending:— *1836–1846, 1850* descending.— *1849 (probable worn plate)*

1305–1307 *MS. 1836/45 drafts:*

~~and, as the rustic Dame~~
And in the Matrons countenance
~~Approached,—upon her~~ countenance might be read
Plain intimation that the words, which *on facing flyleaf to Book V*

1306 aspect] countenance *MS. 1836/45, 1845–*

1307 A plain assurance] Plain indication *MS. 1836/45, 1845–*

1315 slept] lay *alt MS. 1836/45, adopted 1845–*

1318 thoughts] minds *alt MS. 1836/45*

1319 *MS. 1832/36 has three lines of illeg pencil, eras, at page foot* *MS. 1836/45 has draft:*

and
Inviting ease, to quietness [?injured] suffering
Till every thought as gently as a flower
That shuts its eyes at fall of evening dew
Had folded up itself in dreamless [?life] *page foot, del in pencil*

THE PASTOR.

FAREWELL deep Valley, with thy one rude House,
And its small lot of life-supporting fields,
[3] And guardian rocks!—With unreverted eyes
I cannot pass thy bounds, attractive Seat!
[4] To the still influx of the morning light
[5] Open, and day's pure chearfulness, but veiled
From human observation, as if yet
Primæval Forests wrapped thee round with dark
Impenetrable shade; once more farewell
Majestic Circuit, beautiful Abyss,
[10] By Nature destined from the birth of things
For quietness profound!
Upon the side
[12] Of that green Slope, the outlet of the Vale,
[14] Lingering behind my Comrades, thus I breathed
[15] A parting tribute to a spot that seemed
[16] Like the fixed centre of a troubled World.
[19] And now, pursuing leisurely my way,
[20] How vain, thought I, it is by change of place
To seek that comfort which the mind denies;
Yet trial and temptation oft are shunned
Wisely; and by such tenor do we hold
Frail Life's possessions, that even they whose fate
[25] Yields no peculiar reason of complaint
Might, by the promise that is here, be won
To steal from active duties, and embrace
Obscurity, and calm forgetfulness.
—Knowledge, methinks, in these disordered times,

3–4 And guardian rocks!—Farewell, attractive Seat! *1827– ; so MS. 1814/27 but* Farewell attractive Seat!] seat! *MS. 1832/36–*
6 and] to *MS. 1814/27*
13 green] brown *MS. 1814/27–* Slope, the] ridge, sole *MS. 1832/36–*
13/14 Which foot of boldest stranger would attempt, *MS. 1832/36–*
17 Again I halted with reverted eyes;
The chain that would not slacken, was at length
Snapt,—and, pursuing leisurely my way, *1836–; so MS. 1832/36 but* eyes: / The Chain, . . . way *ink over pencil; earlier drafts in MS. 1832/36:*
Again I halted, casting back a look,
And yet another of [?interest & regard;]
The chain that would not slacken
Snapped *pencil at bottom of facing page*
Again I halted with reverted [?eye]
[?And feet] [?]
[? where my] [?] *pencil, partially eras, top of page*
18 it is] is it *1836–*
26 calm forgetfulness] undisturbed repose *ink over pencil MS. 1836/45, 1845–*

Should be allowed a privilege to have
Her Anchorites, like Piety of old;
Men, who, from faction sacred, and unstained
By war, might, if so minded, turn aside
Uncensured, and subsist, a scattered few
Living to God and Nature, and content
With that communion. Consecrated be
The Spots where such abide! But happier still
The Man, whom, furthermore, a hope attends
That meditation and research may guide
His privacy to principles and powers
Discovered, or invented; or set forth
Through his acquaintance with the ways of truth,
In lucid order; so that, when his course
Is run, some faithful Eulogist may say,
He sought not praise, and praise did overlook
His inobtrusive merit; but his life,
Sweet to himself, was exercised in good
That shall survive his name and memory.

Acknowledgments of gratitude sincere
Accompanied these musings;—fervent thanks
For my own peaceful lot and happy choice;
A choice that from the passions of the world
Withdrew, and fixed me in a still retreat,
Sheltered, but not to social duties lost,
Secluded, but not buried; and with song
Cheering my days, and with industrious thought,
With the ever-welcome company of books
By virtuous friendship's soul-sustaining aid,
And with the blessings of domestic love.

Thus occupied in mind I paced along,
Following the rugged road, by sledge or wheel
Worn in the moorland, till I overtook
My two Associates, in the morning sunshine
Halting together on a rocky knoll,
From which the road descended rapidly
To the green meadows of another Vale.

Here did our pensive Host put forth his hand
In sign of farewell. "Nay," the Old Man said,
"The fragrant Air its coolness still retains;
The Herds and Flocks are yet abroad to crop

---

44 inobtrusive] unobtrusive *1820E–*
50 world] crowd *pencil alt MS. 1836/45*
55 the ever-welcome] ever-welcome *MS. 1814/27–1832*
56 By] With *MS. 1832/36–*
63 From which the] Whence the bare *MS. 1836/45, 1845–*

The dewy grass; you cannot leave us now,
[72] We must not part at this inviting hour."
To that injunction, earnestly expressed,
[73] He yielded, though reluctant; for his Mind
Instinctively disposed him to retire
[75] To his own Covert; as a billow, heaved
Upon the beach, rolls back into the Sea.
—So we descend; and winding round a rock
Attain a point that shewed the Valley—stretched
In length before us; and, not distant far,
[80] Upon a rising ground a grey Church-tower,
Whose battlements were screened by tufted trees.
And, tow'rds a chrystal Mere, that lay beyond
Among steep hills and woods embosomed, flowed
A copious Stream with boldly-winding course;
[85] Here traceable, there hidden—there again
To sight restored, and glittering in the Sun.
On the Stream's bank, and every where, appeared
Fair Dwellings, single or in social knots;
Some scattered o'er the level, others perched
[90] On the hill sides, a cheerful quiet scene,
Now in its morning purity arrayed.

"As, 'mid some happy Valley of the Alps,"
Said I, "once happy, ere tyrannic Power
Wantonly breaking in upon the Swiss,
[95] Destroyed their unoffending Commonwealth,
A popular equality doth seem
[97] Here to prevail; and yet a House of State
Stands yonder, one beneath whose roof, methinks,
[98] A rural Lord might dwell." "No feudal pomp,"
[99] Replied our Friend, a Chronicler who stood
Where'er he moved upon familiar ground,
[99/100] "Nor feudal power is there; but there abides,
[100/101] In his allotted Home, a genuine Priest,
[102] The Shepherd of his Flock; or, as a King
Is stiled, when most affectionately praised,
The Father of his People. Such is he,
[105] And rich and poor, and young and old, rejoice

---

71 *del MS. 1814/27, om 1827–*

95–97 A popular equality reigns here, / Save for one House of State beneath whose roof *1827– but* house . . . state *MS. 1832/36–1843* one *del to* yon *MS. 1836/45* Save for yon stately House beneath whose roof *1845– ; MS. 1814/27 drafts toward 1827: interlined* doth seem *del to* reigns here, Here . . . yet a *del to* Save for one House of State, beneath whose roof *and l. 97 del* Save for one House of state beneath whose roof *pencil, eras, at page foot*

99–102 Or power," replied the Wanderer, "to that House
Belongs, but there in his allotted Home
Abides, from year to year, a genuine Priest, *1845– ; so MS. 1836/45 but no quots, and* home . . . Priest *pencil variant, del, at page foot in MS. 1836/45 reads:* Home / From year to year, abides a genuine Pries

Under his spiritual sway, collected round him
[106] In this sequestered Realm. He hath vouchsafed
To me some portion of his kind regard;
And something also of his inner mind
Hath he imparted—but I speak of him
[110] As he is known to all. The calm delights
Of unambitious piety he chose,
And learning's solid dignity; though born
[113] Of knightly race, nor wanting powerful friends.
This good to reap, these pleasures to secure,
[114] Hither, in prime of manhood, he withdrew
[115] From academic bowers. He loved the spot,
Who does not love his native soil? he prized
The ancient rural character, composed
Of simple manners, feelings unsuppressed
And undisguised, and strong and serious thought;
[120] A character reflected in himself,
With such embellishment as well beseems
His rank and sacred function. This deep vale
[123] Is lengthened out by many a winding reach,
Not visible to us; and one of these
[124/125] A turretted manorial Hall adorns;
[125/126] In which the good Man's Ancestors have dwelt
[126] From age to age, the Patrons of this Cure.
To them, and to his decorating hand,
The Vicar's Dwelling, and the whole Domain,
Owes that presiding aspect which might well
[130] Attract your notice; statelier than could else
Have been bestowed, in course of common chance,
On an unwealthy mountain Benefice."

This said, oft halting we pursued our way;
Nor reached the Village Church-yard till the sun,
[135] Travelling at steadier pace than ours, had risen
Above the summits of the highest hills,
And round our path darted oppressive beams.

As chanced, the portals of the sacred Pile

107–108 Under his spiritual sway. He hath vouchsafed *MS. 1814/27–*
109 his] a *MS. 1814/27–*
116 *del MS. 1814/27, om 1827–*
126–130 Winds far in reaches hidden from our eyes,
And one a turreted manorial Hall
Adorns, in which the good Man's Ancestors
Have dwelt through ages—Patrons of this Cure. *1827–* but eyes,] sight, *MS. 1832/36–* hall *MS. 1832/36–* good] good's *1832* ancestors *MS. 1832/36– ; MS. 1814/27 as 1827 but interlined* Winds on *rev to* Winds far And one, *ink over illeg pencil* Adorns,] Adorns *ink over illeg eras pencil* ages Patrons *no punct*
131 decorating] own judicious *MS. 1814/27–* hand] pains, *1827–*
135 in] through *MS. 1814/27–*
137 halting] pausing *MS. 1832/36* pausing, *1836–*

Stood open, and we entered. On my frame,
[140] At such transition from the fervid air,
A grateful coolness fell, that seemed to strike
The heart, in concert with that temperate awe
And natural reverence, which the Place inspired.
Not framed to nice proportions was the Pile,
[145] But large and massy; for duration built.
With pillars crowded, and the roof upheld
By naked rafters intricately crossed,
Like leafless underboughs, in some thick grove,
All withered by the depth of shade above.
[150] Admonitory Texts inscribed the walls,
Each, in its ornamental scroll, enclosed,—
Each also crowned with winged heads—a pair
Of rudely-painted Cherubim. The floor
Of nave and aisle, in unpretending guise,
[155] Was occupied by oaken benches, ranged
In seemly rows; the chancel only shewed
[157] Some inoffensive marks of earthly state

---

144 such] this *MS. 1836/45*
148 framed to] shaped in *MS. 1814/27* raised in *1827–*
152 in] mid *MS. 1814/27, 1827* 'mid *1832–1843* grove,] wood, *MS. 1836/45, 1845–*
161–162 Some vain distinctions, marks of earthly state
By immemorial privilege allowed;
Though with the Encincture's special sanctity
But ill according. An heraldic shield,
Varying its tincture with the changeful light,
Imbued the altar-window; fixed aloft
A faded hatchment hung, and one by time
Yet undiscoloured. A capacious pew *1845– ; MS. 1836/45 has a series of drafts:* inoffensive] pitiable *l. 161 alt* and one by time
Yet undiscoloured. A capacious *interlined* And vain distinction *del to* But ill-according *l. 162 interlined*

vain distinctions
Some ~~pitiable~~ marks of earthly state,
Objects with its peculiar sanctity
But ill according—a capacious Pew *del top of page*
Some vain distinctions—marks of earthly state
their presence
Allowed by antient privelege, though ~~in sooth~~
With that Encinctures special sanctity
But ill according—a capacious [?P] *page foot, del by cross and vertical lines; illeg letter in margin may be a copy instruction*
Some vain distinctions marks of earthly state
By antient privelege, ~~in sooth~~ allowed
In sooth
Though with the spots peculiar sanctity *del left margin over* In sooth *in pencil*
Some [?inoffensive] and, with these [?are mixed]
ill according
Some pitiable marks of eartly state
And *del right margin*
Though with the spots peculiar sanctity
But ill according *inverted right margin*
Some vain distinctions—an heraldic shield
In tincture varying as the sun might shine
Imbued its eastern window and aloft
A faded hatchment hung and one by time
Yet undiscoloured, marks of earthly state *top of facing page; entry continues, below*

[157/164] And vain distinction. A capacious pew
[165] Of sculptured oak stood here, with drapery lined;
And marble Monuments were here displayed
Upon the walls; and on the floor beneath
Sepulchral stones appeared, with emblems graven,
And foot-worn epitaphs, and some with small

161–162 *Further MS. 1836/45 drafts:*
Some vain distinctions, marks of earthly state
Allowed by antient privelege though in truth
With that Encinctures special sanctity
But ill according. A capacious pew *del at bottom of facing page*
Some vain distinctions marks of earthly state
By customary ~~privelege~~ allowed
Though with the spots ~~especial~~ peculiar sanctity
But ill according. *pencil in right margin of facing page*
[?By the] [?] of [?antient stones]
So privele[?ged], [?] marks of earthly state *pencil in left margin of facing page, overwritten in ink as follows:*
marks of earthly state
By immemorial privelege is allow d
Though with the encinctures special sanctity
But ill according. A capacious pew *left margin of facing page*
the chancel only showed
Some vain distinctions marks of earthly state
usual to the place
By ~~customary~~ pride [?] allowed
its own
Though with ~~the spots~~ peculiar sanctity
But ill according *recto of second free front endpaper*
The chancel only showed
So priveleged of yore, without offence
earth⎱
To piety, some marks of [?]⎰ly state
Some vain distinctions marks of earthly state
~~And vain distinctions~~
~~Alowed by antient pre/ilege, tho~~ugh in sooth
~~With the [?pure] sanctity the P~~lace should breathe
~~But ill according.~~ A capacious pew
Of sculptured oak, stood here, with drapery lined
And curtained closely round. [?Obnoxiousless]
[?pious] ~~censure~~ blame or brotherly ~~reg~~ regret
To ~~blame~~ or unavoidable regret
A [?high-fix'd] hatchment, time-discolour'd, told
Of man's mortality and its own decay
A⎱
[?]⎰nd marble monuments were display d
Thronging the walls, and on the floor beneath
Sepulchral stones appeared with emblems graven
And footworn epitaphs & some with small
And shining effegies of brass inlaid.
with drapery lined
Obnoxiousless to brotherly regret
A [?High] fix d Hatchment, [?~~disc~~] time-discolourd told
Of man's mortality & its own dec *entered on verso of second front free endpaper; ll. 6–8a above ("Alowed . . . ill-according") del in pencil; passage from the fourth line ("Some vain . . .") del by a vertical stroke*
only showed
In the simplicity of antient times,
[?So] priveledged—some marks
of earthly state
And vain distinction *in pencil on recto of half title*

165 Upon] Thronging *MS. 1814/27–*

And shining effigies of brass inlaid.
—The tribute by these various records claimed,
Without reluctance did we pay; and read
The ordinary chronicle of birth,
Office, alliance, and promotion—all
Ending in dust; of upright Magistrates,
Grave Doctors strenuous for the Mother Church,
And uncorrupted Senators—alike
To King and People true. A brazen plate,
Not easily decyphered, told of One
Whose course of earthly honour was begun
In quality of page among the Train
Of the eighth Henry, when he crossed the seas
His royal state to shew, and prove his strength
In tournament, upon the fields of France.
Another Tablet registered the death,
And praised the gallant bearing of a Knight
Tried in the sea-fights of the second Charles.
Near this brave Knight his Father lay entombed;
And, to the silent language giving voice,
I read,—how in his manhood's earlier day
He, 'mid the afflictions of intestine War
And rightful Government subverted, found
One only solace, that he had espoused
A virtuous Lady tenderly beloved
For her benign perfections: and for this
Yet more endeared to him, that in her state
Of wedlock richly crowned with heaven's regard,
She with a numerous Issue filled his House,
Who throve, like Plants, uninjured by the Storm
That laid their Country waste. No need to speak
Of less particular notices assigned
To Youth or Maiden gone before their time,
And Matrons and unwedded Sisters old;
Whose charity and goodness were rehearsed
In modest panegyric. "These dim lines,
What would they tell?" said I,—but, from the task
Of puzzling out that faded Narrative,
With whisper soft my venerable Friend
Called me; and looking down the darksome aisle
I saw the Tenant of the lonely Vale
Standing apart; with curved arm reclined

---

170 We paid to each with due respect *alt MS. 1836/45* Duly we paid, each after each, and read *1845–*

180 [?What] [? ? ?] / [?These] [? ? ? ?] *pencil, eras, at page foot MS. 1832/36*

193–194 For her benign perfections; and yet more / Endeared to him, for this, that in her state *MS. 1814/27– but* that, *1845–* yet more *del to* further *del to* for this *l. 193;* First *del to* Further *l. 194 left margin and* Endeared *rev to* endeared *and* for this *del MS. 1836/45*

205 faded] broken *MS. 1836/45*

On the baptismal Font; his pallid face
Upturned, as if his mind were rapt, or lost
In some abstraction;—gracefully he stood,
[215] The semblance bearing of a sculptured Form
That leans upon a monumental Urn
In peace, from morn to night, from year to year.

Him from that posture did the Sexton rouze;
Who entered, humming carelessly a tune,
[220] Continuation haply of the notes
That had beguiled the work from which he came
With spade and mattock o'er his shoulder hung;
To be deposited, for future need,
In their appointed place. The pale Recluse
[225] Withdrew; and straight we followed,—to a spot
Where sun and shade were intermixed; for there
A broad Oak, stretching forth its leafy arms
From an adjoining pasture, overhung
Small space of that green church-yard with a light
[230] And pleasant awning. On the moss-grown wall
My ancient Friend and I together took
Our seats; and thus the Solitary spake,
Standing before us. "Did you note the mien
Of that self-solaced, easy-hearted churl,
[235] Death's Hireling, who scoops out his Neighbour's grave,
Or wraps an old Acquaintance up in clay,
[237/238] As unconcerned as when he plants a tree?
I was abruptly summoned by his voice
[240] From some affecting images and thoughts
And from the company of serious words.
[242/243] Much, yesterday, was said in glowing phrase
Of our sublime dependencies, and hopes
[245] For future states of Being; and the wings
Of speculation, joyfully outspread,
Hovered above our destiny on earth;
But stoop, and place the prospect of the soul
In sober contrast with reality

225 its] his *rev restored to* its *by del MS. 1814/27*

235 All unconcerned as he would bind a sheaf, / Or plant a tree. And did you hear his voice? *1836–; so MS. 1832/36 but* sheaf,] sheaf

236 his voice] the sound *MS. 1832/36–*

238 *del MS. 1836/45, om 1845–*

238/239 Which then were silent; but crave utterance now. / Much," he continued, with dejected looks, *with para at* Much," *1836– but* Much, *1845–* looks,] look, *MS. 1836/45, 1845–* *MS. 1832/36 draft for ll. 238/239–239:*

Which then were silent; but crave
~~Which in those moments, craving~~
utterance now.
"Much" he continued with dejected looks,
"Much, yesterday

And Man's substantial life. If this mute earth
Of what it holds could speak, and every grave
Were as a volume, shut, yet capable
Of yielding its contents to eye and ear,
We should recoil, stricken with sorrow and shame,
To see disclosed, by such dread proof, how ill
That which is done accords with what is known
To reason, and by conscience is enjoined;
How idly, how perversely, Life's whole course,
To this conclusion, deviates from the line,
Or of the end stops short, proposed to all
At its aspiring outset. Mark the Babe
Not long accustomed to this breathing world;
One that hath barely learned to shape a smile,
Though yet irrational of Soul to grasp
With tiny fingers, to let fall a tear,
And, as the heavy cloud of sleep dissolves,
To stretch his limbs, bemocking, as might seem,
The outward functions of intelligent Man;
A grave Proficient in amusive feats
Of puppetry, that from the lap declare
His expectations, and announce his claims
To that inheritance which millions rue
That they were ever born to! In due time
A day of solemn ceremonial comes;
When they, who for this Minor hold in trust
Rights that transcend the unblest heritage
Of mere Humanity, present their Charge,
For this occasion daintily adorned,
At the baptismal Font. And when the pure
And consecrating element hath cleansed
The original stain, the Child is there received
Into the second Ark, Christ's Church, with trust
That he, from wrath redeemed, therein shall float
Over the billows of this troublesome world
To the fair land of everlasting Life.
Corrupt affections, covetous desires,
Are all renounced; high as the thought of man
Can carry virtue, virtue is professed;
A dedication made, a promise given
For due provision to controul and guide,
And unremitting progress to ensure
In holiness and truth."
"You cannot blame,"
Here interposing fervently I said,

257 its] her *MS. 1814/27–*
261 fingers,] finger— *MS. 1832/36–*
272 unblest] humblest *1827–1843* loftiest *1845–*

"Rites which attest that Man by nature lies
Bedded for good and evil in a gulph
Fearfully low; nor will your judgment scorn
Those services, whereby attempt is made
To lift the Creature tow'rds that eminence
On which, now fallen, erewhile in majesty
He stood; or if not so, whose top serene
At least he feels 'tis given him to descry;
Not without aspirations, evermore
Returning, and injunctions from within
Doubt to cast off and weariness; in trust
That what the Soul perceives, if glory lost,
May be through pains and persevering hope
Recovered; or, if hitherto unknown,
Lies within reach, and one day shall be gained."

"I blame them not," he calmly answered—"no;
The outward ritual and established forms
With which Communities of Men invest
These inward feelings, and the aspiring vows
To which the lips give public utterance
Are both a natural process; and by me
Shall pass uncensured; though the issue prove,
Bringing from age to age its own reproach,
Incongruous, impotent, and blank.—But oh!
If to be weak is to be wretched—miserable,
As the lost Angel by a human voice
Hath mournfully pronounced, then, in my mind,
Far better not to move at all than move
By impulse sent from such illusive Power,
That finds and cannot fasten down; that grasps
And is rejoiced, and loses while it grasps;
That tempts, emboldens—doth a while sustain,
And then betrays; accuses and inflicts
Remorseless punishment; and so retreads
The inevitable circle: better far
Than this, to graze the herb in thoughtless peace,
By foresight or remembrance, undisturbed!

Philosophy! and thou more vaunted name
Religion! with thy statelier retinue,
Faith, Hope, and Charity—from the visible world
Choose for your Emblems whatsoe'er ye find

---

308 vows] views *1814* vows *errata 1814, MS. 1814/27*
316 mind,] mind. *1814* mind, *errata 1814*
320 it *del to illeg rev which in turn is del MS. 1814/27*
321 That tempts, emboldens—for a time sustains, *MS. 1832/36–*

Of safest guidance and of firmest trust,—
The Torch, the Star, the Anchor; nor except
The Cross itself, at whose unconscious feet
The Generations of Mankind have knelt
Ruefully seized, and shedding bitter tears,
And through that conflict seeking rest—of you,
High-titled Powers, am I constrained to ask,
Here standing, with the unvoyageable sky
In faint reflection of infinitude
Stretched overhead, and at my pensive feet
A subterraneous magazine of bones
In whose dark vaults my own shall soon be laid,
Where are your triumphs? your dominion where?
And in what age admitted and confirmed?
—Not for a happy Land do I enquire,
Island or Grove, that hides a blessed few
Who, with obedience willing and sincere,
To your serene authorities conform;
But whom I ask, of individual Souls,
Have ye withdrawn from Passion's crooked ways,
Inspired, and thoroughly fortified?—If the Heart
Could be inspected to its inmost folds
By sight undazzled with the glare of praise,
Who shall be named—in the resplendent line
Of Sages, Martyrs, Confessors—the Man
Whom the best might of Conscience, Truth, and Hope,
For one day's little compass, has preserved
From painful and discreditable shocks
Of contradiction, from some vague desire
Culpably cherished, or corrupt relapse
To some unsanctioned fear?"
"If this be so,
And Man," said I, "be in his noblest shape
Thus pitiably infirm; then, He who made,
And who shall judge the Creature, will forgive.
—Yet, in its general tenor, your complaint
Is all too true; and surely not misplaced.
For, from this pregnant spot of ground, such thoughts
Rise to the notice of a serious Mind
By natural exhalation. With the Dead
In their repose, the Living in their mirth,
Who can reflect, unmoved, upon the round
Of smooth and solemnized complacencies,
By which, on Christian Lands from age to age

---

331 and] or *MS. 1836/45, 1845–*
356 Conscience, Truth, and Hope,] faith wherever fixed, *pencil MS. 1836/45* faith, wherever fix'd, *1845–*
357 has] have *1814* has *errata 1814*

Profession mocks Performance. Earth is sick,
And heaven is weary, of the hollow words
Which States and Kingdoms utter when they talk
Of truth and justice. Turn to private life
And social neighbourhood; look we to ourselves;
A light of duty shines on every day
For all; and yet how few are warmed or cheered!
How few who mingle with their fellow-men
And still remain self-governed, and apart,
Like this our honoured friend; and thence acquire
Right to expect his vigorous decline,
That promises to the end a blest old age!"

"Yet," with a smile of triumph thus exclaimed
The Solitary, "In the life of Man,
If to the poetry of common speech
Faith may be given, we see as in a glass
A true reflection of the circling year,
With all its seasons. Grant that Spring is there,
In spite of many a rough untoward blast,
Hopeful and promising with buds and flowers;
Yet where is glowing Summer's long rich day,
That *ought* to follow, faithfully expressed?
And mellow Autumn, charged with bounteous fruit,
Where is she imaged? in what favoured clime
Her lavish pomp, and ripe magnificence?
—Yet, while the better part is missed, the worse
In Man's autumnal season is set forth
With a resemblance not to be denied,
And that contents him; bowers that hear no more
The voice of gladness, less and less supply
Of outward sunshine and internal warmth;
And, with this change, sharp air and falling leaves,
Foretelling total Winter, blank and cold.

How gay the Habitations that adorn
This fertile Valley! Not a House but seems
To give assurance of content within;
Embosomed happiness, and placid love;
As if the sunshine of the day were met
With answering brightness in the hearts of all
Who walk this favoured ground. But chance-regards,
And notice forced upon incurious ears;
These, if these only, acting in despite

406 aged Winter's desolate sway *pencil alt to last five words of 1814, overwritten in ink by* Prelude to coming Winter's desolate sway— *MS. 1836/45* Foretelling aged Winter's dreary sway. *1840– but* dreary] desolate *1845–*

407 adorn] bedeck *MS. 1814/27–*

[420] Of the encomiums by my Friend pronounced
On humble life, forbid the judging mind
To trust the smiling aspect of this fair
And noiseless Commonwealth. The simple race
Of Mountaineers, by Nature's self removed
[425] From foul temptations, and by constant care
Of a good Shepherd tended, as themselves
Do tend their flocks, These share Man's general lot
With little mitigation. They escape,
Perchance, guilt's heavier woes; and do not feel
[430] The tedium of fantastic idleness;
Yet life, as with the multitude, with them,
Is fashioned like an ill constructed tale;
That on the outset wastes its gay desires,
Its fair adventures, its enlivening hopes,
[435] And pleasant interests—for the sequel leaving
Old things repeated with diminished grace;
And all the laboured novelties, at best
Imperfect substitutes, whose use and power
Evince the want and weakness whence they spring."

[440] While in this serious mood we held discourse,
The reverend Pastor tow'rds the Church-yard gate
Approached; and, with a mild respectful air
Of native cordiality, our Friend
Advanced to greet him. With a gracious mien
[445] Was he received, and mutual joy prevailed.
Awhile they stood in conference, and I guess
That He, who now upon the mossy wall
Sate by my side, had vanished, if a wish
[449] Could have transferred him to his lonely House
[451] Within the circuit of those guardian rocks.
—For me, I looked upon the pair, well pleased:
Nature had framed them both, and both were marked
By circumstance with intermixture fine
[455] Of contrast and resemblance. To an Oak
Hardy and grand, a weather-beaten Oak,
Fresh in the strength and majesty of age,
One might be likened: flourishing appeared,
Though somewhat past the fulness of his prime,

---

423 These share] partake *MS. 1814/27–*
425 Perchance, the heavier woes of guilt; feel not *MS. 1832/36–*
445–446 Could have transferred him to the flying clouds,
Or the least penetrable hiding-place
In his own valley's rocky guardianship. *1836–; so MS. 1832/36 which also has an earlier pencil draft:*

the clouds or lodged
Mid
~~In~~ the least penetrable hiding-place
In his own valley's rock

The Other—like a stately Sycamore,
That spreads, in gentler pomp, its honied shade.

A general greeting was exchanged; and soon
The Pastor learned that his approach had given
A welcome interruption to discourse
Grave, and in truth full often sad.—"Is Man
A Child of hope? Do generations press
On generations, without progress made?
Halts the Individual, ere his hairs be grey,
Perforce? Are we a Creature in whom good
Preponderates, or evil? Doth the Will
Acknowledge Reason's law? A living Power
Is Virtue, or no better than a name?
Fleeting as health or beauty, and unsound!
So that the only substance which remains,
(For thus the tenor of complaint hath run)
Among so many shadows, are the pains
And penalties of miserable life,
Doomed to decay, and then expire in dust!
—Our cogitations this way have been drawn,
These are the points," the Wanderer said, "on which
Our Inquest turns.—Accord, good Sir! the light
Of your experience, to dispel this gloom.
By your persuasive wisdom shall the Heart
That frets, or languishes, be stilled and cheered."

"Our Nature," said the Priest, in mild reply,
"Angels may weigh and fathom: they perceive,
With undistempered and unclouded spirit,
The object as it is; but, for ourselves,
That speculative height we may not reach.
The good and evil are our own; and we
Are that which we would contemplate from far.
Knowledge, for us, is difficult to gain—
Is difficult to gain and hard to keep—
As Virtue's self; like Virtue is beset
With snares; tried, tempted, subject to decay.
Love, admiration, fear, desire, and hate,
Blind were we without these; through these alone
Are capable to notice or discern
Or to record; we judge, but cannot be
Indifferent judges. 'Spite of proudest boast
Reason, best Reason, is to imperfect Man
An effort only, and a noble aim;
A crown, an attribute of sovereign power,

456 gentler] gentle *1836–*
460 full] too *MS. 1814/27–*

Still to be courted—never to be won!
—Look forth, or each man dive into himself,
What sees he but a Creature too perturbed,
That is transported to excess; that yearns,
Regrets, or trembles, wrongly, or too much;
Hopes rashly, in disgust as rash recoils;
Battens on spleen, or moulders in despair.
Thus truth is missed, and comprehension fails;
And darkness and delusion round our path
Spread, from disease, whose subtile injury lurks
Within the very faculty of sight.

Yet for the general purposes of faith
In Providence, for solace and support,
We may not doubt that who can best subject
The will to Reason's law, and strictliest live
And act in that obedience, he shall gain
The clearest apprehension of those truths,
Which unassisted reason's utmost power
Is too infirm to reach. But—waiving this,
And our regards confining within bounds
Of less exalted consciousness—through which
The very multitude are free to range—
We safely may affirm that human life
Is either fair or tempting, a soft scene
Grateful to sight, refreshing to the soul,
Or a forbidding tract of cheerless view;
Even as the same is looked at, or approached.
Permit me," said the Priest continuing, "here
To use an illustration of my thought,
Drawn from the very spot on which we stand.
—In changeful April, when, as he is wont,
Winter has reassumed a short lived sway
And whitened all the surface of the fields,
If—from the sullen region of the North
Towards the circuit of this holy ground
Your walk conducts you, ere the vigorous sun,
High climbing, hath attained his noon-tide height—
These Mounds, transversely lying side by side

---

506 Thus comprehension fails, and truth is missed; *1836–*
507 And] Thus *1836–*
513 and] can *MS. 1832/36–*
522 or] and *1827–; so MS. 1814/27 but* &
526–536 Thus, when in changeful April snow has fallen,
And fields are white, if from the sullen north
Your walk conduct you hither, ere the Sun
Hath gained his noontide height, this church-yard, filled
With mounds transversely . . . *1827– but* snow has fallen, / And fields are white,] fields are white / With new-fallen snow, *MS. 1832/36–* Sun] sun *MS. 1832/36–* church-yard,] churchyard, *1836–; MS. 1814/27 as 1827 but*—Thus when . . . fallen / And . . . North / Your . . . you, hither ere vigorous sun, / Hath . . . height—this Church-yard filled / With Mounds, transversely . . .

From east to west, before you will appear
A dreary plain of unillumined snow,
With more than wintry cheerlessness and gloom
[539] Saddening the heart. Go forward, and look back;
On the same circuit of this church-yard ground
[540] Look, from the quarter whence the Lord of light,
Of life, of love, and gladness, doth dispense
His beams; which, unexcluded in their fall,
Upon the southern side of every grave
Have gently exercised a melting power,
[545] *Then* will a vernal prospect greet your eye,
All fresh and beautiful, and green and bright,
[547] Hopeful and cheerful:—vanished is the snow,
[549] Vanished or hidden; and the whole Domain,
[550] To some, too lightly minded, might appear
A meadow carpet for the dancing hours.
—This Contrast, not unsuitable to Life,
Is to that other state more apposite,
Death, and its twofold aspect; wintry—one,
[555] Cold, sullen, blank, from hope and joy shut out;
The other, which the ray divine hath touched,
Replete with vivid promise, bright as spring."

"We see, then, as we feel," the Wanderer thus
With a complacent animation spake,
[560] "And, in your judgment, Sir! the Mind's repose
On evidence is not to be ensured
By act of naked Reason. Moral truth
Is no mechanic structure, built by rule;
And which, once built, retains a steadfast shape
[565] And undisturbed proportions; but a thing
Subject, you deem, to vital accidents;
And, like the water-lilly, lives and thrives;
Whose root is fixed in stable earth, whose head
Floats on the tossing waves. With joy sincere
[570] I re-salute these sentiments, confirmed
By your authority. But how acquire
The inward principle, that gives effect
To outward argument; the passive will
Meek to admit; the active energy,
[575] Strong and unbounded to embrace, and firm

---

538 An unillumined, blank, and dreary plain, *1827– but* dreary, *1845–; MS. 1814/27 as 1827 but* unillumined blank &

541 *om 1827–*

543 dispense] suspense *1836* dispense *restored in errata 1836, MS. 1836/45, 1840–*

549 snow,] pall *MS. 1832/36–*

549/550 That winter cast over the sacred turf, *MS. 1832/36* That overspread and chilled the sacred turf, *1836–*

To keep and cherish? How shall Man unite
A self-forgetting tenderness of heart
And earth-despising dignity of soul?
Wise in that union, and without it blind!"

"The way," said I, "to court, if not obtain
The ingenuous Mind, apt to be set aright;
This, in the lonely Dell discoursing, you
Declared at large; and by what exercise
From visible nature or the inner self
Power may be trained, and renovation brought
To those who need the gift. But, after all,
Is aught so certain as that Man is doomed
To breathe beneath a vault of ignorance?
The natural roof of that dark house in which
His soul is pent! How little can be known,
This is the wise man's sigh; how far we err,
This is the good man's not unfrequent pang.
And they perhaps err least, the lowly Class
Whom a benign necessity compels
To follow Reason's least ambitious course;
Such do I mean who, unperplexed by doubt
And unincited by a wish to look
Into high objects farther than they may,
Pace to and fro, from morn till even-tide,
The narrow avenue of daily toil
For daily bread."
"Yes," buoyantly exclaimed
The pale Recluse—"praise to the sturdy plough,
And patient spade, and shepherd's simple crook,
And ponderous loom—resounding while it holds
Body and mind in one captivity;
And let the light mechanic tool be hailed
With honour; which, encasing, by the power
Of long companionship, the Artist's hand,
Cuts off that hand, with all its world of nerves,
From a too busy commerce with the heart!
—Inglorious implements of craft and toil,
Both ye that shape and build, and ye that force,
By slow solicitation, Earth to yield
Her annual bounty, sparingly dealt forth
With wise reluctance, you would I extol
Not for gross good alone which ye produce,
But for the impertinent and ceaseless strife

---

578 A] With *1827–*
579 And] An *1827–*
604 And patient spade; praise to the simple crook, *MS. 1832/36–*

Of proofs and reasons ye preclude—in those
Who to your dull society are born,
And with their humble birth-right rest content.
—Would I had ne'er renounced it!"
A slight flush
Of moral anger previously had tinged
The Old Man's cheek; but, at this closing turn
Of self-reproach, it passed away. Said he,
"That which we feel we utter; as we think
So have we argued; reaping for our pains
No visible recompense. For our relief
You," to the Pastor turning thus he spake,
"Have kindly interposed. May I entreat
Your further help? The mine of real life
Dig for us; and present us, in the shape
Of virgin ore, that gold which we by pains
Fruitless as those of aery Alchemists
Seek from the torturing crucible. There lies
Around us a Domain where You have long
Held spiritual sway, have guided and consoled,
And watched the outward course and inner heart.
Give us, for our abstractions, solid facts;
For our disputes, plain pictures. Say what Man
He is who cultivates yon hanging field;
What qualities of mind She bears, who comes,
For morn and evening service, with her pail,
To that green pasture; place before our sight
The Family who dwell within yon House
Fenced round with glittering laurel; or in that
Below, from which the curling smoke ascends.
Or rather, as we stand on holy earth
And have the Dead around us, take from them
Your instances; for they are both best known,
And by frail Man most equitably judged.
Epitomize the life; pronounce, You can,
Authentic epitaphs on some of these
Who, from their lowly mansions hither brought,
Beneath this turf lie mouldering at our feet.
So, by your records, may our doubts be solved;
And so, not searching higher, we may learn
To prize the breath we share with human kind;
And look upon the dust of Man with awe."

---

637 *del MS. 1814/27, om 1827–*
638 And watched] Watched both *MS. 1814/27–*

648–649 For WW's end-of-volume note, see p. 302, below.

The Priest replied.—"An office you impose
For which peculiar requisites are mine;
Yet much, I feel, is wanting—else the task
Would be most grateful. True indeed it is
That They whom Death has hidden from our sight
Are worthiest of the Mind's regard; with these
The future cannot contradict the past:
Mortality's last exercise and proof
Is undergone; the transit made that shews
The very soul, revealed as it departs.
Yet, on your first suggestion, will I give,
Ere we descend into these silent vaults,
One Picture from the living.—
You behold,
High on the breast of yon dark mountain—dark
With stony barrenness, a shining speck
Bright as a sun-beam sleeping till a shower
Brush it away, or cloud pass over it;
And such it might be deemed—a sleeping sun-beam;
But 'tis a plot of cultivated ground,
Cut off, an island in the dusky waste;
And that attractive brightness is its own.
The lofty Site, by nature framed to tempt
Amid a wilderness of rocks and stones
The Tiller's hand, a Hermit might have chosen,
For opportunity presented, thence
Far forth to send his wandering eye o'er land
And ocean, and look down upon the works,
The habitations, and the ways of men,
Himself unseen! But no tradition tells
That ever Hermit dipped his maple dish
In the sweet spring that lurks mid yon green fields;
And no such visionary views belong
To those who occupy and till the ground,
And on the bosom of the mountain dwell—
A wedded Pair, in childless solitude.
—A House of stones collected on the spot,
By rude hands built, with rocky knolls in front,
Backed also by a ledge of rock, whose crest
Of birch-trees waves above the chimney top;
In shape, in size, and colour, an abode
Such as in unsafe times of Border war
Might have been wished for and contrived—to elude

669 it] she *MS. 1814/27–*
693 High on that mountain where they long have dwelt *1845–*
698 above] over *MS. 1832/36–*
699 A rough abode—in colour, shape, and size, *1827–*

The eye of roving Plunderer, for their need
Suffices; and unshaken bears the assault
Of their most dreaded foe, the strong South-west,
In anger blowing from the distant sea.
—Alone within her solitary Hut;
There, or within the compass of her fields,
At any moment may the Dame be found,
True as the Stock-dove to her shallow nest
And to the grove that holds it. She beguiles
By intermingled work of house and field
The summer's day, and winter's; with success
Not equal, but sufficient to maintain,
Even at the worst, a smooth stream of content,
Until the expected hour at which her Mate
From the far-distant Quarry's vault returns;
And by his converse crowns a silent day
With evening cheerfulness. In powers of mind,
In scale of culture, few among my Flock
Hold lower rank than this sequestered Pair.
But humbleness of heart descends from heaven;
And that best gift of heaven hath fallen on them;
Abundant recompence for every want.
—Stoop from your height, ye proud, and copy these!
Who, in their noiseless dwelling-place, can hear
The voice of wisdom whispering scripture texts
For the mind's government, or temper's peace;
And recommending, for their mutual need,
Forgiveness, patience, hope, and charity!"

"Much was I pleased," the grey-haired Wanderer said,
"When to those shining fields our notice first
You turned; and yet more pleased have from your lips
Gathered this fair report of those who dwell
In that Retirement; whither, by such course

---

721 But true humility descends from heaven; *1845–; MS. 1836/45 has several drafts:*
among my flock
Few only, in the scale of culture hold
~~A humbler r~~ *bottom of facing page above similar pencil draft but lacking the del line*
true humility of heart descends
From heaven, and that best gift of heaven is their *interlined*
But true humility of heart descends
good gift hath fallen on
From heaven, and that best gift of heaven is theirs *top of page*
But upon them, a blessing that descends
'}
From heaven, hath falle}n/ humility of heart
Abundant recompense for every want *right margin of facing page*
But [?~~true~~] humility of heart descends
From heaven, and that good gift hath fallen on them
on them hath fall'n; *top of facing page*

733 those] them *MS. 1814/27–*

Of evil hap and good as oft awaits
[734] A lone way-faring Man, I once was brought.
[736] Dark on my road the autumnal evening fell
[735] While I was traversing yon mountain-pass,
[737] And night succeeded with unusual gloom;
So that my feet and hands at length became
Guides better than mine eyes—until a light
[740] High in the gloom appeared, too high, methought,
For human habitation; but I longed
To reach it, destitute of other hope.
I looked with steadiness as Sailors look
On the north star, or watch-tower's distant lamp,
[745] And saw the light—now fixed—and shifting now—
Not like a dancing meteor, but in line
Of never-varying motion, to and fro.
It is no night-fire of the naked hills,
Said I, some friendly covert must be near.
[750] With this persuasion thitherward my steps
I turn, and reach at last the guiding Light;
Joy to myself! but to the heart of Her
Who there was standing on the open hill,
(The same kind Matron whom your tongue hath praised)
[755] Alarm and disappointment! The alarm
Ceased, when she learned through what mishap I came,
And by what help had gained those distant fields.
Drawn from her Cottage, on that open height
Bearing a lantern in her hand she stood,
[760] Or paced the ground—to guide her Husband home,

735–738 *MS. 1832/36 has these drafts:* oft awaits] oftentimes *del, then*
Of evil hap and good as oftentimes
Awaits a lone wayfaring man, I once
Was brought, while travelling yon mountain-pass.
Dark on my road the [?~~shades~~]
autumnal evening fell
And night *page foot, then entire preceding passage del*
as oft awaits
A tired way-faring man, once I was brought
While traversing alone yon mountain pass.
Dark on my road the autumnal evening fell *bottom of facing page; see also V, 736–738, below*
736–738 A tired way-faring man, once *I* was brought
While traversing alone yon mountain pass.
Dark on my road the autumnal evening fell, *1836–*
739–741 *MS. 1836/45 has two drafts:*
And night succeeded—with unusual gloom
hands
eyes }
So hazardous that feet and hands } became
Guides safer than— *del, page foot*
And with the night succeeded a thick gloom
So hazardous that feet and hands became
Guides—safer than ~~my eyes~~ mine eyes *right margin; see l. 740, below*
740 So hazardous that feet and hands became *1845–*
751 Said] Thought *1827–*
760 open] aery *MS. 1832/36* aëry *1836–*

By that unwearied signal, kenned afar;
[762] An anxious duty! which the lofty Site,
Far from all public road or beaten way
[763] And traversed only by a few faint paths,
Imposes, whensoe'er untoward chance
[765] (Such chance is rare) detains him till the night
Falls black upon the hills. "But come," she said,
[767] "Come let me lead you to our poor Abode.
Behind those rocks it stands, as if it shunned,
In churlishness, the eye of all mankind;
But the few Guests who seek the door receive
[768] Most hearty welcome."—Entering I beheld
A blazing fire—beside a cleanly hearth
[770] Sate down; and to her office, with leave asked,
The Dame returned.—Before that glowing pile
Of mountain turf required the Builder's hand
Its wasted splendour to repair, the door
Opened, and she re-entered with glad looks,
[775] Her Helpmate following. Hospitable fare,
Frank conversation, made the evening's treat.
Need a bewildered Traveller wish for more?
[778] But more was given; the eye, the mind, the heart,
Found exercise in noting, as we sate
[779] By the bright fire, the good Man's face—composed
[780] Of features elegant; an open brow
Of undisturbed humanity; a cheek
Suffused with something of a feminine hue;
Eyes beaming courtesy and mild regard;
But, in the quicker turns of the discourse,
[785] Expression slowly varying, that evinced
A tardy apprehension. From a fount
Lost, thought I, in the obscurities of time,
But honoured once, these features and that mien

---

765 *del MS. 1814/27, om 1827–*

766 Traversed but by a few irregular paths, *1827–; so MS. 1814/27 but* transversed

768–774 Detains him after his accustomed hour
When night lies black upon the hills. 'But come,
Come,' said the Matron, 'to our poor Abode;
Those dark rocks hide it!' Entering, I beheld *1827– but* When . . . hills.] Till . . . ground. *1832–* Abode;] abode; *MS. 1832/36–; MS. 1814/27 as 1827 but* After his accustomed hour ~~when~~ *and* Detains him *added left margin* "Come let me lead you *del to* [?Follow behind, the Matron] *eras and rev to* "Come" said the Matron "to our poor Abode. . . . Those . . . hide it"—Entering I beheld hide it] conceal *alt in pencil partially eras*

777 Before] Or ere *1827–* Or *para MS. 1832/36–*

780 [?soul] *pencil, eras, possible alt for* looks *MS. 1814/27*

784–785 But more was given; I studied as we sate *MS. 1814/27–*

786–787 an open brow] a smooth marble *l. 787 MS. 1832/36*
By the bright fire, the good Man's form, and face
Not less than beautiful; an open brow *1845–; but MS. 1836/45 draft:* face—composed *del to* countenance *and* Of features elegant *del to* Not less than beautiful, form, and face

795 these] those *1836–*

May have descended, though I see them here.
In such a Man, so gentle and subdued,
Withal so graceful in his gentleness,
A race illustrious for heroic deeds,
Humbled, but not degraded, may expire.
This pleasing fancy (cherished and upheld
By sundry recollections of such fall
From high to low, ascent from low to high,
As books record, and even the careless mind
Cannot but notice among men and things)
Went with me to the place of my repose.

Rouzed by the crowing cock at dawn of day,
I yet had risen too late to interchange
A morning salutation with my Host,
Gone forth already to the far-off seat
Of his day's work. "Three dark mid-winter months
"Pass," said the Matron, "and I never see,
"Save when the Sabbath brings its kind release,
"My Help-mate's face by light of day. He quits
"His door in darkness, nor till dusk returns.
"And, through heaven's blessing, thus we gain the bread
"For which we pray; and for the wants provide
"Of sickness, accident, and helpless age.
"Companions have I many; many Friends,
"Dependants, Comforters—my Wheel, my Fire,
"All day the House-clock ticking in mine ear,
"The cackling Hen, the tender Chicken brood,
"And the wild Birds that gather round my porch.
"This honest Sheep-dog's countenance I read;

---

806 *MS. 1836/45 has a series of drafts elaborating upon the narrator's sleep:*
Sweetened the moment of good night & went
Along with me to the place of my repose *page foot*
Sweetened for me our mutual good night
{soothed me—
And {[? ?] in the place
[?sanctified] of my repose *pencil right margin*
disappear
and [?soothed]
Nor left my mind till every thought like flower
T}
A}hat shut their leaves at fall of evening dew
Was folded up and lost in [?lonely] sleep *pencil at top of page*
Nor disappeared till every *pencil, interlined*
[?receded] quietly
{a
Where every thought as gently as {[?] [?] flower
That shuts its eyes at fall of evening dew
Soon folded up itself in dreamless sleep *bottom of facing page*
Sweetened, for me, our mutual good night,
Nor left me, on a lowly [?palleat] stretch'd
Till slumber had given way to dreamless sleep *pencil in left margin on facing page*
816 heaven's] God's *MS. 1836/45*

"With him can talk; nor seldom waste a word
"On Creatures less intelligent and shrewd.
[820] "And if the blustering Wind that drives the clouds
"Care not for me, he lingers round my door,
"And makes me pastime when our tempers suit;
[823] "—But, above all, my Thoughts are my support."
[827] The Matron ended—nor could I forbear
To exclaim—"O happy! yielding to the law
Of these privations, richer in the main!
[830] While thankless thousands are oppressed and clogged
By ease and leisure—by the very wealth
And pride of opportunity made poor;
While tens of thousands falter in their path,
And sink, through utter want of cheering light,
[835] For you the hours of labour do not flag;
For you each Evening hath its shining Star,
And every Sabbath-day its golden Sun."

"Yes!" said the Solitary, with a smile
That seemed to break from an expanding heart,
[840] "The untutored Bird may found, and so construct,
And with such soft materials line her nest,
Fixed in the centre of a prickly brake,
That the thorns wound her not; they only guard.
Powers, not unjustly likened to those gifts
[845] Of happy instinct which the woodland Bird
Shares with her species, Nature's grace sometimes
Upon the Individual doth confer,
Among the higher creatures born and trained
To use of reason. And, I own, that tired

---

825 seldom] blush to *MS. 1814/27–*
830/831 'My comfort:—would that they were oftener fixed
'On what, for guidance in the way that leads
'To heaven, I know, by my Redeemer taught.' *1845– ; MS. 1836/45 has several drafts:*
u ⎱ of mirth long fled
Now glancing [?]⎰pon freaks of [?little]
[?~~mirth~~]
dreaming over schemes to ease the wants
Long ~~fled, or [?little] schemes~~ to ease the wants
Of this short life; would they were oftener fixed
On what of guidance in the way that leads *over illeg pencil at page foot*
⎧ould
My comfort—w⎩hi that they were oftener fixed
On what for guidance in the way that leads
To heaven, I know, by my redeemer taught *pencil in right margin*
would they were oftener fixed
on
On what of guidance ~~in~~ the way that leads
To heaven, I know, by my Redeemer taught *bottom of facing page*
833 these] your *alt MS. 1836/45*
837 in their path,] each in his path, *alt MS. 1836/45*
852 the] her *pencil MS. 1814/27–*
853 *MS. 1836/45 drafts:* And I own that tired *pencil at page foot and illeg pencil at top of page; see nonverbals*

[850] Of the ostentatious world—a swelling stage
With empty actions and vain passions stuffed,
And from the private struggles of mankind
Hoping for less than I could wish to hope,
Far less than once I trusted and believed—
[855] I love to hear of Those, who, not contending
Nor summoned to contend for Virtue's prize,
Miss not the humbler good at which they aim;
Blest with a kindly faculty to blunt
The edge of adverse circumstance, and turn
[860] Into their contraries the petty plagues
And hindrances with which they stand beset.
—In early youth among my native hills
I knew a Scottish Peasant who possessed
A few small Crofts of stone-encumbered ground;
[865] Masses of every shape and size, that lay
Scattered about beneath the mouldering walls
Of a rough precipice; and some, apart,
In quarters unobnoxious to such chance,
As if the moon had showered them down in spite,
[870] But he repined not. Though the plough was scared
By these obstructions, "round the shady stones
A fertilizing moisture," said the Swain,
"Gathers, and is preserved; and feeding dews
"And damps, through all the droughty Summer day,
[875] "From out their substance issuing, maintain
"Herbage that never fails; no grass springs up
[877] "So green, so fresh, so plentiful, as mine!"
See, in this well conditioned Soul, a Third
To match with your good Couple that put forth
Their homely graces on the mountain side.
[878] But thinly sown these Natures; rare at least
The mutual aptitude of seed and soil
[880] That yields such kindly product. He—whose bed
Perhaps yon loose sods cover, the poor Pensioner
Brought yesterday from our sequestered dell
Here to lie down in lasting quiet—he,
If living now, could otherwise report
[885] Of rustic loneliness: that grey-haired Orphan—
So call him, for humanity to him
No parent was—could feelingly have told,

---

857 for] far *MS. 1832/36–*
861–864 Miss not the humble good they aim at, blest
With kindly faculties to blunt the edge
Of adverse circumstance; disarm, or turn
Into their contraries *del MS. 1832/36*
870 beneath] under *1832–*
882–884 *del MS. 1814/27, om 1827–*
894 could feelingly] feelingly could *1832–*

In life, in death, what Solitude can breed
Of selfishness, and cruelty, and vice;
Or, if it breed not, hath not power to cure.
—But your compliance, Sir! with our request
My words too long have hindered."
Undeterred,
Perhaps incited rather, by these shocks,
In no ungracious opposition, given
To the confiding spirit of his own
Experienced faith, the reverend Pastor said,
Around him looking, "Where shall I begin?
Who shall be first selected from my Flock
Gathered together in their peaceful fold?"
He paused—and having lifted up his eyes
To the pure Heaven, he cast them down again
Upon the earth beneath his feet; and spake.
—"To a mysteriously-consorted Pair
This place is consecrate; to Death and Life,
And to the best Affections that proceed
From their conjunction. Consecrate to faith
In Him who bled for man upon the Cross;
Hallowed to Revelation; and no less
To Reason's mandates; and the hopes divine
Of pure Imagination;—above all,
To Charity, and Love; that have provided,
Within these precincts, a capacious bed
And receptacle, open to the good
And evil, to the just and the unjust;
In which they find an equal resting-place:
Even as the multitude of kindred brooks
And streams, whose murmur fills this hollow vale,
Whether their course be turbulent or smooth,
Their waters clear or sullied, all are lost
Within the bosom of yon chrystal Lake,
And end their journey in the same repose!

And blest are they who sleep; and we that know,
While in a spot like this we breathe and walk,
That All beneath us by the wings are covered
Of motherly Humanity, outspread
And gathering all within their tender shade,
Though loth and slow to come! A battle-field,
In stillness left when slaughter is no more,
With this compared, is a strange spectacle!

---

910 mysteriously-consorted] mysteriously-united *pencil and ink MS. 1836/45, 1845–*
913 From their conjunction] from out their union *alt MS. 1836/45*
915 no less] therewith *MS. 1836/45*
936 is] yields *MS. 1832/36–1843* makes *MS. 1836/45, 1845–*

[930/931] A rueful sight the wild shore strewn with wrecks
[931/932] And trod by people in afflicted quest
Of friends and kindred, whom the angry Sea
Restores not to their prayer! Ah! who would think
[935] That all the scattered subjects which compose
Earth's melancholy vision through the space
Of all her climes; these wretched—these depraved,
To virtue lost, insensible of peace,
From the delights of charity cut off,
[940] To pity dead—the Oppressor and the Oppressed;
Tyrants who utter the destroying word,
And Slaves who will consent to be destroyed;
Were of one species with the sheltered few,
Who with a dutiful and tender hand
[945] Did lodge, in an appropriated spot,
This file of Infants; some that never breathed
The vital air; and others, who, allowed
That privilege, did yet expire too soon,
Or with too brief a warning, to admit
[950] Administration of the holy rite
That lovingly consigns the Babe to the arms
Of Jesus, and his everlasting care.
These that in trembling hope are laid apart;
And the besprinkled Nursling, unrequired
[955] Till he begins to smile upon the breast
That feeds him; and the tottering Little-one
Taken from air and sunshine when the rose
Of Infancy first blooms upon his cheek;
The thinking, thoughtless School-boy; the bold Youth
[960] Of soul impetuous, and the bashful Maid
Smitten while all the promises of life
Are opening round her; those of middle age,
Cast down while confident in strength they stand,
Like pillars fixed more firmly, as might seem,
[965] And more secure, by very weight of all
That, for support, rests on them; the decayed
And burthensome; and, lastly, that poor few
Whose light of reason is with age extinct;
The hopeful and the hopeless, first and last,
[970] The earliest summoned and the longest spared,

937–938 A dismal prospect yields the wild shore strewn
With wrecks, and trod by feet of young and old
Wandering about in miserable search *1836–; so MS. 1836/45 but* yields *del to* makes *then* yields *restored by* stet

939 and] or *1836–*

951 Did lodge, in an] Lodged in a dear *MS. 1832/36– but* Lodged, *1845–*

953 and others, who] others, which, though *MS. 1832/36–*

973 lastly, that poor] that unconscious few *pencil and ink MS. 1836/45*

Are here deposited, with tribute paid
Various; but unto each some tribute paid;
As if, amid these peaceful hills and groves,
Society were touched with kind concern,
And gentle "Nature grieved that One should die;"
Or, if the change demanded no regret,
Observed the liberating stroke—and blessed.
—And whence that tribute? wherefore these regards?
Not from the naked *Heart* alone of Man
(Though framed to high distinction upon earth
As the sole spring and fountain-head of tears,
His own peculiar utterance for distress
Or gladness) No," the philosophic Priest
Continued, "'tis not in the vital seat
Of feeling to produce them, without aid
From the pure Soul, the Soul sublime and pure;
With her two faculties of Eye and Ear,
The one by which a Creature, whom his sins
Have rendered prone, can upward look to heaven;
The other that empowers him to perceive
The voice of Deity, on height and plain
Whispering those truths in stillness, which the Word,
To the four quarters of the winds, proclaims.
Not without such assistance could the use
Of these benign observances prevail.
Thus are they born, thus fostered, and maintained;
And by the care prospective of our wise
Forefathers, who, to guard against the shocks,
The fluctuation and decay of things,
Embodied and established these high Truths
In solemn Institutions:—Men convinced
That Life is Love and Immortality,
The Being one, and one the Element.
There lies the channel, and original bed,
From the beginning, hollowed out and scooped
For Man's Affections—else betrayed and lost,
And swallowed up mid desarts infinite!
—This is the genuine course, the aim, and end,
Of prescient Reason; all conclusions else
Are abject, vain, presumptuous, and perverse.
The faith partaking of those holy times,

977–978 *MS. 1836/45 drafts:* Are *del to* [?Were] *interlined in pencil, and* Were here deposited as the like shall be / Through ages yet to come with tribute paid *pencil at page foot*
986 framed to] claiming *1827–*
995 can upward] upward can *pencil MS. 1836/45*
1002 and] thus *MS. 1832/36–*

---

981 For WW's end-of-volume note, see p. 302, below.
984 For WW's end-of-volume note, see pp. 302–313, below.

Life, I repeat, is energy of Love
Divine or human; exercised in pain,
In strife, and tribulation; and ordained,
If so approved and sanctified, to pass,
Through shades and silent rest, to endless joy."

END OF THE FIFTH BOOK.

BOOK THE SIXTH.

THE CHURCH-YARD AMONG THE MOUNTAINS.

HAIL to the Crown by Freedom shaped—to gird
An English Sovereign's brow! and to the Throne
Whereon he sits! Whose deep foundations lie
In veneration and the People's love,
Whose steps are equity, whose seat is law.
—Hail to the State of England! And conjoin
With this a salutation as devout,
Made to the spiritual Fabric of her Church;
Founded in truth; by blood of Martyrdom
Cemented; by the hands of Wisdom reared
In beauty of Holiness, with order'd pomp,
Decent, and unreproved. The voice, that greets
The majesty of both, shall pray for both;
That, mutually protected and sustained,
They may endure as long as sea surrounds
This favoured Land, or sunshine warms her soil.
—And, O, ye swelling hills, and spacious plains!
Besprent from shore to shore with steeple-towers,
And spires whose "silent finger points to Heaven;"
Nor wanting, at wide intervals, the bulk
Of ancient Minster, lifted above the cloud
Of the dense air, which town or city breeds
To intercept the sun's glad beams—may ne'er
That true succession fail of English Hearts,
That can perceive, not less than heretofore
Our Ancestors did feelingly perceive,
What in those holy Structures ye possess
Of ornamental interest, and the charm
Of pious sentiment diffused afar,
And human charity, and social love.
—Thus never shall the indignities of Time
Approach their reverend graces, unopposed;
Nor shall the Elements be free to hurt
Their fair proportions; nor the blinder rage
Of bigot zeal madly to overturn;
And, if the desolating hand of war
Spare them, they shall continue to bestow—

15 as long as] long as the *1832–*
25–26 Who, with Ancestral feeling, can perceive *MS. 1814/27– but* ancestral *MS. 1832/36–*

19 For WW's end-of-volume note, see p. 313, below.

Upon the thronged abodes of busy Men
(Depraved, and ever prone to fill their minds
Exclusively with transitory things)
An air and mien of dignified pursuit;
Of sweet civility—on rustic wilds.
—The Poet, fostering for his native land
Such hope, entreats that Servants may abound
Of those pure Altars worthy; Ministers
Detached from pleasure, to the love of gain
Superior, insusceptible of pride,
And by ambition's longings undisturbed;
Men, whose delight is where their duty leads
Or fixes them; whose least distinguished day
Shines with some portion of that heavenly lustre
Which makes the Sabbath lovely in the sight
Of blessed Angels, pitying human cares.
—And, as on earth it is the doom of Truth
To be perpetually attacked by foes
Open or covert, be that Priesthood still,
For her defence, replenished with a Band
Of strenuous Champions, in scholastic arts
Thoroughly disciplined; nor (if in course
Of the revolving World's disturbances
Cause should recur, which righteous Heaven avert!
To meet such trial) from their spiritual Sires
Degenerate; who, constrained to wield the sword
Of disputation, shrunk not, though assailed
With hostile din, and combating in sight
Of angry umpires, partial and unjust.
And did, thereafter, bathe their hands in fire,
So to declare the conscience satisfied:
Nor for their bodies would accept release,
But, blessing God and praising him, bequeathed,
With their last breath, from out the smouldering flame,
The faith which they by diligence had earned,
And through illuminating grace received,
For their dear Country-men, and all mankind.
O high example, constancy divine!

Even such a Man (inheriting the zeal
And from the sanctity of elder times
Not deviating,—a Priest, the like of whom,
If multiplied, and in their stations set,
Would o'er the bosom of a joyful Land
Spread true Religion, and her genuine fruits)

39 their minds] the mind *MS. 1832/36–*
48 ambition's] ambitious *1827–*
73 And] Or *MS. 1814/27* Or, *1827–*

Before me stood that day; on holy ground
Fraught with the relics of mortality,
Exalting tender themes, by just degrees
To lofty raised; and to the highest, last;
[85] The head and mighty paramount of truths;
Immortal life, in never-fading worlds,
For mortal Creatures, conquered and secured.

That basis laid, those principles of faith
Announced, as a preparatory act
[90] Of reverence to the spirit of the place;
The Pastor cast his eyes upon the ground,
Not, as before, like one oppressed with awe,
But with a mild and social chearfulness;
Then to the Solitary turned, and spake.

[95] "At morn or eve, in your retired Domain,
Perchance you not unfrequently have marked
[97] A Visitor—intent upon the task
Of prying, low and high, for herbs and flowers:
[98] Too delicate employ, as would appear,
For One, who, though of drooping mien, had yet,
[100] From Nature's kindliness, received a frame
Robust as ever rural labour bred."

The Solitary answered. "Such a Form
Full well I recollect. We often crossed
Each other's path; but, as the Intruder seemed
[105] Fondly to prize the silence which he kept,
And I as willingly did cherish mine,
We met, and passed, like shadows. I have heard,
From my good Host, that he was crazed in brain
By unrequited love; and scaled the rocks,
[110] Dived into caves, and pierced the matted woods,
In hope to find some virtuous herb, of power
To cure his malady!"
The Vicar smiled,
"Alas! before to-morrow's sun goes down
His habitation will be here: for him
That open grave is destined."

---

90 act] work *alt, then del MS. 1836/45*
91 to] done to *1845– ; so MS. 1836/45 but with* [?of] *in margin and ink over pencil at page foot:* Of reverence done paid to the Spirit
paid
98–99 A Visitor—in quest of herbs and flowers; *1827– ; so MS. 1814/27 but* flowers: *MS. 1836/45 has an illeg word in the right margin of l. 98*
105 We often crossed] Often we crossed *pencil MS. 1836/45*
110 he was] being *MS. 1832/36–*
111 and] he *MS. 1832/36–*

[115] "Died he then
Of pain and grief," the Solitary asked,
"Believe it not—oh! never could that be!"

"He loved," the vicar answered, "deeply loved,
Loved fondly, truly, fervently; and pined
[120] When he had told his love, and sued in vain,
—Rejected—yea repelled—and, if with scorn
Upon the haughty maiden's brow, 'tis but
[123] A high-prized plume which female Beauty wears.
[127] *That* he could brook, and glory in;—but when
The tidings came that she whom he had wooed
Was wedded to another, and his heart
[130] Was forced to rend away its only hope,
Then, Pity could have scarcely found on earth
An Object worthier of regard than he,
In the transition of that bitter hour!
Lost was she, lost; nor could the sufferer say
[135] That in the act of preference he had been
[136] Unjustly dealt with; but the Maid was gone!
She, whose dear name with unregarded sighs
He long had blessed, whose Image was preserved—
Shrined in his breast with fond idolatry,
[137] Had vanished from his prospects and desires;
Not by translation to the heavenly Choir
Who have put off their mortal spoils—ah no!
[140] She lives another's wishes to complete,
"Joy be their lot, and happiness," he cried,
"His lot and hers, as misery is mine!"

Such was that strong concussion; but the Man
Who trembled, trunk and limbs, like some huge Oak
[145] By a fierce tempest shaken, soon resumed
The stedfast quiet natural to a Mind
Of composition gentle and sedate,
[148] And in its movements circumspect and slow.
Of rustic Parents bred, He had been trained,
(So prompted their aspiring wish) to skill
In numbers and the sedentary art
Of penmanship,—with pride professed, and taught

---

119 "Do not believe it; never could that be!" *MS. 1832/36–*
121 pined] dared *MS. 1814/27–*
122 At length to tell his love, but sued in vain; *1827– ; so MS. 1814/27 but* vain,
125/126 In wantonness of conquest, or puts on
To cheat the world, or from herself to hide
Humiliation, when no longer free. *1827– ; so MS. 1814/27 but* world or . . . Humiliation when . . . free
136–138 *del MS. 1814/27, om 1827–*
144 as misery] hence forth *pencil MS. 1836/45* is] must be *1845–*
151–156 *del MS. 1814/27, om 1827–*

By his endeavours in the mountain dales.
Now, those sad tidings weighing on his heart,
[149] To books, and papers, and the studious desk,
[151/153] He stoutly readdressed himself—resolved
[152] To quell his pain, and enter on the path
Of old pursuits with keener appetite
And closer industry. Of what ensued,
[155] Within his soul, no outward sign appeared
Till a betraying sickliness was seen
To tinge his cheek; and through his frame it crept
With slow mutation unconcealable;
Such universal change as autumn makes
[160] In the fair body of a leafy grove
Discoloured, then divested. 'Tis affirmed
By Poets skilled in nature's secret ways
That Love will not submit to be controlled
By mastery:—and the good Man lacked not Friends
[165] Who strove to instil this truth into his mind,
A mind in all heart-mysteries unversed.
"Go to the hills," said one, "remit awhile
"This baneful diligence:—at early morn
"Court the fresh air, explore the heaths and woods;
[170] "And, leaving it to others to foretell,
"By calculations sage, the ebb and flow
"Of tides, and when the moon will be eclipsed,
"Do you, for your own benefit, construct
"A calendar of flowers, plucked as they blow
[175] "Where health abides, and chearfulness, and peace."
The attempt was made;—'tis needless to report
How hopelessly:—but Innocence is strong,
And an entire simplicity of mind
A thing most sacred in the eye of Heaven,
[180] That opens, for such Sufferers, relief
Within their souls, a fount of grace divine;
And doth commend their weakness and disease
To Nature's care, assisted in her office
By all the Elements that round her wait
[185] To generate, to preserve, and to restore;
And by her beautiful array of Forms
Shedding sweet influence from above, or pure

157–160 To books, and to the long-forsaken desk,
O'er which enchained by science he had loved
To bend, he stoutly re-addressed himself,
Resolved to quell his pain, and search for truth
With keener appetite (if that might be) *1827– ; so MS. 1814/27 but* To books & to the long forsaken desk *del* In *pencil alt, del by eras, for* To Oer which enchain'd . . . lov'd . . . bend the . . . readdress'd . . . pain & . . .

162 his] the *1827–* soul,] heart *MS. 1814/27–*

188 Within the soul, fountains of grace divine; *MS. 1832/36–*

Delight exhaling from the ground they tread."

"Impute it not to impatience, if," exclaimed
[190] The Wanderer, "I infer that he was healed
By perseverance in the course prescribed."

"You do not err: the powers, which had been lost
By slow degrees, were gradually regained;
The fluttering nerves composed; the beating heart
[195] In rest established; and the jarring thoughts
To harmony restored.—But yon dark mold
Will cover him; in height of strength—to earth
Hastily smitten, by a fever's force.
Yet not with stroke so sudden as refused
[200] Time to look back with tenderness on her
Whom he had loved in passion,—and to send
Some farewell words; and, with those words, a prayer
That, from his dying hand, she would accept,
Of his possessions, that which most he prized;
[205] A Book, upon the surface of whose leaves
[205/206] Some chosen plants, disposed with nicest care,
In undecaying beauty were preserved.
Mute register, to him, of time and place,
And various fluctuations in the breast;
[210] To her, a monument of faithful Love
Conquered, and in tranquillity retained!

Close to his destined habitation, lies
[213] One whose Endeavours did at length achieve
A victory less worthy of regard,
[214] Though marvellous in its kind. A Place exists
[215] High in these mountains, that allured a Band
Of keen Adventurers to unite their pains,
[217] In search of treasure there by Nature formed,
And there concealed: but they who tried were foiled,
[218] And all desisted, all, save he alone;

---

199 which] that *1827–*
204 Will cover him, in the fulness of his strength— *1832– but* strength, *MS. 1832/36–*
208 send *overwritten by illeg pencil, eras MS. 1814/27*
209 Some farewell words—with one, but one, request, *1827– but* request; *1836– ; MS. 1814/27 as 1827 but* with one—but one—request
212–213 A Book, upon whose leaves some chosen plants / By his own hand disposed . . . *1827– but* book, *MS. 1832/36–* plants, *1845– but* plants *1849 (probable worn plate); MS. 1814/27 as 1827 but* hand] hands
220–221 One who achieved a humbler victory, *1827– ; so MS. 1814/27 but* One whose achiev'd a humbler victory
222 exists] there is *MS. 1814/27–*
225–226 In search of precious ore: who tried were foiled, *1827– but* tried, . . . foiled— *1832–* who] they *1836– ; MS. 1814/27 as 1827 but* ore who tried,
227 he] him *MS. 1814/27–*

Who taking counsel of his own clear thoughts,
[220] And trusting only to his own weak hands,
Urged unremittingly the stubborn work,
Unseconded, uncountenanc'd; then, as time
Passed on, while still his lonely efforts found
No recompence, derided; and, at length,
[225] By many pitied, as insane of mind;
By others dreaded as the luckless Thrall
Of subterraneous Spirits, feeding hope
By various mockery of sight and sound;
Hope, after hope, encouraged and destroyed.
[230] —But when the Lord of seasons had matured
The fruits of earth through space of twice ten years,
[232] The mountain's entrails offered to the view
Of the Old Man, and to his trembling grasp,
[233] His bright, his long-deferred, his dear reward.
Not with more transport did Columbus greet
[235] A world, his rich discovery! But our Swain,
A very Hero till his point was gained,
Proved all unable to support the weight
Of prosperous fortune. On the fields he looked
With an unsettled liberty of thought,
[240] Of schemes and wishes; in the day-light walked
Giddy and restless; ever and anon
Quaffed in his gratitude immoderate cups;
And truly might be said to die of joy!
—He vanish'd; but conspicuous to this day
[245] The Path remains that linked his Cottage-door
To the Mine's mouth; a long, and slanting track,
Upon the rugged mountain's stony side,
Worn by his daily visits to and from
The darksome centre of a constant hope.
[250] This Vestige, neither force of beating rain,
Nor the vicissitudes of frost and thaw
Shall cause to fade, 'till ages pass away;
And it is named, in memory of the event,
The PATH OF PERSEVERANCE."
"Thou, from whom
[255] Man has his strength," exclaimed the Wanderer, "oh!
Do Thou direct it!—to the Virtuous grant
The penetrative eye which can perceive
In this blind world the guiding vein of hope,

---

228 Who] He *MS. 1814/27* He, *1827–*
236 subterraneous] subterranean *MS. 1814/27–*
241 the] his *1827– but* the view *del to* his *MS. 1814/27*
242–243 And trembling grasp his long-deferred reward. *MS. 1814/27–but* his] the 1827– reward.] reward *1840 (probable worn plate)*
250 Wishes and endless schemes; by daylight walked *1836–*

That, like this Labourer, such may dig their way,
"Unshaken, unseduced, unterrified;"
Grant to the Wise *his* firmness of resolve!"

"That prayer were not superfluous," said the Priest,
"Amid the noblest relics, proudest Dust,
That Westminster, for Britain's glory, holds,
Within the bosom of her awful Pile,
Ambitiously collected. Yet the sigh,
Which wafts that prayer to Heaven, is due to all,
Wherever laid, who living fell below
Their virtue's humbler mark; a sigh of *pain*
If to the opposite extreme they sank.
How would you pity Her who yonder rests;
Him, farther off; the Pair, who here are laid;
But, above all, that mixture of Earth's Mold
Whom sight of this green Hillock to my mind
Recalls.—*He* lived not till his locks were nipped
By seasonable frost of age; nor died
Before his temples, prematurely forced
To mix the manly brown with silver grey,
Gave obvious instance of the sad effect
Produced, when thoughtless Folly hath usurped
The natural crown which sage Experience wears.
—Gay, volatile, ingenious, quick to learn,
And prompt to exhibit all that he possessed
Or could perform; a zealous actor—hired
Into the troop of mirth, a soldier—sworn
Into the lists of giddy enterprize
Such was he; yet, as if within his frame
Two several Souls alternately had lodged,
Two sets of manners, could the youth put on;
And, fraught with antics as the Indian bird
That writhes and chatters in her wiry cage,
Was graceful, when it pleased him, smooth and still
As the mute Swan that floats adown the stream,
Or, on the waters of the unruffled lake,
Anchors her placid beauty. Not a Leaf,
That flutters on the bough, more light than He;
And not a Flower, that droops in the green shade,
More winningly reserved! If Ye inquire
How such consummate elegance was bred
Amid these wilds; a Composition framed

279 virtue's] *so 1820E–* virtues *1814*
291 which] that *MS. 1814/27–*
306 more light] lighter *pencil MS. 1836/45, 1840–*
308 winningly] willingly *1820E*
310–313 Amid these wilds, this answer may suffice, *1827– but* suffice; *1836–; MS. 1814/27 as 1827 but* wilds;

Of qualities so adverse—to diffuse,
Where'er he moved, diversified delight;
A simple answer may suffice, even this,
'Twas Nature's will; who sometimes undertakes,
For the reproof of human vanity,
Art to outstrip in her peculiar walk.
Hence, for this Favourite, lavishly endowed
With personal gifts, and bright instinctive wit,
While both, embellishing each other, stood
Yet farther recommended by the charm
Of fine demeanor, and by dance and song,
And skill in letters, every fancy shaped
Fair expectations; nor, when to the World's
Capacious field forth went the Adventurer, there
Were he and his attainments overlooked,
Or scantily rewarded; but all hopes,
Cherished for him, he suffered to depart,
Like blighted buds; or clouds that mimicked Land
Before the Sailor's eye; or diamond drops
That sparkling decked the morning grass; or aught
That *was* attractive—and hath ceased to be!
—Yet, when this Prodigal returned, the rites
Of joyful greeting were on him bestowed,
Who, by humiliation undeterred,
Sought for his weariness a place of rest
Within his Father's gates.—Whence came He?—clothed
In tattered garb, from hovels where abides
Necessity, the stationary Host
Of vagrant Poverty; from rifted barns
Where no one dwells but the wide-staring Owl
And the Owl's Prey; none permanently house
But many harbour; from these Haunts, to which
He had descended from the proud Saloon,
He came, the Ghost of beauty and of health,
The Wreck of gaiety! But soon revived
In strength, in power refitted, he renewed
His suit to Fortune; and she smiled again
Upon a fickle Ingrate. Thrice he rose,
Thrice sunk as willingly. For He, whose nerves
Were used to thrill with pleasure, while his voice
Softly accompanied the tuneful harp,
By the nice finger of fair Ladies, touched
In glittering Halls, was able to derive
Not less enjoyment from an abject choice.

341–342 And the Owl's Prey; from these bare Haunts, to which *MS. 1814/27– but* owl's prey; . . . haunts, *MS. 1832/36–*
349 sunk] sank *MS. 1814/27–*
354 Not] No *1832–*

Who happier for the moment?—Who more blithe
Than this fallen Spirit; in those dreary Holds
His Talents lending to exalt the freaks
Of merry-making Beggars,—now, provoked
[345] To laughter multiplied in louder peals
By his malicious wit; then, all enchained
With mute astonishment, themselves to see
In their own arts outdone, their fame eclipsed,
As by the very presence of the Fiend
[350] Who dictates and inspires illusive feats,
For knavish purposes! The City, too,
(With shame I speak it) to her guilty bowers
Allured him, sunk so low in self-respect
As there to linger, there to eat his bread,
[355] Hired Minstrel of voluptuous blandishment;
Charming the air with skill of hand or voice,
Listen who would, be wrought upon who might,
[358] Sincerely wretched Hearts, or falsely gay.
—Truths I record to many known, for such
[359] The not unfrequent tenor of his boast
[360] In ears that relished the report;—but all
Was from his Parents happily concealed;
Who saw enough for blame and pitying love.
They also were permitted to receive
His last, repentant breath; and closed his eyes,
[365] No more to open on that irksome world
Where he had long existed in the state
Of a young Fowl beneath one Mother hatched,
Though from another sprung—of different kind:
Where he had lived, and could not cease to live,
[370] Distracted in propensity; content
With neither element of good or ill;
And yet in both rejoicing; man unblest;
Of contradictions infinite the slave,
Till his deliverance, when Mercy made him
[375] One with Himself, and one with those who sleep."

"'Tis strange," observed the Solitary, "strange
It seems, and scarcely less than pitiful
That in a Land where Charity provides
For all who can no longer feed themselves,
[380] A Man like this should choose to bring his shame

373–374 —Such the too frequent tenour of his boast *1827–; so MS. 1814/27 but*—Such . . . tenour] Such . . . tenor
383 sprung—of different kind:] sprung, different in kind: *MS. 1832/36–*
390 those who] them that *del to* them who *MS. 1814/27* them who *1827–1832* them that *MS. 1832/36–*
394 who] that *MS. 1814/27–*

To the parental door; and with his sighs
Infect the air which he had freely breathed
[383] In happy infancy. He could not pine,
Whencee'er rejected howsoe'er forlorn,
[384] Through lack of converse, no, he must have found
[385] Abundant exercise for thought and speech
In his dividual Being, self-reviewed,
Self-catechized, self-punished.—Some there are
Who, drawing near their final Home, and much
And daily longing that the same were reached,
[390] Would rather shun than seek the fellowship
Of kindred mold.—Such haply here are laid?"

"Yes," said the Priest, "the Genius of our Hills
Who seems, by these stupendous barriers cast
Round his Domain, desirous not alone
[395] To keep his own, but also to exclude
All other progeny, doth sometimes lure,
Even by this studied depth of privacy,
The unhappy Alien hoping to obtain
Concealment, or seduced by wish to find,
[400] In place from outward molestation free,
Helps to internal ease. Of many such
Could I discourse; but as their stay was brief
So their departure only left behind
Fancies, and loose conjectures. Other trace
[405] Survives, for worthy mention, of a Pair
Who, from the pressure of their several fates,
Meeting as Strangers, in a petty Town
Whose blue roofs ornament a distant reach
Of this far-winding Vale, remained as Friends
[410] True to their choice; and gave their bones in trust
To this loved Cemetery, here to lodge
With unescutcheoned privacy interred
Far from the Family-vault.—A Chieftain One
By right of birth; within whose spotless breast
[415] The fire of ancient Caledonia burned.
He, with the foremost whose impatience hailed
The Stuart, landing to resume, by force
Of arms, the crown which Bigotry had lost,
Arouzed his clan; and, fighting at their head,
[420] With his brave sword endeavoured to prevent
Culloden's fatal overthrow.—Escaped
From that disastrous rout, to foreign shores
He fled; and when the lenient hand of Time

---

399 *del MS. 1814/27, om 1827–*
407 laid?"] laid." *1814* laid?" *errata 1814*
413 this] his *1845, 1850*

Those troubles had appeased, he sought and gained,
For his obscured condition, an obscure
Retreat, within this nook of English ground.
—The Other, born in Britain's southern tract,
Had fixed his milder loyalty, and placed
His gentler sentiments of love and hate,
There, where they placed them who in conscience prized
The new succession, as a line of Kings
Whose oath had virtue to protect the Land
Against the dire assaults of Papacy
And arbitrary Rule. But launch thy Bark
On the distempered flood of public life,
And cause for most rare triumph will be thine
If, spite of keenest eye and steadiest hand,
The Stream, that bears thee forward, prove not, soon
Or late, a perilous Master. He, who oft,
Under the battlements and stately trees
That round his Mansion cast a sober gloom,
Had moralized on this, and other truths
Of kindred import, pleased and satisfied,
Was forced to vent his wisdom with a sigh
Heaved from the heart in fortune's bitterness
When he had crushed a plentiful estate
By ruinous Contest, to obtain a Seat
In Britain's Senate. Fruitless was the attempt:
And while the uproar of that desperate strife
Continued yet to vibrate on his ear,
The vanquished Whig, beneath a *borrowed* name,
(For the mere sound and echo of his own
Haunted him with sensations of disgust
Which he was glad to lose) slunk from the World
To the deep shade of these untravelled Wilds;
In which the Scottish Laird had long possessed
An undisturbed Abode.—Here, then, they met,
Two doughty Champions; flaming Jacobite
And sullen Hanoverian! You might think
That losses and vexations, less severe
Than those which they had severally sustained,
Would have inclined each to abate his zeal
For his ungrateful cause; no,—I have heard
My reverend Father tell that, mid the calm
Of that small Town encountering thus, they filled,
Daily, its Bowling-green with harmless strife;
Plagued with uncharitable thoughts the Church;

456 Under] Beneath *MS. 1832/36–*
467 beneath] under *MS. 1832/36–*
470 Which] That *MS. 1814/27–*
471 these] those *1836–*

And vexed the Market-place. But in the breasts
Of these Opponents gradually was wrought,
With little change of general sentiment,
Such change towards each other, that their days
By choice were spent in constant fellowship;
And if, at times, they fretted with the yoke,
Those very bickerings made them love it more.

A favourite boundary to their lengthened walks
This Church-yard was. And, whether they had come
Treading their path in sympathy and linked
In social converse, or by some short space
Discreetly parted to preserve the peace,
One Spirit seldom failed to extend its sway
Over both minds, when they awhile had marked
The visible quiet of this holy ground
And breathed its soothing air;—the Spirit of hope
And saintly magnanimity; that, spurning
The field of selfish difference and dispute,
And every care which transitory things,
Earth, and the kingdoms of the earth, create,
Doth, by a rapture of forgetfulness,
Preclude forgiveness, from the praise debarred,
Which else the Christian Virtue might have claimed.
—There live who yet remember here to have seen
Their courtly Figures,—seated on the stump
Of an old Yew, their favourite resting-place.
But, as the Remnant of the long-lived Tree
Was disappearing by a swift decay,
They, with joint care, determined to erect,
Upon its site, a Dial, which should stand
For public use; and also might survive
As their own private monument; for this
Was the particular spot, in which they wished,
(And Heaven was pleased to accomplish the desire)
That, undivided, their Remains should lie.
So, where the mouldered Tree had stood, was raised
Yon Structure, framing, with the ascent of steps
That to the decorated Pillar lead,
A work of art, more sumptuous, as might seem,
Than suits this Place; yet built in no proud scorn
Of rustic homeliness; they only aimed

487 Change tow'rds each other, change so great, their days *alt MS. 1832/36* change] leaning *MS. 1836/45, 1845–* *MS. 1836/45 has drafts at page foot:* Such leaning towards each other *and* Such change in each towards the other that
513 which should] that might *MS. 1814/27–*
514 For public use preserved, and thus survive *1827–; so MS. 1814/27 but* preserv d, &
522 as] than *MS. 1814/27–*
523 Than] To *MS. 1814/27–* suits] suit *1827–*

To ensure for it respectful guardianship.
Around the margin of the Plate, whereon
The Shadow falls, to note the stealthy hours
Winds an inscriptive Legend"—At these words
Thither we turned; and, gathered, as we read,
The appropriate sense, in Latin numbers couched.
"Time flies; it is his melancholy task
"To bring, and bear away, delusive hopes,
"And re-produce the troubles he destroys.
"But, while his blindness thus is occupied,
"Discerning Mortal! do thou serve the will
"Of Time's eternal Master, and that peace,
"Which the World wants, shall be for Thee confirmed."

"Smooth verse, inspired by no unlettered Muse,"
Exclaimed the Sceptic, "and the strain of thought
Accords with Nature's language;—the soft voice
Of yon white torrent falling down the rocks
Speaks, less distinctly, to the same effect.
If, then, their blended influence be not lost
Upon our hearts, not wholly lost, I grant,
Even upon mine, the more are we required
To feel for those, among our fellow men,
Who, offering no obeisance to the world,
Are yet made desperate by "too quick a sense
Of constant infelicity"—cut off
From peace like Exiles on some barren rock,
Their life's appointed prison; not more free
Than Centinels, between two armies, set,
With nothing better, in the chill night air,
Than their own thoughts to comfort them.—Say why
That ancient story of Prometheus chained?
The Vulture—the inexhaustible repast
Drawn from his vitals! Say what meant the woes
By Tantalus entailed upon his race,
And the dark sorrows of the line of Thebes?
Fictions in form, but in their substance truths,
Tremendous truths! familiar to the men
Of long-past times; nor obsolete in ours.
—Exchange the Shepherd's frock of native grey
For robes with regal purple tinged; convert
The crook into a sceptre;—give the pomp
Of circumstance, and here the tragic Muse
Shall find apt subjects for her highest art.

555/556 To the bare rock, on frozen Caucasus; *1845–; so MS. 1836/45 but* To the bare rock on frozen Caukausus?

—Amid the groves, beneath the shadowy hills
The generations are prepared; the pangs,
The internal pangs are ready; the dread strife
Of poor humanity's afflicted will
Struggling in vain with ruthless destiny."

"Though," said the Priest in answer, "these be terms
Which a divine philosophy rejects,
We, whose established and unfailing trust
Is in controuling Providence, admit
That through all stations human life abounds
With mysteries,—for if Faith were left untried
How could the might—that lurks within her—then
Be shewn? her glorious excellence—that ranks
Among the first of Powers and Virtues—proved?
Our system is not fashioned to preclude
That sympathy which you for others ask;
And I could tell, not travelling for my theme
Beyond the limits of these humble graves,
Of strange disasters; but I pass them by,
Loth to disturb what heaven hath hushed in peace."
—Still less, far less am I inclined to treat
Of Man degraded in his Maker's sight
By the deformities of brutish vice:
For, though from these materials might be framed
Harsh portraiture, in which a vulgar face
And a coarse outside of repulsive life
And unaffecting manners may at once
Be recognized by all"—"Ah! do not think,"
The Wanderer somewhat eagerly exclaimed,
"Wish could be ours that you, for such poor gain,
(Gain shall I call it?—gain of what?—for whom?)
Should breathe a word tending to violate
Your own pure spirit. Not a step we look for
In slight of that forbearance and reserve
Which common human-heartedness inspire,
And mortal ignorance and frailty claim,
Upon this sacred ground, if no where else."

"True," said the Solitary, "be it far
From us to infringe the laws of charity.

---

568 beneath] under *1836–*
585 Beyond these humble graves, of grievous crimes *MS. 1814/27–*
586 Of] And *MS. 1814/27–*
591–592 For, in such Portraits, though a vulgar face *1827–but* portraits, *MS. 1832/36–; MS. 1814/27 as 1827 but* For in . . . portraits,
594 may] might *MS. 1814/27, 1820E–*
602 inspire,] inspires, *pencil MS. 1814/27, 1820E–*

Let judgment here in mercy be pronounced;
This, self-respecting Nature prompts, and this
Wisdom enjoins; but, if the thing we seek
Be genuine knowledge, bear we then in mind
How, from his lofty throne, the Sun can fling
Colours as bright on exhalations bred
By weedy pool or pestilential swamp,
As by the rivulet sparkling where it runs,
Or the pellucid Lake."
"Small risk," said I,
"Of such illusion do we here incur;
Temptation here is none to exceed the truth;
No evidence appears that they, who rest
Within this ground, were covetous of praise,
Or of remembrance even, deserved or not.
Green is the Church-yard, beautiful and green;
Ridge rising gently by the side of ridge:
A heaving surface—almost wholly free
From interruption of sepulchral stones,
And mantled o'er with aboriginal turf
And everlasting flowers. These Dalesmen trust
The lingering gleam of their departed Lives
To oral records and the silent heart;
Depository faithful, and more kind
Than fondest Epitaphs: for, if it fail,
What boots the sculptured Tomb? And who can blame,
Who rather would not envy, men that feel
This mutual confidence; if from such source
The practice flow,—if thence, or from a deep
And general humility in death?
Nor should I much condemn it, if it spring
From disregard of Time's destructive power,
As only capable to prey on things
Of earth, and human nature's mortal part.
Yet—in less simple districts, where we see
Stone lift its forehead emulous of stone
In courting notice, and the ground all paved
With commendations of departed worth,
Reading, where'er we turn, of innocent lives,
Of each domestic charity fulfilled
And sufferings meekly borne—I, for my part,
Though with the silence pleased which here prevails,

628 records] records, *MS. 1832/36* record, *1836–*
629 Depository] Depositories *1836–*
630 Epitaphs:] epitaphs: *MS. 1832/36* epitaph: *1836–* it] that *MS. 1814/27–1832* those *1836–*
647 which] that *MS. 1814/27–*

Among those fair recitals also range
Soothed by the natural spirit which they breathe.
And, in the centre of a world whose soil
Is rank with all unkindness, compassed round
With such Memorials, I have sometimes felt
That 'twas no momentary happiness
To have *one* enclosure where the voice that speaks
In envy or detraction is not heard;
Which malice may not enter; where the traces
Of evil inclinations are unknown;
Where love and pity tenderly unite
With resignation; and no jarring tone
Intrudes, the peaceful concert to disturb
Of amity and gratitude."
"Thus sanctioned,"
The Pastor said, "I willingly confine
My narratives to subjects that excite
Feelings with these accordant; love, esteem
And admiration; lifting up a veil,
A sun-beam introducing among hearts
Retired and covert; so that ye shall have
Clear Images before your gladdened eyes
Of Nature's unambitious underwood,
And flowers that prosper in the shade. And when
I speak of such among my flock as swerved
Or fell, those only will I single out
Upon whose lapse, or error, something more
Than brotherly forgiveness may attend:
To such will we restrict our notice, else
Better my tongue were mute. And yet there are,
I feel, good reasons why we should not leave
Wholly untraced a more forbidding way.
For strength to persevere and to support,
And energy to conquer and repel,
These elements of virtue, that declare
The native grandeur of the human Soul,
Are oft-times not unprofitably shewn
In the perverseness of a selfish course:
Truth every day exemplified, no less
In the grey cottage by the murmuring stream
Than the fantastic Conqueror's roving camp,
Or in the factious Senate, unappalled

653 That 'twas] It was *1832–*
672 will I single out] shall be singled out *MS. 1832/36–*
687 Than] That *1832* the] in *MS. 1814/27–*
688 in] 'mid *MS. 1814/27–*

[674] While merciless proscription ebbs and flows.
[675] —There," said the Vicar pointing as he spake,
"A woman rests in peace; surpassed by few
In power of mind, and eloquent discourse.
Tall was her stature; her complexion dark
[679] And saturnine; her port erect, her head
Not absolutely raised, as if to hold
[680] Converse with heaven, nor yet depressed tow'rds earth,
But in projection carried, as she walked
For ever musing. Sunken were her eyes;
Wrinkled and furrowed with habitual thought
Was her broad forehead; like the brow of One
[685] Whose visual nerve shrinks from a painful glare
Of overpowering light.—While yet a Child,
She, mid the humble Flowerets of the vale,
Towered like the imperial Thistle, not unfurnished
With its appropriate grace, yet rather framed
[690] To be admired, than coveted and loved.
Even at that age, she ruled as sovereign Queen
Among her Play-mates; else their simple sports
[693] Had wanted power to occupy a mind
Held in subjection by a strong controul
Of studious application, self-imposed.
Books were her creditors; to them she paid,
With pleasing, anxious eagerness, the hours
Which they exacted; were it time allowed,

688/689 Whoe'er may sink, or rise—to sink again, *added line 1845–; MS. 1836/45 has a number of drafts: ll. 688–689 del to* whoer may sink *interlined* flows *in l. 689 rev to* flows; *and*
~~Vicissitudes which no prudence can foresee~~
~~And nothing less than [?providence] controul~~ *interlined*
board
~~On sovereign council-seat where treason works~~
~~Insidiously, or in the clamourrous hall~~
~~Of a national Senate, by the ebb & flow~~
~~Of merciless proscription, unappalled.~~ *top of page*
~~Shifting its course as no one can forsee~~
~~And [?Providence might] only may controul~~ *page foot*
Or mid ~~th~~ a factious senate unappalled
Whoeer may sink, or rise to sink again
As merciless proscription ebbs and flows. *right margin*
sink
Whoeer may [?rise] or rise to sink again
As merciless proscription ebbs & flows *bottom of facing page*

689 While] As *1845–; so MS. 1836/45 but see l. 688/689, above*

694–695 And saturnine; her head not raised to hold *MS. 1814/27–*

705 framed] seeking *MS. 1814/27–*

707 as] a *1832–*

708 Among her Play-mates;] Mid her companions *MS. 1814/27* 'Mid her Companions; *1827* Over her Comrades; *1832– but* comrades; *MS. 1832/36–*

709–716 Wanting all relish for her strenuous mind,
Had crossed her, only to be shunned with scorn. *1827– but* her,] her *1836–; MS. 1814/27 as 1827 but* scorn *and pencil draft, eras, at page foot:*
all mind
[?~~that~~] wanting relish for her strenuous [?]
And ~~only~~ crossed her only to shunned with scorn

Or seized upon by stealth, or fairly won,
By stretch of industry, from other tasks.
[695] —Oh! pang of sorrowful regret for them
Whom, in their youth, sweet study has enthralled,
That they have lived for harsher servitude,
Whether in soul, in body, or estate!
Such doom was hers; yet nothing could subdue
[700] Her keen desire of knowledge; or efface
Those brighter images—by books impressed
Upon her memory; faithfully as stars
That occupy their places,—and, though oft
Hidden by clouds, and oft bedimmed by haze,
[705] Are not to be extinguished, or impaired.

Two passions, both degenerate, for they both
Began in honour, gradually obtained
Rule over her, and vexed her daily life;
An unrelenting, avaricious thrift;
[710] And a strange thraldom of maternal love,
That held her spirit, in its own despite,
Bound by vexation, and regret, and scorn.
Constrained forgiveness, and relenting vows,
And tears, in pride suppressed, in shame concealed,
[715] To a poor dissolute Son, her only Child.
—Her wedded days had opened with mishap,
Whence dire dependance.—What could she perform
To shake the burthen off? Ah! there she felt,
Indignantly, the weakness of her sex,
[720] The injustice of her low estate.—She mused;
[720/721] Resolved, adhered to her resolve; her heart
[722] Closed by degrees to charity; and, thence
[721/723] Expecting not Heaven's blessing, placed her trust
[724] In ceaseless pains and parsimonious care,
[725/726] Which got, and sternly hoarded each day's gain.

Thus all was re-established, and a pile
Constructed, that sufficed for every end,

---

717 them] those *MS. 1814/27–*
722 or] nor *MS. 1814/27–*
727 or] nor *1832–*
731 unrelenting,] unremitting, *1836–*
740 she] was *MS. 1814/27–*
742–745 She mused—resolved, adhered to her resolve;
The hand grew slack in alms-giving, the heart
Closed by degrees to charity; heaven's blessing
Not seeking from that source, she placed her trust *1827– but* mused—] mused, *MS. 1832/36–; MS. 1814/27 as 1827 but* the hand . . . alms-giving; the heart itself / Closed . . . source she . . .
746–747 In ceaseless pains—and strictest parsimony,
Which sternly hoarded all that could be spared,
From each day's need, out of each day's least gain. *1836– but* parsimony *1840–*
748 Thus] Yet *MS. 1814/27*

Save the contentment of the Builder's mind;
[730] A mind by nature indisposed to aught
So placid, so inactive, as content;
A Mind intolerant of lasting peace,
And cherishing the pang which it deplored.
Dread life of conflict! which I oft compared
[735] To the agitation of a brook that runs
Down rocky mountains—buried now and lost
[737] In silent pools, unfathomably deep;—
Now, in a moment, starting forth again
With violence, and proud of its escape;—
Until it sink once more, by slow degrees,
[739] Or instantly, into as dark repose.

[741] A sudden illness seized her in the strength
Of life's autumnal season.—Shall I tell
How on her bed of death the Matron lay,
To Providence submissive, so she thought;
[745] But fretted, vexed, and wrought upon—almost
To anger, by the malady, that griped
Her prostrate frame with unrelaxing power,
As the fierce Eagle fastens on the Lamb.
She prayed, she moaned—her Husband's Sister watched
[750] Her dreary pillow, waited on her needs;
And yet the very sound of that kind foot
Was anguish to her ears!—"And must she rule,"
This was the dying Woman heard to say
In bitterness, "and must she rule and reign,
[755] "Sole Mistress of this house, when I am gone?
"Sit by my fire—possess what I possessed—
[756] "Tend what I tended—calling it her own!"
[757] Enough;—I fear, too much.—Of nobler feeling
Take this example.—One autumnal evening,
[758] While she was yet in prime of health and strength,
I well remember, while I passed her door,
[760] Musing with loitering step, and upward eye

754 which it] her heart *1836–*
757 rocky mountains—] a rocky mountain, *1836–*
758–762 In silent pools, and now in eddies chained,—
But never to be charmed to gentleness;
Its best attainment fits of such repose
As timid eyes might shrink from fathoming. *1827– but* pools, now in strong eddies *1832–* chained; . . . gentleness: *MS. 1832/36–; MS. 1814/27 as 1827 but* chain'd;— . . . charm'd . . . gentleness and glad of [?its escape] / But never to be charmed by gentleness / [?I] *pencil, eras, at page foot*
770 on *del to* upon *pencil MS. 1836/45*
775 dying] suffering *MS. 1836/45* death-doomed *1845–*
778 *del, then marked* stet *MS. 1836/45, om 1845–*
780–781 Enough;—I fear, too much.—One vernal evening, *1827– ; so MS. 1814/27 and with earlier draft:* Enough;—I fear, too much. Take this example
784 Musing] Alone, *MS. 1836/45, 1845–* *MS. 1836/45 also cancels* ward *perhaps intending* upturned *as in l. 785; see l. 785, below*

Turned tow'rds the planet Jupiter, that hung
Above the centre of the Vale, a voice
Roused me, her voice; it said, "That glorious Star
"In its untroubled element will shine
[765] "As now it shines, when we are laid in earth
[766] "And safe from all our sorrows."—She is safe,

---

785 Turned towards *del to* Fixed on *and then restored by del to* Turned towards *MS. 1836/45*
790 'And safe from all our sorrows.' With a sigh
She spake, yet, I believe, not unsustained
By faith in glory that shall far transcend
Aught by these perishable heavens disclosed
To sight or mind. Nor less than care divine
Is divine mercy. She, who had rebelled,
Was into meekness softened and subdued;
Did, after trials not in vain prolonged,
With resignation sink into the grave; *1845– ; so MS. 1836/45 fair copy entered vertically in margins of previous two pages (continuing through l. 793) but no quots and* She spake the words, yet inwardly sustained   heavens] Heavens   care] love   She, . . . rebelled,] She . . . rebelled   Was . . . subdued; *om*   grave;] grave   *MS. 1836/45 also has a series of complex drafts on which the fair copy, above, is based: in printed l. 790* She is safe, *del to* In the grave *del*
Till She who had at first [? ? ?]
Full oft, rebelled against [? ? ?]
Submitted *pencil partially eras in right margin*
She who had at first
In divine mercy. Her trial was prolong
~~Till She who~~ had through life full oft rebell
rebelled against
As now against the chastisement of [?heaven]
Submitted *pencil at top of page*
~~sorrows. With that sigh~~
Mingled, I question not sustaining faith
~~In revelations, for the immortal Soul~~
~~Guides unto glory that shall far transcend~~ *page foot, del by vertical lines*
~~Aught by these perishable heavens disclosed~~
~~To sight or mind. No less than love divine~~
~~Is divine mercy. She who had rebell'd,~~
~~Submitted, she who had been proud, became~~ *top of facing page del by vertical lines overwriting pencil draft*
[?through]
Full oft rebelled against heavens chastise *pencil draft at top of facing page continued in ink at bottom of facing page*
~~Meek; After trials not in vain prolonged~~
~~With resignation sank into the grave~~
~~And her uncharitable &~~ *del by vertical lines*
an
And safe from all our sorrows. If a wish
[?]
~~Repented~~ the sigh which she spake, that wish
~~After a trial not prolonged in vain~~
Is in the quiet of the grave fulfilled
And her uncharitable *right margin of facing page*
who [?had at first]
Full oft ~~rebelled~~ against Heavens chastisement
Submitted
Did [? ? ?] [?I doubt not]
she who had at first
Rebelled against the chastisement of heaven *pencil in right margin of facing page*
Say more, with exemplary [?thankfulness] *pencil in left margin of facing page*
[?at]
With th{is sigh[?s]
Mingled, I can not doubt a consciousness
Of [?] for guidance i[?s] the way that leads
To heaven, she knew, by her redeemer [?]
And may ye not sustain a [?trust] that She
Is safe, and her uncharatable acts
And [?] unkindnesses are all forgiven *half title*

[775] And her uncharitable acts, I trust,
And harsh unkindnesses, are all forgiven;
Though, in this Vale, remembered with deep awe!"

THE Vicar paused; and tow'rds a seat advanced,
A long stone-seat, framed in the Church-yard wall;
[780] Part under shady sycamore, and part
[781] Offering a place of rest in pleasant sunshine,
Even as may suit the comers old or young
[782] Who seek the House of worship, while the Bells
Yet ring with all their voices, or before
[784] The last hath ceased its solitary knoll.
To this commodious resting-place he led;
[785] Where, by his side, we all sate down; and there
His office, uninvited, he resumed.

"As, on a sunny bank, a tender Lamb
Lurks in safe shelter from the winds of March,
Screened by its Parent, so that little mound
[790] Lies guarded by its neighbour; the small heap
Speaks for itself;—an Infant there doth rest,
The sheltering Hillock is the Mother's grave.
If mild discourse, and manners that conferred
A natural dignity on humblest rank;
[795] If gladsome spirits, and benignant looks,
That for a face not beautiful did more
Than beauty for the fairest face can do;
And if religious tenderness of heart,
Grieving for sin, and penitential tears
[800] Shed when the clouds had gathered and distained
The spotless ether of a maiden life;
If these may make a hallowed spot of earth
More holy in the sight of God or Man;
Then, on that mold, a sanctity shall brood,
[805] Till the stars sicken at the day of doom.

Ah! what a warning for a thoughtless Man,
Could field or grove, or any spot of earth,

---

791 And *and* I trust *in printed text del to* The hope that *del to* She hath found rest—& no one will reprove *MS. 1836/45; see l. 790, above*
793 *illeg word, del, below* deep *MS. 1836/45*
795 framed] fixed *MS. 1814/27–*
796 under shady] shaded by cool *MS. 1814/27–*
797 Offering a sunny resting-place to them *1827–*
798 *del MS. 1814/27, om 1827–*
802–803 Under the shade we all sate down; and there *MS. 1814/27– but* Under] Beneath *1836–* Beneath *in printed text alt* Under *del MS. 1836/45*
822 on] o'er *MS. 1814/27–*
825 or any] could any *1832–*

Shew to his eye an image of the pangs
Which it hath witnessed, render back an echo
[810] Of the sad steps by which it hath been trod!
There, by her innocent Baby's precious grave,
Yea, doubtless, on the turf that roofs her own,
The Mother oft was seen to stand, or kneel
In the broad day, a weeping Magdalene.
[815] Now she is not; the swelling turf reports
Of the fresh shower, but of poor Ellen's tears
Is silent; nor is any vestige left
Upon the pathway, of her mournful tread;
Nor of that pace with which she once had moved
[820] In virgin fearlessness, a step that seemed
Caught from the pressure of elastic turf
Upon the mountains wet with morning dew,
In the prime hour of sweetest scents and airs.
—Serious and thoughtful was her mind; and yet,
[825] By reconcilement exquisite and rare,
The form, port, motions of this Cottage-girl
Were such as might have quickened and inspired
A Titian's hand, addressed to picture forth
Oread or Dryad glancing through the shade
[830] When first the Hunter's startling horn is heard
Upon the golden hills. A spreading Elm
[832] Stands in our Valley, called THE JOYFUL TREE;
An Elm distinguished by that festive name,
[833] From dateless usage which our Peasants hold
Of giving welcome to the first of May
[835] By dances round its trunk.—And if the sky
Permit, like honours, dance and song, are paid
To the Twelfth Night; beneath the frosty Stars
Or the clear Moon. The Queen of these gay sports,
If not in beauty yet in sprightly air,
[840] Was hapless Ellen.—No one touched the ground

---

830 doubtless, on the] on the very *pencil MS. 1836/45* And on the very turf . . . *1845–*
831 *MS. 1836/45 has several pencil alts:* at prayer *right margin, and*
the Mother
Was often seen to stand, or ~~there to~~ kneel at prayer *at top of page; and as above at top of facing page but* stan, or kneel at pray *and as above in right margin of facing page but* The Mother . . . stand or [?there]
833 the swelling turf] now doth roof *pencil alt MS. 1836/45*
836–837 Of the path worn by mournful tread of Her / Who, at her heart's light bidding, once had moved *1827– but* Her] her *MS. 1832/36–; MS. 1814/27 as 1827 in pencil, eras, at page foot but* hearts light bidding *MS. 1814/27 also has several drafts:* [?whereof] [?] *pencil, eras, in left margin; pencil, eras, in right margin illeg except for* [?her mournful tread]*; and* [?Heavy & slow] *pencil, eras, at top of page*
838 a] with *1827–*
840 wet] gemm'd *MS. 1814/27* gemmed *1827–*
848 When first . . . startling] What time . . . earliest *MS. 1814/27–*
849 Upon . . . spreading] Startling . . . wide spread *1827– but* wide-spread *1836–*
850 called] nam'd *MS. 1814/27* named *1827–*
851 *del MS. 1814/27, om 1827–*

So deftly, and the nicest Maiden's locks
Less gracefully were braided;—but this praise,
Methinks, would better suit another place.

She loved,—and fondly deemed herself beloved.
The road is dim, the current unperceived,
The weakness painful and most pitiful,
By which a virtuous Woman, in pure youth,
May be delivered to distress and shame.
Such fate was hers.—The last time Ellen danced,
Among her Equals, round The Joyful Tree,
She bore a secret burthen; and full soon
Was left to tremble for a breaking vow,—
Then, to bewail a sternly-broken vow,
Alone, within her widowed Mother's house.
It was the season sweet, of budding leaves,
Of days advancing tow'rds their utmost length,
And small birds singing to their happy mates.
Wild is the music of the autumnal wind
Among the faded woods; but these blithe notes
Strike the deserted to the heart;—I speak
Of what I know, and what we feel within.
—Beside the Cottage in which Ellen dwelt
Stands a tall ash-tree; to whose topmost twig
A Thrush resorts, and annually chaunts,
At morn and evening, from that naked perch,
While all the undergrove is thick with leaves,
A time-beguiling ditty, for delight
Of his fond partner, silent in the nest.
—"Ah why," said Ellen, sighing to herself,
"Why do not words, and kiss, and solemn pledge;
"And nature that is kind in Woman's breast,
"And reason that in Man is wise and good,
"And fear of him who is a righteous Judge,
"Why do not these prevail for human life,
"To keep two Hearts together, that began
"Their spring-time with one love, and that have need
"Of mutual pity and forgiveness, sweet
"To grant, or be received, while that poor Bird,
"—O come and hear him! Thou who hast to me
"Been faithless, hear him, though a lowly Creature,
"One of God's simple children that yet know not
"The universal Parent, how he sings
"As if he wished, the firmament of Heaven

874 It was the season of unfolding leaves, *1836–*
876–878 And small birds singing happily to mates
Happy as they. With spirit-saddening power
Winds pipe through fading woods; but those blithe notes *1836–*

"Should listen, and give back to him the voice
[885] "Of his triumphant constancy and love;
"The proclamation that he makes, how far
"His darkness doth transcend our fickle light!"

Such was the tender passage, not by me
Repeated without loss of simple phrase,
[890] Which I perused, even as the words had been
Committed by forsaken Ellen's hand
To the blank margin of a Valentine,
Bedropped with tears. 'Twill please you to be told
That, studiously withdrawing from the eye
[895] Of all companionship, the Sufferer yet
In lonely reading found a meek resource.
[897] How thankful for the warmth of summer days,
And their long twilight!—friendly to that stealth
[898] With which she slipped into the Cottage-barn,
And found a secret oratory there;
[900/901] Or, in the garden, pored upon her book
By the last lingering help of open sky,
Till the dark night dismissed her to her bed.
Thus did a waking Fancy sometimes lose
[905] The unconquerable pang of despised love.

A kindlier passion opened on her soul
When that poor Child was born. Upon its face
She looked as on a pure and spotless gift
Of unexpected promise, where a grief
[910] Or dread was all that had been thought of—joy
Far sweeter than bewildered Traveller feels
Upon a perilous waste, where all night long
Through darkness he hath toiled and fearful storm,
When he beholds the first pale speck serene
[915] Of day-spring—in the gloomy east revealed,
And greets it with thanksgiving. "Till this hour,"
Thus in her Mother's hearing Ellen spake,
"There was a stony region in my heart;
"But he, at whose command the parched rock
[920] "Was smitten, and poured forth a quenching stream,

---

917 *del MS. 1814/27, om 1827–*
918 With which she slipped] When she could slip *MS. 1814/27–*
919 found] find *MS. 1814/27–*
920 Or, in the garden, under friendly veil / Of their long twilight, pore upon her book *1827– but* their] the *pencil alt MS. 1836/45; MS. 1814/27 as 1827 but* twilight pore
922 Till the] Until *1845–*
925 opened] kindled *alt in ink and pencil MS. 1836/45*
927 looked] gazed *ink and pencil MS. 1836/45, 1845–*
930 sweeter] livelier *MS. 1814/27–*
931 Upon . . . where] Amid . . . that *MS. 1814/27–*
932 Hath harassed him—toiling through fearful storm, *1827– but* him—] him, *MS. 1832/36* him *1836– ; MS. 1814/27 as 1827 but* harrass'd him toiling thro'

"Hath softened that obduracy, and made
"Unlooked-for gladness in the desart place,
"To save the perishing; and, henceforth, I look
"Upon the light with cheerfulness, for thee
"My Infant; and for that good Mother dear,
"Who bore me,—and hath prayed for me in vain;—
"Yet not in vain, it shall not be in vain."
She spake, nor was the assurance unfulfilled,
And if heart-rending thoughts would oft return
They stayed not long.—The blameless Infant grew;
The Child whom Ellen and her Mother loved
They soon were proud of; tended it and nursed,
A soothing comforter, although forlorn;
Like a poor singing-bird from distant lands;
Or a choice shrub, which he, who passes by
With vacant mind, not seldom may observe
Fair-flowering in a thinly-peopled house,
Whose window, somewhat sadly, it adorns.
—Through four months' space the Infant drew its food
From the maternal breast; then scruples rose;
Thoughts, which the rich are free from, came and crossed
The sweet affection. She no more could bear
By her offence to lay a twofold weight
On a kind parent willing to forget
Their slender means, so, to that parent's care
Trusting her child, she left their common home,
And with contented spirit undertook
A Foster-Mother's office.
'Tis, perchance,
Unknown to you that in these simple Vales
The natural feeling of equality
Is by domestic service unimpaired;
Yet, though such service be, with us, removed
From sense of degradation, not the less
The ungentle mind can easily find means
To impose severe restraints and laws unjust:
Which hapless Ellen now was doomed to feel.

In selfish blindness, for I will not say
In naked and deliberate cruelty,

---

942 look] breathe *MS. 1836/45, 1845–*
943 'The air with cheerful spirit, for thy sake *1845– ; so MS. 1836/45 but no punct and* for thy sweet sake *pencil at top of facing page*
961 sweet] fond *1836–*
966 And undertook with dutiful content *alt MS. 1836/45, adopted 1845–*
976–977 —For (blinded by an over-anxious dread
Of such excitement and divided thought
As with her office would but ill accord) *no para 1827– but* —For] For *MS. 1832/36– ; MS. 1814/27 as 1827 but* —For blinded . . . dread [?~~or~~] / Of . . . & divided thoughts . . . ill accord *MS. 1814/27 also has at page foot two lines of pencil, eras, probably related to this passage*

[960] The Pair, whose Infant she was bound to nurse,
[961] Forbad her all communion with her own.
They argued that such meeting would disturb
The Mother's mind, distract her thoughts, and thus
Unfit her for her duty—in which dread,
[962] Week after week, the mandate was enforced.
—So near!—yet not allowed, upon that sight
To fix her eyes—alas! 'twas hard to bear!
[965] But worse affliction must be borne—far worse;
For 'tis Heaven's will—that, after a disease
Begun and ended within three days' space,
Her Child should die; as Ellen now exclaimed,
Her own—deserted Child!—Once, only once,
[970] She saw it in that mortal malady:
And, on the burial day, could scarcely gain
Permission to attend its obsequies.
She reached the house—last of the funeral train;
And some One, as she entered, having chanced
[975] To urge unthinkingly their prompt departure,
"Nay," said she, with commanding look, a spirit
Of anger never seen in her before,
"Nay ye must wait my time!" and down she sate,
And by the unclosed coffin kept her seat
[980] Weeping and looking, looking on and weeping
Upon the last sweet slumber of her Child,
Until at length her soul was satisfied.

You see the Infant's Grave;—and to this Spot,
The Mother, oft as she was sent abroad
[985] And whatsoe'er the errand, urged her steps:
Hither she came; and here she stood, or knelt
In the broad day—a rueful Magdalene!
So call her; for not only she bewailed
A Mother's loss, but mourned in bitterness
[990] Her own transgression; Penitent sincere
As ever raised to Heaven a streaming eye.
—At length the Parents of the Foster-child
Noting that in despite of their commands
She still renewed, and could not but renew,
[995] Those visitations, ceased to send her forth;
Or, to the garden's narrow bounds, confined.
I failed not to remind them that they erred:
For holy Nature might not thus be crossed,
Thus wronged in woman's breast: in vain I pleaded:

980–982 *del MS. 1814/27, om 1827–*
983 was] they *MS. 1814/27–*
999 "Nay . . . time!"] so *pencil MS. 1814/27, 1820E* "Nay . . . time! *1814* 'Nay, . . . time!' *1827–*
1006 And whatsoe'er the errand,] On whatsoever errand, *1836–*
1007 Hither she came; here stood, and sometimes knelt *1832–*

But the green stalk of Ellen's life was snapped
And the flower drooped; as every eye could see,
It hung its head in mortal languishment.
—Aided by this appearance I at length
Prevailed; and, from those bonds released, she went
Home to her mother's house. The Youth was fled;
The rash Betrayer could not face the shame
Or sorrow which his senseless guilt had caused;
And little would his presence, or proof given
Of a relenting soul, have now availed;
For, like a shadow, he was passed away
From Ellen's thoughts; had perished to her mind
For all concerns of fear, or hope, or love,
Save only those which to their common shame,
And to his moral being appertained:
Hope from that quarter would, I know, have brought
A heavenly comfort; there she recognised
An unrelaxing bond, a mutual need;
There, and, as seemed, there only.—She had raised,
Her fond maternal Heart had built a Nest
In blindness all too near the river's edge;
That Work a summer flood with hasty swell
Had swept away; and now her Spirit longed
For its last flight to Heaven's security.
—The bodily frame was wasted day by day;
Meanwhile, relinquishing all other cares,
Her mind she strictly tutored to find peace
And pleasure in endurance. Much she thought,
And much she read; and brooded feelingly
Upon her own unworthiness.—To me,
As to a spiritual comforter and friend,
Her heart she opened; and no pains were spared
To mitigate, as gently as I could,
The sting of self-reproach, with healing words.
—Meek Saint! through patience glorified on earth!
In whom, as by her lonely hearth she sate,

1039 raised] built *MS. 1814/27–*

1045 —The bodily frame wasted from day to day; *MS. 1836/45, 1845– but MS. 1836/45 ink over pencil alt* wasted more day to day

1048–1051 *lines from* Much *del in MS. 1836/45 but restored by* stet *MS. 1836/45 drafts:* Much did she [?recall] *pencil at top of page*

Unto me
~~Her spiritual Comforter and friend, her heart~~
her heart
She open'd, and no needful pains were spar *page foot*

1049 she brood *pencil alt MS. 1836/45*

1050 To] Unto *del MS. 1836/45*

1051 [?speak] *interlined, then del MS. 1836/45* her heart *alt in right margin MS. 1836/45; see l. 1052, below, and ll. 1048–1051, above*

1052 She opened; and no needful pains were spared *del, then restored by* stet *MS. 1836/45; see ll. 1048–1051, above*

The ghastly face of cold decay put on
A sun-like beauty, and appeared divine!
May I not mention—that, within these walls,
In due observance of her pious wish,
The Congregation joined with me in prayer
For her Soul's good? Nor was that office vain.
—Much did she suffer: but, if any Friend,
Beholding her condition, at the sight
Gave way to words of pity or complaint,
She stilled them with a prompt reproof, and said,
"He who afflicts me knows what I can bear;
"And, when I fail, and can endure no more,
"Will mercifully take me to himself."
So, through the cloud of death, her Spirit passed
Into that pure and unknown world of love,
Where injury cannot come:—and here is laid
The mortal Body by her Infant's side."

The Vicar ceased; and downcast looks made known
That Each had listened with his inmost heart.
For me, the emotion scarcely was less strong
Or less benign than that which I had felt
When, seated near my venerable Friend,
Beneath those shady elms, from him I heard
The story that retraced the slow decline
Of Margaret sinking on the lonely Heath,
With the neglected House in which she dwelt.
—I noted that the Solitary's cheek
Confessed the power of nature.—Pleased though sad,
More pleased than sad, the grey-haired Wanderer sate;
Thanks to his pure imaginative soul
Capacious and serene, his blameless life,
His knowledge, wisdom, love of truth, and love
Of human kind! He was it who first broke
The pensive silence, saying, "Blest are they
Whose sorrow rather is to suffer wrong
Than to do wrong, although themselves have erred.
This Tale gives proof that Heaven most gently deals
With such, in their affliction.—Ellen's fate,
Her tender spirit, and her contrite heart,
Call to my mind dark hints which I have heard
Of One who died within this Vale, by doom
Heavier, as his offence was heavier far.
Where, Sir, I pray you, where are laid the bones

1059 these] those *1827–*
1079 Beneath] Under *pencil MS. 1836/45, 1845–*
1082 in . . . dwelt] to . . . clung *MS. 1814/27–*
1092 although] albeit *MS. 1832/36–*

Of Wilfred Armathwaite?"—The Vicar answered,
[1080] "In that green nook, close by the Church-yard wall,
Beneath yon hawthorn, planted by myself
In memory and for warning, and in sign
Of sweetness where dire anguish had been known,
Of reconcilement after deep offence,
[1085] There doth he lie.—In this his native Vale
He owned and tilled a little plot of land;
Here, with his Consort and his Children, saw
Days—that were seldom crossed by petty strife,
Years—safe from large misfortune; and maintained
That course which minds, of insight not too keen,
Might look on with entire complacency.
Yet, in himself and near him, there were faults
At work to undermine his happy state
By sure, though tardy progress. Active, prompt,
And lively was the Housewife; in the Vale
None more industrious; but her industry,
Ill-judged, full oft, and specious, tended more
To splendid neatness; to a shewy, trim,
And overlaboured purity of house;
Than to substantial thrift. He, on his part,
Generous and easy-minded, was not free
From carelessness; and thus, in lapse of time,
These joint infirmities induced decay
Of worldly substance; and distress of mind,
That to a thoughtful Man was hard to shun,
And which he could not cure. A blooming Girl
Served in the house, a Favourite that had grown
Beneath his eye, encouraged by his care.
Poor now in tranquil pleasure he gave way
To thoughts of troubled pleasure; he became
A lawless Suitor to the Maid; and she
Yielded unworthily.—Unhappy Man!
[1094] That which he had been weak enough to do
[1095] Was misery in remembrance; he was stung,
Stung by his inward thoughts, and by the smiles

1106–1133 There doth he rest.—No theme his fate supplies
For the smooth glozings of the indulgent world;
Nor need the windings of his devious course
Be here retraced;—enough that, by mishap
And venial error, robbed of competence,
And her obsequious shadow, peace of mind,
He craved a substitute in troubled joy;
Against his conscience rose in arms, and, braving
Divine displeasure, broke the marriage-vow. *1827– but* rest.—] rest. *MS. 1832/36– ; MS. 1814/27 pencil as 1827, overwriting mostly illeg pencil, eras, of first draft entered interlinearly with another illeg pencil draft, eras, at page foot of the last page of rev text, but* There doth he lie.— . . . world . . . retrac'd . . . that by . . . error robb'd of competence . . . joy . . . arms & braving . . . displeasure broke . . . marriage vow *MS. 1814/27 drafts:* Is not *pencil, eras, left margin of l. 1107* [?Shall ye] be led *in pencil interlined at ll. 1129/1130, then del and eras*

Of Wife and Children stung to agony.
Wretched at home he gained no peace abroad;
Ranged though the mountains, slept upon the earth,
Asked comfort of the open air, and found
No quiet in the darkness of the night,
No pleasure in the beauty of the day.
His flock he slighted: his paternal fields
Became a clog to him, whose spirit wished
To fly, but whither? And this gracious Church,
That wears a look so full of peace, and hope,
And love, benignant Mother of the Vale,
How fair amid her brood of Cottages!
She was to him a sickness and reproach.
Much to the last remained unknown; but this
Is sure, that through remorse and grief he died;
Though pitied among Men, absolved by God,
He could not find forgiveness in himself;
Nor could endure the weight of his own shame.

Here rests a Mother. But from her I turn
And from her Grave.—Behold—upon that Ridge,
Which, stretching boldly from the mountain side,
Carries into the centre of the Vale
Its rocks and woods—the Cottage where she dwelt;
And where yet dwells her faithful Partner, left
(Full eight years past) the solitary prop
Of many helpless Children. I begin
With words which might be prelude to a Tale
Of sorrow and dejection; but I feel
No sadness, when I think of what mine eyes
See daily in that happy Family.
—Bright Garland form they for the pensive brow
Of their undrooping Father's widowhood,
Those six fair Daughters, budding yet—not one,
Not one of all the band, a full blown Flower!
Depressed, and desolate of soul, as once
That Father was, and filled with anxious fear,
Now by experience taught, he stands assured,
That God, who takes away, yet takes not half
Of what he seems to take; or gives it back,
Not to our prayer, but far beyond our prayer;
He gives it—the boon produce of a soil
Which our endeavours have refused to till,
And Hope hath never watered. The Abode,
Whose grateful Owner can attest these truths,
Even were the object nearer to our sight

1157 Which] That *MS. 1814/27–*
1163 which] that *MS. 1814/27–*

Would seem in no distinction to surpass
The rudest habitations. Ye might think
That it had sprung self-raised from earth, or grown
Out of the living rock, to be adorned
By Nature only; but, if thither led,
Ye would discover, then, a studious work
Of many fancies, prompting many hands.
—Brought from the woods the honeysuckle twines
Around the porch, and seems, in that trim place,
A Plant no longer wild; the cultured rose
There blossoms, strong in health, and will be soon
Roof-high; the wild pink crowns the garden wall,
And with the flowers are intermingled stones
Sparry and bright, the scatterings of the hills.
These ornaments, that fade not with the year,
A hardy Girl continues to provide;
Who, mounting fearlessly the rocky heights,
Her Father's prompt Attendant, does for him
All that a Boy could do; but with delight
More keen and prouder daring: yet hath she,
Within the garden, like the rest, a bed
For her own flowers and favourite herbs—a space,
By sacred charter, holden for her use.
—These, and whatever else the garden bears
Of fruit or flower, permission asked or not,
I freely gather; and my leisure draws
A not unfrequent pastime from the sight
Of the Bees murmuring round their sheltered hives
In that Enclosure; while the mountain rill,
That sparkling thrids the rocks, attunes his voice
To the pure course of human life, which there
Flows on in solitude from year to year.
—But at the closing-in of night, then most
This Dwelling charms me. Covered by the gloom,
Then, in my walks, I oftentimes stop short,
(Who could refrain?) and feed by stealth my sight
With prospect of the Company within,

1195 the scatterings] rough scatterings *MS. 1814/27–*
1208 sight] hum *MS. 1836/45, 1845–*
1209–1210 Of bees around their range of sheltered hives
Busy in that enclosure; while the rill, *1845– ; so MS. 1836/45 interlined, with two drafts:*
Of bees around their range of sheltered hive
Busy
~~Whurring~~ in that Enclosure, while *pencil at top of page*
from the hum
Of bees around their range of sheltered hives
Busy in that enclosure *pencil at page foot*
1213–1216 Flows on in solitude. But, when the gloom
Of night is falling round my steps, then most
This Dwelling charms me; often, I stop short; *1827– but* often, . . . short;] often . . . short, *1832–* often I] often do I *MS. 1836/45; MS. 1814/27 as 1827 but* solitude But when . . . steps then

Laid open through the blazing window:—there
I see the eldest Daughter at her wheel
Spinning amain, as if to overtake
The never-halting time; or, in her turn,
Teaching some Novice of the Sisterhood
That skill in this, or other household work;
Which, from her Father's honoured hand, herself
While she was yet a little One, had learned.
—Mild Man! he is not gay, but they are gay;
And the whole House seems filled with gaiety.
—Thrice happy, then, the Mother may be deemed,
The Wife, who rests beneath that turf, from which
I turned, that ye in mind might witness where,
And how her Spirit yet survives on Earth.

The next three Ridges—those upon the left—
By close connexion with our present thoughts
Tempt me to add, in praise of humble worth,
Their brief and unobtrusive history.
—One Hillock, ye may note, is small and low,
Sunk almost to a level with the plain
By weight of time; the Others, undepressed,
Are bold and swelling. There a Husband sleeps,
Deposited, in pious confidence
Of glorious resurrection with the just,
Near the loved Partner of his early days;
And, in the bosom of that family mold,
A second Wife is gathered to his side;
The approved Assistant of an arduous course
From his mid noon of manhood to old age!
He also of his Mate deprived, was left
Alone—'mid many Children; One a Babe
Orphaned as soon as born. Alas! 'tis not
In course of nature that a Father's wing
Should warm these Little-ones; and can he *feed?*
That was a thought of agony more keen.
For, hand in hand with Death, by strange mishap
And chance-encounter on their diverse road,
The ghastlier shape of Poverty had entered
Into that House, unfeared and unforeseen.
He had stepped forth, in time of urgent need,
The generous Surety of a Friend: and now
The widowed Father found that all his rights
In his paternal fields were undermined.
Landless he was and pennyless.—The dews
Of night and morn that wet the mountain sides,

1230 The Wife, from whose consolatory grave *1832–*
1233–1308 *del indicated by horizontal pencil mark in MS. 1814/27, om 1827–*

The bright stars twinkling on their dusky tops,
Were conscious of the pain that drove him forth
From his own door, he knew not when—to range
He knew not where; distracted was his brain,
His heart was cloven; and full oft he prayed,
In blind despair, that God would take them all.
—But suddenly, as if in one kind moment
To encourage and reprove, a gleam of light
Broke from the very bosom of that cloud
Which darkened the whole prospect of his days.
For He, who now possessed the joyless right
To force the Bondsman from his house and lands,
In pity, and by admiration urged
Of his unmurmuring and considerate mind
Meekly submissive to the law's decree,
Lightened the penalty with liberal hand.
—The desolate Father raised his head, and looked
On the wide world in hope. Within these walls,
In course of time was solemnized the vow
Whereby a virtuous Woman, of grave years
And of prudential habits, undertook
The sacred office of a wife to him,
Of Mother to his helpless family.
—Nor did she fail, in nothing did she fail,
Through various exercise of twice ten years,
Save in some partial fondness for that Child
Which at the birth she had received, the Babe
Whose heart had known no Mother but herself.
—By mutual efforts; by united hopes;
By daily-growing help of boy and girl,
Trained early to participate that zeal
Of industry, which runs before the day
And lingers after it; by strong restraint
Of an economy which did not check
The heart's more generous motions tow'rds themselves
Or to their neighbours; and by trust in God;
This Pair insensibly subdued the fears
And troubles that beset their life: and thus
Did the good Father and his second Mate
Redeem at length their plot of smiling fields.
These, at this day, the eldest Son retains:
The younger Offspring, through the busy world,
Have all been scattered wide, by various fates;
But each departed from the native Vale,
In beauty flourishing, and moral worth."

END OF THE SIXTH BOOK.

BOOK THE SEVENTH.

THE CHURCH-YARD AMONG THE MOUNTAINS
CONTINUED.

WHILE thus from theme to theme the Historian passed,
The words he uttered, and the scene that lay
Before our eyes, awakened in my mind
Vivid remembrance of those long-past hours;
When, in the hollow of some shadowy Vale,
(What time the splendour of the setting sun
Lay beautiful on Snowdon's craggy top,
On Cader Idris, or huge Penmanmaur)
A wandering Youth, I listened with delight
To pastoral melody or warlike air,
Drawn from the chords of the ancient British harp
By some accomplished Master; while he sate
Amid the quiet of the green recess,
And there did inexhaustibly dispense
An interchange of soft or solemn tunes
Tender or blithe; now, as the varying mood
Of his own spirit urged,—now, as a voice
From Youth or Maiden, or some honoured Chief
Of his compatriot villagers (that hung
Around him, drinking in the empassioned notes
Of the time-hallowed minstrelsy) required
For their heart's ease or pleasure. Strains of power
Were they, to seize and occupy the sense;
But to a higher mark than song can reach
Rose this pure eloquence. And, when the stream
Which overflowed the soul was passed away,
A consciousness remained that it had left,
Deposited upon the silent shore
Of memory, images and precious thoughts;
That shall not die, and cannot be destroyed.

"These grassy heaps lie amicably close,"
Said I, "like surges heaving in the wind
Upon the surface of a mountain pool;
—Whence comes it, then, that yonder we behold
Five graves, and only five, that lie apart,

---

heading CHURCH-YARD] so *1820E–* CHURCHYARD *1814*
7 craggy top,] sovereign brow, *MS. 1814/27–*
33 Upon] Along *MS. 1832/36–*
35–37 Five graves, and only five, that rise together / Unsociably sequestered, and encroaching *1827– ; so MS. 1814/27 but* sequestered and

[36] Unsociable company and sad;
And, furthermore, appearing to encroach
[37] On the smooth play-ground of the Village-school?"

The Vicar answered. "No disdainful pride
In them who rest beneath, nor any course
[40] Of strange or tragic accident, hath helped
To place those Hillocks in that lonely guise.
—Once more look forth, and follow with your eyes
The length of road which from yon mountain's base
Through bare enclosures stretches, 'till its line
[45] Is lost among a little tuft of trees,—
Then, reappearing in a moment, quits
The cultured fields,—and up the heathy waste
Mounts, as you see, in mazes serpentine,
Towards an easy outlet of the Vale.
[50] —That little shady spot, that sylvan tuft,
By which the road is hidden, also hides
A Cottage from our view,—though I discern,
(Ye scarcely can) amid its sheltering trees,
The smokeless chimney-top.—All unembowered
[55] And naked stood that lowly Parsonage
(For such in truth it is, and appertains
To a small Chapel in the Vale beyond)
When hither came its last Inhabitant.

Rough and forbidding were the choicest roads
[60] By which our Northern wilds could then be crossed;
And into most of these secluded Vales
Was no access for wain, heavy or light.
So, at his Dwelling-place the Priest arrived
With store of household goods, in panniers slung
[65] On sturdy horses graced with jingling bells,
And on the back of more ignoble beast;
That, with like burthen of effects most prized
Or easiest carried, closed the motley train.
Young was I then, a school-boy of eight years;
[70] But still, methinks, I see them as they passed
In order, drawing tow'rds their wished-for home.
—Rocked by the motion of a trusty Ass
Two ruddy Children hung, a well-poised freight,
Each in his basket nodding drowsily;

---

43 eyes] sight *MS. 1814/27–*
44 which] that *1827–*
46 among] within *MS. 1814/27–*
50 Towards] Led towards *MS. 1832/36–*
61 then be crossed] in those days *MS. 1836/45*
62 Be crossed, and into this *interlined as intended replacement for* And . . . these *MS. 1836/45* Vales] vale *MS. 1836/45*

Their bonnets, I remember, wreathed with flowers
Which told that 'twas the pleasant month of June;
And, close behind, the comely Matron rode,
A Woman of soft speech and gracious smile,
And with a Lady's mien.—From far they came,
Even from Northumbrian hills; yet theirs had been
A merry journey—rich in pastime—cheered
By music, prank, and laughter-stirring jest;
And freak put on, and arch word dropped—to swell
The cloud of fancy and uncouth surmise
That gathered round the slowly-moving train.
—"Whence do they come? and with what errand charged?
"Belong they to the fortune-telling Tribe
"Who pitch their Tents beneath the green-wood Tree?
"Or are they Strollers, furnished to enact
"Fair Rosamond, and the Children of the Wood,
"And, by that whiskered Tabby's aid, set forth
"The lucky venture of sage Whittington,
"When the next Village hears the Show announced
"By blast of trumpet?" Plenteous was the growth
Of such conjectures, overheard; or seen
On many a staring countenance pourtrayed
Of Boor or Burgher, as they marched along.
And more than once their steadiness of face
Was put to proof, and exercise supplied
To their inventive humour, by stern looks,
And questions in authoritative tone,
From some staid Guardian of the public peace,
Checking the sober steed on which he rode,
In his suspicious wisdom: oftener still,
By notice indirect or blunt demand
From Traveller halting in his own despite,
A simple curiosity to ease.
Of which adventures, that beguiled and cheered
Their grave migration, the good Pair would tell,
With undiminished glee, in hoary age.

A Priest he was by function; but his course
From his youth up, and high as manhood's noon,
(The hour of life to which he then was brought)
Had been irregular; I might say, wild:
By books unsteadied, by his pastoral care
Too little checked. An active, ardent mind;
A fancy pregnant with resource and scheme
To cheat the sadness of a rainy day:

77 Which told that 'twas] Gay offering from *MS. 1814/27* that 'twas] it was *1827–*
89 beneath] under *MS. 1832/36–*
90 'Or Strollers are they, furnished to enact *MS. 1832/36–*

Hands apt for all ingenious arts and games;
[120] A generous spirit, and a body strong
To cope with stoutest Champions of the bowl;
Had earned for him sure welcome, and the rights
Of a prized Visitant, in the jolly hall
Of country Squire; or at the statelier board
[125] Of Duke or Earl, from scenes of courtly pomp
Withdrawn,—to while away the summer hours
In condescension among rural guests.

With these high Comrades he had revelled long,
Had frolicked many a year; a simple Clerk
[130] By hopes of coming patronage beguiled
And vexed, until the weary heart grew sick.
[132] And so, abandoning each higher aim
And all his shewy Friends, at length he turned
[133] For a life's stay, though slender yet assured,
To this remote and humble Chapelry;
[135] Which had been offered to his doubtful choice
By an unthought of Patron. Bleak and bare
They found the Cottage, their allotted home:
Naked without and rude within; a spot
With which the scantily-provided Cure
[140] Not long had been endowed: and far remote
The Chapel stood, divided from that House
By an unpeopled tract of mountain waste.
[145] —Yet cause was none, whate'er regret might hang
On his own mind, to quarrel with the choice
Or the necessity that fixed him here;
Apart from old temptations, and constrained
To punctual labour in his sacred charge.
[150] See him a constant Preacher to the Poor!
And visiting, though not with saintly zeal
Yet when need was with no reluctant will,

---

130 *del in pencil MS. 1814/27* Frolicked industriously, a simple Clerk *1827–*
131 Beguiled by hopes of coming patronage *MS. 1814/27*
132–134 Till the heart sickened. So each loftier aim / Abandoning and all his showy Friends, *1827– but* So . . . Friends] So, . . . friends *1836–; MS. 1814/27 as 1827 but* sicken'd so each lofter . . . Abandoning, & all his shewy Friends
135 *del MS. 1814/27* For a life's stay (slender it was, but sure) *MS. 1832/36–*
136 He turned to this secluded Chapelry; *1827– but* Chapelry;] chapelry *MS. 1832/36* chapelry; *1836–; MS. 1814/27 as 1827 but* secluded] sequestered *pencil, eras, then* sequester'd
137 Which had been offered] Kindly presented *MS. 1814/27* Which] That *1827–*
138 an] *alt* [?some] *pencil, eras, MS. 1814/27*
141–144 With which the Cure not long had been endowed:
And far remote the chapel stood,—remote,
And, from his Dwelling unapproachable,
Save through a gap high in the hills, an opening
Shadeless and shelterless, by driving showers
Frequented, and beset with howling winds. *1836– but* Dwelling, *pencil MS. 1836/45, 1840–*

The sick in body, or distressed in mind;
And, by as salutary change, compelled,
Month after month, in that obscure Abode
To rise from timely sleep, and meet the day
With no engagement, in his thoughts, more proud
Or splendid than his garden could afford,
His fields,—or mountains by the heath-cock ranged,
Or these wild brooks; from which he now returned
Contentedly, to take a temperate meal
At his own board, where sate his gentle Mate
And three fair Children, plentifully fed
Though simply, from their little household farm;
With acceptable treat of fish or fowl
By nature yielded to his practised hand,
To help the small but certain comings-in
Of that spare Benefice. Yet not the less
Their's was a hospitable board, and their's
A charitable door.—So days and years
Passed on;—the inside of that rugged House
Was trimmed and brightened by the Matron's care,
And gradually enriched with things of price,
Which might be lacked for use or ornament.
What, though no soft and costly sofa there
Insidiously stretched out its lazy length,
And no vain mirror glittered on the walls,
Yet were the windows of the low Abode
By shutters weather-fended, which at once
Repelled the storm and deadened its loud roar.
There, snow-white curtains hung in decent folds;
Tough moss, and long-enduring mountain-plants,
That creep along the ground with sinuous trail,
Were nicely braided, and composed a work
Like Indian mats, that with appropriate grace
Lay at the threshold and the inner doors.
And a fair carpet, woven of home-spun wool,
But tinctured daintily with florid hues,
For seemliness and warmth, on festive days,
Covered the smooth blue slabs of mountain stone
With which the parlour-floor, in simplest guise

---

155 *om 1827–*
160 these] the *1827–*
161 Contented to partake the quiet meal *1827–*
162 At] Of *1827–*
165 Nor wanted timely treat of fish or fowl *1836–*
170 (Bear for my sake, with these [?minute] details *MS. 1836/45 draft at page foot, then del, possibly intended as transition for new para; see nonverbals*
177 on] upon *MS. 1836/45, 1845–*
179 which] that *MS. 1814/27*
189 festive] festal *1827–*

Of pastoral home-steads, had been long inlaid.
—These pleasing works the Housewife's skill produced:
Meanwhile, the unsedentary Master's hand
Was busier with his task, to rid, to plant,
To rear for food, for shelter, and delight;
A thriving covert! And when wishes, formed
In youth, and sanctioned by the riper mind,
Restored me to my native Valley, here
To end my days; well pleased was I to see
The once-bare Cottage, on the mountain-side,
Screened from assault of every bitter blast;
While the dark shadows of the summer leaves
Danced in the breeze, upon its mossy roof.
Time, which had thus afforded willing help
To beautify with Nature's fairest growth
This rustic Tenement, had gently shed,
Upon its Master's frame, a wintry grace;
The comeliness of unenfeebled age.
But how could I say, gently? for he still
Retained a flashing eye, a burning palm,
A stirring foot, and head which beat at nights
Upon its pillow with a thousand schemes.
Few likings had he dropped, few pleasures lost;
Generous and charitable, prompt to serve;
And still his harsher passions kept their hold,
Anger and indignation; still he loved
The sound of titled names, and talked in glee
Of long-past banquetings with high-born Friends:
Then, from those lulling fits of vain delight
Uproused by recollected injury, railed
At their false ways disdainfully,—and oft
In bitterness, and with a threatening eye
Of fire, incensed beneath its hoary brow.
—These transports, with staid looks of pure good will
And with soft smile, his Consort would reprove.
She, far behind him in the race of years,
Yet keeping her first mildness, was advanced
Far nearer, in the habit of her soul,
To that still region whither all are bound.
—Him might we liken to the setting Sun
As I have seen it, on some gusty day,
Struggling and bold, and shining from the west

---

193 —These] Those *MS. 1832/36–*
204 upon] chequering *MS. 1832/36–*
206 growth] growths *MS. 1832/36–*
212 and] a *MS. 1814/27–*
216 And] But *MS. 1836/45*
225 —These] —Those *1836–*
232 As seen not seldom on some gusty day, *MS. 1814/27–*

With an inconstant and unmellowed light.
—She was a soft attendant Cloud, that hung
[235] As if with wish to veil the restless orb;
From which it did itself imbibe a ray
Of pleasing lustre.—But no more of this;
I better love to sprinkle on the sod
Which now divides the Pair, or rather say
[240] Which still unites them, praises, like heaven's dew,
[241] Without distinction falling upon both.
—Yoke-fellows were they long and well approved
To endure and to perform.
With frugal pains,
Yet in a course of generous discipline,
Did this poor Churchman and his Consort rear
Their progeny.—Of three—sent forth to try
The paths of fortune in the open world,
One, not endowed with firmness to resist
The suit of pleasure, to his native Vale
Returned, and humbly tilled his Father's glebe.
—The youngest Daughter, too, in duty stayed
To lighten her declining Mother's care.
But, ere the bloom was passed away which health
Preserved to adorn a cheek no longer young,
Her heart, in course of nature, finding place
For new affections, to the holy state
Of wedlock they conducted her; but still
The Bride adhering to those filial cares
Dwelt with her Mate beneath her Father's roof.

[242] Our very first in eminence of years
This old Man stood, the Patriarch of the Vale!
And, to his unmolested mansion, Death
[245] Had never come, through space of forty years;
Sparing both old and young in that Abode.
Suddenly then they disappeared:—not twice
Had summer scorched the fields,—not twice had fallen,
On those high Peaks, the first autumnal snow,—
[250] Before the greedy visiting was closed
And the long-privileged House left empty—swept
As by a plague: yet no rapacious plague

---

240 Which] That, *and* That *alt in pencil MS. 1814/27* That *1827–*
241 Which] That, *and* That *alt in pencil MS. 1814/27* That *1827–*
242 distinction falling] reserve descending *MS. 1814/27–*
243–260 *del by vertical line in left margin MS. 1814/27, om 1827–; MS. 1814/27 has an early attempt at rev:*

With frugal pains,
Yet in a course of generous discipline,
Their progeny was reared.—Of three—that tried *then ll. 248–253 as 1814, rev continues:*
But, ere her bloom had fled by health preserved
To decorate a cheek no longer young, *then continues as 1814*

Had been among them; all was gentle death,
One after one, with intervals of peace.
—A happy consummation! an accord
Sweet, perfect,—to be wished for! save that here
Was something which to mortal sense might sound
Like harshness,—that the old grey-headed Sire,
The oldest, he was taken last,—survived
When the meek Partner of his age, his Son,
His Daughter, and that late and high-prized gift,
His little smiling Grandchild, were no more.

"All gone, all vanished! he deprived and bare,
"How will he face the remnant of his life?
"What will become of him?" we said, and mused
In sad conjectures, "Shall we meet him now
"Haunting with rod and line the craggy brooks?
"Or shall we overhear him, as we pass,
"Striving to entertain the lonely hours
"With music?" (for he had not ceased to touch
The harp or viol which himself had framed,
For their sweet purposes, with perfect skill.)
"What titles will he keep? will he remain
"Musician, Gardener, Builder, Mechanist,
"A Planter, and a rearer from the Seed?
"A Man of hope and forward-looking mind
"Even to the last!"—Such was he, unsubdued.
But Heaven was gracious; yet a little while,
And this Survivor, with his cheerful throng
Of open schemes, and all his inward hoard
Of unsunned griefs, too many and too keen,
Was overcome by unexpected sleep,
In one blest moment. Like a shadow thrown
Softly and lightly from a passing cloud,
Death fell upon him, while reclined he lay
For noon-tide solace on the summer grass,
The warm lap of his Mother Earth: and so,
Their lenient term of separation past,
That Family (whose graves you there behold)
By yet a higher privilege, once more
Were gathered to each other."
Calm of mind
And silence waited on these closing words;
Until the Wanderer (whether moved by fear
Lest in these passages of life were some
That might have touched the sick heart of his Friend

---

299 Of open projects, and his inward hoard *1836–*
313 these] those *1827–*

Too nearly, or intent to reinforce
His own firm spirit in degree depressed
By tender sorrow for our mortal state)
Thus silence broke; "Behold a thoughtless Man
From vice and premature decay preserved
By useful habits, to a fitter soil
Transplanted, ere too late.—The Hermit, lodged
In the untrodden desart, tells his beads,
With each repeating its allotted prayer,
And thus divides and thus relieves the time;
Smooth task, with his compared! whose mind could string,
Not scantily, bright minutes on the thread
Of keen domestic anguish,—and beguile
A solitude, unchosen, unprofessed;
Till gentlest death released him.—Far from us
Be the desire—too curiously to ask
How much of this is but the blind result
Of cordial spirits and vital temperament,
And what to higher powers is justly due.
But you, Sir, know that in a neighbouring Vale
A Priest abides before whose life such doubts
Fall to the ground; whose gifts of nature lie
Retired from notice, lost in attributes
Of Reason,—honourably effaced by debts
Which her poor treasure-house is content to owe,
And conquests over her dominion gained,
To which her frowardness must needs submit.
In this one Man is shown a temperance—proof
Against all trials; industry severe
And constant as the motion of the day;
Stern self-denial round him spread, with shade
That might be deemed forbidding, did not there
All generous feelings flourish and rejoice;
Forbearance, charity in deed and thought,
And resolution competent to take
Out of the bosom of simplicity
All that her holy customs recommend,
And the best ages of the world prescribe.
—Preaching, administering, in every work
Of his sublime vocation, in the walks
Of worldly intercourse 'twixt man and man,
And in his humble Dwelling he appears
A Labourer, with moral virtue girt,
With spiritual graces, like a glory, crowned."

322 In] Amid *1836–*
323 allotted] appointed *MS. 1836/45*
350 of] from *MS. 1836/45*
355 'twixt] between *1836–*

[340] "Doubt can be none," the Pastor said, "for whom
"This Portraiture is sketched.—The Great, the Good,
The Well-beloved, the Fortunate, the Wise,
These Titles Emperors and Chiefs have borne,
Honour assumed or given: and Him, the Wonderful,
[345] Our simple Shepherds, speaking from the heart,
Deservedly have styled.—From his Abode
In a dependant Chapelry, that lies
Behind yon hill, a poor and rugged wild,
Which in his soul he lovingly embraced,—
[350] And, having once espoused, would never quit;
Hither, ere long, that lowly, great, good Man
Will be conveyed. An unelaborate Stone
May cover him; and by its help, perchance,
A century shall hear his name pronounced,
[355] With images attendant on the sound;
Then, shall the slowly-gathering twilight close
In utter night; and of his course remain
No cognizable vestiges, no more
Than of this breath, which frames itself in words
[360] To speak of him, and instantly dissolves.
[363] —Noise is there not enough in doleful war—
But that the heaven-born Poet must stand forth
[365] And lend the echoes of his sacred shell,
To multiply and aggravate the din?
Pangs are there not enough in hopeless love—

---

362 borne] held *MS. 1836/45*

370–371 Into its graveyard will ere long be borne / That lowly, great, good Man. A simple stone *1845– ; MS. 1836/45 has several drafts for ll. 370–372:* Hither, ere long *l. 370 del to* Hither, its graveyard will ere long repose / A simple stone *interlined* perchance *l. 372 del to* belike *del to* belike *del then restored by* stet *interlined and* belike *entered on facing page*

~~of years~~
May cover him; and ~~a century or more~~
Hereby that records help his name pronounced *del by vertical lines bottom of facing page*
Into its graveyard will ere long be borne
G
That lowly great {good Man. A simple stone
Will cover him & by that records help *page foot*
Into its grave-yard will ere, long borne
That lowly great good Man. A simple stone
May cover him & by that record's help *top of page*

373 A century shall] Those fifty years may *MS. 1836/45*

376/377 Even in those peaceful mountain solitudes *interlined then del; repeated at page foot then also del MS. 1836/45*

378 frames] shapes *MS. 1814/27–*

379/380 The Pastor pressed by thoughts which round his theme
Still linger'd, after a brief pause, resumed; *1845– ; MS. 1836/45 has two drafts:*
~~The Pastor, pressed by thoughts that round his theme~~
~~Still lingered, after a brief pause~~
[?ing] ~~resumed~~
~~exlaimed~~ *interlined*
The Pastor pressed by thoughts that round his theme
Still lingered, after a brief pause, resumed, *top of page*

381 must stand] standing *MS. 1832/36* must *del then restored MS. 1836/45*

382 And] Must *MS. 1832/36* And *del to* Must *then* And *restored by* stet *MS. 1836/45*

And, in requited passion, all too much
Of turbulence, anxiety, and fear—
But that the Minstrel of the rural shade
Must tune his pipe, insidiously to nurse
The perturbation in the suffering breast,
And propagate its kind, where'er he may?
—Ah who (and with such rapture as befits
The hallowed theme) will rise and celebrate
The good Man's deeds and purposes; retrace
His struggles, his discomfiture deplore,
His triumphs hail, and glorify his end?
That Virtue, like the fumes and vapoury clouds
Through fancy's heat redounding in the brain,
And like the soft infections of the heart,
By charm of measured words may spread through fields
And cottages, and Piety survive
Upon the lips of Men in hall or bower;
Not for reproof, but high and warm delight,
And grave encouragement, by song inspired.
—Vain thought! but wherefore murmur or repine?
The memory of the just survives in heaven:
And, without sorrow, will this ground receive
That venerable clay. Meanwhile the best
Of what it holds confines us to degrees
In excellence less difficult to reach,
And milder worth: nor need we travel far
From those to whom our last regards were paid
For such example.
Almost at the root
Of that tall Pine, the shadow of whose bare
And slender stem, while here I sit at eve,
Oft stretches tow'rds me, like a long straight path
Traced faintly in the green sward; there, beneath
A plain blue Stone, a gentle Dalesman lies,
From whom, in early childhood, was withdrawn
The precious gift of hearing. He grew up
From year to year in loneliness of soul;
And this deep mountain Valley was to him
Soundless, with all its streams. The bird of dawn
Did never rouse this Cottager from sleep

---

390 where'er] far as *1832–*
392 hallowed theme] sacred call *MS. 1836/45*
393 deeds and purposes;] purposes and deeds; *MS. 1832/36–*
394 discomfiture] discomfitures *1836–*
395/396 Now, and for evermore? Who will do this— *1836–1843, del MS. 1836/45, om 1845–*
399 through fields] o'er field, *MS. 1814/27–*
400 And cottages,] Hamlet, and town; *MS. 1814/27–*
406 this] the *MS. 1836/45, 1845–*
408 it holds] lies here *1845– ; MS. 1836/45 drafts:* it holds *del to* [?of place] *then del to* Of what lies here confines &
414 slender] tender *1820E*

With startling summons; not for his delight
The vernal cuckoo shouted; not for him
Murmured the labouring bee. When stormy winds
Were working the broad bosom of the lake
Into a thousand thousand sparkling waves,
Rocking the trees, or driving cloud on cloud
Along the sharp edge of yon lofty crags,
The agitated scene before his eye
Was silent as a picture: evermore
Were all things silent, wheresoe'er he moved.
Yet, by the solace of his own pure thoughts
Upheld, he duteously pursued the round
Of rural labours; the steep mountain-side
Ascended with his staff and faithful dog;
The plough he guided, and the scythe he swayed;
And the ripe corn before his sickle fell
Among the jocund reapers. For himself,
All watchful and industrious as he was,
He wrought not; neither field nor flock he owned:
No wish for wealth had place within his mind;
Nor husband's love, nor father's hope or care.
Though born a younger Brother, need was none
That from the floor of his paternal home
He should depart, to plant himself anew.
And when, mature in manhood, he beheld
His Parents laid in earth, no loss ensued
Of rights to him; but he remained well pleased,
By the pure bond of independent love
An inmate of a second family,
The fellow-labourer and friend of him
To whom the small inheritance had fallen.
—Nor deem that his mild presence was a weight
That pressed upon his Brother's house, for books
Were ready comrades whom he could not tire,—
Of whose society the blameless Man
Was never satiate. Their familiar voice,
Even to old age, with unabated charm
Beguiled his leisure hours; refreshed his thoughts;
Beyond its natural elevation raised
His introverted spirit; and bestowed
Upon his life an outward dignity
Which all acknowledged. The dark winter night,
The stormy day, had each its own resource;
Song of the muses, sage historic tale,
Science severe, or word of holy Writ

466 had each] each had *MS. 1832/36–*

Announcing immortality and joy
To the assembled spirits of the just,
From imperfection and decay secure.
—Thus soothed at home, thus busy in the field,
To no perverse suspicion he gave way,
No languor, peevishness, nor vain complaint:
And they, who were about him, did not fail
In reverence, or in courtesy; they prized
His gentle manners:—and his peaceful smiles,
The gleams of his slow-varying countenance,
Were met with answering sympathy and love.

At length, when sixty years and five were told,
A slow disease insensibly consumed
The powers of nature; and a few short steps
Of friends and kindred bore him from his home
(Yon Cottage shaded by the woody crags)
To the profounder stillness of the grave.
—Nor was his funeral denied the grace
Of many tears, virtuous and thoughtful grief;
Heart-sorrow rendered sweet by gratitude.
And now that monumental Stone preserves
His name, and unambitiously relates
How long, and by what kindly outward aids,
And in what pure contentedness of mind,
The sad privation was by him endured.
—And yon tall Pine-tree, whose composing sound
Was wasted on the good Man's living ear,
Hath now its own peculiar sanctity;
And, at the touch of every wandering breeze,
Murmurs, not idly, o'er his peaceful grave.

Soul-cheering Light, most bountiful of Things!
Guide of our way, mysterious Comforter!
Whose sacred influence, spread through earth and heaven,
We all too thanklessly participate,
Thy gifts were utterly withheld from Him
Whose place of rest is near yon ivied Porch.
Yet, of the wild brooks ask if he complained;
Ask of the channelled rivers if they held
A safer, easier, more determined course.
What terror doth it strike into the mind

---

470 the just] just men *MS. 1832/36–*
471 Made perfect, and from injury secure. *MS. 1832/36–*
503ff. Thy gifts [? ? ? ? ?]
And in his eyes last hour withheld, from him
This valley [? ? ? ? ? ?]
Were his [? ? ? ?] *pencil, eras, at top and bottom of page MS. 1832/36*

To think of One, who cannot see, advancing
Towards some precipice's airy brink!
But, timely warned, *He* would have stayed his steps;
Protected, say enlightened, by his ear,
And on the very brink of vacancy
Not more endangered than a Man whose eye
Beholds the gulph beneath.—No floweret blooms
Throughout the lofty range of these rough hills,
Or in the woods, that could from him conceal
Its birth-place; none whose figure did not live
Upon his touch. The bowels of the earth
Enriched with knowledge his industrious mind;
The ocean paid him tribute from the stores
Lodged in her bosom; and, by science led,
His genius mounted to the plains of Heaven.
—Methinks I see him—how his eye-balls rolled,
Beneath his ample brow, in darkness paired,—
But each instinct with spirit; and the frame
Of the whole countenance alive with thought,
Fancy, and understanding; while the voice
Discoursed of natural and moral truth
With eloquence, and such authentic power,
That, in his presence, humbler knowledge stood
Abashed, and tender pity overawed."

"A noble—and, to unreflecting minds,
A marvellous spectacle," the Wanderer said,
"Beings like these present! But proof abounds
Upon the earth that faculties, which seem
Extinguished, do not, *therefore*, cease to be.
And to the mind among her powers of sense
This transfer is permitted,—not alone
That the bereft may win their recompence;
But for remoter purposes of love

---

509 who cannot see,] blind and alone, *1845–; MS. 1836/45 drafts:* who . . . advancing *del to* why advancing *del to* blind & alone advancing *interlined* blind and alone, advancing *del right margin*

[?~~H~~] brink,
~~Alone, but timely~~ [?w] ~~e would stopp~~
~~On unknown ground [?have]~~ *page foot*
To think of One blind & alone, advancing
On [?unknown ground] [?] [?precipices] brink *pencil, eras, top of page*
[?blind and]
[?And] [?] [unkown and trackless] [?] *pencil, eras, top of facing page*

510 Towards] Straight toward *MS. 1832/36–*
513 brink] edge *MS. 1814/27–*
517 Or] Nor *MS. 1832/36–*
529 and] or *MS. 1814/27–*
540 That the bereft their recompense may win; *1827–; so MS. 1814/27 but* recompence may win
541 love *del to* faith *then* love *restored by* stet *MS. 1836/45*

And charity; nor last nor least for this,
That to the imagination may be given
A type and shadow of an awful truth,
How, likewise, under sufferance divine,
Darkness is banished from the realms of Death,
By man's imperishable spirit, quelled.
Unto the men who see not as we see
Futurity was thought, in ancient times,
To be laid open, and they prophesied.
And know we not that from the blind have flowed
The highest, holiest raptures of the lyre;
And wisdom married to immortal verse?"

Among the humbler Worthies, at our feet
Lying insensible to human praise,
Love, or regret,—*whose* lineaments would next
Have been pourtrayed, I guess not; but it chanced
That near the quiet church-yard where we sate
A Team of horses, with a ponderous freight
Pressing behind, adown a rugged slope,
Whose sharp descent confounded their array,
Came at that moment, ringing noisily.

"Here," said the Pastor, "do we muse, and mourn
The waste of death; and lo! the giant Oak
Stretched on his bier!—that massy timber wain;
Nor fail to note the Man who guides the team."

He was a Peasant of the lowest class:
Grey locks profusely round his temples hung
In clustering curls, like ivy, which the bite
Of Winter cannot thin; the fresh air lodged
Within his cheek, as light within a cloud;
And he returned our greeting with a smile.
When he had passed, the Solitary spake,
—"A Man he seems of cheerful yesterdays
And confident to-morrows,—with a face
Not worldly-minded; for it bears too much
Of Nature's impress,—gaiety and health,

---

542 *MS. 1836/45 drafts:* charity . . . this *del to* christian charity, & furthermore *del interlined*
~~And, not the least, that here might be set forth~~
~~The type and shadow of that awful truth~~ *bottom of previous page*
Nor least for this/—that here might be perceived
A type and shadow of that awful truth *ink over illeg pencil, eras, top of page*

543 *del MS. 1836/45*

544 an *del to* that *then entire line del and* [?But] [?] *pencil, eras, MS. 1836/45*

545 How, likewise, under] wise, under *ink over illeg pencil, del to* in like sort through *then del and* How, likewise, under *restored by* stet this line *right margin and* stet *left margin MS. 1836/45*

554 [?For who] *pencil, eras, in left margin MS. 1836/45*

Freedom and hope; but keen, withal, and shrewd.
His gestures note,—and hark! his tones of voice
Are all vivacious as his mien and looks."

The Pastor answered. "You have read him well.
Year after year is added to his store
With *silent* increase: summers, winters—past,
Past or to come; yea, boldly might I say,
Ten summers and ten winters of the space
That lies beyond life's ordinary bounds,
Upon his sprightly vigor, cannot fix
The obligation of an anxious mind,
A pride in having, or a fear to lose;
Possessed like outskirts of some large Domain,
By any one more thought of than by him
Who holds the land in fee, its careless Lord!
—Yet is the Creature rational—endowed
With foresight; hears, too, every Sabbath day,
The christian promise with attentive ear,
Nor disbelieves the tidings which he hears.
Meanwhile the incense offered up by him
Is of the kind which beasts and birds present
In grove or pasture; chearfulness of soul,
From trepidation and repining free.
How many scrupulous worshippers fall down
Upon their knees, and daily homage pay
Less worthy, less religious even, than his!

This qualified respect, the Old Man's due,
Is paid without reluctance; but in truth"
(Said the good Vicar with a fond half-smile)
"I feel at times a motion of despite
Towards One, whose bold contrivances and skill,
As you have seen, bear such conspicuous part
In works of havoc; taking from these vales,
One after one, their proudest ornaments.
Full oft his doings leave me to deplore
Tall ash-tree sown by winds, by vapours nursed,
In the dry crannies of the pendant rocks;
Light birch, aloft upon the horizon's edge,
Transparent texture, framing in the east
A veil of glory for the ascending moon;
And oak whose roots by noontide dew were damped,

---

585 the] a *MS. 1814/27–*
595 *del to* Nor will, I trust, the majesty of Heaven *then orig restored by eras of rev MS. 1814/27*
596 Nor will, I trust, the Majesty of Heaven *MS. 1814/27–*
597 Meanwhile] Reject *MS. 1814/27–*
598 Is] Though *MS. 1814/27–*
616 *del MS. 1814/27, om 1827–*

And on whose forehead inaccessible
The raven lodged in safety.—Many a ship
Launched into Morecamb bay, hath owed to him
Her strong knee-timbers, and the mast that bears
[605] The loftiest of her pendants. Help he gives
To lordly mansion rising far or near;
The enormous wheel that turns ten thousand spindles,
And the vast engine labouring in the mine,
Content with meaner prowess, must have lacked
[610] The trunk and body of their marvellous strength,
If his undaunted enterprize had failed
[612] Among the mountain coves, or keen research
In forest, park, or chace. Yon household Fir,
[613] A guardian planted to fence off the blast,
But towering high the roof above, as if
[615] Its humble destination were forgot;
That Sycamore, which annually holds
Within its shade, as in a stately tent
On all sides open to the fanning breeze,
A grave assemblage, seated while they shear
[620] The fleece-incumbered flock;— the Joyful Elm
Around whose trunk the lasses dance in May;—
And the Lord's Oak;—would plead their several rights
[623] In vain, if He were master of their fate.
Not one would have his pitiful regard,
For prized accommodation, pleasant use,
For dignity, for old acquaintance sake,
For ancient custom or distinguished name.
[624] His sentence to the axe would doom them all!
[625] —But, green in age and lusty as he is
And promising to stand from year to year,
Less, as might seem, in rivalship with men
Than with the forest's more enduring growth,
His own appointed hour will come at last;
[630] And, like the haughty Spoilers of the world,
This keen Destroyer, in his turn, must fall.

---

621 hath owed to him] to *him* hath owed *1827–*
623–625 A
The loftiest of her pendants: a|nd the wheel
Enormous round that turns ten thousand spindles *MS. 1814/27*
The loftiest of her pendants; He, from Park
Or Forest, fetched the enormous axle-tree
That whirls (how slow itself!) ten thousand spindles:— *1827– but* Park . . . Forest . . . Spindles:—] park . . . forest . . . spindles: *1836–*
628 their] its *1827–*
630–631 *reduced to* Among the mountain coves. Yon household Fir, *MS. 1814/27– but* Yon *para 1827–* "Yon *1832* Fir] fir *MS. 1832/36–*
640 lasses] maidens *MS. 1814/27* Maidens *1827, 1832* maidens *1836–*
643–646 *del MS. 1814/27, om 1827–*
649 And promising to keep his hold on earth *MS. 1814/27–*

635–636 For WW's end-of-volume note, see p. 313, below.

Now from the living pass we once again;
From Age," the Priest continued, "turn your thoughts;—
From Age, that often unlamented drops,
And mark that daisied hillock, three spans long.
—Seven lusty Sons sate daily round the board
Of Gold-rill side; and when the hope had ceased
Of other progeny, a Daughter then
Was given, the crown and glory of the whole!
Welcomed with joy, whose penetrating power
Was not unfelt amid that heavenly calm
With which by nature every Mother's Soul
Is stricken, in the moment when her throes
Are ended, and her ears have heard the cry
Which tells her that a living Child is born,—
And she lies conscious in a blissful rest
That the dread storm is weathered by them both.
—The Father—Him at this unlooked-for gift
A bolder transport seizes. From the side
Of his bright hearth, and from his open door,
And from the laurel-shaded seat thereby,
Day after day the gladness is diffused
To all that come, and almost all that pass;
Invited, summoned, to partake the cheer
Spread on the never-empty board, and drink
Health and good wishes to his new-born Girl,
From cups replenished by his joyous hand.
—Those seven fair Brothers variously were moved
Each by the thoughts best suited to his years:
But most of all and with most thankful mind
The hoary Grand-sire felt himself enriched;
A happiness that ebbed not, but remained
To fill the total measure of the soul!
—From the low tenement, his own abode,
Whither, as to a little private cell,
He had withdrawn from bustle, care, and noise,
To spend the Sabbath of old age in peace,
Once every day he duteously repaired
To rock the cradle of the slumbering Babe:
For in that female Infant's name he heard
The silent Name of his departed Wife;
Heart-stirring music! hourly heard that name;
Full blest he was, "Another Margaret Green,"

---

662 crown and glory] crowning bounty *MS. 1814/27–*
663–664 And so acknowledged with a tremulous joy / Felt to the centre of that heavenly calm *1827– ; so MS. 1814/27 but* acknowleged *(MS. 1814/27 earlier draft:* Welcomed with [?special] joy, whose [?piercing] power*)*
674 *del MS. 1814/27, om 1827–*
676 and almost] almost to *MS. 1832/36–*
686 the] his *1836–*

Oft did he say, "was come to Gold-rill side."
—Oh! pang unthought of, as the precious boon
[675] Itself had been unlooked for;—oh! dire stroke
Of desolating anguish for them all!
—Just as the Child could totter on the floor,
And, by some friendly finger's help upstayed,
Range round the garden-walk, whose low ground-flowers
[680] Were peeping forth, shy messengers of spring,—
[682/683] Even at that hopeful time,—the winds of March,
[683] One sunny day, smiting insidiously,
Raised in the tender passage of the throat
[685] Viewless obstruction; whence—all unforewarned,
[686] The Household lost their hope and soul's delight.
—But Providence, that gives and takes away
By his own law, is merciful and just;
[687] Time wants not power to soften all regrets,
And prayer and thought can bring to worst distress
Due resignation. Therefore, though some tears
[690] Fail not to spring from either Parent's eye
Oft as they hear of sorrow like their own,
Yet this departed Little-one, too long
The innocent troubler of their quiet, sleeps
In what may now be called a peaceful grave.

[695] On a bright day, the brightest of the year,
[697] These mountains echoed with an unknown sound,
A volley, thrice repeated o'er the Corse
Let down into the hollow of that Grave,
[700] Whose shelving sides are red with naked mold.
Ye Rains of April, duly wet this earth!

703–706 Range round the garden-walk, whose first spring-flowers
Were peeping forth, even at that hopeful time—
The winds of March, smiting insidiously *MS. 1814/27*
Range round the garden walk, while She perchance
Was catching at some novelty of Spring,
Ground-flower, or glossy insect from its cell
Drawn by the sunshine—at that hopeful season
The winds of March, smiting insidiously, *1827– but* She . . . Spring] she . . . spring *MS. 1832/36–*

709 hope] pride *MS. 1814/27–*

710–711 *del MS. 1814/27, om 1827–*

712 Time wants not] —But Time hath *MS. 1814/27– but* Time] time *1836– ; MS. 1814/27 earlier draft*: But [?time hath not] *pencil, eras*

713 and thought *del in pencil and then restored, illeg pencil eras in left margin MS. 1814/27*

719 grave] bed *MS. 1832/36–*

720 On a bright day—so calm and bright, it seemed
To us, with our sad spirits, heavenly-fair— *1836– ; MS. 1832/36 draft:*
On a bright day, so calm and bright it
~~seems~~
seemed
sad
To us, with our spirits, heavenly-fair,

721 with] to *MS. 1832/36–*

Spare, burning Sun of Midsummer, these sods,
That they may knit together, and therewith
Our thoughts unite in kindred quietness!
[705] Nor so the Valley shall forget her loss.
Dear Youth! by young and old alike beloved,
To me as precious as my own!—Green herbs
May creep (I wish that they would softly creep)
Over thy last abode, and we may pass
[710] Reminded less imperiously of thee;—
The ridge itself may sink into the breast
Of earth, the great abyss, and be no more;
Yet shall not thy remembrance leave our hearts,
[714] Thy image disappear. The mountain Ash,
[717] Decked with autumnal berries that outshine
[718] Spring's richest blossoms, yields a splendid show,
Amid the leafy woods; and ye have seen,
[719] By a brook side or solitary tarn,
[720] How she her station doth adorn,—the pool
Glows at her feet, and all the gloomy rocks
Are brightened round her. In his native Vale
Such and so glorious did this Youth appear;
A sight that kindled pleasure in all hearts
[725] By his ingenuous beauty, by the gleam
Of his fair eyes, by his capacious brow,
By all the graces with which nature's hand
Had bounteously arrayed him. As old Bards
Tell in their idle songs of wandering Gods,
[730] Pan or Apollo, veiled in human form;
Yet, like the sweet-breathed violet of the shade,
Discovered in their own despite to sense
Of Mortals, (if such fables without blame
May find chance-mention on this sacred ground)
[735] So, through a simple rustic garb's disguise,
And through the impediment of rural cares,
In him revealed a Scholar's genius shone;

738–741 The mountain Ash
No eye can overlook, when mid a grove
Of yet unfaded trees she lifts her head
Decked with autumnal berries that outshine
Spring's richest blossoms; and ye may have marked *para 1827–but* The] "The *1832* mountain Ash] Mountain-ash *1836–* mid] 'mid *1832–* Spring's] pring's *corr* Spring's *errata 1827* marked] marked, *1832–*; *MS. 1814/27 has three rev: (1)* yields . . . leafy *del to* [?dazzles from afar] / The yet unfaded *pencil interlined; (2)* The mountain . . . seen, *del to*
—Have ye not marked
Mid yet unfaded woods the mountain ash
Decked with autumnal berries that outshine
The richest blossoms of the spring, or seen *a* P *to the left of* Have *indicates a new para; (3) first three lines of the second rev and drafts are del by the last rev:*
The mountain Ash
Ye may have mark'd mid yet unfaded woods
Decked with autumnal berries that outshine *page foot*

751 bounteously] lavishly *MS. 1814/27–*

And so, not wholly hidden from men's sight,
In him the spirit of a Hero walked
[740] Our unpretending valley.—How the coit
Whizzed from the Stripling's arm! If touched by him
The inglorious foot-ball mounted to the pitch
Of the Lark's flight,—or shaped a rain-bow curve,
Aloft, in prospect of the shouting field!
[745] The indefatigable Fox had learned
To dread his perseverance in the chace.
With admiration he could lift his eyes
To the wide-ruling Eagle, and his hand
Was loth to assault the majesty he loved;
[750] Else had the strongest fastnesses proved weak
To guard the royal brood. The sailing glead,
The wheeling swallow, and the darting snipe,
The sportive sea-gull dancing with the waves,
And cautious water-fowl, from distant climes,
[755] Fixed at their seat—the centre of the Mere,
[756] Were subject to young Oswald's steady aim.

[757/758] From Gallia's coast a Tyrant's threats were hurled;
Our Country marked the preparations vast
[760] Of hostile Forces; and she called—with voice
That filled her plains and reached her utmost shores
And in remotest vales was heard—to Arms!
—Then, for the first time, here you might have seen
The Shepherd's grey to martial scarlet changed,
[765] That flashed uncouthly through the woods and fields.
Ten hardy Striplings, all in bright attire
And graced with shining weapons, weekly marched,
From this lone valley, to a central spot
Where, in assemblage with the Flower and Choice
[770] Of the surrounding district, they might learn
The rudiments of war; ten—hardy, strong,

768–769 *MS. 1836/45 has two drafts:*
The fox, in mazy wiles however vers'd
Or confident in strength for onward flight
Over hill [?&] vale, and stream, was taught to dread
His voice, and indefagitable feet
Still foremost, longest, in the obstinate chase *at page foot, del by vertical lines*
Fleeing for life, the fox was taught to dread
t]
His voice, and indefag]igable feet
~~Still foremost, longest, in the resolute chase~~ *ink over pencil in right margin*

770 he could] would he *MS. 1814/27–*

771 and] *alt* for *del MS. 1836/45*

779–780 aim. . . . hurled;] aim, . . . / And lived by his forbearance. From the coast / Of France a boastful Tyrant hurled his threats; *with para at* From *MS. 1832/36–*

780 From Gallia's coast a Tyrant hurled his threats; *MS. 1814/27–1832 but* From] "From *1832; see ll. 779–780 above*

781 the] a *MS. 1814/27* preparations] preparation *MS. 1814/27–*

783 and] that *1832–*

And valiant; but young Oswald, like a Chief
And yet a modest Comrade, led them forth
From their shy solitude, to face the world,
With a gay confidence and seemly pride;
Measuring the soil beneath their happy feet
Like youths released from labour and yet bound
To most laborious service, though to them
A festival of unencumbered ease;
The inner spirit keeping holiday,
Like vernal ground to sabbath sunshine left.

Oft have I marked him, at some leisure hour,
Stretched on the grass or seated in the shade
Among his Fellows, while an ample Map
Before their eyes lay carefully outspread,
From which the gallant Teacher would discourse,
Now pointing this way and now that.—"Here flows,"
Thus would he say, "the Rhine, that famous Stream!
"Eastward, the Danube tow'rds this inland sea,
"A mightier river, winds from realm to realm;—
"And, like a serpent, shews his glittering back
"Bespotted with innumerable isles.
"Here reigns the Russian, there the Turk; observe
"His capital city!"—Thence—along a tract
Of livelier interest to his hopes and fears
His finger moved, distinguishing the spots
Where wide-spread conflict then most fiercely raged;
Nor left unstigmatized those fatal Fields
On which the Sons of mighty Germany
Were taught a base submission.—"Here behold
"A nobler race, the Switzers, and their Land;
"Vales deeper far than these of ours, huge woods,
"And mountains white with everlasting snow!"
—And, surely, he, that spake with kindling brow,
Was a true Patriot, hopeful as the best
Of that young Peasantry, who, in our days,
Have fought and perished for Helvetia's rights,—
Ah not in vain!—or those who, in old time,
For work of happier issue, to the side
Of Tell came trooping from a thousand huts,
When he had risen alone! No braver Youth
Descended from Judea's heights, to march
With righteous Joshua; or appeared in arms
When grove was felled, and altar was cast down,

---

800 laborious] labourious *1814* laborious *errata 1814, but errata gives page number incorrectly as 282 (it is actually 345)*
819 then most fiercely raged;] was most fiercely raging; *MS. 1832/36*
834 Judea's] Judean *MS. 1814/27–*
835 or] nor *MS. 1832/36–*

And Gideon blew the trumpet, soul-enflamed,
And strong in hatred of Idolatry."

This spoken, from his seat the Pastor rose,
And moved towards the grave;—instinctively
His steps we followed; and my voice exclaimed,
"Power to the Oppressors of the world is given,
A might of which they dream not. Oh! the curse,
To be the Awakener of divinest thoughts,
Father and Founder of exalted deeds,
And to whole Nations bound in servile straits
The liberal Donor of capacities
More than heroic! this to be, nor yet
Have sense of one connatural wish, nor yet
Deserve the least return of human thanks;
Winning no recompence but deadly hate
With pity mixed, astonishment with scorn!"

When these involuntary words had ceased,
The Pastor said, "So Providence is served;
The forked weapon of the skies can send
Illumination into deep, dark Holds,
Which the mild sunbeam hath not power to pierce.
Why do ye quake, intimidated Thrones?
For, not unconscious of the mighty debt
Which to outrageous Wrong the Sufferer owes,
Europe, through all her habitable Seats,
Is thirsting for *their* overthrow, who still
Exist, as Pagan Temples stood of old,
By very horror of their impious rites
Preserved; are suffered to extend their pride,

839–841 The Pastor, even as if by these last words
Raised from his seat within the chosen shade,
Moved toward the grave;—instinctively his steps
We followed; and my voice with joy exclaimed: *1836– but* toward] towards *1850; MS. 1832/36 has three versions: (1) a draft at page foot, ink overwriting erased pencil, as 1836 above except* Pastor,] Pastor grave;] grave: exclaimed:] exclaimed *continuing to* "Power &c *l. 842; (2) an interlined draft in ink as 1836 but*

Raised from our seat ~~beneath our chosen~~ {~~shade~~ / tree} *(3) a single line in pencil at bottom of facing page:* This spoken, strait the Pastor rose he [?rose]

853 these involuntary words] this involuntary strain *MS. 1832/36–*

858 Ye Thrones that have defied remorse, and cast / Pity away, soon shall ye quake with *fear! 1836–; MS. 1832/36 has several versions of these lines: (1) page foot as 1836 but* and] & away,] away *fear!*] fear, *continuing to l. 860* For, not &c *(2) pencil at bottom of facing page* that have defied / Well may ye quake with fear *(3) errata leaf verso as 1836 but* remorse, and cast] remorse & flung *fear!*] fear *(4) at the top of two and three leaves on from l. 858 are pencil drafts, eras, possibly related to this passage*

861 Seats,] bounds, *MS. 1832/36–*

862 still] yet *MS. 1832/36–*

863 Stand, like those pagan temples of old, *MS. 1832/36, as part of the draft of ll. 864–865 below* Exist . . . old] Survive . . . yore *1836–*

864–865 By horror of their impious rites, preserved; / Are still permitted to extend their pride, *MS. 1832/36–*

Like Cedars on the top of Lebanon
Darkening the sun.—But less impatient thoughts,
And love "all hoping and expecting all,"
This hallowed Grave demands; where rests in peace
[850] A humble Champion of the better Cause;
A Peasant-youth, so call him, for he asked
No higher name; in whom our Country shewed,
As in a favourite Son, most beautiful.
In spite of vice, and misery, and disease,
[855] Spread with the spreading of her wealthy arts,
England, the ancient and the free, appeared,
In him, to stand before my swimming eyes
Unconquerably virtuous and secure.
—No more of this, lest I offend his dust:
[860] Short was his life, and a brief tale remains.

One summer's day, a day of annual pomp
And solemn chace; from morn to sultry noon
His steps had followed, fleetest of the fleet,
The red-deer driven along its native heights
[865] With cry of hound and horn: and, from that toil
Returned with sinews weakened and relaxed,
[867] This generous Youth, too negligent of self,
(A natural failing which maturer years
Would have subdued) took fearlessly—and kept—
His wonted station in the chilling flood,
[868] Among a busy company convened
[869/870] To wash his Father's flock. Convulsions dire
Seized him, that self-same night; and through the space
Of twelve ensuing days his frame was wrenched,
Till nature rested from her work in death.
—To him, thus snatched away, his Comrades paid
[875] A Soldier's honours. At his funeral hour
Bright was the sun, the sky a cloudless blue,
A golden lustre slept upon the hills;
And if by chance a Stranger, wandering there,
From some commanding eminence had looked
[880] Down on this spot, well pleased would he have seen
A glittering Spectacle; but every face
Was pallid,—seldom hath that eye been moist

---

881 One day—a summer's day of annual pomp *MS. 1836/45, 1845–*

888–892 Plunged—'mid a gay and busy throng convened
To wash the fleeces of his Father's flock—
Into the chilling flood. Convulsions dire *1827*–but Father's] father's *MS. 1832/36* Convulsions] "Convulsions *1832* Convulsions *no para 1836–; MS. 1814/27 is as 1827 but* Plung'd, mid a gay & . . . father's flock, *continued as*
Into the chilling flood, & void of fear
His station there maintain'd. Convulsions dire *then* & void . . . maintain'd. *del and* flood, *rev to* flood.

With tears—that wept not then; nor were the few
Who from their Dwellings came not forth to join
In this sad service, less disturbed than we.
They started at the tributary peal
Of instantaneous thunder, which announced
Through the still air the closing of the Grave;
And distant mountains echoed with a sound
Of lamentation, never heard before!"

The Pastor ceased.—My venerable Friend
Victoriously upraised his clear bright eye;
And, when that eulogy was ended, stood
Enwrapt,—as if his inward sense perceived
The prolongation of some still response,
Sent by the ancient soul of this wide Land,
The spirit of its mountains and its seas,
Its cities, temples, fields, its awful power,
Its rights and virtues—by that Deity
Descending; and supporting his pure heart
With patriotic confidence and joy.
And, at the last of those memorial words,
The pining Solitary turned aside,
Whether through manly instinct to conceal
Tender emotions spreading from the heart
To his worn cheek; or with uneasy shame
For those cold humours of habitual spleen,
Which, fondly seeking in dispraise of Man
Solace and self-excuse, had sometimes urged
To self-abuse, a not ineloquent tongue.
—Right tow'rds the sacred Edifice his steps
Had been directed; and we saw him now
Intent upon a monumental Stone,
Whose uncouth Form was grafted on the wall
Or rather seemed to have grown into the side
Of the rude Pile; as oft-times trunks of trees,
Where Nature works in wild and craggy spots,
Are seen incorporate with the living rock;
To endure for aye. The Vicar, taking note
Of his employment, with a courteous smile
Exclaimed, "The sagest Antiquarian's eye
That task would foil." And, with these added words,
He thitherward advanced, "Tradition tells
That, in Eliza's golden days, a Knight
Came on a War-horse sumptuously attired,

919–920 its . . . its . . . its] her . . . her . . . her *pencil MS. 1814/27*
930 Which,] That *1827–1832* That, *1836–*
944–945 That task would foil;" then, letting fall his voice / While he advanced, thus spake: "Tradition tells *1827–*

And fixed his home in this sequestered Vale.
'Tis left untold if here he first drew breath,
Or as a Stranger reached this deep recess,
Unknowing and unknown. A pleasing thought
I sometimes entertain, that, haply bound
To Scotland's court in service of his Queen,
Or sent on mission to some northern Chief
Of England's Realm, this Vale he might have seen
With transient observation; and thence caught
An Image fair, which, brightening in his soul
When years admonished him of failing strength
And he no more rejoiced in war's delights,
Had power to draw him from the world—resolved
To make that paradise his chosen home
To which his peaceful Fancy oft had turned.
—Vague thoughts are these; but, if belief may rest
Upon unwritten story fondly traced
From sire to son, in this obscure Retreat
The Knight arrived, with pomp of spear and shield,
And borne upon a Charger covered o'er
With gilded housings. And the lofty Steed—
His sole companion, and his faithful friend,
Whom he, in gratitude, let loose to range
In fertile pastures—was beheld with eyes
Of admiration and delightful awe,
By those untravelled Dalesmen. With less pride,
Yet free from touch of envious discontent,
They saw a Mansion at his bidding rise,
Like a bright star, amid the lowly band
Of their rude Homesteads. Here the Warrior dwelt,
And in that Mansion Children of his own,
Or Kindred, gathered round him. As a Tree
That falls and disappears, the House is gone;

---

952 *MS. 1836/45 has* stet *in both margins after attempting* I sometimes *and* haply *del to* In vacant hours I *pencil interlined in ink, both del to* A pleasing thought I sometimes have that bound *interlined, then del; see ll. 966–968 below*

957 An image fair *del then restored by* stet *then replaced by* Fair images *MS. 1836/45*

958–959 When joy of war and pride of Chivalry / Languished beneath accumulated years, *1827– but* Chivalry] chivalry *MS. 1832/36– ; MS. 1814/27 draft:* When joy of war & pride of chivalry / Long crush'd beneath accumulated years;

963 thoughts *del to* fancies *del to* notions *interlined* Vague notions these *left margin MS. 1836/45*

965–966 in this Retreat arrived / The Knight with pomp of helmet spear and shield *MS. 1827/32C*

966–968 The Knight arrived, with spear and shield, and borne
Upon a Charger gorgeously bedecked
With broidered housings. And the lofty Steed— *1845– ; MS. 1836/45 as 1845 but* pomp of *del to* & borne *l. 966 interlined* And borne *del and* Charger covered o'er *del to* [?] gorgeously bedeckd *l. 967 interlined* gilded *del to* broider'd *interlined and* broider'd *l. 968 left margin*
in vacant hours
A pleasing thought I sometimes have—that bound *del to*
Upon a Charger gorgeously bedeckd
With broidered Housings. *page foot, see l. 967 above*

And, through improvidence, or want of love
For ancient worth and honourable things,
The spear and shield are vanished, which the Knight
Hung in his rustic Hall. One ivied arch
Myself have seen, a gateway, last remains
Of that Foundation in domestic care
Raised by his hands. And now no trace is left
Of the mild-hearted Champion, save this Stone,
Faithless memorial! and his family name
Borne by yon clustering cottages, that sprang
From out the ruins of his stately Lodge:
These, and the name and title at full length,—
Sir Alfred Irthing, with appropriate words
Accompanied, still extant, in a wreath
Or posy—girding round the several fronts
Of three clear-sounding and harmonious bells,
That in the steeple hang, his pious gift."

"So fails, so languishes, grows dim, and dies,"
The grey-haired Wanderer pensively exclaimed,
"All that this World is proud of. From their spheres
The stars of human glory are cast down;
Perish the roses and the flowers of Kings,
Princes and Emperors, and the crowns and palms
Of all the Mighty, withered and consumed!
Nor is power given to lowliest Innocence
Long to protect her own. The Man himself
Departs; and soon is spent the Line of those
Who, in the bodily image, in the mind,
In heart or soul, in station or pursuit,
Did most resemble him. Degrees and Ranks,
Fraternities and Orders—heaping high
New wealth upon the burthen of the old,
And placing trust in privilege confirmed
And re-confirmed—are scoffed at with a smile
Of greedy foretaste, from the secret stand
Of Desolation, aimed: to slow decline
These yield, and these to sudden overthrow;
Their virtue, service, happiness, and state
Expire; and Nature's pleasant robe of green,
Humanity's appointed shroud, enwraps
Their monuments and their memory. The vast Frame
Of social nature changes evermore
Her organs and her members, with decay
Restless, and restless generation, powers
And functions dying and produced at need,—

1002 For WW's end-of-volume note, see p. 314, below.

And by this law the mighty Whole subsists:
With an ascent and progress in the main;
Yet oh! how disproportioned to the hopes
And expectations of self-flattering minds!
—The courteous Knight, whose bones are here interred,
Lived in an age conspicuous as our own
For strife and ferment in the minds of men;
Whence alteration, in the forms of things,
Various and vast. A memorable age!
Which did to him assign a pensive lot,
—To linger mid the last of those bright Clouds,
That, on the steady breeze of honour, sailed
In long procession calm and beautiful.
He, who had seen his own bright Order fade,
And its devotion gradually decline,
(While War, relinquishing the lance and shield,
Her temper changed and bowed to other laws)
Had also witnessed, in his morn of life,
That violent Commotion, which o'erthrew,
In town, and city, and sequestered glen,
Altar, and Cross, and Church of solemn roof,
And old religious House—Pile after Pile;
And shook the Tenants out into the fields,
Like wild Beasts without home! Their hour was come;
But why no softening thought of gratitude,
No just remembrance, scruple, or wise doubt?
Benevolence is mild; nor borrows help,
Save at worst need, from bold impetuous force,
Fitliest allied to anger and revenge.
But Human-kind rejoices in the might
Of Mutability, and airy Hopes,
Dancing around her, hinder and disturb
Those meditations of the soul, which feed
The retrospective Virtues. Festive songs
Break from the maddened Nations at the sight
Of sudden overthrow; and cold neglect
Is the sure consequence of slow decay.
—Even," said the Wanderer, "as that courteous Knight,
Bound by his vow to labour for redress
Of all who suffer wrong, and to enact
By sword and lance the law of gentleness,
If I may venture of myself to speak,
Trusting that not incongruously I blend
Low things with lofty, I too shall be doomed
To outlive the kindly use and fair esteem
Of the poor calling which my Youth embraced

1048 shook the] shook their *MS. 1832/36–*
1058 which] that *1827–*

With no unworthy prospect. But enough;
—Thoughts crowd upon me—and 'twere seemlier now
To stop, and yield our gracious Teacher thanks
For the pathetic Records which his voice
Hath here delivered; words of heartfelt truth,
Tending to patience when Affliction strikes;
To hope and love; to confident repose
In God; and reverence for the dust of Man."

END OF THE SEVENTH BOOK.

END OF THE SEVENTH BOOK.] *so 1820E–1843, 1846; om 1814 (which announces end of other books, except for the final one), 1845, 1850*

THE PARSONAGE.

THE pensive Sceptic of the lonely Vale
To those acknowledgments subscribed his own
With a sedate compliance, which the Priest
Failed not to notice inly pleased, and said,
[5] "If Ye, by whom invited I commenced
Those Narratives of calm and humble life,
Be satisfied, 'tis well,—the end is gained;
And, in return for sympathy bestowed
And patient listening, thanks accept from me.
[10] —Life, Death, Eternity! momentous themes
Are these—and might demand a Seraph's tongue,
Were they not equal to their own support;
And therefore no incompetence of mine
Could do them wrong. The universal Forms
[15] Of human nature, in a Spot like this,
Present themselves, at once to all Men's view:
Ye wished for act and circumstance, that make
The Individual known and understood;
And such as my best judgment could select
[20] From what the Place afforded have been given;
[21] Though apprehensions crossed me, in the course
Of this self-pleasing exercise, that Ye
[21/22] My zeal to his would liken, who, possessed
[23] Of some rare gems, or pictures finely wrought,
[23/24] Unlocks his Cabinet, and draws them forth

2–3 *MS. 1832/36 has interlined illeg rev, eras; partly decipherable is draft at page foot:*
{~~ose~~
~~To th~~ {e ~~acknowledgments, by the [?Vicar]~~
paid
~~In [? ? ? ? ?]~~
5 commenced] began *MS. 1832/36–*
6 Those] These *1827–* Narratives] *so 1820E–1832* Naratives *1814* narratives *MS. 1832/36–*
11 these] they *1827–*
23–26 My zeal to his would liken, who unlocks
A Cabinet with gems or pictures stored,
And draws them forth—soliciting regard *1827; so MS. 1814/27 but* who, . . . Cabinet, . . . forth, *see ll. 21–23, 21–26, below, for later variants*
21–23 in the course . . . liken, *del through* Ye *and rev to* that my zeal / Might well to his be likened *interlinear rev MS. 1827/32C* Though apprensions crossed me that my zeal / To his might well be likened, who [ ] *page foot MS. 1827/32C, last words trimmed in process of rebinding*
21–26 Though apprehensions crossed me that my zeal
To his might well be likened, who unlocks
A Cabinet with gems or pictures stored,
And draws them forth—soliciting regard *1832– but* A cabinet stored with gems and pictures—draws / His treasures forth, soliciting regard *1836– ; MS. 1832/36 as 1836 but* pictures draws

One after one,—soliciting regard
To this—and this, as worthier than the last,
Till the Spectator, who a while was pleased
More than the Exhibitor himself, becomes
Weary and faint, and longs to be released.
—But let us hence! my Dwelling is in sight,
And there—"
At this the Solitary shrunk
With backward will; but, wanting not address
That inward motion to disguise, he said
To his Compatriot, smiling as he spake;
—"The peaceable Remains of this good Knight
Would be disturbed, I fear, with wrathful scorn,
If consciousness could reach him where he lies
That One, albeit of these degenerate times,
Deploring changes past, or dreading change
Foreseen, had dared to couple, even in thought,
The fine Vocation of the sword and lance
With the gross aims and body-bending toil
Of a poor Brotherhood who walk the earth
Pitied, and where they are not known, despised.
—Yet, by the good Knight's leave, the two Estates
Are graced with some resemblance. Errant Those,
Exiles and Wanderers—and the like are These;
Who, with their burthen, traverse hill and dale,
Carrying relief for Nature's simple wants.
—What though no higher recompence they seek
Than honest maintenance, by irksome toil
Full oft procured! Yet Such may claim respect,
Among the Intelligent, for what this course
Enables them to be, and to perform.
Their tardy steps give leisure to observe;
While solitude permits the mind to feel;
And doth instruct her to supply defects
By the division of her inward self,
For grateful converse: and to these poor Men,
(As I have heard you boast with honest pride)
Nature is bountiful, where'er they go;
Kind Nature's various wealth is all their own.
Versed in the characters of men; and bound,
By tie of daily interest, to maintain

51 they seek] be sought *MS. 1832/36–*
53 Such may claim] may they claim *MS. 1832/36–*
58 And doth instruct] Instructs and prompts *1827– but* Instructs] Instructs, *1836– ; MS. 1814/27 as 1827 but* instructs &
61–62 Nature (I but repeat your favourite boast) / Is bountiful—go wheresoe'er they may; *1836–; so MS. 1832/36 but comma after* bountiful *overwritten by dash; earlier interlined draft in MS. 1832/36* reads Nature, boast)] boast bountiful—] bountiful, wheresoe'er] wheresoeer
65 tie] ties *1832–*

Conciliatory manners and smooth speech;
Such have been, and still are in their degree,
Examples efficacious to refine
Rude intercourse; apt Instruments to excite,
By importation of unlooked-for Arts,
Barbarian torpor, and blind prejudice;
Raising, through just gradation, savage life
To rustic, and the rustic to urbane.
—Within their moving magazines is lodged
Power that comes forth to quicken and exalt
The affections seated in the Mother's breast,
And in the Lover's fancy; and to feed
The sober sympathies of long tried Friends.
—By these Itinerants, as experienced Men,
Counsel is given; contention they appease
With healing words; and in remotest Wilds
Tears wipe away, and pleasant tidings bring;
Could the proud quest of Chivalry do more?"

"Happy," rejoined the Wanderer, "They who gain
A panegyric from your generous tongue!
But, if to these Wayfarers once pertained
Aught of romantic interest, 'tis gone;
Their purer service, in this realm at least,
Is past for ever.—An inventive Age
Has wrought, if not with speed of magic, yet
To most strange issues. I have lived to mark
A new and unforeseen Creation rise
From out the labours of a peaceful Land,
Wielding her potent Enginery to frame
And to produce, with appetite as keen
As that of War, which rests not night or day,
Industrious to destroy! With fruitless pains
Might One like me *now* visit many a tract
Which, in his youth, he trod, and trod again,
A lone Pedestrian with a scanty freight,
Wished for, or welcome, wheresoe'er he came,
Among the Tenantry of Thorpe and Vill;
Or straggling Burgh, of ancient charter proud,
And dignified by battlements and towers
Of some stern Castle, mouldering on the brow
Of a green hill or bank of rugged stream.
The foot-path faintly marked, the horse-track wild,
And formidable length of plashy lane,

69 Rude intercourse; apt Agents to expel, *1827– ; so MS. 1814/27 but* agents . . . expel Agents] agents *MS. 1832/36–*
76 The affections] Affections *MS. 1814/27–*
81 With gentle language; in remotest Wilds, *MS. 1814/27–*
87 'tis] it is *MS. 1832/36–*

(Prized avenues ere others had been shaped
Or easier links connecting place with place)
Have vanished,—swallowed up by stately roads
[110] Easy and bold, that penetrate the gloom
Of England's farthest Glens. The Earth has lent
Her waters, Air her breezes; and the Sail
Of traffic glides with ceaseless interchange,
Glistening along the low and woody dale,
[115] Or on the naked mountain's lofty side.
[117] Meanwhile, at social Industry's command,
How quick, how vast an increase! From the germ
Of some poor Hamlet, rapidly produced
[120] Here a huge Town, continuous and compact,
Hiding the face of earth for leagues—and there,
Where not a Habitation stood before,
The Abodes of men irregularly massed
Like trees in forests—spread through spacious tracts,
[125] O'er which the smoke of unremitting fires
Hangs permanent, and plentiful as wreaths
Of vapour glittering in the morning sun.
And, wheresoe'er the Traveller turns his steps,
He sees the barren wilderness erased,
[130] Or disappearing; triumph that proclaims
How much the mild Directress of the plough
Owes to alliance with these new-born Arts!
—Hence is the wide Sea peopled,—and the Shores
Of Britain are resorted to by Ships
[135] Freighted from every climate of the world
With the world's choicest produce. Hence that sum
Of Keels that rest within her crowded ports,
Or ride at anchor in her sounds and bays;
That animating spectacle of Sails

---

113 England's] Britain's *MS. 1814/27–* Earth [?has ?] *interlined rev MS. 1832/36*
115 interchange,] intercourse, *1836– ; see verbal variants to VIII, 117, below*
117 Or in its progress, on the lofty side / Of some bare hill, with wonder kenned from far. *1836– but* Or, . . . side, *1845–* far.] far *1849 (probable worn plate); MS 1832/36 drafts:*
From stage to stage, lifted or lower'd the Barge
Of traffic glides with ceaseless interchange
Glistening *del at page foot*
the sail
Of traffic glides with ceaseless intercourse,
Glistening along the low and woody dale;
Or in its progress, on the lofty side
Of some bare hill, with wonder kenned from far *top of facing page*
Or in its progress on the lofty side
some
~~Of~~ bare hill, with wonder kenned from far. *bottom of facing page*
124 The Abodes] Abodes *1827–*
134 —and] —hence *MS. 1814/27–*

113–114 For WW's end-of-volume note, see p. 314, below.

[140] Which through her inland regions, to and fro
Pass with the respirations of the tide,
Perpetual, multitudinous! Finally,
Hence a dread arm of floating Power, a voice
Of Thunder, daunting those who would approach
[145] With hostile purposes the blessed Isle,
Truth's consecrated residence, the seat
Impregnable, of Liberty and Peace.

And yet, O happy Pastor of a Flock
Faithfully watched, and by that loving care
[150] And heaven's good providence preserved from taint!
With You I grieve, when on the darker side
[152] Of this great change I look; and there behold,
Through strong temptation of those gainful Arts,
[153] Such outrage done to Nature as compels
The indignant Power to justify herself;
[155] Yea to avenge her violated rights
For England's bane.—When soothing darkness spreads
O'er hill and vale," the Wanderer thus expressed
His recollections, "and the punctual stars,
While all things else are gathering to their homes,
[160] Advance, and in the firmament of heaven
Glitter—but undisturbing, undisturbed,
As if their silent company were charged
With peaceful admonitions for the heart
Of all-beholding Man, earth's thoughtful Lord;
[165] Then, in full many a region, once like this
The assured domain of calm simplicity
And pensive quiet, an unnatural light,
Prepared for never-resting Labour's eyes,
Breaks from a many-windowed Fabric huge;
[170] And at the appointed hour a Bell is heard—
Of harsher import than the Curfew-knoll
That spake the Norman Conqueror's stern behest,
A local summons to unceasing toil!
Disgorged are now the Ministers of day;
[175] And, as they issue from the illumined Pile,
A fresh Band meets them, at the crowded door,—
And in the Courts—and where the rumbling Stream,
That turns the multitude of dizzy wheels,
Glares, like a troubled Spirit, in its bed
[180] Among the rocks below. Men, Maidens, Youths,
Mother and little Children, Boys and Girls,
Enter, and each the wonted task resumes
Within this Temple—where is offered up

141 Which] That, *MS. 1832/36–*
154 *del 1814/27, om 1827–*

To Gain—the Master Idol of the Realm,
Perpetual sacrifice. Even thus of old
Our Ancestors, within the still domain
Of vast Cathedral or Conventual Church,
Their vigils kept; where tapers day and night
On the dim altar burned continually,
In token that the House was evermore
Watching to God. Religious Men were they;
Nor would their Reason, tutored to aspire
Above this transitory world, allow
That there should pass a moment of the year,
When in their land the Almighty's Service ceased.

Triumph who will in these profaner rites
Which We, a generation self-extolled,
As zealously perform! I cannot share
His proud complacency; yet I exult,
Casting reserve away, exult to see
An Intellectual mastery exercised
O'er the blind Elements; a purpose given,
A perseverance fed; almost a soul
Imparted—to brute Matter. I rejoice,
Measuring the force of those gigantic powers,
Which by the thinking Mind have been compelled
To serve the Will of feeble-bodied Man.
For with the sense of admiration blends
The animating hope that time may come
When strengthened, yet not dazzled, by the might
Of this dominion over Nature gained,
Men of all lands shall exercise the same
In due proportion to their Country's need;
Learning, though late, that all true glory rests,
All praise, all safety, and all happiness,
Upon the Moral law. Egyptian Thebes;
Tyre by the margin of the sounding waves;
Palmyra, central in the Desart, fell;
And the Arts died by which they had been raised.
—Call Archimedes from his buried Tomb
Upon the plain of vanished Syracuse,
And feelingly the Sage shall make report
How insecure, how baseless in itself,

196 *MS. 1836/45 drafts:* A moment, though the live long year, to pass *pencil interlined* a single moment of the year should pass *interlined* That ever *pencil in left margin* That a single *pencil in left margin* That a single moment of the year should pass *pencil at page foot* That a single moment / That ever a moment *pencil at top of page* A single moment of the year to pass *pencil at top of facing page*

201 I] do I *MS. 1832/36–*

208 Which] That *MS. 1814/27–1843* That, *1845–*

223 plain] grave *1836–*

Is that Philosophy, whose sway is framed
For mere material instruments:—how weak
Those Arts, and high Inventions, if unpropped
By Virtue.—He with sighs of pensive grief,
Amid his calm abstractions, would admit
That not the slender privilege is theirs
To save themselves from blank forgetfulness!"

When from the Wanderer's lips these words had fallen,
I said, "And, did in truth these vaunted Arts
Possess such privilege, how could we escape
Regret and painful sadness, who revere,
And would preserve as things above all price,
The old domestic morals of the land,
Her simple manners, and the stable worth
That dignified and cheered a low estate.
Oh! where is now the character of peace,
Sobriety, and order, and chaste love,
And honest dealing, and untainted speech,
And pure good-will, and hospitable cheer;
That made the very thought of Country-life
A thought of refuge, for a Mind detained
Reluctantly amid the bustling crowd?
Where now the beauty of the Sabbath kept
With conscientious reverence, as a day
By the Almighty Law-giver pronounced
Holy and blest? and where the winning grace
Of all the lighter ornaments attached
To time and season, as the year rolled round?"

"Fled!" was the Wanderer's passionate response,
"Fled utterly! or only to be traced
In a few fortunate Retreats like this;
Which I behold with trembling, when I think
What lamentable change, a year—a month—
May bring; that Brook converting as it runs
Into an Instrument of deadly bane
For those, who, yet untempted to forsake
The simple occupations of their Sires,
Drink the pure water of its innocent stream
With lip almost as pure.—Domestic bliss,
(Or call it comfort, by a humbler name,)

---

226 that] the *MS. 1814/27–* whose sway is framed] that only rules *MS. 1814/27* whose sway depends *1827–*

227 For mere *del to* Over *and* On *pencil, eras, in left margin MS. 1814/27* On mere *1827–*

229 By virtue.—He, sighing with pensive grief, *1845– ; so MS. 1836/45 but with pencil exclam after* He

234 these] those *1836–*

236 Sadness and keen regret, we who revere, *MS. 1832/36–*

How art thou blighted for the poor Man's heart!
Lo! in such neighbourhood, from morn to eve,
The Habitations empty! or perchance
The Mother left alone,—no helping hand
To rock the cradle of her peevish babe;
No daughters round her, busy at the wheel,
Or in dispatch of each day's little growth
Of household occupation; no nice arts
Of needle-work; no bustle at the fire,
Where once the dinner was prepared with pride;
Nothing to speed the day, or cheer the mind;
Nothing to praise, to teach, or to command!
—The Father, if perchance he still retain
His old employments, goes to field or wood,
No longer led or followed by his Sons;
Idlers perchance they were,—but in *his* sight;
Breathing fresh air, and treading the green earth;
'Till their short holiday of childhood ceased,
Ne'er to return! That birth-right now is lost.
Economists will tell you that the State
Thrives by the forfeiture—unfeeling thought,
And false as monstrous! Can the Mother thrive
By the destruction of her innocent Sons?
In whom a premature Necessity
Blocks out the forms of Nature, preconsumes
The reason, famishes the heart, shuts up
The infant Being in itself, and makes
Its very spring a season of decay?
The lot is wretched, the condition sad,
Whether a pining discontent survive,
And thirst for change; or habit hath subdued
The soul depressed; dejected—even to love
Of her dull tasks, and close captivity.
—Oh, banish far such Wisdom as condemns
A native Briton to these inward chains,
Fixed in his soul, so early and so deep,
Without his own consent, or knowledge, fixed!
He is a Slave to whom release comes not,
And cannot come. The Boy, where'er he turns,
Is still a prisoner; when the wind is up
Among the clouds and in the ancient woods;
Or when the sun is rising in the heavens,
Quiet and calm. Behold him—in the school
Of his attainments? no; but with the air

---

280 his] the *1820E–*
298 dull . . . close] close . . . long *MS. 1832/36–*
306 in] roars through *MS. 1832/36–*
307 rising in the heavens,] shining in the east, *1827– ; so MS. 1814/27 but* East,

Fanning his temples under heaven's blue arch.
His raiment, whitened o'er with cotton flakes,
[310] Or locks of wool, announces whence he comes.
Creeping his gait and cowering—his lip pale—
His respiration quick and audible;
And scarcely could you fancy that a gleam
From out those languid eyes could break, or blush
[315] Mantle upon his cheek. Is this the form,
Is that the countenance, and such the port,
Of no mean Being? One who should be clothed
With dignity befitting his proud hope;
Who, in his very childhood, should appear
[320] Sublime—from present purity and joy!
The limbs increase; but, liberty of mind
[322] Thus gone for ever, this organic Frame,
Which from heaven's bounty we receive, instinct
[323] With light, and gladsome motions, soon becomes
Dull, to the joy of her own motions dead;
[325] And even the Touch, so exquisitely poured
Through the whole body, with a languid Will
Performs its functions; rarely competent
To impress a vivid feeling on the mind
Of what there is delightful in the breeze,
[330] The gentle visitations of the sun,
Or lapse of liquid element—by hand,

---

316 Could break from out those languid eyes, or a blush *MS. 1832/36–*
324 Thus] Is *MS. 1814/27–1832; see ll. 323–326 below for later variants*
325–326 So joyful in her motions, is become *1827– ; see ll. 323–326 below for later variants; MS. 1814/27 first deletes comma after* receive *l. 325 before del of entire line, and*

So joyful in {her / its own} is
~~With light, and gladsome~~ motions, ~~soon~~ becomes

323–326 The limbs increase; but this organic Frame,
So gladsome in its motions, is become *1836–1843*
The limbs increase; but liberty of mind
Is gone for ever; and this organic frame, *1845–*

MS. 1832/36 drafts as rev of ll. 323–326 toward 1836:
Liberty was, and it is gone forever *interlined, then del* liberty of mind *del to* this organic Is gone . . . this *del, see l. 324 above* So joyful . . . become *del to* So gladsome in its motions is become *see ll. 325–326 above*

The limbs encrease, but this organic frame
So gladsome in his motions is [?become] *rev of lines immediately below*
~~Liberty was, and it is gone forever~~
The limbs increase, but this organic Frame,
~~Which from Heaven's bounty we receive~~ instinct
~~With prompt and gladsome motions~~ is become *page foot*

MS. 1836/45 drafts as rev of ll. 323–327 toward 1845:
while with freedom lost *l. 323 del interlined* is *del to* soon *del* becomes *l. 324 interlined* Thought pines *l. 324 left margin* but while with freedom lost / Thought pines & dwindles this organic frame *at page foot and del by vertical lines*

The limbs increase, but liberty of mind
Is gone for ever and this organic frame
So joyful in its motions, soon becomes
Dull, *left margin*

330 its] her *MS. 1814/27–1832*

Or foot, or lip, in summer's warmth—perceived.
—Can hope look forward to a manhood raised
On such foundations?"
"Hope is none for him,"
The pale Recluse indignantly exclaimed,
"And tens of thousands suffer wrong as deep.
Yet be it asked, in justice to our age,
If there were not, before those Arts appeared,
These Structures rose, commingling old and young,
And unripe sex with sex, for mutual taint;
Then, if there were not, in our far-famed Isle,
Multitudes, who from infancy had breathed
Air unimprisoned, and had lived at large;
Yet walked beneath the sun, in human shape,
As abject, as degraded? At this day,
Who shall enumerate the crazy huts
And tottering hovels, whence do issue forth
A ragged Offspring, with their own blanched hair
Crowned like the image of fantastic Fear;
Or wearing, we might say, in that white growth
An ill-adjusted turban, for defence
Or fierceness, wreathed around their sun-burnt brows,
By savage Nature's unassisted care.
Naked and coloured like the soil, the feet
On which they stand; as if thereby they drew
Some nourishment, as Trees do by their roots,
From Earth the common Mother of us all.
Figure and mien, complexion and attire,
Are framed to strike dismay, but the outstretched hand
And whining voice denote them Supplicants
For the least boon that pity can bestow.
Such on the breast of darksome heaths are found;
And with their Parents dwell upon the skirts
Of furze-clad commons; and are born and reared
At the mine's mouth, beneath impending rocks,
Or in the chambers of some natural cave;
And where their Ancestors erected huts,
For the convenience of unlawful gain,
In forest purlieus; and the like are bred,

---

344 If there were not, *then*, in our far-famed Isle, *1836–; so MS. 1832/36 but no italics*
351 own blanched] upright *1836–*
353 we might say,] (shall we say?) *1836–*
356 By savage Nature? Shrivelled are their lips; *1836–*
362 framed . . . but the] leagued . . . but *1827–; so MS. 1814/27 but* leagu'd
366 dwell upon] occupy *MS. 1832/36–*
367 and] such *MS. 1814/27–*
368 beneath] under *MS. 1832/36–*
369 in the] dwell in *MS. 1832/36–*
370 And] Or *MS. 1832/36–*

[370] All England through, where nooks and slips of ground,
Purloined in times less jealous than our own,
From the green margin of the public way,
A residence afford them, mid the bloom
And gaiety of cultivated fields.
[375] —Such (we will hope the lowest in the scale)
Do I remember oft-times to have seen
'Mid Buxton's dreary heights. Upon the watch,
Till the swift vehicle approach, they stand;
Then, following closely with the cloud of dust,
[380] An uncouth feat exhibit, and are gone
Heels over head like Tumblers on a Stage.
—Up from the ground they snatch the copper coin,
And, on the freight of merry Passengers
Fixing a steady eye, maintain their speed;
[385] And spin—and pant—and overhead again,
Wild Pursuivants! until their breath is lost,
Or bounty tires,—and every face, that smiled
Encouragement, hath ceased to look that way.
—But, like the Vagrants of the Gypsy tribe,
[390] These, bred to little pleasure in themselves,
Are profitless to others. Turn we then
To Britons born and bred within the pale
Of civil polity, and early trained
To earn, by wholesome labour in the field,
[395] The bread they eat. A sample should I give
Of what this stock produces to enrich
[397] And beautify the tender age of life,
A sample fairly culled, ye would exclaim,
[398] "Is this the whistling Plough-boy whose shrill notes
Impart new gladness to the morning air?"
[400] "Forgive me! if I venture to suspect
That many, sweet to hear of in soft verse,
Are of no finer frame:—his joints are stiff;
Beneath a cumbrous frock that to the knees
Invests the thriving churl, his legs appear,
[405] Fellows to those which lustily upheld
The wooden stools, for everlasting use,
On which our Fathers sate. And mark his brow!
Under whose shaggy canopy are set
Two eyes, not dim, but of a healthy stare;

---

380 Upon the] In earnest *MS. 1832/36–*
399 produces] hath long produced *MS. 1832/36–*
400–401 The tender age of life, ye would exclaim, *MS. 1814/27–*
403 new] now *1846*
406 Are of no finer frame. Stiff are his joints; *1836–*
409 which] that *MS. 1814/27–*
411 On which] Whereon *MS. 1814/27–*
413 healthy *del to* vacant *MS. 1836/45*

[410] Wide, sluggish, blank, and ignorant, and strange;
Proclaiming boldly that they never drew
A look or motion of intelligence
From infant conning of the Christ-cross-row,
Or puzzling through a Primer, line by line,
[415] Till perfect mastery crown the pains at last.
—What kindly warmth from touch of fostering hand,
What penetrating power of sun or breeze,
Shall e'er dissolve the crust wherein his soul
Sleeps, like a caterpillar sheathed in ice?
[420] This torpor is no pitiable work
Of modern ingenuity; no Town
Nor crowded City may be taxed with aught
Of sottish vice or desperate breach of law,
[424/425] To which in after years he may be rouzed.
[425/426] —This Boy the Fields produce: his spade and hoe,
[427] The Carter's whip which on his shoulder rests
In air high-towering with a boorish pomp,
The sceptre of his sway; his Country's name,
[430] Her equal rights, her churches and her schools,
What have they done for him? And, let me ask,
For tens of thousands uninformed as he?
In brief, what liberty of mind is here?"

This cheerful sally pleased the mild good Man,
[435] To whom the appeal couched in those closing words
Was pointedly addressed; and to the thoughts
Which, in assent or opposition, rose
Within his mind, he seemed prepared to give
[439] Prompt utterance; but, rising from our seat,
The hospitable Vicar interposed
[440] With invitation earnestly renewed.
—We followed, taking as he led, a Path
Along a Hedge of stately hollies framed,

414 blank, and ignorant, and] blank— eyes ignorant and *MS. 1832/36* *line om 1836, restored 1840–* wide, sluggish, blank, and ignorant, and strange *pencil, then del MS. 1836/45*
419 perfect] [?slow formed] *pencil, eras, MS. 1814/27*
426 may] can *MS. 1832/36–*
428–429 To which (and who can tell where or how soon?)
He may be roused. This Boy the fields produce:
His spade and hoe, mattock and glittering scythe, *1836– ; so MS. 1832/36 but* produce:] produce may] might *interlined*
430 which] that *MS. 1814/27–*
437 cheerful] earnest *in pencil, eras, then* ardent *MS. 1814/27* ardent *1827–*
438 those] its *1827–*
440 Which,] That, *MS. 1814/27–*
442–443 Prompt utterance; but the Vicar interposed *MS. 1832/36–*
444 earnestly] urgently *MS. 1814/27–*
446 stately hollies framed,] hollies, dark and tall *1827– but* hollies,] hollies *MS. 1832/36– ; MS. 1814/27 as 1827 but* and] &

Whose flexile boughs, descending with a weight
Of leafy spray, concealed the stems and roots
That gave them nourishment. How sweet methought,
When the fierce wind comes howling from the north,
How grateful, this impenetrable screen!
Not shaped by simple wearing of the foot
On rural business passing to and fro
Was the commodious Walk; a careful hand
Had marked the line, and strewn the surface o'er
With pure cerulean gravel, from the heights
Fetched by the neighbouring brook.—Across the Vale
The stately Fence accompanied our steps;
And thus the Pathway, by perennial green
Guarded and graced, seemed fashioned to unite,
As by a beautiful yet solemn chain,
The Pastor's Mansion with the House of Prayer.

Like Image of solemnity conjoined
With feminine allurement soft and fair
The Mansion's self displayed;—a reverend Pile
With bold projections and recesses deep;
Shadowy, yet gay and lightsome as it stood
Fronting the noon-tide Sun. We paused to admire
The pillared Porch, elaborately embossed;
The low wide windows with their mullions old;
The cornice richly fretted, of grey stone;
And that smooth slope from which the Dwelling rose,
By beds and banks Arcadian of gay flowers
And flowering shrubs, protected and adorned.
Profusion bright! and every flower assuming
A more than natural vividness of hue,
From unaffected contrast with the gloom
Of sober cypress, and the darker foil
Of yew, in which survived some traces, here
Not unbecoming, of grotesque device
And uncouth fancy. From behind the roof

---

447 descending] low bending *1836–; so MS. 1832/36, which also has a series of drafts:*

prest
Whose flexile branches with a weight descending
pressed down
low bending

then at page foot:

boughs low bending with a weight
Whose flexile ~~branches, with a weight pressed [?down]~~

449–451 That gave them nourishment. When frosty winds
Howl from the north, what kindly warmth, methought
Is here, how grateful this impervious screen! *1827– but* methought] methought, *1832–* here,] here— *MS. 1832/36–*

455 the surface] its surface *MS. 1832/36–*

457 by the] by a *MS. 1832/36–*

460 seemed *del to* was *del and* seemed *restored by* stet *MS. 1836/45*

Rose the slim ash and massy sycamore,
Blending their diverse foliage with the green
[480] Of ivy, flourishing and thick, that clasped
The huge round chimneys, harbour of delight
For wren and red-breast,—where they sit and sing
Their slender ditties when the trees are bare.
Nor must I pass unnoticed (leaving else
[485] The picture incomplete, as it appeared
Before our eyes) a relique of old times
[486] Happily spared, a little gothic niche
Of nicest workmanship; which once had held
The sculptured Image of some Patron Saint,
Or of the blessed Virgin, looking down
[490] On all who entered those religious doors.

But lo! where from the rocky garden mount
Crowned by its antique summer-house—descends,
Light as the silver fawn, a radiant Girl;
For she hath recognized her honoured Friend,
[495] The Wanderer ever welcome! A prompt kiss
The gladsome Child bestows at his request,
And, up the flowery lawn as we advance,
Hangs on the Old Man with a happy look,
And with a pretty restless hand of love.
[500] —We enter;—need I tell the courteous guise
In which the Lady of the place received
Our little Band, with salutation meet
[501] To each accorded? Graceful was her port;
A lofty stature undepressed by Time,
Whose visitation had not spared to touch
The finer lineaments of frame and face;
[505] To that complexion brought which prudence trusts in
And wisdom loves.—But when a stately Ship
Sails in smooth weather by the placid coast
On homeward voyage, what—if wind and wave,
And hardship undergone in various climes,
[510] Have caused her to abate the virgin pride,
And that full trim of inexperienced hope
With which she left her haven—not for this,
Should the sun strike her, and the impartial breeze

488–490 Nor must I leave untouched (the picture else / Were incomplete) a relique of old times *1827–; so MS. 1814/27 but* untouch'd the . . . incomplete,)

492 which] that *1827–*

505–508 —We enter—by the Lady of the Place / Cordially greeted. Graceful was her port: *1827–but* place *MS. 1832/36–; MS. 1814/27 as 1827 but* Place . . . greeted.] place . . . greeted

510 Whose gentle visitation had not spared *MS. 1814/27* Whose visitation had not wholly spared *1827–*

511 frame] form *MS. 1814/27–*

Play on her streamers, doth she fail to assume
Brightness and touching beauty of her own,
That charm all eyes. So bright to us appeared
This goodly Matron, shining in the beams
Of unexpected pleasure. Soon the board
Was spread, and we partook a plain repast.

Here in cool shelter, while the scorching heat
Oppressed the fields, we sate, and entertained
The mid-day hours with desultory talk;
From trivial themes to general argument
Passing, as accident or fancy led,
Or courtesy prescribed. While question rose
And answer flowed, the fetters of reserve
Dropped from our minds; and even the shy Recluse
Resumed the manners of his happier days.
He in the various conversation bore
A willing, and, at times, a forward part;
Yet with the grace of one who in the world
Had learned the art of pleasing, and had now
Occasion given him to display his skill
Upon the stedfast 'vantage ground of truth.
He gazed with admiration unsuppressed
Upon the landscape of the sun-bright vale,
Seen, from the shady room in which we sate,
In softened pèrspective; and more than once
Praised the consummate harmony serene
Of gravity and elegance—diffused
Around the Mansion and its whole domain;
Not, doubtless, without help of female taste
And female care.—"A blessed lot is yours!"
He said, and with that exclamation breathed
A tender sigh;—but, suddenly the door
Opening, with eager haste two lusty Boys
Appeared,—confusion checking their delight.
—Not Brothers they in feature or attire,
But fond Companions, so I guessed, in field,
And by the river-side—from which they come,

---

521 doth she fail] fails she *MS. 1814/27–*
523 bright to us] bright, so fair, *1827–; so MS. 1814/27 but* bright so fair
527–528 Here, resting in cool shelter, we beguiled *1827–; so MS. 1814/27 but* Here resting
534 Dropping from every mind, the Solitary *1827–; so MS. 1814/27 but* Solitary [?res]
536 He] And *MS. 1814/27* And, *1827, 1832* And *1836–*
537 and,] nay, *MS. 1814/27–*
551–553 The words escaped his lips with a tender sigh
Breathed over them;—but suddenly the door
Flew open, and a pair of lusty Boys *1827– but* them;—] them; *1832* them: *1836–* lips] lip, *MS. 1832/36–; MS. 1814/27 draft:* ~~The [? ? ? ?] [?tender sigh breath'd~~] / A sigh;—but, suddenly [?~~appeared~~] two lusty Boys *del by eras, and one or two illeg words in pencil, eras, above l. 532*
557 river-side—from which] river's margin whence *MS. 1814/27* river's margin—whence *1827–*

[550] A pair of Anglers, laden with their spoil.
One bears a willow-pannier on his back,
[552/553] The Boy of plainer garb, and more abashed
In countenance,—more distant and retired.
[553/554] Twin might the Other be to that fair Girl
Who bounded tow'rds us from the garden mount.
[555] Triumphant entry this to him!—for see,
Between his hands he holds a smooth blue stone,
On whose capacious surface is outspread
Large store of gleaming crimson-spotted trouts;
[559] Ranged side by side, in regular ascent,
One after one, still lessening by degrees
[560] Up to the dwarf that tops the pinnacle.
Upon the Board he lays the sky-blue stone
With its rich spoil;—their number he proclaims;
Tells from what pool the noblest had been dragged;
And where the very monarch of the brook,
[565] After long struggle, had escaped at last—
Stealing alternately at them and us
(As doth his Comrade too) a look of pride.
And, verily, the silent Creatures made
A splendid sight, together thus exposed;
[570] Dead—but not sullied or deformed by Death,
That seemed to pity what he could not spare.

But oh! the animation in the mien
Of those two Boys! Yea in the very words
With which the young Narrator was inspired,
[575] When, as our questions led, he told at large
Of that day's prowess! Him might I compare,
His look, tones, gestures, eager eloquence,
To a bold Brook which splits for better speed,
And, at the self-same moment, works its way
[580] Through many channels, ever and anon

558 their] fresh *MS. 1814/27* Anglers elated with unusual spoil. *1827, 1832* Keen anglers with unusual spoil elated. *MS. 1832/36–*

560–564 The Boy of plainer garb, whose blush survives
More deeply tinged. Twin might the other be
To that fair Girl who from the garden Mount
Bounded—triumphant entry this for him. *1827– but* him.] him! *1832–* Girl . . . garden Mount] girl . . . garden-mount *MS. 1832/36–* Boy . . . Bounded—] boy . . . Bounded:— *1836–; MS. 1814/27 as 1827 but l. 560 as 1814 except* abashed *del and then restored, and l. 561* In countenance *del and then restored, and* twin might the Other be . . . Garden mount / Bounded, triumphant entry this to him!

566 is] lies *del to* see *MS. 1814/27* see *1827–*

568–569 Ranged side by side, and lessening by degrees *1827–; so MS. 1814/27 but* &

572 spoil;—] freight;— *MS. 1814/27, 1832* freight; *1836–*

587 look,] looks, *1836–*

588 which] that *MS. 1814/27–*

589 at the self-same moment *del to* [?amid flowery islets] *then orig restored by eras of rev MS. 1832/36*

Parted and reunited: his Compeer
To the still Lake, whose stillness is to the eye
As beautiful, as grateful to the mind.
—But to what object shall the lovely Girl
Be likened? She whose countenance and air
Unite the graceful qualities of both,
Even as she shares the pride and joy of both.

My grey-haired Friend was moved; his vivid eye
Glistened with tenderness; his Mind, I knew,
Was full; and had, I doubted not, returned,
Upon this impulse, to the theme—erewhile
Abruptly broken-off. The ruddy Boys
Did now withdraw to take their well-earned meal;
And He—(to whom all tongues resigned their rights
With willingness, to whom the general ear
Listened with readier patience than to strain
Of music, lute or harp,—a long delight
That ceased not when his voice had ceased) as One
Who from truth's central point serenely views
The compass of his argument,—began
Mildly, and with a clear and steady tone.

END OF THE EIGHTH BOOK.

592 the eye] sight *MS. 1814/27–*

597 Even as to spurious sensibility / Untrained, she shares the pride of joy *pencil (with* of *overwritten by* &*) MS. 1836/45*

603 Withdrew, on summons to their well-earned meal; *1827– ; so MS. 1814/27 but* Withdrew on

BOOK THE NINTH.

DISCOURSE OF THE WANDERER, AND AN EVENING VISIT TO THE LAKE.

"To every Form of Being is assigned,"
Thus calmly spake the venerable Sage,
"An *active* principle:—howe'er removed
From sense and observation, it subsists
In all things, in all natures, in the stars
Of azure heaven, the unenduring clouds,
In flower and tree, in every pebbly stone
That paves the brooks, the stationary rocks,
The moving waters, and the invisible air.
Whate'er exists hath properties that spread
Beyond itself, communicating good,
A simple blessing, or with evil mixed;
Spirit that knows no insulated spot,
No chasm, no solitude; from link to link
It circulates, the Soul of all the Worlds.
This is the freedom of the Universe;
Unfolded still the more, more visible,
The more we know; and yet is reverenced least,
And least respected, in the human Mind,
Its most apparent home. The food of hope
Is meditated action; robbed of this,
Her sole support, she languishes and dies.
We perish also; for we live by hope
And by desire; we see by the glad light,
And breathe the sweet air of futurity,
And so we live, or else we have no life.
To-morrow—nay perchance this very hour,
(For every moment has its own to-morrow!)
—Those blooming Boys, whose hearts are almost sick
With present triumph, will be sure to find
A field before them freshened with the dew
Of other expectations;—in which course
Their happy year spins round. The Youth obeys
A like glad impulse; and so moves the Man
Mid all his apprehensions, cares, and fears,—
Or so he ought to move. Ah! why in age
Do we revert so fondly to the walks
Of Childhood—but that there the Soul discerns
The dear memorial footsteps unimpaired

7–9 in every . . . waters *del but restored by* stet *MS. 1836/45*
28 has] hath *1820E–*

Of her own native vigour—but for this,
That it is given her thence in age to hear
Reverberations; and a choral song,
Commingling with the incense that ascends
Undaunted, tow'rds the imperishable heavens,
From her own lonely altar?—Do not think
That Good and Wise will ever be allowed,
Though strength decay, to breathe in such estate
As shall divide them wholly from the stir
Of hopeful nature. Rightly is it said
That Man descends into the VALE of years;
Yet have I thought that we might also speak,
And not presumptuously I trust, of Age,
As of a final EMINENCE, though bare
In aspect and forbidding, yet a Point
On which 'tis not impossible to sit
In awful sovereignty—a place of power—
—A Throne, which may be likened unto his,
Who, in some placid day of summer, looks
Down from a mountain-top,—say one of those
High peaks, that bound the Vale where now we are.
Faint, and diminished to the gazing eye,
Forest and field, and hill and dale appear,
With all the shapes upon their surface spread.
But, while the gross and visible frame of things
Relinquishes its hold upon the sense,
Yea almost on the mind itself, and seems
All unsubstantialized,—how loud the voice
Of waters, with invigorated peal
From the full River in the vale below,
Ascending!—For on that superior height
Who sits, is disencumbered from the press
Of near obstructions, and is privileged
To breathe in solitude above the host
Of ever-humming insects, mid thin air
That suits not them. The murmur of the leaves
Many and idle, touches not his ear;
This he is freed from, and from thousand notes
Not less unceasing, not less vain than these,—
By which the finer passages of sense
Are occupied; and the Soul, that would incline
To listen, is prevented or deterred.

---

40 but for this,] thence can hear *MS. 1814/27–*
41 *om MS. 1814/27–*
46 will ever] ever will *1832–*
57 which] that *MS. 1814/27–*
63 upon] over *1845–*
66 itself,] herself, *MS. 1814/27–*
76 touches] visits *MS. 1814/27–*

And may it not be hoped, that, placed by Age
In like removal tranquil though severe,
We are not so removed for utter loss;
But for some favour, suited to our need?
What more than this, that we thereby should gain
Fresh power to commune with the invisible world,
And hear the mighty stream of tendency
Uttering, for elevation of our thought,
A clear sonorous voice, inaudible
To the vast multitude; whose doom it is
To run the giddy round of vain delight,
Or fret and labour on the Plain below.

But, if to such sublime ascent the hopes
Of Man may rise, as to a welcome close
And termination of his mortal course,
Them only can such hope inspire whose minds
Have not been starved by absolute neglect;
Nor bodies crushed by unremitting toil;
To whom kind Nature, therefore, may afford
Proof of the sacred love she bears for all;
Whose birth-right Reason, therefore, may ensure.
For me, consulting what I feel within
In times when most existence with herself
Is satisfied, I cannot but believe,
That, far as kindly Nature hath free scope
And Reason's sway predominates, even so far,
Country, society, and time itself,
That saps the Individual's bodily frame
And lays the generations low in dust,
Do, by the Almighty Ruler's grace, partake
Of one maternal spirit, bringing forth
And cherishing with ever-constant love,
That tires not, nor betrays. Our Life is turned
Out of her course, wherever Man is made
An offering, or a sacrifice, a tool
Or implement, a passive Thing employed
As a brute mean, without acknowledgment
Of common right or interest in the end;
Used or abused, as selfishness may prompt.
Say, what can follow for a rational Soul
Perverted thus, but weakness in all good,
And strength in evil? Hence an after-call
For chastisement, and custody, and bonds,
And oft-times Death, avenger of the past,
And the sole guardian in whose hands we dare

---

86 What more than that the severing should confer *MS. 1814/27–*

Entrust the future.—Not for these sad issues
Was Man created; but to obey the law
Of life, and hope, and action. And 'tis known
That when we stand upon our native soil,
[130] Unelbowed by such objects as oppress
Our active powers, those powers themselves become
Strong to subvert our noxious qualities:
They sweep away infection from the heart;
And, by the substitution of delight,
[135] Suppress all evil; whence the Being moves
In beauty through the world; and all who see
Bless him, rejoicing in his neighbourhood."

"Then," said the Solitary, "by what power
Of language shall a feeling Heart express
[140] Her sorrow for that multitude in whom
We look for health from seeds that have been sown
In sickness and for increase in a power
That works but by extinction. On themselves
They cannot lean, nor turn to their own hearts
[145] To know what they must do; their wisdom is
To look into the eyes of others, thence
To be instructed what they must avoid:
Or rather let us say, how least observed,
How with most quiet and most silent death,
[150] With the least taint and injury to the air
The Oppressor breathes, their human Form divine,
And their immortal Soul, may waste away."

The Sage rejoined, "I thank you—you have spared
My voice the utterance of a keen regret,
[155] A wide compassion which with you I share.
[156] When, heretofore, I placed before your sight
A most familiar object of our days,
[157] A Little-one, subjected to the Arts
Of modern ingenuity, and made
The senseless member of a vast machine,
[160] Serving as doth a spindle or a wheel;
Think not, that, pitying him, I could forget
The rustic Boy, who walks the fields, untaught;
The Slave of ignorance, and oft of want,
And miserable hunger. Much too much

134–136 They sweep distemper from the busy day,
And make the Vessel of the big round Year
Run o'er with gladness; whence the Being moves *1827– but* Vessel] Chalice *1832* chalice *MS. 1832/36–* Year] year *MS. 1832/36–*
139 power] force *1827–*
158 *del MS. 1814/27, om 1827–*

Of this unhappy lot, in early youth
We both have witnessed, lot which I myself
Shared, though in mild and merciful degree:
Yet was my mind to hindrances exposed,
Through which I struggled, not without distress
And sometimes injury, like a Sheep enthralled
Mid thorns and brambles; or a Bird that breaks
Through a strong net, and mounts upon the wind,
Though with her plumes impaired. If they, whose souls
Should open while they range the richer fields
Of merry England, are obstructed less
By indigence, their ignorance is not less
Nor less to be deplored. For who can doubt
That tens of thousands at this day exist
Such as the Boy you painted, lineal Heirs
Of those who once were Vassals of her soil,
Following its fortunes like the beasts or trees
Which it sustained. But no one takes delight
In this oppression; none are proud of it;
It bears no sounding name nor ever bore;
A standing grievance, an indigenous vice
Of every country under heaven. My thoughts
Were turned to evils that are new and chosen,
A Bondage lurking under shape of good,—
Arts, in themselves beneficent and kind,
But all too fondly followed and too far;
To Victims, which the merciful can see
Nor think that they are Victims; turned to wrongs
Which Women who have Children of their own
Regard without compassion, yea with praise!
I spake of mischief which the wise diffuse
With gladness, thinking that the more it spreads
The healthier, the securer we become;
Delusion which a moment may destroy!
Lastly I mourned for those whom I had seen
Corrupted and cast down, on favoured ground,
Where circumstance and nature had combined
To shelter innocence, and cherish love;
Who, but for this intrusion, would have lived,
Possessed of health, and strength, and peace of mind;
Thus would have lived, or never have been born.

---

170 my] the *MS. 1814/27–*
171 I] she *MS. 1814/27*
172 Sheep] Lamb *MS. 1814/27, 1832* lamb *1827, 1836–*
195 Which] By *MS. 1814/27–*
196 Regard] Beheld *MS. 1814/27–*
197 which . . . diffuse] by . . . diffused *MS. 1814/27–*

Alas! what differs more than man from man!
And whence that difference? whence but from himself?
For see the universal Race endowed
With the same upright form!—The sun is fixed,
[210] And the infinite magnificence of heaven,
Within the reach of every human eye;
The sleepless Ocean murmurs for all ears;
The vernal field infuses fresh delight
Into all hearts. Throughout the world of sense
[215] Even as an object is sublime or fair,
That object is laid open to the view
Without reserve or veil; and as a power
Is salutary, or an influence sweet,
Are each and all enabled to perceive
[220] That power, that influence, by impartial law.
Gifts nobler are vouchsafed alike to all;
Reason,—and, with that reason, smiles and tears;
Imagination, freedom in the will,
Conscience to guide and check; and death to be
[225] Foretasted, immortality presumed.
[229] Strange, then, nor less than monstrous might be deemed
[230] The failure, if the Almighty, to this point
Liberal and undistinguishing, should hide
The excellence of moral qualities
From common understanding; leaving truth
And virtue, difficult, abstruse, and dark;
[235] Hard to be won, and only by a few;
Strange, should he deal herein with nice respects,
And frustrate all the rest! Believe it not:
The primal duties shine aloft—like stars;
The charities that soothe, and heal, and bless,
[240] Are scattered at the feet of Man—like flowers.
The generous inclination, the just rule,
Kind wishes, and good actions, and pure thoughts—

---

213 Within the] Fixed within *MS. 1814/27– but* Fixed, *MS. 1832/36–*
227 presumed.] conceived *del right margin and* stet *left margin MS. 1836/45* conceived *adopted 1845–*
227/228 By all,—a blissful immortality,
To them whose holiness on earth shall make
The Spirit capable of heaven, assured. *1845– ; MS. 1836/45 drafts:*
a blissful immortality,
By all to them
em
~~By all~~ to th[?o] who holiness on earth shall make
The spirit capable of heaven, assured *del by two crosses right margin*
conceived
By all—a blissful immortality
To
~~B~~ them whose holiness on earth shall
The spirit capable of heaven assured *page foot, pencil, del by ink cross*
230 Liberal and] Bountiful *MS. 1836/45*

No mystery is here; no special boon
For high and not for low, for proudly graced
And not for meek of heart. The smoke ascends
To heaven as lightly from the Cottage hearth
As from the haughty palace. He, whose soul
Ponders this true equality, may walk
The fields of earth with gratitude and hope;
Yet, in that meditation, will he find
Motive to sadder grief, as we have found,—
Lamenting ancient virtues overthrown,
And for the injustice grieving, that hath made
So wide a difference betwixt Man and Man.

But let us rather fix our gladdened thoughts
Upon the brighter scene. How blest that Pair
Of blooming Boys (whom we beheld even now)
Blest in their several and their common lot!
A few short hours of each returning day
The thriving Prisoners of their Village school;
And thence let loose, to seek their pleasant homes,
Or range the grassy lawn in vacancy,
To breathe and to be happy, run and shout
Idle,—but no delay, no harm, no loss;
For every genial Power of heaven and earth,
Through all the seasons of the changeful year,
Obsequiously doth take upon herself
To labour for them; bringing each in turn
The tribute of enjoyment, knowledge, health,
Beauty, or strength! Such privilege is theirs,
Granted alike in the outset of their course
To both; and, if that partnership must cease,
I grieve not," to the Pastor here he turned,
"Much as I glory in that Child of yours,
Repine not, for his Cottage-comrade, whom
Belike no higher destiny awaits
Than the old hereditary wish fulfilled,
The wish for liberty to live—content
With what heaven grants, and die—in peace of mind,

---

242 no special] Here is no *MS. 1832/36–; MS. 1832/36 drafts:* mysteries here! [?There] is no special boon [?] *interlined, then:*

Here
~~No mysteries here! [?There] is no special~~ boon
~~For high~~
No mysteries here!—Here is no special boon
For high & *page foot*

243 and] yet *1836–*
244 And] Yet *1836–*
246 haughty] haughtiest *MS. 1832/36–*
253 betwixt] between *1836–*
254 But] Then *1836–* fix] turn *1827, 1832*

Within the bosom of his native Vale.
At least, whatever fate the noon of life
Reserves for either, this is sure, that both
Have been permitted to enjoy the dawn;
Whether regarded as a jocund time
That in itself may terminate, or lead
In course of nature to a sober eve.
Both have been fairly dealt with; looking back
They will allow that justice has in them
Been shewn—alike to body and to mind."

He paused, as if revolving in his soul
Some weighty matter, then, with fervent voice
And an impassioned majesty, exclaimed,
"Oh for the coming of that glorious time
When, prizing knowledge as her noblest wealth
And best protection, this Imperial Realm,
While she exacts allegiance, shall admit
An obligation, on her part, to *teach*
Them who are born to serve her and obey;
Binding herself by Statute to secure
For all the Children whom her soil maintains
The rudiments of Letters, and to inform
The mind with moral and religious truth,
Both understood, and practised,—so that none,
However destitute, be left to droop
By timely culture unsustained, or run
Into a wild disorder; or be forced
To drudge through weary life without the aid
Of intellectual implements and tools;
A savage Horde among the civilized,
A servile Band among the lordly free!
This right, as sacred almost as the right
To exist and be supplied with sustenance
And means of life, the lisping Babe proclaims
To be inherent in him, by Heaven's will,
For the protection of his innocence;
And the rude Boy—who, having overpast
The sinless age, by conscience is enrolled,
Yet mutinously knits his angry brow,
And lifts his wilful hand on mischief bent,

281 this is sure,] sure it is *MS. 1832/36–*
285–286 *MS. 1832/26 has pencil, eras, at page foot:* [? ? ? ? ?] them / B[?een] [? ?] alike to body & [?mind]
300 to inform] inform *MS. 1814/27–*
306 weary . . . aid] a weary . . . help *MS. 1832/36–*
310–312 This sacred right, the lisping Babe proclaims *MS. 1814/27– but* babe *MS. 1832/36–*

298 For WW's end-of-volume note, see p. 314, below.

Or turns the sacred faculty of speech
To impious use—by process indirect
Declares his due, while he makes known his need.
—This sacred right is fruitlessly announced,
This universal plea in vain addressed,
To eyes and ears of Parents who themselves
Did, in the time of their necessity,
Urge it in vain; and, therefore, like a prayer
That from the humblest floor ascends to heaven,
It mounts, to reach the State's parental ear;
Who, if indeed she own a Mother's heart,
And be not most unfeelingly devoid
Of gratitude to Providence, will grant
The unquestionable good; which, England, safe
From interference of external force,
May grant at leisure; without risk incurred
That what in wisdom for herself she doth,
Others shall e'er be able to undo.

Look! and behold, from Calpe's sunburnt cliffs
To the flat margin of the Baltic sea,
Long-reverenced Titles cast away as weeds;
Laws overturned,—and Territory split;
Like fields of ice rent by the polar wind
And forced to join in less obnoxious shapes,
Which, ere they gain consistence, by a gust
Of the same breath are shattered and destroyed.
Meantime, the Sovereignty of these fair Isles
Remains entire and indivisible;
And, if that ignorance were removed, which acts
Within the compass of their several shores
To breed commotion and disquietude,
Each might preserve the beautiful repose
Of heavenly Bodies shining in their spheres.
—The discipline of slavery is unknown
Amongst us,—hence the more do we require
The discipline of virtue; order else
Cannot subsist, nor confidence, nor peace.
Thus, duties rising out of good possessed,
And prudent caution needful to avert
Impending evil, do alike require

---

319 sacred] god-like *MS. 1814/27* godlike *1827–*
343 Which,] That, *1836–*
347 acts] breeds *MS. 1814/27–*
349–350 Dark discontent, or loud commotion, each / Might still preserve the beautiful repose *1827–; so MS. 1814/27 but overwriting illeg eras, and* discontent or discontent, *del in pencil to* discontent *restored by eras of del MS. 1836/45*
353 Amongst] Among *MS. 1832/36–*
358 do alike] equally *MS. 1814/27–*

That permanent provision should be made
[358] For the whole people to be taught and trained.
So shall licentiousness and black resolve
[360] Be rooted out, and virtuous habits take
Their place; and genuine piety descend,
Like an inheritance, from age to age.

With such foundations laid, avaunt the fear
Of numbers crowded on their native soil,
[365] To the prevention of all healthful growth
Through mutual injury! Rather in the law
Of increase and the mandate from above
Rejoice!—and Ye have special cause for joy.
—For, as the element of air affords
[370] An easy passage to the industrious bees
Fraught with their burthens; and a way as smooth
For those ordained to take their sounding flight
From the thronged hive, and settle where they list
In fresh abodes, their labour to renew;
[375] So the wide waters, open to the power,
The will, the instincts, and appointed needs
Of Britain, do invite her to cast off
Her swarms, and in succession send them forth;
Bound to establish new communities
[380] On every shore whose aspect favours hope
Or bold adventure; promising to skill
And perseverance their deserved reward.
—"Yes," he continued, kindling as he spake,
"Change wide, and deep, and silently performed,
[385] This Land shall witness; and, as days roll on,
Earth's universal Frame shall feel the effect
Even 'till the smallest habitable Rock,
Beaten by lonely billows, hear the songs
Of humanized Society; and bloom
[390] With civil arts, and send their fragrance forth,
A grateful tribute to all-ruling Heaven.
From Culture, universally bestowed
[393] On Britain's noble Race in freedom born;
From Education, from that humble source,
[394] Expect these mighty issues; from the pains

359–360 That the whole people should be taught and trained. *MS. 1814/27– but* trained.] trained *1849 (probable worn plate)*
363/364 Upon the humblest member of the State *with* subject *alt for* member *MS. 1836/45*
392 and] that *MS. 1814/27–* With civil arts, that shall breathe forth their fragrance, *1845–*
394 universally] unexclusively *MS. 1814/27–*
395 Britain's] Albion's *MS. 1814/27–*
396 *del MS. 1814/27, om 1827–*

And quiet care of unambitious Schools
Instructing simple Childhood's ready ear:
Thence look for these magnificent results!
Vast the circumference of hope—and Ye
Are at its centre, British Lawgivers,
Ah! sleep not there in shame! Shall Wisdom's voice,
From out the bosom of these troubled Times
Repeat the dictates of her calmer mind,
And shall the venerable Halls ye fill
Refuse to echo the sublime decree?
Trust not to partial care a general good;
Transfer not to Futurity a work
Of urgent need.—Your Country must complete
Her glorious destiny.—Begin even now,
Now, when Oppression, like the Egyptian plague
Of darkness stretched o'er guilty Europe, makes
The brightness more conspicuous, that invests
The happy Island where ye think and act:
Now, when destruction is a prime pursuit,
Shew to the wretched Nations for what end
The Powers of civil Polity were given!"

Abruptly here, but with a graceful air
The Sage broke off. No sooner had he ceased
Than, looking forth, the gentle Lady said,
"Behold, the shades of afternoon have fallen
Upon this flowery slope; and see—beyond—
The Lake, though bright, is of a placid blue;
As if preparing for the peace of evening.
How temptingly the landscape shines!—The air
Breathes invitation; easy is the walk
To the Lake's margin, where a Boat lies moored
Beneath her sheltering tree."—Upon this hint
We rose together: all were pleased—but most
The beauteous Girl, whose cheek was flushed with joy.
Light as a sun-beam glides along the hills
She vanished—eager to impart the scheme
To her loved Brother and his shy Compeer,
—Now was there bustle in the Vicar's house
And earnest preparation.—Forth we went,
And down the Valley on the Streamlet's bank
Pursued our way, a broken Company,

---

398 quiet] faithful *1827–*
424 The silvery lake is streaked with placid blue; *1836–; so MS. 1832/36 but* blue, is streaked with *del to* streaked with a *MS. 1836/45*
429 Beneath her] Under a *1845–*
437 And down the Vale along the Streamlet's edge *1827– but* vale . . . streamlet's *1836– ; MS. 1814/27 as 1827 but* Vale,

Mute or conversing, single or in pairs.
Thus having reached a bridge, that overarched
The hasty rivulet where it lay becalmed
In a deep pool, by happy chance we saw
[440] A two-fold Image; on a grassy bank
A snow-white Ram, and in the crystal flood
Another and the same! Most beautiful,
On the green turf, with his imperial front
Shaggy and bold, and wreathed horns superb,
[445] The breathing Creature stood; as beautiful,
Beneath him, shewed his shadowy Counterpart.
Each had his glowing mountains, each his sky,
And each seemed centre of his own fair world:
Antipodes unconscious of each other,
[450] Yet, in partition, with their several spheres,
Blended in perfect stillness, to our sight!

"Ah! what a pity were it to disperse,
Or to disturb, so fair a spectacle,
And yet a breath can do it!"
These few words
[455] The Lady whispered, while we stood and gazed
Gathered together, all, in still delight,
Not without awe. Thence passing on, she said
In like low voice to my particular ear,
"I love to hear that eloquent Old Man
[460] Pour forth his meditations, and descant
On human life from infancy to age.
How pure his spirit! in what vivid hues
His mind gives back the various forms of things,
Caught in their fairest, happiest attitude!
[465] While he is speaking I have power to see
Even as he sees; but when his voice hath ceased,
Then, with a sigh I sometimes feel, as now,
[468] That combinations so serene and bright,
[471] Like those reflected in yon quiet Pool,

---

453 Yet] But *pencil alt del MS. 1836/45*
455 Ah!] yet *pencil alt del MS. 1836/45*
457 faintest breeze *written in pencil over eras* Yet [? ?] *then all del MS. 1836/45*
470 I sometimes] sometimes I *1832–*
472–474 Like those reflected in yon quiet pool,
Cannot be lasting in a world whose pleasure
(And whose best beauty, beautiful as it is)
Seems but a fleeting sun-beam's gift, whose peace
The sufferance only of a breath of air!" *MS. 1832/36, 1836*
Cannot be lasting in a world like ours,
One whose best beauty, beautiful as it is,
Like that reflected in yon quiet pool,
The sufferance only of a breath of air!" *1840– but* One whose best] Whose highest *1845–;*
entry continues, below

[469] Cannot be lasting in a world like ours,
To great and small disturbances exposed."
[474] More had she said—but sportive shouts were heard;
[475] Sent from the jocund hearts of those two Boys,
Who, bearing each a basket on his arm,
Down the green field came tripping after us.
—When we had cautiously embarked, the Pair

472–474 *MS. 1836/45 drafts:*
~~on which~~
[?that] [~~? ? ?~~]
Like those reflected in yon quiet pool
like that reflected yon quiet pool
And whose *with arrow to l. 472; illeg pencil del by eras above l. 472*
avid
Cannot be lasting in a world ~~whose ^pleasure^~~, like ours *with* avid *and added final comma in pencil and* like ours *ink over pencil*
[?one] W highest
~~(And~~ w}hose ~~best~~ beauty, beautiful as it is~~)~~
,
Seems but a fleeting sun-beam's gift, whose peace } *with added comma eras; then pencil draft at top of page:*
Like those on which a moment pas'd we gazed
[?Contrast] not with our world, whose liveliest pleasure *pencil, del by ink cross and pencil wavy lines; then draft at page foot:*
Whose highest beauty beautiful as it is
Like that reflected in yon quiet pool
Seems but a fleeting &c
473–491a *MS. 1832/36 has ll. 473–491 (as printed in 1836) copied on an inserted leaf*
479–484 With caution we embarked; and now the pair
For prouder service were addrest; but each,
Wishful to leave an opening for my choice,
Dropped the light oar his eager hand had seized.
Thanks given for that becoming courtesy
Their place I took—and for a grateful office *MS. 1832/36–but* For] To *MS. 1836/45* courtesy] courtesy, *1845– ; there are several drafts in MS. 1832/36:*
Cautiously we embark d—and now the pair
For prouder service were address d but
Or
[? ?] dropp d with prompt hand his oar
That I myself might undertake the grateful
Droppd *pencil on free endpaper at back of book*
Cautiously we embarked, & now the pair
For prouder service were addressed, but each
[?For]
ped
Drop t the light oar which he with eager hand
Had seized *del, at page foot*
Was clear [?] I [?droppd,] with [?arms] *pencil at page foot*
Cautiously we embarked, and now the pair
For prouder service were addrest; but each
[? ?] to leave an opening for my choice,
Dropp'd the light oar which he with eager hand
Had seized Had seized; & so I entered on a task *interlined*
I undertook the grateful task — a labour *top of facing page*
Thanks given [? ? ?]
[? ? ? ? ? ? ? ?]
I entered in that [? ? ?]
I undertook the [? ? ?]
Was cleared, I dipp [? ? ?]
[? ?oars] *pencil, eras, top and bottom of facing page; entry continues, below*

[479] Now for a prouder service were addrest;
But an inexorable law forbade,
[479/481] And each resigned the oar which he had seized.
[483] Whereat, with willing hand I undertook
The needful labour; grateful task!—to me
[484] Pregnant with recollections of the time
[485] When, on thy bosom, spacious Windermere!
A Youth, I practised this delightful art;
Tossed on the waves alone, or mid a crew
Of joyous Comrades.—Now the reedy marge
Cleared, with a strenuous arm I dipped the oar,
[490] Free from obstruction; and the Boat advanced
Through crystal water, smoothly as a Hawk,
That, disentangled from the shady boughs
Of some thick wood, her place of covert, cleaves
With correspondent wings the abyss of air.
[495] —"Observe," the Vicar said, "yon rocky Isle
With birch-trees fringed; my hand shall guide the helm,
While thitherward we bend our course; or while
We seek that other, on the western shore,—
Where the bare Columns of those lofty Firs,
[500] Supporting gracefully a massy Dome
Of sombre foliage, seem to imitate
A Grecian Temple rising from the Deep."

"Turn where we may," said I, we cannot err
In this delicious Region."—Cultured slopes,
[505] Wild tracts of forest-ground, and scattered groves,
And mountains bare—or clothed with ancient woods,
Surrounded us; and, as we held our way
Along the level of the glassy flood,
They ceased not to surround us; change of place,
[510] From kindred features diversly combined,
Producing change of beauty ever new.
—Ah! that such beauty, varying in the light
Of living nature, cannot be pourtrayed
By words, nor by the pencil's silent skill;

479–484 *Drafts in MS. 1832/36 continue:*
~~Thanks~~
~~[?] given for that becoming courtesy~~ *top of page*
Cautiously we embarke[ ] air
For prouder service [ ] but each,
Wishful to leave an ope[ ] my choice,
his
~~Dropp'd the light oar wh~~[ ]~~e with eager~~ hand
had siez[?]
Had seized, & I entered on a task *top of page; brackets indicate gaps caused by paper that has peeled off*

489 Now] Soon as *MS. 1832/36–*
490 Was cleared, I dipped, with arms accordant, oars *MS. 1832/36–*
498 bend] shape *MS. 1832/36–*
502 sombre] darksome *MS. 1836/45*

But is the property of him alone
Who hath beheld it, noted it with care,
And in his mind recorded it with love!
Suffice it, therefore, if the rural Muse
Vouchsafe sweet influence, while her Poet speaks
Of trivial occupations well devised,
And unsought pleasures springing up by chance;
As if some friendly Genius had ordained
That, as the day thus far had been enriched
By acquisition of sincere delight,
The same should be continued to its close.

One spirit animating old and young,
A gypsy fire we kindled on the shore
Of the fair Isle with birch-trees fringed—and there
Merrily seated in a ring, partook
The beverage drawn from China's fragrant herb.
—Launched from our hands the smooth stone skimmed the Lake;
With shouts we roused the echoes;—stiller sounds
The lovely Girl supplied—a simple song,
Whose low tones reached not to the distant rocks
To be repeated there, but gently sank
Into our hearts; and charmed the peaceful flood.
Rapaciously we gathered flowery spoils
From land and water; Lillies of each hue—
Golden and white, that float upon the waves
And court the wind; and leaves of that shy Plant,
(Her flowers were shed) the Lilly of the Vale,
That loves the ground, and from the sun withholds
Her pensive beauty, from the breeze her sweets.

Such product, and such pastime did the place
And season yield; but, as we re-embarked,
Leaving, in quest of other scenes, the shore
Of that wild Spot, the Solitary said
In a low voice, yet careless who might hear,
"The Fire, that burned so brightly to our wish,
Where is it now? Deserted on the beach

---

529 fair] [?selected] *del MS. 1836/45* and there] and soon *del* with stet *right margin MS. 1836/45*
530 And *del MS. 1836/45*
531 A choice repast—served by our young companions
With rival earnestness and kindred glee. *MS. 1832/36–*
P|
by youthful p|ages served
our young *page foot MS. 1836/45*
533 roused] raised *1836–*
536 there,] thence, *MS. 1814/27–*

It seems extinct; nor shall the fanning breeze
Revive its ashes. What care we for this,
Whose ends are gained? Behold an emblem here
[555] Of one day's pleasure, and all mortal joys!
And, in this unpremeditated slight
Of that which is no longer needed, see
The common course of human gratitude!"

This plaintive note disturbed not the repose
[560] Of the still evening. Right across the Lake
Our pinnace moves: then, coasting creek and bay,
Glades we behold—and into thickets peep—
Where couch the spotted deer; or raised our eyes
To shaggy steeps on which the careless goat
[565] Browzed by the side of dashing waterfalls.
Thus did the Bark, meandering with the shore,
Pursue her voyage, till a point was gained
[568] Where a projecting line of rock, that framed
A natural pier, invited us to land.
[569] —Alert to follow as the Pastor led
[570] We clomb a green hill's side; and thence obtained,
[572] Slowly, a less and less obstructed sight
Of the flat meadows, and indented coast
Of the whole lake—in compass seen! Far off,
[575] And yet conspicuous, stood the old Church-tower,
In majesty presiding o'er the Vale
And all her Dwellings; seemingly preserved
From the intrusion of a restless world
By rocks impassable and mountains huge.

[580] Soft heath this elevated spot supplied,
With resting-place of mossy stone;—and there

---

552 It seems extinct; nor] Dying, or dead! Nor *MS. 1832/36–*
564 Aloft *pencil del by eras MS. 1814/27*
566 Thus did] And thus *MS. 1832/36–*
567–569 Pursue her voyage, till a natural pier / Of jutting rock invited us to land. *MS. 1814/27– but* Pursued *MS. 1832/36–*
571–572 We clomb a green hill's side; and as we clomb,
The Valley, opening out her bosom, gave
Fair prospect, intercepted less and less, *1827– but* and as] and, as *1836–; MS. 1814/27 as 1827 but* clomb / The valley, . . . prospect intercepted less & less
573 Of] O'er *1836–*
574 whole] smooth *MS. 1814/27–*
576 o'er the Vale] over fields *MS. 1814/27–*
577 all her Dwellings;] habitations; *MS. 1814/27* habitations, *1827–1836* habitations *pencil MS. 1836/45, 1840–*
578 the . . . a] all . . . the *1845–*
581–584 And choice of moss-clad stones, whereon we couched
Or sate reclined—admiring quietly
The general aspect of the scene; but each
Not seldom over anxious to make known *1827–; MS. 1814/27 readings: (1) ll. 581–582 as 1827, interlined (but* stones,] stone *and* [?Where we] *in pencil, eras, above l. 582); (2) l. 583 as 1814 (but* The frame and *del to* Admiring greatly*); (3) l. 584 as 1827; illeg pencil drafting, eras, at page foot, above l. 583, and in left margin*

We sate reclined—admiring quietly
The frame and general aspect of the scene;
And each not seldom eager to make known
His own discoveries; or to favourite points
Directing notice, merely from a wish
To impart a joy, imperfect while unshared.
That rapturous moment ne'er shall I forget
When these particular interests were effaced
From every mind!—Already had the sun,
Sinking with less than ordinary state,
Attained his western bound; but rays of light—
Now suddenly diverging from the orb
Retired behind the mountain tops or veiled
By the dense air—shot upwards to the crown
Of the blue firmament—aloft—and wide:
And multitudes of little floating clouds,
Pierced through their thin etherial mould, ere we,
Who saw, of change were conscious, had become
Vivid as fire—clouds separately poized,
Innumerable multitude of Forms
Scattered through half the circle of the sky;
And giving back, and shedding each on each,
With prodigal communion, the bright hues
Which from the unapparent Fount of glory
They had imbibed, and ceased not to receive.
That which the heavens displayed, the liquid deep
Repeated; but with unity sublime!

While from the grassy mountain's open side
We gazed, in silence hushed, with eyes intent
On the refulgent spectacle—diffused
Through earth, sky, water, and all visible space,
The Priest in holy transport thus exclaimed—

"Eternal Spirit! universal God!
Power inaccessible to human thought
Save by degrees and steps which Thou hast deigned
To furnish; for this Image of Thyself,
To the infirmity of mortal sense
Vouchsafed; this local, transitory type
Of thy paternal splendors, and the pomp
Of those who fill thy courts in highest heaven,
The radiant Cherubim;—accept the thanks
Which we, thy humble Creatures, here convened,
Presume to offer; we, who from the breast

598–599 Ere we, who saw, of change were conscious, pierced / Through their ethereal texture, had become *1827, 1832; so MS. 1814/27 but* pierced / Pierced through their etherial Through their ethereal texture pierced—ere we, / Who saw, of change were conscious—had become *1836–*

617 Image] Effluence *MS. 1814/27* effluence *1827–*

Of the frail earth, permitted to behold
The faint reflections only of thy face,
Are yet exalted, and in Soul adore!
Such as they are who in thy presence stand
Unsullied, incorruptible, and drink
Imperishable majesty streamed forth
From thy empyreal Throne, the elect of Earth
Shall be—divested at the appointed hour
Of all dishonour—cleansed from mortal stain.
—Accomplish, then, their number; and conclude
Time's weary course! Or, if by thy decree
The consummation that will come by stealth
Be yet far distant, let thy Word prevail,
Oh! let thy Word prevail, to take away
The sting of human nature. Spread the law,
As it is written in thy holy book,
Throughout all Lands; let every nation hear
The high behest, and every heart obey;
Both for the love of purity, and hope
Which it affords, to such as do thy will
And persevere in good, that they shall rise,
To have a nearer view of Thee, in heaven.
—Father of Good! this prayer in bounty grant,
In mercy grant it to thy wretched Sons.
Then, nor till then, shall persecution cease,
And cruel Wars expire. The way is marked,
The guide appointed, and the ransom paid.
Alas! the Nations, who of yore received
These tidings, and in Christian Temples meet
The sacred truth to acknowledge, linger still;
Preferring bonds and darkness to a state
Of holy freedom, by redeeming love
Proffered to all, while yet on earth detained.
So fare the many; and the thoughtful few,
Who in the anguish of their souls bewail
This dire perverseness, cannot choose but ask,
Shall it endure?—Shall enmity and strife,
Falsehood and guile, be left to sow their seed;
And the kind never perish? Is the hope
Fallacious, or shall Righteousness obtain
A peaceable dominion, wide as earth
And ne'er to fail? Shall that blest day arrive
When they, whose choice or lot it is to dwell
In crowded cities, without fear shall live
Studious of mutual benefit; and he,
Whom morning wakes, among sweet dews and flowers

---

670 Whom Morn awakens, among dews and flowers *1836–; so MS. 1832/36 but* and] &

Of every clime, to till the lonely field,
Be happy in himself?—The law of faith
Working through love, such conquest shall it gain,
Such triumph over sin and guilt achieve?
[675] Almighty Lord, thy further grace impart!
And with that help the wonder shall be seen
Fulfilled, the hope accomplished; and thy praise
[678] Be sung with transport and unceasing joy.

[682] Once, while the Name, Jehovah, was a sound,
Within the circuit of this sea-girt isle,
Unheard, the savage Nations bowed their heads
[695] To Gods delighting in remorseless deeds;
Gods which themselves had fashioned, to promote
Ill purposes, and flatter foul desires.
Then, in the bosom of yon mountain cove,
To those inventions of corrupted Man
[690] Mysterious rites were solemnized; and there,
Amid impending rocks and gloomy woods,
Of those dread Idols, some, perchance, received
Such dismal service, that the loudest voice
Of the swoln cataracts (which now are heard
[695] Soft murmuring) was too weak to overcome,
Though aided by wild winds, the groans and shrieks
Of human Victims, offered up to appease
Or to propitiate. And, if living eyes
Had visionary faculties to see
[700] The thing that hath been as the thing that is,
Aghast we might behold this spacious Mere
Bedimmed with smoke, in wreaths voluminous,
Flung from the body of devouring fires,
To Taranis erected on the heights
[705] By priestly hands, for sacrifice, performed
Exultingly, in view of open day
And full assemblage of a barbarous Host;
Or to Andates, Female Power! who gave
(For so they fancied) glorious Victory.
[710] —A few rude Monuments of mountain-stone
Survive; all else is swept away.—How bright
The appearances of things! From such, how changed

678/679 Once," and with mild demeanour, as he spake,
On us the Venerable Pastor turned
His beaming eye that had been raised to Heaven, *para 1827– but* Once,"] "Once," *1832* Venerable] venerable *MS. 1832/36–* had been raised to Heaven,] Heavenward had been raised *MS. 1836/45; MS. 1814/27, overwriting illeg erased pencil, as 1827 but* "Once" & . . . turn'd

681 their heads] the head *MS. 1814/27–*

689 dread] terrific *MS. 1814/27* Of those terrific Idols, some received *1827– but* Idols,] Idols *1836–*

695 eyes] sight *pencil del by eras MS. 1832/36*

698 spacious] crystal *MS. 1814/27–*

The existing worship; and, with those compared,
The Worshippers how innocent and blest!
So wide the difference, a willing mind,
At this affecting hour, might almost think
That Paradise, the lost abode of man,
Was raised again; and to a happy Few,
In its original beauty, here restored.
—Whence but from Thee, the true and only God,
And from the faith derived through Him who bled
Upon the Cross, this marvellous advance
Of good from evil; as if one extreme
Were left—the other gained.—O Ye, who come
To kneel devoutly in yon reverend Pile,
Called to such office by the peaceful sound
Of Sabbath bells; and Ye, who sleep in earth,
All cares forgotten, round its hallowed walls!
For You, in presence of this little Band
Gathered together on the green hill-side,
Your Pastor is emboldened to prefer
Vocal thanksgivings to the eternal King;
Whose love, whose counsel, whose commands have made
Your very poorest rich in peace of thought
And in good works; and Him, who is endowed
With scantiest knowledge, Master of all truth
Which the salvation of his soul requires.
Conscious of that abundant favour shower'd
On you, the Children of my humble care;—
On your Abodes, and this beloved Land,
Our birth-place, home, and Country, while on Earth
We sojourn,—loudly do I utter thanks
With earnest joy, that will not be suppressed.
These barren rocks, your stern inheritance;
These fertile fields, that recompence your pains;
The shadowy vale, the sunny mountain-top;
Woods waving in the wind their lofty heads,
Or hushed; the roaring waters, or the still;
They see the offering of my lifted hands—
They hear my lips present their sacrifice—
They know if I be silent, morn or even:
For, though in whispers speaking, the full heart
Will find a vent; and Thought is praise to Him,

---

713 Might almost think, at this affecting hour, *1836–; so MS. 1832/36 but* hour,] hour

737–740 And this dear Land, our Country while on earth
We sojourn,—loudly do I utter thanks
Joy giving voice to fervent gratitude. *MS. 1814/27*
And this dear Land, our Country, while on Earth
We sojourn, have I lifted up my soul,
Joy giving voice to fervent gratitude. *1827– but* land, . . . country, . . . earth *MS. 1832/36–*

745 or] and *1827–*

Audible praise, to Thee, Omniscient Mind,
From Whom all gifts descend, all blessings flow!"

This Vesper service closed, without delay,
From that exalted station, to the plain
Descending, we pursued our homeward course,
In mute composure, o'er the shadowy lake,
Beneath a faded sky. No trace remained
Of those celestial splendors; grey the vault,
Pure, cloudless ether; and the Star of Eve
Was wanting;—but inferior Lights appeared
Faintly, too faint almost for sight; and some
Above the darkened hills stood boldly forth
In twinkling lustre, ere the Boat attained
Her mooring-place;—where, to the sheltering tree
Our youthful Voyagers bound fast her prow,
With prompt yet careful hands. This done, we paced
The dewy fields; but ere the Vicar's door
Was reached, the Solitary checked his steps;
Then, intermingling thanks, on each bestowed
A farewell salutation,—and, the like
Receiving, took the slender path that leads
To the one Cottage in the lonely dell,
His chosen residence. But, ere he turned
Aside, a welcome promise had been given,
That he would share the pleasures and pursuits
Of yet another summer's day, consumed
In wandering with us through the Vallies fair,
And o'er the Mountain-wastes. "Another sun,"
Said he, "shall shine upon us, ere we part,—
Another sun, and peradventure more;
If time, with free consent, be yours to give,—
And season favours."
To enfeebled Power,
From this conmunion with uninjured Minds,
What renovation had been brought; and what
Degree of healing to a wounded spirit,
Dejected, and habitually disposed
To seek, in degradation of the Kind,
Excuse and solace for her own defects;
How far those erring notions were reformed;
And whether aught, of tendency as good

---

757 Beneath] Under *MS. 1832/36–*

773–774 But turned not without welcome promise given, *1827– but* given,] given *1836–1843* made *MS. 1836/45, 1845–*

776–777 Of yet another summer's day, consumed / In wandering with us through the valleys fair, *1836– but* consumed] given up *MS. 1836/45* not loth *1845–* In] To *MS. 1836/45, 1845–* wandering] wander *1845–* valleys fair] fertile vales MS. *1836/45, 1845–*

781 be] is *MS. 1814/27–1843*

And pure, from further intercourse ensued;
This—(if delightful hopes, as heretofore,
Inspire the serious song, and gentle Hearts
Cherish, and lofty Minds approve the past)
My future Labours may not leave untold.

795/ END OF THE NINTH BOOK. *1836– but om 1845, 1850*

NOTES.

PREFACE.

[Preface, *Prospectus*, ll. 83–84]
Page xi.—*"Come thou prophetic Spirit, that inspir'st*
The human soul, &c."

Not mine own fears, nor the prophetic Soul
Of the wide world dreaming on things to come.
Shakespeare's Sonnets.

[Book I, l. 370]
Page 20. Line 10. "———*much did he see of men.*"

In Heron's Tour in Scotland is given an intelligent account of the qualities by which this class of men used to be, and still are, in some degree, distinguished, and of the benefits which Society derives from their labours. Among their characteristics, he does not omit to mention that, from being obliged to pass so much of their time in solitary wandering among rural objects, they frequently acquire meditative habits of mind, and are strongly disposed to enthusiasm poetical and religious. I regret

---

no variants

1–9 *om, replaced by:* At the risk of giving a shock to the prejudices of artificial society, I have ever been ready to pay homage to the Aristocracy of Nature; under a conviction that vigorous human-heartedness is the constituent principle of true taste. It may still, however, be satisfactory to have prose-testimony how far a Character, employed for purposes of imagination, is founded upon general fact. I therefore subjoin an extract from an author who had opportunities of being well acquainted with a class of men, from whom my own personal knowledge emboldened me to draw this Portrait.

"We learn from Cæsar and other Roman Writers, that the travelling merchants who frequented Gaul and other barbarous countries, either newly conquered by the Roman arms, or bordering on the Roman conquests, were ever the first to make the inhabitants of those countries familiarly acquainted with the Roman modes of life, and to inspire them with an inclination to follow the Roman fashions, and to enjoy Roman conveniences. In North America, travelling merchants from the Settlements have done and continue to do much more towards civilizing the Indian natives, than all the Missionaries, Papist or Protestant, who have ever been sent among them.

"It is farther to be observed, for the credit of this most useful class of men, that they commonly contribute, by their personal manners, no less than by the sale of their wares, to the refinement of the people among whom they travel. Their dealings form them to great quickness of wit and acuteness of judgment. Having constant occasion to recommend themselves and their goods, they acquire habits of the most obliging attention, and the most insinuating address. As in their peregrinations they have opportunity of contemplating the manners of various Men and various Cities, they become eminently skilled in the knowledge of the world. *As they wander, each alone, through thinly-inhabited districts, they form habits of reflection and of sublime contemplation.* With all these qualifications, no wonder, that they should often be, in remote parts of the country, the best mirrors of fashion, and censors of manners; and should contribute much to polish the roughness, and soften the rusticity of our peasantry. It is not more than twenty or thirty years, since a young man going from any part of Scotland to England, of purpose to *carry the pack,* was considered, as going to lead the life, and acquire the Fortune, of a Gentleman. When, after twenty years' absence, in that honourable line of

that I have not the book at hand to quote the passage, as it is interesting on many accounts.

[Book III, l. 116]
Page 100. Line 15.—*"Lost in unsearchable Eternity!"*

Since this paragraph was composed I have read with so much pleasure, in Burnet's Theory of the Earth, a passage expressing correspondent sentiments, excited by objects of a similar nature, that I cannot forbear to transcribe it.

"Siquod verò Natura nobis dedit spectaculum in hâc tellure, verè gratum, et philosopho dignum, id semel mihi contigisse arbitror; cùm ex celsissimâ rupe speculabundus ad oram maris mediterranei, hinc æquor cæruleum, illinc tractus Alpinos prospexi; nihil quidem magìs dispar aut dissimile, nec in suo genere, magìs egregium et singulare. Hoc theatrum ego facilè prætulerim Romanis cunctis, Græcísve; atque id quod natura hîc spectandum exhibet, scenicis ludis omnibus, aut amphitheatri certaminibus. Nihil hîc elegans aut venustum, sed ingens et magnificum, et quod placet magnitudine suâ et quâdam specie immensitatis. Hinc intuebar maris æquabilem superficiem, usque et usque diffusam, quantum maximùm oculorum acies ferri potuit; illinc disruptissimam terræ faciem, et vastas moles variè elevatas aut depressas, erectas, propendentes, reclinatas, coacervatas, omni situ inæquali et turbido. Placuit, ex hâc parte, Naturæ unitas et simplicitas, et inexhausta quædam planities; ex altera, multiformis confusio magnorum corporum, et insanæ rerum strages: quas cùm intuebar, non urbis alicujus aut oppidi, sed confracti mundi rudera, ante oculos habere mihi visus sum.

"In singulis ferè montibus erat aliquid insolens et mirabile, sed præ cæteris mihi placebat illa, qua sedebam, rupes; erat maxima et altissima, et quâ terram respiciebat, molliori ascensu altitudinem suam dissimulabat: quà verò mare, horrendum præceps, et quasi ad perpendiculum facta, instar parietis. Prætereà facies illa marina adeò erat lævis ac uniformis (quod in rupibus aliquando observare licet) ac si scissa fuisset à summo ad imum, in illo plano; vel terræ motu aliquo, aut fulmine, divulsa.

"Ima pars rupis erat cava, recessúsque habuit, et saxeos specus, euntes in vacuum montem; sive naturâ pridem factos, sive exesos mari, et undarum crebris ictibus: In hos enim cum impetu ruebant et fragore, æstuantis maris fluctus; quos iterum spumantes reddidit antrum, et quasi ab imo ventre evomuit.

employment, he returned with his acquisitions to his native country, he was regarded as a Gentleman to all intents and purposes."

Heron's Journey in Scotland, Vol. i. p. 89.

1827–but [2] aristocracy of Nature; *MS. 1832/36* aristocracy of nature; *1836–* [*4*] prose testimony *1845–* [5] I, therefore, *1832–* [7] portrait. *1836–* [*8*] 'We *MS. 1836/45, 1845–1849, 1850* [*12*] conveniencies. *1832* [*14*] civilising *1845–1849, 1850* missionaries, Papist or Protestant, *MS. 1832/36* missionaries, papist or protestant, *1836–* [*16*] "It] It *1836–* [22] men and various cities, *1836–* [27] years,] years *1845–* [*28*] considered,] considered *1845–* life,] life *1845–* [*29*] fortune, *1836–1843* fortune *1845–* [*29–31*] gentleman. . . . as a gentleman *1836–* [*31*] purposes.' *MS. 1836/45, 1845, 1850*

2–3 correspondent] corresponding *1845, 1850*

"Dextrum latus montis erat præruptum, aspero saxo et nudâ caute; sinistrum non adeò neglexerat Natura, arboribus utpote ornatum: et prope pedem montis rivus limpidæ aquæ prorupit; qui cùm vicinam vallem irrigaverat, lento motu serpens, et per varios mæandros, quasi ad protrahendam vitam, in magno mari absorptus subito periit. Denique in summo vertice promontorii,commodè eminebat saxum, cui insidebam contemplabundus. Vale augusta sedes, Rege digna: Augusta rupes, semper mihi memoranda!" P. 89. *Telluris Theoria sacra, &c. Editio secunda.*

[Book III, l. 940]
Page 137. Line 13.—*"Of Mississippi, or that Northern Stream."*

"A Man is supposed to improve by going out into the *World,* by visiting *London.* Artificial man does; he extends with his sphere; but alas! that sphere is microscopic: it is formed of minutiæ, and he surrenders his genuine vision to the artist, in order to embrace it in his ken. His bodily senses grow acute, even to barren and inhuman pruriency; while his mental become proportionally obtuse. The reverse is the Man of Mind: He who is placed in the sphere of Nature and of God, might be a mock at Tattersall's and Brookes's, and a sneer at St. James's: he would certainly be swallowed alive by the first *Pizarro* that crossed him:—But when he walks along the River of Amazons; when he rests his eye on the unrivalled Andes; when he measures the long and watered Savannah; or contemplates from a sudden Promontory, the distant, vast Pacific—and feels himself a Freeman in this vast Theatre, and commanding each ready produced fruit of this wilderness, and each progeny of this stream—His exaltation is not less than Imperial. He is as gentle, too, as he is great: His emotions of tenderness keep pace with his elevation of sentiment; for he says, "These were made by a good Being, who, unsought by me, placed me here to enjoy them." He becomes at once a Child and a King. His mind is in himself; from hence he argues, and from hence he acts; and he argues unerringly and acts magisterially: His mind in himself is also in his God; and therefore he loves, and therefore he soars."—From the Notes upon *The Hurricane,* a Poem, *by William Gilbert.*

The Reader, I am sure, will thank me for the above Quotation, which, though from a strange book, is one of the finest passages of modern English Prose.

[Book IV, ll. 130–131]
P. 147. L. 7.—*"'Tis, by comparison, an easy task*
Earth to despise, &c."

See, upon this subject, Baxter's most interesting review of his own opinions and sentiments in the decline of life. It may be found (lately reprinted) in Dr. Wordsworth's *Ecclesiastical Biography.*

[Book IV, ll. 205–206]
P. 150. L. 13.—*"Alas! the endowment of immortal Power,*

Is matched unequally with custom, time, &c."

This subject is treated at length in the Ode at the conclusion of the second volume of Poems by the Author.

[Book IV, l. 325]
P. 155. L. 22.—*"Knowing"—(to adopt the energetic words."*

The passage quoted from Daniel is taken from a poem addressed to the Lady Margaret, Countess of Cumberland, and the two last lines, printed in Italics, are by him translated from Seneca. The whole Poem is very beautiful. I will transcribe four stanzas from it, as they contain an admirable picture of the state of a wise Man's mind in a time of public commotion.

Nor is he moved with all the Thunder-cracks
Of Tyrants' threats, or with the surly brow
Of Power, that proudly sits on others' crimes;
Charged with more crying sins than those he checks.
The storms of sad confusion that may grow
Up in the present for the coming times,
Appal not him; that hath no side at all,
But of himself, and knows the worst can fall.

Although his heart (so near allied to earth)
Cannot but pity the perplexed state
Of troublous and distress'd mortality,
That thus make way unto the ugly Birth
Of their own Sorrows, and do still beget
Affliction upon Imbecility:
Yet seeing thus the course of things must run,
He looks thereon not strange, but as fore-done.

And whilst distraught Ambition compasses,
And is encompass'd, while as Craft deceives:
And is deceiv'd: whilst Man doth ransack Man,
And builds on blood, and rises by distress;
And th'Inheritance of desolation leaves
To great-expecting Hopes: He looks thereon,
As from the shore of Peace, with unwet eye,
And bears no venture in Impiety.

1–2 This subject is treated at length in the Ode—Intimations of Immortality, page 441. *1845, 1850 but* Vol. v. page 148. *1850*

2 second volume of Poems by the Author.] fourth volume. *1827, 1832* fifth volume. *1836–1843, 1846*

"Knowing"—(to adopt the energetic words."] *"Knowing the heart of Man is set to be," &c. 1827–1836 'Knowing the heart of Man is set to be,' &c. MS. 1836/45, 1840–*

Thus, Lady, fares that Man that hath prepared
A Rest for his desires; and sees all things
Beneath him; and hath learn'd this Book of Man,
Full of the notes of frailty; and compar'd
The best of Glory with her sufferings:
By whom, I see, you labour all you can
To plant your heart; and set your thoughts as near
His glorious Mansion as your powers can bear.

[Book V, ll. 648–649]

P. 230. Line 18.—*"Or rather, as we stand on holy earth*
And have the Dead around us."

Leo. You, Sir, would help me to the History
Of half these Graves?
Priest. For eight-Score winters past,
With what I've witnessed, and with what I've heard,
Perhaps I might; . . . .
By turning o'er these hillocks one by one
We two could travel, Sir, through a strange round,
Yet all in the broad high-way of the world.

Author's Poem of the Brothers,
Published in the Lyrical Ballads in the year 1800.

[Book V, l. 981]

P. 245. Line 13.—*"And suffering Nature grieved that one should die."*
Southey's Retrospect.

[Book V, l. 984]

P. 245. Line 16.—*"And whence this tribute? wherefore these regards?"*

The sentiments and opinions here uttered are in unison with those expressed in the following Essay upon Epitaphs, which was furnished by the author for Mr. Coleridge's periodical work, the Friend; and as they are dictated by a spirit congenial to that which pervades this and the two succeeding books, the sympathizing reader will not be displeased to see the Essay here annexed.

[Book V, ll. 648–649]
1 would] could *MS. 1836/45, 1840–*
9–10 *Author's Poem . . . 1800.*] *See Vol. I. p. 132. 1827–1832* See The Brothers *MS. 1832/36* See *The Brothers*, Vol. I. *1836–1843, 1846* See *The Brothers. 1845, 1850*

[Book V, l. 984]
opening quotation this] *that 1827–*
3 the author] me *1845–*

ESSAY UPON EPITAPHS.

It needs scarcely be said, that an Epitaph presupposes a Monument, upon which it is to be engraven. Almost all Nations have wished that certain external signs should point out the places where their Dead are interred. Among savage Tribes unacquainted with Letters, this has mostly been done either by rude stones placed near the Graves, or by Mounds of earth raised over them. This custom proceeded obviously from a twofold desire; first, to guard the remains of the deceased from irreverent approach or from savage violation; and, secondly, to preserve their memory. "Never any," says Cambden, "neglected burial but some savage Nations; as the Bactrians which cast their dead to the dogs; some varlet Philosophers, as Diogenes, who desired to be devoured of fishes; some dissolute Courtiers, as Mecænas, who was wont to say, Non tumulum curo; sepelit natura relictos.

I'm careless of a Grave:—Nature her dead will save."

As soon as Nations had learned the use of letters, Epitaphs were inscribed upon these Monuments; in order that their intention might be more surely and adequately fulfilled. I have derived Monuments and Epitaphs from two sources of feeling: but these do in fact resolve themselves into one. The invention of Epitaphs, Weever, in his discourse of funeral Monuments, says rightly, "proceeded from the presage or fore-feeling of Immortality, implanted in all men naturally, and is referred to the Scholars of Linus the Theban Poet, who flourished about the year of the World two thousand seven hundred; who first bewailed this Linus their Master, when he was slain, in doleful verses then called of him Œlina, afterwards Epitaphia, for that they were first sung at burials, after engraved upon the Sepulchres."

And, verily, without the consciousness of a principle of Immortality in the human soul, Man could never have had awakened in him the desire to live in the remembrance of his fellows; mere love, or the yearning of Kind towards Kind, could not have produced it. The Dog or Horse perishes in the field, or in the stall, by the side of his Companions, and is incapable of anticipating the sorrow with which his surrounding Associates shall bemoan his death, or pine for his loss; he cannot pre-conceive this regret, he can form no thought of it; and therefore cannot possibly have a desire to leave such regret or remembrance behind him. Add to the principle of love, which exists in the inferior animals, the faculty of reason which exists in Man alone; will the conjunction of these account for the desire? Doubtless it is a necessary consequence of this conjunction; yet not I think as a direct result, but only to be come at through an intermediate thought, viz. that of an intimation or assurance within us, that some part of our nature is imperishable. At least the precedence, in order of birth, of one feeling to the other, is unquestionable. If we look back upon the

1 needs] need *1850*

days of childhood, we shall find that the time is not in remembrance when, with respect to our own individual Being, the mind was without this assurance; whereas, the wish to be remembered by our Friends or Kindred after Death, or even in Absence, is, as we shall discover, a sensation that does not form itself till the *social* feelings have been developed, and the Reason has connected itself with a wide range of objects. Forlorn, and cut off from communication with the best part of his nature, must that Man be, who should derive the sense of immortality, as it exists in the mind of a Child, from the same unthinking gaiety or liveliness of animal Spirits with which the Lamb in the meadow, or any other irrational Creature, is endowed; who should ascribe it, in short, to blank ignorance in the Child; to an inability arising from the imperfect state of his faculties to come, in any point of his being, into contact with a notion of Death; or to an unreflecting acquiescence in what had been instilled into him! Has such an unfolder of the mysteries of Nature, though he may have forgotten his former self, ever noticed the early, obstinate, and unappeaseable inquisitiveness of Children upon the subject of origination? This single fact proves outwardly the monstrousness of those suppositions: for, if we had no direct external testimony that the minds of very young Children meditate feelingly upon Death and Immortality, these inquiries, which we all know they are perpetually making concerning the *whence*, do necessarily include correspondent habits of interrogation concerning the *whither*. Origin and tendency are notions inseparably co-relative. Never did a Child stand by the side of a running Stream, pondering within himself what power was the feeder of the perpetual current, from what never-wearied sources the body of water was supplied, but he must have been inevitably propelled to follow this question by another: "towards what abyss is it in progress? what receptacle can contain the mighty influx?" And the spirit of the answer must have been, though the word might be Sea or Ocean, accompanied perhaps with an image gathered from a Map, or from the real object in Nature—these might have been the *letter*, but the *spirit* of the answer must have been *as* inevitably,—a receptacle without bounds or dimensions;—nothing less than infinity. We may, then, be justified in asserting that the sense of Immortality, if not a co-existent and twin birth with Reason, is among the earliest of her Offspring: and we may further assert, that from these conjoined, and under their countenance, the human affections are gradually formed and opened out. This is not the place to enter into the recesses of these investigations; but the subject requires me here to make a plain avowal that, for my own part, it is to me inconceivable, that the sympathies of love towards each other, which grow with our growth, could ever attain any new strength, or even preserve the old, after we had received from the outward senses the impression of Death, and were in the habit of having that impression daily renewed and its accompanying feeling brought home to ourselves, and to those we love; if the same were not counteracted by those communications with our internal Being, which are anterior to all these experiences, and with which revelation coincides, and has through that coincidence alone (for otherwise it could not possess it) a power to affect us. I confess, with me the conviction is absolute, that, if the impression and sense of Death were not thus counterbalanced, such a hollowness would pervade the whole system of things, such a want of correspondence and consistency, a disproportion so astounding betwixt means and ends, that there could be no repose, no joy. Were we to grow up unfostered by this genial warmth, a frost would chill the spirit, so penetrating and powerful, that there could be no motions of the life of love; and infinitely less could we have any wish to be remembered after we had passed away from a world in which each man had moved about like a shadow.—If, then, in a Creature endowed with the faculties of foresight and reason, the social affections could not have unfolded themselves uncountenanced by the faith that Man is an immortal being; and if, consequently, neither could the individual dying have had a desire to survive in the remembrance of his fellows, nor on their side could they have felt a wish to preserve for future times vestiges of the departed; it follows, as a final inference, that without the belief in Immortality, wherein these several desires originate, neither monuments nor epitaphs, in affectionate or laudatory commemoration of the Deceased, could have existed in the world.

Simonides, it is related, upon landing in a strange Country, found the Corse of an unknown person, lying by the Sea-side; he buried it, and was honoured throughout Greece for the piety of that Act. Another ancient Philosopher, chancing to fix his eyes upon a dead Body, regarded the same with slight, if not with contempt; saying, "see the Shell of the flown Bird!" But it is not to be supposed that the moral and tender-hearted Simonides was incapable of the lofty movements of thought, to which that other Sage gave way at the moment while his soul was intent only upon the indestructible being; nor, on the other hand, that he, in whose sight a lifeless human Body was of no more value than the worthless Shell from which the living fowl had departed, would not, in a different mood of mind, have been affected by those earthly considerations which had incited the philosophic Poet to the performance of that pious duty. And with regard to this latter, we may be assured that, if he had been destitute of the capability of communing with the more exalted thoughts that appertain to human Nature, he would have cared no more for the Corse of the Stranger than for the dead body of a Seal or Porpoise which might have been cast up by the Waves. We respect the corporeal frame of Man, not merely because it is the habitation of a rational, but of an immortal Soul. Each of these Sages was in Sympathy with the best feelings of our Nature; feelings which, though they seem opposite to each other, have another and a finer connection than that of contrast.—It is a connection formed through the subtle progress by which, both in the natural and the moral world, qualities pass insensibly into their contraries, and things revolve upon each other. As, in sailing upon the orb of this Planet, a voyage, towards the regions where the sun sets, conducts gradually to the quarter where we have been accustomed to behold it come forth at its rising; and, in like manner, a voyage towards the east, the birth-place in our imagination of the morning, leads finally to the quarter where the Sun is last seen when he departs from our eyes; so, the contemplative

Soul, travelling in the direction of mortality, advances to the Country of everlasting Life; and, in like manner, may she continue to explore those cheerful tracts, till she is brought back, for her advantage and benefit, to the land of transitory things—of sorrow and of tears.

On a midway point, therefore, which commands the thoughts and feelings of the two Sages whom we have represented in contrast, does the Author of that species of composition, the Laws of which it is our present purpose to explain, take his stand. Accordingly, recurring to the twofold desire of guarding the Remains of the deceased and preserving their memory, it may be said, that a sepulchral Monument is a tribute to a Man as a human Being; and that an Epitaph, (in the ordinary meaning attached to the word) includes this general feeling and something more; and is a record to preserve the memory of the dead, as a tribute due to his individual worth, for a satisfaction to the sorrowing hearts of the Survivors, and for the common benefit of the living: which record is to be accomplished, not in a general manner, but, where it can, in *close connection with the bodily remains of the deceased:* and these, it may be added, among the modern Nations of Europe are deposited within, or contiguous to their places of worship. In ancient times, as is well known, it was the custom to bury the dead beyond the Walls of Towns and Cities; and among the Greeks and Romans they were frequently interred by the way-sides.

I could here pause with pleasure, and invite the Reader to indulge with me in contemplation of the advantages which must have attended such a practice. I could ruminate upon the beauty which the Monuments, thus placed, must have borrowed from the surrounding images of Nature—from the trees, the wild flowers, from a stream running perhaps within sight or hearing, from the beaten road stretching its weary length hard by. Many tender similitudes must these objects have presented to the mind of the Traveller, leaning upon one of the Tombs, or reposing in the coolness of its shade, whether he had halted from weariness or in compliance with the invitation, "Pause Traveller!" so often found upon the Monuments. And to its Epitaph also must have been supplied strong appeals to visible appearances or immediate impressions, lively and affecting analogies of Life as a Journey—Death as a Sleep overcoming the tired Wayfarer—of Misfortune as a Storm that falls suddenly upon him—of Beauty as a Flower that passeth away, or of innocent pleasure as one that may be gathered—of Virtue that standeth firm as a Rock against the beating Waves;—of Hope "undermined insensibly like the Poplar by the side of the River that has fed it," or blasted in a moment like a Pine-tree by the stroke of lightening upon the Mountain top—of admonitions and heart-stirring remembrances, like a refreshing Breeze that comes without warning, or the taste of the waters of an unexpected Fountain. These, and similar suggestions must have given, formerly, to the language of the senseless stone a voice enforced and endeared by the benignity of that Nature, with which it was in unison.—We, in modern

---

163 I could] We might *1827–*

times, have lost much of these advantages: and they are but in a small degree counterbalanced to the Inhabitants of large Towns and Cities, by the custom of depositing the Dead within, or contiguous to, their places of worship; however splendid or imposing may be the appearances of those Edifices, or however interesting or salutary the recollections associated with them. Even were it not true that Tombs lose their monitory virtue when thus obtruded upon the notice of Men occupied with the cares of the World, and too often sullied and defiled by those cares, yet still, when Death is in our thoughts, nothing can make amends for the want of the soothing influences of Nature, and for the absence of those types of renovation and decay, which the fields and woods offer to the notice of the serious and contemplative mind. To feel the force of this sentiment, let a man only compare in imagination the unsightly manner in which our Monuments are crowded together in the busy, noisy, unclean, and almost grassless Church-yard of a large Town, with the still seclusion of a Turkish Cemetery, in some remote place; and yet further sanctified by the Grove of Cypress in which it is embosomed. Thoughts in the same temper as these have already been expressed with true sensibility by an ingenuous Poet of the present day. The subject of his Poem is "All Saints Church, Derby:" he has been deploring the forbidding and unseemly appearance of its burial-ground, and uttering a wish, that in past times the practice had been adopted of interring the Inhabitants of large Towns in the Country.—

"Then in some rural, calm, sequestered spot,
Where healing Nature her benignant look
Ne'er changes, save at that lorn season, when,
With tresses drooping o'er her sable stole,
She yearly mourns the mortal doom of man,
Her noblest work, (so Israel's virgins erst,
With annual moan upon the mountains wept
Their fairest gone) there in that rural scene,
So placid, so congenial to the wish
The Christian feels, of peaceful rest within
The silent grave, I would have stray'd:
. . . .
—wandered forth, where the cold dew of heaven
Lay on the humbler graves around, what time
The pale moon gazed upon the turfy mounds,
Pensive, as though like me, in lonely muse,
'Twere brooding on the Dead inhum'd beneath.
There, while with him, the holy Man of Uz,
O'er human destiny I sympathiz'd,
Counting the long, long periods prophecy
Decrees to roll, ere the great day arrives
Of resurrection, oft the blue-eyed Spring

188 appearances] appearance *1827–*

11 stray'd] stayed *1836–*

Had met me with her blossoms, as the Dove
Of old, return'd with olive leaf, to cheer
The Patriarch mourning o'er a world destroy'd:
And I would bless her visit; for to me
'Tis sweet to trace the consonance that links
As one, the works of Nature and the word
Of God."——

John Edwards.

A Village Church-yard, lying as it does in the lap of Nature, may indeed be most favourably contrasted with that of a Town of crowded Population; and Sepulture therein combines many of the best tendencies which belong to the mode practised by the Ancients, with others peculiar to itself. The sensations of pious cheerfulness, which attend the celebration of the Sabbath-day in rural places, are profitably chastised by the sight of the Graves of Kindred and Friends, gathered together in that general Home towards which the thoughtful yet happy Spectators themselves are journeying. Hence a Parish Church, in the stillness of the Country, is a visible centre of a community of the living and the dead; a point to which are habitually referred the nearest concerns of both.

As, then, both in Cities and in Villages, the Dead are deposited in close connection with our places of worship, with us the composition of an Epitaph naturally turns still more than among the Nations of Antiquity, upon the most serious and solemn affections of the human mind; upon departed Worth—upon personal or social Sorrow and Admiration—upon Religion individual and social—upon Time, and upon Eternity. Accordingly it suffices, in ordinary cases, to secure a composition of this kind from censure, that it contains nothing that shall shock or be inconsistent with this spirit. But, to entitle an Epitaph to praise, more than this is necessary. It ought to contain some Thought or Feeling belonging to the mortal or immortal part of our Nature touchingly expressed; and if that be done, however general or even trite the sentiment may be, every man of pure mind will read the words with pleasure and gratitude. A Husband bewails a Wife; a Parent breathes a sigh of disappointed hope over a lost Child; a Son utters a sentiment of filial reverence for a departed Father or Mother; a Friend perhaps inscribes an encomium recording the companionable qualities, or the solid virtues, of the Tenant of the Grave, whose departure has left a sadness upon his memory. This, and a pious admonition to the Living, and a humble expression of Christian confidence in Immortality, is the language of a thousand Church-yards; and it does not often happen that any thing, in a greater degree discriminate or appropriate to the Dead or to the Living, is to be found in them. This want of discrimination has been ascribed by Dr. Johnson, in his Essay upon the Epitaphs of Pope, to two causes; first, the scantiness of the Objects of human praise; and, secondly, the want of variety in the Characters of Men; or to use

---

226 contains] contain *1836–*

his own words, "to the fact, that the greater part of Mankind have no Character at all." Such language may be holden without blame among the generalities of common conversation; but does not become a Critic and a Moralist speaking seriously upon a serious Subject. The objects of admiration in Human Nature are not scanty but abundant; and every Man has a Character of his own, to the eye that has skill to perceive it. The real cause of the acknowledged want of discrimination in sepulchral memorials is this: That to analyse the Characters of others, especially of those whom we love, is not a common or natural employment of Men at any time. We are not anxious unerringly to understand the constitution of the Minds of those who have soothed, who have cheered, who have supported us: with whom we have been long and daily pleased or delighted. The affections are their own justification. The Light of Love in our Hearts is a satisfactory evidence that there is a body of worth in the minds of our friends or kindred, whence that Light has proceeded. We shrink from the thought of placing their merits and defects to be weighed against each other in the nice balance of pure intellect: nor do we find much temptation to detect the shades by which a good quality or virtue is discriminated in them from an excellence known by the same general name as it exists in the mind of another; and, least of all, do we incline to these refinements when under the pressure of Sorrow, Admiration, or Regret, or when actuated by any of those feelings which incite men to prolong the memory of their Friends and Kindred, by records placed in the bosom of the all-uniting and equalizing Receptacle of the Dead.

The first requisite, then, in an Epitaph is, that it should speak, in a tone which shall sink into the heart, the general language of humanity as connected with the subject of Death—the source from which an Epitaph proceeds; of death and of life. To be born and to die are the two points in which all men feel themselves to be in absolute coincidence. This general language may be uttered so strikingly as to entitle an Epitaph to high praise; yet it cannot lay claim to the highest unless other excellencies be superadded. Passing through all intermediate steps, we will attempt to determine at once what these excellencies are, and wherein consists the perfection of this species of composition. It will be found to lie in a due proportion of the common or universal feeling of humanity to sensations excited by a distinct and clear conception, conveyed to the Reader's mind, of the Individual, whose death is deplored and whose memory is to be preserved; at least of his character as, after death, it appeared to those who loved him and lament his loss. The general sympathy ought to be quickened, provoked, and diversified, by particular thoughts, actions, images,—circumstances of age, occupation, manner of life, prosperity which the Deceased had known, or adversity to which he had been subject; and these ought to be bound together and solemnized into one harmony by the general sympathy. The two powers should temper, restrain, and exalt each other. The Reader ought to know who and what the Man was whom he is called upon to think of with interest. A distinct

---

271 life.] *so 1820E–* life, *1814*

conception should be given (implicitly where it can, rather than explicitly) of the Individual lamented. But the Writer of an Epitaph is not an Anatomist who dissects the internal frame of the mind; he is not even a Painter who executes a portrait at leisure and in entire tranquillity: his delineation, we must remember, is performed by the side of the Grave; and, what is more, the grave of one whom he loves and admires. What purity and brightness is that virtue clothed in, the image of which must no longer bless our living eyes! The character of a deceased Friend or beloved Kinsman is not seen, no—nor ought to be seen, otherwise than as a Tree through a tender haze or a luminous mist, that spiritualizes and beautifies it; that takes away indeed, but only to the end that the parts which are not abstracted may appear more dignified and lovely, may impress and affect the more. Shall we say then that this is not truth, not a faithful image; and that accordingly the purposes of commemoration cannot be answered?—It *is* truth, and of the highest order! for, though doubtless things are not apparent which did exist, yet, the object being looked at through this medium, parts and proportions are brought into distinct view which before had been only imperfectly or unconsciously seen: it is truth hallowed by love—the joint offspring of the worth of the Dead and the affections of the Living!—This may easily be brought to the test. Let one, whose eyes have been sharpened by personal hostility to discover what was amiss in the character of a good man, hear the tidings of his death, and what a change is wrought in a moment!—Enmity melts away; and, as it disappears, unsightliness, disproportion, and deformity, vanish; and, through the influence of commiseration, a harmony of love and beauty succeeds. Bring such a Man to the Tomb-stone on which shall be inscribed an Epitaph on his Adversary, composed in the spirit which we have recommended. Would he turn from it as from an idle tale? Ah! no—the thoughtful look, the sigh, and perhaps the involuntary tear, would testify that it had a sane, a generous, and good meaning; and that on the Writer's mind had remained an impression which was a true abstract of the character of the deceased; that his gifts and graces were remembered in the simplicity in which they ought to be remembered. The composition and quality of the mind of a virtuous man, contemplated by the side of the Grave where his body is mouldering, ought to appear, and be felt as something midway between what he was on Earth walking about with his living frailties, and what he may be presumed to be as a Spirit in Heaven.

It suffices, therefore, that the Trunk and the main Branches of the Worth of the Deceased be boldly and unaffectedly represented. Any further detail, minutely and scrupulously pursued, especially if this be done with laborious and antithetic discriminations, must inevitably frustrate its own purpose; forcing the passing Spectator to this conclusion,—either that the Dead did not possess the merits ascribed to him, or that they who have raised a monument to his memory and must therefore be supposed to have been closely connected with him, were incapable of perceiving those merits; or at least during the act of composition had lost sight of

317–318 Ah! no—] No— *1827, 1832* No;— *MS. 1832/36–*

them; for, the Understanding having been so busy in its petty occupation, how could the heart of the Mourner be other than cold? and in either of these cases, whether the fault be on the part of the buried Person or the Survivors, the Memorial is unaffecting and profitless.

Much better is it to fall short in discrimination than to pursue it too far, or to labour it unfeelingly. For in no place are we so much disposed to dwell upon those points, of nature and condition, wherein all Men resemble each other, as in the Temple where the universal Father is worshipped, or by the side of the Grave which gathers all Human Beings to itself, and "equalizes the lofty and the low." We suffer and we weep with the same heart; we love and are anxious for one another in one spirit; our hopes look to the same quarter; and the virtues by which we are all to be furthered and supported, as patience, meekness, good-will, temperance, and temperate desires, are in an equal degree the concern of us all. Let an Epitaph, then, contain at least these acknowledgments to our common nature; nor let the sense of their importance be sacrificed to a balance of opposite qualities or minute distinctions in individual character; which if they do not, (as will for the most part be the case) when examined, resolve themselves into a trick of words, will, even when they are true and just, for the most part be grievously out of place; for, as it is probable that few only have explored these intricacies of human nature, so can the tracing of them be interesting only to a few. But an Epitaph is not a proud Writing shut up for the studious; it is exposed to all, to the wise and the most ignorant; it is condescending, perspicuous, and lovingly solicits regard; its story and admonitions are brief, that the thoughtless, the busy and indolent, may not be deterred, nor the impatient tired; the stooping Old Man cons the engraven record like a second horn-book;—the Child is proud that he can read it—and the Stranger is introduced by its meditation to the company of a Friend: it is concerning all, and for all:—in the Church-yard it is open to the day; the sun looks down upon the stone, and the rains of Heaven beat against it.

Yet, though the Writer who would excite sympathy is bound in this case more than in any other, to give proof that he himself has been moved, it is to be remembered, that to raise a Monument is a sober and a reflective act; that the inscription which it bears is intended to be permanent and for universal perusal; and that, for this reason, the thoughts and feelings expressed should be permanent also—liberated from that weakness and anguish of sorrow which is in nature transitory, and which with instinctive decency retires from notice. The passions should be subdued, the emotions controlled; strong indeed, but nothing ungovernable or wholly involuntary. Seemliness requires this, and truth requires it also: for how can the Narrator otherwise be trusted? Moreover, a Grave is a tranquillizing object: resignation, in course of time, springs up from it as naturally as the wild flowers, besprinkling the turf with which it may be covered, or gathering round the monument by which it is defended. The very form and substance of the monument which has received the inscription, and

349–350 good-will, temperance,] good-will, justice, temperance, *MS. 1832/36–*
365 by its] through its *MS. 1832/36–*

the appearance of the letters, testifying with what a slow and laborious hand they must have been engraven, might seem to reproach the Author who had given way upon this occasion to transports of mind, or to quick turns of conflicting passion; though the same might constitute the life and beauty of a funeral Oration or elegiac Poem.

These sensations and judgments, acted upon perhaps unconsciously, have been one of the main causes why Epitaphs so often personate the Deceased, and represent him as speaking from his own Tomb-stone. The departed Mortal is introduced telling you himself that his pains are gone; that a state of rest is come; and he conjures you to weep for him no longer. He admonishes with the voice of one experienced in the vanity of those affections which are confined to earthly objects, and gives a verdict like a superior Being, performing the office of a Judge, who has no temptations to mislead him, and whose decision cannot but be dispassionate. Thus is Death disarmed of its sting, and affliction unsubstantialized. By this tender fiction the Survivors bind themselves to a sedater sorrow, and employ the intervention of the imagination in order that the reason may speak her own language earlier than she would otherwise have been enabled to do. This shadowy interposition also harmoniously unites the two worlds of the Living and the Dead by their appropriate affections. And I may observe, that here we have an additional proof of the propriety with which sepulchral inscriptions were referred to the consciousness of Immortality as their primal source.

I do not speak with a wish to recommend that an Epitaph should be cast in this mould preferably to the still more common one, in which what is said comes from the Survivors directly; but rather to point out how natural those feelings are which have induced men, in all states and ranks of Society, so frequently to adopt this mode. And this I have done chiefly in order that the laws, which ought to govern the composition of the other, may be better understood. This latter mode, namely, that in which the Survivors speak in their own Persons, seems to me upon the whole greatly preferable: as it admits a wider range of notices; and, above all, because, excluding the fiction which is the ground-work of the other, it rests upon a more solid basis.

Enough has been said to convey our notion of a perfect Epitaph; but it must be observed that one is meant which will best answer the *general* ends of that species of composition. According to the course pointed out, the worth of private life, through all varieties of situation and character, will be most honourably and profitably preserved in memory. Nor would the model recommended less suit public Men, in all instances save of those persons who by the greatness of their services in the employments of Peace or War, or by the surpassing excellence of their works in Art, Literature, or Science, have made themselves not only universally known, but have filled the heart of their Country with everlasting gratitude. Yet I must here pause to correct myself. In describing the general tenour of thought which Epitaphs ought to hold, I have omitted to say, that, if it

---

403 I may observe,] it may be observed, *1832–*
418 observed] borne in mind *1832–*

be the *actions* of a Man, or even some *one* conspicuous or beneficial act of local or general utility, which have distinguished him and excited a desire that he should be remembered, then of course, ought the attention to be directed chiefly to those actions or that act; and such sentiments dwelt upon as naturally arise out of them or it. Having made this necessary distinction I proceed.—The mighty Benefactors of mankind, as they are not only known by the immediate Survivors, but will continue to be known familiarly to latest Posterity, do not stand in need of biographic sketches, in such a place; nor of delineations of character to individualize them. This is already done by their Works, in the Memories of Men. Their naked names, and a grand comprehensive sentiment of civic Gratitude, patriotic Love, or human Admiration; or the utterance of some elementary Principle most essential in the constitution of true Virtue; or an intuition, communicated in adequate words, of the sublimity of intellectual Power,—these are the only tribute which can here be paid—the only offering that upon such an Altar would not be unworthy!

What needs my Shakespeare for his honoured bones
The labour of an age in piled stones,
Or that his hallowed reliques should be hid
Under a star-y-pointing pyramid?
Dear Son of Memory, great Heir of Fame,
What need'st thou such weak witness of thy name?
Thou in our wonder and astonishment
Hast built thyself a live-long Monument.
And so sepulchred, in such pomp dost lie,
That Kings for such a Tomb would wish to die.

[Book VI, l. 19]
P. 250. Line 9.—*"And spires whose silent Finger points to Heaven."*

An instinctive taste teaches men to build their churches in flat countries with spire-steeples, which as they cannot be referred to any other object, point as with silent finger to the sky and stars, and sometimes when they reflect the brazen light of a rich though rainy sunset, appear like a pyramid of flame burning heaven-ward. See "The Friend," by S. T. Coleridge, No. 14. p. 223.

[Book VII, ll. 635–636]
P. 338. Line 1.—*"That Sycamore, which annually holds*
Within its shade, as in a stately tent."

This Sycamore oft musical with Bees;
Such Tents the Patriarchs loved.

S. T. Coleridge.

441–442 Virtue; or an intuition] virtue;—or a declaration touching that pious humility and self-abasement, which are ever most profound as minds are most susceptible of genuine exaltation—or an intuition *1836*–

[Book VII, l. 1002]
P. 354. Line 7.—*"Perish the roses and the flowers of Kings."*

The "Transit gloria mundi" is finely expressed in the Introduction to the Foundation Charters of some of the ancient Abbies. Some expressions here used are taken from that of the Abbey of St. Mary's Furness, the translation of which is as follows.

"Considering every day the uncertainty of life, that the roses and flowers of Kings, Emperors, and Dukes, and the crowns and palms of all the great, wither and decay; and that all things with an uninterrupted course, tend to dissolution and death: I therefore," &c.

[Book VIII, ll. 113–114]
P. 364. Line 12.—*"Earth has lent her Waters, air her breezes."*

In treating this subject, it was impossible not to recollect, with gratitude, the pleasing picture, which in his Poem of the Fleece, the excellent and amiable Dyer has given of the influences of manufacturing industry, upon the face of this Island. He wrote at a time when machinery was first beginning to be introduced, and his benevolent heart prompted him to augur from it nothing but good. Truth has compelled me to dwell upon the baneful effects arising out of an ill-regulated and excessive application of powers so admirable in themselves.

[Book IX, l. 298]
P. 400. Line 19.—*"Binding herself by Statute."*

The discovery of Dr. Bell affords marvellous facilities for carrying this into effect, and it is impossible to overrate the benefit which might accrue to humanity from the universal application of this simple engine under an enlightened and conscientious government.

THE END.

Historical Collations of Nonverbal Variants

The nonverbal differences from the 1814 reading text listed here include variants in spelling, punctuation, capitalization, and paragraphing found in post-publication, authorially influenced manuscripts and in lifetime editions through 1849–1850, except for (1) those that appear in manuscripts fully transcribed in this volume or in other volumes in this series; (2) those that are integral parts of verbal changes and thus appear in the *apparatus* below the 1814 reading text; (3) those that are editorial emendations or changes made in the errata to the 1814 edition; line references for such emendations and errata changes are listed in the headnote to the 1814 reading text, and they appear in the *apparatus* below the reading text. Also not recorded are ampersands, single-letter miswritings (corrected by the copyist), reinforcements of punctuation marks when no change is made, and changes in the various internal page references in successive printed editions.

Manuscripts are identified in the Manuscript Census, above. Abbreviations of lifetime printings are given in the Editorial Procedure, above, as is an account of the methods used to report variants in lifetime editions and in the annotated printings used as part of the process of revision (MS. 1814/27, MS. 1827/32C, MS. 1832/36, MS. 1836/45).

[Dedicatory Poem]

dedicatory poem directly follows title page in all editions except 1832 and 1832E, where poem follows Prospectus

5 Now] Now, *1820E–*

12 produced] produced, *1836–*

14 Offering] offering *1845–*

16 Westmorland] Westmoreland *1827–*

26 Poem] poem *1836–*

27 The] the *1845, 1850*

28 Poet] poet *1836–*

29 Poem] poem *1836–*

34 Anti-chapel] ante-chapel *MS. 1832/36–* gothic] Gothic *1820E–1832* Church] church *1836–*

38 Cells, Oratories] cells, oratories *1836–*

39 Recesses . . . Edifices] recesses . . . edifices *1836–*

45 please, and] please and, *1836–*

47 the] The *1832–*

47–48 Person] person *1836–*

49 Characters] characters *1836–*

55 mean time] meantime *1820E*

56 Book] book *1820E–* the] The *1832–*

57 scope] scop *1820E*

PREFACE

1 Portion] portion *some copies 1836E* por tion *some copies 1836E* portion *1836–* Poem] poem *1836–*

2 apprized] apprised *1827–*

3 laborious] labouriou s *some copies 1836E* Author] Au thor *some copies 1836E and 1836* Aut hor *some copies 1836* Au thor *corr to* Author *MS. 1836/45*

6 World] world *1832–*

10 Poem] poem *1836–*

14 Pages] pages *1836–*

15 Poem] poem *1836–*

17 Mountains] mountains *1836–*

19 Mind] mind *1836–*

21 Verse] verse *1836–*

Prospectus

type of Prospectus *italic except 1845, 1850; for clarity, text below given in roman*

1 "On] 'On *1836–* Life] Lif *1827* Life, *1832*

2 Solitude] solitude *1836–*

12 herself,] herself— *1836–*
13 Verse] verse *1836–*
14 —Of] Of *1820E–* Hope—] Hope, *1836–*
17 power] Power *1820E–*
22 all;] all— *1836–*
23 "fit . . . few!"] 'fit . . . few!' *1827–*
24 So] "So *1827, 1832* Bard,] Bard— *1845–*
32 form;] form— *1836–*
34 thrones,] thrones— *1820E–*
35 them,] them *1820E–*
37 vacancy—] vacancy, *1836–*
38 dreams,] dreams— *1836–*
40 Man,] Man— *1836–*
41 Song] song *1836–*
44 composed] compose *misprint 1845*
49 Main,] Main— *1836–*
57 chaunt] chant *1827–*
66 too,] too— *1836–*
67 Men,] men— *1836–*
80 Cities;] cities— *1836–*
81 comment,—] comment; *1836–* that,] that *1820E–*
82 forlorn!] forlorn!— *1845–*
83 Spirit,] Spirit *1820E* Spirit! *1827–* inspir'st] inspirest *1820E, 1832* inspir'st *MS. 1832/36–*
86 Temple] temple *1836–*
87 Poets;] Poets: *1836–*
89 shine;] shine, *1836–*
90 influence,—] Influence, *1836–* secure,] secure *1836–1843*
96 Contemplating;] Contemplating, *1827, 1832* was,] was— *1836–*
98 Vision,—] Vision; *1836–*
100 then, . . . Power,] then— . . . Power! *1836–*
102 illumination,] illumination— *1836–*
107 end!"] end!' *1836–*

SUMMARY OF CONTENTS/ARGUMENT

Book I Summary of Contents

1 forenoon—] forenoon.— *1836–*
3 account— . . . Wanderer] account.— . . . Wanderer, *1836–*
4 Cottage] Cottage, *1836–*

Book II Summary of Contents

2 illustrated— . . . Wake—] illustrated.— . . . Wake.— *1850*
3 visit—] visit.— *1850*
5 retreat—] retreat.— *1850*
6 below—a . . . procession— . . . Valley—] below.—A . . . procession.— . . . Valley.— *1850*
7 Book] book *1836–*
8 Valley—] Valley.— *1850*
9 Solitary—] Solitary.— *1850*
10 district—] district.— *1850*
11 Individual] individual *1836–* Cottage—] cottage; *1836–1843, 1846* cottage— *1845* cottage.— *1850*
12 Cottage . . . description] cottage . . . Description *1836–* entered—] entered.— *1850*
13 apartment—] apartment.— *1850* repast] Repast *1836–* there—] there.— *1850* View] View, *MS. 1836/45, 1840–* Window] window *1836* window, *MS. 1836/45, 1840–*
14 summits—] summits; *1836–* Companionship] companionship *1836–*
15 him—] him.— *1850* account . . . Inmate] Account . . . inmate *1836–* Cottage—] cottage— *1836– but* cottage.— *1850*
15–16 description] Description *1836–*
17 mind—] mind.— *1850* House] house *1836–*

Book III Summary of Contents

1 Valley— . . . described—] Valley, . . . described.— *1836–*
2 sensations— . . . objects—] sensations.— . . . objects.— *1836–*
3 these— . . . reproved—] these.— . . . reproved.— *1836–*
5 length—] length.— *1836–* felicity—] felicity.— *1850*
5–6 afflictions—] Afflictions.— *1836–*
6 dejection— . . . roused . . . Revolution—] Dejection.— . . . Roused . . . Revolution.— *1836–*
7 disgust— . . . America— . . . disappointment] disgust.— . . . America.— . . . Disappointment *1836–*
8 him—his return—] him.—His return.— *1836–*

Book IV Summary of Contents

1 Narrative—] Narrative.— *1850*
2–3 affliction—] affliction.— *1850*
3 Account] account *1827, 1832; see verbals*
7 faith— . . . sorrow—] faith.— . . . sorrow.— *1850*
9 Exhortations— . . . received—] Exhortations.— . . . received.— *1850*
11 mind—] mind.— *1850* disappointment] Disappointment *1836–*
12 Revolution—] Revolution.— *1850* hope—] hope, *1836–*
14 revolutions] revolutions.— *1850*
15 tranquillity—] tranquillity.— *1850*

16–17 Creatures— . . . recommended] Creatures; . . . recommended; *1836–*
18 Exhortation . . . Communion] exhortation . . . communion *1836–*
19 Nature—] Nature.— *1850*
20 exerted—] exerted, *pencil MS. 1814/27*
21 apathy— . . . society—] apathy.— . . . society.— *1850*
22 it—] it.— *1850* illustrated] Illustrated *1836–*
23 Chaldean] Chaldean, *1820E–* belief—] belief.— *1850*
24 interposes—] interposes.— *1850*
25 society,] society— *1827, 1832*
26 times—] times.— *1850*
27 recal] recall *1827, 1832*
28 popery—] popery.— *1850*
30 Philosophers,] Philosophers— *1827– but* Philosophers.— *1850*
31 guides—] guides.— *1850*
32 herself—] herself; *1836–* how—] how.— *1850*
33 appeal—] appeal.— *1850*
34 Slavery] slavery *1827, 1832; see verbals*
36 Body] body *1827–* renewed—] renewed.— *1850*
39 discourse—] discourse.— *1850* Evening—] Evening; *1836–*

Book V Summary of Contents

1 Valley—Reflections—] Valley.—Reflections.— *1850*
2 described—] described.— *1850*
3 him—] him.— *1850* Church-yard—] Churchyard— *1832; see verbals*
3–4 Monuments—] Monuments.— *1850*
4 where—Roused—] where.—Roused.— *1850* Church-yard] Churchyard *1836–*
6 mind—] mind.— *1850*
7 to—] to.— *1850*
8 life—Inconsistency] *type deteriorates in the press run to* life I n consistency *and eventually to* life[n consistency *1814*
9 men—] men.— *1850*
10 mind— . . . falling-off] mind.— . . . falling off *1850*
11 youth—] youth.— *1850*
12 illusive— . . . approaches—] illusive.— . . . approaches.— *1850*
13 him—His answer— . . . him—] him.—His answer.— . . . him.— *1850*
14 Inquirers] enquirers *1845, 1850* Enquirers *1846* error—] error.— *1850*
15 Portraits] portraits *1836–*
16–17 purpose—] purpose.— *1850*
17 consents— . . . cottage—] consents.— . . . cottage.— *1850*
18 Inhabitants—] Inhabitants.— *1850*
19 kind—] kind.— *1850*
20 Persons] persons *1836–* Church-yard—] Churchyard— *1845* Churchyard.— *1850*
21 unbaptized Infants—] unbaptised Infants.— *1850* Funereal] Funeral *1820E–*
22 Observances—] Observances, *MS. 1814/27–1832* observances, *1836–* Whence—] whence— *1827– but* whence.— *1850* Establishments—Whence] Establishments, Whence *MS. 1814/27* Establishments, whence *1827–*
23 derived—] derived.— *1850* Belief] belief *1836–*

Book VI Summary of Contents

1 England—] England.— *1850*
2 Church—] Church.— *1850*
3 Instance] instance *1836–* love—] Love— *1827– but* Love.— *1850* mind] Mind *1832*
4 subdued—] subdued, *1845, 1850* how—] how.— *1850*
4–5 Miner, an Instance of Perseverance, which] Miner—An Instance of perseverance—Which *MS. 1832/36– but* Miner.— . . . perseverance.— *1850 and* instance *1836–*
5 Example] example *1836–*
6 weakness—] weakness.— *1850*
7 Instance] instance *1836–*
8 here—] here.— *1850*
8–9 harmonizing] harmonising *1832–*
9 Men] men *1836–*
10 life—] life.— *1850* Rule] rule *1836–*
11 expressed—] expressed, *1836–* where—] where.— *1850*
12 Fatality— . . . Pastor—] Fatality.— . . . Pastor.— *1850*
13 Narratives— . . . this—] Narratives.— . . . this.— *1850*
14 Character] character *1820E–* Female—] Female, *MS. 1814/27, 1836–* given—] given.— *1850*
15 Sufferer] sufferer *1836–* Love—] love— *1820E– but* love.— *1850*
16 guilt—] guilt, *MS. 1814/27–* Offender—] Offender.— *1850*
17 Instance] instance *1836–*
18 Wife] wife *1827–*
19 Children—] Children. *1827–*

Book VII Summary of Contents

heading MOUNTAINS,] MOUNTAINS. *1820E* MOUNTAINS *1827–*
1 mind—] mind.— *1850*
2 apart—] apart.— *1850*
3 Family—] Family.— *1850* situation—] situation.— *1850*
4 age—] age.— *1850* Virtue—] Virtue.— *1850*
5 misdirected] mis-directed *1820E–* applause—] applause.— *1850*
6 Man—] man— *1820E– but* man.— *1850* blind Man—] blindman— *1820E* blind man— *1827– but* blind man.— *1850*
7 Blindness—] Blindness.— *1850*
8 vivacity—] vivacity.— *1850*
9–10 Trees— . . . Grave— . . . Birth— . . . Departure—] Trees.— . . . Grave.— . . . Birth.— . . . Departure.— *1850*
11 Death—] death— *1832– but* death.— *1850*
12 Picture— . . . affected—] Picture.— . . . affected.— *1850*
13 Knight— . . . him—] Knight.— . . . him.— *1850*
15 society— . . . Calling—] society.— . . . Calling.— *1850*

Book VIII Summary of Contents

2 long—] long, *1836–*
3 Wanderer;] Wanderer— *MS. 1832/36–*
6 spirit— . . . effects—] spirit.— . . . effects.— *1850*
7 classes—] classes.— *1850*
9 worth—] worth.— *1850*
10 itself—] itself.— *1850*
11 Society—] Society.— *1845, 1850*
12 Cotton-mill—] Cotton-mill.— *1850*
13 reviewed—] reviewed.— *1850*
14 Pastor— . . . House—] Pastor.— . . . House.— *1850*
15 described—] described.— *1850* Daughter—His Wife—] Daughter.—His Wife.— *1850*
16 Companion— . . . appearance—] Companion.— . . . appearance.— *1850*

Book IX Summary of Contents

1 Universe— Its] Universe, its *MS. 1832/36–*
2 soul—] soul.— *1850* Childhood—] childhood— *MS. 1832/36–1843, 1846* Childhood— *1845* Childhood.— *1850*
3 old] Old *1820E–1832* age] Age *1820E–* childhood—] Childhood— *1820E– but* Childhood.— *1850*
4 asserted—] asserted.— *1850*
5 government—] government.— *1850*
6 Instrument—] Instrument.— *1850*
8 shew] show *1832; see verbals* deplored] deplored, *1832* deplored— *1836– but* deplored.— *1850*
11 light—] light.— *1850*
12 to—] to.— *1850*
14 Government— . . . foretold—] Government.— . . . foretold.—*1850*
15 Lake—] Lake.— *1850*
16 hill—] hill.— *1850*
17 Course] course *1832–*
18 him—] him.— *1850*
19 Christianity—] Christianity.— *1850* Flock] flock *1836–*
20 dead— . . . Almighty— . . . Lake—] dead.— . . . Almighty.— . . . Lake.— *1850*
21 Solitary—] Solitary.— *1850*

READING TEXT OF *THE EXCURSION*

Book I

1 'Twas] Twas *1831 (but* 'Twas *1834)*
2 Southward,] Southward *1820E–*
4 shew'd] show'd *1827* showed *1832–*
5 shadows,] shadows *1820E–*
9 interposed.] interposed; *1827–*
14 wren] Wren *1832* wren *MS. 1832/36–* warbles; . . . Man] warbles, . . . man *1836–*
26 Grove] grove *MS. 1832/36–*
27 wished-for] wish'd-for *1827* Port] port *1820E–*
28 there—] there, *1820E–*
29 elms—] elms, *1820E–*
30 Appeared] Appear'd *1827* Hut;] hut; *1820E*
31 other!] other!— *1836–*
34 unimpaired] unimpair'd *1827*
35 Cottage bench] cottage bench *MS. 1832/36* cottage-bench *1836–*
38 marked] mark'd *1827*
41 Turned] Turn'd *1827* tow'rds] tow'rd *1827* toward *1832–*
42 Afforded] Afforded, *pencil MS. 1836/45, 1840–*
43 Detained] Detain'd *1827*
46 Unrecognized] Unrecognised *1832–*
47 slacken'd] slackened *1832–*
60 *no para 1827–* Boys] boys *MS. 1832/36–*
62 looks—] looks, *1836–*
63 up] up, *1827–*

64 Comrade] comrade MS. 1832/36–
65 woods,] woods: 1827–
67 pleas'd] pleased 1820E; *see verbals*
68 touch'd] touched 1832–
70 Turned] Turn'd 1827
71 songs—] songs, 1836–
74 Water] water 1836–
76 parched] parch'd 1827
78 learn'd] learned 1832–
82 Men] men 1836– endowed] endowd 1827 endow'd 1831 (*MS. 1827/32C has an inverted caret in margin indicating need for corr*)
83 divine,] divine; 1832–
84 Verse,] Verse 1827, 1832 verse, MS. 1832/36–
85 (Which . . . youth] (Which, . . . youth, 1820E–
89 shame),] shame); 1827 shame) 1832–
92 favored] favour'd 1827 favoured 1832–
98 unrevealed . . . unproclaimed] unreveal'd . . . unproclaim'd 1827
99 filled] fill'd 1827
108 rise,] rise 1832–
112 born:] born; 1832–
113 Farm] farm 1836–
128 Household] Household, 1827, 1832 household, 1836–
129 Livers] livers 1836–
130 Children] children 1836–
132 maintained] maintain'd 1827
135 Hills] hills MS. 1832/36–
137 repaired] repair'd, 1827 repaired, 1832–
139 Building] building MS. 1832/36–
140 City] city MS. 1832/36–
141 Minster . . . Tenement] minster . . . tenement MS. 1832/36–
142 evening] evening, 1827–
143 Hills] hills MS. 1832/36–
144 darkness,] darkness; *pencil* MS. 1836/45, 1840–
146 travelled] travell'd 1827
148 *para* MS. 1832/36– (*MS. 1827/32C has a check mark perhaps indicating intended para*)
150 Child] child 1836–
152 impress'd] impressed 1832–
155 seemed] seem'd 1827; *see verbals*
162 attained] attain'd 1827
167 Child, . . . Child's] child, . . . child's MS. 1832/36–
170 appetite:] appetite 1840 (*probable worn plate*) appetite— 1845–
171 after day] after-day 1845–
172 Boyhood] boyhood 1836–
174 fix'd] fixed 1820E, 1832–
177 oppress'd] oppressed 1832–
178 fix'd] fixed 1832–
180 informed] inform'd 1827
181 Tale] tale MS. 1832/36–
183 Legend] legend MS. 1832/36–
186 recognize] recognise 1832–
189 Minister's . . . Shelf] minister's . . . shelf MS. 1832/36–
190 Martyrs] martyrs MS. 1832/36– sustained] sustain'd 1827
192 displayed] display'd 1827
193 Persecution, . . . Times] persecution, . . . times 1836–
195 there . . . hap] there, . . . hap, 1820E–
198 Giants] giants 1836– Fiends] Fiends, 1820E–1832 fiends, 1836–
201 Sharp-knee'd] Sharp-kneed 1836–
203 heart] heart, 1820E–
204 cherished] cherish'd 1827
206 diffused] diffus'd 1820E
221 looked] look'd 1827
224 touch'd] touched 1832–
228 spectacle;] spectacle: 1827– form] form, *pencil* MS. 1836/45, 1840– (*MS. 1827/32C has inverted caret in margin, possibly indicating intended comma after* form)
229 swallowed] swallow'd 1827
231 life.] life, 1840 *but not* 1841E
234 *MS. 1827/32C has an inverted caret in margin, possibly indicating intended rev*
242 *possessed] possess'd 1827*
243 Oh] O 1827– bright] bright, *pencil* MS. 1836/45, 1840– appeared] appear'd 1827
244 Promise] promise 1836– learned] learn'd 1827
245 Volume] volume 1836–
246 die:] die; 1827–
247 faith;] faith. 1827–
249 life] life, 1820E–
250 infinite;] infinite: *pencil* MS. 1836/45, 1840–
252 Seemed] Seem'd 1827
258 called] call'd 1827 extacies] ecstacies 1827 ecstasies 1832–
259 flowed] flow'd 1827
260 through] thro' 1820E– learned] learn'd 1827 (*MS. 1827/32C has inverted caret in margin, probably indicating restoration to* learned)
263 Self-questioned] Self-question'd 1827
265 passed] pass'd 1827 town] Town 1832
268 Book] book MS. 1832/36–
269 Stall] stall MS. 1832/36–
270 Orb] orb 1836– Song] Song, 1832 song, 1836–
276 nature] Nature 1827, 1832

277 suppressed,)] suppress'd) *1827* suppressed) *1832–*
280 hours,] hours *1831*
282 do] do, *1827–*
284 Yet still uppermost] Yet, still uppermost, *1827–*
291 lingered] linger'd *1827*
295 th'] the *1832–*
297 shews] shows *1827–*
299 it's] its *1827– ; see verbals*
300 storm,—] storm, *1820E–*
302 thus,] thus *1831, 1832–*
303 pressed] press'd *1827*
304 o'erpower'd] o'erpowered *1820E, 1832–*
305 Nature,] Nature; *pencil MS. 1836/45, 1840–*
308 Universe] universe *MS. 1832/36–*
309 wished] wish'd *1827*
310 silent;] silent: *MS. 1832/36–*
313 darkness:—from] darkness. From *MS. 1832/36–*
317 scanned] scann'd *1827*
326 reared;] reared. *1820E; see verbals*
328 more;] more, *1820E–*
330 Strengthened] Strengthen'd *1827*
331 wholesome] wholesome, *1836–*
334 summoned] summon'd *1827*
344 stern . . . kindly] stern, . . . kindly, *pencil MS. 1836/45* spirit] Spirit *1827–* Who] who *1820E–*
347 attached] attach'd *1827*
348 stedfast] steadfast *1832– but* stedfast *1845, 1850* clouds)—] clouds) *1827–*
349 Mind] mind *1832–*
353 Travellers] travellers *1836–*
354 deemed] deem'd *1827*
356 Squire, and Priest] squire, and priest *1836–*
357 sequestration, all,] sequestration—all *1820E–* dependant] dependent *1827–*
359 fancies,] fancies *1832–1836* fancies, *pencil MS. 1836/45, 1840–*
361 Countrymen] countrymen *MS. 1832/36–*
362 Track] track *1832–*
363 ease;—] ease:— *1845–*
370 wandered] wander'd *1827* Men] men *MS. 1832/36–*
372 passions,] passions *1832–*
374 mid] 'mid *1836–*
378 passed] pass'd *1827*
382 Nature] nature *1836–*
386 unvexed, unwarped] unvex'd, unwarp'd *1827*
387 course] course, *1820E–*
390 it's own] its own, *1827–*
391 Nature] nature *1836–*
393 Man] man *1836–*
394 enjoyed] enjoy'd *1827* went;] went, *1832–*
395 for] for, *pencil MS. 1836/45, 1840–*
396 chearfulness] cheerfulness *1827–*
406 History . . . Families] history . . . families *MS. 1832/36–*
407 prospered] prosper'd *1827*
408 mischance;] mischance, *pencil MS. 1836/45, 1840–*
410 groan.—] groan. *1836–* course,] course *1827–* This *para MS. 1832/36–*
414 days—] days, *1836–* untasked] untask'd *1827*
415 services,—] services— *1827, 1832* services, *1836–*
416 Calling] calling *1832–*
421 endeared] endear'd *MS. 1814/27, 1827*
423 worldly-mindedness] worldly-mindedness, *1820E, 1827*
424 refreshed] refresh'd *1827*
425 day;—] day; *1831, 1836–*
430 watched] watch'd *1827*
431 remembered] remember'd *1827*
436 Whate'er . . . youth] Whate'er, . . . youth, *1820E–*
438 away:] away; *1836–* this] this, *1827–*
439 seemed] seem'd *1827*
440 woods;] woods, *1820E*
442 belief,] belief *1827, 1832*
445 Man] man *1832–*
446 teazing] teasing *1827–* Children] children *MS. 1832/36–* vexed] vex'd *1827* him,] him; *1827–*
451 addressed] address'd *1827*
452 garb] garb; *1820E–*
453 sire] Sire *1832–*
454 Man] man *1836–*
455 passed] pass'd *1827*
458 compressed] compress'd *1827*
459 red] red, *1820E–*
460 eye;] eye, *1831* that] that, *1820E–*
461 grey] grey, *1820E–*
463 wondrous] wond'rous *1827*
465/466 *half rule del in pencil MS. 1836/45*
466 *para 1845, 1850*
467 Appendage] appendage *1836–* Staff,] Staff *1827* staff, *1836–*
468 relinquish'd] relinquished *1820E–*
469 Cottage bench] cottage-bench *1836–*
470 Screened] Screen'd *1827*
476 hailed] hail'd *1827*
478 scooped] scoop'd *1827* scooepd *1832* scoop'd *errata 1832* scooped

MS. 1832/36–
480 day;] day: *1832–*
481 parched] parch'd *MS. 1814/27, 1827*
486 garden-ground] garden ground *1832–* it's] its *1827–*
487 Marked] Mark'd *1827* pass'd] passed *1820E, 1832–*
489 currants] currants, *1820E–* stems] stems, *1836–*
491 looked] look'd *1827*
493 Joined] Join'd *1827* Well] well *1836–*
495 and] and, *pencil MS. 1836/45, 1840–* chearless] cheerless *1827–*
496 returned] return'd *1827*
497 Old] old *1836–* Cottage bench] cottage bench *MS. 1832/36* cottage-bench *1836–*
498 while,] while *1831* uncovered] uncover'd *1827*
505 changed;] chang'd *MS. 1814/27*
510 rocks; nor idly;] rocks! nor idly: *1831*
516 Spring] spring *MS. 1832/36–*
517 seemed] seem'd *1827*
522 minister'd] ministered *1832–*
526 years;] years, *1820E; see verbals*
530 Daughter's . . . me;] daughter's . . . me, *1827–*
531 O] ——————"O *Friend (excerpt starts here)* Oh, *1827–*
532 dust] dust, *Friend*
533 socket.] socket."—————— *Friend (excerpt ends here)* Passenger] passenger *MS. 1832/36–*
534 blessed] bless'd *1827*
536 Spring;] Spring: *1832* spring; *1836–*
538 seemed] seem'd *1827*
539 extinguished] extinguish'd *1827* Hut] hut *1836–*
540 Hut] hut *1836–* abandoned] abandon'd *1827*
541 She] she *1836–* grave!] grave. *1840–*
542 "I] I *pencil MS. 1836/45, 1840–*
543 bloom'd] bloomed *1820E–*
545 love,] love; *1836–*
549 Being—] Being *MS. 1832/36* Being, *1836–*
551 lacked] lack'd *1827*
556 Mower] mower *MS. 1832/36–*
558 Star] star *1836–* vanished . . . passed] vanish'd . . . pass'd *1827*
562 failed] fail'd *1827*
564 Boy] boy *1836–*
565 hope,—] hope, *MS. 1832/36–* Heaven] heaven *1836–*
566 Not] "Not *1832*
568 seasons] seasons, *1827– but* seasons *pencil MS. 1836/45*
569 heaven] Heaven *1820E–*
570 war;] war: *pencil MS. 1836/45, 1840–*
572 Cottages] cottages *MS. 1832/36, 1836* cottages, *pencil MS. 1836/45, 1840–*
574 season;] season: *1836–*
576 be] be, *1820E–*
577 Meanwhile] Meanwhile, *1827–* abridg'd] abridged *1820E–*
581 chearful hope:] cheerful hope, *1827–* but] but, *1820E; see verbals* autumn] autumn, *1820E–*
582 Help-mate] Helpmate *1820E; see verbals*
584 lingered] linger'd *1827* and] and, *pencil MS. 1836/45, 1840–* return'd] returned *1820E, 1832–*
590 turn'd] turned *1820E; see verbals*
594 Kite] kite *1836–*
595 Rocks] rocks *1836–*
596 A] "A *1832* Him] him *1836–*
597 filled] fill'd *1827* possess'd] possessed *1820E, 1832–*
604 ornament;] ornament, *1841– (possible worn plate) but* ornament; *1845, 1850*
605 uneasy] uneasy, *1836–*
611 drooped] droop'd *1827*
612 Town,] town, *MS. 1832/36, 1836* town *pencil MS. 1836/45, 1840–*
615 Babes] babes *1836–*
617 toss'd] tossed *1820E, 1832–*
619 "Every smile,"] 'Every smile,' *1832–*
621 "Made . . . bleed."] 'Made . . . bleed.'" *1832–*
622 Elms] elms *1836–*
623 noon.—] noon. *MS. 1832/36–*
625 hour,] hour *1832–*
626 chearful] cheerful *1827–*
628 Old] old *1836–*
631 away,] away; *1836–*
632 ears,] ears; *1836–*
637 chearfulness] cheerfulness *1827–*
639 recollection,] recollection; *pencil MS. 1836/45, 1840–* Tale] tale *1836–*
640 Passed] Pass'd *1827*
642 despite] despite, *1827–*
645 Tale] tale *1836–*
648 Seemed] Seem'd *1827* relax'd] relaxed *1820E, 1832–*
654 return'd] returned *1820E, 1832–*
655 begged] begg'd *1827* Old] old *1836–*
656 story.—] story. *1836–* *extra vertical space added between parts of split line 1836–*
657 "It . . . wantonness,] It . . . wantonness *Friend*
658 reproof,] reproof *Friend* Men] men *Friend, 1836–*

661 marked] mark'd *Friend, 1827*
664 found,] found *Friend*
665 friendly;] friendly.— *Friend (excerpt ends here)* were't] wer't *1845, 1850*
666 Dreamer] dreamer *1832–*
667 Dreamer! . . . Tale] dreamer . . . tale *1836–*
668 Man's] man's *1836–*
670 But, . . . bidding,] But . . . bidding *1832–*
671 proceed.—] proceed. *1827– extra vertical space after* proceed. *1836– but not 1845, 1850* While] "While *1832*
672 Cottage] cottage *1836–*
674 Country] country *MS. 1832/36–* remote.] remote; *1827–*
678 chear'd] cheered *1820E; see verbals*
680 knock'd] knocked *1820E; see verbals*
682 turn'd] turned *1820E, 1832–*
683 and] and, *1832–* chair] chair, *1832–*
687 name.—] name:— *1832–*
690 seemed] seem'd *1827*
691 Husband] husband *1836–*
692 surprize] surprise *1820E–*
694 disappear'd] disappeared *1820E, 1832–*
695 House] house *MS. 1832/36–* pass'd] passed *1820E* past *1832–*
696 rais'd] raised *1820E–*
702 open'd] opened *1820E, 1832–*
704 gold.—] gold. *1836–* "I] 'I *1832–* shuddered] shudder'd *1827* sight,"] sight,' *1832–*
705 "for] 'for *1832–*
709 joined] join'd *1827; see verbals*
710 Soldiers] soldiers *MS. 1832/36–* Land] land *1836–*
712 me;] me: *1831* fear'd] feared *1820E, 1832–*
713 Babes] babes *1836–*
714 Life."] Life.' *1832* life.' *1836–*
715 This] "This *1832* Tale] tale *1836–*
716 And . . . ended] And, . . . ended, *1820E–*
719 chear] cheer *1827–* both:—] both. *1836–* but] But *1836–* talked] talk'd *1827*
721 look'd] looked *1820E, 1832–*
725 looked] look'd *1827, 1832*
727 Called] Call'd *1827*
728 chearfulness;] cheerfulness; *1827, 1832* cheerfulness, *1836–*
729 seem'd] seemed *1820E, 1832–*
730 I] "I *1832* roved] rov'd *1831*
731 accustomed] accustom'd *1827*
732 wood,] wood *1836–*
734 Drooping,] Drooping *1827–*
736 "trotting brooks"] 'trotting brooks' *1832–*
738 pass'd] passed *1820E, 1831, 1832–*
739 disappeared.—] disappear'd.— *1827* disappeared. *1836–* I *para MS. 1832/36* journey'd] journeyed *1820E, 1832–* way] way, *1827–*
741 grass] grass, *1832–*
742 afresh] afresh, *1832–*
746 Cottage] cottage *MS. 1832/36–* chearful] cheerful *1827–* Object] object *1836–*
749 tufts:] tufts; *1836–*
750 suffered] suffer'd *1827*
751 grew,] grew *1840–*
752 turned] turn'd *1827*
753 strolled . . . appeared] stroll'd . . . appear'd *1827*
761 heads—] heads, *1827–*
763 pease] peas *1836–*
764 dragged] dragg'd *1827* earth.—] earth. *1836–* Ere *para MS. 1832/36–*
765 turned] turn'd *1827* steps,] steps; *1827–*
767 Stranger] stranger *1836–* passed] pass'd *1827*
771 Infant] infant *1836–*
772 self-stilled] self-still'd *1827*
776 remained] remain'd *1827* remained, *1836–* desolate.] desolate: *1827–*
778 unnotic'd] unnoticed *1820E; see verbals*
779 discolour'd] discoloured *1820E, 1832–*
780 Sheep] sheep *MS. 1832/36–*
781 Common] common *1820E*
782 Familiarly;] Familiarly, *pencil MS. 1836/45, 1840–*
784 elms;—] elms; *1836–* Cottage-clock] cottage-clock *MS. 1832/36–*
785 turned] turn'd *1827*
786 thin, her figure too] thin—her figure, too, *1832–*
787 unlocked] unlock'd *1827*
788 "It] 'It *1832–*
789 wandered] wander'd *1827* late,] late; *1836–*
790 sometimes,— . . . speak,] sometimes— . . . speak— *1827–*
791 again."] again.' *1832–*
792 meal] meal, *1820E–*
793 me,—] me— *1827–*
794 hands,] hands— *1820E–*
795 Child] child *1836–*
796 Master] master *1827–*
797 apprenticed—] apprenticed.— *1827–* "I] 'I *1832–*
801 find.] find, *1820E* find; *1827–*
803 myself,] myself," *MS. 1814/27, 1827*

myself,' *1832–* have] "have *MS. 1814/27, 1827* 'have *1832–*
804 Infant] infant *1836–*
806 flowed] flow'd *1827*
809 hope," . . . "that] hope,' . . . 'that *1832–* heaven] Heaven *1820E, 1827; see verbals*
811 home."] home.' *1832–* It *para MS. 1832/36–*
812 her;] her. *1836–*
813 heart:] heart; *1827–*
817 presence,] presence; *1836–*
821 asleep;—] asleep; *pencil MS. 1836/45, 1840–*
825 suffered] suffer'd *1827*
827 drooped] droop'd *1827*
831 house affairs] house-affairs *1836–* appeared] appear'd *1827*
834 sighed] sigh'd *1827*
839 Ere] "Ere *1832* departure] departure, *1820E–*
840 Son's] son's *1832–*
841 She] she *1820E–*
843 prayer.] prayer *1847 (probable worn plate)*
844 and] and, *pencil MS. 1836/45, 1840–* kissed] kiss'd *1827* babe] babe, *1836–*
846 give;] give: *pencil MS. 1836/45, 1840–*
847 thanked] thank'd *1827* wish;—] wish:— *1831*
848 I] "I *1832* returned] return'd *1827*
851 Peeped] Peep'd *1827*
852 drooping;] drooping: *1836–* learned] learn'd *1827*
853 Husband] husband *1836–* lived] lived, *1827–*
854 dead] dead, *1827–*
855 seem'd] seemed *1820E, 1832–*
856 House] house *1836–*
857 negligence.] negligence; *1827–*
860 Cottage window] cottage-window *1836–*
864 Infant] infant *1827–*
866 sighed] sigh'd *1827*
867 garden gate] garden-gate *1836–1843; see verbals* saw,] saw *1836*
869 her:] her; *1831*
870 harden'd] hardened *1820E, 1832–* wither'd] withered *1820E–* grass;] grass: *1827–*
871 appeared] appear'd *1827* mold] mould *1831*
873 flowers,] flowers *1831* seemed . . . gnawed] seem'd . . . gnaw'd *1827*
876 root;] root, *1827–1836* root; *1831, pencil MS. 1836/45, 1840–*
877 Sheep] sheep *1836–*
878 Infant] infant *1836–*
880 "I] 'I *1832–*
881 again."] again.' *1832–* House] house *1836–1843*
882 returned] return'd *1827*
883 hope:—] hope;— *1831* Babe] babe *1836–*
884 Boy] boy *1836–*
887 Sunday] sunday *1836–*
889 undisturbed] undisturb'd *1827* And *para MS. 1832/36–*
891 Babe] babe *1836–*
894 Wilds] wilds *1836–* gain'd] gained *1820E* gained, *1832–*
895 hemp] hemp, *1832–*
896 Boy] boy *1836–*
899 walked] walk'd *1827* road] road, *1827–*
900 and,] and *1827–1836* and, *pencil MS. 1836/45, 1840–*
901 begged] begg'd *1827*
903 then,] then— *1820E–*
905 return'd] returned *1820E, 1832–*
906 Nine] "Nine *1832*
908 lingered] linger'd *1827*
912 Sabbath-day,] Sabbath-day; *1827* Sabbath day; *1832* sabbath day; *1836–*
913 And] And, *1827–* passed] pass'd *1827* by] by, *1827–*
914 Bench] bench *1836–*
921 long drawn] long-drawn *pencil MS. 1836/45, 1840–*
922 pass'd] passed *1820E, 1832–*
923 shewed] shew'd *1827* showed *1832–*
924 Mendicant in Sailor's] mendicant in sailor's *1836–*
925 Child] child *1836–*
926 Ceas'd] Ceased *1820E–* faultering] faltering *1827–*
930 Traveller's] traveller's *1836–*
931 Horseman] horseman *1836–* came] came, *1827–*
932 wistfully;] wistfully: *1820E–*
933 discovered] discover'd *1827 (but* discovered *1831)*
936 decay:] decay; *1836–* gone—] gone, *1820E–*
939 Chequered] Chequer'd *1827*
941 House] house *1836–*
942 sapped] sapp'd *1827* slept] slept, *1832–*
944 tattered] tatter'd *1827* wind;] wind, *1836–*
948 endeared] endear'd *1827*
949 Friend,] Friend,— *1836–*
950 remained;] remain'd; *1827* remained, *1849* died,] died; *1836–*
951 Tenant] tenant *1832–* Walls."] walls!" *1836–*

952 Old] old *1836–*
953 Bench] bench *MS. 1832/36–*
954 turn'd] turned *1820E–*
955 Tale] tale *MS. 1832/36–*
956 and] and, *pencil MS. 1836/45* Garden] garden *MS. 1832/36–* wall,] wall *pencil MS. 1836/45, 1840–*
957 Reviewed . . . seemed] Review'd . . . seem'd *1827*
958 Brother's] brother's *MS. 1832/36–*
959 bless'd] blessed *1832–* her—] her *MS. 1832/36–*
960 returned] return'd *1827*
963 mid] 'mid *1845–*
964 Nature] nature *1827–* mid] 'mid *1845–*
966 Old] old *1836–*
968 more;] more: *1845–*
969 chearful] cheerful *1827–1843; see verbals*
970 eye.] eye? *1845–*
974 silver'd] silvered *1820E, 1832–*
975 passed] pass'd *1827*
977 looked] look'd *1827*
978 filled] fill'd *1827* mind,] *some copies of 1814 have final letter and comma as a partially uninked impression; MS. 1814/27 reinforces the "d" but not the comma*
981 shews] shows *1827–*
982 Appeared] Appear'd *1827*
983 turned] turn'd *1827* away] away, *1827–*
984 walked] walk'd *1827*
987 while . . . trees] while, ... trees, *1820E–*
988 Bench] bench *1836–*
989 Admonished] Admonish'd *1827*
993 Old] old *1836–*
994 grasped] grasp'd *1827* Staff:] staff: *MS. 1832/36* staff; *1836–*
996 Shade] shade *MS. 1832/36–*
997 Stars] stars *1832–* reached] reach'd *1827*
998 Village Inn,— our Evening] village-inn,—our evening *1836–*

Book II

2 Hall to Hall] hall to hall *MS. 1832/36–*
3 Court] court *1836–* Royal] royal *MS. 1832/36–* cheered] cheer'd *1827*
4 Ladies'] ladies' *1836–*
5 Knight] knight *1836–*
6 Pilgrim] pilgrim *1836–*
7 Abbey's] abbey's *MS. 1832/36–*
8 next] next, *1836–*
9 Humbly,] Humbly *1832–* Hospital] hospital *MS. 1832/36–*
10 Outlaws] outlaws *1836–*
11 Hermit's] hermit's *1836–*
12 Robber] robber *1836–*
13 walked] walk'd *1827*
14 Instrument] instrument *MS. 1832/36–*
15 Harp . . . Traveller's] harp . . . traveller's *MS. 1832/36–*
16 Companion] companion *MS. 1832/36–*
17 Land to Land] land to land *MS. 1832/36–*
19 honoured] honour'd *1827*
20 empassioned] empassion'd *1827* empassioned, *pencil MS. 1836/45, 1845–*
29 pace.] pace *1849 (probable worn plate)*
30 School] school *1836–*
33 Looked] Look'd *1827* Guide] guide *1836–*
35 journey—] journey, *MS. 1832/36–*
37 Hamlet] hamlet *MS. 1832/36–*
38 House] house *MS. 1832/36–*
42 Nature's] nature's *1836–*
48 dog,] dog— *1836–*
49 mind—] mind, *1836–*
52 Herd] herd *MS. 1832/36–*
53 walk] walk; *1827–1836, 1841–*
55 Brute's] brute's *MS. 1832/36–*
63 cottage hearth] cottage-hearth *1845–*
65 Huts] huts *1836–*
67 Friend] friend *1836–*
68 sometimes,] sometimes— *pencil MS. 1836/45, 1840–* Poor Man] poor man *1836–*
70 Impatience,] Impatience *1820E–*
73 it,] it; *1836–* perplexed,] perplex'd, *1827; deteriorating comma after* perplexed *looks like a period in some copies of 1843 and 1844E*
76 heaven] Heaven *1827–*
77 men;] men— *pencil MS. 1836/45, 1840–*
78 Him] him *1836–*
79 allayed] allay'd *1827*
80 listened] listen'd *1827*
83 softened] soften'd *1827* spirit,—] spirit— *1820E–1832* spirit, *1836–* condemned] condemn'd *1827*
84 witnessed] witness'd *1827* roved] roved, *1827–*
89 called] call'd *1827*
90 Fellow Traveller] Fellow traveller *1827* Fellow-traveller, *1832–*
94 hills;] hills, *1832–*
97 But . . . distance] But, . . . distance, *1820E–*
99 aerial] aërial *1827–*

101 Wealthy, the Luxurious] wealthy, the luxurious *1836–*
106 They] they *1836–* blessed] blest *MS. 1814/27–*
108 our's] ours *1827–*
109 Could . . . leisure] Could, . . . leisure, *1820E–*
111 air,] air; *MS. 1814/27–*
112 will;] will— *MS. 1814/27–*
115 slowly] slowly, *1820E– ; see verbals*
118 Pilgrim's] pilgrim's *1836–*
122 tow'rds] tow'rd *1827* toward *1832–*
123 Vale] vale *1836–*
124 People] people *MS. 1832/36–*
126 thrilled] thrill'd *1827*
127 answer:] answer; *1836–*
128 Pipe] pipe *MS. 1832/36–*
130 Rustic;] Rustic, *1849*
131 Knot] knot *1836–*
132 formed] form'd *1827* Village green] village green *MS. 1832/36– but* village-green *pencil MS. 1836/45, 1845, 1850*
134 glistened] glisten'd *1827*
135 Assemblage] assemblage *1836–*
140 sun-beams] sunbeams *1827–*
143 reanimate] re-animate *1820E–*
145 "the] "The *1832–*
146 road] road, *1827–*
151 Sun] sun *MS. 1832/36–*
152 skimmed:] skimm'd; *1827* skimmed; *1832–*
153 contend:—] contend: *1820E–*
162 imparted.] imparted:— *1836–*
163 concealed] conceal'd *1827*
165 recompence,] recompense, *1827–* toil—] toil, *pencil MS. 1836/45, 1840–*
168 forestal] forestall *1832–*
169 himself,)] himself) *1832–*
171 Though] "Though *1832*
173 Scotland;] Scotland, *1820E–*
174 sheltered] shelter'd *1827*
178 displayed] display'd *1827*
186 Military Troop] military troop *MS. 1832/36–*
187 Cheered] Cheer'd *1827* Bagpipe] bagpipe *MS. 1832/36–* marched] march'd *1827*
188 Fellow-countrymen] fellow-countrymen *MS. 1832/36–*
189 Office] office *MS. 1832/36–*
190 inclination,] inclination *pencil MS. 1836/45, 1840–*
191 Ruler] ruler *1836–*
192 vanity—] vanity, *1836–* walked] walk'd *1827* World] world *MS. 1832/36–*
194 Pastor . . . Flock] pastor . . . flock *MS. 1832/36–*
195 Soldier . . . Soldiers] soldier . . . soldiers *MS. 1832/36–* roamed] roam'd *1827*
197 wanderer's] Wanderer's *1832* wanderer's *MS. 1832/36–* Friend] friend *MS. 1832/36–*
198 Flower] flower *MS. 1832/36–*
202 For] "For *1832*
203 endowed] endow'd *1827*
204 Office] office *MS. 1832/36–* relinquished] relinquish'd *1827*
205 Home] home *MS. 1832/36–*
208 decay;] decay, *1827–1843; see verbals*
209 abate,] abate; *1836–1843; see verbals* till] 'till *1827–1843; see verbals*
210 year] year, *1836– but* year *1846 (possible worn plate)*
211 all.—] all. *1836–*
212 possessed!] possess'd! *1827*
213 followed] follow'd *1827*
214 prayed] pray'd *1827*
215 dismissal;] dismissal, *pencil MS. 1836/45, 1845–* compelled] compell'd *1827*
217 Eternity.] eternity. *1836–*
222 But] "But *1832*
223 world's] worlds, *1840* appeared] appear'd *1827*
224 unlooked-for] unlook'd-for *1827*
229 reached] reach'd *1827*
230 repaired] repair'd *1827*
231 Emporium] emporium *MS. 1832/36–*
234 transferred] transferr'd *1827*
235 And] And, *1820E–* Pulpit] Pulpit, *1820E–1832* pulpit, *MS. 1832/36–* maintained] maintain'd *1827*
237 one;] one, *1832–*
242 That] "That *1832*
244 Etherial] Ethereal *1832–* Natures . . . Slaves] natures . . . slaves *MS. 1832/36–*
245 by] from *1836* by *restored in errata 1836 and in MS. 1836/45 (pencil)* Advocates] advocates *MS. 1832/36–*
247 seemed] seem'd *1827*
248 gained] gain'd *1827*
250 transcendent] transcendant *1820E*
253 power,] power *1832–*
255 revealed] reveal'd *1827*
257 out,—] out, *1832–*
267 hypocrisy,] hypocrisy— *1836–*
272 wisest,] wisest *1827–* stooped] stoop'd *1827*
273 restraints:] restraints; *pencil MS. 1836/45, 1840–*
278 His] "His *1832*

279 enjoyed] enjoy'd *1827*
280 Layman's] layman's *1836–*
282 him;—] him; *1836–*
283 displayed] display'd *1827*
284 Unhallowed] Unhallow'd *1827*
287 retained] retain'd *1827*
289 nature—] nature, *MS. 1832/36–*
290 weak] weak, *1827–*
291 appeared,] appear'd, *1827*
292 coloured] colour'd *1827*
293 Lover's] lover's *1836–*
295 keener— . . . less.] keener, . . . less: *MS. 1832/36–*
299 showed] show'd *1827* shewed *1836– but* showed *1850* happiness; but] happiness. But *MS. 1832/36–*
301 hope.] hope: *1832–*
303 Life] life *1836–*
307 vain] vain, *pencil MS. 1836/45, 1845–*
308 The] "The *1832* away,] away— *1836–*
309 splendor] splendour *1832*
310 hallowed . . . veiled] hallow'd . . . veil'd *1827*
311 sight,—] sight— *MS. 1832/36–*
313 vexed] vex'd *1827*
314 galled] gall'd *1827*
315 Men] men *1836–*
320 last,] last *1820E; see verbals*
324 life,] life— *pencil MS. 1836/45, 1840–* fixed] fix'd *1827* Home] home *MS. 1832/36–*
327 hours] hours, *1845–*
331 a] 'a *1836–* "world] 'world *1832* world *1836–*
332 mind."] mind.'" *1832–*
335 Vale] vale *1836–*
340 Mountains, Cavern, Fall] mountains, cavern, fall *MS. 1832/36–*
341 water—] water, *1836–* Eminence] eminence *MS. 1832/36–*
342 Renowned] Renown'd *1827* wide.] wide) *1827–*
343 steps;] steps, *1827–*
347 *Guide 1835 selection begins with* "Behold!
348 Vale] vale *1836– but not Guide 1842*
349 Vale] vale *1836– but not Guide 1842*
351 been,] been *pencil MS. 1836/45, 1840– but not Guide 1842* time] time, *pencil MS. 1836/45, Guide 1842* theirs,] theirs *1836– but not Guide 1842;* theirs, *pencil MS. 1836/45*
352 placed,—] placed, *1832–*
353 Urn] urn *MS. 1832/36– but not Guide 1842*
354 encompassed,] encompass'd *1827* South] south *MS. 1832/36– but not Guide 1842*
356 close.] close; *1827–*
358 glittered] glitter'd *1827* sun,] sun *Guide 1846*
359 Dwelling; one Abode] dwelling; one abode *1836– but not Guide 1842*
360 seemed] seem'd *1827* toil] toil, *1827–*
363 House] house *MS. 1832/36– but not Guide 1842*
364 Cock] cock *MS. 1832/36– but not Guide 1842*
366 them;] them: *Guide 1846* Vales] vales *MS. 1832/36– but not Guide 1842*
367 Cuckoo] Cuckoo, *1820E–1832* cuckoo, *MS. 1832/36– but not Guide 1842* tops] tops, *1820E–*
368 place.] place." *Guide 1835, which ends here*
374 secure:] secure; *1836–*
376 furnished] furnish'd *1827*
381 nakedness;] nakedness: *1836–*
383 single] single, *pencil MS. 1836/45, 1840–*
385 no where;] nowhere; *1827–*
387 uncalled] uncall'd *1827*
388 life,] life. *1820E*
392 silent:] silent; *1836–*
393 Abyss . . . Voice] abyss . . . voice *MS. 1832/36–*
394 Voices] voices *1832–*
395 heard—] heard *MS. 1832/36–* ascending:] ascending; *1836–*
396 cadence] Cadence *1832* cadence *MS. 1832/36–* Psalms] psalms *MS. 1832/36–*
397 listened] listen'd *1827* Hut] hut *MS. 1832/36–*
398 One] one *MS. 1832/36–*
400 recognize] recognise *1832–*
401 words;—] words:— *1820E–* "Shall] 'Shall *1836–* Grave] grave *MS. 1832/36–*
402 Death] death *MS. 1832/36–* faithfulness?"] faithfulness?' *1836–* Soul,"] Soul!" *1827* soul!" *1832–*
403 silence,] silence,— *1827–*
406 appeared] appear'd *1827*
407 Persons] persons *MS. 1832/36–*
408 Coffin] coffin *MS. 1832/36–*
410 Valley;] valley; *MS. 1832/36* valley, *1836–*
411 Men] men *MS. 1832/36–*
418 so.] so, *1820E–*
420 One] one *MS. 1832/36–*
421 performed] perform'd *1827*
422 Tenant] tenant *1836–* Solitude] solitude *MS. 1832/36–*

427 Outlet] outlet MS. 1832/36– disappeared] disappear'd 1827
430 Comrade] comrade 1820E–1832 Comrade 1836–
434 platform;] platform— 1827–
436 Recess] recess 1836–
437 For,] For 1836–
445 Children's] children's MS. 1832/36–
446 thronged] throng'd 1827
451 sight] sight, 1820E–
454 on;] on: 1820E; *see verbals* exclaimed] exclaim'd 1827
455 and,] and 1820E, 1827, 1836–1843
456 Book] book MS. 1832/36– moss] moss, 1827
457 earthen-ware,] earthen-ware 1832
461 gone!"] gone?" 1832 Book] book MS. 1832/36–
462 itself,] itself 1832–
466 Tongue] tongue 1836–
468 Friend;] Friend: 1820E–
472 Children; here no doubt] children: here, no doubt, 1827–
478 work;] work! 1827–
479 Darlings] darlings 1836– turned] turn'd 1827
480 memorial] Memorial 1827, 1832 memorial MS. 1832/36– Friend] friend 1836–
481 "Me, . . . most] "Me," . . . "most 1820E– surprize] surprise 1827–
482 Book] book 1827– place!"] place!"— 1832– "A Book] "A book MS. 1832/36–
484 things;] things: 1836–
489 Shepherd] shepherd 1836– world!] world!— 1845–
490 away] away, 1827–
492 your's;] yours; 1827, 1832, 1841, 1846 yours, 1836, 1840, 1845, 1850
493 Him] him 1836–
493/494 *vertical space closed up but indent in l. 494 kept 1850*
494 this] this, 1820E– Book] book MS. 1832/36– Old] old 1836–
496 scorn.] scorn; 1827, 1832 scorn:— 1836– Lover] lover MS. 1832/36– doomed] doom'd 1827
497 failed] fail'd 1827
501 Kings] kings MS. 1832/36–
502 Servant] servant MS. 1832/36–
503 may,] may 1847 *(probable worn plate)*
504 Master's] master's MS. 1832/36–
510 Scoffer's] scoffer's MS. 1832/36–
512 Hardened] Harden'd 1827
514 stepped] stepp'd 1827
518 *para MS. 1814/27–*
519 followed] follow'd 1827
521 opened] open'd 1827
527 rustic,] rustic— 1845–
533 walked] walk'd 1827
534 Grave] grave MS. 1832/36–
535 little One] little one 1836– *but* Little-one 1845, 1850 *(MS. 1836/45 has* One *in pencil, interlined, and* Little one *in pencil in margin)*
537 Heaven] heaven MS. 1832/36–
545 Passed] Pass'd 1827; *see verbals*
546 joined] join'd 1827
547 and,] and 1832– space,] space,— *pencil* MS. 1836/45, 1840–1843 space— 1845–
549 vanished] vanish'd 1827 returned] return'd 1827; *see verbals*
550 retained] retain'd 1827
555 charge—"] Charge"— 1832
557 Child] child 1836–
558 Mourner] Mourner, 1827, 1832 mourner, 1836–
559 Ye] ye? 1836–
561 feet] feet, 1820E–
562 Funeral Train] funeral train MS. 1832/36–
563 disappeared] disappear'd 1827 Child] child 1836–1843
564 Old] old 1836–
566 distressed,] distress'd, 1827 distressed 1832– overpowered] overpower'd 1827
568 Orphan's] orphan's MS. 1832/36–
569 sustained] sustain'd 1827
570 answered] answer'd 1827
572 Other] other 1836–
573 Crag] crag MS. 1832/36–
574 dropped] dropp'd 1827 Vale] vale MS. 1832/36–
576 anywhere,] any where, 1827, 1832 any where; 1836–
580 stopped] stopp'd, 1827; *see verbals*
582 Life] life MS. 1832/36–
583 Corse] corse MS. 1832/36–
584 decency,] decency; 1836–
587 Traveller] traveller 1827–
588 Stranger] stranger MS. 1832/36–
590 Procession,] Procession 1820E–1832 procession MS. 1832/36– road,] road; 1827–
592 clustered] cluster'd 1827
595 Body] body MS. 1832/36– consigned] consign'd 1827
596 bequeathed] bequeath'd 1827
600 Yea] Yea, 1820E– Mourners] mourners MS. 1832/36–
601 Coffin] coffin MS. 1832/36–
606 seen?—Ye] seen—ye MS. 1832/36– have seen] have seen— 1827– *but* have seen? *pencil* MS. 1836/45

607 Husband, Brothers—Brothers] husband, brothers—brothers *MS. 1832/36–*
608 Son . . . Father] son . . . father *MS. 1832/36–*
611 Supporters . . . Weight] supporters . . . weight *MS. 1832/36–*
613 towards] tow'rds *1836–1843* tow'rd *pencil MS. 1836/45*
615 faces;] faces: *1836–* most] most, *pencil MS. 1836/45, 1840–*
617 eye!] eye!— *1836–*
619 mourned] mourn'd *1827*
620 to day] to-day *1820E–*
632 desart] desert *1827–*
633 At *para MS. 1832/36–*
638 love"—] love" *1832–*
639 man] Man *1836–*
641 Associates] associates *MS. 1832/36–*
644 resolve."—] resolve." *MS. 1832/36–*
649 Solitude,] Solitude *MS. 1814/27* solitude, *MS. 1832/36–*
653 Which] Which, *1832–*
654 Friend] friend *MS. 1832/36–*
655 Advocate] advocate *MS. 1832/36–*
656 undeterred] undeterr'd *1827*
658 soul] Soul *1827, 1832*
659 enriched] enrich'd *1827*
663 this] this, *1827, 1832; see verbals*
664 homely] Homely *1845–*
665 reached] reach'd *1827*
668 appeared] appear'd *1827*
669 looked] look'd *1827*
672 Ticked,] Tick'd, *1827* ticked *1845–; see verbals*
673 Guide] Guide, *1827–* cottage stairs] cottage-stairs *1836–*
674 reached] reach'd *1827*
675 entered] enter'd, *1827*
677 cabin,] cabin,— *1827, 1832* will.—] will— *1827–*
679 Ye] ye *1836–*
680 *para MS. 1832/36–*
684 looked] look'd *1827* Friend] Friend, *1832–*
685 returned] return'd *1827*
686 Cheered] Cheer'd *1827* Cheered, *1832–*
687 scattered] scatter'd *1827*
689 withered] wither'd *1827*
690 moss;] moss: *1832* moss. *1836–; see verbals*
693 angling-rod] angling rod *1820E*
694 shattered . . . linked] shatter'd . . . link'd *1827*
698 —But] But *1836–* fulfilled,] fulfilled; *1820E, 1832–* fulfill'd; *1827*
702 bleached] bleach'd *1827*
703 half-covered] half-cover'd *1827*
704 cream,] cream. *1832* cream; *MS. 1832/36–*
705 embossed] emboss'd *1827*
706 tinge,] tinge *1827; see verbals*
709 lacked] lack'd *1827*
710 Table] table *MS. 1832/36–*
712 stilled] still'd *1827*
713 Comforter] comforter *1836–*
714 moved] moved, *1832–*
715 mood] mood, *1820E–*
717 Cell] cell *MS. 1832/36–*
718 not . . . anon] not, . . . anon, *1827–*
719 Peaks] peaks *1836–1843*
720 Vale] vale *MS. 1832/36–* peered] peer'd *1827*
723 Companions] companions *MS. 1832/36–*
724 Which . . . course] Which, . . . course, *1820E–*
726 Brethren] brethren *MS. 1832/36–*
730 blast] blast, *1820E–*
735 greeting:—nor] greeting. Nor *MS. 1832/36–* Nature's] nature's *1836–*
744 sun] Sun *1832* himself] himself, *1827–*
745 day] day, *1827–*
746 Orb] orb *MS. 1832/36–*
749 Stars] Stars, *1827, 1832* stars, *1836–*
751 Agents] agents *MS. 1832/36–*
754 Tale] tale *1836–* threatened] threaten'd *1827*
755 unawares] unawares; *1827, 1832* unawares: *MS. 1832/36–*
760 looked] look'd *1827*
761 Mountain] mountain *1827–*
763 world,] world; *pencil MS. 1836/45, 1840–*
764 Cottage] cottage *MS. 1832/36–*
765 Relinquished] Relinquish'd *1827* dependant] dependent *1827–*
768 distilled] distill'd *1827*
769 Opened] Open'd *1827*
772 nook] nook, *MS. 1832/36–*
773 had—] had, *MS. 1832/36–*
775 life;] life, *1827, 1832* life; *MS. 1832/36–*
783 Old] old *1836–*
785 One] one *1820E–*
789 Housewife] housewife *1836–* possess'd] possessed *1820E, 1832–*
790 Vassal] vassal *MS. 1832/36–* tilled] till'd *1827*
791 fetched] fetch'd *1827* Kine] kine *MS. 1832/36–*
793 Hay-makers] hay-makers *MS. 1832/36–*
794 Maintained] Maintain'd *1827*

796 Child] Child, 1827, 1832 child, MS. 1832/36 child 1836–
798 Shadow] shadow 1836– performed] perform'd 1827
800 reward!] reward!— 1845– Moon] moon 1836–
801 Dame] dame 1836– Queen] queen MS. 1832/36–
803 rushed,] rush'd— 1827 rushed— 1832–
804 humanized] humanised 1850
805 dismay.—] dismay. MS. 1832/36–
806 but] but, 1827–
810 seen] seen, 1832–
811 Friend,] Friend— *pencil MS.* 1836/45, 1840–
814 fuel,] fuel— *pencil MS.* 1836/45, 1840–
817 "Inhuman!" . . . "was] 'Inhuman!' . . . 'was 1832– Old] old 1836–
819 late."] late.' 1832–
820 Husband] husband 1836– Vale] vale MS. 1832/36–
822 Veteran] veteran 1836– dropped,] dropp'd 1827
823 looked] look'd 1827
827 *para MS.* 1832/36–
829 Cell] cell MS. 1832/36–
832 Vale] vale MS. 1832/36–
833 renewed] renew'd 1827
836 vain.] vain: MS. 1832/36–
837 Till] 'Till MS. 1832/36–
838 ruin,] ruin— *pencil MS.* 1836/45, 1840– walls] walls, 1827, 1832 walls MS. 1832/36–
852 Child] child 1820E–
853 Mid] 'Mid 1827–
857 *para MS.* 1832/36–
861 opened] open'd 1827
869 Appearance] appearance 1836–
870 City] city 1836–
872 wondrous] wond'rous 1827
875 spires;] spires, 1820E–
876 terrace] terrace, 1827–
878 there,] there 1827, 1832
887 O] Oh 1832–
895 enwrapp'd] enwrapped 1820E, 1832–
896 appeared] appear'd 1827
899 fixed; and fixed] fix'd; and fix'd 1827
903 power,] power 1832–
905 Vale] vale 1836–1843 Vale, 1845– ; *see verbals*
908 revealed] reveal'd 1827
909 Spirits] spirits 1820E–1832 Spirits MS. 1832/36–
910 Swelled] Swell'd 1827 "I . . . dead,"] 'I . . . dead,' 1832–
911 "And] 'And 1832– do] *do MS.* 1832/36– live?"] live?' 1832–
912 prayed] pray'd 1827
914 gazed;] gazed: 1836–
916 descended.—] descended. MS. 1832/36– Having *para MS.* 1832/36– reached] reach'd 1827 House] House, 1827, 1832 house, MS. 1832/36–
917 Inmate] inmate 1836–
919 seemed] seem'd 1827
921 shew] show 1827– Housewife] housewife 1836–
925 seemed] seem'd 1827
928 shewed] show'd 1827 showed 1832– itself;] itself: 1836– lingered] linger'd 1827
929 Cottage] cottage MS. 1832/36– to-day.] *some copies of 1814 lose period during printing*
930 So] "So 1827, 1832 Tale] tale 1836–
931 turned] turn'd 1827
933 Cupboard] cupboard MS. 1832/36–
934 this] this, 1827–
935 grey-haired] grey-hair'd 1827
936 Hermit] hermit MS. 1832/36–

Book III

1 humming] HUMMING 1827– Bee] bee MS. 1832/36 BEE 1836– Rill—] rill MS. 1832/36 rill— 1836–
2 Falcons,] falcons, MS. 1832/36–1843 falcons 1845– wing,] wing MS. 1832/36
4 Citadel] citadel MS. 1832/36–
7 Cottage-threshold] cottage-threshold MS. 1832/36– passed] pass'd 1827
8 Valley,] Valley 1832 valley 1836 valley, *pencil MS.* 1836/45, 1840–
9 more,] more *pencil MS.* 1836/45, 1840–
10 Anon!] "Anon!" 1836 Anon! *pencil MS.* 1836/45, 1840– exclaimed] exclaim'd 1827
13 gathered] gather'd 1827 Cell] cell 1820E–
15 Prisoners] prisoners 1836–
17 Spot] spot MS. 1832/36– endowed] endow'd 1827
19 recompence] recompense 1827–
20 looked . . . perplexed] look'd . . . perplex'd 1827
21 grey-haired] grey-hair'd 1827
23 Upwards] Upward MS. 1814/27–
24 fashioned] fashion'd 1827
26 yew-tree;] Yew-tree; 1827, 1832 yew-tree, 1836–1843 Yew-tree, *pencil MS.* 1836/45, 1845–

30 Streamlet] streamlet *1836–*
31 earthy] earthly *corr* earthy *errata 1832*
33 crowned] crown'd *1827*
34 Infant] infant *1836–*
35 Life] life *1836–*
37 encumbered] encumber'd *1827*
39 Vale] vale *MS. 1832/36–*
40 Rill] rill *MS. 1832/36–*
42 Crag] crag *MS. 1832/36–*
43 Tower] tower *MS. 1832/36–*
44 barred] barr'd *1827*
46 detained] detain'd *1827*
49 Waterfall] waterfall *MS. 1832/36–*
50 quiet] quite *corr* quiet *errata 1832*
52 discovered] discover'd *1827*
53 Mass] mass *1827–*
55 Ship] ship *MS. 1832/36–* upturned,—] upturn'd,— *1827* upturned, *MS. 1832/36–*
56 Stones] stones *1836–*
58 these] these, *MS. 1814/27* and,] and *1832*
59 disjoined] disjoin'd *1827*
60 That,] That *1827–*
61 Fragment . . . Altar] fragment . . . altar *MS. 1832/36–* smooth.] smooth *1827* smooth: *1832–*
62 appeared,] appear'd *1827* appeared *1832–*
64 Holly] holly *1836–*
66 hand,] hand *1827–*
69 entered] enter'd *1827*
70 high, or low,] high or low *1832–* appeared] appear'd *1827*
71 Water] water *MS. 1832/36–*
72 Barrier] barrier *MS. 1832/36–*
75 chrystal] crystal *1827–* Lake] lake *1832–*
76 Cabinet . . . Sages] cabinet . . . sages *MS. 1832/36–*
77 Kings] kings *MS. 1832/36–*
78 Old] old *1836–*
79 turned] turn'd *1827*
83 Rocks . . . Stones] rocks . . . stones *MS. 1832/36–*
85 Nature's] Nature s *1832* nature's *1836–*
89 Shrub] shrub *1836–*
96 Stream] stream *1836–* gulph] gulf *1827–*
97 Strait] strait *1836–*
101 through,] through; *1836–* Abyss] abyss *MS. 1832/36–*
102 Stars] stars *1836–*
106 Reared] Rear'd *1827* Art] art *1832–*
107 air,] air *1832–*
108 turbulence,] turbulence *1820E–*
110 Lodge] lodge *1836–*
111 mayest] may'st *1827* mayst *pencil MS. 1836/45, 1840–*
112 Thou] thou *MS. 1832/36–* depth,] depth *1820E, 1827*
113 Mayest] May'st *1827* Mayst *pencil MS. 1836/45, 1840–* Truth] truth *1836–*
115 time] Time *1820E–1832* Nature] nature *1836–*
116 Eternity] eternity *1836–*
118 scanned] scann'd *1827*
119 Vale] vale *MS. 1832/36–*
122 Retirement] retirement *MS. 1832/36–*
123 Nook] nook *MS. 1832/36–*
125 enterprize] enterprise *1827–*
126 Hunter] hunter *MS. 1832/36–*
127 disdained] disdain'd, *1827*
128 eyes,] eyes *1832–*
129 deemed] deem'd *1827*
130 Chance] Chance, *1820E*
132 Shaft] shaft *MS. 1832/36–*
134 Titles] titles *MS. 1832/36–*
135 Pillar] pillar *1836–* that] that *MS. 1814/27 that 1827*
136 Obelisk] obelisk *1836–*
137 Cromlech] cromlech *1836–*
141 But,] But *1832–* oppressed] oppress'd *1827*
145 aggravate,] aggravate— *1827–*
149 Diadem] diadem *MS. 1832/36–* pendant] pendent *1832–*
152 plain;—] plain— *1845–* Pyramid] pyramid *1832–*
153 undissolved;] undissolved— *1845–*
154 Ruins] ruins *MS. 1832/36–*
155 Desart] Desert *1827, 1832* desert *MS. 1832/36–*
157 appearance,] appearance *1832–*
158 pitch,] pitch *1832–*
163 happier,] happier *1832–* you,] you *1827–*
164 transports,] transports *1827–* deemed] deem'd *1827*
170 Floweret . . . Plant] floweret . . . plant *MS. 1832/36–*
173 Hound] hound *MS. 1832/36–*
176 quest!] quest!— *1836–*
178 envied] envied, *1832–*
180 heaven] Heaven *1820E–*
182 He,] He *1832–* pocket hammer] pocket-hammer *1836–*
187 chip,] chip *1832–* splinter,—] splinter— *1827–*
191 interveined] intervein'd *1827*
192 chrystal] crystal *1827–*
193 enriched] enrich'd *1827*
195 Entrusted] Intrusted *1827–*

safely—] safely *1832–* pursuit,] pursuit *1827* pursuit, *MS. 1827/32C*
199 near] near, *1820E–*
202 Cottage-boy] cottage-boy *1836–*
203 Pupil . . . Form] pupil . . . form *MS. 1832/36–*
204 Apprentice . . . School . . . Art] apprentice . . . school . . . art *MS. 1832/36–*
205 entered] enter'd *1827* Glen] glen *MS. 1832/36–*
208 dam,] dam *1836–*
212 answered] answer'd *1827*
214 Imagination] imagination *MS. 1832/36–*
215 Question . . . Earth] question . . . earth *MS. 1832/36–*
216 Heaven's . . . Vault] heaven's . . . vault *MS. 1832/36–* suffered] suffer'd *1827*
221 space;] space— *1836–* one] one, *1820E–*
225 no where] nowhere *1827–*
228 attained,] attain'd, *1827* attained,— *1832–*
229 sorrow] sorrrow *1832 (corr in ink to* sorrow *in some copies)* sorrow *MS. 1832/36–*
230 grey-haired] grey-hair'd *1827*
232 Child] child *1836–*
233 Consolations] consolations *1836–*
236 oft-times] oftimes *Huntington MS.*
237 soar."—] soar— *Huntington MS., which ends here* *MS. 1814/27 has a vertical line after dash, possibly intended to eliminate para; MS. 1836/45 has a pencil bracket indicating second half-line should be moved left*
238 replied—] replied.— *1827*
240 inquisition] Inquisition *1832* inquisition *MS. 1832/36–*
242 World!] World— *1827, 1832* World. *MS. 1832/36* world. *1836–*
246 Men] men *1836–*
247 Cave] cave *MS. 1832/36–*
248 Parents] parents *1836–* Mankind!] Mankind: *1827, 1832* mankind: *1836–*
251 insects—] insects *MS. 1832/36–*
253 Chuse] Choose *1827–*
261 Stream . . . Life] stream . . . life *MS. 1832/36–*
262 Power] power *1820E–*
263 Existence] existence *MS. 1832/36–*
264 Sun] sun *MS. 1832/36–*
266 lost] lost, *1820E; see verbals*
269 Not *para MS. 1832/36–*
271 spirit—] spirit *MS. 1832/36–*
276 not:—] not;— *1820E–*
278 regret] regret, *MS. 1832/36–*
283 day] Day *1832* day *MS. 1832/36–* acceptable;—] acceptable; *1832–*
288 Yet] "Yet *1832*
290 kind;] kind, *1827, 1832* kind *1836–*
291 Not] (Not *1827–*
295 feed;] feed) *1827–*
302 dark,] dark *1827–*
306 Spirits,] Spirits! *pencil MS. 1836/45, 1840–*
313–330 *all double quots become single quots 1832–*
313 Autumn] autumn *MS. 1832/36–*
316 Clouds] clouds *1827–*
317 Brooks] brooks *MS. 1832/36–* sway,"] sway, *1836–*
325 fair,] fair *1832*
326 Fancy] fancy *1836–* Golden Age] golden age *MS. 1832/36–*
329 year] Year *1827, 1832* year *MS. 1832/36–*
330 hush'd] hushed *1820E–*
331 Age we know] Age, we know, *1820E–*
335 entertainment—] entertainment:— *1836–* hence!"] hence! *1827*
338 thoughts,] thoughts *1827–1843*
341 Poesy,] Poesy *MS. 1832/36–*
344 stiled] styled *1827–*
345 Dreamer] dreamer *MS. 1832/36–*
346 Dreamer] dreamer *MS. 1832/36–*
347 "shall] "Shall *1820E; see verbals*
350 Her] her *1836–*
353 Gardens] gardens, *1820E; see verbals*
354 Brotherhood] brotherhood *1836–*
356 secure,] secure *1820E*
359 She] she *1836–*
364 Countenance] countenance *MS. 1832/36–*
369 Man's] man's *1836–*
375 drove] drove, *1840–*
376 Hermit] hermit *1836–* Cell] cell *MS. 1832/36–*
379 desart] desert *1827–*
380 sword—] sword, *MS. 1832/36–*
385 agony:—] agony;— *1832–*
394 evermore!] evermore!— *1836–*
395 Life] life *1832–*
398 Nature's] nature's *1836–* steadfast] stedfast *1845–*
399 What] "What *1832*
400 Brotherhood;] Brotherhood, *1832* brotherhood, *1836–* Rock] rock *MS. 1832/36–*
401 Aerial] Aërial *1827–* Vale] vale *MS. 1832/36–*
403 Fellowship] fellowship *MS. 1832/36–*
406 sublime:—] sublime: *MS. 1832/36–*
408 Soul] soul *1836–1843; see verbals*

410 meditation,] meditation *1832–* quietness!] quietness!— *1836–*
411 scheme:—] scheme: *1836–*
412 And,—] And, *MS. 1832/36–1843; see verbals*
413 none,—] none, *MS. 1832/36–1843; see verbals*
417 them,] them *1836–* Voice] voice *MS. 1832/36–*
419 Youth:—] youth— *1836–*
424 suffering—] suffering, *MS. 1832/36–*
425 Hostility,] Hostility— *MS. 1832/36–*
427 A] "A *1832* Child] child *1836–*
436 Enlivened] Enliven'd *1827*
441 are] *are 1836–*
443 Men] men *1836–*
444 heaven,] heaven? *1820E–*
445 flower?] flower?— *1836–*
447 solitude,] solitude: *1836–*
449 Priest] priest *1836–* seat;] seat: *1832–*
451 Poet] poet *1836–* Lyre] lyre *1832–*
459 tremble] tremble, *1832–* Ye] Ye, *1832* ye, *1836–*
462 both,] both *1820E–*
464 hope.] hope: *1820E–*
466 will] *will 1832–*
467 Ye] ye *1836–*
468 But,] But *1832–*
469 heart;] heart. *1820E* heart: *1827–*
472 Nature] nature *1836–*
473 Proficient] proficient *MS. 1832/36–* scene,] scene *1820E–*
477 stem,] stem *1820E–* Speaker's] speaker's *MS. 1832/36–*
478 Place] place *MS. 1832/36–*
481 need,] need; *1820E*
482 Men's] men's *MS. 1832/36–*
483 but,] but *1832, 1836* but, *pencil MS. 1836/45, 1840–*
484 turf, . . . sun;] turf . . . sun, *1827–*
485 And,] And *1836– but* And, *MS. 1836/45* couch] couch, *MS. 1836/45*
488 "You] You *1836*
489 Form] form *MS. 1832/36–* loved.—] loved:— *1827–*
491 honored] honoured *1827–* Friend,] Friend! *1820E–*
499 bareness,] bareness *1832– but rev to* barrenness *then restored to* bareness *MS. 1832/36*
505 You] "You *1832, 1840–*
506 Compatriot;—] Compatriot— *pencil MS. 1836/45, 1840–* Sir] Sir, *1820E–*
507 Stranger] Stranger, *1827, 1832* stranger, *MS. 1832/36–*
509 Vale)] vale) *MS. 1832/36–* told,] told,— *1836* told— *pencil MS. 1836/45, 1840–*
511 One,] One *1827–*
512 all,] all *1820E–* Bride—] Bride, *1827–1836* Bride— *pencil MS. 1836/45, 1840–*
513 Love] Love, *1820E–1832* love, *MS. 1832/36–*
514 Parents] parents *MS. 1832/36–*
516 sights,] sights *1832–*
523 Cottage . . . Bay] cottage . . . bay *MS. 1832/36–*
526 Hold] hold *MS. 1832/36–*
529 Abode, . . . Seat,] Abode— . . . Seat— *1820E–1832* abode— . . . seat— *MS. 1832/36–*
531 Myrtle] myrtle *MS. 1832/36–*
533 Myrtle's] myrtle's *MS. 1832/36–*
534 overlooked] overlooked, *1827* regard] regard, *1827–*
535 Holly . . . Yew] holly . . . yew *MS. 1832/36–*
538 Myrtle] myrtle *MS. 1832/36–*
540 walks] Walks *1827, 1832*
541 track,] Track, *1827, 1832* track; *1836–*
542 gorse] gorse, *MS. 1814/27, 1836–*
543 never-ending] never ending *1836–* line,] line *1827–*
548 Wanderers] wanderers *1836–*
549 Giver . . . Day] giver . . . day *MS. 1832/36–*
550 brightness,] brightness *1832–*
551 desires,] desires; *1836–*
552 enjoyments] enjoyments, *1832–* Heights] heights *MS. 1832/36–*
553 Combs] combs *MS. 1832/36–*
555 seats] seats, *1827–*
557 "That . . . ours."] 'That . . . ours.' *1832–*
558 But . . . season] But, . . . season, *1820E; see verbals*
565 There,] There *1827–*
566 Voyager] voyager *1836–*
570 of,] of *MS. 1832/36–*
571 Her—] Her *MS. 1832/36–*
572 restraint,] restraint— *1820E–* Guardian;—] Guardian— *1820E–1832* guardian— *1836–*
576 addressed] address'd *MS. 1814/27*
578 source,] source *1820E*
581 Father] Father, *1827–* king . . . judge,] King . . . Judge, *1827, 1832*
583 spirit,—] spirit— *1832–*
584 observations—] observations *1820E–*
589 nourishment,—] nourishment— *1832– ; see verbals*

590 Mother's] mother's *1836–* kiss,] kiss *1832–*
591 Infant's] infant's *1836–* smile,] smile *1832–*
592 In] "In *1832* dwelt—] dwelt, *MS. 1832/36–* pair] pair— *1827, 1832* pair, *MS. 1832/36–*
597 Twain] twain *1836–*
602 One] one *1836–*
607 It] "It *1832*
609 But] But, *1820E–*
610 peace] peace, *1845–*
611 Though] Though, *1820E–* Nation] Nation, *1820E–1832* nation, *MS. 1832/36–*
612 Historian's] historian's *MS. 1832/36–*
616 need] need, *1820E–*
617 done] done, *1820E–*
618 things?] things, *1820E–1832* things; *1836–*
620 interests!] interests? *1820E–*
622 diurnal] diurnal, *1845–*
626 imperceptible,] imperceptible; *1827–1843; see verbals*
627 for,] for; *1836–*
629 good,] good *1836–*
630 endeared—] endeared *MS. 1832/36– but* endeared, *MS. 1836/45*
631 Seven] "Seven *1832*
637 grateful,] grateful— *pencil MS. 1836/45, 1840–*
639 sphere,] sphere *1832*
642 support)] support)— *pencil MS. 1836/45, 1840–*
644 have;] have: *1849 (probable worn plate)*
645 But at once] But, at once, *1820E–*
646 Power] power *MS. 1832/36–*
647 Girl] girl *1836–*
648 Death] death *1836–*
651 us,] us *1832– ; see verbals*
653 Man] man *1836–*
654 soon] soon, *1820E–*
655 between] between, *1820E–*
658 Brother] brother *1836–*
659 Calm] "Calm *1832* Lake . . . Winds] lake . . . winds *1836–*
671 heaven's] Heaven's *1820E–1832* heaven's *MS. 1832/36–* etherial] ethereal *1832–*
673 far;] far *MS. 1832/36–*
674 (And] (And, *1820E–1832*
676 And] And, *1820E–*
678 Partner] partner *1836–*
679 Luminary] luminary *1836–*
681 Glory] glory *1836–*
683 Ambition] ambition *1836–*
684 gulph] gulf *1827–*
687 She] she *1836–*
688 disconsolate.] disconsolate! *1836–*
689 What] "What *1832*
690 She] she *1836–*
691 Blameless; . . . joy,] Blameless, . . . joy *1832–*
692 Soul] soul *MS. 1832/36–*
693 stand?] stand! *1820E* stand— *1827–*
694 dependant] dependent *1827–* destitute!] destitute? *1820E–*
695 called] call'd *1827*
697 Ghost] ghost *1836–*
698 Grave] grave *1820E–*
701 Star] star *1836–*
702 Spirit] spirit *1836–* Abode] abode *MS. 1832/36–*
704 Soul] soul *1836–*
706 Life] life *1836–*
709 Power] power *1836–*
715 From] "From *1832* rouzed] roused *1827–*
716 Shepherd] shepherd *MS. 1832/36–*
717 lightening] lightning *1827–*
719 Towers] towers *MS. 1832/36–*
720 o'erthrown] overthrown *ink and pencil MS. 1836/45, 1845–*
723 Palace] palace *1836–*
724 Seat . . . Law] seat . . . law *MS. 1832/36–*
725 Sway] sway *MS. 1832/36–*
726 felt;] felt: *1820E–*
731 soul!] soul. *1832–*
732–741 *double quots become single quots 1832–*
735 Tree] tree *1836–*
736 Voice] voice *MS. 1832/36–*
737 Nations,] nations, *1836–1843* nations; *1845–* Lands] lands *MS. 1832/36–*
738 joy] Joy *1827, 1832* joy *MS. 1832/36–*
740 all] all, *MS. 1832/36–*
741 wealth."] wealth, *1832–*
742 Thus] "Thus *1832*
743 Bride] bride *1836–*
744 Children] children *1836–*
753 Men] men *1836–*
762 Enthusiasts] enthusiasts *1832–*
764 Rule] rule *1836–*
771 Inspiration] inspiration *MS. 1832/36–*
773 Foretold;] Foretold, *1820E–*
774 crowd,] crowd; *1820E–*
776 Scorn] "Scorn *1832*
777 Time's . . . Scribe] time's . . . scribe *MS. 1832/36–*
778 Zealots] zealots *MS. 1832/36–*
781 Disgusted,] Disgusted *1836–*
782 Zealots . . . Confusion] zealots . . . confusion *MS. 1832/36–*
784 "Liberty,] 'Liberty, *1832–*

785 "I . . . Shade!"] 'I . . . Shade!' *1832–* Thee] thee *MS. 1832/36–*
786 Such] "Such *1832*
792 came,] came; *1836– but* came *1846*
793 And] And, *1820E–*
800 own,] own *1846 (probable worn plate)*
803 seized] seize *1846 (probable worn plate)*
816 Thee] thee *MS. 1832/36–*
817 rejected,] rejected— *1827–*
821 perhaps,] perhaps *1840–*
829 —But] But *para MS. 1832/36–*
833 Action, . . . Power] action, . . . power *MS. 1832/36–*
843 Fresh] "Fresh *1832*
844 Ship] ship *1836–* crew:] crew; *1827–*
850 mast,] mast *1832–* streaming!] streaming:— *1827, 1832* streaming. *MS. 1832/36–* But] but *1827, 1832* But *MS. 1832/36–*
851 sense—] sense *MS. 1832/36–*
855 Plague . . . Memory] plague . . . memory *MS. 1832/36–* out,] out; *1827–*
856 things,] things *1840–1843*
857 Spirit] spirit *1836–*
858 Conscience] conscience *1836–* They] they *1832–*
862 Mother,] Mother *1836–*
865 Objects] objects *MS. 1832/36–*
870 Volume] volume *MS. 1832/36–*
871 Nations] nations *MS. 1832/36–*
874 winds,] winds; *1827–*
875 currents, . . . sick,] currents; . . . sick; *1827–*
876 tired,] tired; *1827–*
877 Nature's] Nature's, *1827, 1832* nature's, *1836–* dismayed.] dismayed! *1820E–*
878 Long-wished-for] Long-wish'd-for *1827* "Long-wished-for *1832* Long wished-for *1850*
879 Ship] ship *MS. 1832/36–* leapt] leaped *1832–*
880 Man] man *1836–*
883 Lord] lord *MS. 1832/36–*
884 endured.] endu *1840 (worn plate)* endured. *1841, 1846* endured: *1845, 1850*
885 So] So, *MS. 1814/27–* Fugitive] fugitive *MS. 1832/36–*
886 Followers] followers *MS. 1832/36–*
887 chace] chase *1827–*
888 Sun] sun *MS. 1832/36–*
889 Breeze] breeze *MS. 1832/36– ; see verbals*
891 Stream] stream *MS. 1832/36–*
892 Desart] Desert *MS. 1814/27, 1820E–1832* desert *MS. 1832/36–* behold,] behold *MS. 1814/27–* City] city *1836–*
895 He] he *1836–*
900 feel;] feel *1840–*
908 Passions] passions *MS. 1832/36–*
909 Spectator] spectator *MS. 1832/36–*
914 folly,—] folly, *MS. 1832/36–*
916 Yet,] Yet *1836–1843* crowd] crowd, *1820E–*
920 Mankind] mankind *1836–*
922 vexation.—] vexation. *1836–* Let *para MS. 1832/36–*
924 Regions] regions *MS. 1832/36–*
928 Child. A Creature] child. A creature *1836–*
929 combination] combination, *1832–*
932 himself,] himself; *1827–*
934 Intelligence] intelligence *1836–* Art] art *1836–*
935 Forefathers] forefathers *1836–*
939 Independence] independence *MS. 1832/36–*
940 Northern] northern *MS. 1832/36–* Stream] stream *1836–*
944 or, when] or when, *pencil MS. 1836/45, 1840–*
945 Eminence] eminence *MS. 1832/36–*
947 Savannah] savannah *MS. 1832/36–*
950 Sun . . . Sun] sun . . . sun *MS. 1832/36–*
952 living,] living *1845–* World] world *1836–*
953 So] "So *1832* tow'rd] toward *1832–1843* Woods] woods *MS. 1832/36–*
954 wide,] wide *1840–1843*
956 And] And, *1827–*
957 Bird's . . . Grove] bird's . . . grove *MS. 1832/36–*
959 sympathized] sympathised *1845, 1850*
960 Archetype] archetype *MS. 1832/36–*
962 Creature] creature *MS. 1832/36–*
965 —Enough] Enough *para MS. 1832/36–* Ye] ye *1836–*
967 Fellow-beings] fellow-beings *MS. 1832/36–*
969 regain;] regain: *1836–1843* regain. *1845–* how] How *1845–*
970 World] world *MS. 1832/36–*
973 exist—] exist, *1836–*
974 myself—] myself, *1836–* tenor] tenour *1827–*
976 Brook] brook *1836–*
984 imperceptible; meanwhile] imperceptible. Meanwhile *MS. 1832/36–*
991 wanderer] Wanderer *1827, 1832* wanderer *MS. 1832/36–*
995 allow'd:] allowed; *1820E–*

998 gulph] gulf *1827–*

Book IV

1 Vale] vale *1827–*
2 Narrative] narrative *MS. 1832/36–*
5 minds;] minds, *1820E* minds *1846*
7 due.] due *1827*
8 voice,] voice *1832–*
9 falter] falter, *1827; see verbals*
10 said—] said:— *1836–*
12 Exists,] Exists— *1836–* only;—] only; *MS. 1832/36–*
14 disturbed,] disturbed. *1847 (probable worn plate)*
15 power,] power; *1832–*
17 Good] good *1827–*
20 Supreme] supreme *MS. 1832/36–*
21 Time . . . Eternity] time . . . eternity *MS. 1832/36–*
26 Impatiently;] Impatiently, *1820E, pencil MS. 1836/45, 1840–*
27 Name] name *MS. 1832/36–*
28 souls] Souls *1827–*
29 Thou] thou *MS. 1832/36–*
30 recal] recall *1827– but* recal *MS. 1836/45, 1845, 1850*
31 Thee,] Thee *1827, 1832* thee *MS. 1832/36–*
32 *indented but no vertical space 1827* Then,] Then *1827* Nook] nook *MS. 1832/36–*
33 continued—] continued, *MS. 1832/36–*
34 Heaven.—] Heaven— *1832* heaven:— *MS. 1832/36–* sky,] sky; *1836– but* sky, *1846*
35 fixed] fix'd *1827*
37 Thee] thee *MS. 1832/36–*
38 can,] can, *with comma deteriorating 1843, 1846*
39 empassioned] impassioned *1832–*
41 Thou] thou *MS. 1832/36–*
43 Priest] priest *MS. 1832/36–*
44 Temple] temple *MS. 1832/36–*
46 everywhere] every where *1827– but* everywhere *pencil MS. 1836/45* One] one *MS. 1832/36–*
52 mid] 'mid *1832–*
54 Paradise] paradise *MS. 1832/36–* transplanted.] transplanted, *1827* transplanted; *MS. 1814/27, 1832* transplanted: *1836–* Wintry] wintry *MS. 1814/27–*
57 —Come] —Come, *1827–* Labour] labour *MS. 1832/36–*
58 come] come, *1827–*
60 Thee] thee *MS. 1832/36–*
63 things—] things, *MS. 1832/36*
66 And] "And *1832* Eternal . . . Powers] eternal . . . powers *MS. 1832/36–*
67 steadfastly] stedfastly *1845, 1850*
69 Opinions] opinions *1820E–*
70 Passions] passions *MS. 1832/36–*
75 Intelligence] intelligence *MS. 1832/36–*
76 Time and Space] time and space *MS. 1832/36–* not:] not. *1832–*
77 converse,] converse *1832–*
79 more,] more *1832–* perish?] perish?— *1836–* Source] source *MS. 1832/36–*
80 Cause and End of all,] cause and end of all *MS. 1832/36–*
81 That,] That *1836–* Being,] Being *1832* being *MS. 1832/36–* place,] place; *MS. 1832/36–*
83 Thou—] thou, *1836–* who] Who *1820E–1832*
84 Infancy] infancy *MS. 1832/36–* Thyself,] thyself, *MS. 1832/36– but* thyself. *1840 (possible worn plate; 1841 reads* thyself,*), 1846*
85 awhile] a while *1827– but* awhile *pencil MS. 1836/45, 1845, 1850*
86 Might'st] Mightest *1832* Might'st *MS. 1832/36–* undisturbed—] undisturbed; *1836–*
90 Restor'st] Restorest *1832* Restor'st *MS. 1832/36–* sense,] sense *1840 (possible worn plate; 1841 reads* sense,*), 1845, 1850*
91 steadfast] stedfast *1845, 1850* thou, thou] Thou, Thou *1820E–1832* thou, thou *MS. 1832/36–*
93 Sea her Waves] sea her waves *MS. 1832/36–*
94 endurest] endur'st *MS. 1814/27–*
97 Intellect] intellect *MS. 1832/36–* laws,] laws *1836–*
100 Universe] universe *MS. 1832/36–*
102 Thee] thee *MS. 1832/36–*
104 Meditation] meditation *MS. 1832/36–*
106 these,] these; *1836–* unimprisoned] unimprison'd *1827*
114 Sun] sun *MS. 1832/36–*
115 sleep,] sleep; *1836–*
116 him,] him *1827–* tow'rds] tow'rd *MS. 1814/27, 1827* toward *1832–* Deep] deep *MS. 1832/36–*
117 Sink— . . . Clouds] Sink, . . . clouds *MS. 1832/36–*
118 Spirit] spirit *1836–*
123 Those] "Those *1832*
124 Soul] soul *1836–*
125 better,] better *1832–*
128 necessity,] necessity *1836–*

129 Nature,] Nature *1832* nature *MS. 1832/36–* above,] above *1832–*
131 but] but, *1820E–* Heaven,] Heaven— *1820E–1832* heaven— *MS. 1832/36–*
133 joy,—] joy, *1820E–*
134 world;] world, *1827–*
135 arduous:—] arduous; *MS. 1832/36–*
137 Soul's] soul's *MS. 1832/36–*
139 Soul] soul *1827–*
140 etherial] ethereal *1827–* Hopes] hopes *1820E–*
142 Pillar] pillar *1827–*
147 not;—] not; *MS. 1832/36–*
148 Grief] grief *MS. 1832/36–*
149 meet,] meet— *rev to* meet, *MS. 1832/36*
151 Conscience] conscience *1836–*
156 Object] object *MS. 1832/36–*
159 imperishable] imperishable, *1845–*
160 Reason . . . Writ] reason . . . writ *1836–* holy] Holy *1827, 1832* holy *MS. 1832/36–*
161 Believers] believers *MS. 1832/36–*
163 less.] less; *MS. 1832/36–*
167 transmute,] transmute; *1836–*
175 Vision] Vision, *1820E–1832* vision, *MS. 1832/36–*
176 overconstant] over-constant *1832–* yearning—] yearning;— *1836–*
182 extacy] ecstasy *1827, 1832* extasy *1836* ecstasy *pencil MS. 1836/45, 1840–*
187 They] they *WW to Mrs. J. M. Müleen, MS. 1832/36–*
190 Hope,—] Hope *1820E*
191 mercy] mercy, *1820E–*
193 Hope,—] Hope *1820E* Hope, *1827–*
194 Wisdom . . . Power] wisdom . . . power *1836–*
195 Will] will *1836–*
196 Here] "Here *1832* rest:] rest; *1836–*
201 immoveably] immovably *1827–*
203 Soldiers] soldiers *MS. 1832/36–*
204 Sailor] sailor *MS. 1832/36–*
205 Power] power *MS. 1832/36–*
209 temptations—] temptations; *1836–* vanities] vanities, *1827–*
216 helps, . . . near,] helps . . . near *MS. 1832/36–*
219 prayer,] prayer— *MS. 1832/36–*
220 Stream] stream *MS. 1832/36–* heart,] heart *1832–*
221 Issuing . . . no where] Issuing, . . . nowhere *1827–*
224 Him] him *MS. 1832/36–*
226 Conscience; Conscience] conscience—conscience *MS. 1832/36–*
227 Presence] presence *MS. 1832/36–*
228 Image] image *MS. 1832/36–*
229 regard,] regard; *1820E–*
230 steadfast] stedfast *1845, 1850*
232 earth] earth, *1827–*
233 Part] part *MS. 1832/36–*
239 Grave] grave *MS. 1832/36–*
242 House] house *MS. 1832/36–*
244 Nature's] nature's *MS. 1832/36–* scattered] scatter'd *1827*
246 but . . . steps] but, . . . steps, *1820E–*
246 space!] *some copies of 1814 lose exclam during printing*
248 Mariner] mariner *MS. 1832/36–*
249 pastime;] pastime, *1820E–* Mates] mates *MS. 1832/36–*
250 Friends] friends *MS. 1832/36–*
251 Ship] ship *MS. 1832/36–*
252 Voice,] voice *MS. 1832/36–*
253 spake,] spake *MS. 1832/36–*
254 Tow'rds] Tow'rd *1827* Toward *1832–*
255 He] he *MS. 1832/36–*
259 feels, . . . exhort,] feels . . . exhort *1836–*
261 continued.—] continued— *1832* continued:— *1836–* "For *para MS. 1832/36–*
262 Man] man *MS. 1832/36–*
263 Age] age *MS. 1832/36–*
264 thought—] thought, *1836–*
265 Kind—] Kind *1832* Kind, *1836–*
266 superfluous;] superfluous— *1836–*
268 despair:] despair; *1827, 1832* despair: *1836–*
278 Children . . . World,] children . . . world: *MS. 1832/36–*
279–295 *double quots become single quots 1832–*
281 Progenitors . . . Ye] progenitors . . . ye *MS. 1832/36–*
282 recompence] recompense *1827–*
287 slowly-moving] slowly moving *1820E* Years of Time] years of time *MS. 1832/36–*
289 Nature's] nature's *MS. 1832/36–* taught,] taught; *1820E–*
290 Story] story *MS. 1832/36–* confounded.] confounded! *1820E–*
296 *para MS. 1832/36–* Such] "Such *1820E, 1827*
297 Voice] voice *MS. 1832/36–*
298 Tartarian] Tartarean *pencil MS. 1836/45, 1840–*
299 Impious] impious *MS. 1832/36–*
301 Good] good *MS. 1832/36–*
305 Mankind] mankind *1836–*
308 Bad] bad *MS. 1832/36–*
310 inconsistent] inconsistent, *MS. 1832/36 (MS. 1836/45 has a pencil*

caret after inconsistent *but no added punct)* Good] good *MS. 1832/36–*
312 Cause] cause *MS. 1832/36–*
313 Defenders] defenders *MS. 1832/36–*
314 They] they *1832–*
315 Will . . . efforts] Will, . . . efforts, *1820E–*
317 etherial] ethereal *1827–*
318 Spirit] spirit *1836–* Mankind] mankind *MS. 1832/36–*
319 Spirit] spirit *1836–* appear] appear, *1827–*
320 their's] theirs *1827–*
321 Wise] wise *MS. 1832/36–*
327 "Knowing] 'Knowing *MS. 1814/27, 1832–* Man] man *MS. 1832/36–*
328 World] world *MS. 1832/36–*
334 Man!"] Man!' *1832–*
335 He] he *MS. 1832/36–* understand!] *some copies of 1814 lose exclam during printing* understand— *1827, 1832* understand, *1836–*
336 human] <u>human</u> *MS. 1814/27* Nature] nature *MS. 1832/36–*
337 Natures] natures *MS. 1832/36–*
344 Class] class *MS. 1832/36–*
345 Commonwealth] commonwealth *MS. 1832/36–*
347 Converse] converse *MS. 1832/36–*
348 Spirit] spirit *MS. 1832/36–* love;] love: *1836–*
350 love;] love: *1832–*
353 Love] love *MS. 1832/36–*
355 Life] life *MS. 1832/36–*
357 He] he *MS. 1832/36–*
358 Man] man *MS. 1832/36–*
361 Kinds] kinds *MS. 1832/36–*
364 care,—] care, *MS. 1832/36–*
365 bond,—] bond, *MS. 1832/36, 1836* bond; *pencil MS. 1836/45, 1840–*
370 sustain] sustain, *pencil MS. 1836/45, 1840–*
372 City . . . Seas] city . . . seas *MS. 1832/36–*
373 unfelt,— . . . recommend,] unfelt; . . . recommend,— *1836* unfelt; . . . recommend, *1840–*
374 endear,] endear *1836* endear, *pencil MS. 1836/45, 1840–*
375 Retreat] retreat *MS. 1832/36–*
378 groveling] grovelling *1832–*
379 Man] man, *1836–*
383 transgress;] transgress: *1836–*
385 behold, . . . register,] behold; . . . register; *1820E–*
387 You] you *MS. 1832/36–*
390 box perchance] box, perchance, *1827–*
391 Wren] wren *MS. 1832/36–*
393 Abiding-place] abiding-place *MS. 1832/36, 1836* abiding place, *1840–*
394 Butterfly—] butterfly; *MS. 1832/36–*
395 Creature] creature *MS. 1832/36–* flowers] flowers, *1840–*
399 Eagle] eagle *MS. 1832/36–*
401 leaves,—] leaves, *MS. 1832/36* leaves; *1836–*
402 hills,—] hills, *MS. 1832/36–*
404 heard,] heard *1840*
405 bleat;] bleat, *1836– ; see verbals*
406 Mountain's] mountain's *MS. 1832/36– ; see verbals*
407 Mountain] mountain *MS. 1832/36–*
409 expressed;] expressed: *1836–*
412 life.] life: *1827, 1836–1843* life; *1832, MS. 1836/45; see verbals*
413 Lamb] lamb *MS. 1832/36– ; see verbals*
414 Spirit . . . Solitude!—] spirit . . . solitude! *MS. 1832/36–*
417 best,—] best, *MS. 1832/36–*
419 And,] And *1832*
424 dependance] dependence *1827–*
427 Flower] flower *MS. 1832/36–*
428 Worm] worm *MS. 1832/36–*
429 These] "These *1832* wilds,] wilds *1827–1836* wilds, *pencil MS. 1836/45, 1840–*
431 Mole] mole *MS. 1832/36–*
432 ground;] ground: *1836* Emmet] emmet *MS. 1832/36–*
433 foresight;] foresight, *1827–*
434 Creatures] creatures *MS. 1832/36–*
438 labour— . . . Lake] labour, . . . lake *MS. 1832/36–* covered] cover'd *1827*
439 Cities] cities *MS. 1832/36–* desart] desert *1827–*
442 Creatures,] Creatures *1832–*
444 dependance] dependence *1827–*
447 be,] be *1832–*
448 Flies] flies *MS. 1832/36–*
451 obviously,] obviously *MS. 1832/36–*
452 Fieldfare's] fieldfare's *MS. 1832/36–*
453 Rooks,] rooks; *MS. 1832/36* rooks, *1836–* Sea-mews] sea-mews *MS. 1832/36–*
454 Solitudes] solitudes *MS. 1832/36–*
457 Fowl] fowl *MS. 1832/36–*
458 Pool] pool *MS. 1832/36–*
459 rouzed] roused *1820E–*
461 etherial] ethereal *1827–* arch] arch, *1820E, 1827; see verbals*
463 —Bright apparition . . . forth] Bright apparition, . . . forth, *1836–*
464 Rainbow,] rainbow *MS. 1832/36–*
466 Sun . . . Lord] sun . . . lord *MS. 1832/36–*
467 How] "How *1832*

471 You . . . Heights] you . . . heights *MS. 1832/36–*
472 Shew] Show *1832* show *MS. 1832/36–*
473 revealed!] revealed!— *pencil MS. 1836/45, 1840–* Swains] swains *MS. 1832/36–*
474 not;] not: *1836–* perceived.] perceived, *MS. 1832/36* perceived *1836–*
477 Spleen] spleen *MS. 1832/36–*
479 unthankfully;] unthankfully: *1836–*
480 thoughts;] thoughts: *1820E–* Frame] frame *MS. 1832/36–*
481 Soul's . . . Couch] soul's . . . couch *MS. 1832/36–*
482 Cell] cell *MS. 1832/36–*
483 Powers] powers *1836–*
487 Hollow;] Hollow, *1832–*
490 Nature's] nature's *MS. 1832/36–*
491 Lark . . . Matins] lark . . . matins *MS. 1832/36–*
493 her's] hers *1827–*
495 tops,— . . . Bee] tops, . . . bee *MS. 1832/36–*
498 Watch-tower] watch-tower *MS. 1832/36–*
499 mountains:] mountains; *printed text of MS. 1814/27, 1836–*
500 Goat . . . Deer] goat . . . deer *MS. 1832/36–* and,] and *1836–*
502 pursuit:] pursuit; *1836–*
503 Hut] hut *MS. 1832/36–*
504 repose. *MS. 1814/27 adds close quots which are lacking in its printed text; see verbals*
505 towards] toward *MS. 1814/27 (see verbals);* tow'rd *1827* toward *1832–*
508 "Oh! *para in MS. 1814/27 printed text and quots supplied in MS. 1814/27 (whose printed text lacked quots); see verbals, IV, 506–507*
509 Body] body *MS. 1832/36–* Frame] frame *1827–*
511 blood)] blood.) *1840, 1846* blood) *1841, 1844E, 1845, 1850*
513 Spirit] spirit *MS. 1832/36–*
514 mortal] mortal, *1845–*
520 Presence] presence *MS. 1832/36–* Motion] motion *1827–*
521 and,] and *1836–* Mists] mists *MS. 1832/36–*
522 Vapours . . . Shapes] vapours . . . shapes *MS. 1832/36–*
523 Phantoms] phantoms *MS. 1832/36–*
524 Musician] musician *MS. 1832/36–*
525 instrument;] instrument: *1836* instrument; *pencil 1836/45, 1840–* and,] and *1836–* Streams—] streams *MS. 1832/36–*
528 clouds] clouds, *1820E* Clouds, *1827, 1832* clouds *MS. 1832/36–*
530 moment—] moment, *1820E–*
531 them,] them— *1820E–*
532 Equal] equal *1827–* Energies] energies *MS. 1832/36–*
535 aloud] aloud, *1827–*
536 Be] 'Be *1827–1843; see verbals*
537 month!"] month! *printed text of MS. 1814/27* month!" *MS. 1814/27 adds quots in early rev (adopted 1814) preceding verbal rev to II, 536–537*
538 the] t *1847E (worn plate)*
541 delight,] delight; *MS. 1814/27 printed text; see verbals*
542 long;] long, *1832–*
548 Compatriot,] "Compatriot, *1832* Compatriot *1836–* Hills] hills *MS. 1832/36–*
549 Streams . . . Glen] streams . . . glen *MS. 1832/36–*
550 form] Form *MS. 1814/27 printed text* Image] image *MS. 1832/36–* express'd] expressed *1820E–*
553 leads,] leads— *MS. 1832/36* leads; *pencil MS. 1836/45, 1840–* day by night] day, by night, *1820E–*
559 Remembrance . . . Prince] remembrance . . . prince *MS. 1832/36–*
563 your's] yours *1827–*
567 which . . . need] which, . . . need, *1820E–*
569 will:] will; *MS. 1814/27 printed text*
570 touch,—] touch, *1832–*
571 Shepherd . . . Heights] shepherd . . . heights *MS. 1832/36–*
572 thus] thus, *1827–*
574 A] "A *1832*
575 He—] He, *MS. 1832/36–*
576 Pleasures] pleasures *MS. 1832/36–*
581 One] one *MS. 1832/36–*
582 fancy] fancy, *1827–*
583 That . . . consumption] That, . . . consumption, *1820E–*
587 contemplation,—] contemplation; *1836–*
589 groves,] groves *1827–*
594 Altars . . . Throne] altars . . . throne *MS. 1832/36–*
595 Fortresses] fortresses *MS. 1832/36–*
597 Nature] nature *MS. 1832/36–*
599 *double quots become single quots 1832–*
600 Systems—] systems, *MS. 1832/36–*
601 Substantial—] Substantial, *MS. 1832/36–*
602 Systems] systems *MS. 1832/36–*
603 work—] work, *MS. 1832/36–*
604 once,] once *1836–*
605 Innocents] innocents *MS. 1832/36–*

606 Pupil] pupil *MS. 1832/36–*
607 Superstition] superstition *MS. 1832/36–*
608 Life's] "Life's *1832* Autumn . . . Winter's] autumn . . . winter's *MS. 1832/36–* verge,] verge; *1836–*
614 death-watch,—] death-watch: *1836–*
615 way;] way;— *1836–*
620 ends:] ends; *1836–*
621 Or . . . inward] Or, . . . inward, *1827–* Mind] mind *MS. 1832/36–; see verbals*
623 Heart . . . Heart] heart . . . heart *MS. 1832/36–*
624 Peace . . . Consciousness] peace . . . consciousness *MS. 1832/36–* dwell,] dwell; *1827*
627 Upon] "Upon *1832* Earth] earth *MS. 1832/36–*
629 Solitude] solitude *MS. 1832/36–*
630 Voice] voice *MS. 1832/36–*
631 appeared,] appeared *1845–*
632 Paradise] paradise *MS. 1832/36–*
635 winged] wingèd *1827, 1832* winged *1836–* Messengers] messengers *MS. 1832/36*
636 Island] island *MS. 1832/36–* etherial] ethereal *1827–*
637 Heights] heights *MS. 1832/36–*
642 Intuitions] intuitions *MS. 1832/36–*
646 Solitude] solitude *MS. 1832/36–*
650 localized] localised *1845, 1850* heaven,] heaven; *1820E–*
655 Land] land *MS. 1832/36–*
658 unacknowledged] unacknowledged, *pencil MS. 1836/45, 1845–* Sovereignty] sovereignty *MS. 1832/36–*
662 engulphed,] engulfed, *1827, 1832* engulfed; *1836–*
663 Creature] creature *MS. 1832/36–*
666 power:] power:— *1836–*
667 —Whether] Whether *1836–*
668 Image] Image, *1827, 1832* image, *MS. 1832/36–*
669 Temples] temples *MS. 1832/36–* hands,] hands— *1820E–*
671 Tiara] tiara *MS. 1832/36–* brows—] brows, *1820E; see verbals*
672 Moon and Stars] moon and stars *MS. 1832/36–*
673 Mother Elements] mother elements *MS. 1832/36–*
674 Circle of the Heavens] circle of the heavens *MS. 1832/36–*
675 Existence] existence *MS. 1832/36–*
677 Sense] sense *MS. 1832/36–*
678 Soul] soul *MS. 1832/36–*
679 Shape] shape *MS. 1832/36–*
680 Plain] plain *MS. 1832/36–*
681 Tower;] tower, *MS. 1832/36–*
682 Couch] couch *MS. 1832/36–*
683 Height] height *MS. 1832/36–*
685 City] city *MS. 1832/36–*
686 Worshippers] worshippers *MS. 1832/36–* far-stretched;] far-stretched, *1820E–*
687 grove, and field, and garden,] grove and field and garden *1845–*
688 Town . . . Region] town . . . region *MS. 1832/36–*
689 beleaguring] beleaguering *1836–*
690 Chaldean] "Chaldean *1832*
693 Polar Star . . . Guide] polar star . . . guide *MS. 1832/36–*
694 Guardian] guardian *MS. 1832/36–*
695 steadfast] stedfast *1845, 1850* Planetary] planetary *MS. 1832/36–*
697 flocks,] flocks *1827–1836* flocks, *pencil MS. 1836/45, 1840–*
699 Ether] ether *MS. 1832/36–*
703 Imaginative Faculty . . . Lord] imaginative faculty . . . lord *MS. 1832/36–*
705 Shepherds . . . Stars] shepherds . . . stars *MS. 1832/36–*
709 Constellations] constellations *MS. 1832/36–* earth] earth, *1827–*
710 sight,] sight *1827–*
711 Dead] dead *MS. 1832/36–*
712 Messengers,] Messengers *1827, 1832* messengers *MS. 1832/36–*
713 Judges] judges *MS. 1832/36–*
714 The] "The *1832* Land] land *MS. 1832/36–*
715 Rivers,] Rivers *1836–* shores,] shores,— *MS. 1832/36–*
719 Countries—] countries, *MS. 1832/36–*
720 Adventurers] adventurers *1832–*
723 Operations] operations *1836–* Shape] shape *1832–*
724 Stone] stone *MS. 1832/36–*
726 Art . . . Sense] art . . . sense *MS. 1832/36–*
728 fictions,] fictions *1832–* chaunted] chanted *1827–*
731 Schools] schools *MS. 1832/36–*
732 Region . . . Towns and Farms] region . . . towns and farms *MS. 1832/36–*
733 Temples . . . Tombs] temples . . . tombs *MS. 1832/36–*
737 Philosopher] philosopher *MS. 1832/36–*
738 Warrior] warrior *MS. 1832/36–*
739 prevailed] prevailed, *1820E–*
741 "Take, . . . mine"] 'Take, . . . mine' *1827–* River . . . Locks] river . . . locks *MS. 1832/36–*
742 "this] 'this *1827–* hair,] hair *1820E*

742–748 *double quots become single quots 1827–*
743 Vow] vow *1820E–*
744 Child's] child's *1836–*
746 chrystal] crystal *1827–*
747 lip,] lip *1846*
748 fields."] fields!' *1827–*
751 Life . . . Being] life . . . being *MS. 1832/36*
753 known,] known. *1820E; see verbals*
757 Man] man *1836–*
758 Mankind] mankind *1836–*
760 We] "We *1832* admiration, hope, and love] Admiration, Hope, and Love *1836–*
761 And] And, *1832–*
763 error?] error?" *1827–*
764 exclaimed,] exclaimed: *1832–*
765 Hope, and Admiration] hope, and admiration *MS. 1832/36*
766 Vassals] vassals *MS. 1832/36–* Life] life *1832–*
767 Pioneers] pioneers *MS. 1832/36–*
769 Reason's] reason's *MS. 1832/36–*
777 You] you *MS. 1832/36–*
782 Hath . . . hearing] Hath, . . . hearing, *1827–*
783 Men's Children] men's children *MS. 1832/36–*
786 your's] yours *1827–*
788 Cabins . . . Mother's] cabins . . . mother's *MS. 1832/36–*
789 Dwelling] dwelling *MS. 1832/36–*
790 Torrent] torrent *MS. 1832/36–*
792 or] or, *1827–* Snow] snow *MS. 1832/36–*
793 Wind] wind *MS. 1832/36–*
794 Labourer] labourer *MS. 1832/36–*
795 Fearful,] Fearful; *1836–*
796 Infant] infant *1832–*
797 Shepherd Lad] Shepherd-lad *MS. 1832/36–*
800 adapt] adapt, *1836–*
803 perceives,] perceives *1841– but* perceives, *1845, 1850*
805 Sun of Truth] sun of truth *MS. 1832/36–*
806 Mankind] mankind *MS. 1832/36–*
807 Experience,] Experience *MS. 1814/27–*
808 Nature's] nature's *MS. 1832/36–*
810 recompence] recompense *1827, 1832, 1840–*
816 Worldling's] worldling's *1832–*
830 Illusions] illusions *MS. 1832/36–*
832 Ministers] ministers *MS. 1832/36–*
833 Conscience] conscience *MS. 1832/36–*
838 Phantoms] phantoms *MS. 1832/36–*
841 space] space, *1827–*
843 Once] "Once *1832* 'Once *1836* Once *pencil MS. 1836/45, 1840–* Ages] ages *MS. 1832/36–*
845 Solitude] solitude *MS. 1832/36–*
846 Swains] swains *MS. 1832/36–*
847 Clime . . . Herdsman] clime . . . herdsman *MS. 1832/36–*
853 Fancy] fancy *MS. 1832/36–*
854 Chariot . . . Sun] chariot . . . sun *MS. 1832/36–*
857 Hunter] hunter *MS. 1832/36–*
858 Moon] moon *MS. 1832/36–*
859 wanderer] wanderer, *pencil MS. 1836/45*
862 grove,] grove *1827–1836* grove, *pencil MS. 1836/45, 1840–*
863 (Not] Not *pencil MS. 1836/45, 1840–*
864 cave)] cave,) *1820E* cave, *pencil MS. 1836/45, 1840–*
865 chase,] chase; *1836–* Moon and Stars] moon and stars *MS. 1832/36–*
867 Traveller] traveller *MS. 1832/36–*
868 Rill . . . Fount] rill . . . fount *MS. 1832/36–*
869 Naiad.—] Naiad. *1836–* Hills] hills *MS. 1832/36–*
870 Shadows] shadows *MS. 1832/36–*
873 Zephyrs, fanning] Zephyrs fanning, *1836–*
874 Objects,] objects *MS. 1832/36–*
875 Boughs] boughs *MS. 1832/36–*
880 Deer, or Goat's] deer, or goat's *MS. 1832/36–* beard;] beard— *MS. 1814/27* beard,— *1827–*
882 Deities!] Deities; *1820E–*
883 Shepherd's] shepherd's *MS. 1832/36–* God."] God!" *1820E–*
888 interpose] interpose, *1827–*
889 exclaimed—] exclaimed:— *1836–*
891 Land] land *MS. 1832/36–*
892 Mansions] mansions *MS. 1832/36–*
893 Descendants] descendants *1836–* Men] men *MS. 1832/36–*
895 Altar, Image . . . Piles] altar, image . . . piles *MS. 1832/36–*
896 Souls] souls *1836–*
897 after Race] after-race *MS. 1832/36–*
900 such,] such— *1820E–*
902 propensities?] propensities, *1827–*
904 Phantasy] phantasy *MS. 1832/36–*
905 Wells] wells *MS. 1832/36–*
907 recal] recall *1827– but* recal *pencil MS. 1836/45, 1845, 1850*
909 crags.] crags! *1820E* crags? *1827–*
910 restoration] restoration, *1827–*
911 Patron . . . Priests] patron . . . priests *MS. 1832/36–*
912 streets;] streets *1836–*

913 Powers] powers *MS. 1832/36–*
914 Science, and Philosophy, and Sense] science, and philosophy, and sense *MS. 1832/36–*
917 Idolatry] idolatry *MS. 1832/36–*
918 observances] observances, *1820E–*
920 food;] food: *MS. 1832/36; see verbals*
922 moved] moved, *1827–*
923 Presence] presence *MS. 1832/36–* misconceived;] misconceived, *pencil MS. 1836/45, 1840–*
924 dependance] dependence *1827–*
927 praise] praise, *1820E–*
931 Natures] natures *MS. 1832/36–*
933 Sun solicited—and Earth] sun solicited, and earth *MS. 1832/36–*
936 overstepped] overstepp'd *1827*
937 Now] "Now *1832*
939 Sense and Reason . . . These] sense and reason . . . these *MS. 1832/36–*
940 Men . . . Age] men . . . age *MS. 1832/36–*
944 Earth] earth *MS. 1832/36–*
947 They] they *MS. 1832/36–*
949 They] they *MS. 1832/36–*
952 Heaven] heaven *MS. 1832/36–*
953 Enquire] Inquire *1827–*
958 disconnection] disconnexion *1827–*
964 Souls!—] souls!— *1827, 1832* souls! *1836–* And *para MS. 1832/36–*
966 He] he *MS. 1832/36–* design,] design *1827–*
968 Power] power *MS. 1832/36–*
969 Earth . . . Sky] earth . . . sky *MS. 1832/36–*
970 reveals,] reveals; *1836–*
971 Mystery] mystery *MS. 1832/36–*
972 Frame] frame *MS. 1832/36–*
973 Soul] soul *MS. 1832/36–*
977 Nature] nature *MS. 1832/36–1843*
982 Men] men *MS. 1832/36–*
984 Soul] soul *MS. 1832/36–*
987 Soul . . . Universe] soul . . . universe *MS. 1832/36–*
988 Mirror] mirror *MS. 1832/36–*
990 one] One *1820E–1832* one *1836–* finite] infinite *corr* finite *errata 1832, MS. 1832/36* Object] object *1836–* Abyss] abyss *MS. 1832/36–*
992 Nor] "Nor *1832* Him] him *MS. 1832/36–*
993 Compeers—] compeers *MS. 1832/36–*
994 He . . . Memory] he . . . memory *MS. 1832/36–*
996 Wit] wit *MS. 1832/36–* atchieved,] achieved, *1827, 1832* achieved *1836–*
997 Wisdom] wisdom *MS. 1832/36–* conferred.] conferred, *1827, 1832* conferred; *MS. 1832/36–*
1001 Old] old *MS. 1832/36–* vain] vain, *1845–*
1002 People] people *MS. 1832/36–*
1003 Faith] faith *MS. 1832/36–*
1008 Book] book *MS. 1832/36–*
1011 contempt] contempt, *1820E–*
1012 Friend,"] Friend, *1846 (possible worn plate)*
1014 Lights and Guides] lights and guides *MS. 1832/36–* these—] these. *1836–*
1016 Mind] mind *MS. 1832/36–*
1017 Opinion] opinion *MS. 1832/36–*
1018 Passion] passion *MS. 1832/36–*
1020 Soul] soul *MS. 1832/36–*
1023 Notion] notion *MS. 1832/36–*
1026 life] life, *1820E–1832*
1027 hope] hope, *1836–*
1031 Majesty] majesty *MS. 1832/36–*
1032 *para MS. 1832/36–* —O . . . Mind] O . . . mind *MS. 1832/36–*
1036 Youth's] youth's *MS. 1832/36–*
1037 Manhood's] manhood's *MS. 1832/36–*
1038 Wisdom] wisdom *MS. 1832/36–* shews] shows *1836–*
1039 leisure] Leisure *1827, 1832* leisure *MS. 1832/36–*
1041 chrystal] crystal *1827–*
1043 muse,—] muse, *MS. 1832/36–*
1045 Pride] pride *MS, 1832/36–*
1046 Transgression] transgression *MS. 1832/36–*
1049 Manhood] manhood *MS. 1832/36–* couch,] couch *1827–*
1050 Soft . . . seem;] Soft, . . . seem, *1827–*
1051 past,] past *1836–*
1055 Within] "Within *1832* Faculty] faculty *MS. 1832/36–*
1057 deal,] deal *1845–*
1058 Contingences] Contingencies *1820E–*
1059 As] —As *Cornell MS. 2* Moon] moon *MS. 1832/36–*
1060 summer even] summer Even *MS. 1814/27, Cornell MS. 2* summer even, *Cornell MS. 1* Summer Even *1827, 1832* summer even *MS. 1832/36–*
1061 Grove,] grove *Cornell MS. 2* grove, *MS. 1814/27–*
1062 Burns] Burns, *1836–* light,] light *Cornell MS. 1, Cornell MS. 2*
1065 substance] substance, *Cornell MS. 1*
1066 Yea] Yea, *1836–* incorporated,] incorporated *Cornell MS. 1*
1067 serene.] serene; *Cornell MS. 1, Cornell MS. 2, MS. 1814/27–1836*

serene: *pencil MS. 1836/45, 1840–1843* Like] like *Cornell MS. 1, Cornell MS. 2, MS. 1814/27–1843*

1068 Man's . . . Virtue] man's . . . virtue *MS. 1832/36–* Spirit;] Spirit: *Cornell MS. 1* spirit; *MS. 1832/36–*

1070 calm, a beautiful,] calm a beautiful *Cornell MS. 2* fire,] fire *Cornell MS. 1, Cornell MS. 2*

1071 incumbrances] encumbrances *1832–* life,] life; *Cornell MS. 1*

1072 disappointment,—nay] disappointment, nay *Cornell MS. 1* disappointment—nay, *1836–*

1073 And] And, *Cornell MS. 2* Justice] justice *MS. 1832/36–*

1074 Despair."] despair. *Cornell MS. 1, Cornell MS. 2* despair." *MS. 1832/36–*

1076 exclaimed,] exclaimed; *1836–*

1077 The] 'The *1836–* free,] free; *1820E–1832* free— *MS. 1832/36–*

1077–1079 *rewritten by WW in pencil at page foot, then erased MS. 1832/36*

1078 Resolve—] Resolve," *MS. 1832/36* Resolve,' *1836–*

1079 This . . . demand.] "This . . . demand." *MS. 1832/36* 'This . . . demand.' *1836–*

1080 Creature] creature *MS. 1832/36–*

1082 Friendship] friendship *MS. 1832/36–*

1084 Boat] boat *MS. 1832/36–*

1087 One] one *MS. 1832/36*

1089 needs;] needs: *1845–*

1091 not] not, *1836–*

1092 Love] love *MS. 1832/36–*

1093 Him] him *MS. 1832/36–*

1097 tone] tone, *1820E–*

1098 mien] mien, *1820E–* spake;] spake: *1836–*

1099 Men . . . Men] men . . . men *MS. 1832/36–*

1100 Do] Do, *1820E–* Souls] Souls, *1820E–1832* souls, *MS. 1832/36–*

1104 shame,] shame; *1836–*

1105 So,] So *1827–*

1108 point,—] point, *MS. 1832/36–* all;] all— *1836–*

1111 You] you *MS. 1827/32C, MS. 1832/36–*

1113 Eye] eye *MS. 1832/36–*

1114 Altar . . . Heaven] altar . . . heaven *MS. 1832/36–*

1119 Sun] sun *MS. 1832/36–*

1121 Imaginative] imaginative *MS. 1832/36–*

1125 changing!—] changing! *MS. 1832/36–* I *para MS. 1832/36–*

1126 Child] child *1836–*

1128 Shell] shell *MS. 1832/36–*

1132 heard,—] heard, *MS. 1832/36–; see verbals* whereby,] whereby *1820E–1832* whereby, *MS. 1827/32C*

1133 Monitor] monitor *MS. 1832/36–*

1134 Sea] sea *MS. 1832/36–*

1135 Shell the Universe] shell the universe *MS. 1832/36–*

1137 You] you *MS. 1832/36–*

1146 Man] man *MS. 1832/36–*

1147 Power] power *MS. 1832/36–*

1148 Eye] eye *MS. 1832/36–*

1149 Ear] ear *MS. 1832/36–*

1150 Soul, the Being] soul, the being *MS. 1832/36–* Life] Life, *1827, 1832* life, *MS. 1832/36–*

1152 Rocks] rocks *MS. 1832/36–*

1153 Sky] sky *MS. 1832/36–*

1154 walls;] walls: *1831*

1155 Temple] temple *MS. 1832/36–*

1161 Here,] Here,— *1836–* Nightingale] nightingale *MS. 1832/36–* mute] mute, *1820E–*

1162 Woodlark] woodlark *MS. 1832/36–* chaunt] chant *1827–*

1163 vespers,] vespers,— *1836–*

1164 Air] air *MS. 1832/36–*

1167 Rills, and Waters] rills, and waters *MS. 1832/36–*

1168 day-light] daylight *1827–*

1169 Streams] streams *MS. 1832/36–*

1170 Stars] stars *MS. 1832/36–*

1171 Fabric] fabric *MS. 1832/36–*

1172 Voice . . . Raven] voice . . . raven *MS. 1832/36–*

1173 dark-blue] dark blue *1836–*

1175 afar,] afar *1820E–*

1180 expire,] expire; *1836–* Abyss] abyss *MS. 1832/36–*

1181 But] "But *1832*

1182 Imaginative Heights] imaginative heights *MS. 1832/36–*

1183 Eternity] eternity *MS. 1832/36–*

1189 Throng] throng *MS. 1832/36–*

1191 City] city *MS. 1832/36* City, and town, and tower,— and sea with ships *MS. 1832/36–*

1192 Sprinkled,—] Sprinkled;— *1827–*

1197 chearfulness] cheerfulness *1820E–*

1198 Things, and Things] things, and things *MS. 1832/36–*

1200 Reason's] reason's *MS. 1832/36–*

1201 —For] For *1827, 1836* "For *1832* For, *pencil MS. 1836/45, 1840–* Man,] Man— *pencil MS. 1836/45, 1840–*

1203 Nature] nature *1836–* heart,] heart *1827–*

1204 love,] love *1827, 1832; see verbals* Objects] objects *MS. 1832/36–*

1206 hatred,] hatred— *pencil MS. 1836/45, 1840–*
1207 love] Love *1820E–1832; see verbals*
1211 Fellow-natures,] Fellow-natures *1827, 1832* fellow-natures *MS. 1832/36–*
1212 Accordingly,] Accordingly *1827–* degrees] degrees, *1820E*
1217 Fountain] fountain *MS. 1832/36–*
1220 hear] hear, *1827–*
1221 speak,] speak *1849 (probable worn plate)*
1223 feeling,] feeling *1820E*
1224 And] "And *1832*
1225 Man] man *MS. 1832/36–*
1228 Presences] presences *MS. 1832/36–* Things,] Things. *MS. 1814/27, 1827, 1832* things. *MS. 1832/36–*
1231 Instructed] Instructed, *1820E–1832* instructed, *MS. 1832/36–*
1238 rouze, . . . and . . . will] rouse, . . . and, . . . will, *1820E–*
1243 Sense] sense *MS. 1832/36–*
1246 Spirit] spirit *MS. 1832/36–*
1248 Visitant] visitant *MS. 1832/36–*
1249 name.] name: *1836–*
1250 Heart . . . Eye] heart . . . eye *MS. 1832/36–*
1259 treacherous,] treacherous *1832* treacherous, *MS. 1832/36–* Mind's . . . Power] mind's . . . power *MS. 1832/36–*
1261 Soul] soul *MS. 1832/36–* Things] Things, *1832* things, *MS. 1832/36–*
1262 and] and, *MS. 1832/36–*
1263 choice,] choice— *MS. 1832/36, 1836* choice, *pencil MS. 1836/45, 1840–*
1268 indirect] indirect, *1832; see verbals*
1269 faculties,] faculties; *1836–1843; see verbals* seats] seats, *1836* seats *1840–1843; see verbals*
1271 Soul] soul *1832–*
1273 stream;] stream *1840–1843* stream, *1845–*
1274 remote] remote, *1832–* 'mid] mid *1827–*
1276 Tribes] tribes *MS. 1832/36–*
1279 woods.—] woods. *end of Book IV excerpt 1831*
1280 away;] away *MS. 1832/36–*
1281 me—] me *MS. 1832/36* me, *1836–*
1282 One] one *MS. 1832/36–*
1285 One] one *MS. 1832/36–*
1286 Tree] tree *MS. 1832/36–* Life,] Life; *1827, 1832* life; *MS. 1832/36–*
1288 One] one *MS. 1832/36–*
1291 Earth] earth *MS. 1832/36–*
1295 Dell] Dell, *1827, 1832* dell, *1836–*
1299 seemingly] seemingly, *1827–*
1300 bequest,] bequest; *MS. 1832/36–* lights] lights, *1827–*
1302 Glen] glen *MS. 1832/36–*
1303 Train] train *MS. 1832/36–*
1304 descending;—] descending:— *1836–1846, 1850* descending.— *1849 (probable worn plate)*
1305 Page;] Page: *1836–* Pair] pair *MS. 1832/36*
1307 words] words, *pencil MS. 1836/45, 1840– ; see verbals*
1308 sent,] sent *MS. 1814/27–*
1309 time,] time *1827–*
1310 wrong.] wrong: *1827–*
1311 welcomed;] welcomed— *MS. 1814/27–*
1314 Couch] couch *MS. 1832/36–*
1315 Mountaineers] mountaineers *MS. 1832/36–*
1317 Torrents] torrents *1832–* night,] night; *MS. 1832/36, 1836* night, *pencil MS. 1836/45, 1840–*
1318 And . . . thoughts] And, . . . thoughts, *pencil MS. 1836/45, 1840–*

Book V

1 FAREWELL] FAREWELL, *1827, 1832* "FAREWELL, *MS. 1832/36–*
6 chearfulness] cheerfulness *1820E–*
8 Primæval] Primeval *1827–* Forests] forests *MS. 1832/36–*
9 farewell] farewell, *1827–*
10 Circuit . . . Abyss] circuit . . . abyss *MS. 1832/36–*
12 profound!] profound!" *MS. 1832/36–*
13 Vale,] vale *MS. 1832/36–*
14 Comrades] comrades *1836–*
16 World] world *MS. 1832/36–*
21 tenor] tenure *MS. 1814/27–* hold] hold, *1836–*
22 Life's] life's *MS. 1832/36–*
27 methinks,] methinks *1827, 1832*
29 Anchorites . . . Piety] anchorites . . . piety *MS. 1832/36–*
33 Nature] nature *1836–*
35 Spots] spots *MS. 1832/36–*
39 Discovered, . . . forth] Discovered . . . forth, *1827–*
42 Eulogist] eulogist *MS. 1832/36–*
48 musings;—] musings; *MS. 1832/36–*
51 retreat,] retreat; *1836–*
54 thought,] thought *1836* thought; *pencil MS. 1836/45, 1840–*
55 books] books, *MS. 1814/27–1832* books; *MS. 1832/36–*
64 Vale] vale *1836–*
66 Old] old *MS. 1832/36–*
67 Air] air *MS. 1832/36–*
68 Herds and Flocks] herds and flocks *MS. 1832/36–*
72 Mind] mind *MS. 1832/36–*

74 Covert] covert *MS. 1832/36–*
75 Sea] sea *MS. 1832/36–*
76 descend;] descend: *1836–*
77 shewed] showed *1832–* Valley] valley *MS. 1832/36–*
79 Church-tower] church-tower *MS. 1832/36–*
81 And,] And *1836–* tow'rds] towards *1832–* chrystal] crystal *1827–*
83 Stream] stream *MS. 1832/36–*
85 Sun] sun *MS. 1832/36–*
86 Stream's] stream's *MS. 1832/36–*
87 Dwellings] dwellings *MS. 1832/36* single] single, *1827–*
91 "As,] "As *1836–* 'mid] mid *1827* Valley] valley *MS. 1832/36–*
92 Power] Power, *1827, 1832* power, *MS. 1832/36–*
94 Commonwealth] commonwealth *MS. 1832/36–*
98 Lord] lord *MS. 1832/36–* dwell."] dwell."— *1832–* pomp,"] pomp,' *1832* pomp," *MS. 1832/36* pomp, *1845–*
99 Friend, a Chronicler] friend, a chronicler *MS. 1832/36–1843; see verbals*
100 moved] moved, *MS. 1832/36–1843; see verbals*
102 Home] home *MS. 1832/36–1843; see verbals*
103 Shepherd . . . Flock . . . King] shepherd . . . flock . . . king *MS. 1832/36–*
104 stiled] styled *1832–*
105 Father . . . People] father . . . people *MS. 1832/36–* he,] he; *1827–*
112 The calm *para MS. 1832/36–*
118 spot,] spot— *MS. 1832/36–*
119 soil?] soil?— *1836–*
121 unsuppressed] unsuppress *MS. 1832/36–*
132 Dwelling . . . Domain] dwelling . . . domain *MS. 1832/36–*
138 Village Church-yard] Village Churchyard *1832* Village-churchyard *MS. 1832/36* village-churchyard *1836–* sun,] sun *1836–*
142 portals] Portals *1820E–1832*
143 open,] open; *1836–*
147 reverence,] reverence *1836–* Place] place *MS. 1832/36–*
148 Pile] pile *MS. 1832/36–*
149 built.] built; *1827–*
153 above.] above *1832*
154 Texts] texts *MS. 1832/36–*
155 enclosed,—] enclosed, *1827, 1832* enclosed; *1836–*
159 benches,] benches *1836–*
160 shewed] showed *1832–*
164 Monuments] monuments *MS. 1832/36–*
166 graven,] graven *MS. 1814/27–*
169 —The] The *para MS. 1832/36–*
173 Magistrates] magistrates *MS. 1832/36–*
174 Doctors . . . Mother Church] doctors . . . mother-church *MS. 1832/36–*
175 Senators—] Senators, *1820E–1832* senators, *MS. 1832/36–*
176 King and People] king and people *MS. 1832/36–*
177 decyphered] deciphered *1827–* One] one *MS. 1832/36–*
179 Train] train *MS. 1832/36–*
181 shew] show *1832–*
182 fields] Fields *1832*
183 Tablet] tablet *MS. 1832/36–*
184 bearing] bearing, *1827–*
189 'mid] mid *1827* War] war *MS. 1832/36–*
190 Government] government *MS. 1832/36–*
191 solace,] solace— *MS. 1814/27–*
195 heaven's] Heaven's *1820E–*
196 Issue . . . House] issue . . . house *MS. 1832/36–*
197 Plants . . . Storm] plants . . . storm *MS. 1832/36–*
198 Country] country *MS. 1832/36–*
203 "These *para MS. 1832/36–*
205 Narrative] narrative *MS. 1832/36–*
207 and . . . aisle] and, . . . aisle, *1820E–*
208 Vale] vale *MS. 1832/36–*
209 curved] curvèd *1827–* reclined] reclin'd *MS. 1814/27*
210 Font] font *MS. 1832/36–*
211 Upturned] Upturn'd *MS. 1814/27* rapt] wrapt *1832* rapt *errata 1832*
213 Form] form *MS. 1832/36–*
214 Urn] urn *MS. 1832/36–*
215 peace,] peace,— *1836–1843*
216 rouze] rouse *1827–*
219 came] came, *1820E–*
220 hung;] hung, *1820E–1832*
224 intermixed] intermix'd *then restored to* intermixed *MS. 1814/27*
225 Oak] oak *MS. 1832/36–*
227 church-yard] churchyard *1832–*
231 us.] us:— *1836– but* us— *MS. 1832/36* "Did *para MS. 1827/32C, MS. 1832/36–*
232 churl] Churl *MS. 1814/27–1832*
233 Hireling . . . Neighbour's] hireling . . . neighbour's *MS. 1832/36–*
234 Acquaintance] acquaintance *MS. 1832/36–*
237 thoughts] thoughts, *1820E–*
238 words.] words, *1836–1843 but* words

MS. 1832/36; see verbals
239 Much] "Much *1836–*
241 Being] being *MS. 1832/36–*
243 earth;] earth:— *1827, 1832* earth: *MS. 1832/36–*
245 reality] reality, *1820E–*
246 Man's] man's *MS. 1832/36–*
254 Life's] life's *MS. 1832/36–*
257 Mark *para MS. 1832/36–* Babe] babe *MS. 1832/36–*
259 smile,] smile; *MS. 1814/27–1843*
260 Soul] soul *MS. 1832/36–1843* soul, *1845–*
261 fingers,] fingers— *MS. 1814/27–1832; see verbals* tear,] tear; *MS. 1814/27–*
264 Man] man *MS. 1832/36–*
265 Proficient] proficient *MS. 1832/36–*
269 In] "In *Cornell MS. 1 (excerpt begins here)*
271 they, . . . Minor] they . . . minor *Cornell MS. 1*
273 Humanity] humanity *Cornell MS. 1, MS. 1832/36–* Charge,] charge *MS. 1832/36* charge, *Cornell MS. 1*
274 adorned,] adorned *Cornell MS. 1*
275 baptismal Font. And] Baptismal Font—& *Cornell MS. 1* baptismal font. And *MS. 1832/36–*
276 element . . . cleansed] Element . . . cleans'd *Cornell MS. 1*
277 Child] child *Cornell MS. 1, MS. 1832/36–*
278 Ark] ark *Cornell MS. 1, MS. 1832/36–* Church,] church *Cornell MS. 1* church, *MS. 1832/36–*
279 he, . . . redeemed,] he . . . redeem'd *Cornell MS. 1*
281 everlasting] Everlasting *Cornell MS. 1* Life.] Life *Cornell MS. 1* life. *MS. 1832/36–*
282 desires,] desires *Cornell MS. 1*
283 man] Man *Cornell MS. 1*
284 professed;] professed *Cornell MS. 1*
285 dedication made,] Dedication made *Cornell MS. 1*
286 controul and guide,] controul & guide *Cornell MS.* 1 control and guide, *1827–*
287 progress] Progress *Cornell MS. 1*
288 truth."] Truth—" *Cornell MS. 1 (excerpt ends here)*
291 gulph] gulf *1827–*
294 Creature] creature *MS. 1832/36–* tow'rds] tow'rd *MS. 1814/27, 1827* toward *1832–*
302 be . . . hope] be, . . . hope, *1820E–*
305 "I] I *MS. 1832/36*
307 Communities of Men] communities of men *MS. 1832/36–*
313 But] But, *1820E–*
318 Power,] power, *MS. 1832/36* power,— *1836–*
327 Philosophy] "Philosophy *1832*
329 Hope, and Charity] hope, and charity *MS. 1832/36*
330 Emblems] emblems *MS. 1832/36–*
331 trust,—] trust— *MS. 1832/36–*
332 Torch . . . Star . . . Anchor] torch . . . star . . . anchor *MS. 1832/36–*
333 Cross] cross *MS. 1832/36–*
334 Generations of Mankind] generations of mankind *MS. 1832/36–*
341 bones] bones, *1827–*
345 Land] land *MS. 1832/36–*
346 Grove] grove *MS. 1832/36–*
349 whom] whom, *1820E–*
350 Passion's] passion's *MS. 1832/36–*
351 Heart] heart *MS. 1832/36–*
355 Sages, Martyrs, Confessors—the Man] sages, martyrs, confessors—the man *MS. 1832/36–*
356 Conscience, Truth, and Hope] conscience, truth, and hope *MS. 1832/36–1843; see verbals*
357 compass,] compass *pencil MS. 1836/45*
363 He] he *MS. 1832/36–*
364 Creature] creature *MS. 1832/36–*
366 misplaced.] misplaced: *1827–*
368 Mind] mind *MS. 1832/36–*
369 Dead] dead *MS. 1832/36–*
370 Living] living *MS. 1832/36–*
373 Lands] Lands, *1820E–1832* lands, *MS. 1832/36–*
374 Performance] performance *MS. 1832/36–*
375 heaven] Heaven *1820E–*
383 friend] Friend *MS. 1814/27–*
387 In] in *1827–* Man] man *MS. 1832/36–*
395 follow,] follow *1820E–*
400 Man's] man's *MS. 1832/36–*
406 Winter] winter *MS. 1832/36, 1836; see verbals*
407 How] "How *1832* Habitations] habitations *MS. 1832/36–*
408 Valley . . . House] valley . . . house *MS. 1832/36–*
419 Commonwealth] commonwealth *MS. 1832/36–*
420 Mountaineers,] Mountaineers *MS. 1814/27–1832* mountaineers *MS. 1832/36–* by] (by *1827–* Nature's] nature's *MS. 1832/36–*
422 Shepherd] shepherd *MS. 1832/36–* tended,] tended *1827–*
423 flocks,] flocks) *MS. 1814/27–*

Man's] man's MS. 1832/36–
426 idleness;] idleness: MS. 1832/36–
427 them,] them 1836–
428 ill constructed] ill-constructed 1820E–
433 novelties,] novelties MS. 1814/27–
437 tow'rds] tow'rd 1827 toward 1832– Church-yard] church-yard MS. 1832/36–
443 He] he MS. 1832/36–
449 circumstance] circumstance, MS. 1814/27–
450 Oak] oak MS. 1832/36–
451 Oak] oak MS. 1832/36–
455 Other . . . Sycamore] other . . . sycamore MS. 1832/36–
456 honied] honeyed 1836 honied MS. 1836/45, 1840–
461 Child] child MS. 1832/36–
463 Individual] individual MS. 1832/36–
464 Creature] creature MS. 1832/36–
465 Will] will MS. 1832/36–
466 Reason's . . . Power] reason's . . . power MS. 1832/36–
467 Virtue] virtue MS. 1832/36– name?] name, 1820E–
468 unsound!] unsound? 1820E–
476 Inquest] inquest MS. 1832/36–
477 experience,] experience 1832– gloom.] gloom: 1827–
478 Heart] heart MS. 1832/36–
480 Nature] nature MS. 1832/36–
484 we] we MS. 1832/36–
488 gain] gain, 1832–
489 Virtue's . . . Virtue] virtue's . . . virtue MS. 1832/36–
492 these;] these: 1820E–
495 boast] boast, 1820E–
496 Reason . . . Man] reason . . . man MS. 1832/36–
499 won!] won 1840–1843 won. 1845–
500 himself,] himself; 1820E–
501 Creature . . . perturbed,] creature . . . perturbed; MS. 1832/36–
504 rashly, . . . disgust] rashly . . . disgust, 1820E
505 despair.] despair? 1820E–
508 subtile] subtle 1836–
510 Yet] "Yet 1832
513 Reason's] reason's MS. 1832/36–
516 reason's] Reason's 1832
517 But—] But, MS. 1832/36–
519 consciousness—] consciousness, MS. 1832/36–
520 range—] range, MS. 1832/36–
532 North] North, 1820E; see verbals
533 ground] ground, 1820E; see verbals
539 wintry] wintery 1827
542 Lord] lord 1832–
543 gladness,] gladness 1827–
546 power,] power; 1836–
550 Domain] domain MS. 1832/36–
551 some, . . . minded,] some . . . minded 1832
553 Contrast] contrast 1827– Life] life MS. 1832/36–
555 Death,] Death 1832– twofold] two-fold 1820E– aspect;] aspect! 1836– wintry—] wintery— 1827, 1832
556 Cold, sullen] Cold sullen 1832 Cold, sullen errata 1832, MS. 1832/36
561 "And,] "And 1832– Mind's] mind's MS. 1832/36–
563 Reason] reason MS. 1832/36–
565 steadfast] stedfast 1827, 1845, 1846, 1850
568 water-lilly . . . thrives;] water-lily . . . thrives, 1820E–
571 sentiments,] sentiments 1832–
573 principle,] principle 1827–
577 How] how 1845, 1850 Man] man MS. 1832/36–
579 earth-despising] earth-depising 1832
582 Mind] mind MS. 1832/36–
583 Dell] dell MS. 1832/36–
585 nature] nature, 1836–
588 Man] man 1827–
591 known,] known— 1820E–
592 err,] err— 1820E–
593 pang.] pang! 1820E–
594 Class] class MS. 1832/36–
596 Reason's] reason's MS. 1832/36–
597 doubt] doubt, 1827–
608 encasing,] encasing 1827–
609 Artist's] artist's MS. 1832/36–
614 Earth] earth MS. 1832/36–
616 reluctance,] reluctance; 1836– extol] extol, 1827–
621 birth-right] birthright 1827–
624 Old] old MS. 1832/36–
633 we] we, 1827–
634 aery] aëry 1827– Alchemists] Alchemists, 1827, 1832 alchemists, MS. 1832/36–
636 Domain] domain 1832– You] you MS. 1832/36–
638 heart.] heart; MS. 1814/27–1832 heart: 1836–
640 Man] man MS. 1832/36–
642 She] she MS. 1832/36–
645 Family . . . House] family . . . house MS. 1832/36–
648 earth] earth, 1820E–
649 Dead] dead MS. 1832/36–
651 Man] man MS. 1832/36–
652 Epitomize] Epitomise 1820E– You] you MS. 1832/36–

655 feet.] feet: *1836–*
658 *line ital 1827–*
659 Man] man *1827– line ital 1827–*
660 replied.—] replied— *1836–*
664 They . . . Death] they . . . death *MS. 1832/36–*
665 Mind's] mind's *MS. 1832/36–*
668 shews] shows *1832–*
669 soul] Soul *MS. 1832/36–*
672 Picture . . . living.—] picture . . . living. *MS. 1832/36–*
673 mountain—] mountain, *MS. 1832/36–*
675 sun-beam] sunbeam *1827–*
677 sun-beam] sunbeam *1827–*
681 Site] site *MS. 1832/36–*
683 Tiller's . . . Hermit] tiller's . . . hermit *MS. 1832/36–*
689 Hermit] hermit *MS. 1832/36–*
690 mid] 'mid *1832–*
693 dwell—] dwell *1827, 1832* dwell, *MS. 1832/36–1843; see verbals*
694 A] —A *1827, 1832* Pair,] Pair *1827, 1832* pair *MS. 1832/36– but* pair, *MS. 1836/45*
695 —A House] A house *MS. 1832/36–*
698 top;] top: *1820E–1832*
700 Border war] border-war *MS. 1832/36–*
701 contrived—] contrived, *MS. 1814/27–*
702 Plunderer,] Plunderer— *MS. 1814/27–1832* plunderer— *MS. 1832/36–*
704 South-west,] South-west *1827–*
706 Hut] hut *MS. 1832/36–*
709 Stock-dove] stock-dove *MS. 1832/36–*
714 content,] content. *1846 (possible worn plate)*
716 Quarry's] quarry's *MS. 1832/36–*
719 Flock] flock *MS. 1832/36–*
720 Pair.] Pair; *1827, 1832* Pair: *MS. 1832/36* pair: *1836–*
721 heaven] Heaven *1820E–1832*
722 heaven] Heaven *1820E–1832*
723 recompence] recompense *1827–*
726 scripture] Scripture *1827, 1832*
728 recommending,] recommending *1836–*
734 Retirement] retirement *1832–*
736 way-faring] wayfaring *1827, 1832; see verbals*
738 mountain-pass,] mountain-pass *1820E; see verbals*
739 gloom;] gloom, *1845–*
742 methought,] methought *1832*
745 Sailors] sailors *MS. 1832/36–*
751 I,] I— *MS. 1832/36–*
753 Light] light *MS. 1832/36–*
754 Her] her *MS. 1832/36–*
760 Drawn *rev to para rev to no para MS. 1832/36* Cottage] cottage *MS. 1832/36–* height] height, *1820E–*
763 kenned] kenn'd *MS. 1814/27*
764 Site,] site *MS. 1832/36–*
765 way] way, *1820E; see verbals*
777 returned.—] returned. *MS. 1832/36–*
778 Builder's] builder's *MS. 1832/36–*
781 Helpmate] helpmate *1820E*
782 treat.] treat: *1827–*
783 Traveller] traveller *MS. 1832/36–*
797 Man] man *MS. 1832/36–*
807 Rouzed] Roused *1820E, 1827, 1836–* "Roused *1832*
811–832 *double quots become single quots 1827–*
813 Sabbath] sabbath *MS. 1832/36–*
814 Help-mate's] Helpmate's *1827–*
816 heaven's] Heaven's *1820E– ; see verbals*
819 Friends] friends *MS. 1832/36–*
820 Dependants] Dependents *1827* Comforters . . . Wheel . . . Fire] comforters . . . wheel . . . fire *MS. 1832/36–*
821 House-clock] house-clock *MS. 1832/36–*
822 Hen . . . Chicken] hen . . . chicken *MS. 1832/36–*
823 Birds] birds *MS. 1832/36–*
824 Sheep-dog's] sheep-dog's *MS. 1832/36–*
826 Creatures] creatures *MS. 1832/36–*
827 Wind] wind *MS. 1832/36–*
829 suit;] suit;— *1836–*
830 "—But . . . Thoughts . . . support."] '—But . . . Thoughts . . . support.' *1827– but* 'But *and* thoughts *1836– and* support, *1845–*
833 main!] main!— *1836–*
834 oppressed] opprest *1827–*
835 leisure—] leisure, *MS. 1832/36* leisure; *1836–*
837 falter] falter, *MS. 1836/45*
838 light,] light; *1820E–*
840 Evening . . . Star] evening . . . star *MS. 1832/36–*
841 Sabbath-day] sabbath-day *MS. 1832/36–* Sun."] Sun.'" *1827, 1832* sun.'" *MS. 1832/36–*
842 Solitary,] Solitary *1820E– indented but no additional vertical space 1832*
844 Bird] bird *MS. 1832/36–*
845 line her nest,] line, her nest *MS. 1832/36–*
848 Powers,] Powers *1827–*
849 Bird] bird *MS. 1832/36–*
850 Nature's] nature's *MS. 1832/36–*

851 Individual] individual *MS. 1832/36–*
853 And,] And *pencil MS. 1836/45* own, that] own that, *pencil MS. 1836/45, 1840–*
859 Those] those *MS. 1832/36–*
860 Virtue's] virtue's *MS. 1832/36–*
861 aim;] aim *1836–1843* aim, *1845–*
866 —In] In *MS. 1832/36–* youth . . . hills] youth, . . . hills, *1820E–*
868 Crofts] crofts *MS. 1832/36–*
873 moon] Moon *1827, 1832* spite,] spite; *1820E–1832* spite. *MS. 1832/36–*
875–881 *double quots become single quots 1827–*
876 fertilizing] fertilising *1827–*
878 Summer . . . day,] summer . . . day *MS. 1832/36–*
879 issuing,] issuing *1832*
880 fails;] fails: *MS. 1832/36–*
881 plentiful,] plentiful *1846*
885 Natures] natures *MS. 1832/36–* rare . . . least] rare, . . . least, *1820E–*
887 He—] He, *MS. 1832/36–*
890 quiet—] quiet, *MS. 1832/36–* he,] he— *MS. 1832/36*
895 Solitude] solitude *MS. 1832/36–*
904 looking,] looking; *1836–*
905 Flock] flock *MS. 1832/36–*
908 Heaven] heaven *MS. 1832/36–*
909 spake.] spake— *MS. 1832/36* spake:— *1836–*
910 —"To . . . Pair] "To . . . pair *para MS. 1832/36–*
911 Death . . . Life] death . . . life *MS. 1832/36*
912 Affections] affections *MS. 1832/36–*
913 conjunction.] conjunction;— *1832–1843, 1846* conjunction; *1845, 1850* Consecrate] consecrate *1832–*
914 Him . . . Cross] him . . . cross *MS. 1832/36–*
915 Revelation] revelation *MS. 1832/36–*
916 Reason's] reason's *MS. 1832/36–*
917 Imagination] imagination *MS. 1832/36–*
918 Charity] charity *MS. 1832/36–* Love;] Love, *1820E–1832* love, *MS. 1832/36–*
927 chrystal] crystal *1827–*
929 And] "And *1832, MS. 1832/36* know,] know. *1846 (possible worn plate)*
931 All] all *MS. 1832/36–*
932 Humanity] humanity *MS. 1832/36–*
937 wrecks] wrecks, *1827, 1832; see verbals*
939 Sea] sea *MS. 1832/36–*
943 climes;] climes— *1836–* wretched—] wretched, *1827–*
946 dead—] dead, *1827–* Oppressor] oppressor *MS. 1832/36–* Oppressed] Opprest *1827, 1832* oppresst *MS. 1832/36–*
948 Slaves] slaves *1820E–* destroyed;] destroyed— *1827–*
950 Who . . . hand] Who, . . . hand, *1820E–*
952 Infants] infants *1836–*
957 Babe] babe *MS. 1832/36–*
960 Nursling] nursling *MS. 1832/36–*
962 Little-one] little-one *MS. 1832/36, 1845–* little one *1836–1841*
964 Infancy] infancy *MS. 1832/36–*
965 thoughtless] thoughtless, *1845–* School-boy . . . Youth] school-boy . . . youth *MS. 1832/36–*
966 Maid] maid *MS. 1832/36–*
973 and,] and *1832–*
976 spared,] spared— *1827–*
978 Various;] Various, *1827–*
980 concern,] concern *MS. 1814/27* concern; *1827, 1832*
981 *double quots become single quots 1827–* grieved] grieved, *MS. 1814/27–* One] one *MS. 1832/36–*
984 —And] And *para MS. 1832/36–*
989 gladness)] gladness). *1832* gladness) *MS. 1832/36* gladness)— *1836–*
992 Soul . . . Soul] soul . . . soul *MS. 1832/36–*
993 Eye . . . Ear] eye . . . ear *MS. 1832/36–*
994 Creature] creature *MS. 1832/36–*
995 heaven] Heaven *1832*
997 plain] plain, *1832–*
998 Word] WORD *1827–*
1001 prevail.] prevail: *1836–*
1004 shocks,] shocks *MS. 1832/36–*
1006 Truths] truths *MS. 1832/36–*
1007 Institutions:—Men] institutions:—men *MS. 1832/36–*
1008 Life . . . Love . . . Immortality] life . . . love . . . immortality *MS. 1832/36–*
1009 Being . . . Element] being . . . element *MS. 1832/36–*
1012 Affections] affections *MS. 1832/36–*
1013 mid] 'mid *1820E–* desarts] deserts *1827–*
1014 —This] This *1836–* end,] end *1820E–*
1015 Reason] reason *MS. 1832/36–*
1018 Love] love *MS. 1849, MS. 1832/36–*
1019 human;] human, *MS. 1849*
1020 In strife and tribulation, and ordained *MS. 1849*
1021 sanctified,] sanctified *MS. 1849*
1022 joy."] joy *MS. 1849*

Book VI

1 Crown] crown *MS. 1832/36–*
2 Throne] throne *MS. 1832/36–*
3 foundations] Foundations *1820E–1832*
4 People's] people's *MS. 1832/36–* love,] love; *1820E– but* love: *1849 (probable worn plate)*
8 Fabric] fabric *1836–*
11 Holiness] holiness *MS. 1832/36–* order'd] ordered *1820E–*
12 Decent,] Decent *1845–*
16 soil.] soil *1849 (probable worn plate)*
17 —And,] —And *1820E–1832* And *para MS. 1832/36–*
19 "silent] 'silent *1836–* Heaven;"] heaven;' *1836– but* heaven; *1846 (probable worn plate)*
21 Minster,] minster, *MS. 1832/36– but* minster *pencil MS. 1836/45, 1845, 1850*
24 Hearts] hearts *MS. 1832/36–*
27 Structures] structures *1836–*
31 Time] time *MS. 1832/36–*
33 Elements] elements *MS. 1832/36–*
37 bestow—] bestow, *1836–*
38 Men] men *MS. 1832/36–*
42 civility—] civility, *1836–*
43 —The] The *para MS. 1832/36–* Poet] poet *1832*
44 Servants] servants *MS. 1832/36–*
45 Altars . . . Minsters] altars . . . minsters *MS. 1832/36–*
52 Sabbath] sabbath *MS. 1832/36–*
53 Angels] angels *1832–*
54 Truth] truth *MS. 1832/36–*
56 Priesthood] priesthood *MS. 1832/36–*
57 Band] band *MS. 1832/36–*
58 Champions] champions *MS. 1832/36–*
60 World's] world's *MS. 1832/36–*
62 Sires] sires *MS. 1832/36–*
66 unjust.] unjust; *1820E–*
69 release,] release; *1827–*
70 bequeathed,] bequeathed *1832–*
73 grace] grace, *1827–*
74 Country-men] Countrymen *1827, 1832* countrymen *MS. 1832/36–*
76 Man] man *1832*
78 Priest] priest *MS. 1832/36–*
80 Land] land *MS. 1832/36–*
81 Religion,] religion *MS. 1832/36–*
86 truths;] truths,— *1836–*
88 Creatures] creatures *MS. 1832/36–*
91 place;] place, *1836–*
92 ground,] ground; *1836–*
94 chearfulness;] chearfulness, *1820E* cheerfulness, *1827, 1832* cheerfulness; *1836–*
96 Domain] domain *MS. 1832/36–*
101 One,] one, *MS. 1832/36– but* one *pencil MS. 1836/45* yet,] yet *1827–*
102 Nature's] nature's *MS. 1832/36–* kindliness,] kindliness *1832–*
104 answered.] answered: *1820E–*
110 that] that, *pencil MS. 1836/45*
111 love;] love *MS. 1832/36* love, *1836–*
113 herb,] herb *1832–*
114 smiled,] smiled,— *1836–*
118 grief,"] grief?" *1832–*
120 vicar] Vicar *1832–*
123 —Rejected—yea repelled—] Rejected, yea repelled, *MS. 1832/36– but* repelled; *1836–*
125 wears.] wears *1827–*
129 hope,] hope; *1836–*
131 Object] object *MS. 1832/36–*
133 sufferer] Sufferer *1827–*
140 Choir] choir *MS. 1832/36–*
142 complete,] complete,— *1827–*
143 "Joy . . . happiness,"] 'Joy . . . happiness,' *1832–*
144 "His . . . mine!"] 'His . . . mine!' *1832–*
145 Such] "Such *1832* Man] Man, *MS. 1836/45, 1840–*
146 Oak] oak *MS. 1832/36–*
148 stedfast] steadfast *1827– but* stedfast *1845, 1850* Mind] mind *MS. 1832/36–*
150 And . . . movements] And, . . . movements, *1836–*
161 ensued,] ensued *1827–*
168 'Tis *para MS. 1832/36–*
169 Poets] poets *MS. 1832/36–* nature's] Nature's *1827, 1832*
171 Man] man *MS. 1832/36* Friends] friends *MS. 1832/36–*
174–182 *double quots become single quots 1827–*
174 awhile] a while *1832–*
182 chearfulness] cheerfulness *1827–* peace."] peace.' *1827– but* peace. *1840 (possible worn plate; 1841, 1843 read* peace.'*) and 1849*
184 hopelessly:— . . . Innocence] hopelessly; . . . innocence *MS. 1832/36–*
185 mind] mind, *1836– but* mind *1845, 1850*
186 Heaven,] Heaven; *1836–*
187 Sufferers] sufferers *1836–*
191 Elements] elements *1836–*
193 Forms] forms *1836–*
194 above,] above; *1836–*
203 mold] mould *1827–*
204 him;] him, *1827–*

205 smitten,] smitten *MS. 1832/36–* force.] force; *1827–*
208 passion,—] passion; *MS. 1832/36–*
210 accept,] accept *1832–*
211 possessions,] possessions *1832–*
214 preserved.] preserved; *1827–*
217 Love] love *MS. 1832/36–*
219 Close] "Close *1832*
220 Endeavours] endeavours *1820E; see verbals*
222 Place] place *MS. 1832/36–*
223 Band] band *MS. 1832/36–*
224 Adventurers] adventurers *MS. 1832/36–* pains,] pains *1827–*
227 alone;] alone. *MS. 1814/27–*
231 uncountenanc'd] uncountenanced *1820E–*
233 recompence] recompense *1827–* and,] and *1832–*
235 Thrall] thrall *MS. 1832/36–*
236 Spirits,] Spirits *1827–*
238 Hope,] Hope *1832–*
239 But *para MS. 1832/36* Lord] lord *MS. 1832/36–*
246 Hero] hero *MS. 1832/36–*
250 day-light] daylight *1827–; see verbals*
251 Giddy] Giddy, *MS. 1832/36*
254 —He] He *1827–* vanish'd] vanished *1820E–*
255 Path . . . Cottage-door] path . . . cottage-door *MS. 1832/36–*
256 Mine's] mine's *MS. 1832/36–* long,] long *pencil MS. 1836/45, 1840–*
260 Vestige] vestige *MS. 1832/36–*
262 'till] till *1827–*
264 Thou,] Thou *1832–*
266 Thou . . . it!—. . . Virtuous] thou . . . it! . . . virtuous *MS. 1832/36–*
268 hope,] hope; *MS. 1832/36–*
270 "Unshaken, . . . unterrified;"] 'Unshaken, . . . unterrified;' *1827–*
271 Wise] wise *MS. 1832/36–*
273 Dust] dust *1832–*
274 holds,] holds *1832–*
275 Pile] pile *MS. 1832/36–*
277 Heaven] heaven *MS. 1832/36–*
281 Her] her *MS. 1832/36–*
282 Pair] pair, *MS. 1832/36–*
283 Earth's] earth's *MS. 1832/36–* Mold] Mould *1827, 1832* mould *MS. 1832/36–*
284 Hillock] hillock *MS. 1832/36–*
285 Recalls.—] Recalls!— *1827, 1832* Recalls! *1836–1843, 1846* Recals! *pencil MS. 1836/45, 1845, 1850* *He*] He *1827, 1832 He para MS. 1832/36–*
292 —Gay] Gay *MS. 1832/36–*
294 actor—] actor, *MS. 1832/36–*
295 soldier—] soldier, *MS. 1832/36–*
296 enterprize] enterprize— *1820E, 1827* enterprise— *1832–*
298 Two] Too *1836* Two *errata 1836, pencil MS. 1836/45–* Souls] souls *MS. 1832/36–*
299 manners, . . . youth] manners . . . Youth *1827–*
301 cage,] cage; *1832*
303 Swan] swan *MS. 1832/36–*
305 Leaf] leaf *MS. 1832/36–*
306 He] he *MS. 1832/36–*
307 Flower] flower *1832–*
308 Ye] ye *1827–* inquire] enquire *1832–*
317 Favourite,] Favourite— *pencil MS. 1836/45, 1840–*
321 demeanor] demeanour *1827–*
322 letters,] letters— *pencil MS. 1836/45, 1840–*
323 World's] world's *MS. 1832/36–*
328 Land] land *MS. 1832/36–*
329 Sailor's] sailor's *MS. 1832/36–*
331 attractive—] attractive, *MS. 1832/36–*
332 —Yet] *para MS. 1832/36– but* Yet *1836–*
336 He] he *MS. 1832/36–*
338 Host] host *MS. 1832/36–*
339 Poverty] poverty *MS. 1832/36–*
340 Owl] owl *MS. 1832/36–*
343 Saloon] saloon *MS. 1832/36–*
344 Ghost] ghost *MS. 1832/36–*
345 Wreck] wreck *MS. 1832/36–*
349 He,] he, *MS. 1832/36, 1836* he— *pencil MS. 1836/45, 1840–*
352 Ladies,] ladies *MS. 1832/36–*
353 Halls,] halls, *MS. 1832/36, 1836* halls— *pencil MS. 1836/45, 1840–*
355 moment?—Who] moment—who *MS. 1814/27–*
356 Spirit;] Spirit? *MS. 1814/27–* Holds] holds *MS. 1832/36–*
357 Talents] talents *MS. 1832/36–*
358 Beggars,—] beggars,— *MS. 1832/36–*
365 City] city *MS. 1832/36–*
369 Minstrel] minstrel *MS. 1832/36–*
372 Hearts] hearts *MS. 1832/36–*
379 breath;] breath, *pencil MS. 1836/45*
382 Fowl . . . Mother] fowl . . . mother *MS. 1832/36–*
390 Himself] himself *MS. 1832/36–*
392 pitiful] pitiful, *1820E–*
393 Land . . . Charity] land . . . charity *MS. 1832/36–* That] that, *pencil MS. 1836/45*
395 Man] man *MS. 1832/36–*
400 converse, no,] converse; no— *1836–*
401 speech] speech, *1832–*

402 Being] being *1836–*
403 Self-catechized] Self-catechised *1827–*
404 Home] home *MS. 1832/36–*
407 mold] mould *1827–*
408 Hills] Hills, *1820E–1832* hills, *1836* hills— *pencil MS. 1836/45, 1840–*
410 Domain] domain *MS. 1832/36–*
412 progeny,] progeny— *pencil MS. 1836/45, 1840–*
414 Alien] alien *1836–*
415 find,] find *1820E, 1827*
418 brief] brief, *1827–*
421 Pair] pair *MS. 1832/36–*
423 Strangers . . . Town] strangers . . . town *MS. 1832/36–*
425 Vale . . . Friends] vale . . . friends *MS. 1832/36–*
427 Cemetery] cemetery *MS. 1832/36–*
429 Family-vault . . . One] family-vault . . . one *MS. 1832/36– but* family vault *1836–*
431 burned.] burned: *MS. 1832/36–*
434 Bigotry] bigotry *MS. 1832/36–*
435 Arouzed] Aroused *1820E–*
437 overthrow.—] overthrow. *MS. 1832/36–*
439 Time] time *1832–*
443 —The Other] The Other *para MS. 1832/36– but* other *1836–*
446 they] *they 1827–*
447 Kings] kings *MS. 1832/36–*
448 Land] land *MS. 1832/36–*
449 Papacy] papacy *MS. 1832/36–*
450 Rule . . . Bark] rule . . . bark *MS. 1832/36–*
454 Stream] stream *MS. 1832/36–*
455 Master . . . He,] master . . . He— *MS. 1832/36–*
457 Mansion] mansion *MS. 1832/36–*
458 moralized] moralised *1832–*
459 satisfied,] satisfied— *MS. 1832/36–*
461 bitterness] bitterness, *1820E–*
463 Contest . . . Seat] contest . . . seat *MS. 1832/36–*
464 Senate] senate *MS. 1832/36–*
467 *borrowed*] borrowed *1845–*
470 World] world *MS. 1832/36–*
473 Abode.—] abode. *MS. 1832/36–*
474 Champions] champions *MS. 1832/36–*
480 mid] 'mid *1832–*
481 Town] town *MS. 1832/36–*
482 Bowling-green] bowling-green *MS. 1832/36–*
483 Church] church *MS. 1832/36–*
484 Market-place] market-place *MS. 1832/36–*
485 Opponents] opponents *1836–*
491 A] "A *1832*
496 Spirit] spirit *MS. 1832/36–*
498 ground] ground, *1827–*
499 Spirit] spirit *MS. 1832/36–*
500 that,] that— *pencil MS. 1836/45, 1840–*
503 Earth,] Earth *1836–* earth,] earth *1836* earth, *pencil MS. 1836/45, 1840–* create,] create— *pencil MS. 1836/45, 1840–*
506 Virtue] virtue *MS. 1832/36–*
507 —There] There *para MS. 1832/36–*
508 Figures,—] figures, *MS. 1832/36–*
509 Yew] yew *MS. 1832/36–* favourite] favourite— *1820E* resting-place] resting place *1836–1843*
510 But, . . . Remnant . . . Tree] But . . . remnant . . . tree *MS. 1832/36–*
513 Dial] dial *MS. 1832/36–*
515 monument;] monument: *1836–*
516 wished,] wished *1832–*
518 Remains] remains *MS. 1832/36–*
519 Tree] tree *MS. 1832/36–*
520 Structure] structure *MS. 1832/36–*
521 Pillar] pillar *MS. 1832/36–*
522 art, . . . sumptuous, . . . seem,] art . . . sumptuous . . . seem *1827–*
523 Place] place *MS. 1832/36–*
526 Plate] plate *MS. 1832/36–*
527 Shadow] shadow *MS. 1832/36–* falls, . . . hours] falls . . . hours, *1820E–*
528 Legend"—] Legend."— *1832* legend."— *MS. 1832/36–*
529 and,] and *pencil MS. 1836/45, 1840–*
530 couched.] couched: *1836–*
531–537 *entire passage ital, quots om before each line 1827– but in l. 531* "Time] 'Time *1836–, and in l. 537* confirmed!"] confirmed!' *pencil MS. 1836/45, 1840–*
536 peace,] peace *1827–1843*
537 World . . . Thee] world . . . thee *MS. 1832/36–*
540 Nature's] nature's *MS. 1832/36–*
546 those,] those *1836–* fellow men] fellow-men *1827–*
548 "too] 'too *1827–*
549 infelicity"—] infelicity'— *1827* infelicity,'— *1832* infelicity,' *MS. 1832/36–*
550 Exiles] exiles *MS. 1832/36–*
552 Centinels] Sentinels, *1827, 1832* sentinels *MS. 1832/36–*
554 them.—] them. *MS. 1832/36–*
555 chained?] chained *pencil MS. 1836/45, 1845–*
556 Vulture—] vulture, *MS. 1832/36–*
557 vitals!] vitals? *1820E–*

562 times;] times, *1832–*
563 —Exchange . . . Shepherd's] Exchange . . . shepherd's *MS. 1832/36–*
565 sceptre;—] sceptre; *MS. 1832/36–*
566 circumstance,] circumstance; *pencil MS. 1836/45, 1840–*
568 —Amid] Amid *MS. 1832/36–* hills] hills, *1827–*
570 pangs] pangs, *pencil MS. 1836/45, 1840–*
576 controuling] controlling *1827–*
577 That . . . stations] That, . . . stations, *1820E–*
578 mysteries,—] mysteries;— *1827–* for . . . untried] for, . . . untried, *1820E–*
579 might— . . . her—] might, . . . her, *1827–*
580 shewn?] shown? *1832–*
587 heaven . . . peace."] Heaven . . . peace. *pencil MS. 1814/27, 1820E–*
588 less] less, *1827–*
595 recognized by all"—] recognised by all—" *1832–*
604 no where] nowhere *1827–*
609 but,] but *1836–*
611 Sun] sun *MS. 1832/36–*
614 Lake] lake *MS. 1832/36–*
618 they,] they *1827–*
619 ground] ground *pencil MS. 1836/45*
621 green;] green, *1832–*
622 ridge:] ridge, *1832–*
623 surface—] surface, *MS. 1832/36–*
627 Lives] lives *MS. 1832/36–*
629 faithful,] faithful *1836–*
630 for,] for *1836–*
631 Tomb] tomb *MS. 1832/36–* And] and *1827, 1832*
633 if . . . source] if, . . . source, *1820E–*
637 Time's] time's *MS. 1832/36–*
640 Yet— *para MS. 1832/36–*
642 notice,] notice; *1836–*
643 worth,] worth; *1827–*
645 fulfilled] fulfilled, *1827–*
648 range] range, *1827–*
652 Memorials] memorials *MS. 1832/36–* felt] felt, *1832–*
654 enclosure] Enclosure *1827–*
664 esteem] esteem, *1827–*
666 sun-beam] sunbeam *1827–*
668 Images] images *1827–*
669 Nature's] nature's *MS. 1832/36–*
674 attend:] attend; *1832–*
675 notice,] notice; *1820E, 1827* notice— *1832*
676 And *para MS. 1832/36–*
679 For] For, *pencil MS. 1836/45, 1840–*
680 repel,] repel;— *1827–1836* repel— *pencil MS. 1836/45, 1840–*
682 Soul,] soul, *MS. 1832/36, 1836* soul— *pencil MS. 1836/45, 1840–*
683 shewn] shown *1832–*
687 Conqueror's] conqueror's *MS. 1832/36–*
688 Senate,] senate *MS. 1832/36–*
690 —There] There *para MS. 1832/36–* Vicar] Vicar, *1827–*
691 woman] Woman *1827, 1832*
696 heaven] Heaven *1820E–1832* depressed] deprest *1827–* tow'rds] towards *1836–*
700 One] one *MS. 1832/36–*
702 Child] child *MS. 1832/36–*
703 mid] 'mid *MS. 1814/27, 1820E–* Flowerets] flowerets *MS. 1832/36–*
704 Thistle] thistle *MS. 1832/36–*
707 age, . . . ruled] age . . . ruled, *1832–* Queen] queen, *MS. 1832/36–*
708 sports] sports, *MS. 1814/27–*
722 knowledge;] knowledge, *1832–*
723 images—] images *MS. 1832/36–* impressed] imprest *1832–*
724 memory;] memory, *1832–*
725 places,—] places; *MS. 1832/36* places, *1836–*
728 Two] "Two *1832*
734 Bound] Bound— *1827, 1832, 1840– but* Bound, *pencil MS. 1836/45* scorn.] scorn, *1820E–*
736 concealed,] concealed— *1827–*
737 Child] child *MS. 1832/36–*
739 dependance.—] dependence.— *1827, 1832* dependence. *MS. 1832/36–*
741 sex,] sex. *1827–*
748 Thus] "Thus *1832*
749 end,] end *1832*
750 Builder's] builder's *MS. 1832/36–*
751 mind] Mind *1820E–1832*
753 Mind] mind *MS. 1832/36–*
757 mountains—] mountains, *MS. 1832/36; see verbals*
763 A] "A *1832*
767 upon—] upon, *MS. 1832/36–*
768 malady,] malady *1832–*
770 Eagle] eagle *MS. 1832/36–* Lamb.] Lamb? *1827, 1832* lamb? *MS. 1832/36–*
771 moaned— . . . Sister] moaned;— . . . sister *1836– (ink blot obscures changes, if any, in MS. 1832/36)* Husband's] husband's *1832–*
774–779 *double quots become single quots 1827–*
774 ears!—] ears! *MS. 1832/36–*
778 fire— . . . possessed—] fire, . . . possessed, *MS. 1832/36–1843; see verbals*

779 tended—] tended, MS. 1832/36–
783 door,] door 1845–
785 tow'rds] towards 1836– Jupiter,] Jupiter 1832–
786 Vale] vale MS. 1832/36–1843
787–790 *double quots become single quots* 1827–
787 Star] star 1845–
789 earth] earth, 1827
790 safe,] safe; 1840–1843; *see verbals*
792 unkindnesses, . . . forgiven;] unkindnesses . . . forgiven, 1845–
793 Though, . . . awe!"] Tho', . . . awe." 1845– Vale] vale 1836–1843
794 tow'rds] tow'rd 1832 toward 1836–
799 Bells] bells MS. 1832/36–
800 ring] ring, MS. 1836/45
805 "As,] "As 1820E– Lamb] lamb MS. 1832/36–
807 Parent] parent MS. 1832/36–
809 itself;— . . . rest,] itself; . . . rest; MS. 1832/36–
810 Hillock] hillock MS. 1832/36–
815 do;] do: 1832
822 mold] mould 1827– brood,] brood 1832–
824 Ah] "Ah 1832 Man] man MS. 1832/36–
826 Shew] Show 1832–
827 witnessed,] witnessed; 1820E–
842 —Serious] Serious *para* MS. 1832/36
844 motions] motions, *pencil* MS. 1836/45, 1840–
846 addressed] addrest 1827–
848 Hunter's] hunter's MS. 1832/36–
849 A] *para* 1836– Elm] elm MS. 1832/36–
850 Valley] valley MS. 1832/36–
852 Peasants] peasants MS. 1832/36–
854 dances] dances, 1827
856 Night;] Night, 1832– Stars] stars MS. 1832/36–
857 Moon . . . Queen] moon . . . queen MS. 1832/36–
860 Maiden's] maiden's MS. 1832/36–
863 She] "She 1832 loved,—] loved, MS. 1814/27–
864 The] —The MS. 1814/27–
866 Woman] woman MS. 1832/36–
869 Equals] equals 1836–
874 Sweet,] Sweet MS. 1832/36; *see verbals*
875 tow'rds] tow'rd 1832 toward 1836–
879 heart;—] heart; MS. 1832/36–
881 Cottage] cottage 1832–
883 Thrush] thrush MS. 1832/36– chaunts] chants 1827–
884 evening,] evening 1832–
885 undergrove] under-grove 1846
888–906 *double quots become single quots* 1827–
890 Woman's] woman's MS. 1832/36–
891 Man] man MS. 1832/36–
892 him] Him 1827, 1832 Judge,] judge; MS. 1832/36–
894 Hearts] hearts MS. 1832/36– began *worn type appears as* oegan *in some copies* 1820E
897 received,] received; MS. 1814/27– Bird,] bird, MS. 1832/36, 1836 bird— *pencil* MS. 1836/45, 1840–
898 "—O] 'O *pencil* MS. 1836/45, 1840–
899 Creature,] creature, MS. 1832/36– *but* creature 1846 *(possible worn plate)*
902 wished,] wished 1832– Heaven] heaven MS. 1832/36–
907 Such] "Such 1832
915 resource.] resource; 1832 resource: 1836–
918 Cottage-barn] cottage-barn MS. 1832/36–
921 sky,] sky 1845–
922 bed.] bed! 1827–
923 Fancy] fancy MS. 1832/36–
925 A] "A 1832
929 of—] of, MS. 1832/36 of,— 1836–
930 Traveller feels] traveller feels, 1836–
931 waste,] waste 1836–
934 day-spring—] day-spring, 1827– east] east, 1836–
935 *double quots become single quots* 1827–
937–946 *double quots become single quots* 1827–
936 Thus] Thus, 1832–
937 heart;] heart 1820E *(probably damaged type)*
938 he . . . parched] He . . . parchèd 1827–
941 desart] desert 1827–
944 Infant;] Infant! 1827–
945 me,—] me; MS. 1832/36–
946 vain,] vain; 1836–
947 unfulfilled,] unfulfilled; 1836–
948 return] return, 1827–
951 nursed,] nursed; *pencil* MS. 1836/45, 1840–
958 —Through] Through *para* MS. 1832/36–
964 means,] means; MS. 1814/27–1832 means: 1836–
967 Foster-Mother's] Foster-mother's MS. 1832/36–
968 Vales] vales MS. 1832/36–
974 unjust:] unjust, 1832–
975 feel.] feel: 1836–
978 Pair . . . Infant] pair . . . infant MS. 1832/36–
979 own.] own; 1827, 1832 own: MS. 1832/36–

984 near!—] near! *1836–*
989 Child] child *MS. 1832/36–*
990 Child] child *MS. 1832/36–*
991 malady:] malady; *1832–*
992 burial day] burial-day *1836–*
994 house—] house, *MS. 1832/36–*
995 One] one *MS. 1832/36–*
997 "Nay,"] 'Nay,' *1827–*
1001 weeping] weeping, *1827–*
1004 You] "You *1832, MS. 1832/36* Grave;— . . . Spot,] Grave; . . . spot, *1836– but* spot *MS. 1832/36*
1005 abroad] abroad, *1827–*
1008 day—] day, *MS. 1832/36–*
1010 Mother's] mother's *MS. 1832/36–*
1011 transgression;] transgression, *1832, MS. 1832/36* Penitent] penitent *MS. 1832/36–*
1012 Heaven . . . eye.] heaven . . . eye *MS. 1832/36– but* eye! *1836–*
1013 Parents] parents *1836–* Foster-child] Foster-child, *1827, 1832* foster-child, *MS. 1832/36–*
1015 renewed, . . . renew,] renewed . . . renew *1827–*
1018 erred:] erred; *1827–*
1020 pleaded:] pleaded— *1827–*
1021 snapped] snapped, *1820E–*
1024 appearance] appearance, *1827–*
1026 The *para MS. 1832/36–*
1027 Betrayer] betrayer *MS. 1832/36–*
1033 love,] love *pencil MS. 1836/45*
1035 being] being, *1836– but* being *1845, 1850*
1039 only.—] only. *1836–* She *para MS. 1832/36–*
1040 Heart] heart *MS. 1832/36–* built] built, *1827–* Nest] Nest, *1827* nest *MS. 1832/36–*
1042 Work] work *MS. 1832/36–*
1044 Heaven's] heaven's *MS. 1832/36–*
1050 unworthiness.—] unworthiness. *MS. 1832/36–*
1055 —Meek] Meek *MS. 1832/36–*
1061 Congregation] congregation *MS. 1832/36–*
1062 Soul's] soul's *MS. 1832/36–*
1063 Friend] friend *MS. 1832/36–*
1067–1069 *double quots become single quots 1827–*
1070 through] though *typesetting error 1831* through *1834*
1071 love,] love *1832–*
1075 Each] each *MS. 1832/36–*
1078 When,] When *1845–*
1081 Margaret] Margaret, *ink over pencil MS. 1836/45, adopted 1845, 1850* Heath,] heath, *MS. 1832/36– but* heath *pencil MS. 1836/45, 1845, 1850*
1082 House] house *MS. 1832/36–*
1084 power] Power *1827, 1832*
1087 serene,] serene; *1836–*
1090 saying,] saying,— *MS. 1832/36* saying:— *1836–* "Blest] "Blessed *1820E* "Blest *para MS. 1832/36–*
1093 Tale] tale *MS. 1832/36–*
1097 One . . . Vale] one . . . vale *MS. 1832/36–*
1099 Where,] Where *1832–1843*
1100 Armathwaite?"—] Armathwaite?" *end of Book VI excerpt 1831* —The] The *para MS. 1832/36–*
1105 offence,] offence— *MS. 1832/36–*
1109 strife,] strife; *1820E; see verbals*
1137 Wife . . . Children] wife . . . children *MS. 1832/36–*
1138 home] home, *1827–*
1145 fly,] fly— *pencil MS. 1836/45, 1840–* whither?] whither! *1832–*
1146 peace, . . . hope,] peace . . . hope *1832–*
1147 Mother . . . Vale] mother . . . vale *MS. 1832/36–*
1148 Cottages] cottages *MS. 1832/36–*
1150 unknown;] unknown: *1820E–*
1152 Men] men *MS. 1832/36–*
1155 Here] "Here *1832*
1156 Grave . . . Ridge] grave . . . ridge *MS. 1832/36–*
1158 Vale] vale *MS. 1832/36–*
1159 Cottage] cottage *MS. 1832/36* dwelt;] dwelt *1827, 1832*
1163 Tale] tale *MS. 1832/36–*
1166 Family] family *MS. 1832/36–*
1167 Garland] garland *MS. 1832/36–*
1170 full blown] full-blown *1820E–* Flower!] flower! *MS. 1832/36, 1836* flower. *pencil MS. 1836/45, 1840–*
1171 Depressed] Deprest *1832–*
1173 Now] Now, *1827–*
1179 Hope] hope *MS. 1832/36–*
1180 Owner] owner *MS. 1832/36–*
1181 sight] sight, *1820E–*
1186 Nature] nature *MS. 1832/36–*
1189 —Brought] Brought *para MS. 1832/36–*
1191 Plant] plant *MS. 1832/36–*
1193 garden wall] garden-wall *1820E–*
1198 Who,] Who *1827* heights,] heights *1832*
1199 Attendant] attendant *MS. 1832/36–*
1200 Boy] boy *MS. 1832/36–* do;] do, *1832–*
1201 daring:] daring; *1832–*
1203 herbs—] herbs, *MS. 1832/36–*
1209 Bees] bees *MS. 1832/36–*
1210 Enclosure] enclosure *MS. 1832/36–*
1212 life,] life *MS. 1832/36–*

1218 Company] company *MS. 1832/36–*
1222 time] Time *1832*
1223 Sisterhood] sisterhood *MS. 1832/36–*
1224 this, . . . work;] this . . . work, *1832–*
1225 herself] herself, *1832–*
1226 little One] little-one *1827–*
1227 —Mild] Mild *MS. 1832/36–*
1228 House] house *1820E–*
1231 where,] where *1832*
1232 how] how, *1827–*   Earth.] Earth." *1832* earth!" *MS. 1832/36–*
1239 Others] others *1820E; see verbals*

Book VII

heading MOUNTAINS] MOUNTAINS— *1820E*
1 passed,] passed *1849 (probable worn plate)*
5 Vale] vale *MS. 1832/36–*
6 splendour] splendor *MS. 1832/36– but* splendour *1845, 1850*
12 Master;] Master, *1832–*
15 tunes] tunes, *1827–*
16 tender] tender, *MS. 1836/45*
18 Youth . . . Maiden,] youth . . . maiden *MS. 1832/36* youth . . . maiden, *1836–*   Chief] chief *1836–*
20 empassioned] impassioned *1827–*
29 thoughts;] thoughts, *1827–*
33 pool;] pool: *MS. 1832/36–*
34 —Whence] Whence *MS. 1832/36–*   it,] it *1820E–1836*
38 Village-school] Village school *1820E–1832* village-school *MS. 1832/36–*
39 answered.] answered,— *1845–*
42 Hillocks] hillocks *MS. 1832/36–*
46 trees,—] trees; *MS. 1832/36–*
47 Then,] Then *1832*
48 fields,—] fields; *MS. 1832/36–*   waste] waste, *1820E–*
50 Vale] vale *MS. 1832/36–*
51 —That] That *MS. 1832/36–*
53 Cottage . . . view,—] cottage . . . view; *MS. 1832/36–*   discern,] discern *1832–*
54 trees,] trees *1832–*
55 All *para 1836–*
58 Vale] vale *MS. 1832/36–*
60 Rough] "Rough *1832 no para 1836–*   *MS. 1836/45 has the numeral "2" (or the letter "Q" for "Query") in margin, possibly intending a return to para break as in 1814–1832*
61 Northern] northern *MS. 1832/36–*
62 Vales] vales *MS. 1832/36–*
64 Dwelling-place] dwelling-place *MS. 1832/36–*
72 tow'rds] tow'rd *1832* toward *1836–*
73 Ass] ass *MS. 1832/36–*
74 Children] children *MS. 1832/36–*
76 flowers] flowers, *1827– but* flowers. *1846 (probable worn plate)*
79 Woman] woman *MS. 1832/36–*
80 Lady's] lady's *MS. 1832/36–*
82 journey— . . . pastime—] journey, . . . pastime, *MS. 1832/36–*
87–95 *double quots become single quots 1827–*
88 Tribe] tribe *MS. 1832/36–*
89 Tents] tents *1832–*   Tree] tree *MS. 1832/36–*
91 Wood] wood *MS. 1832/36*
92 Tabby's] tabby's *MS. 1832/36–*
94 Village . . . Show] village . . . show *MS. 1832/36–*
96 overheard;] overheard— *1832* overheard, *MS. 1832/36–*
97 pourtrayed] portrayed *1832–*
98 Boor . . . Burgher] boor . . . burgher *MS. 1832/36–*
103 Guardian] guardian *MS. 1832/36–*
105 wisdom:] wisdom; *1832–*
106 indirect] indirect, *1820E–*
107 Traveller] traveller *MS. 1832/36–*
108 ease.] ease: *1832–*
110 Pair] pair *MS. 1832/36–*
112 A] "A *1832*
115 irregular; . . . wild:] irregular, . . . wild; *1827–*
119 day:] day; *1832–*
122 Champions] champions *MS. 1832/36–*   bowl;] bowl;— *1836* bowl; *pencil MS. 1836/45, 1840–*
124 Visitant,] Visitant; *1820E, 1827* visitant, *MS. 1832/36–*
125 Squire] 'squire *MS. 1832/36–*
126 Duke . . . Earl] duke . . . earl *MS. 1832/36–*
129 With] "With *1832*   Comrades] comrades *MS. 1832/36–*
138 unthought of] unthought-of *1832–*   Patron] patron *MS. 1832/36–*
139 Cottage] cottage *MS. 1832/36–*   home:] home; *1827–*
140 without] without, *1827–*
141 scantily-provided] scantily provided *1820E, 1832; see verbals*
143 Chapel . . . House] chapel . . . house *MS. 1832/36; see verbals*
145 —Yet] Yet *with para MS. 1832/36– but no para 1836–*   whate'er] what'er *1832*
150 Preacher . . . Poor] preacher . . . poor *MS. 1832/36–*
151 zeal] zeal, *1820E–*
152 Yet] Yet, *1827–*   was] was, *1820E–*
153 distressed] distrest *1827–*
154 compelled,] compelled *1827–*

159 fields,—] fields, *MS. 1832/36–*
162 sate] sat *1836–* Mate] mate *MS. 1832/36*
163 Children,] children *MS. 1832/36*
166 hand,] hand— *1827, 1832* hand;— *1836–*
168 Benefice] benefice *MS. 1832/36–*
169 Their's . . . their's] Theirs . . . theirs *1827–*
170 door.—] door. *MS. 1832/36–* So *para MS. 1832/36–*
171 House] house *MS. 1832/36–*
178 Abode] abode *MS. 1832/36–*
181 There,] There *1827– but* Their *1850*
182 mountain-plants] mountain plants *1832–*
184 braided,] braided; *1836–*
186 doors.] doors; *1827– but* doors: *MS. 1832/36*
187 carpet,] carpet *1836–1843*
home-spun] homespun *1832–*
wool,] wool *1836–*
190 mountain stone] mountain-stone *1836–*
192 home-steads] homesteads *1832–*
193 *para MS. 1832/36–* Housewife's] housewife's *MS. 1832/36*
194 Meanwhile,] Meanwhile *1832–*
Master's] master's *MS. 1832/36*
195 task,] task— *1827–*
199 Valley] valley *MS. 1832/36–*
201 Cottage] cottage *MS. 1832/36–*
202 Screened] Screen'd *1832–*
206 Nature's] nature's *MS. 1832/36–*
207 Tenement] tenement *1836–*
208 Master's] master's *MS. 1832/36*
210 *para MS. 1832/36–*
216 hold,] hold— *1836–*
217 indignation; still] indignation. Still *MS. 1832/36–*
219 Friends] friends *MS. 1832/36–*
225 good will] good-will *1832* good-will, *1836–*
226 Consort] *illeg rev eras MS. 1832/36* consort *1836–*
228 mildness] mildnesss *1836–1843, 1846*
231 —Him . . . Sun] Him . . . sun *MS. 1832/36–*
234 light.] light; *1827–*
235 —She] She *1827–* Cloud] cloud *MS. 1832/36–*
240 Pair, . . . say] pair, . . . say, *1836–*
259 Bride . . . cares] Bride, . . . cares, *1820E; see verbals*
261 Our] "Our *1832*
262 Patriarch] patriarch *MS. 1832/36–* Vale] vale *MS. 1832/36*
263 Death] death *MS. 1832/36–*
265 Abode] abode *MS. 1832/36–*
266 disappeared:—] disappeared: *1827–*
267 fields,—] fields; *1827–*
268 Peaks] peaks *MS. 1832/36–*
snow,—] snow, *1827–*
269 closed] closed, *1827–*
270 House] house *MS. 1832/36–*
271 plague: yet] plague. Yet *MS. 1832/36–*
274 —A] A *MS. 1832/36–*
275 perfect,—] perfect— *1832* perfect, *MS. 1832/36–*
277 Sire] sire *MS. 1832/36*
278 last,—] last, *MS. 1832/36–*
279 Partner . . . Son] partner . . . son *MS. 1832/36*
280 Daughter] daughter *MS. 1832/36*
281 Grandchild] grandchild *MS. 1832/36*
282–296 *double quots become single quots 1827–*
282 "All] "'All *1832* 'All *1836–*
285 conjectures,] conjectures— *1827–*
293 Gardener, Builder, Mechanist] gardener, builder, mechanist *MS. 1832/36–*
294 Planter . . . Seed] planter . . . seed *MS. 1832/36–*
295 Man] man *MS. 1832/36–*
305 noon-tide] noontide *1832–*
306 Mother Earth] mother earth *1836–*
308 Family] family *1832–*
309 privilege,] privilege *1832–*
316 depressed] deprest *1827–*
318 broke;] broke: *1827* broke:— *1832–*
321 Transplanted,] Transplanted *1827–* Hermit] hermit *MS. 1832/36–*
322 desart] desert *1827–*
323 prayer,] prayer *1840– but* prayer, *1841, 1841E*
325 his] his *MS. 1832/36 his 1836–*
compared!] compared, *1820E–*
327 anguish,—] anguish; *MS. 1832/36–*
329 him.—] him. *MS. 1832/36–* Far *para MS. 1832/36–*
334 Vale] vale *MS. 1832/36–*
336 nature] Nature *MS. 1814/27–1832*
338 Reason,—] Reason— *1832* reason— *MS. 1832/36* reason, *1836–*
342 shown] shewn *1827*
356 Dwelling] dwelling, *1820E–*
357 Labourer] labourer *MS. 1832/36–*
360 "This] This *1827–* Portraiture is sketched.—The Great, the Good] portraiture is sketched.—The great, the good *MS. 1832/36– but* sketched.—] sketched. *1836–*
361 beloved] belov'd *MS. 1814/27*
Well-beloved . . . Fortunate . . . Wise,]

well-beloved . . . fortunate . . . wise, *MS. 1832/36– but* wise,— *1836–*
362 Titles Emperors and Chiefs] titles emperors and chiefs *MS. 1832/36–*
363 Him] him *MS. 1832/36–* Wonderful] WONDERFUL *1827–*
364 Shepherds] shepherds *MS. 1832/36–*
365 Abode] abode *MS. 1832/36–*
366 dependant] dependent *1827–* Chapelry,] chapelry, *MS. 1832/36–1843* chapelry *1845–*
368 embraced,—] embraced, *MS. 1832/36–*
371 Stone] stone *MS. 1832/36–*
375 slowly-gathering] slowly gathering *1827–1843*
379 dissolves.] dissolves." *1845–*
380 —Noise] Noise *para MS. 1832/36–1843* "Noise *1845– ; see verbals* war—] war, *1820E–*
381 Poet . . . forth] poet . . . forth, *1820E–*
387 Minstrel] minstrel *MS. 1832/36–*
393 Man's] man's *MS. 1832/36–*
395 end?] end *1836–1843* end— *MS. 1836/45* end; *1845–*
396 Virtue] virtue *MS. 1832/36–*
397 fancy's] Fancy's *1820E–1832*
400 Piety] piety *MS. 1832/36–*
401 Men] men *MS. 1832/36–*
403 inspired.] inspired? *1836–*
405 heaven] Heaven *1832*
411 paid] paid, *1820E–*
413 Pine] pine *1836–*
415 tow'rds] toward *MS. 1832/36–*
416 green sward;] greensward; *1827–*
417 Stone,] stone *MS. 1832/36–*
421 mountain Valley] mountain valley *MS. 1832/36–1843* mountain-valley *1845–*
437 Ascended] Ascended, *pencil MS. 1836/45, 1840–*
442 not;] not: *MS. 1832/36–*
445 *para MS. 1832/36–* Brother] brother *MS. 1832/36–*
449 Parents] parents *MS. 1832/36–*
451 love] love, *1836–*
452 family,] family; *1836–*
456 Brother's house,] brother's house; *MS. 1832/36–*
457 tire,—] tire; *1836–* tire: *1846 (probable worn plate)*
458 the] he *1820E (type for initial "t" has dropped out)*
468 holy] Holy *1827, 1832*
477 manners:—] manners: *MS. 1832/36–*
480 At] "At *1832*
482 nature;] nature: *1820E–*
484 Cottage] cottage *MS. 1832/36–*
489 Stone] stone *MS. 1832/36–*
494 Pine-tree] pine-tree *MS. 1832/36–*
499 Soul-cheering] "Soul-cheering *1832* Things] things *MS. 1832/36–*
500 Comforter] comforter *MS. 1832/36–*
503 Him] him *MS. 1832/36–*
504 Porch] porch *MS. 1832/36–*
507 determined] determined, *MS. 1832/36–*
509 One] one *MS. 1832/36–*
510 Towards] Toward *1832; see verbals*
511 steps;] steps, *pencil MS. 1836/45, 1840–*
512 ear,] ear; *pencil MS. 1836/45, 1840–*
514 Man] man *MS. 1832/36–*
515 gulph] gulf *1827–*
523 Heaven] heaven *MS. 1832/36–*
544 truth,] truth; *1827–*
546 Death] death *MS. 1832/36–*
549 thought, . . . times,] thought . . . times *MS. 1836/45*
552 holiest] holiest, *1827–*
557 pourtrayed] portrayed *1832–*
558 That . . . sate] That, . . . sate, *1832–*
559 Team] team *MS. 1832/36–*
564 Oak] oak *MS. 1832/36–*
565 bier!—] bier;— *1820E, 1827* bier— *1832–*
567 Peasant] peasant *MS. 1832/36–*
570 Winter] winter *MS. 1832/36–*
573 spake,] spake; *1820E–*
574 —"A] "A *MS. 1832/36–*
575 to-morrows,—] to-morrows; *MS. 1832/36–*
576 worldly-minded;] worldly-minded, *1832–*
578 hope] Hope *1820E*
587 vigor,] vigour *1827–*
590 Domain] domain *MS. 1832/36–*
592 Lord] lord *MS. 1832/36–*
593 Creature] creature *1820E–* —Yet . . . rational—] Yet . . . rational, *MS. 1832/36–*
594 Sabbath] sabbath *MS. 1832/36–*
595 christian] Christian *1827, 1832* ear,] ear; *1827–*
597 him] him, *1827–*
599 chearfulness] cheerfulness *1827–*
604 This] "This *1832 indented but no vertical space 1832, 1836; vertical space restored MS. 1836/45, 1840–* Old] old *MS. 1832/36–*
605 truth"] truth," *1827–*
608 Towards] Tow'rds *1827, 1832* One] one *MS. 1832/36–*
613 ash-tree] ash-tree, *MS. 1832/36–*
614 pendant] pendent *1827–*
620 ship] Ship *1820E–1832*
621 Morecamb bay] Morecamb Bay *1827, 1832* Morecamb-bay *MS. 1832/36–*

629 enterprize] enterprise 1827–
634 forgot;] forgot— 1836–
635 Sycamore] sycamore MS. 1832/36–
639 fleece-incumbered] fleece-encumbered 1832– flock;—] flock— 1836– ELM] ELM, 1827–
640 May;—] May— 1836–
641 OAK;—] OAK— 1836–
642 He] he MS. 1832/36– fate.] fate; 1827–
646 custom] custom, 1820E; *see verbals*
647 all!] all. 1827–
648 —But] But 1836– is] is, 1827–
655 Now] "Now 1832 again;] again. 1820E again: 1827–
656 thoughts;—] thoughts; 1827–
658 long.] long! 1827–
660 and] and, 1832–
662 whole!] whole; 1827–
665 Mother's Soul] mother's soul MS. 1832/36–
666 stricken,] stricken 1836–
668 Child . . . born,—] child . . . born; MS. 1832/36–
669 conscious . . . rest] conscious, . . . rest, 1827–
671 —The] "The *indented as para but no extra vertical space* 1832 The MS. 1832/36– *but para with extra vertical space* 1836– Him] him MS. 1832/36–
679 Girl] girl MS. 1832/36–
680 hand.] hand, 1820E
681 Brothers] brothers MS. 1832/36–
684 Grand-sire] Grandsire 1827, 1832 grandsire MS. 1832/36–
690 Sabbath] sabbath MS. 1832/36–
692 Babe] babe MS. 1832/36–
693 Infant's] infant's MS. 1832/36–
694 Name . . . Wife] name . . . wife MS. 1832/36–
696–697 *single quots* 1827–
698 —Oh!] Oh! *para* MS. 1832/36–
699 unlooked for;—] unlooked-for; MS. 1832/36–
701 Child] child MS. 1832/36
708 whence—] whence, 1836–
709 Household] household MS. 1832/36–
720 On] "On 1832; *see verbals*
721 sound,] sound; 1836–
723 Grave] grave MS. 1832/36–
724 mold] mould 1827–
725 Rains] rains MS. 1832/36–
726 Sun . . . Midsummer] sun . . . midsummer MS. 1832/36–
730 Youth!] Youth, 1827– beloved,] beloved 1832
738 disappear.] disappear! 1827–; *see verbals*
739 berries] berries, 1827–
742 brook side] brook-side 1836–
743 adorn,—] adorn? MS. 1814/27 adorn;— 1827, 1832 adorn: MS. 1832/36–
745 Vale] vale MS. 1832/36–
750 nature's] Nature's 1820E–1832
751 Bards] bards 1836–
752 Gods] gods 1836–
753 form;] form: 1836–
754 shade,] shade 1840–
756 Mortals,] Mortals 1827, 1832 mortals MS. 1832/36–
760 Scholar's] scholar's MS. 1832/36–
762 Hero] hero MS. 1832/36–
763 coit] quoit 1845–
764 him] him, 1827–
766 Lark's] lark's 1827– rain-bow] rainbow 1827– *but misprint* rainboy 1850
768 Fox] fox 1827–
769 chace] chase 1827–
771 Eagle,] eagle, 1827– eagle, *rev to* eagle; MS. 1836/45
772 loved;] loved: 1832–
778 seat—] seat, *pencil* MS. 1814/27–
779 aim.] aim, MS. 1832/36–
782 Forces] forces MS. 1832/36–
783 plains] plains, 1832– shores] shores, 1827–
784 Arms] arms MS. 1832/36–
786 Shepherd's] shepherd's MS. 1832/36–
787 fields.] fields 1827
788 attire] attire, 1827–
791 Flower and Choice] flower and choice MS. 1832/36–
794 Chief] chief MS. 1832/36–
795 Comrade] comrade MS. 1832/36–
799 youths] Youths MS. 1814/27– labour] labour, 1827–
804 Oft] "Oft 1832
805 grass . . . shade] grass, . . . shade, 1836–
806 Fellows . . . Map] fellows . . . map MS. 1832/36–
808 Teacher] teacher MS. 1832/36–
809–825 *double quots become single quots* 1827–
809 way] way, MS. 1832/36–
810 the] The 1845, 1850 Stream] stream MS. 1832/36–
811 tow'rds] tow'rd MS. 1814/27–1832 toward 1836–
812 realm;—] realm; 1836–
813 shews] shows 1832–
814 "Bespotted] 'Bespotted— MS. 1832/36– isles.] isles: 1832–
816 —Thence—] Thence, MS. 1832/36–
817 fears] fears, *pencil* MS. 1836/45, 1840–

820 Fields] fields *MS. 1832/36–*
821 Sons] sons *MS. 1832/36–*
823 Land;] land, *MS. 1832/36–*
827 Patriot] patriot *MS. 1832/36–*
828 Peasantry] peasantry *MS. 1832/36–*
829 rights,—] rights— *MS. 1832/36–*
830 Ah] Ah, *1827–*
837 soul-enflamed] soul-inflamed *1832–*
838 Idolatry] idolatry *1820E–*
844 Awakener] awakener *MS. 1832/36–*
845 Founder] founder *MS. 1832/36–* deeds,] deeds; *1836–*
846 And] And, *1836–* Nations] nations *1820E–* straits] straits, *1836–*
847 Donor] donor *MS. 1832/36–*
851 recompence] recompense *1827–*
854 said,] said: *1836–* served;] served: *1840– (probable worn plate) but* served; *1845, 1850*
855 forked] forkèd *1827–*
856 Holds] holds *MS. 1832/36–*
860 Wrong . . . Sufferer] wrong . . . sufferer *MS. 1832/36–*
861 Seats] seats *1827, 1832; see verbals*
863 Pagan] pagan *1832–* Temples] temples *MS. 1832/36–*
866 Cedars] cedars *MS. 1832/36–*
867 sun.—] sun. *MS. 1832/36–* But *para 1836–*
868 "all . . . all,"] 'all . . . all,' *1827–*
869 Grave] grave *MS. 1832/36–* demands;] demands, *1832–*
870 Champion . . . Cause] champion . . . cause *MS. 1832/36–*
872 Country] country *MS. 1832/36–* shewed] showed *1832–*
873 Son] son *MS. 1832/36–*
876 appeared,] appeared *1836–*
877 him,] him *1827–* stand] stand, *1827* eyes] eyes, *1827–*
881 One] "One *1832* day,] day— *1827–*
883 chace;] chase— *1827–*
885 horn:] horn; *1820E–*
896 —To] To *1836–* Comrades] comrades *MS. 1832/36–*
897 Soldier's] soldier's *MS. 1832/36–*
898 blue,] blue— *1827–*
900 Stranger] stranger *MS. 1832/36–*
903 Spectacle] spectacle *MS. 1832/36–*
904 pallid,—] pallid: *MS. 1832/36–*
905 tears—] tears, *1832–* few] few, *pencil MS. 1836/45, 1840–*
906 Dwellings] dwellings *MS. 1832/36–*
909 announced] announced, *1836–*
910 air] air, *1836–*
916 Enwrapt,—] Enrapt,— *1827, 1832* Enrapt, *1836–*
918 soul] Soul *1827–* Land] land *MS. 1832/36–*
919 spirit] Spirit *1827–*
922 Descending;] Descending, *1832–*
925 aside,] aside; *1836–*
929 spleen,] spleen *1836–*
930 Man] man *MS. 1832/36–*
932 self-abuse,] self-abuse *1832–*
933 tow'rds] tow'rd *1827, 1832* toward *1836–*
935 Stone] stone *MS. 1832/36–*
936 Form] form *MS. 1832/36–* wall] wall, *1820E–*
938 Pile:] pile; *MS. 1832/36–*
939 Nature] nature *MS. 1832/36–*
940 rock;] rock— *1827–*
943 Exclaimed,] Exclaimed— *MS. 1832/36–* "The *para 1836–* Antiquarian's] antiquarian's *MS. 1832/36*
947 War-horse] war-horse *1832–*
948 Vale] vale *MS. 1832/36–*
950 Stranger] stranger *MS. 1832/36–*
952 that,] that *1836–*
955 Realm . . . Vale] realm . . . vale *MS. 1832/36–*
957 Image] image *MS. 1832/36–* which,] which *1832*
960 world—] world, *MS. 1832/36–*
962 Fancy] fancy *MS. 1832/36–*
963 —Vague] Vague *para MS. 1832/36–*
965 Retreat] retreat *MS. 1832/36–*
975 Mansion] mansion *MS. 1832/36–*
977 Homesteads] homesteads *MS. 1832/36–* dwelt,] dwelt; *1832–*
978 And] And, *1820E–* Mansion] Mansion, *1820E–1832* mansion, *MS. 1832/36–* Children] children *MS. 1832/36–*
979 Kindred . . . Tree] kindred . . . tree *MS. 1832/36–*
980 House] house *MS. 1832/36–*
981 improvidence,] improvidence *1827–*
984 Hall] hall *MS. 1832/36–*
986 Foundation] foundation *MS. 1832/36–*
988 Stone] stone *MS. 1832/36–*
991 Lodge] lodge *1832–*
993 Sir Alfred Irthing] Sir Alfred Irthing *1827– (underlined with "BL" in pencil in margin MS. 1814/27)*
995 posy—] posy, *MS. 1832/36–*
1000 World] world *MS. 1832/36–*
1002 Kings] kings *MS. 1832/36–*
1003 Princes] Princes, *1827–* Emperors] emperors *MS. 1832/36–*
1004 Mighty] mighty *MS. 1832/36–*
1005 Innocence] innocence *MS. 1832/36–*
1006 Man] man *MS. 1832/36–*
1007 Line] line *MS. 1832/36–*

1010 Ranks,] ranks, *1836–* ranks *MS. 1832/36*
1011 Orders] orders *1836–*
1017 overthrow;] overthrow: *1836–*
1019 Nature's] nature's *MS. 1832/36–*
1022 nature] Nature *1827, 1832*
1023 members,] members *1827–*
1026 Whole] whole *MS. 1832/36–*
1028 Yet] Yet, *1827–*
1030 —The] The *para MS. 1832/36–* interred,] interred *1831*
1032 men;] men, *1849 (probable worn plate)*
1033 alteration,] alteration *1836–*
1035 lot,] lot— *1832–*
1036 —To] To *1832–* mid] 'mid *1820E–* Clouds,] clouds *MS. 1832/36–*
1039 He,] He *1827–* Order] order *MS. 1832/36–*
1041 War] war *MS. 1832/36–*
1042 changed] changed, *1827–*
1044 Commotion] commotion *MS. 1832/36–*
1045 town, . . . city,] town . . . city *1836–*
1046 Cross . . . Church] cross . . . church *MS. 1832/36–*
1047 House—Pile . . . Pile] house—pile . . . pile *MS. 1832/36–*
1048 Tenants] tenants *MS. 1832/36–*
1049 Beasts] beasts *MS. 1832/36–*
1056 Mutability, . . . Hopes] mutability, . . . Hopes *MS. 1832/36* mutability; . . . hopes *1836–*
1058 soul,] soul *1832–*
1059 Virtues] virtues *1836–*
1060 Nations] nations *1836–*
1063 —Even] Even *para MS. 1832/36–*
1067 If] (If *1832–*
1069 lofty,] lofty) *1832–*
1071 Youth] youth *MS. 1832/36–*
1075 Records] records *MS. 1832/36–*
1077 Affliction] affliction *MS. 1832/36–*

Book VIII

1 Vale] vale *MS. 1832/36–*
2 own] own, *1820E– but* own. *1849 (probable worn plate)*
4 notice] notice, *1820E–* said,] said:— *MS. 1832/36–*
5 Ye] ye *1836–*
8 And,] And *1850*
10 Death, Eternity] death, eternity *MS. 1832/36–*
11 Seraph's] seraph's *1836–*
14 Forms] forms *1820E–*
15 Spot] spot *MS. 1832/36–*
16 themselves, at once,] themselves at once *1820E–* Men's] men's *MS. 1832/36–* view:] view *1841, 1843 (probable worn plate)*
18 Individual] individual *1836–*
20 Place] place *1820E–* afforded] afforded, *MS. 1832/36–*
27 this—] this, *1820E–*
28 Spectator] spectator *MS. 1832/36–* a while] awhile *1832–*
29 Exhibitor] exhibitor *MS. 1832/36–*
31 Dwelling] dwelling *MS. 1832/36–*
35 spake;] spake: *MS. 1832/36– but* spake; *1845, 1850*
36 Remains] remains *MS. 1832/36–*
39 One] one *MS. 1832/36–*
42 Vocation] vocation *MS. 1832/36–*
44 Brotherhood] brotherhood *MS. 1832/36–*
45 and] and— *MS. 1814/27* and, *MS. 1832/36–* known,] known— *MS. 1814/27*
46 —Yet . . . Estates] Yet . . . estates *with para 1836–*
47 Those] those *MS. 1832/36–*
48 Wanderers] wanderers *MS. 1832/36–* These] these *1832–*
50 Nature's] nature's *MS. 1832/36–*
51 recompence] recompense *1827–*
53 procured! Yet] procured, yet *1827–*
54 Intelligent] intelligent *MS. 1832/36–*
55 be,] be *MS. 1832/36–*
56 observe;] observe, *1827–*
59 self,] self *MS. 1832/36–*
60 Men,] Men *1827, 1832* men *MS. 1832/36–*
63 Nature's] nature's *MS. 1832/36–*
70 Arts] arts *MS. 1832/36–*
76 Mother's] mother's *MS. 1832/36–*
77 Lover's] lover's *MS. 1832/36–*
78 long tried] long-tried *1827–* Friends] friends *MS. 1832/36–*
79 Men] men *MS. 1832/36–*
81 and] and, *1820E; see verbals* Wilds] Wilds, *1820E–1832* wilds, *MS. 1832/36–*
83 Chivalry] chivalry *MS. 1832/36–*
84 They] they *1827–*
87 gone;] gone. *1836–*
92 Creation] creation *MS. 1832/36–*
93 Land,] Land *rev to* land *rev to* Land *MS. 1832/36* Land *1836–*
94 Enginery] enginery *MS. 1832/36–*
96 War] war *MS. 1832/36–*
98 One] one *1827–*
100 Pedestrian] pedestrian *MS. 1832/36–*
101 Wished for . . . came,] Wished-for . . . came— *MS. 1832/36–*
102 Tenantry . . . Thorpe . . . Vill] tenantry . . . thorpe . . . vill *MS. 1832/36–*
103 Burgh] burgh *MS. 1832/36–*

105 Castle] castle *MS. 1832/36–*
111 vanished,—] vanished— *MS. 1832/36–*
113 Glens] glens *MS. 1832/36–*
114 Sail] sail *MS. 1832/36–*
116 dale,] dale; *MS. 1832/36–*
118 *para MS. 1832/36–*
120 Hamlet] hamlet *MS. 1832/36–*
121 Town] town *MS. 1832/36–*
123 Habitation] habitation *MS. 1832/36–*
125 forests—] forests,— *1832–*
129 Traveller] traveller *MS. 1832/36–*
133 Arts] arts *1836–*
134 Sea . . . Shores] sea . . . shores *MS. 1832/36–*
135 Ships] ships *MS. 1832/36–*
138 Keels] keels *MS. 1832/36–*
140 Sails] sails *MS. 1832/36–*
141 Which] Which, *1827, 1832; see verbals*
144 Power] power *1836–*
145 Thunder,] Thunder *1827, 1832* thunder *MS. 1832/36–*
148 Impregnable,] Impregnable *1827–* Liberty . . . Peace.] liberty . . . peace *MS. 1832/36*
149 And] "And *1832* Flock] flock *MS. 1832/36–*
150 and] and, *1827–*
151 heaven's] Heaven's *1820E–* providence] providence, *1827–*
152 You] you *MS. 1832/36–*
153 behold,] behold *1832–*
155 Nature] nature *1836–*
156 Power] power *1836–*
157 Yea . . . rights] Yea, . . . rights, *1827–*
163 undisturbed,] undisturbed; *1827–*
166 Lord] lord *MS. 1832/36–*
169 light,] light *1832–*
170 Labour's] labour's *1836–1843* eyes,] eyes *pencil MS. 1836/45, 1840–*
171 Fabric] fabric *MS. 1832/36–*
172 Bell is heard—] bell is heard, *1832–*
173 Curfew-knoll] curfew-knoll *MS. 1832/36–*
174 behest,] behest— *1820E–*
176 Ministers] ministers *MS. 1832/36–*
177 Pile] pile *MS. 1832/36–*
178 Band] band *MS. 1832/36–* door,—] door— *1827–*
179 Courts . . . Stream] courts . . . stream *MS. 1832/36–*
181 Spirit] spirit *MS. 1832/36–*
182 Maidens, Youths] maidens, youths *MS. 1832/36–*
183 Children, Boys and Girls] children, boys and girls *MS. 1832/36–*
185 Temple—] Temple, *1832* temple, *MS. 1832/36–*
186 Gain— . . . Idol] Gain, . . . idol *MS. 1832/36–* Master] master *1827–* Realm,] Realm— *1832* realm, *MS. 1832/36–*
188 Ancestors] ancestors *MS. 1832/36–*
189 Cathedral or Conventual Church] cathedral or conventual church *MS. 1832/36–*
193 Men] men *MS. 1832/36–*
194 Reason] reason *MS. 1832/36–*
197 Service] service *MS. 1832/36–*
198 Triumph] "Triumph *1832*
199 We] we *MS. 1832/36–*
201 complacency;] complacency:— *MS. 1832/36–*
203 Intellectual] intellectual *MS. 1832/36–*
204 Elements] elements *MS. 1832/36–*
206 Matter] matter *1836–*
207 powers,] powers *1845–*
208 Mind] mind *MS. 1832/36–1843* mind, *1845–*
209 Will] will *1832–*
212 When] When, *1832–*
213 Nature] nature *MS. 1832/36–*
215 Country's] country's *MS. 1832/36–*
218 Moral] moral *1827–* Thebes;] Thebes, *1832–*
219 Tyre] Tyre, *1836–* waves;] waves, *1832–*
220 Desart] Desert *1827, 1832* desert *MS. 1832/36–*
222 Tomb] tomb *MS. 1832/36–*
226 Philosophy,] philosophy, *MS. 1832/36* Philosophy *1836–*
227 instruments:—] instruments;— *1832–*
228 Arts . . . Inventions] arts . . . inventions *MS. 1832/36–*
229 Virtue] virtue *MS. 1832/36–* He] He, *1845–*
234 Arts] arts *MS. 1832/37*
238 land] Land *MS. 1832/36*
240 estate.] estate? *1827–*
245 Country-life] country-life *MS. 1832/36–*
246 Mind] mind *MS. 1832/36–*
248 Sabbath] sabbath *MS. 1832/36–*
250 Almighty] almighty *MS. 1832/36–* Law-giver] Lawgiver *1832–*
256 Retreats] retreats *MS. 1832/36–*
259 Brook] brook *MS. 1832/36–*
260 Instrument] instrument *MS. 1832/36–*
262 Sires] sires *MS. 1832/36–*
264 bliss,] bliss *1836–*
266 Man's] man's *MS. 1832/36*
268 Habitations] habitations *MS. 1832/36–*
269 Mother] mother *MS. 1832/36*
278 —The] The *para MS. 1832/36–*

280 Sons] sons *MS. 1832/36*
283 'Till] Till *1827*
284 birth-right] birthright *1827–*
287 Mother] mother *1836–*
288 Sons?] sons *MS. 1832/36–*
289 Necessity] necessity *MS. 1832/36–*
290 Nature] nature *MS. 1832/36–*
292 infant] Infant *1820E–1832* infant *MS. 1832/36–*
293 decay?] decay! *MS. 1814/27–*
297 depressed;] depressed, *1827* deprest, *1832–*
299 —Oh] —Oh *para MS. 1832/36* Oh *para MS. 1832/36–* Wisdom] wisdom *1820E–*
301 deep,] deep; *1836–*
303 Slave] slave *MS. 1832/36–*
304 Boy] boy *MS. 1832/36–*
306 clouds] clouds, *MS. 1832/36–*
311 whitened] whiten'd *1820E* cotton flakes,] cotton-flakes *MS. 1832/36–*
313 cowering— . . . pale—] cowering, . . . pale, *MS. 1832/36–*
322 Sublime—] Sublime *MS. 1832/36–*
323 increase;] increase, *1832* but,] but *1827– ; see verbals*
324 ever, this] ever. This *MS. 1814/27* ever; this *1827, 1832; see verbals ll. 324–326*
325 heaven's] Heaven's *1820E; see verbals*
328 Touch] touch *MS. 1832/36–*
329 Will] will *MS. 1832/36–*
337 him,"] him!" *1827–*
341 not,] not *MS. 1836/45* Arts] arts *MS. 1832/36–*
342 Structures] structures *1832–*
353 growth] growth, *MS. 1832/36, 1836*
357 Naked] Naked, *1832–*
359 Trees] trees *MS. 1832/36–*
360 Earth . . . Mother] earth . . . mother *MS. 1832/36– but* earth, *1836–*
362 dismay,] dismay; *1836–*
363 Supplicants] supplicants *MS. 1832/36–*
366 Parents] parents *MS. 1832/36–*
368 mouth, . . . rocks,] mouth . . . rocks; *MS. 1832/36–*
370 Ancestors] ancestors *MS. 1832/36–*
373 ground,] ground *1836–*
374 Purloined] Purloined, *MS. 1814/27–*
376 mid] 'mid *1820E–*
378 —Such] Such *para MS. 1832/36* Such *no para 1836–*
380 dreary] drearv *1840 (worn plate)*
384 head] head, *1832–* Tumblers . . . Stage] tumblers . . . stage *MS. 1832/36–*
386 Passengers] passengers *MS. 1832/36–*
389 Pursuivants] pursuivants *MS. 1832/36–*
390 tires,—] tires— *1827–*
392 Vagrants] vagrants *MS. 1832/36–* Gypsy] Gipsy *1827, 1832* gipsy *MS. 1832/36–*
394 Turn *para 1836–*
402 "Is] 'Is *MS. 1814/27–* Plough-boy] plough-boy *MS. 1832/36–*
403 air?"] air!' *MS. 1814/27, 1836–* air!" *1832*
404 "Forgive me!] Forgive me *MS. 1814/27–*
406 frame:— His] frame. His *MS. 1832/36; see verbals*
407 frock] frock, *1827–*
408 churl] Churl *1827, 1832*
410 stools,] stools *1827–*
411 Fathers] fathers *MS. 1832/36–*
413 eyes, . . . stare;] eyes— . . . stare— *1836–*
414 strange;] strange— *1840–*
417 infant conning] infant-conning *1836–*
418 Primer] primer *MS. 1832/36–*
425 Town] town *MS. 1832/36–*
426 City] city *MS. 1832/36–*
428 rouzed] roused *1820E– ; see verbals*
429 hoe,] hoe— *1827, 1832; see verbals*
430 Carter's] carter's *MS. 1832/36–*
432 Country's] country's *1836–*
433 schools,] schools— *1827–*
436 mind] *mind MS. 1832/36–*
445 Path] path *MS. 1832/36–*
446 Hedge] hedge *1832–*
447 boughs,] boughs *MS. 1832/36–*
451 grateful,] grateful *1820E– ; see verbals*
452 Not] —Not *1836–*
454 Walk;] walk: *MS. 1832/36–*
457 Vale] vale *MS. 1832/36–*
458 Fence] fence *MS. 1832/36–*
459 Pathway] pathway *MS. 1832/36–*
462 Mansion . . . House . . . Prayer] mansion . . . house . . . prayer *MS. 1832/36–*
463 Image] image *MS. 1832/36–* solemnity] solemnity, *1820E–*
464 fair] fair, *1820E–*
465 Mansion's . . . Pile] mansion's . . . pile *MS. 1832/36–*
468 noon-tide] noontide *1827–* Sun] sun *MS. 1832/36–*
469 Porch] porch *MS. 1832/36–*
471 cornice] cornice, *pencil MS. 1836/45, 1840–*
472 Dwelling] dwelling *MS. 1832/36–*
474 adorned.] adorned; *1827, 1832* adorned: *MS. 1832/36–*
486 red-breast] redbreast *1827–*
491 gothic] Gothic *1820E–*

493 Image . . . Patron Saint] image . . . patron-saint, MS. 1832/36–
494 blessed] Blessed 1827, 1832 blessed MS. 1832/36–
496 garden mount] garden Mount 1827, 1832 garden-mount MS. 1832/36–
499 recognized . . . Friend] recognised . . . friend MS. 1832/36–
501 request,] request; 1827–
503 Old] old MS. 1832/36–
508 port;] port: 1820E– ; *see verbals*
509 Time] time MS. 1832/36–
513 Ship] ship MS. 1832/36–
525 pleasure.] pleasure.— 1836–
532 prescribed.] prescribed 1827 *(type of period has probably dropped out)*
535 days.] days; 1827–
536 conversation] conversation, 1827, 1832
540 skill] skill, 1820E–
541 stedfast] steadfast 1820E– *but* stedfast 1845, 1850   'vantage ground] 'vantage-ground 1836–
542 gazed . . . unsuppressed] gazed, . . . unsuppressed, MS. 1832/36–
545 pèrspective] perspective 1820E pérspective 1832–
547 elegance—] elegance, MS. 1832/36–
548 Mansion] mansion MS. 1832/36–
554 Appeared,—] Appeared— 1827, 1832 Appeared, MS. 1832/36–
555 Brothers] brothers MS. 1832/36–
556 Companions] companions MS. 1832/36–
563 tow'rds] towards 1820E; *see verbals*
571 Board] board MS. 1832/36–
577 Comrade] comrade MS. 1832/36–   pride.] pride; 1832 pride: 1836–
578 Creatures] creatures MS. 1832/36–
580 Death] death 1836–
582 oh!] O, 1827–
583 Boys! Yea] boys! Yea MS. 1832/36 boys! yea 1836–
584 Narrator] narrator MS. 1832/36–
588 Brook] brook MS. 1832/36–
589 And,] And 1836–
591 reunited: . . . Compeer] re-united: . . . compeer MS. 1832/36–
592 Lake,] lake MS. 1832/36–
593 beautiful,] beautiful— 1836–
594 Girl] girl MS. 1832/36– *but* Girl 1845, 1850
599 Mind] mind MS. 1832/36–
602 broken-off.] broken off. 1832–   Boys] boys MS. 1832/36–
604 He—] He MS. 1832/36   (to] to 1836–
607 harp,—] harp, MS. 1832/36–
608 ceased)] ceased— 1836–   One] one MS. 1832/36
610 argument,—] argument— 1832–

Book IX

1 Being] being 1832–
3 principle] Principle MS. 1832/36–
5 natures,] natures; 1836–
15 Worlds] worlds MS. 1832/36–
16 Universe] universe MS. 1832/36–
19 respected,] repected, 1832 respected 1836–
21 this,] this 1820E–
24 light,] light 1836–
25 futurity,] futurity; 1836–
27 hour,] hour,— 1832 hour 1836–
29 —Those] Those 1832–
33 Youth] youth 1832–
34 Man] man MS. 1832/36–
35 Mid] 'Mid 1820E–
38 Childhood] childhood MS. 1832/36–
40 vigour—] vigour; MS. 1832/36–
43 ascends] ascends, 1836–
44 tow'rds] tow'rd 1827, 1832 toward 1836–
45 altar?—] altar? 1836–   Do *para* MS. 1832/36–
46 Good and Wise] good and wise MS. 1832/36–
52 presumptuously] presumptuously, 1827–
53 EMINENCE,] EMINENCE; 1836–
54 Point] point MS. 1832/36–
56 sovereignty— . . . power—] sovereignty; . . . power, MS. 1832/36–
57 —A] A 1832–   Throne] throne MS. 1832/36–
60 peaks] Peaks 1827, 1832 peaks MS. 1832/36–   Vale] vale 1827–
62 *caret eras after* dale *and comma in margin in pencil eras* MS. 1836/45
63 spread.] spread: 1827–
66 mind] Mind 1832–
69 River] river MS. 1832/36–
70 Ascending!—] Ascending! MS. 1832/36–
73 solitude] solitude, 1845–
74 ever-humming] ever humming 1820E   mid] 'mid 1820E–
76 ear;] ear: 1836–
78 Not . . . these,—] (Not . . . these,) MS. 1832/36–
82 And] "And 1832   Age] age MS. 1832/36–
83 removal] removal, 1836–
93 Plain] plain MS. 1832/36
94 But] "But 1832
95 Man] man MS. 1832/36
96 course,] course; 1836–

102 birth-right] birthright *1832–*
107 predominates,] predominates; *1836–*
109 Individual's] individual's *MS. 1832/36–* frame] frame, *1820E–*
111 Almighty] almighty *MS. 1832/36–*
114 Life] life *MS. 1832/36–*
115 Man] man *MS. 1832/36–*
117 Thing] thing *MS. 1832/36–*
121 Soul] soul *MS. 1832/36–*
140 Heart] heart *1836–*
143 sickness] sickness, *1820E–*
144 extinction.] extinction? *1832–*
149 rather] rather, *1832–*
152 Oppressor . . . Form] oppressor . . . form *MS. 1832/36–*
153 Soul] soul *MS. 1832/36–*
159 Arts] arts *MS. 1832/36–*
164 Boy] boy *MS. 1832/36*
165 Slave] slave *MS. 1832/36–*
166 Much] Much, *1820E–* much] much, *1836–*
170 hindrances] hinderances *1827–*
172 Sheep] sheep *1820E; see verbals*
173 Mid] 'Mid *1820E–* Bird] bird *MS. 1832/36–*
178 less] less, *1820E–*
181 Boy . . . Heirs] boy . . . heirs *MS. 1832/36–*
182 Vassals] vassals *MS. 1832/36–*
185 oppression;] oppression, *1836–1843, 1846*
186 name] name, *1827–*
190 Bondage] bondage *MS. 1832/36–*
192 far;] far;— *1836–*
193 Victims] victims *MS. 1832/36–*
194 Victims;] victims; *MS. 1832/36* victims— *1836–* wrongs] wrongs, *pencil MS. 1836/45, 1840–*
195 Women] Women, *1832* women, *MS. 1832/36–* Children] children *MS. 1832/36–* own] own, *1832–*
199 securer] securer, *1827–*
201 Lastly] Lastly, *1827– but* Lastly *1850*
208 Alas!] "Alas! *1832*
212 heaven,] heaven *MS. 1832/36–*
214 Ocean] ocean *MS. 1832/36–*
216 sense] sense, *1827–*
224 Reason,—] Reason, *1845–* tears;] tears, *1846*
225 will,] will; *MS. 1832/36–*
228 monstrous] monstrous, *MS. 1832/36–*
235 strange] stange *1832* he] He *1832–*
242 here;] here! *1836–*
243 high] high— *pencil MS. 1836/45, 1840–* low, . . . graced] low; . . . graced— *1836–*
245 Cottage hearth] cottage-hearth *MS. 1832/36–*
250 found,—] found; *MS. 1832/36–*
253 Man and Man] man and man *MS. 1832/36–*
254 But] "But *1832; see verbals*
255 Pair] pair *MS. 1832/36–*
257 lot!] lot. *1849 (probable worn plate)*
259 Prisoners] prisoners *MS. 1832/36–* Village school;] Village school: *1827, 1832* village-school: *MS. 1832/36–*
260 homes,] homes *1820E–*
261 vacancy,] vacancy; *MS. 1832/36–*
264 Power] power *1836–*
273 Child] child *MS. 1832/36–*
274 not, . . . Cottage-comrade] not . . . cottage-comrade *MS. 1832/36–*
276 fulfilled,] fulfilled; *MS. 1832/36–*
278 heaven] Heaven *1820E–*
279 Vale] vale *MS. 1832/36–*
283 time] time, *1827–*
288 shewn—] shown— *1832* shown, *MS. 1832/36–*
289 as] at *misprint 1832*
290 matter,] matter; *1845–*
291 exclaimed,] exclaimed— *MS. 1832/36–*
292 "Oh] "O *MS. 1814/27–* *para MS. 1832/36–*
294 Imperial] imperial *MS. 1832/36–*
298 Statute] statute *MS. 1832/36–*
299 Children] children *MS. 1832/36–*
300 Letters] letters *MS. 1832/36–*
302 understood,] understood *1836–*
304 unsustained,] unsustained; *1820E–*
308 Horde] horde *MS. 1832/36–* civilized] civilised *1845, 1850*
309 Band] band *MS. 1832/36–*
315 Boy—] Boy,— *1827, 1832* boy— *MS. 1832/36–*
324 Parents] parents *MS. 1832/36–*
328 mounts,] mounts *1827–*
329 Mother's] mother's *MS. 1832/36–*
332 good;] good— *1836–* which,] which *1832*
337 Look!] "Look! *1832*
339 Titles] titles *MS. 1832/36–*
340 overturned,—] overturned;— *1827, 1832* overturned; *MS. 1832/36–* Territory] territory *1836–* split;] split, 1827–
341 wind] wind, *1827–*
342 shapes,] shapes *1836–*
345 Meantime,] Meantime *1827–* Sovereignty] sovereignty *MS. 1832/36–*
346 indivisible;] indivisible: *1836–*
347 removed, *comma del in pencil then restored MS. 1836/45*
351 Bodies] bodies *MS. 1832/36–*

356 possessed,] possest, *MS. 1832/36* possest *1836–*
363 descend,] descend *1832, 1836* descend, *pencil MS. 1836/45, 1840–*
365 With] "With *1832*
370 Ye] ye *MS. 1832/36–*
376 abodes,] abodes— *1836–*
385 —"Yes] —Yes *1832* Yes *para MS. 1832/36–*
387 and,] and *1827–*
388 Frame] frame *MS. 1832/36–* effect] effect; *1836–*
389 'till] till *1827–* Rock] rock *MS. 1832/36–*
391 humanized] humanised *1845, 1850* Society] society *MS. 1832/36–*
394 Culture] culture *MS. 1832/36–*
395 born;] born, *1827–*
397 issues;] issues: *1836–*
398 Schools] schools *MS. 1832/36–*
399 Childhood's] childhood's *MS. 1832/36–*
401 Vast . . . Ye] —Vast . . . ye *MS. 1832/36–*
402 Lawgivers,] Lawgivers; *1827–*
403 voice,] voice *1827–*
404 Times] times *MS. 1832/36–*
406 Halls] halls *MS. 1832/36–*
409 Futurity] futurity *MS. 1832/36–*
411 destiny.—] destiny. *1836–*
412 Oppression] oppression *MS. 1832/36–*
413 darkness] darkness, *1827–*
414 conspicuous,] conspicuous *MS. 1832/36–*
415 act:] act; *1832–*
416 destruction] Destruction *1820E–1832*
417 Shew] Show *1832–* Nations] nations *MS. 1832/36–*
418 Powers . . . Polity] powers . . . polity *MS. 1832/36–* given!"] given." *1836–*
419 air] air, *1832–*
422 Behold,] Behold *1832–*
426 landscape] Landscape *1820E–1832* shines!—] shines! *MS. 1832/36–*
428 Lake's . . . Boat] lake's . . . boat *MS. 1832/36–*
429 tree."—] tree.— *1820E*
430 pleased—] pleased; *MS. 1832/36–*
431 Girl] girl *MS. 1832/36–* joy.] joy *1840, 1841, 1846 (possible worn plate)*
432 sun-beam] sunbeam *1827–*
434 Brother . . . Compeer] brother . . . compeer *MS. 1832/36–*
438 Company] company *MS. 1832/36–*
443 Image] image *MS. 1832/36–*
444 Ram] ram *MS. 1832/36–*
447 wreathed] wreathèd *1827–*
448 Creature] creature *MS. 1832/36–*
449 Counterpart] counterpart *MS. 1832/36–*
456 disturb,] disturb *1820E, 1827*
459 all,] all *1836–*
462 Old] old *MS. 1832/36–*
467 happiest] happiest, *MS. 1832/36–*
468 speaking] speaking, *1827–*
470 sigh] sigh, *1820E–*
471 bright,] bright *pencil MS. 1836/45, 1840–*
472 Pool] pool *MS. 1832/36– ; see verbals*
475 *para MS. 1832/36–* heard;] heard *1836–*
487 Youth] youth *1836* Youth *pencil MS. 1836/45, 1840–*
488 mid] 'mid *1820E–*
489 Comrades.—] comrades. *MS. 1832/36–* Now] Now, *1827, 1832; see verbals*
491 Boat] boat *MS. 1832/36–*
492 Hawk] hawk *MS. 1832/36–*
496 "yon] yon *1820E* "Yon *1832* Isle] isle *MS. 1832/36–*
499 shore,—] shore; *MS. 1832/36–*
500 Columns . . . Firs] columns . . . firs *MS. 1814/27–*
501 Dome] dome *MS. 1832/36–*
503 Temple] temple *MS. 1832/36–*
504 I, we] I, "we *1820E–*
505 Region] region *MS. 1832/36–*
507 bare—] bare, *MS. 1832/36–*
511 diversly] diversely *1820E–*
514 pourtrayed] portrayed *1832–*
528 gypsy fire] gipsy fire *1827, 1832* gipsy-fire *1836–*
529 there] there, *1827–*
532 —Launched] Lanched *1832* Launched *MS. 1832/36–* Lake] lake *1827–*
539 Lillies] Lilies *1820E–1832* lilies *MS. 1832/36–*
540 waves] waves, *1832–*
541 Plant] plant *MS. 1832/36–*
542 Lilly] Lily *1820E–1832* lily *MS. 1832/36–* Vale] vale *MS. 1832/36–*
544 beauty,] beauty; *1836–*
545 pastime] pastime, *1836–*
548 Spot] spot *MS. 1832/36–*
550 Fire] fire *1820E–*
551 now? . . . beach] now?— . . . beach— *MS. 1832/36–* Deserted] deserted *MS. 1832/36*
560 Lake] lake *MS. 1832/36–*
561 moves:] moves; *1836–*
562 behold— . . . peep—] behold, . . . peep, *MS. 1832/36–*

565 Browzed] Browsed *1827–* waterfalls.] waterfalls; *1836–*
566 Bark] bark *MS. 1832/36–*
570 —Alert] Alert *para MS. 1832/36–* led] led, *1827–*
573 meadows,] meadows *1827–*
574 lake—] lake, *MS. 1832/36–* seen! Far] seen:—far *MS. 1814/27–*
582 reclined—] reclined; *MS. 1832/36–; see verbals*
588 ne'er] never *MS. 1832/36–*
596 aloft—] aloft, *MS. 1832/36–*
600 fire—] fire; *MS. 1832/36–* poized,] poised, *1827, 1832* poised,— *MS. 1832/36–*
601 Forms] forms *MS. 1832/36–*
605 Fount] fount *MS. 1832/36–*
609 *no extra vertical space before para 1832*
611 spectacle—] spectacle, *MS. 1832/36–*
613 exclaimed—] exclaimed: *MS. 1832/36–*
615 thought] thought, *1827–*
616 Thou] thou *MS. 1832/36–*
617 Thyself] thyself *MS. 1832/36–*
619 local,] local *1832–*
620 splendors] splendours *1827–*
624 who] who— *1836–* breast] breast— *1836* breast *pencil MS. 1836/45, 1840–*
626 face,] face— *1836–*
627 Soul] soul *1820E–*
631 Throne . . . Earth] throne . . . earth *MS. 1832/36–*
633 dishonour—] dishonour, *MS. 1832/36–*
634 then,] then *1820E*
635 Or,] Or *1832–* if . . . decree] if, . . . decree, *1820E–*
639 law] Law *1820E–1832*
640 book] Book *1820E–1832*
641 Lands;] Lands: *1820E, 1827* lands: *1832–*
643 purity,] purity *1820E*
646 Thee] thee *MS. 1832/36–*
647 Good] good *MS. 1832/36–*
648 it] it, *pencil MS. 1836/45, 1840–* Sons] sons *MS. 1832/36–*
650 Wars] wars *MS. 1832/36–*
652 Nations] nations *MS. 1832/36–*
653 Temples] temples *MS. 1832/36–*
658 *para MS. 1814/27–* So] "So *1832*
664 Righteousness] righteousness *1820E–*
665 earth] earth, *1827–*
678 transport] transport, *MS. 1836/45*
679 Once,] Once," *1827–* sound,] sound *1832–*
680 isle,] isle *1832–*
681 Nations] nations *1820E–*
685 mountain cove] mountain-cove *1836–*
686 Man] man *MS. 1832/36–*
687 solemnized] solemnised *1845, 1850* there,] there— *1836–*
688 woods,] woods,— *1836* woods— *pencil MS. 1836/45, 1840–*
694 Victims,] victims *MS. 1832/36–*
702 sacrifice,] sacrifice *1832–*
704 Host] host *MS. 1832/36–*
705 Female] female *MS. 1832/36–*
706 Victory] victory *MS. 1832/36–*
707 Monuments] monuments *MS. 1832/36–*
710 and,] and *1832–*
711 Worshippers] worshippers *MS. 1832/36–*
712 mind,] mind *MS. 1832/36–*
714 Paradise] paradise *MS. 1832/36–*
715 again;] again: *1820E–* Few] few *MS. 1832/36–*
717 —Whence] Whence *para MS. 1832/36–* Thee] thee *MS. 1832/36–*
719 Cross] cross *MS. 1832/36–*
721 left— . . . Ye] left, . . . ye *MS. 1832/36–*
724 Sabbath . . . Ye] sabbath . . . ye *MS. 1832/36–*
726 You . . . Band] you . . . band *MS. 1832/36–*
729 eternal] Eternal *1827, 1832*
730 commands] commands, *MS. 1832/36–*
732 Him] him *MS. 1832/36–*
733 Master] master *MS. 1832/36–*
735 shower'd] showered *1820E–*
736 Children] children *MS. 1832/36–* care;—] care, *1827–*
742 recompence] recompense *1827–*
745 still;] still— *MS. 1832/36–*
746 hands—] hands, *MS. 1832/36–*
747 sacrifice—] sacrifice, *MS. 1832/36–*
750 Thought . . . Him] thought . . . him *MS. 1832/36–*
751 Thee, Omniscient] thee, omniscient *MS. 1832/36–*
752 Whom] whom *MS. 1832/36–*
753 Vesper service] vesper-service *MS. 1832/36–*
754 station,] station *1827–*
758 splendors] splendours *1827–* vault,] vault *1820E* vault— *1836–*
759 cloudless] cloudless, *1836–* Star of Eve] star of eve *MS. 1832/36–*
760 wanting;—] wanting; *1836–* Lights] lights *MS. 1832/36–*
763 Boat] boat *MS. 1832/36–*
764 mooring-place;—] mooring-place; *1836–* tree] tree, *1845–*

770 salutation,—] salutation; *MS. 1832/36–*
772 Cottage] cottage *MS. 1832/36–* dell,] dell; *1827, 1832* dell: *MS. 1832/36–*
777 Vallies] Valleys *1827, 1832* valleys *MS. 1832/36–*
778 Mountain-wastes] mountain-wastes *MS. 1832/36–*
779 part,—] part; *MS. 1832/36–*
781 give,—] give, *MS. 1832/36–*
789 reformed;] *in some copies of 1814, punct deteriorates in printing to appear as comma*
792 (if] if *pencil MS. 1836/45, 1840–*
794 past)] past— *pencil MS. 1836/45, 1840–*
795 Labours] labours *MS. 1832/36–*

[Note to Preface, *Prospectus*, ll. 83–84]

opening quotation inspir'st] inspirest 1832– but inspir'st MS. 1836/45 soul, &c."] soul," &c. 1832, 1836 soul,' &c. MS. 1836/45, 1840–
1 Not] 'Not *MS. 1836/45, 1840–*
2 come.] come.' *MS. 1836/45, 1840–*
3 *Shakespeare's] Shakspeare's 1827–*

[Note to Book I, l. 370]

opening quotation "——much] '——much MS. 1836/45, 1840– men."] Men." 1827–1836 Men.' MS. 1836/45, 1840–

[Note to Book III, l. 116]

opening quotation "Lost . . . Eternity!"] 'Lost . . . Eternity!' MS. 1836/45, 1840–
1 composed] composed, *1820E–*
5 "Siquod] 'Siquod MS. *1836/45, 1845, 1850* spectaculum] spectaculum, *1827–*
7 mediterranei] Mediterranei *1820E–*
10 Græcísve] Græcisve *1820E–*
18 altera] alterâ *1836–*
22 "In] In *1836–*
23 qua] quâ *1820E–*
25 horrendum] horrendúm *1836–*
29 "Ima] Ima *1836–* recessúsque] recessusque *1820E–*
34 "Dextrum] Dextrum *1836–*
36 prorupit;] prorupit, *1849 (possible worn plate)*
41 memoranda!"] memoranda!' *1845, 1850*

[Note to Book III, l. 940]

opening quotation "Of . . . Stream."] 'Of . . . Stream.' MS. 1836/45, 1840–
1 "A] 'A *MS. 1836/45, 1845, 1850* Man] man *1820E–*
2 but] but, *1827–*
3 microscopic:] microscopic; *1832–*
7 He] he *1836–*
10 River] river *MS. 1832/36–*
11 Savannah] savannah *MS 1832/36–*
12 contemplates] contemplates, *1836–* Promontory] promontory *MS. 1832/36–*
13 Freeman] freeman *1836–* Theatre] theatre *MS. 1832/36–*
14 His] his *1836–*
15 Imperial] imperial *MS. 1832/36–*
16 His] his *1836–*
17 "These] 'These *1827–*
18 them."] them.' *1827–* Child] child *MS. 1832/36–* King] king *MS. 1832/36–*
19 acts;] acts, *1820E–*
20 unerringly] unerringly, *1827–* His] his *1836–*
21 soars."] soars.' *MS. 1836/45, 1845, 1850*
22 Notes] notes *1820E–*
23 Quotation] quotation *1836–*
25 Prose] prose *1820E–*

[Note to Book IV, ll. 130–131]

opening quotation "'Tis] ''Tis MS. 1836/45, 1840– despise, &c."] despise," &c. 1827–1836 despise,' &c. MS. 1836/45, 1840–

[Note to Book IV, ll. 205–206]

opening quotation "Alas!] 'Alas! MS. 1836/45, 1840– time, &c."] time," &c. 1827–1836 time,' &c. MS. 1836/45, 1840–

[Note to Book IV, l. 325]

variants to poem by Daniel:
1 Thunder-cracks] thunder-cracks *1827–*
2 Tyrants'] Tyrant's *1820E–1832* tyrant's *MS. 1832/36–*
11 distress'd] distressed *1820E–*
12 Birth] birth *1836–*
13 Sorrows] sorrows *1836–*
17 Ambition] ambition MS. *1832/36–*
18 encompass'd] encompassed *1820E–* Craft] craft *1836–* deceives:] deceives, *1827–*
19 deceiv'd] deceived *1820E–* Man . . . Man] man . . . man *1836–*
22 Hopes] hopes *1836–*
23 Peace] peace *1836–*
25 Man] man *1836–*

26 Rest] rest *1836–*
27 learn'd] learned *1820E–*   Book of Man] book of man *1836–*
28 compar'd] compared *1820E–*
29 Glory] glory *1836–*
31 heart;] heart! *1832–*
32 Mansion] mansion *1836–*

[Note to Book V, ll. 648–649]
opening quotation *"Or] 'Or MS. 1836/45, 1840–*   *earth] earth, 1827, 1832*   *Dead] dead 1836–*   *us.'] us.' MS. 1836/45, 1840–*
1 History] history *MS. 1832/36–*
2 Graves] graves *MS. 1832/36–*
3 eight-Score] eight-score *with entire line moved to the right 1827–*
5 *half-line of periods after* might; *om 1820E* might; — — — — — — *1827–*
6 by one] by one, *1827–*
7 round,] round; *1827–*
8 high-way] highway *1836–*

[Note to Book V, l. 981]
opening quotation *"And . . . die."] 'And . . . die.' MS. 1836/45, 1840–*

[Note to Book V, l. 984]
opening quotation *"And . . . regards?"] 'And . . . regards?' MS. 1836/45, 1840–*
3 work, the] work, The *1846*
5 sympathizing] sympathising *1827–*

variants to "Essay upon Epitaphs":
opening para not indented 1832–1843, 1846
1 It] IT *1820E–*
3 Dead] dead *MS. 1832/36–*
4 Tribes] tribes *MS. 1832/36–*   Letters,] letters, *1832* letters *1836–*
5 Graves] graves *MS. 1832/36–*
6 Mounds] mounds *MS. 1832/36–*
7 first,] first *1820E*
8 violation;] violation: *1820E–*
9 "Never any,"] 'Never any,' *MS. 1836/45, 1845, 1850*   Cambden] Camden *1827–*   "neglected] 'neglected *MS. 1836/45, 1845, 1850*
10 Nations] nations *1836–*   Bactrians] Bactrians, *1827–*
11 Philosophers] philosophers *MS. 1832/36–*
12 Courtiers] courtiers *1832–*   Mecænas] Mæcenas *1836–*
14 Grave] grave *1832–*   save."] save.' *MS. 1836/45, 1845, 1850*
15 Nations . . . Epitaphs] nations . . . epitaphs *MS. 1832/36–*
16 Monuments] monuments *MS. 1832/36–*
17 Monuments] monuments *MS. 1832/36–*
17–18 Epitaphs] epitaphs *MS. 1832/36–*
19 Epitaphs] epitaphs *MS. 1832/36–*   discourse of funeral] Discourse of Funeral *1827–*
20 "proceeded] 'proceeded *1836–*
21 Immortality] immortality *MS. 1832/36–*   Scholars] scholars *MS. 1832/36–*
22 Poet] poet *MS. 1832/36–*   World] world *MS. 1832/36–*
24 verses] verses, *1827–*
26 Sepulchres."] sepulchres." *MS. 1832/36* sepulchres.' *1836–*
27 Immortality] immortality *MS. 1832/36–*
29 fellows;] fellows: *1827–*
29–30 Kind towards Kind] kind towards kind *1836–*
30 it.] it *1846 (possible worn plate)*   Dog or Horse] dog or horse *MS. 1832/36–*
31 Companions] companions *1820E–*
32 Associates] associates *1836–*
36 love,] love *1836–*
45–46 Friends or Kindred after Death, . . . Absence] friends or kindred after death, . . . absence *MS. 1832/36–*
49 Man] man *MS. 1832/36–*
51 Child] child *MS. 1832/36–*   Spirits] spirits *1836–*
52 Lamb] lamb *1836–*   Creature,] creature *MS. 1832/36–*
54 Child] child *MS. 1832/36–*
55 Death] death *MS. 1832/36–*
57 Nature] nature *MS. 1832/36–*
59 Children] children *MS. 1832/36–*
61 Children] children *MS. 1832/36–*
62 Death and Immortality] death and immortality *MS. 1832/36–*
65 Child] child *MS. 1832/36–*
66 Stream] stream *MS. 1832/36–*
69 "towards] "Towards *1832–*
71 Sea or Ocean] sea or ocean *MS. 1832/36–*
72 Map] map *MS. 1832/36–*
73 Nature—] nature— *MS. 1832/36–*
76 asserting] asserting, *1827–*   Immortality] immortality *MS. 1832/36–*
77 Offspring] offspring *MS. 1832/36–*
81 avowal] avowal, *1827–*
85 Death] death *MS. 1832/36–*
91 Death] death *MS. 1832/36–*
99 Creature] creature *MS. 1832/36–*
106 Immortality] immortality *MS.*

1832/36–
108 Deceased] deceased *MS. 1832/36–*
109 Country] country *MS. 1832/36–*
110 Corse . . . Sea-side] corse . . . seaside *MS. 1832/36–*   person,] person *1836–*
111 Act] act *MS. 1832/36–*
112 Body] body *MS. 1832/36–*
113 "see] "See *1832–*   Shell] shell *1836–*
114 Bird] bird *1836–*
118 Body . . . Shell] body . . . shell *MS. 1832/36–*
122 latter,] latter *1827–*
124 Nature . . . Corse] nature . . . corse *MS. 1832/36–*
125 Stranger . . . Seal . . . Porpoise] stranger . . . seal . . . porpoise *MS. 1832/36–*   body] hody *1827 (a misprint)*
126 Waves] waves *MS. 1832/36–*
128 Sympathy] sympathy *MS. 1832/36–*
129 Nature] nature *MS. 1832/36–*
133 Planet] planet *MS. 1832/36–*
134 voyage,] voyage *1827–*   sun] Sun *1832* sun *MS 1832/36–*
136 east] East *1832* east *MS. 1832/36–*
138 Sun] sun *MS. 1832/36–*   so,] so *1827–*
139 Country] country *MS. 1832/36–*
140 Life] life *MS. 1832/36–*
145 Laws] laws *MS. 1832/36–*
147 Remains] remains *MS. 1832/36–*
148 said,] said *1827–*
148–149 Monument . . . Man] monument . . . man *MS. 1832/36–*
149 Being] being *MS. 1832/36–*
Epitaph,] Epitaph *1832* epitaph *MS. 1832/36–*
153 Survivors] survivors *MS. 1832/36–*
156 Nations] nations *MS. 1832/36–*
Europe] Europe, *1832–*
157 to] to, *1827–*
158 Walls of Towns and Cities] walls of towns and cities *MS. 1832/36–*
163 Monuments] monuments *MS. 1832/36–*
164–165 Nature] nature *MS. 1832/36–*
168 Traveller,] Traveller *1827, 1832* traveller *MS. 1832/36–*   Tombs] tombs *MS. 1832/36–*
170 "Pause Traveller!"] "Pause, Traveller!" *1827, 1832* 'Pause, Traveller!' *1836–*
171 Monuments . . . Epitaph] monuments . . . epitaph *MS. 1832/36–*
173 Life as a Journey—Death as a Sleep] life as a journey—death as a sleep *MS. 1832/36–*
174 Wayfarer—of Misfortune as a Storm] wayfarer—of misfortune as a storm *MS. 1832/36–*
175 Beauty as a Flower] beauty as a flower *MS. 1832/36–*   pleasure] Pleasure *1832*
176 Virtue . . . Rock] virtue . . . rock *MS. 1832/36–*
177–178 Waves;—of Hope . . . Poplar] waves;—of hope . . . poplar *MS. 1832/36–*   "undermined] 'undermined *1836–*
178–179 River . . . Pine-tree] river . . . pine-tree *MS. 1832/36–*   it,"] it,' *1836–*
179 lightening] lightning *1820E–*
Mountain top] Mountain-top *1820E–1832* mountain-top *MS. 1832/36–*
180 Breeze] breeze *MS. 1832/36–*
182 Fountain] fountain *MS. 1832/36–*
suggestions] suggestions, *1827–*
184 Nature,] Nature *1827, 1832* nature *MS. 1832/36–*
185 advantages:] advantages; *1820E–*
186 Inhabitants . . . Towns and Cities] inhabitants . . . towns and cities *MS. 1832/36–*
187 Dead] dead *MS. 1832/36–*
189 Edifices] edifices *MS. 1832/36–*
190 Tombs] tombs *1832–*
191 notice] Notice *1827, 1832* notice *MS. 1832/36–*   Men] men *MS. 1832/36–*
192 World] world *MS. 1832/36–*
193 Death] death *MS. 1832/36–*
194 Nature] nature *MS. 1832/36–*
198 Monuments] monuments *MS. 1832/36–*
199 Church-yard . . . Town] church-yard . . . town *MS. 1832/36–*
200–201 Cemetery . . . Grove] cemetery . . . grove *MS. 1832/36–*
201 Cypress] cypress *MS. 1832/36–*
203 Poem] poem *MS. 1832/36–*
206 Inhabitants . . . Towns] inhabitants . . . towns *MS. 1832/36–*
207 Country] country *MS. 1832/36–*

variants to poem by Edwards:
1 "Then] 'Then *1836–*
8 gone)] gone,) *MS. 1832/36–*
11 stray'd] strayed *1820E–1832, see verbal variants*
16 Dead] dead *1832–*   inhum'd] inhumed *1820E–*
17 There,] There *1827–*   Man] man *1820E–*
18 sympathiz'd,] sympathized, *1820E* sympathised, *1827–*
22 Dove] Dove, *1827–1836, 1845, 1850*

Dove. *1840–1843, 1846 (probable worn plate)*

23 return'd] returned *1820E–*

24 o'er] over *1827* destroy'd] destroyed *1820E–*

28 God."] God.' *1836–*

variants to "Essay on Epitaphs," continued:

208 Village Church-yard . . . Nature] village church-yard . . . nature *MS. 1832/36–*

209 Town] town *MS. 1832/36–*

209–210 Population] population *MS. 1832/36–*

210 Sepulture] sepulture *MS. 1832/36–*

213 Sabbath-day] sabbath-day *MS. 1832/36–*

214 Graves of Kindred and Friends] graves of kindred and friends *MS. 1832/36–*

215 Home . . . Spectators] home . . . spectators *MS. 1832/36–*

216 Parish Church . . . Country] parish-church . . . country *MS. 1832/36–*

219 Cities . . . Villages, the Dead] cities . . . villages, the dead *MS. 1832/36–*

221 Epitaph . . . Nations of Antiquity] epitaph . . . nations of antiquity *MS. 1832/36–* turns] turns, *1827–*

223 Worth] worth *MS. 1832/36–* Sorrow . . . Admiration] sorrow . . . admiration *1836–*

224 Religion] Religion, *1827, 1832* religion, *MS. 1832/36–* Time] time *MS. 1832/36–* Eternity] eternity *1827, MS. 1832/36–* Accordingly] Accordingly, *1832–*

227 Epitaph] epitaph *MS. 1832/36–*

228 Thought or Feeling] thought or feeling *MS. 1832/36–*

229 Nature] nature *MS. 1832/36–*

231–232 Husband . . . Wife; a Parent] husband . . . wife; a parent *MS. 1832/36–*

232–233 Child; a Son] child; a son *MS. 1832/36–*

233–234 Father or Mother; a Friend] father or mother; a friend *MS. 1832/36–*

235 Tenant . . . Grave] tenant . . . grave *MS. 1832/36–*

236 This,]This *1836–*

237 Living] living *MS. 1832/36–* Immortality] immortality *MS. 1832/36–*

238 Church-yards] church-yards *MS. 1832/36–*

239 any thing] anything *1850*

240 Dead . . . Living] dead . . . living *MS. 1832/36–*

241 Epitaphs] epitaphs *MS. 1832/36–*

242 causes;] causes, *1820E* Objects] objects *MS. 1832/36–*

243 Characters of Men] characters of men *MS. 1832/36–* or] or, *1827–*

244 "to . . . Mankind] 'to . . . mankind *1836–*

245 Character] character *1820E–* all."] all.' *1836–*

246–247 Critic and a Moralist] critic and a moralist *MS. 1832/36–*

247 Subject] subject *MS. 1832/36–*

248 Human Nature] Human-nature *1827, 1832* human-nature *MS. 1832/36–* scanty] scanty, *1827–* abundant;] abundant: *1836–*

249 Man] man *MS. 1832/36–* Character] character *1836–*

251 Characters] characters *MS. 1832/36–*

252 Men] men *MS. 1832/36–*

254 Minds] minds *MS. 1832/36–*

256–257 Light of Love in our Hearts] light of love in our hearts *MS. 1832/36–*

258 Light] light *MS. 1832/36–*

260 intellect:] intellect; *1820E–*

264–265 Sorrow, Admiration, or Regret] sorrow, admiration, or regret *MS. 1832/36–*

266 Friends and Kindred] friends and kindred *MS. 1832/36–*

267 equalizing] equalising *1827–* Receptacle . . . Dead] receptacle . . . dead *MS. 1832/36–*

270 Death . . . Epitaph] death . . . epitaph *MS. 1832/36–*

271 proceeds; of death] proceeds—of death, *1836–*

273 Epitaph] epitaph *MS. 1832/36–*

274–275 excellencies] excellences *1820E, 1827*

277 composition.] composition.— *MS. 1832/36–*

280 Reader's . . . Individual] reader's . . . individual *MS. 1832/36–*

285 Deceased] deceased *MS. 1832/36–*

286 solemnized] solemnised *1832–*

288–289 Reader . . . Man] reader . . . man *MS. 1832/36–*

291 Individual] individual *MS. 1832/36–* lamented] lamented.— *1836–* Writer . . . Epitaph] writer . . . epitaph *MS. 1832/36–*

292 Anatomist] Anatomist, *1832* anatomist, *MS. 1832/36–*

293 Painter] Painter, *1832* painter, *MS. 1832/36–*

294 Grave] grave *MS. 1832/36–*
297–298 Friend . . . Kinsman] friend . . . kinsman *MS. 1832/36–*
299 Tree] tree *MS. 1832/36–*
299–300 spiritualizes . . . away] spiritualises . . . away, *1832–*
301 lovely,] lovely; *MS. 1832/36–*
302 say then] say, then, *1827–*
303 that accordingly] that, accordingly, *1832–*
304 order!] order; *1836–*
305 exist,] exist; *1820E–*
309 Dead . . . Living!—] dead . . . living! *MS. 1832/36–*
312 moment!—] moment! *MS. 1832/36–*
315 Man] man *MS. 1832/36–* Tomb-stone] Tombstone *1832* tombstone *MS. 1832/36–*
316 Epitaph . . . Adversary] epitaph . . . adversary *MS. 1832/36–*
320 Writer's] writer's *MS. 1832/36–*
324 Grave] grave *MS. 1832/36–*
325 Earth] earth *MS. 1832/36–*
327 Heaven] heaven *MS. 1832/36–*
328 Trunk . . . Branches] trunk . . . branches *MS. 1832/36–*
329 Worth . . . Deceased] worth . . . deceased *MS. 1832/36–*
332 Spectator] spectator *MS. 1832/36*
333 Dead] dead *MS. 1832/36–*
334 memory] memory, *1827–*
337 Understanding] understanding *MS. 1832/36–*
338 Mourner] mourner *1836–*
339–340 Person . . . Survivors, the Memorial] person . . . survivors, the memorial *MS. 1832/36–*
343 Men] men *MS. 1832/36–*
344 Temple] temple *MS. 1832/36–*
345 Grave . . . Human] grave . . . human *MS. 1832/36–*
346 "equalizes . . . low."] 'equalizes . . . low.' *1836– but* 'equalises *1845, 1850*
349 good-will,] good-will *1820E*
354 case)] case,) *1836–*
359 Epitaph] epitaph *MS. 1832/36–* Writing] writing *MS. 1832/36–* studious;] studious: *1832–*
360 all,] all— *1836–*
362 busy] busy, *1827–*
363 tired;] tired: *1827–* Old Man] old man *MS. 1832/36–*
364 Child] child *MS. 1832/36–* it—] it;— *1832–*
364–365 Stranger . . . Friend] stranger . . . friend *MS. 1832/36–*
366 Church-yard] church-yard *MS. 1832/36–*
367 Heaven] heaven *MS. 1832/36–*
368 Writer] writer *MS. 1832/36–* case] case, *1832–*
370 Monument] monument *MS. 1832/36–*
373 permanent] permanent, *1827–*
376 strong] strong, *1832–*
377 involuntary] involuntarily *1820E (probably a misprint)*
378 Narrator . . . Grave] narrator . . . grave *MS. 1832/36–*
378–379 tranquillizing] tranquillising *1845, 1850* resignation,] resignation *1827–* time,] time *1820E–*
384 Author] author *MS. 1832/36–*
387 Oration . . . Poem] oration . . . poem *MS. 1832/36–*
389 Epitaphs] epitaphs *MS. 1832/36–*
390 Deceased . . . Tomb-stone] deceased . . . tomb-stone *MS. 1832/36–*
395 Judge] judge *MS. 1832/36–*
396 dispassionate.] dispassionate *1849 (probable worn plate)*
397 Death] death *MS. 1832/36–* unsubstantialized] unsubstantialised *1845, 1850*
398 fiction] fiction, *1827–* Survivors] survivors *MS. 1832/36–*
399 imagination . . . reason] Imagination . . . Reason *1832*
402 Living . . . Dead] living . . . dead *MS. 1832/36–*
405 Immortality] immortality *MS. 1832/36–*
406 Epitaph] epitaph *MS. 1832/36–*
408 Survivors] survivors *MS. 1832/36–*
410 Society] society *MS. 1832/36–*
413 Survivors . . . Persons] survivors . . . persons *MS. 1832/36–*
414 preferable:] preferable *1849 (possible worn plate)*
415 ground-work] groundwork *1832–*
417 Epitaph] epitaph *MS. 1832/36–*
422 Men] men *MS. 1832/36–*
424 Peace or War . . . Art] peace or war . . . art *MS. 1832/36–*
425 Literature, or Science] literature, or science *MS. 1832/36–*
426 Country] country *1836–*
428 Epitaphs] epitaphs *MS. 1832/36–* that,] that *1832–*
429 Man] man *MS. 1832/36–*
430 him] him, *1827–*
432 act;] act: *1832–*
434 distinction] distinction, *1827–* Benefactors] benefactors *1820E–*
435 Survivors] survivors *MS. 1832/36–*
436 Posterity] posterity *MS. 1832/36–*
437–438 individualize] individualise *1845, 1850*

438 Memories of Men] memories of men *MS. 1832/36–*
439–440 Gratitude . . . Love] gratitude . . . love *MS. 1832/36–* Admiration;] admiration; *MS. 1832/36* admiration— *1836–*
441 Principle] principle *MS. 1832/36–* Virtue;] virtue; *MS. 1832/36* virtue;— *1836–*
443 Power,] power, *MS. 1832/36* power; *1836–*
444 Altar] altar *MS. 1832/36–* unworthy!] unworthy. *1836–*

variants to poem by Milton:
1 What] "What *1832* 'What *1836–* Shakespeare] Shakspeare *1827–*
4 star-y-pointing] star-ypointing *1832, 1850* star y-pointing *1836–1843, 1846* starry-pointing *MS. 1832/36, 1845*
8 live-long Monument.] live-long Monument, *1820E, 1827* livelong Monument, *1832* livelong monument, *MS. 1832/36–*
10 Kings . . . Tomb] kings . . . tomb *MS. 1832/36–* die.] die." *1832* die.' *1836–*

[Note to Book VI, l. 19]
opening quotation "And] 'And MS. 1836/45, 1840– silent] 'silent 1832– Finger] finger 1827– Heaven."] Heaven.'" 1832, 1836 Heaven." 1840–
3 sometimes] sometimes, *1827–*
6 14.] 14, *1836–*

[Note to Book VII, ll. 635–636]
opening quotation "That . . . shade, . . . tent."] 'That . . . shade . . . tent.' 1836–
1 This] 'This *1836–*
2 loved.] loved.' *1836–*

[Note to Book VII, l. 1002]
opening quotation "Perish . . . Kings."] 'Perish . . . Kings.' 1836–
1 "Transit . . . mundi"] 'Transit . . . mundi' *1836–*
2 Foundation Charters] Foundation-charters *1836–* Abbies] Abbeys *1827–*
3 Mary's] Mary's, *1845*
4 follows.] follows:— *1832–*
5 "Considering] 'Considering *1836–*
7 things] things, *1827–*
8 therefore,"] therefore,' *1836–*

[Note to Book VIII, ll. 113–114]
opening quotation "Earth has lent] ————"Earth has lent 1827, 1832 ————'Earth has lent 1836– Waters, air] waters, Air 1827– breezes."] breezes."—— 1827 breezes." 1832 breezes.' 1836–
2 which] which, *1827–*
3 industry,] industry *1827–*

[Note to Book IX, l. 298]
opening quotation "Binding . . . Statute."] 'Binding . . . Statute.' 1836–
2 effect,] effect; *1832–* overrate] over-rate *1827–*

Editors' Notes
The Excursion, 1814

In addition to providing here our notes to *The Excursion*, we also briefly refer to Wordsworth's notes that are fully presented elsewhere in this volume. The notes that the poet appended to *The Excursion* in 1814 are given on pp. 298–314, above, together with historical collations of the verbal changes he made to those notes in lifetime editions of his works. The *Excursion* section of the notes that Wordsworth dictated to his friend and neighbor Isabella Fenwick in 1843 is presented in full in Appendix III, below.

Abbreviations of lifetime printings cited are listed at the end of the Editorial Procedure. Manuscripts are identified in the Manuscript Census.

Dedicatory poem

The opening sonnet is dedicated to the Earl of Lonsdale, Sir William Lowther, an important benefactor of WW's. The Lowthers were one of the most important families in the northwest of England. WW's father had worked as land agent to Sir James Lowther, the previous earl, and on his death had money owing to him. In fact, the claim made for this sum by the orphaned Wordsworth children was ignored by Sir James and only settled after his death in 1804. WW met Sir William Lowther (through Sir George Beaumont) in July 1807. In 1812 WW asked Lowther for financial assistance and was first offered £100 a year by the earl, who then arranged for him to be appointed as Distributor of Stamps working for the revenue service with a small regular income of £90 a year. WW also campaigned for the Tory Party on behalf of the Lowthers against the liberal Henry Brougham in the 1818 general election, when he wrote *Two Addresses to the Freeholders of Westmorland.*

1 thy fair domains] The grounds of Lowther Castle, situated on the northeastern side of the Lake District, below Penrith. As a child WW probably visited it with his father.

4 swift-flowing Lowther's current] The river Lowther runs into the river Eamont.

Rydal Mount] In 1813 the Wordsworths moved to Rydal Mount, a house owned by Lady Fleming, who lived quietly opposite them in Rydal Hall.

July 29, 1814] In fact the dedicatory sonnet was almost certainly written in June, not July, since WW was on holiday in Scotland from July 18 to September 9, 1814 (see *Chronology: MY*, p. 554).

Preface

1 a Portion of a Poem] *Exc* was the only section of *The Recluse*, which was to be in three parts, to be published in WW's lifetime (see note to "Preface," l. 16, below).

7–8 passing events] The effects of the French Revolution (see *Prose*, III, 10).

13 some valued Friends] Among others, Sir George and Lady Margaret Beaumont, whom WW had known since 1803 and who urged him to publish *Exc*. Beaumont, himself an artist and a major patron of the arts, supported a number of writers and artists of the time; WW dedicated his next publication (*Poems*, 1815) to him.

16 THE RECLUSE] The *Recluse* project was worked out between WW and STC in 1797–98 with STC providing much of the stimulus for this intended epic. It was to be a philosophical poem, offering a complete metaphysical system. In practice, for WW, it was

to consist of three parts, excluding the preparatory poem (*The Prelude*). The first and third parts were to be given in the poet's own voice and the middle section, *Exc*, presented as a dramatic utterance. Most of WW's lengthiest pieces of poetry are part of this endeavor, as WW makes clear in his discussion of it here.

16–17 when the Author returned to his native Mountains] WW settled in Grasmere in December 1799. *Prose*, III, 10, suggests that WW is also here referring to Milton's preface to *The Reason of Church Government*. WW commented upon Milton's work in a letter written at the time of the completion of *Exc* (see *MY*, II, 146) and perhaps read it shortly before April 28, 1814 (see Wu, *Reading I*, p. 148).

15–20 The account given here is "not strictly accurate" (see *PW*, V, 363). *The Recluse* scheme was begun in 1798 at Alfoxden, and WW did not retire to Grasmere until 1799.

23 addressed to a dear Friend] STC.

26–27 containing views of Man, Nature, and Society] WW first describes this intention in his letter of March 6, 1798, announcing *The Recluse*: "My object is to give pictures of Nature, Man, and Society" (*EY*, p. 212). Cf. STC's description of his own intended long poem, *The Brook*: "I sought for a subject that should give equal room and freedom for description, incident, and impassioned reflections on man, nature and society, yet supply in itself a natural connection to the parts and unity to the whole" (*STCBL*, I, 195–196); and John Thelwall's 1793 publication *The Peripatetic, or Sketches of the Heart, of Nature and* Society. See also *H at G*, p. 20, and our introductory note to Book III, below.

32 the two Works] *The Prelude* and *The Recluse*.

32–39 WW attempts to relate all his works to this model, suggesting a strongly holistic sense of the development of his poetic oeuvre, which is also reflected the following year in the arrangement of his *Poems*, 1815 (see Frances Ferguson, *Language as Counter-Spirit* [New Haven, 1977], pp. 35–95).

43 the Public] A loaded term for WW, as is seen at the end of his *Essay Supplementary to the Preface* (1815), in which he distinguishes between the reception of his work by the "Public" of his day and by the "People" of the future: "Towards the Public, the Writer hopes that he feels as much deference as it is entitled to: but to the People, philosophically characterised, . . . his devout respect, his reverence is due" (*Prose*, III, 84).

51 a system] WW, ambiguous at this crucial point, evades a clear definition of what exactly the "philosophy" in his philosophical poem amounts to, suggesting instead that the reader "will have no difficulty extracting the system for himself." Disapproval of WW's "peculiar system" (Jeffrey, p. 1) is a constant note in the attacks upon him by Francis Jeffrey. For discussion of the poem's resistance to "systems," see Hickey, pp. 16–17 and 166–178. Cf. *Exc*, IV, 600–603.

55–56 taken from the conclusion of the first Book of the Recluse] The *Prospectus* is taken from the end of *Home at Grasmere*, the surviving portion of the intended first part of the poem (see *H at G*, pp. 100–107).

Prospectus

The *Prospectus* could have been written as early as 1798 or as late as March 1804 (see *Chronology: MY*, p. 663) but is now thought probably to have been written at some time between spring 1800 and 1802. For the difficulty of dating the lines, see *H at G*, pp. 20–22; for manuscript work, see *H at G*, pp. 255–267, 394–403.

1–2 The syntax of the opening lines, with the delayed employment of the main verb, establishes a Miltonic tone from the outset. See note to I, 470, below.

7–8 whose presence soothes / Or elevates the Mind] Cf. *Tintern Abbey*, ll. 26–31, and *Prelude*, I, 625.

13 numerous Verse] *PW*, V, 372, draws attention to the quotation of *PL*, V, 150, the first of frequent Miltonic references in the *Prospectus*, prefiguring many more such allusions in *Exc* itself.

23 "fit audience let me find though few!"] A quotation from *PL,* VII, 31, where Milton also addresses Urania as his heavenly muse.

25 Urania] Daughter of Zeus and Mnemosyne and muse of astronomy; in the seventeenth century Urania's name was quite commonly used for the title of a poem dealing with celestial themes.

30 heaven of heavens] The same phrase appears in *PL,* VII, 553.

33 Jehovah] Cf. Exodus 6: 3. See also *Exc,* IV, 648, and IX, 679.

34 empyreal thrones] The same phrase appears in *PL,* II, 430.

36 The darkest pit of lowest Erebus] The proper name for the murky place between earth and Hades. Cf. *PL,* II, 882–883: "the lowest bottom shook / Of *Erebus.*"

40 Into our Minds, into the Mind of Man] The *Prospectus* draws upon the late eighteenth-century idea that the external world is internalized in an almost physical sense.

63–68 Cf. WW's description of the poet in his 1802 addition to the "Preface" to *Lyrical Ballads,* in which he states that "He considers man and nature as essentially adapted to each other, and the mind of man as naturally the mirror of the fairest and most interesting qualities of nature" (*Prose,* I, 140; *LB, 1797–1800,* p. 752).

79 barricadoed evermore] *PW,* V, 372, notes the echo of *PL,* VIII, 241: "barricado'd strong."

83–84 WW's end-of-volume note in *Exc* (see p. 298, above) here refers the reader to the opening lines of Shakespeare's Sonnet 107.

87 mighty Poets] Cf. WW's *Resolution and Independence,* l. 123 (1807 text).

90–93 Shedding benignant influence] *PW,* V, 372, points out the echo of *PL,* VII, 375 ("Shedding sweet influence") and that the rest of WW's passage can be compared to *PL,* X, 660–662, in its account of planetary influence. See also *Prelude* (1850 text), I, 102–103, and *Exc,* I, 287.

93–96 Cf. editors' note to *Exc,* I, 81–82, below.

Summary of Contents

WW gives a prose summary for each book in a manner typical of eighteenth-century descriptive poems such as James Thomson's *The Seasons* or William Cowper's *The Task.* In the first and second editions of *Exc* (1814, 1820), these summaries were printed together at the front of the poem, but they were divided up to preface individual books from 1827 onward. The summaries reward some attention, often suggesting a certain line of reading or points of comparison that may not be explicit in the poem itself.

BOOK I: "The Wanderer"

Book I has a complicated history. It was first written as *RC* in 1797–1798 and then reworked as *The Pedlar* in 1802–1804. See *RC & Pedlar* (and *Chronology: MY,* pp. 22, 665–667, 676–677) for an account of the composition of *RC* up to 1804. See *M of H* for literary sources for *RC* and the Wanderer (including Goethe's *Der Wandrer*). The first surviving copy of these lines written as part of *Exc,* probably between 1809 and 1812, is to be found in MS. 71. (For all MSS. of the separate poem, see *RC & Pedlar.*)

The last MS. in which the narrative that became *Exc* Book I is still a separate work is *RC/Pedlar* MS. M. Though *Exc* Book I for the most part quite closely resembles the MS. M text, the most obvious changes are the removal of an explicit division of the poem into parts (although breaks in the text remain); the omissions of the little girl to whom the Pedlar told his stories (MS. M, ll. 71–93) and of the Pedlar's elder brother, already a packman (MS. M, ll. 334–341); and the additions of earlier images from *RC* MSS. B and D of the "Dreaming Man" at the start of the poem (MS. B, ll. 9–17; MS. D, ll. 10–18) and of the passage at *Exc,* I, 81–111, which celebrates the "Poets sown by Nature" (cf. *RC/Pedlar* MS. M, ll. 100–102). Notes below record other significant changes in *Exc* from what is in *RC* and *Pedlar* MSS.

WW's changes to the name of his central character across these texts are also significant. In MS. B he is called simply "an aged Man" (l. 36); in MS. D he is named "The venerable Armytage" (l. 38), and in one of the drafts in that MS. he is named Patrick Drummond (58r; *RC & Pedlar,* p. 331). Otherwise, in MS. B he is called the "old Man," and in MS. M again he is introduced and described simply as the "Old Man" (l. 21). Thus, although his profession is clearly recognizable, and although DW's *Journals* repeatedly refer to the poem as *The Pedlar,* the character is not given this title within the poem itself. Only in drafts for *Exc* does WW directly begin to call him by any title. In MS. 71 the name "Wanderer" first appears at I, 470, in a line of rev at the top of 16r; at I, 622 on 20r, WW changes "the Old Man" in pencil to "Wan." The first use of "Wanderer" in the base text of MS. 71 is in MW's hand on 80r; this section of the MS. dates from the fifth stage of *Exc* composition. In subsequent rev to *1814,* his title was reinforced by use of "Wanderer" in Book I at ll. 55 and 383 (see verbal variants to the reading text, above).

The decision to present the character in *Exc* as having left his trade (I, 416) is important in stressing his social role as one who makes connections between all people and places. The deflection of criticism of the low status of WW's hero may also have been an intention, but as contemporary critics made clear, this attempt was not successful. Hazlitt states, "[W]e take leave of him when he makes pedlars and ploughmen his heroes, and the interpreters of his sentiments. It is, we think, getting into low company, and company, besides, that we do not like" (Hazlitt, p. 636).

The act of "wandering" is also significant. WW states of RS, "*Books* . . . were in fact *his passion; & wandering,* I can with truth affirm, was mine" (IF; p. 1215, below). The importance of a man's occupation in shaping his mind and spirit is also strongly felt in WW's own note on the Wanderer at I, 370 (see below). WW directly identifies himself with the Wanderer, stating that "the character I have represented in his person is chiefly an idea of what I fancied my own character might have become in his circumstances" (IF; pp. 1215–1216, below), but he also gives two other models for him. These are a packman, whom WW knew as a boy, and a Scotsman, James Patrick, who was married to MW's cousin, Margaret Robison, and who had looked after cattle in Perthshire before becoming a pedlar and finally a draper in Kendal. Patrick died in 1787 at the age of 71 and was buried in Kendal churchyard. SH often stayed with this couple, and in *The Grasmere Journals* (January 27, 1802) DW describes a letter from SH, "a sweet long letter, with a most interesting account of Mr Patrick" (*Journals,* p. 59). The account of the Wanderer's childhood also bears many similarities to WW's own as represented in *The Prelude.*

2–3 glared / Through a pale steam] James Butler points out (see *RC & Pedlar,* p. 42) that the opening lines are "an adaptation of a passage from *An Evening Walk* (1793), along with rev made of it at Windy Brow in 1794"; see *EW,* pp. 34, 132–133.

10–18 WW opens the poem with a metaphorical image of the "dreaming Man" who at first seems to be associated with the poet but is dissociated from him at l. 18. Cf. Lucretius, *De Rerum Natura (On The Nature of the Universe),* bk. II, ll. 1–20, with its image of the wise man elevated and remote from the world. Wu suggests that WW had read *De Rerum Natura* by 1794 and notes the possibility that it may have been a model for *The Recluse* (Wu, *Reading I,* p. 90; *Reading II,* p. 256). Epicurean images of the pleasure to be found in withdrawal recur in the Wanderer's final speech at IX, 52–81. See also *Exc,* III, 355, and *Prelude,* VIII, 711–727. Other images of "dreaming" in the poem occur at I, 440, 666–667, 982; and III, 345–346.

14 Where the wren warbles] Cf. *Prelude,* II, 125–126: "and that single Wren / Which one day sang so sweetly in the Nave."

21 Across a bare wide Common] WW changes the setting of the tale from Salisbury Plain to the Lakes when he resituates it in *Exc,* I. WW freely acknowledges the need for poetic license: "The scene of the first book of the Poem is, I must own, laid in a tract of country not sufficiently near to that which soon comes into view in the second book to

agree with the fact" (IF, p. 1217, below).

29 a brotherhood of lofty elms] Cf. *Memorials of a Tour in Scotland, 1803; Sonnet: Composed at —— Castle,* l. 6: "A brotherhood of venerable Trees."

37 An iron-pointed staff lay at his side] In *RC* MS. B the pedlar also has a "long white pack" (l. 44); in MS. D he has a "pack of rustic merchandize" (l. 44); and in *Pedlar* MS. E both of these descriptions are given (ll. 28, 377). The Pedlar has, of course, retired and so become a Wanderer in *Exc* (see pp. 437–439, below, and note to I, 416, below).

51 He by appointment waited for me here] Cf. I, 27, and I, 33. In *Pedlar* MSS. E and MS. M, the pedlar is also met by arrangement, as he is here; but in the earlier *RC* MSS. B and D, it is represented as more of a chance meeting.

55 A market-village] Hawkshead, where WW lived from the ages of nine to seventeen while attending the grammar school. The specific place names in *Pedlar* MSS. are removed for *Exc* (see p. 433, below).

81–82 Oh! many are the Poets that are sown / By Nature] Perhaps a central point in *Exc,* which seeks to represent not just the mind of the poet but also those of other men with fine sensibilities. See also *Prospectus,* ll. *93–96.* Cf. Thomas Gray's *Elegy Written in a Country Churchyard,* ll. 45–96, for similar sentiments.

92 These favored Beings] Cf. *Lines Left Upon a Seat in a Yew Tree,* l. 16 (text of 1800): "a favored being."

95–97 *Exc* intends to speak on behalf of those too easily overlooked. Cf. VIII, 391–395, where the Pastor asks that the good man's deeds be recorded.

106 I will here record in verse] In Book I the role of the Poet as a writing figure is felt far more strongly than it is later in the poem. The story of the Wanderer's history is the only tale that the Poet tells directly.

112 the hills of Athol] Hills in the Grampian highlands of Scotland. This specific description of the Pedlar/Wanderer's birthplace is only finally settled upon for *Exc.* In *RC* MS. B the Pedlar is born "on Cumbrian hills" (l. 48), in *Pedlar* MSS. E (ll. 102–103) and M (l. 123) "Among the hills of Perthshire" (the hills of Athol are in Perthshire). WW first visited Scotland in 1801 and then went on a six-week walking tour in 1803 with DW and STC, as recorded in DW's *Recollections of a Tour in Scotland.* In a letter to Walter Scott of November 7, 1805, WW declared, "I long much to see more of Scotland, both North and South; it is (not excepting the Alps) the most poetical Country I ever travelled in" (*EY,* p. 641). Lyon goes so far as to suggest that one of the aims of the poem was "to glorify Scotland" (Lyon, p. 66).

112–138 STC attacked these lines in *Biographia Literaria* as examples of "minute matters of fact" (*STCBL,* II, 134), and WW may have been responding to this criticism when he altered the lines in 1827, removing ll. 115–127 (see also p. 19, above).

129 Pure Livers] *PW,* V, 411, compares *Resolution and Independence,* ll. 104–105 (text of 1807): "Such as grave Livers do in Scotland use, / Religious men, who give to God and Man their dues."

129–133 The account of the Wanderer's early childhood suggests a strict, possibly Calvinist, upbringing. See also note to I, 427–430, below.

134–239 At this point the Poet gives us a biography of the Wanderer. The description of the Wanderer's childhood strongly resembles WW's account of his own early years in *The Prelude.*

138 To his Step-father's School] In alterations for *PW,* 1845, WW removes any familial connection to the Schoolmaster.

143–144 Cf. *Prelude,* I, 406–413.

149 not from terror free] Cf. *Prelude,* I, 307; I, 632; XIII, 143–147. See also *Exc,* I, 204.

152–166 This very physical delineation of external effects upon the mind looks back to David Hartley's writings on association in *Observations on Man* (1749). When *RC* was first written, WW was still a firm supporter of Hartley's ideas, which he would have come across as a Cambridge undergraduate. See Wu, *Reading I,* p. 72. Cf. *Prelude,* I, 628–631; II, 367–371.

160–166 *PW* Knight, V, 34, compares *Ode: Intimations of Immortality,* ll. 142–148 (text of 1807).

163 active power] Cf. *Exc* IX, 3, 132.

190 The life and death of Martyrs] Probably John Foxe's *Book of Martyrs* (1641). In *RC* MS. B, the Pedlar "read & read again . . . The life & death of Martyrs" (*RC & Pedlar,* pp. 162–163; see Wu, *Reading I,* p. 59; *Reading II,* p. 89).

197 That left half-told] *PW,* V, 441, compares the reference in Milton's *Il Penseroso,* ll. 109–110, to Chaucer and the *Squire's Tale*: "Or call up him that left half told / The story of *Cambuscan* bold."

197–203 As in WW's self-depiction in *The Prelude,* the value of chapbook stories and characters for developing the child's imaginative powers is emphasized. Cf. *Prelude,* V, 364–369.

204 Where Fear sate thus] The relationship between fear and love of nature in the young Wanderer echoes that of the child in *The Prelude.* See note to I, 149, above.

223 And ocean's liquid mass, beneath him lay] *PW* Knight, V, 36, notes here: "The sea is not visible from the hills of Athole, except from the summit of Ben y' Gloe, where it can be seen to the south-east in the clearest weather. Wordsworth did not care for local accuracy in this passage. It was quite unnecessary for his purpose."

220–239 Cf. *Prelude,* IV, 330–345.

227–228 his spirit drank / The spectacle] Cf. *Exc,* IV, 1265, and *Prelude,* I, 590–592, as well as *Lines written at a small distance from my house . . .* [*To my Sister*], ll. 27–28.

240–241 on the lonely mountain tops, / Such intercourse was his] Lyon, p. 53, compares *Prelude,* I, 446, 450.

244–250 Here WW directly contrasts revealed and natural religion within the Wanderer's education. See also notes to I, 439–440, and IV, 43, below.

260–263 Cf. *Tintern Abbey,* ll. 88–93 (text of 1798).

274 The purer elements of truth] WW refers to Euclid's *Elements,* which established the mathematical science of geometry and was a central text in an eighteenth-century education. The grammar school at Hawkshead, which WW attended, had a high reputation for mathematics and under the headmaster William Taylor sent a number of successful scholars to Cambridge. See Ben Ross Schneider, *Wordsworth's Cambridge Education* (Cambridge, 1957) pp. 4–6; Wu, *Reading I,* p. 54. See also *Prelude,* V, 64, 88.

287 sweet influence] Cf. note to WW's *Prospectus,* l. 90, above, and *PL,* VII, 375 ("sweet influence").

337–340 WW tries to present the Wanderer in relatively classless terms, suggesting he could have been a schoolmaster had he wished it. See also WW's note to *Matthew*: "Like the Wanderer in the Excursion, this Schoolmaster was made up of several both of his class & men of other occupations" (IF, p. 38).

345 The Savoyard] Native of Savoy (a region in South East France, south of the Lake of Geneva).

346 The free-born Swiss] A reminder that Switzerland was invaded by Napoleon in February 1798. The significance of this event, to which WW refers more than once in *Exc,* can be felt in a letter to James Losh of December 4, 1821, when WW states: "I abandoned France, and her Rulers, when they abandoned the struggle for Liberty, gave themselves up to Tyranny and endeavoured to enslave the world . . . after Buonaparte had violated the Independence of Switzerland, my heart turned against him, and the Nation that could submit to be the Instrument of such an outrage" (*LY,* I, 97). See also WW's poem of 1807, *Thought of a Briton on the Subjugation of Switzerland* and STC's poem *France: An Ode* (a more immediate response to the same event). The invasion of Switzerland is referred

to elsewhere at *Exc,* V, 93–95, and VII, 829.

348–349 did now impel / His restless Mind] In his copy of the first edition of *Exc* (now at Cornell University), Benjamin Robert Haydon wrote the word "Caledonia!" opposite this line in the margin. For other Haydon annotations, see notes to I, 399; IV, 186; IV, 854.

350 In *Pedlar* MSS. E and M at this point, the pedlar is described as having an older brother who is already in the profession, and this example encourages him in his desires (MS. E, ll. 286–291; MS. M, ll. 334–340; see *RC & Pedlar,* pp. 406–407). The lines are removed in MS. 71 (see p. 457, below).

370–387 The description of the Wanderer's life makes clear its attractions for WW in the way it allows direct contact with the simple peasant life, and also emphasizes that the individual is shaped by the kind of life he leads. The Wanderer develops a necessary balance, a "just equipoise of love," which makes him the ideal spokesman for others' lives in the poem. See also WW's end-of-volume note to I, 370 (p. 298, above), which quotes from Robert Heron's *Observations Made in a Journey Through the Western Counties of Scotland* (1793) to illustrate this point: "as they wander each alone, through thinly-inhabited districts, they form habits of reflection and of sublime contemplation (I, 89)." (In fact WW's own references as given in his notes are slightly inaccurate, since he actually quotes from Heron, I, 89–90, 91.) WW had probably read Heron as early as 1800 (Wu, *Reading I,* p. 4); in his notes to *Exc,* WW paraphrases the passage from Heron in his editions of 1814 and 1820 but quotes in full from 1827 onward. See also *RC & Pedlar,* pp. 479–480.

374–376 These lines, with their mention of rural folk who "speak a plainer language," can clearly be compared to WW's first critical statement of poetic intention in the "Preface" to *Lyrical Ballads* (1800): "Low and rustic life was generally chosen because in that situation the essential passions of the heart find a better soil in which they can attain their maturity, are less under restraint, and speak a plainer and more emphatic language" (*LB, 1797–1800,* p. 743).

381 Cf. IV, 299.

399–400 He could *afford* to suffer / With those whom he saw suffer] Cf. Shakespeare, *The Tempest,* I.ii.5–6: "O! I have suffered / With those that I saw suffer." In Haydon's copy of *Exc* he writes in the margin by these lines "But not to help them." (For other Haydon comments, see notes to I, 348–349; IV, 186; IV, 854.) This point is an important one in relation to the Wanderer. His distance and relative objectivity in relation to the tales he hears is valuable (and contrasts later with the Solitary, who cannot "afford" such suffering). BF also records WW's own reputed comment on STC: "He had always too much personal and domestic discontent to paint the sorrows of mankind. He could not 'afford to suffer / With those whom he saw suffer'" (BF, p. 100).

416 His Calling laid aside, he lived at ease] At the time that the events of the poem record, the Wanderer has retired from his active profession and now "wanders" purely from choice. See note to I, 37, above.

427–430 These lines and the description of "fear or darker thought" at I, 437, suggest a Calvinist upbringing. Cf. I, 129–133.

439–440 This account of the Wanderer as coming from a strongly hierarchical religious background but as having formed beliefs more personal and pantheistic is significant for the poem as a whole and the nature of his teaching. So, for example, in Book IV when he tries to console the Solitary, the Wanderer is willing to call upon examples from Natural Religion as much as from biblical teachings. Cf. I, 244–250; IV, 43. For other images of the dreamer, see I, 10–18; I, 666–667; I, 982; and III, 345–346.

441–443 This passage is not in the versions of Book I that appear in *RC* and *Pedlar* MSS.

452–465 For unused drafts from 1798 possibly related to the history of the Pedlar/Wanderer, see *RC & Pedlar,* pp. 112–115, 118–125, and *PW,* V, 413.

465 In *Pedlar* MS. E this line is followed by the words "End of Part First."

470 Supine the Wanderer lay] This highly Miltonic construction is the first direct naming of the central figure in the poem. This line is not in any of the *RC* or *Pedlar* MSS.

507–513 The classical and elegiac mood of these lines and the idea expressed in them looks back to a number of classical sources. Strongest comparison can be made with Theocritus, *Idylls,* I and III; Virgil, *Eclogues,* V, 13–44; and *Georgics,* I, 475–489 (see *PW* Knight, V, 48).

525–526 Cf. *EW,* ll. 255–256 ("For hope's deserted well why wistful look? / Chok'd is the pathway, and the pitcher broke") and Ecclesiastes 12:6 ("or the golden bowl be broken, or the pitcher be broken at the fountain").

531 the good die first] Cf. *Plutarch's Moralia: A Letter of Condolence to Appolonius* in which he quotes Menander as saying "Whom the gods love dies young" (II, "A letter of condolence to Appolonius," sec. 119, 34E).

531–533 These lines were published in *The Friend,* no. 15, January 25, 1810 (*STCF,* II, 292) and also by Percy Bysshe Shelley as a title quotation to *Alastor; or The Spirit of Solitude.* On the whole, however, Shelley was disappointed by *Exc.* See also VIII, 571–575.

538 At this point (with slight variations) *RC* MSS. B and D describe the animal inhabitants of the cottage: "The unshod Colt, / The wandring heifer and the Potter's ass" (MS. D, ll. 111–112); see *RC & Pedlar,* pp. 50–51.

544–550 A draft of these lines appears in *Peter Bell* MS. 2 (MS. 33, 50^{v}); see *RC & Pedlar,* p. 418n. for that draft. The lines are not found in *RC* MSS. B or D but are added to the poem in *Pedlar* MS. E. WW comments specifically on this section, stating that the lines "faithfully delineate as far as they go, the character possessed in common by many women whom it has been my happiness to know in humble life" (IF, p. 1217, below).

555 Robert is a weaver, using a handloom and employed in preindustrial domestic industry.

566 Not twenty years ago] In *RC* MSS. B and D, the story is set "now some ten years gone" (MS. B, l. 185; MS. D, l. 133); in *RC/Pedlar* MSS. E and M, this dating is changed to "some twenty years ago" (MS. E, l. 465; MS. M, l. 514); see *RC & Pedlar,* pp. 52–53, 420–421).

568 Two blighting seasons] WW refers to the bad harvests of 1794–1795. Butler notes that "wheat that normally cost about fifty shillings per British imperial quarter (eight bushels) climbed to ninety-two in 1795, an increase that led to bread riots" (*RC & Pedlar,* p. 4). At the time of writing *RC,* these events were almost contemporaneous (although WW set them in a more distant past); by 1814 and the publication of *Exc,* they had occurred sixteen years earlier. Thus the chronology of I, 566, is almost accurate.

576–577 *PW,* V, 414, points out that "And their place knew them not" is an indirect echo of *PL,* VII, 144 and of Psalms 103:16. The biblical phrasing is perhaps intended to universalize and give authority to the tale of Margaret that follows.

593–594 Cf. *Old Man Travelling; Animal Tranquility and Decay,* ll. 1–2: The little hedgerow birds, / That peck along the road, regard him not."

596 Him] In the *RC* and *Pedlar* MSS., Margaret's husband is named Robert at this point (MS. B, l. 213; MS. D, l. 161; MS. E, l. 495; MS. M, l. 544): see *RC & Pedlar,* pp. 54–55, 422–423).

624 deepest noon] *PW,* V, 414, compares *The Waggoner,* l. 6: "In silence deeper far than that of deepest noon."

634/635 The space left here in *Exc* reflects a division at this point into a "Second Part" in *RC* MSS. B and D and into "Part Third" in *Pedlar* MS. E.

646–647 an eye / So busy] Cf. STC's *Rime of the Ancyent Marinere.* "He holds him with his glittering eye" (l. 17, text of 1798). Both STC and WW were interested in the power of the speaker to hold the audience. See STC on animal magnetism: "in which the enkindling Reciter, by perpetual comment of looks and tones, lends his own will and apprehensive faculty to his Auditors" (*STCBL*, II, 239). For other references to *Rime*, see II, 683, 798; III, 860–861; VI, 109.

657–666 These lines are quoted as an epigraph to *The Friend*, no. 13, November 16, 1809 (*STCF*, II, 172).

666–667 This image of the "dreamer" looks back to the Poet's opening image (I, 10–18). Cf. also I, 440, 982, and III, 345–346.

700–704 Just what Margaret sees when she realizes Robert has left her changes in the rewriting of drafts across the *RC* and *Pedlar* MSS. and into *Exc*; for discussion of this point, see Bushell, chapter 4.

703–704 The gold is Robert's payment for enlisting. The government offered a bounty of ten guineas to any men enlisting for service in Europe only (see J. Steven Watson, *The Reign of King George III, 1760–1815* [Oxford, 1960], p. 376).

736 "trotting brooks"] Cf. Burns's poem *To W. S****** [*Simpson*], *Ochiltree*, stanza XV: "adown some trotting burn's meander" (l. 87). In his "Postscript" to *The River Duddon*, WW also quotes these lines from Burns, which are, he says, "chosen, if I recollect right, by Mr. Coleridge, as a motto for his embryo 'Brook'" (*Sonnet Series*, p. 77).

741 bladed grass] *PW*, V, 414, points out use of the same phrase in *A Midsummer Night's Dream*, I.i.211.

777–783 The Wanderer refers to the red dye used by farmers to mark their sheep. Cf. DW in the *Alfoxden Journal*: "The moss rubbed from the pailings by the sheep that leaves locks of wool, and the red marks with which they are spotted, upon the wood" (see *RC & Pedlar*, p. 64).

840 some tokens of regard] Money.

892–895 Margaret turns to domestic industry to support herself, spinning hemp, but she is exploited as a cottage worker with far less profitable self-sufficiency than Robert previously had as a weaver.

906 Nine tedious years] "Five tedious years" in *RC* MSS. B and D (MS. B, l. 482; MS. D, l. 447); see *RC & Pedlar*, pp. 68–69.

906–951 WW recalls these lines as being first written for the poem and composed at Racedown, Dorset, in 1795 (IF; see p. 1215, below). In fact there is some uncertainty about this dating, since DW speaks of *RC* as a "new poem" in a letter of 1797 (*EY*, p. 189), and STC quotes from the end of the original poem in a letter of June 10, 1797 (*STCL*, I, 327). It seems likely that WW's memory is two years out.

917–920 The physical track of the individual on the landscape is also emphasized in the stories of the Miner (VI, 255–264) and of Ellen (VI, 824–828, 836–840) later in *Exc.*

919–922 A sense of Margaret's occupation here is provided in Patricia Baines's *Spinning Wheels, Spinners, and Spinning* (London, 1977): "[T]he long fibres [of flax or hemp] are more difficult to manage when held in the hand, so they were tied round the spinner's waist. . . . A child was employed to turn the wheel by means of this pole from one side while the spinners walked backwards from the rotating hooks on the other side, playing out fibres with each hand as they went and so making two yarns at a time which, on the return journey, were twisted together" (pp. 63–64).

929–932 Cf. *The Old Cumberland Beggar*, ll. 32–36.

951 Last human Tenant] As is pointed out in *PW*, IV, 414, the emphasis on "human" would have been more strongly felt after the Book I descriptions of various animal tenants of the cottage in earlier versions of the poem (see note to I, 538, above). This line was the end of the poem in an early state of *RC* MS. B.

952–984 See *RC & Pedlar*, pp. 256–259, 278–279, for earlier alternative versions of an attempted ending in *RC* MSS. B and D.

959 the impotence of grief] Some critics are uneasy over the ending to Margaret's tale, suggesting that the consolation offered by the Wanderer in ll. 967–984 does not

successfully counterbalance the suffering described in the tale itself. See James Averill, *Wordsworth and the Poetry of Human Suffering* (Ithaca, 1980), pp. 55–61.

968/969 At this point in the reworking of *Exc* for *PW*, 1845, WW added seven lines of far more explicitly Christian expression in relation to Margaret's suffering (see the verbal variants to the reading text, above). For discussion of those and similar additions, see the Introduction, pp. 21–22, above, and Lyon, pp. 24–27. See also William Hale White, *An Examination of the Charge of Apostasy Against Wordsworth* (1898) for Victorian discussion of WW's alterations. The major "Christian additions," which will be commented on throughout these notes, can be found at I, 969, 982; III, 408; V, 161–162; V, 830; VI, 790; IX, 227.

982 At this point in *PW*, 1845, WW changed the lines to refer to sorrow, despair, ruin, and grief as appearing but "an idle dream" and to indicate that "meditative sympathies repose / Upon the breast of faith" (see the verbal variants to the reading text, above). For images of the dreamer compare I, 10–18; I, 440; I, 666–667; III, 345–346.

Book II: "The Solitary"

The second book of *Exc* contains the strongest sense of the poem as a journey that is actually "going somewhere" in physical terms, with the Wanderer and the Poet covering ground and responding to their environment. It also marks the true opening of the new poem moving beyond the earlier *RC* material and translates the surroundings from Margaret's tale in southwest England to the very different topography of the Lake District in a manner that WW vividly describes in IF: "The scene of the first book of the Poem is . . . laid in a tract of country not sufficiently near to that which soon comes into view in the second book to agree with the fact . . . it would require more than seven leagued boots to stretch in one morning from a common in Somersetshire or Dorsetshire, to the heights of Furness Fells & the deep vallies they embosom" (see p. 1217, below). There is a strong sense of rootedness in Book II: we are given examples of different local customs in the village wake and the traditional funeral service, and this book also depicts immediately recognizable landmarks of the Lakes such as the Langdale Pikes that loom over the Solitary's valley, although those mountains are not named as such. At the same time the physical excursion frames the narratives with tales being told in close relationship to their natural setting. A strong sense of topography is also used to reinforce character: the Wanderer is a traveler, recognized and welcomed in many communities as he travels up the valleys. The Solitary, by contrast, lives in a place that is bleak, self-contained, remote and hidden.

1–2 In days of yore how fortunately fared / The Minstrel] The opening section (ll. 1–29), and ll. 1–2 in particular, bear comparison with James Beattie's two-book poem *The Minstrel; or the Progress of Genius* (1771, 1774), which describes "How forth the Minstrel fared in days of yore, / Right glad of heart" (I, 21–22). WW had read *The Minstrel* at school in Hawkshead and was certainly influenced by it (see Wu, *Reading I*, p. 11, and Everard H. King, *James Beattie's "The Minstrel" and the Origins of Romantic Autobiography* (Lewiston, NY, 1992). Beattie's central character, Edwin, with his naturalized Scottish education among the hills, could certainly be compared with the Wanderer. In a letter of May 20, 1767, Beattie discusses his poem in terms that may also bear on WW's: "My hero was to be born in the south of Scotland; which you know was the native land of the English minstrels; I mean of those minstrels who travelled into England, and supported themselves there by singing their ballads to the harp" (*Memoir of Beattie* by Alexander Dyce, *Poetical Works of James Beattie* [London 1871], p. xxi). The description of the traditional minstrel could also be compared to Sir Walter Scott's wandering figure as portrayed in the "Introduction" to the *Lay of the Last Minstrel* (1805), where he seeks "Ladies' praise" in order to perform his work. Scott's poem emphasizes the social value of such a figure, linking communities by his travel and encountering all kinds of people, which clearly compares with the Wanderer's role. Cf. VII, 9–22; VIII, 606–607.

Draft material toward this opening description of the Minstrel was originally written for *The Prelude* and can be found in MS. 48 (15^{v}; *13-Bk. Prelude*, II, 374–375). In that early draft the description is applied to the poet himself, but when the account is reworked for *Exc* in MS. 47 (33^{v}), there is a shift from first to third person. The comparison to the Minstrel is finally used for the Wanderer in MS. 71 (as in the published *Exc*); see p. 430, below.

15 His Harp, suspended at the Traveller's side] Cf. Beattie, "His harp, the sole companion of his way" (*The Minstrel*, I, 25).

17 Opening from Land to Land an easy way] Cf. STC's *Rime of the Ancyent Marinere*, l. 619: "I pass, like night, from land to land" (text of 1798).

36–87 These lines are not in the earliest version of Book II (MS. 47), where earlier material on the Minstrel leads straight on into line 88 (on 33^{v}). This description of responses to the Wanderer by local people first appears in the fair-copy text of MS. 71, where it is clearly being drafted and written into the main body of the text (see MS. 71, 35^{v}, 36^{v}).

44–49 This passage is an expanded version of lines found in *Pedlar* MSS. E (ll. 359–360) and M (ll. 407–409); see *RC & Pedlar*, pp. 412–313. In terms of its original context, the section should occur in Book I after "Self-taught, as of a dreamer in the woods" (l. 440). WW's decision to move the lines to this point in Book II was possibly made to bulk out this second briefer description of the Wanderer (see also *PW*, V, 415).

88–89 But when the rising sun / Had three times called us] The Wanderer and the Poet have thus been walking together for three days.

124–144 See also DW's *Journals* (p. 20) for September 2, 1800, in which she describes a village fair.

162–163 The Solitary's cottage is situated in Little Langdale at the top of the Great Langdale Valley. See WW's account in *Select Views* (1810), where he describes Langdale as "austere but reconciled and rendered attractive to the affections by the deep serenity that is spread over every thing" (*Prose*, II, 269).

164–334 These lines give the Wanderer's account of the Solitary's life. The narrative does not appear in the first version of Book II (MS. 47). It is copied out into MS. 70 without the account of the Solitary's marriage and children, and then rewritten as part of the fair copy of MS. 71. For discussion of the complexities in relation to this section, see pp. 439–440, below.

166 From sight of One] The Solitary. The Wanderer now proceeds to tell the Poet a brief account of the Solitary's life as preparation for their meeting and to explain the reason for the Solitary's withdrawal into a remote valley. This procedure seems to imitate the structure of Book I, in which the Poet gave the reader the Wanderer's biography before introducing him.

168–169 The Wanderer's disclaimer here anticipates the fuller retelling of the Solitary's tale by himself in Book III.

171 he, like myself] The shared Scottish origins of the Wanderer and Solitary are referred to elsewhere in the poem. See III, 506; IV, 548; and VIII, 35.

196–222 The very heart of the Solitary's tragedy as told by the Wanderer (the deaths of the Solitary's wife and children) first appears in MS. 71 in a late rev on inserted leaves 39^{v}–40^{v}; WW clearly wrote this material after the deaths of his own two children in 1812. Although this Book II account of the Solitary's tragedy precedes the fuller account of the tale that WW includes in Book III, the Book III materials were written first. For discussion of this sequence of composition, see pp. 453–455, below.

222–277 The account of the Solitary's entrancement with the French Revolution and its ideals can be directly compared with WW's account of his own involvement in Books IX and X of *The Prelude*. The Wanderer's attack on the radical thinkers of the Revolution is quite severe, and WW reworks this passage a number of times in DC MSS. 47, 70, and 71.

224 the unlooked-for dawn] The start of the French Revolution. Cf. IV, 263.

224–225 Cf. *Prelude* IX, 388–392; X, 539–544, 689–736.

236 The cause of Christ] One of the first published edition's two direct references to Christ (the other occurs at V, 278). "Jesus" is used at V, 958, and "Redeemer" occurs at IV, 1097; at V, 914, and IX, 718–719, the Pastor speaks of "Him who bled" on "the Cross." For contemporary dissatisfaction with what some saw as a paucity of references to Christ, see Montgomery and Wilson. Later changes made to the 1814 text increase the number of such direct references by other characters, as when the Matron describes herself as "by my Redeemer taught" (see verbal variant to V, 830/831, of the reading text, above). See also Lyon, pp. 116–117, and pp. 21–22, above.

245–246 Cf. *Prelude,* X, 309–314.

250–260 WW here comments on the excessive hopes and optimism created in response to the Revolution and the dangerous effects they could have upon the life of an individual who invested in them fully only to be let down. WW in IF relates the Solitary to a particular individual, Joseph Fawcett (1758–1804), a dissenting preacher, who was affected in just this way: "his Xtianity was probably never very deeply rooted; &, like many others in those times of like shewy talents, he had not strength of character to withstand the effects of the French Revolution & of the wild and lax opinions which had done so much towards producing it & far more in carrying it forward in its extremes" (see p. 1216, below).

258 Plague from this union spread] Here, and at II, 260, political ideals are described as a kind of sickness. See also the Solitary's own use of such imagery to describe his personal suffering at III, 855.

266 Life, like that Roman Janus, double-faced] In Roman religion Janus was the god of gates and doorways and, by extension, of beginnings. His symbol was a double-faced head that looked both ways. See also STC's comment on WW's religion that "it conjures up to *my* fancy a sort of *Janus*-head of Spinoza and Dr Watts" (*STCL,* V, 95).

275 false philosophy] WW again refers to those who developed optimistic philosophical hopes for mankind out of the French Revolution. The attack seems particularly directed against William Godwin's *Political Justice* (1793)—with its arguments for reason as the means by which man could achieve perfectibility—which WW himself was first deeply impressed by and then, like many others, turned against. See also Wu, *Reading I,* pp. 66–67. Cf. *Prelude,* X, 765–768, 805–829.

290–291 Again, images of infection, and a personification of Liberty as a sick woman, are used to describe the political disease of the times. The division of the Solitary's life into a personal and political phase (more marked in his own telling of his story in Book III) might also suggest a parallel here between his first crisis when his wife and children die of some kind of "plague" and the second, more universal, political malady by which he is infected.

305 of Him] An indirect reference to Christ. See note to II, 236, above, for more direct references.

331–332 a "world / Not moving to his mind."] The quotation is from George Dyer's poem *On the death of Gilbert Wakefield. Meditated in a Garden, near a Churchyard, At the Close of Autumn,* in *Poems* (1802): "When man, quite wearied with a world, perhaps, / Not moving to his mind" (I.ii.118–119). WW had read this poem by 1810 (see Wu, *Reading II,* p. 82). *PW* Knight, V, 80, compares *Ode: Intimations of Immortality*: "Moving about in worlds not realiz'd," l. 148 (text of 1807).

335–359 The description of the journey by the Wanderer and the Poet is given geographical specificity by WW in IF: "In the Poem I suppose that the Pedlar & I ascended from a plain country up the vale of Langdale & struck off a good way above the Chapel to the Western side of the Vale we ascended the hill & thence looked down upon the circular recess in which lies Blea Tarn chosen by the Solitary for his retreat" (p. 1217, below). In topographical terms they climb Lingmoor, the hill that separates Langdale from Little Langdale, but of course *Exc* is a work of fiction and not of geography.

347–368 WW quotes these lines in *A Guide through the District of the Lakes* (*Prose,* II, 159–160), adding this note to II, 357 ("A quiet treeless nook"): "No longer strictly applicable, on account of recent plantations."

358 A liquid pool] Blea Tarn. In *Select Views* WW described Blea Tarn as "not an object of any beauty in itself, but it is situated in a small, deep circular Valley of peculiar character; for it contains only one Dwelling-house and two or three cultivated fields" (*Prose,* II, 270).

393 Of that profound Abyss] A Miltonic construction. Cf. *PL,* II, 438 ("void profound"); II, 405 ("The dark unbottom'd infinite Abyss").

401–402 "*Shall in the Grave thy love be known, / In Death thy faithfulness?*"] The quotation refers indirectly to Psalms 88:11 ("Shall thy loving kindness be declared in the grave? or thy faithfulness in destruction?").

406–414 The funeral described is a traditional one in which the bearers carry the coffin from the house to the grave. WW expressly requested that this traditional practice be followed at his own funeral rather than using the more recent hearse vehicle: "the latter has been the means of introducing a change much to be lamented in the mode of conducting funerals among the Mountains. . . . I beg to be excused for giving utterance here to a wish that should it befall me to die at Rydal Mount, my own body may be carried to Grasmere Church . . . on the shoulders of neighbours no house being passed without some words of a funeral Psalm being sung" (IF, p. 1219, below). This procedure was duly followed on WW's death, and the "coffin walk" from Rydal to Grasmere can still be followed today. See also *Journals,* September 3, 1800 (p. 20) for an account of John Dawson's funeral: "The corpse was then borne down the hill & they sang till they had got past Town-end." Lyon, p. 54, suggests that DW's account here may have been the model for this *Exc* passage. See also DW's account of the tragic death of George and Sarah Green and their funeral in a letter of March 23, 1808 (*MY,* I, 201–202), and in her *George & Sarah Green, a Narrative,* ed. Ernest de Selincourt (Oxford, 1936).

466–467 a Novel of Voltaire, / His famous Optimist] The novel is *Candide,* in which Voltaire made fun of the optimistic philosophy of Leibniz's *Theodicy.* The Wanderer disapproves of such reading since it adopts a cynical stance in relation to human suffering rather than offering any kind of positive teaching. Various critics, including Hazlitt, criticized WW for this attack on Voltaire (see also notes to II, 510, and IV, 993, below). WW read *Candide* in the early 1790s (Wu, *Reading I,* p. 142).

469 Retreat within retreat] Cf. *Prelude,* VIII, 335: "Shelter'd within a shelter" (in which such withdrawal is seen as a positive rather than a negative move).

501 summoned Kings to scaffolds] The Wanderer seems to be looking gloomily ahead, but the line clearly also refers back to the beheading of Louis XVI, on January 21, 1793, and possibly of Charles I on January 30, 1649.

504 A kerchief sprinkled with his Master's blood] It was the custom at beheadings throughout the seventeenth and eighteenth century to stain some piece of cloth as a memento. In his account of the execution of Louis XVI, Thomas Carlyle in *The French Revolution* describes "dipping of handkerchiefs, of pike-points in the blood" (*The Works of Thomas Carlyle: Centenary Edition* (New York, 1898–1901), IV, 111; chapter 3.2.VIII: "Place de la Révolution").

510 this dull product of a Scoffer's pen] Hazlitt commented of this line that "we conceive that it would have been more in character, that is, more manly, in Mr. Wordsworth . . . if he had blotted out the epithet after it had peevishly escaped him" (Hazlitt, p. 556). In a letter to WW, September 19, 1814, CL describes his defending of WW's line: "That objection which M Burney had imbibed from him [Hazlitt] about Voltaire I explaind to MB (or tried) exactly on your principle of it being a characteristic speech" (*CLL,* III, 112). Cf. note to IV, 993.

523 The Solitary makes his entrance.

542–544 *PW* Knight, V, 89, compares *Resolution and Independence,* ll. 97–98: "He answer'd me with pleasure and surprise; / And there was, while he spake, a fire about his eyes" (text of 1807).

563 This blooming Child] Cf. III, 647; VI, 1127.

577–580 For WW's own valuing of such customs, see note to II, 406–414, above. WW comments expressly on ll. 577–580 in IF: "little did I foresee that the observance & mode of proceeding w[h]. had often affected me so much would so soon be superceded" (p. 1219, below).

596 Ashes to ashes, dust bequeathed to dust] "An Order for the Burial Service" in The Book Of Common Prayer indicates that these lines are to be spoken as the coffin is lowered into the grave: "ashes to ashes, dust to dust." The Solitary has presumably just heard these lines at the funeral of the old Pensioner.

604 We shall not sleep, but we shall all be changed] Again, this line refers to the "Burial Service" from The Book of Common Prayer: "we shall not all sleep but we shall all be changed" (which in turn draws on 1 Corinthians 15:51).

620 That poor Man] The old Pensioner, whose funeral the visitors witnessed on their arrival in the valley and whose tale the Solitary goes on to tell. Cf. the shepherd in *SBC* (see pp. 1212–1213, below).

621–622 with a faint sarcastic smile / Which did not please me] The Poet is far less sympathetic toward the Solitary than is the Wanderer. Such responses perhaps raise the question of how far WW is to be directly identified with the Poet. On this issue see, for example, William Howard, "Narrative Irony in *The Excursion*," *Studies in Romanticism* 24 (1985): 511–530.

639 the sick man] The Solitary.

646 my benign Companion] The Wanderer.

648–652 The Solitary attacks idealization of country living, suggesting that those who live in this remote community do not always act in good ways. Presumably he is referring to the behavior of the housewife, which he returns to at ll. 767–773, 789–791, and 921–924. Cf. Hazlitt's more extreme attack in the third part of his review of *Exc* where he states, "All country-people hate each other" (Hazlitt, p. 637). Cf. V, 420.

683 My eyes were busy] Cf. notes to I, 646–647; II, 798; III, 860–861; VI, 109.

701–708. This kind of heightened description of everyday objects left WW open to parody. James Hogg in *The Poetic Mirror* (1816), which makes much use of *Exc,* seems to be parodying II, 706–708, in his poem *The Stranger*, where he describes the butter as "One roll of yellow treasure, all as pure / As primrose bud reflected in the lake" (p. 136).

719 on two huge Peaks] The Langdale Pikes loom up behind the valley in which the Solitary is supposed to live. In fact, because of the rim of the valley behind, you cannot actually see the Pikes from the cottage that is situated there. *PW* Knight, V, 96, points out that "if the three were seated, as described, in the upper room of the cottage (which has one small window looking towards the Pikes), they could not possibly see them. . . . [T]he realism of the narrative here gives way" (96). Again, though, it should be remembered that *Exc* is a poetic text, not a factual one.

744–746 *PW* Knight, V, 97, notes, "This is strictly accurate. On and about the 21st June, the sun, as seen from Blea Tarn, sets just between the Langdale Pikes."

780 slow and torpid] See also the Solitary's later description of the rural mind and the peasant boy at VIII, 71, and VIII, 424. His point is that country life, with all its hardships, can have a negative effect on its inhabitants.

791 Kine] An archaic plural of "cow."

798 like a Shadow] This Coleridgean image (cf. *Rime of the Ancyent Marinere*: "I pass, like night, from land to land, l. 619 [text of 1798]) recurs in *Exc*; cf. VI, 109: "We met and passed like Shadows." For other references to *Rime,* see note to II, 683.

840 a Chapel, a small Edifice] WW in IF gives a specific location: "The Ruins of the old Chapel, among which the old man was found lying, may yet be traced, & stood upon

the ridge that divides Paterdale from Boardale & Martindale" (see p. 1218, below).

846–850 The account of the old man, lost and seeking shelter in the storm, seems to echo Act III of *King Lear,* as well as WW's play of 1798–99, *The Borderers,* IV.i and V.ii. DW also gives the story of the old man in some detail in a journal entry (November 9, 1805) on an "Ullswater Excursion." In DW's version the old man did not die: "he was at first stupefied, & unable to move, yet after he had eaten and drunk, & recollected himself a little he walked down the Mountain, and his health did not afterwards seem to have suffered" (*Prose,* II, 373–374). See note to II, 928–929, below.

860–863 The Solitary's stumbling out of the mist to see the view echoes the Snowdon passage in *The Prelude* (XIII, 36–40). His vision of the city in the clouds also has much in common with the biblical vision of a New Jerusalem in Revelation 21:10–25. Line 862 of Book II is identical to III, 729.

860–916 According to WW in IF, "The glorious appearance disclosed above & among the mountains was described partly from what my friend M[r]. Luff who then lived in Paterdale witnessed upon this melancholy occasion & partly from what Mary & I had seen . . . above Hartshope Hall in our way from Paterdale to Ambleside" (p. 1218, below). CL also seems to recall the same sky in a letter of August 9, 1814, thanking WW for sending him a copy of *Exc*: "that gorgeous Sunset is famous, I think it must have been the identical one we saw on Salisbury plain five years ago, that drew Phillips from the card table where he had sat from rise of that luminary to its unequall'd set; but neither he nor I had gifted eyes to see those symbols of common things glorified" (*CLL,* III, 95). The cloud formation may or may not have actually occurred at sunset, however, since CL notes in a later letter that "I find I miscalld that celestial splendour of the mist going off, a sunset. That only shews my inaccuracy of head" (III, 112).

907 I saw not, but I felt that it was there] Cf. l. 14 of *Conclusion* (later *After-thought*), Sonnet XXXIII (later XXXIV) in *The River Duddon*: "We feel that we are greater than we know."

928–929 The old man survives his night on the mountain but dies quietly three weeks later. Cf. note to II, 846–850. WW in IF gives us additional details concerning the characters in this tale: "all that belongs to the character of the Old Man was taken from a Grasmere Pauper who was boarded in the last house quitting the Vale on the road to Ambleside; the character of his hostess, & all that befell the poor man upon the mountain, belongs to Paterdale. The woman I knew well; her name was Ruth Jackson, & she was exactly such a person as I describe" (p. 1218, below).

Book III: "Despondency"

As with Book II, the first half of Book III maintains a strong sense of location and places dialogue within a natural context in a way that allows responses to nature to reveal more about what is being said, and about the attitudes and characters of the speakers, than they intend. This technique is strongly felt, for example, in the different responses of the three characters to the great rocks at the foot of the waterfall that they look down upon. Such scenes are reminiscent of John Thelwall's *The Peripatetic* (1793), in which the disaffected "Belmour" journeys with and is offered consolation by his companions. Cf. notes to "Preface," ll. 26–27, above, and to III, 835, below.

The Solitary's tale in Book III is closely linked both to the book that precedes and the one that comes after it. In Book II the reader was presented with the Wanderer's third-person account of the Solitary's life; in Book III that story is told again, this time by the Solitary himself (his story is the only first-person narrative of the poem). These two versions of the same story reward comparison in terms of emphasis, intention, and the responses of the listeners within the poem and of the reader beyond. In telling his own tale, the Solitary makes clear the reasons for his withdrawal from the world and his apathetic response to life. This account then leads directly into Book IV, where the Wanderer responds to the Solitary's difficulties point by point, almost seeming to translate retrospectively the Solitary's narrative into a discursive text. In these ways, then, Book III looks backward and forward to unite the early books of the poem.

Finally, Book III is perhaps one of the most interesting books with regard to WW's compositional method because of the changes made to it by the poet in response to events in his own life. These changes are focused on the Solitary's telling of the loss of his family, which occurs in MS. 71 as an eight-page insertion added by WW after the deaths of his own children. See pp. 448–453, below, for a full discussion.

10 our Host] The Solitary.

21 my grey-haired Friend] The Wanderer.

51–162 In this passage each of the three onlookers (the Poet, the Wanderer, and the Solitary) interprets the natural scene according to his own inner state and philosophical or religious beliefs. The Solitary explicitly comments on this procedure at III, 156–160.

53–75 "The local allusions in this passage, and in what follows, are most exact and literal. . . . There are many fragments of ice-borne rock, high up the flank of Blake Rigg to the west, and on the slopes of Lingmoor to the east . . . but this particular mass of rock lay 'Right at the foot of that moist precipice,' and there it still lies" (*PW* Knight, V, 108).

97 With timid lapse] *PW*, V, 420, compares the use of the word "lapse" to describe the falling water with that of Milton in *PL*, VIII, 263 ("liquid Lapse of murmuring streams"), with l. 4 of Sonnet XX from *The River Duddon* ("the liquid lapse serene"), and with *Exc*, VIII, 334.

116 See WW's lengthy Latin note to this line on pp. 299–300, above, quoting from Thomas Burnet's *Telluris Theoria Sacra* (2nd ed., 1688–89), I, 89; see also Wu, *Reading II*, pp. 36–37. The first English version (*Sacred Theory of the Earth*, I, 1684; II, 1690) does not directly correspond to the Latin text; we are indebted to Brother Gabriel Fagan, F.S.C. (La Salle University) and James Shiel (University of Sussex) for their assistance in translating Burnet's rhapsodic prose:

"If, indeed, anything on this earth gives us a spectacle truly pleasing to and worthy of a philosopher, I can attest that Nature touched me in such a way; when I, looking out from the loftiest cliff, viewed the Mediterranean shore, then the cerulean surface of that sea, and finally certain Alpine regions; nothing truly more disparate and strange, nor of its kind more extraordinary and remarkable. This was a theater I could easily prefer to all the Roman ones and all the Greek ones, and this show put on by nature to all the stage performances or contests in the amphitheater. Nothing here is simply elegant and pretty, but huge and magnificent because it pleases by both its vastness and its immensity. Here I behold the uniform surface of the sea, spread out from end to end, so great a line of sight can be seen; hence to great eruptions on the face of the earth, and immense variegated masses standing high or sinking down: lofty, hanging down, leaning back, heaped together—all placed wild and uneven. The unity and simplicity of Nature, the inexhaustible plains, are pleasing from this vantage point; from another view the diverse complexities of great bodies as well as chaotic debris of all sorts: which, to my eye, seem the rubble not of any given city or town, but of a destroyed world.

"There was something unusual and marvelous on each specific mountain, but above all the rest, that ledge, on which I sat, was most pleasing to me; it was very sheer and high, and when looking up from the ground, disguised its height by a somewhat gradual ascent: looking down to the sea, a fearsome, headlong plunge as if it were a true perpendicular stately wall. Beyond that seaside view, it was smooth and uniform (a situation sometimes noticeable in mountains) and then there was a rupture in that surface from top to bottom rent asunder by either some upheaval of the earth, or by a lightning bolt.

"The bottom portion of the steep was a cave, which had a space containing grottos entering into the hollow mountain; whether made long ago by Nature, or eaten away by the sea and the relentless pounding of the waves. Into these the surgings of the sea entered with great force and noise, and then the cave turned them into foam and thrust them out again as if vomiting them from its deep maw.

"The right side of the mountain was steep, with sharp rock and naked crag; the left was not neglected by Nature, inasmuch as it was adorned by trees: and a stream of clear water rushed toward the foot of the mountain: which irrigated a nearby valley, creeping along slowly, through various twistings, as if attempting to prolong its life, and suddenly disappeared into the great sea. At the highest point of the promontory, pleasantly situated on a rock, I sat in contemplation. Farewell, awesome seat, fit for a king. Majestic rock, forever part of my remembrance!"

119 the Tenant of that lonely Vale] The Solitary.

135 Pompey's Pillar] Pompey was a Roman general who fought against Julius Caesar for the control of Rome in defense of the republic. After his defeat by Caesar, Pompey fled to Egypt; later travelers to Alexandria incorrectly believed that a granite column erected in honor of the Emperor Diocletian was in fact the burial marker for Pompey.

136 My Theban Obelisk] Thebes was the main city of Boeotia in Ancient Greece. It was famous as the birthplace of Heracles, among others. The kings of Thebes were descended from Cadmus and famously included Oedipus among their doomed number. See also note to VI, 559.

137 A Druid Cromlech] Cf. *The Vale of Esthwaite,* ll. 31–34, and n., in *Early Poems, 1785–1797,* p. 424. A cromlech is a prehistoric stone structure involving a large stone lying horizontally upon three or more upright stones (as at Stonehenge).

147 that huge Pile] Stonehenge.

150–152 The description of the eddying wind echoes that of WW's *Adventures on Salisbury Plain,* ll. 154–157 (see *SPP,* p. 127).

152 On Sarum's naked plain] Salisbury Plain. Cf. WW's *Adventures on Salisbury Plain,* l. 1 ("on the skirt of Sarum's Plain"; *SPP,* p. 123).

154 Syria's marble ruins] *PW*Knight, V, 112, suggests that this reference is to Palmyra, a city in an oasis of the Syrian desert once famous for its ruins. In ancient times great trade routes crossed in Palmyra. Cf. VIII, 220.

152–156 If these lines sound faintly anticipatory of Shelley's poem *Ozymandias,* it is probably because WW and Shelley are both drawing upon a common source in C. F. Volney's *The Ruins: or a Survey of the Revolutions of Empires* (1791; trans. from the French, 1795).

166 The wandering Herbalist] The Unrequited Lover (whose tale is told beginning at VI, 98) is also a lover of plants.

177 that Fellow-wanderer] The Solitary gives a generalized portrait of another figure, that of the geologist.

214–229 In the brief debate that follows, the Solitary holds on to his position: that questioning man's origins, seeking to find purpose in life or spiritual development is pointless, since all ends in death. He denies the immortality of the soul.

230–237 The Wanderer refers to the initial encounter with the Solitary at II, 532–537, when the Solitary was comforting the grieving child with Christian consolation (suggesting belief in the immortal soul). He counters the Solitary's abstract and negative philosophizing with a more grounded practical response to life's troubles.

239–243 The Solitary returns to the same point made at III, 214–215.

245–248 A Native American creation myth. This account is the first of a series of examples given by the Solitary of the search for man's origins in different religions and cultures. *PW*Knight, V, 115, notes: "The Navagos and several other American tribes have this legend." See also *PW*Knight, V, 392–393.

253–256 *PW*Knight, V, 116, tells us: "Before the time of Solon, the Athenians wore golden . . . brooches, or pins with a golden cicada for the head . . . since the grasshopper . . . was supposed to spring out of the ground."

260 holy Ganges] The great sacred river of northern India, formed by the drainage of the southern Himalayas.

265 a living Ocean] Cf. *Tintern Abbey*, l. 99 ("And the round ocean, and the living air," text of 1798) and *Prelude*, III, 626–627 ("Itself a living part of a live whole, / A creek of the vast sea."

267 Like Niger, in impenetrable sands] This great river of West Africa is the only one that affords a route into the interior. In his appendix to Mungo Park's *Travels* (1799), the leading British geographer James Rennell suggested that the Niger ended by evaporation. WW had read Mungo Park by 1804 (see Wu, *Reading I*, p. 162).

269–287 At the end of this disquisition, the Solitary makes it clear that his own position is not one of contented acceptance and resolution but a more negative apathetic state of simply existing without wanting to think about it.

283–285 Cf. Despaire's speech in Spenser's *Faerie Queene*, bk. 1, canto IX, 40, ll. 8–9: "Sleepe after toyle, port after stormie seas, / Ease after warre, death after life, does greatly please."

305–312 The Solitary thinks back to an earlier time when he was able to respond imaginatively and openly to the world around him.

324–326 The Solitary rejects poetic idealism, preferring a direct response to Nature to an imaginative one.

326 the Golden Age] Cf. *Prelude*, VIII, 185: "So ancient Poets sing, the golden Age." According to Hesiod in *Theogony*, this age was the period of the first race of man living under the reign of Cronos (Saturn). Men lived like gods without sorrow, illness, or old age; spring was eternal.

328 In Arcady] Cf. *Prelude*, VIII, 183: "Not such as in Arcadian Fastnesses." In strict geographical terms, Arcadia was a mountainous area in the central Peloponnesus, but the pastoral character of Arcadian life made it the traditional setting for classical pastoral.

345–346 a Dreamer] Cf. I, 10–18, 440, 666–667, 982. Cf. *Prelude*, III, 28: "I was the Dreamer, they the Dream."

338–346 The Poet takes up the Solitary's argument to state that if poetry is to be attacked, then so should philosophy. He considers different approaches to life's suffering and concludes by questioning the Solitary's dismissiveness.

355 Epicureans] The followers of Epicurus believed that man should dedicate himself to the pleasures of friendship, simple living, and withdrawal from the world in order to achieve inner calm and wisdom. *Exc* does at times seem to touch upon Epicurean sentiments. See Wu, *Reading II*, p. 256. Cf. I, 10–18, and IX, 52–81.

362 The Stoic's heart] The Stoics believed that man should submit without complaint to the necessities of life. The wise man must be without passion (though not without feeling) with human conduct conforming to natural laws. The poem can be read as advocating to some extent this Stoic position. For discussion of this point, see chapter 3 of Jane Worthington, *Wordsworth's Reading of Roman Prose* (New Haven, 1947).

374–410 This passage was originally written for the *Tuft of Primroses* in 1808. WW had some difficulty positioning the section when he integrated it into *Exc*, placing it first at the opening of Book V (MS. 70, 6^{r}) with the Poet looking wistfully back at the Solitary's valley as they leave it, and then moving the passage to its final position in Book III (MS. 71, 75^{r}–76^{r}). The lines when spoken by the Poet still seem to articulate a positive sense of solitude, but in the mouth of the Solitary they read more as a justification of negative withdrawal. Changes in anticipation of this move can be seen in the original MS. (MS. 65, 43^{v}–45^{r}; *Tuft*, pp. 244–249). See also Bushell, pp. 68–73, for discussion of these changes.

400 the monastic Brotherhood] The passage as originally written for *Tuft* is followed by an account of the life of St. Basil. This reference thus anticipates the material that was to follow in the original context.

408 In *PW*, 1845, "the human soul" became "the immortal Soul." See also note to I,

968/969, for Christian additions to the poem.

443–445 Clearly reflecting his own experiences, the Solitary makes the point that one of life's central truths is that happiness is not lasting.

481 for confession] *PW* Knight, V, 124, compares WW's Sonnet VI: *The Trosachs* in *Yarrow Revisited and Other Poems,* l. 2, "an apt confessional."

489 Her whom once I loved] The Solitary's wife.

506 Revered Compatriot] The Wanderer (who, like the Solitary, comes from Scotland). See also II, 171; IV, 548; VIII, 35.

526–557 The setting of the Solitary's married life in Devon perhaps draws upon WW's recollection of his early adult years (1795–1797) with DW in Racedown, Dorset (which was close to the sea) and then at Alfoxden (1797–98), near the Bristol Channel and on the edge of the Quantocks. In a copy of *Exc* 1814 annotated by STC, this passage is marked with a vertical line; Beer, p. 462, speculates that STC (provided he drew the line) may have been struck by the similarity to his own early married life and also remembered the time he spent in the Quantocks with WW and DW. For other STC annotations to this volume (now at Victoria University Library, Toronto), see notes to IV, 13–17, 40–42, 97–99, 279–289, 306–310, 617, 629.

539 In MS. 71 (83^r–84^v) there is a passage here, omitted from the final poem, in which the Solitary compares his early married life with his wife to that of Adam and Eve (see pp. 451, 642–643, below).

540–557 This description of the landscape matches experiences of WW and DW at Racedown, Dorset, as recorded by DW in a letter of August 14, 1797: "From the end of the house we have a view of the sea, over a woody meadow-country . . . wherever we turn we have woods, smooth downs, and valleys" (*EY,* p. 191).

548 unmolested Wanderers] There are many "Wanderers" of different sorts within *Exc.* Cf. *Prelude,* XII, 135–184.

557 "That all the grove and all the day was ours"] Like earlier editors of *Exc,* we have been unable to identify the source of WW's quotation.

607–609 Reluctant to come to the tragic heart of his tale, the Solitary breaks off to address his sympathetic listeners.

612 Cf. note to III, 777, below. The Solitary has a negative view of history as a world force destroying his life and beyond his control.

631 The Solitary experiences seven years of happy married life.

647 Our blooming Girl] Cf. II, 563; VI, 1127.

647–658 The deaths of the Solitary's son and daughter (and the Solitary's subsequent suffering) were added to the poem after WW's loss of two of his own children in 1812. In MS. 71 this section appears on an eight-page insertion that includes the shorter pieces *MG* and *CC.* The former, WW tells us, "was in part an overflow from the Solitary's description of his own & his wife's feelings upon the decease of their children" (IF, p. 67). It is also clearly an overflow of his and MW's feelings. Cf. II, 212. See also pp. 448–453, below.

678 O heavy change] Cf. Milton, *Lycidas,* l. 37: "But O the heavy change."

695–704 The Solitary turns away from the living in an attempt to find communion with his dead loved ones.

709–710 These lines first appear in WW's *The Borderers* (IV.ii.102–103, p. 236), where they describe Rivers's state of mind after his crime and before his apparent "recovery" by convincing himself of the powers of rationalism. Here the Solitary uses them to represent his desperation at the loss of his family, but the echo of *The Borderers* perhaps also indirectly anticipates his imminent political enthusiasm and despair. The lines are also quoted by STC in *Biographia Literaria* at the end of chapter 5 (*STCBL,* I, 105). See also CL's essay "The Praise of Chimney-Sweepers," which gives this description: "he went sounding on through so many dark stifling caverns" (*The Works of Charles and Mary Lamb,* ed. E. V. Lucas [London, 1903–1905], II, 124).

718–722 The Bastille, prison and symbol of tyranny, fell on July 14, 1789. Cf. *Prelude* IX, 63–67.

727–731 The Solitary recalls his vision as described at II, 859–907.

729 This line is identical to II, 862, as the Solitary here recalls his earlier vision and makes a comparison with his previous feelings about the Revolution.

731–732 prophetic harps / In every grove were ringing] The French Revolution was heralded as a new dawn for mankind. During the 1790s numerous prophets and mystics, such as Richard Brothers and Joanna Southcott, emerged to predict that the apocalypse was imminent and that a new world was about to be born.

735 "The Tree of Liberty"] *PW* Knight, V, 132, notes, "During the American War of Independence, trees were planted as symbols of freedom. This custom passed over to France. The Jacobins planted the first tree of Liberty in Paris in 1790, and the practice spread rapidly."

737 Be joyful all ye Nations in all Lands] Cf. Psalms 100:1 ("Make a joyful noise unto the LORD, all ye lands").

743–744 The Solitary makes a direct parallel between his previous personal life and the political one into which he is "reborn."

764 Saturnian Rule] Saturn was the Roman god of agriculture associated with the Greek god Cronos, who established the golden age (see note to III, 326, above). In Roman religion the festival of Saturn was a time of feasting and merrymaking. Saturnian rule therefore is one of liberty and joy for all.

769–770 A long-suspended office in the House / Of public worship] The Solitary had originally trained as a church minister. See II, 182.

777 History, Time's slavish Scribe] Cf. note to III, 612, above.

782 fiercer Zealots] The Jacobins. Cf. *Prelude,* X, 456–457; X, 468–469.

784–785 Dion Cassius in his *Roman History* states that Brutus at the end of his life "first uttered aloud this sentence of Heracles: O wretched Valour, thou wert but a name, / And yet I worshipped thee as real indeed; / But now, it seems thou wert but Fortune's slave" (*Dio's Roman History,* vol. V, bk. XLVII, sec. 49.2).

822–823 Cf. *PL,* IV, 391–392: "compels me now / To do what else though damn'd I should abhor."

825 that Land] France, which the Solitary compares to a bird plucking at its own breast as its various factions fight among themselves in the course of the Revolution.

829–830 —But all was quieted by iron bonds / Of military sway] Control over revolutionary instability was finally asserted by Napoleon, who seized power in November 1799.

835 —In Britain, ruled a panic dread of change] There is ample evidence of this "panic dread" in responses to the French Revolution by the British government in the 1790s. In 1794 Parliament temporarily suspended the Habeas Corpus Act, thus allowing political suspects to be held without trial. Radical leaders such as Horne Tooke, Thomas Hardy, and John Thelwall were arrested and indicted for high treason in the Treason Trials of 1794, although they were ultimately acquitted. See also *Prelude,* X, 645–656, where WW attacks Pitt's government.

855 like a Plague, will Memory break out] The Wanderer originally used this image at II, 258, to describe the negative influence of false philosophy upon the Solitary.

860 The vengeful Furies] Figures from Greek myth also known as the Eumenides or Erinyes. These avenging deities were the personification of a curse pronounced upon a wrongdoer whom they would then hunt without mercy.

860–861 The Solitary's imagining of faces turned upon him here seems to echo STC's mariner, reproached by his dead companions (*Rime of the Ancyent Marinere,* ll. 441–444, text of 1798). Cf. I, 646–647; II, 683, 798; VI, 109.

870 That Volume] The Bible.

891 this gigantic Stream] *PW* Knight, V, 138, indicates that the reference is to the

Hudson River, the principal river of New York State, flowing from the Adirondack wilderness into the Atlantic. But the description is generic and would fit, among other possibilities, the Delaware River at Philadelphia, a larger city than New York in 1800. As with many of his Lake District locations, WW here avoids specific names.

892 a City] *PW* Knight, V, 138, indicates New York; see, however, note to III, 891, above.

924–952 The Solitary sets off into the West in search of the noble savage.

938–949 EdeS, in his notes to Book VIII of *The Prelude*, makes a comparison between draft material in MS. 48 and this section of *Exc.* In each case the text gives a description of a Native American looking down from an eminence (*The Prelude or Growth of a Poet's Mind*, ed. Ernest de Selincourt [2d ed. rev. Helen Darbishire, Oxford, 1959]), p. 558; cf. MS. 48, 24r, in *13-Bk Prelude*, II, 386).

940–941 that Northern Stream / Which spreads into successive seas] *PW* Knight, V, 139, indicates the "Stream" is the St. Lawrence, which seems a good possibility; see, however, the note to III, 891, above, about WW's generic place references. WW's Note to III, 940 (see p. 300, above), gives a lengthy quotation from William Gilbert's Notes on *The Hurricane* to describe the potentially negative effect of travel on the mind. See also Wu, *Reading I*, p. 63; *Reading II*, p. 92.

955 the merry Mocking-bird] Also known as the mock bird or mock nightingale. "Mockingbird" is the popular name for this American bird belonging to the thrush family, so named because of its ability to imitate other birds' cries and its great range of song.

956 Muccawiss] Also known as the "whip-poor-will" or whipperwill, this bird is a species of goatsucker. A correspondent of Knight's tells us that Muccawiss is the Algonquin (Native American) name for it (see *PW* Knight, V, 393–396). *PW*, V, 423, suggests that WW got his knowledge of the bird from Jonathan Carver's *Travels Through the Interior Parts of North-America in the Years 1766, 1767, and 1768* (London, 1778), which contains in its final chapters a large catalog of Native American beasts and birds. Carver states, "The Whipperwill, or as it is termed by the Indians, the Muckawiss. . . . It acquires its name by the noise it makes, which to the people of the colonies sounds like the name they give it Whipper-will; to an Indian ear Muck-a-wiss. The words, it is true, are not alike, but in this manner they strike the imagination of each" (Carver, p. 468). See also Wu, *Reading II*, p. 44. Cf. WW's *A Morning Exercise*, l. 16: "And, in thy iteration, 'WHIP POOR WILL.'"

960 that pure Archetype of human greatness / I found him not] The Solitary's hopes are shattered once again. Primitive man turns out to be a base creature, almost resembling, from the Solitary's warped perspective, the "Yahoos" of Swift's *Gulliver's Travels.*

965–971 The Solitary concludes by summing up his central difficulties: a loss of faith in man, a loss of inner faith, and an apathetic response to life. The Wanderer in his response in Book IV will address all these points. See also Lyon, p. 77.

974–998 The Solitary's story ends with the metaphor of his life as a river. Cf. *Prelude*, IV, 247–264, in which the image of the multiple depths and surfaces of the river is used as metaphor for the poem itself and the poet's recollections. This image exists as a single discrete entry in MS. 73 (8r–9r); it is then copied out into MS. 71, 109r–110r (see pp. 829–830, 670–671, below).

Book IV: "Despondency Corrected"

The fourth book of *Exc* was much admired by WW's contemporaries. The first review of the poem by William Hazlitt in *The Examiner* set this trend, quoting from Book IV and drawing attention to the "succession of splendid passages, equally enriched with philosophy and poetry, tracing the fictions of Eastern mythology to the immediate intercourse of the imagination with Nature" (Hazlitt, p. 556). Those sections in particular were influential upon second-generation Romantics (Keats, Shelley, and Byron) in the model they presented of the imagination as a vital force linking man to the external world and providing moral understanding independent of reason. In a letter to Haydon of January 10, 1818, Keats declared the poem to be one of "three things to rejoice at in this Age" (*LJK*, I, 203), and the influence of Book IV is strongly felt in *Endymion*. See H. W. Piper, *The Active Universe* (London, 1962).

In terms of the philosophical content of Book IV, the Wanderer appeals to the Solitary by arguing for feeling and imagination as principles of natural religion. He is antimechanistic and antirationalist at various points in the argument as he tries to restore the Solitary by reawakening his response to nature. It is in Book IV that WW draws closest to fulfilling STC's (disappointed) expectations for the philosophical poem, outlined by him in the letter of May 30, 1815, discussed on p. 4, above. For STC the goals of *Exc* should have involved "removing the sandy Sophisms of Locke, and the Mechanic Dogmatists, and demonstrating that the Senses were living growths and developments of the Mind & Spirit in a much juster as well as higher sense, than the mind can be said to be formed by the Senses" (*STCL*, IV, 574). However, WW is neither willing to condemn rationalism absolutely nor to turn toward pure transcendentalism (as STC had done). Instead, the Wanderer's philosophy tries to offer a balance of reason tempered by an imaginative response to the natural world with a strong basis in sensory experience.

Within the dramatic context of the poem, the argument of Book IV consists of the Wanderer's response to the Solitary's autobiography of Book III. Lyon summarizes the Wanderer's argument as falling into three main parts: "First he states his faith . . . then he applies it to the problems of the Solitary . . . and finally he shows the Solitary how to restore his faith in God and man" (p. 77). For discussions of WW and philosophy, see also Newton P. Stallknecht, *Strange Seas of Thought* (Bloomington, 1958) and Keith G. Thomas, *Wordsworth and Philosophy* (Ann Arbor, 1989).

Summary of Contents *PW* Dowden, VI, 362, points out that the "Summary of Contents" for Book IV was given in great detail in 1814 but condensed in *PW*, 1827, and again in *PW*, 1836.

2–3 commenced in pain, / In pain commenced] *PW*, V, 423–424, describes this line as "an obvious imitation of the common Miltonic repetition."

10ff. The Wanderer's speech throughout Book IV is given as a direct response to the Solitary's account of his life in Book III (as the two book titles of "Despondency" and "Despondency Corrected" make clear). His argument responds point by point to the Solitary, drawing upon a range of philosophical positions to try to make him adopt a more positive outlook. See Lyon, pp. 78–79, for a clear overview of this procedure.

12–20 As part of the affirmation of his own beliefs, the Wanderer here suggests a stoical response to life's suffering. See also Jane Worthington, *Wordsworth's Reading of Roman Prose* (New Haven, 1946), pp. 43–74. See note to III, 362.

13–17 In a copy of *Exc* 1814 annotated by STC, this passage had an annotation now eras and illeg; see Beer, p. 462. For other STC annotations to this volume (now at Victoria University Library, Toronto), see notes to III, 526–557; IV, 40–42, 97–99, 279–289, 306–310, 617, 629.

28 Soul of our souls] As with much of the Wanderer's language, this has a strongly biblical sense while not referring to any specific passage. *PW* Knight, V, 146, points out that WW in January 1849 copied out IV, 28–31, for "a lady in America" and suggests that the poet selected those lines to copy because of the death of his daughter Dora in 1847.

40–42 In a copy of *Exc* 1814 annotated by STC, l. 41 is marked with an X and a note (now partially eras) is at page foot. Beer, pp. 461–462, reads that note as "Remembered, unconsciously I [?doubt not,] from a mss drama of mine," followed by four verse lines that Beer suggests are from STC's unfinished *The Triumph of Loyalty* (1800; excerpt published as "The Night-Scene" in *Sybilline Leaves* [1817]). See further discussion of STC's note in Beer, p. 462. For other STC annotations to this volume (now at Victoria University Library, Toronto), see notes to III, 526–557; IV, 13–17, 97–99, 279–289, 306–310, 617, 629.

43 Me didst thou constitute a Priest of thine] The Wanderer's description of himself seems to combine natural and revealed religion and hints at Methodism. Such a combination is also felt in WW's comment about a possible sequel to the poem involving "a sacrament say, in the open fields, or a preaching among the Mountains" (IF; p. 1224, below). See also the note, below, to IX, 773–778, and the Poet's account of the Wanderer at I, 244–250, 439–440.

51 The particle divine remained unquenched] A Neoplatonic view of childhood, suggesting the possibility of preexistence. Lyon, p. 94, stresses the antimechanistic point of such comments, with WW's affirming the existence of innate ideas in opposition to Locke and Hartley. Cf. notes, below, to IV, 83–84, 205–206.

76 Whose kingdom is, where Time and Space are not] Lyon, p. 77, notes that the poem is "shot through with Kantian-Coleridgean transcendentalism in the passage on the eternal forms of duty."

83–84 Thou—who didst wrap the cloud / Of Infancy around us] Again, a Neoplatonic image of childhood strongly reminiscent of the *Ode: Intimations of Immortality*, ll. 64–66. Cf. notes to IV, 51, 205–206.

97–99 In a copy of *Exc* 1814 annotated by STC, this passage is marked with a vertical line and may have had a brief note, now eras and illeg; see Beer, p. 462. For other STC annotations to this volume (now at Victoria University Library, Toronto), see notes to III, 526–557; IV, 13–17, 40–42, 279–289, 306–310, 617, 629.

111–112 The Wanderer's recalling of his youth echoes the Poet's description of him at I, 134–166; cf. WW's description of himself in *Prelude*, II, 330: "Thence did I drink the visionary power."

114 The Sun rise up] *The Prelude*, IV, 330–345.

123 Cf. *Tintern Abbey*, 84–86 (text of 1798); *The Prelude*, XI, 336–339.

130–131 See WW's note (p. 300, above); WW there refers to Christopher Wordsworth's *Ecclesiastical Biography* (1810), which in turn quotes from part I of Richard Baxter's *Narrative of the Most Memorable Passages of his Life and Times*: "To despise earth is easy to me; but not so easy to be acquainted and conversant in Heaven" (*Ecclesiastical Biography*, V, 585). WW owned a copy of his brother's book (see Wu, *Reading II*, pp. 246–247).

142 like a Pillar of smoke] The Wanderer constantly uses biblical images metaphorically without specific reference. Cf. Song of Songs 3:6, Judges 20:40.

173–184 The Wanderer begins to address particular points made by the Solitary in Book III, arguing against desire for transcendence and the longing to be united with his dead family.

178 Cf. *Hamlet* I.ii.129 (First Folio): "O that this too too solid flesh would melt."

186 Nor rapt, nor craving] Haydon's copy in the Cornell library has WW's correction of "sleep" to "rapt" (as in the errata to *1814*) and a note by Haydon: "This Wordsworth corrected himself, the day he sat to me for My Picture [*Christ's Entry into Jerusalem*]—that is to be put in by Newton & Voltaire—Dec. 22, 1817 while he was reading the passage aloud." Cf. notes to I, 348–349, 399; IV, 854.

187 They whom you deplore] That is, the Solitary's dead family whose loss he deplores (mourns).

205–206 See WW's Note (pp. 300–301, above), which directs the reader to make a comparison with his *Ode: Intimations of Immortality*. Again, the Wanderer asserts that the soul contains innate powers and comparison to the *Ode* suggests a Platonic belief in the soul's preexistence. Cf. notes to IV, 51, 83–84, above.

231–232 Cf. *PL*, VII, 13–14 ("Into the Heav'n of Heav'ns I have presum'd, / An Earthly Guest, and drawn Empyreal Air") and STC's *Religious Musings*, l. 415: "Soaring aloft I breathe th' empyreal air" (*STCPW*, I, part I, 191).

233 Sons of the morning] Cf. Milton, *On the Morning of Christ's Nativity*, l. 119 ("the sons of morning sung") and *PL*, V, 716 ("Among the sons of Morn"). Reginald Heber

used the phrase in the first line of his Epiphany hymn "Brightest and best of the sons of the morning" (1811).

261 For that other loss] The Wanderer continues to address the causes of the Solitary's despondency, shifting here from his personal sense of loss to his political one.

263 the unexpected transports of our Age] The Solitary (like WW) has been first wildly caught up in, and then deeply disappointed by, the events of the French Revolution. Cf. notes to II, 222–277, 250–260.

279–289 In a copy of *Exc* 1814 annotated by STC, a note opposite these lines reads, "Might not Providence have addressed the same language to Luther? Dr. Bell? To every bold benefactor of the Human Race?" See Beer, p. 460. For Andrew Bell, see our introductory note to Book IX, p. 419, below. For other STC annotations to this volume (now at Victoria University Library, Toronto), see notes to III, 526–557; IV, 13–17, 40–42, 97–99, 306–310, 617, 629.

294 Wisdom of her sons] *PW*, V, 424, compares to Matthew 11:19 ("wisdom is justified of her children").

298 Tartarian darkness] In Greek myth Tartarus, which held the confined Titans, was the abyss below Hades. Cf. *PL*, II, 69: "*Tartarean* Sulphur."

299 groaning nations] Cf. I, 381.

306–310 In a copy of *Exc* 1814 annotated by STC, a note to these lines reads, "compare this with the same Truth announced in 'The Friend.'" Beer, p. 461, suggests that STC's reference is to *The Friend* of September 7, 1809 (see *STCF*, II, 55–60). For other STC annotations to this volume (now at Victoria University Library, Toronto), see notes to III, 526–557; IV, 13–17, 40–42, 97–99, 279–289, 617, 629.

308–310 As *PW*, V, 424, points out, DW refers to these lines as "an admirable comment upon the conduct of the Allies from beginning to end" in a letter to Catherine Clarkson of April 11, 1815 (*MY*, II, 229), commenting upon the government's handling of Napoleon.

325–334 See WW's note (pp. 301–302, above), referring to his quotation from the poem "To the Ladie Margaret, Countesse of Cumberland" by the "time-hallowed Poet" (l. 326) Samuel Daniel (1561–1619). See also Wu, *Reading II*, pp. 68–69.

335–353, 357–371 These lines first occur in *Home at Grasmere* MS. R (MS. 28: 148/149i^{r}–150/151i^{r}). See *H at G*, pp. 187–199.

349 For knowledge is delight] Cf. *The Prelude*, II, 306 ("all knowledge is delight") and *The Cuckoo at Laverna*, l. 61 ("so fraught with knowledge and delight").

404–414 These lines are first drafted in MS. 48 (36^{r}, 36^{v}, 50^{v}) for *The Prelude*; see *13-Bk Prelude*, II, 402–403, 420. See IF for *To Joanna*, in which WW states, "There is in the Excursion an allusion to the bleat of a lamb thus reechoed and described without any exaggeration, as I heard it on the side of Stickle Tarn" (IF, p. 18). In a letter to WW of January 30, 1801, CL also comments on "the description of the continuous Echoes in the story of Joanna's laugh, where the mountains and all the scenery absolutely seem alive" (*CLL*, I, 265).

442 Creatures, that in communities exist] The Wanderer pragmatically uses the interruption of the lamb to shift his argument and draw upon examples from nature to show the importance of fellowship and society for all creatures.

460 while with their clang the air resounds] *PW*, V, 426, compares *PL*, VII, 421–422: "and soaring th'air sublime / With clang despis'd the ground."

467–469 he shall find / Who seeks not] Cf. Matthew 7:8 and Luke 11:10, both of which read, "For every one that asketh receiveth; and he that seeketh findeth; and to him that knocketh it shall be opened."

471–474 The Wanderer refers to the Solitary's account of his vision at II, 871–907, reinterpreting its meaning for him.

488 in a lonely pool] Blea Tarn.

491–504 *PW*, V, 426, provides the following information: "In W's Commonplace Book of 1800 Thomas Wilkinson has written after the passage which suggested *The Solitary Reaper* . . . the following: 'But take courage, return to thy Father, rise with the lark, climb the summits of thy surrounding Hills, roll the Stone in thunder from the mountain, and follow with all thy might the Wild Goats of Ben Vorlach, so shalt thou return weary to thy Cottage, and thy rest will be as quiet as mine.'"

526–531 These lines were first drafted for *The Prelude* in MS. 48 (55[v]); see *13-Bk Prelude*, II, 427.

539 The strain of transport] The attempt to persuade by argument in the context of a natural setting and to work upon the auditor by "enthusiasm" and "transport" is reminiscent of the Earl of Shaftesbury's writings, as is the argument that man possesses an innate moral sense. WW refers to Shaftesbury in the *Essay, Supplementary to the Preface* (1815) as "an author at present unjustly depreciated" (*Prose*, III, 72). See also Wu, *Reading II*, p. 62.

545 tranquillizing power] Cf. RS, *To Contemplation*, "Come, tranquillizing Power!" (l. 12).

548 Compatriot, Friend, remote are Garry's Hills] Again, the Wanderer reminds the Solitary of their common Scottish origins. Garry's Hills form part of the Grampian Mountains in Perthshire. The "hills of Athol" (see I, 114), among which the Wanderer grew up, are close by. Cf. II, 171; III, 506; VIII, 35.

556 the great Artificer] Cf. William Cowper, *The Task*: "The great Artificer of all that moves" (VI, 207).

564–569 Cf. WW's "Poor earthly casket of immortal Verse," in *Prelude*, V, 164.

587 parterres] A level space in a garden consisting of ornamental flower beds.

599 "the dreadful appetite of death?"] WW gives this line in quotation marks, but there is no obvious source for it. A play of 1775, *The Heroine in the Cave* by Henry Jones and Paul Hiffernan, contains the line "Oh, tyranny! Thou horrid, hateful pest! / Who gratifiest thy appetite of death" (II.iii).

600–603 Cf. "Preface" to *Exc*, l. 49, in which WW states, "It is not the Author's intention formally to announce a system." The poem is throughout opposed to rational philosophic systems that deny and destroy feeling—and lead to brooding introspection. The Solitary makes this point more clearly at IV, 617–626.

606 A Pupil in the many-chambered school] Cf. Keats's letter to Reynolds for May 3, 1818: "I compare human life to a large Mansion of Many Apartments. . . . The first we step into we call the infant or thoughtless Chamber" (*JKL*, I, 280).

607 Where Superstition weaves her airy dreams] The Wanderer argues that even superstitious belief is preferable to apathy and lack of feeling.

617 In a copy of *Exc* 1814 annotated by STC, the word "sense" is underlined; a note is now eras and illeg; see Beer, p. 462. For other STC annotations to this volume (now at Victoria University Library, Toronto), see notes to III, 526–557; IV, 13–17, 40–42, 97–99, 279–289, 306–310, 629.

627 new-created Earth] Milton uses the phrase "new created World" four times in *PL* at III, 89; IV, 937; VII, 554; and X, 481. WW may also be remembering William Cowper's *The Task* (1785): "To gratulate the new-created earth" (V, 820); on WW's familiarity with Cowper, see Wu, *Reading I*, pp. 38–39, and Wu, *Reading II*, pp. 65–67.

627–759 At this point, to show the importance of having an active and emotionally based philosophy of response to nature, the Wanderer gives a series of descriptions of primitive man illustrating a natural spiritual and moral instinct. These descriptions were much admired by WW's contemporaries.

629 In a copy of *Exc* 1814 annotated by STC, the word "Solitude" is underlined; a note is now erased and illegible; see Beer, p. 462. For other STC annotations to this volume (now at Victoria University Library, Toronto), see notes to III, 526–557; IV, 13–17, 40–42, 97–99, 279–289, 306–310, 617.

630–631 *PW* Knight, V, 168, compares Genesis 3:8 ("And they heard the voice of the LORD God walking in the garden in the cool of the day").

633 gliding like morning mist] *PW*, V, 426, compares *PL*, XII, 629: "Gliding meteorous, as Ev'ning Mist."

643 to banishment condemned] Cf. *PL*, XI, 108–109 ("To them, and to their Progeny from thence / Perpetual banishment"); *PW* Knight, V, 169, compares Genesis 3:24 ("So he drove out the man").

649 or blaze of light] *PW*, V, 426, compares *PL*, III, 377–378: "Thron'd inaccessible, but when thou shad'st / The full blaze of thy beams."

650 cloud of darkness] *PW* Knight, V, 169, compares Exodus 33:9 ("the cloudy pillar descended").

651 the wandering ark] *PW* Knight, V, 169, compares the portable ark described in Exodus 37:1–29.

653 Between the Cherubim] *PW* Knight, V, 169, compares Exodus 25:22 ("between the two cherubims which are upon the ark of the testimony").

654 Showered miracles] *PW* Knight, V, 169, gives an example from Exodus 16:4 ("Behold, I will rain bread from heaven for you")

662–665 The Wanderer again argues against a reliance upon rationalism unbalanced by feeling and imagination.

667–759 The Wanderer now turns to other religions and examples of individuals of all races whose belief drew upon an imaginative response to the natural world.

681 Tower] The Temple of Belus, or Bel or Baal, a great god in Babylonian religion. The Chaldeans were priests of this god. See Herodotus, *The Histories*, vol. I, bk. I, sec. 182). WW owned a copy of *The History of Herodotus* (Wu, *Reading II*, pp. 108–109).

690 Chaldean Shepherds] The Chaldeans were an ancient Babylonian people particularly associated with knowledge of astrology (hence, as described here, their interest in the skies); they also reputedly possessed magical powers.

695 The Planetary Five] The five planets, besides Earth, known to the ancients: Mercury, Venus, Mars, Jupiter, and Saturn.

698 radiant Mercuries] *PW* Knight, V, 171, points out that all five planets are called "Mercuries" because, like the god, they all act as messengers carrying—as WW says at IV, 700—"Decrees and resolutions of the Gods."

699 in perpetual round] *PW*, V, 427, notes use of the same phrase in *PL*, VI, 6.

703–704 At this point the poem explicitly presents an account of the imaginative interaction between pagan man and the natural world. Read in the context of Book IV, however, it is an example of an active and imaginative philosophy (in opposition to cold reason) rather than a whole-hearted endorsement of pagan myth—though second generation Romantic poets may have understood it as such an endorsement. See Alex Zwerdling, "Wordsworth and Greek Myth," *University of Toronto Quarterly* 33 (1963–64): 341–354; Alan G. Hill, "New Light on 'The Excursion,'" *Ariel* 2 (1974): 37–47.

714–759 Leigh Hunt, reviewing Keats's 1817 volume in the *Examiner*, noted how deeply Keats was influenced by *Exc*, in particular by IV, 714–759, and IV, 844–884 (*PW*, V, 427). See also note to IV, 854–855, below.

715 sounding shores] *PW* Knight, V, 172, compares Milton, *Lycidas*, l. 154: "the shores and sounding Seas."

729 wandering Rhapsodists] Greek strolling minstrels.

741–748 See Pausanias, *Description of Greece* (I, 37, 3): "Before you cross the Cephisus, there is the monument of Theodorus, who excelled all his contemporaries as an actor in tragedy; and near to the river, there are [two] statues, one of Mnesimache, another of her son, in the act of cutting off his hair [over the stream and presenting it] as a votive offering to the Cephisus" (*PW* Knight, V, 173; see also V, 396–398). *PW*, V, 427, also notes, after Knight, that WW's source may have been Pope's note on the *Iliad*, XXIII, 175, which refers to Achilles' votive offering of a lock of hair for Patroclus when it had been vowed to the river Spercheius. Copies of Pope's *Homer* and Thomas Taylor's translation of Pausanias were both to be found in WW's library. See also Wu, *Reading II*, p. 112.

757–759 While Man grows old, and dwindles, and decays . . . trod] Cf. Keats's *Ode to A Nightingale*, "Where youth grows pale, and spectre-thin, and dies" (l. 26).

760 We live by admiration, hope, and love] Cf. note to V, 1018.

760–762 This passage is first drafted in MS. 48 (4[v], 18[r]) for *The Prelude* (see *13-Bk Prelude*, II, 359, 378).

785–786 Cf. The Lord's Prayer. See Matthew 6:9–13, Luke 11:2–4.

797–799 The Shepherd Lad . . . hours] *PW*, V, 428, compares *Henry VI, Part 3*, II.v.21–25.

802–806 The Wanderer argues for the existence of natural good in man and the positive force of the imagination in relation to this natural good.

854–855 B. R. Haydon's copy of *Exc* (now at Cornell University Library) has a marginal note opposite these lines: "Poor Keats used always to prefer this passage to all others." Cf. notes to I, 348–349; 399; IV, 186, 714–759.

884 Verbal changes introduced to this line in *PW*, 1827, and in *PW*, 1845 (see the verbal variants to the reading text) should be considered in light of the following comment by BF: "I remember to have heard the poet, one evening at Mr Lamb's, read the whole passage with his usual unction; and, himself condemning the harshness of the original line, he altered it to 'The strain was aptly chosen: I could mark–' for the sake of the pause in the middle of the line, which was a relief after the full period of the preceding lines, ending 'The Simple shepherd's awe-inspiring god.' We all thought this a great improvement, and a learned harmony. Why was the short pause thrown away again?" (BF, pp. 46–47, which also identifies the evening as possibly May 23, 1815).

893 those godly Men] The Solitary is referring to the Covenanters. There were two covenants. The attempt by Charles I to introduce changes into Scottish liturgy led to the signing of the National Covenant in Edinburgh in 1638. This affirmed a resistance in Scotland to Anglicizing and Romanizing influences. In 1643 the National Covenant was followed by the Solemn League and Covenant by which Scots entered the Civil War on the side of Parliament in return for the protection of Presbyterianism in Scotland and (as they thought) its furtherance in England and Ireland. After the beheading of Charles I, the Covenanters supported Charles II, who was forced to subscribe to the covenants. Many of the key events and characters of this period are depicted in great detail by Sir Walter Scott in *Old Mortality* (1816).

903–904 to sow afresh / The weeds of Romish Phantasy] The Covenanters were concerned to resist all Anglican and Roman Catholic influences.

906–907 Saint Fillan . . . Saint Anne . . . Saint Giles] Three saints revered in Scotland. There are two Scottish saints called Saint Fillan, the most famous being an Irish missionary who came to Scotland in the eighth century and was associated with the battle of Bannockburn. Saint Anne was the mother of the Virgin Mary. Saint Giles was a Greek who settled in France and founded a Benedictine society there. The parish church of Edinburgh was dedicated to him, and his arm bone was one of the treasures of the church. This relic was carried through Edinburgh in procession on the Saint's day (September 1). See *PW* Knight, V, 179; *PW*, V, 428.

916 Upon our brave Progenitors] Another reference to the Covenanters. The Wanderer's positive view of them supports the idea, suggested earlier (see note to I, 129–133) that his own original religion was strictly Presbyterian.

929–930 such, in their degree, / Were those bewildered Pagans] The Wanderer's comment here makes it clear that the pagan examples given earlier were intended largely to illustrate their instinctive sense of moral good.

937–964 This passage has been read as WW's speaking out against science, but his position may be more clearly understood from a dispute over the representation of science in *Exc* recorded in Robert Perceval Graves's *Life of Sir William Rowan Hamilton* (Dublin, 1882–1889). Hamilton describes WW as standing in defense of "Science, that raised the mind to the contemplation of God in works . . . but as for all other science, all science which put this end out of view, all science which was a bare collection of facts for their own sake . . . it *degraded* instead of raising the species. All science which waged war with and wished to extinguish Imagination in the mind of man and to leave it nothing of any kind but the naked knowledge of facts, was, he thought, much worse than useless" (I, 313). See also Lyon, pp. 104–106.

952 *PW*, V, 428, compares *PL*, XII, 59, where "great laughter was in Heav'n" on the building of the tower of Babel.

954–964 This passage was originally part of the Pedlar's discourse in *RC* MSS. B (49ʳ, 50ʳ) and D (68ᵛ); see *RC & Pedlar*, pp. 266–269, 373–374.

972 so fearfully devised] *PW*, V, 428, compares Psalms 139:14, "I am fearfully and wonderfully made."

993 the laughing Sage of France] Voltaire, whose novel *Candide* the Wanderer found abandoned by the Solitary at II, 466. At the Comédie Française, Voltaire, aged eighty-four, was crowned—as the Athenian poets used to be. Cf. notes to II, 466–467, and 510; *PW* Knight, V, 183.

1020–1021 As he does throughout this book, the Wanderer asserts an antimechanistic position.

1062 Cf. Exodus 3:2 ("Behold, the bush burned with fire, and the bush was not consumed"). Such complex, indirect use of biblical image as part of a natural metaphor for the soul is typical of the ways in which the Wanderer works upon the Solitary through his own religious belief and language while appearing to give arguments based on the relationship between man and nature. In his review of *Exc* for the *Quarterly Review* (October 1814), CL described IV, 1057–1076, as "a kind of Natural Methodism" (p. 105). See also the discussion of the use of types and emblems in the poem by Alan G. Hill in "Wordsworth's 'Grand Design,'" *Proceedings of the British Academy* 72 (1986): 187–204.

1075–1077 This point is an important one in the poem since the Solitary shows himself to be moved for the first time. For different critical responses, see George Myerson, *The Argumentative Imagination: Wordsworth, Dryden, Religious Dialogues* (Manchester, 1992), p. 50, and Susan Wolfson, *The Questioning Presence: Wordsworth, Keats, and the Interrogative Mode in Romantic Poetry* (Ithaca, 1986), p. 119.

1097 Redeemer's feet] One of the rare references to Christ in the 1814 text of the poem, and the only use of word "Redeemer." See also II, 236; V, 278, 914, 958; IX, 718.

1111 we have heard from You a voice] The climax of the Wanderer's argument is to assert that he can see goodness in the Solitary of which he is not himself aware and that human sympathy and love of nature still exist within him.

1123 the inferior Faculty] Reason uncolored by imagination.

1125–1134 Walter Savage Landor accused WW of plagiarizing these lines from *Gebir* (1798), I, 169–176, although it is not clear whether WW had read Landor's poem before writing *Exc* (see Wu, *Reading II*, p. 131). Landor attacked WW in "An Imaginary Conversation: Southey and Porson" in *Blackwood's Edinburgh Magazine*, December 1842, 687–715. WW's son-in-law EQ responded in the same periodical in April 1843, with an "Imaginary Conversation Between Walter Savage Landor and the Editor of Blackwood's Magazine" (pp. 518–536) that defended WW against the charge of plagiarism, stating "what a coil have you made about that eternal sea-shell, which you say he stole from you, and which, we know, is the true and trivial cause of your hostility towards him!" (p. 533). In IF to *Composed by the Sea-shore* ("What mischief cleaves to unsubdued regret"), WW expressed his surprise at Landor's charge; as a child, WW had himself listened for the ocean in a seashell "scores of times & it was a belief among us that we could know from the sound whether the tide was ebbing or flowing" (p. 74). In the context of *Exc*, the extended metaphor is again used here to tell the Solitary that he is more spiritually alive than he can himself recognize.

1147 false conclusions of the reasoning Power] Again, the Wanderer asserts the necessity of combining rational understanding with imaginative and emotional response to the natural world.

1172 One Voice—the solitary Raven] Cf. DW's journal entry of July 26, 1800 (*Journals*, p. 14). See also IF to *Evening Voluntaries* in which WW states, "there is a passage in the Excursion towards the close of the 4th. Book where the voice of the Raven in flight is traced thro' the modifications it undergoes as I have often heard it in that Vale [Grasmere] & others of this district" (IF, p. 55) and WW's letter to Catherine Clarkson, January 1814, indicating that someone who has not heard such a sound may not "be able to relish that illustration" (*MY*, II, 190).

1194 o'er printless sands we march] Cf. Milton, *Comus*, l. 897: "my printless feet."

1201–1271 These lines draw upon *RC* MSS. B (20v–21r, 46r–49r) and D (67v–69r); see *RC & Pedlar*, pp. 120–123, 260–267, 372–374. According to WW, "The lines towards the conclusion of the 4th. book . . . were in order of time composed the next either at Race Down or Allfoxden, I do not remember which" (IF, p. 1215, below).

1213–1214 The man who responds positively to Nature will also find himself reintegrated into society. The excursion that forms the basis of the poem's action has this intention in relation to the Solitary.

1259 the Mind's *excursive* Power] The Wanderer ends with an idealized vision of the mind's union of imagination and reason, emotion and understanding, in response to the natural world. WW draws our attention to the connection between the external and internal journeying of the protagonists by italicizing "excursive."

1260–1271 EdeS compares this passage (and the *RC* composition that it draws upon; see note to IV, 1201–1271, above) to two speeches in *Hamlet*: II.ii.318–327 and IV.iv.33–39.

1264–1266 *PW*, V, 431, notes the echo of *PL*, V, 528 ("Inextricable, or strict necessity"). The Wanderer here outlines a necessitarian view of man's position, though without subscribing to it.

1286 Tree of Life] Cf. Genesis 3:22, 3:24; Proverbs 13:12,15:4; Revelation 2:7, 22:2, 22:14.

Book V: "The Pastor"

Book V marks a change of direction in the poem as a whole, proceeding from discussion and argument into a series of narratives. In the first half of the book, the Solitary revives the argument of Book IV, but—such debate leading nowhere—the Wanderer draws a halt to it (ll. 642–643) and invites the Pastor to adopt a different approach. The book then shifts into a series of epitaphic tales that are intended, in part at least, to continue addressing the issues of the argument through narrative, though their relevance is not always immediately apparent. The ideas expressed in Books V–VII were also being explored by WW in other forms of writing in 1809–1810, when many of the churchyard narratives were probably written. Comparison can be made with WW's translation of Chiabrera's epitaphs for STC's *The Friend* and with WW's three *Essays on Epitaphs*, the first of which is given in the poet's own notes to *Exc*.

CL was a great admirer of WW's writing on epitaphs (his comment in *Rosamund Gray*—"Where are all the *bad* People buried?"—is quoted by WW at the start of his second *Essay on Epitaphs*). In a letter to WW of August 9, 1814, discussing *Exc*, CL remarked, "The part (or rather main body) which has left the sweetest odour on my memory . . . is the Tales of the Church yard" (*CLL*, III, 95). Hazlitt in the second part of his *Examiner* article, however, takes an opposite position: "[W]hy introduce particular illustrations at all, which add nothing to the force of the general truth" (Hazlitt, p. 555). If the poem is read with the emphasis purely on philosophical content, then these books can appear marginal. For positive discussion of the significance of the epitaph form for WW's later poetics, see particularly Frances Ferguson, *Language as Counter-Spirit* (New Haven, 1977); W. J. B. Owen, *Wordsworth as Critic* (London, 1969); Bushell, chapter 6.

Regarding settings in this section of the poem and the books that follow, it is important to remember that "Wordsworth's topography, though founded on fact, is ideal, and not literal" (*PW* Dowden, VI, 348). In IF on a number of occasions, WW himself emphasizes this characteristic of the poem, particularly pointing out the imaginative combining of Langdale Valley and Grasmere Church "by the waving of a magic wand" (p. 1217, below).

1–57 In revising MS. 74A (1r–1v; rev on loose bifolium, 1v–2v), WW drafts an expanded but ultimately unused opening to Book V that includes a comparison of "happy Britain" with a "haughty France" whose topography is as appealing as Britain's but whose people are not free. MS. 74A reinforces the poet's nationalistic tone in its unpublished rev of l. 47 ("Nor would I, as a Patriot and a Man," loose bifolium, 2v).

9 Impenetrable shade] Cf. III, 557. "Impenetrable shade" seems to be a common phrase in the period, used by, among others, Thomas Chatterton in *A Hymn for Christmas Day*, l. 4, and William Gilbert in *A Solitary Effusion in a Summer's Evening*, l. 22 (a poem subjoined to *The Hurricane*, which WW refers to in his note at III, 940).

59 by sledge or wheel] *PW* Knight, V, 198, notes: "The sledge used for bringing down peats or bracken from the uplands. The 'sledge' has not yet entirely given way to the 'wheel.'"

74 as a billow] In correspondence concerning alterations made by WW to his poetry, BF criticized this image, to which WW replied in a letter of October 24, 1828: "I cannot accede to your objection to the billow. The point simply is, he was cast out of his element and falls back into it, as naturally and necessarily as a billow into the sea. There is imagination in fastening solely upon that characteristic point of resemblance, stopping there, thinking of nothing else" (*LY*, I, 646).

79–80 Cf. Milton, *L'Allegro*, ll. 77–78: "Towers and Battlements it sees / Bosom'd high in tufted trees." *PW*, V, 431, notes that the fir trees that had screened the Grasmere churchyard were cut down in 1807, as mentioned by DW (*MY*, I, 159).

87–89 Cf. Sonnet XIII of *The River Duddon*, l. 1: "Hail to the fields—with Dwellings sprinkled o'er."

92–94 This "tyrannic Power" refers to Napoleon's invasion of Switzerland in February 1798. Cf. notes to I, 346; VII, 829.

94 unoffending Commonwealth] Cf. "noiseless Commonwealth," V, 419, where WW is making a comparison between the Swiss people and those of the Lakes.

95 A popular equality] Cf. *Prelude*, IX, 218–232, where the poet describes how the experience of equality in his native mountains prepared him to admire and support the early democratic principles of the French Revolution.

99 a Chronicler] The Wanderer, whose life as a Pedlar has made of him a natural historian of people's lives. Cf. the description of the Pastor as "the Historian" at VII, 1.

102 a genuine Priest] WW's description of the Priest's role and relation to his community given in his *Guide through the District of the Lakes* is relevant here: "They had, as I have said, their rural chapel, and of course their minister, in clothing or in manner of life, in no respect differing from themselves, except on the Sabbath-day" (*Prose*, II, 200–201). Cf. note to VI, 44–53.

114–115 though born / Of knightly race] WW in IF describes the Pastor as "a country clergyman of more than ordinary talents, born & bred in the upper ranks of society . . . brought by his pastoral office & his love of rural life into intimate connection with the peasantry of his native district" (p. 1217, below).

143–147 As *PW*, V, 431–432, points out, CL commented on this passage in a letter to WW of August 9, 1814: "One feeling I was particularly struck with as what I recognised so very lately at Harrow Church on entering in it after a hot & secular day's pleasure, the instantaneous coolness and calming, almost transforming properties of a country church just entered—a certain fragrance which it has, either from its holiness, or being kept shut all the week, or the air that is let in being pure country—exactly what you have reduced into words" (*CLL*, III, 96–97)

161–162 In MS. 1836/45 (and *PW*, 1845–), the lines are altered to: "marks of earthly state / By immemorial privilege allowed." See also note to I, 968/969, for Christian additions to the poem. In *PW*, 1845, WW also made additions to this passage (in particular adding the word "Encincture," which the *OED* cites as an example of a rarely used word, giving *Exc* as the first use of it). The word is defined in the *OED* as "The process of surrounding as with a girdle; the fact of being so surrounded."

164 marble Monuments were here displayed] *PW* Knight, V, 203, notes that "The details of this description apply in most particulars to the Church at Grasmere, although some are probably borrowed from Wordsworth's recollections of Hawkshead and of Bowness." For a description of the church and churchyard, see also IF, pp. 1218–1219, below).

173–175 WW seems to be making a series of puns here to emphasize the contrast between the living and dead in "upright Magistrates," "Grave Doctors," and "Uncorrupted Senators." Cf. *A Poet's Epitaph* in *Lyrical Ballads* (1800) in terms of tone.

176–182 This passage refers to Henry VIII's celebration of alliance with Francis I of France in June 1520, which took the form of a great tournament known as "The Field of Cloth of Gold."

185 the sea-fights of the second Charles] Presumably the Anglo-Dutch naval wars during the reign of Charles II.

189 intestine War /And rightful Government subverted] These lines refer to the English Civil Wars of 1642–1651.

208 the Tenant of the lonely Vale] The Solitary.

217 humming carelessly a tune] *PW* Knight, V, 205, compares *Hamlet,* V.i.61–66.

231–235 The description of the gravedigger by the Solitary again echoes Hamlet's responses in Act V.i. Hartman (p. 307) asks of the Solitary "Who is the Solitary, if not the Hamletian man in black . . . ?"

239 Much, yesterday, was said] The Solitary here revives the previous day's debate. Although Book IV ended positively, with some sense that his despondency had been in part "corrected," the Solitary now reverts to his former misanthropy.

257 Mark the Babe] Cf. *Prelude,* II, 237–243 ("Bless'd the infant Babe . . .)."

260–288, 290, 291–326, 327–361, 387–391, 392, 413–414, 423, 428–431, 432–435, 600–620, 892–894 These lines were originally written as part of *TPL*; they are reproduced in *PW*, V, 432–441, with the remark that *TPL* "was never revised and was ultimately rejected as disproportionate" (p. 432). See pp. 470–473, below, and Appendix II, below.

260–288, 269–288 The Solitary attacks baptism on the grounds that the belief that it can literally wash away sin is an ironic comment upon man's overly high ideals and expectations, as well as on the hollowness of such rituals. On November 6, 1817, Crabb Robinson comments, "The passage about baptism in *The Excursion,* it is not easy to defend" (*Henry Crabb Robinson on Books and Writers,* ed. Edith J. Morley (3 vols.; London, 1938; rpt. New York, 1967), I, 212). The origin of this passage is in the context of the cyclical life of the peasant in *TPL* (see transcriptions, below, of MS. 74, 33^{v}–35^{v}; cf. MS. 74A, 7^{r}–8^{v}).

278 Christ's Church] The second use of the word "Christ" in the poem, the other being at II, 236. See also IV, 1097; V, 914, 958; IX, 718.

289–305 This passage was originally written to be spoken by the Solitary in *TPL*; ll. 309–320 were added when the passage was instead given to the Poet (see transcriptions, below, of MS. 74, 35^{v}–36^{v}; cf. MS. 74A, 7^{v}–8^{v}). WW divides the argument into two voices in order to avoid possible contradiction in first criticizing and then defending the rites of organized religion.

306–313 The Solitary acknowledges man's need to look up to the ideals of Philosophy and Religion but sees them as hollow and pointless.

314–316 The Solitary here refers to *PL*, I, 157, where Satan tells Beelzebub "Fall'n Cherub, to be weak is miserable."

325 to graze the herb in thoughtless peace] *PW*, V, 442, compares *PL*, IV, 253: "Grazing the tender herb."

329 Faith, Hope, and Charity] See 1 Corinthians 13:13: "And now abideth faith, hope, charity, these three; but the greatest of these is charity." The Solitary draws upon core Christian values only to suggest that they have not helped man much in the search for contentment. His tone here is hard to read. Cf. V, 269, 603–611.

332–333 The Torch, the Star, the Anchor . . . The Cross itself] Emblems of organized religion.

338 unvoyageable sky] Cf. *PL*, X, 366: "this unvoyageable Gulf obscure."

343 The Solitary here inverts the reassurance of immortality offered by the lines "death hath no more dominion over him" (Romans 6:9). As with "Faith, Hope, and Charity" at V, 329, he calls upon fundamental tenets of Christianity only to dismiss them.

351–361 The Solitary returns to his earlier theme of ll. 246–253: if we could see each other clearly, we would be shocked at what was revealed.

365–366 The Poet's response, interestingly, agrees with the Solitary to some extent, in distrusting the ritual and show of organized religion. See note to V, 374–385, below.

374–385 The Poet criticizes the hollowness of church ritual but unlike the Solitary offers a positive alternative, asserting the importance of day-to-day links between people. WW's own attitude toward organized religion was ambivalent in 1814. On May 13, 1812, Crabb Robinson records WW's defending the Church but also confessing that "he knew not when he had been in a church at home—'All our ministers are such vile creatures'" (*Diary, Reminiscences, and Correspondence*, ed. Thomas Sadler [London, 1869], I, 90). Cf. DW's letter of 1811: "I assure you we are become regular church-goers (we take it in turn) for the sake of the children, and indeed Mr Johnson, our present curate, appears to be so much in earnest . . . that I think we should go even if we had not the children, who seem to make it a duty to us" (*MY*, I, 487). See also Lyon, pp. 113–116.

386–406 The Solitary now shifts his ground to complain at the curtailing of life for the ordinary working man.

419–420 The simple race / of Mountaineers] At the same time, the Solitary suggests that life in the country and the individuals who inhabit it are far from perfect. Cf. II, 648–652.

437 The reverend Pastor] Of the introduction of this character and his role CL remarked, "Nothing can be conceived finer than the manner of introducing these tales. With heaven above his head, and the mouldering turf at his feet—standing betwixt life and death—he seems to maintain that spiritual relation which he bore to his living flock, in its undiminished strength, even with their ashes" (Lamb, p. 108). See also IF (p. 1217, below).

455 like a stately Sycamore] *PW* Knight V, 214, notes, "The sycamore is the favourite tree at the Mountain Farms of Cumberland and Westmoreland, as it affords the best shelter from rain, and the most thorough protection from the heat of the sun, during sheep-shearing. A special feature of the valley as you go down Langdale from Blea Tarn, is the abundance of sycamore." WW in IF also comments on the comparison between man and tree used here (see p. 1217, below). See also note to VII, 635–636.

460–473 The Wanderer sums up the key points in the debate so far. The passage is important for the context of the tales that follow, since the Pastor does, to some extent, address those issues in the individual lives he relates.

480–495 The Pastor's first point is central to his whole attempt to move the Solitary, since he emphasizes that man's judgment is primarily subjective and colored by individual weaknesses or emotions. The implication is that there is little point in trying to argue in order to change someone's mind.

484 That speculative height] *PW,* V, 442, compares William Cowper, *The Task,* I, 289 ("on this speculative height") and *PL,* XII, 588–589 ("Let us descend now therefore from this top / Of Speculation").

487–490 As the Wanderer did throughout Book IV, the Pastor again draws attention to the necessary limits that should be placed upon Reason.

512–517 The Pastor (like the Wanderer) is not totally antirationalist. The higher mind, he admits, may helpfully be aided by Reason, but it is of little use to the ordinary man.

563–570 Lyon, p. 95, notes that the Wanderer makes an explicitly antimechanistic point here, arguing that moral intuition is innate, in opposition to the ideas of David Hartley, who states "the Moral Sense is therefore generated necessarily and mechanically" (*Observations on Man, His Frame, His Duty, and his Expectations. In Two Parts* [London, 1749], II, 504).

572–574 This question could be seen as one of the core issues of the poem.

603–611 The Solitary's tone here is hard to read (as it also is at V, 269, and 329). His "buoyant" response is actually an ironic attack on the idea that the simple country life is ideal. He suggests instead that hard physical labor is mind dulling, and he values it only insofar as it can offer an escape by working too hard to be able to think.

603 praise to the sturdy plough] Reminiscent of Virgil's *Georgics,* Book I, but not a direct reference. See also Wu, *Reading I,* pp. 140–142 and *Reading II,* pp. 231–233, and Hartman, pp. 296–298.

626–628 At this point the Wanderer acknowledges the absolute subjectivity of each speaker's position, which means that argument is an ineffective tool.

634–635 Throughout the Middle Ages, alchemists had tried to transmute baser metals into gold or silver.

639–640 The Wanderer here explicitly turns from argument to narrative in an attempt to act upon the Solitary.

648–649 See WW's note (p. 302, above), where he quotes a comparable passage from *The Brothers,* ll.184–191 (text of 1800). See also note to VI, 626–631, below.

672–729 WW in IF describes Jonathan and Betty Yewdale, on whom the narrative is based (see p. 1218, below). Their daughter Sara was the Wordsworths' servant in Grasmere.

673 yon dark mountain] According to *PW* Knight, V, 222, "Silver How is the only 'dark mountain' visible to the west from the moss-grown seat in the Grasmere Churchyard; but here again the realism of the narrative gives way, and not Silver How but Lingmoor is described with Hackett Cottage at its south-eastern foot"; Knight's note is another reminder that the topography of *Exc* is not to be taken literally.

700 unsafe times of Border war] The Border wars between Scotland and England began in 1296 when Edward I removed the Stone of Destiny and claimed conquest of the kingdom. This state of conflict lasted for the next three hundred years until in 1603 James VI of Scotland also became James I of England. Raiding and spoiling was a way of life on the Borders. Sir Walter Scott was, of course, a Borderer by birth and drew upon Border traditions in *The Lay of the Last Minstrel* and *Marmion,* as well as collecting oral poetry in the *Minstrelsy of the Scottish Border.* WW visited the region with DW as part of their tour of Scotland in 1803, with MW in 1814, and with Dora in 1831. See also WW's early dramatic work *The Borderers* (1796).

708 the Dame] *PW,* V, 442, quotes from unpublished notes of WW's conversation with Christopher Wordsworth concerning the original for this character: "Betty Yewdale died this morning, Sunday, Jan. 12th, 1834. She lived originally in Langdale, and was the woman who in my poem lights her husband Jonathan from the quarry. She talked the dialect of these parts in its purest and most ancient form. Much of her language is older than the Conquest."

723 Abundant recompence] Cf. *Tintern Abbey*, l. 89 (text of 1798).

747 saw the light] *PW* Knight, V, 225, compares WW's sonnet beginning "Even as a dragon's eye."

763 By that unwearied signal] Cf. WW's sonnet beginning "The fairest, brightest, hues of ether fade" and IF in which WW states, "The cottage of Hackett was often visited by us, & . . . was occupied by the husband & wife described in the Excursion, where it is mentioned that she was in the habit of walking in the front of the dwelling with a light to guide her husband home at night" (IF, p. 19). See also IF to *Epistle to Sir George Howland Beaumont. Bart.* (IF, p. 64).

768 till the night] For rev to this phrase, see WW's letter to BF discussing changes to *Exc*, October 24, 1828 (*LY*, I, 647).

789 a feminine hue] *PW* Knight, V, 226, notes this "feminine complexion of the Cumbrian peasants who work in the higher mines, is probably in part due to the continual mists and moisture of the heights."

830/831 In *PW*, 1845– , WW here places some explicitly Christian lines in the mouth of the Matron; see the verbal variants to the reading text, above. See also note to I, 968/969, for Christian additions to the poem.

885 But thinly sown] Cf. Mark 4:16–17.

888 Pensioner] The old man, whose death the Solitary described at II, 755–929.

914 Direct references to Christ are rare in the 1814 text of *Exc*; see note to II, 236. Cf. IV, 1097; V, 278; V, 958; IX, 718–719.

929–1022 In the draft of this speech in MS. 75 and in the fair copy in MS. 74A (stub 25, leaves 26^{r}–27^{v}), the passage continues at l. 940b with the words "This Contrast yet / A little longer may our thoughts pursue" (MS. 75, E1^{r}) and then gives a lengthy description of men being wrongfully imprisoned or mistreated by tyrannical rulers. The passage returns home with an attack on society when it ignores the poor:

> In our own Christian land by penury driven
> Hopeless of all relief and unrelieved
> Retire, like Birds to holes & corners (MS. 75, E2^{r}).

958 of Jesus] The only use of this name in the poem. Cf. II, 236; IV, 1097; V, 278, 914, 958; IX, 718–719.

959 trembling hope] Cf. Thomas Gray's *Elegy Written in a Country Churchyard*: "There they alike in trembling hope repose" (l. 127).

981 "Nature grieved that One should die;"] The quotation is from RS's poem *The Retrospect*: "Affection then will fill the sorrowing eye / And suffering Nature grieve that one should die" (ll. 139–140). See WW's Note on p. 302, above.

984 See WW's note on pp. 302–313, above, where WW gives the first *Essay upon Epitaphs* in full, indicating that the *Essay* has a "spirit congenial to that which pervades this and the two succeeding books" of *Exc*. The quotation on p. 313, above, is from Milton's "On Shakespeare," ll. 1–8, 15–16. For commentary on the first *Essay upon Epitaphs*, see *Prose*, II, 100–105.

990–999 Lyon, p. 97, indicates that this passage is "the most explicit statement of the doctrine of the senses of the soul."

998 the Word] Cf. John 1:1 ("In the beginning was the Word, and the Word was with God, and the Word was God").

1002–1007 The Pastor here defends church ritual (responding to the Solitary's earlier attack).

1014–1016 Again, Reason is placed within clear limits and given a specific aim, now within a more explicitly Christian context.

1018–1022 Unsurprisingly, this Christian belief lies at the heart of the Pastor's position. These lines were frequently anthologized in the nineteenth century. Cf. MS. 1849 in the Manuscript Census, above, and IV, 760.

Book VI: "The Church-yard among the Mountains"

Book VI of *Exc* works alongside Book VII to give a series of stories based on those who lie in the unmarked graves of the churchyard. These stories are largely told by the Pastor but prompted by the requests of his listeners. Of particular interest in relation to this section of the poem are IF, since WW there gives background information about the real inhabitants of Grasmere and Langdale upon whom the stories are based. In critical terms, however, these stories have tended to be dismissed as mere illustration coming after the argument. Hartman (p. 319), for example, describes them as the "heaping up of exempla in the medieval manner" but also acknowledges "many . . . are deeply moving."

The stories look back partly to Chaucer but should also be read in the context of the eighteenth-century epitaphic tradition. Eighteenth-century interest in graveyards produced poems such as Thomas Gray's *Elegy Written in A Country Churchyard* (1751) and Edward Young's *The Complaint, or Night Thoughts on Life, Death and Immortality* (1742–1745); other writers on epitaphs included Samuel Johnson with his *Essay on Epitaphs* (1740) and William Godwin with his *Essays on Sepulchres* (1809), both of which may have influenced WW's thinking on the subject. (For Godwin, see Wu, *Reading II*, pp. 93–94.) A more immediate poetic source is George Crabbe's poem *The Parish Register* (1807). A comparison between Crabbe and WW (at WW's expense) had been made by Francis Jeffrey in his 1807 review of Crabbe's *Poems* (*The Edinburgh Review* 12 [1808]: 131–151), so the two poets were well aware of each other. In a letter of 1808, WW comments that "nineteen out of 20 of Crabbe's Pictures are mere matters of fact" (*MY*, I, 268)—the same criticism that STC was to make against WW (see note to I, 112–138, above). It seems highly likely that WW was responding to Crabbe's *Parish Register* in this section of *Exc.* There are some clear resemblances between the works, such as the uses of a parson as narrator and of a pastor as teller of tales about his predecessors. Furthermore, there are specific similarities between Crabbe's "Rambler" and WW's "Miner" and between Crabbe's "Phoebe Dawson" and WW's "Ellen." See also Wu, *Reading II*, p. 67, and Lyon, pp. 37–40.

This section of *Exc* is strongly anticipated by WW's earlier poem "The Brothers," published in *Lyrical Ballads* (1800). *Exc* also incorporates narratives (at the end of Book VI) originally written for *Home at Grasmere*; in terms of mood and of the relation of topography to a man's life, many of the stories in Books VI and VII bear comparison not only with *Home at Grasmere* but also with *The Tuft of Primroses* (written in 1808). Beth Darlington reminds us, "During his years of work on *The Excursion*, 1810 to 1814, the manuscripts of *Home at Grasmere* were frequently before WW's eyes" (*H at G*, p. 24).

1–42 The opening apostrophe to church and state—given here by the Poet—is illustrative of the later WW's more conservative Anglican position and his desire in the poem to make connections between his representation of a local community and a national one. That passage thus also anticipates the Wanderer's proclamations of the need for national education in Book IX. STC cites ll. 1–80 as an example of WW's "occasional prolixity, repetition, and an eddying instead of progression of thought" (*STCBL*, II, 136).

11 In beauty of Holiness] Cf. 1 Chronicles 16:29; 2 Chronicles 20:21; Psalms 29:2; Psalms 96:9; Psalms 110:3.

14 mutually protected and sustained] "Note Wordsworth's love for the Established Church of England, and compare the Ecclesiastical Sonnets" (*PW* Knight, V, 236).

19 "silent finger points to Heaven;"] See WW's note on p. 313, above. As WW indicates, the phrase is a quotation from STC's essay in *The Friend* (November 23, 1809): "point as with silent finger to the sky and stars" (*STCF*, II, 195).

23–30 The Poet envisages a model of church influence that is partly orthodox, with its emphasis on charity and social love, but also partly secularized with its presentation of an instinctive natural response to architecture.

43 The Poet] Since it is "the Poet" making this statement, the use of the third person address here operates as a formal declaration. The "Summary of Contents" for

the books of the poem refers to the Poet as "The Author," apart from at this point.

44–53 The description clearly relates to the Pastor but also echoes the model of the ideal minister in *Guide through the District of the Lakes.* Cf. note to V, 102, above.

56–75 The Poet's plea is that the priesthood will be able to follow the examples of past Anglican martyrs, not "degenerate" from their "spiritual Sires." WW's fears of Catholic emancipation, combined with his increasing respect for the Church of England, are consistent with such views (see *LY,* II, 32–33, 36–46).

67 bathe their hands in fire] *PW* Knight, V, 237, asks "Was he thinking of Cranmer?" On the day of his death by burning (March 21, 1556), Thomas Cranmer retracted his recantations and thrust his fist into the fire calling out, "This hand has offended."

98–218 The first of the stories in Book VI describes The Unrequited Lover. All these portraits refer to actual local people, whom WW or his family knew and whom WW describes in IF (see pp. 1219–1223, below). Cf. note to III, 166, above.

109 We met, and passed, like shadows] In relation to the Solitary's sense of himself as self-appointed exile, see also STC's *Rime of the Ancyent Marinere*: "I pass, like night, from land to land" (l. 619; text of 1798) and Mortimer in WW's *The Borderers* "I will go forth a wanderer on the earth, / A shadowy thing" (V.iii.265–266; text of 1797–99). Cf. note to II, 798. For other references to *Rime,* see I, 646–647; II, 683, 798; III, 860–861.

121–122 *PW,* V, 457, suggests that these lines were altered in 1827, "so as to avoid invidious comparison with Viola in *Twelfth Night,* II.iv.110–112 'She never told her love, But . . . pin'd in thought.'"

141 their mortal spoils] Cf. *Hamlet,* III.i.67: "When we have shuffled off this mortal coil."

168–171 *PW,* V, 458, finds such a sentiment expressed in Chaucer's *The Franklyn's Tale* (ll. 36–38) as well as in *The Faerie Queene,* bk. 3, canto I, 25. WW translated several of Chaucer's tales in 1801–1802, with later rev (see *Translations of Chaucer and Virgil, by William Wordsworth,* ed. Bruce E. Graver [Ithaca, 1998], pp. 11–19). See Wu, *Reading II,* pp. 47–48.

194 Shedding sweet influence] *PW,* V, 458, points out this direct quotation from *PL,* VII, 375.

219–264 The second story in Book VI is that of The Persevering Miner.

221–222 The Pastor's uncertainty about the Miner's tale is also echoed by WW in his later description of the man upon whom it was based: "In reviewing his story one cannot but regret that such perseverance was not sustained by a worthier object" (IF, p. 1220, below).

255–264 WW also employs an image of the physical mark left by the individual on the landscape as a kind of naturalized epitaph at I, 917–920, and at VI, 824–828, 836–840. See also Hickey's discussion (pp. 89–96) of the miner's path as a figure for narrative.

270 "Unshaken, unseduced, unterrified;"] A direct quotation from *PL,* V, 899.

283 that mixture of Earth's Mold] Cf. Milton, *Comus,* l. 244: "any mortal mixture of Earth's mold."

285–390 The third oral epitaph is the story of The Adventurer, or The Prodigal Son. See also IF, pp. 1220–1221, below. WW, later in IF, tells us that this figure was the older brother of Oswald (whose tale is told in Book VII; see note to VII, 720–838).

332 when this Prodigal returned] Cf. Luke 15:20–24. As in the biblical tale, the Pastor's version celebrates the openness of parental love. The Solitary, in his sullen response, seems almost to adopt the role of the disgruntled elder brother of the Bible.

340 the wide-staring Owl] *PW,* V, 458, compares *Love's Labour's Lost,* V.ii.925: "Then nightly sings the staring owl."

365–367 The Solitary's description of the city's corrupting influence could be compared to its effect upon Luke in WW's *Michael*: "He in the dissolute city gave himself / To evil courses" (ll. 453–454; text of 1800).

388 contradictions infinite] Cf. Thomas Heywood, *The Hierarchie of the Blessed Angells* (1635): "Warring with contradictions infinite" (bk. IX, "The Angell," l. 11,766). WW owned a copy of Heywood's poems (see Wu, *Reading II*, p. 110).

397 Infect the air] The "Summary of Contents" for Book VI states that at this point in the Solitary's reaction to the tale he is "applying this covertly to his own case." Unsurprisingly, then, he uses the image of infection here to describe the effect of the Prodigal's return to his own past, which he had previously applied to himself and his own memory (see III, 855–857).

402 dividual Being] The phrase appears in *PL*, XII, 85.

421–537 The next tale is that of The Two Men of Opposite Principles: The Jacobite and Hanoverian Whig. WW tells us in IF that he had this story from Ann Tyson, the dame with whom he lodged in Hawkshead (see pp. 1220–1221, below).

433 The Stuart] Charles Edward Stuart, the Young Pretender, or Bonnie Prince Charlie, the grandson of James II exiled in France after the English throne was taken by William of Orange and Mary in the Bloodless Revolution of 1688. After an abortive French invasion of England in 1744, he went alone to Scotland in 1745 to gather the Scottish clans around him and attempt to recapture the English throne.

437 Culloden's fatal overthrow] Bonnie Prince Charlie was defeated (and forced to flee again into exile) at the battle of Culloden Moor, April 16, 1746. The Jacobites were pursued by government troops under the Duke of Cumberland with orders to kill every survivor.

447 The new succession] The Hanoverian line began with George I, who took the throne in 1714 after Queen Anne.

449 the dire assaults of Papacy] James II's strong Catholic beliefs, and in particular the birth of a son to his Catholic wife, which would assure a Catholic succession, prompted the invitation to William of Orange to come to England in November 1688.

499 the Spirit of hope] The Pastor continually emphasizes Christian virtues.

513 a Dial] A sundial.

530 in Latin numbers couched] The Poet silently translates these for us.

535–537 These lines—with their direct address to the passing traveler—are reminiscent of the epitaphs of Chiabrera that WW had been translating for STC's *The Friend* in 1809–1810 and that he praises in the second and third *Essays on Epitaphs* (see *Prose*, II, 79, 89–91). See also Wu, *Reading II*, p. 49.

539 the Sceptic] The Solitary.

548–549 "too quick a sense / Of constant infelicity"] From Jeremy Taylor's *The Rule and Exercises of Holy Dying* (1651): "If we could but hear . . . how many People there are that weep with Want, and are mad with Oppression, or are desperate by too quick a Sense of constant infelicity" (ch.1, sec. 5.2). See also Wu, *Reading II*, pp. 208–209.

555–557 Prometheus was one of the Titans who gave men the gift of fire by stealing it from heaven. Zeus punished him for this transgression by having him chained to a cliff in the Caucasus Mountains. Each day an eagle tore at his liver, while each night the liver grew again so that the torment could continue. Prometheus was eventually released by Heracles (who shot the eagle). The story is the basis of Aeschylus's *Prometheus Bound* and Shelley's *Prometheus Unbound*.

558 Tantalus] Tantalus, the son of Zeus, was a favorite of the gods until he offended them in various ways. As a result he suffered eternal punishment in the Underworld. He was placed in a lake with water up to his chin (which receded if he tried to drink it) and with fruit above his head (which leapt from his hand if he tried to pluck it).

559 line of Thebes] The house of Thebes was cursed for three generations. Laius, King of Thebes, and his wife, Jocasta, were told by an oracle that their son (Oedipus) would kill his father and marry his mother. After unwittingly fulfilling the prophecy, Oedipus blinded himself and went into exile, where the Furies pursued him to his death.

The curse was passed on to his two sons, Eteocles and Polyneices, who killed each other while fighting over their right to rule Thebes. See Sophocles, *The Theban Plays.* See also note to III, 136.

565–566 give the pomp / Of circumstance] Cf. *Othello,* III.iii.354: "Pride, pomp, and circumstance of glorious war!"

570–572 The Solitary's view is of a predetermined universe with a hostile God in control.

586 Of strange disasters] Cf. *Prelude,* VIII, 217–218: "the tragedies of former times / Or hazards and escapes." There is a sense in which the portraits of men's lives given in *Exc* are the fullest expression of the aim of Book VIII in *The Prelude* to speak of "High thoughts of God and Man, and love of Man" (VIII, 64).

611–614 *PW,* V, 459, compares *PL,* V, 185–187.

623–624 almost wholly free / From interruption] WW emphasizes that the churchyard contains unmarked graves. See IF to *Epistle to Sir George Howland Beaumont. Bart.,* where WW declares his dislike of "iron palisades to fence off family burying grounds" and himself directs attention to *Exc* at this point: "See the lines in the vi[th] book of the Excursion, beginning 'Green is the Church yard'" (IF, p. 66). Ironically, WW's strong feelings on this subject have not been able to be respected at his own grave, which suffers from just such "fencing off" from tourists.

626–631 The reminder that these are oral epitaphs looks directly back to *The Brothers.* In that poem Leonard comments that "Your dalesmen, then, do in each other's thoughts / Possess a kind of second life" (ll. 182–183; text of 1800). See also note to V, 648–649, above.

646–661 The Poet's feelings at this point in the poem directly echo lines in the second *Essay on Epitaphs*: "It is such a happiness to have, in an unkind World, one Enclosure where the voice of detraction is not heard; where the traces of evil inclinations are unknown; where contentment prevails, and there is no jarring tone in the peaceful Concert of amity and gratitude" (*Prose,* II, 63–64).

690–793 The tale of The Unamiable Woman follows. Critical response to this tale was largely negative. Hazlitt in particular commented that it "carries that concentration of self-interest and callousness to the feelings of others to its utmost pitch" (Hazlitt, p. 637). See also IF on p. 1221, below. *PW,* V, 460, adds some further details about her: "The woman was Aggy Fisher, sister-in-law of Molly, servant of the W.'s 1800–1804. In D.W.'s *Journal* will be found a hint of her parsimony (May 16, 1800) and examples of her gift for conversation (June 3 and 21, 1802). She died in 1804."

755–762 The comparison of the woman's life to the flow of the river (a typically Wordsworthian image) partly echoes the Solitary's use of such an image for himself at III, 974–998. Cf. *Prelude,* IV, 247–264.

785 the planet Jupiter] There may be some significance in the woman's looking at this particular planet since it is associated with negative characteristics such as ambition, haughtiness, and insolence. Jupiter was WW's "own beloved star" (*Prelude,* IV, 247).

790 In the addition made here in *PW,* 1845 (see verbal variants to the reading text, above), not only does the woman now die resignedly rather than rail against death, but the Pastor's confident belief in "divine mercy" assures her of Christian salvation in spite of her flaws. See note to I, 969, above, for Christian additions to the poem.

794–795 Cf. *The Brothers*: "Upon the long stone-seat beneath the eaves," l. 18. *PW,* V, 460, also compares "seats in the rude wall" (see *EW,* l. 41; p. 132).

805–1073 The tale of Ellen. Contemporary reviewers responded warmly to this story, including Francis Jeffrey, who, in his negative review of the poem, nonetheless acknowledged this tale as "that of a simple, seduced and deserted girl, told with great sweetness, pathos and indulgence by the Vicar at the parish" (Jeffrey, p. 22). As Jeffrey's response suggests, the portrait could be seen as taking part in a tradition of sympathetic portraits of fallen women including Cowper's "Crazy Kate" in *The Task* and Crabbe's Phoebe Dawson in *The*

Parish Register (with whom Ellen bears some close comparison). WW's account in IF places great emphasis on his sources: "The story that follows was told to Mrs. Wordsworth & my Sister by the Sister of this unhappy young woman" (p. 1221, below). See also discussion of Ellen's tale in Hickey, pp. 84–88.

824–828 The Wanderer notes the relationship between the silent landscape and those who have lived out their tragedies upon it. Cf. I, 917–920; VI, 255–264, 836–840.

832 a weeping Magdalene] See note to VI, 1008, below.

834 of poor Ellen's tears] The importance of the tale in *Exc* is marked by giving the character a name, as few are in the epitaphic tales.

836–840 A specific image of Ellen's physical path, worn by her daily and no longer to be seen. Cf. I, 917–920; VI, 255–264, 824–828.

846 A Titian's hand] Tiziano Vecellio (1485–1576), the great Italian painter of the Venetian school.

848 Cf. Milton, *Lycidas*: "What time the Gray-fly winds her sultry horn," l. 28.

856 To the Twelfth Night] The Pastor's account of January 6, feast of the Epiphany, continues his description of local customs that at different times of year involve dances round a tree.

911 The poem reminds us of the natural origins of the Valentine—originally the song of mating birds to one another at the opening of spring—in the parallel Ellen draws between her own situation and that of the thrushes she hears outside.

924 pang of despised love] Cf. *Hamlet,* III.i.72: "The pangs of dispriz'd love."

938–942 Ellen's metaphor refers to the moment when Moses finds water in the desert for his people; see Numbers 20:11 ("And Moses lifted up his hand, and with his rod he smote the rock twice: and the water came out abundantly, and the congregation drank, and their beasts also").

969–970 The Pastor outlines the egalitarian nature of life in the Lakes; cf. *Prelude,* IX, 218–226. The treatment of Ellen by her employers, who try to forbid her attending even her own child's funeral, stands as a notable exception.

1008 A rueful Magdalene] Cf. VI, 832. The Pastor explains his use of the comparison here—perhaps because she is clearly now a "fallen," though repentant, woman. Cf. Luke 7:37–50.

1026 Home to her mother's house] *PW,* V, 460–461, notes this as "an unconscious reminiscence of the last line [IV, 639] of *Paradise Regained*: 'Home to his Mother's house private return'd.'"

1100–1232 The story of Wilfred Armathwaite and the next tale were originally written as part of a series of narratives for work on *Home at Grasmere*; the two tales were then altered for incorporation in *Exc* at some point between 1810 and 1814 (see MS. 28, 132–138/141i^{v}; MS. 59, 21^{v}–27^{r}; *H at G,* pp. 144–165, 322–343).

1106–1133 In *PW,* 1827– , the story of Wilfred Armthwaite was reduced when these lines were removed (see p. 20, above).

1127 A blooming Girl] Cf. I, 563; III, 647.

1154 *PW,* V, 461–462, suggests, "Here, it seems probable, W. intended to place the story of the Shepherd of Bield Crag." (See Appendix II, below.)

1155–1232 At this point comes the tale of The Widower (with six daughters), a second passage originally written as part of *Home at Grasmere* (see note to VI, 1100–1232, above).

1220–1226 The images are those of domestic industry, still existent in the early part of the nineteenth century but shortly to be destroyed by industrialization. Cf. VIII, 267–284, where the Wanderer gives an image of destruction of domestic happiness and employment by industry.

1233–1308 The story of The Second Marriage of a Widower. In *PW,* 1827– , this story is removed (see p. 20, above).

Book VII: "The Church-yard among the Mountains Continued"

Book VII continues in much the same vein as Book VI. It is still set in the churchyard with further epitaphic stories being shared. This book does, however, contain stories of the living as well as the dead. The section on past pastors of the valley is strongly reminiscent of the final section of "Burials" in Crabbe's *The Parish Register,* in which Crabbe's parson gives a series of portraits of his predecessors. Unsurprisingly, in Crabbe's poem these portraits are less respectful and more satiric than those of WW's Pastor.

1–30 As at the start of Book VI, the opening lines give the Poet's internal thoughts, in this case describing his overall response to the narratives he has heard so far.

1 the Historian] Cf. the labeling of the Pastor here, in recording the lives of others, to the description of the Wanderer as "Chronicler" at V, 99.

7–8 Snowdon's craggy top . . . Cader Idris, or huge Penmanmaur] Welsh mountains that WW had visited in the summers of 1791 and 1793 with Robert Jones on walking tours of North Wales. See also the well-known description of the ascent of Snowdon in *Prelude,* XIII, 1–65.

9–22 The comparison of the effect on the Poet of the Pastor's narratives to that of a minstrel's song is an echo of an extended comparison of the Wanderer with the figure of the wandering minstrel at II, 1–29, and at VIII, 606–607.

37–38 Because the school building was located on the edge of the Grasmere churchyard, that churchyard was also used as the school playground. Ground nearest the school was not used for burial until lack of space eventually compelled it to be. After the death of WW's son Thomas in 1812, DW commented on the disturbing proximity of the school and churchyard, a fact that partly caused the family to move from Grasmere Parsonage, where they were living at the time, to Rydal Mount: "above all the view of that school, our darling's daily pride and joy—that church-yard his playground—all oppressed us and do continue to oppress us with unutterable sadness" (*MY,* I, 60).

41 Of strange or tragic accident] Cf. *Prelude,* VIII, 217–218: "the tragedies of former times, / Or hazards and escapes."

42–46 In these lines the poem merges the landscape of the churchyard's "hillocks" with the landscape beyond, moving from microcosm to the wider scene almost imperceptibly.

50 an easy outlet of the Vale] *PW* Knight, V, 285, identifies this "outlet" as the road to Keswick, passing north out of Grasmere Valley over Dunmail Raise.

56–58 "The cottage in which the parson of Wytheburn then lived still stands on the right or eastern side of the road, as you ascend the Raise, beyond the Swan Inn" (*PW* Knight, V, 286). *PW,* V, 464, adds, "The 'Cottage' where the Sympsons lived, still known as Broadrain, is situated some 300 yards above the bridge over Tongue Ghyll; the 'vale beyond' is Wytheburn."

63 wain] a wagon.

64–309 The first depiction is of the Clergyman and his Family. It is based upon Rev. Joseph Sympson, curate of Wytheburn, who died at the age of ninety-two and was buried in Grasmere churchyard on July 2, 1807 (see *PW,* V, 464). DW's *Journals* record the Wordsworths' regular visits to the Sympson family (see, for example, entries for May to June 1800). In a note to Sonnet VI of *The River Duddon,* WW praises the eldest son of the family, also named Joseph ("a man of ardent feeling, and his faculties of mind, particularly his memory, were extraordinary") and prints one of his poems (*Sonnet Series,* p. 83; see also pp. 101–102). WW in IF has more about Joseph Sympson, the son, and asserts the accuracy of his poetic portrait of the family: "the whole that I have said of them is as faithful to the truth as words can make it" (p. 1222, below).

70 The Pastor reminds us of his own history as one born and bred in the valley.

87–95 Onlookers conjecture that the family may be traveling players who will act out popular stories such as those circulated in chapbooks by pedlars. Cf. *Prelude,* V, 364–367; VII, 114–117, 303–307.

163 three fair Children] "Joseph Sympson had, in fact, six children, three boys and three girls" (*PW*, V, 464).

175–176 no soft and costly sofa there / Insidiously stretched out its lazy length] A direct reference to the opening of Cowper's *The Task*: "I sing the Sofa" (I, 1) and to another line later in the same book "The sedentary stretch their lazy length" (I, 389).

190 smooth blue slabs of mountain stone] Such stones from the local quarries were common in the cottages at this time.

261–309 This account of the Sympson family was originally written for the *Tuft of Primroses* (1808) in MS. 65 (36^r–38^v) and later redrafted there in preparation for incorporation into *Exc.* See *Tuft*, pp. 27, 43–45, 151, 214–225. See also pp. 1111–1113, below.

262 the Patriarch of the Vale] The clergyman's story shows his integration into the community to the point at which he is named as a kind of natural monument in his own right and given a particular local identity that overrides his vocational one.

274 A happy consummation] Cf. "'tis a consummation / Devoutly to be wish'd" *Hamlet*, III.i.63–64.

314–315 That might have touched the sick heart of his Friend / Too nearly] The Wanderer is anxious that the story of the man losing all his family may be upsetting to the Solitary because of its similarity to his own tragedy.

318 Behold a thoughtless Man] The Wanderer is still describing the previous character, summing up his life.

321 The Hermit] Cf. III, 376.

334–335 The story of Another Clergyman. The second clergyman, described in the "Summary of Contents" to this book as "a character of resolute Virtue," refers to WW's friend Robert Walker. WW in IF (see p. 1222, below) simply refers us to his notes for *The River Duddon* where he gives a lengthy *Memoir* of Walker's life, including praise of him in letters from others, and states that "An abstract of his character is given in the author's poem of The Excursion" (*Sonnet Series*, pp. 86–98).

363 the Wonderful] This appellation seems to have been commonly applied to Robert Walker as WW tells us in the *Memoir* in his *The River Duddon*: "the epithet of WONDERFUL is to this day attached to his name" (*Sonnet Series*, p. 91).

370–376 The Pastor describes his fellow priest as if he is still alive in the poem although Robert Walker had in fact died on June 25, 1802, and was buried in Seathwaite chapel. This is one of two examples within this book in which the people on whom characters are based are represented as if dead when still alive or vice versa. See note to VII, 503, below.

380–395 The Pastor makes a statement against poetry and demands instead that the poet should celebrate the deeds of the good man. This passage should be compared with the Poet's lines upon "Poets that are sown / By Nature" (see I, 81–82), in particular his comment that "Strongest minds / Are often those of whom the noisy world / Hears least" (I, 95–97).

412–498 The next story is that of the Deaf Man who lost his hearing in childhood. It is based upon Thomas Holme of Chapel Hill, who died in 1773 at the age of sixty-seven. On his epitaph was written, in part, "HE WAS DEPRIVED OF THE SENSE OF HEARING IN HIS YOUTH AND LIVED ABOUT 50 YEARS WITHOUT THE COMFORT OF HEARING ONE WORD. HE RECONCILED HIMSELF TO HIS MISFORTUNE BY READING AND USEFUL EMPLOYMENT" (*Prose*, II, 118–119). The tale in this case seems to actually represent what all the tales purport to be: an expansion of the man's epitaph into narrative. WW makes this expansion clear when he quotes ll. 413–498 at the end of the third "Essay on Epitaphs" as an example of "a concise Epitaph which I met with some time ago in one of the most retired vales among the Mountains of Westmoreland. There is nothing in the detail of the Poem which is not either founded upon the Epitaph or gathered from enquiries concerning the Deceased made in the neighbourhood" (*Prose*, II, 93–94). See also IF, p. 1222, below.

489–490 that monumental Stone preserves / His name] The Dalesman's grave is not unmarked, although his name is not given to us.

503–532 The story of A Blind Man. This portrait is based upon the blind mathematician and botanist John Gough (1757–1825). *PW* Knight, V, 398–399, directs us to pp. 355–368 of Cornelius Nicholson's *Annals of Kendal* (1861). This text gives a fascinating account of Gough's examination of plants: "The plant to be examined was held by the root or base in one hand, while the fingers of the other travelled slowly upwards over the stem, branches, and leaves, till they reached the flower. . . . [I]f it proved to be a novelty, its class was first determined by the insertion of the tip of his tongue within the flower. . . . It was truly wonderful to witness the rapidity with which his fingers ran among the leaves." STC also refers to Gough as "not only an excellent mathematician; but an infallible botanist and zoologist. He has frequently at the first feel corrected the mistakes of the most experienced sportsman, with regard to the birds or vermin which they had killed, when it chanced to be a variety or rare species" (*Shorter Works and Fragments*, ed. H. J. Jackson and J R. de J. Jackson [2 vols.; Princeton, 1995], I, 335). Since Gough was still alive in 1814, this epitaphic portrait is premature and again shows WW's artistic freedom in dealing with his real-life subjects (see note to VII, 370–376, above). It is also worth noting that WW himself suffered from trachoma and was worried that he might go blind. An attack occurred in the summer of 1810 when he would have been working on *Exc* and may have partly prompted the comments on blindness in this section. See also IF on p. 1222, below.

513 on the very brink of vacancy] The risk of falling over the edge recalls James's fate in WW's poem *The Brothers*, as well as Mortimer in his play *The Borderers*, V.i.

526 instinct with spirit] The phrase appears in *PL*, VI, 752. As *PW*, V, 465, points out, "In his description of the blind man W. instinctively falls into Miltonic phraseology and rhythm." The series of textual allusions at this point (see the following notes) reinforces such a Miltonic sense.

528 Fancy and understanding] The phrase appears in *PL*, V, 486.

531–532 humbler knowledge stood / Abashed, and tender pity overawed] Cf. *PL*, IV, 846–847: "abasht the Devil stood / And felt how awful goodness is."

548 men who see not as we see] Prophets and seers, often portrayed as being blind.

551–553 Presumably WW is referring here to Milton's blindness, as well as alluding to his *L'Allegro* ("Married to immortal verse," l. 137) in the reference at VII, 533, to "wisdom married to immortal verse."

560 adown a rugged slope] *PW*, V, 465, points out "There is no 'rugged slope' with a 'steep descent' near Grasmere churchyard." Since WW tells us that the setting is a combination of Grasmere and Langdale (see our introductory note to Book V, above), the poem has clearly reverted to the topography of the latter at this point.

557–654 The epitaphic stories are broken off temporarily by the interruption of the living in the form of "a Peasant who passes" (see "Summary of Contents" for Book VII)—the tree feller.

585–586 In the early draft of this passage in the Houghton MS., the man's age is given as seventy-seven.

610–611 Cf. the Pastor's dislike of having trees cut down with DW's remarks upon returning from Coleorton in 1807: "All the trees in Bainriggs are cut down, and even worse, the giant sycamore near the parsonage house, and all the finest firtrees that overtopped the steeple tower" (*MY*, I, 159).

635–636 That Sycamore] WW's note (see p. 313, above) to this line quotes from a similar image of the tree as a tent in STC's poem *Inscription for a Fountain on a Heath*, ll. 1–2 (see *STCPW*, I, part 2, 663). At V, 455, the Pastor is also compared to the sycamore, a popular tree in the Lake District; see WW's comments on this comparison in IF, p. 1217, below.

648–654 *PW*, V, 466, indicates that in early draft work (MS. 75, B1ʳ, B2ʳ), "W's description of the old Woodsman assumed that he was already dead." Furthermore, the Woodsman passage must have been written earlier than the "Patriarch of the Vale" section (VII, 261–309), since lines are transferred from the account of the Woodsman into the "Patriarch of the Vale" passage for the *Tuft of Primroses* (and then later moved to *Exc*). For discussion of the complexities here, see pp. 459–461, below.

659–719 The Pastor now speaks of "A female Infant's Grave" (see "Summary of Contents" for Book VII) and tells the story of the family with seven sons and one daughter. This tale is based upon the Green family, who had lived in Grasmere for many generations. In her *Journals* (November 24, 1801; p. 40), DW describes how "John Greens house looked pretty under Silver How." See also IF, p. 1222, below.

720–838 Here is the story of Oswald, "A youthful Peasant" (see "Summary of Contents" for Book VII). That the tale is significant in some way is indicated by the fact that, like Margaret in Book I and Ellen in Book VI, the protagonist is named within the poem. See IF, pp. 1222–1223, below, where WW tells us that this boy was of the Dawson family and actually the younger brother of the Prodigal whose tale is told at VI, 285. WW himself attended the funeral of that model for his "youthful Peasant." See also DW's letter on returning to Grasmere in July 1807: "Many persons are dead, old Mr. Sympson, his son the parson, young George Dawson, the first young Man in the vale" (*MY*, I, 158). WW's feelings of dismay at changes felt on his return prompted him to write the *Tuft of Primroses*, and such emotions also partly lie behind the epitaphic books of this poem. See also James A. Butler, "Wordsworth's *Tuft of Primroses*: 'An Unrelenting Doom,'" *Studies in Romanticism* 14 (1975): 237–248.

720 Cf. George Herbert, *Sunday* ("O Day, most calme, most bright, " l. 1) and *Vertue* ("Sweet day, so cool, so calm, so bright," l. 1); see Wu, *Reading II*, p. 108.

774 glead] A bird of prey; "More usually glede or gled, is a name, chiefly north-country, for the Kite" (*PW* Smith, p. 563).

780 The Tyrant is Napoleon, preparing France for aggressive war against other nations.

785–793 In response to the threat of invasion from France, Thomas Wedgwood paid for the equipping of a company of men from the Lake District known as "Wedgwood's Mountaineers" (*PW* Knight, V, 312).

794 young Oswald, like a Chief] Cf. WW's *The Borderers*. In the 1842 version of the text the villain of the play, Rivers, is renamed Oswald. David Erdman has pointed out that the change of name connects WW's villain to John Oswald, an English Jacobin who suggested to the convention the idea of a "law of suspects," which was adopted on September 19, 1793, and then applied to the Girondists. (See "Wordsworth as Heartsworth; or, Was Regicide the Prophetic Ground of Those 'Moral Questions'?" *The Evidence of the Imagination*, ed. Donald H. Reiman, Michael C. Jaye, and Betty T. Bennett [New York, 1978], pp. 39–40; see also David Erdman, *Commerce des lumières: John Oswald and the British in Paris, 1790–1793* [Columbia, Missouri, 1986].) Apart from his name, however, "Oswald" of *Exc* seems to bear more resemblance to the gullible hero (Marmaduke) of *The Borderers* than to WW's villain.

818–822 Oswald is using the map to point out to his companions the sites of recent Napoleonic victories: his defeat of the Russians and Austrians at Austerlitz on December 2, 1805 (by which he gained control of German states, northern Italy, and the Adriatic coast) and of the Prussians at Jena on October 14, 1806.

826–838 The Pastor first identifies the shepherds of the mountainous Lake District with the sturdy peasantry of Switzerland and then extends their bravery, personified by Oswald, to biblical proportions, by making comparison with Old Testament examples.

829 After conquering northern Italy, Napoleon invaded Switzerland and occupied Bern on March 5, 1798. The French established the Helvetic Republic, which lasted

from 1798 to 1803. The occupiers treated Switzerland as a vassal state. See also I, 346, and V, 93–95.

832 Of Tell] William Tell, the legendary Swiss hero of the thirteenth and early fourteenth centuries, who symbolized the struggle for personal and political freedom. According to tradition, Tell, a famous marksman, was forced by a tyrannical Austrian governor to shoot an apple from his son's head from eighty paces away. Later he killed the governor, which helped spur the people to rise up against Austrian rule and led eventually to Swiss independence.

834–835 to march / With righteous Joshua] Cf. Joshua 1:2–11; 8:1–3.

836 When grove was felled, and altar was cast down] Cf. Judges 6:25–34.

837 And Gideon blew the trumpet] Cf. Judges 6:34: "But the Spirit of the LORD came upon Gideon, and he blew a trumpet."

868 "all hoping and expecting all"] A reference to 1 Corinthians 13:7 ("Beareth all things, believeth all things, hopeth all things, endureth all things").

881–882 Cf. *PL*, I, 742–744: "from Morn / To Noon he fell, from Noon to dewy Eve, / A Summer's day."

908 the tributary peal / Of instantaneous thunder] The guns saluting the dead youth.

913–932 As at the end of Ellen's tale (see VI, 1074), the Poet records the different emotional responses of the listeners in some detail.

945–997 This final tale is of Sir Alfred Irthing, the Elizabethan knight, an ancestor of the Knott family. On February 18, 1815, DW tells us: "William and Mary and little Willy paid a visit to old Mrs Knott yesterday with the Exn. in hand, William intending to read to the old Lady the history of the Grasmere Knight" (*MY*, II, 202–203). See IF, p. 1223, below.

946 in Eliza's golden days] In the reign of Queen Elizabeth I.

989–990 his family name / Borne by yon clustering cottages] These cottages were called Nott houses after the family from which the knight came. See IF, p. 1223, below.

992–997 This account of the three bells bearing the knight's name seems to be fictitious. *PW* Knight, V, 323, tells us that two of the three bells were probably provided by the Flemings of Rydal Hall, although the third was a recasting by Dorothy Knott made in 1808 but not bearing the name "Sir Alfred Irthing."

1002 See WW's note on p. 314, above. WW comments upon this "Transit gloria mundi" in his notes, giving Furness Abbey as a general source for his expression here.

1002–1004 These lines are redrafted from part of WW's rendition of St. Basil's address to St. Gregory Nazianzen in the *Tuft of Primroses*, MS. 65 (58[r]; *Tuft*, pp. 27, 50, 290–291).

1044–1049 The Wanderer describes the violent acts of the Reformation, which the knight would have experienced in his youth.

Book VIII: "The Parsonage"

The final two books take the poem away from its previously localized concerns into a wider application of moral ideals to the nation as a whole and to changes in society. Dialogue and debate are no longer used in relation to any endeavor to help the Solitary, and there is a shift to wider issues. WW attempts, through the Wanderer, to address a wider audience and national themes in terms of industrial change and a call for universal education. For particular discussion of these themes in Books VIII and IX, see Hickey, pp. 105–129; Mary Wedd, "Industrialization and the Moral Law in Books VIII and IX of *The Excursion*," *Charles Lamb Bulletin*, n.s., 81 (1993): 5–25; and Connell, pp. 160–181.

The speeches of Books VIII and IX are probably those sections of the poem that most gave it its didactic reputation. Francis Jeffrey is referring to these when he describes the poem as: "decidedly didactic; and more than nine tenths of it are occupied with a species of dialogue, or rather a series of long sermons or harangues" (Jeffrey, p. 5). At the same time, however, Jeffrey later praises Book IX's "animated exhortation to the more general diffusion of education among the lower orders" (p. 27).

1 The pensive Sceptic] The Solitary.

3 Cf. I, 163; IX, 132.

35 his Compatriot] The Wanderer. Cf. II, 171; III, 506; IV, 549.

36 this good Knight] Sir Alfred Irthing, whose tale was the last to be told in Book VII.

44 a poor Brotherhood who walk the earth] Packmen like the Wanderer.

52 irksome toil] The same phrase appears in *PL*, IX, 242.

71 Cf. II, 780; VIII, 424.

89 An inventive Age] WW in IF gives a lengthy account of changes to rural life caused by industrialization and states, "Reviewing at this later period, *1843*, what I put into the mouths of my Interlocutors a few years after the commencement of the Century, I grieve that so little progress has been made in diminishing the evils deplored, or promoting the benefits of education which the Wanderer anticipates" (p. 1223, below).

92 A new and unforeseen Creation] Industrialization. The Wanderer's (and WW's) attitudes seem to be ambivalent as he partly admires and partly fears the consequences. Such a position is typical of the time, expressing contemporary fears of insurrection and potential moral depravity in the new industrial towns (see Connell, pp. 63–67).

102 of Thorpe and Vill] Homestead; small house or farm. Cf. *Ecclesiastical Sketches*, Part 1, Sonnet XXII, l. 13.

113–114 The Earth has lent / Her waters] See WW's note on p. 314, above. In that note, he compares his tempered praise of industrialization with John Dyer's wholehearted support for it in *The Fleece*, a poem that WW admired. See Wu, *Reading II*, p. 83.

125 Like trees in forests] WW uses naturalistic imagery to describe the spread of industrialization.

132 Cf. I, 163; IX, 3.

144–145 The linking of localized change to wider changes in society and to Britain's status as a nation—particularly as a naval power—anticipates the Wanderer's later speech in Book IX.

168–175 The Wanderer now views the effects of industrialization far more negatively in terms of its destruction of rural peace and social ties.

174 the Norman Conqueror's stern behest] William the Conqueror introduced the curfew bell to England in 1068 as a means of suppressing rebellion against him.

185–187 The Wanderer paints a picture of idolatry, a kind of false religion of exploitation, created by the manufacturing system.

201 yet I exult] An example of the Wanderer's mixed feelings on the subject, as he returns to praise the "Intellectual mastery" represented by advances in the manufacturing industry.

218 Upon the Moral law] Ultimately the Wanderer's point is that industry will only be a great good for the country as a whole if it is underpinned by moral values.

Egyptian Thebes] The ancient capital of Upper Egypt. It contained various magnificent tombs and temples, including that of Tutankhamen, and stood on the Nile where Luxor now stands. The examples that follow are of those ancient civilizations that did not have "moral law" at their heart and so fell into ruins.

219 Tyre] The oldest city of Phoenicia, it consisted of a town on the mainland and two islands opposite. Magnificent and luxurious, it was partly destroyed by Alexander the Great but remained important until the Middle Ages. Where part of one island sank, its ruins were to be seen under the water. Citing an earlier source, *PW* Knight, V, 335, indicates "in the end of the twelfth century, towns, markets, streets, and halls might be observed at the bottom of the sea."

220 Palmyra] The city of palms. This city was either enlarged or built by Solomon in the tenth century B.C. It existed in an oasis in the Syrian desert, its wealth coming from control of the desert trade routes between northern Syria and Babylonia. Cf. III, 154.

222 Call Archimedes from his buried Tomb] Cicero states: "When I was quaestor I tracked out his grave which was unknown to the Syracusans (as they totally denied its existence) and found it enclosed all round and covered with brambles and thickets. . . . So you see, one of the most famous cities of Greece, once indeed a great school of learning as well, would have been ignorant of the tomb of its one most ingenious citizen" (*Tusculan Disputations*, bk. V, sec. XXIII.64–67)

258 what lamentable change] Cf. *King Lear*, "The lamentable change is from the best" (IV.i.5).

267–284 The Wanderer now paints a bleak portrait of the social effects of the Industrial Revolution. This description could be compared with the positive depiction of domestic industry at VI, 1220–1226.

285–287 An attack on Adam Smith's *Wealth of Nations* (1776), which WW had read by 1804 (see Wu, *Reading II*, p. 193). WW disapproved of the economists for being more concerned with manufacturing efficiency than with the effects of such efficiency upon the individual. Cf. *Prelude*, XII, 79–87.

289–294, 304–308, 317–330 These lines are first found as draft material in DC MSS. 15 (stub 25) and 16 (79^r–80^r); *see LB, 1797–1800*, pp. 307–308, 718–719, 728.

299–305 *PW*, V, 471, suggests that WW's interest in the evils of child labor stems from conversations with the radical John Thelwall, who visited him in Alfoxden in 1797. See also our introductory note to Book III, above.

334 Cf. III, 97.

351 The Solitary counters the Wanderer's depiction of the imprisoned factory child with portraits of rural poverty in the gypsies and then later in the native poor of Britain. Cf. WW's *Gipsies*.

380 'Mid Buxton's dreary heights] "The heights between Buxton and Macclesfield, at the top of the Valley of the Gite" (*PW* Knight, V, 342).

417 the Christ-cross-row] The alphabet. It was called this either because it had a cross prefixed to it in the hornbooks or because of a superstition of writing the alphabet itself in the form of a cross.

424 Cf. II, 780; VIII, 71.

441–442 he seemed prepared to give / Prompt utterance] The Wanderer is interrupted at this point but returns to answer the Solitary's questions at IX, 181.

571–575 Shelley ridiculed this description of the piled-up fish in his Wordsworthian parody, *Peter Bell The Third*, part VI, stanza XXVI. In a note, Shelley refers to this depiction in *Exc*: "See the description of the beautiful colours produced during the agonizing death of a number of trout, in the fourth part of a long poem in blank verse, published within a few years. That poem contains curious evidence of the gradual hardening of a strong but circumscribed sensibility, of the perversion of a penetrating but panic-stricken understanding" (ll. 127–131n).

583 those two Boys] The portrait of the two boys and their naturalized and coequal education in part seems to stimulate the Wanderer's call for national education in Book IX. See also note to IX, 259.

606–607 with readier patience than to strain / Of music, lute or harp] Again, the Wanderer's speech seems to be compared with the song of the traditional minstrel. Cf. II, 1–29; VII, 9–22.

Book IX: Discourse of the Wanderer, and an Evening Visit to the Lake

Book IX is distinguished by the call for national education, with the Wanderer's speech clearly being used to offer a direct address to the readership and the government of

Britain. WW supported a particular educational model developed by Andrew Bell in his work as superintendent of the Madras Male Orphan Asylum. Bell's system was built upon the idea of pupil-teachers, in which each class consisted of children teaching each other. STC, WW, and RS were all supporters of this Church of England system in opposition to Bell's rival, Joseph Lancaster, a Quaker who advocated free education on more general Christian principles; for STC on Bell, see note to IV, 279–289, above. WW read Bell's book in 1808 and became an increasingly enthusiastic supporter, as he wrote to Thomas Poole in March 1815: "If you have read my Poem, the 'Excursion,' you will there see what importance I attach to the Madras System. Next to the art of Printing it is the noblest invention for the improvement of the human species" (*MY,* II, 210). WW intended to send his son John to Charterhouse because it used Bell's methods. Grasmere school was also run on the "Madras System" at this time, and WW taught there briefly and spent some time with Bell during his visit to the school in 1811–1812. For discussions of Bell and Lancaster and the involvement of Romantic poets with their systems, see Alan Richardson, *Literature, Education, and Romanticism: Reading as Social Practice, 1780–1832* (Cambridge, 1994), pp. 91–108, and R. A. Foakes "'Thriving Prisoners': Coleridge, Wordsworth and the Child at School," *Studies in Romanticism* 28 (1989): 187–206. The way in which Book VIII ends in direct anticipation of the Wanderer's speech, as well as the fact that these two books are half the length of the earlier ones, encourages us to read them together. The positioning of the Wanderer's speech at the opening of Book IX also gives it dramatic emphasis.

1–26 The first part of the Wanderer's speech is found in draft material in DC MSS. 15 (63^r) and 16 (77^v–78^v); see *LB, 1797–1800,* pp. 309–310, 721, 728. See also note to IX, 129–138,142–153, below.

3 An *active* principle] This phrase is to be found in a number of texts that may or may not be directly referred to here. For example, Isaac Newton explains the continuity of motion on the basis of "active principles," stating: "And if it were not for these principles the bodies of the earth, planets, comets, Sun, and all things in them would grow cold and freeze" (*Optics,* 4th ed. [London, 1730], bk. III, part I, pp. 399–400). Perhaps a more significant source for WW is the use of the term by Anthony Ashley Cooper, Third Earl of Shaftesbury, in *The Moralists*: "The active Mind, infus'd thro' all the Space, Unites and mingles with the mighty Mass" (*Characteristicks of Men, Manners, Opinions, Times,* ed. Philip Ayres [Oxford, 1999], II, 78). Cf. also *Tintern Abbey,* ll. 94–103 (text of 1798); *Exc* I, 163; IX, 132. See also Lyon, pp. 108–109.

38–40 The depiction of "the Soul" here seems to tend toward Neoplatonism.

51–81 The Wanderer's account of withdrawal from the world accords with an Epicurean sense of life's ambition. Cf. I, 10–18; III, 355.

82–93 These lines are drawn from 1798 draft toward the character of the Pedlar in MS. 14, the Alfoxden Notebook (see *RC & Pedlar,* pp. 114–115); see also, below, the transcriptions of MS. 75, $C2^r$; MS. 74, 47^v–48^r.

88 the mighty stream of tendency] Cf. Hazlitt on "Mr. Malthus" in *The Spirit of the Age,* where—in arguing against Godwinian perfectibility—he describes "'the mighty stream of tendency' as Mr Wordsworth in the cant of the day calls it" (*Complete Works of William Hazlitt,* ed. P. P. Howe [London, 1930–34], XI, 106). Matthew Arnold also later uses the phrase: "That *stream of tendency by which all things seek to fulfil the law of their being*" (*St. Paul and Protestantism With Other Essays* [London, 1892], p. 7).

97–99 These lines lay down the basis of the Wanderer's argument: man can only achieve his fullest potential, and the wisdom of old age, if intellectual freedom has not been denied him. The same point is made again at IX, 114–120, in asking that man should not abuse other men.

132 our active powers] Cf. I, 163; IX, 3.

129–138, 142–153 This material was also part of the earlier draft found in DC MSS. 15 and 16 and referred to in the note to IX, 1–26, above.

152 human Form divine] This phrase appears in *PL,* III, 44.

163–164 The Wanderer refers back to the Solitary's argument at VIII, 351–436, that the rural as well as the industrial poor should be pitied.

181 Such as the Boy you painted] In Book VIII the Solitary described the intellectual torpor of the uneducated Plough-Boy, concluding "what liberty of mind is here?" (VIII, 436). The Wanderer now addresses this issue.

198–200 In his comments in IF, when WW is looking back from a Victorian perspective, he adopts these lines as advice in relation to the action of the Chartists, recommending "wiser and more brotherly dealing towards the many on the part of the wealthy few" (see p. 1224, below). The "People's Charter" was published in May 1838 and made demands for the rights of working men. When the government ignored these demands, Chartism became increasingly active as desperate men destroyed machinery and attacked factory owners. Since 1837–1842 were the years in which Chartism had most political force, WW is using *Exc* to make a point of contemporary relevance when dictating those comments in 1843.

227 In *PW,* 1845– , the Wanderer gives a much more direct expression of belief in immortality at this point (see verbal variants to the reading text, above). See note to I, 968/969, for Christian additions to the poem.

228–237 In sentiments opposed to the philosophy of William Godwin, the Wanderer here refuses to believe that moral understanding can be achieved only through abstruse reasoning and is not available to all. The Wanderer reverts instead to a Shaftesburian expression of belief in natural moral sense: even the simplest man can be naturally good.

259 thriving Prisoners] In *The Prelude* WW attacked models of supervised education based on the philosophies of Rousseau and Godwin (V, 226–232). *Exc* marks a swing toward support of more formal, and strongly hierarchical, models of education. At the same time, the depiction of the two boys, naturally learning together outdoors, remains a powerful counterbalance to this model and suggests that the main attraction of Bell's system for WW may have been the concept of mutual learning. Cf. VIII, 583.

296–336 The Wanderer builds to the climax of his speech in which he calls upon the state to provide free national education for all. In fact, partly because of the religious issues involved in the Bell-Lancaster debate, a national education system was not put in place until W. E. Forster's Education Act of 1870.

298 Binding herself by Statute] See WW's note on p. 314, above, in which he praises Dr. Bell directly. WW, along with many other Romantics, was very taken with Andrew Bell's monitorial system of education in which the children of each class taught each other. See our introductory note to Book IX, above, and Wu, *Reading II,* pp. 20–22.

306 To drudge through weary life] Cf. *Hamlet,* "To grunt and sweat under a weary life" (III.i.77).

308 A savage Horde] At this point *Exc* echoes many of the sentiments of RS's article on Poor Laws in the *Quarterly Review* (December 8, 1812), where he expressed fears of a descent into mob rule. See Connell, pp. 165–166.

337 Calpe's sunburnt cliffs] Gibraltar, the ancient name for which is "Calpe."

337–340 The Wanderer describes the subjection of Europe to Napoleon, in contrast to Britain's resistance to the oppressor. *Exc* was, of course, first published the year before Napoleon's defeat at Waterloo.

365–366 avaunt the fear / Of numbers crowded on their native soil] A reference to Thomas Malthus's *Essay on Population* (1798) and his fears of overpopulation. The Wanderer's solution to such problems seems to be to send people out to the colonies.

377–400 The Wanderer's optimistic vision sees national education as providing Britain with the moral backbone from which to go forth and spread good across the globe. Indirectly, WW seems to see himself as a kind of poetic prophet at this point, with the power to expand his teaching from the poetic text into a force for good in society at large.

412–413 Another reference to Napoleonic subjection, here making a comparison with the subjection of the Israelites by the Egyptians and the biblical plagues by which they were finally released. See Exodus 10:21–23.

434 his shy Compeer] Cf. *PL*, I, 127: "his bold Compeer."

440–451 The vision of the ram reflected in the water draws on early draft material for *The Prelude* in MS. 48, 34r–34v, 36v, 37r (see *13-Bk Prelude*, II, 399–400, 403). For discussion of changes made to those lines when incorporated into *Exc*, see pp. 465–466, below.

484–489 Here is a rare moment in *Exc* when the "Poet" seems to be directly identified with WW himself, as the text refers to his own autobiographical accounts in *Prelude* of rowing alone or with others. See *Prelude*, I, 373–428, and II, 170–180.

520 Vouchsafe sweet influence] Cf. *PL*, VII, 375: "Shedding sweet influence."

531 The beverage drawn from China's fragrant herb] Tea. In a letter discussing changes made to various texts in 1828, WW admits to BF, "My line is (I own) somewhat too pompous, as you say" (*LY*, I, 647). WW altered this line in *PW*, 1836, to "A choice repast—served by our young companions / With rival earnestness and kindred glee."

548 the Solitary said] The Solitary's pessimistic thoughts show him to be as yet still unreconciled to society; these thoughts prepare in part for the inconclusive ending of the poem.

575 the old Church-tower] Presumably Grasmere Church.

590–608 See IF, pp. 1217 and 1224, below. *PW*, V, 474, points out that the description of the sunset contains a number of Miltonic expressions; see the next six notes.

596 Of the blue firmament] The same phrase occurs in *PL*, XI, 206.

605 the unapparent Fount of glory] Cf. *PL*, VII, 103: "Of Nature from the unapparent Deep."

609 The party is supposed to be seated upon Loughrigg-fell, above the lake in Grasmere, looking down upon the village.

620 paternal splendors] Cf. *PL*, VII, 219: "Paternal Glory."

625 the frail earth] Cf. *PL*, II, 1030: "this frail World."

631 empyreal Throne] Cf. *PL*, II, 430: "Empyreal Thrones."

639–640 Spread the law, / As it is written in thy holy book] Unsurprisingly, the Pastor gives value to biblical truth. This valuing of scripture contrasts with the Wanderer's emphasis upon natural rather than revealed religion.

687 Mysterious rites were solemnized] The Pastor looks back to pre-Christian religion in Britain and seems to be referring to druidical practices. Cf. *Prelude*, XII, 320–336; *The Vale of Esthwaite*, ll. 25–34 (see *Early Poems, 1785–1798*, p. 424); *Salisbury Plain*, ll. 424–427, and *Adventures on Salisbury Plain*, ll. 158–159 (see *SPP*, pp. 35 and n., 127).

695–697 The Pastor's nightmarish druidical vision could be compared with the Solitary's account of human graves speaking forth the true characters of the dead at V, 246–253.

701 To Taranis] An ancient thunder god of Gaul identified by the Romans with Jupiter. Taranis is Gaelic for "Tara" or "Tharan," meaning "thunder." He is mentioned by Lucan in *The Civil War (Pharsalia)*, bk. I, l. 446 (see *PW*, V, 474).

705 to Andates] According to *PW* Knight, V, 379, "The Greeks seem to have considered her as *Nemesis*, or the goddess of revenge."

718–719 through Him who bled / Upon the Cross] One of the rare references to Christ in the poem. Cf. II, 236; IV, 1097; V, 278, 914, 958.

748 They know if I be silent, morn or even] Cf. *PL*, V, 202: "Witness if I be silent, Morn or Even."

768 the Solitary checked his steps] The poem ends with divided paths, as the Solitary returns home, unconverted. Religious readers of the poem were unhappy with this outcome. Montgomery, p. 31, noted the lack of explicit teaching of Christian salvation and concluded that "wanting this 'one thing,' this 'one thing needful,' all the glories of

philosophy . . . vanish like a florid sunset, leaving the forlorn and disconsolate sinner wandering in darkness, and *still* crying—'What shall I do to be saved?'" For discussion of a possible classical model (*Octavius* by Minucius Felix) for this open-ended conclusion, see Hill, *Ariel.*

771–773 The path leads back to the Solitary's home at the top of the Langdale Valley. Cf. II, 359.

773–777 Montgomery, p. 21, picks up this "promise" of a future meeting: "Mr Wordsworth could so sing of Christ's kingdom, if it has indeed come into his heart, as would for ever set the question at rest; and we hope that in the promised prelude or sequel to his volume, he *will.*" WW in IF quotes IX, 773–777, and states: " When I reported this promise of the Solitary, & long after, it was my wish, & I might say intention, that we should resume our wanderings & pass the borders into his native country where as I hoped he might witness in the Society of the Wanderer some religious ceremony—a sacrament say, in the open fields, or a preaching among the Mountains, which . . . might have dissolv'd his heart into tenderness & so done more towards restoring the Christian Faith in which he had been educated" (p. 1224, below). In making such a suggestion WW was probably responding to the criticism of Montgomery (an article he is known to have read) as well as to that of Wilson. For discussion of Wilson and WW, see pp. 21–22, above. Alan G. Hill makes an interesting comment on the nonexistent sequel when he suggests "the real sequel to *The Excursion* is surely the *Ecclesiastical Sketches* (1822) when Wordsworth illustrates a redemptive spirit working through the forms of organized religion" (Hill, *Proceedings,* p. 197). See also Wu, *Reading II,* pp. 150–151. Cf. IV, 43.

The Excursion

Manuscripts

Prologue
Eight Stages of *Excursion* Composition
The Manuscript History of *The Excursion*
Transcriptions and Selected Photographic Reproductions

Prologue

In this section are provided (1) a table listing "Eight Stages of *Excursion* Composition"; (2) an account of "The Manuscript History of *The Excursion*"; (3) complete leaf-by-leaf transcriptions of the pre-publication manuscripts of *The Excursion* prepared by William Wordsworth or under his supervision; (4) photographs of selected manuscript pages.

The manuscripts transcribed here are discussed in the Manuscript Census, pp. xxi–xxvii, above, and the transcriptions are presented in accordance with the principles outlined in the Editorial Procedure, pp. 29–30, above. Each of the transcriptions is headed by a list of cross-references to the various accounts of that manuscript in the prefatory "Manuscript History of *The Excursion*." The "Key to Manuscript Transcriptions" in Appendix I, pp. 1203–1207, below, enables readers to locate all manuscript passages that contribute to a particular passage in *The Excursion*.

The selected photographs illustrate particularly important, interesting, or representative manuscript pages. DC MS. 47, the early manuscript in which Wordsworth decided how to develop *The Excursion* from his previously written *The Ruined Cottage*, is fully shown in photographs, as is DC MS. 70 (another early and central manuscript). All ten pages in DC MS. 80 where Wordsworth worked on *The Peasant's Life*, lines excluded from *The Excursion* and then copied (in a shortened form) as a free-standing work, are also given in photographs. DC MSS. 71, 73, 74, and 75 are partially represented in photographs; the headnotes to these four manuscripts' transcriptions provide lists of selected photographs. We include photographs of all manuscript pages containing work toward Book IV—with the exception of four lines on DC MS. 69, 220^{v}—because of the significance of this book. The Dove Cottage manuscripts of *The Excursion* are, in general, of two sizes, the first about 16 cm. in height and the second between 18.7 and 22 cm. The smaller-format manuscripts are here ordinarily presented in two facing pages per photograph and the larger-format ones in a single page per photograph.

Given that Wordsworth wrote the poem over an eight-year period in nine major manuscripts and also drew on material elsewhere that dates as early as the 1790s, the history of the eight stages of *Excursion* composition is not a straightforward one to trace. The following table, prefatory account of the manuscripts, transcriptions, and photographs aim at providing readers with guidance for finding their way through the complex manuscript development of Wordsworth's epic poem.

Eight Stages of *Excursion* Composition

(1) Pre-*Excursion* Material

For each manuscript, we list in the far right column the Cornell Wordsworth volume where it is discussed and transcribed; see also the Manuscript Census, pp. xx–xxi, above, for details about what passages in these notebooks contribute to *The Excursion.*

1798	DC MS. 14	Alfoxden Notebook	*RC & Pedlar*
	DC MS. 17	*Ruined Cottage* MS. B	*RC & Pedlar*
1798–1799	DC MS. 15	*Christabel* Notebook	*LB, 1797–1800*
	DC MS. 16	*Ruined Cottage* MS. D	*LB, 1797–1800*
1800 or 1806	DC MS. 28	*Home at Grasmere* MS. R	*H at G*[1]
1803–1804	DC MS. 37	*Ruined Cottage* MSS. E, E^2	*RC & Pedlar*
1804	DC MS. 44	*Ruined Cottage* MS. M	*RC & Pedlar*
	DC MS. 48	*Prelude* MS. Y	*13-Bk Prelude*
1806	DC MS. 59	*Home at Grasmere* MS. B	*H at G*
1808	DC MS. 65	*Tuft of Primroses*	*Tuft*

(2) *Excursion* Manuscripts

Difficulties of specific dating for many of these manuscripts mean that delineating "stages" of the poem's development has less to do with possible dates of composition than with the shape of the material at a given stage. (The relative order of the manuscripts and sections within them can be fairly clearly determined, but the exact dates—and length of time between stages of development—frequently cannot).[2]

First Stage: Either September 1806 or from December 1809

DC MS. 47	Book II, ll. 1–789
DC MS. 69	Book III, ll. 1–330

[1]The part of MS. 28 that contributes to *Exc* is dated 1800 by Jonathan Wordsworth in "On Man, on Nature, and on Human Life," *Review of English Studies* 31 (1980): 17–29; Beth Darlington leans toward an 1806 date in *H at G*, pp. 11–12.

[2]The dates correspond to evidence in the letters and to the account given in *Chronology: MY*, pp. 656–686; our division of *Exc* composition into stages, however, slightly differs from *Chronology: MY* (see note to "Fourth Stage," below).

Second Stage: Between December 1809 and March 1812

DC MS. 69	Book I copied mainly from *Ruined Cottage/Pedlar* MS. M
DC MS. 71	Fair copy of Books I, II, and III (lines 1–330)
DC MS. 70	Reworking from DC MS. 47 for Book II insert for DC MS. 71
DC MS. 71	Book II Insert A—now partially removed—sewn in as leaves 42–45; insert draws on DC MS. 70, which reworks DC MS. 47
[MS. not extant	Books VI, VII, and VIII passages]
DC MS. 67	Book VI, ll. 412–498, copied (probably from a MS. not extant) at end of *Essay on Epitaphs III*
Commonplace Book	Book VI, ll. 412–498, copied, presumably from a letter sent by the Wordsworths to the Beaumonts

Third Stage: Between December 1809 and March 1812

DC MS. 70	Book IV (work from l. 335 onward)
DC MS. 73	Book IV (work on the near-conclusion of the book)
DC MS. 73	Book III (work toward the end-of-book image of life as a river)
DC MS. 70	Book V (work toward the beginning of the book)

Fourth Stage: Between late August 1811 and May 1814[3]

DC MS. 74	Book V, including *The Peasant's Life* and *The Shepherd of Bield Crag*
DC MS. 69	Book V sections reworked from DC MS. 74

Fifth Stage: Between January 3, 1813, and May 1814

DC MS. 71	Book III expansion from l. 331 to end of book
DC MS. 71	Book II Insert B (leaves 36–41) added; Insert A (leaves 42–45) partially torn out)
DC MS. 69	Book IV reworked (ll. 1–334 added)
DC MS. 71	Book III Insert C (leaves 75–76), drawing on *Tuft of Primroses*, possibly now added
WW to Lord Lonsdale	Draft for III, 592–607
DC MS. 71	Book III Insert D (leaves 87–90), drawing on WW to Lord Lonsdale, now added
DC MS. 71	Book III Insert E (leaves 102–105), a fair-copy version in WW's hand of the text in the manuscript around it, probably now added

[3]This stage is difficult to place. The work could have taken place either before or after the fifth stage (prompted by the children's deaths). The assumption is that WW would work continuously on related material rather than jumping between two stages of the poem's development, and our fourth and fifth stages reconstruct composition on this basis. As such, they slightly differ from Mark Reed's sequence at this point (see the account of these stages on pp. 446–455, below, and in *Chronology: MY*, pp. 673–681).

Sixth Stage: Possibly from late August 1811; probably between January 3, 1813, and May 1814

[MS. not extant	Work on Books VI, VII, VIII and IX, preceding DC MS. 74]
DC MS. 74	Work on Books VI and VII, incorporating material from *Home at Grasmere* and *Guide to the Lakes*
DC MS. 75	Work on Books VI, VII, VIII
Berg MS.	Draft for Book VIII (ll. c. 463–c. 523)
Houghton MS.	Draft for Book VII (ll. 554–603, 648–654)
DC MS. 74	Reworking of parts of Books VI–VIII

Seventh Stage: Between January 3, 1813, and May 1814

DC MSS. 74 and 75	Entry of Book IX material
DC MS. 73	End of Book IX

Eighth Stage: Between January 3, 1813, and May 1814

[MS. not extant	Book V without *The Shepherd of Bield Crag* and *The Peasant's Life* copied from DC MSS. 69, 70, 74, 75 bifolium E]
DC MS. 74A	Fair copy version of Book V (probably mid-1814)
DC MS. 80	Separate version of *The Peasant's Life*
Morgan MS.	Revision of *The Peasant's Life* from DC MS. 80
DC MS. 73	First half of Book VI written
[MS. not extant	Full fair copy for printer]

The Manuscript History of *The Excursion*

First Stage: Either September 1806 or from December 1809

DC MS. 47	Book II, ll. 1–789
DC MS. 69	Book III, ll. 1–330

The earliest manuscript for *The Excursion* (excluding earlier material for *The Ruined Cottage* contributing to Book I) is DC MS. 47. It contains a large part of the material for Book II but does not include the expansion of the Solitary's tale concerning his personal life, the story of the Old Pensioner, and the Solitary's hilltop vision. Since Book I was already written in the form of *The Ruined Cottage*, this work for Book II represents Wordsworth's first fresh writing for the new poem. However, the question of exactly when this material might have been entered is a difficult one; it may have been written in September 1806 as an early phase of work on the poem, or it may not have been composed until 1809–10.

We have two pieces of external evidence from Wordsworth himself concerning sources for Book II. Material that comes at the end of the book in the final published poem includes the Solitary's hilltop vision of the city in the clouds, the origins of which Wordsworth gives us in the Fenwick Notes:

> The glorious appearance disclosed above & among the mountains was described partly from what my friend Mr. Luff who then lived in Paterdale witnessed . . . & partly from what Mary & I had seen in company with Sir G. & Lady Beaumont above Hartshope Hall in our way from Paterdale to Ambleside. (p. 1218, below)

Reed dates this incident no earlier than September 5, 1807 (*Chronology: MY*, p. 362); thus this particular section of Book II—describing the Solitary's vision—cannot have been written before this date. The Solitary's vision, however, is not present in DC MS. 47 and could easily have been added later: "The description of the vision of the cloud-city at the conclusion of the story of the Old Man Lost can not have been composed before 5 Sept 1807 . . . but the rest of the story need date only after 8 Nov 1805" (*Chronology: MY*, p. 661). Second, we need to consider the tale of the Old Pensioner himself. Reed tells us that this story could not have been written before November 8, 1805, since this is the date when Charles Luff told Wordsworth the story and showed the poet the ruins of the chapel where the old man was found (see *Chronology: MY*, p. 304). In DC MS. 47 the tale of the Old Pensioner is not told, but it is clearly anticipated in various ways: on 12^{v} a housewife is described as treating the Old Pensioner cruelly; the Wanderer and Poet witness the funeral of the old man (although we are told little about him); and the Solitary anticipates that he will go on to tell the story, stating, "I will tell" and "you shall hear" on 45ʳ. After some description of the inside of the cottage and the view behind it, work for Book II ends toward the back of the notebook on 49ʳ with two pages on the Housewife entered afterward. Wordsworth possibly then went on to work on the tale elsewhere before incorporating it later into the full version of Book II in DC MS. 71.

It is therefore conceivable that Wordsworth could have been working on Book II in 1806, as suggested in evidence from the letters. Reed debates this point and seemingly favors the later composition time of 1810: "the apparent connection between the sort of tale told for the Old Man and the kind of composition probably going on c. early 1810 makes a date about the latter time an attractive likelihood for those verses" (*Chronology: MY,* p. 662). However, since this tale of the Old Pensioner does not actually occur in DC MS. 47, the possibility of the manuscript's having been written earlier than 1810 still remains. DC MS. 47 may well represent an important early stage in the development of the poem, rather than coming in with the bulk of work in 1809–10.

It is helpful to consider DC MS. 47 in relation to the story of *The Ruined Cottage,* thinking about what the poem represents at this stage, rather than anticipating what is to come after it. The work for Book II in this manuscript begins with the Minstrel passage. This passage is copied into the notebook from a passage of draft material in DC MS. 48 (*Prelude* MS. Y). In the original version of the passage in DC MS. 48, the description of the Minstrel is applied not to the Wanderer (as in Book II) but to the poet:

Yet such a Man so favour'd could not
draw
By his glad faculties more earnest
bliss
From that ~~his vagrant &~~ wanfaring life
Than I unknown uncountenancd & obscure
Accoutred with a knapasack &
a staff
(*13-Bk Prelude,* II, 374–375: DC MS. 48, 15ᵛ)

In DC MS. 47 this passage is reworked and altered from first into third person, but the lines remain very close to the original in their description of the Wanderer rather than the poet: "Than this same Man uncountenanc'd & obscure" (33ᵛ). The comparison of an individual to the wandering Minstrel of former times thus shifts from being applied to the poet himself, in the autobiographical context of *The Prelude,* to the dramatic context of *The Excursion* in which the image is applied to a character. If we consider that at this stage all Wordsworth has for *The Excursion* is Book I, in its *Ruined Cottage/Pedlar* form (MS. M), then this reattribution of lines represents an important point of connection backward, and development ahead, for the kind of poem Wordsworth wants to write. The reattribution outlined here is highly representative of the differences between Wordsworth's first long poem (*The Prelude*) and his second (*The Excursion*). In the first, the only possible comparison is with Wordsworth himself; in the second, the image of the wandering minstrel is shown to apply not, as we might anticipate, to the figure designated as "Poet" but to another character, to one of the "Poets that are sown / By Nature" (I, 81–82). Wordsworth seems to imply, then, that the Wanderer's life is "poetic" in its own right. Such an idea was implicitly present in MS. M of *The Ruined Cottage* (which forms the basis of Book I), but this opening to Book II explicitly asserts the Wanderer's own authority as a "natural" poet.

In the text as it is ordered at this stage in DC MS. 47, the opening description is clearly intended to lead on into the description of the Wanderer and the Poet's ascent, their view of the Solitary's valley, and their witnessing of the funeral of the Old Pensioner (which the Wanderer thinks is that of the Solitary). It is only on 38^r, after they have begun to descend the valley, that the Wanderer tells the Solitary's tale, giving an account of his political disappointment and loss of faith (38^r–40^v). On arrival they then meet the Solitary and return to his cottage, which is described in some detail, including the peaks above it. This first version in DC MS. 47 differs from the final poem in two ways: (1) the telling of the Solitary's tale occurs after the travelers have seen the valley rather than on the way up to it; and (2) there is an absence of any personal account of the Solitary's life.[1]

As it stands then in DC MS. 47, Book II reaffirms the relation of character to place that is felt so strongly and tragically in Margaret's tale of Book I. At this point in the development of the poem, the motive for characterization is largely topographical. People are defined by place, and this kind of definition is what Books I and II are about. Indeed, it is what *The Excursion* is about at this early stage of writing. Book II opens by affirming the Wanderer's character as an individual who has no fixed place but is in no way diminished by this lack; the value of his wandering life is confirmed as he guides the rather touristic Poet over unknown ground. The Solitary, too, is very strongly located in his own valley, though in different ways. He at first seems to be defined by mess and clutter—first in the remnants found on the hillside and then in his own small hut—but the Solitary locates himself in relation to the massive Langdale Pikes behind him, his "good Companions" (47^v). Interestingly, the most significant definition of him in the final poem—which is implicit in the Poet's response to the valley as he looks down from above ("So plac'd to be shut out from all the world" [34^r])—does not work in this version, because the description of place is given before rather than just after the Solitary's story has been told.

The second manuscript used in the early composition of the poem, DC MS. 69, lies between DC MS. 47 and DC MS. 71 in terms of the development of the first three books. Materials relating to Books I and III in DC MS. 69 directly anticipate the next manuscript in sequence, DC MS. 71 (which gives a full version of Books I, II, and III). At the same time, DC MS. 69 also contains drafts for Books IV and V, which relate to the fourth and fifth stages of work on the poem and will be discussed below. Much of DC MS. 69 is blank or contains stubs with only occasional pages of text. Material is entered from both the front and

[1] The significance of changes made from MS. 47 to MS. 71 will be treated below in the discussion of MS. 71.

the back of the notebook, with the lines for later Books IV and V inverted and written to proceed forward from the back of the notebook toward the middle. Book III material in DC MS. 69 exists on five surviving pages (7^{r}–7^{v}, 72^{r}–72^{v}, and 84^{r}) and on stubs whose surviving letters suggest that work toward most of Book III, lines 1–330, was probably present (*Chronology: MY*, p. 677).[2] The surviving material indicates that DC MS. 69 directly formed the basis for Book III in DC MS. 71. Mark Reed dates Books I and III in this manuscript on the basis of their relation to DC MS. 71 (which they precede), concluding "these probably date by Mar. 1812" (*Chronology: MY*, p. 678). There is, however, no evidence that rules out the possible early (1806) entry of Book III material, which is entered on the first pages of the notebook and in front of the copied Book I text.

II

Second Stage: Between December 1809 and March 1812

DC MS. 69	Book I copied mainly from *Ruined Cottage/Pedlar* MS. M
DC MS. 71	Fair Copy of Books I, II, and III (lines 1–330)
DC MS. 70	Reworking from DC MS. 47 for Book II insert for DC MS. 71
DC MS. 71	Book II Insert A—now partially removed—sewn in as leaves 42–45; insert draws on DC MS. 70, which reworks DC MS. 47
[MS. not extant	Books VI, VII, and VIII passages]
DC MS. 67	Book VI, ll. 412–498, copied (probably from a MS. not extant) at end of *Essay on Epitaphs III*
Commonplace Book	Book VI, ll. 412–498, copied, presumably from a letter sent by the Wordsworths to the Beaumonts

The particular importance of DC MS. 69 in the history of the development of *The Excursion* is that it is the first document in which *The Ruined Cottage* is treated as Book I of the completed poem. The loss of the section of text between the two surviving leaves of 114^{v} and 120^{r} is frustrating because it represented the first reworking of *Ruined Cottage/Pedlar* MS. M (1804) for Book I, as surviving evidence shows.[3]

In his discussion of changes made at an earlier stage to *Ruined Cottage* material (from MS. E to MS. M), James Butler noted that Wordsworth cut out part of his description of the Pedlar singing to a little girl because "the Pedlar's singing songs . . . and crying over her innocence are more suited to the characterization of *The Pedlar*, 1802, than to the philosophical function the Pedlar's history once again served in 1804" (*RC & Pedlar*, p. 35). In revising MS. M in DC MS. 69, Wordsworth returned to this section and now removed it altogether. In fact

[2]Leaf 84^{r} contains the last Book III entry for ll. 309–330. (Reed's line numbers *in Chronology: MY* refer to the 1850 text in *PW*, V, rather than to the 1814 reading text in our edition; his 1850 line numbers have accordingly been adjusted to 1814 ones where relevant).

[3]In his headnote to *RC* MS. D, James Butler notes that "the number of variants between . . . [MS. 71] and the immediately preceding MSS. E, E^{2} and M suggests the possibility of an intervening manuscript, now lost" (*RC & Pedlar*, p. 283). MS. 69 probably represents this stage.

there is some gesturing toward this future omission in MS. M itself where the description of the girl is introduced by these lines:

> and though, in truth,
> This incident be something like a nook
> Or pleasant corner which from my right path
> Diverts me. . . .
> (MS. M, 7^{r}; *RC & Pedlar*, pp. 387, 389)

Apart from the reason Butler gives, a second reason for removing this passage is probably that it took the focus away from the relationship between the younger Poet and the Wanderer. It is also worth noting that the specificity of "that same Town of Hawkshead" (MS. M, 7^{r}, *RC & Pedlar*, p. 387), which was given with the description of the girl, is lost. This removal of place-specific references is a significant change relating to the entire *Excursion*. Although the poem as a whole is firmly rooted in Grasmere and its neighbouring towns and valleys, places in the poem are described in considerable topographical detail rather than being directly named. We see an example of this technique in the description of the Langdale Pikes, which rise up behind the Solitary's cottage but are described only as "two huge Peaks / That from some other Vale peered into this" (II, 719–720). In Book I, then, the poem does not name "Hawkshead" as the Poet's boyhood town partly because of this decision not to relate the poetic landscape directly to the real one, but also, presumably, because a boy who had lived in Hawkshead was hardly likely to be unfamiliar with the Langdale Valley and Little Langdale where the Solitary is situated. These changes further contribute to the presentation of the Poet as a figure not native to the region.

The second surviving page from Book I in DC MS. 69 is much closer to *Ruined Cottage/Pedlar* MS. M than the first, and it looks very much as if the base text on this page is copied directly from MS. M, 8^{r}, the two being identical down to the line "The Mother married to a second Mate" (DC MS. 69, 120^{r}). On this page Wordsworth's crossings out and the replacements of lines clearly show DC MS. 69 as intermediary between the earlier *Ruined Cottage/Pedlar* MS. M and the later DC MS. 71. One line here can serve to illustrate development across the manuscripts:

> Among the Hills of Perthshire he was born
> (MS. M, 8^{r}; *RC & Pedlar*, p. 393)
> ~~Among the hills of Perthshire he was~~
> born
> (DC MS. 69, 120^{r})
> Among the hills of Athol he was born.
> (DC MS. 71, 6^{r})
> Among the hills of Athol he was born:
> (*Exc*, I, 112)

In DC MS. 69 Wordsworth copies the line from *Ruined Cottage/Pedlar* MS. M but is not satisfied with it. At this stage he makes no replacement, instead appearing to omit the line (the text still reads coherently without it). In DC MS. 71 the line is altered to the sense it has in the final text.[4]

From the evidence of the two surviving pages in DC MS. 69 (114^{v}, 120^{r}), it seems likely that the material between them concerned the Poet's biography of the Wanderer. It seems possible, too, that the recto pages in DC MS. 69 contained a copy of the *Ruined Cottage/Pedlar* MS. M text and the verso pages a reworking of this material. (Such usage of rectos and versos would explain why 114^{v} differs more from *Ruined Cottage/Pedlar* MS. M than does 120^{r}). These two pages in DC MS. 69, however, are only nineteen lines apart in terms of their content in relation to the final text of *The Excursion,* despite having the stubs of five leaves between them. This discrepancy makes it hard to be sure what the intervening material actually contained.

DC MS. 71 represents a significant stage of the poem's development, the point at which a number of other manuscripts were brought together. Reed points out that this notebook provides the "longest surviving continuous MS of any portion of the poem" (*Chronology: MY,* p. 676). DC MS. 71 contains a neat and continuous copy of Books I through III in Mary Wordsworth's hand and, as such, draws upon all earlier draft material toward these books in DC MSS. 47 and 69, as well as upon later additional material written in DC MS. 70 and reinserted here. Work in DC MS. 71 up to III, 330, was probably entered some time in 1809–1810, though this date is not certain. However, material in the base copy text (Mary Wordsworth's hand, except for the inserts) still contains no version of the Solitary's personal tragedy, as told by the Wanderer. The absence of this material confirms that the main entry must have taken place before the deaths of the Wordsworths' children (after which the personal material for the Solitary was written). For this reason Reed dates the base copy in DC MS. 71 as being probably written by March 1812 (*Chronology: MY,* p. 677), which leaves the time of entry very open. The manuscript could have been copied quite a bit earlier and written out in its original state up to Book III, line 330, including material from DC MS. 69. It is likely that when Wordsworth returned to *The Excursion* some time in 1809–10, he would have begun by pulling together the material already written elsewhere, and this activity seems to be what DC MS. 71 initially represents. Later work (from III, 330, onward) relates to a later stage of the poem's development.

Overlap with both DC MS. 47 and DC MS. 69 is clearly present in DC MS. 71. After the first block of inserted pages, involving the expansion of the Solitary's life (material not present in DC MS. 47), the text from 46^{r} to 58^{r} is clearly copied from DC MS. 47.[5] This material concerns the section of Book II describing the journey to the Solitary's valley and conversation with him. The Book II text continues cleanly in Mary Wordsworth's hand until 64^{r}. The last section of it in DC MS. 71, from 58^{r} to 64^{r}, concerns the tale of the Old Pensioner and his vision. No manuscript source for this material survives, but it was almost certainly drafted elsewhere, before this clean copy of it. Material for the first 330 lines of Book III in DC MS.

[4]If this section of MS. 69 had reworking of the recto on the preceding verso page, then WW might have already changed this section on 120^{r} by using the torn-out page opposite (119^{v}).

[5]Text on 34^{r}–34^{v} for the opening section on "The Minstrel" is also copied from MS. 47.

71 is almost certainly copied from work that was in DC MS. 69; the copied text in DC MS. 71, 74^r, breaks off at the same line that concludes the surviving copy on 84^r of DC MS. 69: "Night hush'd as night & day serene as day."

The internal construction of DC MS. 71 is fairly complex. Since the manuscript pulls together material scattered among previous notebooks, Wordsworth is careful to keep the text coherent, continuous, and in the right order. It is therefore not surprising that DC MS. 71 also contains five inserted sections, here given in the order in which they occur in the notebook:

Stubs 42–43, Leaves 44–45	Insert A, for Book II. Wanderer's account of the Solitary's life; on surviving leaves. Fair copy in Mary Wordsworth's hand draws on DC MS. 70, which in turn draws on DC MS. 47. The original text in DC MS. 71, before this insert, continued from leaf 35^v to leaf 46^r. Inserted at second stage of composition; see below in this section.
Leaves 36–45	Insert B, for Book II. Expanded account of the Solitary's life, partially replacing Insert A. Fair copy in MW's hand. Postdates DC MS. 70 work. Inserted at fifth stage of composition; see below.
Leaves 75–76	Insert C, for Book III. Copied in WW's hand and drawn from *Tuft of Primroses*. Probably inserted at fifth stage of composition (see p. 446, below).
Leaves 87–90	Insert D, for Book III. First section copied in WW's hand from WW to Lord Lonsdale. Probably inserted at fifth stage of composition; see below.
Leaves 102–105	Insert E, for Book III. Fair-copy version in WW's hand of the text in the manuscript around it. Probably inserted at fifth stage of composition to provide a cleaner copy of messy revision; see below.

The inserts represent either the introduction of material from other sources or the expansion of certain sections for the final text.

One significant way in which DC MS. 71 moves on from DC MS. 69 is in the changes made to material originally written for *The Ruined Cottage* or *The Pedlar*. The opening of Book I in DC MS. 71 looks back earlier than *Ruined Cottage/Pedlar* MS. M to *Ruined Cottage* MSS D, E, and E^2. The reason for this use of earlier material is probably that the first leaf of MS. M is missing.[6] From line 62 (4^v) onward, the text in DC MS. 71 largely follows MS. M except where redrafting occurs in DC MS. 69. The two surviving pages of DC MS. 69 that contain working for Book I are both used in DC MS. 71 at 5^r and 6^r.

[6]The text in MS. 71 follows *RC* MS. D to halfway through l. 23 on 3^v, at which point it seems to shift briefly to MS. E^2 and then to a reworking of MS. E (see *RC & Pedlar*, p. 453). MS. E provides the text for ll. 26–36, at which point MS. 71 returns to MS. E^2 for ll. 37–61, and then finally goes to MS. M at l. 62 (4^v).

Our previous discussion of Book I in DC MS. 69 indicated that one element of revision was the removal of named locations from *The Excursion*. Unsurprisingly we see this same kind of revision occurring in DC MS. 71. So in MS. E^2 the text reads as follows:

> ~~a~~ [?~~shelterd~~] a little town obscure,
> In ~~the heart of Fur~~ness Fells
> hidden
> Or market village ^ ~~seated~~ in a tract
> ~~At Hawks~~head, where my school-boy days were
> pass'd
> (MS. E^2, 1^v; *RC & Pedlar*, pp. 385, 387)

These revisions in *Ruined Cottage/Pedlar* MS. E^2 already suggest the ways the lines are altered in DC MS. 71:

> In a little Town obscure
> A market Village seated in a tract
> Of mountains
> (DC MS. 71, 4^v)

Such changes were discussed earlier insofar as they related to the Poet, but they also have the effect of making the Wanderer's movements and journeying seem both more wide-ranging and unknowable. As such they perhaps contribute to the desired presentation of him as an almost mythic, or biblical, figure—what Charles Lamb described as "*Palmer*, or *Pilgrim*" (Lamb, p. 111). Certainly there is evidence of Wordsworth's trying to make his Wanderer acceptable as an authority figure here. Similar artistic considerations underlie the way that Wordsworth directly addresses the question of the Wanderer's rank in lines that are not present in MS. M but are copied from DC MS. 69, 120^r:

> Though born in low estate and earning bread
> By a low Calling, yet this mild good Man
> Rank'd with the prime and choice of sterling Minds.
> (DC MS. 71, 6^r)

These lines in DC MS. 71 are then crossed out, and they are replaced by a less explicit authorization of the Wanderer, an account that survives into the published *Excursion*:

> But as the mind was filled with inward light
> So not without distinction had he lived
> Beloved & honoured far as he was known
> (DC MS. 71, 6^r)

These examples give us clear evidence that Wordsworth was well aware of the class implications of his choice of hero and was trying to address it by giving his figure a different kind of authority. When we consider the problems involved in redefining the Pedlar as the Wanderer in *The Excursion*, one of the most significant, clearly, is that the character no longer is simply the subject of a casual encounter and a shared tale but has become the moral guide and authority for the whole long poem. Contemporary critical response to the Wanderer, forcefully articulated by Francis Jeffrey, suggests that this difficulty is one that Wordsworth did not successfully resolve:

> What but the most wretched and provoking perversity of taste and judgment, could induce any one to place his chosen advocate of wisdom and virtue in so absurd and fantastic a condition? Did Mr Wordsworth really imagine, that his favourite doctrines were likely to gain any thing in point of effect or authority by being put into the mouth of a person accustomed to higgle about tape, or brass sleeve-buttons? (Jeffrey, p. 30)

Other alterations to the presentation of the Wanderer in DC MS. 71 occur at the point where Wordsworth in MS. M had originally described him as having a brother. Although these lines are copied into DC MS. 71 from MS. M, they are partly crossed out:

who had left his home
He had a Brother ~~elder than himself~~
~~Six years, who long before had left his home~~
To journey far and wide with Pedlar's Wares.
(DC MS. 71, 12^{v}–13^{r})

The reason for this change may again be a subtle one in relation to the Wanderer. The lines in MS. M suggest a matter-of-fact reason for his choosing the profession of Pedlar; his elder brother did it, so why shouldn't he? Indeed, the manuscript tells us as much:

"What should hinder now"
Said he within himself, "but that I go
And toil in the same calling."
(DC MS. 71, 13^{r})

Part of the poem's point is that the Wanderer has become the kind of person he is as a result of his way of life, as well as choosing that way of life because of who he is; thus his decision to "wander" loses some significance when attributed, at least partially, to doing whatever his brother did. We also have to bear in mind the importance that wandering holds for Wordsworth himself, who states in the Fenwick Notes that wandering is "*his passion*" (see IF, p. 1215, below). There is a sense in which the life of the traveler is to be seen as a kind of vocation, a "Calling" (DC MS. 71, 15^{v}; l. 416). These details relating to the brother's influencing of the Wanderer's choice of profession are therefore removed from DC MS. 71 and from the published poem.

A far more obvious alteration from *Ruined Cottage/Pedlar* MS. M, seen throughout DC MS. 71, answers the question of what the difference really is between Pedlar and Wanderer: the difference is simply that the Wanderer seems to have retired. In all earlier *Ruined Cottage* MSS., the central figure necessarily carries the tokens of his profession with him and is introduced in relation to them.

These base text lines are copied out into DC MS. 71 from DC MS. E^2 (*RC & Pedlar*, p. 385) but are then crossed out and rewritten to eliminate the pedlar's pack:

> while that Staff
> {ed figure
> Afford{ing to his ~~person~~ as he stood
> ~~Behind him fixed upheld a long white Pack~~
> Detained for contemplation or repose
> ~~That crossed his shoulders, wares for them who~~ live
> Graceful support; the countenance of the Man
> ~~In lonely Villages and straggling Huts~~.
> Was hidden from my view, & he himself
>
> (DC MS. 71, 4^{r})

Similar alterations occur throughout DC MS. 71. On 15^{v}, for example, the Wanderer is described as traveling with his staff as "one memorial of his former toils"; there is also the substitution of "freight" for "Pack" on 18^{v} and the alteration on 31^{v} from "The old Man rose and lifted up his load" to what becomes in the final text (part of which is drafted at the bottom of the page) "The Old Man rose, and with a sprightly mien" (I, 993). Now the Wanderer no longer carries his workman-like "Pack" but only his biblical staff. Much follows from this alteration. In DC MS. 71 Wordsworth strongly emphasizes the point that the Wanderer is no longer working in order to travel (or having to travel in order to work) but choosing to do so. He is no longer traveling by necessity; instead his profession is described as a "Calling laid aside" (15^{v}). Immediately afterward on 16^{r} in DC MS. 71, Wordsworth revises the text and—for the first time in the poem—includes the name "Wanderer."[7] This character is now titled not according to his former profession but according to his present mode of life.

Comparing the Wanderer's involvement with Margaret in Book I to his relationship with the Solitary in Book II illustrates the difference between his roles as Pedlar and as Wanderer. Although he narrates Margaret's tale as the Wanderer, he figures within it very strongly as a working Pedlar. In recalling her story the Wanderer views her life from the perspective of the traveling salesman on his rounds, sampling her changes of fortune as she samples his wares. Any feelings he has toward her, and even his ability to help, are necessarily circumscribed by his professional life and the need to move on. In relation to the Solitary in Book II, though, the Wanderer is now a free agent, and it shows. He decides to engineer a meeting between the two men (Poet and Solitary) for his own reasons. He specifically goes to the aid of his friend and has the luxury of staying as long as he wishes or feels he can help. The nature of the Wanderer's engagement with another's life is subtly changed; more important he is in a position to offer more, and more sustained, moral support than he could ever give to Margaret.

[7]In MS. 71 the Wanderer is first called by this title at I, 470, in a line of rev at the top of 16^{r}. At l. 622 on 20^{r}, WW changes "the Old Man" in pencil to "Wan." The first use of "Wanderer" in the base text of MS. 71 is in MW's hand on 80^{r}; this section of the MS. dates from the fifth stage of *Exc* composition.

If the Wanderer of *The Excursion* is presented as having greater moral authority than the original Pedlar, it is in part because retirement allows it to be so.

As Book I shifts focus from the Wanderer to Margaret, the nature of the changes made in DC MS. 71 also alters, and these changes become more localized. One such change, relating to the naming of characters, is worth touching upon. A small alteration occurs on 19ᵛ with the line describing Margaret's husband: "Ill fared it now with Robert, he who dwelt / Here in this Cottage." On the manuscript page there is a cross above "Robert," and this mark seems to anticipate the change made for the published poem in which Robert's name is removed at this point so that the lines read instead "A sad reverse it was for Him who long / Had filled with plenty" (I, 596–597). Names in *The Excursion* are significant things. The lack of identifying place names in the poem was noted above in discussing DC MS. 69, and something similar is also at work in relation to the principal speakers: Wanderer, Poet, Solitary, and Pastor. They are all identified by their social or professional functions rather than by personal names. When a character is named—as with Margaret, Ellen, or Oswald—this naming usually signifies the value of their tale, and of their lives.[8] Thus the removal of Robert's name at this point in DC MS. 71 is presumably intended to keep the focus more sharply upon Margaret, and he is not finally called by name until I, 881. This delay makes that single naming more emphatic. Moreover, when the word "Robert" finally occurs in the text, it is through Margaret speaking his name, in the last line she utters, as an expression of her fear that he will never return.

Such changes from *Ruined Cottage/Pedlar* MS. M to Book I of *The Excursion* are not major alterations, but they are worth close consideration. Prior to our edition of *The Excursion*, James Butler has given the complete history of this early material up to 1804 in detail, but the subsequent manuscript history to 1814 has not been comprehensively presented.[9] Now, however, we can fill in the missing pieces of a work begun in its earliest form in 1797 and finally published in 1814, and see, at last, all the stages of development of one of Wordsworth's greatest poems. DC MS. 71 is the most significant surviving manuscript for revealing how changes to *The Ruined Cottage* not only produced Book I of *The Excursion* but also laid the foundations for the entire poem.

In turning to the Book II material in DC MS. 71, we see that Mary Wordsworth copied a large part of it directly from DC MS. 47. DC MS. 71 closely follows DC MS. 47 up to some point before l. *384*, where l. *384*a of DC MS. 47 leads directly into l. *67*b as part of the same line on 38ʳ of DC MS. 47.[10] In the original state of DC MS. 71, pagination and line numbering continued consecutively from leaf 35 to leaf 46 (which originally followed leaf 35 before inserted leaves). Line *55* of DC

[8]There are exceptions to this valuing of names, however. Wilfred Armathwaite and Sir Alfred Irthing are also named, even though they are not particularly significant characters. In the case of the latter, naming relates to the recording of his name on the bells of the church, but there is no obvious reason for naming Wilfred Armathwaite (other than the fact that his tale was originally written for *Home at Grasmere* and the name may carry over from that text).

[9]See *RC & Pedlar*. *PW*, V, contains some of that *Exc* compositional history.

[10]Italic line numbers in this paragraph (which match those in the right-hand margins of the transcriptions of MS. 71, below) refer not to *1814* but to the state of Books I, II, and III (up to l. 330) as they existed before the death of WW's children in 1812. The poet then revised the text to incorporate a similar tragedy into the Solitary's life.

MS. 71 led in this state directly into l. *206*, thus following the original sequence in DC MS. 47, in which the Wanderer tells the Poet about the Solitary as the two men descend toward the valley. Sometime before Mary Wordsworth reached l. *384* in DC MS. 71 (perhaps when she came to 41^{r} in DC MS. 47, where, in a revision of DC MS. 47's previous sequence, l. *384* leads into ll. *386ff.*), she discovered that DC MS. 47 already had implicitly restructured the book. Although there are no specific instructions for that restructuring in DC MS. 47, the Solitary's history was clearly to be moved to an earlier position in the narrative (see DC MS. 47, 41^{r}) and to be told to the Poet by the Wanderer not as they descended the valley but instead as they climbed toward it, as in the published poem. In this implied revision, l. *67b* was no longer to follow directly from l. *384a* but to follow l. *55* or some yet-to-be-expanded variant. Since something now had to be done to remedy the error in copying the early section of Book II into DC MS. 71, a decision was then probably made to employ the back pages of DC MS. 70 to revise the sequence of lines and consolidate ll. *56–210*. DC MS. 70 thus forms the basis for Insert A, leaves 42–45. It is, however, possible to conjecture another sequence in which the structural revisions implied in DC MS. 47 are coterminous with the copying of DC MS. 71, so that work in DC MS. 47, from 41^{r} onward, was undertaken during the copying of MS. 71; DC MS. 70 would then be used to consolidate ll. *56–210*. Although this alternate conjecture cannot be ruled out, the nature of the continuous drafting in DC MS. 47 suggests that it was more likely that Mary and William discovered the implied sequential revision in DC MS. 47 during copying of DC MS. 71; they would then have revised and consolidated the crucial, intervening lines (*56–210*) to bridge l. *55* in 35^{v} and l. *211* in 45^{r}, the original manuscript sequence in DC MS. 71. The necessity for such complicated alterations may suggest that some time had passed between the original composition in DC MS. 47 and the subsequent copying of it into DC MS. 71; when WW and MW returned to DC MS. 47 for that recopying of it, WW seems no longer to have had clearly in mind its implied structural revision. In any event, inserted leaves 42–43 (now stubs) probably reflected WW's work in DC MS. 70 related to ll. *56–130*, which—at nineteen lines per page—would comprise approximately seventy-five lines, leading into ll. *131–210* on inserted leaves 44–45. Later, after the death of Wordsworth's children and at the fifth stage of *Excursion* composition, the poet returned to Book II in DC MS. 71 to replace his original Insert A (leaves 42–45) about the Solitary's life with an expanded, much more personal, account incorporating information about his character's family tragedies (Insert B, leaves 36–45).

Besides that complex second-stage revising of the Wanderer's account of the Solitary in Book II, this stage of the poem involved Mary Wordsworth's incorporating new material at the end of Book II concerning the Old Pensioner and the Solitary's hilltop vision. It seems highly likely that this new work had been drafted elsewhere, since it appears in DC MS. 71 in a fair-copy version with little correction. Book III material up to line 330 was also almost certainly copied from DC MS. 69 into DC MS. 71 at the second stage of composition, and it appears in Mary Wordsworth's hand (which ceases to be continuous and fluent at l. 330 on 74^{r} in DC MS. 71). It seems reasonably safe to conclude that this block of copied text from Books I and II and part of Book III in DC MS. 71 constitutes the second stage of the poem's development, a stage of recopying and consolidation. At the same time, though, Wordsworth was probably also writing (in a manuscript that does not survive) a first version of many of the tales in Books VI, VII, and VIII, coming out of his growing interest in the epitaph form. Further evidence of Wordsworth's work at this time on epitaphic verse material is Sara Hutchinson's copy—from a no-longer-extant manuscript—of the story of the deaf dalesman (VI, 412–498). Her passage appears at the end of the third *Essay on Epitaphs* in DC MS. 67 (which was definitely written by February 28, 1810).[11] The same lines are written, in an unknown hand, into the Commonplace Book kept by the Beaumonts.

III

Third Stage: Between December 1809 and March 1812

DC MS. 70	Book IV (work from l. 335 onward)
DC MS. 73	Book IV (work on the near-conclusion of the book)
DC MS. 73	Book III (work toward the end-of-book image of life as a river)
DC MS. 70	Book V (work toward the beginning of the book)

It looks as though, after the transcription work in DC MS. 71, Wordsworth was uncertain how to tell the Solitary's tale or even how he intended to develop the rest of Book III after l. 330, and he therefore put it aside and turned instead to work on Book IV in DC MS. 70. Work toward Book IV—which forms the bulk of the material in DC MS. 70—is tortuous in its progression. The notebook contains virtually no stretches of fluent and continuous writing but instead an endless circling advance, with continual reworking along the way. Such compositional characteristics are partly a reflection of the content, however, since Book IV is the most heavily philosophical section of the poem. DC MS. 70 also contains material for two other main sections of the poem: (1) a passage for Book II entered on the last pages of the notebook and continuing on the inside back cover (see the second stage, above); (2) material for the opening of Book V.

When we consider the Book IV material in DC MS. 70, we can immediately tell from the content alone whether such material was written before or after the completion of Book III in DC MS. 71. In the published poem, it is in the opening section of Book IV (ll. 1–334) that the Wanderer directly addresses the Solitary's troubles as raised by him in the story of his personal tragedy in Book III. Without doubt this section of Book IV could not have been written until the later, personal material in Book III had been added. And, tellingly, DC MS. 70 contains Book IV material that begins only at IV, 335 (16^r). It thus seems likely that Wordsworth reached III, 330, of DC MS. 71 and then left this manuscript and began work on Book IV in DC MS. 70. DC MS. 70 is thus a parallel manuscript to DC MS. 71, probably being written a short time after the copying out

[11]See *Chronology: MY,* pp. 443, 676.

of Books I–III, 330, in DC MS. 71 but certainly before the writing of the later part of Book III in that notebook.

There are a number of points in DC MS. 70 where much earlier material is integrated into what became Books IV and V of *The Excursion.* The first such passage for Book IV occurs on 2ʳ and consists of only three lines:

> We live by admiration & by love
> And even as these are well & wisely fixed
> To
> ~~In~~ dignity of being we ascend
> (DC MS. 70, 2ʳ)

These lines appear in DC MS. 48 as part of *The Prelude* (see *13-Bk Prelude,* II, 359, 378). In the context of Book IV material here, the lines are entered on the first blank recto page and in the hand of Mary Wordsworth. A second example of the recycling of a much earlier passage in *The Excursion* occurs at 19ʳ–19ᵛ and 20ᵛ–21ʳ with the description of the "Lamb in Solitude." Again, this passage is found in drafts in DC MS. 48 (*13-Bk Prelude,* II, 402, 420). Finally, on 16ʳ–17ʳ, written in fair copy in Mary Wordsworth's hand, come the lines beginning "Happy is he who lives to understand," which occur in the published poem at IV, 335–353. These lines are taken from DC MS. 28, a manuscript for *Home at Grasmere* (see *H at G,* pp. 196–197). The passage stands alone in DC MS. 70 and looks to have been copied directly from the earlier piece, incorporating changes made to the earlier draft. At this point that work for Book IV probably starts in DC MS. 70. Again, just as the earlier "Minstrel" passage from *Prelude* manuscript DC MS. 48 provided the starting point for Book II in DC MS. 47, so the lines from the *Home at Grasmere* manuscript seem to provide the necessary stimulus for the poet to go on to write Book IV.[12]

As work on Book IV advanced, it looks as though Wordsworth ran out of space in DC MS. 70 and therefore went on to another empty notebook, DC MS. 73. DC MS. 73 is a notebook that contains endings: the near-conclusion of Book III; the near-conclusion of Book IV (the close of the Wanderer's speech); and the end of Book IX and thus of the whole poem. Toward the front of DC MS. 73 is material for Book IV that follows on from DC MS. 70,[13] as well as material toward the end of Book III that precedes the same passage at the end of DC MS. 71. It seems likely that the Book IV material was entered first (with Wordsworth carrying on here after running out of room in DC MS. 70); the Book III material comes next. DC MS. 73, however, is another manuscript—like DC MS. 69—that contains entries clearly added at different times and relating in this case to two different stages of work on the poem. DC MS. 73 was left blank, apart from these entries at the front of the notebook, until a major block of work on DC MSS. 74 and 75 had been completed. Toward the end of the compositional process,

[12] Internal evidence for the order of entry of Book IV material in MS. 70 is given in more detail in the notes to the transcriptions, below.

[13] In terms of the consecutive order, the main block of work in MS. 70 ends at IV, 1096 (56ʳ), with the Solitary asking questions; MS. 73 starts at IV, 1152 (3ᵛ). However, the section between these two points (containing natural metaphors of Faith) is reworked elsewhere in both MSS., as discussed below.

Wordsworth returned to DC MS. 73 and entered a large amount of work there for Book IX, including the ending of the poem and work on the opening of Book VI. These materials in DC MS. 73 for Books VI and IX will be discussed at the seventh and eighth stages of composition, below.

Book IV material in DC MS. 73 seems to work in close interaction with DC MS. 70. So, for example, the image of the burning altar that occurs in DC MS. 73, 6^{r}, is then copied back into DC MS. 70 on 22^{v}. The image of the child with a shell in DC MS. 70, 16^{v} (ll. 1126–1140) provides a passage not present on DC MS. 73, 6^{r} (where copy jumps from l. 1125 directly to l. 1141). In both manuscripts the content consists of natural metaphors by which the Wanderer seeks to return the Solitary to a belief in Christian religion. DC MS. 73 takes us to the end of the Wanderer's speech in Book IV but not to the very end of the book as it is given in the published poem (the manuscript does not contain the Poet's response to the Wanderer nor the description of the natural scene as they return to the cottage).[14] In the published text, a lengthy section is inserted here between the natural images and the end of the Wanderer's speech, and this passage looks back to material originally written for *The Ruined Cottage.*[15] Lines 1201 and 1260, which frame that passage, are found in DC MS. 73 on 5^{v} and 7^{r} but not the passage itself. As far as we can tell, this missing section was probably fully integrated into Book IV only for the final fair copy, now lost, sent to the printer in 1814.

When Book III in DC MS. 71 was broken off at line 330, that manuscript and Book III itself were left incomplete until the deaths of the children prompted Wordsworth to return to it. However, one descriptive passage, which appears at the very end of Book III as it is published, is found in DC MS. 73. That passage in DC MS. 73 stands as a distinct image and may have been written as such without the poet's having a clear place in mind for it at first.[16] On 8^{r}–9^{r} of DC MS. 73, Wordsworth writes lines 976–995 out twice (the second version on 8^{v}–9^{r} clearly being a cleaner rewriting of the piece immediately preceding it). This passage contains the Solitary's own self-presentation of his life as a river, which he looks at and along and through, considering the river in terms of length and of surfaces and depths. This wonderful image, with which Wordsworth eventually concluded the Solitary's narrative in Book III, is written out in DC MS. 73 as a single extended metaphor, which Wordsworth later draws upon directly in DC MS. 71. The text in DC MS. 73 ends three lines short of the conclusion of the final poem, at line 995, and the last three lines are then added on the copy of this passage on 110^{r} of DC MS. 71.

These facts are important since they tell us two things about the overall development of the poem. After Wordsworth ran out of space in DC MS. 70, he continued his Book IV material in DC MS. 73, which then runs to the end of the Wanderer's speech. The image for Book III is entered on the following page

[14]MS. 73 ends on 7^{v} at l. 1284; Book IV as published in 1814 ends at l. 1319.

[15]*RC* MSS. B (20^{v}–21^{r}, 46^{r}–49^{r}) and D (67^{v}–69^{r}); see *RC & Pedlar,* pp. 120–123, 260–267, 372–374.

[16]Mark Reed's date for this Book III passage (January 3, 1813–May 1814; see *Chronology: MY,* p. 683) is later than our suggested placing of it within the third stage of composition (between December 1809 and March 1812). His later date is possible if WW jumped out of MS. 71 to write the first version of the passage in MS. 73 and then returned to MS. 71, but—because of the self-contained nature of the passage—an earlier entry is equally possible. (See also *Chronology: MY,* p. 679.)

in DC MS. 73, strongly suggesting that it was written in after the Book IV work. Since we also know that this image was written before Wordsworth's completion of Book III in DC MS. 71, we can be reasonably sure that Book IV material was more or less complete (from l. 335 onward) before the deaths of Wordsworth's children in 1812—and thus before he returned to Book III in January 1813. This analysis also supports the argument that the development of the poem progresses from DC MS. 71 (Books I, II, III up to l. 330) to DC MSS. 70 and 73 (Book IV) and then returns back to DC MS. 71 (conclusion of Book III).

Finally, we should note that early work toward Book V in DC MS. 70 was also probably entered at this stage. This material is the first written for Book V, and it starts with the line "Farewell, deep Valley with thy lonesome house" (DC MS. 70, 4^{v}) before leading into a passage, originally located here within Book V but later moved to Book III, revised from *The Tuft of Primroses.* All of this material is written quite messily in Wordsworth's hand, with considerable reworking on 7^{r}–7^{v} and 8^{r} concerning the introduction of the Pastor. Here, a number of possible titles and descriptions of him are entered, ranging from the Poet's speculations concerning "a little Empire—is it ruled / By a wise prince" (7^{r}) to "A [?man]," "a [?thane]," "a Pries by function," and "a keeper" (all tentatively entered on 7^{r}), and finally, on 7^{v}, to the following:

shepher {,
A consci[?n]tious ~~pastor of~~ { ~~his~~ flock
[?in] ~~and [?as kings are]~~
{ ~~ter,~~
~~Of holy charc~~ {a a shepherd
[?pries]
(DC MS. 70, 7^{v})

Wordsworth finally settles on "A father of his people" and "as good kings / Are said to be" (7^{v}), lines that survive with slight alterations into the published text (V, 103–105). These various drafts show Wordsworth's anxiety over the introduction of the Pastor and, as with the Wanderer, the problem of giving to him an authority that overrides status and class. Wordsworth is clearly keen to naturalize his role, with the Christian image of "The shepherd of his flock" (on 8^{r} and in the published text) being particularly appropriate for the region that the Pastor inhabits. A few following pages in DC MS. 70 (8^{v}–10^{r}) still concern Book V and the description of the interior of the church but the entries appear to have been added at a different time.

The earliest work for Book V, then, seems to be constructed around the leaving of one particular location (the Solitary's valley) and anticipation of the next one (the Pastor's valley) that Poet, Solitary, and Wanderer gaze down upon. The construction of Book V therefore resembles that of Book II and to some extent Book I. In each case, the new character is introduced at the start by one who knows him well; we then meet the character in person, and what develops later in each book in terms of conversation or narrative is strongly colored by that character. That Wordsworth was anxious to get this character of the Pastor right is strongly felt on pages 7^{r}–8^{v} of DC MS. 70 and also suggests that the construction of the poem is both linear and radial: the journey takes us forward to new encounters, and each point of encounter leads to the generation of narrative, dialogue, and the stories of others.

Finally, in relation to Book V in DC MS. 70, Wordsworth begins to incorporate passages from *The Tuft of Primroses.* This material originates in DC MS. 65, where there is evidence of reworking on 43^{v}–45^{r} that is clearly in preparation for repositioning the text within *The Excursion* (see *Tuft*, pp. 244–249). In DC MS. 70, the lines are first placed within Book V as the Poet and Wanderer leave the Solitary's valley; however, only part of the passage as it appears in the published poem appears here.[17] The Poet utters the image of withdrawal as he looks back upon the Solitary's place of abode:

> In a low Voice & with reverted eyes
>   a
>   [?~~at~~]
> A parting tribute to th [?] spot
>   that seemed
>   or
> Like the fix'd centre of a troubled wr ld
> Backward I looked & lookd again
>   with hope
> To imprint a final Image on my mind
>   (DC MS. 70, 6^{r})

Those lines are followed shortly afterward by an account of the kind of natural temptation to withdrawal that such a place presents, which leads directly into "What impulse drove the Hermit to his cell" at the bottom of 6^{r}. This idea as expressed in DC MS. 70 follows the redrafting of the passage in the earlier DC MS. 65, redrafting where the lines are given to the Poet to voice in *The Excursion*:

> I said, no wonder that your hapless Friend
> Was fancy smitten by this calm retreat
> . . . .
> By this temptation might be lured, to quit
> The empty turmoils of a bustling world
>   (DC MS. 65, 43^{v}; *Tuft*, p. 245)

The image of the Hermit is originally written as a positive image of reclusion in *The Tuft of Primroses*, where the passage stands between an account of the poet's own self-presentation as one who has withdrawn to the mountains and the ensuing portrait of spiritual withdrawal presented by St. Basil. At this stage of reworking the passage for *The Excursion*, it is still a largely positive image being uttered by the Poet and suggestive of some sympathy with the Solitary's position. As with the Minstrel passage drawn from *Prelude* manuscript DC MS. 48 for use in Book II of *The Excursion*, revisions are also connected to a change in

---

[17]The horizontal line across the page on 6^{v} where the piece breaks off (at a line corresponding to III, 385, of the published text) could indicate that WW was aware of the need to move the lines even as he entered the passage here. Equally, it might just be a way of marking off potential Book V entries from a passage of earlier working from Book IV that occurs on 6^{v}–7^{r}.

voice from first to third person—as is seen in the reworking on DC MS. 65, 43^{v}, when the words are put into the mouth of the Poet. This passage finds its final resting place in DC MS. 71, probably at the fifth stage of composition, when it is sewn in as Insert C (75^{r}–76^{r}) and given in full, relating to III, 374–410, of the published text. However, as the passage is shifted from the opening of Book V to the middle of Book III—and from the mouth of the Poet to the mouth of the Solitary—the image that began positively becomes a negative one. The passage itself hardly changes, but the altered context changes its meaning. The lines are now given as part of a debate with the Poet, in which the Solitary asks, "What impulse, did in later ages drive / The Hermit to his Cell" (75^{r}). Although the Solitary expresses admiration for such "impulses," the image is now being used *against* the Poet, and in part as a mistaken justification for the negative model of unhealthy retreat that the Solitary himself represents. The Hermit passage is a fine example of an earlier passage being gradually transformed in meaning by its repositioning from one text (*The Tuft of Primroses*) to another (*The Excursion*).[18]

IV

Fourth Stage: Between late August 1811 and May 1814[19]

DC MS. 74	Book V, including *The Peasant's Life* and *The Shepherd of Bield Crag*
DC MS. 69	Book V sections reworked from DC MS. 74

As we have seen in the third stage of composition, the very beginnings of Book V are found in DC MS. 70 (4^{v}, 6^{r}–10^{r}), probably added later than work on Book IV. This Book V material included passages describing the journey from the Solitary's valley to the Pastor's, the description of the Pastor, the account of the inside of his church, and the Solitary standing alone in the church. In spite of the fact that this material was not written as a continuous whole, Wordsworth must have been reasonably content with it, since he did not copy it out or rework it in DC MS. 74 along with the other Book V material. The work on the opening of Book V in DC MS. 70 almost certainly precedes DC MS. 74; DC MS. 70 ends at V, 227 (10^{r}), and the lowest-numbered Book V passage in DC MS. 74 contains material within it from line 260 (33^{v}).[20] Book V was now developed by Wordsworth at some length in DC MS. 74, where material toward it is found scattered throughout the notebook. It was then reworked, partly in DC MS. 69 and at a relatively early stage, and then sometime later in a manuscript now lost, in preparation for the clean copy of Book V in DC MS. 74A.

The first material entered for Book V in DC MS. 74 appears to be on 28^{r} starting

[18]For critical discussion of such acts of translation across the MSS. of the *Exc*, see Bushell, pp. 59–73; for a listing of the various inserts added to MS. 71, see p. 435, above.
[19]See n. 3 on p. 427, above.
[20]There is work on the inside cover of MS. 74 for V, 257–266, but it is probably a later entry.

with the line "Our Nature, said the Priest, in mild reply" (V, 480).[21] However, we need also to bear in mind that Book V material at this stage is closely connected both with *The Peasant's Life*—a lengthy narrative of the rural everyman told by the Solitary but (largely) cut from the published poem—and with *The Shepherd of Bield Crag,* a much shorter piece, also later omitted from the poem.[22] Although the brief opening work for Book V in DC MS. 70 seemed to focus very strongly on the presentation of the Pastor by the other characters, the Pastor is not the focus of the book as it develops in DC MS. 74. Instead, Book V in DC MS. 74 is built up initially around *The Peasant's Life.* The sections relating to the Pastor's character had been roughed out in DC MS. 70 and are not copied here in DC MS. 74; the section relating to the Pastor's arrival first emerges in DC MS. 69 (where it was probably entered on stubs 242–244).[23]

DC MS. 69 makes its final appearance in relation to the Book V material in its reworking of DC MS. 74: stubs at the back of DC MS. 69 contain enough fragments of letters to make it clear that V, 300–676, were once copied there from DC MS. 74. The appearance of DC MS. 69, with no back cover and loose binding threads, also allows for the possibility of further leaves in front of those that survive here as stubs (the original leaves at the back were used with the notebook inverted and thus proceed from the back toward the middle of the notebook). It is therefore possible—although there is no firm evidence—that DC MS. 69 also contained a version of V, 1–299, leading into the surviving stubs. Stubs in DC MS. 69 show the one-time presence of those sections of *The Peasant's Life* that were retained for Book V; the stubs do not suggest the presence of passages from *The Peasant's Life* omitted from the published *Excursion.* This fact suggests—although the remaining evidence on the stubs is inconclusive—that this material in DC MS. 69 may have been a reworking of DC MS. 74 related to removing most of the story of *The Peasant's Life* from Book V.

Before we turn away from DC MS. 69, the textual cohabitation of work for the *Guide to the Lakes* and *The Excursion* within this notebook is worth considering. In the front of the notebook, the prose material comes after the poetry, on the opposite page with one blank page between (7^r–8^v); at the back of the notebook, the prose is written with the notebook inverted. In both cases, too, material for the *Guide* is written in the same direction as the poetry (front and back entries both proceed toward the middle of the notebook), and this fact is particularly interesting in relation to the inverted text at the back of the book. It would seem logical that material for the *Guide* may have been entered after *Excursion*

---

[21]MS. 74 will be discussed more fully in terms of its contents and its relation to the poem's overall development in the sixth stage of composition, below.

[22]Although *TPL* and *SBC* are clearly written at this stage of the poem's development, they are discussed below at the eighth stage of composition, the point when they are removed from the poem, partly in order to keep the development of the MSS. as clear as possible but also because the discussion is necessarily focused on the reasons for their removal.

[23]Book V in MS. 74 includes material for ll. 257–266, 260–362, 387–406, 419–420, 429–433, 480–558, 607–620, 660–663, 904–928, 984–985, 989, 1010–1022. There are thus a number of gaps in the text, some of which are partially filled by looking back to MS. 70 (fragmentary material for ll. 1–223) or ahead to MS. 69 (ll. 300–676), but the rest of which are entered only in the fair copy of MS. 74A. This fact strongly suggests the possibility of an interim MS. (now lost) to bring this material together.

work, but if this were the case why would Wordsworth not enter both sections together at the front of the book? As Mark Reed puts it, "Appearance does not permit confident conjecture about the relative priority of entry of *G*[*uide*] and *Exc* materials" (*Chronology: MY*, p. 678). It does, however, encourage conjecture about the parallel writing of different texts in DC MS. 69. The fact that the entry of the *Guide* material almost seems to mirror the material for *The Excursion* (some entered at the front, the right way up, some entered at the back, inverted) suggests that Wordsworth was working simultaneously on very different materials. At the same time that he was reworking *The Excursion*, he was apparently also working on his *Guide*. Although the placement of poetry and prose alongside each other is in one sense merely physical juxtaposition, reflecting parallel work on a number of pieces, in another sense it also represents—at a deeper level—a kind of interplay between people and landscape that the published poem reflects.

With regard to the overall development of *The Excursion*, the key questions about the fourth stage of composition are how far Wordsworth would have taken the writing of Book V before going on to later books and at what point the decision to remove *The Peasant's Life* was made. On the whole, it seems likely that Wordsworth had roughed out all of this material in DC MS. 74 and recopied at least some of it in DC MS. 69 but was then interrupted in 1812 by the death of his children. The poet was then led away from Book V and back to earlier books.

V

Fifth Stage: Between January 3, 1813, and May 1814

DC MS. 71	Book III expansion from l. 330 to end of book
DC MS. 71	Book II Insert B (leaves 36–41) added; Insert A (leaves 42–45) partially torn out)
DC MS. 69	Book IV reworked (ll. 1–334 added)
DC MS. 71	Book III Insert C (leaves 75–76), drawing on *Tuft of Primroses*, possibly now added[24]
WW to Lord Lonsdale	Draft for III, 592–607
DC MS. 71	Book III Insert D (leaves 87–90), drawing on WW to Lord Lonsdale, now added
DC MS. 71	Book III Insert E (leaves 102–105), a fair-copy version in WW's hand of the text in the manuscript around it, probably now added

Wordsworth's work on the poem was quite advanced when the deaths of his two children sent him back to Book III and the tale of the Solitary. As we know from family letters, on June 4, 1812, Wordsworth's young daughter Catherine died unexpectedly of a seizure. Dorothy's letters describe in detail the despair and guilt felt by Mary Wordsworth: "her spirits are much improved—yet her dejection

[24]On Insert C, see p. 446, above; for more on the various inserts added to MS. 71, especially Insert A, see pp. xxiv, 435, and 440, above.

is miserable at times—I would give the world that she had been at home—for I am convinced that she would have felt very differently" (*MY*, II, 45). But just as the mother was beginning to recover, a second child died in December 1812. Thomas was the "darling of the house, and of everyone who looked at him" (*MY*, II, 61), as well as being the child who showed the most likelihood of intellectual aptitude.[25] This second death was not only a terrible trial to Mary but was also very deeply felt by Wordsworth. In a letter to Southey he states, "For myself dear Southey I dare not say in what state of mind I am; I loved the Boy with the utmost love of which my soul is capable, and he is taken from me . . . " (*MY*, II, 51). When the children died, the Wordsworths lived in the Parsonage House at Grasmere, directly opposite from the churchyard. But the proximity of the living to the dead—in many ways the positive focus of *The Excursion*—proved too much for the family, as Dorothy makes clear: "Our present Residence, which is close to the Church-yard and the school which was our darling's Daily pride and pleasure is become so melancholy that we have resolved to remove from it . . . " (*MY*, II, 68). The deaths of the children precipitated the move to Rydal Mount, where Wordsworth was to finish his work on *The Excursion* and where he lived until his death.

The latter part of DC MS. 71 bears the heavy weight of Wordsworth's first response to this family tragedy, as Wordsworth now returned to continue Book III from where he had stopped at l. 330 in the second stage of composition. In the light of his own terrible personal experiences, Wordsworth wrote of the Solitary's marriage and the loss of his family. These autobiographically based additions to *The Excursion* have implications for how we respond to the Solitary in the final poem—as well as for the relationship between the first telling of his story by the Wanderer and the second telling of it by the Solitary himself.[26]

As we have seen in considering the second stage of composition, Book III almost certainly existed in the form of lines 1–330 in DC MS. 69; this evidence (deduced from stubs and odd surviving leaves) is strongly supported by the existence of a continuous text in DC MS. 71, 65^r–74^r (almost certainly copied from DC MS. 69). After this point in DC MS. 71, the material becomes increasingly fragmentary, involving reworking and first-draft material in Wordsworth's hand (see particularly 86^v–96^v). From 97^r onward there are some blocks of more continuous text (still in Wordsworth's hand), which may have been copied from an earlier source for Book III that has not survived. The major section of new work focuses on the Solitary's life, expanding it to include a personal tragedy as well as the political one previously outlined in Book II. The changes made to this narrative in Book III have obvious implications for rewriting the Solitary's tale in Book II when the Wanderer tells it for the first time.

It is worth looking in some detail at the least stable section of DC MS. 71—perhaps the most disturbing and moving part of any Wordsworth manuscript. On the reverse side of a draft letter to Lord Lonsdale dated January 8, 1813, Wordsworth

[25]In the same letter, Dorothy describes him as "peaceable, affectionate, yet lively and ardent in the pursuit of knowledge in the most extraordinary degree" (*MY*, II, 61).

[26]On our transcription pages for MSS. 47, 69, 70, and 71 (see below), the italic line numbers in the right-hand margins designate the state of Books I–III, *299*, as they existed before the deaths of WW's children.

composed material for III, 592–607, involving an expansion of the Solitary's life story. This draft appears to have been written before (and to have contributed to) another version of the same passage, part of the inserted material sewn into DC MS. 71 as leaves 87–90.[27] When we turn to the notebook itself, DC MS. 71 is pleasantly domestic and may even be homemade, since it consists of a thick card cover with a piece of brown-and-white spotted cloth used as the binding. On the inside back cover and on one other page are a number of child's scribbles and the initials "D.W" clumsily made, presumably by Dora. Such details, reminding us of the familial context in which the poem was written, have a direct and poignant bearing on the content of this particular notebook. Much of the notebook, as we have seen in discussing the second stage of composition, contains fair copy written by Mary Wordsworth. However, after approximately eighty leaves of clear and clean writing in Mary's hand, the manuscript suddenly becomes far less ordered, jumping from Mary's writing to Dorothy's for four pages, back to Mary briefly for two and a half pages, then to Dorothy for a further three before Wordsworth takes over and continues in his own hand for the rest of the notebook. Here is a listing of this crucial section of DC MS. 71, showing the changes of hands:

81^{r}	Mary
81^{v}	William
82^{r}–82^{v}	Dorothy
83^{r}	Dorothy, then Mary
83^{v}–84^{r}	Mary
84^{v}	Mary, then William; end of Mary's copying in DC MS. 71
85^{r}–85^{v}	Dorothy
86^{r}	Dorothy, then William; end of Dorothy's copying in DC MS. 71
86^{v}	William
87^{r}	William; beginning of insert and reworking of WW to Lord Lonsdale
87^{v}	William, who writes the rest of Book III

Unsurprisingly, the content at the point where the writers repeatedly change concerns the Solitary's autobiography and the section in which the account of his idyllic married life moves on to describe the sudden deaths of his wife and children. The manuscript reveals the gradual withdrawal of amanuenses as first Mary stops and then, when the material comes closer to the actual account of the children's deaths, Dorothy, too, withdraws, until there is only William to continue onward. This creative response to grief strongly resembles Wordsworth's account of his reaction to his brother John's death, written to Sir George Beaumont on May 1, 1805: "I composed much, but it is all lost except a few lines, as it came from me in such a torrent that I was unable to remember it; I could not hold the pen myself, and the subject was such, that I could not employ Mrs Wordsworth or my Sister as my amanuensis" (*EY*, p. 586).

In DC MS. 71 Mary first stops writing at the bottom of 81^{r}, just before the Solitary begins to speak of his wife and his early marriage in Devon. Leaf 81^{v} is written

[27]Because the passage in MS. 71 is considerably longer than the extract on the back of the draft letter to Lord Lonsdale, this work in MS. 71 may also represent copy from an intermediate MS. that does not survive.

in Wordsworth's hand, and then Dorothy takes over for the next two and a half pages, which describe the happiness of the Solitary's life with "Anna"—as he calls his wife here in material left out of the published text. Somewhat unexpectedly, Mary's hand then returns from 83^{v} to 84^{v} (perhaps either she or William decided that this material was not too troubling); then she breaks off—significantly—at the most explicitly heightened comparison of the Solitary's past to an Edenic state: "Finished & fair as Paradise itself / Where the first Adam dwelt with happy Eve" (DC MS. 71, 84^{v}). The rest of 84^{v} is filled with rewriting for this section in William's hand; then on 85^{r} Dorothy takes over again. The reason for Mary's withdrawal can immediately be seen from the first four lines on this page:

> But on the freedom of that wedded life
> Which we enjoy'd in common Nature laid
> Welcome restraint my tender Mate became
> The thankful Captive of maternal bonds
> (DC MS. 71, 85^{r})

It seems likely that William, knowing what the next section of the poem was to be, brought a halt to Mary's involvement in order not to cause pain over the recent deaths and the untimely breaking of her own "maternal bonds." At this point, then, Dorothy takes over for two and a half pages, until the point at which the Solitary pauses and addresses his audience, before finally going on to describe the deaths of his children and wife. Dorothy's copying in DC MS. 71 ends with these lines:

> the Mother's kiss
> And Infant's smile awaited my return
> ~~Your hearts I feel are with [?me,] I perceive~~
> withholds not from my words
> Your courtesy ~~provides for what I say~~
> (DC MS. 71, 86^{r})

On the next page, William then goes on to describe "two Little-ones that bless'd our love" (86^{v}). Such material was clearly considered by the poet to be too charged for either of the two women to be able to write out, and so he is on his own from this point on.

Wordsworth's entries very clearly represent his attempts to come to terms with the losses. DC MS. 71 contains among the lines for Book III two passages that later became separate poems (*Maternal Grief* and *Characteristics of a Child three Years old*). The process of the poet's working through his own grief on these pages often introduces a strongly personal note into the text, particularly in terms of the relationship between father and mother, their two responses to the loss, and the inability of one to help the other. So, for example, Wordsworth has the Solitary lament how little he could comfort his wife:

> grievous
> To my Copartner in this bitter loss
> Support I could not yield who did myself

support
Require^from others less disturbed
(DC MS. 71, 94^{v})

This section becomes, then, a kind of dialogue with the self. Wordsworth the poet tries to offer succor to Wordsworth the husband, who feels himself to be failing and as desperate in his own way as is the deeply grieving mother. The difference is that his guilt and grief concern his wife as much as the lost children, but he is at least able to write about it. In this section of Book III, we hear the alternating voices of Wordsworth, of the Solitary (who speaks in first person here), and of Wordsworth's attempt to voice Mary's feelings on her behalf.

Sometimes those voices are hard to distinguish. In one draft describing the death of the Solitary's daughter, for example, Wordsworth writes as follows:

Would ye not shriek at such a Spectacle.
—Ah but ~~a mother saw~~ it—it was seen
A claim that shatterd all
~~And by a Father felt~~
(DC MS. 71, 92^{r})

At such times Wordsworth's writing out of his own grief seems to be loaded with a sense of guilt that he can at least write; Mary is not only unable to have such an outlet but is also necessarily remote from him, and from him as a writer, as he puts his feelings down on paper. As a result, the act of coming to terms with his own loss through composition and the reworking of the text alone also seem to involve some attempt to voice that loss on behalf of the mother, who is only able to "see" what the father can "feel." Out of such feeling comes the writing of *Maternal Grief,* initially embedded in passages for *The Excursion.* The development of *Maternal Grief* feels deeply autobiographical:

Wringing of hands & in the Mothers breast
Conflicts of agonizing thoughts like these.
—Departing Child I could forget thee once
Though at my bosom nurs'd
(DC MS. 71, 92^{v})

Looking back again to Wordsworth's writing after the death of his brother John, we see that, although he failed to memorialize his brother in verse at that time, the attempt to do so acted as a prompt and stimulus, returning Wordsworth afresh to composition of *The Prelude.* In a letter to Sir George Beaumont he makes this fact clear: "Unable to proceed with this work, I turned my thoughts again to the Poem on my own life, and you will be glad to hear that I have added 300 lines to it in the course of last week" (*EY,* p. 586). The dramatic mode of *The Excursion* may also have helped Wordsworth to continue his work on the poem by distancing him slightly from the events. It seems possible, again, that in responding to death and grief in this way he gains from it a source of stimulus by which to take the poem forward. DC MS. 71, as now expanded, thus tells two tragic tales: one of the Solitary and the other of the Wordsworths. The first story is given in the words of the text, and the second is woven into the fabric and structure of the notebook itself. It seems, too, that the emotional conflict of the Solitary, reflected in textual strategies within the final poem, is a direct extension of the emotional and textual difficulties in the environment within which this section of the poem was produced.

The decision to add this new material to Book III had consequences both for the opening of Book IV and for the first telling of the Solitary's tale in Book II. Wordsworth must now have responded in two ways: by writing in DC MS. 69 the opening linking section for Book IV (ll. 1–334) and by writing a passage to be inserted and sewn into DC MS. 71 for Book II (adjusting the first version of the Solitary's life to match the second expanded one in Book III). We cannot be sure in which order he made these changes, but evidence suggests that the insert for Book II in DC MS. 71 was probably made later.

In the published version of the opening of Book IV, the Wanderer makes such statements as these: "Endeavour thus to live; these rules regard" (IV, 229) and "For that other loss, / The loss of confidence in social Man" (IV, 261–262). Such phrases make clear the intention of the whole opening section of Book IV: a direct address by the Wanderer to the Solitary, which contains a detailed attempt to answer the personal difficulties raised by the Solitary in his narrative of Book III. Having completed Book III in DC MS. 71, Wordsworth was now in a position to link the two books closely in this way. DC MS. 70, which had already been filled at the third stage of composition with work for Book IV, does not contain any of this opening material: Wordsworth instead turned back to the earlier DC MS. 69. DC MS. 69 probably contained most of Book IV, 1–759 (incorporating the new opening and some cleaner copied text from DC MS. 70), but all that survives of this Book IV work in DC MS. 69 is material on stubs and one fragment of text on 220^{v}. When we compare that fragment with DC MS. 70, however, the DC MS. 69 text is, without question, a reworking of what is in DC MS. 70. The heavily reworked and unstable text of DC MS. 70 was thus cleanly written out in DC MS. 69, together with the new opening for Book IV that responded to revisions made to Book III in DC MS. 71.[28]

Besides altering Book IV by adding the Wanderer's response to the expanded account of the Solitary's difficulties as expressed in Book III, Wordsworth also had to revise Book II in the light of the new Book III material about the tragic deaths in the Solitary's family. Thus Wordsworth now—after the death of his own two children—added (as Insert B) to his account in DC MS. 71 of the Solitary's life. That account of the Solitary in Book II of DC MS. 71 actually has five stages of development:

(1) Drafting DC MS. 47, which places the Solitary's tale as Poet and Wanderer descend to the Solitary's mountain valley, but which also strongly intimates a future restructuring of Book II by moving the tale earlier (to a point when Poet and Wanderer ascend toward his valley);

(2) Copying the base text for Book II from DC MS. 47 into DC MS. 71, work that seems to

[28]For a complete listing of what remains of IV, 1–755, on the stubs of MS. 69, see pp. 526–529, below.

have stopped before reaching the Solitary's tale, probably because Mary Wordsworth realized that passages in DC MS. 47 implied a restructuring of the book that would require moving the story earlier;

(3) Using the back pages of DC MS. 70 to consolidate what is in DC MS. 47 and produce a fair copy of the Solitary's tale, covering only his political despair, in preparation for revising DC MS. 71;

(4) Copying this account of the Solitary from DC MS. 70 and adding it to DC MS. 71 as Insert A (now stubs 42–43 and leaves 44–45);

(5) Writing—some time later and after the deaths of Wordsworth's children—of leaves containing a second version of the tale, taking into account the expansion of Book III by combining revised DC MS. 70 material, the text of Insert A, and a brief account of the Solitary's familial tragedies;

(6) Removing part (leaves 42–43) of Insert A and sewing the new leaves into DC MS. 71 as Insert B (leaves 36–41).[29]

This new material on Insert B thus replaced Insert A's opening two leaves (now stubs 42–43); the final two pages of that first insert (44–45) remain—heavily reworked—after the end of the Insert B in DC MS. 71.

The only part of the Wanderer's account of the Solitary's tale not found in DC MS. 70 is the passage relating to the personal tragedy in the Solitary's life (DC MS. 71, 39^{v}–40^{r}). There are no other manuscripts for this succinct Book II account of the painfully full tale told in Book III. It looks as though Wordsworth drew back from the Book III material at this point and simply summarized it for Book II. So, for example, on DC MS. 71, 40^{r}, the Wanderer tells us:

How full their joy
How free their love. Oh pitiable state
In the short course of one undreaded year
Death blasted all—Death suddenly oerthrew
Two lovely Children—all that they possessed
The Mother followed

The extreme brevity and compactness of this account presumably rendered it acceptable for Mary Wordsworth to write it out when it was copied into DC MS. 71 as part of Insert B. This chronology of composition also has clear implications for the way the two tales of the Solitary read in the published *Excursion*: the Wanderer's third-person account in Book II appears almost callous in the rapidity of its telling in comparison with the Solitary's long and painful first-person version in Book III. The complex process of Wordsworth's revising of Books II and III strongly colors the kinds of narrative told and the reader's responses to them.

In conclusion, we can see that DC MS. 71 contains three distinct periods of work, spanning at least two major stages of the poem's development. The first is the fairly straightforward copying out of Books I to III, 330. The second is the additional work on the second half of Book III in DC MS. 71 after the children's

[29]More detailed discussion of the complexities surrounding the inserted material can be found in the notes to the relevant transcription pages of MS. 71 (see below). For more information on the first four stages of the Solitary's story in Book II, see pp. 439–440, above; a complete list of all inserts in MS. 71 is given on p. 435, above.

deaths, followed by the opening to Book IV in DC MS. 69 in response to it. Then finally comes the Wanderer's brief tale of the Solitary, taking into account the death of his children, with Insert B replacing Insert A in order to maintain the status of DC MS. 71 as a "complete" manuscript of the early books.[30]

VI

Sixth Stage: Possibly from late August 1811; probably between January 3, 1813, and May 1814

[MS. not extant	Work on Books VI, VII, VIII, and IX, preceding DC MS. 74]
DC MS. 74	Work on Books VI and VII, incorporating material from *Home at Grasmere* and *Guide to the Lakes*
DC MS. 75	Work on Books VI, VII, VIII
Berg MS.	Draft for Book VIII (ll. c. 463–c. 523)
Houghton MS.	Draft for Book VII (ll. 554–603, 648–654)
DC MS. 74	Reworking of parts of Books VI–VIII

Further discussion of the manuscripts may be assisted by some consideration of the ways in which individual books of *The Excursion* move forward. Wordsworth has a number of ways of developing a book. One is to begin with a "set piece." In this case the opening passage marks the book off from the previous material, creating the confidence to begin writing a new book without worrying about making a connection with material that came before. This kind of opening structure clearly occurs for Books II and IX, where the opening passages also draw on a much earlier piece of writing (the "Minstrel passage" for Book II, the Wanderer's speech on the "active principle" for Book IX).

A second method for beginning a book is to start someplace in the middle at what frequently turns out to be two or three hundred lines into the book as eventually completed. Sometime later, Wordsworth will return to write the opening of the new book and to connect it with the preceding book. The most striking example of this approach occurs with Book IV, where the opening section is written last because it is dependent upon the expansion of the end of Book III. The same procedure also occurs with Book VI, where the opening half is written into DC MS. 73, in what appears to be the last piece of composition for *The Excursion*, sometime after the composition of the middle of the Book VI.

Books VII and VIII stand as exceptions to these two main modes of composition, since they run directly on from the conclusions of the previous books in DC MS. 74 (see 75^r, 7^r–7^v). This model is unusual but probably reflects the facts that the contents of Books VI and VII are extremely similar (containing a series of epitaphic tales set in the churchyard) and that the opening of Book VIII follows on logically from that material. Such fluid continuity also suggests a previ-

[30]WW may also at this time have added to MS. 71 another insert, drawing on a passage from *The Tuft of Primroses* entered at the third stage of composition into MS. 70 and seemingly there intended for Book V. In MS. 71 this passage (leaves 75–76) becomes part of Book III.

ous, less continuous—and now missing—manuscript for some of this material. A range of compositional openings thus occurs in the next stage of the poem's development.[31]

The most significant manuscript for this stage of the poem's composition is DC MS. 74, which presents us with a series of difficulties in terms of trying to ascertain both the order within the notebook itself and the wider order and development of *The Excursion*. The manuscript contains a large amount of material. Apart from an uncut page leaving 106^v–107^r blank, all 125 leaves of the notebook are full, with material relating to Books V, VI, VII, VIII, and IX; as a result, DC MS. 74 is the most substantial of all *Excursion* notebooks. The manuscript operates within the overall structure of composition in a way similar to that of DC MS. 71: a stage at which a number of other manuscripts are pulled together (although DC MS. 74 does so in a less clear and cohesive way than does DC MS. 71). Important in representing the scope of the poem, DC MS. 74 clearly signifies a drive toward completion. Material is not all entered at the same time, but it does seem likely, as Mark Reed suggests, that "[DC] MS. 74 appears on balance . . . likely to have been filled with the bulk of its *Exc* materials within a short space of time" (*Chronology: MY*, p. 681).

Certain distinctive characteristics of DC MS. 74 clearly indicate that it is written at a relatively late stage of the poem's composition. The most obvious of these characteristics is that the notebook contains a large number of important sections moving across books as much as working within them. Thus DC MS. 74 contains the end of Book VI, which runs straight on into Book VII (75^r); the end of Book VII, which runs straight on into Book VIII (7^r–7^v); and the end of Book VIII, which runs straight on into Book IX (26^r). The notebook itself does not contain the whole of any of these books, and so it seems to be used expressly for the purpose of linking books together.

A second characteristic of DC MS. 74 is the way in which it connects to DC MS. 75. The nature of this relationship is not merely one of reworking—copying from one text to another—but quite often operates something like a jigsaw, with DC MS. 74 containing most of the pieces of a text, but with a missing part to be found in DC MS. 75. We see examples of this interlocking of manuscripts with the tale of "Oswald" and with the passage describing the Pastor's son and his friend in Book VIII. Such a structure suggests that Wordsworth's simultaneous use of DC MSS. 74 and 75 represents an important and quite rapid stage of composition.

These details lead us on to one final, and frustrating, characteristic of DC MS. 74: the indirect evidence that there must have been in concurrent use another notebook, or at least considerably more scraps of material, not now extant. Evidence for this missing material exists in examples such as the tale of Ellen, which is copied out cleanly at some length in DC MS. 74 with only very brief prior drafting for it in DC MS. 75; or Oswald's tale, allowed for but not

[31]The two openings not mentioned above are of Book III (probably in MS. 69) and of Book V (in MS. 73). In both of these cases, WW seems to work distinctly and discretely on the opening sections of the books with the bulk of work for subsequent passages being left for a later MS. stage.

included in DC MS. 74 and existing only in a short draft section in DC MS. 75. These gaps, and the jump from sketchy early drafting to a complete and clean text, must lead us to suppose that there were other lengthier workings for this material elsewhere. It seems highly likely that at least one other notebook existed and contained some of the churchyard stories (particularly those of Ellen and of Oswald). Furthermore, on 111ʳ in DC MS. 74 the lines describing the deaf dalesman are omitted as the text jumps from line 417 to line 499, with a mark "&c" after l. 417. The missing lines 418–498 clearly existed in a final form elsewhere; one place they appear is in DC MS. 67, a manuscript for the third *Essay on Epitaphs*, copied by Sara Hutchinson by February 28, 1810 (see second stage of composition, p. 441, above). All of these facts again suggest the existence of now-missing manuscript material—written earlier than DC MS. 74—for the churchyard books. To speculate, it seems possible that this notebook might have been partly filled in 1809–10 and might then have been used in the expansion of Books VI and VII along with DC MS. 75 material, at which point Wordsworth returned to DC MS. 74 and wrote most of this material into it, arranging those passages in sequence. A final phase of work might then have occurred for Books VIII and IX with the missing notebook holding early drafting, for Book VIII particularly, and those drafts then being reworked in DC MS. 74.

The relationship of DC MS. 74 to surviving manuscripts is also quite complex. The loose bifolia of DC MS. 75, closely connected to DC MS. 74, contain materials that both precede and rework what is in that manuscript. DC MSS. 74A and 80 are developed later than DC MS. 74 but in close relation to its work on Book V. Finally, DC MS. 73 is also involved, having as its final entries the copying out of material for Books VI and IX from DC MS. 74. At this point in the poem's development, then, we need to distinguish three groupings of work involving DC MS. 74 and other manuscripts: (1) work for Books VI and VII and the overlap between DC MSS. 74 and 75; (2) work for Book IX and overlap among DC MSS. 74, 75, and 73, discussed below in the seventh stage of *Excursion* composition; (3) work for Book V and *The Peasant's Life* (discussed below in the eighth stage of composition, together with the removal of *The Peasant's Life* from Book V). Work for Books VI and VII in DC MS. 74 may have partly overlapped with Book V composition: the entry of *The Peasant's Life* and Book V material suggests the existence of other passages already present in the notebook. *The Shepherd of Bield Crag* and possibly Book VI material for the story of Ellen appear to have been entered earlier than the Book V work.[32] After the bulk of *The Peasant's Life* and Book V material had been written into DC MS. 74, Wordsworth appears to have expanded Book VI and continued on into Book VII, writing out a fair copy of VII, 2–111, immediately after his first entry of VII, 2–253 (see 75ʳ–81ᵛ). (This material concerns the story of one of the previous pastors, who becomes in later years the Old Patriarch.)

Other material relating to Books VII, VIII, and IX in DC MS. 74 can be found in an earlier form in the sets of leaves that constitute DC MS. 75. DC MS. 75 does

[32]The fact that the Wanderer is still called the Pedlar in MS. 74, 69ʳ, suggests early entry, possibly before rev of MS. 71 when the Pedlar is changed to the Wanderer.

not exist in bound form; it instead consists of a series of seven loose bifolia of paper similar to what is in DC MS. 74; these bifolia are now arbitrarily assigned letters from "A" to "G." For the most part these bifolia precede DC MS. 74. The only exceptions occur with bifolia F and G, which are written on a thicker, bluer paper, and are also distinguished in that they are neatly copied by Mary Wordsworth (bifolia A–E and the Berg MS. are, for the most part, in Wordsworth's hand); this heavier paper most closely resembles that of DC MS. 74. Work on the lighter paper (bifolia A–E and the Berg MS) precedes the text in DC MS. 74; composition on the heavier paper (bifolia F–G) postdates that notebook.[33] Here are the contents of DC MS. 75 (and the Berg MS):

A	Story of Oswald (Book VII)
B	Stories of Ellen, Patriarch (brief mention, later omitted), and Woodsman (Books VI and VII)
C	Entry of two boys, Wanderer's Speech (Books VIII and IX)
D	Wanderer's Speech (Book IX)
E	Pastor's summing up (Books V, VII)
F	Description of churchyard / Patriarch's Tale (Book VII)
G	Description of churchyard / Patriarch's Tale (Book VII)
Berg MS	Description of Pastor's daughter (Book VIII)

Much about DC MS. 75 is uncertain. We cannot be sure, for example, of how much more of it there might have been, of the relative order of the materials, or of whether these materials were all written at the same time. Wordsworth's writing on separate bifolia rather than in a notebook suggests that the DC MS. 75 work has an intermediary status. It is written alongside DC MS. 74, but it is also possible that the DC MS. 75 sheets held some transitional material from another manuscript, now lost, or that there were originally far more DC MS. 75 bifolia than now remain. In practical terms the latter possibility may be less likely (if there were a large number of bifolia, Wordsworth would probably have bound or stitched them together). The argument for another manuscript, now missing, seems stronger.

When we look at the material in DC MS. 75, we can see that the appearance of the writing is not consistent. On bifolia A and B (the material describing Oswald and Ellen), the text is roughly written with many crossings out; that composition is clearly early draft. Passages such as that for the Woodsman and for the description of the two boys in B and C are on the whole much cleaner, though still with some crossings out; the Berg MS. has a similar appearance. Text on D and E looks like copied text, written out in preparation for reworking. Finally, the material later than DC MS. 74 on F and G is a neat fair copy by Mary Wordsworth. The material on bifolium E is particularly interesting: the first two pages are a copying out of text in Mary Wordsworth's hand, and the second two contain reworking of the same material in a much rougher form by Wordsworth. That the earliest text is fair copy strongly supports the argument for a prior and now-lost manuscript from which Mary Wordsworth worked. Furthermore, if we look

[33] See also *Chronology, MY,* p. 682, to which we are here indebted.

at the tale of Ellen, we find a fairly rough draft of it on the DC MS. 75 bifolium but a neatly copied version in DC MS. 74 (from 58^{r} to 68^{r}), which includes the DC MS. 75 material as its starting point but is considerably longer than what is on the bifolium. The additional material in DC MS. 74 is surely copied from somewhere, but no previous version of it survives.

The tale of Ellen, the only Book VI material in DC MS. 75, contains on $B1^{r}$ and $B1^{v}$ work toward the beginning of the tale. One interesting feature of Ellen's tale at this stage is that Wordsworth calls her "Emma," even tentatively giving her a full name at one point:

> The Queen of these gay sports
> If not in beauty yet in spritely air
> Ellen A[?]
> Was ~~Emma~~ Dalton
>
> (DC MS. 74, 60^{r})

The change to "Ellen" is indicated here, but the previous choice of "Emma" has some significance, since Emma is the name that Wordsworth often uses to represent Dorothy in his poetry.[34] At the very least, this early use of "Emma" signals that her story is important and one about which Wordsworth himself cares. This impression is confirmed at a dramatic level within the poem when, at the tale's conclusion, the Poet compares his emotions to how he felt at the end of Margaret's tale. At a personal level, Wordsworth's own emotional response is clear from a letter of 1815 to Mrs Clarkson, in which he responds to the criticism of a friend of hers:

> Could the anger of Ellen before she sate down to weep over her babe, though she were but a poor serving-maid, be found in a book, and that book be said to be without passion, then, thank Heaven! that the person so speaking is neither my wife nor my Sister . . . (*MY*, II, 190).

In work that became part of Book VII, DC MS. 75 contains the tale of the Woodsman in an early version in which he is described as if already dead (in *The Excursion* the living man walks past the travelers). Later draft toward this description can also be found in the Houghton MS., where lines from Book VII are entered on both sides of a sheet originally containing just the address panel of a letter addressed to "Capt. Luff." The Houghton MS. develops the portrayal much more fully and has the Woodsman striding past the characters, as in the published text. The survival of this scrap again reminds us that there must have been much more manuscript material for these stories.

Also in DC MS. 75, on $B1^{r}$ and $B2^{r}$, is material relating to the Patriarch of the Vale, perhaps once part of the description of the old Woodsman. This material for Book VII is then expanded in DC MS. 74, before part of the Patriarch of

---

[34]For an explicit example of the use of "Emma," see our discussion at this sixth stage of composition of *The Tuft of Primroses* in MS. 65, below. See also James Butler, "William and Dorothy Wordsworth, 'Emma,' and a German Translation in the Alfoxden Notebook," *Studies in Romanticism* 36 (1997): 157–171.

the Vale is copied out again in bifolia F and G of DC MS. 75. The story has its origins in *The Tuft of Primroses,* where revisions to the tale of the old man and his family—almost certainly dating from the time when the story was being prepared for inclusion in *The Excursion*—can be seen on the pages of DC MS. 65 (see *Tuft,* pp. 214–225). Relationships among DC MS. 74, the base text of DC MS. 65, reworking in DC MS. 65 for *The Excursion,* and DC MS. 75 are complex indeed.[35]

The story of the Patriarch of the Vale concerns the life of one of the earlier Pastors in the valley who lives to become its oldest inhabitant. In extreme old age, however, his family is tragically killed by plague, leaving him the only survivor. The tale is worthy of note for the way in which a sense of audience is bound up with its telling across the different texts. In the first version for *The Tuft of Primroses,* at the point at which all the family has died and only the old man is left, Wordsworth had envisaged an audience outside his tale (where Dorothy is again given her literary identity as "Emma"):

> Methinks that Emma hears the murmuring song
> pure
> And the ~~glad~~ Ether of her Maiden soul
> Is overcast, and thy maternal eyes
> Mary, are wet, but not with tears of grief
> (DC MS. 65, 37^{r}; *Tuft,* p. 219)

In such details about the audience's response, *The Tuft of Primroses* anticipates, in terms of form and intention, the later epitaphic books of *The Excursion.* Although *The Tuft of Primroses* is a first-person piece, it incorporates into the narratives both a response to them and a sense of a wider audience, techniques that become even more important in the dramatic context of *The Excursion.* In the version of the tale revised for *The Excursion,* those lines about Emma and Mary are omitted, but passages on the verso pages of DC MS. 65 and in DC MS. 75 give the comments of those looking on as the tragedy occurred:

> How will he face the remnant of his life
> What will become of him we said, & mused
> In vain conjectures
> (DC MS. 65, 36^{v}; *Tuft,* p. 217)

[35]The entire final version of the Patriarch of the Vale as it appears in *Exc* is present in MS. 65, although the text is constructed in a quite complicated way. The first two lines "Our very first in eminence of years / The Patriarch of the Vale" are taken from 37^{r} (see *Tuft,* p. 219). The text then jumps back to halfway down 36^{r} at "Death to the happy House" and follows through to 37^{r}, to the line "And little smiling Grandchild were no more." At this point it jumps across to the verso reworking on 36^{v} (p. 217) all of which is used, and then ahead to the last page of verso reworking on 38^{v} (see *Tuft,* p. 225), which begins halfway through a line with "too many & too keen." The half-line missing from this page ("Of unsunn'd griefs") can be found on 38^{r}. It is evident from the comprehensiveness of this material that it was rewritten to follow text in MS. 74 (anticipating its entry into the poem at a later point), although the tale is not actually entered in this MS. The only place where the Patriarch's tale appears copied out for inclusion into *Exc* is in MS. 75 on the last two leaves of bifolium G. This version runs continuously on at points where material jumps from original recto to reworked verso material in MS. 65, thus clearly showing the incorporation of the new work.

This version creates an audience within the story itself, as well as the audience outside the tale.

Finally, that outer level of audience also changes in intriguing ways as the story of the Patriarch develops in *The Excursion*. In DC MS. 74, before telling the tragic part of the tale, the Pastor breaks off in a passage not retained in the published poem:

> This said, abruptly from his seat he rose
> Nor, at that moment, were his audience free
> from some uneasy feeling of regret
>   kind
> That he in ~~fond~~ compliance with their wish
> A Task had undertaken which must needs
> Excite some painful and disturbing thoughts
> Unfit for Strangers to participate
>   (DC MS. 74, 82^r)

Here the reason for a break in the story is the Pastor's personal knowledge of the family and the closeness of the material to him. The nature of this breaking off, immediately before the tragic heart of the tale, also resembles similar moments as the Wanderer in Book I recounts Margaret's story, and as the Solitary in Book III tells of his own tragedy. In the published poem the Pastor's pause is omitted, and audience reaction occurs at the end of the tale: a calm silence is broken by the Wanderer, whom the Poet thinks may be "moved by fear":

> Lest in these passages of life were some
> That might have touched the sick heart of his Friend
> Too nearly. . . .
>   (VII, 312–315)

In the final version of the Patriarch's story, then, uneasiness remains. Instead of being connected with the Pastor's feelings, however, it is—unsurprisingly in terms of its content—related to the Solitary.

Much of Book VII is to be found in DC MS. 74 in three main blocks of work, with the opening of the poem written first roughly and then rewritten immediately afterward. Some of this material draws on texts originally written for other purposes. After the tale of Ellen ends in DC MS. 74, for example, comes another section of epitaphic material on 70^r to 73^r, this time taken not from *The Tuft of Primroses* but from *Home at Grasmere*. This reused material becomes the Pastor's account of Wilfred Armathwaite, and it begins in DC MS. 74 with the description of a "green nook close by the churchyard wall." The origins of the passage that follows can clearly be seen in revisions made on the blank verso pages opposite the original text on the recto pages in *Home at Grasmere* MS. B (DC MS. 59, 21^v–27^r; *H at G*, pp. 322–343). As with the work from *The Tuft of Primroses*, revisions on the pages in *Home at Grasmere* MS. B clearly work toward incorporation of the text into *The Excursion*. Wordsworth reused two stories from *Home at Grasmere* MS. B, that of the unfortunate Wilfred (who has an adulterous affair with his maid) and that of the widowed Father with Six Daughters. The immediately following tale in DC MS. 74, that of the Husband with Two Wives, was clearly written in the same vein as the recycled *Home at Grasmere* stories.[36]

Two other passages in DC MS. 74 have their origin even before Wordsworth found a home at Grasmere in December 1799. The first such passage concerns the "Cottage Boy" and his poverty of mind as described by the Solitary (VIII, 289–294, 304–308, 317–330). These lines draw on "There is a law severe of penury," one of several blank verse fragments composed in Germany in 1798 or 1799 (see *LB, 1797–1800*, pp. 307–308). DC MS. 74 follows "There is a law severe of penury" for its first twenty-six lines, at which point in *The Excursion* the Wanderer digresses to the example of the Pastor's sons and the value of childhood and then leads into a description of age "As of a final eminence" (DC MS. 74, 46^v). When he returns to his opening subject, the necessary liberty of mind and body for each man, the text then returns to the 1798 material from lines 129–138 and 142–153. The second fragment, "There is an active principle," immediately follows "There is a law severe of penury" in DC MS. 16; "There is an active principle" is prominently positioned as the opening to *Excursion*, Book IX, and is discussed at the seventh stage of composition, below.

The Book VII story of Oswald stands out, with the story of Ellen, as one of the lengthier churchyard stories in which the main character is named and the response given in some detail. In DC MS. 74 one block of text takes *The Excursion* up to the end of the story of Margaret Green that precedes Oswald's tale, and another block of text elsewhere in the manuscript picks up the story of the Elizabethan knight that follows it. Of Oswald himself, however, there is only a slight trace. DC MS. 74 begins the block of work on the Elizabethan Sir Alfred Irthing with the ending of Oswald's tale and the response to it, thus suggesting that the story of Oswald was written somewhere else (now not extant) in a reasonably full version. Work on bifolium A of DC MS. 75 for Oswald's tale is in some way connected (and presumably prior) to that missing manuscript, but we have only a very fragmentary sense of his story in surviving manuscripts. In any case, the articulation of a response to Oswald's tale in DC MS. 74 seems to act as a link passage for Wordsworth, leading him to begin new material in that manuscript.[37]

Other material for Book VIII occurs on $C1^r$, $C1^v$, and $C2^v$ of DC MS. 75 (the description of the Pastor's two boys and of the fish they have caught piled high upon a stone) and in the Berg MS. Book VIII work in DC MS. 74 jumps a little over a hundred lines from a description of the Pastor's cottage on 25^v to the conclusion of the Book and the withdrawal of the boys, who have otherwise not been mentioned in DC MS. 74:

> Abruptly broken off. The ruddy Boys
> Did now withdraw to take their

[36]In his revision of *Exc* for the edition of 1827, WW omitted the tale of the Husband with Two Wives (see p. 20, above).

[37]Something similar occurs on 82^r–82^v, where WW breaks off from the Patriarch's Tale by describing the Pastor's pause (and the audience's response) and then restarts Book VII with the Poet's grateful description of the effect of the tales upon him.

{[?~~well~~]
{[?] [?~~earned~~]
well-earn'd meal.
(DC MS. 74, 26^r)

Between Wordsworth's copy on 25^v (which ends at l. 491) and on 26^r (beginning at l. 602), several pages—perhaps eight in four conjugate leaves—are missing; those leaves almost certainly contained a version of intervening lines 492–601 (see Chronology: MY, p. 679). He elsewhere wrote out materials contributing to this account of the Pastor's boys—on bifolium "C" of DC MS. 75 certainly, and probably at a greater length than what has survived.[38] As with the lines describing the Patriarch of the Vale, the DC MS. 75 passages do not directly overlap with DC MS. 74 but represent a close working relationship between the two manuscripts.

The Berg MS. is certainly closely related to DC MS. 75, bifolium C; both manuscripts are written on the same kind of paper and contain lines related to the Pastor's family. Entries in the Berg MS. describe the walk down to the Pastor's cottage and the meeting with his daughter and wife. This draft corresponds loosely to lines 463–523 of Book VIII of the final poem, a section that comes before the passage (ll. 552–581) on DC MS. 75, bifolium C. Also, since lines in DC MS. 75, $C1^v$, compare one of the Pastor's boys to his daughter and mention that meeting ("The Other might be twin to that fair Girl / Who bounded toward us from the garden mount"), it seems highly likely that these two pieces were written at about the same time, with the Berg MS. slightly earlier.

Finally, in DC MS. 74 we also have another kind of textual overlap, between prose and poetry, similar to that which occurred in DC MS. 69 with material for *Guide to the Lakes.* On leaves 37^v and 125^r of DC MS. 74, there are passages of prose toward the introduction of the first *Essay on Epitaphs* into the notes to *The Excursion* and from the *Essay* itself. Leaf 37^v contains at its top a fair-copy writing out of the line of poetry (V, 984) to which the note will apply and then a continuation in prose:

But whence this tribute wherefor these
regards
The sentiments and opinions ~~here~~
here uttered in unison
~~uttered that follow~~ are ~~so much in~~
~~the same spirit~~ with those expressed
in the following essay upon epitaphs

According to Mark Reed, "The presence of this introductory sentence, an apology for the reprinting of the *Essay*, tends to imply . . . that the NB was in use during the late stages of preparation of the poem for the press" (*Chronology: MY*, p. 680). The nature of the entry itself supports this reading, although its position alone on a single page may mean that it was added at a later time than other

[38]MSS. 74 and 75 do not directly interlock: MS. 75, bifolium C, contains work for just thirty lines (VIII, 552–581) of what became one hundred in the published text.

material in the notebook.[39] The second prose passage relating to the *Essays on Epitaphs* occurs toward the back of the notebook on 125r. It begins, "If then in a creature endowed with the faculties of foresight & reason" and goes on to assert the belief in immortality necessary for the existence of monuments.[40] This long sentence is not in the first *Essay* as published in Coleridge's *The Friend* in 1810 and appears for the first time when the *Essay* was reprinted in Wordsworth's notes to *The Excursion.* The position of the sentence here, within the poetic manuscript, may suggest that this prose emerges as Wordsworth's own response to the poetry. It seems, then, that *The Excursion* can feed into other works just as other works feed into it.

The work leading from Book VII into VIII and then from Book VIII into IX was probably added at the next stage of composition, the seventh—slightly later within the manuscript development of DC MSS. 74 and 75. In terms of content, these materials shift away from the churchyard stories to wider issues concerning national education and industrial change.

VII

Seventh Stage: Between January 3, 1813, and May 1814

DC MSS. 74 and 75	Entry of Book IX material
DC MS. 73	End of Book IX

One of the last stages of composition for *The Excursion* is work for Book IX, which finds its opening lines in the much earlier passage written in 1798–99 in Germany, beginning "There is an active principle."[41] The first twenty-three lines of the text of 1798–99 are now placed in the mouth of the Wanderer. As they do elsewhere, DC MSS. 74 and 75 seem to work together in integrating the earlier text. It looks as though Wordsworth first copied the early passage from DC MS. 16 into DC MS. 74 on 26r–27r; this DC MS. 74 material is certainly closer to DC MS. 16 than to the published poem. Having copied that first block of text (IX, 1–26) into DC MS. 74, Wordsworth next turned to DC MS. 75 to extend *The Excursion* material that was to be incorporated within it before returning to DC MS. 74 and writing in the second block (IX, 129–138, 142–153), drawing again on DC MS. 16. So the writing on bifolia C2r and D1r of DC MS. 75 corresponds to the Wanderer's discussion of old age, which in the published text comes between the two passages copied into DC MS. 74 from DC MS. 16. On the other hand, the text on DC MS. 75, D1v–D2v, works toward the passage that follows what Wordsworth copied into DC MS. 74 from DC MS. 16.[42] There is also an

[39]The line of poetry above the note is probably copied back into this notebook from the text in MS. 74A (28v).

[40]See *Prose,* II, 52, ll. 102–112, and p. 305, above.

[41]See *LB, 1797–1800,* pp. 309–310, 728.

[42]The integration of the MS. 16 material thus develops across the MSS. as follows: MS. 74 (26r–27r, ll. 1–26); MS. 75 (C2r, ll. 57–94; D1r, ll. 106–131); MS. 74 (48v–50r, ll. 129–138; 50r–50v, ll. 142–153); MS. 75 (D1v–D2r, ll. 157–166).

echo of earlier material on DC MS. 75, C2^{r}, in the description of the Wanderer looking down from the mountaintop upon "the mighty stream of tendency." This passage loosely relates to material on the character of the Pedlar in DC MS. 14 (16^{r}; see *RC & Pedlar,* pp. 114–115), but only this single line is copied directly into DC MS. 75—and later into DC MS. 74, 47^{v}.

Book IX work is obviously the last stage of composition in DC MS. 74, because it is entered around the earlier material already present in the rather full manuscript. For example, at the end of the first entry, on 27^{r}, Wordsworth notes "See Mark" and makes a distinctive symbol (an elaborate letter "H"), a mark that refers to a similar one to be found at the top of 46^{v} where the text continues. Where Book IX material overlaps with DC MS. 75, the DC MS. 75 passages (on bifolia C and D) precede DC MS. 74; in general, though, the work for Book IX in DC MS. 74 is quite rough, with fairly heavy reworking in places. Book IX thus begins with copying into DC MS. 74 work from a manuscript of 1798–99 (with revisions toward *The Excursion* marked on DC MS. 16 in crossed-out lines [see *LB, 1797–1800,* p. 310n]), then moves to writing on loose bifolia (some or all of which have survived as part of DC MS. 75), and next returns to DC MS. 74 (where there is not really room for the entire Book IX).

Faced with this shortage of space in DC MS. 74, Wordsworth turned back to DC MS. 73, which at this point had only leaves 2^{v}–9^{r} used for Books III and IV work during the third stage of composition. In DC MS. 73 as it now stands, these Book III and IV passages are followed by the lines describing the ram reflected in the lake (9^{r}–9^{v}) and then the Book IX material beginning on 14^{v}. Continuous copy of the Book IX text in DC MS. 74 had broken off toward the end of the Wanderer's speech around line 358 (122^{v}, 124^{v}), which is not at an obvious stopping point. The lowest-numbered full entry of Book IX text in DC MS. 73 begins at line 292 on 19^{r}: "O for that happy period." In the published poem this passage in DC MS. 73 is the last part of the Wanderer's speech, separated by a pause from what precedes it, and represents his final fervent outpouring on behalf of national education. In DC MS. 74, the last block of text (119^{v}–124^{v}) also concerns this section but is quite scrappy, with a number of reworked lines. It seems possible that a little time may have elapsed between filling in DC MS. 74 and moving on into DC MS. 73, judging from the nature of this quite lengthy overlap between the manuscripts (i.e., Wordsworth probably did not just continue writing on from one notebook into the other). A theory of some lapse in time between notebooks may be supported by the entry of the passage about the ram into DC MS. 73 before the reworking and completion of Book IX.

The first entry of Book IX material into DC MS. 73—the ram passage—is another example of much earlier work being incorporated into *The Excursion.* It occurs on 9^{r}–9^{v} of DC MS. 73 with a passage relating to IX, 440–457, of the final text. This ram passage is clearly copied from DC MS. 48, where, as with some other early material incorporated into what became Book IV, it was a reworking of lines originally written toward *The Prelude.* An important difference between this passage in DC MS. 48 and DC MS. 73 occurs at the end of the description. DC MS. 48 reads as follows:

A strong temptation seiz'd me to dissolve
The vision but I could not & the Stone
[ ]natched up for that intent droppd
from my hand
(DC MS. 48, 34^{v}; *13-Bk Prelude,* II, 400)

In the passage as revised for Book IX of *The Excursion,* this change is made:

Ah pity twere to destroy
Or to disturb [?a] so fair a spectacle
And yet a breath can do it—these
few word
The {Lady / [?]} {whispered / [?]}
(DC MS. 73, 9^{r}–9^{v})

Again, we have a change of voice from the Poet's own to a character—this time the wife of the Pastor. There is also an interesting contrast between the masculine, active, and destructive impulse of the young poet in the first version, eager to destroy what he sees, and the passive, reflective voice of the female, content to look on, in the second.

After this passage about the ram, the main entry of Book IX in DC MS. 73 starts with the final section of the Wanderer's speech, entered at first quite cleanly (for the part that overlaps with DC MS. 74) and then from 21^{r} onward (around l. 358) with far more revisions on the pages.[43] For the most part, the later material looks like first draft, which Wordsworth then immediately recopied, more cleanly. Mark Reed reminds us that the content here—in particular, the remarks on national education—reflects Wordsworth's interest in the educational methods of Dr Andrew Bell ("the impassioned character of Book IX's advocacies is particularly likely to reflect the intense concern of late 1811" [*Chronology: MY,* p. 679]); the passage almost certainly dates after that time. The section of DC MS. 73 concerning educational ideas seems to be more emphatic than what is in DC MS. 74. We see this increased strength of feeling particularly in the call for the state to offer education to all. So, for example, DC MS. 74 reads as follows:

Binding herself by statute to secure
To all ~~the~~ the Children whom her Soil
[?~~Pl~~] maintains
forever within
Or place ~~at least well within~~ the reach
of all
The rudiments of Learning—
(DC MS. 74, 120^{r})

In this version the rather tentative "at least well within the reach" is replaced by the more affirmative "forever within," but the whole line still rather undermines

[43]An exception to this rough working occurs on 23^{r}–23^{v} with clean and continuous ll. 364–400, possibly suggesting an earlier version of them elsewhere, now lost.

the firmness of the desire that the state "Bind herself." In DC MS. 73, though, the same ideas are much more forcefully expressed:

> Binding herself by statute to secure
> For all the Children whom her soil maintains
> The rudiments of Letters & to inform
> The mind with moral & religious truth
> Both understood and practised
>
> (DC MS. 73, 19^{r}–19^{v})

Here the weak qualifying line has been removed altogether, and now Wordsworth is much more specific about what that teaching should concern itself with—not only practically ("the rudiments of Letters" rather than the more abstract "Learning") but also in terms of the moral aims of education.

Wordsworth turned back to the early pages in DC MS. 73 (14^{v}–18^{r}) to rewrite as fair copy the section running from the Pastor's hillside prayer to the very end of the poem (IX, 678–795). Presumably, the encompassing of a heightened and bloody description of pagan sacrifice within an extemporized Christian sermon at this point caused Wordsworth some difficulties in his drafting on 40^{r}–46^{r}. However, the second main reason for recopying this section is to clarify and confirm the very ending of the poem. One of the major criticisms of *The Excursion* by Wordsworth's contemporaries concerned the inconclusiveness of the ending, in which the Solitary walks away, his problems not explicitly resolved within the poem and himself unconverted.[44] In looking at the conclusion in manuscript form, then, it is interesting to consider how strongly Wordsworth is committed to ending in this way and whether there is a range of possible endings being considered. The ending appears—in two versions—in DC MS. 73 but nowhere else in the manuscripts. The first version, which looks like first-draft material, is on 46^{r}; the second, a revision of it, is written at the end of the recopied section on 18^{r}. They are reproduced here for comparison:

And gentle hearts & lofty minds approve,
                                        may
                                        [?may] { leave
My future Labours ~~shall~~ not { [?le]
                                                untold
                End.

This { (
        { if delightful hopes, as heretofor
[?Approved] }
        [?of] }
        Inspire verse   gentle
Sustain the serious song & ~~lofty~~ hearts
[?~~Be~~] Cherish
~~Are touchd~~, & lofty souls approve the
)
                                past {

---

[44]See particularly Montgomery, whose praise for *Exc* is tempered by his dissatisfaction with the role of Christianity in the poem and its ending.

My future Labours may not leave
untold
(DC MS. 73, 46^{r})

And whether aught of tendency as good
And pure from further intercourse ensued,
This, (if delightful hopes as heretofore
Inspire the serious song, and gentle
Hearts
Cherish, and lofty minds approve the past)
untold
My future Labours may not leave ~~untold~~,
Finis—
(DC MS. 73, 18^{r})

The version on 18^{r}, above, incorporates the revision at the bottom of the passage on 46^{r}, but there is, on the whole, remarkably little reworking for the very end of a nine-book epic. Wordsworth seems to be sure that he wants to end in this way, and at this point. The poem's final line—a very open-ended statement—does not change, and at the end of each version Wordsworth asserts "End" or "Finis." There is no sense of the poem's petering out into an inconclusive conclusion. Rather, the decision to leave the poem open in this way is strongly affirmative. The final page of working on 46^{r} also contains in almost its entirety (one half line is at the bottom of 45^{v}) the complex Miltonic final sentence of the ending. This sentence consists of thirteen and a half lines of syntax left hanging and delayed by subclause after subclause, to be resolved only by the main clause and the conditional structure ("if delightful hopes . . . may not leave untold") of the final line. As well as being important for recapitulating the kind of open communication involved in *The Excursion* itself, this indefinite conclusion may also reflect Wordsworth's personal desire to go on and complete *The Recluse.* These lines are voiced by the character of the Poet, to the reader, but there is also a sense that Wordsworth is willing *himself* into the belief that his own "future Labours" may not be left "untold."

VIII

Eighth Stage: Between January 3, 1813, and May 1814

[MS. not extant	Book V without *The Shepherd of Bield Crag* and *The Peasant's Life* copied from DC MSS. 69, 70, 74, 75 bifolium E]
DC MS. 74A	Fair-copy version of Book V (probably mid-1814)
DC MS. 80	Separate version of *The Peasant's Life*
Morgan MS.	Revision of *The Peasant's Life* from DC MS. 80
DC MS. 73	First half of Book VI written
[MS. not extant	Full fair copy for printer]

Wordsworth at the seventh stage of composition had concluded *The Excursion* but without having finished it. The middle section concerning Books V and VI was still unresolved; it was thus probably at this point that he turned back to Book V and *The Peasant's Life* and made the decision to separate the two.[45] About the same time, he also decided not to include in *The Excursion* the drafting in DC MS. 74 for what we have called *The Shepherd of Bield Crag*. Neither *The Shepherd of Bield Crag* nor *The Peasant's Life* has been discussed in any detail so far, but it is necessary to do so now, bearing in mind that although the material was removed at this point, it was actually written at the fourth stage of the poem's development. Both pieces are to be found in DC MS. 74, with one part of *The Peasant's Life* also copied into DC MS. 80 (with a few lines then revised in the Morgan MS.). In our edition *The Shepherd of Bield Crag* (as it appears in two versions in DC MS. 74) and *The Peasant's Life* (in its DC MS. 80 state) are given as reading texts in Appendix II, below.

The Shepherd of Bield Crag is strongly reminiscent of Wordsworth's stories of local shepherding life in Book VIII of *The Prelude* and also bears some resemblance to the account in *The Brothers* of the shepherd falling to his doom. Here the shepherd of Bield Crag also falls to his death, and his neighbors find his body guarded by his dog. De Selincourt and Darbishire compare *The Shepherd of Bield Crag* to Wordsworth's poem *Fidelity* (published in 1807), and they offer a possible reason for the poet's omitting it from *The Excursion*: "Perhaps W. concluded that the tale bore too close a resemblance to that of Gough and his faithful dog" (*PW*, V, 463). The pages where *The Shepherd of Bield Crag* occurs in DC MS. 74 (43^v–46^r) were once carefully removed from the actual notebook (i.e., the pages are now present but are not physically attached to their stubs). On those pages are an initial copy of the tale, followed by revision, another copy of the story, and then more revision.

In the context of *The Excursion*, there are a number of possible reasons for omission of *The Shepherd of Bield Crag*. When the tale begins on 44^r in DC MS. 74, it is clearly being situated within *The Excursion*; this first complete copy gives a straightforward account of the shepherd's life and death. Revision at the top of the facing 43^v reveals different starting points for the piece, with Wordsworth seeming to alter the focus of his tale as he revised. In the middle of 43^v, he apparently seeks to honor the shepherd as a worthy protector of his animals: "Venturing to take his well known way in quest / Of some endangered straggler of his flock" (43^v). Only at the bottom of that page does the focus shift from the man himself to his dog and its devotion: "To thy sad mishap / A word shall be devoted for the sake / Of a dumb Friend and servant" (43^v). There is then a slight sense of uncertainty whether the center of this tale is the man or the dog, or both; subsequent revision rearranges major sections of the narrative, and places both the tale and a moralizing comment in the mouth of the priest.

In addition to this initial uncertainty over focus is the ambiguity of the story's potential positioning within *The Excursion*. De Selincourt and Darbishire suggest that the story was intended to come after the tale of Wilfred Armathwaite in Book VI, thus contrasting the guilty adulterer roaming the hillside in torment

[45]This decision could have been made earlier but probably not much earlier, since the first half of Book VI (which cannot have been written until the decision was made) is entered after the Book IX material in MS. 73.

and abandoning his duties to the shepherd who "range[s] the Coves and Heights with different aim, / Far different thoughts" (44^r, ll. 4–5). The use of "Far different" here certainly suggests that the shepherd's portrait stands as a positive contrast to whatever has gone before. The Old Pensioner of Book II, however, is also referred to in drafting for *The Shepherd of Bield Crag* ("More hapless than the Old Man whom we this day / Have given to earth!" [44^r, ll. 7–8]).

Reed suggests that the two first pieces to be written into DC MS. 74 were the story of Ellen and *The Shepherd of Bield Crag*. If so, it seems possible that, at a relatively fluid stage of composition, Wordsworth was keeping his options open. Although De Selincourt's and Darbishire's suggestion for its placement after Wilfred Armathwaite's tale in Book VI is convincing, the fact remains that *The Shepherd of Bield Crag* could, potentially, come after a number of other tales: that of the Unrequited Lover at the start of Book VI (who wanders the hills searching for plants for himself and his beloved); and, less convincingly (since they are not shown to "range the hills"), the Persevering Miner or the Unamiable Woman. It seems possible, then, that *The Shepherd of Bield Crag* might have been more valued in relation to its context than in its own right.

When we turn from *The Shepherd of Bield Crag* to *The Peasant's Life*, we are confronted with a much more significant change to the draft text in preparation for publication. *The Shepherd of Bield Crag*, one brief story among many, is easily removable. Work for *The Peasant's Life*, on the other hand, is present throughout DC MS. 74 (with sections reworked in DC MS. 80 and the Morgan MS.). The point to bear in mind is that *The Peasant's Life* at the time of first composition was draft for Book V and becomes a separate text only by virtue of Wordsworth's removal of it.[46] *The Peasant's Life*, told by the Solitary, is unusual in the context of *The Excursion* in not being centered on a single, known individual but in presenting a far more "generic" portrait. At this stage the story seems to be integral to Book V, and yet when we turn to the fair copy of Book V in DC MS. 74A, most of it has been removed with the remainder "translated" into a different kind of voice. We are not presented here with a narrative that is simply cut from the later version of the poem. Instead, *The Peasant's Life* is a substantial piece of poetry that is written in one form, for one purpose and function within the poem, and that has that function completely altered by the later context in which it is presented. We could consider *The Peasant's Life*, then, as having a kind of double existence—as narrative and as discourse—both parts of which this edition enables us to consider. As *The Peasant's Life* develops and moves away from the narrative account of the Peasant boy's birth and into a more satiric attack on church ritual and on the hard life of rural toil, that material overlaps with Book V and is retained in the final poem. Where the poetry swerves off into elements describing the cycle of the peasant's life, this narrative material is not retained.[47] In the transcriptions in this edition of DC MS. 74, DC MS. 80, and

---

[46]The title is not WW's but editorial. EdeS and Darbishire edited an eclectic version of the text in *PW*, V, 432–441; for our shorter text of *TPL* (taken from MS. 80), see Appendix II, below.

[47]Passages retained for Book V that were originally written as part of *TPL* are (in the order in which they occur within *TPL*) V, 892–894; V, 413–414; V, 259–288; V, 290, 291–326; V, 600–611; V, 327–361; V, 612–620; V, 387–391, 392, 394–406; V, 423, 428–431, 432–435.

the Morgan MS., we provide right-margin, italic line numbers (labeled *TPL*) to show 551 lines of *The Peasant's Life* corresponding to the version entered in DC MS. 74 before a large part of the tale was removed from *The Excursion.*

In *The Peasant's Life* as it exists in DC MS. 74, the whole piece comes from the mouth of the Solitary and gives us a narrative with a double purpose. Primarily it is intended to make a political statement about the poverty of rural life that others tend to idealize; but at the same time (whether the Solitary originally intends it or not), the account becomes in part a kind of celebration of the life of the peasant, which contains simple pleasures in spite of its difficulties. The narrative presents a universalized, cyclical depiction of a peasant's life. The Solitary states of the graves, "I know no more what Tenant each contains / Than doth the grass that roofs it" (DC MS. 74, 33^r, ll. *20–21*). Thus the Solitary tells a very different tale from any other in *The Excursion* and marks a clear distinction between his tale and the Pastor's tales, which depend upon the Pastor's having known the living men and women who now reside beneath the turf.

The core description of the Peasant is a fine and sensitive piece of writing and paints a touching portrait of rural life. In the end, however, in the context of *The Excursion,* there were strong reasons for Wordsworth to remove the narrative from his final text. The first such reason relates to the depiction of the Solitary, who narrates the tale. On the inside back cover of DC MS. 74 come a few lines of unused draft clearly related to *The Peasant's Life,* in which the Solitary states, "Such the [?condition] of mankind, yet once / Out of myself I speak & [?nearly touched]." In the published *Excursion* the Solitary always, and only, speaks "of himself," a fact that emphasizes his damaged, self-centered personality. But in *The Peasant's Life*—as in the two lines just quoted—we see the Solitary not only as conscious of his own limitations but also attempting "yet once" to articulate in a different way. The story of the Peasant, as it exists in manuscript form, does not show the Solitary as empathizing with a particular individual, but it does, nonetheless, present him as being capable of strong feeling on behalf of others not related to him. As such, the account of *The Peasant's Life* works against the Solitary's character, which is more narrowly presented in the published text.

A second reason for removing *The Peasant's Life* relates to the possible positioning of this lengthy tale. Some of its early lines (see DC MS. 74, 32^r, ll. *5–14*) compare directly with Book VI, 607–615, a point in the final poem at which the churchyard narratives are interrupted by a disquisition upon the graves. It seems possible that the first half of Book VI was one intended position for *The Peasant's Life* but that the story grew much too large to fit there. De Selincourt and Darbishire give its extreme length as the reason *The Peasant's Life* was dropped, stating that it "was ultimately rejected as disproportionate" (*PW,* V, 432). With the passage amounting to the approximate length of a third of a book, its length is clearly a problem; even worse, *The Peasant's Life* must be intended to come somewhere in Books V and VI, books that themselves are already beginning to overflow with other stories by the stage of DC MS. 74.

But it is not simply a question of the length of *The Peasant's Life* in relation to Book VI; there is also the issue of the wider intentions of the other stories within these books. The Solitary's tale of the Peasant has its cyclical elements but ultimately makes the point that the rural poor are not able to see that cycle through to the end. Even though the Peasant experiences a full "Spring," the Solitary asks:

> Yet where is glowing Summers long rich day
> That ought to follow faithfully express d
> And mellow Autumn . . .
> (DC MS. 74, 102^r^, ll. *483–485*)

The Peasant is cheated of his natural inheritance: a long and full life. In comparison with the Pastor's tales of the churchyard, which would form the material to be put alongside *The Peasant's Life* in some way, this latter story can have only a negative effect. If the Pastor is trying to celebrate the individual lives of the dead, however humble, and to take lessons from them, the Solitary's narrative of the Peasant seems to present a direct challenge to such an attempt. The question of what the living can gain from the dead is thus supplanted by that of what the living should be doing for the living. *The Peasant's Life,* then, has the potential to subvert one of the central messages of the poem as a whole, and this fact seems a strong reason for removing it.

We do need to bear in mind, though, that Wordsworth does not simply "remove" the whole text. Instead, he cuts into it, breaks it up, and retains the points at which the Solitary is more discursive, while removing the core narrative of the *Life* itself. The main passages that Wordsworth takes out of *The Peasant's Life* and then reemploys in sections of debate in Book V are the description of the Peasant boy as a baby and his baptism (*TPL,* ll. *92–287*); the Solitary's attack on such rituals (ll. *132–166* and *185–218*); the Solitary's sarcastic praise for rural labour (ll. *173–184*); and short passages dealing with the failure of the full natural cycle (ll. *466–470, 483–495, 504–508,* and *514–517*).

As it expanded, Wordsworth may have considered some of *The Peasant's Life* material for Book VI. If so, it might also explain why Wordsworth begins his earliest work for Book VI (apart from the story of Ellen entered in DC MS. 74 before Book V work) with a discussion between characters that comes halfway through the book in the published poem (VI, 590; DC MS. 74, 89^r^). He was perhaps contemplating placing *The Peasant's Life* narrative in the first half of Book VI prior to that discussion. Wordsworth's beginning with the second half of Book VI may have occurred because the poet already had the story of Ellen written elsewhere (in a manuscript now missing) and, having inserted this story into DC MS. 74, he continued on from it. Starting in the middle, however, may also have been necessary because Wordsworth was not certain how much space Book V and *The Peasant's Life* material were going to take up—or whether *The Peasant's Life* was going to extend beyond Book V and become part of Book VI. Such uncertainty would explain the fact (which otherwise seems strange) that the first half of Book VI in DC MS. 73 is added *after* Book IX and the conclusion of the whole poem within that book.

It follows that the first half of Book VI in DC MS. 73 could have been written only after Wordsworth's decision not to include *The Peasant's Life* in *The Excursion.* At about the same time, Book V would have been copied into an interim manuscript (now lost), which must have drawn upon the opening lines in DC MS. 70, on DC MS. 74, and on the reworking of that material in DC MS. 69. From this consolidation of material, Mary produced a fair-copy version of the whole of Book V, without *The Peasant's Life*, in DC MS. 74A. The shortened version of *The Peasant's Life* entered in DC MS. 80 may have been written out either at this point or slightly later, after Wordsworth had decided not to use the material in Book V but with the possible intention of using or publishing it elsewhere. So Books V and VI, in spite of being quite fully drafted in DC MSS. 74 and 75, still needed additional work at this final stage of composition.

DC MS. 74A exists as an unbound set of four gatherings and a loose bifolium; the loose bifolium, at one time sewn at the front of the four gatherings, contains revision of what appears in the opening gathering. Fair-copy text in DC MS. 74A, largely in Mary Wordsworth's hand, contains most of Book V as it exists in the published *Excursion* but with some additions and omissions. The manuscript brings together work from DC MSS. 69, 70, 74, and 75 E; DC MS. 74A was clearly written at a relatively late stage of the poem's development. Mark Reed points out that the paper of DC MS. 74A is similar to that of DC MS. 75, and he dates both manuscripts to "perhaps early 1814" (*Chronology: MY*, p. 682).

DC MS. 74A seems to have been dictated to Mary, as occasional errors suggest.[48] An interesting mistake creeps into that manuscript in the naming of the Wanderer by his earlier title of "Pedlar" on 13^{r} (l. 475) and 14^{v} (l. 559). Since all Book V material was written after the decision to change the name had occurred, the error may have come about as a result of Wordsworth's oral dictation to Mary in which he momentarily forgot the name change.[49] Another characteristic of DC MS. 74A makes clear that its writing comes near the end of the compositional process: the increased use of punctuation and speech identifications within the manuscript. So, for example, we are given the final version of lines first entered in DC MS. 74:

> The narrow avenue of daily toil
> For daily bread"
>   "Yes!" buoyantly exclaimed
> The pale Recluse– "Praise to the sturdy plough
>   (V, 601–603; DC MS. 74A, 15^{v}–16^{r})

> The narrow avenue of daily toil
> For daily bread. Praise to the sturdy plough
>   (V, 601–603; DC MS. 74, 37^{r})

Comparison of the passage in DC MS. 74A with what is in DC MS. 74 (where it occurs as part of *The Peasant's Life*) immediately shows how DC MS. 74A clarifies voice, speaker, and breaks in speech—an essential element in the poem that

---

[48]Examples of possible dictation errors include "Troubles" for "Trembles" and "two" for "too" (13^{v}, l. 503) and the partial entry of "Divine" on the previous line before Mary realizes her mistake (29^{v}; ll. 1018–1019).

[49]The same error occurs in MS. 74 on 69^{r}–69^{v}.

earlier *Excursion* manuscripts in general pay little attention to.[50] In this example we also see a change from the single voice of DC MS. 74 to the division of the same speech into two voices in DC MS. 74A and the published poem. This clear distinguishing of speakers occurs surprisingly late in the poem's manuscript history. The lack of attention throughout the compositional process to the dramatic framework almost certainly has consequences for the presentation of the published poem, in which the speakers are not always absolutely distinct.

DC MS. 74A is important in that it creates a clean final version of Book V with most of *The Peasant's Life* removed and the remainder fully integrated. The development of Book V thus occurs in this order: DC MS. 74—DC MS. 69—possibly missing MS.—DC MS. 75—DC MS. 74A. Unfortunately, key stages here concern the work (now existing only as stubs) in DC MS. 69 and the material contained in the possibly lost manuscript. DC MS. 69 probably represented an early "holding" document for Book V work, before Wordsworth sorted out this section and finally decided to remove *The Peasant's Life.* The major decisions about what to remove and what to retain for Book V (and how to keep the book coherent after all those changes) may have occurred in a missing manuscript but also directly bear upon DC MS. 74A. At certain points DC MS. 74 is used in preparation for the fair-copy text in DC MS. 74A. An example of that close relationship occurs on the inside front cover of DC MS. 74, where the description of the peasant babe is copied out from its original integrated position as work for *The Peasant's Life* at 33^{v}–34^{r} and then revised on 12^{r} and 13^{r}. That section on the inside front cover treats the passage as a distinct block, separated from the original narrative context, and thus anticipates (closely though not exactly) its final repositioning in Book V in DC MS. 74A (7^{r}–7^{v}).

DC MS. 74 also shows the process of separation of Book V material from *The Peasant's Life.* Evidence for that major splitting up occurs in the continuous block of work for Book V running from 28^{r} to 40^{r} in DC MS. 74; Wordsworth there crossed out material (mainly on the recto pages) from the long account of *The Peasant's Life*; the crossed-out sections became part of a revised Book V. So on 28^{r}, for example, two blocks kept in the final Book V text (ll. 480–499) at the top and bottom of the page are crossed out, while a boxed extract in the middle is revised on the opposite page (27^{v}). The crossed-out sections closely resemble the Book V material copied into DC MS. 74A, but the revised lines are omitted. A number of pages that follow (29^{r}, 30^{r}, 31^{r}, 32^{r}, 35^{v}–36^{v}) also contain similar large-scale crossings out, frequently right across the whole page. Much of this work in DC MS. 74 is very close to the corresponding sections in DC MS. 74A.[51] DC MS. 74A also incorporates revisions written on the pages of DC MS. 74 throughout this section (V, 480–556, of the published text). The conclusion of Book V given at the back of DC MS. 74 (108^{r}) is also directly copied in DC MS. 74A (29^{v}) from line 1014 to the end. Elsewhere, however, DC MS. 74 is

[50]Another example of this kind of clarification occurs on MS. 74A, 14^{r}, where WW adds at l. 526 the words "The Priest continued" to indicate who is speaking.

[51]For example, the fair-copy text in MS. 74A on 13^{v}–14^{r} follows exactly the text in MS. 74 (29^{r}), but WW adds in MS. 74A (bottom of 13^{v} and top of 14^{r}) what became ll. 512–520 of the published poem.

considerably more fragmented and discontinuous than DC MS. 74A, suggesting the presence of interim material between the two manuscripts.

For the opening section of Book V, DC MS. 74A looks back to DC MS. 70, but it seems likely that an interim manuscript of some sort existed between these two surviving versions. Another version of the opening to Book V exists on the loose bifolium of DC MS. 74A, a revision of DC MS. 74A, 1^{r}–1^{v}. The expanded description given in those two sources describes the Poet's looking back on the Solitary's valley and being suddenly filled with a joyous impulse to speak: "A livelier strain of feeling thus broke forth / Transition such as animates the Grove" (DC MS. 74A, 1^{r}). The passage below, omitted from the final poem, is one in which Wordsworth attempts to widen the focus:

> [ ] happy Britain! heaven protected Isle,
> From that immense Metropolis through all
> Her
> {~~Her~~   {C   { ies
> {Thy humbler {cit {[?es] Towns and Villages
>   her
> To the bare rock upon ~~thy~~ sounding shores
>   her   { [?P]
> And ~~thy~~ remotest Dwelling- {places—blest
> Oh my beloved Country, favoured, blest
>   (DC MS. 74A, loose bifolium, 1^{v})

The attempt to unite the nation through the Poet's vision here and his nationalistic feelings strongly resemble those of the Wanderer toward the end of his speech in Book IX (ll. 387–391). These additional lines for Book V go on to contrast the liberty of Britain with the slavery of France. France may possess hidden valleys similar to those of the Solitary's, but the French ones are inhabited by a people "Born to be Slaves and ripened for the Sword" (DC MS. 74A, loose bifolium, 2^{r}). Again, this debate over man's freedom and liberty, the birthright of all, is the focus of the Wanderer's speech concerning "Britain's noble Race in freedom born" (IX, 395). The closeness in subject and tone between these rejected lines for Book V and the climactic declamation of *The Excursion* seems one possible reason for removing the lines from Book V. Another reason for that removal could be that the Poet's declaiming in this way makes the opening to Book V very similar to that of Book VI, where the Poet directly apostrophizes: "Hail to the Crown by Freedom shaped" (VI, 1).

DC MS. 74A also draws upon material in the surviving leaves of DC MS. 75, bifolium E (which is written on the same kind of paper as DC MS. 74A). That bifolium contains material for the end of Book V and the Pastor's summing up. A long additional passage for the concluding section of Book V appears on bifolium $E1^{r}$–$E2^{r}$; it is retained and reworked in DC MS. 74A (26^{r}–27^{v}) but is not included in the published poem.

The Peasant's Life is reworked in DC MS. 80, which includes a revision from DC MS. 74 of the core of the tale, describing the peasant's stealthy lovemaking, marriage, and child. This section of about ninety lines, omitted from DC MS. 74A, is without doubt one of the most attractive sections of *The Peasant's Life* in its 551-line state in DC MS. 74. Wordsworth wrote out the shortened version in DC MS. 80, with some revision; further revision to a few lines occurs on the single leaf of the Morgan MS. It seems likely that the copy of *The Peasant's Life* in DC MS. 80 was produced at about the same time that DC MS. 74A was copied with this material omitted. De Selincourt and Darbishire include one account of these lines within their composite version of *The Peasant's Life* (see *PW,* V, 432–441). The state in DC MS. 80 has been reproduced here (in Appendix II) as its own reading text: Wordsworth's reworking of the fragment in DC MS. 80 suggests that this version is what Wordsworth wished to preserve of *The Peasant's Life.* Since we also know that DC MS. 80 was used to collect a number of pieces in preparation for Wordsworth's edition of his *Poems* (1815), the presence of *The Peasant's Life* in that manuscript offers the possibility that the poet was thinking of publishing this shortened version in 1815.

The final area of overlap among DC MSS. 74, 75, and 73 concerns Book VI. The first half of Book VI seems to be the very last section of the poem to be written; it was apparently added to DC MS. 73 after the conclusion of the poem (Book IX) had been entered. At first glance, such delayed writing of the first half of Book VI seems strange, since there is nothing remarkable about it that might necessitate such a delay. However, as already suggested, it seems likely that the real reason for postponement has to do with questions concerning what was actually going to be included in Book V and whether *The Peasant's Life* material might be placed as the first half of Book VI. The final decision about the contents of Books V and VI seems to have occurred only after Book IX had been completed. At this point Wordsworth apparently decided to remove *The Peasant's Life* and therefore had Book V written out again in fair copy by Mary Wordsworth in DC MS. 74A. Having finally made this decision to omit *The Peasant's Life,* the poet then saw that he had to go back to Book VI, which had been written only from lines 590 onward in DC MS. 74.

The first half of Book VI (ll. 1–537) makes its appearance on leaves 46^{v}–65^{v} in DC MS. 73 (leaf 46^{r} is the last one of Book IX material). If we look at the content of Book VI, we can immediately see that the late date of its writing is felt in the published poem. Book V ends with a speech by the Pastor, anticipating the epitaphic stories, but Book VI opens with a slightly dislocated "Poet's Address to the State and Church of England." When we realize that this opening was probably written after Book IX (with the Wanderer's call upon the state to take care of its people), then the start of Book VI can be seen to come out of a slightly different mood than the churchyard stories around it. That opening represents a sudden shift into a high poetic and monologic mode, uttered as an apostrophe by the Poet, and the sense that it is slightly out of place remains in the published poem. Otherwise, there is nothing remarkable about the rest of the material in the first half of Book VI, since it consists of a series of epitaphic tales: that of the Unrequited Lover, the Miner, the Prodigal Son, and the Hanoverian and the Jacobite. Book VI entries in DC MS. 73 end at the conclusion of the story of the Hanoverian and the Jacobite (l. 537). The text in DC MS. 73 thus does not run up to the point at which the Book VI material begins in DC MS. 74 (l. 590). Book VI in DC MS. 73 instead breaks off at the point where a brief discussion occurs in the published text, a discussion that concludes where the main entry in DC MS. 74 begins (88^{v}–89^{r}), with lines that were originally linked to *The Peasant's Life.* The material in DC MS. 73—apart from the opening section that contains some crossings out (particularly on 47^{v})—is cleanly written, largely in Wordsworth's hand. At least some of that material was probably in the missing manuscript that also contained earlier versions of the stories of Ellen and Oswald. So although the first half of Book VI may have been the last material to be entered into the "active" manuscripts in order to be located within the poem's final structure, much of its content could have been written at an earlier time.

Finally, the Wordsworth household prepared a final and neat manuscript—or series of manuscripts—of *The Excursion* to be used by the printer because the poem could not have been typeset from the messy manuscripts we have been considering. That printer's manuscript does not survive.

Transcriptions and Selected Photographic Reproductions

DC MS. 47

DC MS. 47—in use at the first stage of *Excursion* composition for work on Book II—is described in the Manuscript Census, p. xxii, above. For a discussion of this manuscript and the composition of *The Excursion*, see pp. 429–431, above.

Italic line numbers in the right-hand margins of the transcriptions and in the transcription notes refer not to the 1814 reading text in this edition but to the underlying pre-1813 text of *Excursion*, I–III, c. *299*; i.e., the state before Wordsworth revised this material following the death of his two children. This state of the underlying pre-1813 text reaches its fullest development in DC MS. 71. Bracketed line numbers at the top right of the pages of transcription in DC MS. 47 provide cross-references to the line count in the 1814 reading text.

For a complete photographic representation of the leaves of *Excursion* work in DC MS. 47, see pp. 504–521, below. The image size of the photographs of DC MS. 47 on pp. 504 and 521 is 114 percent of actual size; the image size of photographs on pp. 505–520 is 75 percent of actual size.

[12v] [II, 767–789]

The Housewife tempted by such slender gains II, 621
As might from that occassion be distill'd 622
Contriv'd as she before had done for me 623
d
A place to harbour also this Olm} man 624
Food gave him for his meals a blind dull 625
nook
Such as she had a kennel for his rest 626
This of itself not ill, would yet have been 627
{is was
Ill-borne in earlier life but h{e ~~had~~ now 628
The still contentedness of eighty years 629
And more than that that more torpid & 633
{;
more slow{,
He moved about beneath a Double Cloud
The punishment if punishment it were 634
Of spendthrift feats excesses of his prime 635
A duty & a heavy task to [?me] 637
It would have been to hold discourse 637, 638
with him
But he was a cheap pleasure to my eye 639
Calm inoffensive ready in his way 640
And useful to his utmost power and there 641
Our Dame knew what she had 642

[32v] [II, 398–401]

from below II, 269
{S
The {strain continued spiritual as 270
before,
[?partly]
Though, [?~~partly~~], I could recogniz the words: 271
{ey
The {[?] sang "shall in the grave thy love 272
be known
Though now I partly recogniz'd the [271]
words:

621ff. Rev of 49v, 49r. Cf. MS. 71, 58v–59v.

269ff. Alt for 35r. These lines are entered below draft of *Prelude*, VII, 616–622 (cf. *13-Bk Prelude*, I, 492; II, 354–355). Rev on 32v and 35r are in the same ink, but those on 35r are generally closer to MS. 71. Cf. MS. 71, 48r.

[33[r]] [II, 1–20]

In days of old how fortunately far'd II, 1
The Minstrel wandering on from Hall to Hall 2
e
Baronial Court or Royal cher{r'd with gifts 3
Munificent & love & Ladys praise 4
Now meeting on his road an armed Knight 5
beneath s roof
A Pilgrim now ~~within~~ an Abbey^ ~~lodg'd~~ 6, 7
lodg'd
One evening sumptuously / the next ~~perhaps~~ 8
{H
Humbly in a religiously {hospital 9
Or with some merry Outlaws of the wood 10
Or hapy shrouded in a Hermits cell 11
Withal from Robbers & from danger safe 12
By melody & by the charm of Verse 14
And with his Harp still pendent at his side 15
Familiarly as now our Labourers wear
Their Satchels when they plod to distant fields.
{One
Yet such a {Man so favour'd could not draw 19, 20
{faculties
By his glad {[?] more earnest bliss 20

[33[v]] [II, 21–35, 88–96]

From that eventful & wayfaring life II, 21
Than this same Man uncountenanc'd & obscure 22
Accoutred with his Burthen & a Staff 24
extract
And nothing better had the skill to ~~draw~~ 25
By grace of Heav'n from many a ramble, far 26
{L
And wide protracted through the tamer {land 27
{d
Of these our unimaginative {Days.— 28

He was a Man whom many sympathies
Had made me cleave to & we now pursued 33
Our journey beneath favorable Heavens 34
At leisure resting reading in the shade

The opening twenty-four lines of Book II draw upon draft in *Prelude* MS. Y (MS. 48); see *13-Bk Prelude,* II, 374–375.

Two words ("That in") at top left of page are related to *Prelude* draft on facing verso.

1ff. Cf. MS. 71, 34[r]–34[v].

6–8 Rev in rust-tinted ink. In l. *8*, the mark after "sumptuously" signals the insertion.

21ff. Cf. MS. 71, 34[v]–35[v].

Or talking of such matter as occurred
But when the Sun had for the third time 46
risen
My Fellow-traveller said with earnest voice 47
As if the thought were but a moment old 48
That leaving all encumbrances behind 49
{L
The day should be a day of {liberty 50
And I must yield myself without reserve 51
To his disposal. Glad was I of this 52
We started & he led towards the hills 53
Up through an ample vale with higher hills 54
At distance
~~Before us~~ crags austere and desolate. 55

[34[r]] [II, 335–359]

Along this Vale till noontide we advanc'd *II, 206*
When suddenly upturning he began 207
To climb upon one side of it a ridge 208
Of steep ascent his object being, I guess d 209, 210
{S
{some secret of the mountains Cavern, Fall 211
{W
Of {water or some boastful Eminence 212
Renown'd for splendid Prospect far & wide 213
We clomb without a Track to guide our 214
reach'd a heathy plain
steps
And on the summit ~~to a [?He] heathy Plain~~ 215
With a tumultuous waste of huge hill tops 216
~~Were brought a [?] region which I trod~~
~~In front~~ a savage region & I walked 217
Before us
With weariness when all at once behold 218
Beneath our feet a little lowly Vale 219
A lowly Vale & yet uplifted high 220
{M
Among the {mountains even as if the Spot 221
Had been from eldest time by wish of 222
theirs
So plac'd to be shut out from all the world 223
Urn like it was in shape deep as an Urn 224
Encompass'd round about with highest rocks 225
Which but in one small Opening to the 226
south
Sloped gently back elsewhere abrupt & 227
close.
A quiet treeless Nook with two green fields 228

206ff. Cf. MS. 70, inside back cover, and MS. 71, 45[v]–46[v].
215 "[?He]" is del by eras.

And one bare Dwelling one Abode no
more 229

[34ᵛ] [II, 360–381]

{P {T
It seem'd the home of {poverty & {toil II, 230
{W
Though not of {want: the little Fields made
green 231
By husbandry of many thrifty years 232
Paid chearful tribute to the moorland House 233
s}
There crow'd} the Cock single in his domain 234
do not find a coverts
The small Birds found no thicket there 235
find in spring
~~To shroud them~~ only from the neighbouring
Vales 236
The Cuckoo straggling up to the Hill-tops 237
{th
Shoute{d faint tidings of some gladder
place. 238
recess
Ah what a sweet thought I is here 239
Instantly throwing down my limbs at ease 240
Upon a bed of heath full many a Spot 241
Of hidden beauty have I chanc'd to espy 242
Among the mountains never one like this 243
So lonesome & so perfectly secure 244
Not melancholy no for it is green 245
And bright & fertile furnished in itself 246
With the few needful things which Life
requires 247
In rugged arms how soft it seems to lie 248
!}{F
How tenderly protected }{far & near 249
We have an image of the pristine earth 250
The planet in its nakedness were this 251

[35ʳ] [II, 382–402]

{sole
Man's only Dwelling {[?] appointed seat II, 252
{W
First, last, & single in the breathing {world 253

230ff. Cf. MS. 71, 46ᵛ–47ᵛ.
235 Rev below line is in rust-tinted ink.
239 Word "recess" is added in rust-tinted ink; "abyss" is entered in same ink as alt for "recess", 35ʳ, l. *264*.

252ff. Cf. MS. 71, 47ᵛ–48ʳ.

Without a Fellow near it or remote 254
It could not be more quiet: peace is here 255
Or no where days unruffled by the gale 256
Of public News or private years that pass 257
Forgetfully uncalled upon to pay 258
The common penalties of mortal life 259
Sickness or accident, or grief or pain. 260
  On these & other kindred thoughts intent 261
In silence by my Comrades side I lay 262
He also silent when from out the heart 263
abyss
Of that profound recess a solemn Voice 264
Or several Voices in one solemn sound 265
Was heard ascending mournful deep 266
and slow
{as ps} a s}
The Cadence {[?] of [?p]l}alms ~~the~~ pl}alm of 267
death
We listen'd looking down towards the Hut 268
But seeing no one meanwhil from below 269
{s [?now could hear]
The {Strain continued & I ~~recogn~~iz'd 270
solemn as before
Though now I [?shortly recognizd] 271
{y
These Words, "Shall in the grave th{[?er] 272
love be known
In death thy faithfulness." God rest his 273
Soul

[35v] [II, 403–423]

The Old Man exclaim'd abruptly breaking II, 274
silence
He is then dead God give him peace at 275
last.
  He scarce had spoken when those holy Strains 276
Not ceasing forth appeared in view a Band 277
Of rustic Persons from behind the Hut 278
Bearing a Coffin in the midst with which 279
They shaped their course towards the sloping 280
side
Of that small Valley singing as they moved 281
A sober Company & few the Men 282
Bareheaded & all decently attired 283
Some steps they thus advanc'd & then the 284
~~Pl~~ Psalm
Ended and from the stillness which ensued 285

---

264 See note to 34v, l. *239*.
269–272 Alt for 32v.

274ff. Cf. MS. 71, 48r–48v.

Recovering to my Friend I said, "You spake 286
{[?~~fancid~~] i}
I {[?thought] fanc {e'd with emotion as of one 287
Who must have been well known to you." 288
He was so
But let us to the House for I would have 289
Assurance of the manner of his death 290
Perhaps too tis not he but some one 291
else
Some other Tenant of the solitude. 292
So down a steep & difficult descent 293

[36r] [II, 424–443]

~~along~~ the
Tr}
We}usting ourselves, II, 294
we wound from crag to
crag
Where passage could be found & when the Train 295
r}
Who bore the Body having g}each'd the top 296
Of that offsloping Outlet disappear'd 297
I upon easy ground & there
~~We~~ landed ~~safely upon easy ground~~ 299
Stood waiting for my Comrade whe 300
And now were hasting forward when I
saw
{An invited me aside
{[?Is] object that ~~entic d my steps~~ a side 301
It was an Entry narrow as a door 302
Which after some short windings open'd out 303
ch}
Into a platform that by work of ar}ance 304
As seem'd & not design was, sheep-fold 305
wise
Enclos'd ~~within~~ between a single mass of rock 306
And one stone wall the floor was smooth & green 307
{C
And the small {compass of the space within 308
Shut out from view of any thing but sky 309
And passing clouds & where the rock & wall 310
Met in an angle hung a tiny roof 311
Or Penthouse which had been most quaintly 312
framed
By thrusting two rude sticks into the 313
wall
And overlaying them with mountain sods 314
Screen for a low sod seat beneath of width 315

294ff. Cf. MS. 71, 48v–49v.

And barely so to hold a full-grown 316
Man

{in
I les deliberate {[?f] the course I took 298
had landed upon easy ground [299]

[36v] [II, 445–467]

the whole
But which was plainly work of Childrens II, 318
hands
~~Both seat & little Canopy above~~
was throng'd
And here & there upon the grassy floor 319
With chiefly
{With
{[?Were] Baby houses ~~built of~~ small loose 320
stones
Together rang'd in circle or in square. 321
g }
The Old Man who to my summons [?h]}iving 322
way
Had enter'd look'd about him carelessly 323
when stooping down
stoopin[?g]
And now would have pass'd on^: ~~when I exclai~~m'd 324
With such ejaculation as attends
o}
~~Lo what is here & stooping dr}wn dr~~ew 325
forth
Upon some chance discovery I drew
A Book which in the midst of stones & moss 326
W }
And wreck of party colour'd earthen [?]}are 327
Finding a useful place had help'd 328
to build
One of those Baby structures. Gracious Heaven 329
Cried
~~Said~~ the Old Man ~~while In my hands~~ I 330, 331
held
The ~~Volume forth~~ it cannot but [?h]e is 330
which in my hand
And he is gone". The Book ^ ~~was swoln~~ 331, 332
Had open'd of itself for it was swolnd 332
~~with rain~~
~~Mouldy & damp & opening it I found~~ 333
With rain & damp I found to be a work [333]
~~With much surpriz a work in the French~~ 334
~~tongue~~

318ff. Cf. MS. 71, 49v–50r, 1r.
330 Phrase "he is" is a miswriting for "be his"; cf. MS. 71, 49v.

In the French tongue
~~No other than~~ a Nove of Voltaire
Un
His famous Optimist. [?f]}happy Man

[37r] [II, 468–489]

Exclaimed my Friend here then has been to
him
Retreat within retreat a sheltering place
had fits
Within how deep a shelter: he was one
Even to the last of genuine tenderness
Not lost to genuine tenderness of heart
And lov'd the haunts of Children here no doubt
He sometimes play'd with them & here hath
sate
Far oftener, by himself. This Book I guess
Hath been forgotten in his careless way
Left here when he was occupied in mind
And so must by the Children have been
found.
Heaven bless them & their innocent work
To what odd purpose have the darlings
turn'd
This monument of their unhappy Friend
8
17}o
Me said I the device surprizes less
I know not for what reason than to find
a book it is
Such Book in such a place". "~~The Book~~
replied
He answer'd not
~~My Friend is not~~^ ill suited to the man
at sight : str
And I was mov'd in seeing of it [?]} tis [?]}ange
I grant & yet more strange had been to see
{O
The Man who was its {owner dwelling here
With one poor Shepherd far from
all the world

336ff. Cf. MS. 71, 50r–50v.

348 The corrected line count, "180", appears to be in the same ink as the paragraph beginning at l. *349*; it is the only contemporary line count in the MS. and probably precedes resumption of composition at l. *349*. The actual number of primary lines through l. *348* is 178. WW may have rounded to the nearest multiple of ten or included two lines of rev.

[37v] [II, 490–513]

Our errand has it seems been thrown away II, 357
And I am griev'd less for my sake than yours 359
And least of all for him who is no more. 360
d} h}
By this the Book was in the Ol[?]} Man's [?]}ands 361
glancin on the
And he continu'd ~~on the open page~~ leaves 362
.}
~~Glancing~~ an eye of scorn } the Lover, said he, 363
doom
him
To love when hope hath fail'd whom no 364
dept
~~abyss~~
Of privacy is deep enough to hide 365
Hath yet his bracelet or his lock of hair 366
And that is joy to him: when change of times 367
Hath summon'd Kings to scaffolds do but give 368
faithful ~~loyal~~
The Servant who henceforth must hide his 369
head
Henceforth
~~His head~~ in whatsoever nook he may 370
his
{~~his~~ ste}
A Kerchief sprinkled with {the Marty}rs blood 371
a
And he too hath his comforter: how poor 372
Beyond all poverty how destitute 373
Must that Man have been left who hither 374
driv'n
Flying or seeking could yet bring with him 375
No dearer relique & no better stay 376
Than such a Book as this. I did 377, 379
not fear

[38r] [II, 513–517, 170–189]

{pd
To tax you with this journey as we step{t II, 380
covert ~~into~~ light
Fort from that viewless to open day 381
Said chearfully my venerable Friend 382
For I have knowledge that you do not 383
shrink

357ff. Cf. MS. 71, 50v–51v.

380–384 Cf. MS. 71, 51v.

From moving spectacles: Few words *384, 67*
may serve
To tell his story he was like my self *68*
Born on the hills of Scotland we had this *70*
In Common too that both of us were sprung *69*
From poor & lowly parentage & hence [*69*]
And from some noble personal qualities
He had awaken'd in me more concern
Than might seem just yet not so for his
Powers
Were bright & rare: but let me be more brief.
In piety and innocence he spent *74*
A studious youth & after proper course *78*
Of studies to the ministry was call'd *79*
pes
And went abrod for lack of better ho[?] *80*
As military Chaplain to a band [?] *83*
Of highlanders, his fellow country men *84, 85*
knowledge
In learni first in talents far the *88*
first

[38^{v}] [II, 192–196, 224–239]

Subjet to vanities yet [?prompt] *II, 91*
s
In every generoul feeling among these, *92*
Youn ardent less a pastor with his Flock *94*
many years
Than a Soldier among Soldiers ~~here &~~ there *95*
He went where fortune Led
~~He wander'd many years where fort~~une led *96*
~~By such communications [?well] prepar'd~~
To stifle tender scruples & take up
~~A virtue or vice as might befall~~
From ~~those with whom he lived.~~ But
nobler days
Open'd upon him & a nobler life. *97*
The vision that enchanted all mankind *98*
Save some few selfish hearts appeared *99*
in France

67ff. Cf. MS. 70, 58^{v}, 59^{r}, 60^{r}, 59^{v} and MS. 71, missing leaves 42–43 (see notes to 35^{v}–36^{r}), 39^{r}–39^{v}.

384a Repetition of this half-line on 41^{r} indicates repositioning of the Solitary's history (ll. *67–167*), which was originally placed after l. *384a*; see note to l. *384a* on 41^{r} and pp. 439–440, above, for repositioning of this history earlier in Book II.

74 The use of a different pen and ink begins here.

91ff. Cf. MS. 70, 59^{v}, 60^{r}, 61^{r}, 60^{v} and MS. 71, missing leaves 42–43 (see notes to 35^{v}–36^{v}, 41^{v}, 44^{r}), 39^{v}, 40^{v}.

97–101 Since these lines are not extant in MS. 71 (although they were probably once entered on missing leaves 42–43), line numbering is based on MS. 70.

Him did it rouze to a surpassing Joy 100
[?~~It rou~~]
~~Nor was it that a~~
Who was by nature fervent to disease 101
~~Than his of whom I speak. In joy & pride~~
{b
He {Broke from out his narrow sphere repair d 102
To London then a fountain of great hopes 103, 105
And there with popular talents preach'd 106, 107
the cause
Of Christ & of the new born Liberty 108
As one & leading to one glorious end 109
Intoxicating service! more than a that
A happy service for he was sincere

[39r] [II, 240–247, 257–268]

As vanity & fondness for applause would
~~suffer him~~ to
M}
Would suffer him to be. So}eanwhile the ship
Sail'd fairly [?flattering] course & he was blithe
Deeming himself a resting mariner
That righteous cause of freedom the old II, [110]
Man
Continue'd, now insensibly seduced
Beyond his first intention did we know
~~That righteous & most holy cause we know~~ 110
Combined in one hostility as friends 111
{av
Etherial natures & the worst of sl{[?]es 112
Was serv'd as seem d by advocates that 113
came
From regions opposite as heaven & hell [114]
One courage seemd to animate them both 115
From regions opposite as heav n & hell. 114
A victory had been atchieved & [?hope]
By perfect love of truth that cast out fear 130
~~Plagues follow'd on such mixture sprea~~ding 131
~~plagu~~es
While [?other] are advancing day by days
[?Stole b]
The strongest did not easily escape 132
And he what wonder? took a mortal 133
taint

---

100 "Joy" overwrites "in" above.
100/101 "[?It rou]" is del by eras.
109 The two unnumbered lines below l. *109* and the first two lines on 39r (all related to *1814*, II, 238–241), are omitted in MS. 70 and thus may also have been omitted in the first version of the passage copied in MS. 71 (on missing leaves 42–43); consequently, they are not given line numbers here, although a variant of these unnumbered lines is included on inserted leaves 40v and 41r in MS. 71.

Concerning the unnumbered lines at the top of 39r, see the note to 38v, l. *109*.
110ff. Cf. MS. 70, 60v, 61r–62r and MS. 71, missing leaves 42–43 (see notes to 35v–36v, 40v), 44r, 41r–41v.

i
An [?d] nfidel contempt of sacred truth 134
Stole by degrees into his heart & hence 135
For him & for his individual ~~loss~~ harm 136
faced
Life lik that Roman Janus double [?d] 137
Vilest hypocrisy the laughing, gay 138
a fear
Hypocrisy not leg gu'd with ~~pride~~ but 139
pride

[39[v]] [II, 269–288, 296–299]

[?There] all ~~was~~ / p~~u~~rity & ~~there~~
The sensual talker was the lib~~e~~ral man
Smooth words he had to wheedle simple souls *II, 140*
[?&] [?higher]
[?for] those ~~better~~] [?lessons]
for t
But to the ini[?] iate [?~~often~~] ~~of~~ the inner s[~~?~~] 141
was
Old freedom ~~seemd~~ old servitud & he 142
Was wisest whose opinions stoop d the least 143
To tried authority & known restraints 144
Whose creed for this at bottom was the truth 145
hy
Did in the light of false philosop [?r]y 146
Spread like a halo round a misty moon 147
Widening its circle as the storms advance 148

X
I do not wish to wrong him for his heart 153
light
Though vain in midst of such debasement still 159
Was generously disposed made more human
In a mix'd sort by [?poverty] itself
[?More sanguine]
And flattering views of outward circumstance
[?that quick to feel]
Public or personal: of feeling quick
Sanguine in temper
He still continued when worse days were come 167
To deal about his sparkling eloquence 168
Strugglin[?g] against the strange reverse with zeal 169
The look'd like happiness: but in despite 170

140ff. Cf. MS. 70, 62[r]–62[v], 59[v], 57[v] and MS. 71, missing leaf 43 (see note to 40[v]), 44[r]–44[v], 41[v].
153 The X signals the expansion and rev of ll. *153–167* on 40[v].

[40^{r}] [II, 300–320, 331–332]

Of all this outside bravery within *II, 171*
He neither had encouragement nor hope *172*
For moral fortitude & strength of mind *173*
Were wanting & simplicity of life *174*
And reverence for himself & last & best *175*
The love & fear of God the sense of God *176*
Sole feeling by the which we can sustain
True comprehensivenessess of intellect
The glory of the times [?fading] away *179*
The splendour which had given a festal *180*
air
To self importance hallow'd it & [?~~even~~] *181*
veiled
[?~~Con~~] From sight of his own eye this gone he lost *182*
~~All feeling of conviction~~
All joy in human nature was consumd *183*
And toss d about by liev[?e]ty & spleen *184*
[?fruitles]
And fruitles indgnation galled by pride *185*
Made desperate by contempt of men who gain [?d] *186, 187*
Without desert what he deserv d weak men *188*
Too weak even for his envy or his hate *189*
And thus beset & finding in himself *190*
Nor pleasure nor tranquillity at last *191*
For want of better prospect he [?withrew]
Into this place, as farthest from a *202*
world
Not moving to his mind *203*

[40^{v}] [II, 282–296]

I would not wrong him for he was a man *II, 153*
Of generous wishes & retain d in midst *158*
Of much debasement what he had received *159*
From nature an intense & glowing mind *160*
[?strength] of Liberty flow d past
[?was gone]
And when the strength of Liberty ~~decayed~~ *161*
And mortal sickness on her face appeared *162*

171ff. Cf. MS. 70, 62^{r}, inside back cover, and MS. 71, 44^{v}–45^{v}.
180 The page is torn above and through the "f" in "festal".
184/185 Pencil rev.
203 WW appears to have interrupted composition here, expanding and revising ll. *153–167* on 40^{v}, shifting the Solitary's history earlier in Book II between l. *55*, 33^{v} and l. *206*, 34^{r} (the passage is much rev in MS. 70). Composition resumed at l. *384*, 41^{r}, revising 38^{r} where the half-line *384* was followed by the half-line *67*. After l. *203*, the manuscript takes on the character of work in progress, with rougher drafts than earlier copy. See pp. 439–440, above.

153ff. Rev of 39^{v}. Cf. MS. 70, 62^{r}–62^{v}, 59^{v}, 57^{v} and MS. 71, 44^{v}.
161 Rev seems to have taken place in two stages: first, "decayed" is rev to "[?was gone]" and l. *162* entered; second, the rev above the line was entered.

He colour'd objects to his own desire
As with a Lovers passion, Yet his moods
Of pain were keen as those of better
men
And keener for his fortitude was less
Thus he continued when worst days
were come
And he continud when the evil day
Was

[41[r]] [II, 517–537]

From moving spectacles. But let us on
[?~~till~~] till
I follow'd, ~~but~~ he made a sudden stand
For full in view approaching through the
gate
That open d from the enclosure of green fields
Into the rough uncultivate'd ground
Behold the Man whom he had fancied dead
I knew from the appearance & the dress
That it could be no other, a pale face
{A t}
{[?T T]} all & meagre person, in a garb
Not rustic, dull & faded like himself
He saw us not though distant but
{sy few steps
For he was bu{[?isi~~ed~~] dealing from a store
Which on a leaf he carried in his hand
S} {nts by
[?Of]}trings of ripe curra{t ~~gift~~ with
which he strove
~~Mingling as I could hear endearing~~ word
With intermixture of endearing word
To chear a weeping Child a ruddy boy
That tottered by his side. They to the
grave
[?he]
Are bearing him my little Boy [?he] said
To the dark pit but he will feel
no p[?ai]
His body is at rest his soul
in he[?v]

384a This half-line, the same one as on 38[r], indicates later repositioning of the Solitary's history, so that it is not told as it is here while descending into the valley but earlier in Book II while ascending to the valley. See note to l. *384a* on 38[r] and pp. 439–440, above. Cf. DC MS. 71, 51[v]–52[r].

386/387 Pen testing here is in a darker ink and sharper point than previously used on the page but is similar to that beginning the half-line [*418*] on 41[v].

396 The overwriting "sy" is entered in darker ink, perhaps over partial eras.

398 In rev, WW inadvertently crossed out "gift" instead of "by".

403 The last word of the line in MS. 71 reads "pain".

404 The last word, written off the foot of the page, is almost certainly "heaven" as in MS. 71.

[41^v] [II, 538–555]

Glad was my Comrade now though he II, 405
at first
I doubt not had been more surprized than 406
glad
But now recovered from the shock & calm 407
& to ~~the~~
{&
He soberly advanc d{[?] ~~gave~~ the man 408
Gave}
{The}
{A Chearful greeting. Vivid was the light 409
Which flashed at this from out the 410
others eye
He was all fire the sickness from his face 411
Pass'd like a fancy that is swept away 412
Hands joined he with his Visitant a grasp 413
An eager grasp & many moment space 414
v}
Long after what was f}amishd had 415
return d
~~Amiab~~
the life
An amicable smile retained ~~its life~~ 416
~~Upon his hollow cheek~~ 418
Which it had unexpectedly received 417
Upon his hollow cheek. How kind, [418]
said
he
Nor could your coming have been better timed 419
world
For this you see is in our little Spot 420
^
A day of sorrow I have here a charge 421

[42^r] [II, 556–563, 573–583]

And speaking this he patted
e} tender[?ly]
~~Affectionately~~ And ten[?d] }rly he patte[?d] as he II, 422
spoke
{the
The sun-burnt forehead of {that weeping Child 423
A little Mourner whom it is my task 424

405ff. Cf. MS. 71, 52^r–52^v.
[*418*] "How kind" begins the use of a darker ink and sharper pen.

422ff. Cf. MS. 71, 52^v–53^v.
422 The line drawn below "as he" is in the same ink as the rev "tenderly" and may signal adoption of the original reading of the first line in MS. 71: "And speaking thus he patted tenderly".

om}
To co[?]}fort, but how came you, which your road 425
You cannot well have miss'd the funeral 426
train
[?h]}
They scarcely yet are out of sight, we [?th]}eard 427
The old man answer'd from yon rock 437
above
whose steep sides we
[?f} {~~reed~~]
~~Down which we~~ [?f}o{und] ~~a~~ passage to the [?plain] 438
down whose steeps we dropped into the Vale
The Hy[?m] they sang a solemn sound [?itruth] 439
Whereve[?er] heard but in a place like this 440
{than
Tis more {hu human. ~~Nothing is to me~~ 441
~~So chearing so ennobling so [?]~~
Many antient [?rights] [441]
of our [?rural ancs]
And customs ~~of the venerable~~ time [?~~are~~] 442
[~~?] [?grieve~~]
Pal
{Are
{[?Have] ~~gone;~~ or stealing from us; this I hope 443
[?will last]
~~To [?lose] the~~ [?least]
Forever; what a [?moving sig]
Will last forever. Who that has a heart 444
And does not feel the awfulness of life 446
whe
That moment ~~that~~ the corpse is lifted 447
up
In that one moment when

[42v] [II, 584–606]

In silence with a hush of decency II, 448
And from the threshold moves with song 449
of peace
{ome
And confidential yearnings to its h{[?ouse] 450
w}
Its final home in God. And [?t]}hen they go 451, 453
r}
A mute procession on thes lonely [?w]}oad 454
As is I know the manner in the hills
And pass some single tenement or lot 455
Of cluster d dwellings taking up again 456

427–439 Rev on 45r–45v.
443 The two lines below, for which conjectured readings are offered, have been formed in part by the scratching of a pen that has run dry of ink.

448ff. Cf. MS. 71, 53v–54r, 113v, 33v, 32r.

The monitory Voice. But most of all 457
Then when the body soon to stir no 459
more
From the church aisl is raised and 461
f}
b}orward
borne
Upon the shoulders of the next in love 462
The nearest in affections or in blood 463
[?also]
Have I not seen ye ~~too~~ my friend 464
[?must]
[?both]

[44[r]] [II, 633–644]

at this *II, 494*
I interpos'd though loth to speak and said 495
Can it be so among so small a band 496
As ye must neeb be here in such a place 497
I would willingly methinks lose sight 498
[?]
[?retiring]
Of a departing cloud. ~~We see replied~~ 499
~~The solitary even as we have eye~~
[?T] Twas not for Love [499]
~~an ardent~~
{a
Answer'd the Sick man ~~with~~ {[?] [?~~stead~~] voice 500
[?~~with~~] a careless
That I cam hither; ~~nor have~~ I found 501
neither have I found
Among my Comrade rational or [?] 502
t}
Enough of [?feeling a} enderneness or]
[?mood] love
[?in]
[?~~suff~~]
To} o}
[?]} undermine my firs resl}lve 505
Among my comrades that have power of speec [502]
Or o}
[?That]}ther conversation that is here 503
~~Enough of feeling~~
Temptation [?change] 504
~~Love so [?abund~~ant] as to ~~under~~mine [505]
~~My first resolve~~ [505]
My [?mood] or undermine my first [505]
resolves
Nor in such other converse [503]

The following leaf, 43, which has been torn out, presumably contained a draft of ll. *465–494*.

494ff. Cf. MS. 71, 54[v]–55[r].

494 The two words begin a new paragraph in MS. 71 and assume the missing lines on the torn-out leaf 43. See note to 42[v].

The bottom right of the page is torn.

as is here
prevailing
temp[?tion] . [504]

[44v] [II, 645–649]

I said said he speaking with like careless *II, 506*
voice
[~~?~~]
[?i]
a [?] [?f he had]
To that benign Old Man, great pity tis *507*
To [?treat] here ~~chearfully~~
~~Ye were not here~~ though [?in kindness] *508*
That ~~This your journey is~~
a [?ek]
[?e] [?we] [?sore]
That you are come a ~~little~~ *508, 509*
[?~~though scarcely can~~]
Though you & I [?have] different [?eyes]
That you are come too late else [?had] *[508, 509]*
you
That you
A few [?daily earlier] would have shew to *509*
you
What twas [?my] *510*
pity tis *[507]*
That with a word I cannot to this spot *[508]*
Transport you at my will an earlier *[508, 509]*
day
Had shewn you what it was [?Had] *509, 510*

[45r] [II, 647–663, 563, 568, 573]

That Fortune did not guide you to this *II, 508*
house
then
A few days earlier you would ~~then~~ have seen *509*
What stuff the dwellers in this solitude *510*
This little tempting innocent solitude *511*
Are made of an ungracious matter this *512*
yet
Which for truths sake & in remembrance *513*
too
Of former conversations with my friend *514*
I will tell nakedly and undeterred *515*
By reverence which is due to his grey *516*
hairs

506ff. Rev on 45r. Cf. MS. 71, 55r.

508ff. Cf. MS. 71, 55r–56r, inside front cover, 53r.
508–510 Rev of 44v.

but} ye
And venerable life yet} ~~you~~ shall hear. 517
{& {e
—I talk {[?] y{ou are standing in the sun 518
Without refreshment—let us in 519
[?Haven]
[?of] this little Child 427
An orphan, ~~then or [?one] of your~~ [?small friend] 432
or so I fear, [?~~for we~~ could]
Is ~~taken from you~~
[?] [?I could not] [432]
[?tell]
~~That [?twas] the coffin~~
—I [?that] from the hill [? ? ?] 437
[?could] [?]

[45v] [II, 563–575, 662–668]

[?I this] child II, 427
An Orphan so I fear & you yourself 432
Must have sustained a loss.— 433
~~It could not~~
~~well~~
The hand of death
Has answerd he been here but could not 434
well
Have fallen more lightly if It had not 435
fallen
~~Upon myself. No doubt you had fears~~ 436
Which had [?] [?been] better on myself
no doubt ~~when you had~~ [?heard] ?439
[?seen]
if from the hill 437
~~The [?]~~ [?~~th~~] ~~[?]~~ [?~~leave~~] this [?dear]
From sun &c 518
f]
[?~~You would bear little hope if] of of~~] ~~inding~~
Without refreshment saying this he led 519
Towards the Cottage: homely was the spot 520
And to my feeling ere we reach'd the door 521
Had almost a forbidding nakedness 522
{ly
Less fair I grant [?was] painful{y less fair 523
Than it appeared when from the 524
valleys brink

518–519 Continued on 45v.
427–437 Rev of 42r; rev on 45v.

427ff. Cf. MS. 71, 53r, 55v.
427–433 Rev of 45r, 42r.
518 Continued from 45r.
436, 439, 518/519 In these lines the Solitary refers to the Wanderer's misapprehension that the funeral was the Solitary's; see 35v, l. 275.

[46^r] [II, 669–680]

I had looked down upon it, all within II, 525
[?As by the] funeral train it had [?been] 526
Was silent & the solitary Clock 527
Tick'd as I thought with melancholy 528
And yet the little Dwelling did not want
A formal comeliness fireside & chair
Were orderly & cleanly as the Man
Who /to the chapel with the funeral
train
Was/[?gone] had
the
[?Were dress d thus] for ~~that~~ Day
[?~~er er~~]
Ere to the distant Church they took their 532
way
We clomb the Cottage stairs as we were led 533
n|
And reacsh'd a little Room &|arrow & low 534
And reach'd a small appartment dark & low [534]
Which we no sooner enter'd than our Host 535
Said gayly this is my domain, my cell 536
My Hermitage my Cabin what you will 537
I love it better than a snail his House 538
But you shall now be feasted with 539
our best
So with more ardour than an 540
unripe Girl

[46^v] [II, 681–700]

Left one day mistress of her Mothers II, 541
stores
He went about his hospitable task. 542
My eyes were busy & my thoughts no less 543
And pleas'd I look d upon my grey-hair'd 544
Friend
As if to thank him he took looks & look'd 545
plainly
Chear'd [?~~rested~~] & yet serious. What a 546
wreck
We had about us scatter'd was the floor 547
With Books maps minerals wither'd plants 549
& flower.
{c
Mechani{[?l] tools, the shavings & the dust 551

525ff. Cf. MS. 71, 55^v–56^r.

528/532 WW's first description is of an "orderly & cleanly" cottage. This is in marked contrast to the description of disorder that is soon drafted and adopted in later versions. The description undergoes further heavy rev in MS. 71.

532 Conjectured readings above this line may be pen testings.

541ff. Cf. MS. 71, 56^r–56^v.

{woods
From {[?diver] of divers colours, trinket toys 552
Loose scraps of paper, some as I could see 553
Scribbled with verse, a broken angling rod 554
For neighborhood a cob-web'd telescope 555
And instruments of of music some half 556
made
Some in disgrace hung dangling from 557
the walls
{of
But from such entertainment {[?ou] our eyes
And such employment of our thoughts we soon
Were summon d, for the promise was fulfilld 558
A feast before us & a happy host 559
Inviting us in glee to sit & eat 560

[47r] [II, 701–714]

w}
A Napkin wh}hite as foam of that rough *II, 561*
brook
By which it had been bleachd oerspread the 562
board
{And
{[?That] was itself half coverd with a load 563
Of ~~pastoral dainties oaten cakes & cheese~~ 564
Curds cream, ~~& [?]~~ ~~prints~~ of butter (by that 565
name
~~The Houswifes called them) & figured~~ oer, the
stamp
Of ~~curious moulds moulds in what the~~y had
been cast
oa} br}
Of pastoral dainties ot}ten [?pr]}ead curd cream [564]
{kes
And ca{tes of Butter curiouslly impress d [565]
Bu}
[?By] [?]t}tter that [?richly] had imbibed the 566
[?tinge]
[?e]
Of meadow flowers its native meadow flow'rs 567
Nor lacked for more delight on that warm 569
day
Our table small parade of garden fruit 570
And whortle-berries from the mountain 571
side
The Child who long ere this had still'd 572
his sobs
Was now a help to his late Comforter 573
Mov d like a willing Page as he 574
was bid

561ff. Cf. MS. 71, 57r.

[47[v]] [II, 715–726, 735–744, 750–752]

~~Obedient to our ey~~
Ministering to our need. While thus II, 575, 576
we sate
Fronting the window, ever & anon 577, 578
I glanced an upward look (the sight till 579
now
I had not see on two huge mountain peaks 580
some
That from ~~an~~other vale, peep'd into this. 581
s
~~Yes~~ [?a] ~~aid our Host~~ those lusty Twins 583, 582
Those lusty Twins
and I
Are good Companions many ~~are the [?fair~~] 584
are sounds
Which the wind fashions in his tuneful 585
voice
Among the peaks & rock & dashin [?waves] 586
[?w]
[?s] av
Thes Creature have their harmony for I so 587, 595, 596
be the [?hand]
So do I call it though it ~~be [?work~~] [?o] 597
there e
Of silence though [?] b [?ee] no voice. The 598
Cloud
of golden suns
Th mist the shadow ~~light of setting~~ 599
M[?oontion] of m[?outai] light all come ther 600
& touch
An instrument which though it does not
[?~~speak~~]
[?] speak
Tho~~ughts are not busier in the mind of~~
m[?e]
&
I yet a language [?to] a [?harmony] 602
~~Unto~~
[?To a] ~~sick & weary~~ mind & spirit 602, 603
&
To [?sick] spirit her I sit [?] look 602, 603, 607
[?]
~~Till eyes [?ar~~]

583, 582ff. Rev on 48[r]–49[r]. Cf. MS. 71, 57[r]–58[r].
600/602 The canceled line, "Thoughts are not busier . . . ," found also on 48[r] and 48[v], although om in MS. 71, is included in *1814*; cf. *1814*, II, 750–752.

[48^r] [II, 741–744, 750–752]

Upon the [?charges] that
And [?drive] about the [?charges that shape]
{Forth
{[?] a quiet interchange they [?sha]
Thoughts are not bus[?ieier] in the mind
o }
[?f]}f man
& hope
[?And] [?]
[?There]
A language ~~which an idle Spirit~~ [?lov] *II, 602*
not unwelcome to sick heart
Or idle spirits here I sit ~~& look~~ & watch *603, 607*
The quiet [?unremitting] interchange
Thght are not busier in the mind ~~of [?the~~]
[?man]
But [?the] is [?hidden]
they touch *600*
And have a [?answer] there they come & shape *601*
[?there] [?] I sit & [?watc]
{[?is]
Thought {[?are] not busier in the mind of
man
W }
[?No]}ork is not busier in the
No work is busier in the mind of man
~~That is the [?work~~ done there]
Than work that [?is done th]

[48^v] [II, 721–726, 735–744, 750–752]

Those lusty twins & I exclaimed our Host *II, 582, 583*
Are good Companions: many are the *584*
sounds
Which the wind fashions in his tuneful course *585*
Among the rocks & heaths & dashing shores *586*
{of upper sky
These Creatures also {[?have] the silent sky *587*
These also have their harmony for so *595, 596*
{I {e
So do {[?it] call though there b{[?een] no voice *597, 598*
Clouds mists & shadow light of golden *599*
sun[?s]
{ither
Motions of moonlight all come th{[?ere &] the[?re] *600*
touch

602ff. Cf. MS. 71, 57^v–58^r.
The drafts on the page attempt a rev of 47^v; in turn, these are rev on 48^v–49^r. Concerning the fourth line and the last five lines, see note to 47^v, l. *600/602*.

582ff. Rev of 48^r, 47^v; rev on 49^r. Cf. MS. 71, 57^v–58^r.
597, 598 WW elides two lines from 47^v before restoring them whole on 49^r.

And have an answer, thither come & shape *601*
A language not unwelcome to sick hearts *602*
And idle spirits here I sit & watch. *603, 607*
not
~~No work is busier in the mind of man~~
Thoughts are not busier in the mind of
man
s}
This} is the work done there.

[49^r] [II, 738–740, 775–782]

g}
For so I call it thou[?h]}h it be the hand *II, 597*
Of silence though there be no voic The clouds *598*
The mist the shadow *599*

His was th still conten[?t]tedness of age *628, 629*
more [?languid] & more
And more than that ~~for he was~~ *631, 633*
torpid
[?slo]
B[?reath a]
~~Paying~~ by [?dimness] of a [?clouded twin] *633*
He moved about the Double Cloud
The penalty if penalty it [?were] *634*
Of Spendthrift [?deeds] ~~the~~ excesses of *635*
his prime

[49^v] [II, 767–778]

The Huswi[?f]wife tempted by such *II, 621*
slender
gain
[?g]} from this occasion be distill d
As mi[?h]}t [?~~be ther~~ be] distill d *622*
Contrived had done for
A nook— As she before ~~contrived~~ for *623*
me
A} place {to
To} ~~nook to~~ harbour {[?har] harbour also this *624*
old man
gave for
Food for his meals a blind dull [?nook] *625*
the {of
such as she {or {[?]
~~The best~~ she had {[?a] kennel for his rest *626*
Thi Man of four score winters as I said

603, 607 On the passage below this line, see note to 47^v, l. *600/602*.

597ff. Rev of 48^v, 47^v. Cf. MS. 71, 58^r, 59^r.
628, 629ff. This pencil draft continues from 49^v and is then rev on 12^v.

621ff. Pencil draft continues on 49^r and is then rev on 12^v. Cf. MS. 71, 58^v–59^r.

[?And]
ill
not ill, would ~~bad~~ [?hard]
This, of its self [?lacked ~~not~~ not] [?] 627
an
To his hard [?fortune] & in [?his] earlier 628
[?time]
[?~~period~~]
[?ever as he]
But [?~~when~~ not] a man of [?idle life] 629
[?was now transformd]
And look d for nothing better than he
foun[?d]
Moreover his was not a [?quie] old age 631
For he [?had been a farmer]
[?His]

The stub of 51^{v} contains erased or badly rubbed pencil draft, largely illegible, of which a few final words of three lines possibly related to II, *763–764* (see MS. 71, 63^{r}) can be conjectured: [?dead, ?cloud, ?closed] / [?r]ied / [?lived].

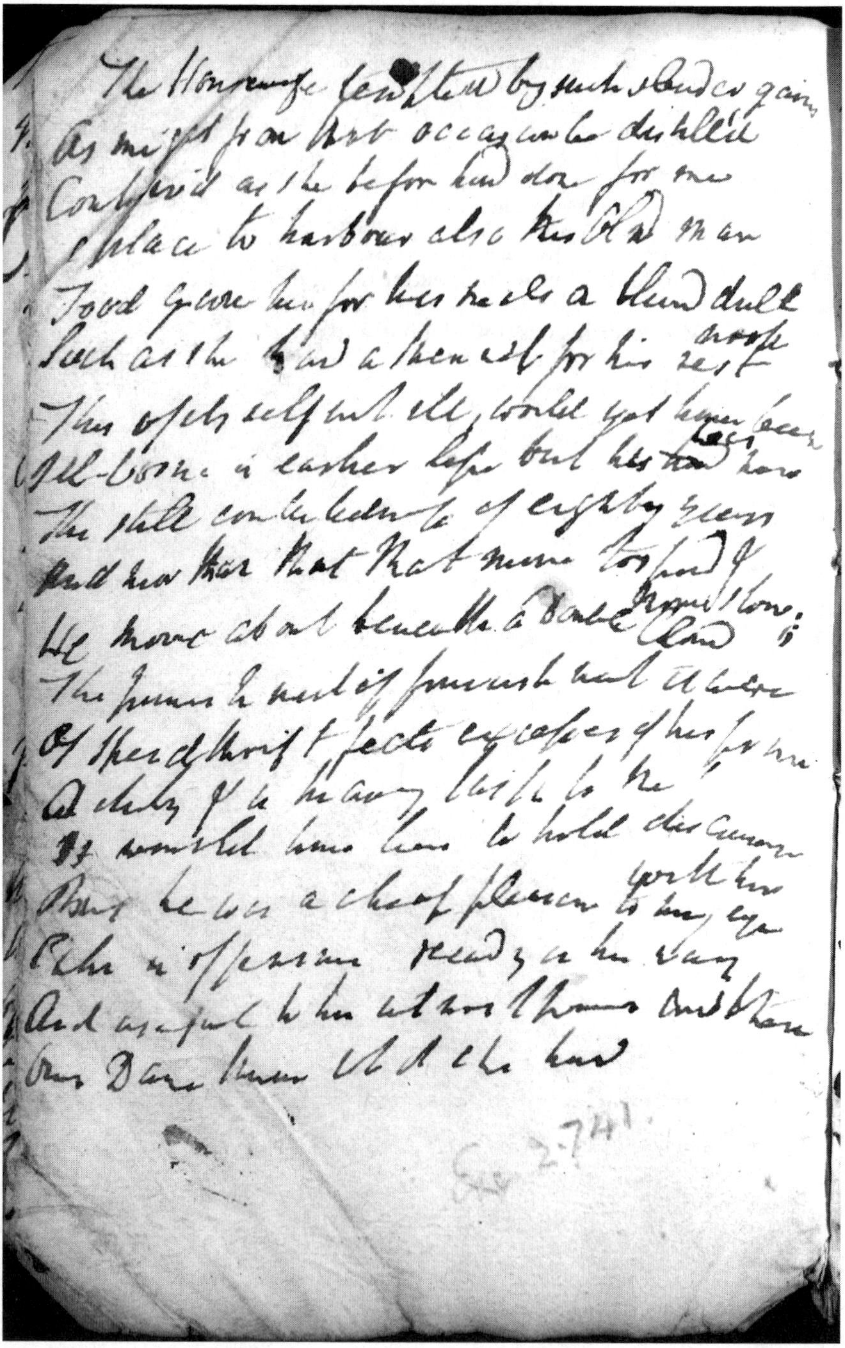
The Homestead [illegible] by such slender gains
As might from that occasion be distilled
Contrived as she before had done for one
A place to harbour also this old man
Food gave him for his meals a blind dull
Such as she had a [illegible] for his rest
Thus [illegible] well [illegible] would yet [illegible]
All-borne in earlier life but [illegible]
The still contentedness of eighty years
[illegible]
He moves about beneath a double [illegible]
The [illegible]
Of [illegible]
A [illegible]
It would have been to hold discourse
But he was a [illegible]
[illegible]
And [illegible]
[illegible]

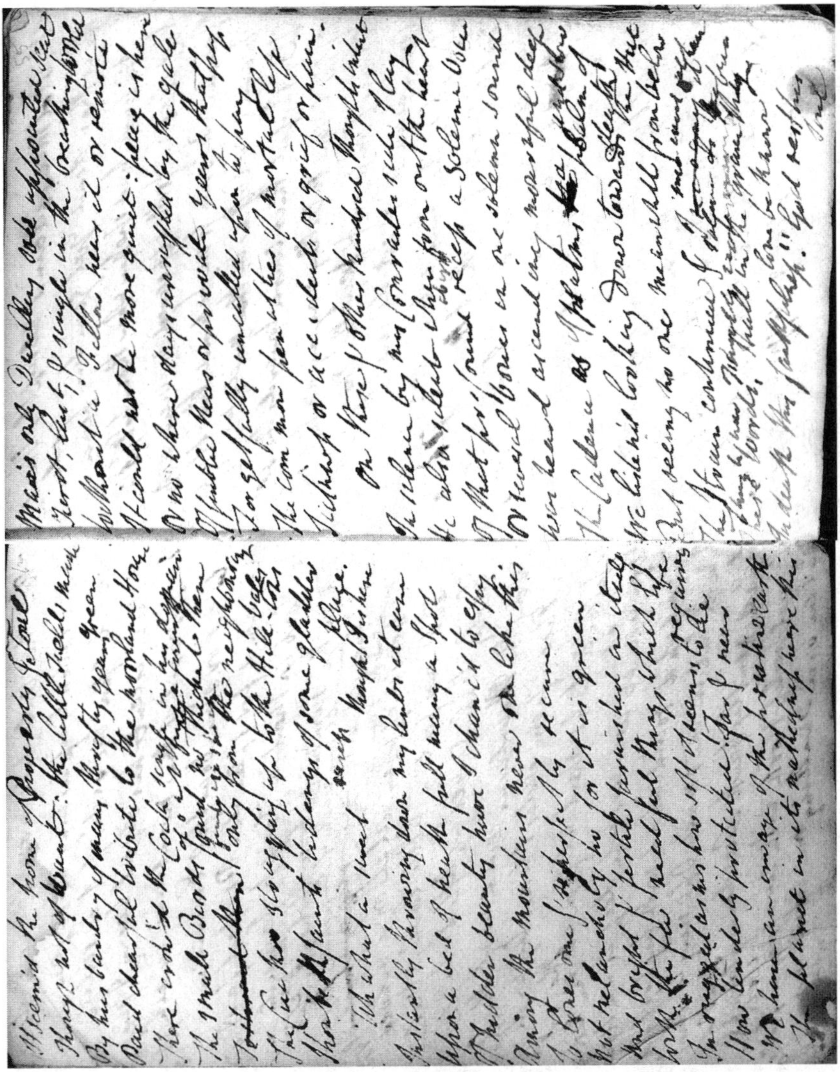

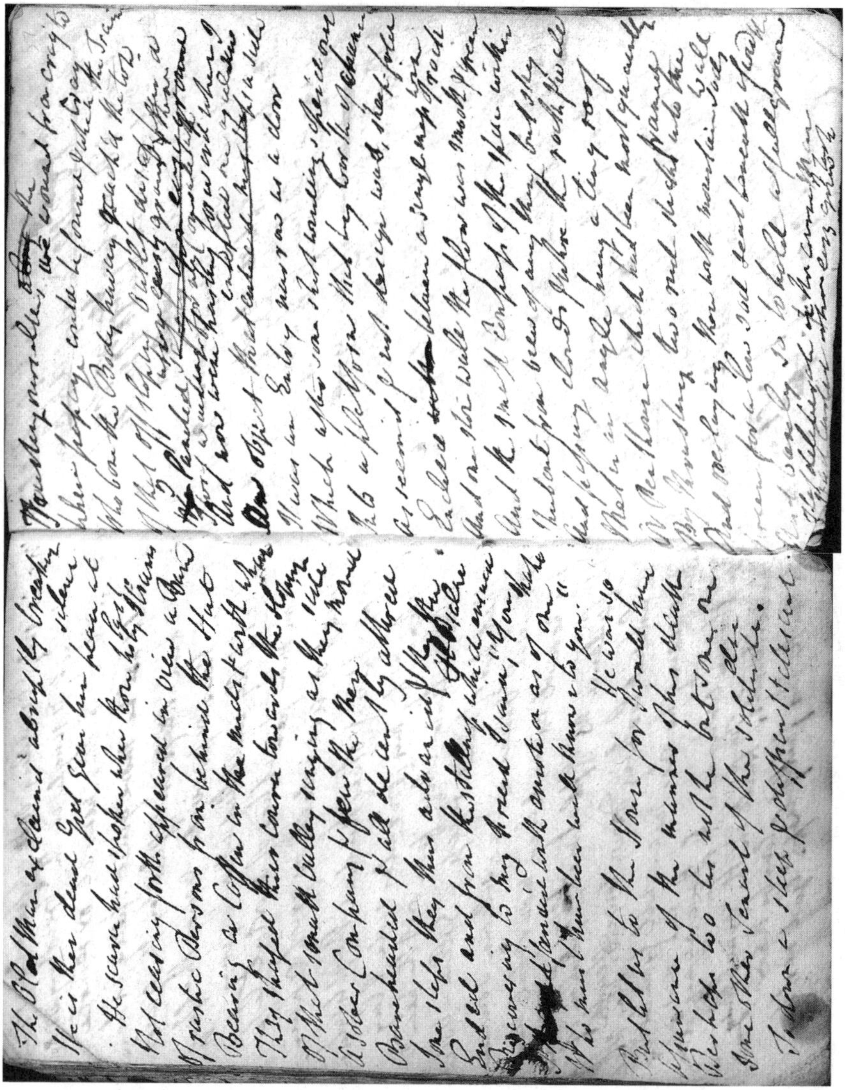

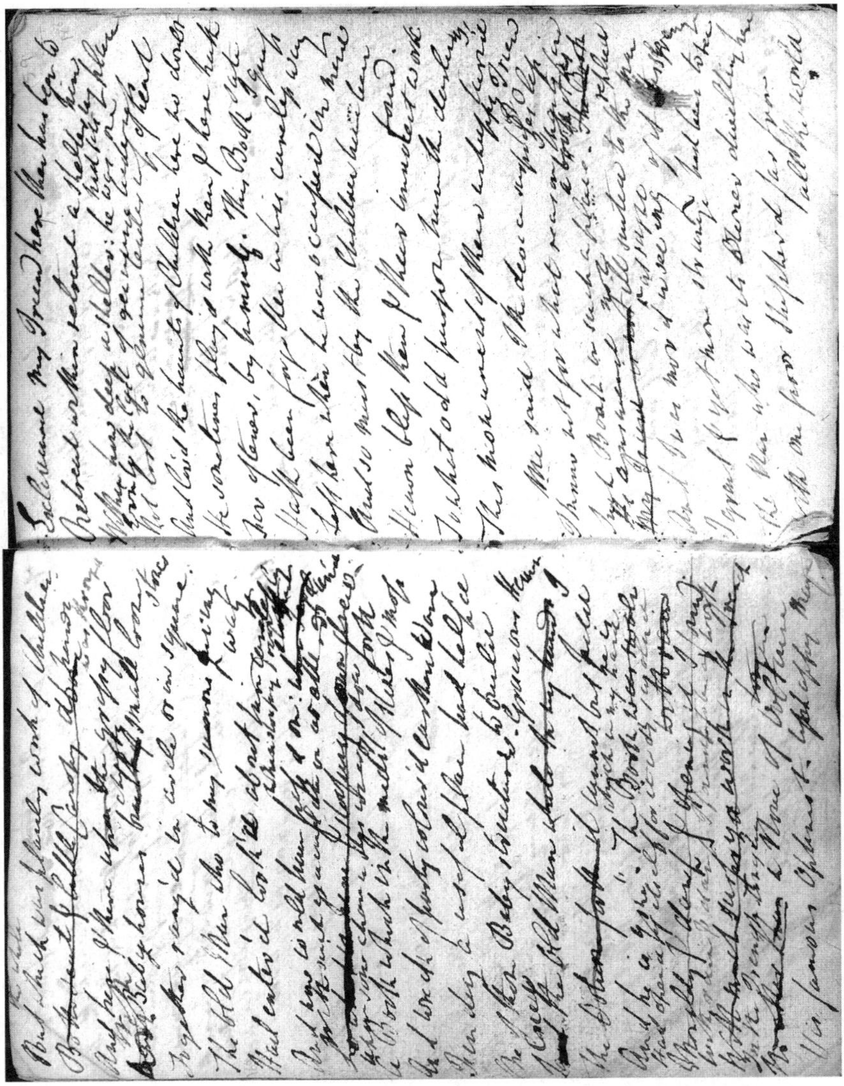

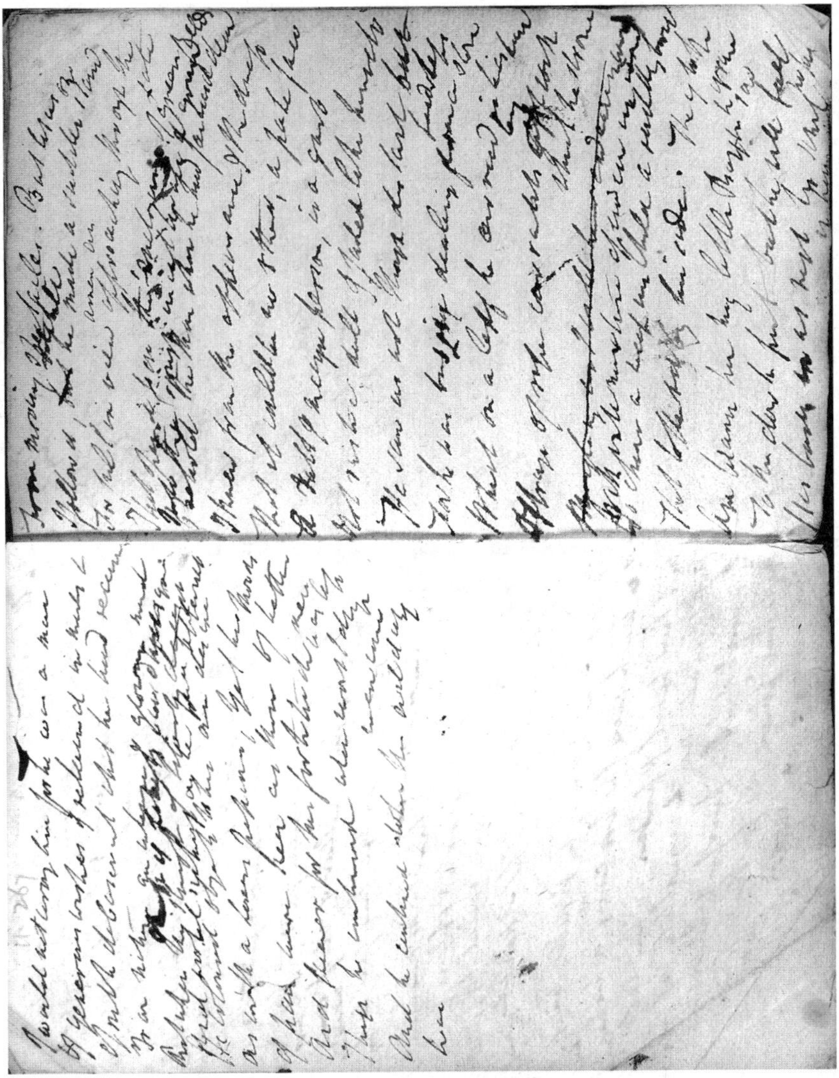

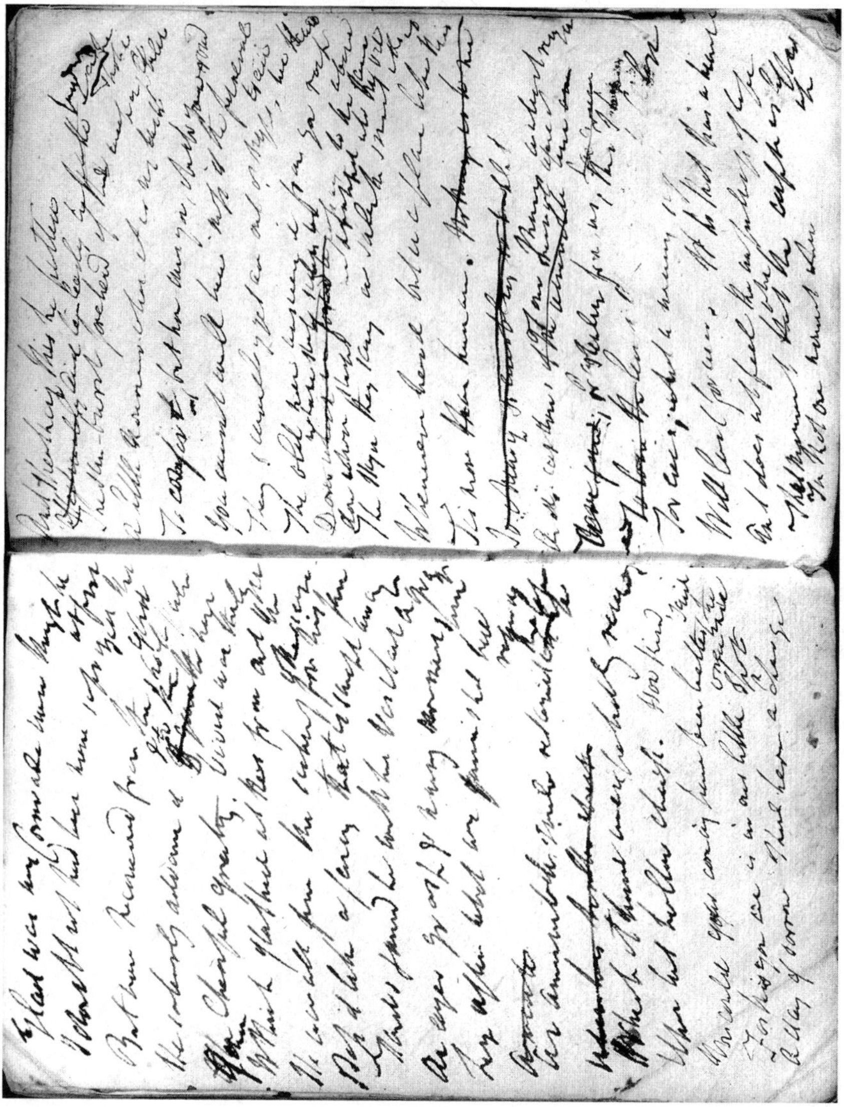

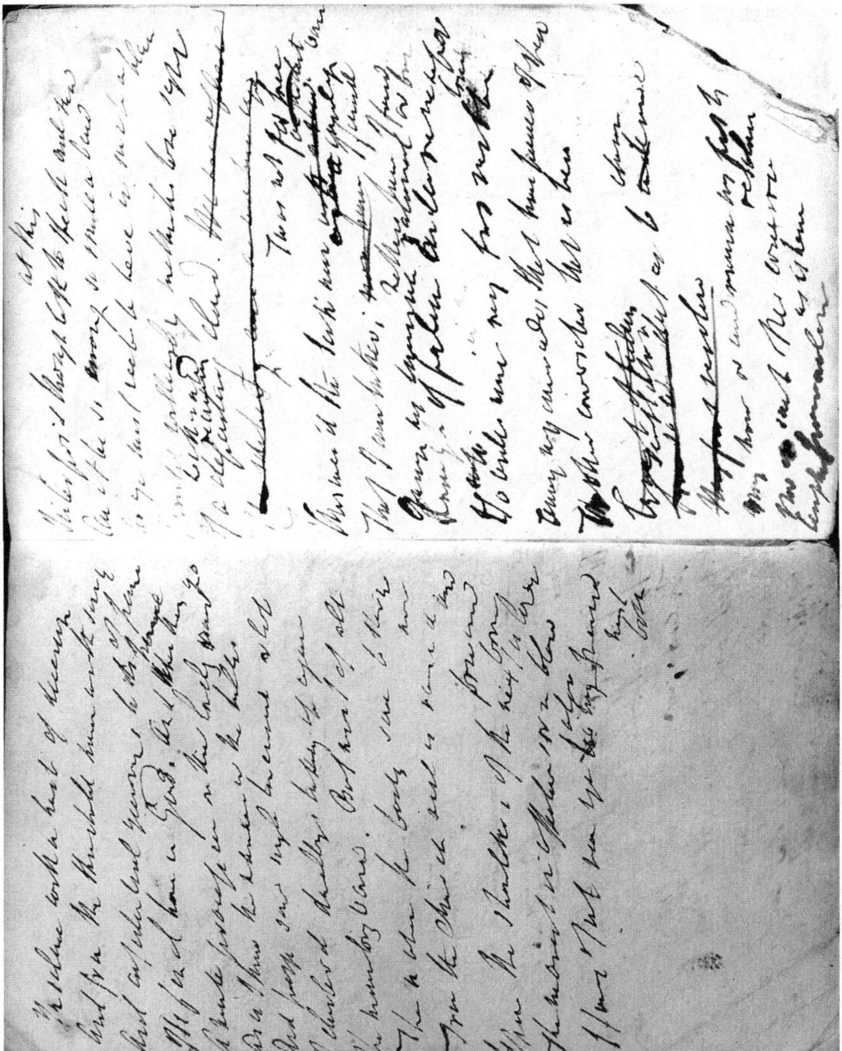

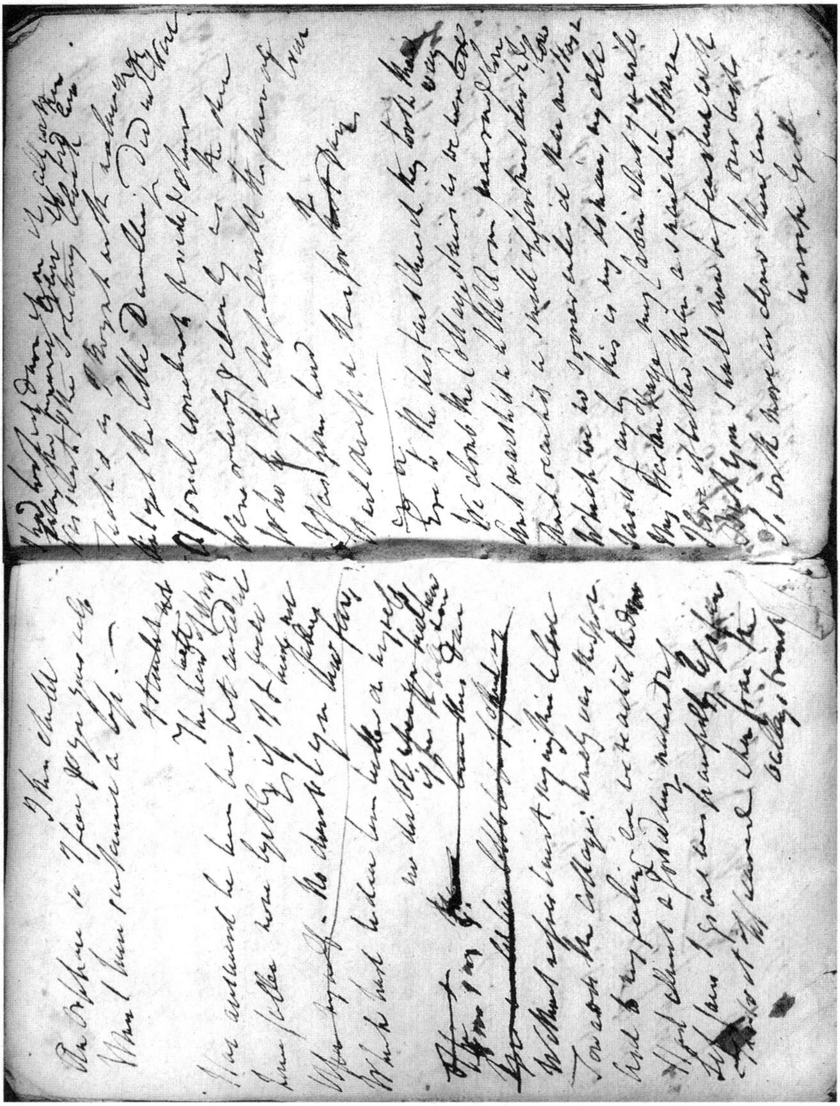

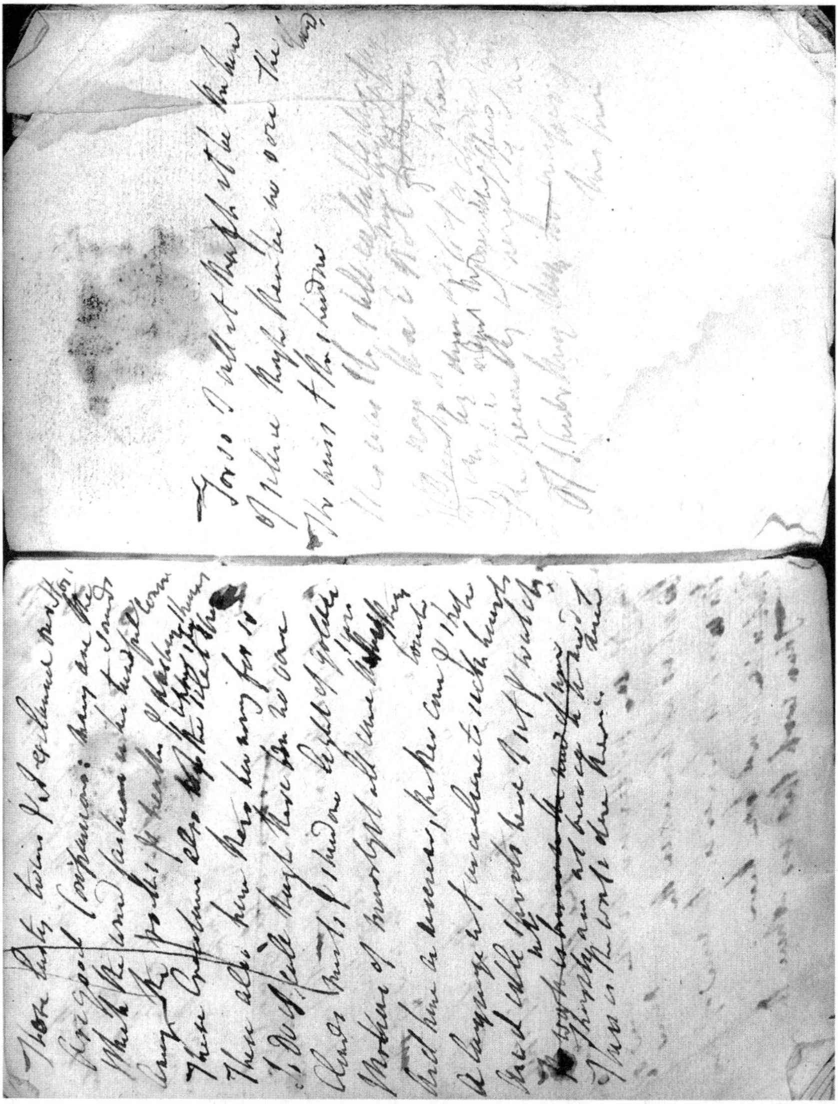

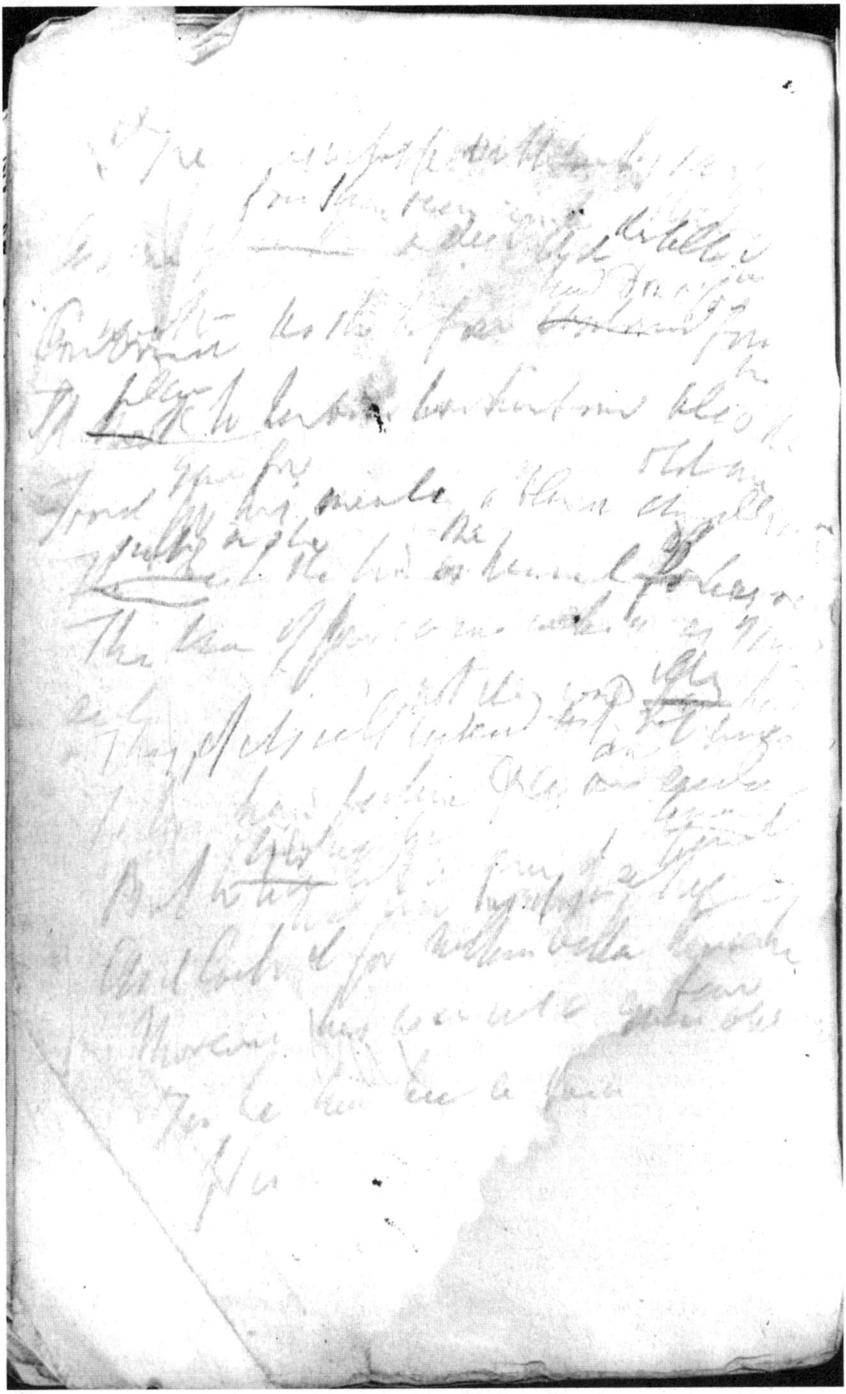

DC MS. 69

DC MS. 69—in use at the first, second, fourth, and fifth stages of *Excursion* composition for work on Books I, III, IV, and V—is described in the Manuscript Census, pp. xxii–xxiii, above. For a discussion of this manuscript and its role in the composition of *The Excursion*, see pp. 431–435, 447–448, 453, above.

DC MS. 69 is a complex manuscript for two major reasons: (1) its entries proceed from both ends of the notebook, with the notebook inverted to write the latter sequence; (2) many of the leaves have been torn from the notebook, frequently leaving on the stubs initial or terminal letters that suggest the original contents. We thus preface transcription of the relatively few surviving leaves with a full report on the leaves and stubs remaining in DC MS. 69, beginning with the work proceeding from the front of the notebook.

Although the inverted stubs and leaves at the back of the notebook are here designated as rectos or versos reading from the front (that is, from the direction of the earliest material entered in this notebook), inverting the notebook also in effect reverses rectos and versos. All work is in Wordsworth's hand unless otherwise stated.

Italic line numbers in the right-hand margins of the transcriptions, in the transcription notes, and in the following listing refer not to the 1814 reading text in this volume but to the underlying pre-1813 text of *Excursion,* I–III, c. *299*; i.e., the state before Wordsworth revised this material following the death of his two children. This state of the underlying pre-1813 text reaches its fullest development in DC MS. 71. Bracketed roman line numbers at the top right of each page of Book I or Book III manuscript transcription provide cross-references to the line count in the 1814 reading text; underlying pre-1813 numbers in the following listing of stubs can be converted to 1814 reading text numbers by using the cross-references that we provide to the transcription of DC MS. 71.

In addition to the references to *Excursion* manuscripts in the notes to the transcriptions, we provide where appropriate references to *Ruined Cottage/ Pedlar* MS. M (DC MS. 44; see Manuscript Census, above).

[Stub 1]

Nothing decipherable.

[Stubs 2–3]

Inverted (see report below).

[Stub 4^r]

Initial letters of three words can be conjectured: [?An] / [?So] / [?inf].

[Stub 4^v]

No legible traces of writing.

[Stub 5]

Inverted (see report below).

[Stub 6^r]

Work related to Book III, c. *120*–c. *130* (cf. stub 77^r; MS. 71, 68^v–69^r); initial letters correspond to III, *125–130*: Of Time & [?con] / [?A] / [?W] / [?A] / O / On / [?Wi *rev*].

[Stub 6^v]

Blank.

[Leaf 7^r–7^v]

Book III, *154–168*, probable rev and expansion of work on stub 78^r (cf. MS. 71, 69^v–70^r).

[Leaves 8^r–21^v]

Prose description entitled "Borrowdale" (see *Prose*, II, 148, 340–348; MS. 69 is here referred to by its earlier number, MSS. Verse 57).

[Leaves 22–63]

Blank.

[Leaves 64–70]

Inverted with work toward Book IV proceeding from the back of the notebook (see below).

[Stub 71^r]

Work on Book III picks up with copy entered successively on the rectos (with rev on the versos) of stubs and leaves 71–84; versos remain unreported unless entries are detectable. On stub 71^r is work probably related to III, *1–19*, possibly rev of 72^r (cf. MS. 71, 65^r–65^v); initial letters on the bottom inch and a half of the page correspond to III, *16–19*: B / In *added* / T[?h] / Some *del* / Some *added*.

[Stub 71^v]

Possible rev of 72^v; terminal letters correspond to III, *46–47*: [?that] / [?detained] / [?he] / [?led].

[Leaf 72^r]

III, *20–45* (cf. MS. 71, 65^v–66^v).

[Leaf 72^v]

III, *43–48* (cf. MS. 71, 66^r–66^v).

[Stub 73]

Nothing detectable, but possibly some version of III, c. *46*–c. *62* was once entered on the recto, bridging 72^r and 74^r (cf. MS. 71, 66^v–67^r).

[Stub 74^r]

Work related to III, c. *63*–c. *80* (cf. MS. 71, 67^r–67^v); initial letters correspond to III, *63–64*: [?A] / ? / [?Co] / A.

[Stub 75^r]

Work related to III, c. *81*–c. *103* (cf. MS. 71, 67^r–68^r); initial letters correspond to III, *82–84*: Of / A / M [*rev*] / Of.

[Stub 76^r]

Work related to III, c. *104*–c. *124* (cf. MS. 71, 68^r–69^r); initial letters correspond to III, *104–106*: O[?f] / [?] / [?].

[Stub 77^r]

Work related to III, c. *125*–c. *143*, (cf. 6^r, ll. *125–130*; MS. 71, 68^v–69^v); initial letters correspond to III, *131*: [?On] / ? / [?H].

[Stub 78^r]

Work related to III, c. *144*–c. *180* (cf. 7^r–7^v; MS. 71, 69^v–71^r); initial letters correspond to III, *145–147*: T / P / [?N].

[Stub 79^{r}]

Work related to III, c. *181*–c. *196* (cf. MS. 71, 70^{v}–71^{r}); initial letters correspond to III, *182–183*: H[?e] / [?T *rev*] / H.

[Stub 80^{r}]

Work related to III, c. *197*–c. *218* (cf. MS. 71, 71^{r}–71^{v}); initial letters correspond to III, *198–199*: T[?o] / [?F].

[Stub 81^{r}]

Work related to III, c. *219*–c. *240* (cf. MS. 71, 72^{r}–72^{v}); initial letters correspond to III, *220–221*: B / O.

[Stub 82^{r}]

Work related to III, c. *241*–c. *265* (cf. MS. 71, 72^{v}–73^{r}); initial letters correspond to III, *242–244*: In / B / B.

[Stub 82^{v}]

One terminal word can be read: "said."

[Stub 83^{r}]

Work related to III, c. *266*–c. *277* (cf. MS. 71, 73^{r}–73^{v}); initial letters correspond to III, *267–270*: Or *rev* / W / A / I.

[Leaf 84^{r}]

III, *278–299* (cf. MS. 71, 73^{v}–74^{r}).

[Leaves 84^{v}–114^{r}]

Blank.

[Leaf 114^{v}]

I, *72–84* (cf. MS. 71, 5^{r}–5^{v}).

[Stubs 115^{r}–119^{v}]

There is nothing decipherable on these stubs, although they may have contained some Book I material bridging 114^{v} and 120^{r}.

[Leaf 120^{r}]

I, *103–132* (cf. MS. 71, 6^{r}–6^{v}).

[Leaves 120^{v}–197]

Blank.

[Leaf 198^{r}]

Lines provided in transcription, below, and as a reading text in Appendix II, below: "As when, upon the smooth pacific deep."

[Leaves 198^{v}–215^{v}]

Blank.

Work proceeds from the other end of the notebook, inverted, on stubs and leaves 248–216, 70–64, 5, 3, 2. Book V copy begins with c. 300 on 248^{v}, inverted; for the possibility that missing leaves may have included Book V, 1–c. 299, see pp. xxii–xxiii, above.

[Stub 248^{v}]

Work related to V, c. 300–c. 315, drawing upon MS. 74, 36^{v}, 36^{r} (cf. MS. 74, 35^{v}, 36^{r}, 36^{v}; 74A, 8^{r}–8^{v}); initial letters correspond to V, 300–314: O / T[?h] / [?] / R / Li / I *rev* / The / With / These / To / Are / Sha / B / I[?n] / I.

[Stub 248^{r}]

Work relating to V, c. 315–c. 328, drawing upon MS. 74, 36^{r}–36^{v} (cf. MS. 74, 35^{v}, 36^{r}, 36^{v}; 74A, 8^{v}); terminal letters correspond to V, 322: [?ts] *or* [?ds].

[Stub 247^{v}]

Draft possibly related to V, 605ff., probably drawing upon some rev of MS. 74, 36^{v}, 37^{r} (cf. MS. 74A, 16^{r}); this would follow the sequence of MS. 74 that has lines running from

V, 321 variant, into V, 607ff., as part of an expansion of *TPL*; initial letters correspond to V, 605–607: [?F] / [?A] / An / B / [?A].

[Stub 247^r]

No letters appear on this stub, but possibly work related to V, c. 327–c. 349 was entered here and on the bottom half of 247^v (cf. MS. 74, 38^r; MS. 74A, 8^v–9^r).

[Stub 246^v]

Draft relating to V, c. 350–c. 364, drawing upon MS. 74 and incorporating its rev (cf. MS. 74, 39^r, where l. 361 has a cross in the left margin indicating where to leave off copy; MS. 74A, 9^v); initial letters correspond to V, 350–361: [?H] / I *overwriting* [?O] / Co / By / Wh / Of sa[?g] / Whom / For / From / Of / [?L *rev*] / Or / Sin *rev* / [?Th] / [?sin *del*] / [?to *rev*] / [?s *rev*].

[Stub 246^r]

Work probably related to rev of V, c. 365–c. 375 (cf. MS. 74A, 9^v–10^r); terminal letters related to V, 367, 371–372: [?se *del*] / [?hts] / [?] / [?he] / [?ies].

[Stub 245^v]

Work related to V, c. 375–c. 390 (cf. MS. 74A, 10^r–10^v); the last three lines (which are added) are probably related to ll. 385–390 but are not incorporated in MS. 74A, and are possibly related to rev on 244^v, ?V, 426/427; initial letters correspond to V, 377–384, 388–391: Of / A *added* / A / Fo / [?]o *rev to* Ho / And / Lik / Rig / [?Hi *del*], *a cross in the left margin signals rev at page foot*] / With *added* / If / F / A / W / Th *added* / No[?w] *added with a cross in left margin* / I *added.*

[Stub 245^r]

Work related to V, c. 391–c. 419 (cf. MS. 74, 1^r, 28^v; MS. 74A, 10^v–11^r); terminal letters correspond to V, ?398: [?ce, ?se, *or* ?re].

[Stub 244^v]

Work related to V, c. 420–c. 433, with added last two lines not incorporated in MS. 74A (cf. MS. 74, 1^r, 105^r; MS. 74A, 11^r–11^v); initial letters correspond to V, 420–433: O[?f] / T / [?O] / D / W / Ma *del* / The *added* / D *rev to* Th [*del*] / Nov *added* / Yet / Is / Th[?a] / It / An / Ol / A / G[?u] *added* / Th *added.*

[Stub 244^r]

Work probably related to a longer version of V, c. 434–c. 440 than is found in MS. 74A (cf. MS. 74A, 11^v), whose terminal letters are: [?l] / [?ild] / st / - / - / - / nt[?] / - / [?e] / [?ls].

[Stub 243^v]

Work related to V, c. 441–460 in hand of MW (cf. MS. 74A, 12^r–12^v); initial letters correspond to V, 443–451: Th / Sa / Cou / Wi *added* / For / And *del* / Li / B / Of / Ha.

[Stub 243^r]

Work in hand of MW probably related to V, c. 460–c. 479, expanded and revised by WW on stub 242^v (cf. MS. 74A, 12^v–13^r); terminal letters correspond to V, 466, 479: er / - / - / - / [?] / [?] / [?] / red.

[Stub 242^v]

Work in hand of MW related to V, c. 490–c. 499 (cf. MS. 74, 28^r), and V, 470–475 in hand of WW expanding and revising stub 243^r (cf. MS. 74A, 13^r–13^v). Initial letters in hand of MW correspond to V, 491–499: Lo / B / A / O / R / A / A / St; initial letters in hand of WW correspond to V, 470–475: Fo / Am / And / Doo / Our / Thes.

[Stub 242^r]

Work related to V, c. 500–511ff. in hand of MW (cf. MS. 74, 29^r; MS. 74A, 13^v); terminal letters correspond to V, 508, 511: [?ks] / - / - / - / id.

[Stub 241^v]

Work related to V, c. 527–c. 542 in hand of MW and WW (cf. MS. 74, 29^r, 29^v, 30^r;

MS. 74A, 14^r–14^v). Initial letters in hand of MW correspond to V, 530–542: W / A / If / Towa / Your / High / These / From / A dre / With / Sadde / On th / Look fr; in hand of WW added at page foot, possibly as rev of stub 242^r: To use / Drawn (V, 527–528).

[Stub 241^r]

Work related to V, c. 543–c. 566 in hand of MW (cf. MS. 74, 29^v, 30^r; MS. 74A, 14^v–15^r); terminal letters correspond to V, 549–561: ow / - / - / urs / [?f]e / - / e / out / ched / spring / thus / ke / d's repose.

[Stub 240^v]

Work related to V, c. 566–c. 580 in hand of MW (cf. MS. 74A, 15^r); initial letters correspond to V, 568–579: A / Wh / Flo / I re / By / This [*del*] / The / To ou / Meek / Strong / To keep / Wise in *added WW* / a self— / And ea.

[Stub 240^r]

Work related to V, c. 580–c. 600 in hand of MW and WW (MS. 74A, 15^r–15^v); terminal letters in hand of MW correspond to V, 597–598: - / - / - / the / - / ubt / [?k]. Terminal letters corresponding to V, 599–600, 592–594, in hand of WW are beneath horizontal line: for aught *del to* err / we know *del* / [?] / [?s]ly class / [?are] found.

[Stub 239]

Nothing legible on either side of this stub, but possibly lines related to V, 601–628 once stood here (cf. MS. 74, 36^v, 39^r–40^r; MS. 74A, 15^v–16^r).

[Stub 238^v]

Work related to V, c. 629–642 (cf. MS. 74A, 16^v–17^r); initial letters correspond to V, 631–642: [?] / I / Yo / Dig / Of virg / Fruit *added* / Seeks / To fr *del to* Seeks / Around / Held / And [?th] / Give u / For our / He is who / Wha.

[Stub 238^r]

Work related to V, c. 643–662, revised on stub 237^v (cf. MS. 74A, 17^r–17^v); terminal letters correspond to V, ?644–653, 661–662: t / ds / them / [?] / own / d / told / n·/ [?hese] / nce. / - / info[?rm] / [?ns] to rest / re mind / But the task *del* / ask *added.*

[Stub 237^v]

Work related to V, c. 659, 666–669, 652–659, rev of stub 238^r (cf. MS. 74A, 17^v); initial letters correspond to V, c. 659, 666–669, 652–659: A *del* / Loo *del* / The / Mort / Is un / The [?v] *bracket in left margin signals transposition of "The" through "The," V, 666–669, to stub 236^r* / [?the *added*] / auth / Who *del* / Who *added and del* / Who f / Benea / So by / And so, / From the / To prize / And look.

[Stub 237^r]

Work possibly related to V, 719ff. (cf. MS. 74A, 18^v); less likely, the conjectured reading "pair" may be related to V, 905 in MS. 74, 32^r; terminal letters correspond to V, ?719–720: [?nd] / [?oft] / [?ir] / - / - / [?flock] / [?pair].

[Stub 236^v]

The leaf is torn and the few legible initial letters provide no exact correspondence to Book V lines; they may be part of a rejected draft of the Pastor's reply at V, 660ff., with the initial letters "Dep[?r]" the start of "Depressed" or "Depresses" because a mark on the tear may be the initial "s" of a double "s." Initial letters: [?] / [?]pa / Dep[?r] / I me[?et] / And.

[Stub 236^r]

Work related to V, c. 668–676 (cf. MS. 74A, 17^v); terminal letters correspond to V, 668–676: shews / [?t]s / I give / vaults / hold / bare / k / [?k] / till a shower / it.

Book IV copy begins with 235^v, inverted.

[Stub 235^v]

Work related to IV, c. 1–25; there is a tear in the upper left corner of the leaf; initial letters correspond to V, 7–12, 16–17, 22, 24–25: [ ]ile / [ ]uch / That / The Wa / For / Exist / Whose / All ac / Faith / Of his pe / Of all aug *with* all *del.*

[Stub 235r]

Work related to IV, c. 26–41; terminal letters correspond to IV, 33–41: [?es] / [ ]ome sky / fixed / [ ]ll the / [ ][?v]l / - / who / who can / mpassioned voice / [ ]ll in / [ ]e crowd / where / hast built *del to* built.

[Stub 234v]

Work related to IV, c. 42–58; initial letters correspond to IV, 49–58: [?om] / nd from / The p / And m / Thy [?b] / From [?p] / Impend *added* / Is come / And if / Come [?s] / And sa / Come labou / Perpetua.

[Stub 234r]

Work related to IV, c. 112–122 (IV, 79–91 found in MS. 73, 7r–7v); terminal letters correspond to IV, 114–122: [?] / [?urned] / [?ith] day / s the [?day] *rev to* deep / s *with* [?riched] *added*] / ced. / joy / air / with light / ificence / ss / filled / with love.

[Stub 233v]

Draft possibly related to IV, 122–141; initial letters: In / W[?h] / —O[?h] / Th[?e].

[Stub 233r]

Illeg, possibly draft toward IV, 122–142.

[Stub 232v]

Work related to IV, c. 141–c. 150; initial letters correspond to IV, ?142–145: [?] / [?w *added*] / Th[?a] / Ris / [?Closes] *del to* [?M].

[Stub 232r]

Work related to IV, c. 150–c. 170; terminal letters "[?ld]" correspond to IV, 150 ("hold) or IV, 168 ("withheld"):

[Stub 231v]

Initial letters correspond to IV, ?149–150: I[?f] / An / Th[?ro] / To [?tho].

[Stub 231r]

Terminal letters correspond to IV, ?187–192: [?lore] / [?ake] / joy *added above* [? ?s love] / - / [?] / [?ts].

[Stub 230v]

Work related to IV, c. 159–c. 190, in hand of MW, probably copy of 232r–231r; initial letters correspond to: IV, 159–163, ?187: [?Of] / [?W] / In[?s] / Is of / No n / I do n.

[Stub 230r]

Work related to IV, c. 190–c. 207; terminal letters correspond to: IV, ?202–207: [? *del*] / [?] / [?eal] / [?th] / [?t]regth / [?]ring / al power / [?me] / [?ens].

[Stub 229v]

Work related to IV, c. 208–c. 228; initial letters related to IV, ?226–228: [?O] / [?A *del*] / A[?s] / A[?n].

[Stub 229r]

Work related to IV, c. 215–c. 222; terminal letters correspond to IV, 216–222: [?ear] / [?yer] / [?h]eart / [?ws] / [?tr]ength.

[Stub 228v]

Work related to IV, c. 206–217; initial letters correspond to IV, ?206–207, 216–217: Is[?] / And / Those / Who.

[Stub 228r]

Work related to IV, c. 217–c. 236; terminal letters correspond to IV, ?236: [?] / [?] / [?] / [?eft].

[Stub 227v]

Work related to IV, c. 200–c. 220; initial letters correspond to IV, 204–208: Of / A[?l]

/ Is / And / In.

[Stub 227^{r}]

Work related to IV, c. 220–c. 238; terminal letters correspond to IV, 226–230: [?d] / [?S]oul / rld / regard / [? ?spot *del*] / t.

[Stub 226^{v}]

Work related to IV, c. 238–250, 238–239; initial letters related to IV, 247–250, 238–239: Sm / W[?h] / To / Or h / And *added* / In th *added.*

[Stub 226^{r}]

Work related to IV, c. 250–c. 270 (cf. MS. 70, 45^{r}); terminal letters correspond to IV, 261, 263: [?loss] / ed / an.

[Stub 225^{v}]

Work related to IV, c. 270–c. 290 in hand of MW; initial letters related to IV, 279–286: [?] / [?] / Va / On / Fro[?m] / Fit r / What *del to* Are / For y / And / Recla.

[Stub 225^{r}]

Work related to IV, c. 300–322; terminal letters correspond to IV, 314–316, 320–322: virtue / g / theirs / the wise *added* / eace.

[Stub 224^{v}]

Work related to IV, c. 630–644, 329–332 (cf. MS. 70, 29^{r}, 29^{v}–30^{r}, 6^{r}); initial letters correspond to IV, 639–644, 329–332 (added lines in hand of MW; probably related to rev of stub 225^{r} and to ll. 335–626): [?T] / [?] / Com / And / Fell / That / Those *added* / Still *added* / Predom *added* / As he *added.*

[Stub 224^{r}]

Work related to IV, c. 645–c. 670; cf. MS. 70, 30^{r}–30^{v}; terminal letters correspond to IV, 658–661: [?] / ty / ame / rew / [?ar]d.

[Stub 223^{v}]

Work related to IV, c. 670–c. 680; cf. MS. 70, 30^{v}–31^{r}; initial letters correspond to IV, 672–676: P / And / And / And / A se / With.

[Stub 223^{r}]

Work related to IV, c. 680–c. 700; cf. MS. 70, 34^{v}, 32^{v}–33^{r}; terminal letters correspond to IV, 690–691: [?ess] / is / [?kies].

[Stub 222^{v}]

Work related to IV, c. 700–715; initial letters correspond to IV, 702, 706–707: Of / [?] / - / In / Betw / [?] *rev* And.

[Stub 222^{r}]

Work related to IV, c. 715–c. 730; terminal letters correspond to IV, 720–722: [?] / [?alled] / [?] / [?ints] / [?estow] / [?].

[Stub 221^{v}]

Work related to IV, c. 730–c. 750; initial letters correspond to IV, 736–740: [?] / A / An / [?Wh] *rev* As / And / Wh[?e].

[Stub 221^{r}]

Work related to IV, c. 750–c. 759; terminal letters correspond to IV, 754–755: [?s]ed / t.

[Leaf 220^{v}]

IV, 756–759.

[Leaf 220^{r}]

Blank.

[Stub 219]

Nothing legible.

[Leaves 218^{v}–216^{r}]

Prose, in MW's and WW's hands, "From Ambleside to Keswick" (see *Prose,* II, 148;

340–341, n. to l. 1591/1592; MS. 69 is here referred to by its earlier number, MSS. Verse 57).

The Book IV material on stubs 70^{v}–64^{r} below is later than that on stubs 235–221, and follows the sequence established in those drafts.

[Stub 70^{v}]
Illeg pencil.
[Stub 70^{r}]
Illeg, possible rev of material entered on 69^{v}–63^{r}.
[Stub 69^{v}]
Work related to IV, c. 160–c. 175; probably supplies missing ll. c. 164–184 from earlier stubs 230^{v}–230^{r} (IV, 163, 187–215), continuing on to stub 66^{r} which supplies lines related to c. 184–215; initial letters correspond to IV, 164–169: [?A] / Eve / Of a / T[?o] / [?I] / [?] *del to* [?W] / So / [?].
[Stub 69^{r}]
Work related to IV, 1–c. 20; terminal letters correspond to IV, 1–3: [?le] / [?p]lain, / e; / s.
[Stub 68^{v}]
Work related to IV, c. 27–c. 40; initial letters correspond to IV, 27–31: To th / Sou / Su / Re / Th.
[Stub 68^{r}]
Work related to IV, c. 41–c. 60; terminal letters correspond to IV, 45, 47: [?nd] / [?] / tread.
[Stub 67^{v}]
Work related to IV, c. 60–66, 109–c. 120 (IV, 79–91 found in MS. 73, 7^{r}–7^{v}); initial letters correspond to IV, ?65–66, 109–114: And / An *added* / If *del to* A / Th / [?s *added*] / Wh / In / Of s / T[?h].
[Stub 67^{r}]
Illeg, probably some version of IV, c. 120–c. 140.
[Stub 66^{v}]
Work related to IV, c. 140–c. 160; initial letters correspond to IV, 148–155: If G / If, [?i] / th[?r] / In / [?F]o / Of / In / A.
[Stub 66^{r}]
Illeg, possibly supplies missing lines from earlier stubs 230^{v}–230^{r} (IV, 163, 187–215) related to c. 185–215ff., continuing from stub 69^{v}, which supplies ll. c. 164–184.
[Stub 65^{v}]
Work related to IV, c. 210–c. 225; initial letters correspond to IV, 216–221: Tho / Who / On / Vig / A / I / [?].
[Stub 65^{r}]
Work related to IV, c. 225–c. 240; terminal letters correspond to IV, ?244–245: [?es] / [?th].
[Stub 64^{v}]
Work related to IV, c. 240–c. 260; initial letters correspond to IV, 248–253: W / To / Or / W[?h] / S / T.
[Stub 64^{r}]
Illeg, possibly related to IV, c. 260ff.
[Stub 5^{v}]
Work on stubs 5, 3, and 2 is entered with the notebook inverted; initial letters on stub 5^{v} in the right margin in the hand of MW can be conjectured: Of w / [?w]i / Of / w /

[?T].

[Stub 5^r]

Terminal letters in the hand of MW, probably prose, can be conjectured: [?team] / [?wn] / id.

[Stub 3^v]

Initial letters in hand of MW remain unidentified: And / An / A / He / To / On / Fo.

[Stub 3^r]

The terminal letters of four lines probably relate to the prose narrative of the journey from Ambleside to Keswick (cf. 218^v–216^r): elling / first / main / [?arm].

[Stub 2^v]

Traces of two indecipherable letters remain.

[Stub 2^r]

No traces of writing remain.

[7^r] [III, 147–164]

~~Or Syrias Marble Ruins towering high~~ *III, 154*
~~Above the sandy desart in the light~~ *155*
~~Of sun or Moon. Forgive me if [?I] say~~ *156*
~~in your~~
~~That this Appearance which for your minds~~ *157*
hath raisd
{ [?~~Exaltations~~] { ~~the same cause~~
{[? ? ? ?] ~~inspirations~~ ({[?is for me] *158*
~~Different effect producing~~) is for me *159*
Not less than that huge Pile (from some abyss *147*
{mortal {P
Of {[?] {power unquestionably sprung) *148*
Whose hoary diadem of pendant rocks *149*
Confines
{[?~~tains~~]
D[?e]{[?] the shrill voice whirlwind, round & round *150*
Eddying within its vast circumference *151*
On Sarum's naked Plain—than Pyramid *152*
Of Egypt unsubverted undissolved *153*
Or Syrias marble Ruins towering high [*154*]
Above the sandy desart in the light [*155*]
Of sun or Moon. Forgive me if I say [*156*]
{an
That {this Appearance which hath raised your [*157*]
minds
To an exalted pitch—(the self same cause [*158*]
Different effect producing) is to me [*159*]
Rather a place of penance than delight *160*
Though at this moment I can look around me *161*
By the reflection of your pleasure pleased. *162*
Yet happier, in my judgement, even than you *163*
With your bright transports fairly may be *164*
deem

[7^v] [III, 165–168]

Is he, (if such have ever entered here) *III, 165*
The wandering Herbalist, ~~who in like~~ course *166*
who clear alike
of vain
Of in~~conclusive thought [?unoccupied~~]
who free alike
From vain, and that worse evil, vexing thought *167*
Casts on these uncouth forms a slight regard *168*

151–168 Probable continuation from stub 6^r; continued on 7^v; probable rev and expansion of work on stub 78^r; cf. MS. 71, 69^v–70^r.

165–168 See note to 7^r above.

[72r] [III, 20–45]

~~Sequestered though it be with jealous care~~
~~Is slenderly endowed, a little gem~~
~~Which might by no incurious search be miss'd;~~
~~But if discover'd and once seen tis then~~
~~Seen to the heart and thoroughly possess'd.~~
So saying, round he look'd as if perplex'd, III, 20
And, to remove those doubts, my grey-haired 21
Friend
Said, 22
or let "Let us trace this Streamlet to its source 30
Feebly it tinkles with an earthy sound 31
a few
And easy steps may bring us to the spot 32
Where haply crown'd with Flowerets & green herbs 33
{M
The {mountain-infant to the Sun comes forth 34
Like human life from darkness." ~~At the~~ word 35
sharp
~~We followed as he led a~~ sudden ~~A sharp~~ turn 36
Through a strait passage of encumbered ground 37
Proved that this hope was vain. For now we stood 38
Shut out from prospect of the open Vale 39
And saw the Water that composed this Rill 40
Descending, disembodied, and diffused 41
{~~crag~~
ample [? sc{ope] crag
Oer the smooth surface of a ~~lofty rock~~. 42
Lofty, and steep and naked as a tower 43
and who
All further progress here was barred. ^ ~~I turn~~'d 44
Stranger, or Inmate of the lonesome Vale
What living Man, thought I within myself 45

[72v] [III, 43–48]

as a Tower III, 43
All further progress here was barred.—And who, 44
vacant
Thought I, ~~they~~ if Master of a ~~leisure~~ hour 45

Probably continued from stub 71r; rev and expanded on 72v. The first five canceled lines of the Solitary's description of this hidden valley world appear to be replaced by *1814*, ll. 13–19 (cf. MS. 71, 65v), probably drafted as rev at the bottom of stub 71r, MS. 69.

20–22a, *30*b–*45* Cf. MS. 71, 65v–66v.

22, 30 Phrase "or let" is in pencil. "Said" possibly signals the continuation of rev on the bottom of stub 71r.

32 Rev in pencil.

35–36 "A sharp" is del in pencil and ink. The rev, from "At the word," is entered first in pencil, overwritten in ink, and del in pencil. The rev "sharp" is in pencil, possibly intended to restore the original reading and rejecting the rev "a sudden turn." MS. 71 and *1814*, however, adopt the first rev, "At the word / We followed as he led:—a sudden turn."

43–45 Rev on 72v; another attempt at drafting related to these lines may have been made on stub 73v.

43–48 Rev and expansion of 72r; cf. MS. 71, 66r–66v.

Here would not linger willingly detained 46
Whether to such wild objects he were led 47
When copious rains &c 48

[84^r] [III, 309–330]

And with the Imagination be content *III, 278*
Not wishing more, repining not to tread *279*
The little twining path of earthly care *280*
By flowers embellish'd and by springs refreshed. *281*
Blow winds of Autumn—let your chilling *282*
breath
live
Take the green herbage from the Mead, and strip *283*
variegated rob garb
The forest of its beautiful attire *284*
And let the bursting clouds to fury rouze *285*
The gentle Brooks—Your desolating sway *286*
Thus I exclaimed no sadness sheds on *287*
me
And no disorder in your rage I find{. ,} *288*
{What dignity change
{[?How its gravity] what beauty in this [?~~course~~] *289*
From mild to angry and from sad to gay *290*
{~~With~~
{[?That] ~~intermixture and unceasing change~~
Alternate and revolving—how benign *291*
How rich in animation & delight *292*
How bountiful these elements compare *293*
{th as
Wi{ght aught of more desireable or fair *294*
Devized by fancy for the golden age *295*
Or
~~With~~ that perpetual warbling that *296*
{i
preva{ ls
In Arcady beneath unaltered skies *297*
Through the long year in constant quiet *298*
bound
Night hush'd as night & day serene as day *299*

[114^v] [I, 69–81]

mind *I, 72*
[?Tur]n'd inward[?s,] or at my request he sang *73*

278–299 Cf. MS. 71, 73^v–74^r, where this passage concludes the first stage of copying.
294 Word "as" in pencil.

72–84 See 120^r. Cf. MS. M, ll. 60–65, 100 (*RC & Pedlar*, pp. 387, 391); MS. 71, 5^r–5^v. The brackets at the beginning of the lines represent tears in the page; the torn pieces are stuck to the next full leaf, 120^r, which provides the conjectured readings.

O[ld] songs—the product of his native hills 74
A [ski]llful distribution of sweet sounds 75
Feeding the soul and eagerly imbibed 76
As cool refreshing water by the care 77
[Of] the industrious Husbandman diffused 78
[Th]rough a parch d meadow ground in time 79
of drou[?th.]
e
[?Still] deeper wl{lcome found his pure discourse 80
[?H]ow precious when in riper days I learnd 81
To weigh with care his words & to rejoice 82
In the plain presence of his dignity 83

Oh many are the Poets &c 84

[120r] [I, 101–127]

Though born in low estate and earning br[ea]d I, 103
{C
By a low {calling, yet this mild good M[an] 104
Ranked with the prime and choice of sterling 105
minds.
I honour'd him, respected, nay revered; 106
And some small portion of his eloquent speech 107
And some things that may serve to set in 108
view
The feeling pleasures of his loneliness 109
The doings, observations which his mind 110
[?~~stile~~]
Had dealt with—I will here record in ~~verse~~ 111
strains
if with truth they
Which, ~~if it~~ correspond ~~with truth~~, and sink 112
Or rise, as venerable nature leads, 113
accept
The high and tender Muses shall ~~approve~~ 114
With gracious smile deliberately pleased 115
And listening Time reward with sacred praise 116
~~Among the hills of Perthshire he was~~ 117
born
[?An]
His Father, he being yet an Infant, died 120
S
In poverty and left three s{ons behind. 120, 122

---

74 "Old" supplied from MS. M, l. 62, and MS. 71, 5r.
75 Word "skillful" supplied from MS. 71, 5r; at this point MS. 69 diverges from MS. M.
78–81 Initial readings in brackets supplied from MS. 71, 5r.
84 The opening line signals the inclusion of the passage beginning at l. 100 in MS. M.

103–117, 120–132 Cf. MS. M, ll. 114–130 (*RC & Pedlar*, pp. 391, 393); MS. 71, 6r–6v. For speculation on what may have been entered between 114v and 120r of MS. 69, see p. 524, above.
103–104 Pieces of the torn leaf, 114v, are stuck to the upper right margin and obscure the readings at the end of ll. *103* and *104;* readings in brackets are supplied from MS. M, ll. 114, 115, and MS. 71.
112 Word "they" is in pencil, as is the deletion of "it".

The widowed Mother for a second Mate
~~The Mother married to a second Mate~~ 125
Espoused the Teacher of the Village School
~~The Teacher of the Village School, a Man~~ 126
~~A blameless Man~~
{~~to~~
~~Of blameless life who~~ {[?] ~~her Children gave~~ 127
{C
Who on her {children zealously bestowed
Needful instruction, not alone in arts 128
Which to his humble duties appertained 129
But in the lore of right and wrong, the law 130
in the peaceful ways
Of human kindness, ~~peace, and [?love], the~~ [?ways] 131
Of honesty and holiness severe. 132

[198r]

As when, upon the smooth pacific deep,
Dense fogs, to sight impervious, have withheld
A gallant vessel from some bold Emprize
Day after day deferred, till anxious hope
Yields to despair if chance a sudden
breeze
V}
Spring up and dissipate the v}eil all hearts
Throb at the change, and every sail is
T}   spread
[?]}o speed [?~~the~~] her course along the dazzling
waves
For recompense of glorious ~~vic~~ conquest
soon
To be atchieved upon the astonish'd foe.

---

131 The conjectured word at the end of the line, supplied from MS. M, l. 129, and MS. 71, 6v, is obscured by a pink gummy substance (perhaps sealing wax) which caused leaf 114 to stick to 112 and the subsequent tearing of leaf 114.

See Appendix II for reading text.

[220v]

age
IV, 756 From diminution safe & time & age
757 While Man grows old & dwindles
& decays
758 And countless generations of mankind
759 Depart & leave no vestige where
they trod—
130
693

This page seems to represent the furthest point in Book IV in MS. 69. Some version of Book IV, 627–755, amounting to 130 lines (including ll. 756–759), perhaps drawn from MS. 70 (29r–37r), preceded this (see the contents listing of leaves and stubs of MS. 69, above).

756–759 Cf. MS. 70, 37r.

The line count "693" is in pencil in the hand of WW below the "130"; it probably takes into account either another 563 or 693 lines based on revised copy of MS. 70 that probably once stood on leaves, now undecipherable stubs, of MS. 69 or in another, now missing, MS., giving a total for Book IV, revised, of either 693 or 823 lines.

DC MS. 71

DC MS. 71—in use at the second and fifth stages of *Excursion* composition for work on Books I, II, and III—is described in the Manuscript Census, pp. xxiii–xxiv, above. For a discussion of this manuscript and its role in the composition of *The Excursion,* see pp. 434–441, 448–455, above.

There are three categories of italic line numbers in the right-hand margins of the transcriptions: (1) numbers consisting of Roman numerals for books followed by Arabic numerals for lines refer not to the 1814 reading text in this edition but to the underlying pre-1813 text of *Excursion,* I–III, c. *299;* i.e., the state before Wordsworth revised this material following the death of his two children; (2) line numbers preceded by *CC* (all on leaves 93^{v}–94^{r}) refer to lines included in the poem *Characteristics of a Child three Years old* after the passages were omitted from *The Excursion;* (3) line numbers preceded by *MG* (all on leaves 91^{v}, 92^{v}–93^{v}, 94^{v}–95^{v}) refer to lines included in the poem *Maternal Grief* after the passages were omitted from *The Excursion.* Left-hand margin line numbers in roman type on the transcriptions of DC MS. 71 provide cross-references to the line count in the 1814 reading text. These references to the 1814 reading text are given at intervals of five (more frequently in complex passages) up to the end of the underlying pre-1813 reading text (at III, *299*); after that point, a number is assigned to every line that has an equivalent in the 1814 reading text.

In addition to the references to *Excursion* manuscripts in the notes to the transcriptions, we provide where appropriate references to *Ruined Cottage/ Pedlar* MS. M (DC MS. 44; see Manuscript Census, p. xxi).

On pp. 674–683, below, we present sample photographs of these leaves of DC MS. 71:

DC MS. 71, inside front cover and 1^{r}
DC MS. 71, 12^{v} and 13
DC MS. 71, 14^{v} and 15^{r}
DC MS. 71, 15^{v} and 16
DC MS. 71, 32^{v} and 33^{r}
DC MS. 71, 34^{v} and 35^{r}
DC MS. 71, 41^{v} and 44^{r}
DC MS. 71, 53^{v} and 54^{r}
DC MS. 71, 56^{v} and 57^{r}
DC MS. 71, 112^{v} and 113^{r}

The image size of the photographs of DC MS. 71 is 71 percent of actual size.

[Inside front cover]

this zealous Friend
II, 654 Of past discussions with ~~my Fri~~end
[?I now]
655 [?And by example of pure life,] [?]
[?Will]
656 [?Shall] force upon his notice [?undeterrd]
Will force [?u] undeterrd
657 By the example of his own pure ~~life~~
[?soul]
658 And that respect & deference
which [?a soul]
659 May fairly claim by niggard
age
enriched
it
660 In what values most the love of god
661 And his frail Creature man—

[?best]
(age that commands the wealth
of other minds
[660] In what he [?v]

this zealous Friend
[654] Of past discussions wi
[655] And advocate of humble life I now
[656] Will force upon his notice undeterred
[657] By the example of his pure ~~life~~ course
[658] And that respect and deference which
a Soul
[659] May fairly claim by niggard Age enriched
[660] In what it values most the love of God
[661] And his frail Creature Man

[1^r]

II, 446 Whose simple skill had throngd the grassy
floor
less
447 With work of frame {[?half] solid a proud shew
448 ~~With~~ baby houses studiously arranged
Of
449 Nor wanting ornament of walks between
450 With mimic trees inserted in the turf

Rev of 55^v, 56^r. Ll. 654–661/[660] are in pencil and are overwritten by ll. [654]–[661] in ink, below. At the bottom of the page are lines (here not transcribed) beginning "Then, (last wish." The passage continues on 1^r and is recopied on 1^v; it is related to the post-preamble of *Prelude*, I, 229–236; see *13-Bk Prelude*, II, 9, 19–20.

II, 446–454 are in pencil and are a rev of 49^v; I, 696–702 are a rev of 22^v–23^r. At page foot are five lines (here not transcribed) that continue *Prelude*, I, material from the inside front cover. Leaf 1^v has a version of *Prelude*, I, 229–236. See note to inside front cover.

451 And gardens interposed. pleased
with the sight
452 I could not choose but beckon to my
guide
453 Who having enter'd carelessly lookd
round
454 And now would have pass d on

I, 696 And on the third as wistfully she raised
697 Her head from off her pillow to look forth
698 Like one in trouble for returning light
699 Within her chamber casement she espied
700 A folded paper lying as if placed
tremblingly
701 To meet her waking eyes—This ~~she strai~~tway
e
702 Open'd & found no writing but ~~with~~ the[?i]rein

[2r]

I, 410 ~~as makes the nations~~ groan
422 As makes the nation groan.—Vigourous in health
—
[410] And to his purpose true, this humble course
maintained
~~Of toilsome~~ rural traffic he pursued
~~Till due~~
[410] As makes the nations groan. This active
C course,
411 [?c]hosen in youth, through manhood he pursued
412 Till due provision for his modest wants
413 Had been obtained & thereupon resolved
[?untasked]
414 To pass the remnant of his days ~~untainted~~
With hardship
415 ~~By~~ needless services from ~~labour~~ free
416 His calling laid aside he lived at ease
[?to] [?to]
417 But still he loved [?] [?p] pace the public
ways
418 And the wild paths & when the summers warmth
would leave
419 Invited him ~~he~~ often left his home
420 And journeyed far revisiting those scenes
421 —Which to his memory were most endeard.
[422] Vigorous in health of hopeful Spirits, untouch'd
423 By worldly mindedness or anxious care

Rev of 14r–14v and 15v; see note to l. *393/394*, 14v.

[2ᵛ]

~~dimly~~ seen I, 2
[?~~indistin~~]
&
Th[?er] rough strong refractions ~~of~~ [?oppressive] 3
light
As ~~through~~ a
~~A baffling haze~~
Glanced on the sight
From many a brooding cloud with 6

[3ʳ]

I
ted high
'Twas summer and the sun was moun I, 1
Southward the in[?s]di[?nc]tly
~~*Along the South the uplands feebly glared*~~ 2
Southward, the Landscape indistinctly
downs
Through a pale steam; but all the nothern 3
~~a clear~~ {*st*
In cleare {[?*r*] *air ascending shew'd far off* 4
{er
{o{[?] with sh }
A surface dappled {[?] [?sh]}adows flung
~~*Their surfaces with shadows dappled oer*~~ 5
With sha[?d]dows flung from many
[?a]
~~*Of deep embattled clouds*~~*: far as the sight* 6
From many a brooding cloud
{\
~~*Could reach*~~{ ~~*those many shadows lay in spots*~~ 7
~~*Determined and unmo*~~*ved, with steady beams* 8
bright
Of ~~*clear*~~ *and pleasant sunshine interposed* 9
Pleasant to him who on the soft cool moss 10
Extends his careless limbs along the front 11
Of some huge cave whose rocky ceiling casts 12
A twilight of its own an ample shade 13

Pencil rev of 3ʳ.
3 Del by eras.

Rev on 2ᵛ.
The base text of 3ʳ–74ʳ is in MW's hand.
1–13 Cf. MS. M, ll. 1–3; because MS. M is missing its first leaf, "MS. E2 (the original first gathering of MS. M is thus transcribed up to l. 51" (*RC & Pedlar*, p. 383).
1/3 Rev in pencil.
3/4 Phrase "a clear" is in pencil, then del in ink.
4/5 The conjectured rev overwritten by "oer with sh" is in pencil.
5/6 Rev in pencil.
7–8 Del in pencil.
9 Del in pencil. WW's pencil rev overwritten in ink by MW.

[3^v]

{M
{man
2 {warbles while the}
Where the Wren {[?l] [?] [?to warble]} dreaming
the
Half-conscious of ~~that~~ soothing melody
With side-long eye looks out upon the scene
By that impending Covert made more soft
More low and distant. Other lot was mine
Yet with good hope that soon I should obtain
s
A ^ grateful resting-place and livelier joy. 20
Across a bare wide Common I was toiling
With languid feet which by the slippery ground
i
Were baffled, nor could my weak arm de{sperse
The host of insects gathering round my face
And ever with me as I paced along.
Upon that open Level stood a Grove
bound.
The wished for Port to which my steps were
Thither I came, and there amid the gloom
Spread by a brotherhood of lofty Elms

[4^r]

3
Appeared a roofless Hut four naked Walls
That stared upon each other. I looked round
And to my wish and to my hope espied
Him whom I sought a Man of reverend age
[?~~tal~~]
But stout and hale for travel unimpaired
There was he seen upon the Cottage bench
Recumbent in the shade as if asleep
feet
An iron-pointed Staff lay at his ~~side~~.
marked
Him had I ~~seen~~ the day before—alone
And in the middle of the public Way 40
Stationed, as if to rest himself, with face
[~~-?-~~]
Turn'd tow'rds the Sun then setting; while that
Staff

20 WW's pencil rev overwritten in ink by MW.
21–29 Cf. MS. M, ll. 4–16 (see *RC & Pedlar*, pp. 383, 385).
26–36 Draft toward these lines appears in a late rev of MS. E; see *RC & Pedlar*, p. 453.

Rev on this page is part of redefining the Pedlar of *RC* as the Wanderer of *Exc.* Cf. 6^r; 15^v–16^r; 20^r, l. 582.
30–44 Cf. MS. M, ll. 18–32 (see *RC & Pedlar*, p. 385).
33/34 Rev del by eras.
40/41 Del (of two illeg letters) by eras.

{ed figure
Afford{ing to his ~~person~~ as he stood
~~Behind him fixed upheld a long white Pack~~ 42
Detained for contemplation or repose
~~That crossed his shoulders; wares for them who~~ 43
live
Graceful support; the countenance of
the Man
~~In lonely Villages and straggling Huts.~~ 44
45 Was hidden from my view, & he himself
[?so] [?I had beheld]
The face of him who thus ~~before me stood~~ 45
Standing before me in the public way
Detained for Contemplation or Repose 46
Was hidden from my view, the Man himself 47
While in that [?sort] the Man before [45]
me stood
[45] His face was hidden from my view & he [47]

[4ᵛ]

4
46 *Unrecognized; but striken by the sight* I, 48
With slack'ned footsteps I advanced and soon 49
A glad congratulation we exchanged
~~As I came up to him great joy was ours~~ 50
At such unthought of meeting.— For the night 51
50 *We parted nothing willingly, and now* 52
He by appointment waited for me here 53
Beneath the shelter of these clustering Elms. 54
We were tried Friends. I from my Childhood 55
up
Had known him. In a little Town obscure 56
55 *A market Village seated in a tract* 57
~~past~~
Of mountains, where my school-day time was 58
pass'd.
One Room he owned the fifth part of a House *60* 59
A place to which he drew from time to time 60
{or
And found a kind of home {*and harbour there.* 61
60 *—He loved me, from a swarm of rosy Boys* 62
Singled out me, as he in sport would say 63
62 *For my grave looks too thoughtful for my years.* 64
~~Glad was I when he from his rounds returned.~~ 65

45/[47] The queried words of rev above l. *45*, the rev line below l. *45*, and ll. [*45*] and [*47*] at page foot are in pencil.

49–65 Cf. MS. M, ll. 34–52 (see *RC & Pedlar*, pp. 385, 387).
58 Del by eras.
65 Line count at 5ʳ, l. *81*, may take into account del of this line.

[5^{r}]

5
As I grew up it was my best delight
To be his chosen Comrade. Many a time
On holidays we wandered throught the Woods
A pair of random Travellers—we sate
We walked; he pleased me with his sweet dis
course
Of things which he had seen; and often~~er~~ touch'd
Abstrusest matter, reasonings of the mind
Turned inward, or at my request he sang
Old Songs—the product of his native hills
A skillful distribution of sweet sounds
Feeding the soul and eagerly imbibed
As cool refreshing Water by the care
Of the industrious Husbandman diffused
Through a parched meadow-ground in time of
drought.
Still deeper welcome found his pure discourse
How precious when in riper days I learn'd 80
To weigh with care his words and to rejoice
In the plain presence of his dignity.
~~mine eager~~

[5^{v}]

6
Oh! many are the Poets that are sown
By Nature, Men endowed with highest gifts
The Vision and the faculty divine,
Yet wanting the accomplishment of Verse
Which in the docile season of their youth
It was denied them to acquire through lack
Of culture and the inspiring aid of Books
Or haply by a temper too severe
Or a nice backwardness afraid of shame
Nor having e'er as life advanced been led
By circumstance to take unto the height
The measure of themselves these favored Beings
All but a scattered few, live out their time
Husbanding that which they possess within
And go to the grave unthought of. Strongest
minds

66–74, 83 Cf. MS. M, ll. 53–62, 99 (see *RC & Pedlar*, pp. 387, 391).
72–84 Cf. MS. 69, 114^{v}, which draws on MS. M, ll. 60–65, 98–100ff. (see*RC & Pedlar*, pp. 387, 391).
81 MW's count appears to miss a line. Possibly she intended to exclude del l. *65* on 4^{v}, but the del of l. *65* is in a dark ink similar to other dels that MW's line counts do not recognize. Subsequent line counts differ from the base text numbering by one until 12^{v}, l. *341*.
Aborted rev at page foot may be related to l. *76*.

84–98, 101 Cf. MS. M, ll.100–112 (see *RC & Pedlar*, p. 391).
84 Cf. MS. 69, 114^{v}.

Are often those of whom the noisy world 99
Hears least; else surely this Man had not left, 100
~~*Nor others of like mold whom I have known,*~~ 101
100

[6^r^]

7

His graces unrevealed and unproclaimed. I, 102
~~*But honoured was he far as he was known*~~
~~*Though born in low estate*~~ *and* ~~*earning bread*~~ 103
But as the mind was filled with inward light
~~*By a low Calling, yet this mild good Man*~~ 104
So not without distinction had he lived
~~*Rank'd with the prime and choice of sterling M*~~*inds.* 105
Beloved & honored far as he was known
~~*I honour'd him, respected, nay*~~ *revered:* 106
And some small portion of his eloquent speech 107
And something that may serve to set in view 108
The feeling pleasures of his loneliness 109
The doings, observations which his mind 110
verse
Had dealt with—I will here record in ~~*strains*~~ 111
it
Which if with truth ~~*they*~~ *correspond, and sink* 112
Or rise, as venerable Nature leads 113
The high and tender Muses shall accept 114
With gracious smile deliberately pleased 115
And listening Time reward with sacred praise. 116
Among the hills of Athol he was born. 117
There on a small hereditary Farm 118
And unproductive slip of rugged ground 119

[6^v^]

8

His Father dwelt; and died in poverty. I, 120
While He, whose lowly fortune I retrace 2} 121
10}0
The youngest of three Sons, was yet a Babe 122
A little One unconscious of their loss 123
But eer he had outgrown his infant days 124
His widowed Mother for a second Mate 125
Espoused the Teacher of the Village School 126

102–105 Rev is part of redefining the Pedlar as the Wanderer. Cf. 4^r^ and notes.
102–111, 117 Cf. MS. M, ll. 113–123, which reads "Perthshire" for "Athol" (see *RC & Pedlar,* pp. 391, 393).
103–117 Cf. MS. 69, 120^r^, which draws on MS. M, ll. 114–130.
107 Eras may be of "words"; cf. MS. M, l. 118.

120–122, 125–137 Cf. MS. M, ll. 124–135 (see *RC & Pedlar,* p. 393). From l. *133, Exc* Book I in MS. 71 appears to be based on MS. M, ll. 131ff., as MS. 71 follows rev in MS. M, except as noted, although punct, spelling, and caps may differ.
120–132 Cf. MS. 69, 120^r^.

~~carefully~~
Who on her Offspring zealously bestowed
Needful instruction not alone in arts
Which to his humble duties appertained
But in the lore of right or wrong the rule
Of human kindness in the peaceful ways
Of honesty and holiness severe.
A virtuous household though exceeding
poor,
Pure livers were they all, austere and grave
And fearing God, the very Children taught
~~*& Piety maintained with*~~
Stern self-respect, a reverence for God's word,
strict[?*ly*]
132 *an habitual Piety—maintained* [?*with strictness*]
{ly
~~*And piety*~~ *scarce* { *known on English Land.*
With
Strictne[?*snss*]

[7ʳ].

9
Nor was he lot[?*h*] ~~*when winter came*~~
that freedom to resign
When winter came for then he might I, [140]
repair
With book in hand & satchel [?*on his back*]
134 *From his sixth year, the Boy of whom I speak*
In summer tended Cattle on the Hills,
thro' the {*inclement & the* / [?*barren season*] *he* [?*resigned*]} *perilous days*
~~*But in the winter time he duly went*~~
Of long continuing winter he repaired
To his Step-father's School that stood alone, 140
Sole Building on a Mountain's dreary edge,
Far from the sight of City Spire, or sound
.}
Of Minster Clock ,} *From that bleak Tenement*
He, many an evening, to his distant home
retur}
In solitude saw} *ning, saw the hills*
Grow larger in the darkness, all alone
Beheld the Stars come out above his head
And travelled through the wood with no one
near
To whom he might confess the things he saw.
So the foundations of his mind were laid.

135–137 Interlinear rev is in hand of DW and continues at the top of 7ʳ.

138–154 Cf. MS. M, ll. 136–152 (see *RC & Pedlar*, pp. 393, 395).
Rev at the top of the page, continued from the bottom of 6ᵛ, is in the hand of DW. DW entered a later version of these lines at page foot. MW copied the lines interlinearly at l. *140* to form ll. 136–137 of *1814*. MW's rev overwrites an earlier partial rev of l. *140*, "[?barren season] he [?resigned]," which is in the same ink as the base copy.
144 Eras is probably of a copying error: MS. M, l. 142, agrees with the rev reading.

In such communion, not from terror free,
While yet a Child, and long before his time,
He had perceived the presence and the power

days
X *But thro' the inclement & perilous ~~months~~*
Of long continuing-winter he repaired

[7ᵛ]

10
Of greatness, and deep feelings had impress d
o
Great objects on his mind, with pr}rtraiture
And colours so distinct that on his mind they lay
Like substances, and almost seemed
To haunt the bodily sense. He had received
native genious
(Vigorous in ~~mind by Nature~~ as he was)
A precious gift; for, as he grew in years,
With these impressions would he still compare
r
All his {[?R] emembrances, thoughts, shapes and forms
And being still unsatisfied with aught
Of dimmer character, he thence attained
An active power to fasten images
ur
Upon his brain, and on their pict[?]}ed lines
e
Intensly brooded, even till they acquired
The liveliness of dreams. Nor did he fail,
While yet a Child, with a Child's eagerness
Incessantly to turn his ear and eye,
On all things which the moving seasons brought

[8ʳ]

11
To feed such appetite: nor this alone
Appeased his yearning. In the after day
Of Boyhood, many an hour in caves forlorn,
mid
And ∧ ~~in~~ the hollow depths of naked crags
He sate, and even in their fixed lineaments
Or from the power of a peculiar eye,
Or by creative feeling overborne,
Or by predominance of thought oppressed,
Even in their fixed and steady lineaments,
He traced an ebbing and a flowing mind
Expression ever varying.
Thus informed

155–172 Cf. MS. M, ll. 153–170 (see *RC & Pedlar*, p. 395).

173–189 Cf. MS. M, ll. 171–187 (see *RC & Pedlar*, pp. 395, 397).

He had small need of books; for many a Tale
Traditionary round the mountains hung:
And many a legend peopling the dark woods
Nourished Imagination in her growth
185 *And gave the mind that apprehensive power*
By which she is made quick to recognise

[8ᵛ]

who sustaind
[190] X *With will inflexible those fearful pangs*
191 12 *Triumphantly displayed in records left*
192 *The moral properties and scope of things.*
eagerly
But ~~greedily~~ he read and read again
Whate'er the Ministers old Shelf supplied,
~~chiefly those~~
who suppli ed
190 *The life and death of Martyrs ~~who sustained~~*
who sustained
~~Whose sufferings are displayed in~~
~~Intolerable pangs~~, ~~the Records left~~ who sustaind x
193 *Of Persecution and the Covenant, times*
194 *Whose echo rings through Scotland to this hour*
~~might be~~
~~Nor haply was there wanting here and there~~
195 *And there by lucky hap had been preservd*
A straggling Volume torn and incomplete
That left half-told the preternatural Tale,
ie
Romance of Giants, Chronicle of Fei nds,
Profuse in garniture of wooden cuts, 200
200 *Strange and uncouth, dire faces, figures dire*
Sharp-knee'd, sharp-elbow'd and lean ancled
too,
With long and ghostly shanks, forms which once
seen
Could never be forgotten.
In his heart

[9ʳ]

wanting 13
Where fear sate thus a cherished Visitant
205 *Was ^ yet the pure delight of love*
A milder Spirit yet had found no place
Love yet was wanting the pure joy of love

190–205 Cf. MS. M, ll. 188–203 (see *RC & Pedlar,* p. 397).
196 Eras is probably of a copying error: "hour" is the reading of MS. M, l. 193 as rev.
205–208 Draft toward these lines is found in a late rev of MS. E (see*RC & Pedlar,* p. 454).

206–222 Cf. MS. M, ll. 204–218 (see *RC & Pedlar,* pp. 397, 399).
206/207 The caret signals the inclusion of "wanting" above l. *206.*

By sound diffused or by the breathing air,
Or by the silent looks of happy things
Or flowing from the universal face
Of earth and sky. But he had felt the power
Of Nature, and already was prepared
By his intense conceptions to receive
Deeply the lesson deep of love, which he
Whom Nature, by whatever means, has taught
To feel intensly, cannot but receive.
hath been
From early childhood, even as ~~I have~~ said,
From his sixth year, he had been sent abroad
In summer to tend herds: such was his task
.
Henceforward till the later day of youth 220
Oh! then what soul was his when on the tops

[9^v]

14
Of the high mountains he beheld the sun
Rise up, and bathe the world in light. He
Ocean & earth, the sold frame of earth
looked;
~~The ocean and the earth~~ beneath him lay
And oceans liquid mass .
In gladness and deep joy : The clouds were
touched
And in their silent faces did he read
Unutterable love. Sound needed none,
Nor any voice of joy: his spirit drank
The spectacle; sensation, soul and form
All melted into him; they swallowed up
His animal being: in them did he live,
And by them did he live: they were his life.
In such access of mind, in such high hour
Of visitation from the living God
Thought was not in enjoyment it expired
~~In joy exalted to beatitude~~
No thanks he breathed, he proffered no request
Rapt into still communion that transcends
The imperfect offices of prayer and praise
were breathed

223–239 Cf. MS. M, ll. 219–233 (see *RC & Pedlar*, pp. 399, 401).
228 Eras is probably of a copying error: MS. M, l. 224, reads "needed."
235–241 Two sets of draft toward these lines (ll. *238–239* and *235–241*) are found in a late rev of MS. M, ll. 231–235 (see *RC & Pedlar*, pp. 456–457).
Rev "were breathed," at page foot, seems intended for l. *237*, but it was not adopted in *1814*.

[10r]

15
His mind was a thanksgiving to the power I, 240
That made him, it was blessedness and love 240 241
—A Herdsman on the lonely mountain tops, 242
Such intercourse was his, and in this sort 243
Was his existence oftentimes possessed 244
Oh! then how beautiful, how bright appeared 245
The written Promise! he had early learned 246
To reverence the Volume which displays 247
The mystery, the life which cannot die: 248
But in the mountains did he feel his faith. 249
There did he see the writing. All things there 250
mo
Breathed im{*mo* / [?*ort*]}*rtality, revolving life* 251
And greatness still revolving: infinite. 252
There littleness was not; the least of things 253
Seemed infinite, and there his spirit shap'd 254
Her prospects, nor did he believe, he saw. 255
What wonder if his being thus became 256
Sublime and comprehensive! Low desires, 257
Nor bound nor [?immeasurable] there
appeared
[?spirits]

[10v]

16
Low thoughts had there no place yet was his I, 258
heart
~~mind~~
Lowly; for he was meek in gratitude. 259
~~those ectasies were called to mind~~
Oft ~~as he called to mind these extasies~~ 260
those extacies to mind
And whence they flowed, and from them he 260 261
acquired
Wisdom which works through patience thence he 262
learned
In many a calmer hour of sober thought 263
To look on Nature with a humble heart 264
Self questioned where it did not understand, 265
And with a superstitious eye of love. 266
Thus pass'd the time, yet to the neighbouring 267
duly *Town*
He ~~often~~ went with what small overplus 268
His earnings might supply, and brought away 269

240–257 Cf. MS. M, ll. 234–251 (see *RC & Pedlar*, p. 401).
248 Eras is probably of a copying error: MS. M, l. 242, reads "cannot."
Rev at page foot may be related to l. 245 or an attempt to extend the argument of l. 255. The word "[?spirits]" is in different ink from the rev above.

258–274 Cf. MS. M, ll. 252–268 (see *RC & Pedlar*, pp. 401, 403).

The Book which most had tempted his desires 270
While at the Stall he read. Among the hills 271
He gazed upon that mightly Orb of Song, 272
The divine Milton. Lore of different kind, 273
The annual savings of a toilsome life, 274

[11^r]

17

His Step-father supplied, books that explain I, 275
The purer-elements of truth involved 276
In lines and numbers, and by charm severe, 277
Especially perceived where nature droops 278
res
And feeling is supp[? lied] } *s'd, preserves the mind* 279
Busy in solitude and poverty 280
occ } {*ied* *deceived*
[? occ] } *up* {*ations oftentimes*
T } {*ese*
~~*And*~~*, t* } *h* {*us* ~~*employed*~~*,* ^ ~~*he many a time o'erlookd*~~ 281
{*ile* *280*
The listless hours wh {*en in the hollow vale,* 282
Hollow and green, he lay on the green turf 283
In pensive idleness. What could he do, 284
With blind endeavours in that lonesome life 285
Thus thirsting daily? Yet still uppermost,
Nature was at his heart, as if he felt, 287
{ *how*
Though yet he knew not { *[? long], a wasting power* 288
In all things which from her sweet influence 289
Might tend to wean him. Therefore with her 290
{ *Her* } *hues*
{ *[? With her]* } *forms, and with the spirit of her forms* 291
He clothed the nakedness of austere truth 292

[11^v]

T }
18 [?] } he history
Wind rain & cleaving thunder
~~engaged with [?rudimental]~~ tasks
While yet ~~*he lingered in the elements*~~ I, 293
~~While [?in]~~ *he lingered in the rudimets*

275–292 Cf. MS. M, ll. 269–286 (see *RC & Pedlar*, p. 403).
279 Eras is probably of a copying error: MS. M, l. 273, reads "suppress'd."
280/281 Word "deceived" is in pencil overwritten in the same ink as MW's other revs of this line. *1814* adopts MW's first rev, "occupations."
288 Eras is probably of a copying error: MS. M, l. 282, reads "how."
291 Eras is probably of a copying error: MS. M, l. 285, reads "Her."

293–309 Cf. MS. M, ll. 287–303 (see *RC & Pedlar*, pp. 403, 405).
The first two lines are in pencil; these lines and related pencil interlinear drafting at l. *303*, at page foot, and on 12^r appear intended to follow l. *302* but were not adopted in *1814*.

laws
Of science, and among her simplest {[?],
His triangles they were the stars of Heaven
This silent Stars: oft did he take delight
'
295 *To measure th*{*e altitude of some tall crag*
Which is the Eagle's birth-place, or some peak
Familiar with forgotten years, which shews
Inscribed, as with the silence of the thought
Upon its bleak and visionary sides 300
300 *The history of many a winter storm,*
[?~~Tempests~~] ~~[?]~~
Or obscure records of the path of fire.
or
~~And the commotion of inter~~nal
[?]
And thus before his eighteenth year was ~~gone~~
told
Accumulated feelings pressed his heart
With an encreasing weight: he was o'erpowered
305 *By ~~his own~~ Nature, by the turbulence subdued*
mind
Of his own ~~heart~~, by mystery, and hope
soul
307 *And the first virgin passion of a ~~mind~~*
[?~~The wind~~ cloud wind]
The cleaving thunderbolt [?~~the brook~~]
Or}, or [?rain]
Of} water spirit descended from the [?cloud]

[12[r]]

[?That with a] *19*
Intelligible trace of wrath appeared
W}
A}hirlwind & rain & cleaving thunderbolt
308 *Communing with the glorious Universe.*
Or water spirit descended from the clouds
309 *Full often wished he that the winds might rage*
310 *When they were silent; far more fondly now*
i
Than [?*h*]}*n his earlier season did he love*
conflict
Tempestuous nights, the ~~uproar~~ and the sounds
That live in darkness: from his intellect,
And from the stillness of abstracted thought,
and
315 *He sought repose ~~in vain~~. I have hear him say*

---

294 Eras is probably of a copying error: MS. M, l. 288, reads "laws."
297 Added apos restores "th'altitude," which is the reading of MS. M, l. 291.
302/303 Rev in pencil; del in ink.
303/304 Rev in pencil; "the commotion of inter" del in ink.
Draft at page foot is in pencil; see note above.

310–325 Cf. MS. M, ll. 304–319 (see *RC & Pedlar*, p. 405).

All rev above l. *311* and below l. *325* are in pencil. First line on the page continues draft from the facing 11[v]; next three lines of rev from "Intelligible" through "clouds" appear to be rev of draft at page foot and imply inclusion of last line on page or l. *303* on 11[v] (see note to 11[v]).

often failing at this time to gain
That ~~at this time he scanned the laws of light~~
The peace he sought he scannd the laws of light
Amid the roar of torrents, where they send
From hollow clefts up to the clearer air
to
320 *A cloud of mist which ~~in~~ the shining sun* 320
322 *Varies its rainbow hues. But vainly thus,*
~~But~~ And thus, & vainly by all other
{t
323 *And{ vainly, ~~by all other~~ means he strove*
324 *To mitigate the fever of his heart*
325 *In dreams, in study and in ardent thought*
Whirlwind
of ~~wind~~ & rain & cleaving thunder
Or water spirit descending from the cloud
Or the commotions of internal fire

[12v]

328 yet gaining more
[329] 20 And every moral feeling of his soul
[330] Strengthened & braced ~~by [?breat]~~
[?~~while nature~~]
[330] by breathing [?in content]
326 *Thus, even from Childhood, upward, was he rear'd,*
~~yet [?every day~~]
yet [?every wind]
327, 328 *Doubtless in want of much, ~~yet gaining more~~,*
[330] Strengthend & braced by breathing in
[? ?subtle] content
~~Breathing a piercing air of poverty~~,
{the
[331] The keen {& wholesome air of poverty
{f
332 *And drinking {rom the well of homely life.*
334 *—Now came the time that summond him to fix*
~~And now brought near to manhood~~, ~~he began~~
335 *Upon the course of humble industry,*
~~To think upon life's future course and how~~
~~best might earn~~
~~He best might earn his worldly maintenance~~. ^
336 *By which his maintence might best be gaind*
His Mother strove to make her Son perceive
With what advantage he might teach a School
{ joining
In the ad{ [?vantage] Village, but the Youth,
340 *Who of this service made a short essay*

326–341 Cf. MS. M, ll. 320–335 (see *RC & Pedlar*, p. 407).

328–332 Rev of this passage probably began with pencil draft at page foot, ll. 330–331, then entered interlinearly between ll. *326–329*. Another draft at page foot, ll. 329–[332], overwrites the earlier pencil draft, but its reading for l. 331 is not adopted. The draft at the top of the page appears to be the final rev with the "And" of l. [329] overwriting the "o" of the page number. All eras are probably of copying errors, since they restore readings of MS. M; in ll. *327, 329, 331*, they coincide with revs to MS. M. Cf. MS. M, ll. 320–323.

329 Word "of" possibly underlies "from" as in MS. M, l. 323.

Found that the wanderings of his thoughts were
then
A misery to him, that he must resign
343 *A task he was unable to perform.*
who had left his home
He had a Brother ~~elder than himself~~
~~Six years, who long before had left his home~~
yet every day *330*
330 Strengthend [?& braced] by breathing
[?in content]
wholesome [?air]
331 The [?keen &] [? ?] of poverty
329 And every moral feeling of his soul
[330] Strengthened & brac d by breathing in content
{air
[331] The unindulgent {[?] of poverty
{from
[332] And drinking {[?] the well

[13r]

21

To journey far and wide with Pedlar's Wares
{*&* *on English ground*
~~In England, where~~ {*he trafficked at that time,* ^
Healthy and prosperous. "What should hinder now"
Said he within himself, "but that I go
And toil in the same calling." And in truth,
This plan, long time had been his favourite thought
and
365 *He asked his Mother's blessing, ~~did~~ with tears*
ing *second* *from him*
Thank ^ *~~the good Man~~, his* ^ *Father, asked* ^
367 *~~From him~~ paternal blessings, ~~and set forth~~*
bestowd
[367] *~~A Traveller bound to England~~. The good Pair* ^
Their farewell benediction
~~Offered up prayers, and blessed him~~, but with hearts
Foreboding evil. From his native Hills
370 *He wandered far, much did he see of Men,*
Their manners, their enjoyments and pursuits,
Their passions and their feelings, chiefly those
Essential and eternal in their heart
Which, 'mid the simpler forms of rural life,

---

340 Rev in hand of DW.
340–347 These lines do not appear in *1814*.
341 MW's line count is ten short here onward to 13v; cf. 12r, l. *321*.

342–358 Cf. MS. M, ll. 336–352 (see *RC & Pedlar*, pp. 407, 409). Rev in the hand of DW except as noted.
349 Word "second," in the hand of MW, restores the reading of MS. M, l. 343.
350–351 "The good Pair bestowed" of l. *351* is connected by a line so as to follow "blessings" of l. *350* and to form l. 367 of *1814*.

[13[v]]

22

Exist more simple in their elements, I, 359
And speak a plainer language. In the woods, 360
A lone enthusiast, and among the fields, 361
i
It{enerent in this labour, he had passed 362
The better portion of his time, and there 340 363
Spontaneously *thriven*
~~From day to day~~ had his affections ~~breathed~~ 364
Upon the Bounties of the year & felt
~~The wholesome air of Nature~~, there he kept 365
The Liberty of Nature
In solitude and solitary thought 366
His mind in a just equipoise of love. 367
Serene it was unclouded by the cares 368
Of ordinary life, unvexed, unwarped 369
By partial bondage. In his steady course 370
No piteous revolutions had he felt, 371
No wild varieties of joy or grief, 372
Unoccupied by sorrow of its own 373
His heart lay open; and by Nature tuned 374
And constant disposition of his thoughts 375

[14[r]]

23

To sympathy with Man, he was alive I, 376
To all that was enjoyed where'er he went 377
for
And all that was endured, ~~and~~ in himself 378
Happy, and quiet in his chearfulness, 379
He had no painful pressure from without 380
That
~~Which~~ made him turn aside from wretchedness 381
With coward fears. He could afford to suffer 382
those *came*
With ~~them~~ whom he saw suffer. Hence it ~~was~~ 383
That in our best experience he was rich 360 384
And in the wisdom of our daily life: 385
various
For hence minutely in his ~~daily~~ rounds 386
He had observed the progress and decay 387
Of many minds, of minds and bodies too, 388
y
The historie[?s]} of many families, 389

359–375 Cf. MS. M, ll. 353–369 (see *RC & Pedlar*, p. 409).
363–366 Rev in hand of DW.
363 MW's line count is twelve less than the number of base lines entered since the last line count at 12[v], l. *341*. Subsequent line counts differ from the reading text numbering by twenty-three until l. *420*, 15[r]. There is no apparent explanation for the error.

376–392 Cf. MS. M, ll. 370–386 (see *RC & Pedlar*, pp. 409, 411).
380 Butler notes that MSS. B and D of *RC* read "within"; he conjectures a copying error in MSS. E and M, l. 374 (see *RC & Pedlar*, p. 411).
389–390 Rev in hand of DW.

had
~~And~~ how they ^ prospered; how they were oerthrown 390
By passion or mischance, or such misrule 391
Among the unthinking Masters of the earth 392
[?~~humble~~]
410 This ~~toilsome~~ course
[?toil]} [?~~wand~~]
O [?lone]} some rural
travel
~~labour~~
traffic
411 Of unambitious ~~industry~~ he pursued
412 Till due provision for his modest wants
413 Had been obtaind & thereupon

[14^v]

With steadfast mind
410 24 And bless d with vigo[?uru]s hea[?lt] this humble
course
411 of toilesom rural traffic he pursu[?e]
410, 422 *As makes the nations groan. Untouch'd by* I, 393
H *taint*
423 *Of worldly-mindedness or anxious care* 394
Observant, studious, thoughtful, and refreshed 395
425 *By knowledge gathered up from day to day:* 396

Thus had he lived a long and innocent life{. 397
The Scottish Church both on himself & those 398
With whom from Childhood he grew up, had held 399
The strong hand of her purity, and still 400
430 *Had watched him with an unrelenting eye.* 401
age
This he remembered in his riper ~~years~~ 402
With gratitude and reverential thoughts. 403
But by the native vigour of his mind, 380 404
By his habitual wanderings out of doors, 405
435 *By loneliness, and goodness and kind works,* 406
~~ere in docile~~
' *n*
Whate{ver in ~~his~~ childhood or ~~h~~is} youth 407
437 *He had imbibed of fear or darker thought* 408
~~utterly dispers'd~~

410–413 Draft at page foot is part of a sequence of rev first intended as a new beginning to the second part of Book I on 15^v, further rev on 14^v and 2^r, and finally indicated as following l. *393* on 14^v. See notes to 15^v and 14^v.

393–408 Cf. MS. M, ll. 387–402 (see *RC & Pedlar*, pp. 411, 413).
Draft at top of page del by a cross appears to be rev of drafts at bottoms of 14^r and 15^v; additional rev is on 2^r. "And" of l. 410 overwrites the page number. See notes to 14^r, 15^v.
393/394 Mark appears to signal insertion of some version of draft of ll. 410–423 on 2^r. The first version of these lines is entered on 15^v and appears to be an attempt at a new beginning for the second part of Book I. It is rev on 14^r and the top of 14^v.
406/407 Phrase "ere in docile" in pencil; "docile" overwritten in ink by MW.
407 Word "his" del in pencil; "h" in the second "his" del by eras.
408/409 Rev in pencil; overwritten and del in ink. The rev is also entered in pencil at page foot.

438 *Was melted all away: so true was this* 409
439 *That sometimes his religion seemed to me* 410
440 *Self-taught, as of a dreamer in the woods* 411
utterly dispers'd

[15^{r}]

441 *Who to the model of his own pure heart* I, 412
25
442 *Framed his belief, as grace divine inspired* 413
443 *Or human reason dictated with awe* 414
438 ~~*Was melted all away: so true was this*~~ 409
439 ~~*That sometimes his religion seemed to me*~~ 410
440 ~~*Self-taught, as of a dreamer in the woods*~~ 411
444 *—And surely never did there live on earth* 415
M *of kindlier nature* end of Book
445 *A m*] *an of* ~~*sweeter temper.*~~ ~~*Birds and*~~ *beasts,* 416
He loved them all, chickens and household dogs, 417
~~*And to the Kitten of a neighbours house*~~ 418
453 *Such as might suit a rustic Sire prep*[*?ard*]
~~*Would carry crumbs and feed it.*~~ 419
449 ~~nor was he less indulgent to the tong[?e]~~
450 of ~~garrulous age~~

2

{*lain his garb*
452 P{*oor and plain*
[449] Nor listened he less patiently to those
[450] Whom age had rendered garrulous
{*And*
454 {*Was his appearance, yet he was a Man* 420

409–411 Copied from del lines on 15^{r} as part of an expansion of MS. M, ll. 392ff. Ll. *412–414*, not in MS. M, continue at the top of 15^{r}. The line count on 15^{r}, l. 423, includes this early rev on 14^{v}.

409–426 Cf. MS. M, ll. 403–417 (see *RC & Pedlar*, p. 413).

This page and 15^{v}—with their related revs on 113^{r}, 112^{v}, 36^{r}, 35^{r}–35^{v}—reveal a series of shifting conceptions and complex revs of the end of the first part and the beginning of the second part of Book I, which ultimately sees the "Birds and beasts" passage transferred to II, 41–64; see note to 35^{r}. Earliest rev on the page was del of ll. *409–411* and expansion of these lines at the bottom of 14^{v} and top of 15^{r} in pen and ink similar to that of the base copy. This expanded version was included in the line count at l. *423*. Rev by eras to ll. *419–420* are probably also early. Next stage of rev, expanding ll. *416–419* into *1814*, I, 445–452, and II, 41–64, was made after at least part of Book II was copied, probably in the fifth stage of *Exc* composition (see pp. 383 [n. 44–49] and 453–454, above). The last rev on 15^{r} was the addition of l. 453 between ll. *418/419*; the addition assumes the *1814* rev to l. 454, "For sabbath duties," which is not entered in MS. 71. Lines related to I, 445–450 are entered interlinearly and at page foot. Two versions of Book I and Book II lines expanding the work on 15^{r} are entered on 113^{r} and 112^{v}. Both appear intended to follow l. *416* at one stage or another; 113^{v} appears to be initially intended toward rev in Book I, but 112^{v} seems intended as rev and expansion of Book II. Sometime after the opening pages of Book II were copied, most probably in 1813 or 1814, the lines related to Book II, 44–64, were added on 35^{r}–35^{v} and rev and recopied on inserted leaf 36^{r}. WW seems to have resolved his concern over the division of parts one and two of Book I; *1814* restores the dividing line below l. 465, and no significant rev occurs after *1814*.

412–414 These added lines at the top of the page are continued from ll. *409–411* at the bottom of 14^{v}.

415/416 Phrase "kindlier nature" is in pencil overwritten in ink. The reference "end of Book" is probably to the rev of ll. 445–452 on 113^{r}, which was first drafted at page foot and interlinearly between ll. *419–420*. A closely related rev is entered on 112^{v}.

416–419 Expanded on 112^{v} and 113^{r}. The "2" (or possibly a "Q") probably signals the inclusion of the lines on 113^{r} which are marked in the same way and follow the expansion of ll. 444–452 immediately preceding these lines on 113^{r}. The expansion of ll. *416–419* on 113^{r} and 112^{v} become II, 44–61.

455 *Whom no one could have passed without*
remark 421
Active and nervous was his gait; his limbs 422
And his whole figure breathed intelligence 423
400
Time
~~*Age*~~ *had compressed the freshness of his*
cheek 424
Into a narrower circle of deep red 425
460 *But had not tamed his eye, which under*
brows 426
The rough sports
[445]
446 And teazing ways of Children vexd not him
{Nor
447 {[?] could he bid them from his presence, tired
448 With questions & importunate demands
[449] ~~He was a ready listener~~ to the tongue
Indulgent listener was he
[450] Of garrulous age nor did the Sick man's tale

[15[v]]

{*& such*
[466] *So was he framed* {*wh*[?] *his course of life*
[467] *Who now with no appendage of a staff*
26
[468] *The prized memorial of relinquishd toils*
469 *Upon that Cottage bench reposed his limbs*
461 *Shaggy and grey had meanings which it*
brought I, 427
From years of youth, which like a being made 428
Of many beings he had wondrous skill 429
To blend with knowledge of the years to come 430
465 *Human, or such as lie beyond the grave.* 431
f} *408*
Such was in brief the History o[?r]} my Friend
on}
[466] So was he framed. This [?]}ly let me add
412 That due provision for his modest wants
413 No sooner had been made than he resol[?v]d
414 To pass the remnant of his days untasked
415 With needless service & from hardship free
at ease
416 His Calling laid aside he lived ~~in peace~~
[?haunt]
417 But still he love to [?~~pace~~] the public way

---

423 MW's line count includes the rev on 14[v]–15[r], ll. *409–414*.

427–436 Cf. MS. M, ll. 418–427 (see *RC & Pedlar*, pp. 413, 415).
Rev, continued on to the top of 16[r], is part of redefining the Pedlar as the Wanderer. Cf. 4[r] and note.

Rev on 15[v] and 16[r] appears to take place in three stages. The first is interlinear at page foot between ll. *433* and *436*, resulting in ll. 466, 468, 467, and the unnumbered rev between ll. *435–436* ending "meanwhile." The second rev, ll. 412–421, adopting the opening line and a half of ll. *432–433*, is entered in the space left between the horizontal line at l. *431* (demarcating the end of the first part of this book) and l. *432* (the opening of the second part). These demarcations between the first and second parts follow MSS. E and M, l. 422 (cf. *RC & Pedlar*, pp. 412, 413); *1814* and MS. M also have a horizontal line, while MS. E concludes "End of Part First." This second rev continues interlinearly through l. *433* and concludes with ll. 419–421 at page foot. It is subsequently rejected as a new opening for the second part of the book, and instead used for an expansion of ll. *392–393* on 14[r], 14[v], and 2[r]. The third and final rev, ll. [466]–469 at the top of the page, is a rev of the first, interlinear rev at page foot, and continues on to the top of 16[r] through l. 472.

~~Such was in brief the~~ history of my Friend:

{[?warmth]
418 And the wild paths & ~~of~~ when the summer[?s] {[?]

466 *So was he framed. Now on the bench he lay*

468 And one memorial of his former toils

And of his pack of Merchandise had made

467 A staff with ~~iron~~ iron filleted & forked

A pillow for his head: his eyes were shut

Lay at his ~~side~~ side meanwhile

472 *The shadows of the breezy Elms above*

Invited}
419 And the} him ~~abroad~~ he often left his his home

tr
420 And ~~wandere~~ far revisiting those scenes

421 Which to his memory were most endeared

[16r]

e}
470 *Skren} 'd from the sun. supine the Wanderer lay*

27

His eyes as if in drowsiness half shut

472 *The shadows of the breezy Elms*

{ing
473 *Dappl{ed his face. He had not heard my steps*

As I approached; and near him did I sit

475 *Unnoticed in the shade some minutes space*

At length I hailed him, seeing that his hat

Was moist with water drops, as if the brim

Had newly scooped a running stream. He

ro}
[?]} *se,*

And ere the pleasant greeting that ensued

said I
480 *Was ended, "Tis a burning day" ~~said I~~*

"My lips are parched with thirst, but you I

guess

Have somewhere found relief." He, at the word,

Pointing towards a sweet-briar, bade me climb

aspiring
The fence hard by, where that ~~tall slender~~ shrub

485 *Looked out upon the road. It was a plot*

Of garden-ground run wild, its matted weeds

Marked with the steps of those, whom as they

passed, 20

The gooseberry trees that shot in long lank slips

Or currants hanging from their leafless stems

437–453 Cf. MS. M, ll. 428–444 (see *RC & Pedlar*, p. 415).

470–472 Rev continued from top of facing verso, 15v.

442 Overwriting of "rose" is probably the result of a copying error.

451 Line count begins anew at l. *433* with what in MSS. of *RC* opens the second part (see MS. M, l. 422). That count precedes all the major revs on 15v–16r and thus does not include them.

[16^v]

28

490 *In scanty strings had tempted to oerleap* I, 454

Here casting round my eye

around

The broken wall. ~~I looked about, and there,~~ 455

I look'd around & there

Where two tall hedge-rows of thick alder boughs 456

espied

Joined in a damp cold nook, I ~~found~~ a Well, 457

plumy fern

Half covered up with willow flowers and ~~grass~~. 458

495 *My thirst I slaked and from the chearless spot* 459

upon the ~~Cottage bench~~

Cottage

496 *Withdrew, and while ~~beside the~~ ^ shady bench* 460

He sate & near him

497, 498 *~~I yet was standing~~ with uncovered head* 461

499 {I yet was standing freely to respire
{[? ? ? ?]

~~Intent to catch the motion of the air~~ 462

500 And cool my temples in the fanning air

{*p*

The Old Man s{[?*t*] *ake, "I see around me here* 463

Things which you cannot see: we die, my Friend, 464

Nor we alone, but that which each man loved 465

And prized in his peculiar nook of earth 466

s} *him*

505 *Die* } *with ~~us~~, or is changed; and very soon* 467

Even of the good is no memorial left. 468

The Poets in their elegies and songs, 469

Lamenting the departed call the groves, 470

They call upon the hills and streams to 471

mourn

[498] He sate & near him with uncovered head
[499] I yet was standing freely to respire
[500] And cool my temples in the fanning

[17^r]

29

510 *And senseless rocks; nor idly; for they speak* I, 472

In these their invocations with a voice 40 473

Obedient to the strong creative power 474

454–471 Cf. MS. M, ll. 445–461 (see *RC & Pedlar*, pp. 415, 417).

455 Rev appears to be in three stages: First, "about" is del and rev to "around" above the line. Second, "I ... there" is del in pencil and the rev above the line entered in pencil. Third is the rev below the line.

460 "Cottage" immediately above "shady" is in pencil.

460–463 Rev at page foot.

461/462 Rev overwrites illeg pencil, which is partially eras..

467 Pencil rev to "him" is overwritten in ink.

[498]–[500] Pencil rev of interlinear rev of ll. *461–462* above. The last word in l. [500], "air," is entered opposite at bottom of facing 17^r.

472–487 Cf. MS. M, ll. 462–477 (see *RC & Pedlar*, p. 417).

473 There is no obvious explanation for MW's miscount of "40" when 42 is the accurate figure.

exist
Of human passion. Sympathies there are 475
More tranquil, yet perhaps of kindred 476
birth
That steal upon the meditative mind 477
And grow with thought. Beside yon Spring 478
I stood,
And eyed its waters till we seemed to feel 479
{.
One sadness, they and I{, *For them a bond* 480
Of brotherhood is broken: time has been 481
When every day the touch of human hand 482
Dislodged the natural sleep that binds them 483
up
In mortal stillness and they ministered 484
As
To human comfort. ~~*When*~~ *I stooped to drink* 485
Upon the slimy foot-stone I espied 486
{*less* *wo*} {*d*}
The use {*ful*[*?ly*] *fragment of a br*} {*ok*} *en bowl;* 487
air

[17[v]]

30 pensive that
Green with the moss of years, a ^ *sight* ~~*it was*~~ I, 488
days
That moved my heart, recalling former ~~*times*~~ 489
When I could never pass that road but she 490
Who lived within these walls, when I appeared, 491
A daughter's welcome gave me, and I loved 492
her
As my own Child. O Sir! the good die first, *60* 493
And they whose hearts are dry as summer dust 494
Burn to the socket. Many a Passenger 495
Hath blessed poor Margaret for her gentle 496
looks
When she upheld the cool refreshment, drawn 497
From that forsaken Spring; and no one came 498
But he was welcome; no one went away 499
him
But that it seemed she loved ~~*them*~~. *She is dead,* 500
{~~*of the*~~ {:"
~~*Forgotten in the quiet*~~ {*grave* ~~*grave*~~} {. 501
The light extinguished of her lonely Hut
{The Hut itself abandoned to decay
of one who [?dwelt beneath this roof]}

---

475 Alt "exist" is in pencil.
At page foot "air," in pencil, is the last word of l. [500] on the facing 16[v].

488–504 Cf. MS. M, ll. 478–493 (see *RC & Pedlar*, pp. 417, 419).
488 Pencil rev with "pensive" overwritten in ink.
491 Rev corrects a probable copy error: reading of MS. M, l. 480, is "when I appeared."
500 Del and rev in pencil overwritten in ink.

~~*I speak of a poor Woman who dwelt here*~~
And She forgotten in the quiet grave
~~*This Cottage was her home and she the best*~~
{O
I speak of {one ~~who dwelt beneath this Roof~~
~~*Of many thousands who are good and poor.*~~
continued he of one whose
stock
Of virtues bloomd beneath
this lo[?*ne*]*ly roof*

[18^{r}]

31
She was a Woman of a steady mind,
Tender and deep in her excess of love,
Not speaking much, pleased rather with the joy
Of her own thoughts: by some especial care
Her temper had been framed as if to make
A being who by adding love to peace
Might live on earth a life of happiness.
Her wedded Partner lacked not on his side
The humble worth that satisfied her heart. 100
sober withal {*al*
Frugal, affectionate ^ *and ~~therewith~~*{
She with pride would tell
Keenly industrious. ~~I have heard her say~~
often seated
That he was ~~up and busy~~ at his loom
In summer ere the Mower was abroad
Among the grass, and oft in early Spring
Ere the last Star had vanished. —They who passed
At evening, from behind the garden fence
Might hear his busy spade which he would
ply

[18^{v}]

32 *un* *of day*
After his daily work ^*till the ~~day~~-light*^
Had failed
~~*Was gone*~~*, and ~~every~~ leaf and flower were*
lost
In the dark hedges. So their days were spent
In peace and comfort, and a pretty Boy
Was their best hope next to the God in Heaven.
Some twenty years ago, but you, I think

---

502 Pencil del overwritten in ink. Overwritten rev above the line, "of one … [?roof]" (see rev following l. *501*, above), is in pencil.

505–521 Cf. MS. M, ll. 494–508 (see *RC & Pedlar*, p. 419).

513 MW's line count inexplicably adds twenty lines, which are carried forward in her subsequent line counts.

514 WW's "withal" is in pencil.

522–538 Cf. MS. M, ll. 509–525 (see *RC & Pedlar*, pp. 419, 421).

Can scarcely bear it now in mind, there came
Two blighting seasons when the fields were
left
With half a harvest. It pleased Heaven to
add
570 *A worse affliction in the plague of war:*
571 *A happy Land was striken to the heart;*
'Twas a sad time of sorrow and distress:
120
572 *A wanderer among the Cottages,*
freight
I, with my Pack of winter raiment, saw
The hardships of that season; many rich
575 *Sank down, as in a dream, among the poor,*
And of the poor did many cease to be

[19r]

33
And their place knew them not. Meanwhile
abridged
Of daily comforts, gladly reconciled
To numerous self-denials, Margaret
580 *Went struggling on through those calamitous*
years
With chearful hope: but ere the second autumn
on lay
~~*Her husband*~~ ~~*to*~~ *a sick-bed was* ~~*confined*~~
~~Oppress'd~~ Smitten
~~*Labouring*~~ *with perilous fever. In disease*
He lingered long; and when his strength retur
ned
585 *He found the little he had stored to meet*
The hour of accident or crippling age
Was all consumed. Two Children had they now,
One newly born. As I have said, it was
A time of trouble; shoals of Artisans
590 *Were from their daily labour turned adrift*
To seek their bread from public charity,
They and their wives and children, happier far
Could they have lived as do the little birds *140*
[582] *Her lifes true help mate on a sick*
bed lay

[19v]

596, 597 *34* *Long had filled with plenty*
& possessed in peace
594 *That peck along the hedges, or the kite*

539–555 Cf. MS. M, ll. 526–541 (see *RC & Pedlar*, pp. 421, 423).
545 Word "Smitten" is entered in ink different from that of other rev.

556–572 Cf. MS. M, ll. 542–558 (see *RC & Pedlar*, p. 423).
596, 597 Pencil addition is rev at page foot.

[?*who*]
595 *That makes his dwelling on the mountain* 557
X *rocks*
Ill fared it now with Robert, he who X 558
This lonely *dwelt*
598 ~~*Here in this*~~ *Cottage. At his door he stood* 559
599 *And whistled many a snatch of merry tunes* 560
600 *That had no mirth in them; or with his knife* 561
Carved uncouth figures on the heads of sticks, 562
Then idly sought about through every nook 563
In house or garden any casual work 564
Of use or ornament, and with a strage 565
yet
605 *Amusing,* ~~*but*~~ *uneasy novelty* 566
He blended, where he might, the various tasks 567
Of summer, autumn, winter, and of spring 568
But this endured not, his good humour soon 569
Became a weight in which no pleasure was 570
610 *And poverty brought on a petted mood* 571
611 *And a sore temper: day by day he drooped,* 572
X
596 he who long
[597] Had filled with plenty and possess'd in
peace
[598] This lonely Cottage

[20r]

35
And he would leave his home and to the Town I, 573
Without and errand would direct his steps *160* 574
And wander here and there among the 575
fields.
615 *One while he would speak lightly of his Babes* 576
And with a cruel tongue: at other times 577
He tossed them with a false unnatural joy 578
And 'twas a rueful thing to see the looks 579
Of the poor innocent Children. "Every smile" 580
620 *Said Margaret to me, here, beneath these Trees,* 581
"Made my heart bleed." 582
Wan
At this the Old Man paused
And looking to those enormous Elms, 583
hour of {*n* {*on*
He said, "tis now the^ *deepest* {*ho*{*ur.* 584
At this still season of repose and peace 585

---

558 Crosses indicate the last rev at page foot. Cross above "dwelt" is in pencil. Cross above "Robert" may indicate a further rev or intention to rev, not recorded in MS. 71; the name "Robert" is not in *1814* at this point. L. 596 in *1814* reads, "A sad reverse it was for Him who long."
559, 566 Del and rev in pencil.

573–589 Cf. MS. M, ll. 559–575 (see *RC & Pedlar*, pp. 423, 425).
582 "Wan" is in pencil. This abbreviation for Wanderer is part of redefining the Pedlar as the Wanderer. Cf. 4r and note.

This hour when all things which are not at
rest
Are chearful; while this multitude of flies
Is filling all the air with melody
Why should a tear be in an Old Man's eye?

[20ᵛ]

36
Why should we thus with an untoward mind
And in the weakness of humanity
From natural wisdom turn our hearts
away,
To natural comfort, shut our eyes and ears
And, feeding on disquiet, thus disturb *180*
The calm of nature with our restless thoughts.
181

{*He*
{*He spake with somewhat of a solemn tone*
But when he ended there was in his face
Such easy chearfulness, a look so mild
That for a little time it stole away

[21ʳ]

37
All recollection, and that simple Tale
{*sound*
Passed from my mind like a forgotten {[?*dream*]
A while on trivial things we held discourse,
To me soon tasteless. In my own despite
I thought of that poor Woman as of one
Whom I had known and loved. He had rehears'd
Her homely Tale with such familiar power,
With such an active countenance, an eye
So busy, that the things of which he spake
Seemed present, and, attention now relaxed,
There was a heartfelt chillness in my veins.
I rose, and, turning from that breezy shade,
Went forth into the open air, and stood
{*the*
To drink {[?*of*] *comfort of the warmer sun*

590–599 Cf. MS. M, ll. 576–585 (see *RC & Pedlar*, p. 425).

595/596 The horizontal rule signals end of the second part, as it does in MS. M, l. 581. MW's line count, "181," totals the number of lines in the second part, but because of earlier errors in counting lines, the actual number here should be eighteen fewer, or "163." Cf. 17ʳ, l. *473* and 18ʳ, l. *513*. There is a space of approximately six lines between the rule and l. *596*.

596 "He" partially erased and then overwritten.

596ff. Third part of Book I has less rev, perhaps because Margaret's story remained relatively fixed, whereas the Pedlar's character undergoes changes as and when he becomes the Wanderer.

600–616 Cf. MS. M, ll. 586–602 (see *RC & Pedlar*, pp. 425, 427).

601 MS. M, l. 587, reads "sound."

613 Probable copy error: MS. M, l. 599, reads "the."

Long time I had not staid e're looking round *614*
Upon that tranquil Ruin, I returned 20 *615*
And begged of the Old Man that for my sake *616*

[21^v]

38
[?]
He would resume his story. He replied, *I, 617*
"It were a wantonness and would demand *618*
Severe reproof if we were Men whose hearts *619*
Could hold vain dalliance with the misery *620*
Even of the dead; conten[?]*ted thence to draw* *621*
A momentary pleasure, never marked *622*
By reason, barren of all future good. *623*
But we have known that there is often found *624*
In mournful thoughts, and always might be found *625*
A power to virtue friendly, wer't not so *626*
I am a dreamer among Men, indeed *627*
An idle dreamer. 'Tis a common Tale, *628*
An ordinary sorrow of Man's life, *629*
A Tale of silent suffering, hardly clothed *630*
,
In bodily form{. *But without further bidding* *631*
I will proceed. *632*

[22^r]

39
While thus it fared with them *I, 632*
To whom this Cottage till those hapless years *633*
Had been a blessed home it was my chance *634*
To travel in a Country far remote 40 *635*
And glad I was, when, halting by yon gate *636*
once more
That leads from the green lane, ~~again~~ I saw *637*
These lofty Elm-trees. Long I did not rest: *638*
With many pleasant thoughts I cheared my *639*
way
Oer the flat Common. At the door arrived, *640*
I knocked, and when I entered, with the hope *641*
Of usual greeting, Margaret looked at me *642*
A little while, then turned her head away *643*
Speechless, and sitting down upon a chair, *644*
Wept bitterly. I wist not what to do *645*

617–632 Cf. MS. M, ll. 603–618 (see *RC & Pedlar*, p. 427).
617 MW seems to have entered the first stroke of "H" before beginning her copy one line lower.
621 A probable copy error in the middle of "contented" is del by eras.
631 The period of MS. M, l. 617, is retained in *1814*, which also adds a dash before "But."

632–647 Cf. MS. M, ll. 618–633 (see *RC & Pedlar*, pp. 427, 429).
637 Del and rev in pencil.

Or how to speak to her. Poor Wretch! at last
She rose from off her seat, and then, O Sir!

[22v]

[696] *as wistfully she raised*
Her head from off her pillow
[697] *To lo* *to look forth*
40
I cannot tell how she pronounced my name:
With fervent love, and with a face of grief
Unutterably helpless, and a look
That seemed to cling upon me she enquired
If I had seen her Husband. As she spake
A strange surprize and fear came to my
heart
Nor had I power to answer, ere she told
not
That he had disappeared ~~just~~ two months gone *60*
He left his house: two wretched days had passed
as {wistfully / [? ?] to raise
696 *And on the third, by the first ~~break~~ of light*
697 Her head from off her pillow to look fort
699 *Within her casement full in view she saw*
X *~~A letter, such it seemed, which she forthwith~~*
702 *Opened, and found no writing, but therein*
enclosed
Pieces of money carefully ~~wrapped up~~,
shudderd
Silver and gold, "I ~~trembled~~ at the sight"
Said Margaret "for I knew it was his hand
coming of the morning
698 For the sure ~~comfort of returning~~ light
chamber
[699] Within her ~~cottage~~ casement she espied
700 A folded paper lying as if placed

[23r]

[?endd]
41
~~The~~ ere that day
was [?~~done~~]
706 *Which placed it there; and on that very day,*

648–663 Cf. MS. M, ll. 634–649 (see *RC & Pedlar*, p. 429).
All del and rev are in pencil unless otherwise noted.
[696]–[697] Rev of interlinear rev at ll. *656–658*; continued page foot, ll. 698–700, and at page foot of facing 23r (ll. 701–702). Rev on 1r.
656/657 Oblong circle in right margin probably signals further rev on 1r. Diagonal cancellation line is in ink.
659/660 The X in the left margin indicates the resumption of the text at l. 702 after rev on 23r, and possibly 1r, both of which conclude with l. 702.
700ff. Line at page foot is continued at page foot of facing 23r; cf. note above.

664–680 Cf. MS. M, ll. 650–666 (see *RC & Pedlar*, pp. 429, 431).
All del and rev are in pencil unless otherwise noted.
Queried word at top of the page is probably "ended" as in *1814*, I, 706.

By One who from my Husband had been sent,
The tidings came that he had joined a Troop
Of soldiers going to a distant Land.
He could not gather
—He left me thus—~~Poor Man!~~ ~~he had not~~ heart
for
To take a farewell of me; ~~and~~ he feared
That I should follow with my Babes, and sink
Beneath the misery of that wandering life".
This Tale did Margaret tell with many tears
And when she ended I had little power
To give her comfort, and was glad to take
Such words of hope from her own mouth as
served *80*
To chear us both: but long we had not talked
Ere we built up a pile of better thoughts,
And with a brighter eye she looked around
As if she had been shedding tears of joy.
We parted. It was then the early spring;
To meet her waking eyes. This she
[?str straitway]
~~forthwith~~
Open'd & found no writin

[23v]

42
I left her busy with her garden tools;
And well remember, o'er that fence she look
ed
And, while I paced along the foot-way path
Called out, and sent a blessing after me
With tender chearfulness, and with a voice
That seemed the very sound of happy thoughts
I roved o'er many a hill and many a dale
accustomed
With ~~this~~ my ~~weary~~ load, in heat and cold
Through many a wood and many an open ground
In sunshine and in shade, in wet and fair,
{blithe of heart as mi}
Drooping or {gay as might befal} ght befal,
My best companions now the driving winds
And now the "trotting brooks" and whispering trees,
{ad
And now the music of my own s{[?hort] steps,
With many a short lived thought that passed
between

100

667/668 Pencil rev is overwritten in ink.
701–702 Continued from page foot of facing 22v; rev on 1r.

681–695 Cf. MS. M, ll. 667–681 (see *RC & Pedlar*, pp. 431, 433).
688 Del and rev in pencil.
691 In MS. M, l. 677, WW changes his initial rev "gay and" to "blithe of heart."
694 Probable copy error: MS. M, l. 680, reads "sad."

[24r]

43

.} journeyed back
And disappeared,} I ~~came~~ this way ~~again~~ I, 696
Towards the wane of summer, when the wheat 697
Was yellow and the soft and bladed grass 698
ing had
Sprang ~~up~~ afresh ~~and~~ o'er the hay-field spread 699
Its tender green. When I had reached the door 700
I found that she was absent. In the shade 701
Where now we sit I waited her return 702
Her Cottage wore its customary look; 703
As chearful as before; but that I thought 704
{ng porch
~~The honeys~~uckle crowde{d round the ~~door~~ 705
~~And from the wall hung down in heavier tu~~fts 706
And knots of worthless stone-crop started out 707
[752] *Blinding the lower panes*
751 *~~Along the window's edge and grew like w~~eeds* 708
~~Against the lo~~wer panes. I turned aside 709
And strolled into her garden. It appeared 710
To lag behind the season, and had lost 711
Its pride of neatness. From the border lines 712
[749] *Hung down in heavier tufts & that*
bright weed
[750] *The yellow stone crop suffered*
to take root
[751] *Along the windows edge profusely*

[24v]

44
Composed of daisy and resplendant thrift I, 713
Flowers straggling forth had on those paths 714
encroached

696–712 Cf. MS. M, ll. 682–698 (see *RC & Pedlar*, p. 433). All del and rev are in pencil unless otherwise noted.

700 Eras is probably of a copying error; MS. M, l. 686, reads "reach'd the."

706–708 Rev at page foot.

712–719 Draft toward these lines, continuing on 24v, is found in a late rev of MS. M, ll. 698–701 (see *RC & Pedlar*, p. 457). See note to 24v, ll. *726ff.* below.

[752] Rev continued from page foot, l. [751].

713–727ff. Cf. MS. M, ll. 699–710, and late rev in MS. M, 23r (see *RC & Pedlar*, pp. 433, 435, 457).

718 Del and rev in pencil.

726ff. Complex and ultimately redundant series of rev on 24v–25r probably took place in three stages. The most probable sequence was that MW first copied as one continuous passage the five lines found in MS. M, ll. 708–712, corresponding to the erased and overwritten ll. 769, 770, 771, 775 at page foot, and probably l. 776 on the top of 25r. Second, these lines were del by eras, and ll. *736–738* entered following l. *735* on 25r, and ll. *726–727* on 24v over the erased ll. 769, 770, drawing upon WW's rev in MS. M, 23r (see *RC & Pedlar*, p. 457). MW's line count on 25r at l. *735* seems to confirm this sequence, as do her subsequent line counts. This second stage thus forms the early base text for MS. 71 and is numbered accordingly. Third, ll. *735–740* were del on 25r and ll. *726–727* del on 24v, with all del on both pages in similar wavy strokes. Ll. [769] and [770] would then seem to have been written over the eras, and ll. [770], [771], 772–773 entered on 24v, continuing with ll. 774–776 at the top of 25r, with l. 776 probably overwriting its own earlier eras. These lines are all in a different ink from that used throughout, as are the wavy cancellation lines. MW's line count through the end of the book suggests that this third stage of rev took place after her complete fair copy was made.

Which they were used to deck: carnations, once 715
Prized for surpassing beauty, and no less 120 716
760 *For the peculiar pains they had required,* 717
declind [?] {*d*
~~*Hung down*~~*n their lanquis*{~~*hed*~~ *heads without* 718
support.
The cumbrous bind-weed with its wreaths 719
and bells
Had twined about her two small rows of peas 720
And dragged them to the earth. Ere this an hour 721
765 *Was wasted. Back I turned my restless steps* 722
And as I walked before the door it chanced 723
A Stranger passed, and guessing whom I sought 724
768 *He said that she was used to ramble far.* 725
[775] {~~*The spot, though fair, seem'd very desolate*~~} 726
769 {[? *The sun was sinking in the west; and now*]}
776 {~~*The longer I remained more desolate,*~~} 727
770 {*I* [? *sate with*] *sad* [? *impa*] *tience. Fro*[? *m within*]}
[769] {*The sun was sinking in the west and now*}
771 {[? *Her*] *solitary Infant* [? *cried aloud*].}
[770] {*I sate with sad impatience from within*}
775 {[? *The*] *spot though* [? *fair seemed very desolate*],}
[771] *Her solitary Infant cried aloud*
772 *Then like a blast that dies away self-stilled*
773 *The voice was silent. From the bench*
I rose

[25^r]

45

774 *But neither could divert nor soothe my thoughts*
was
775 *The spot though fair* ~~*seemed*~~ *very desolate*
776 *The longer I remained more desolate*
And looking round I saw the corner stones, I, 728
Till then unnoticed, on either side the door 729
{*ains*
With dull red st{[? *ones*] *discoloured and stuck* 730
oer
780 *With tufts and hairs of wool, as if the sheep* 731
{*C*
That fed upon the {*common thither came* 732
Familiarly, and found a couching-place 733
drawing to the spot
783 *Even at her threshold;* ~~*resting there at will*~~ 734

718, 726ff. See notes on p. 568.

728–747 Cf. MS. M, 713–726 (see *RC & Pedlar*, p. 435).
774–776 Rev continued from 24^v (see note there).
775 Del and rev in pencil.
776 Eras line may be the same as the line that overwrites it and follows MS. M, l. 712, as part of the first sequence of composition begun on 24^v. It is erased in the next stage of rev; cf. note to *726ff.* on 24^v.
730 Rev to "stains" restores the original reading of MSS. B and D of *RC* miscopied as "stones" in MSS. E and M, l. 715.
734 Rev above line is in pencil.

[?to]
~~*As if in some wild event of their own.*~~ *140*
769 ~~*The sun was sinking in the west; and now*~~
770 ~~*I sate with sad impatience. From within*~~
771 ~~*Her solitary Infant cried aloud.*~~ *Deeper*
783b *shadows*
772 ~~*Then like a blast that dies away, self-stilled,*~~
F
784a *[?D]* *rom these tall elms*
773a, 784b ~~*The voice was silent.*~~ *The* ~~*house*~~*-clock struck*
cottage *eight,*
785 *I turned and saw her distant a few steps.*
Her face was pale and thin, her figure too
Was changed. As she unlocked the door, she said,
"It grieves me you have waited here so long
But, in good truth, I've wandered much of late
790 *And sometimes, to my shame I speak, have need*
Of my best prayers to bring me back again.

[25ᵛ]

46
While on the board she spread our evening meal *I,*
Sh
793, 795 [?*46*] *e told me she* ~~*had lost her elder Child,*~~
is *is*
~~*'Twas well,—for he was eating chearful bread*~~
~~*may*~~
~~*And useful works might learn, a serving Boy*~~
To
796 *With* *a kind Master on a distant Farm*
[?*That*] *he,* [?*for months had been, a*] *serving Boy*
Now
797 [?] *happily apprenticed*
Apprenticed by [?*the Parish*]. *"I perceive*

734/735 Word "[?to]" is in pencil.

734–740 See note to ll. *726ff.* on 24ᵛ. These lines are included in MW's line count on 45ᵛ, l. *755*. Ll. *734b–740a* are not present in MS. M.

738/740 Rev "Deeper shadows / From these tall elms" is in pencil and entered after del in order to bridge l. 783 above and l. 784 below.

740 Word "house" del in pencil; "cottage" is in pencil.

740–753 Although the text here follows that of MS. M, ll. 713–730 and its rev, ll. 728–730 (see *RC & Pedlar*, p. 457), copy seems to have broken off after the half-line at l. *740* and a space has been left before resumption of copy on 25ᵛ, l. 752. Ll. *740–749* are in the same ink used throughout, while ll. *750–753* are in different ink, suggesting that in a first stage of rev, the underlying text on 25ᵛ, ll. *752–753* (half-line), were meant to follow directly upon l. *749*. Probably, ll. *750–753* were then added and then rev again at the bottom of 25ᵛ to form the basis for *1814*. MW's line count at l. *755* includes ll. *735–755*.

748–753 After leaving space on 25ʳ for lines to be inserted, MW appears to have resumed copy with the underlying text of l. *752* or, less likely, l. *753*. The underlying text at ll. *752–753* follows the unrevised MS. M, ll. 729–730 (see *RC & Pedlar*, p. 435). Ll. *749–751* follow a late rev of MS. M, ll. 728–730 (see *RC & Pedlar*, p. 457). These lines are then partially rev at page foot to form the basis for *1814*, although there is no complete MS. for those readings. MW's line count at l. *755* included ll. *748–753*, although not their expansion at page foot. See note to 25ʳ, *740–753*, above.

749–751 Del in pencil. The angle mark in the left margin probably signals the rev at page foot.

750 The dash after "well" may be added.

752–767 Cf. MS. M, ll. 729–744, and MS. M, 23ʳ, 23ᵛ (see *RC & Pedlar*, pp. 435, 437, 457).

You look at me, and you have cause, Today
I have been travelling far, and many days 160
About the fields I wander, knowing this
Only, that what I seek I cannot find.
And so I waste my time: for I am changed
And to myself," said she "have done much wrong,
And to this helpless Infant. I have slept
Weeping, and weeping I have waked, my tears
Have flowed as if my body were not such
As others are, and I could never die.
But I am now in mind, and in my heart
More easy, and I hope" said she "that Heaven
Will give me patience to endure the things
Which I behold at home". It would have grieved

interrupting not the work
Which gave em. to her listless hands
That she had parted

[26^r]

47
Your very {*Soul* / *heart*} *to see her, Sir! I feel*
The story linger~~s~~ in my heart; I fear
'Tis long and tedious, but my spirit clings
To that poor Woman: so familiarly
Do I perceive her manner and her look
And presence, and so deeply do I feel
Her goodness, that, not seldom, in my walks
A momentary trance comes over me 180
And to myself I seem to muse on One
By sorrow laid asleep, or borne away
A human being destined to awake
To human life, or something very near
To human life when he shall come again
Yes
For whom she suffered. ~~*Sir*~~*, it would have grieved*
Your very soul to see her: evermore
Her eyelids drooped, her eyes were downward cast,
And when she at her table gave me food

793–795 Rev in pencil of l. *749* above. These lines form the basis for *1814* where the abbreviation "em." in l. 794 reads "employment" and l. 795 concludes "with her elder Child."

768–784 Cf. MS. M, ll. 745–761 (see *RC & Pedlar*, p. 437). For related rev, see note to 25^v, ll. *748–753*, above.
768 The correction "Soul" follows MS. M, l. 745, which reads "soul."
769 Del by eras.

[26ᵛ]

48

She did not look at me. Her voice was low, I, 785
830 *Her Body was subdued. In every act* 786
Pertaining to her house affairs appeared 787
less
The care ful stillness of a thinking mind 788
Self-occupied, to which all outward things 789
Are like an idle matter. Still she sighed, 790
835 *But yet no motion of the breast was seen,* 791
No heaving of the heart. While by the fire 792
s
We sate together sighs came on my ear 793
838 *I knew not how, and hardly whence they came.* 794
~~apprentic'd~~ X
~~*I gave her for her Son, the Parish*~~ *Boy,* 200 795
~~*A Kerchief and a book wherewith she seemed*~~ 796
842 *Pleased; and I counselled her to have her* 797
trust
In God's good love, and seek his help by prayer. 798
I took my Staff and when I kissed her Babe 799
845 *The tears stood in her eyes. I left her then* 800
to her care
839 *Ere my departure ^ I gave*
840 *For her Sons use some token of regard*
Wherewith in her distress the Mother
seemd

[27ʳ]

49

846 *With the best hope and comfort I could give* I, 801
wish
She thanked me for my ~~will~~, but for my hope 802
It seemed she did not thank me 803
I returned
And took my rounds along this road again 804
850 *Ere on its sunny bank the primrose flower* 805
[?welcome] to
Peeped forth to give an earnest of the spring 806
I found her sad and drooping; she had 807
learned
No tidings of her Husband: if he lived 808
She knew not that he lived; if he were dead 809

785–800 Cf. MS. M, ll. 762–777 (see *RC & Pedlar,* pp. 437, 439).

793 The "s" in "ears" is added and then del in pencil.

795–796 Del in pencil, but "Parish" first del in ink. The X in the right margin signals the pencil rev, ll. 839–840ff., at page foot.

839–840 Pencil rev of ll. *795–796*. In place of the last line, l. 841 of *1814* reads "And I exhorted her to have her trust." MW's line count "220" on 27ᵛ, l. *817*, appears to exclude the del lines, *795–796*, without taking into account the three added lines at page foot. Possibly, the lines were added after MW's line count.

801–816 Cf. MS. M, ll. 778–793 (see *RC & Pedlar,* p. 439).

802 Del and rev in pencil.

She knew not he was dead. She seemed the same
r
In person and appearance; but ~~*the*~~ *house*
Bespake a sleepy hand of negligence;
The floor was neither dry nor neat, the hearth
Was comfortless, and her small lot of books
Which, one upon the other, heretofore
Had been piled up against the corner panes

[27ᵛ]

50
In seemly order, now, with straggling leaves
Lay scattered here and there, open or shut 220
As they had chanced to fall. Her Infant Babe
Had from its Mother caught the trick of grief
And sighed among its play things. Once again
I turned towards the garden gate, and saw
More plainly still that poverty and grief
weeds defaced
Were now come nearer to her; ~~*the earth was*~~ *hard*
The hardend soil
~~*With weeds defaced*~~ *and knotts of withered grass;*
No ridges there appeared of clear black mold,
No winter greenness; of her herbs and flowers
It seemed the better part were gnawed away
r} {ra into
On} t{hempled ~~*on the*~~ *earth; a chain of straw*
turned about
Which had been ~~*twisted round*~~ *the slender stem*
Of a young Apple-tree lay at its root;
The bark was nibbled round by truant sheep.

[28ʳ]

51
Margaret stood near, her Infant in her arms,
And, seeing that my eye was on the Tree,

---

811 Del by eras.

817–832 Cf. MS. M, ll. 794–809 (see *RC & Pedlar,* pp. 439, 441).
824–825 Del and rev in pencil, with the exception of "hard." Eras may be of a copying error caused by the "rd" being worn away in MS. M, l. 801.
829–830 Del and rev in pencil, except for the overwriting of eras.

833–849 Cf. MS. M, ll. 810–826 (see *RC & Pedlar,* p. 441).
All del and rev are in pencil unless otherwise noted.

~~She~~ *said* she
"I$_\wedge$ *fear*$_\wedge$ *it will be dead and gone"*
Ere Robert came again". Towards the House
Together we returned, and she enquired
If I had any hope? But for her Babe, [?2]*40*
orphan
And for her little ~~*friendless*~~ *Boy, she said*
She had no wish to live, that she must die
Of sorrow. Yet I saw the idle loom
Still in its place: his Sunday garments hung
Upon the self-same nail; his very Staff
Stood undisturbed behind the door. And
{In *when*
{[?] dark december {raced
~~*This way the ensuing winter*~~ *I ret{urned*
this way
She told me that her little Babe was dead
released
And she was left alone. She now, I learned,
from her maternal cares
{~~*After her Infant's death*~~ *had* }
{*Had taken up the employment*} *taken up*
[? ? ?] e} wilds
The employment common through tho}se parts
cold *and gained*
In dark december I retrac'd
this way
In cold december I retraced
[?this] way

[28ᵛ]

52
By spinning hemp a pittance for herself
And for that end had hired a neighbour's
give her needful help *Boy*
To ~~*help her in her work*~~. *That very time*
Most willingly she put her work aside
along the miry road
And walked with me a mile, and, in such
The full space of a mile *sort*
ad a }
That any heart h[?*eart*]}*ched to hear her, begged*
That wheresoe'er I went, I still would ask
{ *w* }
For him {*f*[?*o*]}*hom she had lost. We parted then,*
Our final parting; for, from that time forth, *260*
Did many seasons pass 'ere I returned
Into this Tract again.
Nine tedious years,

835 "She said" and first caret are in ink. Quot after "gone" is del by eras.
848 Overwriting of eras is in ink.
[890] Rev of l. *845*.

850–865 Cf. MS. M, ll. 827–842 (see *RC & Pedlar*, pp. 441, 443).

From their first separations, nine long years, 861
She lingered in unquiet widowhood, 862
A Wife and Widow. Needs must it have been 863
A sore heart-wasting. I have heard, my Friend 864
That in yon arbour oftentimes she sate 865

[29^r]

53
Alone thro half the vacant
~~The idle length of half a a~~ Sabbath-day I, 866
if
And ~~when~~ a dog passed by she still would 867
quit
The shade, and look abroad. On this old Bench 868
For hours she sate; and evermore her eye 869
Was busy in the distance, shaping things 870
That made her heart beat quick. You see that 871
Path
Now faint, the gras has crept o'er its grey line 872
There to and fro she passed through many a day 873
Of the warm summer; from a belt of hemp 874
That girt her waist spinning the long drawn 875
thread
With backward steps. Yet ever as there passed 876
A Man whose garments shewed the Soldier's red, 877
Or crippled Mendicant in Sailor's garb *280* 878
The little Child who sate to turn the wheel 879
Ceased from his task, and she with faultering 880
voice,
Made many a fond enquiry; and when they, 881
Whose presence gave no comfort{ , were gone by 882

[29^v]

54
Her heart was still more sad. And by yon I, 883
gate
That bars the Traveller's road she often stood, 884
And, when a stranger Horseman came, the 885
latch
Would lift, and in his face look wistfully, 886
Most happy if from aught discovered there 887
Of tender feeling she might dare repeat 888

---

861 Word "separations" is probably a copying error; both MS. M, l. 838, and *1814* read "separation."

866–882 Cf. MS. M, ll. 843–860 (see *RC & Pedlar*, p. 443).
866–867 Del and rev in pencil.

883–898 Cf. MS. M, ll. 861–876 (see *RC & Pedlar*, pp. 443, 445).
888 An ink dot occurs after "feeling."

The same sad question. Meanwhile her poor
Hut
Sank to decay: for he was gone, whose hand,
At the first nipping of October frost,
Closed up each chink, and with fresh bands
gr } *of straw*
Chequered the [?*th*]} *een-grown thatch. And so*
she lived
Through the long winter reckless and alone,
Until her house by frost and thaw and rain
{ile
Was sapped; and wh{*en she slept, the night*
damps
Did chill her breast; and, in the stormy day, *300*
Her tattered clothes were ruffled by the wind

[30[r]]

55
Even at the side of her own fire. Yet still
She loved this wretched spot nor would for
worlds
Have parted hence; and still that length of
road,
And this rude Bench one torturing hope endeared
Fast rooted at her heart; and here, my Friend,
In sickness she remained, and here she died,
Last human Tenant of these ruined Walls.
The Old Man ceased: he saw that I was moved;
From that low Bench rising instinctively,
I turned aside in weakness, nor had power
To thank him for the Tale which he had told,
I stood, and leaning o'er the Garden Wall
Reviewed that Woman's sufferings and it
seemed
To comfort me, while with a Brother's love
I blessed her in the impotence of grief.
At length towards the Cottage I returned

[30[v]]

57
Fondly, and traced with interest more mild
That secret spirit of humanity,
Which, mid the calm oblivious tendencies
u } *320*
Of Nat[?*t*]} *re, mid her plants, and weeds, and flowers*

---

896 Rev in pencil.

899–914 Cf. MS. M, ll. 877–892 (see *RC & Pedlar*, p. 445).
912 Comma del by eras.

915–929 Cf. MS. M, ll. 893–907 (see *RC & Pedlar*, p. 447).

And silent overgrowings still survived. 919
The Old Man noting this, resumed, and said 920
"My Friend! enough to sorrow you have 921
given,
The purposes of wisdom ask no more; 922
Be wise and chearful, and no longer read 923
The forms of things with an unworthy eye. 924
She sleeps in the calm earth, and peace is 925
e}
hers}
I well remember that those very plumes, 926
Those weeds and the high spear-grass on that 927
wall
By mist and silent rain-drops silvered oer, 928
As once I passed did to my heart convey 929

[31^r]

58
So still an image of tranquillity, *I,* 930
So calm and still, and looked so beautiful 931
which
Amid the uneasy thoughts ~~that~~ filled my mind 932
That what we feel of sorrow and despair 933
From ruin and from change, and all the grief 934
The passing shows of Being leave behind 935
Appeared an idle dream that could not 936
live
Where meditation was: I turned away *340* 937
And walked along my road in happiness". 938
r }
He ceased. E'[?*v*]}*e long, the sun declining shot* 939
A slant and mellow radiance which began 940
ile
To fall upon us wh~~ere~~ beneath the Trees 941
We sate on that low Bench: and now we felt, 942
Admonished thus, the sweet hour coming on. 943
A linnet warbled from those lofty Elms, 944

[31^v]

59 *o*}
A thrush sang, loud, and other meli}*dies,* *I,* 945
At distance heard, peopled the milder air. 946
The Old Man ~~rose and lifted up his load~~; 947
cast }
Together [?*then*]}*ing then a farewell look* 948

925 Pencil overwriting restores reading of MS. M, l. 903: "here."

930–944 Cf. MS. M, ll. 908–922 (see *RC & Pedlar,* p. 447).
932 Del and rev in pencil restores reading of MS. M, l. 910.
941 Del and rev in pencil.

945–951 Cf. MS. M, ll. 923–929 (see *RC & Pedlar,* pp. 447, 449).
947 Del in pencil; rev at page foot (ll. [993]–994).

Upon those silent Walls we left the shade 949
And ere the Stars were visible had reached 950
998 *A Village Inn, our Evening resting-place* 951

354

[993] *and with a sprightly mien*
994 *Of hopeful preparation graspd*
his staff

[32r]

II, 593 The monit{o / yry} voice. Proceeding thus
The [?ho] {S / acred} Edifice they reach & there
In the church aisle beneath the vested
Priest
599 The nearest in affectio or in blood
601 Kne{lt / e} by the coffin resting on its lid
602 In silent grief their unuplifted
Heads
603 And hear manwhile the Psalmists
mournful Plaint
604 And that most awful scripture that
declares
605 We shall not sleep but we shall all
be changed.
[?~~likewise~~]
606 Have I not seen ye also may have
seen
607 Son Husband, Brothers, Brothers side
by side
608 And son & father also side by side
609 Rise from that posture & in concert
move
611 Four dear Supporters of one senseless
Cors

[32v]

III, 195 Safely entrusted to their own pursuits
2 1
196 This earnest Pair may rove from hill to hill
197, 198 From clime to clime no pain is in their sport
200 Yet one is near who holds in my esteem

593–611 Rev of 113v, 33v, 53v–54r (*1814* adopts the first rev of the passage on 53v–54r). Cf. MS. 47, 49v, 49r, 12v.
606 Del by eras.

195–214 Rev of 68v–69r, 70v, 71r–71v.
195 Numbers below line indicate reversal of word order.

201 Place worthier still of envy. May I
{at name
202 Without offence th{e fair faced Cottage Boy
203 Dame Natures Pupil of the lowest Form
{S
204 Youngest Apprentice in the {school of Art
~~As from the open Vale we enter d here~~
205 ~~Him might you noticed as we enter d~~
here
as ~~we entered from the open glen~~
[?~~earnestly~~]
206 ~~From the Open vally~~, busily engaged
[?] {S {ng
207 Heart {soul & hands in mendi{g the
L} defects
208 l}eft in the fabric of a leaky dam
209 Fram d for enabling this penurious
stream
210 To turn a slender Mill (that new made
play thing
Th} {he
211 For his delight: H}e happiest {[?is] of all
of all
213 If [?th] such as now he is he might remain:
214 Ah what avails imagination high

---

131 Rudely to mock the works of toiling
Man.
132 And Hence, that upright shaft of
stone
unhewn
[?Maintaining] here in solitary state
134 From age to Age hath won from
me the name

[33^r]

III, 134 Hath won from me the venerable name
135 Of Pompey's Pillar, that I gravely stile
136 My Theban obelisk, and there behold
137 A druid Cromlech. Thus I entertain
n
138 The antiquaria humour, & am pleasd
139 To skim along the surfa[?ce]s of things
140 Beguiling harm[?lyss] the tedious
hour[?s]:
141 But if the Spirit be oppressd
{is unhewn
132 And hence th{[?at] upright shaft of stone
133 From Fancy willing to set off her stores

131–134 Rev of 69^v, continued on 33^r.

132–141 Rev of 63^v, 70^r, continued from 32^v.

[134] By sounding titles hath acquired
Pillar the name
[135] Of Pompeys that I gravely style &c

{C
232 To that same {child addressing
tenderly
233 The Consolation of a hopeful mind

[33^v]

II, 594 it touches it confirms & elevates
Then when the Mourners, They who on the
neath floor
Of the church aisle be~~side~~ the vested Priest
601 Knelt by the Coffin resting on its lid
602 In silent grief their unuplifted Heads
603 And heard meanwhile the Psalmists
mournful Plaint
604 And that most awful Scripture which
declares
605 We shall not sleep but we shall all be changed
Then when they rise & on their shoulders
bear
595 The body forth to be consigned to earth
596 Ashes to ashes Dust bequeathed to dust
s} een }
606 Have I not }[?see]}? Ye likewise may
have seen
607 Son Husband Brothers: Brothers side
by side
608 And son & father also side by side
611 ~~Four dear supporters of one~~
609 Rise from that posture & in concert
mov
[609] Rise from that posture, forth in concert
move

[34^r]

[~~?~~] *64*

re }
In days of yo[?ur]} how fortunately fared *II, 1*

232–233 Rev of 71^v.

594–[609] Rev on 32^r; rev of 113^v, 53^v–54^r. Cf. MS. 47, 49^v, 49^r, 12^v.

Cf. MS. 47, 33^r; MS. 48, 15^v (see *13-Bk Prelude*, II, 374–375).

Lines *1–55* are at least partly based on a rev and expanded text of MS. 47 no longer extant. Where MSS. 47 and 71 differ, *1814* often follows MS. 47 in its readings, punct, and caps. Possibly, these differences indicate that some of the copy is based on dictation.

1 Illeg word above line, possibly a false start, del by eras.

The Minstrel, wandering on from Hall to
                                        Hall
Baronial Court or Royale,} cheared with gifts
Magnificient, and Love and Ladies praise,
Now meeting on his road an armed Knight
Now resting with a Pilgrim by the side
Of a clear brook: beneath an Abbey's roof
One evening sumptuously lodged; the next
Humbly in a religious Hospital
                                        s
Or with some merry Outlaw of the Wood
             o
Or haply shr[?r]} uded in a Hermit's Cell.
Him savage Robbers spared asleep or wake

[34v]

65
He walked protected from the sword of War
By virtue of that sacred Instrument
                                        Traveller
His harp suspended at the Wanderer's side
His dear Companion wheresoe'er he went
Opening from Land to Land an easy way
Be melody and by the charm of verse
Yet not the noblest of that honoured Race
                    loftier
Drew happier, ~~purer~~, more empassioned thoughts 20
                    journeying
From his long ~~travels~~ and eventful life
Then this obscure Itinerant an obscure
                    ul e
23 *But an high-so{le [?]}d and tender-hearted Man*
28 *Accoutered with his burden and his staff*
                                        ~~not failed~~
In humblest gui[?ze] been empowerd
24 *And nothing better had ~~the skill~~ to extract*
Had skill to [?extract]
[24] *By grace of Heaven ^ from many a ramble far*
25 *And wide protracted through the tamer ground*
              ile
27 Both wh{en he trod the Earth in humblest
                                        guise
[28] Accoutred with his burthen & his staff

---

4 *1814* reverts to the MS. 47 reading, "Munificent" for "Magnificient."
10 Rev in pencil.

13–15, 19–22, 24–27 Cf. MS. 47, 33r–33v.
All rev and del in pencil unless otherwise noted.
13 From this point the text begins to depart significantly from MS. 47.
15 Rev seeks to avoid confusion with the change in name of the Pedlar to the Wanderer.
18 Rev in ink overwriting eras; MS. 47 reads "melody."
23 The error, corr by overwriting, may suggest that WW was dictating from a revised version of MS. 47.
25 Del of "the skill" is in the same ink as rev "not failed," which is del in pencil.
27–[28] Rev continued on top of 35r.

[35r]

66

29 And now when free to move
with ligter pace
26 *Of these our unimaginative days.* II, 28
~~*What wonder then*~~
30 *What wonder then, if I, whose favourite* 29
school
~~*If I whose favourite school hath been*~~ [~~? ?~~]
and rural
Hath been the fields, the roads {[?*the lanes*] *lanes* 30
win
And pathways [?*lea*]} *ding on from farm to farm* 31
Looked on this guide with reverential love 32
Each with the other pleased we now pursued 33
35 *Our journey beneath favourable skies* 34
o
Turn wheres[?]} *ee'r we would he was light* 35
{*;* could
Unfailing{, *not a hamlet* ~~*did*~~ *we pass* 36
w *n*
Rarely a house [?]} *hich did* [?*h*]} *ot yield to* 37
him
39 or from his tongue call forth
{*i*
Remembrances, while mon {[?] *tory hints* 38
40 Some way-beguiling tale. Nor less regard
~~*By natures various objects were supplied*~~ 39
41 Accompanied those strains of apt discourse
~~*For apt discourse and way-beguiling*~~ 40
~~alling~~ *tales* *40*
~~*Perpetually were flowing from his tongue*~~. 41
43 ~~And in the silence of his face I read~~
44 ~~His overflowing spirit. Birds and beasts~~
~~And~~
45 ~~[?The F]} the mute Fish that glances in the stream~~
~~o~~
46 ~~And harmless Reptile c[?]} iling in the sun~~
~~the~~
47 ~~And gorgeous insect hovering upon air~~
48 ~~The Fowl domestic & the household Dog~~
49 ~~In his capacious mind he loved them all~~

---

29 This pencil rev, continued from the bottom of 34v, is consistent with the major rev in Book I where the Wanderer is retired from trade.

28, 33–34 Cf. MS. 47, 33v.

28/29, 29/30 Canceled lines entered first and then del by eras; "school" overwrites the eras of illeg words below.

41 Word "flowing" rev to "falling" before del of entire line. Inserted leaf 36r continues with l. *42*.

43–60 Rev of 112v–113r, 15r; rev on 36r–36v. Continued on top of 35v, and rev and recopied on 36r as part of the major rev that substituted leaves 36–41. The passage is extended after the insertion of leaves 36–41, providing ll. 64–88, on 64v–65r, between Books II and III. The "Birds and beasts" passage in a much shorter form originally closed the first part of Book I (see note to 15r). It was rev on 113r probably initially as Book I rev, and then on 112v, probably toward Book II, and concludes with the original opening line of 35v (II, *42*). Given the work on this passage at the back of this notebook, it is likely that this was a late 1813 or afterward rev, and thus is not counted as part of the underlying pre-1813 text.

[35v]

50 Their rights acknowledging he felt for all.
52 The quiet pleasures of the pasturing Herd
67
53 To happy Contemplation soothed his walk
54 along the fields and in the shady groves
× ~~How~~
55 ~~And~~ the poor Brute's condition forc d to run
Its course of suffering in the public Road
smote
Sad Contrast all too often^ {smote / [?pierc d]} his heart
With unavailing pity. Rich in love
And sweet humanity he was himself
60 To the degree that he desired beloved.
Greetings and smiles we met with all day long *II, 42*
From faces that he knew; we took our seats *43*
By many a Cottage hearth where he received *44*
64 *The welcome of an Inmate come from far.* *45*
88, 89 *But when the sun had for the third time risen* *46*
90 *My fellow Traveller said with earnest voice,* *47*
91 *As if the thought were but a moment old,* *48*
That leaving all incumbrances behind *49*
The day should be a day of liberty *50*
92 *And I must yield myself without reserve* *51*
To his disposal. Glad was I of this; *52*
We started, and he led towards the hills, *53*
95 *Up through an ample Vale of higer hills* *54*
96 *At distance, crags austere and desolate!* *55*
100 ~~But shining now in mornings~~ chearful light
[50] ~~felt for all~~
[50] Oft was {~~was~~
51 Occasion ~~oft~~ [?is]} given me to perceive
[52] How the calm pleasures of

50–54 Continued from bottom of 35r; rev at page foot. Rev of 35r, 112v, 113r, 15r. Rev on 36r. See notes to 35r, 15r.

46–55 Cf. MS. 47, 33v.

As the line and page count indicate, this page originally continued directly on 46r. The cancellation of the page is related to the recopying of this passage (in 1813 or 1814) on inserted leaf 36r.

54/55 Left margin X probably signals intended rev of the passage.

55 In the first stage of rev, inserted leaves 42–45 followed directly from leaf 35. Leaves 42–43 (now stubs) probably once comprised ll. *56–130* based on MS. 70. See first note to 36r.

100 This line is probably entered last on the page, squeezed between ll. 96 and [50], and related to l. 100 rev on 36v.

[50]–[52] Possibly entered in relation to the recopying on 36r, since l. 51 is an added line on 36r and the rev of l. 52 on 36r follows l. [52] at the bottom of 35v.

[36^{r}]

Which Natures various objects might supply
And in the silence of his face I read
His overflowing Spirit. Birds and beasts
And the mute Fish that glances in the
stream
And harmless Reptile coiling in the sun
And gorgeous Insect hovering on the air
The Fowl domestic and the household Dog
In his capacious mind he loved them all.
Their rights acknowledging he felt for all
Oft was occasion given me to perceive
calm
How The ~~quiet~~ pleasures of the pasturing Herd
To happy Contemplation soothed his walk
Along the fields and in the shady groves
How the poor Brutes condition forced to
run
Its course of suffering in the public road
!
Sad contrast, all too often smote his heart
With unavailing pity. Rich in love
And sweet humanity he was himself
T that he
He ~~was himself~~ t o the degree desired,
beloved.

[36^{v}]

61 *Greetings and smiles we met with all day*
long
From faces that he knew; we took our
seats
By many a Cottage hearth where he received
64 *The welcome of an Inmate come from far.*
88, 89 * *But when the sun had for the third time risn*
90 *My fellow Traveller said with earnest voice,*
91 *As if the thought were but a moment old,*
| *That leaving all incumbrances behind*
| *The day should be a day of liberty*

This is the first leaf in the second group of inserted leaves, 36–41, later than the insertion of leaves 42–45. Leaves 36–41, with their important rev of the Solitary's life to include the death of his wife and children, replace leaves (now stubs) 42–43, sometime in 1813 or 1814, and lead, although with some duplicate text on 41^{v} and 44^{r}, into leaf 44^{v}. See pp. 439–440, 453–454, above, for a discussion of the two groups of inserted leaves (36–41, 42–45). Text on these inserts is transcribed in reduced type.

42–43 Probably entered in space left at top of page. L. 42 assumes continuation from l. 41 on 35^{r}, and provides a bridge between the revised passage on 35^{r} and copy on 36^{r}.

42–60 Rev of 35^{r}–35^{v}, 112^{v}, 113^{r}, 15^{r}. See notes to 35^{r} and 15^{r}.

51–52 Added l. 51 and the rev of l. 52 appear to be dependent on the rev at the bottom of 36^{v}; base text l. 52 follows the reading at the top of 35^{v}.

60 Del by eras.

Inserted leaf. See note to 36^{r}.

61–64 Rev of 35^{v}; 112^{v}.

46–55 Cf. MS. 47, 33^{v}. Although the underlying italic text line numbering on leaves 36–41 does not properly belong to these late inserted leaves because leaves 42–43 have been removed with their contents related to II, *56–130*, they are given as reference to the underlying text as it stood in MSS. 47 and 70. MS. 70 begins with l. *56* (58^{v}).

88, 89 The mark in the left margin signals the inclusion of II, 64–88, on 64^{v}–65^{r}.

91/92 The vertical line in the left margin, which overwrites a shorter wavy vertical line, signals an intended rev or del. *1814* does not include these lines.

That
And I must yield myself without reserve
To his disposal. Glad was I of this;
We started, and he led towards the hills,
Up through an ample Vale with higher
hills
At distance, crags austere and desolate
But now array'd in morning's chearful light
~~*Now beautiful by mornings radiant light.*~~
But
P—The wealthy, the luxurious, by the stress

[37^r]

Of business rowzed, or pleasure, ere their time,
May roll in Chariots or provoke the Hoofs
Of the fleet Coursers they bestride to raise
From earth the dust of morning slow to rise
And They if blesed with health and hearts at ease
Shall lack not their enjoyment;—but how faint
Compared with ours! who pacing side by side
Could with an eye of leisure look on all
That we behold and lend the listening sense
To every grateful sound of earth and air,
at
Pausing {[?*on*] *will; our spirits braced, our thoughts*
Pleasant as roses in the thickets blown
And pure as dew bathing their crimson leaves.
P—Mount slowly Sun! and may our journey lie
Awhile within the shadow of this hill
that shield us
This friendly hill protected from thy beams!
a shelter from

[37^v]

Such is the Summer Pilgrims frequent wish
with
s
And as that wi{*th* ^ *prevalence of thanks*
For present good oer fear of future ill
Stole in among the mornings blither thoughts
chased away *o* '
Twas ~~*banished*~~ *for tw*} *w*{*ards the western side*
Of the broad Vale casting a casual glance
We —
I saw a throng of People{ *wherefore met?*

---

92 Rev in pencil.
100 "But" below line is in pencil. Corresponding rev of this line appears at bottom of 35^v. *1814* has a reading closer to the unrevised line, "And beautified with morning's purple beams."
101 "P," probably in the hand of DW, is a copying instruction for a new para. Cf. l. 115, 37^r.

Inserted leaf. See note to 36^r.
115 "P," probably in the hand of DW, is a copying instruction for a new para, as in *1814*. Cf. l. 101, 36^v.
117 Rev in pencil. *1814* adopts the second rev, "This friendly hill, a shelter from thy beams!"

Inserted leaf. See note to 36^r.
124 *1814* adopts the penciled rev "We."

Blithe notes of music suddenly let loose
On the thrilled ear did to this question yield
{'d
Prompt answer they proclaim{ the annual
Wake
Which the bright season favours. Tabour & Pipe
In purpose join to hasten and reprove
The laggard rustic and repay with boons
Of merryment a party-coloured Knot
formed
{[?~~rm~~] {.
Already ~~fo~~{[?un]~~d~~ upon the Village green{
Beyond the limits of the shadow cast

[38^r]

{'d our
By the broad hill glisten{s upon ~~the~~^ sight
a} {R
The gay Assembly }ge. {round them and above
Glitter with dark recesses interposed
Casement and cottage roof and stems of trees
Half-veiled in vapoury cloud~~s~~ the silver steam
Of dews fast melting on their leafy boughs
By the strong sun beams smitten. Like a
mast
Of gold the May-pole shines as if the
rays
Of morning aided by the exhaling dew
With gladsome influence could re-animate
The faded garlands dangling from his sides
P. Said I the music and the sprightly scene
Invite us shall we quit our road and join
The festive mattins? He replied not loth
Here would I linger and with you partak
t}
Not one hour merely but }ill evening's close
The simple pastimes of the day and place

[38^v]

By the fleet Racers ere the sun be set
The turf of yon large pasture will be skimmed
There too the lusty wrestlers will contend
But know we not that he who intermits
The ~~task and duties of the day untunes~~
~~Full oft the pleasures of the day~~ that cease
~~To flow when purposes are lightly changed~~
The appointed task and duties of the day
Untunes full oft the pleasures of the day
{C {ing
~~And~~ {check{s the finer spirits that refuse

---

127 Rev in pencil.

Inserted leaf. See note to 36^r.
134 Mark below line indicates rev, "our," adopted *1814*.
138 Del of "s" in "clouds" by eras.
145 "P," probably in the hand of DW, is a copying instruction for a new para, as in *1814*. Cf. l. 101 (36^v), l. 115 (37^r).

Inserted leaf. See note to 36^r.

To flow when purposes are lightly changed
We must proceed a length of journey yet
Remains untraced then pointing with his II, 57
staff
Towards those craggy summits his intent 58
P
He thus imparted. X *In a spot that lies* 59
Among yon mountain fastnesses concealed 60
You will receive before the hour of noon 61
Good recompence I hope for this day's toil 62
From sight of one who lives secluded there 63

[39^r]

Lonesome and lost, of whom & whose past life II, 64
e|stall
Not to fort|~~aste~~ such knowledge as may be 65
More faithfully collected from himself 66
This brief communication shall suffice 67
Tho' now sojourning there he like myself 68
Sprang from a stock of lowly Parentage 69
t|
Among the wilds of Scotland, in a track| 70
Where many a sheltered & well tended plant 71
s|t
Upon the humble[?r]| ^ *ground of social life* 72
Doth at this day I trust the blossoms bear 73
Of piety and simple innocence 74
d
Such grateful promises his youth display 75
And as he shewed in study forward zeal 76
All helps were sought all measures strained 77
that he
By due scholastic discipline prepared 78
Might to the ministry be called which 79
done
Partly through lack of better hopes & part 80
Perhaps incited by a curious mind 81
In early life the charge he undertook 82

[39^v]

186 Of Chaplain to a military troop
~~*Of spiritual guide & teacher to a Band*~~ II, 83
Cheered by the Highland Bagpipe as they 84
marched
In plaided Vest his fellow Country men 85
189a *This humble station filling to the world* 86
Such seemed it to his Comrades and himself 87

57ff. Cf. MS. 70, 58^v. The italic line numbers of the underlying text are based on the revised copy of MS. 70; the underlying text in MS. 71 probably once continued from 35^v on the now-removed leaves 42–43. L *56*, "As up this Vale we journeyed side by side," occurs only in MS. 70, 58^v. See notes to 36^v (ll. *46–55*) and 36^r.

59 "P" and the cross-out X above it, both probably in the hand of DW, are copying instructions for a new para, as in *1814*. Cf. l. 101 (36^v), l. 115 (37^v), l. 145 (38^r).

Inserted leaf. See note to 36^r.
64–82 Cf. MS. 70, 58^v–60^r. See notes to 38^v, 36^r.
67–80 Cf. MS. 47, 38^r.

Inserted leaf. See note to 36^r.
83–96 Cf. MS. 70, 60^r; MS. 47, 38^r–38^v. See notes to 38^v, 36^r.

189b *But stored with learning & by native power* 88
190 *And force of native inclination made* 89
An intellectual Ruler in the haunts 90
192a *Of social vanity profuse meanwhile* 91
In kind and generous feeling among these 92
193 *Gay and affecting graceful gaiety* 93
Lax buoyant, less a Pastor with his Flock 94
195 *Than a Soldier among Soldiers long he* 95
roamed
Where fortune led—and Fortune who oft proves 96
The careless Wanderers Friend to him made
known
A blooming Lady a conspicuous flower
Admired for beauty & for sweetness praised
200 *Whom he had sensibility to love*
Ambition to attempt & skill to win

[40[r]]

{For
{From this fair Bride most rich in gifts
Nor spar} *of mind*
Most rich} ingly endowed with wordly wealth
His office he relinquished & retired
205 *From the world's notice to a rural home*
Youth's season yet with him was scarcely
passed
And she was in youth's prime. How full their
{ h *joy*
208, 209 *How free their love. O{ [?p] pitiable state*
210 *In the short course of one undreaded year*
Death blasted all—Death suddenly oerthrew
Two lovely Children—all that they possessed
The Mother followed—miserably bare
The one Survivor stood he wept he pray'd
215 *For his dismissal—day & night compelled*
By pain to turn his thoughts towards the grave
And face the regions of Eternity
An uncomplaining apathy displaced
This anguish & indifferent to delight
To}
220 *A} aim & purpose he consumed his days*
To private interest dead & public care

[40[v]]

So lived he so he might have died. But
now
To the wide world's astonishment appeared
~~*App*~~}
The[?d]} ~~*eared the dawning the unlooked for*~~ *light*
The glorious opening the unlook d for dawn
Which }
225 *That} promised everlasting joy to France*
That sudden light had power to pierce
the gloom
In which his spirit friendless upon earth
In separation dwelt and solitude

Inserted leaf. See note to 36[r].

Inserted leaf. See note to 36[r].

The voice of social transport reached even
him
He broke from his contracted bounds repaired II, 102
To the great City an emporeum then 103
Of golden expectations and receiving 104
Freights every day from a new world of hope 105
Th
H *ither his popular talents he transferred* 106
And from the Pulpit zealously maintained 107
The cause of Christ and civil liberty 108
As one and moving to one glorious end 109
Intoxicating service! I might say
A happy service for he was sincere

[41^{r}]

As vanity and fondness for applause
And new and shapeless wishes would allo[?*w*]
That righteous causes of freedom did we kno[?*w*] II, 110
e
Combing *for one hostility as friends* 111
Etherial natures and the worst of slaves 112
Was served by rival advocates that came 113
and
From regions opposite as heaven [?*from*] 114
hell
One courage seemed to animate them all 115
And from the dazzling conquests daily 116
gained
By their united efforts there arose 117
A proud & most presumtious confidence 118
In the transcendant wisdom of the age 119
i *c*
And its d[?*e*]*s*‸*ernment not alone in rights* 120
And in the origin & bounds of power 121
Social and temporal but in laws divin[?*e*] 122
Deduced by reason or to faith revealed
An overweening trust was raised & fear 129
Cast out alike of person & of thing 130
Plague from this union spread whose subt[?*le*] 131
bane

102–109 Cf. MS. 70, 60^{v}, 61^{r}; MS. 47, 38^{v}–39^{r}. See notes to ll. 238–241, below, and 38^{v}, 36^{r}.

238–241 Although these lines (continuing on 41^{r}) are not found in MS. 70, they do appear in MS. 47, 38^{v}–39^{r}, in a close variant. Whether left out intentionally or not from MS. 70, the lines might have been reinstated in leaves 42–43 and thus formed part of the underlying pre-1813 text. There is, however, no way of determining this, and it seems equally possible that WW went back to MS. 47 to expand this passage for inserted leaves 36–41. Given this uncertainty, and while accepting the possibility that they might have once stood in leaves 42–43, they have not been given underlying text line numbering.

Inserted leaf. See note to 36^{r}.

240–241 See note to ll. 238–241 on 40^{v}. A worn strip at the edge of the leaf (where it was removed from the whole sheet) partially remains. The conjectured last letters of these lines were probably written on that strip.

110–131 Cf. MS. 70, 60^{v}–61^{v}. These lines were probably copied from the removed inserted leaves 42–43. The differences between 41^{r} and MS. 70 are probably a result of rev on those removed inserted leaves.

110–115, 130–131 Cf. MS. 47, 39^{r} (but see note to ll. 238–241 on 40^{v}).

122/129 Although found in MS. 70 and entered on 112^{v}, ll. 124–128 are not present here and in *1814*. They were probably entered on removed inserted leaves 42–43 but not included in the process of rev. The copy on 112^{v} may well signify an intention at a late stage to restore them to the text.

258–281 L. 258 is rev of first line of 44^{r}. Leaf 44^{r}, where this passage continues, was the third inserted leaf of the first, pre-1813, stage of rev. It was rev and subsequently del, probably after the removal of inserted leaves 42–43, so that it follows directly after leaf 41; see pp. 453–454, above.

[41ᵛ]

The strongest did not easily escape II, 132
And he, what wonder, took a mortal taint. 133
How {*s* / [?*S*]} *hall I trace the change how bear to tell*
That he broke faith with those whom he had
laid
In earth's dark chambers with a Christian's
hope
An Infidel's contempt of holy writ 134
Stole by degrees upon his mind & hence 135
Life like that that Roman Janus double faced 137
Vilest hypocricy the laughing, gay 138
Hypocricy not leagued with pride but fear 139
Smooth words he had to wheedle simple souls 140
But for disciples of the inner school 141
Old freedom was old servitude & they 142
The wisest whose opinions stooped the least 143
To known restraints & who most boldly drew 144
Hopeful prognostications from a creed 145
Which in the light of false philosophy 146
Spread like a h{*a* / [?*o*]}*lo round a misty moon,* 147
Widening its circle as the storms advance. 148
His sacred function was at length renounced 149
And every day & every place enjoyed 150
The unshackled Layman's natural liberty 151
Speech, manners, morals all without 152
disguise

[44ʳ]

{*bane* / [?*taint*]}
258 *Plague from this union spread whose subtile* II, 131
The strongest did not easily escape 132
260 *And he what wonder took a mortal taint* 133
[? ?]
261 How shall I trace the change how bear to tell
{[?lodged] / [?laid]}
262 {That he broke faith with th[?ose] whom he had
264 X [?*An infidel*] [?] [?*of sacred truth*]} 134
263 In earths dark chambers with a Christian's hope
265 *Stole by degrees upon his mind and hence* 135
~~*For him and for his individual harm*~~ 136
266 *Life like that Roman Janus double faced* 137

Inserted leaf. See note to 36ʳ.
Rev of 44ʳ; see note to ll. 258–281 on 41ʳ. Continued on inserted leaf 44ᵛ, remaining from the first stage of rev.
132–148 Cf. MS. 47, 39ʳ–39ᵛ.
132–152 Cf. MS. 70, 57ᵛ, 61ᵛ–62ʳ.
264 Adopted from 44ʳ, rev at page foot; *1814* reverts to "infidel contempt."
268 *1814* reverts to the original order, "fear, but pride."

Rev on 41ʳ–41ᵛ. Inserted leaves 42–43 from the first stage of rev, of which only stubs remain, originally preceded inserted leaves 44–45. Replacement leaves 36–41, from rev in 1813 or 1814, lead directly into 44ᵛ. See notes to 36ʳ, 41ᵛ.
131–148 Cf. MS. 47, 39ʳ–39ᵛ.
131–152 Cf. MS. 70, 57ᵛ, 61ᵛ–62ʳ.
134 See rev at page foot. MS. 70, 61ᵛ, reads "An infidel contempt of sacred truth."
264 The X in the left margin probably signals the rev at page foot.

267 *Vilest hypocricy, the laughing, gay* 138

p
Hypocricy not leagued with [?f] ride but fear 139

[?*with*]
268 *Vilest* [?*hypocricy, not leagued* *fear but pride*]

3 2 1

ls
269 *Smooth words he had to wheedle simple sou nd* [?*s*] 140
270 *But for disciples of the inner school* 141

t y
Old freedom was old servitude and he he 142

s ped
The wisest whose opinions too [?*k*] *the least* 143

ho were most bold to
273 X To known restraints, who were most bold to draw
and who most bodly [?took]

X ~~To tried [?authority]~~ [? ? ?] [?*known*] [?] 144
274 Hopeful prognostications from a creed
[?~~Whose~~] [? ? ? ?] [?~~told~~] 145
[?~~Which bountifully just comparisons describd~~)]

Which
275 *Did in the light of false philosophy* 146

, ,
Spread like a halo round a misty moon 147

.
Widening its circle as the storms advance 148
His sacred function was at length renounced 149
280 *And every day and every place enjoyed* 150
The unshackled Layman's natural liberty 151
Speech manners morals all without disguise 152

ls
[264] XXAn infidel [?] Contempt of holy writ [*134*]

drew
[273] To known restraints, and who most bodly
took

[44[v]]

I do not wish to wrong him—though the II, 153

c course
Of private life licent iously displayed 154
Unhallowed actions planted like a crown 155
285 *Upon the insolent aspiring brow* 156
Of spurious notions worn as open signs 157
Of prejudice subdued he still retained 158
Mid such debasement what he had received 159
From Nature an intense and glowing mind 160
290 *And when the strength of liberty decayed* 161

er
And mortal sickness on h is face appeared 162

---

268 Numbers below line indicate reversal to "pride but fear" in rev and on 41[v]. *1814* reverts to the original order, "fear, but pride."

273 The X signals rev at page foot.

144 Del by eras. MS. 70, 62[r], reads "To tried authority & known restraints."

145 Del first by a stroke and then by eras. MS. 70, 62[r], reads, "Whose creed with sorrow be it said."

145/146 Del by eras.

[264] The X's in left margin signal rev of l. 264 above, adopted in 41[v]. *1814* reverts to "infidel contempt."

Cf. MS. 70, 57[v], 62[r]–62[v]; MS. 47, 39[v]–40[v].

162 Rev restores reading of MS. 70, 62[r].

He coloured objects to his own desire 163
As with a Lovers passion yet his moods 164
Of pain were keen as those of better Men 165
And keener as his fortitude was less 166
And he continued when worse days were come 167
To deal about his sparkling eloquence 168
Struggling against the strange reverse with 169
zeal
That showed like happiness but in despite 170
Of all this outside bravery within 171
He neither felt encouragement nor hope 172
For mortal dignity and strength of mind 173

[45^r]

Were wanting and simplicity of life II, 174
And reverence for himself and last and best 175
Confiding thoughts and love and fear of Him 176
Before whose sight the troubles of this world 177
Are vain as billows in a tossing sea 178
ing
The glory of the times fa~~ded~~ ^ away 179
The splendour which had given a festal air 180
To self-importance hallowed it and veiled 181
From his own sight this gone therewith he lost 182
All joy in human nature was consumed 183
scorn
And vexed and chased by levity and ~~spleen~~ 184
And fruitless indignation galled by pride 185
Made desperate by contempt of Men who 186
throve
Before his sight in power or fame and won 187
Without desert what he desired weak men 188
Too weak even for his envy or his hate 189
And thus beset and finding in himself 190
Nor pleasure not tranquillity at last 191
After a wandering course of discontent 192
In foreign lands and inwardly oppressed 193
With malady in part I fear provoked 194

[45^v]

By weariness of life he fixed his home II, 195
Or rather say sate down by very chance 196
Among these rugged hills where now he dwells 197
And wastes the sad remainder of his {*hours* / [?*days*]} 198
In self-indulging spleen that doth not want 199
Its own voluptuousness on this resolved 200
With this content that he will live and die 201
Forgotten at safe distance from a world 202
Not moving to his mind 203

Cf. MS. 70, 62^v–inside back cover.

174–191 Cf. MS. 47, 40^r.

184 In MS. 70 "spleen" is also rev, probably to "scorn," indicating the close relationship of MSS. 70 and 71.

---

198 MS. 70 reads "hours."

206–211 Cf. MS. 70, inside back cover.

202ff. Cf. MS. 47, 40^r, 34^r.

{e These serious words
Closed th{ese preparatory notices 204
With which my fellow-traveller had beguiled 205
The way while we advanced up that wide Vale 206
Now suddenly up-turning he began 207
To climb upon one side of it a ridge 208
Pathless and smooth of long and
~~*A rough and pathless ridge of*~~ *steep ascent* 209
As if the object of his quest had been 210

[46^r]

68
~~*Along this Vale till noon-tide we advanced,*~~ II, 206
~~*When suddenly up-turning, he began*~~ 207
~~*To climb upon one side of it a ridge*~~ 208
~~*Of steep ascent, his object being I guessed*~~ 209, 210
Some secret of the mountains, Cavern, Fall 211
Of water, or some boastful Eminence 60 212
Renowned for splendid prospect far and wide. 213
We clomb without a track to guide our steps, 214
And on the summit reached a heathy plain 215
With a tumultuous waste of huge hill tops 216
Before us, savage region! and I walked 217
In weariness: when all at once behold! 218
{a
Beneath our feet, {A little lowly Vale; 219
A lowly Vale, and yet uplifted high 220

[46^v]

69
Among the Mountains, even as if the spot II, 221
Had been from eldest time by wish of theirs 222
So placed to be shut out from all the world. 223
Urn like it was in shape, deep as an urn, 224
{ rocks
Encompassed round about with highest {[? hills] 225
one
Which, but in ^ small Opening to the south 226
Sloped gently back, elsewhere abrupt and close. 227

Cf. MS. 47, 34^r.

Leaf originally followed leaf 35. Wavy deletion lines cancel first four lines as part of the process of rev that includes insertion of leaves 41–45.

211 Continues from l. *210* on 45^v. MW's line count ("60") proceeds from 35^r, l. *40*, and is discontinued after this "60."

Cf. MS. 47, 34^r–34^v.

225 Eras is probably of a copying error: MS. 47 reads "rocks."

226 Rev and the caret (caused by the omission of MS. 47 reading) are in pencil; rev is overwritten in ink.

A quiet treeless nook with two green fields 228
A liquid Pool that glittered in the Sun
And one bare Dwelling, one Abode, no more 229
It seemed the Home of poverty and toil 230
Though not of want: the little fields made 231
green
By husbandry of many thrifty years 232
Paid chearful tribute to the moorland house 233
There crows the Cock single in his domain 234

[47[r]]

70
[?cov]
The small Birds find in Spring no thicket there II, 235
To shroud them only form the neighbouring 236
vales
The Cuckoo straggling up to the hill tops 237
Shouteth faint tidings of some gladder place 238
! *t*
Ah what a sweet recess{, though{ I is here 239
Instantly throwing down my limbs at ease 240
Upon a bed of heath; full many a spot 241
Of hidden beauty have I chanced to espy 242
Among the mountains; never one like this, 243
So lonesome, and so perfectly secure: 244
n
Not melancholy, f}o, for it is green, 245
And bright, and fertile, furnished in itself 246
With the few needful things which life requires. 247
—In rugged arms how soft it seems to lie, 248
e
How tenderly prot{racted! far and near 249

[47[v]]

71
We have an image of the pristime earth II, 250
nak *d*
The planet in its lon}eli}ness; were this 251
;
Man's only dwelling,} sole appointed seat, 252

---

228 Eras is probably of a copying error: MS. 47 reads "with."
229 Pencil rev overwritten in ink. "S" in "Sun appears to be capitalized in the overwriting.

Cf. MS. 47, 34[v].
235 Rev, in pencil, is probably the beginning of "covert" or "coverts," which forms part of an early rev in MS. 47.
239 The "t" in "thought" is added in pencil and overwritten in ink by MW.
249 Pencil rev and del.

Cf. MS. 47, 34[v]–35[r].
251 MS. 47 reads "nakedness."

First, last, and simple in the breathing world, 253
~~*Without a fellow near it or remote;*~~ 254
It could not be more quiet: peace is here 255
Or no where; days unruffled by the gale 256
Of public news or private; years that pass, 257
Forgetfully; uncalled upon to pay 258
The common penalties of mortal life, 259
Sickness, or accident, or grief, or pain. 260
On these and other kindred thoughts intent 261
In silence by my Comrade's side I lay 262
He also silent when from out the heart 263
Of that profound abyss a solemn Voice 264
Or several Voices in one solemn sound 265

[48[r]]

71

funeral [?hymn]
Chaunted among the solitary hills
Was heard ascending: mournful, deep, and slow II, 266
{*a funeral dirge*
{[?~~hymn~~]
The cadence, as of psalms, ~~a psalm of d~~eath 267
a funeral dirge
Chaunted among the solitary
We listened, looking down towards the hut 268
O}
But seeing no o} ne: meanwhile from below 269
The strain continued spiritual as before 270
Yet
And now distinctly could I recognize 271
There words "Shall in the Grave thy love be known 272
In death thy faithfulness". God rest his soul 273
The old Man exclaimed, abruptly breaking silence 274
{*He is Departed to find* }
{hath departed and finds}
He is then dead ~~and hath fou~~nd peace at last. 275
This scarcely &
~~*He scarce had*~~ *spoken when those holy strains* 276
Not ceasing forth appeared in view a band 277
Of rustic Persons from behind the hut 278

257 Comma after "pass" is faint and may be random mark or eras.

Cf. MS. 47, 32[v], 35[r]–35[v].
All rev and del in pencil unless otherwise noted.

267 Word "psalm" was del first and rev to "[?hymn]" above. A second line deletes "a psalm of d" and "[?hymn]"; then "a funeral dirge / Chaunted among the solitary" is entered below. The final reading in *1814*, "a funeral dirge," is next entered in ink overwriting "[?hymn]."

275 Overwriting is in ink. MS. 47 is uncorrected and reads "He is then dead God give him peace at last." The differences here and at other points between MSS. 47 and 71 suggest WW's revising and dictating at times while MW copied. An alternate explanation (another fair copy between MSS. 47 and 71) is unlikely given the error that necessitated the inserted leaves 42–45.

Bearing a Coffin in the midst with which 279
ha
They sloped their course towards the sloping 280
m *side*
Of that s[? al] all Valley singing as they moved 281

[48^v]

72
A sober Company and few, the Men II, 282
Bare-headed, and all decently attired. 283
Some steps they thus advanced and then 284
dirge
the [? psalm]
Ended and from the stillness that ensued 285
Recovering, to my Friend I said, "you spake 286
Methought, with apprehension that these
rites
Are paid to him upon whose shy retreat
I [? fancied with emotion as] of [? one] 287
This day we purpos'd to intrude." "I did so
Who must have been well known to you " 288
hence that we may learn the truth
[? "He was so]
But let us to the house for I would be 289
Perhaps it is not he but some one else
Assured as to the manner of his death." 290
For whom the pious service is performed
Perhaps too 'tis not he but someone else 291
Some other Tenant of the Solitude" 292
So to a steep and difficult descent 293
Trusting ourselves we wound from crag to 294
crag
Where passage could be won, and as the train 295
Who bore the Body having gained the top 296
ff
Of that out -sloping Outlet disappeared 297
I, more impatient in the course I took 298
X

[49^r]

73
Had landed upon easy ground and there II, 299
Stood waiting for my Comrade, when behold 300
An object that enticed my steps aside. 301

---

280 Rev restores MS. 47 reading: "shaped."
281 Overwriting of eras is in ink.

Cf. MS. 47, 35^v–36^r.
284 Rev to "dirge" is possibly related to rev on 48^r, l. *267*.
288 Closing quot not eras.
298 Pencil X and an additional pencil mark at page foot may indicate rev entered elsewhere since reading in *1814* is rev of ll. *295–296*.

Cf. MS. 47, 36^r.

It was an Entry narrow as a door
Which after some short windings opened
out
434a *Into a Platform, that by work of chance*
434b *As seemed, and not design lay, sheep-fold*
wise
435 *Enclosed between a single mass of rock*
436 *And one stone wall. The floor was smooth and*
green
And the small compass of the space within
Shot out from view of any thing but sky
437 *And passing clouds: and where the rock*
and wall
438 *Met in an angle hung a tiny roof*
Or penthouse which most quaintly had been framed
440 *By thrusting two rude sticks into the wall*
And overlaying them with mountain sods
442 {To weatherfend a little turf [?-wrought seat]
{[?The roof and ceiling of a low sod] [?]
Man might sit nor dread
{In which a full grown {Man might
{[?might sit at]}
443 {In which a full grown Man sitting [?at} ease]
ease
~~sit at ease~~

{~~From sun~~
{[?rain] }
444 Might from} ~~shine guarded~~ or a [?tr]}ssing shower (pa above [?tr])
or might sit secure
The burning sunshine

[49[v]]

a spot
443 On which which a full grown Man
74 might sit at ease
444 And find protection from a transient
show
little turf built
Screen for a low sod seat beneath ~~a seat~~
A spot [?i]n which a full grown migh rest
On which a Man of stature tall might rest

Drafts at page foot are related to rev at the top of 49[v]. Three main stages of drafting are distinguishable. Pencil draft appears to have been entered first and then eras. An ink draft was then entered, partly rev, and then mostly eras:

[?The roof and ceiling of a low sod] [?]
[?might sit at]
In which a full grown Man sitting at ease
[?]}
Might from}

(Possibly the pencil draft at the top of 49[v] intervened at this point.) Another copy overwrites the eras ink draft and is in turn rev. Uncanceled "ease" above del "sit at ease" may be part of the erased line. So, too, "sit at ease" may be del as part of rev of first ink draft. The next-to-last line, "or might sit secure," is an alt, possibly entered earlier, to rev of overwritten line "Man might sit nor dread." *1814* ultimately reads, "Whereon a full-grown man might rest, nor dread."

Cf. MS. 47, 36[r]–36[v].

443–444 Draft at top of page is in pencil and probably rev of second stage of rev at bottom of 48[r]. These lines are rev of pencil del on 49[v] at l. *315* and pencil rev at ll. *315/316*.

Scantily sheltered from a transient shower
wrought by
But the whole plainly ~~work~~ of children's hands
Whose simple skill had thronged
~~*And here and there*~~ *the grassy floor* ~~*was thronged*~~
With work of frame less solid a proud shew
Of⎱ & curiously ~~studious~~ly arranged
Wi⎰~~*th*~~ *Baby-houses, chi*~~*efly small loose stones*~~
Nor wanting ornament of walks between
~~*Together ranged in circle or in square*~~*.*
And mimic trees inserted in the turf
~~*The Old Man who to*~~ *my summons giving way*
And gardens interposed. Pleased with
the sight
~~*Had entered, looked about him carelessly*~~
I could not chuse &c but
And now would have passed on: when I
exclaimed
Lo! what is here and stooping down drew forth
A Book, which in the midst of stones and moss
And wreck of party-coloued earthen ware
~~Finding~~ ⎫
Filling⎭ ~~a [?va]~~
Placed⎫ [?piled]
[?*Finding*]⎭ *as they came to hand had helped to*
make
⎧*heaven*
One of those petty structures. Gracious ⎩[?*shouted*]
⎧*O*
Cried the ⎩*old Man, it cannot but be his*
ornaments of walks
449 Nor wanted walks [? ? ?]
[450] And mimic trees inserted [? ? ?]
451 And gardens interposed [?a pretty sight]
452 [?We] could [?not chuse] but [?beckon to my]
[?guide]
[452] X I could not chuse but beckon to my Guide
453 Who having entered carelessly looked
round
447 With piles of frame less

---

319 Rev and del in pencil; rev is overwritten in ink.
319–324 See note, below, to l. *330*.
450 Rev is continued at page foot, signaled by an X, and is itself a rev of pencil drafting at page foot and at the bottom of 50[r].
328 Conjectured reading "[?piled]" is in pencil.
329 MS. 47 reads "Heaven."
330 The entire passage at page foot is rev on 1[r], most probably before the interlinear rev. First four lines here on 49[v] are in pencil and continue at the bottom of 50[r]. They form the basis for the rev of ll. *319–324*. First two of the pencil lines are overwritten by the fifth and sixth lines below. The X in the margin signals continuation of revision entered at ll. *323/324*. The last line overwrites the fourth line of the pencil draft. Final reading for this last line is added to pencil draft on 1[r].

[50^{r}]

463 With searching damp & seemingly had lain

75

464 To the injurious element exposed
465 From week to week
And he is gone. The Book which in my hand II, *331*
Had opened of itself for it was swoln *332*
[463] X With searching damp & seemingly had lain
work
[465] *With damp and rain I found to be a ~~book~~* *333*
t
In the French Tongue, a novel of Volc} aire *334*
His famous Optimist. "Unhappy Man *335*
Exclaimed my Friend, here then has been to him *336*
Retreat within retreat a sheltering place *337*
470 *Within how deep a shelter: he had fits* *338*
Even to the last of genuine tenderness *339*
And loved the haunts of Children here no doubt *340*
He sometimes played with them and here hath sate *341*
Far oftener by himself. This Book I guess *342*
475 *Hath been forgotten in his careless way* *343*
Left here when he was occupied in mind *344*
Cottage s
And ~~so must~~ by the ^ Children hav}~~e~~ been found *345*
Heaven bless them and their inconsiderate work *346*
453 Who having entered carelessly look[?ed]
451 Pleased with the sight
452 I could not chuse but
464 X To the injurious elements exposed
[465] From week to week I found to be a work

[50^{v}]

76
To what odd purpose have the darlings turned II, *347*
,} sad memorial of their hapless
480 *This} ~~monument of their unhappy~~ ^ Friend* *348*
c
Me, said I, the devis} e surprizes less *349*

Cf. MS. 47, 36^{v}–37^{r}.

Draft at top of page, rev and expansion of l. *333*, is in pencil; it is recopied at ll. *332/333* and as the first three lines (in pencil) at page foot. The X at l. *332/333* indicates continuation of last two lines, also marked with an X, at page foot.

333 Del and rev "work" are in pencil.

346 MS. 47 reads "innocent"; "inconsiderate" is kept through all printed editions.

Cf. MS. 47, 37^{r}–37^{v}.

348 Pencil rev is overwritten in ink.

I know not for what reason than to find
A
Such Book in such a place. "[?*t*] *Book it is*
483 *He answered not ill-suited to the Man*
486 *And I was moved at sight of it: 'tis strange*
I grant and yet not strange had been to see
was i
The Man who is [?] *ts Owner dwelling here,*
With one poor Shepherd far from all the
world
490 *Now if our errand hath been thrown away*
As from these intimations I forbode
Grieved should I be less for my sake than
yours
And least of all for him who is no more.
M
By this the book was in the old Man's hand

[51^r]

77
495 *And he continued glancing on the leaves*
An eye of scorn. "The Lover, said he doomed
To love when hope hath failed him whom
no depth
Of privacy is deep enough to hide
Hath yet his bracelet or his lock of hair
500 *And that is joy to him: when change of times*
Hath summoned Kings to Scaffolds do but give
The faithful Servants who must hide his head
Henceforth in whatsoever nook he may
p r
A Kerchief s[?*tr*] ^*inkled in his Master's blood*
e
505 *And he too hath his comfortu r: how poor*
Beyond all poverty how destitute
Must that Man have been left, who hither
driven
im
Flying or seeking could yet bring with her
No dearer relique and no better stay
510 *Than this dull product of a Scoffer's pen*

---

351 MW may have begun to copy the unrevised line in MS. 47. Possibly the rev in MS. 47 was entered during copying of MS. 71.

Cf. MS. 47, 37^v.
364 The last letters of the erased word seem to be an "l," possibly followed by an "e."
369 Del by eras.

[51^v]

78

m}
In} pure conceits discharging from a heart II, 378
impious
Hardened by ^ pride. "I did not fear 379
To tax you with this journey" as we stepped 380
Forth from that viewless nook to open day 381
513b, 514a *Said chearfully my Venerable Friend* 382
516 *"For I have knowledge that you do not shrink* 383
From moving spectacles; but let us on." 384
So saying on he went, and at the word 385
I followed, till he made a sudden stand 386
For, full in view approaching through the 387
p } *gate*
That o[?]} ened through the enclosure of green fields 388
Into the rough uncultivated ground 389
Behold the Man whom he had fancied dead. 390
I knew from the appearance and the dress 391
That if could be no other; a pale face, 392
g }
A tall and meagre person, in a [?G]} *arb* 393

[52^r]

79

Not rustic, dull and faded like himself II, 394
He saw us not though distant but few steps 395
For he was busy, dealing, from a store 396
Which on a Leaf he carried in his hand, 397
Strings of ripe Currants, gift by which he strove 398
With intermixture of endearing words 399
To chear a weeping Child, a ruddy Boy 400
Who tottered by his side. "They to the grave 401
Are bearing him my little One" he said, 402
"To the dark pit but he will feel no pain 403
{*S*
His Body is at rest, his {*soul in Heaven".* 404
Glad was my Comrade now, though he at first 405

Cf. MS. 47, 41^r, 37^v, 38^r.

378 Pencil rev, possibly of a dictation error; line is not in MS. 47.

379 Pencil rev is overwritten in ink. The line lacked a metrical foot. MS. 47 reads "Than such a Book as this. I did not fear".

381 Eras may have been of "roof." MS. 47 leaves a space for this word but adds "covert into" above the line, with "into" then del.

384 MS. 47 on 38^r continues after l. *384a*, "From moving spectacles," with ll. *67ff.* The rev of this sequence in MS. 47, 41^r, continues with ll. *384ff.* MS. 71 gives no sign of being interrupted at this point, but it is possible that the restructuring of the sequence of lines in Book II that takes place in MS. 47, 41^r, was discovered at this point. That discovery, whenever it occurred, resulted in the insertion of leaves 42–45 to restructure Book II (see first note on 44^r, above).

Cf. MS. 47, 37^v–38^r, 41^r–41^v.

I doubt not had been more surprized than glad
But now recovered from the shock and calm
He soberly advanced and to the Man
Gave chearful greeting. Vivid was the light
Which flashed at this from out the Other's eyes

[52v]

80

He was all fire the sickness from his face
Passed like a fancy that is swept away;
Hands joined he with his Visitant, a grasp
An eager grasp; and many moment's space
Long after what was vanished had returned
An amicable smile retained the life
Which it had unexpectedly received
Upon his hollow cheek "How kind he said
Not could your coming have been better timed
For this you see is in our little world
A day of sorrow, I have here a Charge"
And speaking thus he patted tenderly
The sun-burnt forehead of the weeping Child
{is my task}
"A little Mourner whom it {hath been my task}
To comfort, but how came you which your road
You cannot will have missed the funeral Train

[53r]

{They scar} *81*
"{This Child} cely yet are out of sight". "This Child"
{is of an}
Said the Old Man {[? to weep] age to weep
At any grave or solemn spectacle
Inly distressed or overpowered with awe
He knows not why but he perchance this
day
Is shedding Orphan's tears and you yourself
Must have sustained a loss." "The hand of death
He answered "has been here but could not well
Have fallen more lightly if it had not fallen
Upon myself." The other left these words
Unnoticed thus continuing "From yon crag
Down whose steep sides we dropped into the Vale
We heard the hymn they sang a solemn sound
Heard any where but in a place like this

Cf. MS. 47, 41v–42r.
424 Eras probably amends a copying error: MS. 47 reads "is my task."

Cf. MS. 47, 42r, 45r–45v.
431 Pencil rev supplies the missing foot.
Possibly the copying errors, the missing foot in l. *431*, the awkward meter and difficult syntax of l. *435* are all due to working from the draft rev on 45r and 45v of MS. 47.

T
[?*I*] *is more than human. Many precious rites* 441
And customs of our rural ancestry 442
Are gone or stealing from us this I hope 443

[53ᵛ]

82
Will last forever. Often have I stopped *II, 444*
When on my way I could not chuse but stop 445
So much I felt the awfulness of Life 446
C
In that one moment when the corse is lifted 447
In silence with a hush of decency 448
Then from the threshold moves with song of 449
peace
And confidential yearnings to its home 450
Its final home in Earth. What Traveller, who 451
a Stranger
How far so'eer [?*removed*] *does not own* 452
The bond of Brotherhood when he sees them go 453
A mute processesion on the houseless road 454
Or passing by some single tenement 455
Or clustered Dwellings where again they 456
raise
The monitory Voice. But most of all 457
It touches, it confirms and elevates 458
on
Mourners they who [?at] the floor
Then when the Body soon to [~~? ?~~] 459
of the Church aisle beneath the vested Priest
Ashes to ashes dust bequethed to dust 460
Is raised from the Church aisle and forward 461
borne
Upon the shoulders of the next in love 462
The nearest in affection or in blood 463
very
ose
Yea by thle ~~same, the~~ mourners who
had knelt

Cf. MS. 47, 42ʳ–42ᵛ.

Passage from ll. *451–494* differs significantly from MS. 47, in which the draft for ll. *465–494* was probably entered on a missing leaf 43. Ll. *459–464* are much rev in MS. 71, although *1814* restores one of the early canceled readings.

The earliest rev appears to be eras and del on 54ʳ of ll. *461–463*, which are recopied and expanded at bottom of 53ᵛ and top of 54ʳ. Although ll. *460–463* entered at bottom of 53ᵛ are canceled in pencil and l. *601* at top of 54ʳ is amended, *1814* restores these early readings. The next stage of rev is probably pencil drafts entered on 113ᵛ, followed by pencil drafting and del on 53ᵛ and 54ʳ. A copy of the text based on these pencil rev is copied on 33ᵛ. An alt draft closer to that of the first rev and to *1814* is entered on 32ʳ, incorporating pencil rev to l. 601 on 54ʳ and l. *467*.

459 Del by eras, which tears the page; MS. 47 reads "soon to stir no more." MS. 71 does not follow MS. 47 here. Although erased words are illeg, the few letters that can be made out do not correspond to MS. 47. Rev above and below l. *459* is in pencil.

460ff. Vertical del lines are in pencil.

600 Rev here is in black ink and may be last stage of rev after a decision to restore the earlier reading.

[54^r]

Knelt by the
601 ~~Beside the~~ Coffin, resting on its lid
602 In silent grief their unuplifted heads 83
603 { And heard meanwhile the Psalmist's }
595 {*Is raised from the Church aisle and forward*} II, 461
{ plaint
mourful {*borne*
598 ~~*Upon the Shoulders of the next in love*~~ 462
604 And that most awful scripture that
declares
599 ~~*The nearest in affection or in blood*~~ 463
605 We shall not sleep but we shall all be changed
606 X *—Have I not seen ye likewise may have seen* 464
Son, Husband, Brothers; Brothers side by side 465
also si }
And Son and Father, [?*likewise*]} *de by side* 466
609 Rise from that posture and in { weight
611 *Four dear Supporters of one senseless* {[?*corpse*] 467
concert move
From which they do not shrink and under which 468
They faint not but advance towards the grave 469
Step after step together with their firm 470
615 *Unhidden faces he that suffers most* 471
He outwardly, and unwardly perhaps, 472
617 *The most serene with most undaunted eye* 473
~~*To like composure diciplined but with looks*~~ 474
~~*Downcast they went in dutiful regard*~~ 475
~~*Stationed upon the margin of the grave*~~ 476
~~*Nor finally doth care of other hands*~~ 477
~~*Resign the Body to the hollow ground*~~ 478
and on their shoulders
Then when they rise ~~& bear the body forth~~
bear
595 The body forth to be consigned to earth
596 Ashes to ashes dust bequeathed to dust 460
606 Have I not seen ye like 464

[54^v]

84 {st are they w}
Oh! ble{*ssed are they* }*ho Live and die like* II, 479
these
Loved with such love and with such sorrow 480
mourned"

461–464 Cf. MS. 47, 42^v.
601 Del and rev in pencil.
461–465 See note on 53^v.
606 Pencil X in left margin signals inclusion of rev at page foot, which is partly drafted on 113^v and recopied on 33^v. Other lines, as indicated by the copy on 33^v, are meant to follow after l. 605.
611 Addition of l. 609 above and below is in pencil overwritten in ink; that rev is related to copy on 32^r.
474–478 First three lines of passage canceled by wavy ink marks; last two lines del in pencil. Rev and del at page foot are in pencil, partly based on drafts on 113^v, and are meant to follow l. 605. The complete passage is copied on 33^v.

"That poor Man taken hence today" replied 481
The Solitary with a faint sarcastic smile 482
Which did not please me, "must be deemed I 483
fear,
Of the unblessed for he will surely sink 484
Into his Mother earth without such pomp 485
Of grief, depart without occasion given 486
By him for such array of fortitude. 487
Full seventy winters hath he toiled and mark 488
This simple Child will mourn his one short hour 489
And I shall miss him, scanty tribute, yet 490
This wanting he would leave the sight of men 491
If love were his sole claim upon their care 492
Like a ripe date which in the desart falls 493
Without a hand to gather it." At this 494

[55^r]

85

I interposed, though loth to speak and said II, 495
"Can it be so among so small a band 496
As ye must needs be here: in such a place 497
I would not willingly methinks lose sight 498
Of a departing cloud." "Twas not for love" 499
Answered the sick Man with a careless 500
Voice
"That I came hither neither have I found 501
Among my Comrades who have power of 502
speech
Nor in such other converse as is here 503
Temptation so prevailing as to change 504
That mood or undermine my first resolve" 505
li} k}
Then speaking in e} ss} e careless mood he said 506
To my benign Companion "pity 'tis 507
That Fortune did not guide you to this house 508
A few days earlier then would you have seen 509
W} {at stuff the dwellers in this so} {itude 510
T} h} is tempting, smiling, innocent [?sec]} l} usion 511
~~*This tempting, smiling, innocent solitude*~~ [511]

481–483 Quots added after line entered but in same ink as original copy.
494 MS. 47, 44^r, continues with "at this" after its missing leaf.

Cf. MS. 47, 44^r–44^v, 45^r.
498 Rev may overwrite miscopied "lose."
510–[511] Rev adds l. *510*, left out in copying. In the erased l. *511*, the final word (possibly "seclusion") is probably a copying error, as MS. 47 and the recopied l. [*511*] read "solitude." L. [*511*] is del in pencil, then ink. The first two unnumbered lines at page foot are the first attempt at rev of l. [*511*]. The second line is in pencil and del by eras; the end of that line, now obscured by pencil smudging, might have read "it seems." The first line, partly del in ink and entirely del in pencil, may be intended to overwrite the second line. Original text of the remaining lines at page foot is in pencil (overwritings are in ink) and continues at the top of 55^v.

~~All innocent and tempting as its seems~~
[?~~Innocent & tempting~~ as]
650 {That seems by Nature framed to be the seat}
{That seems [?or looks so innocent & pure]}
651 {And very bosom of pure innocence}
{[?That]} seems by [?] framed to } be
[?Appears]} Nature
the seat

[55v]

[?safe]
651 And very bosom of pure innocence
86 *this*
Are made of, an ungracious matter ~~'tis~~ II, 512
Which for tr }
[?*Th*] [?]} *uths sake yet in remembrance* 513
too
654 *Of former conversations with my Friend* 514
restraind
I will tell nakedly and undeterred 515
distinguishd Soul
By reverence ~~which is~~ due to his grey hairs 516
~~Which~~ Made richer, so it seems by nigg[?ard]
661 *And venerable life: but ye shall hear.* 517
I talk—and ye are standing in the sun 518
Without refreshment"! Saying this he led 519
{S
Towards the Cottage: homely was the {*spot* 520
665 *And to my feeling 'ere we reached the door* 521
Had almost a forbidding nakedness 522
even
Less fair I grant^ *painfully less fair* 523
a }
The} *n it appeared when from the Valleys* 524
brink
We had looked down upon it. All within 525
670 ~~*As by the funeral train it had been left*~~ 526
As left by that departed company
Was silent and the solitary clock 527
659 Made richer (so it seems) by niggard age
660 In what it prize most the love of God
{[?his]
[661] And {[?the] frail creature Man

Cf. MS. 47, 45r–46r.

Rev at top of page continues from 55r and is in pencil; it is recopied in ink at the bottom of 55r.

512 Rev restores reading in MS. 47.

513 Rev is probably of a copying error: MS. 47 reads "Which for truths."

514–517 Rev in pencil at page foot, the top and bottom of 56r, and the inside front cover. An early draft toward this rev is entered in pencil on 61v. In ll. *515–517*, rev and del are in pencil.

523 Rev in pencil, overwritten in ink.

524 Rev in pencil.

[56r]

without restraint
and undeterred 87
656 I will tell nakedly ~~in words [?his history]~~ II, 515
{By
657 {[?And] the example of his own pure life
wh}
658 And that respect and defere [?]}ich
Ticked as I thought with melancholy sound 528
a Soul
~~The chairs were in disorder: on a board~~ 529
659 May fairly claim by niggard age
~~Was seen the remnants of that humble fare~~ 530
[?crease]
~~On which the little Company had fed~~ 531
~~Ere to the distant Church they took their way~~ 532
673 {*Following our Guide we climb the Cottage stairs* }
{*Climbing the Cottage stairs as we were led*} 533
And
~~We~~, reached a small Apartment dark and 534
low
675 *Which was no sooner entered then our Host* 535
Said gaily this is my domain, my cell 536
My hermitage, my cabin what you will 537
it {house
I love ~~him~~ better than a snail his {[?*shell*] 538
But you shall now be feasted with our best 539
{our
680 *So with more ard*{*uous than an unripe Girl* 540
Left one day Mistress of her Mother's stores 541
He went about his hospitable task 542
My eyes were busy and my thoughts no less 543
And pleased I looked upon my grey-haired Friend 544
[658] By that respect & deference which a Soul
[659] May fairly claim by niggard age enriched
660 In what it values most the love of god
661 And his frail Creature Man

Cf. MS. 47, 46r–46v.

Small-type passage at top of page is in pencil (and is continued in pencil and interlinearly at ll. *528/529*, *529/530*, *530/531*, and then at page foot); it is rev of draft at bottom of 55v, and is rev on the inside front cover.

534 Mark after "We" signals rev.

538 Del and rev of "him" in pencil; overwriting of eras is in ink and restores the reading of MS. 47.

[658]–661 This pencil draft is rev of pencil draft at the top of the page and on 55v. The entire passage is rev on the inside front cover.

[56v]

88

l
685 *As if to thank him, he too looked and t looked* II, 545
Cheared plainly and yet serious. What a 546
wreck
He had about us, scattered was the floor 547
688 *And in like sort, chair window-seat and shelf*
~~*Chair window seat and shelve were over*~~ 548
With books, maps, minerals, withered plants
herbs spread
and flowers
689 *With books maps fossils withered ~~plants~~* 549
Green moss, [? tools shavings and dust] *and*
flowers
[690] *And tufts of mountain moss & here & there*
from
dropp'd fr ^
[?A] feather [?from the] hawk's and eagle's
[?*From wood of*] [?] [?*colours*], *trinket toys,* 550
wing
Lychen & tufts of moss
Lay intermingled with mechanic tool[*?s*]
[?*Mechanic*] [? ?] [?*shavings and dust*]
[?*Loose*] [? ? ? ? ?] [?*could perceive*] 551
[691] Lay intermixed with these mechanic
From wood of diverse colours, trinket toys
[?*Scribbled with*] [? ?] [?*broken ang*] *ling* 552
tools
And [?*rod*]
692 ~~*Loose*~~ *scraps of paper some I could perceive* 553
Scribbled with verse: a broken angling-rod 554
Within the quiet of a dusty nook
Stood
695 [?] *neighboured by a cob-web'd telescope* 555
And instruments of music some half made 556
Some in disgrace hung dangling from the 557
walls.
But speedily the promise was fulfilled 558
A feast before us and a courteous Host 559
in glee
700 *Inviting us to eat to sit and eat.* 560
And tufts of
690 ~~Lychens & mou~~ntain moss & here & there
691 Lay, intermixed with these, mechanic tools
[692] and scraps of paper

Cf. MS. 47, 46v.

548 Canceled with wavy del line. Although "herbs" (in pencil) does overwrite "and" in l. *548*, "herbs" is actually a rev of "plants," which is del in pencil in l. *549*.

[690] Del in pencil. This line and ll. 691–[692] are drafted in pencil at page foot.

550/551 "Lychen & tufts of moss" is in pencil, possibly intended to rev l. [690], above.

[691] WW's rev "Lay intermixed with these mechanic" is in pencil.

555 An added stroke on the "w" of "cob-web'd" may be intended to spread out the "w" to hide the hyphen.

690–[692] This pencil draft at page foot is part of the final stages of rev of ll. *549–553*. First line of pencil draft is del and rev in ink.

[57r]

89

A napkin white as foam of that rough brook II, 561
By which it had been bleached o'erspread the
board 562
And was itself half-covered with a load 563
Of dainties, oaten-bread, curds, cheese, and cream 564
And cakes of butter curiously impressed 565
Butter that had imbibed a golden tinge 566
A hue like that of yellow meadow flowers 567
Reflected faintly in a silent pool 568
Nor lacked for more delight on that warm
day 569
Our Table small parade of garden fruits 570
And whortle-berries from the mountain sides. 571
The Child who long 'ere this had stilled his sobs 572
(Was now a help to h{is / [?]} late Comforter) 573
Moved like a willing Page as he was bid 574
Minist{ring / ering} to our need 575
In genial mood
While at our pastoral banquet thus we sate 576

[57v]

90

Fronting the window of that little cell II, 577
I could not ever and anon forbear 578
To glance upward and look {on two huge Peaks / the sight till now} 579
{Right opposite / I had not seen} two Giant g{~~ian~~ / reat} mountain Peaks 580
That from some other Vale pee~~p~~red into this 581
Those lusty Twins on which ~~you cast~~ your [?cast]
eyes are ~~cast~~ 582
Exclaimed our Host if here you dwelt would
be 583
Your prized Companions: many are the notes 584
Which in his tuneful course ^the wind^ draws forth 585
From rocks, woods, caverns, heaths and
dashing shores 586

Cf. MS. 47, 47r–47v.
573 Parens may be added.

Cf. MS. 47, 47v, 48v.
580 Vertical mark after "two" signals insertion of "Giant."
582 Pencil del and rev.

And well these lofty brethern bear their
part
{chiefly when the storm}
In the wild concert {[?*all the upper air*]}
{n {ll
Rides high, the{ a{[?i] the upper air they fill
{With roaring}
{[?*Fill*] [?]} *sound that ceases not to flow*
{*Like smo*}
730 {*Among* [?*the*]}*ke along the level of the blast*
irs}
In mighty current and the song is the[?]}
flood
{ *Of stream and headlong* ɜ}
{*The* [?*utterance*] *of* [?*stream*]^ [?]}~~*tream*~~ *that seldom*
fails
And in the grim and breathless hour of noon

[58r]

91
Methinks that I have heard them echo back
735, 736 *The thunders greeting but they also yield*
Music of finer frame a harmony
So do I call it though it be the hand
Of Silence though there be no voice; the clouds
740 *The mist the shadows, light of golden suns*
t}
Motions of moonlight all come }*hither, touch*
And have an answer thither come and shape
A language not unwelcome to sick hearts
{*there the sun himself*}
And idle spirits: {[?*here I sit and*] *watch*}
745 At the calm close of summers longest day
{; between
Rests his substantial orb{ ~~*and near*~~ *those*
heights
And on the top of either pinnacle
More keenly than elsewhere in nights blue
vault
{.
749 *Sparkle the stars as of their station proud*{
Here do I sit and watch
With brightening face

587–593 These lines are not in MS. 47, although partial rough drafts are on MS. 47, 48v.

594–607 Cf. MS. 47, 47v–49r.
600 Rev in pencil.
603 Colon after "spirits" may be added as part of the overwriting. MS. 47, 48v, has the original base text reading of MS. 71, now eras, following "spirits."
604 Rev above and below line are in pencil, as is the del. Draft toward rev is in pencil at page foot.
606 MS. 47 drafts (48r, 47v, 48v)—a variant of *1814*, ll. 750–751—are not included in MS. 71. In MS. 47, after l. *607a*, are a few pencil drafts toward the remainder of Book II, and possibly more such drafts were on now-missing leaves. But most of the text from which MW copied the rest of Book II into MS. 71 was probably entered in a notebook other than MS. 47.

The Old Man heard him speaking thus 608
and said
[?and twixt] those [?Heig]

[58v]

92
{ith which}
"Now for the Tale w{hich with y} you threatened II, 609
us"
In truth the threat escap d me unawares
"I had forgotten it and 'tis no more ~~than~~ 610
And was forgotten—let this challenge stand
{rustic
Than a bare incident of {homely life 611
For my excuse if what I shall relate
But ye shall have it.—Outcast and cut off 612
Tire your attention.
As we seem here and must have seemed to you 613
When ye looked down upon us from the Crag 614
Islander of a stormy Mountain sea 615
We are not so, perpetually we touch 616
Upon the vulgar ordinance of the world 617
And he whom this our Cottage hath to day 618
Relinquished was dependent for his bread 619
Upon the laws of public charity. 620
The Houswife tempted by such slender gains 621
As might from that occasion be distilled 622
Opened, as she before had done for me, 623
<u>Her doors to admit this homeless Pensioner</u> 624
In truth the threat escaped me unawares
And was forgotten let this challenge stand
For my excuse if what I shall relate
Tire your attention—Outcast & cut
off

[59r]

93
Food gave him for his meals a blind dull nook II, 625
Such as she had the Kennel of his rest 626
This, in itself not ill, would yet have been 627
Ill born, in earlier life; but his was now 628
The still contentedness of seventy years 629
Calm did he sit beneath the wide spread 630
m} tree
Of his old age and yet less call} and meek 631
Winningly meek or venerably calm 632

Cf. MS. 47, 12r, 49v.
609–613 Interlinear rev is in pencil, then copied at page foot in ink.
610 Del by eras.

Cf. MS. 47, 12r, 49r, 49v.

pay |
780 *Than slow and torpid [?press]} ing in this wise* *633*
penalty if
A lingering ^ penalty ~~if such~~ it were *634*
For spendthrift feats excesses of his prime *635*
I loved the old Man for I pitied him *636*
A task it was I own to hold discourse *637*
785 *With One so slow in gathering up his thoughts* *638*
to
But he was a cheap plesure ~~in~~ my eye, *639*
{y
Mild, innofensive, ready in his wa{[?*iy*] *640*
his
And useful to ~~the~~ utmost ~~of his~~ power *641*
and there

[59v]

94
Our Huswife knew full well what she pos-
sessed *II, 642*
790 *He was her Vassal of all labour, nursed* *643*
Her Infants from the Pasture fetched ker Kine *644*
Her plot of garden ground he delved and *645*
orderly array *dressed*
792, 793 *And one among the ~~band of Hay-makers~~* *646*
Of hay makers {,
793 *~~Well as he might~~*{ *beneath the burning sun* *647*
Did he maintain his place with steady *648*
{ins
pa{[?*ce*]
795 *Errands he went at needs to other Vales* *649*
Leading sometimes an inexperienced Child *650*
Too young for any profitable task *651*
So moved he like a Shadow that performed *652*
Substantial service willingly and well *653*
So came and went uninjured and secure *654*
{,
[799] *From all mishap Now mark*{ *~~and I will~~ prove* *655*
~~That we have here a growth of human~~ hearts *656*
Bad as the worst. The moon
801 *~~Unsightly as the worst~~. Our dame the Queen* *657*
800 The moon her mon[?t]ly round, the Moon
[801] The moon hath not completed, Since our Dame
the Queen

---

639 What we read as a comma may possibly be an "s" to form "eyes."

649 On the "s" in "needs," the pencil mark we show as a del may be a reinforcement or a signal for rev.

[60r]

{C 95
Of this one {cottage and this lonely Dale II, 658
~~*At the approach of evening three weeks past*~~ 659
Into my little sanctuary rushed ~~*V*~~ 660
Voice into rueful treble humanized 661
805 *And features in deplorable dismay* 662
I treat the matter lightly but alas! 663
It is most serious: from mid noon the 664
{*Had fallen in* *rain*
{*In torrents all torrents all the mountain-tops* 665
Were hidden and black vapours coursed their 666
sides
r }
810 *This had I seen and saw and from he*[?]} *mouth* 667
that on the heights that aged Man
Now heard, ~~*I heard it with distress of*~~ *mind* 668
815 ~~*That the Old Man alone upon the heig*~~*hts* 669
816 *Lay somewhere at the mercy of the storm* 670
~~*Alone and had been so for many hours*~~ 671
'Twas known to her her only of the house 672
812 *For at her bidding early in the day* 673

[60v]

96
The heights he had ascended to delve turf II, 674
For winter fuel to the noontide meal 675
815 *He came not nor returned though hour* 676
passed by
Hour after hour and still a raging storm 677
Inhuman! said I why not speak eree this 678
Alas! tis now too late. Even at the word 679
820 *Her husband entered from a distant Vale* 680
We sallied forth together found the Spot 681
Where the neglected Man had piled his
work
~~*With difficulty found it where the Old Man*~~ 682
{through
But {[?in] all quarters
~~*Had piled his work but*~~ *looked for him in vain* 683
We shouted but no answer; darkness fell 684
825 *Without remission of the blast or shower* 685
And fears for our own safety drove us home 686
I, who weep little, did, I will confess 687
The moment I was seated here alone 688

---

659 See rev at bottom of 59v.
660 Del by eras.
671–672 The angle bracket possibly signals WW's intention to change the line sequence.

681–683 Interlinear rev is in turn rev at page foot.

found the tools
dropp'd
Where the neglected veteran had [?~~wrap~~]

[61^r]

97
Honour my little Cell with some few tears
Which anger or resentment could not dry
All night the storm endured and soon as help
Had been collected from the neighbouring Vale
With morning we renewed our Quest: the wind
Was fallen, the rain abated but the hills
Lay
~~*Were*~~ *shrouded in impenetrable mist*
And long and hopelessly we sought in vain
Till chancing on yon lofty ridge to pass
a
A he[?*e*]} *p of ruin, almost without walls*
And wholly without roof in ancient time
It was a Chapel a small Edifice
onely } *e* } *l* }
In which the Peasants of these l[?] *l*[?]} *Da*} *le*} *s*
For worship met upon that central Height
{is
Chancing to pass th{*ese wreck of stones we*
{E *there*
~~*We there*~~ {*espied at last the object of our*
search

[61^v]

98
Couched in a nook and seemingly alive
It would have moved you had you seen
the guise
In which he occupied his chosen bed
among tufts of heath
Lay ~~*more than*~~ *three parts buried*^ ~~*under*~~ *load*
a}
Which he, with labour hard hd}d rooted up
2 *1*
~~*Of heath-plant which he with his hands had*~~
~~*pulled*~~
And spread for a protection from the touch
d} *p*}
Of the cold groun[?g]} *and heav*} *ed the covering*
high

---

822 The last word may be an attempt at "wrought."

---

707 First rev is "load" to heath," then l. 708 del, then "more than" and "under" del, then caret and "among tufts of" added.

707/708 Pencil transposition mark and numbers reverse the word order.

850 *To baffle as he might the watery storm,* 711
And there we found him breathing peacefully 712
Snug as a Child that hides itself in sport 713
Mid a green hay cock in a sunny field 714
We spake he made reply but would not 715
stir
855 *At our entreaty less for want of power* 716
Then apprehension and bewildering thoughts 717
[?life]
to his [?simple need]
His lofty spirit & [?experienced] [?]
And [?is] [?] {[? ?]
659 [?By] niggard age [?appears to] {[? ?]
660 In what it prizes most the love of God
661 And [?his frail creature man]

[62r]

was he lif[?e]d *99*
So did we lift him gently from the ground II, 718
And ~~homewards~~ with their freight the Shep- 719
homeward
herds ^ *moved*
Throu } *,* } *,*
Wh[?en a] } *gh the dull mist* } *I following* } *when a step* 720
A }
860 *[?F]* } *single step that freed me from the skirts* 721
Of the blind vapour opened to my view 722
Glory beyond all glory ever seen 723
dreaming
By waking sense or by the ~~living~~ ^ *soul*
863 *Or by the dreaming soul. A [?huge] [?]* 724
A huge and }
870 *Boldly say [?a]* } *mighty City boldly say* 725
A wilderness of buildings sinking far 726
And self-withdrawn into a boundless depth 727
Far sinking into splendour without end 728
Fabric it seemed of Diamond and of gold 729
875 *With alabaster domes and silver spires* 730
And blazing terrace upon terrace high 731
877 *Uplifted and serene pavilions bright,* 732
879 *And battlements that on their restless fronts* 733

Rev at page foot, in smudged pencil, is an early draft toward rev of l. *516* on 55v.

---

718 Rev in pencil. The queried "e" may have been intended as a "t."
719 Del and rev in pencil. The long pencil mark cancels the "s" and transposes "homeward" to read "the Shepherds homeward moved" as in *1814*.
720 Commas are added in pencil.
726 Del of "s" in pencil.

[62v]

100

Bore stars illumination of all gems II, 734
By earthly nature had the effect been wrought 735
Upon the dark materials of the storm 736
Now pacified on them and on the coves 737
And mountain {— *steeps and summits whereunto* 738
The vapours had receeded ta[?] {*k*} *ing there* 739
Their station under a cerulian sk {*y*} [?*ey*] 740
Oh! 'twas an unimaginable sight 741
Clouds mists streams watery rocks and 742
emerald turf
Clouds of all tincture rocks and saffire sky 743
Confused commingled mutually inflamed 744
Molten together and composing thus 745
Each lost in each t {*h*} [?] *at wonderful array* 746
Of temple palace citadel and huge 747
Fantastic pomp of structure without 748
name

[63r]

Right *101*
Right
~~*And*~~ *in the midst where interspace appear* II, 749
ed
Of open court an object like a throne ~~*stood*~~ 750
Stood fixed and shining canopies were seen 751
[—?—]
~~*Of burnished gold as seemed or shining stone*~~ 752
And implements of ordinary use 753
But vast in size in substance glorified 754
Such as by Hebrew prophets were beheld 755
In vision forms uncouth of mightiest power 756
For admiration and misterious awe 757
Below me was the earth this little vale 758
Lay low beneath my feet twas visible 759
I saw not but I felt that it was there 760
That which I saw was the revealed abode 761
Of spirits in beatitude my heart 762
Swelled in my breast I have been dead I cried 763
And now I live oh wherefore do I live 764

---

749 Del and lower "Right" are in pencil.
750 Del by eras.
751 The queried word, probably part of the original line above, is del by eras.
752 Del by wavy lines.

[63v]

102

And with that pang I prayed ~~it~~ to be {*no more* / *so*}
But I forget our charge as utterley
I then forgot him there I stood and gazed
The apparition faded not away
And I descended having reached the house
I found the Shepherd's burden safely lodged
And in serene possession of himself
Beside a genial fire that seemed to spread
{*A gleam of comfort oer his palid face*
[? ? ? ?] [?*he had heard*]}
~~*Our shouts the night before but had not dared*~~
~~*To stir from it and shouted back in vain*~~
Great shew of joy the huswife made and truly
Was glad to find her conscience set at ease
And not less glad for sake of her good name
That the poor Sufferer had escaped with life

[64r]

103

But though he seemed at first to have received
No harm and uncomplaining as before
Went through his usual tasks a silent change
Soon shewed itself, he lingered three short weeks
And from the Cottage ha{*th* / *s*} *been borne today.*
So ends my dolorous tale and I am glad
That it is ended at these words he turned
And with blithe air of open fellowship
Brought from the Cup-board wine and stouter cheer
Like one who would be merry. {*S* / *seeing this*}
My grey-haired^*Friend* *said courteously* "{*N* / *nay nay*}
You have regaled us as a Hermit ought
Now let us forth into the sun: our Host
Rose though reluctantly and forth we went

773–775 Eras and del lines appear to relate the old man's night in the nook covered by heath. Cf. ll. 704–711 on 61v.

785 Transposition mark and numbers are in pencil.

[64v]

Listening well pleas'd, forgetting while he
104 spake
That this was but a record of the past
To some consenting thoughts which have arose
I yielded utterance in words like these
III, 339, 340 "If smiles of Pity be the just reward
I said tempted here to interpose
III, 1 ~~*A humming*~~
III, 339 If smiles
an Inmate come from far *II, 64*
II, 64 Nor was he loth to enter ragged Huts *65*
65 Wherein his charity was bless'd, his voice *66*
Heard as the voice of an experienced Friend *67*
And sometimes, where[?r] the Poor Man held dispute *68*
With his own mind, unable to subdue *69*
II, 70 Impatience through inaptness to perceive *70*
General distress in his particular lot, *71*
Or cherishing resentment, or in vain *72*
Struggling against it with a soul perplexd *73*
And finding in itself no steady power *74*
To draw the line of Comfort that divides *75*
Calamity the chastisement of heaven *76*
From the injustice of our brother Men *77*
~~From wrongs inflicted by our Brother men~~ [77]

[65r]

II, 78 To him appeal was made as to a judge
105
79 Who with an understanding heart allayd
80 The perturbation, listened to the plea,
81 Resolved the dubious point & sentence gave
82 So grounded, so applied, that it was heard
83 With soften'd spirit, even when it
condemn'd.
[?In]
84 Such intercourse I witness'd while we roved
85 Now as his choice determined now as mine
88 But when the Sun &c
III, 1 *A humming Bee—a little tinkling Rill* *III, 1*
A pair of Falcons wheeling on the wing 2
In clamourous agitation round the crest *3*
e
Of a tall Rock their aery Citad[?*a*]} *l* *4*

III, 339, 340 Rev of 74r, 73r, 76r–76v.
III, 1 Del by eras; false start at beginning Book III (see 65r).
II, 64–88 Rev and expansion of 36v; continued on top of 65r.

78–88 Continued from 64v; rev and expansion of 36v.
III, 1–11 Cf. MS. 69, stub 71r.

By each and all of these the pensive ear 5
Was greeted in the silence that ensued 6
When through the Cottage threshold we had 7
passed
And deep within that lonesome Valley stood 8
Once more beneath the concave of the calm 9
                                  cl
Cerulian sky—Anon! ex[*?xc*] *aimed our Host* 10
Triumphantly dispersing with the taunt 11

[65^v]

106
That shade of discontent which on his brow III, 12
Had gathered—Ye have left my Cell, but see 13
How Nature hems you in with friendly arms 14
                  her   Ye
And by my [*?my*] *help* [*?you*] *are my Prisoners still* 15
But which way shall I lead you? how contrive 16
In sport so parsimoniously endowed 17
That the brief hours which yet remain may 18
reap
Some recompense of knowledge or delight 19
So saying round he looked as if perplexed 20
And to remove those doubts my grey-haired 21
          S   *Friend*
Said, "[*?S*] *hall we take this pathway for our guide* 22
Upward it winds as if in summer heats. 23
Its line had first been fashioned by the Flock 24
A place of refuge seeking at the roots 25
Of yon black Yew-tree, whose protruded boughs 26
Darken the silver bosom of the crag 27

[66^r]

                    meagre   *107*
From which it draws its ^ *sustenance* III, 28
There in commodious shelter might we rest. 29
Or let us trace this streamlet to its source 30
Feebly it tinkles with an earthy sound 31
And a few steps may bring us to the spot 32
Where haply crowned with Flowrets and green herbs 33
The mountain Infant to the sun comes forth 34
Like human life from darkness." At the word 35
We followed as he led:—a sudden turn 36
Through a strait passage of encumbered ground 37

12–22a Cf. MS. 69, stub 71^r, leaf 72^r. Ll. *22b–29* do not seem to appear in MS. 69; ll. *13–19* are probably drafted in MS. 69 at the bottom of stub 71^r, as rev of the lines del at the top of 72^r.
17 The word "sport" is a miscopy of "spot."

30b–44 Cf. MS. 69, 72^r.

Proved that such hope was vain; for now we stood
Shut out from prospect of the open Vale
And saw the Water that composed this Rill
Descending disembodied and diffused
{C
Oer the smooth surface of an ample {crag
Lofty and steep and naked as a Tower.
All further prospect here was barred.—And who

[66^{v}]

108
Thought I, if Master of a vacant hour
Here would not linger willingly detained
Whether to such wild objects he were led
fi }
When copious rains have magni[?ed]} ed the Stream
Into a loud and white-robed Waterfall
Or introduced at this more quiet time
Upon a semicirque of turf-clad ground
The hidden nook discovered to our view
A mass of rock resembling as it lay
Right at the foot of that moist precipice
A stranded Ship with keel upturned, that
rests
Fearless of winds and waves. Three several stones
Stood near of smaller size and not unlike
To monumental pillars: and from these
seen
Some little space disjoined a pair were ~~near~~

[67^{r}]

109
That with united shoulders bore aloft
A fragment, like an Altar flat and smooth
Barren the tablet yet thereon appeared
Comspiciously stationed one fair Plant
A tall and shining Holly which had found
A hospitable chink and stood upright
As if inserted by some human hand
In mockery to wither in the sun
Or lay its beauty flat before a breeze
The first that entered. But no breeze did now
Find entrance; high or low appeared no trace

45–48 Cf. MS. 69, 72^{r}–72^{v}; stub 71^{v}.
46–62 Cf. MS. 69, stub 73.
59 Pencil del and rev.

63ff. Cf. MS. 69, stub 74^{r}.

Of motion, save the water that descended ~~steep and high~~ 71
Diffused adown that barrier of steep rock 72
And softly creeping like a breath of air 73
Such as is sometimes seen and hardly seen 74

[67v]

110
To brush the still breast of a crystal lake III, 75
~~Reflecting vividly the neighbour[?ing]~~ [?]
"Behold a Cabinet for sages built 76
Which Kings might envy!" 77
Praise to this effect
Broke from the happy Old Man's reverend lip 78
Who to the Solitary turned and said, 79
In sooth with loves familiar priviledge 80
cried
You have de~~scribed~~ in no unseemly terms 81
Of modesty that wealth which is your own 82
Amon
Upon} g these rocks and stones methinks I see 83
More than the heedless Impress that belongs 84
To lonely Nature's casual work: they bear 85
A semblance strange of power intelligent 86
And of design not wholly worn away. 87
Boldest of Plants that ever faced the wind 88
How gracefully that slender Shrub looks forth 89
From its fantastic birth-place. And I own 90

[68r]

111
Some shadowy notion hangs upon my mind III, 91
That in the fashion of the smooth flat stone 92
The mass from which the careless Holly sprouts 93
And in the fellowship which thus it holds 94
With its untired supporters, and no less 95
In those three others, upright and unhewn 96
li} {d
Each single and yet seemingly aliv} e{ 97
{l it
Yea in that stranded Hulk or rather cal{ led 98

---

71 Pencil del; the words, perhaps introduced as a copy error, add three syllables to the line.

75ff. Cf. MS. 69, stubs 74r, 75r.
75/76 Pencil rev and del. The queried reading may be "hood" rather than "[?ing]" followed by a single letter.
81 Pencil del and rev.

91ff. Cf. MS. 69, stubs 75r, 76r.
91 Ink semicircle and mark above "hangs upon" possibly indicates intention of later rev as in *1814*: "Some shadowy intimations haunt me here." Remainder of passage is much altered in *1814*.

gg
A ~~str~~and|ed Temple thatched with living heath
That punctually renews its splendid flowers
92 *From year to year, I cannot but incline*
92, 93 *To a dim faith that in these various shews*
93 *A chronicle survives a type or remnant*
94 *Of purposes akin to those of Man*
95 *But wrought with mightier arm than now prevails*
—Voiceless the stream descends into the gulph
With timid lapse—and lo! while in this strait
We our
I stand—the chasm of sky above my head

[68v]

112
Is heavens profoundest azure no domain
fickle
100 *For ^short-lived clouds to occupy*
Or to pass through, but rather an abyss
In which the everlasting stars abide
And whose soft gloom and boundless depth
might tempt
The curious eye to look for them by day
105 *Hail Contemplation from the stately Towers*
Reared by the industrious hand of human art
To like thee high above the misty air
And turbulence of murmuring Cities vast
From academic groves that have for thee
110 *Been planted, hither come and find a Lodge*
To which thou mayest resort for holier peace
From whose calm centre thou through height or
depth
May'st penetrate, wherever truth shall lead;
Measuring through all degrees untill the scale
115 *Of time and conscious nature disappear*
199, 200 Yet one there is who holds in my esteem
[?worthier]
201 Place still of envy, May I name
202 Without offence the fair faced
Cottage Boy
203 Dame Nature's pupil of the
lowest Form

99 Del by eras of opening three letters of probable copying error "stranded"; see l. *98*.

120–130 Cf. MS. 69, stub 6r.
Rev at page foot is in pencil and continues at bottom of facing 69r; rev of pencil on 70v–71r, and is rev on 32v.

[69r]

113

Lost in unsearchable eternity III, 126
A pause ensued and with minuter care 127
We scanned the various features of the scene 128
And soon the Tenant of that lonely Vale 129
120 *With courteous voice thus spake* 130
"I should have grieved
Hereafter, should perhaps have blamed myself 131
If from my poor retirement ye had gone 132
Leaving this nook unvisited, but in sooth 133
Your unexpected presence had so rouzed 134
125 *My spirits that they were bent on enterprize* 135
And like an ardent Hunter I forgot 136
Or shall I say disdained the game that lurked 137
before
At my own door. The shapes ^ our eyes 138
And their arrangement doubtless must be deemed 139
130 *The sport of Nature aided by blind chance* 140
204 Youngest apprentice in the school
of art
205, 206 He might you notice [?as we enterd here]
[205, 206] From the open valley [?earnestly]
[?engaged]
207 Heart soul [?&] hands

[69v]

114 *

131 *Rudely to mock the works of toiling Man* III, 141
141 *But if the spirit be oppressed by sense* 142
Of instability revolt decay 143
of Nat[?ure]
143 *And change and emptiness these freaks ~~suffice~~* 144
~~Do then suffice~~ and
145 *~~To quicken and~~ to aggravate, ~~to~~ feed* 145
{do
144 And her blind Helper Chance {[?] then suffice
2
146 *Pity and scorn and melancholy pride* 146
To quicken & to aggravate to feed *1*
Not less than that huge Pile (from some abyss 147
Of mortal Power unquestionably sprung) 148
Whose hoary diadem of pendent rocks 149
150 *Confines the shrill-voiced whirlwind round* 150
and round
Eddying within its vast circumference 151

See rev on 32v and 33r.
127 Eras may be of "by."
204–207 Pencil draft continues from bottom of 68v; see the note there.

---

131 Asterisk seems to signal rev at page foot.
146 Numerals "2" and "1" reverse the line sequence.

On Sarum's naked plain—than Pyramid
Of {*E* / *egypt*} *unsubverted undesolved*
Or Syrias marble Ruins towering high
Above the san[*?t*]} *dy* *desart in the light*
Of sun or moon. Forgive me if I say
I} [?]}magination f[?ee]} [?il]} ls the secret [?]
[131] [?Rudely]
132 And hence that upright shaft of unhewn stone
134 Hath won from me the venerable name
135 of Pompeys pillar—This I gravely stil[?e]

[70[r]]

115
That an Appearance which hath raised your mind
To an exalted pitch (the self same cause
Different effect producing) is to me
Rather a place of penance than delight
Though at this moment I can look around me
By the reflection of your pleasure pleased.
Yet happier in my judgement even than you
With your bright transports, fairly may [*?w*]} b *e deem* ed
Is he (if such have ever entered here)
The wandering Herbalist who clear alike
From vain and that worse evil vexing thoughts
Casts on these uncouth forms a slight regard
Of transitory interest, and peeps round
For some rare flowret of the hills, or plant
Of craggy fountain, what he hopes for wins
Or learns at least, that 'tis not to be won
Then keen an eager as {*a* / *an*} *fine-nosed hound*
136 My Theban obelisk and there behold
137 A druild Cromlech. Thus I entertain
138 The antiquarian humour, and am pleased
139 To skim along the surfaces of things
140 Beguiling harmlessly the lonesome hours

154ff. Cf. MS. 69, 7[r].
[131]–135 This passage, continuing on 70[r], is rev on 32[v]–33[r].
[131] "[?Rudely]" is in pencil, possibly entered before the ink rev. EdeS conjectures "heart" for the last word of the first line of rev; all that is entered are two or three letters, the last probably an "e," preceded by "h" or "li."

157ff. Cf. MS. 69, 7[r]–7[v], stub 78[r].
136–140 Continued from bottom of 69[v] and rev on 32[v]–33[r].

[70ᵛ]

E}
T}ntrusted safely to their own pursuits
116
This eager may roam from hill to hill
From clime to clime, no pain is in their
sport
By soul-engrossing instinct driven along *III, 174*
Through wood or open field, the harmless Man *175*
Departs, intent upon his onward quest *176*
Nor is that fellow-wanderer, so deem I *177*
{(
Less to me envied{, you may trace him oft *178*
By scars which his activity has left *179*
Beside our roads and pathways though thank *180*
heaven
{)
This covert nook reports not on his hand{ *181*
{edge
He who with pocket hammer smites the {[?rocks] *182*
Of the hard rocks by weather stains disguised *183*
Or green and grey with vegetation thin *184*
Natures first growth detaching with the *185*
stroke
A chip or splinter to resolve his doubts *186*
And with that ready answer satisfied *187*
barbar}
Doth to the substance give some [?]}ous *188*
holds *name*
Yet one there is who ~~ranks~~ in my esteem
May I [?name]
Still higher place, for envy. ~~Shall~~ [?Can] ~~I say~~
[?little] [?Cottage] Boy
Without offense that is the fair faced [?~~child~~]
our [?late] attendant—Him you might
observe

[71ʳ]

hurries *117*
And passes on; or from the fragment picks *III, 189*
His specimen, if haply interveined *190*
With sparkling mineral, or crystal tube *191*
e}
Be lodged therein, and thinks himself i}nriched *192*

195–197 This pencil draft is continued in pencil at page foot, at the bottom of 71ʳ, and at the top of 71ᵛ. It is meant to follow l. *193* on 71ʳ and is rev on 68ᵛ–69ʳ and 32ᵛ.
174ff. Cf. MS. 69, stubs 78ʳ, 79ʳ.

189ff. Cf. MS. 69, stubs 79ʳ, 80ʳ.
189 Rev in pencil.

⊗
194 *Wealthier and doubtless wiser than before*
Entrusted &c
214 *A what avails Imagination high*
215 *Or question deep? what profits all that Earth*
Or Heaven's blue vault is suffered to put forth
{l
Of impulse or al{urement for the soul
To quit the beaten track of life and soar
Far as she finds a yielding element
220 *In past or future far as she can go*
Through time or space if neither in the one
Nor in the other region nor in aught
~~*That may by pure abstraction be conceived*~~
223 *That Fancy dreaming oer the map of things*
205, 206 As here we entered [?he] earnestly employed
Heart
207 ~~Soul~~ [?&] soul & hands in mending the defects
208 Let in the fabric of a leaky dam

[71ᵛ]

stream
209 Framed for enabling this penurious
[?that]
210 *118* To turn a slender mill, his new made
play [?t]
211 For his delight. The happies[?t is] of all
Hath placed
224 ~~*To lie*~~ ^*beyond these penetrable bounds*
heard
{ar
225 *Words of assurance can be ~~he~~{re,* ^*if no where*
A habitation for consummate good
Of for progressive virtue by that search
Can be attained, a better sanctuary
229 *From doubt and sorrow than the sensless grave*
240 ~~*But I could waive the thought of whence we*~~
rise
And what when breath hath ceased we may become.
Here are we in a bright and breathing world
Our origin what matters it? in lack

193/194 Rev is entered on top and bottom of 70ᵛ, bottom of 71ʳ, and top of 71ᵛ. Rev on 68ᵛ–69ʳ and again on 32ᵛ. The interlinear words possibly signal the pencil revs on 70ᵛ–71ᵛ and 68ᵛ–69ʳ. The symbol above "before" probably signals inclusion of the last rev on 32ᵛ. The text in *1814*, however, follows the reading of the interlinear rev ("Entrusted') rather than 32ᵛ ("Safely entrusted").

194 *1814* begins "Ah!"

203 Del by continuous wavy ink line.

205, 206ff. Three lines of rev are in pencil and continue from 70ᵛ; see note to l. *193/194*, above. "Let" in the last line reads "Left" in *1814*.

209–211 This pencil draft is entered from 71ʳ and 70ᵛ and is then rev on 32ᵛ. The pencil rev at ll. *216/217* on 71ᵛ may continue the draft.

204ff. Cf. MS. 69, stub 80ʳ.

210 The X and another mark to the left of it signal the rev at page foot and on 72ʳ. Rev on 33ʳ.

Of worthier explanation say at once 214
245 *With the American a thought which suits* 215
The place where now we stand that certain 216
Men
restor d so soon to [?peace] & [?senseless] joy
Leapt out together from a rocky cave 217
e ts
And these were the first par{tn{ers of mankind 218
230 × "Is this," the grey-hair'd Pedlar mildly said,
231 That voice which we so lately over heard
C
232, 233 Consoling tenderly the weeping {child
S}
234 "His body is at rest, his [?]}oul in heaven"
235 These were your words", and verily methinks
236 Wisdom is oftimes nearer when we stoop

[72^r]

119
[?~~*Or if some image by the summer air*~~]
Or if a different image be recalled III, 219
[?~~*Should be recalled in*~~] ~~[? ?]~~
250 *By the warm sunshine and the jocund voice* 220
251 ~~*Of insects sporting in the summer air*~~ 221
of insects
Or chirping out ~~*their brief and*~~ *careless lives* 222
252 *On these soft beds of thyme-besprinkled turf* 223
C
~~*May*~~ {*chuse with the gay Athenian a conceit* 224
As sound with that blithe race who wore ere- 225
while
255 *Their golden grasshoppers in sign that they* 226
Had sprung from out the soul whereon they dwelt 227
But stop, these theoretic fancies jar 228
On serious minds, for doubtless in one sense 229
The theme is serious, then as Hindoos draw 230
iey}
260 *Their holy Ganges from a skyer} fount* 231
Even so deduce the stream of human life 232
From seats of power divine and hope or trust 233
That our existence winds its stately course 234

216/217 Pencil rev. Conjectured "peace" may read "bliss." The line is not adopted in *1814*, and possibly it is meant to continue pencil draft (ll. 209–211) at top of page.

230–236 This rev, marked to follow l. *209* above, is continued on the bottom of 72^r. In l. 230, *1814* reads "Wanderer" instead of "Pedlar." The use of "Pedlar" at this point in MS. 71 is perhaps an unconscious return to a discarded conception or an indication that the change of character's name from "Pedlar" to Wanderer" may have occurred after the fair copy of Book III through MS. 71, 74^r. "Wanderer" first appears in the base text of MS. 71 on 80^r, in copying that seems to date from the fifth stage of composition.

219ff. Cf. MS. 69, stub 81^r.

219 First two lines of base text del by eras. The evidence of immediate correction on this page may suggest dictation and close work with WW as opposed to mere copying.

221 Del in pencil.

222 Del and rev in pencil.

Than when we soar." The Other, not displeased
Promply replied, "My motion is the same
And I, without reluctance, could decline
All act of inquisition whence we rise
And what &c

[72v]

120
Beneath the sun, like Ganges, to make part III, 235
Of a living ocean: or if such may seem 236
Its tendency to be engulphed and lost 237
Like Niger in impenetrable sands 238
And utter darkness: thought which may be faced 239
Though comfortless.—Not of myself I speak 240
Such acquiescence neither doth imply 241
In me, a meekly bending spirit, soothed 242
By natural piety, nor a lofty mind 243
By philosophic dicipline prepared 244
For calm subjection to acknowledged law 245
Pleased to have been contented not to be. 246
Such palms I boast not; No—to me who find 247
Reviewing my past { *way* / [? *life*] }*, much to condemn* 248
Little to praise and nothing to regret 249
~~*If I must take my choice between the*~~ { ~~*pair*~~ / [? *two*] } 250
Save some remembrances of dream-like joys
That scarcely seem to have belong'd to me
If I must take my choice between the pair

[73r]

121
That rule alternately the weary hours III, 251
Night is than day more acceptable; sleep 252
Doth in my estimate of good appear 253
A better state than waking death than sleep 254
Feelingly sweet is stillness after storm 255
Though under covert of the wormy ground 256
Yet be it said in justice to myself 257
That in more genial times when I was free 258
To explore the destiny of himan kind 259
Not as an intellectual game pursued 260

237–241 Rev continues from bottom of 71v.

235ff. Cf. MS. 69, stubs 81r, 82r.
250 Line is replaced by the added lines at page foot.

251ff. Cf. MS. 69, stubs 82r, 83r.

With curious subtilty thereby to cheat 261
Irksome sensations, but by love of truth 262
Urged on, or haply by intense delight 263
In feeding thoughts wherever thought could feed 264
{(
I did not rank with those { *too dull or nice,* 265
{*For*
{[?] *to my judgment such they then appeared* 266
{)
Or too aspiring thankless at the best, { 267
He paused, and I was tempted to [?exclaim]
[?hear]
~~With~~

[73[v]]

122
Who in this frame of human life perceives III, 268
An object whereunto their souls are tied 269
In discontented wedlock nor did e'er 270
From me those dark impervious shades that 271
hang
Upon the region whither we are bound 272
Exclude a power to enjoy the vital beams 273
Of present sunshine. Deities that float 274
spirits
On wings, Angelic Virtues, I could muse 275
Oer what from eldest time we have been told 276
{s
Of your bright form { *and glorious faculties* 277
And with the Imagination be content 278
Not wishing more, repining not to tread 279
[?twisting] sinuous
The little *twining* *path of earthly care* 280
By flowers embellished and by springs refreshed 281
Blow winds of Autumn—let your chilling breath 282
{*mead*
Take the live herbage from the { *field and strip* 283
Or that Elysium fabled to possess
Stars and purpureal sunshine of its own
A place of recompense for [?gliding] Shades
Of Heroes, Bards, and Lovers
myrtle crown

WW's draft at page foot is probably rev of opening lines of his addition at bottom of 74[r].

268ff. Cf. MS. 69, stub 83[r], leaf 84[r].
275 Rev in pencil.
280 Rev in pencil; a pencil line beneath "twining" may indicate del or need for rev.

Rev below the rule is probably meant to follow l. *299* on 74[r]; rev of l. *296* there probably prepares the text for its inclusion. Rev here on 73[v] probably follows eras of first two lines in WW's hand at bottom of 74[r]. The transition is rev on 64[v] and on the inserted leaves 75[v]–76[v]. Another attempt at transition seems to have been made at the bottom of 73[r].

[74r]

shady *123*
The ^*forest of its green attire* III, 284
And let the bursting clouds to fury rouze 285
The gentle brooks—Your desolating sway 286
Thus I exclaimed no sadness sheds on me 287
And no disorder in your rage I find 288
What dignity, what beauty in this change 289
From mild to angry and from sad to gay 290
Alternate and revolving—how benign 291
How rich in animation and delight 292
{d
How bountiful these elements compare{ 293
With aught as more desirable or fair 294
Devised by fancy for the golden age 295
With the
Or ~~*that*~~ ^*perpetual warbling that prevails* 296
In Arcady beneath unaltered skies 297
Through the long year in constant quiet bound 298
Night hushed as night and day serene as day 299
339, 340 {Though pleased to listen I was temp }
{[?If smiles of Pity be the just reward]}
ted [?here]
With self congratul
341 {~~To interrupt the speaker, rather say~~}
{Of [?Poesy] [? ?] [?employ]ed }
To slide into the stream of his discourse
[?I said]
{current
With a consenting {[?voice] & ~~exclaimed~~
I }
[339, 340] [?O]}f smiles of pity be the just reward
[341] Of Poesy thus courteously employed

[74v]

III, 342 In framing models to improve the scheme
343 Of man's existence and recast the world
344 Why should not grave Philosophy be stiled
345 Herself a Dreamer of a kindred stock
346 A Dreamer yet more spiritless and dull?
347 Yes,' said I, 'shall the immunities to which

This page (see "123" at its top) is the last numbered one in MS. 71. Second-stage copying (in MW's hand) probably broke off at l. *299* and resumed as fifth-stage work (in WW's hand), probably at the top of 74v. Cf. MS. 69, 84r, where copying also ends at l. *299*. At l. *299* in MS. 71 ends our editorial right-margin numbering (in ital) used to designate the text as it stood at the conclusion of second-stage work (before the death of WW's two children in 1812). See pp. 432–441, 448–455, above, for second- and fifth-stage work on *Exc.*

341 Queried words of eras line were probably "thus courteously," as in the last line on the page.

For page-foot rev that identifies the narrator as replying earlier than l. 347, see last note to 73v.

342 Here WW probably resumed copy after the break on 74r at l. *299*. At page foot, MW resumes at l. 358 what seems clearly intended as fair copy; her fair copy continues on the originally facing 77r (see first note to 75r), and from 77r through 81r.

348 She doth lay claim the precepts she bestows
349 Establish sounder titles of esteem
{Her
350 For {[?],—who, (all too timid & reserved
351 For onset, for resistance too inert
352 Too weak for suffering and for hope too
tame)
353 Did place in flowery Gardens curtained round
354 With world-excluding groves the Brotherhood
355 Of soft Epicurians,—taught—if they
356 The ends of being would secure & win
357 The crown of wisdom to yield up their
souls
358 *To a voluptuous unconcern preferring*
370 Security from shocks of accident
[?peace]
371 From pain & fear & cherished tranquil day
its as mortal lifes chief good
372 For their own sake ~~the bound of their desires~~
As mortal life's chief good & worthiest hope

[75r]

III, 359 Tranquillity to all things. Or is She,
360 I cried more worthy of regard, the Power
361 Who for the sake of sterner quiet, closed
362 The Stoic's heart against the vain approach
363 Of admiration and all sense of joy.
364 His Countenance gave notice that my zeal
365 Accorded little with his present mind.
~~paused~~ ceased
366 I ~~stopped~~, and he resumed.—Ah! gentle Sir
367 Slight if you will the <u>means</u> but spare to slight
368 The <u>end</u> of those who did, by system, rank
ob} {M
369 As the prime of}ject of a Wise{man's aim
370 Security from shock of accident
ful days
ful days
371 Release from dear and cherished peace ~~of mind~~
* With faithful care
{their own sakes just
372 For {its own sake the bound of their desires
As mortal life's chief good & worthiest hope.
373 And only reasonable felicity
374 What impulse, did in later ages drive
in
375 The Hermit to his Cell ~~mid~~ forest wide
~~With faithful care~~
[372] For their own sakes as mortal life's
chief good

370–372 These lines continue rev on the originally facing 77r and are rev on 75r. Rev of l. 372 is probably related to rev on 75r.

Leaves 75 and 76, inserts added at a late stage in composition of Book III, rev and expand 77r and 74v. Text on these inserts is transcribed in reduced type.

372–376 Asterisk before "With faithful care" probably signals rev of passage at page foot and two added lines at top of 75v.

374–410 Cf. MS. 70, 6r–6v, and *Tuft of Primroses*, MS. 65, 44r and 43v (see *Tuft*, pp. 244–247).

[374] What motive drew—what impulse,
, I would ask

[75^{v}]

III, 375 Through a long course of later ages drove
376 The Hermit to his Cell in forest wide
closing eyes
377 Or whatt detained him, till ~~his days were spent~~
378 Took their last farewell of the sun & stars
379 Fast anchor d in the desart. Not alone
380 Dread of the persecuting sword. Remorse,
381 Wrongs unredress'd or insults unaveng d
382 And unavengeable—defeated pride
383 Prosperity subverted maddening want
384 Friendship betrayed affection unreturnd
385 Love with despair or grief in agony.
386 Not always from intolerable pangs
387 He fled, but compass'd round by pleasure, sigh'd
388 For independent happiness; craving peace
389 The central feeling of all happiness
390 Not as a refuge from distress or pain
391 A breathing-time, vacation, or a truce
392 But for its absolute self, a life of peace,
393 Stability without regret or fear
394 That hath been, is, & shall be evermore.
But, out of matter worthless as myself
See! with what strenuous idleness I spin
331 Most wearisome reflections—Age we
know
332 Is garrulous; and solitude is
apt

[76^{r}]

III, 395 Such the reward he sought & wore out life
396 There, when on few external things his heart
397 Was set, and those his own, or if not his
398 Subsisting under Nature's steadfast law.
399 —What other yearning was the master tie
400 Of the monastic brotherhood, upon rock
401 Aerial or in green secluded vale
402 One after one collected from afar
403 And undissolving fellowship?—What but this
404 The universal instinct of repose
405 The longing for confirmed tranquillity
406 Inward & outward humble or sublime
407 The life where hope and memory are as one
408 Earth quiet and unchanged, the human Soul
409 Consistent in self rule—and heaven revealed

---

[374] Comma after "impulse" is obscured by tear in corner of leaf; comma before "I" may thus reinforce its presence.

Inserted leaf; see note to 75^{r}.

375–376 Rev at top of page is continued from 75^{r}.

380 What we read as a comma after "Remorse" may instead be the apos in "unaveng'd."

Passage below the rule is rev of transition following l. *299* on 74^{r} and continued on 76^{r}–76^{v}, rev of 64^{v}, and bottom of 74^{r}. Possibly, space was intentionally left at the bottom of leaves 75 and 76 for rev.

Inserted leaf; see note to 75^{r}.

410 To meditation in that quietness.
333 to anticipate the privilege of age
From far
334 Far have ye come & surely with a hope
335 Of better entertainment—let us hence
336 Loth to forsake the spot & still
more loth
theme
337 To be diverted from our present
m| Sir with
338 I said [?]|y thoughts agreeing y[?ou]
339 Would push this censure farther

[76v]

III, 411 Such was their scheme: thrice happy he who gaind
412 The end proposed, and though the same were miss d
413 By multitudes perhaps obtained by none
414 They for the attempt & for the pains employed
415 Do in, my present censure stand redeemed
{e {that
From th{at unqualified disdain {[?which] once
~~Would have been cast upon them~~
~~by~~
416 ~~From that [?dispraise] & scorn which from my voice~~
by my voice
417 Would have been cast upon them ^ ~~in the time~~
Delivering its decisions from the seat
solve
{solve
418 Of forward youth:—that scruples not to {weigh
~~a~~
419 Doubts & determine questions by ~~the~~ rules
420 Of inexperienc'd judgement, ever prone
421 To overweening faith, and is inflamed
422 By Courage to demand from real life
423 The test of act & suffering—to provoke
it comes
424 Hostility, how dreadful when ~~provoked~~
{.
425 Whether affliction be the foe or guilt{,
in that stage
{at time
426 A Child of Earth I rested {in that ~~stage~~
427 Of my past course to which these thoughts advert
428 ~~Of my past course to which these thoughts~~
~~advert~~
429 Upon earth's native energies &c
338 I said my thoughts agreeing Sir with yours
339 Would push this censure farther for
if smile
340 Of scornful pity

333–339 Passage below rule continues rev that begins at page foot of 75v; ll. 338–339 are further rev at page foot of 76v.

338 Last word of line, obscured by a blot and partially torn away, was probably "yours" as in *1814*.

This page is the last of the inserted leaves; see note to 75r.

415–429 Rev of 77r–77v.

338–340 Continued from 76r and 75v as rev of 64v and 74r.

[77r]

III, 359 *Tranquillity to all things or is she*
360 *I cried more worthy of regard the Power*
361 *Who for the sake of sterner quiet closed*
362 *The Stoics heart against the vain approach*
363 *Of admiration & all sense of joy*
~~Thus, (he continued is contempt~~ misplaced
[?Extreme] & misapplied contempt [?]
~~*Thus is Contempt misplaced by forward*~~
~~*youth*~~
solve
419 By forward youth, that scruples not to ~~weigh~~
420 {Doubts and determine questions by the rules
{[? ? ? ?] [?*to weigh*]}
421 Of inexperienc'd judgement ever prone
[?by] trial
422 To overweening faith, and is inflamed
By
423 {Of courage to demand from real life
{*Of inexperienced judgments,* [?] [?*sti*]} *rred*
424 {The test of act & suffering,—to provoke
{*By* [? ?] [?*of courage to*] *provoke*}
425 *Hostility how dreadful when it comes*
426 *Whether affliction be the for or guilt*
{[?*E*]
427 *—A Child of* {[?*e*] *arth I rested at that time*
364 His Countenance gave notice that my zeal
365 Was not in concord with his present mind
366 I stopp'd and he exclaimed—oh gentle Sir
367 Slight if you will the means but spare to slight
368 The end of those who did by system, rank
369 As the prime object of a wise man's aim

[77v]

III, 429 *Upon Earths native energies forgetting*
430 *That mine was a condition that required*
431 *Nor energy nor fortitude—a calm*
432 *Without vicissitude, which if the like*
{presented
433 *Had been* {[?*fortaste*] *to my view elsewhere*
434 *I might have even been tempted to dispise*
435 *But that which was serene was also bright*
436 *Enlivened happiness with joy overflowing*
should
437 *With joy & oh that memory* ~~*still*~~ *survives*

MW's copy here on 77r continues from the originally facing 74v.

Text of page is canceled because of rev and expansion on inserted leaves 75–76; see note on 75r.

363/419 In the base text line, "youth" is del by eras and overwritten by "to weigh" in l. 419.

421–422 L. 421 overwrites an earlier rev by WW. Possibly "[?by] trial" is a rev of the underlying text of l. 422 before eras and rev.

364–369 This rev is continued on originally facing 74v, and rev on inserted leaf 75r.

438 *To speak the word with rapture—natures*
{. boon
439 *Lifes genuine inspiration{ happiness*

440 *Above what rules can teach or fancy feign{*
441 *Abused as all possessions are abused*
442 That are not prized according to their worth
443 And yet what worth what good is given to Man
444 More solid than the gilded clouds of heaven
445 What joy more lasting than a vernal flower?
446 None—tis the general plaint of human kind
447 In solitude and mutually addressed

[78^r^]

each all
III, 448 From ~~Man~~ to ~~Man~~ for wisdom's sake.—this truth
449 The Priest announces from his holy seat
450 And crowned with garlands in the summer grove
451 The Poet fits it to his pensive Lyre
at} final }
452 Yet ere th[?is]} [?peace}~~ful~~] resting-place be gaind
442 ~~*That are not prized according to their worth*~~
453 Sharp contradiction hourly shall arise
443 ~~*And yet what worth, what good is giv'n to Man*~~
454 To cross the way, &, we perchance, by doom
444 ~~*More solid than the gilded clouds of heaven*~~
455 Of this same life shall be constrained to griev[?e]
445 ~~*What joy more lasting than a vernal flower*~~
to murmur &
454, 455 ~~*And yet by doom of this same life we*~~
Shall be ~~*grieve*~~
~~*We are*~~ *compelled to grieve & to repine,*
That the prosperities of love & joy
Should be permitted oft times to endure
So long & be at once cast down for ever.
Oh tremble ye to whom hath been assigned
A course of days composing happy months
And they as happy years the present still
So like the past & both so firm a pledge
463 *Of a congenial future that the wheels*

[78^v^]

III, 464 *Of pleasure move without the aid of hope*
465 *For mutability is nature's bane*
466 *And slighted hope will be avenged &*
Ye n} *when*
467 *And }eed her favour ye shall find her*
not

439–440 Added punct is in pencil.
442ff. Rev of middle of 78^r^ is continued on the top of 78^r^.

448–455 Continued from 77^v^; rev and expansion of ll. 442–445.

468 *But in her stead fear doubt & agony*
469 *This was the bitter language of the heart*
470 *But while he spake look gesture tone of voice*
ere
471 *Tho' discomposed & vehement w{as such*
472 *As skill & graceful nature might suggest*
473 *To a Proficient of the tragic scene*
474 *Standing before the multitude beset*
heard
475 *With sorrowful events & we who {[?saw]*
476 *And saw were moved. Desiring to divert*
477 *Or stem the current of the speakers thoughts*

[79[r]]

III, 478 *We signified a wish to leave that place*
479 *Of stillness & close privacy that seemed*
480 *A nook for self-examination framed*
481 *Or for confession in the Sinners need*
482 *Hidden from all Men's eyes. To our attempt*
ank
483 *He yielded not but pointing to a b{*[?]
~~a grassy slope [?def~~]
484 ~~*Or sloping couch*~~ *defended from the Sun*
By the projecting side of that huge rock
Which bore the likeness of a stranded hulk
Or uncouth temple built in some dark age
& on that Couch
485 *For worship & inviting us to sit*
486 *He turned upon that tender-hearted Man*
487 *A serious eye & thus his speech renewed*
488 *You never saw, your eyes did never look*
489 *On the bright form of her whom once I loved*

[79[v]]

III, 490 *Her silver voice was heard upon the earth*
491 *A sound unknown to you else honor'd friend*
492 *Your heart had borne a pitiable share*
493 *Of what I suffered when I wept that loss*
494 *And suffer now not seldom from the thought*
495 *That I remember & can weep no more—*
496 *Stripp'd as I am of all the golden fruit*
497 *Of self-esteem & by the cutting blasts*
498 *Of self-reproach familiarly assailed*
499 *I would not yet be of such wintry bareness*
500 *But that some leaf of your regard should*
hang
501 *Upon my naked branches lively thoughts*

---

484 Rev del by eras.

502 *Give birth full often to unguarded words*
503 *I grieve that in your presence from my*
tongue

[80[r]]

III, [505] you know
[506] Revered Compatriot
504 *Too much of frailty hath already dropped*
505 *But that too much demands still more* X
To you
506 *Revered Compatriot & to you kind Sir*
507 *Not to be deemed a Stranger as you come*
508 *Following the guidance of these welcome feet*
509 *To our secluded Vale I would discourse*
Of what I have been to the end that ye
By evidence from other lips than mine
Not to be gained, may judge of what I am
And what our common nature is in me.
Yet How without humiliation speak
Though
~~*What*~~ *(to the pensive Wanderer this was said)*
Some point between us lie
~~*What if some points there be*~~*, where we may*
meet
In fellow-feeling dare I hope to gain
The requisite indulgence from a Soul
[509] To our secluded Vale it may
be told
510 That my demerits did
not sue in
vain

[80[v]]

So widely parted from me, that hath
moved
Above the unequal ground of hope & fear
Along its own peculiar element
With the unimpeded motion of a cloud
Upon the bosom of the ethereal deep
—To that exclusive bower in which we
dwelt
How shall I draw so free a Spirit down

Rev at top and bottom of page is in pencil, as are vertical cancellation marks. Rev at bottom assumes omission of lines on 80[v] up to l. 510 on 81[v], although this passage on the three leaves is not canceled.

505 Pencil X in right margin signals rev at top of page.

509/[509] In the sixth line, the use of "Wanderer" instead of "Pedlar" clearly distinguishes this fifth-stage portion of MS. 71 from the numbered pages (second-stage work) where use of the name "Wanderer" is limited to rev.

And if that wish succeed
~~*And*~~ *by* ~~*what skill shall*~~ *I detain*
him there
Till he hath seen & knows & understands
What love to souls content with narrow room
A }
[?] } *secret bounty can bestow what life*
Can give & that familiar Spectre
death
Insatiably recurring to his task,

[81r]

At three tremendous moments take away
Yet if extremes degrade a living Soul
Is any calm so perfect as the calm
{though
Of the vast Ocean {yet *the same disturbed*
By sudden visitation of the blast
Frets as if very madness were at large
Amid its lowest depths.—Behold in me
How time & solitude together make
{ lawless
A {[?*tedious*] *Speaker all incapable*
To keep the appointed line. It grieves
me now
Tho' here we sit in stillmess & cool shade
{that
That we were tempted forth & left {*my cell*
X ~~Which as a lonely shipwreck d~~
An instrument hangs there to which my
voice
{that
Could sing of pleasures {*which I dare not speak*
Composure would at least attend the touch
Of those soft strings & then I could relate
Which as a lonely Shipwreck'd Man might say
~~shelter~~
Doth harbour me & mine. Upon its walls
An instrument is hung to which my Voice

[81v]

With progress steady as a flowing stream
How those benignant Spirits that direct
Unsettled Fancies where to fix were pleased
III, 510 That my demerits should not sue in vain
511 To One on whose mild radiance many gazed
512 With hope and all pleasure. This
fair Bride

The X, in the left margin of the thirteenth line on 81r, signals substitution of the passage added at page foot.

513 In the devotedness of youthful love
514 Preferring me to Parents and the choir
515 Of gay companions—to the natal roof
516 And all known places and familiar sights
517 Resigned with sadness gently weighing down
518 Her trembling expectations but no more
519 Than did to her due honour and to me
520 Yielded that day {a confidence sublime
521 In what I had to build upon—{This / I led} Bride
522 Youn modest meek and beautiful I led
523 To a low Cottage on a ~~shelter d~~ sunny Bay
524 Where the salt sea innocuously breaks
525 And the sea breeze as innocently breathes
526 On Devon's leafy shores—a sheltered Hold
527 In a soft clime encouraging the {Soil / [?soul]}

[82r]

III, [528] To a luxuriant bounty. With the Rose
The jasmine intertwined her slender arms
524 ~~Where the sa~~[?t] {l} ~~t sea innocuously breaks~~
~~and sky and air~~
526 ~~On Devon's leafy shores~~, {({~~a gentle clime~~ / [?In essence] [?]}}
~~*Of sun & shower encouraging the earth*~~
528 ~~*The Rose and*~~ ~~*intertwined their arms*~~
~~*To a l*~~
[?With the] ~~*luxuriant bounty*~~*). With the Rose*
~~*The jasmine intertwined her slender arms*~~
Around the windows of our Cot: a weight
Of Woodbine overcanopied the Porch:
530 *See! rooted in the earth, its kindly bed,*
531 *The unendangered Myrtle, deck'd with flowers,*
532 *Before the threshold stands to welcome us;*
533 *While in the flowering Myrtle's neighbourhood*
534 *Not overlook'd, but courting no regard*
535 *Those native plants the Holly & the Yew*
536 *Gave modest intimation to the mind*
537 *Of willingness with which they would unite*
538 *With the* {*g* / *p*} ~~*rized*~~ *green Myrtle to endear the hours*
539 *Of winter, & protect that pleasant place*
~~Invite the Stranger to prolong his stay~~
[528] ~~In a luxuriant Region. With the Rose~~

524–527 Rev of 82r, continued at top of 82r.

524–528 Rev at page foot; after cancellation of this passage on 82r, rev at bottom of 81v and top of 82r, and then further rev before readings appearing in *1814*. Possibly the rev at page foot was intended as rev of the copy on 81v, to follow l. 526.

526b DW begins copying and continues through 83r, l. 552a.

[82^v]

Ah! why so full, so perfect, so mature
Exclaim'd my Anna no deficience left
None—where invention might suggest a
work
For our united hands, presumptuous aim
{B
Such {beauty to reform:—to take away
Is to destroy; and would to thee, dear Spot,
Be an ungrateful wrong; unkind it were
{th
To undo what ha{s so happily been done,
Time, Art, and Nature all consenting here
III, 540 *—Wild were the walks upon those lonely*
Downs
541 *Track leading into track, how mark'd how worn*
542 *Into bright verdure among fern & gorse*
543 *Winding away its never-ending line*
& by what means
How fashion'd first, ~~distinctly [?how]~~ preserved
Whether by tread of man or beast, or touch

[83^r]

Of their supernatural steps invisible,—
III, 544 *On their smooth surface evidence was none*
545 *But there lay open to our daily haunt*
546 *A range of unappropriated earth*
547 *Where Youth's ambitious feet might move at*
large
548 *Whence, unmolested Wanderers, we beheld*
{G
549 *The shining {giver of the day diffuse*
550 *His brightness o'er a tract of sea & land*
551 *Gay as our spirits, free as our desires*
552 *As our enjoyments boundless. From these*
heights
553 *We dropped at pleasure into sylvan coombs*
554 *Where arbours of impenetrable shade*
555 *And mossy seats detained us side by side*
556 *With hearts at ease & knowledge in our*
hearts
557 *That all the grove & all the day was ours*
~~—Thence rising, if a gently falling slope~~
~~Ris'n from such seat of gently sloping gr~~ound

The box may indicate lines del or intended for elsewhere; these lines do not appear in *1814*. Absence of del marks here and elsewhere in MS. 71 suggests that substantial rev took place in a subsequent MS. (or that WW provided detailed instructions for recopying MS. 71).

---

552 MW resumes copying at "From these heights."
Rev at page foot, continued at the top of 83^v, expands the opening base text lines on 83^v.

~~Invited, or the thicket would permit~~
Then ere the measure of repose was full,
Ris'n on
Ris }
[?Aris] }en the impulse of some sudden thought
soft
~~Ris'n from those [?seats]~~] if gently
turf
sloping ~~ground~~
From the dark bower

[83v]

Allured, or tangled woodland would
permit
~~*Thence rising if the woodland would permit*~~
We followed where the infant streamlet led
We took the infant streamlet for our guide
One I remember an indulgent rill
That oft has moistened Annas rosy lip
Brook
With its cool waters—this wild-wandering {~~Brook~~ *Rill*}
And others not less wild or those free tracks
Conducting us not seldom were we smit
By composition ch{*oice* [?*ance*]} *of natures forms*
near
Remote or ~~*vast*~~ *presenting to the eye*
Tasks for the shading pencil which some
day
More patient in the tenour of its joys
see
Should {~~*see*~~ *be accomplished. Mid a fearful store*}
for years unlooked
Of things ~~*unlooked for*~~ *at I possess*
A work in that far distant time performed
: } portraiture,-impressed
~~*By Anna's hand,*~~ } ~~*—a true reflexion traced*~~
~~As on a mirror~~
~~*On the smoorth tablet of the first abode*~~
By Anna's hand;—the Canvas represents
As in a mirror shown, the first Abode
Of man, a clay buit Cottage thatch'd with
Broom

EdeS suggests that "shading pencil," in the tenth base text line on 83v, echoes *PL*, III, 509: "By Model, or by shading pencil drawn."

In the thirteenth base text line, rev "unlooked" is entered diagonally across the line.

Three lines at page foot are rev of base text lines immediately above and on 84r.

[84r]

~~woodman's~~

~~*A little clay built Cottage roofed with thatch*~~

Rill

The first which he who with that ~~stream~~ descends
Ere far descended meets upon the bank
Of its life-feeding waters. As it grew

Piece
{[?Pie]
The mimic {[?*work*] *was quickened by my*
praise
Flowers also have I pictured with a touch
Of skill as fine; the scentless images
Of past delights existing in their forms
And not relinquishing their brilliant hues
Though in their spirit dead. But all was
life

To
~~*With*~~ *us all nature breathing love was filled*
With fragrance universal. Still perhaps
Still may be seen undwindled undecayed
Some bright originals from which she took
Those faithful copies in the ground surviving

with
Whither tranplanted by [?*her*]} *a tender hand*
They from their various birth places were brought

[84v]

And throve assembled in our small domain
Blest occupation pastimes innocent

~~*Thus & by other inoffen*~~[?*i*] ~~*ive ways*~~

Thus
{that {[—?—]
Love {[?*who*] *through* {[?*out*] *the region of thoughts*
Can make that purer which was deemed most
pure
Love that exalts the finest essences
~~*And brightens brightest hues found space*~~
to employ
~~*His busy fingers in that finished spot*~~
~~*Finished & fair as Paradise itself*~~
~~*Where the first Adam dwelt with happy Eve*~~

only
And brightens brieghtest hues not wrought

Enclosures
{at Enclosure
In the {[?ose fair gardens] to redress and guard

First base text line is rev at the bottom of facing 83v. At the top of 84r, "woodman's" is possibly an adjective to describe "Cottage" in the first line of 84r or is perhaps entered as part of the rev on 83v.

MW breaks off copy at the middle of 84v, and DW resumes copy on 85r, leaving half a page on 84v for WW's rev of MW's work and of DW's first two lines on 85r. A draft, probably related to the fourth and fifth lines of rev, is entered at the bottom of 85r.

And to maintain but also could find space
To introduce new touches of his own
'd
Heighten ing the beauties
The ~~charms to a height [?ten]~~ of a finished
spot
Finished and fair as Paradise itself
Where the first Adam dwelt with sinless Eve.
III, 558 But in due season Nature interfered
559 And called my Partner to resign her share
560 In the pure freedom of that wedded life
561 Ejoyed by us in common.—To my hope
562 To my heart's wish my tender Mate
became

[85r]

III, 560 ~~*But on the freedom of that wedded life*~~
561 ~~*Which we enjoy'd in common Nature laid*~~
562 ~~*Welcome restraint my tender Mate became*~~
563 *The thankful Captive of maternal bonds*
p ths
564 *And those wild wa lks were left to me alone*
565 *There could I meditate on follies past*
566 *And, like a weary voyager escaped*
567 *From risk & hardships, inwardly retrace*
s t
568 *A course of vain delight & thoughtless guil[? d]*
569 *And self-indulgence without shame pursued*
570 *There undisturb'd could think of, & could thank*
573 ~~*That earthly Providence whose guiding love*~~
571 *Her whose submissive spirit was to me*
572 *Rule & restraint, my Guardian, shall I say*
i
That harmlessly diversify ed an oft
(at least so seemed [?it] to [?our] partial eyes)
~~ver~~
~~That did di~~[?] ~~sify~~
[?~~h~~]
That did diversify & [?in our] [?] ~~eig[?t]~~ eyes
[?Have]

[85v]

P
III, 573 *That earthly providence whose guiding love*
574 *Within a port of love had lodged me safe,*
575 *Safe from temptation & from danger far*

At the top of 85r, DW resumes copy through l. 608 on 86r.
First three lines on 85r are rev at page foot of 84v.
573 Canceled line on 85r is perhaps a copying error; the line also appears at the top of 85v.
Passage at page foot of 85r seems related to unnumbered lines of rev on 84v.

[?~~proceed~~] ~~[? ?]~~ [?~~walk~~]
576 Strains followed of acknowlegement addressed
[?~~This~~]
~~And saw the threshold crowded with a brood~~
577 To an Authority enthroned ~~where sight~~ above
~~Of ragged Children gazing as I pass'd,~~
578 The reach of sight from whom as from their source
~~There in soft [?whi] sper to myself I said~~
579 Proceed all visible Ministers of good
~~"A cloud hath veil[? ?] her from our sight~~
580 That walk the earth—Father of Heaven & Earth
~~Unhurt will reappe[?ar] & shine again~~
581 Father and King and Judge adored & feared
~~On these hill tops and~~ [?bountifully] *~~yields~~*
582 These acts of mind and memory & heart
~~For you [?&] your Almighty Fa[?ther's] glory~~
[583] And spirit—interrupted & relieved
~~That [?ble] ssed light which ye [?before] have felt~~
~~Gladdening your doors. Such notices, such~~
thoughts
583 ~~Such intrerested notices relievd~~
{By
{[?*nd*]}
584 A[?*re*]} *observations transient as the glance*

[86r]

III, 585 *Of flying sunbeams, or to the outward form*
586 *Cleaving with power inherent & intense*
587 *As the mute insect fix'd upon the plant*
588 *On whose soft leaves it hangs, & from whose cup*
D} imperceptibly
589 *It d} raws ~~invisbly~~ its nourishment*
590 *Endear'd my wanderings; & the Mother's kiss*
591 *And Infant's smile awaited my return*
607 *~~—Your hearts, I feel, are with [?me,] I perceive~~*
withholds not from my words
608 *—Your courtesy ~~provides for what I say~~*
Attentive O Gentle Friends
609 *~~A willing~~ audience. But ~~as times of peace~~*
610 As times of quiet & unbroken peace
611 Though for a nation times of blessedness
612 Give back faint echoes from the Historians
page

The X canceling two-thirds of the page was erased before the interlinear rev were entered. Consequently, some words or letters of the original base text lines were erased along with the X.

576 WW's rev above and below line are del by eras. The first word of the original base text line, now eras, is probably "Oftimes."

578 The word underlying "reach" may be "sight."

580 Eras words were the final ones of the original line, immediately above.

590–591 Pencil diagonal mark cancels two lines, but those lines are in *1814*.

591/607 Intervening passage is first drafted on the back of a copy of WW's letter to Lord Lonsdale, 8 January 1813 (see pp. 1105–1106, below). Rev on inserted leaves 87r–87v.

607 Rev on inserted leaf 87v, where the passage (ll. 607–617) is indicated as following l. 606.

609–615 Rev on 89v and on inserted leaf 87v.

613, 614 ~~Even so I hear how faithless is the voice~~
615 ~~Which those most happy days rever~~
~~berate~~,
613 So in the imperfect sounds of this discourse
614 Depress'd, I hear, how faithless is the voice
[615] Which those most happy days reverberate
× [?fraught]

[86v]

Time with the fairest fruits of time advan
ced
Knowledge & fancy's elegant deli[?g]ts
~~Knowledge and love activity & peace~~
joy
And morning chearfulness & nightly peace
And for two Little-ones that bless'd our love
Encreasing strength and growing comeliness.
III, 631 Seven years of occupation undisturbd
632 Established seemingly a right to hold
633 That happiness, and use and habit gave
{S
634 To what an alien {spirit had acquired
635 A patrimonial sanctity. And thus
636 With thoughts and wishes bounded to this
lif
637 I lived and breathed, most grateful, if
to enjoy
638 Without repining or desire for more
639 For different lot or change to higher sphere
640 (Only except some impulses of pride
activity of mind repose of heart

[87r]

Time with the fairest fruits of time advance[?d]
Knowledge and fancy's elegant delights
Activity of mind repose of heart.
And morning chearfulness and nightly peace.
III, 592 In privacy we dwelt—a wedded Pair
593 Companions daily, often all day long
594 Not placed by fortune within easy reach
595 Of various intercourse, not wishing aught
596 Beyond the allowance of our own fireside

---

[615] Rev and symbol below the line remain unidentified; possibly, they signal a rev no longer extant.

Passage originally continued on 91r, the facing leaf before four inserted leaves were added between 86v and 91r. Rev on inserted leaves 87r, 90r.

Rev at page foot is incorporated into the text (third line) on 87r.

Leaf 87r is the first leaf of the inserted leaves (87–90), containing rev and recension; for discussion of these passages, see p. 450, above, and the note to 91v, below.

Draft for ll. 592ff. (continuing to "Yields her affections" on 87v) is on the back of a copy of WW to Lord Lonsdale, 8 January 1813 (see p. 1106, below).

597 The Twain within our Cottage born
598 Inmates, and Heirs of our united love
599 Graced mutually by difference in sex
600 By the endearing names of nature joined
601 And with no wider interval of time
602 Between their several births than servd
for One

[87ᵛ]

III, 603 To establish something of a Leader's sway
pa
604 Yet left them joined by sym[?pt]thy in age
605 Equals in pleasure fellows in pursuit
606 On these two Pillars rested as in air
It soothes me to perceive
607 Our Solitude.—I speak to minds that
know
The course of Nature.—See we not the Nun,
Within
{[?Within]
{[?Encaged] a ~~Convents~~ wiry grate encaged
A Prisoner, though not wanting choice of grave
B
Or gay Companions to a Captive bird
Yields her affections—occupies the time
In delicate attentions to its needs
Or
In [?fond] obserance of its antic feats
[?d]
And if her lessons rais [?e] to higher pitch
Its ma[?v]ellous accomplishments, she smile
In triumph, gives caresses & receives
when
Nor finds the day too long ^ if so beguiled

[88ʳ]

The hardy Mariner from Indian shores
Returning homeward if the Ship convey
A Leopards cub or brinded Tygers whelp
Drawn from its native forest can in the[?se]
Find ready solace for his leisure hours
And in the busiest casts a glance that
way.
as
Who more delighted more sincerely ple[?s]d ed
e
Than this ungentle wand rrer of the Deep
ile
Whe[?] he admires the gambols & incites

Inserted leaf; see note to 87ʳ.

607 Rev (in darker ink than the base text of l. 607) indicates placement of ll. 607–615, first entered on 86ʳ and continued on 89ᵛ (see note to ll. 608–615 on 89ᵛ).

Vertical line in the right margin probably indicates these lines are to be skipped in later copying. Vertical line in the left margin possibly signals need for rev (and would thus precede decision to cut the entire passage).

Inserted leaf; see note to 87ʳ. Left-margin vertical line probably indicates cutting of these lines from later copying.

e} forbears
To new ext}rtion nor perchance ~~doth spare~~
To lull the Favorite in his rugged arms
Till it ha[?s] learned to love him in return
mid Como's chestnut groves
No otherwise ~~upon the pine clad steeps~~
Or on the pine clad steeps of Appenine
~~Of Appenine~~ the Hermit Monk
The Hermit Monk forth issuing from his cell
Lures down the Squirrel from the
{&
bough {or wins
The Hermit Monk standing before his cell

[88v]

From}
The } the high rock the unrestriced Dove
To perch upon his shoulder—Ah—if then,
Nature & circumstance for one effect
Combining can to such dependence pledge
The human feeling in their several hearts
Judge of a parent's joys in solitude
Among} {[?L]
[?] } his sportive smiling {little-ones
A mothers tenderness, a fathers love
How constant, how habitual, how intense.
{C rewards
The sanguine {chaser of the worlds delights
such
Knows not to measure ~~this~~ affection,—He
Moves in the shouls but never tried its depths
This universal instinct of mankind
Tis solitude that carries to the extreme
Of passion and dominio in the soul
A strengh a weakness inconceivable

[89r]

hence,—at least
The state of Kings is lonely; for this cause
For this cause chiefly is the crowned King
~~They to their infant offspring [?do incline~~]
To a degree unusual among Men
{~~prize~~
~~And~~ {[?love] ~~the Company of Little~~ Ones
the ~~cares of sovereignty~~
~~More than would [?els] be possible~~
[?their]
Pleas'd with the sight of children & holds dear
The company their Innocence affords.
{~~Power~~
~~Grand[?eur] or~~ {[?] ~~would other wise allow~~.
M}
The Spartan [?K]}onarch, once as Story tells

Inserted leaf; see note to 87r. The fourth word in the penultimate line was intended as "dominion."

Inserted leaf; see note to 87r. The right-angled line in the right margin at page foot probably indicates cutting of the passage from later copying.

Surprized whie busy with a Playmates
part
Mid his young
~~Among his~~ children, blush'd not, well
aware
jus
That Nature of hereself is [?]tified
like
But oh he loved not, could not love [?those] those
s ~~glare~~
Who far from armie[?g] & the pomp of Courts
Awake to these calm pleasures every day
On the pla[?in] ground of rural privacies
As I—even I cherished & loved my own

[89v]

supplies
That to my words your courtesy ~~afford~~
III, 608 Your Courtesy witholds not from my words
A willing
609 Attentive audience. But oh gentle Frieds
610 As times of quiet and unbroken peace
N
611 Though for a nation times of blessedness
612 Give back faint echoes from the Histor
ians page
613 So in the imperfect sounds of this discourse
614 Depress'd I hear how faithless is the voice
days
615 Which those most blissful times reverberate.
616 What special record can or need be given
habits
T habits
617 [?]o rules & [?customs ~~bond~~] whereby much
was wroght
All within the sphere
618 But ~~in the circle all~~ ^ of litt[?le] things,
[?Her diurnal]
619 Of humbl though to us important cares
[620] And precious interests. Smoothly did our life
[?You divine the worst]
[620] ~~[?A]nd precious interests—[?changes slowly~~]
~~wrought~~
621 Advance not swerving from the path prescribe
[?If] you imagine changes
[622] Her annual her diurnal round alike
And in their progress imperceptible

623, 624 Faithfully kept. And you divine

Inserted leaf; see note to 87r.

Large diagonal cancellation line on this page may indicate a decision, later changed, to cut the passage. Alternatively, although perhaps less likely, the passage may have been canceled as part of a process of restructuring the book. Cancellation lines here, on 87r,and on pages following are in a distinctive brown ink belonging to a very late stage of rev. WW's instruction on 91v, "Keep this page" (a page that had been canceled in pencil), indicates the late stage of rev this ink belongs to. Dark black ink rev of l. 607 on 87v is probably later than the brown ink.

608–615 Rev of 86r; l. 607 added to 87v indicates that these lines are to follow l. 606 on that page.

617–626 A series of pencil drafts precedes the ink rev. The first pencil drafts, presented at page foot (ll. 620–625) are overwritten in ink by ll. 623–626, shown immediately above. The phrase "[?Her diurnal]" between ll. 618 and 619 is in pencil, overwritten in ink; the pencil line at [620] (beginning "[?A]nd") is rev in ink immediately above; the line between ll. 621 and [622], beginning "[?If]," is in pencil, which is then overwritten in ink by l. 621. These pencil drafts were rev on 113v.

the worst
[625] If you imagine changes slowly wrought
{~~progress~~
626 ~~And in their~~ {[?] ~~imperceptible~~
620 Smooth was the [?path] nor [? ?]
[?]
[?wrought]
622 [?The annual] [?] [?the diurnal round]
625 Through [?] [?changes slowly]

[90[r]]

III, 627 Not wish'd for, sometimes noticed with
a sigh
~~regret~~,
628 (Whate'er of good or lovely thing might br[?ign])
S}
{s}~~ighs~~
{[?Forth]
629 Sighs of regret for the familiar good
630 And loveliness en[?e]deared—which
they removed

631 Seven years of occupation undisturbed
632 Established seemingly a right to hold
633 That happiness & use & habit gave
634 To what an alien Spirit had
acquired
And
{&
635 A patrimonial sanctity.— {[?] thus
636 With thoughts & wishes bounded to this
world
637 I lived and breathed, most grateful if to
i} enjoy
638 Without repeping}ng or desire for more
{F
639 {for different lot or change to higher sphere
{O
640 ({only except some impulses of pride)

[91[r]]

no
III, 641 With~~out~~ determined object, though upheld
642 By theories with suitable support)
643 Most grateful if in such wise to enjoy
644 Be proof of gratitude for what we have
645 Else, I allow, most thankless.—But at once

---

626 Overwriting "progress" probably corrects a copying error or possibly reinforces a few miscopied letters.

Inserted leaf; see note to 87[r].
Page is canceled in the same distinctive brown ink, indicating later rev, as is 89[v] (see note there).
627 What we read as a comma after "regret" may be an "s."
635–640 Rev of 86[v]. The ampersand in l. 635 is possibly del.
Leaf 90[v] is blank.

Passage followed directly from 86[v] before leaves 87–90 were inserted. See next note for comment on ink cross.

646 From some dark seat of fatal power
was urged

shattered
~~shatterd~~
647 A claim that [?blasted] ~~all the claim of~~
death.

The time no doubt has been
—Condemn me not.—~~I might have boasted once~~
When strength of passion would have made me
boast
As each enraptured Lover fondly boasts
And every Husband happy in his choice
That mine was a peculiar blessedness.
And when in pride of passion stronger still
I could have boasted
[?] [?boasted] [?] that the Power which
shook
Pile
[?~~frame~~]
That Pile & having shaken overthrew
To me had dealt a portion of despair
Unmatch'd on earth, and solitary pain.
to
But no—exception from a common fate
Peculiarity of doom would now

all
th
a claim that shattered, ale Spoiler fell
rnd
[?n'd]
Upon our peace & & robb'd us unfor[?w]a[?d]

[91v]

Keep this page
Had kept me silent—as a feeble Man
t
Among a suffering multidude I speak.
—Have you espied upon the dewy lawn *MG*, 27
t
A Pair of Leverens each provoking each 28
To a continuance of their fearless play 29
Two several creatures with their separate gifts 30
see in all
Of sense and Intellect; but ~~note them well~~
~~Observe them nearly and behold~~ in all 31

The text is canceled by two ink crosses (the first in the distinctive brown ink associated with late rev; see note to 89v). The second cancellation is earlier and thus explains the rev on 95v–96r (the two lines at page foot may have been added as part of that rev).

"Keep this page" at the top probably indicates that WW, after rejecting this material for *Exc*, wanted to save it for use elsewhere. This material on 91v–95v seems to have once been thought of as the basis for a single, separate poem but eventually became *Maternal Grief* (published 1842, hereafter *MG*) and *Characteristics of a Child three Years old* (published 1815; hereafter *CC*). Cf. *Poems, 1807–1820*, pp. 522–523. Right-margin line references to these poems are provided to texts in *Poems, 1807–1820*, pp. 118–122. Insertion of leaves 87–90 in MS. 71 was made after WW decided to exclude these passages from *Exc.*

The second, and larger, cancellation X is in pencil.

27 Change of pen and ink.

30/31 Phrase "see in all" is in pencil.

That Nature prompts them to display, their looks 32
Their starts of motion and their fits of rest 33
An undistinguishable stile appears 34
And character of gladness, as if Spring 35
Lodged in their innocent bosoms & the Soul 36
Of the rejoicing morning were their own; 37

{O
Mark what {one is the Other is the same.
Now, should a ravenous Bird a fowl of strength
Such as abide among these craggy wastes,
Before your eyes with sudden sweep descend

[92r]

Such as abide among these Crags descend
From the high quarters where he rules in state
And of these unoffending Playmates seize
One and for ever break their joint delight
Would ye not shriek at such a Spectacle.
—Ah but ~~a mother saw~~ it—it was seen
A claim that shatterd all
III, 647 ~~And by a Father felt~~ / Our blooming Girl
{D
648 Caught in the gripe of {[?d]eath with such brief time
649 To struggle in as scarcely would allow
650 Her cheek to change its colour was conveyed
651 From us to regions inacessible
d}
652 Where height or depth am}mits not the approach
s}
653 Of living man though longing to pur[?p]}ue.
So was the myrtle-shaded Cottage turned
Into a House of mourning from whose doors
All grace and favour were at once withdrawn
No light of gladness shone around the Hearth

[92v]

No music rang within the walls but there
Silence prevailed and undeparting gloom
Suspence of breath and respiration deep,
Prayers yielding short relief or haply none
Wringing of hands & in the Mothers breast
Conflicts of agonizing thoughts like these.
—Departing Child I could forget thee once MG, 1
Though at my bosom nurs'd—this woeful gain 2
Thy dissolution brings that in my soul 3

37ff. Rev at page foot is of first two lines on 92r.

Symbol at top left of 92r probably indicates rev on 91v. Diagonal slash canceling first five lines is in pencil, as is the del in the sixth line and the rev of l. 647. The curved line in the left margin at page foot perhaps marks the lines for consideration for the separate poem that later became *MG*.

s
Perpetually a {Shadow doth abide 4
That never never more shall be displaced 5
S
By the returning {substance, seen or touchd, 6
S
[?D]}een by mine eyes or clasped in my embrace. 7
Absence & death how differ they & how 8
~~by [? ? ?]~~
[~~?Followed] & [?downcast looks] [?&] [?] [?eye~~]

[93r]

Shall I admit that nothing can restore *MG, 9*
What one short sigh so easily removed *10*
Death life and sleep reality and thought *11*
Instruct me, God, their boundaries to know *12*
know
And make my new condition fairly mine
resignation
—O teach me calm submission to thy will. *13*
~~When we were summoned to deplore this loss~~
The Child [?she bewaild]
~~She whom~~ we mourned had overstepp'd the pale *14*
[?s] [?]
Of Infancy, but still did breathe the air *15*
That sanctify its confines and did still *16*
With all the Little-ones on earth partake *18*
Reflected beams of that celestial light *17*
Whose universal influence warmed & cheard *19*
The individual qualities of mind *20*
That in her own bless d nature took *21*
their birth

[93v]

~~And had~~ *MG, 22*
Open'd, before the Mothers wakeful
eye
~~And had begun before her Parents Eyes~~ [22]
Unfolding daily [?their peculiar]
Daily to open and unfold their sweets *23, 24*
When we were summoned to deplore her loss
That point she had attained that single
[?On] point
{[?And] which those powers are given & only those

8ff. Two lines at page foot are del by eras; possibly these lines are related to lines at the bottom of 93r and the top of 93v.

14 Rev to "[?she bewaild]" may be part of altering text once thought of as *Exc* to the separate poem of *MG*, because—if the reading is in fact "she"— it is no longer "we" but just "she" who mourns. Rev, in similar ink, at the top of 93v also suggests this change in focus from parents to mother.

22 Del by eras.

And only in such measure degree
That one so furnished may depart from
earth
And be received into another world
An untransfigured Spirit without change
From grace to be supplied or taint
removed
Or discord needing to be harmonized.
Loving she was and tractable though wild CC, 1
{And
{[?For] Innocence had privilege in her 2
To dignify arch looks & laughing eyes 3
{And feats of cunning and the pretty 4
{In [?voluntary songs/&] [? ?]
round
{Of trespasses affected to provoke 5
{[? ? ? ?] [?or her heart impelld]
Mock chastisment & partnership in play 6

[94ʳ]

{And as a faggot sparkles on the hearth CC, 7
{[? ? ? ?] [?by the]
[?] [?fawn]
{Not less if unattended and alone 8
{[?Or] [?be seen] [?sporting on the dewey field.]
Than when both young & old sit gathered 9
round
And take delight in its activity 10
{of
Even so this happy Creature {in herself 11
Was
All sufficent solitude to her 12
Was blithe society who filled the air 13
With gladness and in voluntary songs 14
{F
Light were her sallies as the tripping {fawn's 15
Forth started from the fern where she lay couched 16
Unthought of unexpected as the stir 17
Of the soft breeze ruffling the meadow-flowers 18
Or from before it chasing wantonly 19
The many coloured images impress d 20
Upon the mirror of a placid Lake.) 21

Partial box at page center separates material not intended for new poem or poems growing out of *Exc* material. *CC* at this point seems to have been part of *MG*; vertical cancellation marks on 93ᵛ–94ᵛ (in same light brown ink as revs to *MG*) seem to be copying instructions to exclude *CC* from later copying of *MG*. Cf. note to 91ᵛ.

Eras lines at page foot here and at the top of 94ʳ may be variants of later ones on 94ʳ comparing the child to the natural world.

Cf. note to 93ᵛ.

The pen ran dry on the upper-left stroke of the canceling X.

[94v]

grievous
To my Copartner in this bitter loss
Support I could not yield who did myself
support
Require ^ from others less disturbed
Or from the blank and calm of solitude
X ~~Darkness was double darkness outward weight~~
Nor in this anguish could the Mother lean
On her surviving Child, as on a Staff
By heaven afforded to uphold her maimed
And tottering Spirit weak & desolate
{[?trouble]
For he to {[?sorrow] and distress unused
Shrunk from her presence shunn'd her sad approach *MG, 51*
With timid heart and stole away to find *52*
In his known haunts of joy whereer he might *53*
{T
A more congenial object. But as {time *54*
{b
Mellowed her pangs & reconciled the {Boy *55*
X Dark became doubly dark to outward weght
Was inward added whe
~~To inward added~~ whensoeer our minds
In converse met—nor could the Mother lean
[?]
{privation
In this {affliction on the Company

[95r]

To what he saw he gradually returned *MG, 56*
encouraged
{ecourage
Like a scared Bird {[?incited] to renew *57*
intercourse
A broken fellowship.—O blessed Child *58*
Thy pure and perfect excellence demands
An everlasting record but I think
{T
And speak of {thee among wild rocks & stones
Nor ask for other audience which this day
Provideth not unthankfully received
Albeit soon to be resigned. Large space,
twice seven years of trouble
troubles
Full ~~twenty years~~ of memory, ~~doth~~ lie
Between us rolling like the stormy deep

Cf. note to 93v.
The small, left-margin X signals the rev at page foot.

In the line two-thirds of the way down the page (beginning "Full"), "troubles " is in pencil, and "doth" is del in pencil.

C
But oh sweet comforter I can perceive
As in the nearness and the perfect light
Of yesterday thy beauty, see thine eyes [58]
(Large eyes of liquid sweetness ever full)
T
On her who bore thee turned with pensive fear 59
And gentle awe who stopping doth imprint 59–61

[95v]

On her who bore thee turned who stoops to imprint MG, 60, 61
A kiss of Chearfulness & hopeful Love 61
That hath recalled the colour to thy cheek 62
mul
And stills thy tre[?mbl]ous lip.—So both were cheared 63, 64
And I with them; and they together breathd 64
Fresh air in open fields, and when the Day 64, 65
Was gone; and Twilight, to the Mother's wish 66
Befriended that observance they would join 67
hose was the lost one
In walks w[?] boundary was the lost ones grave 68
Which he with snowdrops planted finding there 69
Amusement where the Mother did not miss 70
Dear consolation kneeling on the turf 71
In prayer and blending with this solemn rite 72
Of pious hope the vanities of grief 73
If still I linger in these thoughts detained
me
Condemn [?not] not—The time no doubt has been
When strength of passion would have made me boast
As each enraptured Lover fondly boasts
And every Husband happy in his choice
And every Parent tender in his Love

Rev at page foot is of first line on 95v.

60, 61 Rev at bottom of 95r.
68 In-line rev "was the lost ones grave" in pencil, partially rewritten above in ink.
Rev at page foot and continuing on 96r is possibly added in a space left for it; the lines seem to be copied from a passage on 91r–91v.

[96r]

That mine was a peculiar blessedness
And when in pride of Passion stronger still
I could have boasted that the Power which
ver} shook
That Pile & having shaken oer }threw
despair
{spair
To me had dealt a portion of de{light
Unmatch'd on earth & solitary pain
peculiarity of doom
But no—exception to a common fate
Had kept me silent as a feeble man
Among a suffering multitude I speak
{Ah!
{ Therefore, in calmness let me tell that
—Yet can I tell how bear to tell that
he
Who in this sort foretasted of the grave
Not fearfully, but with delight, & gleams
Of fancy scattered among serious thoughts
Before th fondly look'd for time was come
~~Before those~~ snowdrops with their passing
[?Who there loved] Flowers
{Could y}
{[?Did] beautified} the mound to which his pains
Had brought them that this Innocent
was laid
In the green Churchyard by his Sister's side.
ruthless
III, 659 ~~Calm as a frozen Lake when dreary winds~~
660 ~~Blow fiercely, agitating earth~~ & sky
661 The Mother now remained; as if in her
662 Who to the lowest regions of the Soul,
erewhile
663 Before, had been ^unsettled & dist[?urbed]
T

[96v]

III, 664 This second visitation had no power
To shake, but only to bind up & seal
establish thankfulness of heart
And to inspire meek patience & delight
In heavens determinations ever just
[?e]
667 ~~And merciful~~,
And even when most severe most
merciful,
If so interpreted. Behold, said I

Small-type lines at top continued from 95v, possibly in space left for the purpose. In the fifth line, the revs "spair" and "despair" are in pencil. In the seventh line, rev "peculiarity of doom" is in pencil.
The "T" at page foot is probably the aborted beginning of l. 664 on 96v.

Rev on 97r.

669 (Not finding strength within me
to attain
668 The elevation where she stood alone
But not too senseless to admire) beh[?old]
{An
{[?] untranslated Spirit all at once
Cleans'd & made perfect; see in [?Womans]
Form
Ideal truth embodied & enshrined
The weeds of misery put off & faith
Once more by miracle disclosed. O
Thou
677 Ordained at once the Partner of my woes
And comforter, eye hast Thou given
to hope
Benighted suddenly & filled with
joy
The House of mourning—

[97[r]]

III, 669 Immense
severed
670 The space that ~~parted~~ us, but as the
sight
671 Communicates with heaven's etherial
orbs
672 Incalculably distant, so I felt
673 That consololation may descend from
far
674 (And that is intercourse & union too)
This ~~I perceived & have not yet forgotten~~
675 While overcome with gratitude & filled
holiest
676 With encrease pure of ~~holy~~ love,
I lookd
677 One her at once superior to my
woes
O heavy change
678 And partner of my loss. From [?her]
[?~~pure peace~~]
679 Dimness oer that bright luminary crept
~~Proceeded & [?she f]~~
680 Insensibly, the immortal & divine
~~The House of Mourn[?ing.] O th[?e] heavy~~
[?press] Change
681 Yielded to mortal [?~~weak~~]ness ~~smiles [?all]~~
peace

Leaf 97[r] is partial rev of 96[v], rev on 97[v].

669 "Immense" may be intended to follow the last line on 96[v], or it may assume rev of l. 669 there. At ll. 680/681 on 97[r], WW's base text line suggests consideration and then rejection of proceeding with his passage by rev of last line on 96[r].

681 Conjectured rev above the line may have been intended as "pressure."

~~and she~~ fell
pure
her glory
682 As from the pinnacle of wordly state
drops astounded
683 Wretched Ambition ~~falls~~ or sinks ~~she~~ fell
gul[?f] obscure of silent pain
684 Into a ~~culpable [?obs] distress of~~ mind
{keen
685 And {[?] heart anguish of itself ashamed

[97v]

III, 678 o heavy change
Not by successive clouds that overspread
679 Dimness oer this clear luminary crept
This supernatural luminary—no
680 Insensibly, the immortal & divine
[679] Into its very own [?constution] dimness crept
681 Yielded to mortal reflux, her pure
glory
682 As from the pinnacle of wordly state
683 Wretched Ambition drops astounded,
fell
grief
684 Into a gulph obscure of silent ~~pain~~
685 And keen heart anguish of itself
ashamed,
686 Yet obstinately cherishing itself
687 And so consum[?e]d [?the] she melted
from my arms
688 And left me, on this earth, disconsolate.
revived
689 What followed cannot be ~~retraced~~ in
thought
690 Much less retraced in words. If She, so
[?in]
Blameless ~~pure~~
691 Of life, so intimate with love & joy
692 And all the tender motions of the Soul
693 Had been supplanted Could I hope
to stand
~~Could I [?ho~~]
694 Infirm dependent & now destitute

[?I] it wore the [?semblance]
[?]
At first, methought it [?was air]
or [?haze]
That had appear d & would disperse
That supernatural [?luminary but our]
[?soul]

Leaf 97v is rev of 97r.
Lines below the rule may be drafting toward or failed rev of lines on 97r.

[98r]

III, 695 I called on dreams & vision to disclose
696 That which is veiled from waking thought
conjured
697 Eternity as men constrain a Ghost
~~on~~ spake
698 To appear & answer—~~to~~ the Grave I said
Imploringly, looked up & askd the
699 [?~~Unhouse] thy shrouded~~ d ~~Phantoms~~—
~~aske~~d the heaven
700 If Angels traversed their cerulean
floors
If fix'd or wandering Star
701 If they in truth could any tidings
yield
702 Of the departed Spirit, what abode
703 It occupies what consciousness retains
704 Of former loves & interest; then my Soul
705 Turn inward, to examine of what
stuff
706 Time's fetters are composed, and
long life was
707 To inquisition ~~vain~~ & profitless
708 By Pain of heart now check &
now impelld

[98v]

III, 709 The Intellectual Power through
words & things
710 Went sounding on—a dim & perilous
way
&
711 And from these transports, these
toils abstruse
712 Am I entabled to retain some trace
713 Of time else lost, existing unto me
{found
714 Only by records in myself not {[?lost].
at}
715 From this} abstraction I was rouzd—
and How?
716 Even as a Thoughtful Shepherd by a flash
717 Of Lightening startled in a gloomy cave
seized
727 As marvellously rouz d, as when in
volved
728 In blinding mist upon the mountain
tops
{hath erewhile
As {ye were told been told I reachd
the skirts
[728] Of the deep Vapour & beheld at once

729 Glory beyond all glory ever seen
730 Confusion infinite of heaven & earth
731 ~~To mortal eyes display d.—~~P
rophetc
Harps
{t {Soul. {Lo
[731], 718 Dazzling {[?]he [?So{ul] For {[?] the horrid

[99^r]

{In [?field]
III, 732 {O[?] every grove were ringing, war shall
cease
733 Did ye not hear that conquest is abjurd
Bring garlands bring forth choicest
flowers to deck
The tree of Liberty—my heart rebounded
My melacholy Voice the chorus joined
Be joyful all ye Nations, in all land,
Ye that are capable of joy be glad
Henceforth whateer is wanting [?to] your
selves
In others ye shall promptly find and
all
Be rich, by mutual & reflected
wealth.
{To for Lo the dread Bastile
718 {[?For] mortal Men displayd.—The Horrid
Tower
Where wretched Mortals, seldom seen
or heard
From age to age had bee deposi[?]ted
through
As in a treasure house—by proud
command
And for the secret joy of sovregn Power
{e
720 F{[?a]ll to the ground—by violence
oerthrown

[99^v]

{shouts a}
III, 721 Of indignation, and with {[?hoots] th }t
{wnd
dro{[?]
722 The crash they made in falling, from their
wreck
stones

---

[731], 718 Cf. l. 718b on 99^r and l. 731a on 100^v.

---

718 Reading here is as *1814* and is thus probably later than the rev at bottom of 98^v. In the line below l. 718, a mark partly over the "W" may possibly be a false start at rev or a signal for rev, as the passage is altered by *1814*.

723 A golden Palace rose or seemed to rise
724 The appointed seat of equitable Law
725, 731 And mild paternal sway—Prophetic
harps

{nve
742 Thus was I reco{[?]rted to the world
[?Thier]
744 Society became my glittering Bride
And aery hopes my Children: From
{pths
the de{[?]
personal feeling
745 Of natural passion seemingly escap[?e]
746 My soul diffused itself in
wide embrace
747 Of Institutions & the forms of ~~things~~ of power
Upon {[?&]
749 ~~Along~~ lifes surface{, ~~meeting no restr~~aint
748 As they exist in mutable array
No ~~obstacle that did not bow its h~~ead
surface
[749] {Upon lifes
{What though
In my veins ~~there flowed~~
750 There flow d no Gallic blood
nor had I breath
{G
751 The air of France, not less than {gallic
zeal
752 Kindled & bu[?rnt] amid the sapless
twigs

[100[r]]

an
III, 753 Of ~~my~~ exhausted heart—If busy men
weave
sober w
754 In [?~~formal~~] conclave met to [?]eave
w}
{a a [?]}[?eb]
755 Of {[?]mity whose livg thread should
stre[?ct]
756 Beyond the seas & to the farthest
Pol
757 There did I sit, assisting—if with noise
[?n]
758 And acclamation crowds in open
air

725, 731 The second half of the line signals for the "Prophetic harps" passage; see l. 731 on 98[v], continued on 99[r].

---

754 For the last word, WW possibly first wrote "bed" by mistake, or intended "thread," and changed the first letter to form "web," as in *1814*.

755 The last word is intended as "stretch," as in *1814*.

E}
759 [?T] [?]}xpressd the tumult of their minds
my voic
The Power of ~~song~~ verse
[?spirit]
760 There mingled; heard or not; and in
still
& still grove
{un
I left not {[?]invoked [?~~mind~~]
tuned
762 Where mild enthusiast ~~fram~~d a pensive
763 Of thanks & expectation, in accord
I sang Saturnian Rule
764 With their belief—[?I ~~talk~~ d] of gold
765 Return, a prgeny of happier years
766 Permitted to descend & bless mankind.
~~With [?ennobling principle] of peace & [?love~~]
767 With promises the Hebrew Scripture
teem,
768 I fet the Invitation, & resumd
769 A long-suspended office in the house
770 Of Public, wor[?h]ship where the
glowing
phrase

[100v]

Of antient inspiration serving me
III, 771 ~~Of scripture [?borrowing~~] I promised too
I promised too
also, with undaunted trust
772 For'told & add[?ed] pr[?ay]er to prop
hecy,
773 The admiration winnin [?of] the crowd
{dev
774 The help desiring of the pure {[?]
out.

---

fr}
715 [?Fr]}om that abstraction I was rouzed—
a[?n] how
716 Even as a thoughtful Sheph[?e] by a flash
717 Of lightening startled in a gloomy cave
[?Mid]
718 ~~Of~~ those wild hills. For Lo the horrid
Tower
I fel
725 And mild paternal sway. The ~~pot~~ent
shock
726 I ~~felt~~—The tra[?n]formation I perceived,

---

775 Text continues on 101r.
715–718 Rev and transition connecting l. 717 on 98v to passage at bottom of 99r.
725–731 Rev and transition connecting l. 725, 731 on 99v to l. 732 on 99r.

[?or found,]
727 As marvellously seized &c
731 Dazzling the Soul. Meanwhile prop
hetic

[101^r]

III, 776 Scorn & contempt forbid me to proceed
777 But History, Time's slavish Scribe, will
tell
778 How rapidly the zealots of the Cause
779 Disbanded—or in hostile Ranks appeared
S these
780 [?T]ome tired of honest service, ~~some~~
outdone
781 Disgusted therefore, or appaled, by aims
782 Of fiercer Zealots—so Confusion
reignd
more co
783 And the ~~few~~ faithful were [?]mpelld
to exclaim
784 As Brutus spake to virtue, Liberty
785 I worshipp'd Thee, & find thee
but a Shade.
786 Such recantation had for me no
charm
787 Nor would I bend to it, who should
have grieved
788 At aught however fair which bore
the mien
trop
789 Of a conclusion or catas[?]he
790 Why then conceal that when
simpl
the timid good

[101^v]

III, 791 In timid selfishness withdrew, I sought
792 Other support not scrupulous whence
[? ?] it came
it stood
a[?n]
793 [?~~Nor~~] ~~by what compromise~~ [~~?procured~~]
~~not nice~~.
[793] And by what compromise it stood
not nice
if notions seemd to be hi
794 Enough for me if notions were high-pitched

Text on 101^r is continued from l. 775 on 100^v.

Rev on 102^r–102^v. See next note for an account of inserted leaves 102–105 and stubs 106–107.

795 And qualities determined. Ruling such
maintaind a [?stock]
[?think]
796, 798 And with such herding—I began to feel
799 That if the emancipation of the world
missed
800 Were ~~lost~~, I should at least secure
my own
801 An be in part compensated.
797 Hopeless & still more hopeless every hour
798 But in the process I began to feel
[799] That if the mancipation of the world
[800] Were miss'd I should at least secure
my own
[801], 817 And be in part compensated.—I smiled
818 At other's tears in pity and in scorn
se
819 At tho{s[?e] which treacherous
Nature sometimes drew

[102r]

III, 801 And be in part compensated. Of Rights
802 Usurp'd upon I argued, and adopted
803 Among the floating tenets of the day
804 Whateer Abstraction furnished for my
needs
805 Or purposes, nor scrupled to proclaim
806 And propagate by Liberty of life
807 Those new persuasions. Not that I rejoiced
808 Or even found pleasure in such vagrant
course
809 For its own sake, but farthest from the walk
happiness &
~~unoff~~
810 Which I had trod in [?innoc]}~~ending~~ Peace
811 Was most inviting to a troubled mind
812 Which in a struggling & distempered world
813 Beheld a cherish'd Image of itself.
814 Yet mark the contradictions of wh[?ich]
Man

---

[801], 817 Ll. 801–817 are entered on inserted leaf 102r. In all, four leaves (102–105) were inserted after leaf 101, replacing leaves 106 and 107, now stubs. Enough remains on the stubs of leaves 106 and 107 to suggest what once stood there. On the top half of 106r, WW continued drafting from 101v, l. 819; the initial letters of ll. 821–828, preceded by a possible "F," are visible on the stub. Then he redrafted ll. 801–807 on the lower half of 106r (the initial letters of ll. 801, 805, 806 [as rev] are identifiable). On the top of 106v, now a stub, WW perhaps wrote work toward ll. 808–830; terminal letters remaining on the bottom half of stub 106v suggest a version of ll. 831–838, with the endings of lines 837–838 clearly identifiable. The top of stub 107r has too little remaining to speculate on its contents, but some state of ll. 838–846 was certainly present on the lower half (initial letters of ll. 838–840, 842, 845–846 are identifiable). On 107v, now a stub, WW seems to have continued on from 107r, drafting a version of ll. 847–861 (terminal letters of ll. 852, 858, and 859 are identifiable). The passage torn out of MS. 71 at leaves 106–107, ll. 801–861, was recopied by WW, probably from another partial draft at least for ll. 808–830, on inserted leaves 102–103.

Inserted leaf; see note to 101v. Some of the lines extend over the folds of leaves 102–105; copying on these leaves apparently preceded folding them for insertion into MS. 71. Text on the inserted leaves is in smaller type because it is rev of the original lines on leaves now removed.

Is still the Sport. Here Nature was my
guide
The Nature of the Dissolute, but Thee
O fostering Nature I rejected, smiled

[102v]

At others tears in Pity, and in scorn
At Those which thy soft Influence sometimes
drew
From my unguarded Heart. the tranquil
shores
Of Britain circumscribed me, else perhaps
I might have been entangled among deeds
Which now as infamous I should abhor
Despise as senseless: for I strangely relishd
The exasperated Spirit of that Land
B
Which turned an angry [?b]]eak against
the down
Of its own breast, as if it hoped thereby
To disencumber its impatient wings.
but all was quieted by iron bonds
Of military sway. The shifting aims
The moral interests the creative might
functions
The varid organs & high attributes
Of civil action yielded to a Power
Formal & odious & contemptable

[103r]

In Britain ruled a panic dread of
change
The weak were praised rewarded & advancd
And, from the impulse of a just disdain,
Once more did I retire into myself
There [?find]ing no contentment I resolved
{some
To fly for safeguard to {[?a fo] foreign shore
Remote from Europe from her blasted
{Her Hopes
{[?Those] fields of carnage & polluted air.
Fresh blew the Wind when oer the
Atlantic Main
The Ship went gliding with her thoughtless
crew
And who among them but an Exile freed
From discontent, indifferent, pleased to
sit
Among the busily employed, not more
With obligation charge with service
task'd
Than the loose pendant to the idle
wind
Upon the tall mast, streaming—But
Ye Powers

Inserted leaf; see notes to 101v and 102r.

Inserted leaf; see notes to 101v and 102r.
839 In *1814* the line begins "There feeling."

[103v]

III, 851 Of soul & sense mysteriously allied
852 O never let the wretched, if a choice
853 Be left him, trust the freight of
his distress
854 To a long Voyage oer the silent deep
855 For like a Plague will memory break out
856 And in the blank & solitude of things
857 Upon his Spirit with a fevers strength
858 Will conscience prey. Feebly mus[?t] they have
felt
859 Who in old time attired with snakes &
whips
860 The vengeful Furies. Beautiful regards
861 Were turnd on me—the face of her I loved.
862 The Wife & Mother pitifully fixing
863 Tender reproaches insupportable. {c
864 Where now that boasted Liberty? no well{ ome
865 From unknown objects I received, & those
866 Known & familiar which the vaulted
sky

[104r]

III, 867 Did in the placid clearness of the night
868 Disclose, had accusations to prefer
869 Against my peace.—Within the Cabin
stood
870 That Volume, as a compass for the Soul
871 Revered among the nations. I implored
872 Its guidance, but the infallible support
873 Of faith was wanting:—tell me why refused
874 To one by storms annoyd & adverse
winds
875 Perplexd with currents, of his weakness
sick
by
876 Of vain endeavours tired, and ~~of~~ [?His]
own
877 And by his nature's ignorance dismay d.
878 Long wished for sight—the western world
appeared
879 And when the Ship was moored—I leapt ashore
880 Indignantly—resolved to be a Man
e}
881 Who having oer}r the past no power, would
live
882 No longer in subjection to the past
883 With abject mind—from a tyrannic
Lord

Inserted leaf; see notes to 101v and 102r. After completing ll. 801–861 here (recopying what was torn out of MS. 71 at leaves 106–107), WW continued with ll. 862–866, rev of original leaf 108r.

Inserted leaf; see note to 103v. Ll. 867–877 are rev of leaf 108r; ll. 878–936 (continued on inserted leaves 104v–105v) are not present in the original leaves of MS. 71.

[104v]

III, 884 Inviting penance fruitlessly endured.
{cleard
885 So (like a Fugitive whose feet have {[?crossd]
886 Some Boundary, which his Followers may
not cross
887 In prosecution of their deadly chase)
888 Respiring I look d round, How bright the
Sun
produce
889 How promising the breeze, can aught ~~compare~~
compare for power
890 In the old World, thought I, ~~with this [?vast]~~
891 And majesty with this gigantic Stream
{?
892 Child of the Desart{,—& behold a City
893 Fresh youthful & aspiring?—What are these
s }
894 To me, or I to them, a[?t]} much at least
895 As he desires that they should be[?e] whom
winds
896 And waves have wafted to this distant
shore
897 In the condition of a damaged seed
898 Whose fibres, cannot if the would, take
root.
899 Here may I roam at large; my business
is
Roaming at large
900 To observe ~~whateer I may~~ & not to feel
the}
901 And [?]}refore not to act—convincd
that all

[105r]

III, 902 Which bears the name of action, howsoeer
903 Beginning, ends in servitude, still painful
904 And mostly profitless, And, sooth to say,
905 On nearer view a motely spectacel
906 Appeared, of high pretensions un
reproved
907 But by the obstreperous voice of higher still.
908 Big passions strutting on a petty stage.
{ay
909 Which a detach'd Spectator m{ight regard
un }
910 Not [?am]}amused. But ridicule demands
{[?&]
911 Quick change of objects{; and to laugh alone
912 In woods & wilds or any lonely place
913 At a composing distance from the haunts
{f {h
914 Of stri{ve & folly, thoug{[?it] be a treat
915 As choice as musing leisure can bestow
916 Yet, in the very centre of the crowd

Inserted leaf; see note to 104r.

Inserted leaf; see note to 104r.

o}
917 To keep the secret of a poignat scr }rn
918 May suit an airy Demon, but of all
919 Unsosocial courses tis the one least fit

[105v]

kind, the one
{,
III, 920 For the gross spirit of Mans [?~~nature~~]{ [?~~soon~~]
For him doth it become an absolute [?height]
{That to please
921 {[?And] soones faills & quickiliest turns
922 Into vex[?ax]tion—Let us then I said
923 Leave these unknit Republics to the scourge
924 Of their own passion & to Regions haste
Whose shades have never felt the encroaching
~~ich~~} {~~yet~~
925 ~~Wh~~[?ere]} {[?they] ~~have felt not the disturbi~~ng
{Or axe
926 {[?Nor] soil endure a transfer in the mart
~~Of their rapacity~~.
927 Of their rapacity. There Man abides
928 Prim[?o]eval Natures child. a creature
{In weak
929 { Combination (wherefore else driven back
930 So far, and and of his old inher[?i]tance
931 So easily deprived?) but for that cause
932 Mor[?re] dignified, & stronger in himself
judge
933 Whether to act, [?~~think~~], suffer or enjoy
~~What [?must] the workings of the~~
934 True the intelligence of social art
{v
935 Hath o{[?p]erpower d his forefathers & soon
936 Will sweep the remnant of the line away
But can the oppressor shew an inward
soul
That shall with his compare

[108r]

III, 862 The wi[?l]fe & Mother piti[?fi]fully fixing
863 Tender reproaches insupportable.
ere}
864 Wh[?]} now that boasted Liberty? no
welcome
865 From unknown objects I received, & those
w}
866 Known & familiar [?]}hich the vaulted
sky
867 Did, in the placid stillness of the night
868 ~~Displayed~~ had accus[?]sations to prefer
[?~~Reverd~~] disclose
869 Against my peace.—Within the

Inserted leaf; see note to 104r.

The half-line at page foot ("That shall with his compare") keys the text on this last of the inserted leaves to the text at the top of the original leaf 108v.

Rev and incorporated into inserted leaves 103v–104r.

stood
cabin [?lay]
870 That Volume, as a Compass for the soul,
I implord
871 Reverd among the nations—~~Not in~~
~~pride~~
~~But in humiliation did I ask~~
but the
[?~~its in~~]
872 Its guidance,—~~an~~ infalilble support
873 Of faith was wanting—tell me
why refused
874 To one [?~~by~~] in darkness & with storms [?beset]
875 Perplex d with currents, of this weakness
sickend
876 Of [?~~his~~] vain endeavours tired & by his own
877 And by his natures ~~ingnoran[?ce]~~
i
[?d]gnorance dismayed.

[108v]
That shall with his compare. ~~how bright how~~ clear
III, 939 ~~How lofty how [?serene]~~ when side by side
940 Of Missippi or that northern stream
941 That spreads into successive seas, he
walks
freeborn state
942 And not obscurely feels his ~~power[?s] of~~
l mind
sub[?]ime
943 And his [?~~instincti~~] capacities of soul
gained
944 There imaged: or when having the top
945 Of some commanding Eminence which yet
neer beheld
946 Intruder ~~never saw~~ the thence surveys
947 Forest & wide savannah, the expans
expanse [?beheld]
948 ~~The [?territory] of unappr~~opriated earth
949 With mind that sheds a light on what it sees
950 Free as the sun & lonely as the Sun
Pouring
951 Above his head, ~~that~~ pours its rad
iance
down
952 ~~Upon~~ a living & re[?j]oicing worldd.
[948] The expanse of unappr[?]opriated earth
W
[949] In ith mind that sheds a ligt on what
he sees.

The first line, incorporating the rev at the bottom of inserted leaf 105v, appears to be added to key the end of text on inserted leaves to previously existing copy on 108v. Less likely, although possible, is that WW interrupted composition after 108r, copied the inserted leaves 102–105, then returned to a blank 108v to continue copy from his inserted leaves.

{ly ~~the e~~ye
In loneli{ness [?exaltation] like
~~Perceives; exalted~~, lonely as the Sun,
[951] Pouring above his head its radiance
down
[952] Upon a living & rejoicing world

[109r]

{w
III, 953 So, west{erard tow'rd[?s] the unviolated
woods
and [?as] I [?pass along]
954 I bent my way, & verily was cheerd
955 Faild not to greet the merry mocking Bird
y}
B[?]} the blithe mocking Bird & heard
at [?even]
his companion [?in the grove]
{[?bird] cry
957 And heard [?from] {[?]
~~The melancholy cry of Whip~~poorwill,
958 The plaintive cry repeated, [?Whip]
B} {pure
960 [?T]}ut that {[?fair] Archetype of human
greatness
961 I found him not—[?~~I~~] There, in his stead
[?sordi] appeared
962 A creature ~~abject~~ vengeful & impure
~~savage~~
~~Fierce, venge & s~~
963 Remorseless, and submissive to no law
964 But superstitious fear & abject sloth
965, 974 What need of more here am I ~~& [?in~~]
[?~~self~~]
the
Which s} & ~~what~~ course
975 ~~Doth~~ my life hold }—this parallel
will
{you [?shew]
976 Say, have {[?] [?ye] stood to watch
Brook
a mountain [?~~stream~~]
977 In some still passage of its course
& seen
978 With In the depths of its capacious
breast
eminence

Cf. MS. 73, 8r.

The significance of "eminence" at page foot is unclear; conceivably the word is related to l. 945 on 108v.

[109v]

III, 979 Inverted trees & rocks & azure sky
980 And on its glassy surface specks of foam
981 And conglobated bubbles undissolved
982 Numerous as stars, that by their
onward lapse
983 Betray to sight the motion of the stream
984 Else imperceptible; meanwhile is heard
985 Perchance—a roar or murmur,
& the sound
986 Though soothing & the little floating Iles
987 Though beautiful are both by nature
charged
988 With the same pensive office, & make
known
989 Throgh what perplexing Labyrinths & abrupt
990 Precipitations, & untoward Straits
991 The earth-born Wanderer hath pass d
& quickly
992 That respite oer like traverses
& toils

[110r]

again
III, 993 Must be encountered. Such a stream
994 Is human life and so the Spirits fares
owd
995 In the best quiet to its course all[?] },
on
996 And such is mine save [?] [?l]}ly for a
hope
997 That my particular current soon will
reach
998 The unfathomable gulph where all is
still—

[112v]

I, 444 And surely never did there live on Earth
445, II, 45 A Man of kindlier nature. Birds & beasts
II, 45 And the mute fish that glances in the Stream
46 And harmless reptile coiling in the sun

Cf. MS. 73, 8v.

Cf. MS. 73, 9r.

998 This is the last line of Book III of *Exc.* Leaves 110v–112r are blank, with the exception of 111v, which has a pencil triangular shape with an "A" inside.

I, 444ff., II, 45ff. Rev of 15r (see note there), related to and probably later than draft on facing 113r; rev on 35r–36v.

hovering
47 And gorgeous insect ~~soaring~~ on the air
48 The Fowl domestic & the household Dog
mind
49 In his capacious ~~heart~~ he loved them
all
50 Their rights acknowledging he felt
for all
52 The quiet pleasures of the pasturing Herd
53 To happy Contemplation soothed his wa
walk
54 Along the fields and in the shady groves
55 And the poor Brutes condition forced
to run
56 Its course of suffering in the public road
{his
57 Sad Contrast all too often smite {its heart
58 With unavailing pity. Rich in love
59 And sweet humanity he was himself
60 To the degree which he desired, beloved
61 Greetings & smiles we met with &
Religion's high immunities. The grants *II, 124*
Of faith to chosen lands voutchsafed or those *125*
By Deity committed to the heart *126*
Oer the wide plain of universal earth *127*
Mans spiritual hopes dependencies *128*
& fear[?s]
By Deity committted to the heart
Oer the wide plain of universal earth
Mans spiritual hopes dependencies
& fears

[113r]

A man of kindlier nature
I, 445 The rough sports
446 And teazing ways of Children vex'd not
him
{s
447 Nor could he bid them from his pre{zence, tired
448 With questions and importunate demands
449 Indulgent listener was to the tongue
450 Of garrulous age, nor did the sicks
mans tale

53–58 A faint, diagonal pencil slash, perhaps introduced accidentally, may cancel these lines.

Below the rule, inverted in the right margin, appears "Say," false start of WW's sonnet "Say, what is honour," which is partly copied on 113v.

II, *124*–[*128*] Cf. MS. 70, 61v. Although found in MS. 70, these lines are excluded from the sequence on MS. 71, 41r and from *1814*. They were probably entered on the removed inserted leaves 42–43, and canceled in the process of rev. Their presence here may well signify an intention at a late stage to restore them to the text.

Rev of 15r; rev on 112v, 35r–36v.

First line on page is added by squeezing it into the space to the left of the half-line, "The rough sports."

447 Possibly the "z" overwrites the "s."

451 To his fraternal sympathy addressed
452 ~~Exhaust his social patience~~
Obtain reluctant hearing.2 Birds & beasts
A} t}
II, 45 T}nd the mute fish &}hat glances in the
stream
46 And harmless reptile coiling in the sun
47 And gorgeous insect hovering on the air
49 In his capacious mind he loved them all
48 The fowl domestic & the houshold dog
hearth
And to the kitten of a neighbour's house
Would carry crumbs & feed it. But the
course
Of such enjoyment is by nature smooth
{. [?~~the~~]}
I prais him not for this{, ~~but~~ ~~[?that~~ gui} ~~guilt~~]
~~Of [?his own~~] species & their froward ways
I, [445] [?Chilled not him] The boisterous sports
{ed
[446] And teazing ways of childhood vex{[?] not
him

[113ᵛ]

Then when the Mourners, they
who on the
floor
Of the church aisle beneath the vested
priest
II, 601 Knelt by the coffin

595 Then when they rise and bear the
body forth
[?now]
[595] Upon their shoulders soon to be consign

III, 620 Smooth did our Life
621 Advance not swerving from the path
prescribd
622 Her annual & diurnal round alike
623, 624 Faithfully [?kept]. And you div
[?truth]
ine the
625 If you [?imagine]

452/ Cancellation of the "Birds & beasts" passage is probably related to decision to include it in Book II (see 35ʳ–35ᵛ). The numeral "2" (or perhaps it is the letter "Q") corresponds to the same symbol on 15ʳ and signals the continuation of the passage with the partial l. *419*, "Plain his garb."

II, 601, 595, [595] These three lines are pencil rev of 53ᵛ, 54ʳ; rev on 33ᵛ, 32ʳ.
III, 620–625 Pencil rev of 89ᵛ (see the note there to ll. 617–626).
Inverted at page foot are the first three and one-half lines, in ink, of WW's sonnet "Say, what is Honour" (see *Poems, 1807–1820*, pp. 52, 499). Inside back cover has "DW" written on it in pencil.

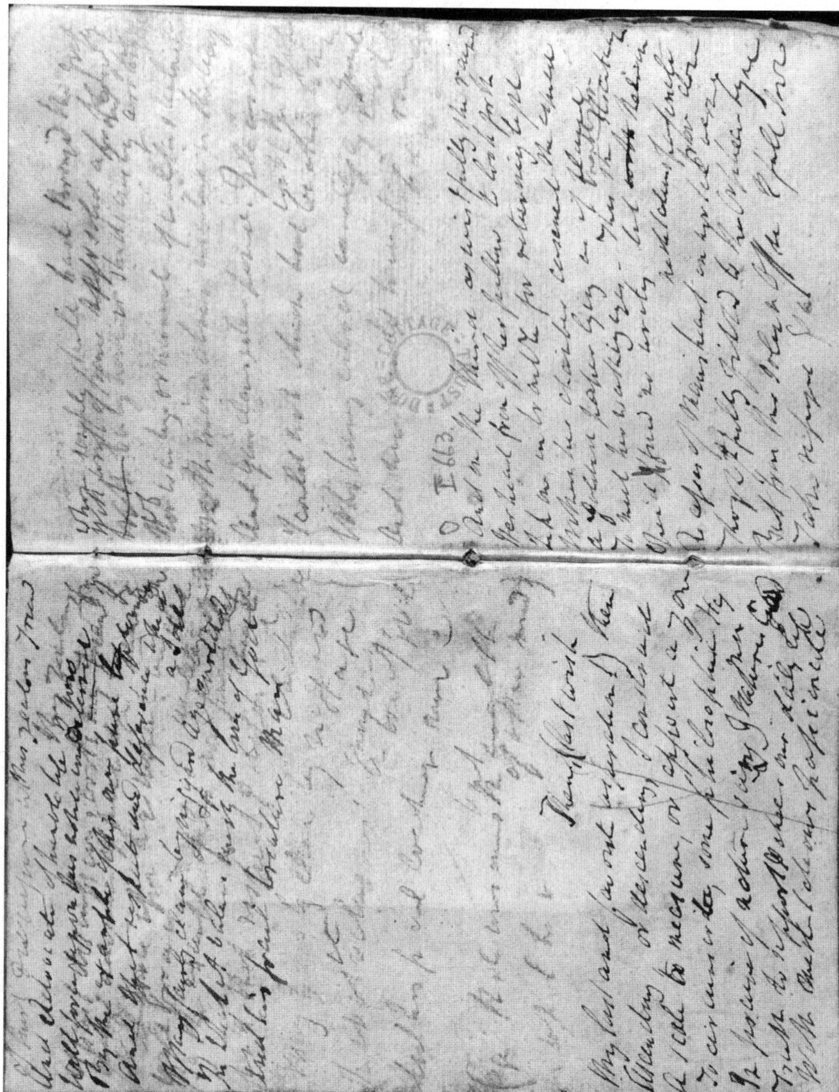

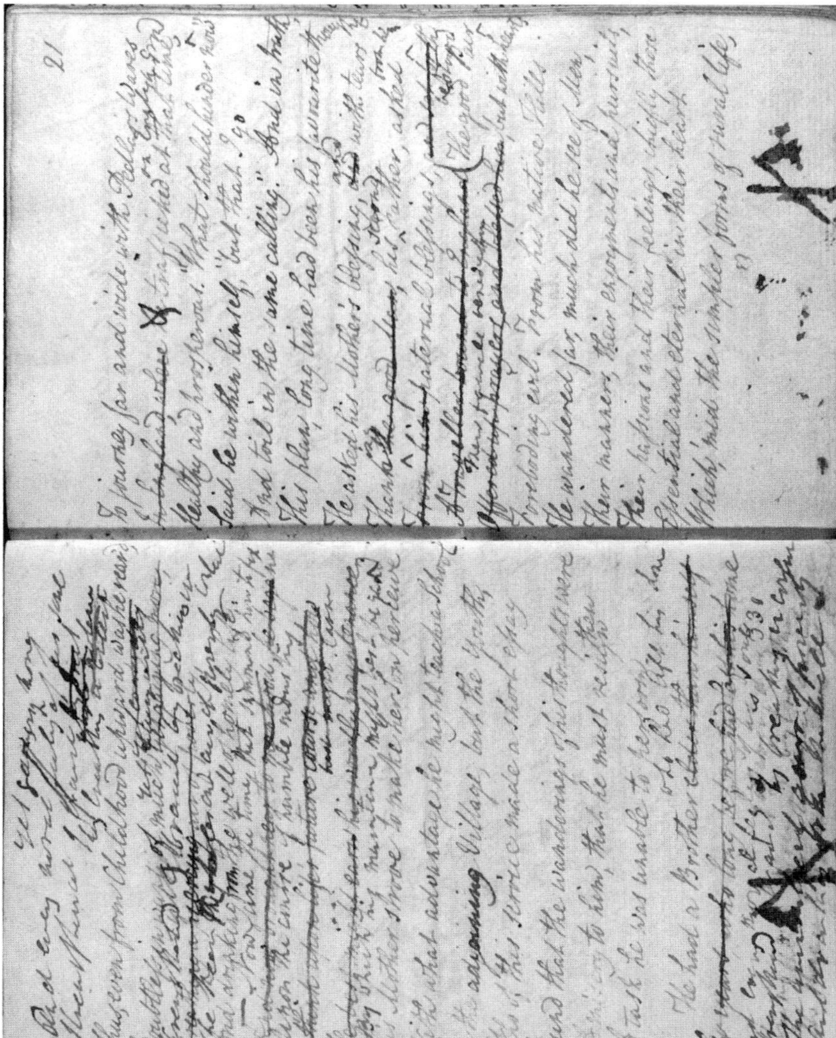

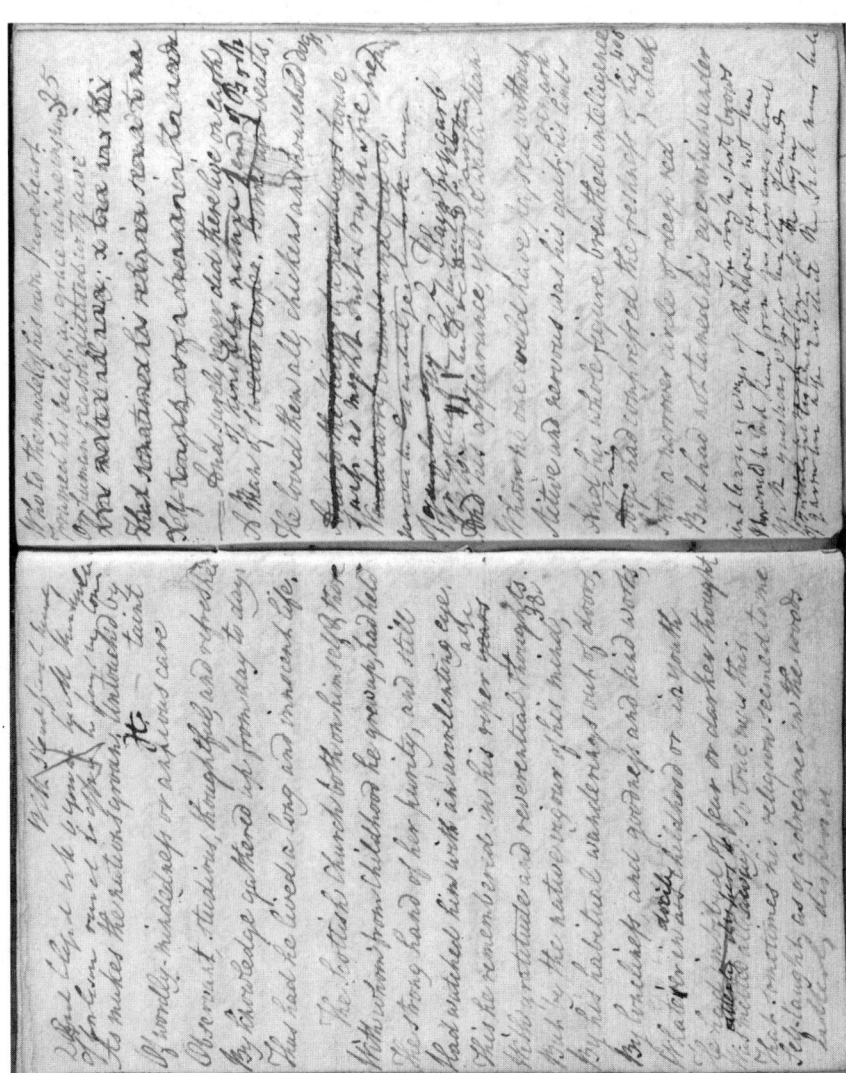

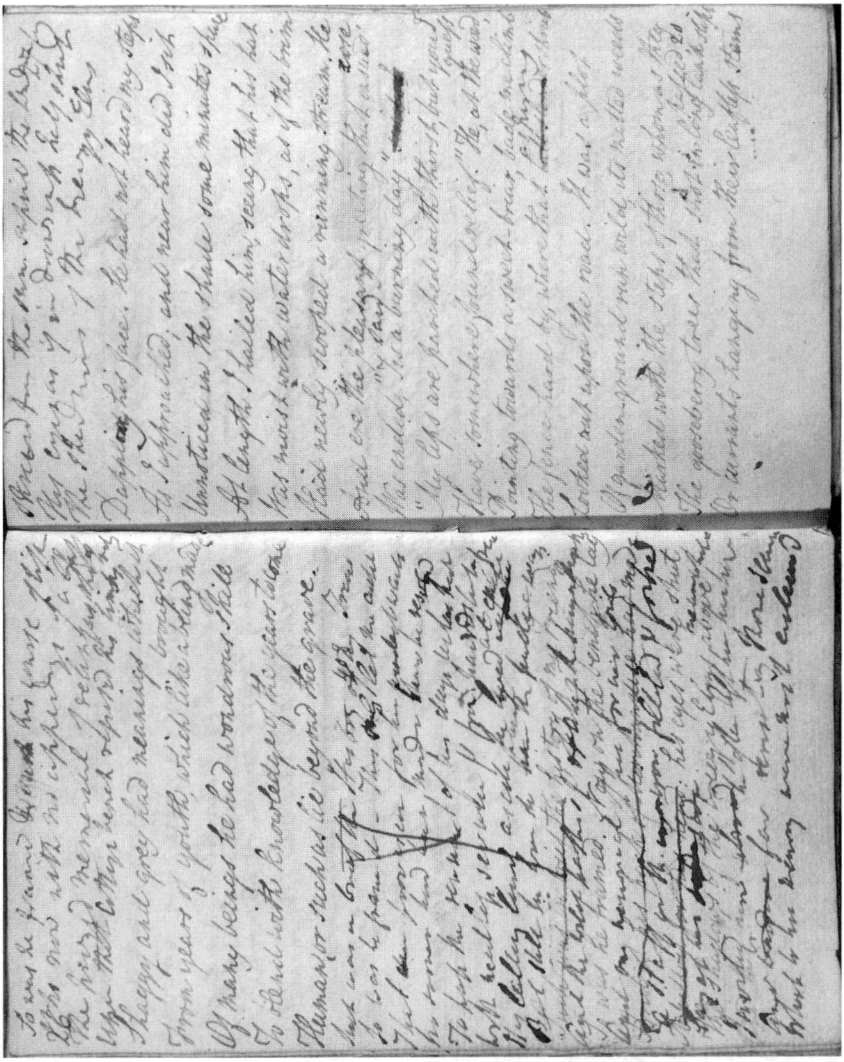

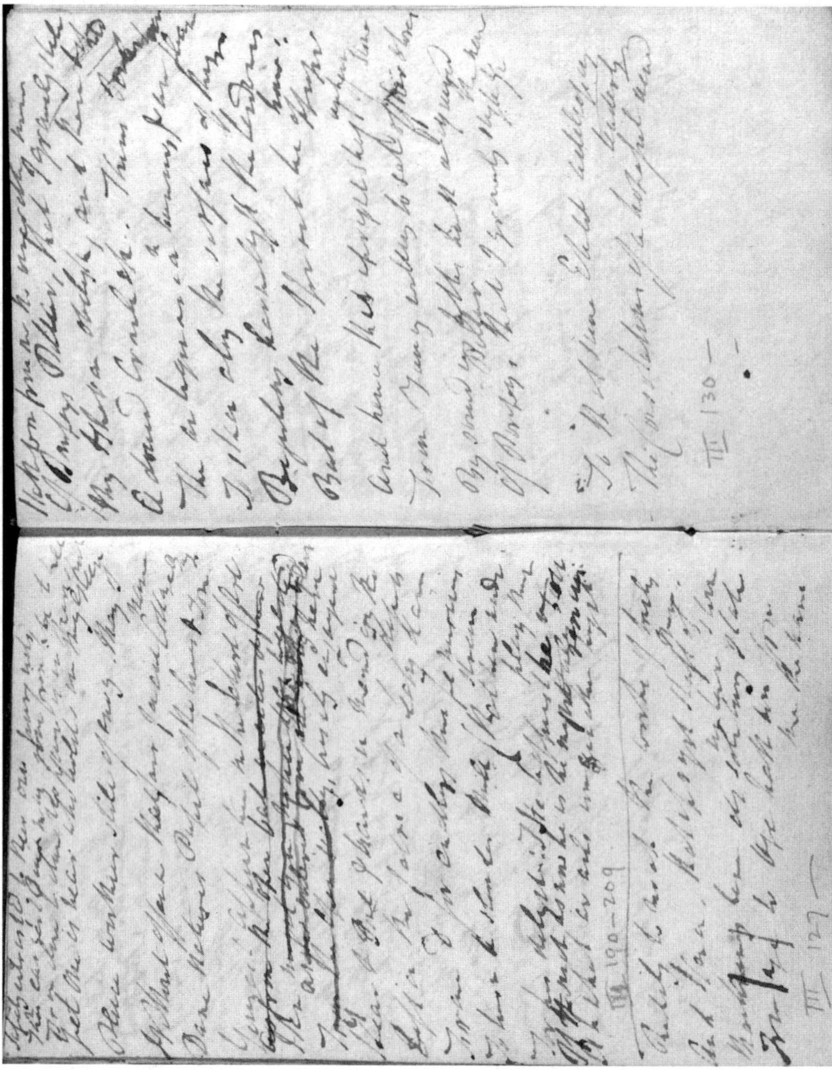

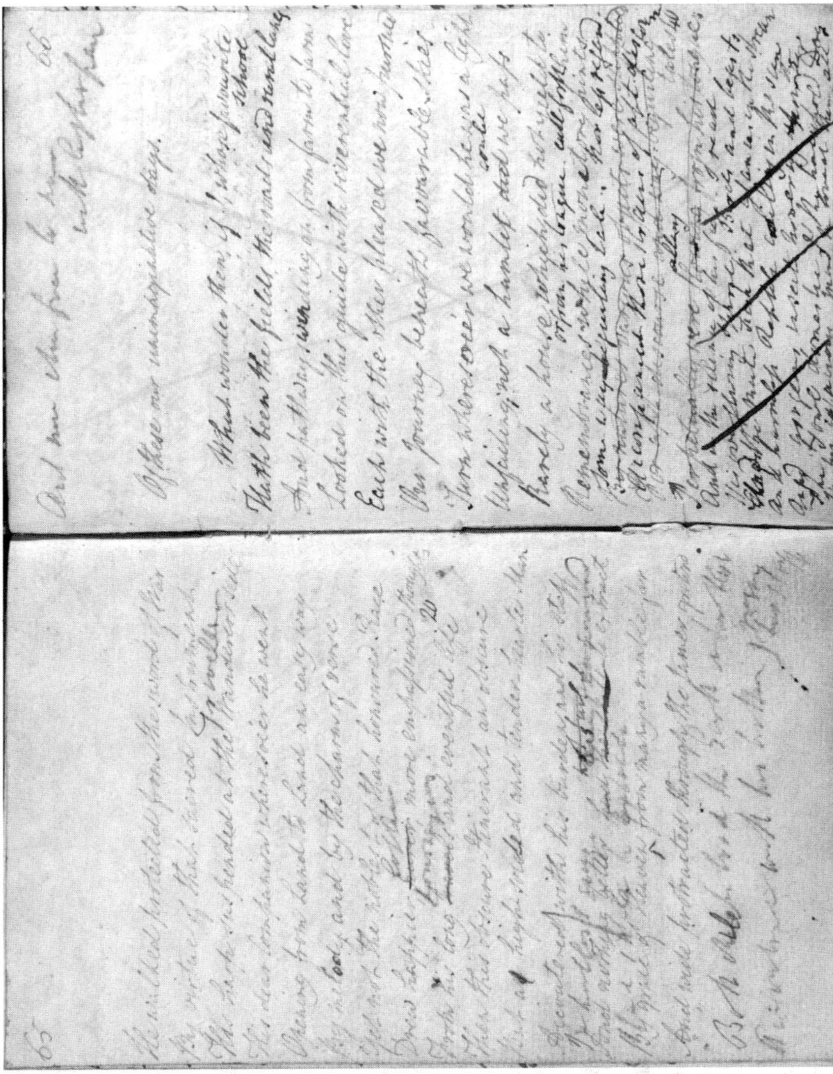

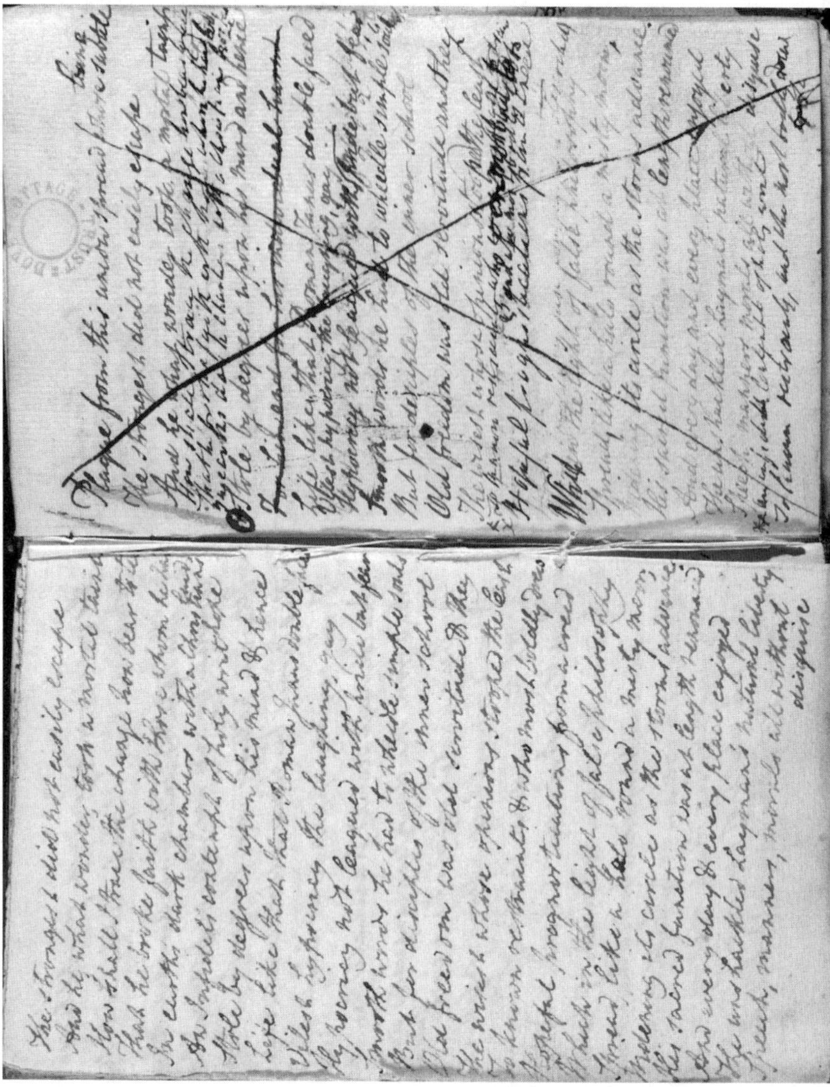

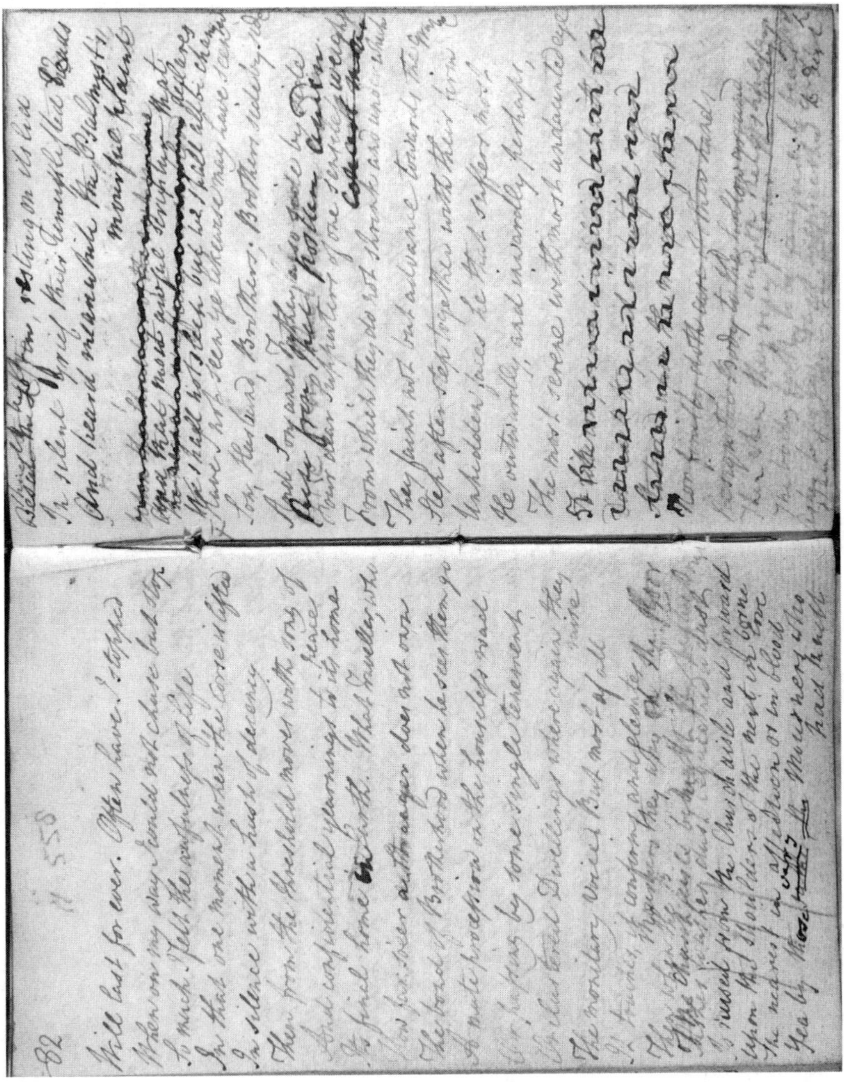

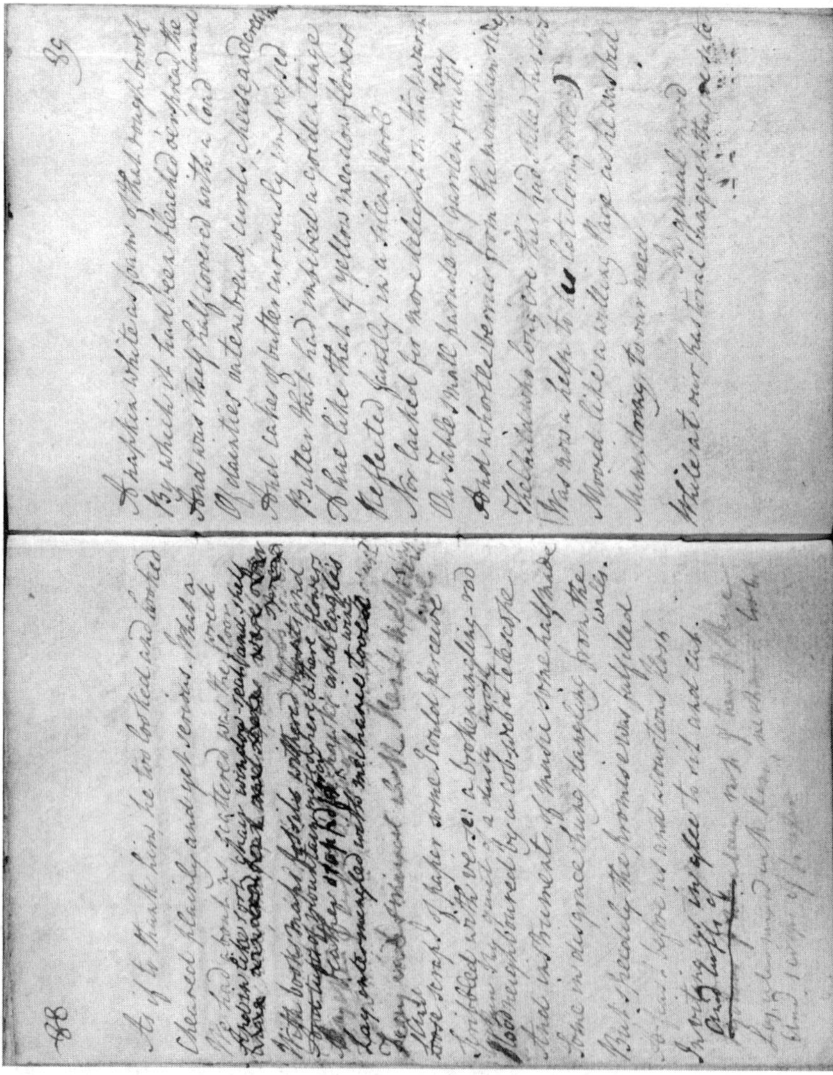

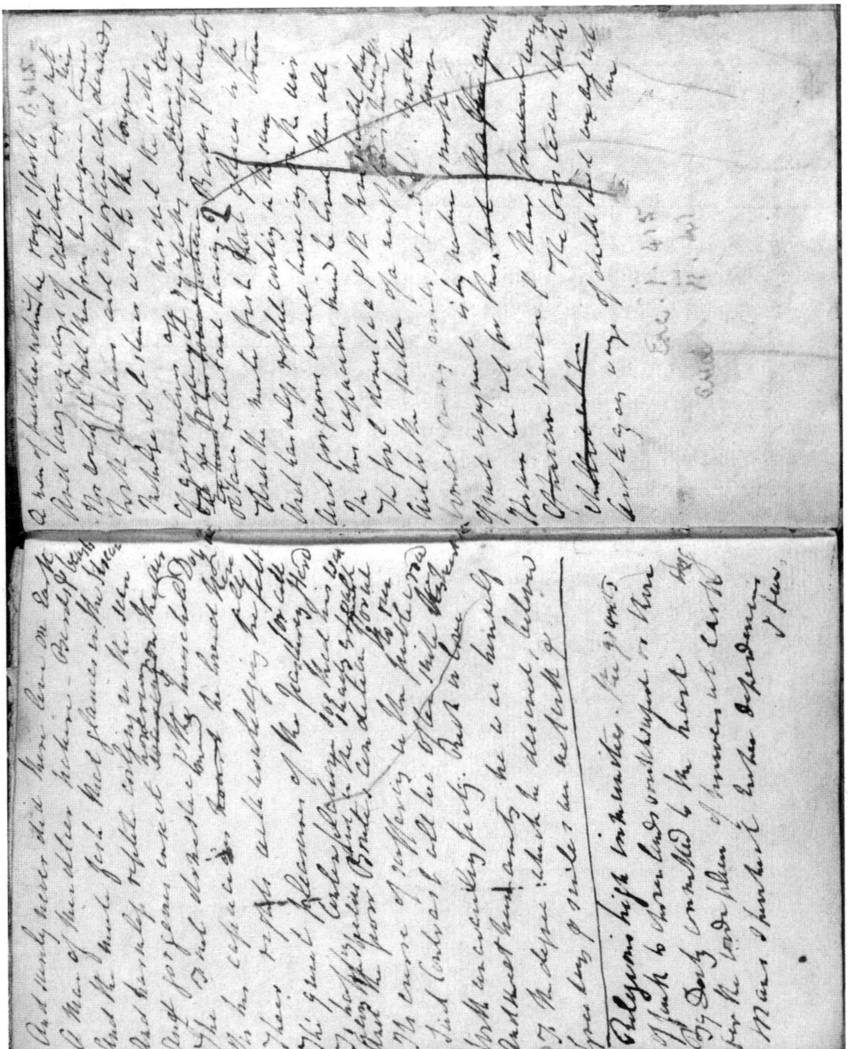

DC MS. 70

DC MS. 70—in use at the second and third stages of *Excursion* composition for work on Books II, III, and IV—is described in the Manuscript Census, p. xxiii, above. For a discussion of this manuscript and its role in the composition of *The Excursion,* see pp. 440–446, above.

Left-hand margin line numbers on the transcriptions of DC MS. 70 provide cross-references to the line count in the 1814 reading text in this edition. On leaves 57^v to the end of DC MS. 70, right-margin italic line numbers refer not to the 1814 reading text in this edition but to the underlying pre-1813 text of *Excursion,* I–III, c. *299;* i.e., the state before Wordsworth revised this material following the deaths of his two children. Bracketed line numbers at the top of leaves 57^v to the end provide cross references to the line count in the 1814 reading text.

For a complete photographic representation of the leaves of *Excursion* work in DC MS. 70, see pp. 759–814, below. The image size of the photographs of DC MS 70 is 75 percent of actual size.

[inside front cover]

                [?induce]
IV, 1015   Be not [~~?]~~ [~~?mis~~led] by anything amiss
in your [?sef to think] — [?favorably] of [?Man]

[?s] inspired [?kno]wledge

[1^{v}]

                i }   no p }
IV, 618   Where soul [?] }s dead and feeling has [?] }lace
                                          in
619   Where knowledge ill begun [?~~with~~] cold remark
620   On outward thing with formal inference ends
                                    { tis
621   Or if the mind inward { [?is] perplexd
                                                  { ss
622   Lost in a gloom of uninspired re { [?ce]earch
623   Meanwhile the heart within the heart, the seat
624   Where peace & happy Conscience ought to dwell
625   On its own axis restless revolves
a [?beam] of chearing
light.

The vertical line, "[?s] inspired [?know]ledge," may be related to IV, 619, 622 on 1^{v}. The horizontal lines are probably related to IV, 1015, on 41^{r}. Beneath the horizontal lines, WW has entered some numbers, possibly a financial calculation: "8" below "19", a line drawn below, and below the line the sum "15 7" with "7" overwriting "3".

In DW's hand on the facing recto of leaf 1 is an unidentified ten-line Latin elegiac poem beginning "*Si mihi, si liceat traducere leniter aevum*" ("If only I am granted to pass my life in peace") and ending "*Quid restat? tandem mihi cura dolorque valete:/Hoc tantum superest, discere 'posse more'*"" ("What else? A last farewell to care and sorrow,/With one task left: to learn how to die"). The content, vocabulary, and scansion suggest this is a transcription of a Christian poet. We are indebted to Dr. James Shiel for the translation and suggestions about the poem's possible sources.

618–626 Rev of 12^{v}, 13^{r}; see also 28^{v}, 29^{r}. MS. 69 once held substantial portions of Book IV material, but most of the leaves have been torn out. The contents of some of the remaining stubs can be conjectured, but cross-references to this MS. 69 material are not given here. A detailed listing of the stubs may be found in the headnote to MS. 69 and in Appendix I.

619, 622 See vertical line on inside front cover.

626 And nowhere finds
the chear[?g] lght of truth

~~torrents~~ [?voce]
789 Heard while the dwelling vibrates to
the din
790 Of the contiguous torrent, swoln with
rains
792 And furious, or while ~~the~~ snow is at the
door

[2r]

IV, 760 *We live by admiration & by love*
761 *And even as these are well & wisely*
fixed
To
762 *~~In~~ dignity of being we ascend*
~~As they are placed erron[?i]ously we fall~~
[?]
763 *But what is error? & of errors which*
b
773 *Doth most de[?f] ase the mind the genuine*
seats
774 *Of power where are they who shall*
regulate
~~ascertain~~
[775] *With ~~just~~ the scale*
th
775 *~~The~~ tru e ~~degrees~~ of intellectual rank?*
that ou
776, 777 *~~Methinks for this office y [?] possess~~*
778 *~~Some rare advantages your early days~~*
~~Remembering you most feelingly must know~~
[776, 777] *Methinks that for this office you possess*
[778] *Some rare advantages your early days*
779 *A feeling recollecting may supply*

[2v]

IV, 780 *Of much exalted good that may attend*
[?Y] feelingly
781 *~~Upon~~ a humble state y ou ~~well~~ must*
know

---

626 Of the two alternate half-lines, *1814* adopts "the cheering light of truth".
789–792 Rev of 2v, 3r.
789 The del "[?voce]" is a miswriting of "voice." Cf. 2v, l. 788.

760ff. Hand of MW to l. 796 on 2v; she also attempts on 3v–4r a fair copy of WW's draft of ll. 784–814 (2v–3v). Most of remainder of Book IV material is all draft in the hand of WW. Ll. 760–762 are based on a passage in MS. 48 of *The Prelude* (see *13-Bk Prelude*, II, 359, 378). See 37r and p. 442, above.

780ff. Rev on 3r, 1v; see also 38v, 3v.

787 *That on the lap religion may be learned*
tongue
788 *In smoky Cabins from a Mother's ~~voice~~*
{~~torrents~~ voic
789 Heard while the rafters vibr{at
[?accents]
Its music blending with the lonesome wind
While showers descend or
792 *~~Fearful & sad while~~* ^ *snow is at the door*
793 *Assaulting & defending & the wind*
794 *A sightless labourer whistles at his [?~~work~~]*
work—
795 *Fearful but resignation tempers fear*
796 *And piety is sweet to Infant minds*
[?~~stretched~~]
797 The shepherd lad who in the sunshine
carves
{ial [?~~fram~~]
798 On the green turf a d{[?] to divide
799 The silent hours, and who to that
report
800 Can portion out his pleasures & can time
is not left
801 His round of pastoral duties [?~~doth~~]
[?~~with lo~~]

[3r]

IV, 802 With less intelligence for moral things
803 Of gravest import; early he perceives
804 Within himself a measure & a rule
805 Which to the sun of truth he can
apply
806 That shines for him, & shines for all
mankind.

---

789 To which the Cottage vibrates while the fields
overflowed {n
Are ~~drenchd with rain~~, or with the wi{[?l]d
be} [?or]
That roar [?wi]}hind the hut with
threatning
807 The knowledge daily pressd upon his mind
808 <u>Of nature's wants how few they are: [?And where]</u>
[808] Few are the wants of nature, what there
are
809 And where they lie, how answered
and appeased
{This pressd
[807] {[?So] knowledge daily ~~force~~d upon his mind

802ff. Rev of 2v; rev on 1v, 3v, 4r.
789/807 The loop of the "l" in "wild" is erased to form "wind".

[?~~Thought] gr[?ow~~]
810 An ample recompense affords
811 For manifold privations, he refers
notions
812 His judgements to this standard
on this rock

[3v]

IV, 813 Rests his desires and hence in after
life
814 Soul strengthing patience & sublime
content

---

807 Experience daily forc[?ing] him to look
808 On Natures wants, and teaching what
they are
[808] ~~How plain & few~~
809, 808 And where they lie how simple & how few
809 Yet only to be answer[?e] and appeased
By hard endeavours keeping pace with
time

---

that Nature wants
784 *He by experience taught can understand*
808, 784 Are few & plain can feel & understand
785 ~~*And feel the wisdom of the prayer that*~~
asks
[785] The wisdom of the prayer that daily ~~*asks*~~
[808] *For daily bread he knows that Natures wants*
808, 809 *Are few and plain yet not to be appeased*
But by endeavours keeping pace with time
810 *This knowledge ample recompense affords*
m *if*
811 *For [?a] andef old privations he refers*
notions
812 *His ~~judgem~~ to this standard on this rock*

[4r]

IV, 813 *Rests his desires & hence in after life*
814 *Soul strengthening patience and sublime content*
784, 807, 808 He by experience taught how few & plai
808, 784 Are natures wants, can feel & understand
785 The wisdom of the prayer that daily asks

813–814 Rev on 4r, 4v.
807–809 Rev of 3r; rev on 4r.
784 Hand of MW, continuing to l. 814 on 4r. Rev of 3r; rev on 4r; cf. 2r.

813–814 Rev of 3v.

786, 808 For daily bread, ~~he knows that Natures~~
wants
[808] ~~Are few & plain~~
~~He only he~~
783 He and his like & only they per[?haps]
simple
784 In^ childhood understand & feel
[785] The wisdom of the prayer that ~~daily~~
asks
Of for
[786, 808] For daily bread; ~~he~~, by experience taught
~~And [?simple~~]
[808] He knows how few & plain are
{ing
807 Experience daily fix{es his regards
[808] On natures wants he knows how few they are
809 And where they lie how answered & appeased
810 This knowledge ample recompense affords
811 For manifold privations, he refers
812 His notions to this standard. On
this rock

[4^v]

IV, 813 Rests his desires and hence in after-
life
814 Soul-strengthening patience & sublime content.
820 Thus girded by [?an unrelaxing] zone
821 That while it binds, invigorates and supports
815 Thus circumscribed, Imagination here
816 Wastes not her powers as in the wordlings
{mind
{[?]
{On
817 {[?A] fickle pleasures & superfluous cares
818 And trivial ostentation but is free,
{t
[820] ~~Gir~~{d ~~by a zone that~~
820, 821 Thus girded by a zone that while it binds
[821] Invigorates & supports [?to]
and [?s]
819, 820 And puissant, ~~thus girded~~ by a zone
{[~~?holds~~] s}
[821] ~~That~~ {[?] ~~it binds~~ invigorates & p}uports
819 to range the solemn walks
[820] Of time & nature; girded by a zone
it
[821] That while [?] binds invgorates & supports

783ff. Rev of 3^v, 3^r; rev on 4^v. See also 49^v.

IV, 813–[821] Rev of 4^r, 3^v; see also 49^v.

V, 1 Farewell, deep Valley with thy lone
some house
2, 4 And fair green fields; farewell
attractive Seat
destined
11 By nature fashioned at the
birth of things

[6r]

V, 12, 13 For quietness profound." Upon
that Slope
13 The sole commodious outlet of the Vale
14 Lingering behind my Comrades thus I
breathed
3 In a low Voice & with reverted eyes
a
{[?~~at~~]
15 A parting tribute to th{[?] spot
that seemed
or}
16 Like the fix'd centre of a troubled wr}ld
Backward I looked & lookd again
with hope
To imprint a final Image on my mind
{.
That should not fade{ ~~away~~.
[?~~Me~~] Thought that
22 Even they, methought, whose
life
23 Yields no peculiar reason for complaint
allurement might be
24 By this ~~temptation~~ [?~~might] be~~ lured
led on
Might be ~~lured~~ to quit
{course
{[?]
25 The ~~road~~ of active duty, and embrace
26 Obscure delights & calm forgetfulness.
III, 374, 376 What impulse drove the
Hermit to his
cell

V, 1ff. Copy continues without interruption on 6r, although leaf 5 has been torn out. On the recto of the stub of leaf 5 nothing can be read; on the verso, two line endings in WW's hand can be conjectured, "[?ty]," and about two line spaces below, "[?ge]." See pp. 444–446, above, for discussion of the relation between Book V and III material on 4v, 6r–6v, 7r–10r and the composition of MS. 71, as well as its relation to MS. 65 of *The Tuft of Primroses* (see *Tuft*, pp. 151).

V, 1–16 Cf. MS. 74A, 1r.

V, 12–13ff. Cf. MS. 74A, 1r and *Tuft of Primroses*, MS. 65, 44r (see *Tuft*, p. 247). See note to 4v.

III, 374, 376 Cf. MS. 71, 75r.

[6v]

III, 377, 378 And what detained him there there
till life was spent
not
379 Fast anchored in the desart, [?al]
alone
380 Dread of the persecuting sword, remorse
or
381 Wrongs unredress'd ~~and~~ insults
unavenged
382 And unavengeable, defeated Pride
383 Prosperity subverted, maddening want
384 Friendship betray'd affection unre
turned
385 Love with despair
steps ow'rds
IV, 1302 Our ~~way~~ directing t|o t the
Villag Church
Occasion soon was offered to resign
The Cottge Youngling to his Mothers
care
[?on her]
Who with an infant arms we
[?he] met
Returning homeards.
1306 In the Maitron face

[7r]

[?]
[?With]
F in
A[?n] lowing & broad & [?] the bulk & [?gait]
IV, 1306 Of her unwieldy person might be read
a
1307 A plain [?] ssurance that the
tale which
[?~~what~~] told
~~How [?she dealt~~]
old
1308 The hapless fate of that ~~poor~~
pension
~~Now pe~~
1309 Whom ~~she this~~
To [?now] peacefully [?interrd]
T
1310 H|e her humanity had done no
wrong

III, 377–385 Cf. MS. 71, 75v and *Tuft of Primroses*, MS. 65, 44r, 43v (see *Tuft*, p. 244–247). See note to 4v.

IV, 1302ff. This concluding passage appears to have been entered after most of the Book IV material was drafted in the notebook. Possibly before this, MS. 73, 7v, concludes its draft of the last part of the book at l. 1284. The intervening lines (1285–1301) are not extant in any MS.

Behold a little Empire—is it
ruled
V, 96 By a wise prince; I said—for
yonder stand
kind of [?]
97, 98 Methinks a ~~rural~~ Palace where a
[?Thane]
[96] a House of state is
[?formal]
~~Or~~ [?~~village~~]
L
98 Or rural [?B] ord might dwell { — [?]
a
~~A [?man]~~] { [?] [?~~thane~~]
a Priest
102 A Pries by function, [?] [?and a ~~keeper~~]

[7^{v}]

~~The old Man [?turnd~~]
[?~~Industrious~~], This [?garnered]
V, 98 [?~~From~~] no feudal pomp
[?power is]
101 ~~Is there~~, or feudal Prince, but [?her a]
abides
102 The old Man said a, Priest, and one
in truth
shepher {,
103 A consci[?n]tious ~~pastor of~~ { ~~his~~ flock
[?in] ~~and [?as kings are~~]
{ ~~ter,~~
[103] ~~Of holy charc~~ {a a shepperd
[?pries]
[?~~C~~]
[?~~When there co~~]
[?When]
105 A father of his people
When [?he] good
104 ~~Is [?Said~~] and ~~as the [?best~~] King
[?~~Is~~ t]
or
[103] [?~~Is told~~] ~~and~~ as good kings
~~Who is said~~
[104] Are said to be be when they
are [?hailed]
[105] The father of his peple, gather d
{ is round [?hi]
108 In th { [?] [?~~al seques~~] spot
sequesterd [?~~Vald~~] realm.

V, 96ff. Rev on 7^{v}, 8^{r}. Cf. MS. 74A, 2^{v}.

98ff. Rev of 7^{r}; rev on 8^{r}. Cf. MS. 74A, 2^{v}. The first two lines may be related to the transition drafted at the foot of 10^{r}.

[8r]

Who [?~~by~~]
~~to who his [?worth~~]
~~Hath g[?ained a pa~~]
Who is in truth
[?~~T]o~~
~~For watchful[?nes] & in[?sensbly wise~~]
V, 103 The shepherd of his flock,
{[~~?~~]
{[?Are] ~~of~~
107 And of saway & influe,
{ or
[103] {[?are] as good king
[107] Are said to of spiritual sway
with influence [?gained]
And temporal influe, a Priest
[?in truth]
~~But see, [?god Sir~~]
{[~~?~~] a [?Sain]
{[?Our ~~Host~~]
102 The old Man said [?In] his [?alloted]
[?al influe]
in due degree
A man of [?spiritu]
Of of [?trust]
~~With~~ temporal influenc [?pater]

[8v]

~~And [?s~~] ea }
V, 166 Sepulcral stones appar[?]}red, with
emblems grave
~~gr~~ {[?some]
167 On the smooth slab and epitaphs, {[?up]
{ies
167, 168 With footworn effig{ey of brass inlaid
169 The tribute ~~which~~ by these various
records [?~~fr~~] claimed
170 Without reluctance did we pay,
and read
171 The ordinary tale of births
172 Office alliance & and promotion,
all
173 Ending in dust; of upright magistrates
174 Grave Doctors stren[?u]s for their Mother Church
175 And uncorrupted Senators, alike

103ff. Rev of 7v, 7r. Cf. MS. 74A, 2v.

166ff. Cf. MS. 74A, 5r. The gap between the draft of V, 98–107 on 7r–8r and the copy of V, 166–214 in the hands of WW and DW on 8v–9r suggests that an earlier draft may have existed with material related to ll. 108–65 leading into V, 166.

br
176 To king & people true. A pl azen plate
ily
177 Not easy decypherd told of
one
178 Whose course of earthly honour
was commenced
179 [?Ar] In the capacity of page
180 To the eighth Henry when he
crossed the
Seas

[9r]

[?in] the fields
V, 181, 182 His [?~~sp pomp~~] to exhibit ~~on the~~ [?a]
shores of france
183 Another table registered the death
And ng
184 Of praised the valiant beari [?g] of
Tried a knight
185 Slai in the sea fights of the 2[?d] Charles
186 Near this brave knight his father
lay entombed
ice
187 And to the silent language giving voce
188 I read of him, who in his early days
189 Amid the afflictions of in[?s]testine
go ware
190 And strife & rght [?] vernment
oerthrown
191 This only comfort had that he espoused
192 A gentle dame, a lady most beloved
193 For her benygn perfections, & for this
[?T] [?That]
196 [?And her] she with numerous issue
filled his house
That and
197 ~~Wh~~o throve like plants, that felt
no storm the while
198 Their country was laid waste—W[?ha]
What need to speak
201 Of infants & unwedded sisters old
~~Who as the [?humble~~]

[9v]

V, 200, 202 blameless & [?good who] lived respected,
died

181ff. Cf. MS. 74A, 5r–5v.

200ff. Cf. MS. 74A, 5v–6r.

Lamented; ~~and with~~ hope that they should
see
A bliss ere resurrection.
206, 207 *Softly [?my] venerable Friend*
I looked
And from the Altar steps where
we stood
208 *Saw at the Western end of th[?at]*
dark pile
209 *The Solitary standing with his*
arm
210 *On the baptismal font reclined*
a gleam
[210] *Shone from a window on his*
pallid face
211 *Upturn'd as if his senses were*
~~*absorb'd*~~
r} {[?t]
[?wr} ap{pd and]
r}
wr} apt or lost
212 *In som*
some abstraction
gracefully he stood

[10r]

V, 213 *Fixed without motion like*
a sculpturd form
214 *Leaning upon a monumen—*
tal Urn

---

223 Withrew & strait we followed.—
~~In the [?sun~~]
[?huge]
225 ~~Beside an overhanging~~ oak a ~~broad~~
S} ~~th~~} oak
T}~~tretched its~~ [?]}~~ick [?brances] from a~~
[?~~neighbo~~uring]
[225] a broad oak
[?~~And~~]
[?~~R]ight~~ leafy {[?nches]
[225] Fronting the door, its ~~shady~~ [?bra{h]
226 From an adjoining field & overhung

206–214 Hand of DW. The corrections in l. 211 suggest WW dictating and closely supervising the copy. DW's sole interventions here and in 19v also support an argument that this material was added after most of Book IV was drafted.

213ff. Cf. MS. 74A, 6r.

214/223 The gap between DW's copy and WW's resumption at l. 223 suggests the existence of an earlier version. The last lines may be related to the first two lines on 7v; see note to 7v. Leaves 10v–12r are blank.

small / to the
s
227, 223 ~~The~~ [?of]}pace of that green church ,} [?a] ~~shade~~
~~ed~~,
To the shade
He turn{[?g] ~~and by~~
[223] To a spot
He turnd

[12v]

IV, 608 Lifes Autumn past I stand on Winters
verge
desire {ish
609 And daily lose what I [?wou] w{[?] to keep
th
610 Yet would I ra[?]}er instantly decline
611 To the traditionary sympathies
612 To a most rustic ignorance and
t
613 A fearful apprehension from o}he owl
614 Or deathwactch &

[612] and take
[?screeching]
[613] Sad apprehension from an owl
[614] Or deathwatch and as readily
[?~~or~~] rejoice
615 If two auspicious magpies cross d my
way
616 This rather would I do than see & hear
617 The repetions wearisome of sense
{hath
618 Where soul is dead and feeeling {as
no
[~~?~~] [?alad]
619 Where knowledge ill begun
in cold remark
Ends worse, as wanting love [?at hand,]
[?pursued]
620 In formal inference [?selfish]
[?doubt] & vain

[13r]

in
IV, 619 Where knowledge ill begun ~~with~~ cold remark
620 On owtward things with formal inference
ends

608ff. Rev of 28v; rev on 13r, 1v.

613–614 These lines are closer to *1814* than ll. [613]–[614] below. The gap between ll. 608–614 at the top third of the page and ll. [612]–620 at the bottom half of the page also suggests that ll. 608–614 were entered after ll. [612]–620 were drafted.

619ff. Rev of 12v; rev on 1v. See also inside front cover, 28v, 29r.

Or
621 [?An] if the mind turn inward, tis perplexed
in
622 Lost [?] a gloom of uni[?s]pired research
∨ The central point of self it cannot quit

~~The central~~
A vapoury atmospher with [?strait]
embrace
♓ [?Defeats] all heavenly influence & the
Soul
625 On its own axis restlessly revol[?ves]
626 And no where finds the che[?e]ring
beams of truth

478 Trust me pronouncing on your own desert
judge
479 You the[?] unthankfully, distempered
nerves
480 Infect the thoughts the languor of the frame
481 Depresses the soul's vigour. Quit your
couch
482 Cleave not so fondly to your moody Cell
i
483 Nor let the Spir ts that maintain
repose

[13ᵛ]

IV, 483 ~~Nor let [?t]~~
p
484 In heaven & earth with disaproving eye
485 Look down upon your taper through a Watch
486 Of midnight hours unseasonably twinkling
In
487 [?Lit] this deep hollow like a sullen
star
488 Dimly reflected in a lonely pool.
d
489 Take Courage, and withr raw yourself
from ways
490 That run not parallel to Natures course.
For they though smooth are treacherous & [?& blind]
To the mild yoke of day [?be tractable]
An[?d] from the morning learn [?humanity]
491 Rise with the Lark, your mattins shall
r obtain
492 G[?] ace be their composition what it may

622/625 The symbol either marks the passage for rev or indicates insertion of lines drafted elsewhere.
478ff. Rev of 22ʳ, 22ᵛ, 21ʳ.

484ff. Rev of 23ʳ, 21ᵛ, 21ʳ.

493 If but with hers performd, climb once again
^
494 Climb every day those ramparts, meet the
breeze
495 Upon their tops; & haply you shall there
[495] Pass in your wanderings an Adventurous Bee
ing
496 From your own Garden murmurg in ~~the~~ beds
yon
[?every] point,
497 Of blooming Heath—let [?its] commanding [?~~Pair~~]
t ~~Peak~~
498 B yon frequented watch Tower, roll
the stone
499 In thunder down the mountains.
with all your might
500 Chase the wild goat & if the bold
red Deer

[14r]

IV, 453 Rooks [?cawling] loud, or as they pass on high
s a g
Announcd by [?] h [?] dows [?f] liding on the
ground
;
[453] In multitude ! And Sea mews from afar
Which on day
~~That~~ at some boisterous time when fleets
of ships
Upon the angry surface of the main
bro
Are str ken & confounded steer their course
[?Fearless], and hover d [?on the]
454 And hover on the troubled Element
above these inland solitude
455 Unscatter d by the wind at whose loud
420 Ah if the heart too confidently raised
421 Perchance too lightly occupied or
lulled
422 Too easily despise or overlook
423 The vassalage that binds her to the earth
424 Her sad dependance upon time and all
425 The trepidations of mortality
place
426 What ~~land~~ so destitute & void but there
427 The little flower her vanity shall check
428 The trailing worm reprove her
thoughtless pride

453–455 Rev of 15r, 15v, 19r.
420–428 Rev of 18v.

harbours
fly to thes [?~~coverts~~]
501 ^ driven by hound & horn
502 Loud echoing, addg your speed to the
pursuit
503 So wearied to you hut shall you re[?tu]
[?urn]
504 And sink at [?evening] into sound repose

[14v]

ao
IV, 429 These craggy regions—these ch[?]}tic wilds
be
430 Does that [?pe]}nignity pervade which warms
en
431 The mole content[?]}ted with her darks
~~ome~~
some walk
432, 433 In the cold ground the intelligence that
makes
[432], 434 The tiny emment strong by social leage
435 Supports the generations multiplies
{eir a spatious plan
436 Th{e tribe till we behold the ~~face of earth~~
[?~~plain~~] all with little Hills
437 ~~Or hill~~ or grassy bottom with ~~their work~~
Their labour, as a lake
438 ~~Of hillocks~~ covered ~~as the~~ sea with waves
439 Thousands of cit[?es] in the desart place
{~~Built~~
440 {[?With] up of life, and food, and means of life
the thought
441 Nor wanting here to entertain ~~your [?sight~~]
&}
~~The sage & fervent commonwel~~ }~~th of~~
Creatures that [?~~bird~~]
{~~roods~~
442 [?~~How b~~{irds] ~~that~~ in communities exist
443 Less as migh seem for general guard
ianship
444 Or through dependence upon mutual
aid
445 That by participation of delight
446 And a strict love of fellowship
combined

[15r]

Herons, or Rooks or Seamews {ar
IV, 453 The flight of rooks & seamews from af{[?]

501–504 Rev of 22r.

429ff. Rev of 15v, 15r, 18v, 19r.

453ff. Rev of 19r, 15v; rev on 14r. See 21r.

455 Unccatter d by the wind at whose
loud call
ow
456, 458 Their voyage was begun the f[?]ls that
[?is] seek
458 Th e lonely pools & there together sit
459 In silent congress or together rouz'ed
460 Take flight while with their clang
the air resounds
that e
461 And over all in [?Heavens] thereal arch
462 The fleecy company of changeful
clouds
463 Brght apparition suddenly put forth
464 The rainbow smiling on the faded storm
465 The mild assembla[?] of the starry
G heavens
great
466 And the ~~brig~~ht Sun earths universal
Lord.

Rooks on the wing
[453] ~~Herons, or Rooks~~ or Seamews from afar
[?boister]
of ships
That at a time when Fleets ~~in helpless~~
[?steer] [?]
On [?the distracted bosom of the main]
steer [?aloft]
Are [?~~broke~~] broken & confounded, ~~sail~~ aloft
[455] Unscattered by th [?waves]
[?s] [?]
On the vex d bosom of the main, dispers[?ed]

[15v]

IV, 442 ~~And those communities~~
[?how] in
[442] ~~And~~ Birds that [?in] communities
[?] exist
general
443 Less as might seem for guardianship
th ai
444 Or [?fr] [?r]gh depe[?danc] up[?o] mutual [?al] d
457, 458 The water fowl that seek the lonely pools
459, 460 And sit together fly or together fly
In sportive congregation; not by [?need]
Or
[444] But from dependenc upon mutual
aid
445 But by participation of delight
446 And a strict love of fellowship [?or]
combined
453 The flight of Rook & seamews from
afar

442ff. Rev of 19r; rev on 14v, 14r, 15r.

455 Unscattered by the wind at whose loud
call
456, 458 Their voyage was begun the fowl that
seek
458 The ^ lonely pools & there together sit
[?thence]
[?they]
459 In silent congress or together [?fly]
460 Take flig[?ht] while with their clang
a
[?]ir resounds

[16^{r}]

IV, 335 *Happy is he who lives to understand*
336 *Not human nature only but explores*
337 *All Natures to the end that he may find*
338 *The law that governs each and where begins*
339 *The union or partition that which makes*
340 *Degree or kind among all visible beings*
341 *The constitutions powers and faculties*
342 *Which they inherit cannot step beyond*
343 *And cannot fall beneath which do assign*
344 *To every class its station and its office*
345 *Thro' all the mighty commonwealth of things*
346 *Up from the creeping plant to sovereign Man*
347 *Such converse if directed by a mild ~~sincere~~*
S
348 *Sincere, and humble spirit teaches love*
349 *For knowledge is delight and such delight*
350 *Breeds love yet suited as it rather is*
351 *To thought and to the climbing intellect*
352 *It teaches less to love than to adore*
353 *If that be not indeed the highest love*

[16^{v}]

IV, 1125 I have see

335ff. Hand of MW, continuing at the top of 17^{r}. It is possible, and perhaps probable, that work in MS. 70 began here and continued on 17^{r}. The verso of leaf 16 and most, if not all, prior leaves were left blank (perhaps purposively) and later used for revisions (cf. 2^{r}–4^{v} but also 10^{v}–12^{r}). To form IV, 335–375, WW drew upon a passage in MS. R of *Home at Grasmere* (see *H at G*, p. 197). The absence of punctuation and capitalization in MW's copy, and WW's, assuming copy and significant rev at l. 358, suggest WW's dictating to MW through l. 357, working on the rev of those lines as he went along.

This verso, left blank in earlier stages of composition, provided space for WW to develop material from 22^{v}. Leaf 22^{v} revises and continues draft found on 21^{r}–21^{v}, 44^{r}, and MS. 73, 16^{r}. Leaf 16^{v} here provides the intervening lines, 1125b–1141a, which do not appear in a consecutive draft of ll. 1111b–1152 found in MS. 73, 6^{r}. The lines in MS. 73, 6^{r} probably intervene between the copy found in MS. 70, 44^{r}, and further work on this sequence of lines in MS. 70, 21^{r}–21^{v}, 22^{v}. MS. 73 continues with consecutive drafts of ll. 1152–1284 and ll. 79–91, 956. Cf. MS 73, 2^{v}–7^{v} and p. 443, above.

1126 A curious Child who dwelt upon
O⎱ tract
1127 I ⎰f inland ground applying to his ear
⎰d
smooth lipd ⎱
1128 The convolutions of a purple shell
1129 To which, in silence hushd, his very
soul
1130 Listend intensely, and his countenance
soon
1131 Brghtend with joy, for Murmurings
from within
sonorous cadence by which
1132, 1133 Were heard ~~by which~~ the monitor [?]
express d
1133 To his belief the monitor ex ⎰ ~~o~~
1134 Misterious union with its native ~~s~~⎱[?on]
sea
1135 Even such a shell the universe
itself
1136 Is to the ear of faith. And there
are times
doth impart
1137 I doubt not, when to you it [?imparts]
1138 Authentic tidings of invisible things
⎰ebb
1139 Of ⎱ever & flow & ever during powr
~~& [?love~~]
1140 ~~And deep peace~~ subsisting in the heart
[1140] And central peace ^
1141 Of endless agitation. Here

[17[r]]

IV, 354 *Yet something hangs about our daily ~~being~~* life
357 *Not to be satisfied with this and he*
M⎱
358 Is yet a happier a⎰an who for those heights
359 Of speculation not unfit descends
~~At Nature's call, to walk in humbler ways~~
& the
At Natures call, in ~~Reasons~~ leisure hours
Of Reason his affections [?entertain]
360 ~~And his affections gently entertains~~
363 ~~With individual objects of regar[?d~~]
361 Among the inferior kinds not merely
those
~~that~~
⎰[?~~that~~]
That s⎱hall
362 ~~Which~~ he may call his own & ~~which~~ depend

354ff. Continued from 16[r]. Rev on 17[v], 19[v]. Cf. MS. R, *Home at Grasmere* (see *H at G*, pp. 190–199). See note to 16[r].

{fro
364 Upon his care {whom whom he also looks
365 For signs and tokens of a mutual bond
366 But others far beyond this narrow sphere
367 Whom for the very sake of love he loves
368 Nor is it a mean praise of rural life
369 And solitude that they do favour
most
370 Most frequently call forth and best
sustain
371 These mild & pure sensations, and to you
loneliness
374, 375 How much might they endear the ~~solitude~~
375 Of this sublime retirement:
371, 373 These pure sensations & ~~to you~~ how
much
that can penetrate
372 Into the heart of Cities [?future minds]

[17v]

IV, 373, 374 How much might they endear & recommend
375 The loneliness of this sublime retreat
the [?mind]
Power they possess to occupy ~~& [?ins~~pir]
384, 374 ~~To teach set forth~~ enliven & inspir[?it]
[384, 374] To [?sooth] to teach enliven & inspir[?it]
388 I guess that welcome to
b}
389 The Redr}reast feeds in winter at your
hand
390 A Box perchance is from your casement
hung
391 For the small wren to build in. Not in vain
392 The barriers disregarding that surround
393 This deep abiding place, before your
sight
394 Mounts on the breeze the butterfly & soars
395 Small Creature as he is, from earths bright
flowers
396 Into the dewy clouds. Ambition reign[?s]
blank [?unreprovd]
397 In the ~~rude~~ wildnessness ~~And [?takes~~]
[?her way]
Along the vacant [?skies]—Ambition free

371, 373; 372 These transitional lines are probably among the latest rev in this complex sequence and are the basis for the opening lines of DW's copy on 19v.

373ff. Rev of 17r; rev on 19r, 19v, 20r, 20v. Related draft on 18r. WW seems to be working back and forth across the opening from the recto of leaf 18 to the verso of leaf 17 and then continuing ll. 396–413 from the middle of 19r to the middle of 19v, probably leaving 18v and the top of 19r blank, before DW makes a try at a fair copy of ll. 371–401 on 19v.

396 A different pen and ink, similar to that used for the rev at the bottom of 17r, is employed from "Ambition" through the last line on the page.

[?envious] strife
From ~~all degrading~~ pride

[18r]

with [?his]
IV, 378 If ~~with the~~ froward will & groveling
offended Sou[?l]
379 Of ~~man, displeased~~ turn
[379] Offended turn to [?these] ~~with [?those~~ converse]
Power they posses to occupy the mind
384, 374 To sooth to teach enliven & inspir[?it]
who never heard
[381] To mark their placid state
382 Of law ~~rule~~ which they have power to
break or rule
383 Which they are temted to tra[?n]gress
with these
[?Converse], ~~the [?spot abides yet] & will~~
[?for]
[379] liberty is yours
381 To mark the state of [?them].
385, 386 May we converse & free from [?envey]
find
387 Complacence there. But wherefore
this to you
[379] liberty is here[?in]
invitation every
[381] And opportunity each hour renewd

[18v]

IV, 420 ~~If~~ Ah if the heart too confidently raisd
421 Perchance too lightly occupied, or lulld
422 Too easily despise or overlook
423 The vassalage that binds her to the earth
and
424 Her sad dependence upon time, [?] [?d] all
425 The trepidations of mortality
426 What place so destitute & void but
there
427, 428 ~~The flower shall check her pri~~de,
~~the trailing worm~~
~~the trailing~~
R [?]
428, 427 [?R]~~eprove his vanity~~.
[427, 428] The little flower shall check her
~~easy~~
thoughtless prid

378ff. Rev on 19v–20r; related draft on 17v. See note to 17v.

420ff. Rev on 14r–14v.

[428, 427] The trailing worm ~~reprove her vanity~~
F| her vanity reprove
427 The little f|lower her vanity shall check
[428] The trailing worm reprove her thoughtle[?s]
r | pride
429 These craggy [?g]|egions [?these] chaotic wilds
430 Why speak of that [?benigty] that warms
431 The mole contented with her darksome
walk
432, 433 In the cold earth the intelligence that
makes
432, 434 The tiny Emmet strong by social leage
435 Supports the generations multiplies
436 The tribes till we behold the
face of eart[?h]

[19r]

i|
IV, 437 On h |ll or grassy bottom with their
work
437, 438 [?Of] hillocks covered in the Sea with wave
439 Ten Thousand in the desart place
440 Built up of life & food & means of life
441 Nor wanting here to entertain [?your] thought
{[?birds]
442 The sage & fervent commonwealth of {[?bees]
453 The flight of Rooks or seamews from far
{Unscatter d }
455 {~~And waterfowl~~} by the wind & whose
{[?~~Their~~] loud call
456 {[?The] In [?company] their voyage was begun
457, 458 The waterfowl that seek the lonely
pool
396 ambition reigns
397 In the blank wilderness. The soul ascends
398 Towards her native firmament of heaven
399 When the fresh Eagle in the month of
401 This shady valley leaves & leaves the dark
{ou
402 Empurpled hill conspicu{[?]sly renews
401, 402 Mount from the [?shadowy] valley & renews
403 A proud communication with the
sun
404 Low sunk beneath the horizon. While
[?r]| I speak
[404] [?a tone to aid me] & [?f|eproach] I hear

437–458 Continued from 18v; rev on 15v, 15r, 14v, 14r.
396ff. Rev of 17v; rev on 20v.
404–412 A draft of IV, 404–412, is found in MS. 48 of *The Prelude* (see *13-Bk Prelude*, II, 402, 420).
[404] Conjectured “a tone” may be “at once.”

405 From yon huge breast of rock
a solemn bleat

[19^{v}]

IV, 406 Sent forth as if it were the Mountain's
voice
407 As if the visible Mountain made the cry.
And hark again that single voice there is
411 No other and the region all around
412 Is silent empty of all [?space] of life
413 It is a lamb left somewhere to itself
371 *These pure sensations which*
can penetrate
~~*Whe*~~
crowded {y
372 *Into the* ~~*heart of*~~ *cit*{*ies* & *how much*
374 *How much might they endear* & *re-*
-commend
375 *The loneliness of this sublime re*
-treat
378 *If the froward will* & *grovelling*
mind
379 *Of man offended liberty is here*
380 *And invitation every hour re—*
-newed
381 *To mark their placid state*
who never heard

[20^{r}]

IV, [382] a comm [?and]
382 *Of Law which they have power to break*
Or Rule *or rule*
383 ^ *Which they are tempted to transgress*
[?~~can~~]| with these
386 ~~*With these may*~~ *we*} ~~*converse* &~~
free from envy find
Instructed, solace & beguild with these
[?re]cord
387 ~~*Complacence* [?*f*]~~
With these {[?]
385 ^ *May we converse, their knowledge* ~~*n*~~{~~*ote*~~
register [?~~*regi*~~]

406–413 Rev on 20^{v}. See note to 19^{r}, ll. 404–412.
412 Leaf 21^{r} and *1814* read "shape" for the conjectured "space".
371 Hand of DW, continuing to l. 401 on 20^{v}.
371–381 Rev of 17^{r}, 17^{v}, 18^{r}.

382ff. Rev of 17^{v}, 18^{r}.

~~*And note*~~
[386] *Observe their ways, & free from*
envy find
[387] *Complacence there; but wherefore*
this to you?
388 *I guess that welcome to your lonely*
hearth
389 *The Red-breast feeds in winter from*
your hand
390 *A box perchance is from your casement*
hung
391 *For the small wren to build in not in*
vain
392 *The barriers disregarding that surround*
393 *This deep abiding-place, before your*
{on *sight*
394 *Mounts* {*in the breeze the Butterfly*
& soars
395 *Small Creature as he is from earths*
bright flowers

[20v]

IV, 396 *Into the dewy clouds. Ambition reigns*
{*l*
397 *In the waste wilderness. the sou*{[?]
ascends
398 *Towards her native firmament of heaven*
399 *When the fresh eagle in the month of*
May
400 Upborne, at evening, with replenished wing
401 *This shady valley leaves, & leaves the*
dark
402 Empurpled hills, conspicuously renewing
403 A proud communication with the sun
404 Low sunk beneath the horizon. While I
trace
Or strive at least imperfectly to trace
These obligations of the human Soul
Mysteriously sustained even now I hear
405 From yon huge breast of rock a solemn bleat
406 Sent forth as if it were the Mountain's voice
407 As if the visible Mountan made the cry.
408, 410 And hark! again that solemn bleat
—there is
411 No other and the region all around

396ff. Rev of 17v, 19r, 19v.
404–414 See note to ll. 404–412 on 19r.

[21^{r}]

IV, 412 Is silent, empty of all shape of life
413 —It is a Lamb left somewhere to itself
414 The plaintve Spirit of the solitude.
467 How bountiful is Nature—he shall find
?468 W
[?]
W
[?F]
?471 Of
?472 A
?473 [?W]
?474 A[?n]
?475 T
[?In]
?1112 A
?1113 By
?1121 Im[?ag]
Of [?ine]
From

[21^{v}]

IV, 1123 By that inferior faculty which molds
1124 With her minute speculative pains
1125, 481 Opinion, ever-changing—Quit your couch
482 [?Cl] [? ? ?] [?t] [?] [?dly] to your moody cell

[?n]
[?]
{[?ll]
{[?]
?498 [?tone]
?499 ight

The leaf has been torn out, leaving only four lines at the top of the page. Ll. 412–414 revise 19^{v}. The remaining line and decipherable letters on the stubs indicate that the passage consisted of some version of ll. 467–478 followed by a version of ll. 1111–1125, 481–499, with ll. 500–504 continued on 22^{r}. The passage is revised on 22^{r}–22^{v}, 23^{r}. Ll. 478–504, dropping the intervening ll. 1111–1125, are then revised on 13^{r}–13^{v}, 14^{r}. For ll. 420–466, see 14^{r}–15^{v}, 18^{v}, 19^{r}. Ll. 1111–1125, probably in an earlier state, are found in MS. 73, 6^{r}. For ll. 1100–1112, see 44^{r}. For ll. 1125–1141, see 16^{v}. See note to 22^{v}.

1123ff. Continued from 21^{r}; cf. note to 21^{r}. A space of approximately eight lines intervenes between l. 482 and the first conjectured line ending.

[22r]

IV, 500 Chase the wild Goat & if the bold red
501 Fly to these harbours driven by hound
Loud echoing & horn
502 ~~With echo~~, add your speed to the pursuit
hut
503 So, ~~sh~~ wearied to your shed shall you
return
504 And sink at evening into timely sleep.
489 Take courage & withdraw yourself from ways
490 That run not pallarell with nature
467 How bountiful is nature he shall find
468 Who seeks not and to him who hath not asked,
469 Large measure shall be given—three sabbath
days
470 Are scarcely told sinc on a service bound
hills
471 Of mere humanity you clomb these [?heights]
472 And what a marvellous & heavenly shew
473 Was to your sight revealed: the Swains
moved on
474 And heeded not—You lingered & perceived.
475 There is a luxury in self dispraise
476 And inward self disparagement affords
477 To meditative spleen a grateful feast—
[478] pronouncing on your own desert
478 Trust me ~~you judge amiss. A death~~less
spirit
479 You judge unthankfully. Distemper'd
nerves
1111 [?~~Abides] within we have heard yo~~ur
[?voice]
480 Infect the thoughts the lang[?ouo]r
of the [?frame]

[22v]

s
IV, 481 Depressed the souls vigour.
1112 At every moment soften d in its course
1113 By tenderness of heart, have seen your eye
1114 Even like an altar lit by fire[?s] from heaven

500–504 Copy appears to have continued directly on 22r from 21v before the entire passage, ll. 467ff., was revised below. See note to 21r.

489–490 These lines may have been entered first on the page as rev of the facing verso of leaf 21. The rule below l. 490 was probably meant to separate ll. 467ff. from the work above and to signal the start of a complete rev after l. 504. Resumption of continuous copy begins with l. 508 on 23r.

467ff. Rev of 21r–21v; rev on 13r–13v, 14r.

1111/480 WW followed the sequence of 21r–21v by having ll. 1111ff. come after l. 478. Some time after completing 22v he abandoned that sequence as indicated by the del and rev on 22r–22v, a process that probably led to the rev on 13r. See notes to 22v, 21r, 21v, 44r, 16v.

---

481 See note to 22r, ll. 1111/480.

1112ff. This is a continuation of the rev on 22r before l. 1111 on that page was del. The sequence incorporates rev found in MS. 73, 6r, which seems to intervene between MS. 70, 44r and 21r. See notes to 21r, 21v, 22r, 44r, 16v.

1115 Kindle before us. Your discourse, this
Lethe day
{Lethe
1116 That like the fabled {[?] wishd to flow
1117 In creeping sadness through oblivious shades
1118 Of death and night has caught at
every turn
1119 The colours of the sun; acess ~~is yet~~ for yo
1120 Is yet preserved to principles of
truth
1121 Which the imaginative will upholds
1122 In seats of power that can not be
approache
&c

[23r]

climb once again
{[?r]ts
IV, 494 These rampar {[?] , daily climb, and rangin round
Their wide circumference inhale thereon
Celestial air, the clefts and caver[?s] seek
F}
498 [?]}illed with the strife of waters—roll the
&c

---

508 Ah what a joy it were in vigorous health
509 To have a body—this our vital frame
510 With shrinking sensibility endued
{ And
511 {[?With] all the nice regard[?s] of flesh & blood
512 And to the elements surrender it
from
m}
513 Ass if it were a spirit, ~~of~~ [?d]}ischance
Secure & unobnoxious to distress
515 What joy to wander in unpeopled vales
m}
516 And [?r]}ountainous retirements only trod
517 By devious footsteps regions consecrate
518 To oldest time and careless of the storm
{R
519 That keeps the {raven quiet in her nest
520 Be as presence or a motion, one
521 Among the many there and while the
~~M[?ist]~~
Mists

1122 "&c" signals continuation, probably to follow the related continuous sequence of ll. 1111b–1152 found in MS. 73, 6r. Ll. 1100–1112 are found on 44r and ll. 1125–1141 on 16v.

494–498 Rev of 21v; rev on 13v. See notes to 21r–22v.

498 The "&c" probably indicates inclusion of the late rev, l. 499 on 21v and ll. 500–504 on 22r.

508ff. These lines begin a new sequence of composition that runs fairly continuously, albeit with some significant rev, through l. 759 on 37r. The introductory lines, 505–507, providing a transition between l. 504 and l. 508, are not present in this notebook.

[23v]

IV, 522 Flying and rainy vapours call out Shapes
523 And Phantoms from the crags and solid
Earth
524 As fast as a Musician scatters sounds
O
525 [?F] ut of an instrument, and while the stream,
526 As at a first Creation and in haste
ied
527 to exercise their untr [?id] facu[?ti]es X
528 Decending from the region of the clouds
529 And starting from the hollows of the earth
530 More multitudinous every moment [?~~rend~~]
rend
531 Their way before them what a joy to roam
532 An equal among mightiest energies
533 And haply sometimes with articulate voice
534 Amid the deafening tumult scarcely heard
535 By him that utters it exclai aloud
536, 537 Be this continued so from month to
month
539 Whoeer hath known such transports
[?in]
ere [?the] youth
540 Hath through the Ambition of his soul given
and way
541 To such desires at graspd at
ch
su [?re] delghts
542 Shall feel the stirring of them late
and long

[24r]

In
IV, 543 [?Its] spite of all the weakness that life
brings
544 Its disappointments griefs & vexing cares
that droops shall
[?ers] he
And heavy sorrow [?s] shall lift ~~the~~
The lids ~~lids~~
545 Of his despondency ~~shall hear~~ & wake
546 Wake sometimes to a noble restlessness
547 Loving the spots which once he gloried
in
548 Compatriot, Friend, remote are
Garrys hills
549 The streams far distant of your native
glens
[?vale]

---

528 The X probably indicates an intention to rev or to insert a passage at this point, possibly satisfied by the addition of l. 529.

543ff. Rev on 24v.

550 Yet is their form & image here expressd
n ~~faithful~~ as by a
551 I [?~~lovely~~] duplicate, at least set forth
{[?here]
[?In] {[?turn] the [?work]
{ i {u {;
552 ~~By~~ brotherly simil{[?y]t{yde{ and ~~here~~
[552] ~~By a fraternal likeness~~
554 Are [?brav incitements] engines not the same
556 But by the great artificer endue[?ued]
{no
557 With {[?a] inferior Power
[552] ~~By a fraternal likeness: for your [?need]~~
~~the [?force]~~
you [?see]
~~Here~~
[?Is here of]
[554] [?~~Dot] here [?abound] of engines, not the~~
{[?ear] same
[554] You [?h{ave] the work of engines
—not the same

[24v]

IV, 548 Compatriot, Friend, remote are
H
Garrys [?str]{ills
549 The Streams far distant of your native
glen
550 Yet is their form and Image here expressd
551 As by a Duplicate at least set forth
552, 553 With a fraternal likeness, whereseer
~~you [?r~~ s]
552 Your steps are turned
[?upraise]
Your turn to quicken & ~~incite the~~
{day mind
By {[?]—beneath the clouds & stars of night
554 Are various engines working, not the same
555 As those by which in youth your
soul was
moved
556 But by the great Artificer endued
557 With no inferior Power.
552 With brotherly resemblance. Turn
your steps
553 Wherever fancy leads, by Day, by night
[554] Are various engines working not
{ich the same
[555] As those by wh{y your Soul in youth
was moved
[556] But by the great artificer endued

548ff. Rev of 24r.

[25ʳ]

IV, 557 With no inferior power. ~~You d~~
Thogh not [?deprived]
[557] The sight of human face you dwell
alone
558 You walk, you live, you speculate
alone
559 Yet doth Remembranc like a sovereign
{G Prince
560 For you a stately {gallery maintain
561 Of gay or tragic pictures. You have seen
562 Have acted suffered travelled far
observd
563 With no incurious eye. And books are
yours
{lay booty
564 Where {[?lie] the treasures of antiquity
t}
568, 570 Enb}ombd, and music waits upon
your touch
571 Sounds which the waderg Shepherd
o} from these h[?e]ghts
572 Hears & f[?r]}rgets his purpose. Furnished
thus
573 How can you droop if will[?n]g to be raised
joy
If earth yet be restored & [?~~truth~~]
return
fresh [?]
With the bright Visitant, to break
the [?ties]

[25ᵛ]

Of habit wisdom to extract
{F {~~of~~
{[?f]~~rom deeds~~ {[?] [?~~fllies~~]
{from
{Long long relinquished follies, to reform
Erroneous judgements, [?give] a steadier
hand
To weigh a clearer insight to perceive
IV, [564] ~~Within whose chamber treasure lies~~
conceal
Within whose chambers ^
564 ~~Where treasure lies conceald~~

557ff. Rev on 25ᵛ, 26ʳ.
573ff. A vertical line in the left margin, which also marks the first five lines of continuous draft on 25ᵛ, indicates rev. Leaf 26ʳ resumes below the rev of ll. 563–567, with l. 574, omitting the marked lines on 25ʳ–25ᵛ.

For the first five lines marked with a vertical line in the margin, see note to 25ʳ, l. 573ff.
564ff. Rev of 25ʳ; rev on 26ʳ.

Preserved thrgh every age {o
565 ~~The~~ ~~[?of every]~~ age more prec{[?]us far
566 That the accumulated store of gold
567 And orient gems which for a day
of need
568 The Sultan hides in his forefather[?s]
tomb
at will
569 These hoards of truth can you unlock
570 And [?love], & music waits upon
{which your touch
571 Sounds {[?] the wanderg Shepherd
from these he[?i]ghts
572 Hears & forgets his purpose, furnished
thus
573 How can you droop if willlg to
be raise.

[26ʳ]

IV, 563 and books are yours
564 Within whose silent Chambers treasure
P} lies
565 [?T]}reserved from age to age, more
precious far
566 Than that accumulated store of gold
or}
567 <u>And [?f]}ient gems.</u>
574 A piteous lot it were to flee from Man
{Nature
575 Yet not rejoice in {[?] . He
whose hours
576 Are by domestic pleasures uncaress d
{whole
577 And unenlived, who exists, {[?~~alo~~]
benefits years
578 Apart from ~~services~~ received or
done
579 Mid the transactions of a bustling
[?fr-] world,
di}
Cut off its [?pa]}scoveries & pursuits
581 And babys passions such a man
hast need
l}[?v]}
582 Of a quick fancy and a}if }ly heart
for ~~each~~ day's Books [?may]
[?the]
583 That ~~books for~~ his consumpttion provide

563–567 Rev of 25ᵛ, 25ʳ.
574ff. Rev on 28ʳ, 27ᵛ.
582 The apos in "day's" below the line may have been first entered as a comma after "fancy".

[?~~bundant~~] { es
584 A ~~daily~~ food of whol{[?so]ome qualit[?y]
584, 585 And earth & air inspire him with
dealght

[26v]

{downcast
{[?] [?to] [?pines]
[?T]} {[?~~occupy~~]
[?I]}hought[?s] {[?despair], & ~~with~~ melancholy
[?~~pin~~]}
{herd [?pla}int]
Een as a Shep{[?] to his satter d flock
Pipes for [?amusemt] though with [?outward love]
fashion
IV, 602 So let [?him] ~~frame~~ [?~~his~~] theories
And smile
t}
603 At his own ~~work~~—d[?e]ss[?o]}roy with a touch
o}
604 If unreligious let him be at P}nc[?e]
605 Among ten thousand[?s] Innocents enrolled
606 A Pupil in the many chabered school
{S
607 Where {suspestition weaves her
airy drea[?m]

{Yew
Else what awaits him but a {sha
tree shade
[?barreness] & death,
Of melancholy killing grass & flower
Within its flowers & banishing
mu } the sun
And the soft [?pi]}sic of the Shepherds
pipe
600, 602 If tiried of systems let him still
[?pursue]
[?its]
[600] each [?in] their
degree
[?mould]
601 Substantial yet all [?~~fadi~~ng like new]
[?Love]
602 New systems let him build
himself & smile

[27r]

IV, 603 At his own work demlisshd with

602ff. Alt and rev on 27r, 27v.
607 Draft below the rule is related to draft at the bottom of 27v and 28r. See note to 28r.

603ff. Alt and rev of 26v; rev on 27v, 28r.

[?r] a touch
No [?t] therefore let him scorn all [?thought]
602 But build new systems of his own
& smile
603 At the fond work demlisshed at a [?touch]

Else what a waits him but a yew
shade
d
Of black & unpro[?tuc]uctive melancholy
Within its circuit killing grass
& flower[?s]
The whole Year through & banishing
the sun
And the soft music of the shepherds
pipe
[?~~Within~~] ~~And~~
[?~~The~~]
[?figure]
[602] ~~A [?bulder] let hi be [?in pure~~ refined]
Revenge & compensation are at hand
h
[602] Let him build systems of [?] is [?ow]
[?n]

[27[v]]

IV, 584 A not unwholesome food & earth & air
585 Inspire his pensive humor with delight
dismal
Else what awaits him but a yew
[?frenzy] tree Shade
[?~~fever~~]
Of ~~bla[?c]ck~~ & unproductive melacholy
Black as the compass of a yewtree [?grove]
~~Within its curcuit k~~illing grass & flowers
[?admitting] neither flower nor herb
The whole year round & banishing the sun
And the sof music of the shepherds pipe
e
600 If tired of systems [?t] ach in its degree
601 Substantial & all [?mouldering] in their turn
Revenge and compensation are at
hand
602 Let him build systems of his own & smile
603 At the fond work demolished with
un l a touch
604 If [?] rei gieo[?g]ous, let him be at once
605 Among ten thousand ennocents enrolld

584ff. Continued from 28[r]. Rev of 27[r], 26[v], 26[r]. Ll. 586–599 are entered on 55[r], at a later stage of rev.

585/600 Alt at bottom of 28[r], 26[v]. See note to 28[r].

606 A Pupil in the many chambered scho{o}l
(o written above)

607 Where Superstit{i}on weaves her airy
dreams

[28^{r}]

IV, 574 A piteous lot it were to flee from Man
575 Yet not rejoice in Nature. He whose hours
576 Are by domestic pleasures uncaressed
577 And unenlivened who exists whole years
578 Apart from benefits received or done
{~~Distress~~
{Mid ~~relieved or injury sustained~~
579 Mid the transactions of the bustling
Crowd
580 Who neither hears nor feels a wish
to hear
good
581 Of the wide worlds commoeton, of its ~~gains~~,
or evil interests {[?~~wrangling~~]
~~Or losses, of its~~ {la[?] ~~laughters~~ tears
{su
~~Inventions & discoveries & pur~~{[?]its
[581] ~~And [?baby] passi~~ons such a one hath
need
582 Of a quick fancy and a stirring heart
consumption
583 That for the days books may yield
&c
584 A not unwholesome food,

~~Black as a yew tree g~~rove
No yew tree grove more [?baleful],
from the [?spot]
Unlucky spot of ground that gave
it birth
Excluding

[28^{v}]

[?S]} on winters
IV, 608 Lifes autumn past [?I]}tand ~~upon the~~ verge
609 And daily lose what I would wish to
keep
610 Yet rather would I instantly decline

574ff. Rev of 26^{r} leads to redrafting of ll. 584–607 on 27^{v}.
584 The draft below the rule is related to drafts on 27^{r}, 26^{v}, never adopted in *1814*.

608–618 Continued from 27^{v}. Rev and expanded to include ll. 619–626 on 12^{v}–13^{r}, 1^{v}; see also inside front cover.

[?r]
611 To the simplicitites of childish ~~life~~
days
Or a mo[?s]
612 [?~~Nursed in~~] most rustic ignorance and
As on the fields I walked or [?public]
take
daw
[?Council or witness] from a [?]
[?~~omen~~] ominous
615 Or pair of magpies ~~hopp~~ing
616 This than only see and hear
617 The repetitions wearisome of sense
618 Where soul is dead & feeling hath
F
no place
[?If] or purposes of widom or delight
635 With wingend Voyager who daily
[?broug]
636 To ~~his small island, to his [?flo~~wering]
[?~~world~~],
From the [?main Continent] of heaven [?news]
From the [?main Continent continent]
of [?hea]
[636] To his small in the ethereal deep
637 Tidings of joy & love
[?and]
And [?impulse]—[?i] companionship
[?of]
[?] man
For [?love] for[~~?~~][?~~ed~~] [?]
[?~~friend~~ one]

[29r]

IV, 627 Upon the breast of new created Earth
~~In that first blissful garden~~
walk
628 and when & wheresoeer he
628, 629 Man walked; ~~alone or mated~~, and wherer
~~In that first blissful garden he repo~~sed
Alone or mate
[629] ~~lod~~
629 ~~Or~~ [?] ~~ged or wandered~~ solitude was
not
630 He heard upon the wind the articulate
voic
631 Of God, and Angels to his sght appeared
632 Crowning the glorious Hills of Paradise

635ff. Continued from facing recto of leaf 29; rev at bottom of 29r and on 29v.

627–634ff. Continued from 28v; continued at bottom of facing verso of 28v and on 29v. For intermediary lines, 608–626, see 12v–13r, 1v.

633 Or through the groves Glidg like mor
ning mist
634 Enkindled by the sun; he sate & talked
{[?dor]
With Heaven Ambassor{[?], ~~familiar~~ guest
o}
In ~~his green bower and heard of~~ [?~~lf~~}ve]

637 from these pure heights
active
638 (whether of ~~actual~~ vision sensible
639 To sght & feeling or a pomp severe
640 Of [?form] & circumstance to shadow forth
[?His]
Of circumstance through
[?Lofty tradition] to set
for

[29[v]]

~~for our infirmity by forms of [?sens~~]
IV, 641 Communications spiritually maintaind
642 And intuitions moral & divine)
e}
643 Fell the first Par[?]}nt, banishment
ensued
For all the race & sorow & [?distress]
{[?time] {for s
645 Were spread by {[?] & Man {of Man
Estate
646 Had cause to mourn but solitude
was not

---

635 With winged Messengers who daily brought
636 To his small Island in the Etherial deep
j} {y
637 Tidings of [?g]}o{[?r] and love. From these
{W pure Heights
638 ({whether of actual vision, sensible
{T
639 {to sight & feeling; or that in this sort
640 Have condescending been shadowed
{ns forth
[641] Communicatio{[?n]d spiritually maintain'd
[642] And intuitions moral & divine)
k}
[643] Fell human [?]}ind to banishment
condemn'd

634/637ff. Continued from bottom of 28[v].

641–646 Continued from 29[r]; rev below and on 30[r].
635ff. Rev of 29[r], 28[v].

[30r]

IV, 644 That flowing years repealed not, and
distress
{for
645 And guilt spread wide & Man {of
Man's estate
646 Had cause to mourn, but Solitude
was not.
shapeless Power above all Power
647 Jehovah, one & single, ~~Shapeless Pow~~er
Single & one {the
648 ~~Above all Powers~~, { omnipresent god
vocal utterance or blaze of light
649 ~~By speaking voice, or blaze of light, or thick~~
Or cloud of
650 ~~Tempestuous~~[?t]ness darkness localized
~~in h~~eaven,
enshrined wanderg ark
651 On earth ~~within the~~ within the
{~~As~~
{~~Or if on mountain Sinai~~
out of
652 Or ~~thunderg~~ Sion thunderg from his throne
race
653 Between the Cherubim, on the chosen
654 ~~His worshippers showe~~r d miracles,
{rd ~~dispens'd~~
[654] Showe{[?d] miracles & ceased not to dispense
655 Judgements that filled ~~the land with~~
the land from age to age
656 With hope and awe and gratitude & fear
657 And with amazement smote thereby
to assert
658 His scorned, or unvenerated, sover
eignty

[30v]

And when
{~~And~~
IV, 659 {[?Nor] ~~when~~ the One ineffable of name
with[?rdew]
660 In nature indivisible, ~~was lost~~
{Mortal
661 To {[?Natur] Admiration or regard
662 Nor then was Deity engulphed, or Man
[?Sole] {l
663 The rational Creature left to fee{[?d] the
weight
664 Of his own reason without sense
or thought
{a
665 Of higher reason, ~~or~~ {[?s] purer will

644ff. Continuation and rev of 29v.

666 To benefit & bless through mightier power
673 He to the mother elements uprais[?ed]
eyes
676 His ~~hands~~ in filial piety stretchd forth
His hands in act of worship
To the whole zealous
667 Whether the Persian ~~tutored~~ to
reject
668 Altar & image and the inclusive
walls
669 And roofs of Temples built by
care
human ~~hands~~,
climbing the loftiest mountain
670 The loftiest hills ascending, from their
tops
671 With myrtle wereathed tiara
on his brows

[31^{r}]

IV, 672 Shall offer sacrifice to Sun & Moon
673 And to the winds & Mother Elements
674 And the whole circle of the heavens, for
him
675 A sensivtive existence & a god
With lifted hands invoked & hymns of praise
676 Invoked with pr[?e]ayer & hymns
of holy praise
680 Or from the plai of Babylon uprose
{above
681 Tower planted {[?up] tower nor [?wanted]
[?pomp]
Of graven images the structure built
To the Celestial Belus from whos t[?o]
{top
{[?]
684 Pure & seren the God might overlook
vast
685 Winding Euphrates & the City [?vast]

665/667 A space may have been left where ll. 673, 676 and 676/667 were added. Ll. 667–671 are in different pen and ink.

666 Added in same pen and ink as ll. 667–671 below.

673ff. Rev on 31^{r}.

---

672 Rev of 30^{v}; rev on 31^{v}, 34^{v}, 32^{v}. This is the first of a complex series of drafts and revisions on 31^{r}–35^{v} toward ll. 677–713. Composition seems to have proceeded in three stages. The first drafts with alternate readings are entered on 31^{r}–32^{r}. A second stage of composition and rev is found on 34^{v}, 35^{r}, 35^{v}. The latest drafts are found on 32^{v}–33^{v}, with rev of ll. 703–705 on 34^{r} contributing to rev on 33^{r}.

681/684 The reference here to "graven images" and similarly on 32^{v}, l. 679/680, to "Metal or stone idolatrously served" are in direct opposition to WW's source, Herodotus, who explicitly points out that the Babylonians had no idols. This may explain the omission of these lines in *1814*. Cf. *PW*, V, 426.

686 Of his brightest worshippers fars[?s]tret
[?ched]
{[?ly]
687 Wi~~th~~ grove & garden infinite{ & [?wold]
690, 691 Chaldean shepherds nghtly from the
ad} stars
[?Learnd] [?]}oration in that coloudness
{field
life support~~ing~~ {[?pl] [?]
Their ~~pastoral~~ [?oeconomies]

[31^v^]

IV, 690, 691 Chaldean Shepherds in that cloudless field
692 Spread like a sea their lifes support
and [?home]
Amid the cool of silent night
~~The cool the~~ silent hours of dewy night
Br}
[?The]}ought peaceful occupation that
All weariness, with grateful hearts
heavens they lookd
693 Upon the central star as on a guide
694 And guardian of their course that
{closed
never {[?hid]
His steadfast eye
[?N]}
695 ~~His shinin~~g face [?]}or could mislead
their steps
[695] Those chiefly round the plan[?e]tary
Five
Reverenced watching
They worshippd ~~follow~~ing with
delight d
{[?~~thought~~]
{[?]
[?heart] [?]
[698] Of those perpetual Mercuries
{ose
698 The course of the{[?e] resplendent Mercuries
Charged [?intentions]
[?intentions] [?their]
{with
700 ~~Bearing~~ {the the ~~purpose~~ of the gods—
T} They [?wait]
[?H]}he [?wanderers hailed the glad]
[?return.]

31^v^, 690ff. Continuation and rev of 31^r^; continued on 32^r^; rev on 34^v^, 35^r^, 32^v^– 33^r^. See note to 31^r^.

695 There may be a dash or a period after "face" that is obliterated by the heavy diagonal cross-out line.

[32r]

IV, 699 In ~~a perpetual~~ everlasting round [?their]
[?circuit]

699, 706 On never resting jour[?nies], to and fro
[?orbits]

Interpreting the

707 Betwixt the ~~lights~~ of our apparent
sphere

708 Performed, and its invisible counterpart

709 The answering Constellation, [?under] earth
~~Hidden~~
{Which
711, 712 {[?O] [?] to the dead are present, who
behold

711, 713 They deem all accidents & judge of all

710 ~~Hidden from us but [?p]~~

710, 711 Removed from us but present to the
dead

713 Who see all accident & judge
of all.

Bold dream[?s] their peaceful
scien did
[?adm]

Dreams [?still] {[?as]
~~And~~ bolder dreams, {[?for] antient Books
report

That early Science did admit
{S {star
Their {science did Admit of {[?that] that
{[?apt] {moving pass
In {[?~~set~~] rotation {[?ro]

699, 706 ~~In everlast g cour~~ses, to and fro
x

[707] Betwi[?st]t the lights of our

[32v]

{less
IV, 677 Or, {yet reluctantly to bond of sense
soul framed

678 Yielding the~~ir minds~~ the Babylonian
for gave

679 ~~To~~ influence undefined a personal
{shape
{[?form]

Metal or stone idolatrously served
did raise

680 And by their labour, from the plain
{[?eared]
upraisd upr{ose

699ff. Rev on 34v, 35r, 35v, 33r–33v, 34r. See note to 31r.

677ff. Rev of 34v, 31r, 31v. This begins the third and last rev of this passage. See note to 31r.
679/680 See note to 31r, l. 681/684.

681 Tower, eight times planted on the top of
his Tower
682 That Belus, nightly to [?the] splendid
couch
683 Descending, there might rest, and
height
at
from the [?e] ~~Seat~~
684 Pure & seren the god[?] did overlook
685 Winding Euprhates & & the City vast
686 Of his devoted Worshippers far
tchd
f stre[?]
688 Their Town, [?&]oodful region of defense
[?]
687 With grove & garden in [?finite]
[?] [?& long]
690 Chaldean Shepherds ranging trackless
fields
691 Beneath the concave of unclouded
skies
[?entwined]

[33^r]

S
IV, 692 spread like a sea their life's support &
light [?home]
693 Looked on the Polar star as on a guide
694 And guardian of their course that never
eye closed
695 His stedfast ~~nor could mislead their steps~~
[695] ~~If danger press d~~; the planetary five
696 With a submissive rever[?e]nce they beheld
697 Watch d from the Centre of their sleeping
flocks
698 Those radiant Mercuries that seemed
to move
699 Carr[?n]g, through ether, in perpetual round
700 Decrees & resolutions of the Gods
701 And by their aspects signifying works
702 Of dim futurity to man revealed
e
Th[?o]se primitive astronnomers pursued
~~Streams bolder still as antient book~~
The motions nightly traceable in heaven
report
With thought of moral inquest bolder [?still]
~~That early Science did admit~~, of star

---

687 The conjectured word at the bottom of the page, "entwined," may be intended as an alternate conclusion for this line.

---

692 Rev of 34^v, 35^r, 31^v, 32^r. See note to 31^r.

702–705 See related draft of ll. 703–705 on 34^r. "Streams" in the second line below l. 702 reads "Dreams" on 35^r.

705 Urged from within they made report
706 In set rotatation passing to & fro
{een
707 Betw{ixt the orbs of our apparent
{he
sp{[?eh]re

[33v]

{[?t]
IV, 708 And its invisible counterpar{[?d], adornd
709 With answering Constellations, under
earth
[710] Removed from all approach sight
710 From inter~~course of~~ livg ~~men concealed~~
711 But present to the dead, who, so they
deemed,
~~Did [?like~~]
712 Like those Celestial Messengers beheld
713 All accident & judges were of all.
[710] Veiled, nor approachable by living
Man

[34r]

IV, 703 The Imaginative faculty is Lord
did lead
704, 705 ~~Of natural observat[?io] led~~ [?lea]
[?~~o~~]
[704, 705] Of observations natural, led on
To moral inquisition bolder
urged still
{[?ur]
Thus {[?~~enj~~] & thus enjoined, ~~repor~~ts
{~~in~~ [?were]
Thus nightly from with{[?] enjoind
& urge
Those first astronomers intermingling
dreams
705 ~~Of their religion made~~ report of stars
A}
T}nd nightly from within enjoined
& urged
Those first astronomers with
the sensuous
~~the truth of~~
[?sense]
[705] Which they discernd, to blend
report of stars

708ff. Rev of 35v, 32r; continued on 36r. See note to 31r.

703ff. See related draft on 33r and note to 31r.

[34v]

a ~~bound~~[?l] {l / ess field
trackles
IV, 690 Chaldean shepherds on ~~the cloudless~~
[?]
~~fields~~
691 Beneath the concave of unclouded skies
692 Spread like a sea, their lifes support
& home
693 Look d on as on a guide
nd
694 A{s [?a] guardian of their course that never
closed
695 His steadfast eye, nor could mislead
their steps
If dagger press d e
[695] Journeying . Th{e plant{tary five
watching
They reverence ~~fol~~lowing with delghted
thought
698 Those radiant Mercuries that seemed
to move
699 Carrying thrgh ether in perpetual
[?~~bearing~~] round
700 ~~From place to place~~ the [?intentions] of the
gods
701 And by their aspects signifying works
702 Of dim futurity to man reavealed

[35r]

And a submiss[?] reverence
IV, 696 ~~With reverential nature~~ they beheld
695 The planetary five, [?~~not idly], wat~~ch d
[?c]
amid their floks
698 ~~Those radiant Mercurie~~
[695] The plant[?ar] five
~~That slept~~
[696] With a submissive rever[?nc] they be
Watch d from the centre of their sleeping
flock
[698] Those radiant Mercuries that seemed
to move
699 ~~Carr ing through ether in perpetual~~
round
[?~~The] Interpreting~~
[699] Carrying thrgh ether in perpetua[?l]

690ff. Rev of 31v, 32r; rev on 35r, 32v, 33r. See note to 31r.
695/[695] Word "dagger" may be a miswriting; 33r, l. [695], reads "danger".

696ff. Rev of 34v, 31v, 32r; rev on 33r, 34r. See note to 31r.

The purposes and [?councils] of the
700 Decrees & resolutions of the Gods

Dreams bolder still as antient
Books report
That early did admit, of star
~~That~~
~~fix d~~ passing
706 In apt rotation ~~mov~~ing to fro
707 Betwixt the lights of our appare
nt speher

[35v]

IV, 708 And its invisible counterpart adornd
709 With answer d constellations, under
eart
o
710 Remove[?d] from intercourse [?] f liv g men
711 But present to the dead, who so
they deemed
712 Like those etherial Messenger [?beheld]
713 All accidents & judges were of all

720 with unrivalled skill
721 As nicest observation furnished
hints
722 For studious Fancy did his hand
bestow
723 On fluent operation

[36r]

sprітely
IV, 714 The lively Grecian in a land of hills
715 Rivers, and fertil pl ns & sounding
Found shores
716 Under a cope of var[?e]gated skies
717 Could find commodious plac for every
God
~~Which bard or sage his trave~~lled
Countries
~~Might chuse to [?in~~]
r
718 P[?] omptly received as prodigally
ll brought
719 To a [?] surrounding Countries at the choice

708ff. Rev of 32r; rev on 33v. See note to 31r.
720–723 Rev of facing recto of leaf 36.

714ff. Continued from 33v. A new sequence of composition begins here of ll. 714–759, which, with rev, runs through 38v. This is followed by a blank leaf, 39r, and ll. 760ff. begin on 2r.

{[?~~Yoke~~]
720 Of all Adventurers~~—to the~~ {[?]
a} he [?bent]
[?~~Pliant & verst~~t}~~ti~~] His Genius gave
[720] ~~With new inventions and unrivalled~~
skill
723 To fluent operations personal form
{[?o]usly
724 Metal or stome idolastor{y served
{And {nt
725 {Ye yet triumpha{l oer this pompous
tangibble show
726 Of art, this ~~palpable~~ array of sense
On every side
727 At every turn enountred;—in despite
c}
728 Of the gross fictions [?s]c}haunted
in the streets

[36ᵛ]

{R
IV, 729 By wanderg {[?r]hapsodists, and in contempt
hourly
t} {[?s]
730 Of doutbs}s and bold denial{s ~~dai~~
[?h]} heard
731 Amid the wrangling s[?c]}ools, A Spirit
{g
hun{d
732 Beautiful Region oer thy Towns
& farms
733 Statues & temples and memorial
And w} fonts
734 ~~Their~~ emanations [?p]}ere perceivd,
and acts
735 Of immortality in Natures course
736 And in her laws, and mysteries
were held
P}
737 As Bonds, by grave [?S] [?]}hilosopher[?s]
and child
738, 739 And armed Warrior, chearfulness
prevailed
{ad
740 When piety more awful h{[?] relax'd.
741 Take running river take these
742 Thus might a votary say, Th
Loocks of [?mind]
y[?e]ld
The votary said I ~~give~~^ them as
thy due

720–723 Rev on facing verso of leaf 35.

729ff. Rev on 37ᵛ, 38ʳ, 38ᵛ.
742ff. Alt on bottom of 37ʳ.

oft
746 For those s[?weet] murmurs & the
tf
gra[?ve]ul ~~lym~~
lymph
[?W]
[?]
747 [?In] which thou refresh the thirsty
lip

[37r]

IV, 748 And moisten all day long th[?at] flowery
field
Nor doubt that
749 ~~And doubtless~~, sometime when the
gift was shed
750 Upon the flowing stream a thought arose
[751] Of life continuous, being unimpaired
751 Of Being unimpaired, ~~and~~ continuous
life
752 That hath been is & where ~~it is &~~ was & is
, fe
753 There shall be ; seen & heard & & [?]lt
r and known
754 And [?s]ecognized; existie[?]ence
b unexposed
755 To the [?]lind walks of mortal accident
d
F di minution
756 Arom [?pr]eser~~vatio~~n] safe of [?time]
a
& [?]ge
dw
757 While Man grows old & [?f]indles
n & [?] decays
758 And co[?ut]tless generations of [?mank]
mankind
759 Depart; and leave no vestige
where they trod

742 Thus might a votary say the severd
[?ations] hair
Pres[?ting]
~~tly~~ i
[?~~Devout~~] [?] ~~offerg~~ ~~ng~~ to his natve stream
[?i] ing [?ed]
Accept th[?u]s offer g yield [?ing]

748ff. Rev on 37v, 38r, 38v.
742ff. Alt on bottom of 36v.
756–759 Cf. MS. 69, 220v.

[37^{v}]

IV, 741 Take running River take these locks of mine
742 Thus might a Votary say the severed
hair
Presenting humbly to his native stream
The consecrated gift has been thy due
a child
Since first upon thy banks I played
746 Thy murmurs heard, and drank the
grateful lymph
747 With which dost refresh the thirsty lip
748 And moisten all day long these flowery
fields
Accept the offering & be ever kind
My prayers grant my wishes to
fulfil[?l]
~~Bathed~~
Such frame of words the Votary might
use
[?Or] And thus perhaps might siletly
prol[?n]g
[?meditation]
His [?i]nwards while he stood and
Ey d the current as it pass d along
The consecrated gift [?hat been thy]

[38^{r}]

[?~~O~~]
[?S] ~~ccasion~~

×
T~~h[?]~~
This for the general rite occasions dear
Of special gratitude perhaps would
[?promt]
Words like to these, This hallow d gift
I bry[?ng]
he
For [?him] whose loss I mourned hath now
returned
IV, 745 Upon thy banks he once again hath trod
746 Thy murmurs heard and drank the
[~~?~~]
[?] lymph[?s]
Or while a Father on the margin stood
Thus might he speak this hallowed gift
I bry[?ng]

741ff. Rev of 36^{v}, 37^{r}; rev on 38^{r}, 38^{v}.
742ff. The two lines are indented because of ink blots on the page.
748ff. See the unnumbered lines at the top of 38^{r} for another version of the unnumbered lines below.

745ff. Rev of 37^{v}, 37^{r}, 36^{v}; rev on 38^{v}. See the unnumbered lines at the bottom of 37^{v} for an alternate version of the unnumbered lines at the top of the page.

~~Bestow~~ {Child
744 Thankful for my beloved {[?sons] return
~~D[?]~~
~~Upon~~ {C
[745] The Banks {cephisus he again hath trod
[746] The murmurs heard & drank the grateful
lymph

[38v]

IV, 741 Take running River take these locks of mine
votary r}
742 Thus might a Fathe say, This seve[?]}'d
[~~?~~] my hair
743 My vow fulfulling, do I here present
744 Thanful for my beloved Chlds return
[?verge]
C} {phisus
745 The ~~banks~~ [?h}e]}{[?] he again hath
trod
746 Thy murmurs heard and drank the
grateful lymph
f} e}
747 With which thou dost re[?]}resh the}~~se~~
lip} ~~flowering fields~~
thirsty [?]}
748 And moisten all day long these flowery
fields
749 And doubtless sometimes when the hair
was shed
750 Upon the flowing stream a thought arose
n}
751 Of life continuous, beig}g unimpaired

[39v]

~~Unerring~~ Unbaffled
IV, 941 ~~A twofold~~ power ~~hat~~ of vision hath prepared
937 Now shall profound Philosophers receive
Less from the awful faculties of sight
And hearing shapeless obtain
937, 938 Now shall profound Philosophers ~~receiv~~
939 ~~From sense from reason~~
[939] From human Sense & reason less than
men
far misled {[?S] ~~these~~
So ~~ignorant~~—{[?s]~~hall they, in truth~~,
be [?poor]

741ff. Rev of 38r, 37v, 37r, 36v. Leaf 39r is blank. Ll. 752–759 are entered on 37r. Ll. 760–821 are entered on 1v–4v. Ll. 847ff. begin on 49v. Leaf 40 begins a new sequence of composition, from ll. 937–1112, running through 45r with rev.

941ff. Rev of facing recto of leaf 40.

940 ~~Compar d with these~~. Shall men for
whom

[40r]

profound
IV, 937 Now shall ~~our sage~~ Philosophers be poor
S} {ll
940 Compared with these. T}ha{t Men for whom
A microscopic vision our Age
941 ~~The optic glass of Scien~~ce hath prepared
{to
T{he explore
942 ~~Both for~~ the world within & world without
{ Gigantic S }
943 Be joyless as the blind. {[?Those] [?M]}ouls
~~at length~~
at this late season
944 Whom Earth as if ~~to recompense the loss~~
for Man
compensates at length
~~Of Bodily stature~~ has producd
The loss of bodily stature,
945 To wage with heer a second war, to weigh
946 The planets in the hollow of their hand
n}
And tame the elemet}ts shall they in
~~truth~~ fact
950, 975 Be but a dwindled race. Accuse me
{ol not
976 Of b{[?]dness unknown Wanderer
as I am
977 If havg walkd with nature three [?s]
score year[?s]
978 And offered much as frailty would allow
c}
979 My heart a daily sar}rific to Truth
980 I do pronounce them such. ~~And~~
~~such was he~~
A worthier name

937ff. Rev on facing verso of leaf 39. Composition resumed here with leaf 39 left blank and continued through l. 1112 on 44r, with rev extending to 45r.

940 Word "these" (later omitted) refers to the ancients, Greeks, and votary of the immediately preceding passages in the MS. ending in l. 759 on 37r, those whose lives are strongly bound to the natural world. The proximity of the reference suggests that much fewer, if any, of the ultimate 178 lines between l. 759 on 37r and l. 937 on 40r were intended to intervene. The blank leaf suggests only a maximum of forty lines may have been intended. For ll. 760–821 see note to 38v; for ll. 847–935 see 49v–54r. Ll. 954–964, although not indicated as following in the MS., are closely related to a passage in the addendum to MS. B and MS. D of *RC* where an X marks the ending of the half-line 964 in MS. D. (See *RC & Pedlar*, pp. 266–269, 373–374.) MS. 73, 7v, has l. 956 directly follow l. 91.

980ff. MW begins copy at bottom of the page and continues through 41v, l. 1021. There is some evidence that the passage is being dictated rather than copied: the lack of punct, corrections in the hand of MW (e.g. 41r, l. 1005), metrical irregularities on 41r, ll. 1019, 1020ff., and the copy error on 41v, ll. 1020–1021.

[40ᵛ]

IV, 984 *Can they deserve who while the human*
soul
985 *Is of a thousand faculties composed*
986 *And twice ten thousand interests prize*
the frame
987 *Of Nature this transcendant universe*
988 *No more than as a mirror that reflects*
989 *To proud self love its own intelligence*
990 *That one poor finite object in the abyss*
infinite
991 *Of ~~Mind & Being~~ twinkling restlessly*
992 *Nor higher title would I yield to him* X
{S
{sage of France
993 *And his compeers ~~the shrewd~~ the laughing*
~~Sage~~^
994 *Crowned was he if my memory doth not err*
995 With laurel planted upon hoary hair
996 *In sign of conquests by his wit atcheivd*
997 *And benefits his wisdom had conferred*
998 *His tottering body was oppressed with flowers*
999 *Far less becoming ornaments than those*
1000 *With which Spring sometimes decks a*
witherd tree

[41ʳ]

IV, 1001 *Yet so it pleased a fond & vain old Man*
1002 *And a most frivolous people Him I mean*
~~overturn~~ ridicule
1003 *Who framed to ~~rectify~~ confiding faith*
1004 *This piteous leg^end ^which by chance we found*
1005 *~~In a blind nook thence piled~~*
through
[1005] *Piled in a nook ~~by~~ malice as might seem*
1006 *Among more innocent rubbish Speaking*
thus
1007 *With a brief notice when & how & where*
1008 *We had espied the book he drew it*
forth
1009 *And courteously as if the act removed*
1010 *At once all traces from the good man's*
{ *Of* *heart*
1011 {[?*An*] *unbenign aversion or contempt*

---

992 The X in the right margin probably signals a new verse para and possibly intended rev of the opening line. Cf. *1814*.

1005 The rev may be caused by an error in dictation. See note to 40ʳ, l. 980ff.

1012 *Restored it to its owner gentle Friend*
{S {nd
1013 Herewith he grasped the {solitarys ha{[?]d
1014 *You have known better lights & guides*
than these
1015 *Ah let not aught amiss within dispose*
practise on
1016 *A noble mind to ~~traffic with~~ itself*
1019 *To invert authority & make appeal*
1019, 1020 *From high to lower judgements seats*
Whate' er looking before or after you perceive

[41v]

IV, 1017 *Tempt not opinion to promote the work*
1018 *Of passion & engage a faithless will*
In services which conscience disapproves
1020 *Or shrinks from Can you question*
Inherits an all } *that the soul*
1021 *That the Soul [?inh]}egiance not by choice*
support
[1017] And tempt opinion to ~~promote~~ the wrongs
is felt or feared
[1018] Of passion whatsoeer ~~you dread or feel~~
2 1
[1019] From higher judgements make no appeal
[1020] To lower: can you question that
the soul
[1021] Inherits an allegiance not by choice
1022 To be cast off upon an oath proposd
each new
1023 By ~~any~~ upstart notion? In the ports
1024 Of levity no refuge can be found
1025 No shelter for a spirit in distress,.
{with
Laugh but sincerely {[?but] mirth's
genuine [?power]
Meet scorn with scorn but seek
for truth elsewhere
disesteem
1026 He who by wilful di[?sestee] of life
1027 And proud insensibility to hope
1028 Affronts the eye of solitude shall
learn

1015 See inside front cover.
1016ff. Rev on 41v.
1919, 1920ff. The metrical irregularities of the last two lines on the page may be due to an error in dictation. See note to 40r, l. 980ff.

1017ff. Rev of 41r.
[1017] Fair copy ends as WW resumes transcription. Successive pages are marked by the process of drafting, rev, and recension.

[42ʳ]

mild
[?~~m~~]
IV, 1029 That her [?]eek nature can be terrible
1030 That neither she nor Silence lack the power
ted
1031 To avenge their own insul[?] Majesty
1032 [?—] blest seclusion
O happy rural days in virtue pass d
And the sobrieties of humble thought
~~Benevolence & chearfulness & faith~~
autumnal
In [?truths] ^ sunshine & the air
1044 Of meek repentanc[?e,] breathing
[1045] ruins of fallen prid
From out the mouldcrd
[1044] ~~wall flower [?scents]~~
1045 ~~From the deserted [?Mansion] of fallen~~ & pride
now ~~decayed~~
forlorn
1046 And chambers of transgression
1047 O calm contented day & peaceful nights
w
1048 Who [?th]ith such good within his reach
his grasp
while such good awaits
would strive
[?coul obt] obtaind
1049 To reconcile his Manhood to a couch
s under that disguis
1050 Soft as may [?b]eem, but ~~inwardly oppr~~essd
Stuffed
1051 [?Oppressed] with the thorny substance
of the past
nd
1052 For fixed annoyance a[?t] full oft
[?~~phantoms~~] beset
1054 ~~vapour of futurity~~
~~With [?favorably~~]
1053 With ~~dre~~ floating dreams dis
consolate & black
[1048] Who while such good
can ~~may~~ be obtained

[42ᵛ]

IV, 1054 The vapoury phantoms of futurity.
1055 Within the Soul a faculty abides
1056 That with interpositions which would
hide
1057 And darken so can deal that they become
ex
1058 Contingencies of pomp and serve to [?]alt

1029ff. Rev on 42ᵛ, 44ᵛ, 45ʳ.
1032 The mark in the right margin probably signals the rev on 44ᵛ.

1054ff. Rev of 42ʳ, 57ʳ, 56ᵛ, 58ʳ; rev on 43ʳ.

H
1059 [?]er native brightness. As, ~~to the eye~~
of him
[1059] ~~Who pauses on his way~~, the ample Moon
1060 In the deep stillness of a summer even
1061 Rising behind a thick & lofty grove
[1062] Burns like a n unconsuming fire of light
1062 Appears to burn, an unconsuming fire
[?~~silent~~]
1063 In the green trees; and kindlg on all
sides
a
1064 The le a[?l]fy umbrage turns the dusky veil
b
1065 Into a sus stance glorious as its own
incorporated by power
1066 Yea with its own, embodied, by a
power
[1067] Like power abides
1067 Capacious & serene. ~~Like~~ influence
~~dwells~~
Celestial t
1068 In Mans ~~immortal~~ spiri t[?s], ~~to pervade~~
~~And to subdue incorporate and a~~bsord

[43^r]

~~Desert and Virtue cannot [?ever] exist~~
~~But in the neighbourhood & by the touch~~
IV, [1068] Virtue thus
~~Of evil, which they overcome, & feed~~
[1069] Sets forth and magnifies herself thus
feeds
1070 A calm a beautiful & silent fire
mortal l
1071 From the incumbrances of ~~adversi~~ [?] ife
[?even]
[?nor]
[?~~nor~~]
1072 From error disappointment, [?yea] ~~even~~
times from guilt
1073 And some^ so relenting Justice wills
F
1074 E[?v] rom palpable oppressions of despair
1068 ~~virtue thus~~
[1068] In ~~mans immortal spirit~~
1069 ~~The touch of evil overcomes & feeds~~

1062 The brackets perhaps indicate WW's indecision about which alternate to select. Cf. 57^r, 58^r.

1063 The del of the conjectured rev "silent" may be related to the repetition of "silent" in l. 1070 on 43^r.

1068 Word "absord" in line at page foot is a miswriting of "absorb"; cf. first line on 56^v.

1070ff. Rev of 42^v, 57^r, 56^v, 56^r.

1074/1077 Ll. 1075–1076 do not appear in any extant MS. before *1814*.

The mind i[?f] free
1077 But how begin & whence, "~~Awake Arise~~
Resolve ~~the~~ haughty Moralist
1078 ~~The haughty Moralist~~ would say
1079 This single act is all that we demand
1080 Alas such Wisdom bids a creature
fly
1081 Whose very sorrow is that Time
{th
ha{s shorn
1082 His natural wings!—to friendship
Let him turn
1083 For succour but perhaps he sits
alone

[43v]

stormy
IV, 1084 On ~~the wild~~ waters in a little Boat
1085 That holds but one & can contain no
more
1086 Religion tells of amity sublime
preclu
1087 Which no condition can ~~ex~~clude
[?him]
of ~~one~~
1088 Who sees all suffering conprehends all
w} wants
1089 All f}eakness fathoms can supply all
;
needs [?]}
1090 But is that bounty absolute, his gifts
{not
1091 Are they {[?] still in some degree rewards
For service done. A
}?
1092 For acts of service[};^ Friend who doth
[?n]}
[?]}eed
{will
Reciprocal observance {[?sha] he own
1093 The heart that owns not him—Will
showers of gr[?ac]
1094 When in the sky no promise can be
seen
1095 Fall to refresh a parch'd & witherd
land
1096 Or shall the groaning Spirit cast her
load
1097, 1099 At the Redeemers feet?—
As Men from Men

1077 *1814* reads "The Mind is free".

1093ff. Rev of 56r, 55v.
Ll. 1097b–1099a do not appear in any extant manuscript before *1814*.

[44r]

IV, 1100 Do in the constitution of their souls
{y {to
1101 Differ, by myster{[?ies] not {be be explain
by various ways & sink
1102 And as we fall ~~from right~~ by varios
1103 One deeper than another self-condemned
ways
1104 Through manifold degrees of guilt & shame
1105 So manifold and various are the
ways
{fashioned
{[?] for the steps
{[?~~though~~]
1106, 1108 Of restoration ; {[?tending] ~~to one~~ point
1109 ~~Peace with ourselves and unity~~
[?~~united~~]
union with God
1107 Of all infirmity and tending all
1108 To the same point attainable by
all
Pe} ~~for~~ in {union
[1109] [?]}ace ~~with~~ our selves and {[?] [?t]
with our God
1110 For him to whom I speak an easy
road
[?o]}
1111 Lies [?]} open: we have heard from you a
voice
1112 At every moment softend in its course

[44v]

IV, 1032 Oh blest seclusion, when the mind
admits
1033 The law of duty, and thereby can live
1034 Through each vicissitude of loss & gain
Link d in entire complacence with its choice
1035 ~~In rational complacence~~ with ~~its choice~~
Youth's
{~~h's~~
1036 When ~~Yout~~{[?h] presuptuousness is
mellowed down
1037 And manhoods vai[?n] anxiety dismissd
{[?When] shows
1038 {[?] Wisdom ~~sh[?ed~~] her seasonabl[?es]
fruit

1111ff. Composition seems to break off here, while WW explores ways of continuing the sequence of lines in MS. 73 in pages left blank in the front of MS. 70, and possibly these or other directions in MSS. no longer extant. MS. 73, 6r, contains a continuous sequence of ll. 1111b–1152, omitting ll. 1125b–1141a, and consecutive drafting through l. 1284. This probably precedes the rev and expansion of 44r on 21r–22v, 16v. Ll. 1302–1310 are found in MS. 70, 6v–7r.

1032 Rev of 42r.

U}
1038 [?Of]}pon the boughs of shelter[?i]g leisure
hung
p}
1040 In sober d}lenty when the spirit
stoops
{[?stoops]
{[?]
1041 To drink with gratitude the [?~~cryt~~]
crystal stream
1042 Of unreproved enjoyment and is pleasd
saluted
{~~saluted~~
1043 ~~With~~ To muse, and be {[?] by the
w}   air
1044 Of meek repentance b}afting wall
s[?weets]
flower [?swe]
1045 From out the mouldered ruins
of fallen pride

[45r]

IV, 1046 And chambers of transgression now
forlorn
calm contented
1047 Oh calm content

[?your]
261 ~~and~~ for ~~that~~ other loss
for earth while
262 The loss of [?~~hope~~] ~~which [?prom~~ised]
~~and [?to mankind~~]
faith
confidence in social
The loss of hope in that [?futurity]
[?~~happin~~]
~~Of [?transfiged] earth~~
Promised [?~~to human kind~~]
[?Perfection]
[?earth] with all [?~~its~~]
Of knowlege wisdom happiness &
joy

1046–1047 Rev of 42r. Leaves 45v–49r are blank.

261ff. Other than ll. 79–91 in MS. 73, 7r, 7v, which in MS. 73 seem to form part of the poem's conclusion, these are the only extant MS. lines related to the first 332 lines of Book IV (DC MS. 69 preserves stubs that contained a version of these lines). The lines seem to presume the context of the first quarter of the book, where the Wanderer contrasts the Solitary's loss of family with the loss of utopian or social idealism. *1814* provides the missing half-line of l. 261, "The Sage continued." The position of these lines at the end of substantial sequence of draft preceding a number of blank pages and their context of dual loss suggest that they are among the latest entries in the notebook, probably post-1812 after the death of WW's children.

[49v]

IV, 847 In thast fair clime the lonely Herdsman
stretch'd
848 On the soft grass through half a sumners
day
849 With music lulled his indolent repose
{And
850 {Or in some fit of weariness if he
851 When his own breath was silent chanced to
hear
852 A distant strain far sweeter than the
sounds
853 Which his poor skill could make, his
{fetched
Fancy {[?]
{S
854 Even from the blazing Chariot of the {sun
855 A beardless Youth who touch d a
ne} golden lute
856 A fill'd th illuming}d groves with
ravishment
eyes
{[?s]
857 The nightly Hunter lifting up his {[?eyes]
858 Towards the crescent Moon with grateful
heart
859 Called on the lovely Wander who bestowed
860 That timely light to share his joyous sport
861 And hence a beaming Goddess with her
Across nymphs
862 ~~Along~~ the lawn & through the darksome grove
863 Not unaccompanied with tuneful notes
864 By echo multiplied from rock or cave
865 Swept in the storm of chase, as Moon
& stars

[50r]

rifted clouds
IV, 866 Glance rapidly along the clouded heavens
867 When winds are bl[?] strong. Each brook
N} upon had then
869 Its n}aiad sunbeams ~~on the~~ distant hills
870 Gliding apace with shadows intermix d
871 Might with small help from fancy be
transformed
872 Into bright Oreads sporting visibly
873 The Zephyrs fanning as they pa[?st]

847ff. Rev of 53r, 53v, 52v. Ll. 618–821 leading up to this sequence are entered on 1v–4v. Ll. 822–846 are not in any extant MS.

866ff. Rev of 53v, 52v, 53r, 54r.
867 Word "bl[?]" obscured by ink blot. *1814* reads "blowing".

[867] The traveller slaked
868 His thirst from rill or gushing fount &
thanked
[869] The Naiad; Sunbeams upon distant Hills
in their train
[870] Gliding apace with shadows ~~inter[?mixed~~]
[871] Might with small help from fancy be
transformed
[872] Into fleet oreads sporting visibly
[873] The Zephyrs, fanning as they past, their
wings
874 Lack d not for love fair objects when
they wooed
875 With gentle whisper. Wither'd boughs
grotesque
876 Stripped of their leaves & twigs
by hoary age
877 From depth of shaggy Covert peeping
e} forth
878 In [?d] wood or on step}p
mountain's side

[50v]

IV, 879 And sometimes intermix d with stir[?ring h]orns
880 Of the live deer or Goats depend[?n]g beard
lurking
{se { [?~~lur~~]
881 The{ [?t] were the {[?hor~~ns] of~~ satyrs a wild
{Pan brood
882 Of gamesome deities of {pa himself
883 The simple Shepherds awe inspiring
God[?]
The pale Recluse, who hitherto had sate
{,
On the grey stone{ —hearkening in silent mood,
888 Like one who listens to a murmuring stream,
now
889 Untired, was tempted ~~here~~ to interpose
890 And with a smile exclaimed.
"Tis well you speak
891 At a safe distance from our native land
892 And from the Mansions where our Youth
was taught.
893 The true desendants of those
godly men

879ff. Rev of 54r.
879 The queried words are obscured by ink blots.
883 What is probably a period after "God" is obscured by an ink blot.
883/888 Although these lines are omitted in *1814*, the reference to the Solitary as "the pale Recluse" takes on something of the nature of an epithet being employed three times: in V, 222, 603, and VIII, 338.

~~Who with a [?fever age~~]
894 Who swept from Scotland in a flame
of zeal
895 Shrine altar image and the
massy piles

[51r]

That gave them harbour retainin[?g]
IV, 896 ~~That harboured them~~ the Souls ~~who~~ yet
churlish retain
897 The ~~unalter~~'d features of that after
race
& wood hollow rock
898 Who fled to caves ~~& clefts of~~ naked
rock
899 In deadly scorn of superstitious rites
900 Or what their Conscience fancied to be suc
901 [?H]ow think you would they tolerate
this scheme
902 of fine propensities, that tends if urged
903 Far as it might be urge to sow afresh
904 The weeds of romish fatasy in vain
would
905 Uprooted—~~to~~ reconsecrate our wells
906 To fair St Helen & to good St Anne
907 And from long banishment recall St Giles
again
908 To watch once more with tutelary love
909 Oer stately Edinborough throne [?on]
{ crags
{ [?yo]
And/bur[?n]g inwardly with white pure light
914 Of sciences & philoso
~~Once more [?t~~]
912 To be once more paraded through
her streets
[?~~Now] seek no protection~~

[51v]

simpl
IV, 913 Now ~~better~~ guarded by the sober
powers
914 Of scieces & phil[?ios]phy & sense
915 This answer followed. my
You have turned ~~our~~
thought[?s]

---

900 Word "such" written off the edge of the page.
901 The conjectured "H" is obscured by an ink blot.
909/914 Expanded and rev on 52r.

913ff. Continued from ll. 910–912 on 52r.

On men who ~~shrank to woods & dis~~mal
Upon } rocks
{[?th] [?]} rose
916 {[?T] our brave progenitors who ~~fought~~
{r
917 Against idolatry with wa{l[?k] like
{~~On~~ mind
{Up~~on those hapless fugitives who shrunk~~
~~F~~ }
[?S]}~~rom vain observances~~
And
918 ~~Who~~ shrunk from vain observances to [?lu]
919 In caves & in the clefts of dismal rock
920 Depri[?ve]d of shelter covering fire & food
921 Why for this very reason that they felt
922 And did acknowledge wheresoer
they moved
923 A spiritual presence oftimes mis
conceived
924 But still a high dependance
a div[?ne]

[52ʳ]

IV, 925 Bounty & government that fill d
their heart
926 With joy and gratitude & fear & love
927 And from their fervent lips drew
hymns of praise
928 With which the desarts rang. Though
favored less
929 Far less than these yet such in their
degree
930 Were those bewilder d pagans of ol[?d]
B } time [?~~den~~]
931 [?T]}eyond their own poor natures
~~ase~~} and above
932 They looked, [?w]}~~mbled worshi~~ppd
& revered
the
were humbly thankful for [?food]
daily [?the]
933 With they receive at natures [?han]d, their
~~will~~
934 ~~They [?shape] and fortified the~~ [?mora]l sense
of [?~~all~~]
[934] ~~And [?as] the [?crown~~] and their moral sense
[?Were] haply chearful

---

918 The conjectured "lu" is probably "lurk" as in *1814*.
920 "Deprived" is obscured by ink blot.
924 *1814* reads "divine".

933–934 Words "hand" and "moral" obscured by ink blot.

935 They fortified with reverence
{G
for the {god
910 A blessed restoratio to behold
911 The saint upon the Shoulders of his
{priests
s{[?ho]
912 Once more paraded through her
crowded streets

[52^{v}]

IV, 850 But in some fit of silence, if he heard
852 A distant strain far sweeter
than the sounds
853 Which his poor skill could make
his fancy [?feign]
or looking back
or cast a look
To [?times more distant of a world]
[?Still early, occupation of mankind]
847 To that fair clime
Each brook had
Sunbeams then
869 Its naiad—Oreads on the distants
hills
871 Might with small help fancy
be [?transfigured]
872 Into bright Oreads sporting [?visibly]

[53^{r}]

[?]
IV, 867 [?The wind blows strong]
[?fresh] [~~?~~]
And the [?~~rough~~] blast [?were ~~deities~~,]
[?smiling deities]
873 The Zephyr fann[?ing] as [?]
{[~~?~~]
?866/867 ~~The travell[?g]~~ {[?]
and [?noble work]
[?age]

910–912 Rev of 51^{r}; continued on 51^{v}. For ll. 937ff. see 40^{r}.

850ff. Drafted in pencil. Rev on 49^{v}, 50^{r}; related draft on 53^{r}, 53^{v}.

867ff. These lines, some of which are in pencil (see below), are part of a complex process of related draft and rev on 52^{v}, 54^{r}, 52^{v}, 49^{v}, 50^{r}.

867–?866/867 The first four lines are in different pen and ink from ll. [847]–856 below. They were probably entered last on the page and are related to draft at the foot of 53^{v} and l. 873 at the top of 54^{r}. Lines related to l. 873 are revised on 54^{r} below the rule. L. ?866/867 may be related to the idea of movement expressed in l. 866 (see 53^{v}, "Charge rapidly," where the "C" overwrites an initial "T"), or to l. 867, "The traveller" (see 50^{r}). The last rev is found on 50^{r}.

?866/867ff. The lines beginning "and [?noble work]" and ending "In that" are in pencil. They were probably entered first on the page and are related to pencil draft on 52^{v}.

The [?simple occupations]
847 In that
[847] The Herdsman streched
848 On the soft grass through half a summers
day
849 With music lulled his indolent
repose;
852 But discontented with the sounds produced
F} fetched
853 By his untutored skill, his [?]}ancy
854 Even from the blazing Chariot of the Sun
855 A beardles Youth who touch d ~~the~~ a
Golden lute
856 And filled the illumined groves
with ravishment

[53^v]

T} [?halting] with
IV, 857 W}he nightly hunter lifting up his eyes
Towards
Fixed}
858 [?To] } on the crescent, moon, with
[?heart]
{Call {W grateful
859 {[?] on the lovely {wanderer who bestowed
shared
860 That timely light, to [?~~chear~~] his joyous
{ [?a beamin]g go} sport
861 And Hence {[? ?] [?]}ddess
Across with her nymphs
~~From hill to hollow vale, oer open~~
862 ~~Along~~ the ~~open~~ lawns & through the shady
woods
plain
And throgh the darksome trail of
863 Not unaccomppanied [?with] tuneful note
leafy woods
865 Swept in the storm of chase, as Moon
C} & stars
866 T}[?harge] rapidily along the clouded
heavens
{o
867 When winds are blowing stro{gng. The
fragran[?t]
[?fruits]
Wafted from [?flowring] orchard that
[?embowerd]
Pomonas ~~visible~~ image filled [?the] heart

847–856 Rev on 52^v, 49^v.

857ff. Rev on 49^v, 50^r; related drafting on 53^r, 54^r, 52^v. Cf. note to 53^r.

With expectation [?unconfined]
{?of
[?And] by the [?season{? ?oft gave visibly]
[?and pure]
[?Touchg all—nor loosened a plant]
[?nor] [?flow]

[54[r]]

Z}
IV, 873 Ear}ephyrs [?wooed]
Earth parched with drought [?obtained]
relief from
The whispering Zephy was a [?voice]
that

{Z
[873] The {[?z]ephyrs fanning as they past
{gs
n} their win{[?d]
874 Lack d f}ot for love fair object whom
{they
{[?sh] wooed
875 With softest whispers. Withered boughs
grotesque
876 Strippd of their leaves & twigs by hoary
{From age,
877 {[?And] depth of shaggy Coverts peeping
forth
878 In [?~~dark]~~ ~~[?~~] wood or on steep mountain
side
{[?&c]
879 And sometimes intermixd with {stirring
{e horns
880 Of the liv{ing deer, or goats depending
Beard
881 These were the lurking Satyrs
a wild brood
882 Of gamesome deities, [?or] Pan himself
883 The simple Shepherds awe
{G
inspirg {god

[55[r]]

IV, 586 Truth has her pleasure grounds—her
haunts ~~walks~~ of ease
587 And easy contemplation, gay parterre[?r]s

873ff. Rev of 53[r]; rev on 50[r], 50[v]. Related drafting on 53[v], 53[r], 52[v]; cf. note to 53[r]. Leaf 54[v] is blank.

586–599 Expansion of draft found on 26[r]–28[r], providing the first text of these lines in the notebook.

                h
588 And labyrint{[?in]ine walks & sunny spots
589 And shady spots for recreation framed
590 These may he rage, if willing & partake
perhaps
en
591 Their soft Indulgences and th{[?ere] ~~at length~~
at
[?comforts]
a[?t] at [?leng]
592 May be recruited for the ~~fearful~~ tasks
And course of
593 ~~And~~ services ~~while~~ truth requires
from those
594 Who tend her Altars wait upon [?he]
her thrones
595 And guard her fortress. Who thinks
& feels
~~Why~~ [?~~The~~]
596 And recognizes ever & anon
597 The breeze of nature stirring in his
soul
598 Why need such man go desperately
astray
599 Or nurse the dreadful appetite of death

[55v]

and wait
IV, 1093 impling showers of grace
i
[1094] Whe{[?n]n the sky no promise can be
Or waiting in [?submision absolute]
~~Till they descend~~
nd
[1093] a{[?] shall we ask imploring showers
of grace
[1095] To fall from heaven upon a thirsty
[?la]
1094 And shall we ask, and wait while
In the sky
1094, 1093 No promise can be seen till showers
freshen of grace
~~to~~ ~~re~~
1095 ~~Decend~~ {[?] [?]}~~novate a wither d~~ land
[1095] Fall to refresh a parch & wither'd land
[?Religi]

1093ff. Rev of 56r; rev on 43v.

1093–[1095] The first six base text lines appear to have been entered after ll. 1094–[1095] below.

At page foot the conjectured "Religi" may be related to l. 1086 (see 43v).

[56^r]

[?where]
IV, 1077 But [?~~where~~ shal] we begin, of holy [?writ]
~~That [?aid] be [?sought imploring~~]
S [?showers]
1093 [?O]}~~hall [?we ask~~ and,] ~~and wait~~
And shall we as [?that] showers of
1095 From heaven descend upon a thirsty
[?the oerburthen] soil
1096 Or shall [?~~dejected~~]
[?~~depression~~] cast her
load
1097 At the Reedemers feet;—o bless d
ar they
[1096] ~~Or shall [?the oerburth~~]
[?~~Whose scheme~~]
[?~~Who in the~~] {had
~~When I exclaim~~, if ~~having~~ I {[?]
[?wholly left]
The ways of faith [~~?~~] through [?which]
my mother had
~~Led me helpless little~~ a[?n]
Laid open to my infant helpless[?n]
{[?]
Bless d who I {[?lov]

[56^v]

And to subdue incorporate & absorb
Dessert & virtue cannot [?ever]
exist
IV, 1068 ~~Virtue [?hath no exis~~tence],
But in the neighbourhood & by the
{. touch
1069 Of evil{, [?~~power majesty] [? ~~]
{[?These]
{[?They] they overcom & [?draw]
A [?ligt] of divine Liberty [?upraised]
~~nor~~
1072 From error disappointment, ~~yea~~
{[?disappointm]
and {[?] [?s]a~~y from~~
guil
1073 And sometimes, so eternal mercy
{[?dark] wills
1074 Een from the {[?]
dim
~~black~~ intervals of despair

1077ff. Continued from 56^v; rev on 55^v, 43^r, 43^v.
The unnumbered lines at the bottom of the page may be an attempt to extend and recast the Solitary's initial response in l. 1077 above, revealing even in these fragments a character perhaps at once more intimate and more forceful. Cf. 43^r, 1077ff.

1068ff. Continued from 57^r; continued on 56^r; rev on 42^v, 43^r.

[1069] Of evil which they overcome & feed
A a
1070 ~~Th~~eir calm ~~their~~ beautiful & silent
[?fire] [?]
{[?flame]
{[?life]
{[?c] {[?of]
1071 From the encumbran{[?tnce] {[?~~earthly~~]
[?~~care~~]
{[?guilt]
[1072] From error, disappointm{[?ent]
{[?yea]
{[?nay] from guilt
[1074] And palpable oppressions
of despair

[57^r]

IV, 1055 within the soul
Within the soul
[1055] The Soul divine a faculty abides
which
1056 That with interpositions ~~that~~ would
hide
1057 And darken so can deal that
{ they
{[?are] become
1058 Contingencies of pomp, and ser [?e] to exalt
to the eye of him
1059 Her native brightness as the ample Moon
Who pauses on his way
{In
1060 {De the deep stillness of a summer
even
1061 Rising behind a thick & shady grove
To the eye of him, who pauses on his way
u }
1062 Burns like an [?in]}nconsuming fire of
light
1063 In the green &.
{[?to]
{[?]
{to
[1062] Appears {[?in] burn in unconsuming
fire, [?&c]
[1063] In the green trees and kindling on all
sides
1064 The leafy umbrge turns the dusky veil

1055ff. Rev of 58^r; continued on 56^v; rev on 42^v, 43^r. Leaf 42^v generally follows 57^r rather than 58^r with the exception of "lofty" for "shady" in l. 1061. Work appears to be contemporaneous on 57^r and 58^r.

1060–1061 Leaf 57^r inverts the line sequence on 58^r.

1061–1063 From "To the eye" to "In the green &." is in different ink.

1063 The "&." signals the continuation of the draft on 58^r.

1065 Into a substanc glorious as its own
1066 Yea with its own embodied by a
power
1067 Capacious & sere[?n] like influence dwells
1068 In mans imortal Spirit, to pervade

[57v] [II, 278–287]

was
His sacred function [?] at length reno
unced
~~At leng[?t] his sacred function was abjured~~. *II, 149*
And every day and every place enjoyed *150*
Th
U } unshackled Laymans natural *151*
Liberty
Speech manners morals all without disguise *152*
I
[?D] } do not wish to wrong him—though *153*
the course
Of private life licentiously display d *154*
Unhallowed actions planted like a *155*
crown
Upon the insolent aspiring brow *156*
Of spurious notions worn as open ~~signs~~ *157*
e signs
Of pr } judice subdued, he still retained *158*
&c
[?I]

[58r]

your [?s exists]
IV, 1055 Within the Soul a faculty abides
Which
T [?]
1056 [?A] } ~~hat~~ with interposit { [?ons] that would hide
1057 And darken, so can deal that they are
her [?means]
1058, 1059 To exalt { its native splendour. As the
moon
1061 Rising behind a thick and lofty grove
Mid
1060 { [?In] the deep stillness of a summer even
Appear
1062 { Burns to burn a[?n] unconsuming fire

149ff. Rev of 59v, 62r. Cf. MS. 47, 39v, 40v; MS. 71, missing leaves 42–43 (see notes to 36r, 41r), 41v, 44r, 44v. See pp. 439–440, above, for general discussion of the sequence of composition of Book II in MS. 70 and its relation to other MSS. From 57v to the end of MS. 70 bracketed line references in the right margin on each leaf refer to *1814*, and right-margin italic line numbers refer to the pre-1813 text of *Exc,* I–III, c. 299.

158 The "&c" signals resumption of the text at l. *159* on 62r.

1055ff. Rev on 57r, 42v; see note to 57r.

1061, 1060 Leaf 57r inverts the lines.

1063 In the green trees, and kindling on all
sides
1064 Their leafy umbrage turns the dusky
veil
1065 Into a substance glorious as its own
1066 Yea with its own embodied by a power
1067 Capacious & ser[?ne].
——Enlivening thoughts
On this aerial voyager attend
w}
By sympathy, the l}asted Spirits find
Soft renovations of admiring love
b}
And [?]}oundless sovereignty participates
Of innocent pleasures.

[58^{v}] [II, 160–180]

As up this Vale we journeyed side by side II, 56
with his staff
My fellow Traveller pointing as he spake 57
Towards those craggy summits thus 58
~~*Made known his purpose to a spot*~~ *that* 59
lies
Concealed among yon mountain solitudes 60
I shall conduct you to receive I hope 61
Ere noon a recompense of this days toil 61, 62
From sight of one who lives secluded there 63
lonesome & lost, of whom & whose past life 64
Not to forestall such knowledge as may be 65
More faithfully collected from himself 66
This brief communication shall suffice 67
There, tho' sequestered he was like myself 68
Born on the hills of Scotland we had this 70
ng}
{[?*n*]*g*}
In common too that both were spru{[?*g*] 69
from poor
And lowly parentage his time of youth 69, 75
In piety & innocence was spent 74
And as he shewed in study forward zeal 76
All helps were sought all means were 77
straind that he

1067ff. The lines below beginning "—Enlivening" are in different pen and ink. The passage may, as *PW, V*, suggests (p. 426), be related to ll. 396ff. See 20^{v} and *PW*, 1850, ll. 394ff.

Hand of MW.

56ff. Rev on 59^{r}; cf. MS. 47, 38^{r}; MS. 71, 38^{v}. Copy in MW's hand continued directly from l. *77* on 58^{v} to l. *78* on 60^{r}, with two intervening leaves left blank for rev. See note to 57^{v}.

56–77ff. Differences from the text on MS. 47, 38^{v}, suggest that another MS., no longer extant, intervenes. Missing leaves 42–43 of MS. 71 probably contained some pre-1813 version of the lines in MS. 70.

64 The rev, in the same pen and ink as MW's copy, is entered in a space left blank.

[59r] [II, 160–178]

As up the vale we journey'd side by side *II, 56*
My Fellow Traveller pointing with his staff *57*
Towards those craggy summits thus made *58*
known
His friendly purpose. "In a spot that lies *59*
Concealed among yon mountain solitude *60*
You will receive before the hour of noon *61*
good
A recompense, I hope for this days toils *62*

16 816
8 7
128 112

There though sequestered he was like myself *68*
9
Sprung from a stock of lowly parentage *69*
Among the wilds of Scotland, in a tract *70*
Where many a sheltered and well- *71*
tended plant
Upon the humblest ground of social life *72*
Doth at this day I trust the blossoms bear *73*
Of piety and simple innocence *74*
His Youth such grateful promises *75*
displayed
20
held forth

[59v] [II, 282–287, 187–193]

D
I do not wish to wrong him though the course *II, 153*
Of private life was sullied & disgraced *154*
By evil actions planted like a crown *155*
Upon the insolent aspiring brow *156*
open
Of spurious notions, worn as signs *157*
Of prejudice subdued he still retained *158*
at length

56ff. Rev of 58v; continued on 60r. Cf. MS. 47, 38r; MS. 71, 38v; and notes to 57v, 58v. Leaves 59r and 59v were left blank when MW continued her copy from 58v directly on 60r.

The multiplication in the center of the page may be an attempt to determine the number of lines that could be entered on seven or eight pages, estimating sixteen lines to a page. Continuous copy, primarily in MW's hand, fills twelve pages including the inside back cover. But approximately four pages in terms of space are given over to rev in one form or another. The line count "9" at ll. *68/69* does not take into account ll. *63–67* on 58v. The line count "20" at the bottom of the page includes ll. *63–67* on 58v.

153–[155] Rev of 62r; rev on 57v. Cf. MS. 47, 38r; MS. 71, missing leaves 42–43 (see notes to 36r, 41r), 41v, 44r, 44v. See notes to 58v, 59r.

Work on this page appears to have begun with l. *88, 89* and the partial line deleted below, "By the," which are in different ink from related lines below and on 60r. Ll. *84–89* are in the same ink as the lines on 60r and appear to have been entered second on the page. Work in MW's hand (ll. *88, 89ff.*) appears to continue directly on 60v. Ll. *153–158* and rev below of 62r are in the hand of WW and revised on 57v; these lines are in different pen and ink from other work on the page and would seem to constitute the third and fourth stages of work on this page.

~~A~~|
T|~~nd now~~ the Preachers office he 158
renounced
I do not wissh to wrong him though the [*153*]
Of private life licentiously [?di] [*154*]
displayed
~~By learning raised above the rest & [?made~~] *88, 89*
Unhallowed actions planted &*c* [*155*]
~~By the~~
Who to the notes of Highland bagpipe~~s~~ *84*
marched
In plaided vest his fellow Country men *85*
t} {e world
This humble station filling to {h}imself *86*
Such}
To the} seemed it to his Comrades & himself *87*
stored with
But ~~raised by~~ learning & by native power *88*
And force of native inclination made *89*
An intellectual Ruler in the haunts *90*
Of social vanity & prompt meanwhile *91*
{To
{In every generous feeling among these *92*
Gay & affecting graceful gaiety *93*

[60r] [II, 181–196, 224–225]

By due scholastic dicipline prepared *II, 78*
Might to the ministry be called which done *79*
Partly through lack of better hopes, and part
~~For want of better hope~~ *80*
[?~~Moved~~] Perhaps incited by a curious mind *81*
[?~~He] went abroad for want of better hope~~ [*80*]
In early life he undertook the charge *82*
spiritual guide & teacher
Of ~~military Chaplain~~ to a band * *83*
to
~~Of Highlander who~~ ^ ~~the Bagpipe marched~~ *84*
Who to the pipes of highland
~~I[?n plai]ded vest his fellow Country men~~ * *85*
~~In learning first in talents far the~~ first *88*
~~An intellectual Ruler in the walks~~ *90*

[*154*] The conjectured "di" is obscured by an ink blot, which may also obscure the last word of the revision l. [*153*], "course."

[*155*] The "&c" may signal resumption of text at l. *155* on 57v, although rev on 59v appears earlier than copy on 57v. Alternately it may refer to a copy of this passage no longer extant.

88, 89ff. Rev of 60r; continued on 60v. Cf. MS. 47, 38r, 38v; MS. 71, missing leaves 42–43, 39r, 39v. See notes to 58v–60r.

78ff. Continued from 58v; continued on top half of 61r; rev on 59v, 60v; cf. MS. 47, 38r, 38v; MS. 71, missing 42–43 (see notes to 36r, 41r), 39r, 39v. See notes to 57v, 58v–59v.

83 The asterisk signals the shift to ll. *84–89* on 59v.

85 The conjectured reading is obscured by an ink blot.

85/88 The asterisk appears to signal the revision of l. *88, 89* on 59v. A period may be obscured by the asterisk and the heavy blotting of the asterisk may be an attempt at del.

~~Of social vanity yet prompt meanwhile~~
To ~~among these~~
~~In every generous feeling~~ [?among th]
~~Gay buoyant less a Pastor with his flock~~
~~Than a Soldier among Soldiers long he~~
roamed
~~Where fortune led but more ambitious~~ aims
~~Opened upon him & more flattering views~~
The Vision that enchanted all mankind
s
Save some few selfi[?] heharts appeared in
fill overflowing France
Him did it ~~rouse~~ to a ~~surpassing~~ joy
n
Who was by [?f] ature fervent to disease

[60v] [II, 194–196, 224–237, 243]

Lax buoyant less a Pastor with his flock
Than a Soldier among Soldiers long he roamed
Where fortune led but more ambitious aims
dazzling
Opened upon him & more ~~flattering~~ views 40
The vision that enchanted all mankind
Save some few selfish hearts appeared in
France
Him did it rouse to a surpassing joy
Who was by Nature fervent to disease
He broke from out his narrow sphere
i repaired
To the great City an empore um then
Of golden expectations & receiving
~~welcome~~
~~From every mind receiving~~ ^ ~~freights~~
Freights every day from a new world of hope
~~Of all that is extravagant in Man~~
Thither he went with popular talents graced
~~And there with popular talents preachd~~
And from the pulpit zealously maintained
~~the cause~~
The cause of Chirst & civil Liberty
Of Christ & ~~of the new born Liberty as one~~

98–101 In different pen and ink. Work here appears to continue on 61r, ll. *102–109*, before breaking off for rev on 61r, 60r, 59v and continuing on 60v, 61r.

94ff. Continued from 59v; rev from 60r, top half of 61r; continued on bottom half of 61r. Cf. MS. 47, 38v, 39r; MS. 71, missing leaves 42–43 (see notes to 36r, 41r), 39v, 40v, 41r. See notes to 57v, 58v–60r.

97 The line count, "40," includes all line rev on 59r, 59v, 60r.

99/100 A mark here (visible in the photograph) is caused by the blotting of the asterisk on 60r.

102–109 Rev from 61r.

As one
And moving to one glorious end. 109
That righteous cause of freedom 110
did we know

[61ʳ] [II, 230–252]

He broke from out his narrow sphere II, 102
repaired
~~*Repaired to the gr*~~
an emporium then
To the great City ~~*fountain*~~ *at that time* 103
Of all that is extravagant in Man
Of schemes and notions & extravagant hopes
~~*And there*~~
From every wind ~~that blew~~ receiving
[?welcome] freights
Of all that is extravagant in man,
And there with popular talents 107
preach'd the cause
Of Christ and of the new-born Liberty 108
As one, and leading to one glorious 109

Combine for one hostility as friends 111
Etherial Natures & the worst of Slaves 112
by rival
Was served ~~*as seemed by*~~ *advocates that* 113
came
From regions opposite as heaven & hell 114
One courage seemed to animate them all 115
flattering Conquests ~~rapid wide-spread~~
And from the ~~*flattering*~~ ∧ *conquests daily* 116
[?*60*] *gained*
did arise
By their united efforts ~~*sprang a faith*~~ 117
A proud & most presumptuous confidence 118
In the transcendant wisdom of the age 119
And its discernment not alone in rights 120

[61ᵛ] [II, 253–266]

And in the origin & bounds of power II, 121
Social and temporal but in nature's laws 122

109/110 MS. 70 omits, possibly inadvertently, four lines from MS. 47 that are included in MS. 71 and later versions as *1814*, ll. 238–241.
110 Continued on bottom of 61ʳ.

102ff. Cf. MS. 47, 38ᵛ, 39ʳ; MS. 71, missing leaves 42–43 (see notes to 36ʳ, 41ʳ), 40ᵛ, 41ʳ. See note to MS. 70, 57ᵛ.
102–109 Continued from 60ʳ; rev on 60ᵛ.
111ff. Continued from 60ᵛ.

121ff. Cf. MS. 47, 39ʳ; MS. 71, missing leaves 42–43 (see notes to 36ʳ, 41ʳ), 41ʳ, 41ᵛ, 44ʳ, 112ᵛ. See note to MS. 70, 57ᵛ.

And in the eternal government of things
Religion's high immunities the grants
Of faith to chosen lands vouchsafed or
those
By Deity committed to the heart
Oer the wide plain of universal earth
Man's spiritual hopes dependencies & needs
trust , [?&] [?*by*]
An overweening ~~confidence~~ was raised
C *alike* *fear*
~~That~~ c|*ast out*^ *fear of person & of thing*
~~In well intentioned minds to action raised.~~
from this *bane*
Plague ~~followed~~ union spread whose subtile ^
[?~~*band*~~]
The strongest did not easily escape
And he what wonder took a mortal taint
An infidel contempt of sacred truth
Stole by degrees upon his mind & hence
For him & for his individual harm 80
Life like that Roman Janus double-faced

[62ʳ] [II, 267–295]

s
Vilest hypocri|*cy the laughing gay*
fear
Hypocricy not leagued with |*pride but pride*
Smooth words he had to wheedle simple souls
But for disciples of the inner school
Old freedom was old servitude & he
s *ped*
The wisest whose opinion| *too*|[?*k*] *the least*
To tried authority & known restraints
Whose creed with sorrow be it said
Did in the light of false philosophy
Spread like a halo round a misty moon
Widening its circle as the storms advaned
Tur back [?~~page~~] [?] D
~~I do not wish to wrong him for his heart~~
he
~~Was generously disposed & still~~ retained
~~In midst~~ of
Mid such debasement what he had receivd
From Nature an intense & glowing mind
And when the strength of liberty decayed
And mortal sickness on her face appeared
He coloured objects to his own desire

124–128 Om in the consecutive text of MS. 71, 41ʳ and *1814*, but copied at the end of MS. 71, 112ᵛ.

136/137 The line count, "80," includes all line rev on 60ᵛ, 61ʳ, 61ᵛ.

138ff. Rev on 59ᵛ, 57ᵛ. Cf. MS. 47, 39ʳ, 39ᵛ, 40ᵛ; MS. 71, 41ᵛ, 44ʳ, 44ᵛ. See note to MS. 70, 57ᵛ.

148/153 The conjectured instruction, "Tur back [?page]," signals the rev on 59ᵛ, 57ᵛ.

As with a Lovers passion yet his moods 100
Of pain were keen as those of better Men
And keener as his fortitude was less

[62ᵛ] [II, 296–316]

worse
And he continued when ~~worst~~ days were
come
To deal about his sparkling eloquence
Struggling against the strange reverse with
zeal
That showed like happiness but in despite
Of all this outside bravery within
He neither felt encouragement nor hope
dignity
For moral ~~fortitude~~ & strength of mind
Were wanting & simplicity of life
And reverence for himself & last & best
Confiding thoughts & love & fear of him
Before whose sight the troubles of the
world
in a
Are vain as billows ~~of the~~ tossing Sea
The glory of the times fading away
The splendour which had given a festal
air
To self importance hallowed it & veiled
therewith
From ~~sight of~~ his own eyes this gone he lost
All joy in human nature was consumed
And vexed & chased by levity & spleen 120
And fruitless indignation galled by pride
Made desperate by contempt of men
who {throve / gained}
Before his sight in power or fame & ~~gained~~ won

164/165 The line count, "100," does not include the rev on 59ᵛ, 57ᵛ.

167ff. Cf. MS. 47, 39ᵛ, 40ʳ; MS. 71, 44ᵛ, 45ʳ. See note to MS. 70, 57ᵛ.

186/187 "Si mihi, si liceat," the opening line of the Latin poem copied on 1ʳ, is entered inverted in the hand of DW. See note to inside front cover.

184/185 The line count, "120," is continued directly from 62ʳ.

[inside back cover] [II, 317–340]

Without desert what he desired weak men
Too weak even for his envy or his hate
And thus beset & finding in himself
Nor pleasure nor tranquillity at last
After a wandering course of discontent
In foreign lands & inwardly oppressed
With malady in part I fear provoked
By weariness of life he fixed his home,
Or rather say sate down by very chance
Among these rugged hills where now he dwells
And wastes the sad remainter of his hours
In self-indulging spleen that doth not want
Its own voluptuousness on this resolved
With this content that he will live & die
Forgotten, at safe distance from a world
Not moving to his mind.
These serious words
{*e* 14
Closed th{*ese preparatory notices* ~~*wi*~~
With which my fellow Traveller had beguiled
The way while we advanced up that wide vale
Now suddenly upturning he began
To climb upon one side of it a ridge
A rough & pathless ridge of steep ascent
As if the object of his quest had been
Some secret 147

188ff. Cf. MS. 47, 40ʳ, 34ʳ; MS. 71, 45ʳ, 45ᵛ, 46ʳ. See note to MS. 70, 57ᵛ. MS. 70 expands the MS. 47 material in some significant ways. Since this page is entirely fair copy, an intervening manuscript, no longer extant, must have been in use.

203/211 The first "14" is an aborted line count; "147" at the foot of the page continues directly from the last line count on 62ᵛ. See note to 59ʳ.

204 Del by eras.

211 WW's inverted signature appears at the bottom of the page, probably entered before most, if not all, of the notebook was used for composition.

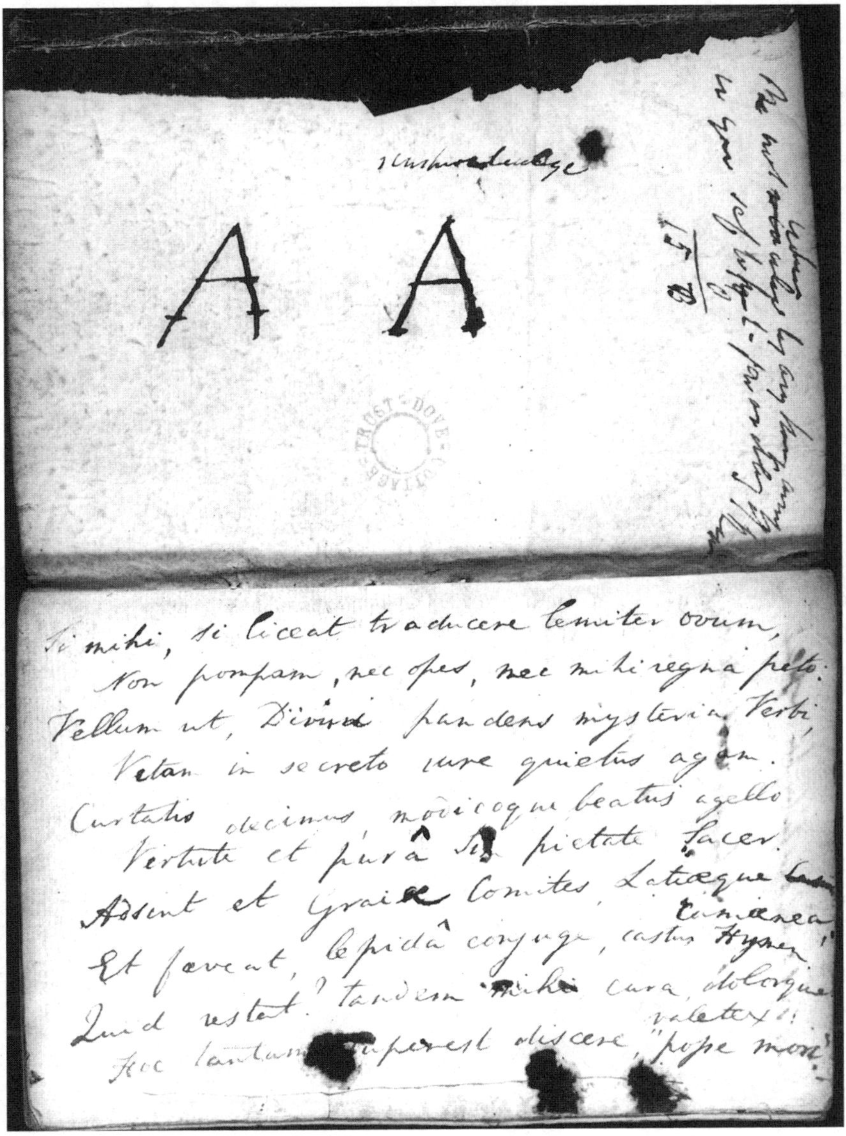

A A

Te mihi, si liceat traducere leniter aevum,
Non pompam, nec opes, nec mihi regna peto.
Vellem ut, Divinae pandens mysteria Verbi,
Vitam in secreto rure quietus agam.
Curtatis decimis modicoque beatus agello
Virtute et purâ sim pietate sacer.
Adsint et Gratiae Comites, Latiaeque Camaenae
Et faveat, lepidâ conjuge, castus Hymen!
Quid restat? tandem mihi cura, doloque valete!!
Hoc tantum superest discere, "pope mori".

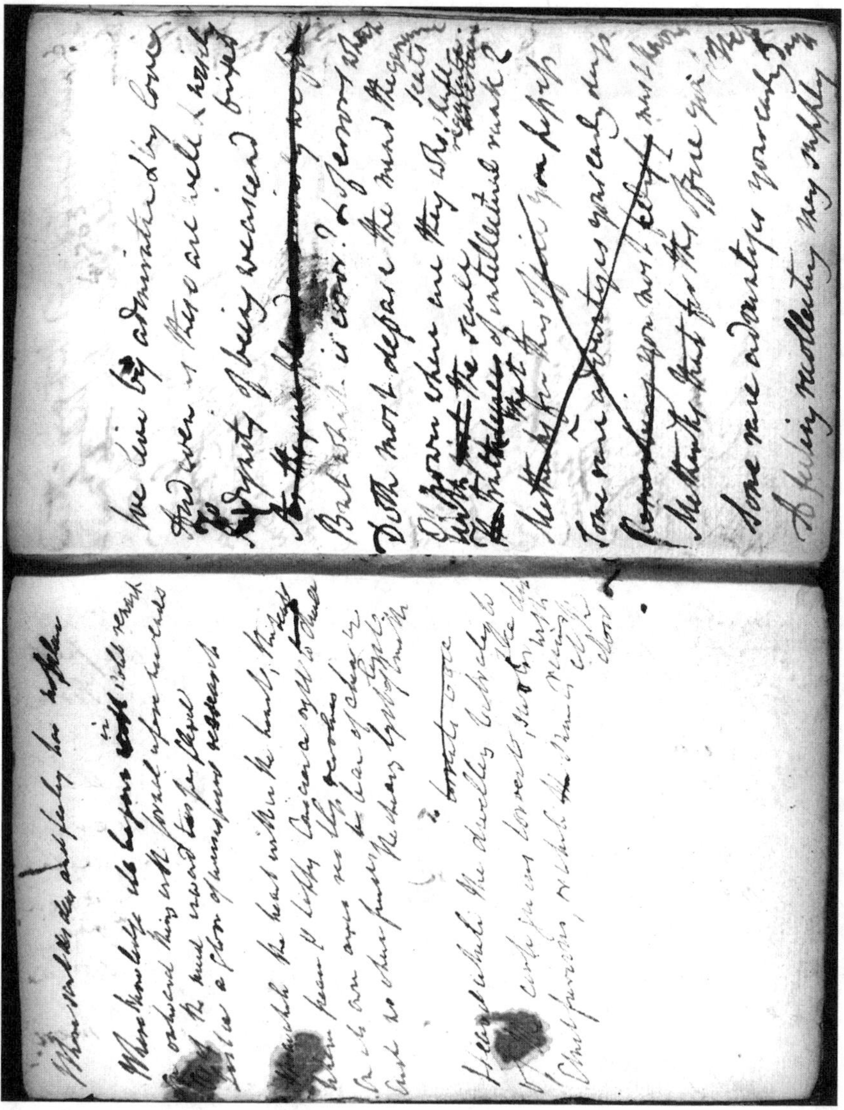

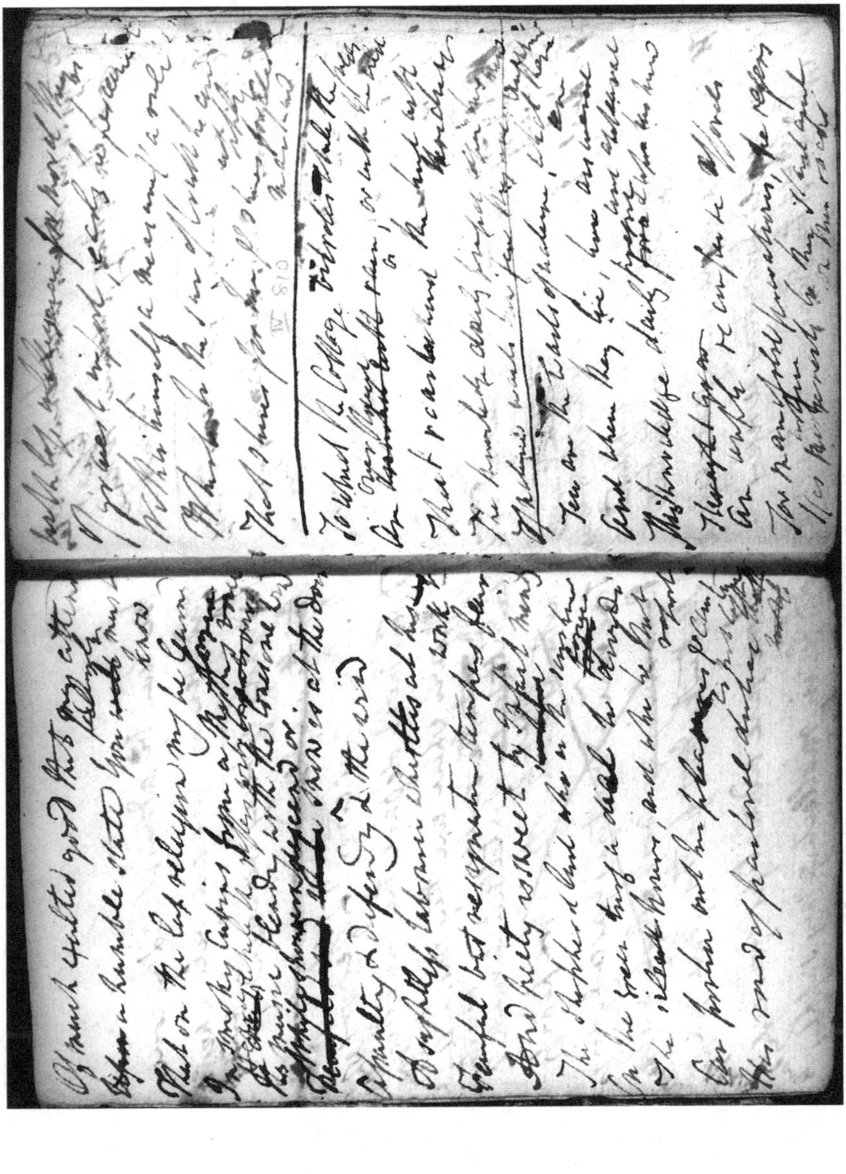

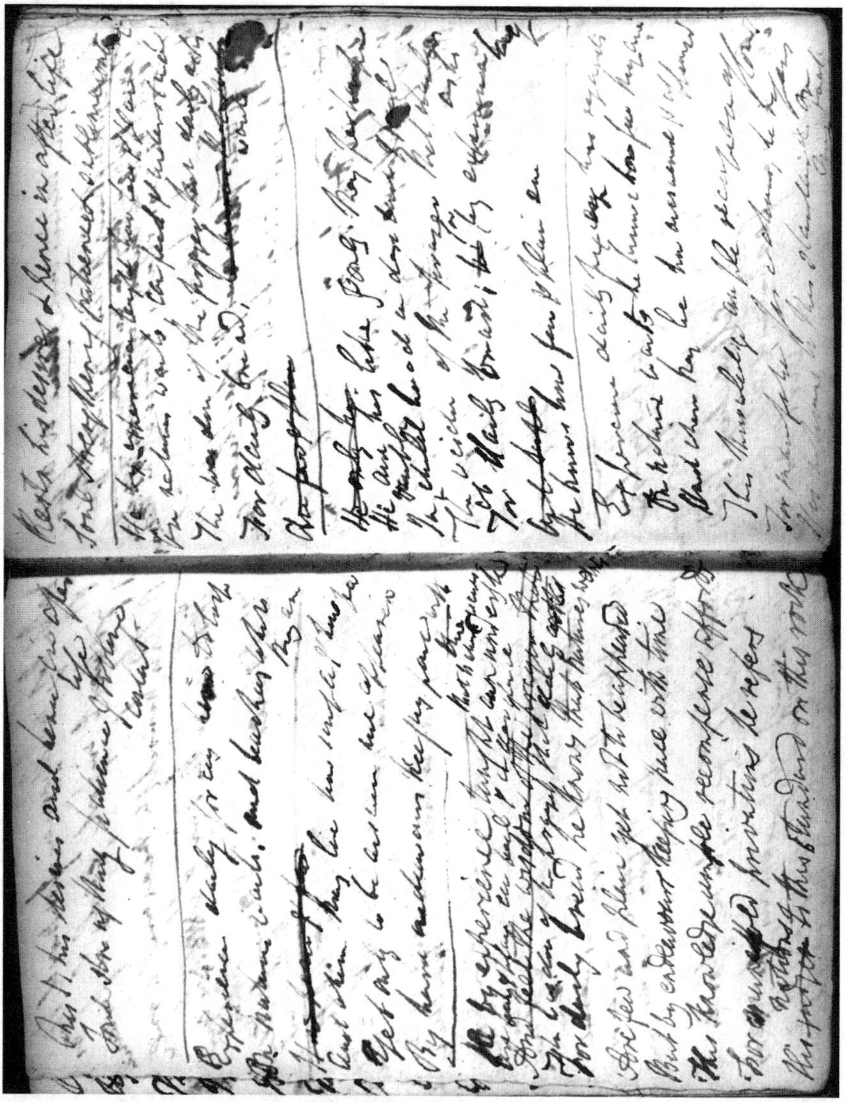

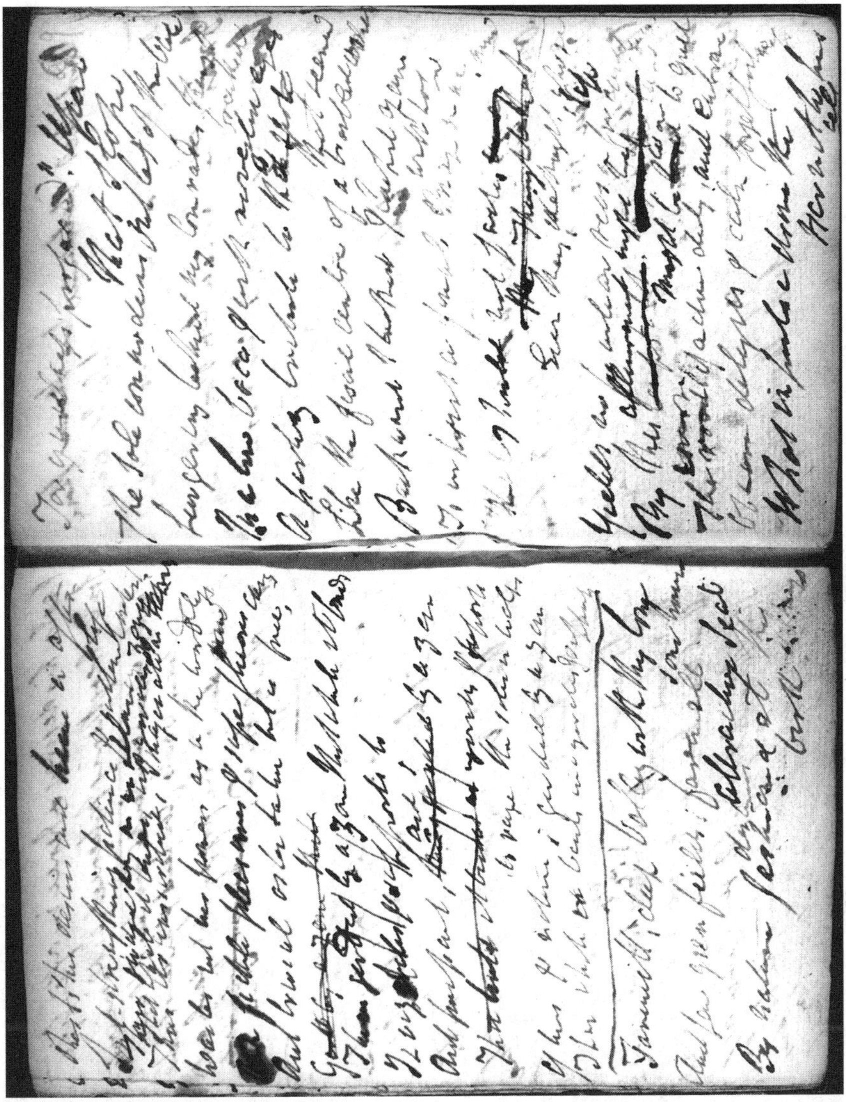

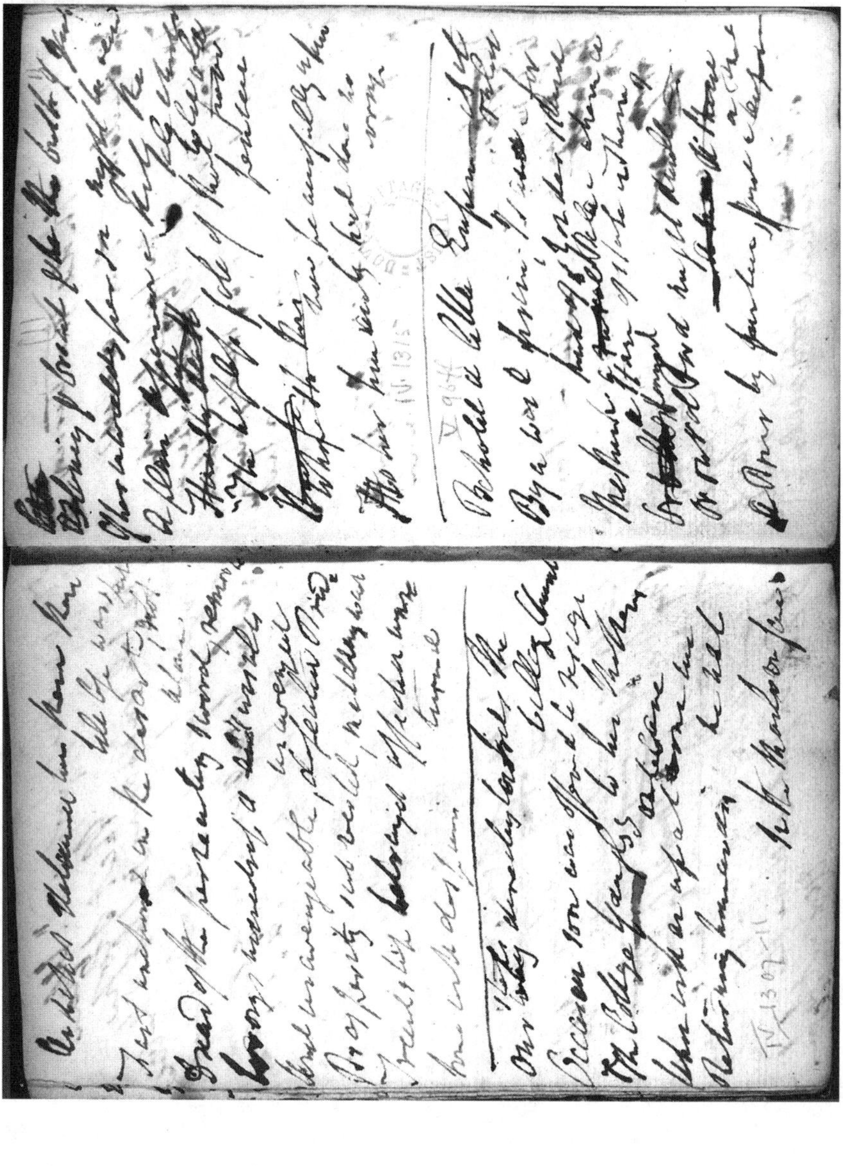

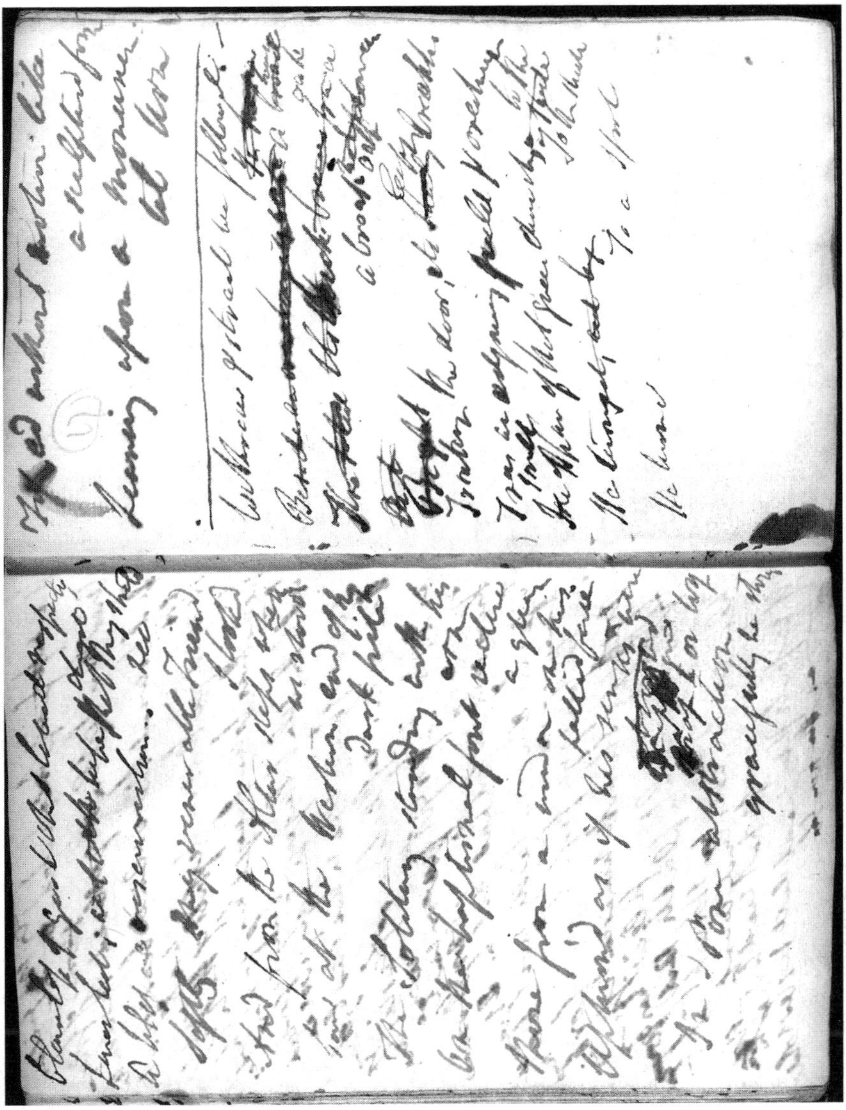

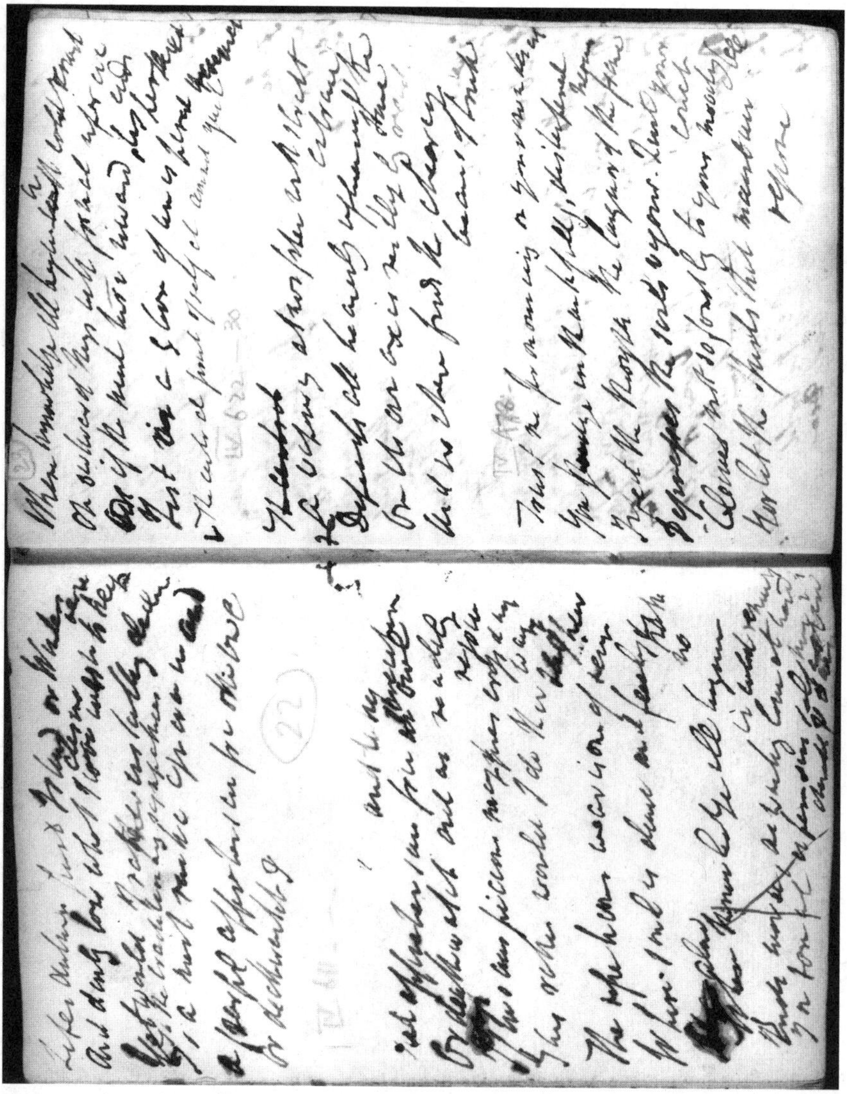

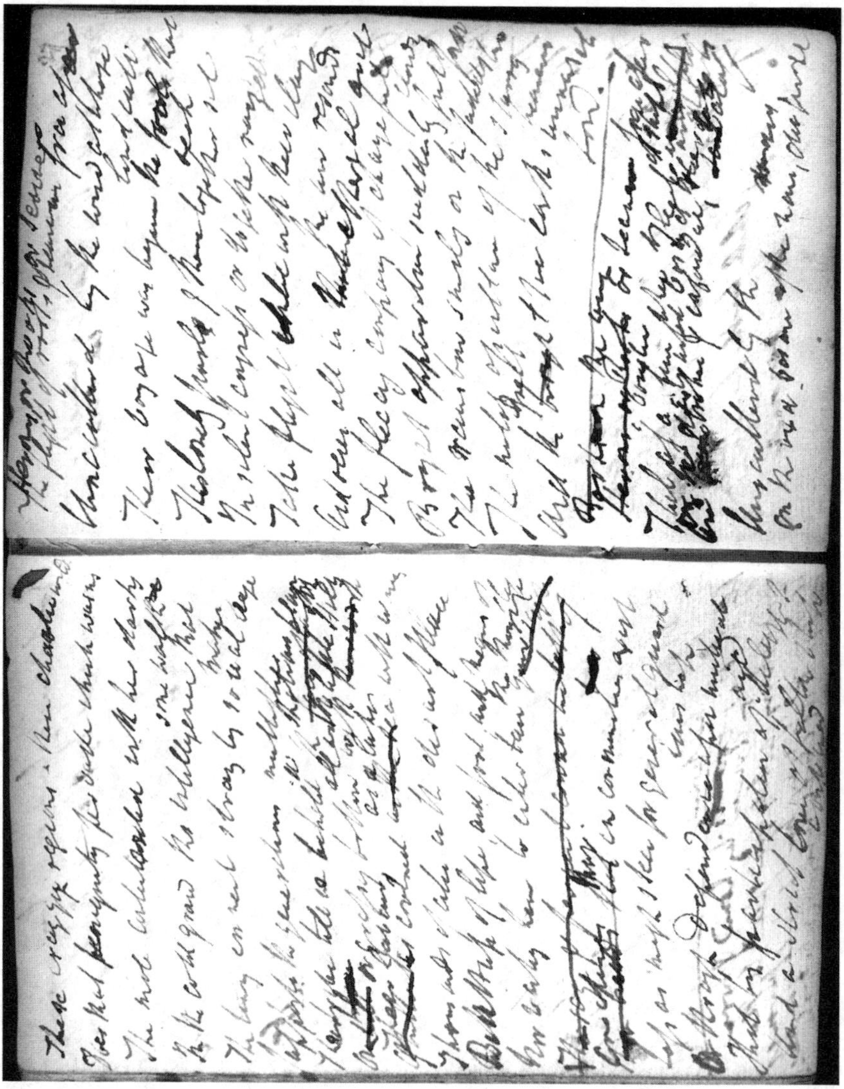

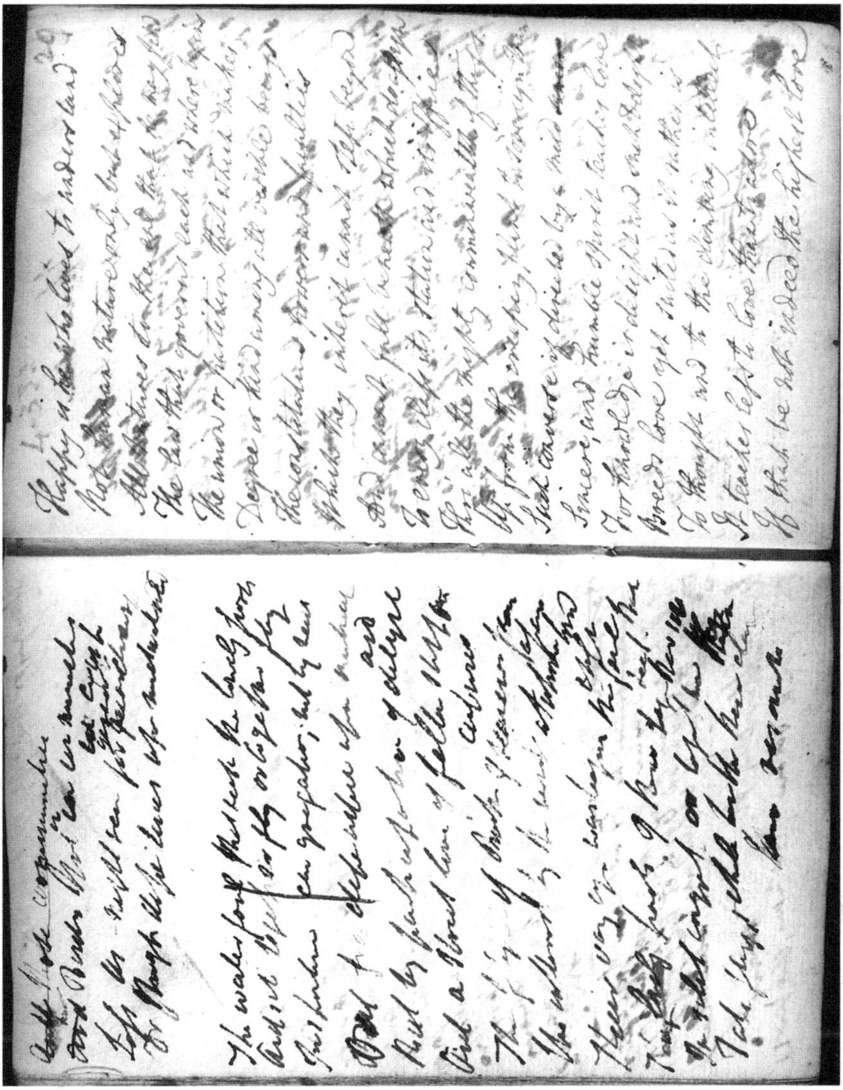

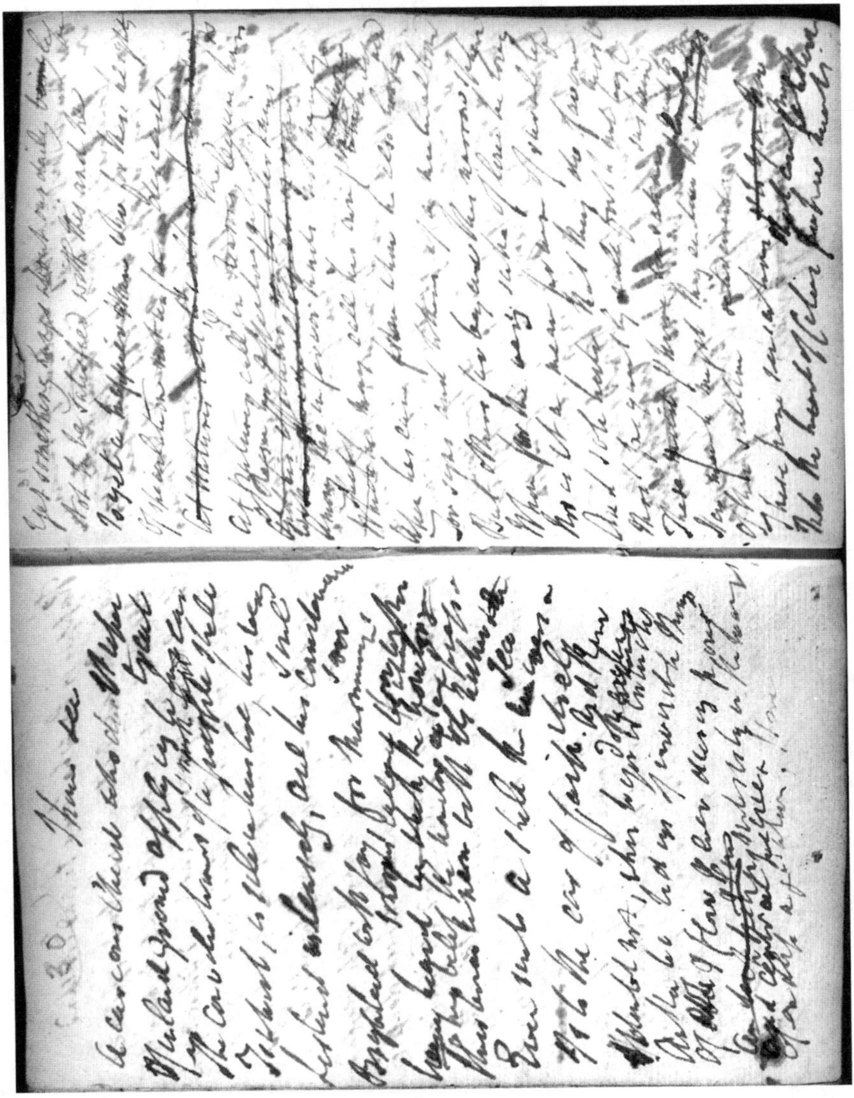

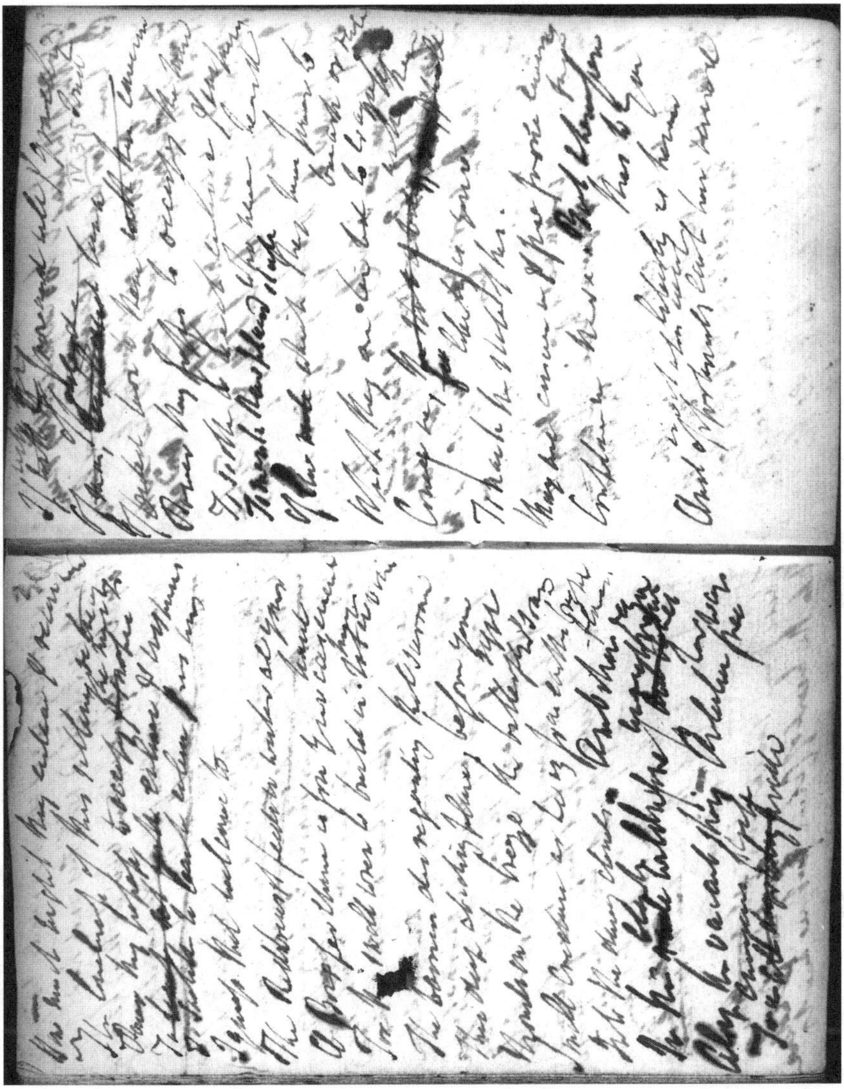

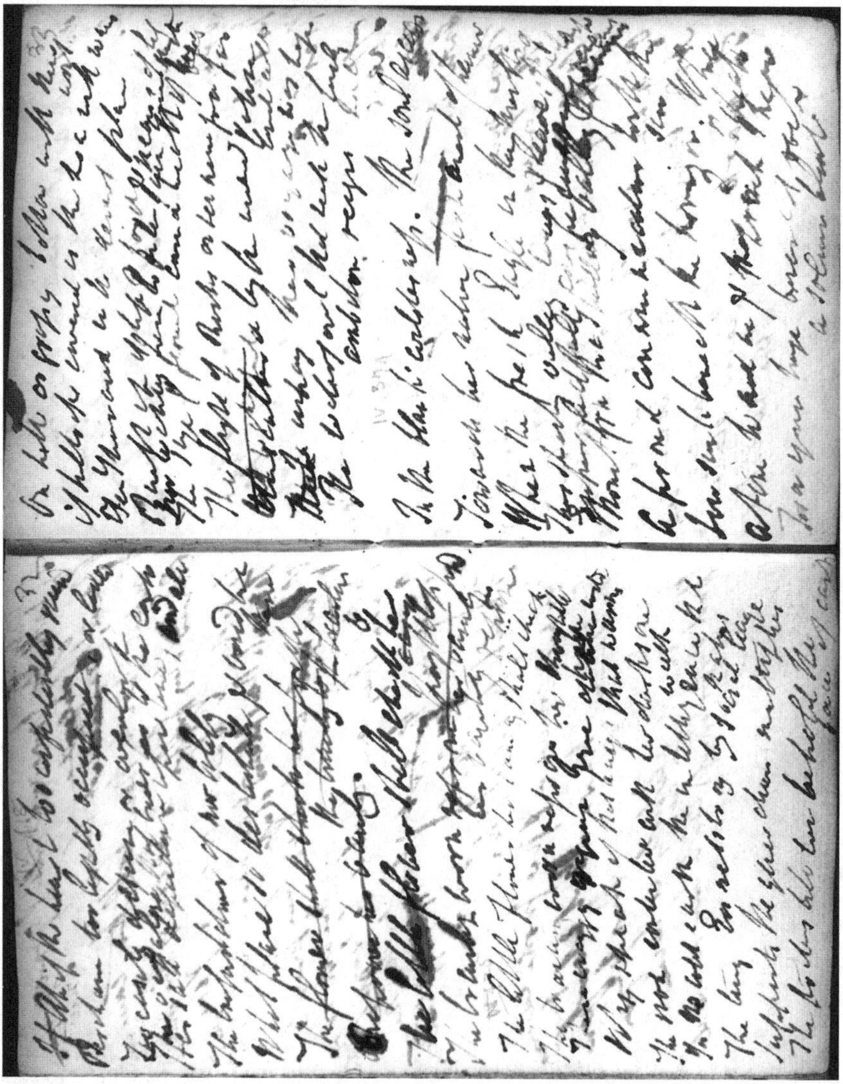

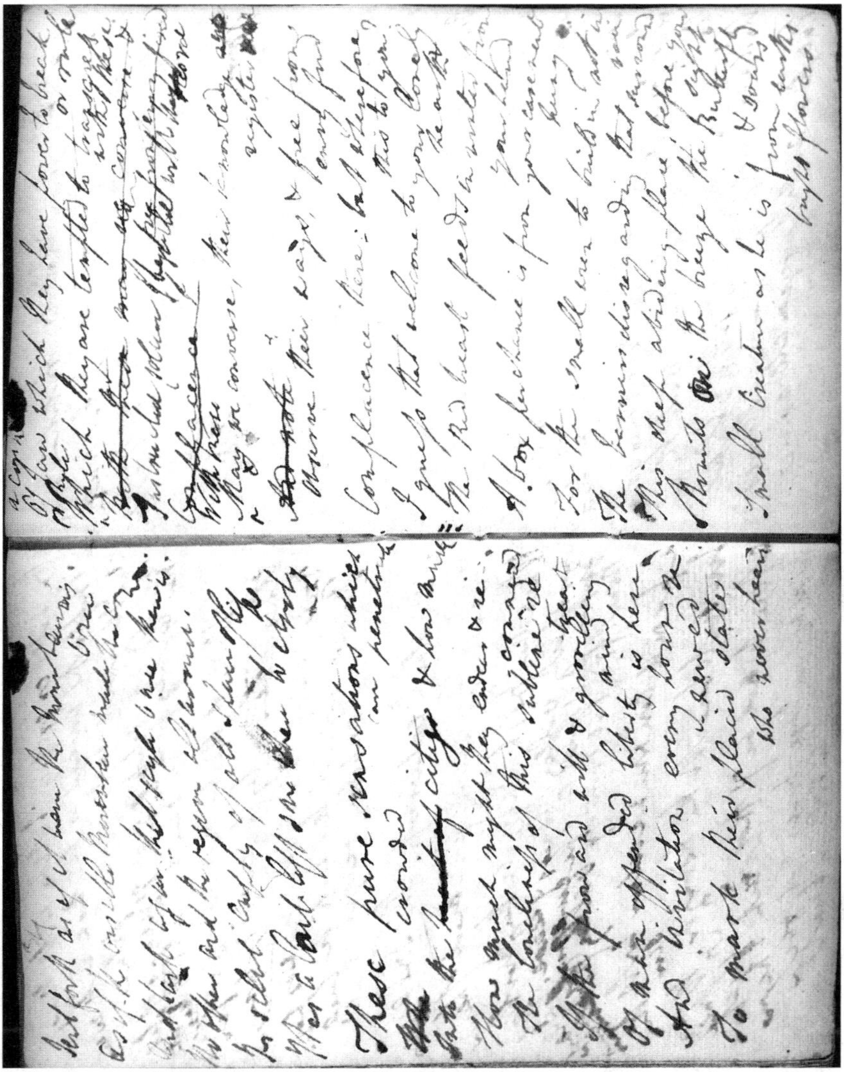

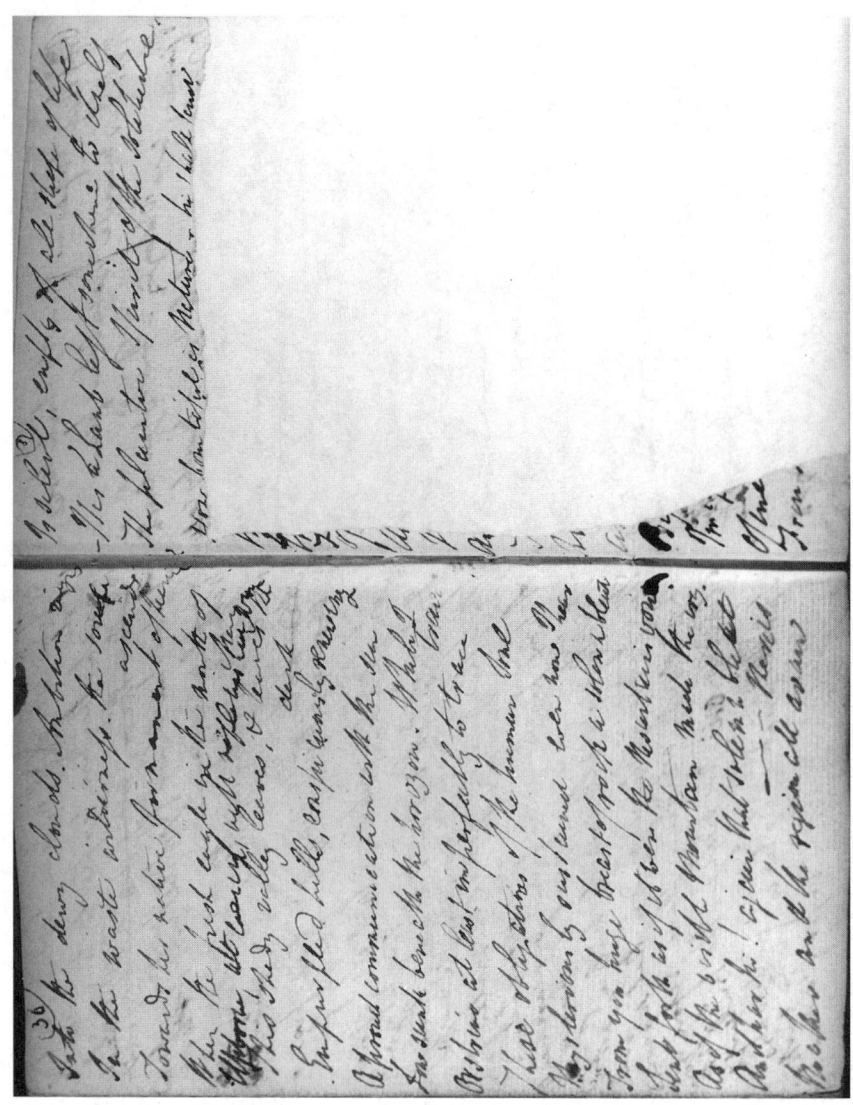

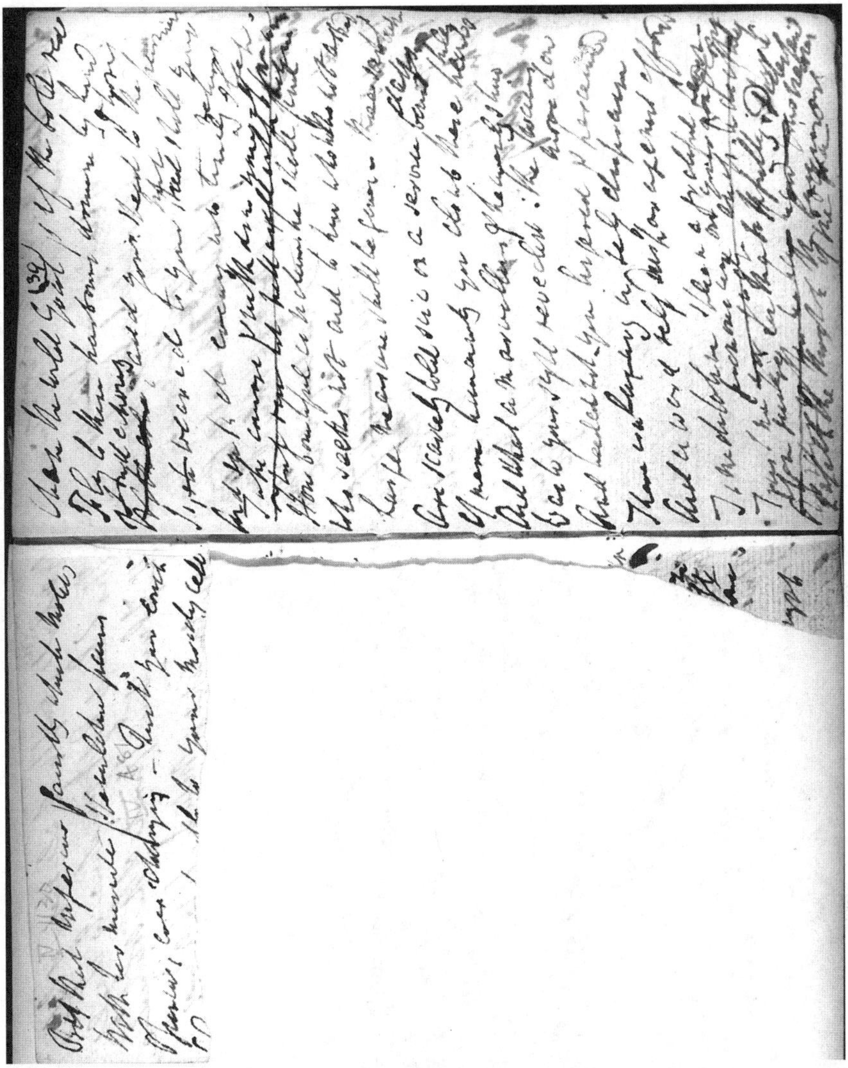

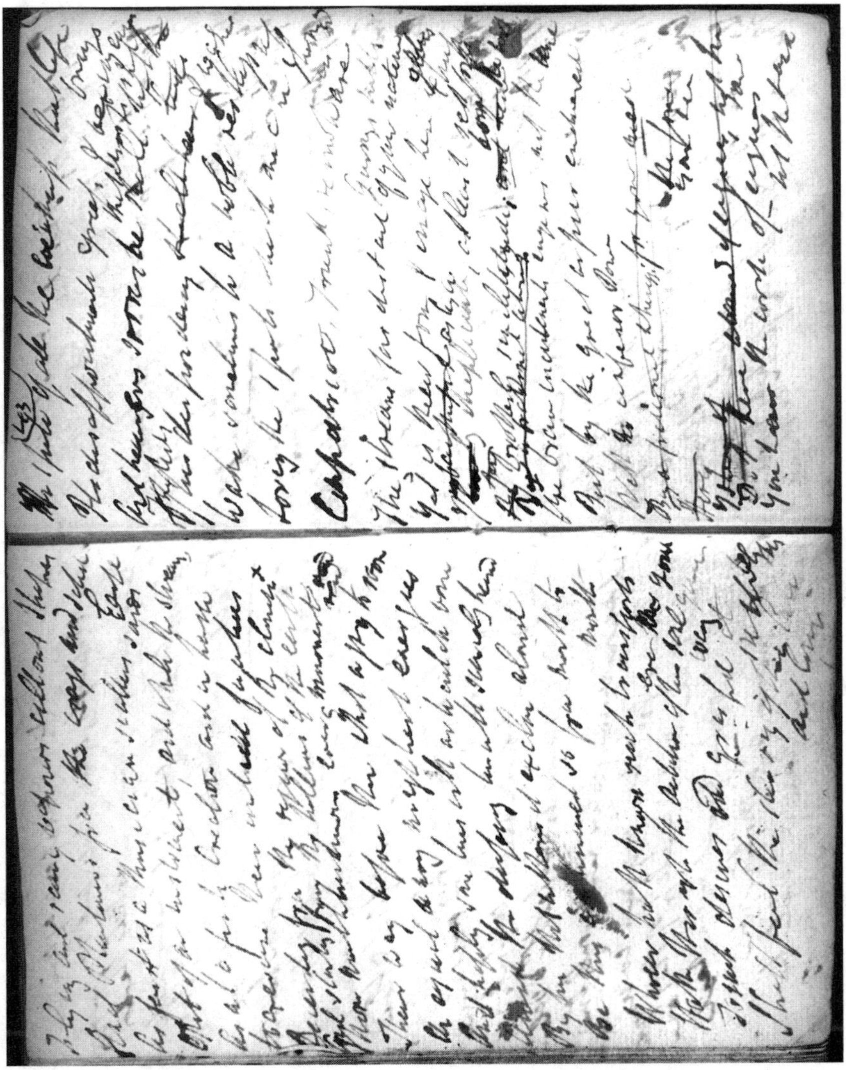

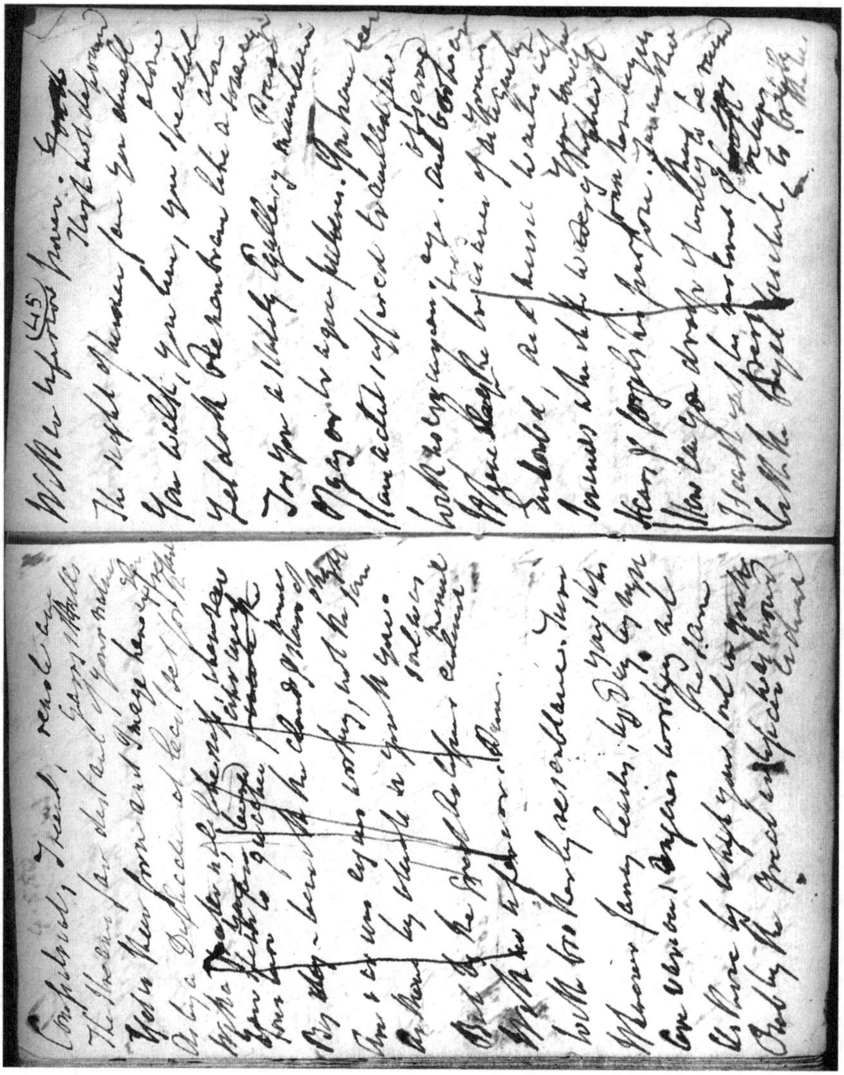

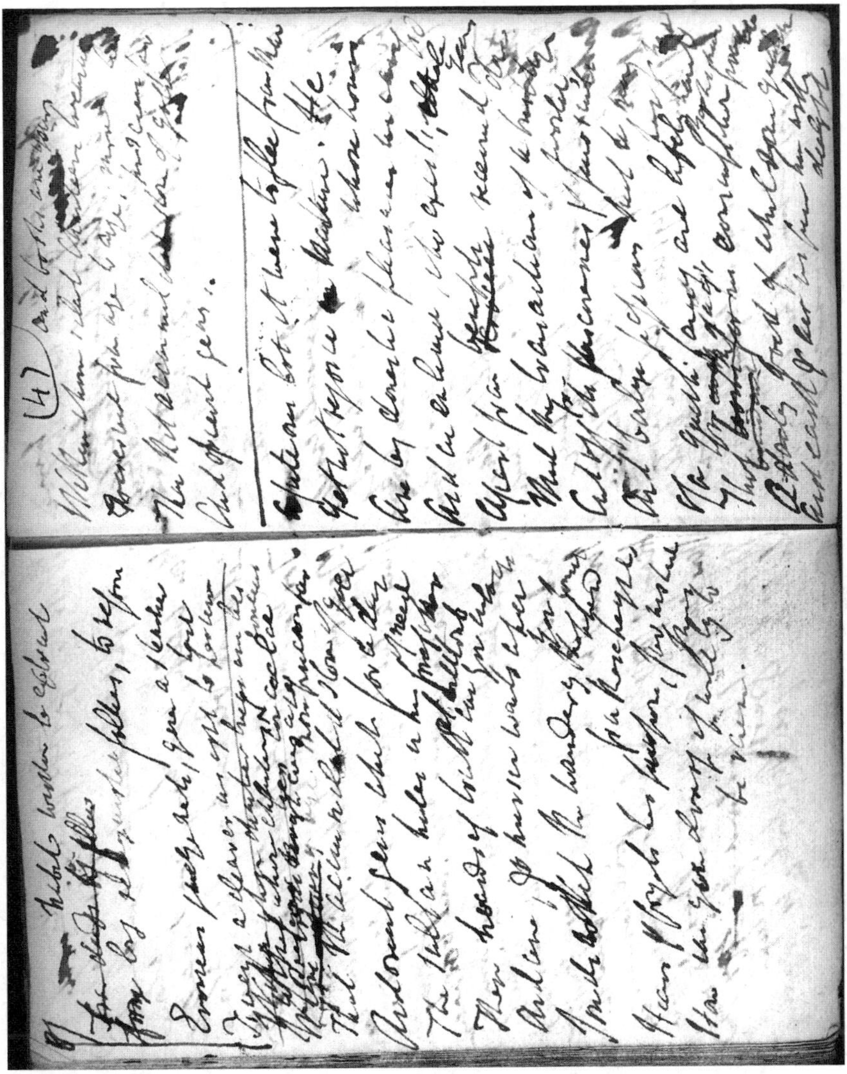

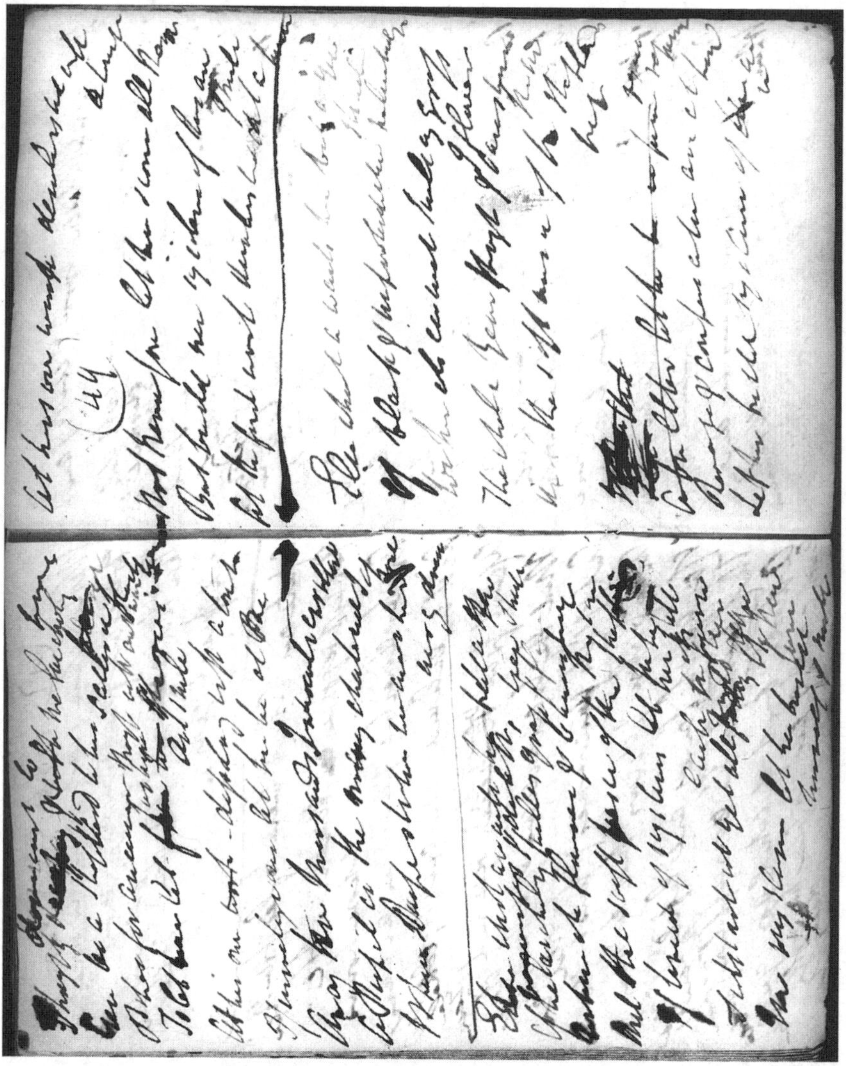

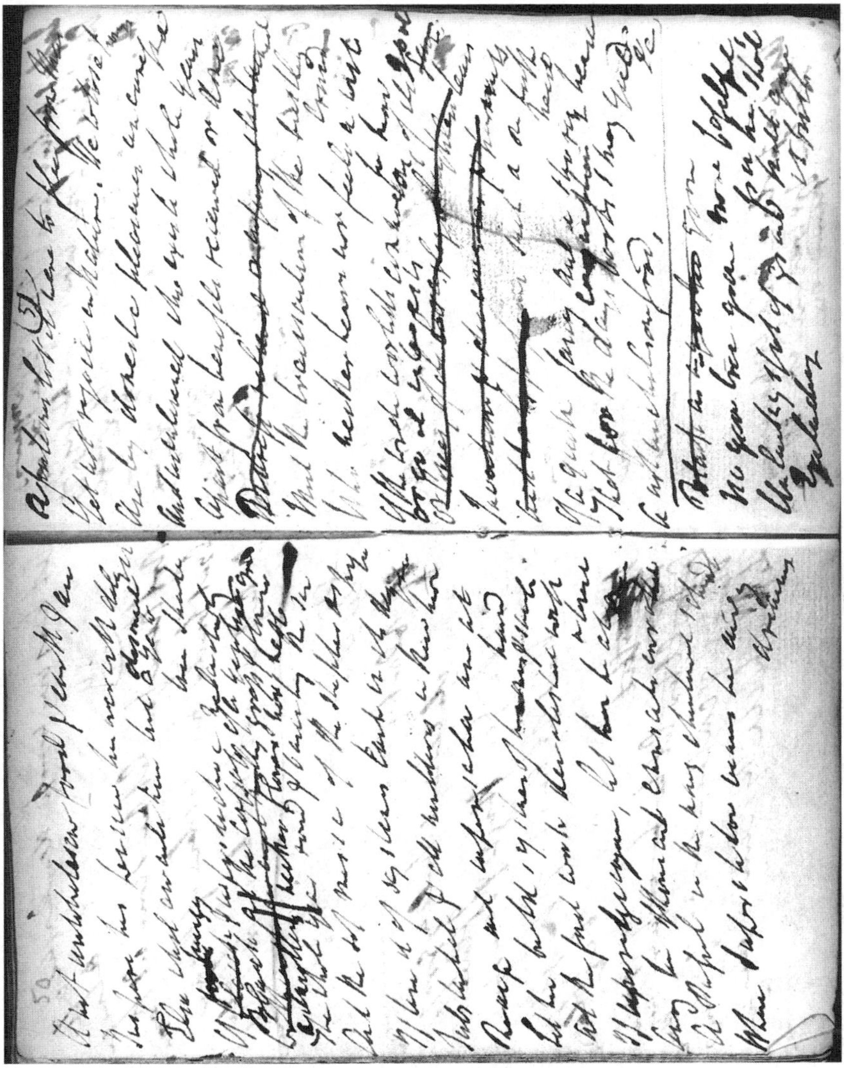

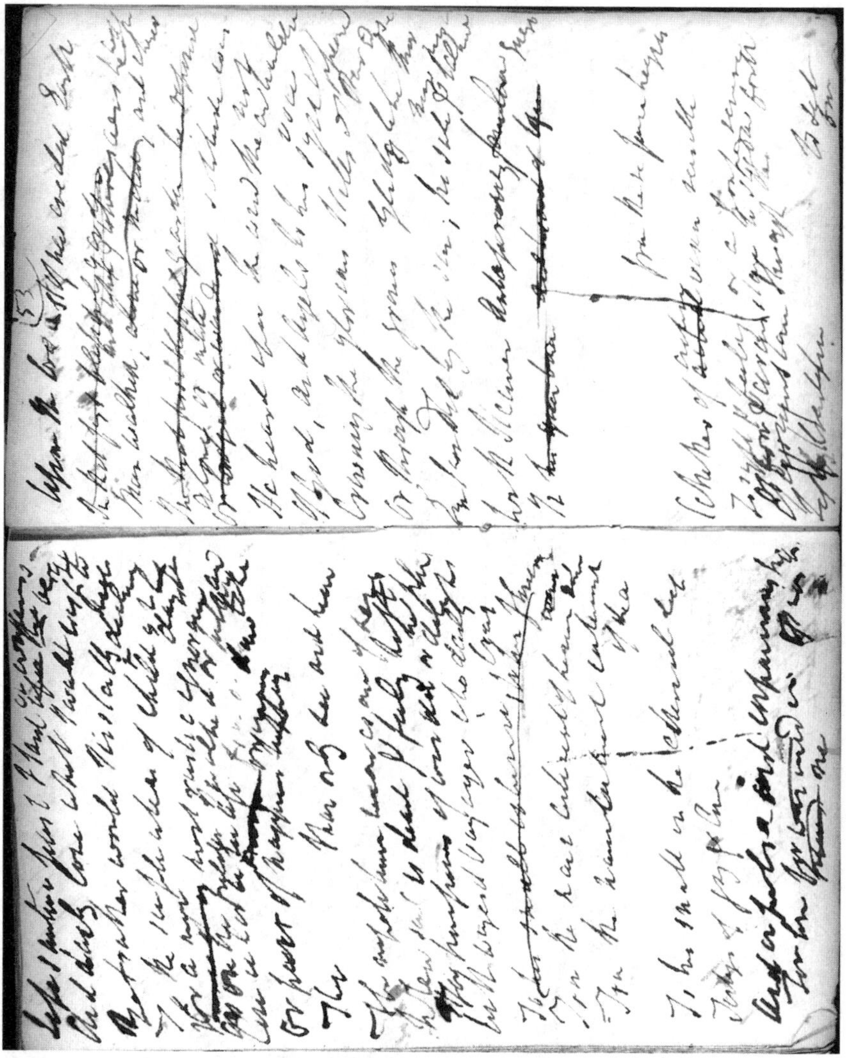

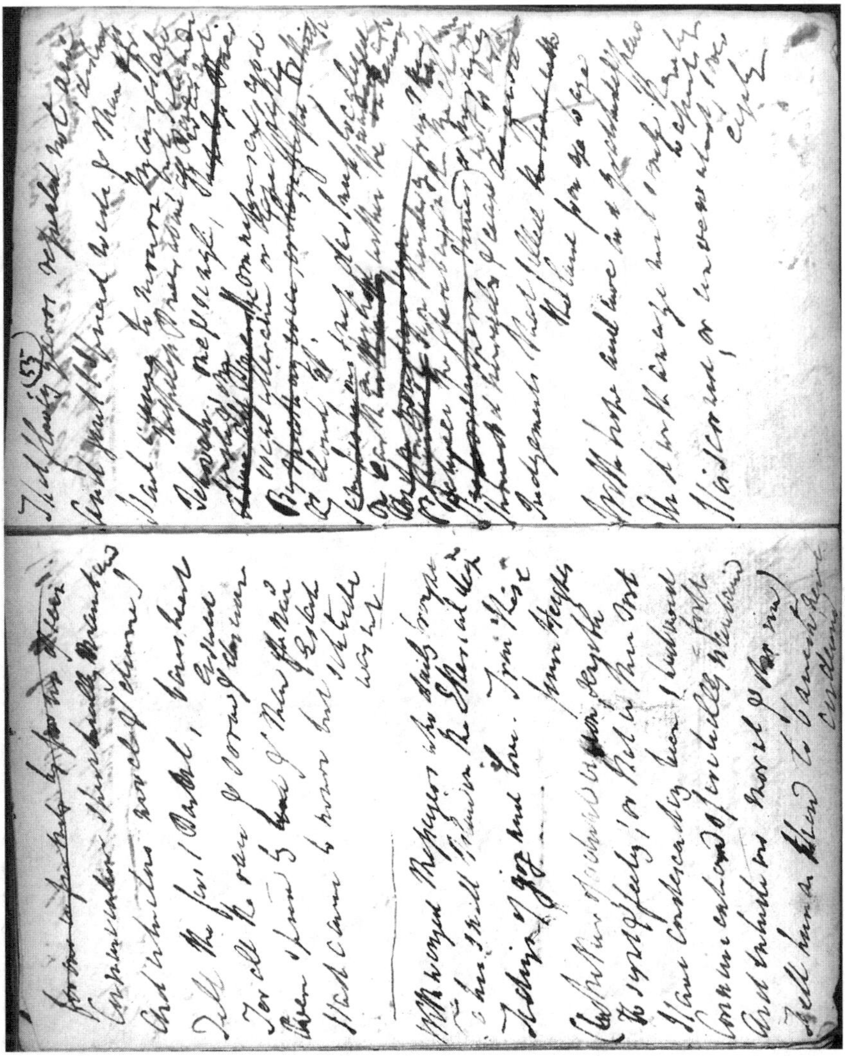

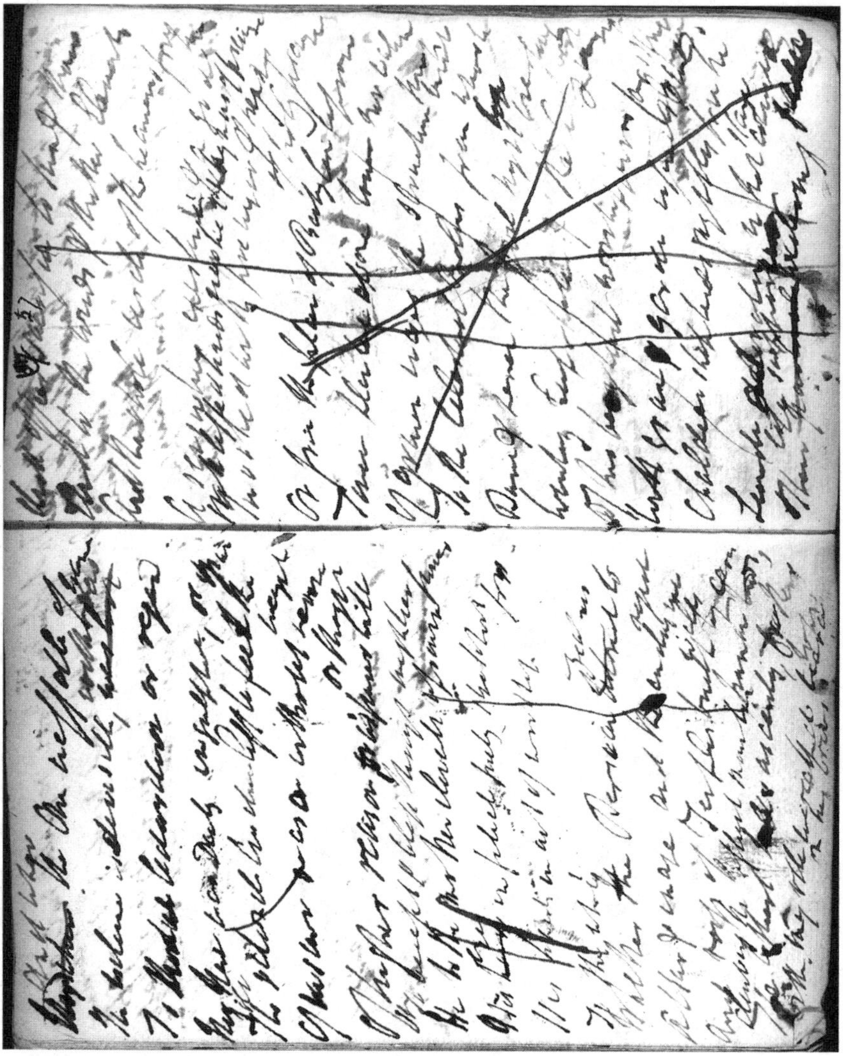

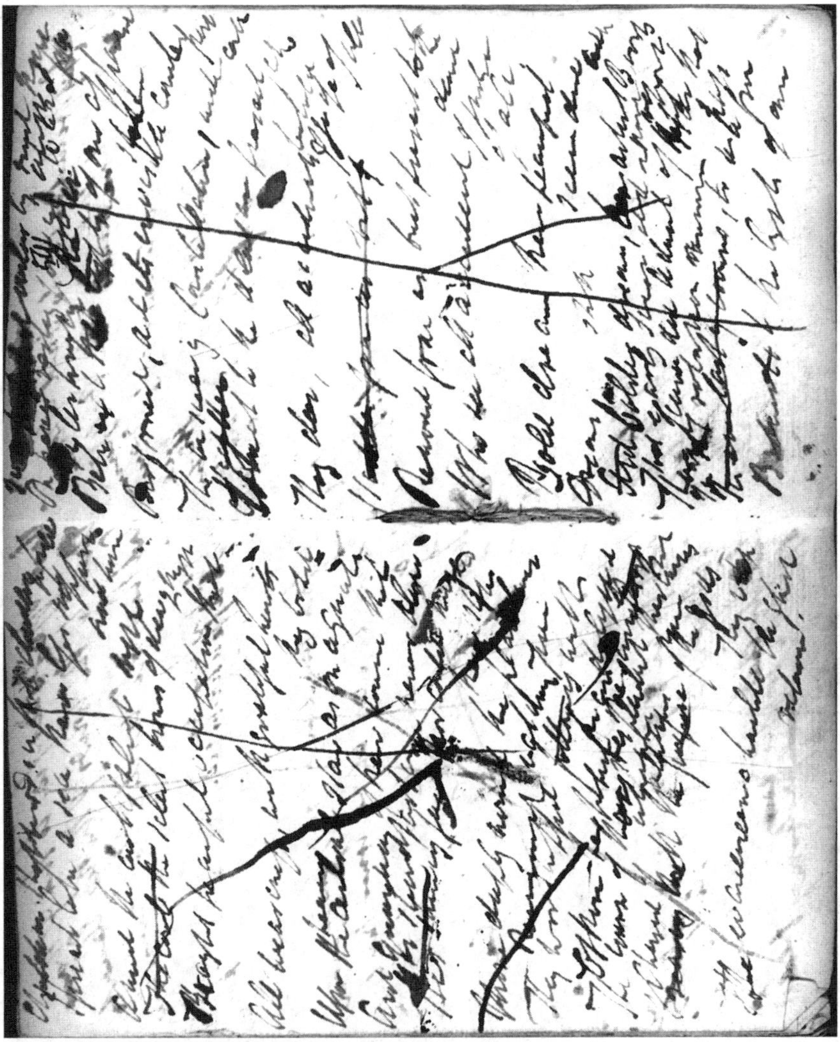

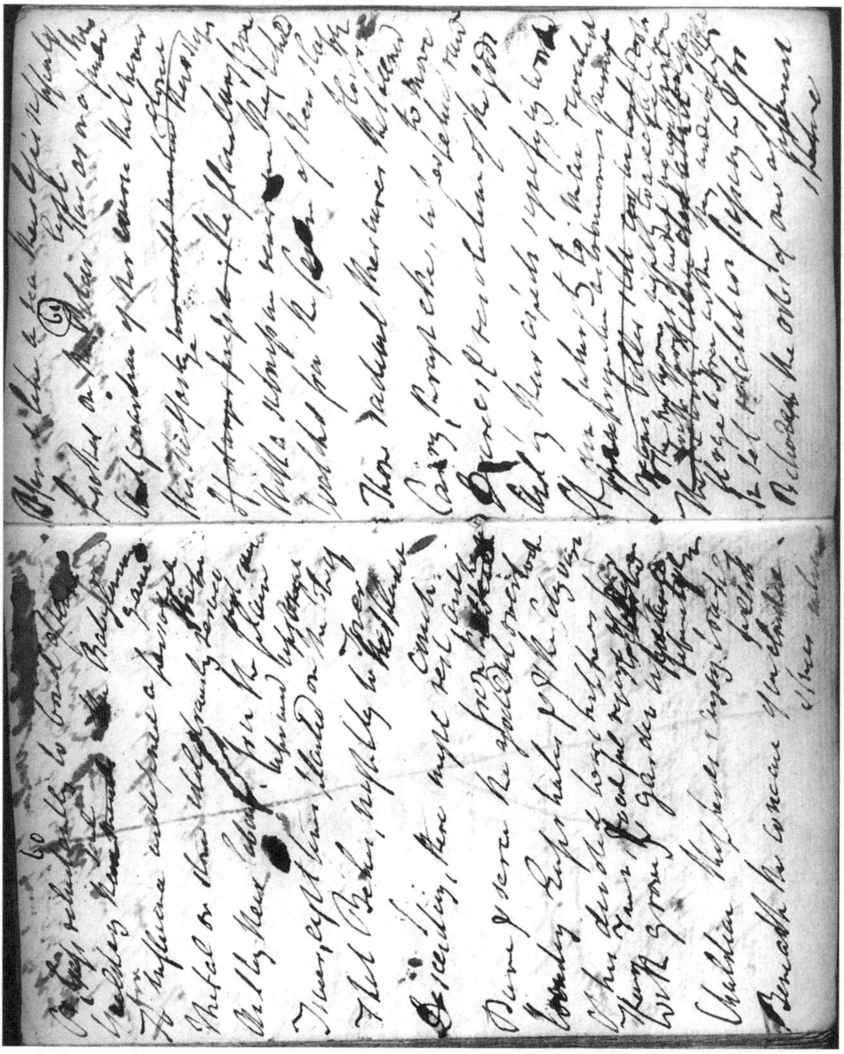

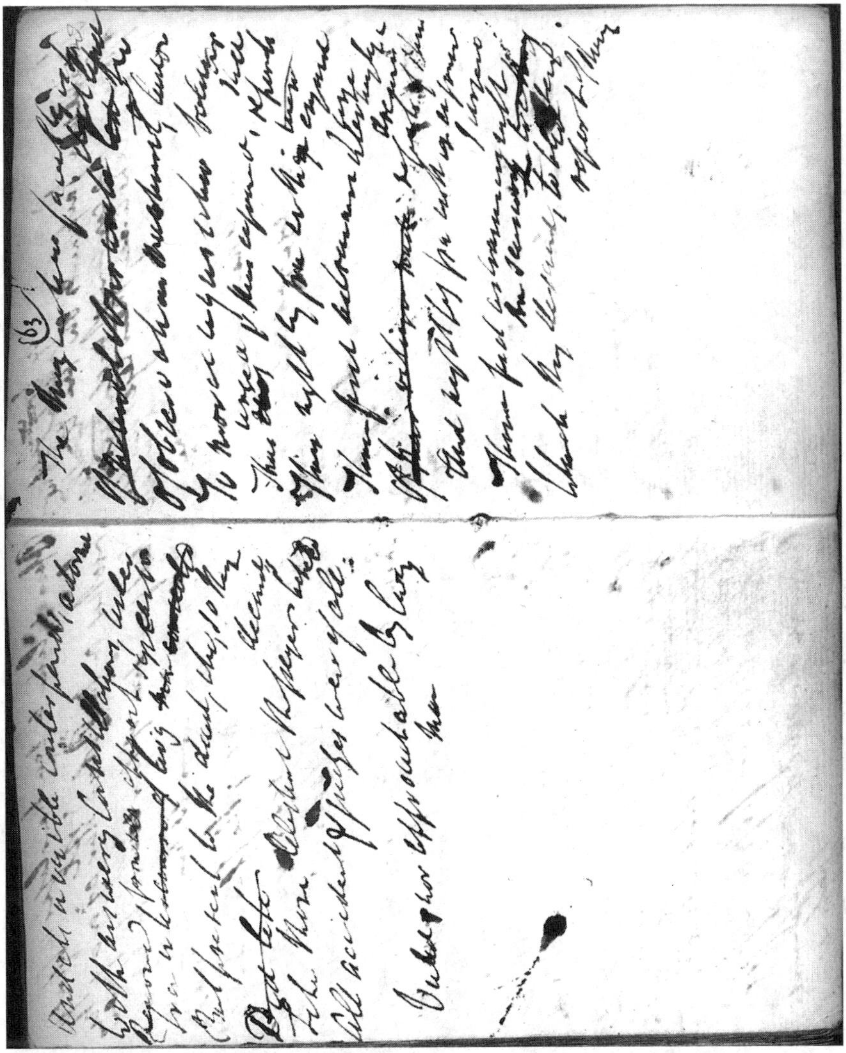

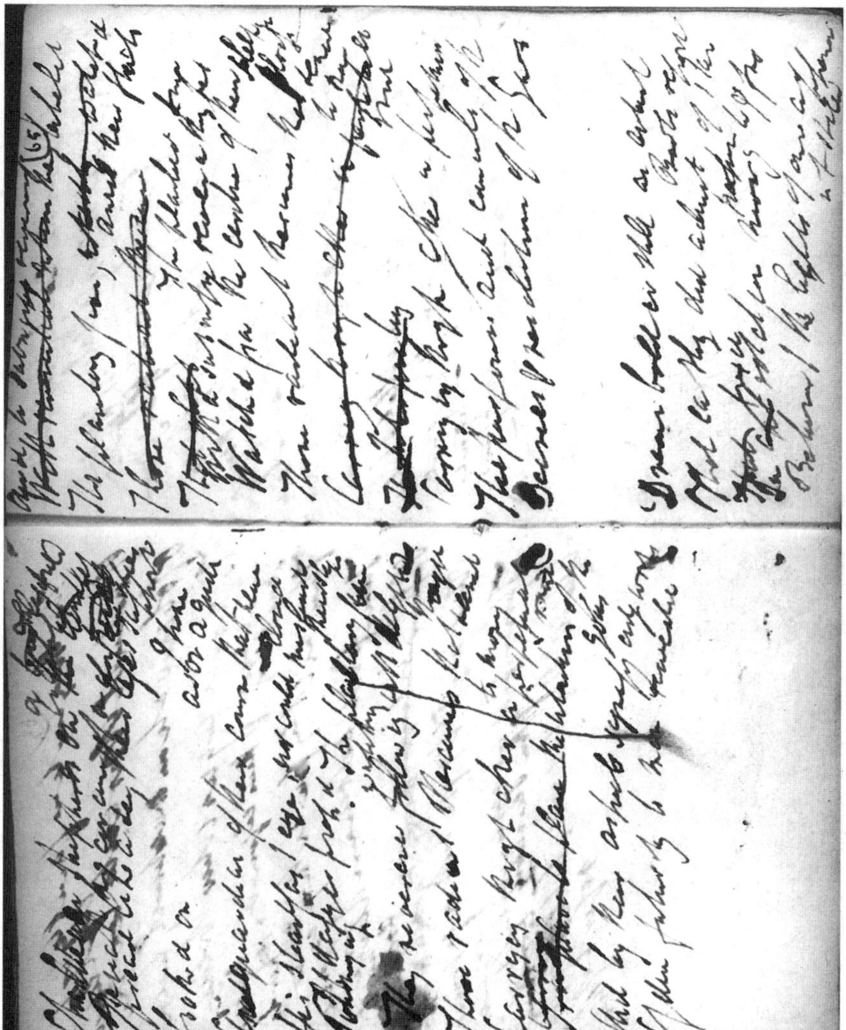

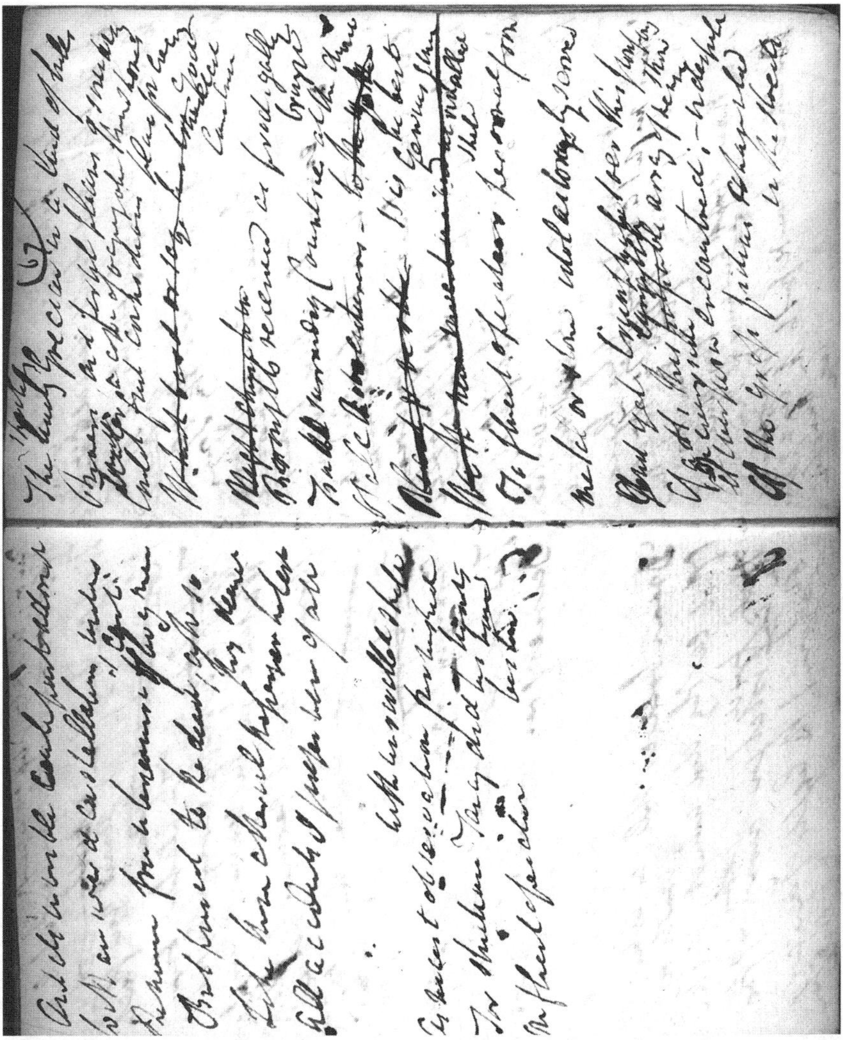

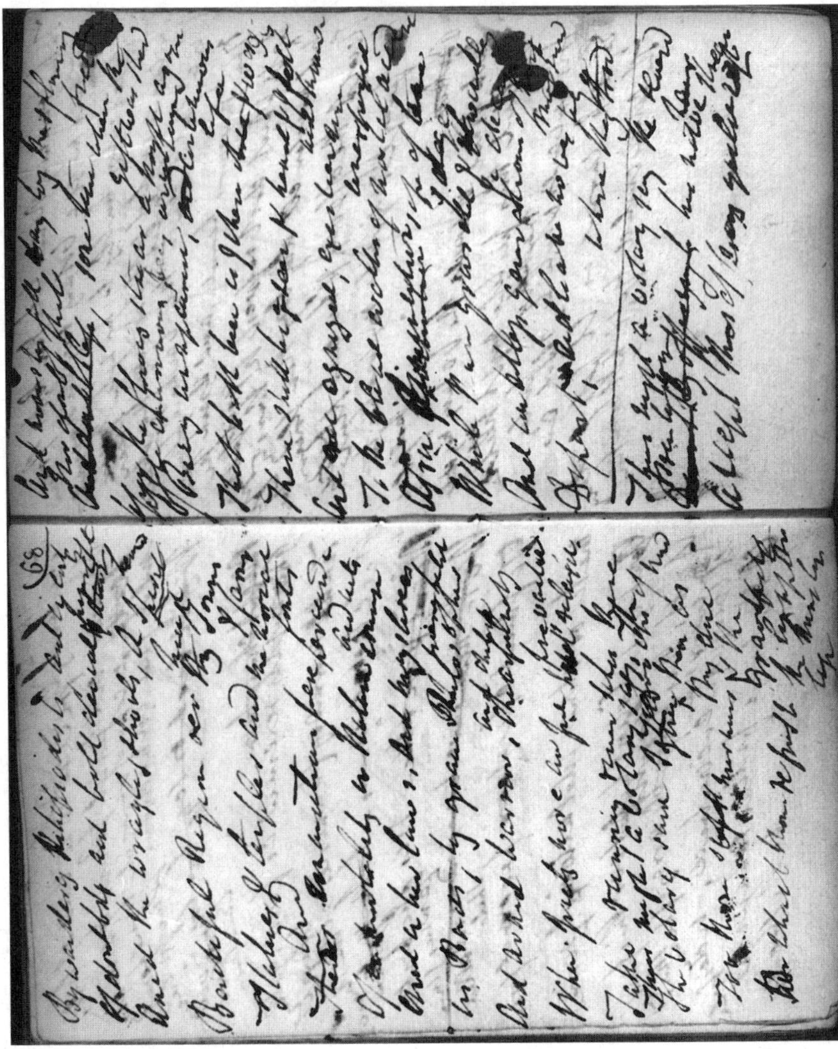

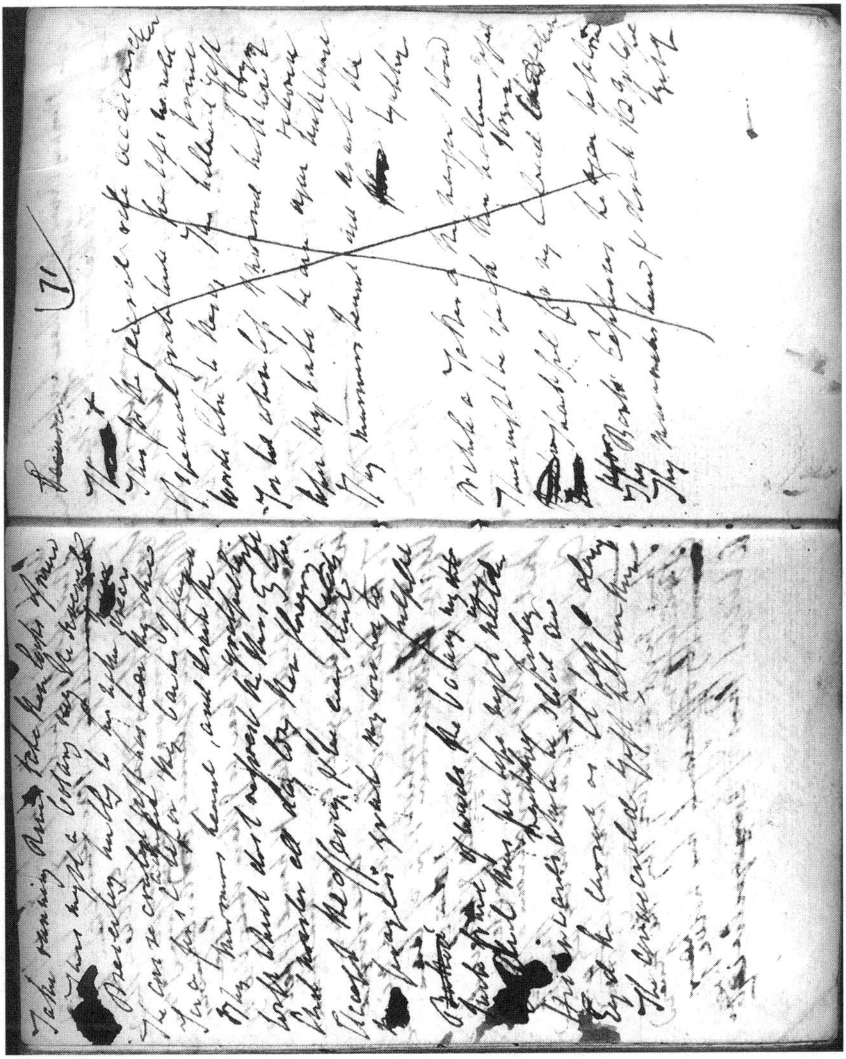

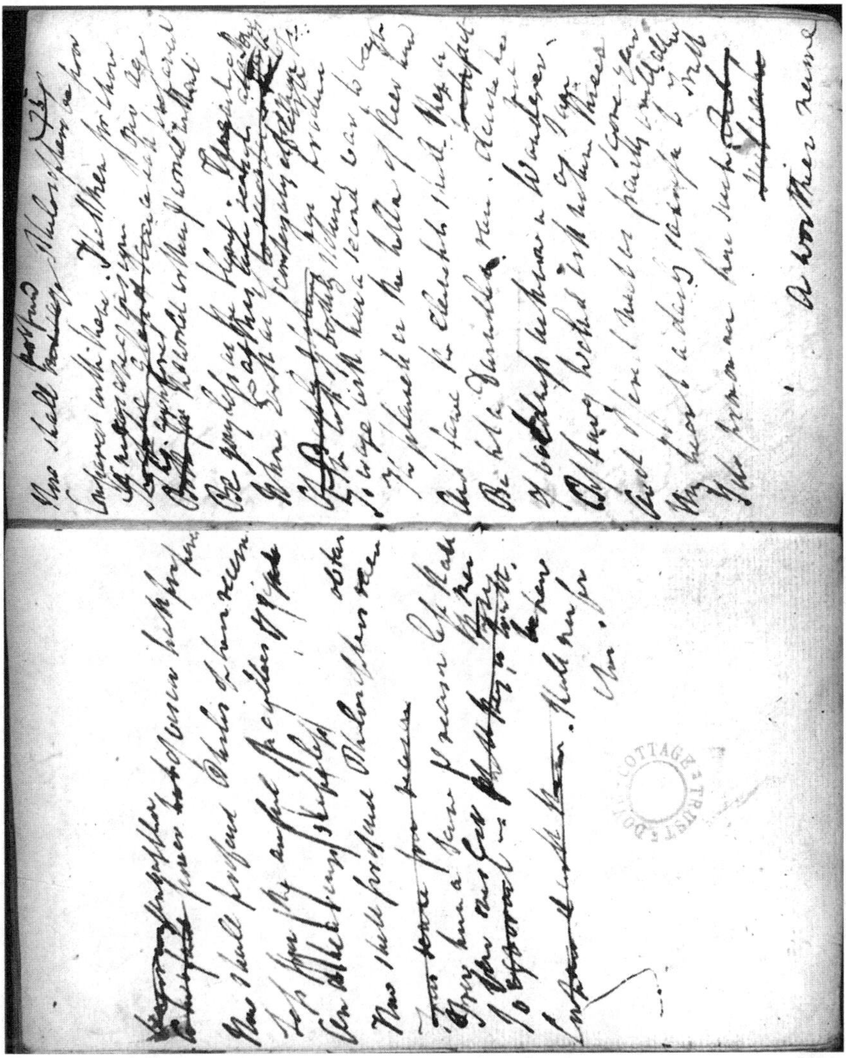

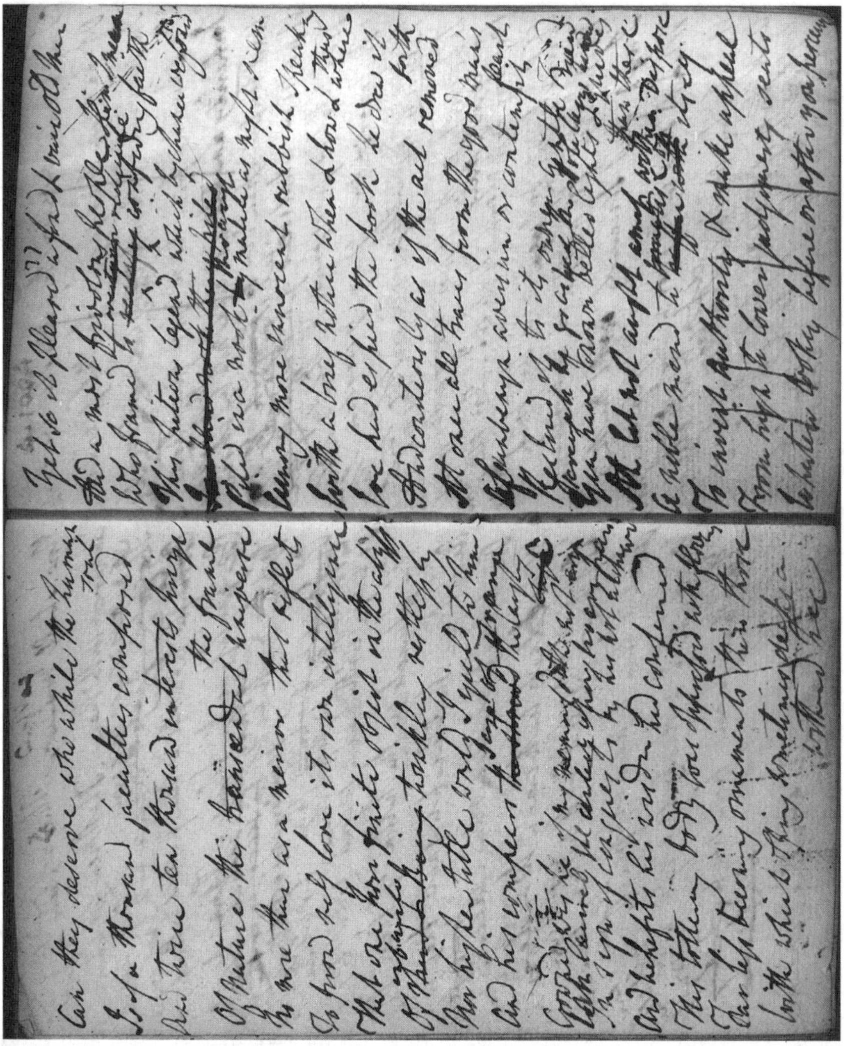

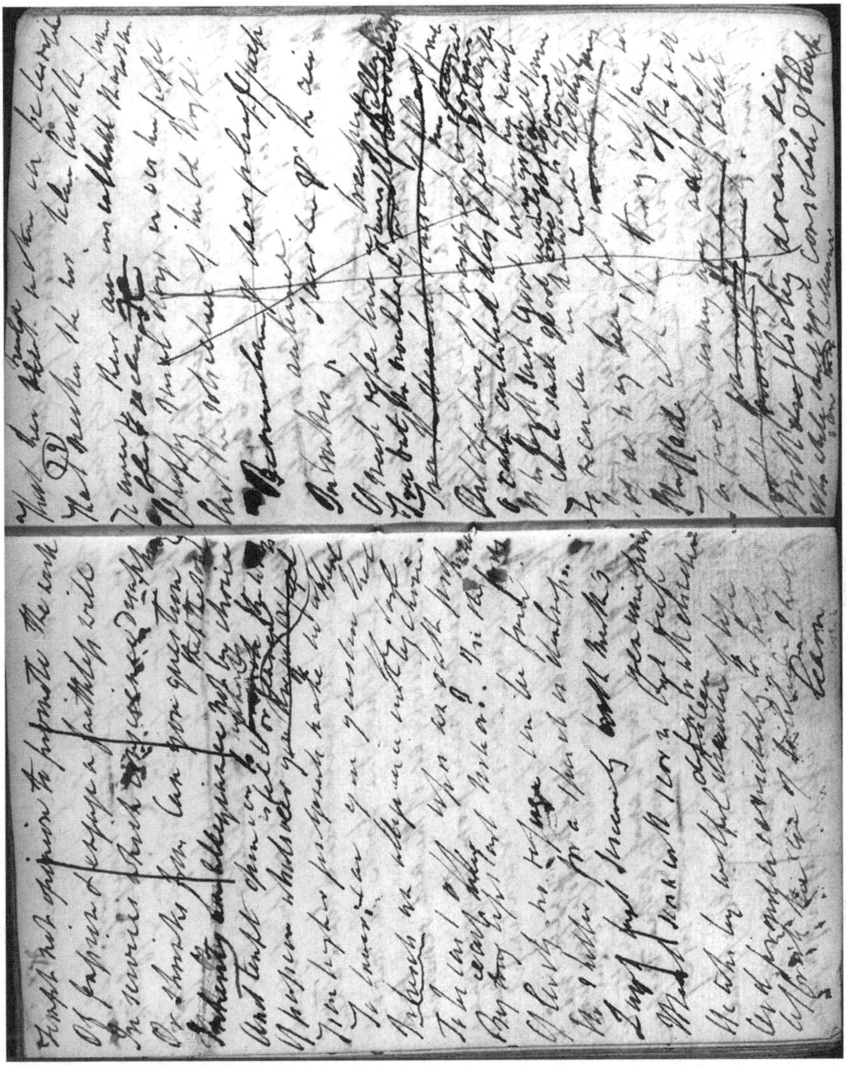

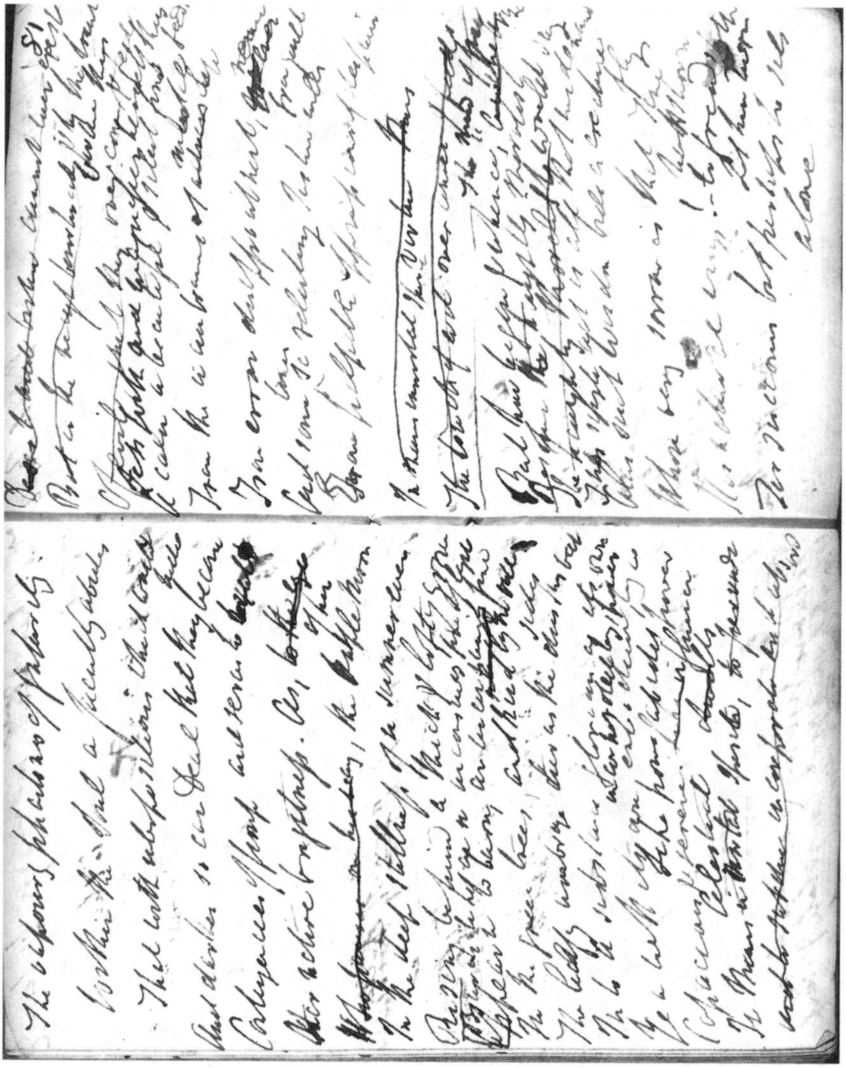

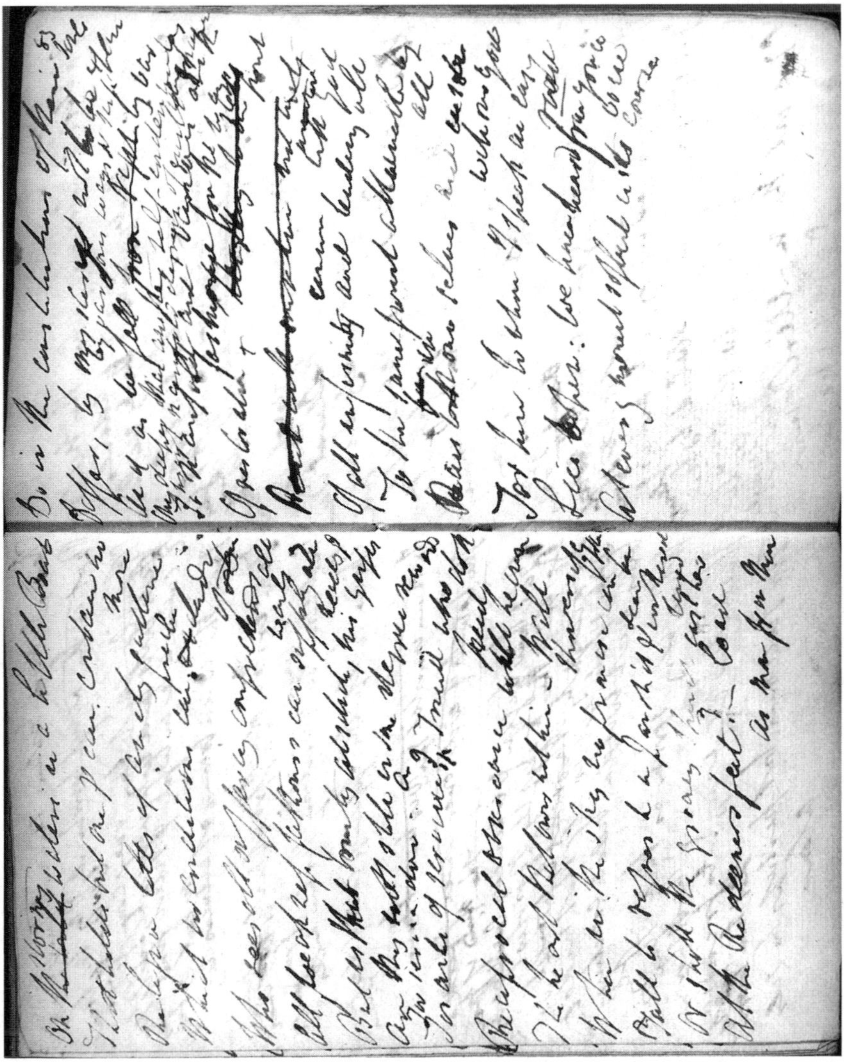

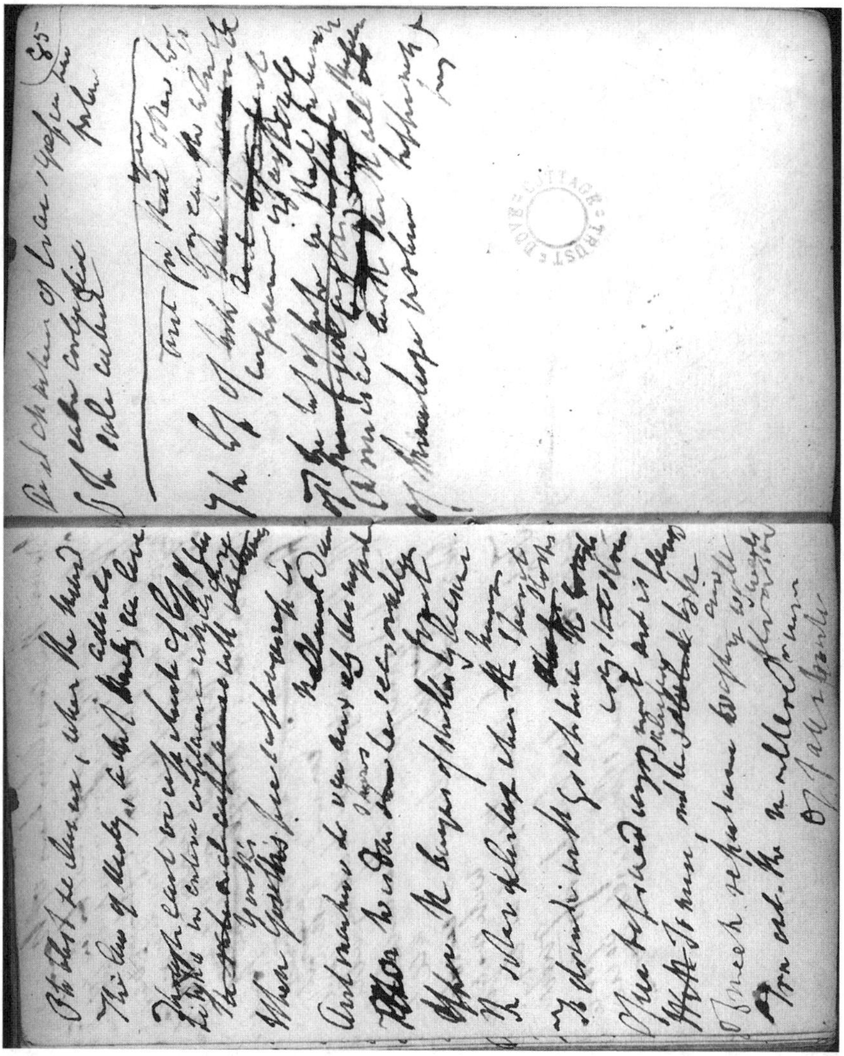

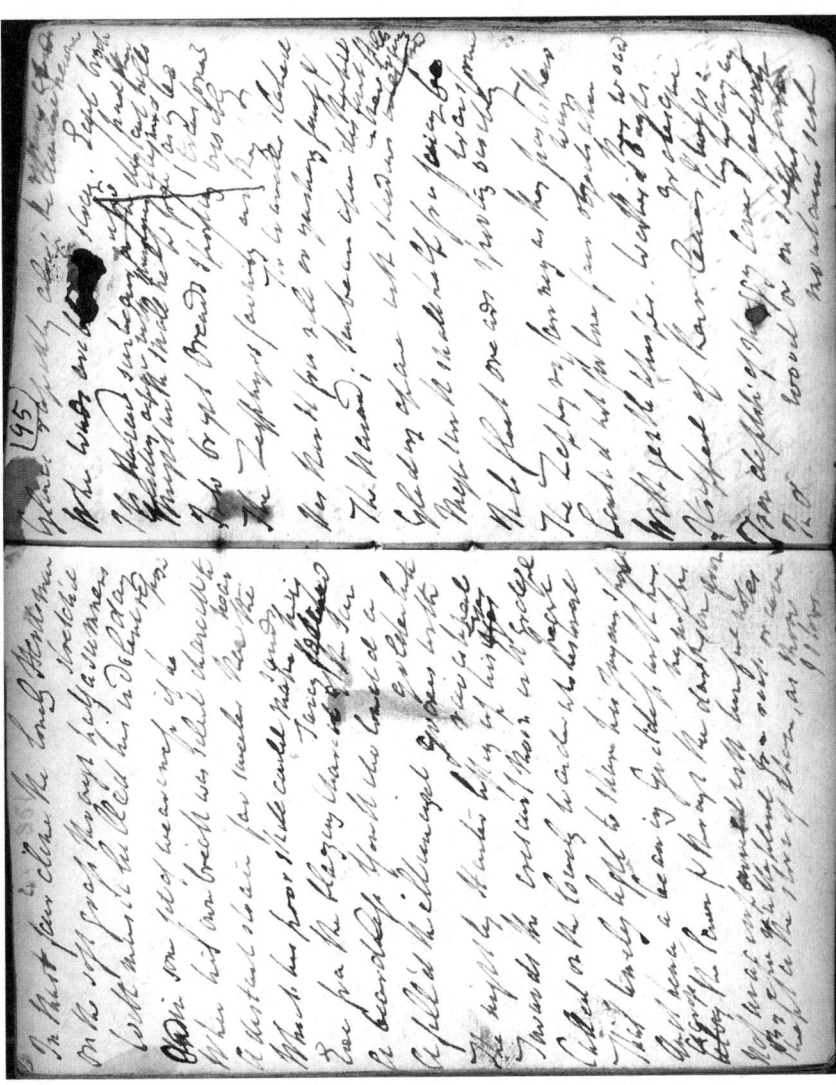

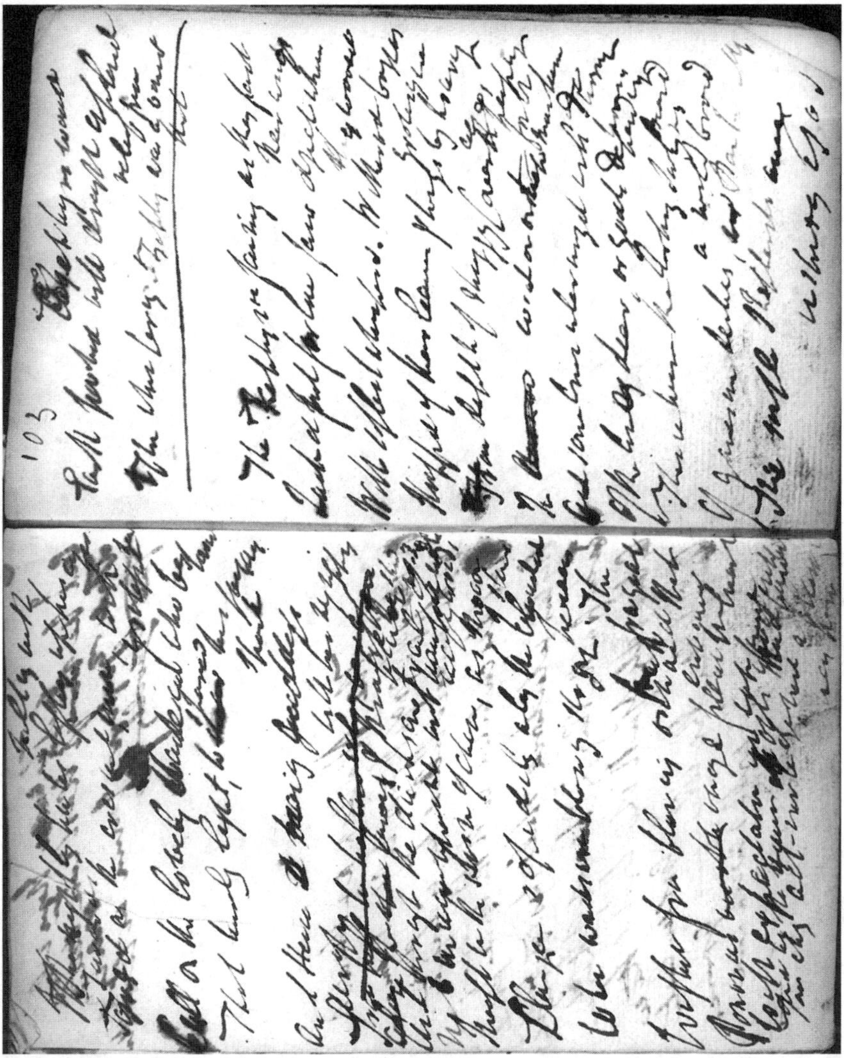

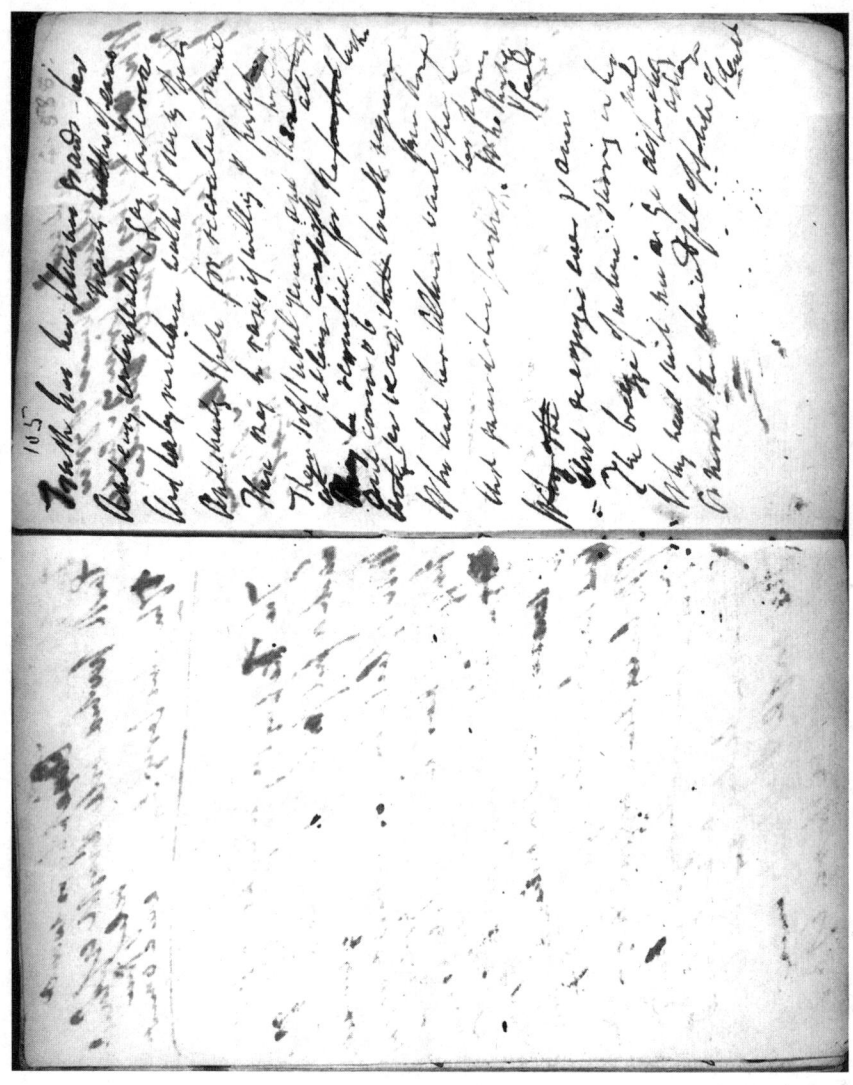

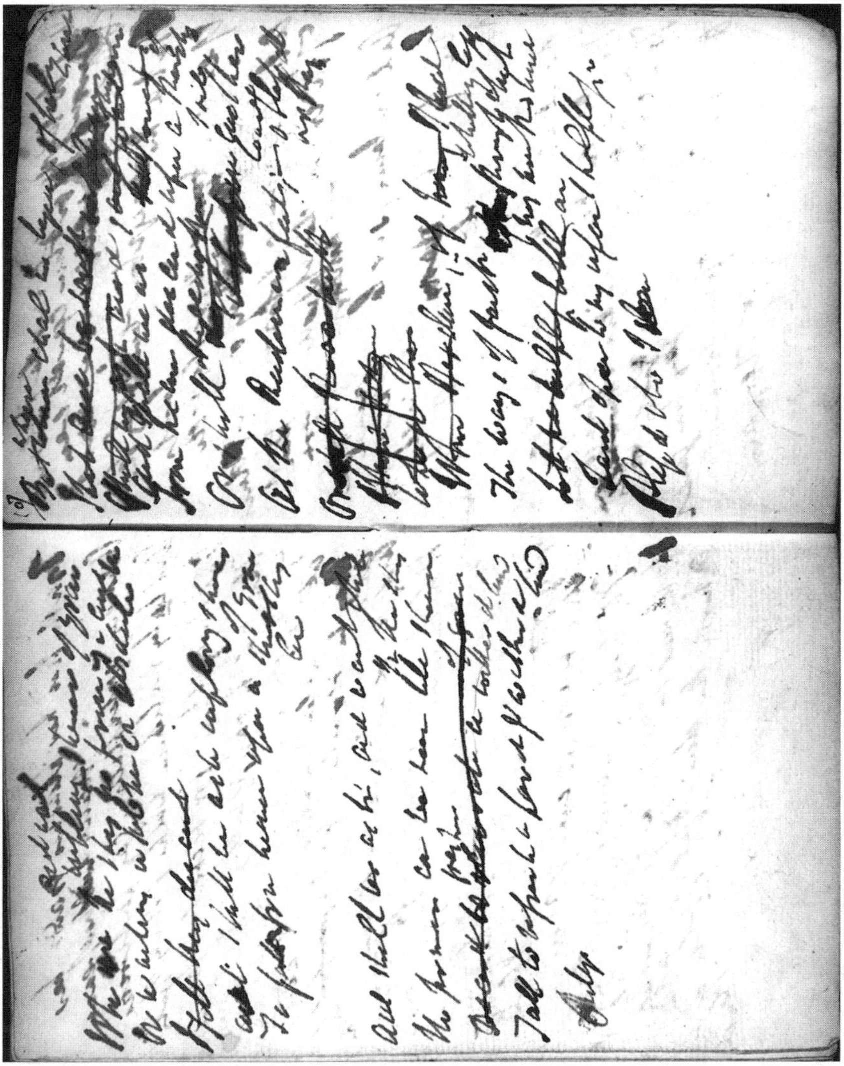

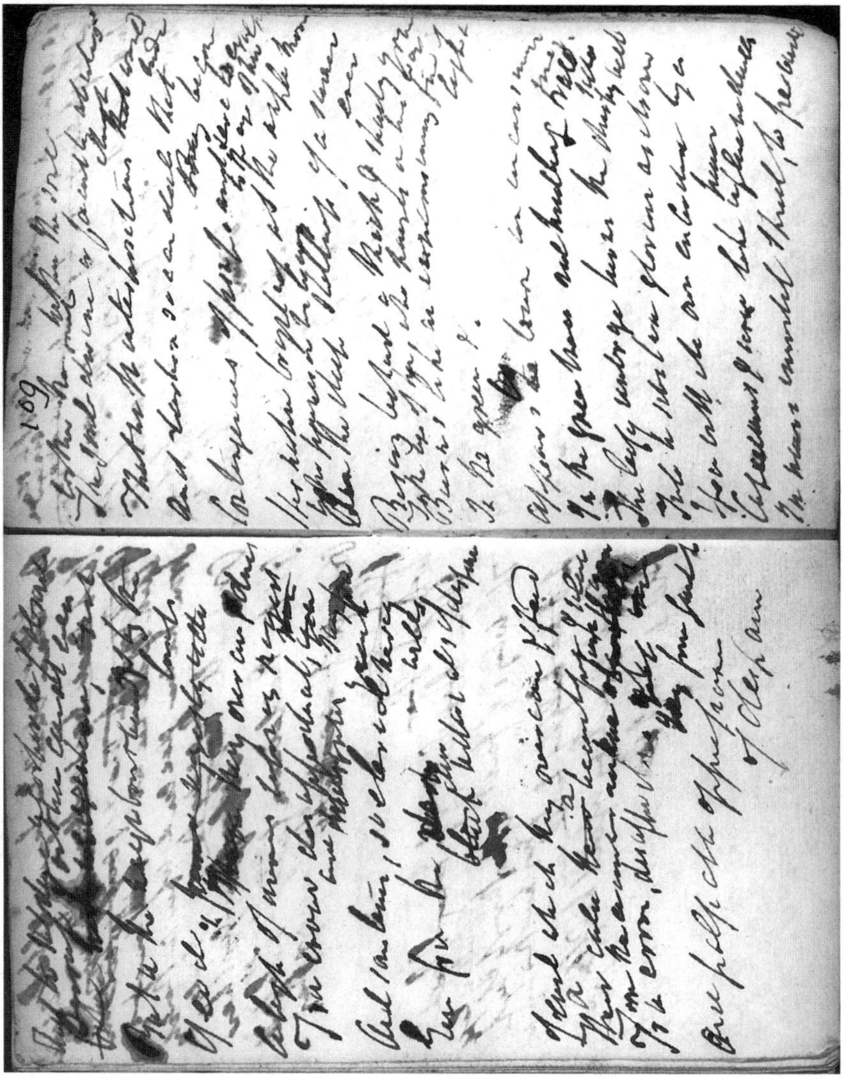

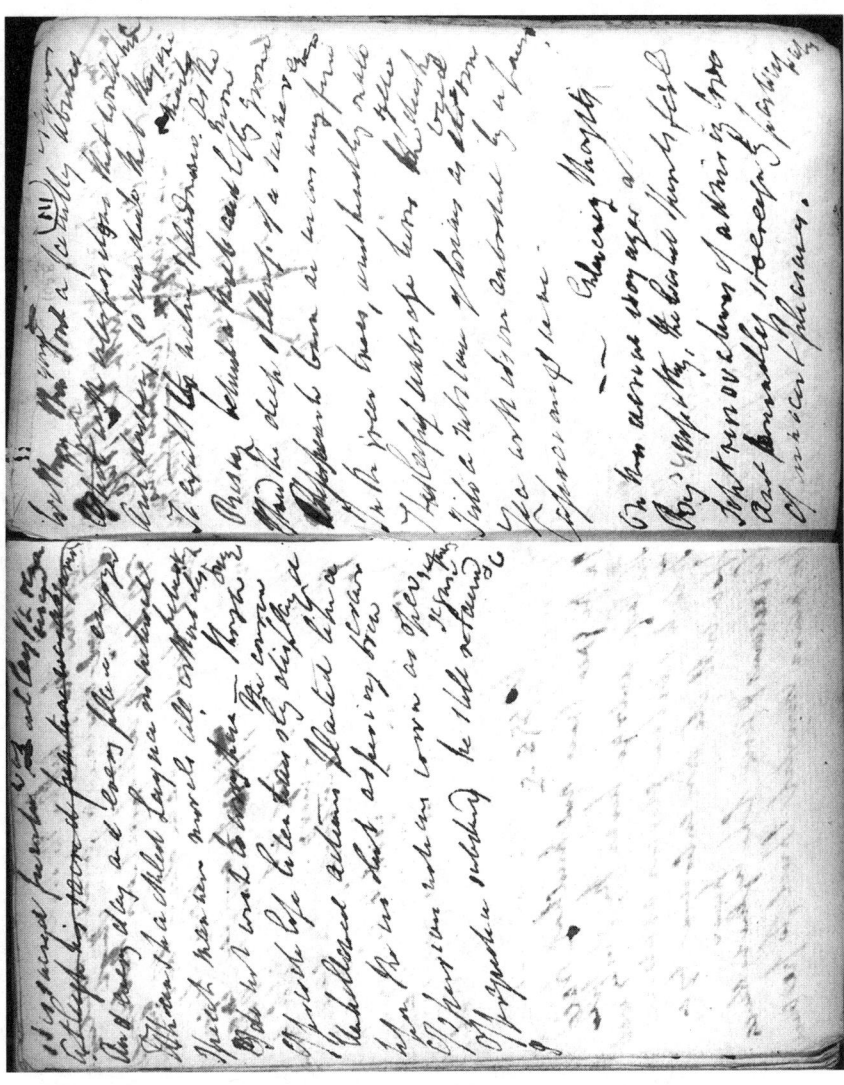

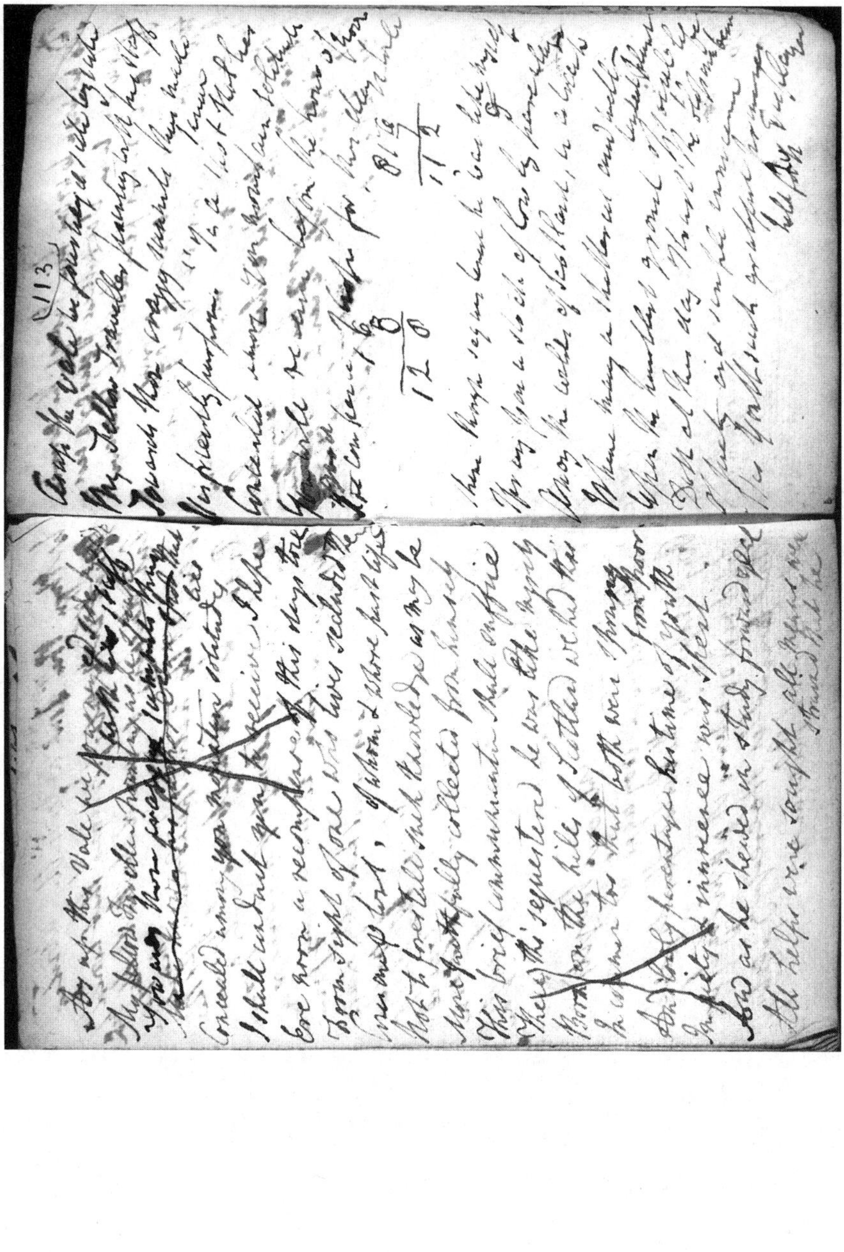

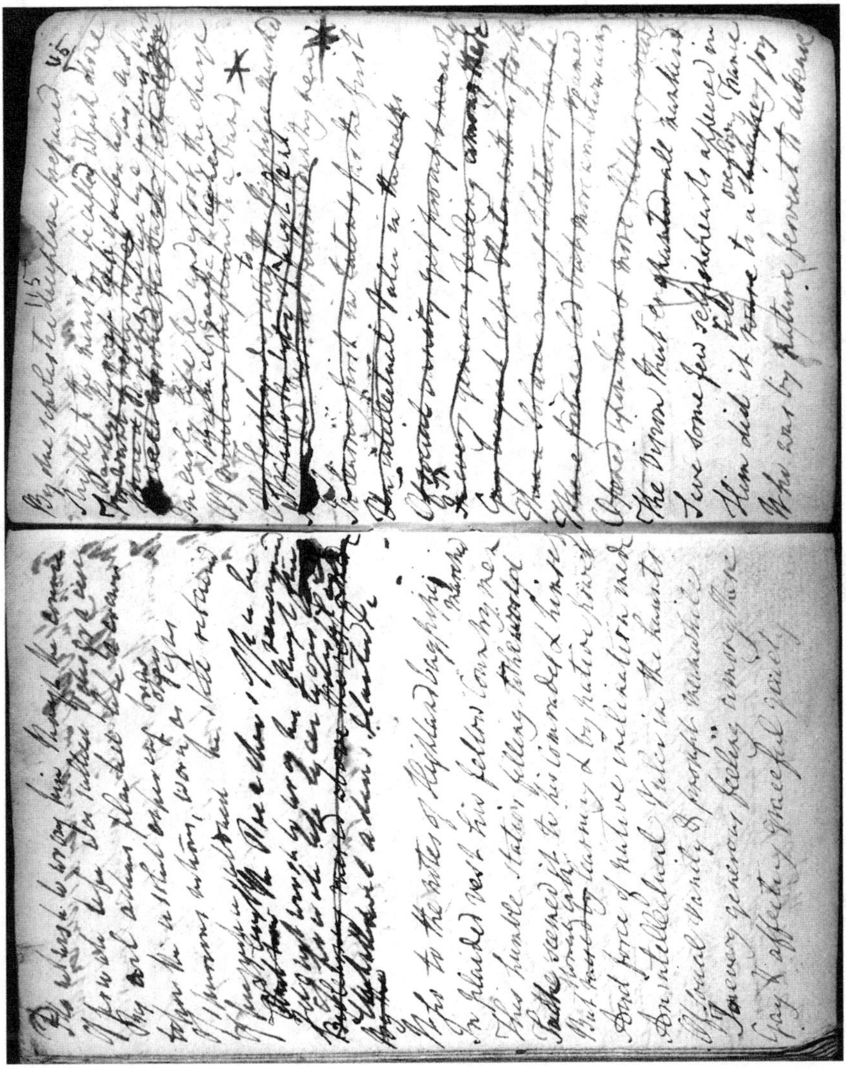

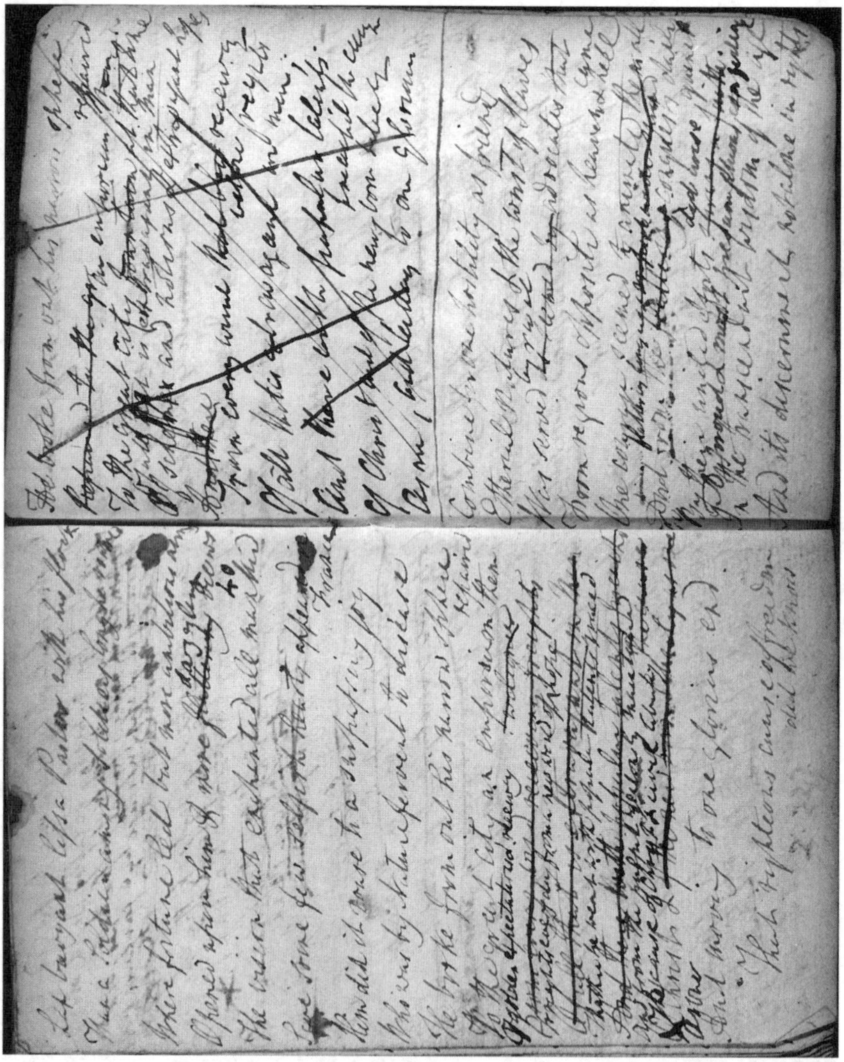

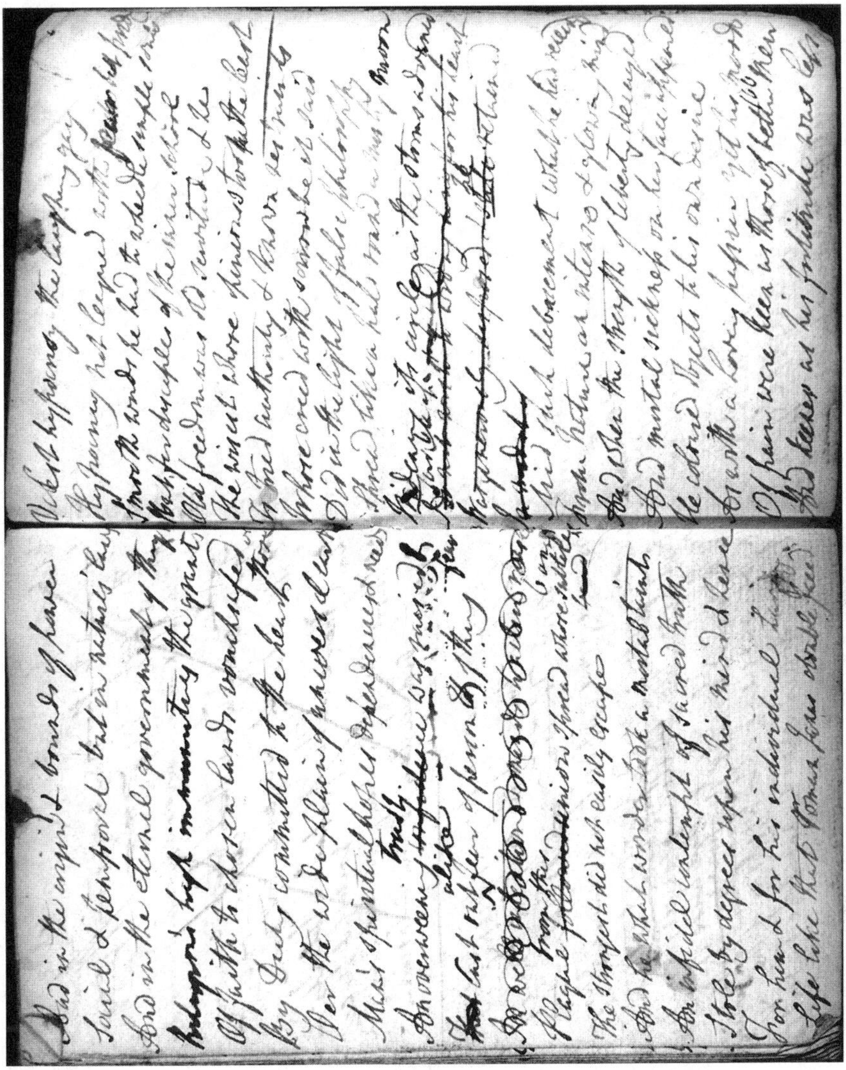

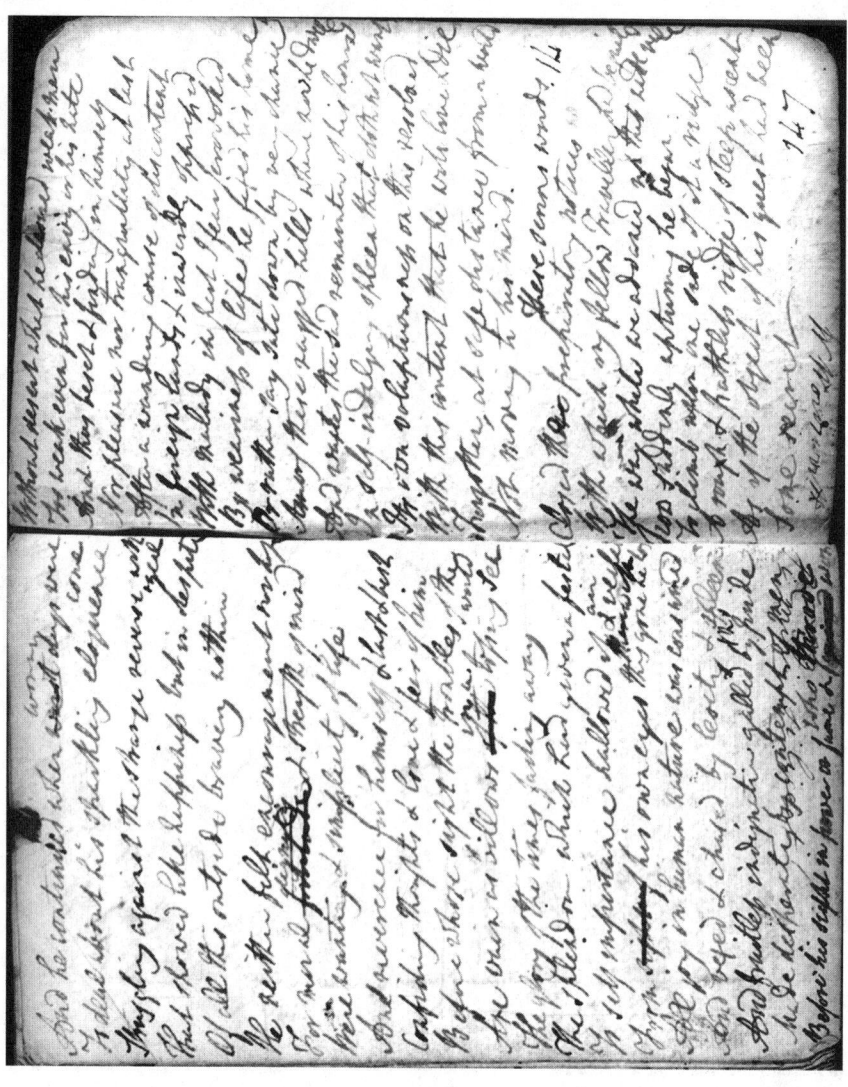

DC MS. 67, with Readings of Commonplace Book

DC MS. 67—whose gathering devoted to *Essay on Epitaphs, III,* contains work toward *Excursion,* VII, 412–498, dating from the second stage of composition on the poem—is described in the Manuscript Census, p. xxii, above. For a discussion of this manuscript and its role in the composition of *The Excursion,* see pp. 441, 457, above. Left-hand margin line numbers on the transcriptions of DC MS. 67 provide cross-references to the line count in the 1814 reading text in this edition.

The same *Excursion* passage that is in DC MS. 67 also appears in the Commonplace Book kept by Lord and Lady Beaumont (for a description of the Commonplace Book, see the Manuscript Census, p. xxii, above). The similarity of the two versions suggests that the Commonplace Book text also dates from the second stage of *Excursion* composition. Below the transcription of the DC MS. 67 passage is presented a record of the verbal and nonverbal differences in the Commonplace Book.

[*Essay upon Epitaphs III,* 6[r]]

VII, 412 *Beneath that Pine which rears its dusky head*
417a *Aloft and covered by a plain blue stone*
417b *Briefly inscribed a gentle Dalesman lies*
418 *From whom in early childhood was withdrawn*
419 *The precious gift of hearing. He grew up*
420 *From year to year in loneliness of soul*
421 *And this deep mountain valley was to him*
422 *Soundless with all its streams. The bird of dawn*
423 *Did never rouze this Cottager from sleep*
424 *With startling summons: not for his delight*
425 *The vernal cuckoo shouted not for him*
426 *Murmured the labouring bee. When stormy winds*
427 *Were working the broad bosom of the lake*
428 *Into a thousand, thousand sparkling waves*
429 *Rocking the trees or driving cloud on cloud*
430 *Along the sharp edge of yon lofty crags*
431 *The agitated scene before his eyes*
432 *Was silent as a picture evermore*
433 *Were all things silent wheresoe'er he moved.*
434 *Yet by the solace of his own calm thoughts*
435 *Upheld he duteously pursued the round*
436 *Of rural labours: the steep mountain side*
437 *Ascended with his staff and faithful dog.*
438 *The plough he guided and the scythe he swayed*
439 *And the ripe corn before his sickle fell*
440 *Among the jocund reapers. For himself*
441 *All watchful and industrious as he was*
442 *He wrought not neither field nor flock he owned*
443 *No wish for wealth had place within his mind*
444 *Nor husband's love nor father's hope or care*
445 *Though born a younger Brother need was none*
446 *That from the floor of his paternal ~~roof~~ home*
447 *He should depart to plant himself anew*
448 *And when mature in manhood he beheld*
449 *His Parents laid in earth no loss ensued*
450 *Of rights to him but he remained well pleased*
451 *By the pure bond of independent love*
452 *An inmate of a second family*

SH wrote the base text.

417a Aloft, and cover'd
417b inscribed,
420 Soul;
422 Soundless, . . . Streams.
425 cuckow shouted;
426 Murmur'd
428 thousand thousand . . . waves,
430 crags,
431 eyes *with no del*
432 picture:
434 Yet, his own calm] his calm
435 Upheld,
437 Dog.
440 himself,
441 was,
442 not; . . . owned,
444 love, . . . care.
445 Brother,
446 paternal home
447 anew;
448 when, . . . manhood,
449 earth,
450 him, . . . pleased,
451 independant
452 Inmate . . . Family,

[*Essay upon Epitaphs III*, 6v]

The fellow-labourer and friend of him
To whom the small inheritance had fallen.
Nor deem that his mild presence was a weight
~~Upon his Brother's house~~
That pressed upon his Brother's house for books
Were ready comrades whom he could not tire
Of whose society the blameless Man
Was never satiate their familiar voice
Even to old age with unabated charm
refresh'd *his*
Beguiled his leisure hours ~~composed~~ thoughts
Beyond its natural elevation raised
His introverted spirit and bestowed
Upon his life an outward dignity
Which all acknowledged. The dark winter night
The stormy day had each its own resource
Song of the muses sage historic tale
Science severe or word of holy writ
Announcing immortality and joy
assembled
To the ~~exalted~~ spirits of the just
^
From imperfection and decay secure
Thus soothed at home thus busy in the field
To no perverse suspicion he gave way
No languor peevishness nor vain complaint
And they who were about him did not fail
In reverence or in courtesy they prized
His gentle manners: and his peaceful smiles
The gleams of his slow-varying countenance
Were met with answering sympathy and love.
—At length when sixty years and five were told
A slow disease insensibly consumed
The powers of nature and a few short steps
Of friends and kindred bore him from his home
Yon Cottage shaded by the woody crags
To the profounder stillness of the grave.
Nor was his funeral denied the grace

455/456 Canceled half-line seems to correct a copying error.
461 WW's del and rev to "refresh'd" is in pencil; SH's added "his" is in ink.

---

453 Fellow-labourer . . . Friend
454 Inheritance
455/456 *om*
456 House,
459 satiate: . . . voice—
461 hours, composed his thoughts
463 spirit,
465 night,
466 day, . . . resource,
467 Muses, . . . tale,
468 severe, . . . Writ
470 the assembled spirits of the Just
471 secure.
472 home, . . . field,
473 way,
474 languor, peevishness, . . . complaint:
476 courtesy:
477 smiles,
478 countenance,
480 length, . . . told,
482 powers of nature] flowers of nature;
483 Friends and Kindred . . . home,
484 (Yon . . . crags)
486 Funeral

Of many tears virtuous and thoughtful grief
Heart-sorrow rendered sweet by gratitude
And now that monumental Stone preserves
His name and unambitiously relates
How long and by what kindly outward aids
And in what pure contendedness of mind
The sad privation was by him endured.

P
And yon tall {*pine-tree whose composing sound*
Was wasted on the good Man's living ear
Hath now its own peculiar sanctity
And at the touch of every wandering breeze
Murmurs not idly o'er his peaceful grave.

---

487 tears, . . . grief,
488 Heart sorrow, . . . gratitude.
490 name,
491 long, . . . aids,
494 Pine-tree,
495 man's
496 sanctity.

DC MS. 73

DC MS. 73—in use at the third, seventh, and eighth stages of *Excursion* composition for work on Books III, IV, VI, and IX—is described in the Manuscript Census, p. xxiv, above. For a discussion of this manuscript and its role in the composition of *The Excursion*, see pp. 442–444, 465–468, 476–477, above.

Left-hand margin line numbers on the transcriptions of DC MS. 73 provide cross-references to the line count in the 1814 reading text in this edition.

On pp. 903–914, below, we present sample photographs of these leaves of DC MS. 73:

DC MS. 73, 2^r
DC MS. 73, 3^r
DC MS. 73, 3^v
DC MS. 73, 4^r
DC MS. 73, 4^v
DC MS. 73, 5^r
DC MS. 73, 5^v
DC MS. 73, 6^r
DC MS. 73, 6^v
DC MS. 73, 7^r
DC MS. 73, 7^v
DC MS. 73, 46^r

The image size of the photographs of DC MS. 73 is 84 percent of actual size.

[2^{v}]

IV —Come ye that are disturb'd this steady voice
Of streams the stillness and the stiller sound
Shall awe you into peace this gleaming lake
These glistening Cottages and hoary fields
And in the midst above and underneath
Shadowy recesses bosoms gloomy Holds
Viewless impenetrable infinite
And tranquil as the abys of deepest sleep
Or that dark world the untrouble home of
death
Lo in the west a solemn sight behold
cresting yon
[?~~High~~]
[?]] ~~on that~~ craggy barriar ~~lofty~~ rigd[?e]
arksome t
A Pageantry of d{arkling {Trees that stand
Single in their aerial solitude
Stand motionless in solitary calm
{And
{Yet greeted gently by the moving clouds
That pass and & pass and ever are to come
Varying their colours slowly in the light
Of an invisible moon ~~but then are gone~~
[?clouds]
~~at length—[?the] the procession~~ closed
[?th]
{No asleep
[?{~~T cloud appears] the [?breezes are life] [?]~~
The firmament [?immov]
T}
~~That [?Twin]~~ t}hat twinkle in their stat{[?on]
ions
self-disturbed

Rev on 4^{r}, 4^{v}, 5^{r}. This passage, intended as an alt and/or continuation to IV, 1152–1179 (3^{r}–4^{r}, 5^{r}–5^{v}), is not adopted in Book IV. Attempts on 4^{r}, and rev at bottom of 3^{r}, may have been intended to join the two passages. MW's copy on 5^{v}, however, indicates the ultimate Book IV sequence as continuing ll.1179ff. with the addendum to MS. B of *RC* (see *RC & Pedlar*, pp. 260–275).

Last two lines appear related to rev at the bottom of 3^{r}, possibly an attempt to join the two passages. Cf. 4^{r}. 4^{v}, however, rejects the apparent attempt to join the passages and adopts the rev on the bottom of 3^{r} and 2^{v} as its conclusion.

[3^{r}]

IV, 1152 when these lofty rocks
1153 At nights approach bring down the cloudless sky
1154 To rest upon their circumambient walls
of dimensions vast
1155 ~~In peace~~ a Temple framing ~~vast and huge~~
1156 And yet not too gigantic for the sound
1157 Of human Anthems choral song and burst
1158 Sublime of instrumental harmony
fy
1159 To glorily the Eternal. What if these
1163 Nature fails not to provide
Be wanting, ~~yet not seldom at such hour~~
1164 Impulse and utterance to the solemn scene
And to the holy passions of [?sweet]
1170 Of stillness, dimness and repose is heard
1169 Accordant chiefly then when at such hour
1171 Within the curcuit of this fabric huge
1172 One Voice—the solitary Raven flying
1173 Athwart the concave of the dark-blue dome
1174 Unseen and high above all power of sight
1175 The Ravens voice an iron knell renew d
[1175] At intervals with echoes from afar
1176 Fainter and fainter echoes as the
1176, 1178 Which the Bird utters fades upon the ear
1179 By distance and yet dies not.—~~all is still~~
earth is stilld
The firmament immoveably composed
stars
Save those celestial lamps the living

[3^{v}]

IV, 1152 when these lofty rocks
1153 At nights approach bring down the cloudless sky
1154 To rest upon their circumambient walls
s
1155 A Temple framing of dimentions vast
1156 And yet not too gigantic for the sound
1157 Of human anthems choral song and burst
1158 Sublime of instrumental harmony
1159 To glorify the Eternal.—What if these
1163 Be wanting Nature fails not to provide
I
1164 [?L]mpulse and utterance, with the solemn
scene
And with the holy passions of the soul

Rev on 3^{v}–4^{r}, 5^{r}–5^{v}. Possibly continued from 6^{r}.
1176 All other copies supply "cry" at end of line.
Rev at page foot appears to be later than 4^{r}, and related to copy at bottom of 2^{r}. Rev incorporated in copy on 4^{v}. Possibly, this rev is an attempt to fuse copy on 3^{r} with 2^{v}.

Rev of 3^{r}; rev on 5^{r}–5^{v}; continued on 4^{r}.

the
1169 Accordant—chiefly then when at such
hour
1170 Of stillness dimness and repose is heard
1171 Within the circuit of this fabric huge
1172 One Voice the solitary Raven flying
1173 Athwart the concave of the dark blue
dome
1174 Unseen and high above all power of sight
1175 The Ravens voice an iron knell renew d
[1175] At intervals with echoes from afar
1176 Fainter and fainter echoes as the cry
1176, 1177 With which the bird accompanies his flight
calm
1178 Through the [?~~wide~~] region fades upon
the ear

[4r]

IV By distance—and yet dies not.—~~all is~~
~~still~~
~~Save the pale stars that twinkle self disturbed~~
~~but~~
~~it pervades~~
[?measure]
~~All space it fills the bosom of all~~ time
~~Or seems to fill—but [?lest] it hath [?ex~~pired]
~~A deeper gloom hath fallen and all thing~~
save those celestial lamps the living stars
That twinkle in their stations self disturbed
all is still
~~All [?el~~]
Earth air and water are at peac no form
~~No image~~ [?touch]
~~Memorial~~, in~~timation vestige~~, ~~thought~~
image [?remains]
Or ~~breathing~~ of disquietude appears
heaven val[?t]
Save in the ~~bl~~ue unfathomable ~~sky~~
Whence those celestial lamps the living
stars
Are twinkling in their station[?s] self disturb
if thy heart
have [?listend] it will fill with [?quite]ness
[?As with moons meek] light a mountain[?s]
val
[?Suduing] all things to its own repose

Leaf 4r continues from 3v; rev of 3r; rev on 5v, 3r, 2v, 4v–5r. Passage beginning with the second line appears to be an attempt to join 1v, l. 1179, with some version of the para on 2v (see note there), probably earlier than the rev at bottom of 3r and 2v.

In the third line from the bottom, another possibility for conjectured "quiteness" (intended as "quietness") is "gentleness."

[4v]

IV Come ye disquieted This steady voice
Of streams the stillness and the stiller sound
you
Shall awe into peace this gleaming lake
These glistening cottages and hoary fields
And in the midst above and underneath
~~Appear the mountains and the scattered hills~~
Shadowy recesses, bosoms, gloomy holds,
Viewless impenetrable infinite
And tranquil as th abys of deepest sleep
Or that dark world the untroubled home of death
—Lo in the west a solemn sight—behold
Upon utmost y
~~Cresting~~ yon craggy barriers ~~loft[?iest]~~ ~~brow~~] ridge
A pageantry of darksome trees that stand
Single in their aerial solitude
Stand motionless in solitary calm
Yet greeted gently by the moving clouds
That pass and pass and ever are to come
Varying their colours slowly in the light
Cloud follows cloud
[?~~length~~]
Of an invisible moon—~~At~~ [?last] ~~ensues~~
as thought succeed to thought ~~but~~ now ensues
Ensues a pause
[?~~I watch~~] the long procession seems to end
~~A pause~~
No straggler left behind—not one appears
last surviving breeze
stirred
The ^breeze that ~~was~~ in heaven hath died
away
And all things are immoveably composed
Save here and there an [?uncomplying] star

[5r]

That twinkles in its station self distubred
That in its station twinkles self-disturbed

IV, 1152 When these lofty rocks
1153 At night's approach bring down the unclouded sky
1154 To rest upon their circumambient walls
of
1155 A Temple framing for dimensions vast
enormous
1156 And yet not too gigantic for the sound
1157 Of human anthems, choral song, and burst
1158 Sublime/of instrumental harmony

Rev of 2v–3r, 4r.

Passage above the rule continued from 4v, rev of 3v, 4r, 3r.
1158 Del of comma by eras.

1159 To glorify the Eternal. What if these
1161 Be wanting; if the Nightingale be mute
1162 And the soft Woodlark never chaunted here
1163 Her vespers, Nature fails not to provide
1164 Impulse & utterance—The ~~breathing~~ passing air
1165 Murmurs devoutly from the shadowy heights
{blind
1166 And {dim recesses of the cavern d rocks
1167 ~~And cavern d rocks; rills~~, waters numberless
[1167] The little rills and waters numberless
1168 Inaudible by day light, blend their notes
the
1169, 1170 With loud streams; and oftentimes is heard
1171 Within the circuit of this fabric huge
1172 One Voice—the solitary Raven flying
1173 Atthwart the concave of the dark blue dome
1174 Unseen, and high above all power of sight
1175 An iron knell with echoes from afar
1176 Fainter & fainter echoes as the cry
1176, 1177 With which the bird accompanies his flight
1178 Through the calm region fades upon the ear

[5v]

IV, 1179, 1181 By distance & yet dies not. *But descending*
a}
1182 *From these imi}ginative heights that yield*
1183 *Far stretching views into eternity ~~with earnest heart~~*
By long experience taught
~~With earnest heart once more~~ I recommend
Those humbler sympathies with things that hold
1201 *An inarticulate language &c as in the red book*
a support
and [?an opportune]
1197 ~~As a support~~ for chearfulness ~~and [?ease~~]
For hearts if not too heavily oppressed
Those softer renovations that proceed
From general natures mild appearances
1198 Those humbler Sympathies with living things
{from {morn
[1198] Or things inan[?ina]mate that {[?to] da {[?wn] to eve
1199 Do speak to eye and ear in every [?field]
I recommend

1171 Ink over pencil.

Continued from bottom of 5r; rev of 4r, 3r. "But descending" begins MW's hand, through l. 1201.

1201 MW's note, "as in the red book," refers the copyist to a red leather pocket notebook—MS. 16—which contains this passage (see *RC & Pedlar*, pp. 372–374, 260ff.).

1197 Change in pen and ink.

[1197] As a resource for indolence & ease
A charm for [?care] an opportune relief
For hearts if not too heavily depressed
Communications sedulously held
An intercourse habitually maintained
[?watc]fully [?maintained]
With general natures mild appearances
~~And~~ } And
[1198] [?Those]} ~~Those~~ humble sympathies with living things
{ate [?E]}
[1198] Or things inani{m that from morn to e}ve
[1199] Do speak to eye and ear in every grove
Reasons
1200 And speak to social ~~interests~~ inner sense
[1201] A[?n universal] language

[6^{r}]

{~~hear~~
IV, 1111 We have {[?] ~~your~~ heard your voice
1112 At every moment soften in its course
1113 By tenderness of heart have seen your eye
1114 Even like an Altar lit by fire from heaven
this day
1115 Kindle before us—your discourse ~~that~~
~~wished~~
1116 That like the fabled Lethe wished to flow
1117 In creeping sadness through oblivious shades
1118 Of death and night hath caught at every
turn
1119 The colours of the sun: access for you
{serve
1120 Is yet pre{[?] to principles of truth
1121 Which the imagination will uphold
{~~In~~
1122 {And ~~seats of power that cannot be approach~~
[1122] In seats of wisdom not to be approached
1123 By the inferior faculty that moulds
1124 With her minute & speculative pains
1125, 1141 Opinion ever changing. ~~X~~ Here you stand,
1142 Adore & worship when you know it not
1143 Pious beyond the intention of your thought
1144 Devout above the meaning of your will
1150 Has not the soul the being of your life

Passage on 6^{r} appears to be later than the corresponding lines entered in MS. 70, 22^{r}–22^{v} and 21^{v}, although added l. 1124 must then be understood as an accidental omission, later added. L. 1122 on MS. 70, 22^{v}, however, follows the early line, del, on 6^{r}. In MS. 70, ll. 1111–1125 first follow IV, 478 and are continued by IV, 482 on 22^{r}–22^{v} and 21^{v}. Later in MS. 70, 44^{r}, ll. 1111–1112 follow ll. 1110–1111 in *1814*. Possibly, copy on 6^{r} in MS. 73 is related to the copy in MS. 70, 44^{r}; the first line, 1111, in MS. 70 is closer to *1814* than MS. 73. If so, then MS. 73 here is later than MS. 70, 22^{r}–22^{v} and 21^{v}; but earlier than MS. 70, 44^{r}; in which case MS. 70 is post-1808. Entry of ll. 1125–1141 in MS. 70, 16^{v}, probably adds weight to the argument that MS. 73 and later stages of MS. 70 were used in conjunction with one another. MS. 70, l. 1141 ("Here"), clearly indicates that MS. 70, 16^{v}, is later than MS. 73, 6^{r}.

1115 Possibly a comma follows the rev "day."

1125, 1141 Symbol indicates insertion, probably of ll. 1125–1141, in MS. 70, 16^{v}.

y tr
1152 ~~Have~~ [~~?~~]} ~~ou not~~ [?]} ~~embled when~~ those
R lofty rocks
1151 [?~~Sou~~]} eceived a shock of awful consciousness
[1152] Mild yet deep searching—When these
lofty

[6v]

Here
IV, 1272 [?Th] closed the Sage
[1272] That musical & eloquent harangue
1273 Which in continuous stream he had poured
forth
1275 Unwearied, like an India orator
1275, 1276 Like a grave Elder among Indian tribe
Amid the assemble
1282 Whom Time & lonely Nature have made
wise
1283 Gracing his language with authority
[?he]
1280 The word [?then] uttered
[1275] Like a grave Indian orator, on a day
Of solemn conference, an experiencd Man
T exhort[?in]
1276 [?A]} he assembled tribes [?addressing] on a day
Of solemn conference—a Man
[1272] Here closed the Sage
[1272] That musical and eloquent harangue
1273 Which in continuous stream he had poured forth
[1275, 1276] Like a Grave Orator the assembled tribes
addressing with a [?word]
1274 Mid Indian wilds ~~exhorting on a day~~
1284 That from the ear of hostile Spirits [?wrung]
~~for~~
[1276] Of ~~solemn conference set apart~~—a Man
[1282] Submissive audience [?asembled]
[1283] Whom Time & lonely [?Natu] made wise
1283/1259 Gracing his language with authority.
the excursive power
Of intellect & thought & to the pure
Yet passionate abstractions of the heart.

[7r]

IV, 1260 So build we up the being that we are
79 For could the Almighty P[?ower] from whose will

Leaf 6v is rev on 7v.
Ink and pen change for rev passage below vertical del stroke.

Rev on 7v.
Drafting suggests that the passages above and below the rule were originally part of same sequence—possibly intended for the end of the book (i.e., about l. 1260).

We take our origin, ~~whose indulgent~~ love
~~Embraces our infirmities, to whom~~
[?~~Throug fallen~~]
deat[?les]
87, 90 ~~From helpless~~ sleep reverses every day
91 To reasons blessed light could he [?design].
[?who]

Beyond providential calculation [?wise]
wrap
83 who ~~made~~ the cloud
84 Of infancy ~~dissolve~~ around us that himself
~~Might there~~
Therein
85 [?~~Therein~~] might with our conscious a while [?~~bring~~]
[?by]
86 Hold undisturb d communion who, [?at} night]
87 When lawless fear has [?garner d] in our sleep
[87] The nightly Anarch who dispels
~~D~~ that disturbs [?our dre]
88, 90 [?] ~~eaths image, sleep, and brings us daily back~~
that embraces our
dream
90 ~~And brings us daily back~~
~~To rea~~
A
[90] D}nd doth restore us every day from sleep
[91] To reasons blessed light
[1260] So build we up the Being that we are.
[79] For could the [?Essential] Spirit from whose
will
[83] We take our origin, who wrapped the cloud
[84] Of infancy around us that himself
~~might hold~~
[85] Therein ~~might~~ with our simplicity [?~~awhile~~]
M a while
[86] [?]ight hold on earth community [?undisturb]

[7v]

doth [?molests]
IV, 87 Whose care ~~di[?d~~] [?chase] th anarch that
[?tracts]
distracts dist{[?urbs]
90 Our dreams & doth restore us every day
91 To reasons blessed light, could he [?design]
956 That we should pore & dwindle while we pore &c
dreaming
chy
[87] Whose care ~~dispels~~ the anarc{y of ^ sleep
~~Or from its~~
[87] Who from the anarchy of dreaming sleep

---

91 Alt to conjectured "design" may be "deign" as in IV, 966.

Continuation and rev of 7r; rev of 6v.
87 Possibly WW started to write "dis" for "dispel" before rev to "doth."
91 Alt for conjectured "design" may be "deign"; cf. note to 7r, l. 91.

~~c~~ | a}
88 ~~Dispels, or from its deathlike V~~[?au{lt}]~~ncy~~
Or from its deathlike void with punctual care
R}
[90] [?D]}estores daily to the vital [?sens]
us
[91] And reasons blessed light
1272 Here closed the Sage
[1272] That musical & eloquent harangue
[1273] Poured forth with fervor in continuous stream
{uous
1273 Which in contin{al stream he had poured
{I forth
1274 Like a grave Orator mid {indian wilds
H}
1275, 1276 [?I]}is thoughts delivering to the assembled tribes
Upon some argument of deep concern
1280 The words
{and
my mind {[?heart] heart obey[?ed]
1279 He had discoursed
w}
1282 Like one whom time & nature have made [?&]}ise
1283 Gracing his language with authority
1284 Which hostile Spirits silently allow

[8r]

~~sometimes~~ stood to
{t
III, 976 So have [?~~I~~] {[?~~sood~~] and watch'd a mountain Brook
977 In some still passage of its course [?,] and seen
{hs
978 Within the dept{[?s] of its unruffled breast
{trees
979 Inverted {[?] and rocks, and azure
And} ~~floating~~ sky
980 [?Sail]} on ~~its~~ surface specks of silver foam,
986 ~~Or all her little floating iles [?entire~~]
982 Numerous as stars, which by the their onward
~~B~~} lapse
981 Of [?]}~~ubbles undissolv, a company~~
983 Betrayed to sight the motion of the stream
m}
984 Else ip}perceptible, and I have heard
984, 985 Meanwhile, a roar, or murmur; and the
sound
{oo little floating isles
986, 980 Though so{[?]thing, and the specks of silver foam
987 Though beautiful were both by nature charged
988 With the same pensive office & made known
989 Through what perplexing labyrinthes, and abrupt

Precedes MS. 71, 109r–110r. Rev on 8v–9r.
982–983 Line in left margin indicates rev.

[?uneasy]
990 Precipitations and untoward straits
{ had
991, 992 The Brooks {[?we] passed:—and soon, that
[?hindrance] respite oer
992 Like traverses [?and] like [?uneasy] straits
again
993 ~~The like~~ must be encountered. Such a stream
994 Is human life and so the spirit fares
995 In its best quiet.
and bubbles
fl}
[986] Making a company of [?]}oating isles

[8v]

glassy [?rafst]
III, 980 And on the surface ~~spec~~ of silver foam
981 And conglobated bubbles undissolved
986 ~~Making a compan~~
[986] A Company of little floating Iles
982 Numerous as stars; that by their onward
lapse

---

to
976 So have I stood, ~~and~~ watch ~~d~~ a Mountain brook
977 In some still passage of its course and seen
978 Within the depth of its capacious breast
rocks
979 Inverted trees, and ~~clouds~~ and azure sky
980 And on its glassy surface specks of foam
981 And conglobated bubbles undissolved
986 ~~A company of little floating Isles~~
982 Numerous as Stars, that by their onward lapse
983 Betrayed to sight the motion of the Stream
984 Else imperceptible; and I have heard
985 Meanwhile a roar, or murmur; and the sound
[986] Though soothing and the little floating Isles
987 Though beautiful were both by nature charge
988 With the same pensive office and made known
T}
989 [?]}hrough what perplexing Labyrinths & abrupt
990 Precipitations and untoward straits

[9r]

~~The Brook~~ o}
III, 991 The earth-born wanderer had passed; & son}n,
992 That respite oer like traverses & toils

Rev of 8r. Contributes to MS. 71, 109r–110r. Continues on 9r.
980–982 Passage above rule is rev below rule.
984 Semicolon may possibly be a comma with an accidental mark above it.

991–995 Continued from 8v; rev of 8r.

993 Must be again encountered—Such a
Stream
994 Is human life and so the Spirit fares
the i
995 In ~~its~~ best quiet to [?]|ts course allow'd
And reaching [?soon]
~~having reached~~
IX, 440 Once ~~coming to~~ a bridge that overlooked
the hasty streaml[?et]
441 A ~~mountain torrent~~ where it lay becalmed
In deep pool[?s] there saw we at a gl[?a]
442 By a flat meadow, at a glance I saw
443 A twofold Image on the grassy bank
white fleecd
w
444 A [?S]now[?h]|hite^Ram and in the peaceful flood
445 An other & the same most beautiful
446 On the green turf with his imperial front
[?~~superb~~]
447 Shaggy & bold & [?horns] [?]
Cre
448 The Breathing [?cre]|ature stood as beautiful
~~were~~ showed
[?~~showd~~] was
449 Beneath him [?stood] his shadowy counterpart
450 Each had his glowing mountains each his
sky
451 And each seem d Centre of his own fair world
u
[447] Shaggy & bold, & wreathed horns s[?]perb
what [?a]
455 Ah pity twere to destroy
456 Or to disturb [?a] so fair a spectacle
457 And yet a breath can do it—these
few word

[9v]

Lady whispered
IX, 458 The [?] [?] ~~softly while we~~
[?stood]
~~as if~~ half afraid

[14v]

IX, 678 unceasing joy
679 Once, while the name, Jehovah, was a sound

---

993 Possibly a period follows "encountered." In eras (probably of a copying error), an initial "S" can be conjectured.

IX, 440ff. Probably continued from 25v; rev on 26r–26v, 18v.

455ff. These lines, continued on 9v, are probably an added attempt to continue this passage, which draws on MS. 48, 34r–34v, 36v–37r (see *13-Bk Prelude*, II, 399–400, 403). Cf. 18v.

Continued from 9r. Leaves 10r–14r are blank, and leaves 11–12 and 13–14 are uncut at the top.

Rev of 40r, 41v, 42r.

678 The phrase "unceasing joy" is the end of the previous verse para; cf. 41v.

Within the limits
680 Amid the forest of this sea-girt Isle
681 Unheard, the savage Nations bowed their heads
682 To Gods delighting in remorseless deeds;
{ ich
683 Gods, wh{[?om] themselves had fashion, to
promote
684 Ill purposes, and flatter foul desires.
bo }
in th [?]}som of yon mountain cove f}
685 Then, ~~mid these mountainous retreats~~, }~~for~~ here
Wh[?er] yet exist
May yet be seen memorials of that age
In unmolested solitude preserved)
686 To those Inventions of corrupted Man
and there
687 Mysterious rites were solemnized, ~~in groves~~
[688] Amid the depths of long departed woods

{hts
688 Gloomy & still selected from the deep{[?s]
Of deepest forests, Natures silent holds
And awe-inspiring fastenesses; secure
{ steel
From all intrusion—till by {[?sword] & flame
They were laid waste the consecrated
Brought oaks
Fell d to the ground & altars overturn d
and some
689 Of those accursed Idols there receved

[15r]

IX, 688 Amid impending rocks & gloomy woods,
{Of
[689] {And those dread Idols some perhaps received
689 ~~There, of the accursed Idols, some received~~
690 Such dismal service, that the loudest
(} Voice
691 Of the swoln cataracts }which now are heard
{)
692 Soft-murmuring{ was too weak to overcome,
693 Though aided by wild winds, the groans & shriek
694 Of human Victims offered up to appease
{:
695 Or to propitiate[?s]{, and, if living Eyes
696 Had visionary faculties to see
697 The thing that hath been as the thing is,

681 Another possibility for "Nations" is "natives"; *1814* reads "Nations."
688/689 The box marks these lines for possible rev or del; see rev on 15r.
689 Rev of 15r; rev on 15r.

Rev of 14v, 40r, 42r–42v.
689 Rev on 14v.

behold | perchance
698 We might perhaps}, ~~perhaps~~, this wide
spread mere
699 Bedimmed with smoke, in wreathes voluminous
700 Flung from the body of devouring fires
{ i
701 To Taranis erected on the he{[?a]ghts
702 By priestly hands, for sacrifice, performed
703 Exultingly, in view of open day
704 And full assemblage of a barbarous Host

[15v]

IX, 705 Or to Andates, Female Power! who gave
706 For so they fancied, glorious Victory.
B |
709 [?W]}ut mark the appearances of things—how changed
709, 710 From such the worship & with those compared
711 The Worshippers how innocent & blest!
712 So wide the difference a willing Mind
713 At this affecting hour might almost think
714 That Paradise the lost abode of Man
715 Was raised again & to happy few
716 In its original beauty here restored.
{G
717 —Whence but from thee, the true & only {god
718 And from the faith derived throgh him who
bled
719 Upon the Cross this marvellous advance
720 Of good from evil as if one extreme
721 Were left—the other gained. O ye who
come

[16r]

{ n
IX, 722 To kneel devoutly in yo{[?ur] reverend Pile
723 Called to such office by the peaceful sound
724 Of sabbath Bells; and Ye who sleep in earth
725 All cares forgotten, round its hallowed Walls
[Living & dead an undivided Flock] Q
726 For you, in presence of this little band
to |
727 Gather [?in]}gether on the green hill side
728 Your Pastor is emboldened to prefer
729 Vocal thanksgivings to the eternal King
730 Whose love whose counsel & commands have
made

Leaf 15v is rev of 42v–43r.

Rev of 43r–43v.

725/726 WW brackets the line, probably for rev or del, marking it with what appears to be a "Q" for "Query."

peace
731 Your very poorest rich in self of thought
732 And in good works, & Him who is endowed
733 With scantiest knowledge Master of
all truth
734 Which the salvation of his soul requires

[16^v]

IX, 735 Cons[?c]ous of that abundant favour showered
736 On you, the children of my humble care,
737 On your Abodes, and this beloved Land
birth place Country
H ~~Countr~~
738 Our C<u>ountry</u>, home & birth pl while on
earth
s
739 We [?] ojourn, loudly do I utter thanks
740 With earnest joy, that will not be suppressed
741, 745 Rocks rivers mountains, woods & watry Plains,
see
~~see~~ [?H]
746 They [?hear] [?~~of my~~] the offering of my lifted
hands
747 They hear my lips present their sacrifice
748 They know if I be silent, morn or even,
749 For though in whispers speaking, the full
heart
750 Will find a vent & thought is praise
to Him,
Thee
751 Audible praise to [?his] omnis[?i]ent
Mind
752 From whom all gifts decend, all
blessings flow.

[17^r]

IX, 753 This Vesper-service closed, without delay,
F
754 [?W] rom that exa[?u]lted station to the plain
755 Descending, we pursued our homeward
course
756 In mute Composure oer the shadowy Lake
757 Beneath a faded sky. No trace appeared
758 Of those celestial splendors; grey the vault
E
759 Pure cloudless ether; and the star of eve[?n]

Rev of 43^v, 44^r.
738 Underlining of "Country" probably indicates need for rev, as in *1814*.

Rev of 44^v–45^r.
759 Semicolon probably reinforced but possibly rev from commas.

{L
Was wanting; but inferior {lights appeared
Faintly, too faint almost for sight, and some
Above the darkened Hills stood boldly forth
In twinkling lustre, ere the Boat attained
Her mooring place—wher to the sheltering
{t
{Tree
Our youth Voyagers bound fast her prow
With prompt & careful hands. This done
we paced
The dewy fields; but ere the Vicars door
Was reached, the Solitary turned aside

[17v]

{e
Th{at single Path invit[?in] him that leads
To the one Cottge in the dell profound
His chosen Residence. He turned aside
But not till welcome promise had been given
That he would share the pleasures & pursuits
Of yet another summer's day consumed
through
In wandering with us ~~oer~~ the valleys fair
{S
And oer the mountain wastes. Another {sun
Said He, shall shine upon us ere we
part
Another sun & peradventure more
If Time with free consent be yours to give
And season favours. To enfeeble Power,
From this communion with uninjured minds
given
What renovation had been brought, & what
Degree of healing to wounded Spirit
Dejected and habitually disposed
To seek in degradation of the Kind

[18r]

Excuse & solace for its own defects
How far those erring notions were reformed
And whether aught of tendency as good
And pure from further intercourse ensued,
This, (if delightful hopes as heretofore
Inspire the serious song, and gentle
Hearts
Cherish, and lofty minds approve the past)

---

760 Semicolon probably reinforced but possibly rev from commas.

Leaf 17v is rev of 44v–45r, 46r, 45v.

Rev of 46r.

untold
795 My future Labours may not leave ~~untold~~.
Finis—

[18v]

IX, 292 A saintly Youth removing from the throne
[?then] to possess
Of England ~~all~~ unworthy ~~of a Prince~~
~~gentle~~ refus
A Prince so ~~truly wise &~~ good, ~~re[?nounce]~~
[?pure] ~~so merciful & wise~~
[?~~in~~]
~~Th~~ [?pre] ~~tended boon~~
With to give effect
To his benignant purpose & [?withold]
The precious boon
450 Each had his glowing Mountains each his sky
451 And each seemed centre of his own fair world,
452 Antipodes unconcious of each other
453 Yet, in partition, with their several spheres
in to our sight
454 Blended ~~with~~ perfect stillness. So to the eyes
Of the rapt Prophet & expiring saints
Thing past, surrounding things & things to come,
indivisible
[?One individual univer compose]
[?solemn]
In [?qu] vision [?quietly] revealed

[19r]

IX, 292 O for that happy period—ages past
Not unforeseen nor unprepared—though Heaven
saintly
A ~~Royal~~ Youth removing from his Throne
His [?beni]
E[?re] [?the] [?] benignnant
Before ~~the~~ Cherished purpose was fulfilled
to e
Did th [?is] Lands unworthiness refuse
e
The pri tious boon!—that [?æ]ra I invoke
293 When prizing knowledge as her noblest wealth
~~Wh[?en] a fr[?ee country]~~
294 Too ~~long deferred when~~ this Imperial Realm
And best protection

Cf. MS. 74, 119v, 56r, 55v.
292ff. Rev of 19r.
450–454 Rev of 26v, 9r. Ll. 440–454 rev of MS. 48, 34r–34v, 36v–37r (see *13-Bk Prelude*, II, 399–400, 403).

Cf. MS. 74, 119v–120r, 156r, 155v.
Rev on 18v. The text is later than MS. 74.

~~On knowledge resting as her surest prop~~
295 While she exacts allegiance shall admit
296 An obligation on her part to teach
297 Them who are born to serve her & obey,
298 Binding herself by statute to secure
299 For all the Children whom her soil maintains
300 The rudiments of Letters & to inform
301 The mind with moral & religious truth

[19v]

IX, 302 Both understood and practised—so that
none
303 However destitute be left to droop
304 By timely culture unsustained, or run
or
305 Into a wild disorder: ~~and~~ be forced
d
306 To druge through weary life without the aid
307 Of intellectual implements and tools
308 A savage Horde among the civilized
309 A servile Band among the lordly free.
310 This right as sacred almost as the
right
311 To exist & be supplied with sustenance
312 And means of life the lisping Babe proclaims
inherent
313, 314 To be invested in his innocence
315 And the Rude Boy who having overpassed
{C
316 The sinless age by {conscience is enrolled
317 Yet mutinously knits his angry Brow

[20r]

IX, 318 And lifts his wilful hand on mischief bent
319 Or turns the sacred faculty of speech
320 To impious use—by process indirect
321 Declares his due while he makes known
his need
322 In vain this right of nature is announced
323 This universal plea in vain addressed
324 To eyes & ears of Parents who themselves
325 Did in the time of their necessity
326 Urge it in vain—& therefore, like
a prayer,
327 That from the humblest floor ascends to
heaven,

Cf. MS. 74, 120r–120v, 55v–56v.

Cf. MS. 74, 120v, 121v–121r.

328 It mounts—to reach the States parental
ear
329 Who if indeed she own a Mothers heart
m
330 And be not [?]|ost unfeelingly devoid
331, 332 Will grant what England happily secure
331 + Of gratitude & providendence will grant
333 From interference of external force
334 May grant at leisure—without
risk incurred
335 That what in wisdom for herself she doth
332 The unquestionable good which England
safe

[20v]

IX, 336 Others shall eer be able to undo.
337 —Look! & behold from Calpes sunbur t cliffs
338 To the flat margin of the Baltic sea
339 Long-reverenced Titles cast away—as weeds,
L
340 [?Of]|aws overturned and Territory split
341 Like fields of ice rent by the polar wind
join in
342 And for[?c]d to ~~take~~ [?a] less obnoxious shapes
[?~~it~~] they
[?~~they~~]
343 Which ere {[?it] gains consistence, by a
gust
344 Of the same breath are shattered & destroyed
345 Meantime the Sovereignty of these fair Isles
346 Remains entire & indivisible
ingnorance were which acts
at ~~as~~
347 And if th{e causes w{ere removed [?~~wit that~~]
~~act~~
348 Within the compass of their several shores
ude
349 To breed commotion and disquiet{ing
350 Each might preserve the beautiful repose

[21r]

IX, 351 Of heavenly Bodies shining in their spheres.
352 The discipline of slavery is unknown

---

331 The X signals added l. 332 at page foot.

Cf. MS. 74, 121v–122v.
337 The pen seems to have run dry at the second "n" in "sunburnt."

Cf. MS. 74, 122v, 124v, 121r.

{A
353 {[?]mongst us, hence the more do we require
354 The discipline of virtue—order else
not
355 Can subsist nor confidence nor peace.
possessed
duties rising out of good ~~bestowed~~
356 Thus ~~gratitude to heaven for good bestowed~~
avert
357 And prudent caution needful to [?advert]
equally do alike
358 Impending evil obviously ^ require
359 That permanent provision should be made
360 For the whole people to be taught & traind.
361 So shall licentiousness & black resolve
362 Be rooted out and virtous habits take
363 Their place & genuine piety descend
364 Like an inheritance from age to age.
~~Rulers~~
{[?~~R~~]
Too ~~thoughtless~~ {[?~~rulers] of this favoured Rea~~lm
[?~~If ye] faithful to your sacred trust~~
365 Instruct the people and avaunt all fear

[21[v]]

IX, 385 Yes, he continued, kindling as he spake
386 Change wide & and deep & silently performd
would
might and as Days roll on
387 The land ~~shall~~ witness ~~nor this land alone~~
{~~h~~
388 ~~For Britain is the whole Ear~~[?ts{] ~~vital~~
heart
Earth's would
388 ~~Whose~~ universal frame ~~shall~~ feel the effect
broad
Through her ~~wide~~ Continents & scattered Isles
389 Even to the smallest habitable Rock
That
{~~That~~ beats waves
390 {Wh[?at] ocean ~~lulls~~ with solitary [?~~voice~~].
371 For as the element of air affords
372 An easy passage to the industrious
bees
373 Fraught with their burthens and a
way as smooth

---

355 What appears to be a period after "peace" is overwritten by the "d" in "possessed" below.
365 Rev and expanded on 22[r], 23[r].

Cf. MS. 74, 124[v].
Rev on 22[r], 23[r]–23[v].

[?~~young brood~~] i
374 ~~For th[?e f]~~ ~~swarms~~ to take the{i/ } r sound
ing flight
For those ordained where {l
375 From the throng'd hive & settle{l/ } e they list
376 In fresh abodes their labours to
renew
wide
377 So ~~are~~ the waters, open to the power
378 The will the instincts & appointed
needs
370 Rejoice imperial Island & be proud
[370] As having special cause for pride & joy

[22[r]]

do
IX, 379 Of britain, & invite her to cast off
380 Her swarms, and in succession send
Bound them forth
381 To establish new communities ~~on shores~~
Wherever found that promise to
mature
For enterprize its merited reward.
382 On every shore whose aspect favours hope
[?~~And~~] or to
383 ~~And~~ bold adventure, promising skill
384 And ~~industr~~
perserverance their deserved
rewards.
365 ~~With such [?facility] avaunt all fear~~
[?foreer that]
Therefore avaunt ~~that over~~-busy fear
{[?such] [?the]
With {[?that] provision [?made] avaunt all fear
366 Of numbers crowded on their native soil
healtfull
367 To the prevention of all ~~natural~~ growth
through
368 ~~By~~ mutual injury rather in the law
369 Of encreas [?~~rather~~] and the mandate from
above
370 Rejoice proceeding to replenish earth
~~With generous [?virtues~~]
children
With [?our superfluous] ~~products~~ of a [?soil]
[?courts ~~of [? ?]~~ [?arts]
Renowned for [?~~seed~~] & liberty & [?~~works~~]
truth.
I} proud
Imperial Br|slands & & be glad
[370] Rejoice: ~~as of [?the land~~]

370–[370] Lines related to those at foot of 22[r]. In l. [370], cap "J" may be intended in "joy."

Rev and expansion of 21[r]. Rev on 23[r]–23[v].

365ff. Change in ink and pen. In rev of next-to-last line, "Man" may be intended as "Mandate," the reading of *1814*.

[?As] of selected to replenish earth
[?customs Man]
And with thy language, [?~~sow or] [? ~~] [?release]
The seeds of virtue liberty & [?Law]

[22ᵛ]

[?Too]
IX, 402, 403 [?For] ~~thoughtless Rulers of these favored Realms~~
410 Rulers assist your country to fulfill
411 Her glorious destiny, — ~~amid the [?cares~~]
~~And manifold anxie[?t]ies of [?war le~~]
war
[?ho]
the [?~~time~~] must [?come]
[?joy to prais]
[?high praise]
[?pursuit while]
And [?be your] [?] [? ?]
[?now]
412 Now when oppression like the Egyptian
plage
guilty suffer[?ing]
413 Of darkness spread oer ~~wretched~~ Europe
[?make]
414 The sunshine more conspicously appear
415 In which we move about & think & act.
417 [?~~Shew] to the [?wretch~~]
[?~~hand] of war~~
[416] Now while ~~the anxieties & cares~~ of war
destruction is a prime pursuit
[?by]
And [?in] the [?urgent wounds]
~~And by the anxieties~~ & cares of war
[412] Your minds are through necessity oppressd
[417] Shew to the wre[?c]thed nations for what
The bonds of social [?intercourse] end
&
418 [?Society] [?f] Government were [?framed].
bestowed
[418] The Powers of civil government [?~~imposed~~] framd

[23ʳ]

IX, 364 Like an inheritance from age to age.
365 With such foundations laid avaunt the
fear
366 Of numbers crowded on their native soil
367 To the prevention of all healtful growth

402, 403 Rev of 21ʳ, 364/365. This line, originally intended to follow l. 364 on 21ʳ and on MS. 74, 124ᵛ, precedes l. 410 here and on 24ʳ.
410–418 Rev on 24ʳ–25ʳ.

Cf. MS. 74, 124ᵛ.
Rev of 22ʳ, 21ʳ.

368 Through mutual injury—rather in the law
369 Of increase and the mandate from above
370 Rejoice!—and Ye have special cause for
joy.
371 —For as the element of air affords
372 An easy passage to the industrious bees
373 Fraught with their burthens and a way as
smooth
374 For those ordained to take their sounding flight
375 From the throng d hive and settle where
they list
376 In fresh abodes their labour to renew
377 So the wide waters open to the power
378 The will the instincts and appointed needs
379 Of Britain do invite her to cast off
380 Her swarms and in succession send them
forth
381 Bound to establish new communities
382 On every shore whose aspect favours hope
383 Or bold adventure, promisin[?g] to skill

[23v]

IX, 384 And perseverance their deserved reward.
385 —Yes, he continued, kindling as he spake
386 Change wide and deep & silently performed
387 This Land shall witness and as days roll on
s} s}
388 Earths universal frame }w}hall feel the effect
Through her broad Continents & scattered Isles
389 Even to the smallest habitable Rock
{O
390 That {ocean beats with solitary waves
394 From culture universally bestowed
395 Upon a noble race in freedom born
humble
396 From education from that ~~simple~~ source
397 Expect these mighty issues from the pai[?n]
398 And quiet care of unambitious shools
~~For childhood [?framed~~]
399 Instructing simple childhoods ready ear
{os
400 Thence look for th{ese magnificent results
So
~~As~~ from the virtues of a petty seed
Which in his thievish bill the flying
Crow
Transports without encumbrance are
evolved

Cf. MS. 74, 124v.
Rev of 95v, 22r–21v.
400 The unnumbered lines following are drafted on 95v.

[24^r]

giant
Trunk limbs & umbrage of the ~~mighty~~ oak
so
Darkening the noontide, ~~as~~ from some
still fount
T Which the exulting Traveller bestrides
{ease
With sportive {[?] & proud complacency
{G
Proceeds the state of {ganges, or the Nile.
IX, 402, 403 Awake, ye Rulers of these favoured
Realms.
[?happy]
410 ~~Awake~~! assist your Country to fulfill
411 Her glorious destiny. begin eve now—
412 Now when oppression like the Egyptian
plague
stretched oer guilty
413 Of Darkness ~~spread oer wretched~~ Europe
makes
414 The Brightness more conspicuously appear
415 In which we move about & think & act
416 Now when destruction is a prime
pursuit
And with the anxieties of beastly war
Your minds are through necessity oppressed
417 Shew to the wre[?cthe]d nations for what
civil Polity end
418 The powers of government were ~~framed~~
given

[24^v]

~~At once descending from the height of~~ zeal
H}
IX, 419, 420 W}ere, gracefully, the impassioned
Sage broke off
By apprehension checked that his dis
listener's course
Might tire the [~~?Pastors] ex~~ patience &
~~exhaust~~
420 His sympathy. No sooner had he ceased
[~~?~~] looking forth
T} {n
421 W}ha{t [?with] ~~soft tone~~ the gentle Lady said
422 Behold the shades of afternoon have fallen

Unnumbered passage at top of 24^r is a rev of 95^v.
Numbered lines are a rev of 22^v
402, 403 A variant of this line originally followed l. 364 on 21^r (see also MS. 74, 124^v). On MS. 73, 22^v, the line precedes l. 410 but is del.
411 Period is possibly a random mark.

slope
[?~~slope~~]
423 Upon this flowery [?] — & see, beyond
424 The Lake though bright is of a placid
blue
425 As if preparing for the peace of Evening.
S
462 T|he loved to hear that eloquent old Man
out
463 Pour forth the meditations of his mind
464 On human life
~~Int~~
Loth to exhaust the Listeners sympathy
419 Abruptly her but with a graceful air
420 The sage broke off
from infancy to age
Far back as he remembered and as far
As
[?And]| he looked forward cheered with ~~pensive~~
pensive hope

[25^r]

And wide in compass as a tender heart
him
Had taught to observe.
~~Abruptly here but with a graceful air~~
~~venerable~~
IX, 419, 420 Here, gracefully, the ~~impassioned~~ Sage
broke
[420] Broke off by modest apprehension check d
~~By apprehension check d that his Disc~~ourse
[?thus]
That his discourse ~~though~~ with an earnest [?mind]
~~Might tire, if inconsiderately prolongd~~
Prolong d in height of zeal might weary out
hearers
The patience of his ~~audience~~ & exhaust
That his discourse prolonged in height of zeal
Might tire the listeners patience and exhaust
o
420 Their sympathy. —N|o[?n] sooner had he
ceased
421 Than looking forth the gentle Lady said
n
after
422 Behold the shades of [?]| noon have fallen
423 Upon this flowery slope, and see—beyond
424 The lake though bright is of a placid
blue

---

464 Rev below, related to ll. 419–420, is a rev of 25^r; see note to 25^r, ll. 419, 420.

Rev of 24^v, rev on 24^v.

419, 420 Rev probably tried first at the page foot, then between the lines of the base text, then in the second rev at the page foot and/or the rev on 24^v following l. 464. Ll. 419, 420 are further rev on 24^v, perhaps the latest in the series of changes.

425 As if preparing for the peace of evening.
426 How temptingly the landscape shines—the
air
~~Whose [?fervent] heat already is allay'd~~
427 Breathes invitation;—easy is the walk
428 To the Lake's margin where a boat
lies moored
429 Beneath its sheltering tree. Upon this [?~~hint~~]
hint
{ all {were
430 We rose together— {[?we] {ros pleased but
most
[419] Abruptly here but with a graceful air
[419, 420] ~~Here with a graceful air the Sage brooke off~~
[420] The sage broke off by apprehension checkd
By ~~apprehension check d that his discourse~~

[25v]

Beauteous
IX, 431 The [?~~loved~~] Girl whose cheek was flushed
eager with joy.
432 Light as a sunbeam gliding along the hills
Seen & not seen within a [?m] {h
433 ~~And forth she hastene~~d to impart the sc{[?]eme
She vanished eager [?the] {C
434 To her loved Brother & his shy {compeer.
there
435 ~~All~~ now was bustle in the Vicar's
earnest {ar house
436 And ~~eager~~ prep{[?]ation. Forth we went,
437 And down the valley on the Streamlets
bank
Pursued {C
438 ~~We took~~ our way—a broken {company
{[?saunter d]
Thus as we {[?] [?down] the [?wild] Brooks [?side]
461 In a soft tone to me the Matron said,
{[?at]
462 I love to hear th{[?is] eloquent Old Man
463 Pour forth the meditations of his mind
464 On human Life from infancy to age,
Far back as he remembers & as far
As he looks forward che[?ere]d by pensive
{[?broad] hope
And {[?] in compass as a tender heart
Hath taught him to observe.
465 How bright his picture—in what lovely
Do } hues
466 [?Ha]}th he reflect the characters of things
Eve[?n like this] image —

Rev on 26r–27r.
431 Another possibility for "loved" is "livid."

[26r]

oer
{ing
IX, 432 Light as a sumbeam glid{es ~~upon~~ the hills
S
[?A]}een & not seen within a moments space
{scheme
433 She vanised, eager to impart the {[?]
434 To her loved Brother & his shy Compeer.
435 Now was there Bustle in the Vicars House
earnest
436 And ~~eger~~ preparation: forth we we went
437 And down the valley on the streamlets bank
438 Pursued our way a broken Company
439 Mute or conversing single or In pairs—
did {down {[?that]
{[?over] through {[?] [?pleasant]
[?field]
Thus ~~as~~ we [?sauntered] ~~down the wild~~
brooks
through the pleasant [?field]
440 And reaching soon a bridge that overlook[?d]
441 The hasty rivulet where it lay becalmed
442 In a deep pool, there saw we at a glance
a
443 A two fold image—on ~~the~~ grassy bank
crystal
444 A snow white Ram and in the ~~peaceful~~
flood
445 Another & the same most beautiful
449 ~~Beneath him showed his shadow~~
446 On the green turf with his imperial front
447 Shaggy & bold & wreathed horns superb
448 The breathing creature stood—
as beautiful
[442] there by chance espied

[26v]

IX, 449 Beneath him show d his shadowy Counterpart
450 Each had his glowing mountain each his
sky
{C
451 And each seem'd {centre of his own
fair world
452 Antipodes unconscious of each other
453 Yet in partition with their several spheres
454 Blended in perfect stillness to our sight
disperse
455 Ah what a pity were it to ~~destr~~oy
456 Or to disturb so fair a spectacle

Rev of 25v and 9r. Rev on 26v.

Rev of 25v, 9r–9v; rev on 18v.

{th
457 And yet a brea{[?t] ca can do it.—
These few words
458 The Lady whispered—while we stood & gazed
together, all,
459 ~~All~~ gathered in still delight
460 Not without awe Thence passing on
low}
she said
461 In a sof} voice to my particular ear
462 I love to hear that eloquent old Man
463 Pour forth his meditations & descant
464 On human life from infancy to age
Far back as he remember & as far
As he looks forward cheerd by pensive
ho[?p]
And wide in compass as a tender heart
Hath by experience taght hi to observe
Or strong Imaginatio to [?con conceive]

[27r]

pure his spirit vivid
IX, 465 How ~~bright his~~ pictures in what ~~lovely~~
hues
His mind various forms of things
466 ~~Doth he~~ reflect the character of things
467 Caught in their fairest happiest attitude
472 ~~Even like that image in the silent pool~~
[472] A mirror faithful as that silent pool.
468 While he is speaking I have power to see
wills b}
469 Even as he see—[?w]}ut when his vo[?ic] hath
ceased
470 Then with a sigh I sometimes feel as now
so serene & bright
471 That combination so divinely fair
~~Ca Cannot be p~~[?er]
473 Cannot be lasting in a world like ours
474 To great & small disturbance exposed
But him they shake not hardly seem to touch
soul hope
His mind as ever fill'd with [~~?~~] & joy
Or with a holy sadness, not less sweet
475 More had she said—but from behind was
sportive {those heard
476 A jocund carol & {[?] Boys appeared
477 With baskets fraught the pages of our
Yet train
~~But~~ him they shake not—hardly seem to touch

Left-margin line at page foot probably indicates rev or del since these lines do not appear in *1814*.

Rev of 25v.

[475] —More had she said—but sportive shouts
jocund we heard
[476] Sent from the merry hearts of those two
Boys

[27[v]]

IX, 477 Who bearing each a basket on his arm
[478] Down the green fiel came tripping after us
~~Appeared and down the meadow ground~~
in haste
478 ~~Came tripping after us. The shore we~~ reachd
~~Embarked—nor [?faild] the Pages of our train~~
{~~C~~ ~~charges~~
479 ~~Our~~ {~~company~~ embarked, ~~and orders given~~
[479] We reached the shore & cautiously embarked
~~And requisite authority put forth~~
{ose
Th{e little ones disburthen d of their charge
~~Those inexperienced voyagers were~~
service} hushed
480 Now for a prouder [?were]} were addressed
~~Into secure composure.—Looks & words~~
~~eager~~
~~Expressed the wishes of that youthful~~
pair
~~Who proferr d now their further services~~
{an
481 But {[?] inexorable law forbad
had
482 And each resigned the oar which he ^ seized.
Whereat
483 ~~Therefo~~re with willing hand I undertook
needful grateful {!
484 The ~~ooarsman's~~ labour, pleasant task{: —
to me
485 Pregnant with recollections of the time
486 When on thy bosom spatious Windermere
487 In youth I practiced this delight art
488 Tossed on the waves alone or with a band
Joyous
489 Of ~~happy~~ Comrades.—
496 Tow'ards yon rocky Ile

---

482 The words from "resigned" are either del in pencil or written over an earlier pencil stroke. In the latter case, that pencil stroke may have been drawn to mark the intended insertion of ll. 489ff. on the facing 28[r].

489 Ll. 489–495 are on 28[r], then rev on 30[v].

496 The "w" in "Tow'ards" may be del with a vertical stroke.

[28r]

IX, 497 Clothed with transparent birch trees ~~steer~~
bend your
course
496 The Vicar said, and pointed as he spake
[?Or]
499 [?] tow'rds that other on the western shore
[?as we soon shall] [?]
bare
500 Where the [?tall] Columns of those lofty firs
gracefully
501 Supporting steadily a massy dome
iage S
502 Of sombre foll[?id] [?]eem to imitate
G
503 A grecian Temple rising from the Deep.
[?~~as~~]
~~Into secure [?]~~
re
489, 490 The ~~we~~edy margin cleared I dippd
the oars
491 Without obstruction & the Boat ad
vanced
492 Through the clear water[?s] smoothly as
[?~~kite~~]
a Hawk
493 That disentangl d from the shady boughs
494 Of some thick wood, its place of Covert,
1 cleaves
495 The abyss of air with correspondent
2 wings
505, 506 Rich field & sylvan slopes & rugged rocks
508 Surrounded us & as we held our course
509 Along the surface of the crystal flood
510 They ceased not to surround us, change of place
features
511 From kindred ~~objets~~ variously combined
512 Producing change of beauty ever new

Rev on 28v, 30v.

503/489, 490 With "Into secure [?]," WW possibly meant to begin rev of the passage that appears on the facing verso (27v, ll. 480/481).

495 Drawn line and numbers indicate transposition of the two half-lines, as in *1814*.

505, 506 Change of ink and pen.

[28v]

~~Here might~~
IX, 520 ⁎ ~~Much~~ could the Poet tell in faithful words
Much ~~could~~ if of willing auditors secure
521 Of objects seen, employments well deviz'd
522 And unsought pleasures springing up by chance
523 As if some friendly Genius had ordained
524 That as the day thus far had been replete
525 With pure enjoyment & serene delight
same
526 The ~~like~~ should be continued to its close
505, 506 ✕Rich fields & sylvan slopes & rugged
rocks ~~hills~~
508 Surrounded us and as we held our course
509 Along the surface of the glassy flood
510 They ceased not to surround us, change of place
511 From kindred features variously combined
512 Producing change of beauty ever new.
[520] ~~Here if of willing auditors secure~~
to
519 ~~In strains from which the Condescending Muse~~
deny to
[520] ~~Would not withold her influen I coul speak~~
538 ~~Of flowery spoils collected egerly~~
[538] Rapaciously [?we] gather d flowery spoils

[29r]

IX, 539 From land & water lillies of each hue
{ float
540 Golden & white—that {[?ride] upon the waves
541, 542 And court the wind, & lilly of the Vale
~~And the sequester d~~ lilly ~~that delights~~
~~of the vale~~
& from the sun witholds
543 That loves the ground, & [?~~fills her shadey~~] [?haunt]
{sun
from the {[?] witholds
With [?~~tender frag~~]
fragrance
~~pensive~~
544 Her ~~beauty [?] from the breeze her s~~weets

Rev of 28r; rev on 29v–31v.

520–526 Left-margin symbol probably indicates passage recopied; see rev on 28v (page foot), 29v–30r, 31r.

521 "Of ob" reinforced.

505 The X indicates another copy of the following passage; see bottom of 28r and also 30v.

538 Continued from bottom of 29r.

Rev on 29v, 30r, 31v.

544 Ink blot obscures third word.

~~Yet [?here] we~~
[544] Her pensive beauty; from the breeze her sweets.
~~There we did [?we gather] — the flowers~~
[?~~less prize~~]
528 A gypsy fire we kindle on the shores
I
529 Of that fairly [?s] land and beneath the trees
[?r]
531 ~~Sipped at the~~ [?] [?~~efreshed] beverage~~
530 In circle seated merrily partook
[531] The beverage drawn from China's fragrant herb
532 With shouts we raiz'd the ecchoes—stiller sound
534 The lovely girl supplied—a simple song
Whose low tones reach not [?t]
535 ~~That to the cavern~~ of the distant rocks
gently
536 To be repeated ~~there~~ but sank [?~~int~~]
~~Reach d not~~
537 into our hearts & charmed the peacful flood

[29^v]

IX, 513 Ah that such beauty &c
Much, if of willing auditors secure
tell
520 The Poet here could in faithful words
521 Of objects seen employments well devized
522 And unsought pleasures sprin[?ging] up by chance
523 As if some friendly Genius had ordained
e
524 That as th [?is] day thus far had been replete
525 With pure enjoyment & serene delight
526 The same should be continued to its close.
528 A Gypsy fire we kindled on the shores
529 Of that fair island, and beneath the trees
merrily seated in a a ring we
530 In circle seated merr[?ied]ly par partook
531 The beverage drawn from Chinas fragrant herb
532 Launchd from our hands the smooth stone skim d the Lake
533 With shouts we raiz d the echoes—stiller sounds
534 The lovely Girl supplied a simple song
535 Whose low tones reached not to the distant rocks

---

537 Continued on l. [538] at bottom of 28^v.

Rev of 30^r, 28^v–29^r; rev on 30^v.
513 See lines added at page foot, rev of 30^r.
522 Ink blot obscures "sprin[?ging]."

513, 514 Ah—that such beauty cannot be portrayed
pencil's
nor can by
[?of]
515 In words, & ~~is the [?propert]~~ ~~amb~~ers happier skill
516 But is the property [?of] of [?him] alone
noted it with care markd
517 Who hath beheld it—[?~~seen~~] it with his
eye
[?noted] it with [?care]
h l
518 And to his mind re[?~~cord~~]ed it wit{[?eye]}ove

[30r]

IX, 536 To be repeated there but gently sank
537 Into our hearts & charmed the peaceful
flood.
u
While lingering yet [?w]}pon the lovely isl
538 Rapaciously we gathered flowery spoils
539 From land & water—lillies of each hue
that float upon the waves
y
540 Golden & white: & ~~lilli~~{es ~~of the~~ vale
And court the wind & lilly of the vale
loves the ground
541, 543 That ~~courts the wind~~ & from the sun
witholds
544 Her pensive beauty from the breeze her sweets{.;
541 Shyest of flowers yet social with
kind [?]
{her
[?]
Modest—yet
[~~?Are modest] [?~~]
513 ~~Ah that such beauty~~
~~Yet her~~
~~And yet th flowers that~~
545 Such product & such pastime did the
place
furnish to th jocund hearts
546 And season yield [?~~such chearfulness~~]
[?~~inspired~~]
[~~ ? ~~]
[546] o ~~with~~ [?jocund ~~hearts~~ em]
~~Of~~ [?]}~~ld & young but as we reem~~barked
Of [?old] [?furnis d] —as we reembark
547 And left the shore the solitary

---

516 Conjectured "of" is obscured by ink blot.
518 Conjectured "cord" is obscured by ink blot.

Continuation of 29v; rev of 29r, 28v; rev on 31v.
513 Del by eras as part of WW's continuing attempt to shape this sequence, related to copy on 29v.

slow
[513] Ah that such beauty, in such sucession smooth
[?en'd]
Thus [?openening] on the view—retiring [?thus]
[513] Insensbly & vary [?in] the light
514 of living Nature cannot be pourtrayed
o
Yet, if [?] f willing auditors secure
[?the] Poet ~~Poet~~
520 Much [?could] ~~the~~ tell of objects seen
[?more]
521 And [?of] of occupations well devized

[30v]

IX, 489, 490 The reedy margin cleared I dipp'd the oars
491 Without obstruction and the Boat advancd
clear
492 Through the ~~smooth~~ water smoothly as a hawk
493 That disentangled from the shady boughs
494 Of some thick wood, her place of covert, cleaves
495 With correspondent wings, the abyss of air.
505 Rich fields & sylvan slopes, & rugged rocks
508 Surrounded us and as we held our course
evel
509 Along the l [?imit] of the glassy flood
510 They ceased not to surround us, change of place
diversly
511 From kindred features ~~variously~~ combined
512 Producing change of beauty ever new.
varyin in the light
513 —Ah that such Beauty ~~cannot be pourtrayed~~
of
514 [?On] living Nature, and presented thus
In smooth succession cannot be poutrayed
On
515 ~~By~~ words, ~~nor by even pencils happier~~
nor by the pencils silent skill
516 But is the property of him alone
~~seen it with his eyes~~
517 Who hath beheld it—noted it with it care
518 And in his mind recorded it with love
[?strive]
Suppressing therefore all desire to ~~aim~~ [?aim]

---

[513]–514 Rev on 29v (page foot), 30v, 31r.
520–521 Rev of 29v, 28v; rev on 31r. Ink blots obscure conjectural readings.

489–512 Rev of 28v–28r.
495/505 The missing ll. 496–504 are drafted as continuation of l. 489 on 27v and 28r.
513–518 Rev of 29v–30r.

{[?For]
{[?At] that which ~~lies [?not within his~~ our power]
is not in our power to [?~~reach~~]
To reach [?] [?]

[31^r]

~~Not, venturing, therefore or attempt so far~~
IX, 520 The Poet will content himself to speak
~~Yet, if of willing auditors secure~~
{aim
Supressing therefor all desire to {[?]
~~Much could the Poet tell of objects seen~~
t} his { reach
A[?n]} that which is not in ~~our~~ power to {[?aim]
~~With Admiration fe[?r]ent & sincere~~,
~~Of little [?petty~~]
[520] ~~The Poet will content himself to~~ speak
521 ~~And [?more~~] of occupations well devized
the Poet
519 ~~Of petty~~ It shall suffice if he speak
522 And unsought pleasures springing up
by chance,
[521] Of trivial occupations well devize
523 As if some friendly Genius had ordained,
524 That, as the Day thus far had bee[?n] replete
sincere
525 With pure enjoyment & serene delight,
526 The same should be continued to its close.
g}
527 One spirit animating old & yound} ✳
528 A g[?u]psey fire we kindled on the shore
{and its
529 Of that fair isl{es, & beneath ~~the~~ trees
530 Merrily seated in a ring partook
531 The beverage drawn from Chinas fragrant
herb.
532 Launchd from our hands the smooth
stone skimmed the Lake
533 With shouts we raized the echoes—stiller sounds
534 The lovely girld supplied—a simple song
535 Whose low tones reached not to the
distant rocks
Con}
519 [?] }tented therefore [?with an humbler]
Therefore relinquishing

[519] Suffice therefore if the rural Muse
[520] Vouchsafe sweet influence while her Poet speaks
[521] Of Trivial occupations well devized

520–535 Rev of 30^v, 30^r, 29^v–29^r, 28^v.

527 Pencil asterisk in the right margin possibly indicates thought of rev, but *1814* follows 31^r reading.

Last two lines on page are rejected or alt drafts toward rev at top of page.

[519]–[521] Vertical entries in left margin overwrite text and correspond to *1814*.

[31v]

IX, 536 To be repeated there but gently sank
537 Into our hearts & charmed the peaceful
flood
{spoils
538 Rapaciously we gathered flowery {[?]
539 From land & water, lillies of each hue
{that}
540 Golden & white {& }1} float upon the
1}
waves
541, 542 And court the wind, and lilly of the Vale
543 That loves the ground, and from the sun witholds
Her her
544 ~~Its~~ pensive Beauty from the breeze ~~its~~ sweets
541 Shyest of plants yet social to her kind.
{did
545 Such product & such pastime {[?&] the
place
546 And season yield—but as we reembar[?e]d
547 Leaving, in quest of other scenes, the shore
548 ~~And left the shore~~, the solitary said
Of that fair Isle,
549 In a low, voice, yet careless who might
hear
550 The fire that burnt so brightly to our wish
551 Where is it now—deserted on the beach
552 It seems extinct; [?~~how soon~~]! nor shall
fanning
the breeze

556 *And in this unpremeditated slight
which is no further needed, see
557 Of that ~~where~~of we have no further nee[?d]
558 The common course of [?living] gratitud

[32r]

embers
IX, 553 Revive its ~~ashes~~—what care we for this
{ends
{needs are gaind
554 Whose ~~needs are~~ served—behold an~~d~~
emblem here
one of
555 Of ~~this~~ days pleasure ~~&~~ all mortal joys
~~D~~
556, 557 # [?] ~~id in this slight of which need [?we need~~ no more]
558 ~~Are emblem too of human gr~~atitude
557 Of that whereof we have no further need

Rev of 30r, 29r, 28v.
556–558 Rev of 32r, where these lines also have a marginal symbol.

Rev of 31v.
556, 557 Marginal symbol signals insertion of lines at bottom of 31v.

~~To kindle prompt as ready to ex~~pire
That kindle promptly and as soon expire
s[?ti
The object ~~out of mind—the~~
[?at]
559 Th[?is] plaintive note disturbed not the repose
e so steered
560 Of the still [?r]vening—[?no]uthward now we
[?~~steered~~]
ing
568 And by assistance of a juttg rock
569 That framed a natural pier we land
all
571 On the main shore, and climbing up the
side
smooth [?water] [?near]
[571] Of a ~~stiff~~ hill that from the ~~waters edge~~
~~Abruptly rose~~
~~Rose, with a bold ascent~~,
[571] Rose, with bold ascent, we [~~?~~] there attaind
A ~~less~~ a~~[?n overview from~~]
[?re] an unobstructed sight
572 By ~~the~~ [?t] by slow degrees ~~a pros~~pect
~~of the pla~~[?~~ce~~]
[572] Slowly, a less & less obstructed sight
574 The whole ~~wide~~ fair Vale & Lake indented
In compass round coast
[572] ~~Slowly a~~ less & less obstructed sight
ale
[574] Of the whole vall & lake indented coast
575 And in the [?~~midst~~] the churchtower
[?stretched round]

[32^{v}]

IX, 573 Of that flat meadows & indented coast
574 Of the whole Lake, in ~~majesty~~ compass seen:—
far of
~~beyond~~
575 And yet conspicuous stood the old Church
Tower
576 In majezsty presiding oer the vale
seemingly preserved
~~shut~~ out
577 And all its dwelling: ~~from the wo~~rld
[?seeming] [?turmoil]
~~shut out~~
the
578 From ~~all~~ intrusion of a rest[?]les world
579 By ~~rocks~~ Rock impassable & mountains
huge.

571–575 Rev on 32^{v}.
575 At page foot of 32^{r}, alt for conjectured "midst" is "majest."

the smooth
571 On the main shore and climbing ~~up~~ the steep
side
dd
green with [?abr] e[?]ge
[571] Of a ~~smoo~~th hill that from the waters [?sid]
sharp [?w thence ob]
[571] Rose with a bold ascent we the[?nc] attained
572 Slowly a less & less obstructed sight
[573] Of the flat meadows & indented coast
[574] Of the whole Lake, in compass seen: far off
[575] And yet conspicuous stood the old
Church
tower
[576] In majesty presiding oer the vale
[577] And all its Dwelling seemin[?]ly [?~~int~~] preservd
[578] From the intrusion of a restless world
[579] By rocks impassable & mountains
huge

[33^r]

we stood
~~Well pleased~~, upon this elevated spot
~~We lingered long~~,
IX, 580 ~~The elevated spot which we had~~
gained
[582] Lingering well pleased, each
580, 581 Supplied commodious seats of moss & stone
there
582 And ~~so~~ we lingered long, —the eye of each
583 Settling upon the features of the scene
[?them]
pleas d [?him] most
Which most attracted him
[?~~times~~]
out
[?~~oft had~~]
each
[?and] ~~some~~times pointing
[?ou]
585 ~~general~~ some discovery of his own
586 T'~~others~~ notice what himself had marked
or[?d] [?~~obj~~]
585 or to some fav [?merely from a] objects
[586] They, haply [?missed], or ~~from a nat~~ural
wish
[?eyes]
[586] ~~Their eyes~~ directing other [?notice from]
587 To impart a joy imperfect while
Untill unshared,
588 ~~At length~~ these acts of mutual regard

571–[575] Rev of 32^r.

Rev on 34^r–34^v, 35^v–36^r.

individual
[?small] particular
589 And little separate notices were lost
In one impression that possessd
the soul
590 Of all who saw. Already had the Sun
591 Sinking with less than ordernary
state
592 Attained his western bound; but
rays of light

[33v]

IX, 594 2 Behind the summit of the [?western] hill
593 1 Now suddenly diverging from the orb
Sunk down,
594, 595 Withrawn or veiled, shot upwards to the
crown
596 Of the blue firmament—aloft & wide
[?darted]
597 Enflaming multitude of cloud
Through [?& separate]
l
600 ~~Light~~ [?] light [?~~clouds~~] and [?separate] ~~of~~ dimension
ultudues small
601 2 Innumerable m ulti of forms,
[600] 1 Separ[?at]ly poised & of dimension ~~small~~
small
602 Scatter d through half the circle of the sky
the H heaven
607 That which [?in] [?] eavend displayd, the
liquid deep
608 Repeated but with unity sublime.
609 While on the grassy mountains open side
610 We gazed, in silence hushe with eyes
intent
611 On the refulgent spectacle diffused
612 Through earth sky & water & all
visib space
613 The Priest in holy rapture thus
Retired exclaimed
[594] ~~Withdrawn~~ behind the mountain tops or veild
595 By the dense air

[34r]

site
IX, 580 Upon that elevated ~~spot~~ ~~spot~~ we stood
582 Lingering well pleased, admiring quietly

Rev on 34r, 35v, 36r–36v.
594–593, 601–[600] Numbers in left margin reverse line order to sequence of *1814*.
602/607 The missing lines 603–606 are drafted on 34r.
609–613 Rev of 34v; then rev on 36v.

Rev of 33r–33v; rev on 35v–36v.

dom make known
584 And each not sel[?~~o~~] eager to ~~point~~ out
585 ~~Discoverys which himself had made~~
[585] His own discoveries, or to favorite points
{[?~~Or~~]
[585] {[?] ~~or to [?some] fav~~orite point
notice merely [?some]
~~ob~~ }
586 Directin [?] }~~serv~~ation from ~~a~~ wish
587 To impart a joy imperfect while
[?~~uns~~] unshared
~~But [? ~~]
Untill these acts of mutual regard
[?their ~~part~~] small ~~was [?obsc~~]
[?~~these~~]
589 And ~~individual~~ partic[?url] interests
~~was [?obscure~~]
were
~~was~~ absorbed
In one impression that possed the soul
~~Of all who~~
603 And giving back & shedding each
{[?ea]
The illustrious on {[?]
[?~~Restraint the bles~~]
unapparent of glory
605 Which from the font of [?~~unapparent~~]
glory
606 They had imbibed & ceased not ~~to [?r~~]
[?to] bright
604 With prod gal communion those [?~~proud~~] hues

[34v]

IX, [609] While on the open [?mountain] side
We ~~stood~~ sate,
[610] In [?silence hushed] ~~we stood~~ with eyes intent
611 On the refulgent spectacle diffused
[?th]
609 While on the mountain side
In [?~~Thou~~]
610 ~~A~~ silent company we stood with eyes
{ fulgent intent
On the re{[?splendent] spectacle intent
613 The Priest in holy rapture thus exclaimd
612 Through earth sky water & all visible space
Eternal Spirit
614 Supreme existence
[614] Almight Father universal God
Spirit
every region
{~~ever~~
Through {all ~~the re~~ of the spatious earth

603–606 Continues draft from l. 602 on 33v.

Rev of 33v; rev on 36v–37r.

And through all worlds whereer the light of life
exists
{ce
Is kindled and intelligen{t abides
{B
Adored & dreaded!—{being infinite,
material
For this ~~reflected~~ ^ image of thyself
617 ~~Eternal, for this Shadow of thyself~~
~~This [?local spir~~]
618 To the infirmity of mortal sense
[?locally]
this local transitory type
619 Voutchsafed, ~~this image visibly express d~~
splendours
620 Of thy paternal Glories and the Pomp
621 Of those that fill thy Courts in highest heaven
622 The Radiant Cher[?a]bim accept the thanks
here convened
623 Of [?us] thy humble Creatures, ~~here convened~~.

[35r]

{ y
IX, 628 Such as they are who in th{[?e] presence stand
in {nd
629 Unsullied uncorruptible a{d drink
I }
630 [?T]}mperishable majesty streamed forth
earth
631 From thy empyreal throne, the elect of eart
632 Shall be, divested at th appointed hour
cleans d
633 Of all Dishonour, cleared of mortal stain.
and conclude
634 Accomplish then their number, ~~or if still~~
{weary or if through laps of year
635 Times {[?] course, of the [?thus] hast [?decreed]
Which no imagination may [?compute]
[~~?~~] ~~[?Contin~~] to be born & die
continue
Man shall ~~be born & die~~, and this great
frame
And this great frame of things be unconsumed
~~Of Things, thy workmanship be unconsumed~~
[?] [?the int]
If such be thy be thy unsearchable decree
638 Oh let thy word prevall to take away
639 The sting of human nature; spread the law
640 As it is written in thy holy book
641 Throughout all lands let every nation hear
642 The high behest & every heart obey

---

623 Phrase "here convened" is partially eras and then del in ink.

Rev on 37r–38r, 39v–40v.

643 Both for the love purity and hope
That [?pain] & mortal fra[?ilties] shall
exist
[?y] [?thy] r
If th[?e] [?in]^scrutable decree od dains

[35[v]]

IX, 580 Commodious resting of [?~~turf~~] & stone
[?]
580, 581 This elevated spot suppli[?d] & there
582 We sate well pleasd—adm
644 That it affords to such as do thy will
645 And persevere in good that they
n shall rise
646 And have a [?h] earer of thee in heaven.
ty
647 Father of good this prayer in boun y grant
~~This prayer fulfilled in mercy to thy Son~~
of good bounty
648 Father of [?in mercy] in mercy ~~grant th[?i]~~
this prayer
649 ~~Then not till then shall persecution cease~~
650 ~~And cruel wars expire~~
[648] In mercy grant it to thy wre[?ch]ed
ons
nor S[?]
nor
[649] Then [?not] till then shall persecution
cease
[650] And cruel wars expire
Mankind must breathe—the world be unconsumed
635 If such by thy inscrutable decree
And for created man & this great frame
earth sky [?marvellous]
Of [?thing] & ~~heaven~~ thy ~~wondrous~~ workmans
Almighty Power [?such issue thou] ordain
1
Mankind shall breathe the wor d be un
consumed
If such [?duration] for this frame of things
[?ma]
Thy [?in] [?rvellous work] & for created Man
[?Such]
[?T]
Almighty Power thy [?Providence] ordain
638 Oh let thy word prevail 1

Last two lines of 35[r] are rev of unnumbered lines at middle of page.

580–582 Rev of 33[r], 34[r], 36[r].
644–650 Rev on 38[r].
635–638 Rev of 35[r], rev on 37[v], 39[v]–40[v].
638 Two pairs of words are marked for transposition. The "1" indicates what should be the opening set; if there is a corresponding "2," it is obscured by an ink blot.

[36^{r}]

mountains huge
IX, 580 —~~Upon this elevate site~~ we stood
[580] This elevated spot of ground supplied
581 Commodious seat of turf & mossy stone
& there we sate
582 ~~Lingering well-pleas d~~—admiring quietly
frame &
583 The general aspect of the scene
584 As each not seldom eager to make known
[?lope]
[580] [?~~Some~~] ~~[?~~] Soft heath this elevated s [?pot] suppli[?d]
With
[581] [?And] resting place of mossy stone & there
585 His own discoveries, or to favorite points
w
[582] ~~We sate~~ ~~pell pleas~~ed
[?their] merely
586 Directing ~~general~~ notice ^ from a wish
admiring
[582] We sate reclined [?]
587 To impart a joy imperfect while unshared;
signs
Untill these ~~acts~~ of mutual regard
each t, absorb[?d]
589 And small particular interes t[?s] were effaced
appearence that alike impressd
By one ~~impression, that possessed the soul~~
The minds of all.
590 Of all who saw. Already had the sun
591 Sinking with less than ordinary state
b
592 Attained his western [?li] ound; but rays of light,
593 Now suddenly diverging from the orb
594 Retired behind the mountain tops or veild
595 By the dense air, shot upwards to the crown
596 Of the blue firmament—aloft—& wide,—
And multitude of little floating clouds
597 ~~Dar[?ted], enflaming multit~~udes of clouds
little
[597] and multitudes of floating Clouds
been seen to glow
598, 599 Pierc'd through their texture [?thin,] became at once
Like purest flame
600 Glorious bright, clouds [?separated] poised
[600] [?Innu] Vivid as fire

[36^{v}]

IX, [598] Pierced through their thin aetherial mould ere we

580–600 Rev of 34^{r}, 33^{v}, 33^{r}; ll. 597–600 rev on 36^{v}.
580–582 Rev on facing 35^{v}.
598, 599 Ink blot obscures "texture [?thin,]."
600 Ink blot obscures "[?separated]."

---

[598]–613 Rev of 36^{r}.

[599] Who saw of change were conscious ha[?d] become
[600] Vivid as fire—clouds separately poised

{~~ois'd~~
600 ~~Separately p~~{[?] ~~full of dimensions~~ small
{e
601 Innumerable multitud{es of forms
[?~~heav~~]
602 Scattered through half the circle of the sky
603 And giving back, and shedding each on
[?each]
604 With prodigal communion, the bright hue
605 Which from the unapparent fount of glory
606 They had imbibed and ceased not to receive
607 That which the heavens display d the liquid
deeps
608 Repeated but with unity sublime.
{from
609 —While {on the grassy mountains open side
610 We gazed, in silence hushed with eyes intent
the
611 On the refulgent spectacle diffused
612 Through earth sky water and all visible
In strains of space
613 The Priest in holy rapture thus exclaimed
596 aloft & wide
597 And multitudes of little floating clouds
598 Pierc d through their thin aetherial mould ere we
become
599 Who saw of change were conscious had ~~be come~~
[600] Vivid as fire clouds [?sepear~~ately~~] poised
separately poised

[37r]

IX, 614 Eternal Spirit universal God
[Through every Region of the spateous earth]
Through
And through all worlds whereer the light
of life
Is kindled and intelligence abides
Adored & dreaded—Being infinite
615 And inacessible to human thought
S}
616 [?]}ave by degrees & steps which thou hast
deigned [?deig]

---

604 Line spacing indicates that "bright" was added after "hue" was written.
596–[600] Rev of 34r, 33v.

Rev of 34v–35r.
614 The brackets around the second line perhaps signal its intended rev or om (and perhaps also the three lines following) as in *1814*.

this
[617] To furnish, for [?]
617 ~~For this material~~ image of thy self
618 To the infirmity of mortal sense
sitory
619 Voutchsafed—this local tran [?] [?tory]
type
620 Of thy paternal glories and the pomp
621 Of those who fill thy courts in highest
heaven
622 The radiant cher[?a]bim accept the
thanks
623 Of us thy humble Creatures, here convened.
628 Such as they are who in the presence
stand
629 Unsullied incorruptible & drink
630 Imperishable majesty streamed forth
empyreal
631 From thy [?~~imperi~~] Throne the elect of
earth

[37ᵛ]

[?sum]
Whose [?~~p~~] no [?poets] knowledge may [?compute]
IX, 632 Shall be divested at the appointed hour
633 Of all dishonour—cleansed of mortal
stain.
634 Accomplish then their number & conclude
[?] or, ~~if~~ that wishd [?release]
[?since]
635 Times weary course, ~~or if through age to~~ age
from he
Though, [?to] the peaceful slumberer of t [?] dark
Divided only by a moments space
[?~~Endure]—whose sum no foresight may~~
[?compute]
y
637 Is f[l]et far off to thoughts of living men
[?nor] [~~?] by~~ power of [?fait]
In faith aspiring, ~~if [?thou hast decreed~~]
~~Mankind shall breathe, the world~~ be
~~Al~~ [?~~unconsumed~~]
[?The] ~~mighty Ruler that through lapse of years~~
~~d~~
~~Which no prophets knowle gge may [?compute~~]
[?insight]
~~If such duration for this frame of things~~
~~Man shall continue to be born & die~~
~~Thy marvellous works & for created Man~~
~~And this great frame of things be [?unconsumed~~]
In faith aspiring nor by power of faith
~~Thy providence almighty Power ordain~~
Made capable to know what thou hast [?veiled]

Rev of 35ʳ and 35ᵛ, perhaps working back and forth on these pages and 37ʳ.

632 Conjectured "poets" in rev may be "priests" or an attempt at "prophets" as in the del fourth line below l. 637.

From faith & prophecy—the [?term prescribd]
638 Oh let thy word prevail ~~to take a~~way
[?is]
For th{[?e] duration of this frame of things
And all who breathe [?these elements—] let the
word
[?e]
639 The sting of human nature—spread th{[?y] law
e
640 As it is written in thy} holy Book
~~I~~ ~~is~~
[635] [?T]}~~f th~~y ~~sovereign purpose has decreed~~
[?Is] [?] through inability to read
The purpose of thy providence—must still
[637] [?remain] far off

[38r]

IX, 641 Throughout all Lands let every Nation
hear
642 The high behest & every heart obey
643 Both for the love of purity & hope
644 Which it affords to such as do thy will
645 And persevere in good that they shall
rise
646 To have a nearer view of thee in heaven
Fa this prayer
647 P[?]}ther of Good in bounty grant
648 In mercy grant it to thy wretched
sons
649 Then nor till then shall persecution
cease
650 And cruel wars expire. The way is
marked
appointed
651 The guide ~~is [?furnished~~] & the ransom
paid
[?But] who
652 {[?T] they who [?knew], the nations {of of yore
653 Heard & erected temples where they meet
654 ~~Do in their souls [?perverse~~ness] linger still
[654] These sacred Truth to acknowled
~~d~~
655 ~~Preferred bonds and~~ [?]}~~arkness to a state~~
[652] Alas the nations who received of Yore
[653] These tidings & within their temples meet
[654] The sacred truth to acknoledge, linger
still
[655] Preferring bonds and darkness to a state

[38v]

IX, 656 Of holy freedom by redeeming love

Rev of 35r–35v; rev on 40v–41r.
652 The "B" possibly overwrites "Tha" to form "But."

657 Proffered to all while yet on earth detaind
658 Thus fare the many: & the thoughtful few
Who{
659 [?]} in the anguish of their souls [?lament]
661 ~~Shall this be so shall [?enimosity] & strife~~
660 This dire pervers ness cannot chuse but ask
[661] Shall it endure? shall enmity &
662 Deceit & guile be left to sow their seed
Falshood
663 And the kind never perish—Is the hope
664 Fallacious or will that blest day arrive
[664] When righteousness shall win & hold
the world
{dominion
665, 666 In peaceable {[?communion], neer to fail
667 When they whose choice or lot it is to
dwell
668 In crowded cities, without fear shall live
{e
669 Studious of mutual benefit, as h{[?im]
among sweet dews & flower
670 Whom morning wakes to ~~till the [?lonely] field~~
[?~~O~~]{
671, 672 [?] } ~~of every clime be happ~~
671 In every clime to till the lonely fields
672 Be happy in himself The law of faith

[39r]

[?triumph]
IX, 673 Working through love such ~~conquest~~ shall
it gain
674 Such conquest over sin & guilt atchieve
658 Thus fare the many & the thoughtful few
{needs
660 Who [?granted] this perverseness {[?]
{Of must ask
{And their own hearts & [?dive] if so they
[?Lovingkindness] [?must]
{[?y]
Into th{[?is] [~~ ? ~~] ~~[?crafts] of [?those]~~] to [?learn]
~~If th[?ey]~~]
[?se] souls are
grieve[?d]
[658] The few the thoughtful few who ~~gri~~
~~grieve~~

Rev on 39r, 41r.

661 Conjectured "enimosity" possibly intended as "enmity."

670 Possibly "lovely" (or "lowerly" or "lowering" intended as "flowerly" or "flowering") is the reading instead of the conjectured "lonely."

673–678 Rev on 41v. Ll. 673–674 run on from 38v; the rule may mark stopping to rev ll. 658–661 from the facing 38v before continuing with ll. 675–678.

658–661 Rev of 38v; rev on 41r.

[660] For this perversen cannot chuse but
ask
661 Shall it endure—
G
675 Almighty P od thy further grace impart
A
676 T nd with that help the wonder shall
be seen
677 Fulfilled the hope accomplished, and
[?name]
thy ~~praise~~
678 Be sung with transport & unceasing
~~joy~~.
praise

[39v]

IX, 634 Accomplish then their number and conclude
635 Times weary course, or [?since] that wished
release
Though from the peaceful slumberer of the
dark
Divided only by a moments space
[?Is] yet far off to thoughts of living men
nor [?~~and~~] by power of faith
In faith aspiring, and by thy decree
Which in truth [?be]
637 [?Ma] [?] none can fathom may ~~be~~ distant
far
[637] [?~~Ages] & countless ages let thy word~~
[?Remain]
[?] For us who [?would] exist on earth
[?~~ages~~]
c [?removed]
Ages & [?] ountless agse. Let thy
In faith aspiring nor by power of faith
Made capable to know what thou hast
veiled
From faith & prophessy the term [?~~appo~~]
e prescri
To th is duration of the
far removed
[637] May yet by thy decree be [?~~placed~~] far off
[637] Ages & countless ages, let thy word
[?T] [?]
To the

---

678 Word "joy" partially eras then del in ink.

Rev of 37^v, 35^v–35^r; rev on 40^r–40^v.
634 Apparent del of "and conclude" is actually blotting of the facing 40^r.

[40r]

~~by a moments space~~
~~May yet by thy decree be far removed~~
IX, 637 ~~Ages & countless ages~~—let thy word
Though from the peaceful slumberer of the dark
Divided only by a moments space
Is yet far off to thoughts of living men
In faith aspiring nor by power of faith
Made capable to know what thou hast
veild
From faith & prophecy—the term [?~~ap~~]
[?]
prescribed
For the duration of the world & all
[637] Who breathe these elements, Let
thy word [?]

in groves
688, 689 Of thickest glo[?m] & some, he said, required
690 Such dismal service that the loudest
Voice
691 Of the swoln cataracts which now are heard
692 Soft murmuring, was too weak to overcome
{ns
693 Though aided by wild winds the gr[?an{d] & shrieks
694 Of human victims, offered up to appease
{ng
695 Or to propitiate; and if livi{g eyes
696 Had visionary faculties to see
697 The that hath been as the thing that is
698 We might behold [?perhaps], this wide
~~spread [?mer~~]
wide spread mere
699 Redding from shore to shore with ghasly blaze

[40v]

IX, 634 Accomplish then their number & conclude
{ or
635 Times weary course! {[?if], if, by thy decree
636 The consummation that will come by stealth
637 Be yet far distant—let thy word prevail
638 O—let thy word prevail to take away
{S
639 The sting of human Nature—{spread the law

Boxed lines are rev of 39v, 37v, 35v, 35r; rev on 40v. The passage may be boxed to indicate its intended om from fair copy.

688–698 Rev of 42r; rev on 14v–15r.

693 Rev forms "groans."

Clean copy incorporates and finalizes several pages of draft on 40r, 39v, 38r, 37v, 35v, 35r.

636 WW after many tries at this passage in MS. 73 appears to have given up on the elaboration of these lines attempted in preceding drafts, and possibly drafted this abbreviated final version somewhere other than MS. 73 as this fair copy line appears in no other version.

As it is written in the holy book
Throughout all Lands let every nation hear
The high behest and every heart obey—
Both for the love of purity & hope
Which it affords to such as do thy will
And persevere in good that they shall rise
To have a nearer view of thee in heaven.
Father of Good this prayer in bounty grant
In mercy grant it to thy wretched Sons
Then, nor till then, shall persecution cease
And cruel wars expire. The way is markd,

[41r]

The guide appointed and the ransom paid
who
Alas the nations of of yore received
[?a] christian[?s]
These tidings and within their Temples meet
still [?til]
The sacred truth to acknowledg linger s [?i]
Preferring bonds and darkness to a state
Of holy freedom by redeeming Love
Proffered to all while yet on earth
detained.
thoughtful
So fare the many—and the [?wort] few
i
Who in the anguish of their souls bewa ll
[?e]
Th is dire perversness cannot chuse but ask
Shall it endure?—shall enmity & strife
Falsehood & guile be left to sow their seed
And the kind never perish?—is the hope
Fallacious? or will that blest day arrive
When righteousness shall win & hold the
world
In peaceable dominion neer to fail
W
[?] he they whose choice or lot it is to d
well
In crowded cities without fear shall live
Of public outrages or private wrong

---

643 Partial eras is probably of a copying error as both earlier draft 38r and *1814* have "purity."

Rev of 39r, 38r–38v.
667 Overwriting may reinforce a partially formed "Wh."

[41^v]

IX, 669 Studious of mutual benefit, and he
morning
670 Whom ~~the sun~~ wakes ~~to be~~ among sweet
{ &
dews {[?of] flowers
671 Of every clime to till the lonely field
672 Be happy in himself? The law of faith
673 Working through love such conquest shall
it gain
674 Such triumph over sin & guilt atchieve.
{L
~~God~~ {lord
675 ~~Almighty~~ ~~Power~~ thy further grace impart
676 And with that help the wonder shall be seen
677 Fulfilld The hope accomplish d & thy praise
678 Be sung with transport & unceasing joy

679 Once, while the name Jehovah was a sound
680 Amid [?~~of~~] the forests of this sea girt Isle
681 Unheard—the savage nations bowed
their heads
{G del} morseless
682 To {gods rej}ighting in re~~vengeful~~ deeds
which [?themse ve] had fashioned
[?who]} ~~created~~
683 Gods [?they} themseselve] ~~invented~~ to promote
l }
684 Iill purposes & f[?]}atter foul desires.
ous retreats
685 Then, mid these mountain ~~fastness~~es, for
here

[42^r]

May yet be seen memorials of that age
In unmolested Solitude preserved
{ ose
IX, 686 To th{[?at] Inventions of corrupted Man
687 Mysterious rite were solemniz d in groves
{[?gloom] receivd
Of thickest {[?] , & [?some], tis said, ~~require~~
And covert places, and, as Records tell,
[?~~terrifi~~]
689 ~~Of those accursed Idols some required~~

669–678 Rev of 38^v–39^r.
678–685 Rev on 14^v.

Rev on 14^v–15^r.
687/689–698 Rev on 40^r.

⊛ that the loudest voice
Such [?apart]
690 ~~This~~ dismal service, ~~not [?in peac] perfor~~med
awe but so loud
~~And~~ with {[?]-inspiring stillness, ~~but [?with~~]
[690] And [?din] the celebration that the voice
(
691 Of the perpetual streams{, which now are heard
)
692 Soft murmuring{, in the season of their rage
[692] And highes fury were too weak to drown
693 Though aided by strong winds, the shrieks & groans
694 Of human victims offered up to appease
695, 698 Or to propitiated—this wide-spread
⊛
mere
[690] Such dismal service that the loudes voice
swoln cataracts
[691] Of the ~~descending stream~~ which now ar heard
[692] Soft murmuring was too weak to overcome
[693] Though aided by strong winds the groans & shrieks

[42[v]]

Of in the quiet of a summer eve
blaz[?e]
[?ghastly]
IX, 699 Redden d from shore to shore with streaming
[?~~ghast~~]
Flung ~~light~~
[?~~F~~] body
700 [?~~Sent~~] ~~that~~ from the heart of those devouring fires
701 To [?ri] Taranis erected on the heights
702 By priestly hands for impious sacrifice.
to
705 Or {[?] Andates, femal Power, who gave
706 For so they fancied glorious victory
[?In]
709 ~~Now see~~ the appear [?ce] of things—how changed
But mark [?os]
710 From such the worship & with th{[?at] compared
711 The worshipper how innocent & blest
712 So wide the difference ~~& that~~ a willing
mind
~~In [?hours~~] this affecting
713 At ~~such an~~ hour as this might almost
think
714 That Paradise, the lost abode of man,
to
715 Was raised again,—& ~~for~~ a happy few
716 In its original beauty here restored

690–693 The marking above l. 690 signals substitution of the rev passage at page foot.

"Of" in first line is perhaps intended as "Oft."
699 Rev on 40[r].
699–717 Rev on 15[r]–15[v].

717 Whence but from thee, the true & only God
[702] By priestly hands for sacrifice performed
703 Exultingly in view of open day
O
[705] T}r to Andates, femal Power, who gave
{ied,
[706] For so they fanc{y glorious victory
704 And full assemblage of a barbarous
Host

[43^r]

{word
{[?]
{him
IX, 718 And from thy truth revealing through {[?]
through bled
the fath derived ~~from~~ him who ~~died~~
719 Upon the Cross—this marvellous advance
720 Of good from evil, as if one extreme
[?there]
[?thy favord ground]
721 Were left, the other gain'd—accord
thy [?]
{li
Upon [?the endeavours] of re{[?g]gious [?men]
[?~~better~~] [?bliss] as
And [?~~happ~~] happier [?~~than~~] this re[?gion is]
[?secure]
When with the countenance of its former [?state]
in opposition [?placed] [?Man]
Contrasted, or ~~the general state of [?Man~~]
As now exist[?ent]
to be read
Yet
[?worthier ha]
Yet ~~far more~~ happy than this [?simple] spot
And more [?protective] of all holy [?thing things]
The universal face of earth shall be
O ye who come
[?~~leave~~]
[721] Were left the other gain. ~~O Ye who quit~~
[?~~come~~]
~~dwellings scattered oer these~~ [?pleasant]
[?field]
~~Your habitations mid these~~
722 ~~T worship God who within yon rever~~end
pile
{ly re}
[722] [?~~The knee~~] devout[?h]{ in that [?]}verend Pile
To kneel

Rev on 15^v–16^r.

721/[721] The unnumbered lines apparently attempt to compare the present happy state with an even more "marvellous" (l. 719) future redemption, just as the present is more enlightened than the barbaric past.

[43v]

IX, 723 Called to such office by the pea[?c]ful sound
724 Of sabbath bells & ye who sleep in earth
s
725 All care forgotten, round its hallowed walls
~~And Ye who sleep around its hallowed walls~~
l
[?For I] [?] living & dead an undivided flock
is
726 For you, in presence of th [?] littl Band
727 Gathered on the green hill side
[?~~speaks~~] prefer
728 Your Pastor ~~is~~ embolded to [?~~assume~~]
Vocal
729 [?~~Praise~~] & thanksgiving to the eternal king
[?&]
730 Whose love whose counsel commands have made
731 Your very poorest rich in peace of thought
[?are]
[?thou] him who [?] [?endowed]
732 And in good works—[?~~Yet thou who~~] ~~[?~~]
and [?thou] who are endowed
all truth
733 With scantiest knowledg master of ~~the~~
734 Which the salvation of his soul requires.
Rocks mountains rivers wood
~~Rivers~~
741 Rocks ~~& mountains rock[?s]~~ & watery Plains
They know
748 ~~Witness~~ if I be silent morn or even
~~For [?in sof]~~
749 For though in whispers speak[?in] the full heart
750 ~~Will utter what she [?feel]~~

[44r]

IX, 750 Will find a vent & thought is praise
A ~~to him~~
751 [?T] udible praise to Thee Omniscient Mind
752 From whom all gifts descend all blessings flow
735 Conscious of that abundant favour shower[?d]
Y entrusted to
736 On y ou the Children of my humble care

Rev on 44r, 16r–16v.
734–749 Passage expanded on 44r.

Rev on 16v.
735–749 Rev and expansion of 43v.

beloved land
{[?~~beloved~~]
737 On your abodes, & this {[?delightf]ul Land
beloved Land

showerd
[735] ~~They know if conscious of the favour~~ shower[?d]
[736] On you the children of my humble care
abode beloved
[737] On your [?~~and on~~] this Land ~~our home~~
[738] Our birthplace, home & country [?shall] on
[?earth]
738 ~~And country~~ [?while] among the
[?this]
[?land]
739 ~~We sojourn [?i]~~
beloved land
738, 737 ~~Our Country home~~
[738] Our birthplace home & country while on earth
S }
[739] We [?j]}oujourn, loudly do I utter thanks
740 With earnest joy; that will not be suppress d
Rocks Rivers mountains woods & watry plains
746 They see the offering of my lifted hand[?s]
747 They hear my lips present their sacrifice
748 They know if I be silent morn or even
749 For though in whispers speaking the full
heart

[44v]

IX, 753 This vesper-service closed—without delay
{~~high~~
~~the~~ {[?] ~~raised ground~~
754 ~~We left that eminence and to the plain~~
[754] From that exalted station to the plain
{ing,
755 Descend{ed [?~~then~~] we pursued our homeward
cours

756 In mute composure oer the shadowy Lake
757 Beneath a faded sky. No trace was left
{plendours,
758 Of those celestial s{ grey the vault
Pure
759 ~~Calm~~, cloudless, ether and the star of Eve
760 Was wanting; but inferior lights appear d
761 Faintly, too faint almost for sight, and some
762 Above the darkend hills stood boldly forth

---

738 Conjectured "land" possibly first written "eart" and the "e" changed to "l" and a "d" added.

Rev on 17r–17v; rev of 45r.

756 Eras under "oer" may be of "along" as on 45r rev.

758 The word "splendours" seems to have been added—in whole or after the initial "s"—in a space left.

763 In twinkling lustre ere the Boat attained
where to
764 Her mooring-place; ~~beneath~~ the sheltering tree
765 ~~To which~~ our youthful Voyagers bound fast her
prompt & prow
766 ~~Her prow~~ with careful hands: this done we
paced
767 The dewy fields but ere the Vicars door
768 Was rea[?ced] the Solitary turned aside,
{e
771 Th{at single Path inviting him that leads
772 To the one Cottage in the dell profound
773 His chosen Residence. He turned aside

[45[r]]

When he had ceased, on that commanding
height
IX, 753 ~~He ceased & from that elevated spot~~
754 We lingered not but straitway to the [?~~shore~~]
{ed, {& plain
755 Descend{ing ~~we~~ {[?] pursued our homeward course
~~along~~
756 In mute composure oer the shadowy
Lake
757 Beneath a faded sky. No trace was left
758 Of those celestial splendours; grey the
~~Pure~~, [?calm] vault
[?~~Of~~] cloudless ether
759 ~~Cloudless & placcid~~; & the star of eve
760 Was wanting; but inferior lights appeared
763 Doubtfully twinkling—ere the Boat
attained
where, to the sheltering tree
764 Her mooring place, ~~beneath the sheltering~~
tree
765 Our youthful voyagers bound fast her [?prow]
[?the] [?tried] prow
765, 766 X ~~To which we [?tied] her fast with~~
{~~we~~ careful hands.
[765] ~~To which~~ {[?] ~~bound her fast~~
766, 767 This done—we quickly paced the dewey
fields
{ door
767 But ere the Vicar's hospitable {[?roof]
768 Was gained, the Solitary turned aside,
a [?scanty]
771 That single Path inviting him that leads
{ the
772 To {[?his] one cottage in the dell profound
[766] X With prompt & careful hands. This done
we paced

Rev on 44[v], 17[r]–17[v].

765, 766 The X signals insertion of l. [766] at page foot.

[45v]

IX, 773 His chosen Residence. He turned aside
{an a}
But not before {[?of] [?]}cceptable word
774 Of unexpected promise had been given
775 That by the morning light he would
random return
[775] And share the pleasure & pursuit
776 Of yet another summers day, consumed
777, 778 In wandering with us through these mountain
wastes
777 And valleys

[773] he turned aside
Though promise
[774] ~~But~~ not till welcome^had been given
[775] That he would share the pleasures & pursuits
[776] Of yet another summers day, consumed
[777] In wandering with us through the valley
fair
778 And oer the mountain wastes. Another
sun
779 Said he, shall shine upon us ere we part
780 Another sun & peradventure more
with
781 If Time ~~&~~ free consent be yours to give
782 And season favours.—~~For~~ To
Power
enfeebled [?~~power~~]

[46r]

this
IX, 783 From ~~such~~ communion with uninjured
renovation minds
784 What ~~restoration~~ had been brought, & what
785 Degree of healing to a wounded spirit
786 Dejected, and habitually disposed
787 To seek in degradation of the Kind
Ex} de
788 [?A]}cuse & solace for its own [?~~fail~~] defects
789 How far those erring judgements were reformed
a}
790 And whether o}ught, of tendency as good
791 And pure, from further intercourse
ensued,

Leaf 45v is rev on 17v.

Leaf 46r is rev on 17v–18r.

I [?h]
792 O f [?animation] & delightful [?~~verse~~] hopes
[?tore]
793 Sustain as here [?f] [?] & the serious verse
Through varying [?measure led]
794 And gentle hearts & lofty minds approve.
may
[?may] leave
795 My future Labours shall not [?le] untold
End.

(
[792] This if delightful hopes, as heretofor
[?Approved]
[?of]
Inspire verse gentle
[793] Sustain the serious song & ~~lofty~~ hearts
[?~~Be~~] Cherish
[794] ~~Are touch~~ d, & lofty souls approve the
)
past
[795] My future Labours may not leave untold

[46[v]]

O
VI, 17 And o Ye swelling Hills & spatious Plains
18 Besprent, from shore to shore, with steeple Towers
19 And Spires, whose silent finger points to heaven,
20 Nor wanting, at wide intervals, the Bulk
rais'd
M lifted reared
21 Of antient [?m] inster, rising above the Cloud
22 Of the dense air which Town or City breeds
23 To intercept the Sun's glad beams, may neer
24 That true succession fail of English Hearts
25 That can perceive not less than heretofore
n
26 Our Ancestors did <u>feeligly</u> perceive
27 What in those holy Structures Ye possess

Rev of 47[v].
17 Ink blot obscures "ing" in "swelling."
23 A faint mark above "neer" may be intended as an apos.

The first three words of Book VI are copied out on 49[r] (see the note there).
1 False start "by" obscured by ink blot.

[47r]

Book—
VI, 1 ~~Hail to the Crown by F~~
[1] Hail to the Crown by Freedom shaped—to gird
! T
2 An English Sovereign's Brow ; and to the throne
Whereon
~~Whereon~~
3 On which he sits whose deep foundations lie
the
4 In veneration and peoples Love
5 Whose steps are equity whose seat is law
to
6 Hail [?] the State of England, and conjoin
7 With this a salutation as devout
8 Made to the Spiritual Fabric of her
C u
ch [?a]rch
9 Founded in truth, by blood of Martyrdom
10 Cemented, by the hands of Wisdom reared
11 In beauty of holiness with ordered pomp,
V
12 Decent, & unreproved. The voice that greets
13 The majesty of both shall pray for both
14 That, mutual protected & sustain d,
15 They may endure as long as sea
surrounds
i f Land ~~fields~~
16 Th es[?e] Fav avoured ~~He~~ or sunshine warms her
soil
[?~~glebe~~]
soil
fields

[47v]

O [?~~often as thy Sons~~]
VI, 17 An Oh ye swelling Hills & wide-spread Plains
[?~~May~~] ~~beholding~~
, ,
~~And oh fair England~~ ~~when~~ thy Sons ~~behold~~
~~In contemplation looking forth behold~~
18 ~~Hill dale & plain besprent~~ with steeple
[?inkle] Towers
[18] ~~Besprent from shore to shore~~
Besprinkled, far & wide, with
19 And Spires whose silent finger points to heaven,
X ~~May they perceive with gratitude to him~~
~~with [?unabated] gratitude perceive~~
25 ~~May they continue to perceive & feel~~
By whose protecting goodness empires stand
27 ~~What to these sacred Structures they~~
[?~~How much] th[?ese] Venerable Rites conferd~~
~~possess~~

17–27 Rev on 46v.
19 Marginal X probably indicates rev at page foot.

28 Of ornamental interest & the charm
29 Of pious sentiment diffused afar
30 And human charity & social love
{Times
31 Thus never shall the indignities {of Time
their reverend graces
32 Approach ~~those [?reverd] Fabrics~~, unopposd,
hurt
33 Nor shall the Elements be free to mar
34 Their fair proportions nor the blinder rage
35 Of bigot zeal madly to overturn
23, 25 May never Hearts be wanting to perceive
25, 26 And feel not less than heretofore was felt
[27] What in those holy Structures ye possess

[48r]

And, if
~~The~~ ~~if~~
VI, 36 ~~And may~~^ the desolating hand of War
[?&] They shall
37 Spare them, ~~and they~~ continue to bestow
38 Upon the throng'd abodes of busy men
39 (Depraved, and ever prone to fill their minds
40 Exclusively with transitory things;)
41 An air and mien of dignified pursuit
42 Of sweet civility,—on rustic wilds
43 Thus wishing, can the Poet fail to add
44 An earnest prayer that Servants may abound
{; {M
45 Of those pure altars worthy{, {ministers
46 Detached from pleasure, to the love of gain
in} { de
47 Superior, ~~in~~}suseptible of Pri{[?ce],
48 And by ambitions longings undisturbed;
49 Men whose delight is where their duty leads
50 Or fixes them; whose least distinguished
day
51 Shines with some portion of that heavenly
lustre
52 That makes the sabbath lovely in the sight
53 Of blessed angels, pitying human cares.

[48v]

VI, 54 And, as on earth it is the doom of truth
[?attacked]
attacked
55 T to be perpetually ~~assailed~~ by foes
be still
56 Open or covert, ~~may~~ that Priesthood ~~yield~~,

---

43 Reinforcement of "can."
47 Change to "Pride" probably corrects a copying error.

replenished with a
57 For her defence, ~~a never-failing~~ Band
strenuous
58 Of ~~zealous~~ Champions in scholastic arts
59 Thoroughly disciplined; nor, (if, in course
60 Of the revolving worlds disturbances
Righteous
61 Cause should recur, which^Heaven avert!
Sires
62 To meet such trial) from their Spiritual
63 Degenerate, who constrained to wield the
sword
64 Of disputation shrunk not, though assailed
65 With hostile din & combating in sight
66 Of angry Umppire, partial & unjust;
after,
67 And did, there{for bathe their hands
in fire,
68 So to declare the conscience satisfied,—

[49r]

VI, 69 Nor for their Bodies would accept release
Book
G
70 But, blessing {god & praising him, bequeath[?d]
1 Hail to the
71 With their last breath from out the
smouldering flame
72 The faith which they by diligence had ear[?n d]
[?An]} earn d
73 [?Di]}d through illuminating grace received
74 For their dear Countrymen & all mankind.
75 Of high example, constancy divine.
ing
76 Even such a Man, (inherit{g the zeal
77 And from the sanctity of elder times
like
78 Not deviating; a Priest, the {[?] of whom
ns
79 If multiplied & in their statio{n set
80 Would oer the bosom of a joyful land
81 Spread true Religion & her genuine fruits)
82 Before me stood that day on holy ground
83 Fraught with the relics of mortality
[?]
84 Exa{[?a]lting tender themes, by just degree

---

68 Possibly a colon is added, following comma at end of line.

The words "Book" (partly overwritten by l. 69) and "Hail to the" (between ll.70 and 71) suggest that WW meant to begin his transcription of Book VI here but then moved it back to 47r.

80, 83 Letters "ful" in "joyful" and of "ty" in "mortality" are reinforced.

84 Queried overwriting in the first word may instead be a deletion of "[?a]."

85 To lofty raised, and to the highest
last

[49v]

VI, 86 The head & mighty Paramount or truths
87 Immortal life in never-fading worlds
88 For mortal Creatures conquered & secured.

{faith
89 That basis laid, those principle of {[?true]
90 Announced, as a preparatory act
91 Of Reverence to the spirit of the place,
92 The Pastor cast his eyes upon the ground
93 Not as before like one oppress'd with [?awe]
B} awe
94 [?An]}ut with a mild & social chearfulness,
~~And thus proceeded—[?Mark] said he~~,
95 Then to the Solitary turnd, and spake.
97 Perchance you not unfrequently have seen
96 At morn or eve—in your retired Domain
98 A Visitor intent upon the task
99 Of prying, low & high, for herbs & flowers.
You cannot but have noticd him he range[?d]
~~You must have notic'd him; through~~
two years space

[50r]

Through two years space these
~~He rang'd these rugg~~ed mountains every [?kind]
VI, 181 Collecting as successively they blow
On rock, in dells, or by the plashy springs
{Too as would appear
100 {Emp delicate employ~~ment as would seem~~
{One
101 For {[?one] who though of drooping mien had
yet
{frame
102 From nature's kindliness receivd a {[?form]
{d
103 Robust as rural Labour ever bre{[?ed]—
[?~~R~~]}
[?T]}[?~~ustic~~] as
104 The Solitary answered. Such a Form
105 Full well I recollect—we often crossd
106 Each other's path but as the Intruder
{S seemed
107 Fondly to prize the {silence which he kept
108 And I as willingly did cherish mine

In the last line on leaf 49v, the semicolon may be a comma.

pass'd
109 We met and ~~crossed~~, like Shadows—
I have heard,
110 From my good Host that he was crazed
in brain
clomb the crags
111 By unrequited love, and ~~rang d~~ the ~~Hills~~
through
112 And pierced the Caverns & ~~the~~ thickest
wood
of power
113 In hope to find some virtuous herb ~~to cure~~
114 To cure his malady."—The Vicar
smiled
~~The V~~

[50ᵛ]

VI, 115 Alas—before tomorrows sun goes down
116 His habitation will be here—for Him
117 That ~~e[?m]~~ open grave is destined.—
Died he then
118 Of pain & grief, the Solitary asked,
119 Believe it not—oh never could that
be.—
120 He loved, the v [?c]ar answered deeply lov[?e]
fervently
121 Lovd fondly, truly ~~hopelessly~~ and pined
122 When he had told his love & sued in
vain
123 Rejected—yea repell'd—and if with scorn
124 Upon the haughty maidens brow—tis but
125 A high-priz'd plume that female
Beauty wears.
b
126 That he could [?p]}rook, and glory in—
but when
he
127 The tidings came that She whom had woo'd
128 Was we[?d]ded to another & his heart
its
129 Was forced to rend away his only hope
130 Then Pity could have scarcely found on
earth

[51ʳ]

VI, 131 An object worthier of regard than He
132 In the transition of that bitter hour.

114 "The V" at page foot is del by eras.

120 Possibly the comma (which is blotted) is a random mark or intended as a dash.
127 The apos in "woo'd" may instead be an accidental mark.

132 Lost was She lost; nor could the
Sufferer say
{e
134 That in th{is act of preference he had been
135 Unjustly dealt with—but the
Maid was
gone
136 She whose Dear name with unregarded
sighs
137 He long had blessed, whose Image he preservd
138 Shrined in his breast with fond Idolatry
va }
139 Had [?was]}nished from his [?s] prospects & desires,
{ ~~her~~
~~Happy~~ {[?th] ~~Husban was & wretched~~
~~He~~.
140 Not by translation to the heavenly Quire
141 Who have put off their mortal spoils—
ah no
142 She lives another wishes to complete.
J }
143 [?S]}oy by their lot & happiness, he cried,
His
144 ~~Her~~ lot and hers, as misery is mine
145 Such was that strong Concussion; but the
Man
146 Who trembled, trunk and limbs, like
~~some huge~~
some huge Oak

[51v]

[?e]}
VI, 147 By a fi }rce tempest shaken—soon resumed
stedfast
148 The outward quiet natural to a Mind
149 Of composition gentle & sedate
150 And, in its movements, circumspect & slow.
born—He had been
151 Of Rustic Parents ~~he was born, but~~ traind
152 So prompted their aspiring wish—to skill
{o
153, 154 In numbers and the lab{[?r]urs of the Pen
earn'd
[?professd]
[153, 154] Mute sedentary Arts by which he ~~earnd~~
a livelihood
154, 155 And taught among the mountain Dales—
~~Teaching the Swains, his maintenance~~, &
now
157 To books and papers & the studious
Desk
{f
158 He stoutly readdress'd himsel{[?ve] —
resolved
159, 160 ~~To cheat his pain by following old~~
pursuits

160, 161 ~~With keener appetite.—Of what might~~
~~pass~~
159 and enter on the path
[159] To quell his pain, or if not quell, deceive
[159] and enter on the path of o
[159, 160] ~~By entering on the path of old pursuits~~
160 Of old pursuits with keener appetite
[160, 161] Wit keener appetite. Of what ensued
161 And closer industry.^
162 Within his Soul no outward sign[?s] appeard

[52r]

was seen
VI, 163 Till a betraying sickness ~~appeared~~
{cheek
164 To oerspread his {[?frame]—& through his frame
crept
it ~~spread~~
unconcealable
165 With slow mutation not to be concealed.
change
166 Such universal^as Autumn makes
leafy
167 In the fair body of a^grove ~~at first~~
{Di
168 {[?]scoloured, then divested. <u>Tis</u>
affirmed
169 By Poets skill in natures secret ways
170 That Love will not submit to be controlld
Man
171 By mastery– —And the good lackd not
friends
172 Who strove to instill this truth into his
mind
173 A mind in all heart-mysteries, unversed.
174 Go to the Hills, said one, remit awhile
baneful {~~ju~~ early
175 This most ~~in~~{[?]~~rous~~ diligence, at^morn
176 Court the fresh air, explore the heaths & woods
177 And leaving it to others to ~~expl~~ foretell
178 By calculation sage the ebb & flow
{Of
179 {And tides, & when the moon will be eclipsd
180 ~~Do you construct a Diary for yourself~~
Do you for your
~~For your~~ own benefit ~~do you~~ construct
181 A calendar of flowers, pluck'd as they
blow
s}
182 Where Healt abide[?d]} & chearfulness & peace

---

159 Ink overwrites pencil half-line.
[159] Ink overwrites pencil words "and enter on the path of o."
160 Ink overwrites pencil line.
161 Ink overwrites pencil phrase. Caret indicates the half-line substitution for l. 161.

[52v]

VI, 183 The attempt was made—"tis needless to report
184 How hopelessly—but Innocence is strong
185 And an entire simplicity of mind
186 A thing most sacred in the eye of Heaven.
~~And [?thee, O] nature Heavens pure minister.~~
193 With all thy beautiful array of forms ×
196 —A[?b]scribe it not {to / [?]} impatience, here exclaimd
197 The Wanderer if I guess'd that he was heald
198 By perseverance in ~~such~~ [?t] the course prescribd
199 you err not
You do not err
[199] ~~The Priest replied~~—the strength which had been lost
200 By slow degrees was gradually regained
201 The fluttering nerves composed the beating heart
the thoughts
[202] In rest established & the jarring [?round]
in rest
202 Establish[?e in] tranquillity. ~~and life~~
~~Restored~~ To harmony restore
203 ~~Brought back~~ to Reasons sway—But yon dark mold
204 Will cover him, in pride of strength to earth
205 Hastily smitten by a fevers force
191 —And all the elements, that round these wait
192 To generate, to preserve & to restore

[53r]

By
VI, 191 ~~With~~ all the elements that round {Her / the[?se]} wait
192 To generate, to preserve & to restore
[?by]
193 And all thy beautiful array of forms
194 Shedding sweet influence—{f / [?F]}rom above, or pure
they
195 Delight exhaling from the ground [?~~we~~] tread

Lines 187–195 drafted and rev on 53r; ll. 187–203 rev on 53v.

186/193 The X in the right margin indicates rev and continuation, probably the draft of ll. 187ff. on facing 53r, or ll. 191–192 at bottom of 52v, or draft of ll. 191–195 and 187–190 as continuous reading on 53r.

201/[202] Phrase "the thoughts" may have been the first rev of l. 202, below.

relief
a
187 That opens for such sufferer [?f]} fount
188 Within their souls a fount of grac divine
189 And doth commend their weakness & disease
190 To nature's care, supported in her office

---

206 Yet not with ~~blow~~ stroke so sudden as refused
{her
207 Time to look back with tenderness on {[?]
in to send
208 Whom he had loved with passion, and ~~he said~~
209 Some farewell words, and with those words
a prayer
210 That from his dying hands he would accept
{h
211 That, which of {[?]is possessions most he
prise'd
212, 213 A Book within whose leaves the forms of Plants
214 In undecaying Beauty were preservd,
[?~~There] leaf & flowers~~
time & place
215 Mute register to him of tenderest thoughts
216 And various fluctuations in the breast
217 To her a monument of faithful love
218 Conquered, and in tranquillity
retain'd

[53^{v}]

VI, 187 That opens for such Sufferers relief
~~Wh[?o~~]
188 Within their souls a fount of grace divine
&
{[?~~and~~]
189 And doth commend their weakness {[?or] diseas
190 To Nature's care assisted in her office
191 By all the elements that round her wait
192 To generate, to preserve, & to restore
{F
193 And by her beautiful array of {forms
194 Shedding sweet influence from above,
and pure
195 Delight exhaling from the ground they
it if tread.
196 —"Impute not to impatience—~~here~~
I infer exclaim'd
197 The Wanderer, ~~if I say~~ that he was heal'd

187–195 Rev of 52^{v}; rev on 53^{v}.
190/206 Missing lines 191–205 are on 52^{v}; passage rev on 54^{r}.
210 On 54^{r}, and in *1814*, the reading is "she" for "he."

Rev of 53^{r}, 52^{v}.
187/188 "Wh[?o]" entered first on page and then del by eras.

198 By perseverance in the course prescribed"

powers
{th,
199 "You do not err, the ~~streng~~{h, which
had been lost
{ere
200 By slow degrees, w{as gradually regained
201 The fluttering nerves composed, the beating
heart
202 In rest establishd, and the jarring thoughts
203 To harmony restored—But
yon dark mold

[54^r]

height
VI, 204 Will cover him—in ~~pride~~ of strength to earth
205 Hastily smitten by a Fevers force,
206 Yet not with stroke so sudden as refused
207 Time to look back with tenderness on her
208 Whom he had loved in passion, and to send
{ [?,]
209 Some farewell words{[?&] & with those words a
prayer
210 That from his dying hands she would accept
211 Of his possessions That which most he
prized
upon the surface of whose leaves
212 A Book within whose leaves the forms of
{S ~~Plants~~
Som{e ome chose
[?~~These lea~~]
{[?sen] {nts
213 ~~Pl~~ cho{[?ice] of pla{[?ces] disposed with nicest care
214 In undecaying beauty were preserved,
215 Mute register to him of time & place
216 And various fluctuations in the breast
217 To her a monument of faithful love
218 Conquered and in tranquillity retain'd.

198/199 Additional space is perhaps left to denote the Pastor's response, which forms a new verse para in *1814*.

204–205 Rev of 52^v.
204 Possible comma eras after "strength."
206–218 Rev of 53^r.

[55v]

Near the Turf
Which hides that strenuous Labourers furrowd
brow
VI, 285 *Lies one who lived not till his locks were*
nipped
286 *By seasonable frost of age nor died*
287 *Before his temples, prematurely forced*
288 *To mix the manly brown with silver grey,*
289 *Gave obvious instance of the sad effect*
290 *Produed when thoughtless folly hath usurped*
291 *The natural Crown that sage experience*
wears
292 *Gay volatile in genius quick to learn*
293 *And prompt to exhibit all that he possessed*
z
294 *Or could perform a* [?j] *ealous Actor hired*
295 *Into the troop of mirth a Soldier sworn*
296 *Into the lists of giddy enterprize*
297 *Such was he yet as if within his frame*

[56r]

d
VI, 298 *Two several souls alternately had loged*
299 *Two sets of manners could the youth put on*
300 *And fraught with antics as the indian bird*
301 *That wreathes & chatters in her wiry cage*
302 *Was graceful when it pleased him smooth*
& still
303 *As the mute Swan that floats adown the*
stream
304 *Or on the Waters of the unruffled Lake*
Not a Leaf
305, 308 *Anchors her placid beauty. If ye ask*
306 That flutters on the bough more light than He
307 And not a Flower that droops in the green
XXX shade
309 *How in these wilds such elegance was bred*
[?~~M~~]
310 *Mid rustic swains a composition framed*
311 *Of qualities so adverse to diffuse*
312 *Whereer he moved diversified delight*
313 *A simple answer may suffice even this*

Leaves 54v and 55r are blank, probably to allow for the intended copying of lines (likely already in draft form) related to VI, 219–283, the Miner's story. The second line of resumption of copy on 55v (in MW's hand) refers to "that strenuous Labourers furrowd brow," an appropriate reference to the Miner. The most likely explanation is that WW instructed MW to begin her copying on 55v because of his intended rev to existing draft of the Miner's story.

MW's fair copy, rev by WW, continues to the top of 57r.

307/309 The left-margin "XXX" signals insertion of line at page foot.

309/310 The conjectured "M," del by eras, may have been an abortive attempt to begin l. 308 (which begins "More").

T}
314 t} *was Nature's will who sometimes under take*[?*s*]
315 *For the reproof of human vanity* [?*a*]
316 *Art to outstrip, in her peculiar walk*
317 *Hence for this favourite lavishly endowed*
{Y
308 X X X More winningly reserv[?e]. If {ye inquire
[309] How

[56v]

and bright
{ ~~&~~
VI, 318 *With personal gifts* {[?*or*] ~~*with*~~∧ *instinctive wit*
319 *While both embellishing each other stood*
320 *Yet further recommneded by the charm*
321 *Of fine demeanour & by dance & song*
every fancy framed
322 *And* ~~*no mean*~~ *skill in letters* ~~*fairest*~~
~~expectations~~
{r ~~*hopes*~~
323 Fair expectations; no{ when to the World's
nor
{: &}
323, 324 ~~*Were entertained*~~{ [?]} *when the A*~~*dvent*~~*urer, went*
[324] Capacious field forth went the Adventurer there
{that
in {[?]
{ ʒ
[323, 324] ~~*Forth to the World*~~{ [?] ~~*capacious field not there*~~
325 *Were he or his attainments overlooked*
wa}
326 *Or scantily retu*}*rded, but all hopes*
he
327 *Cherished for him* ~~*were*~~ *suffered to depart*
328 *Like blighted buds or clouds that mimicd land*
329 *Before the Sailors eye or diamond drops*
330 *That sparkling decked the morning grass or aught*
331 *That was attractive & hath ceased to be*
332 *Yet when this Prodigal returned the rites*
~~*The* [?*rit*]~~

[57r]

VI, 333 *Of joyful greeting were on him bestowed*

---

332 At page foot of 56v, the copying error of "The [?rit]" is del by eras.

334 *Who by humiliation undeterred ~~sought in~~*
~~his weariness~~
for [?port]
335 Sought ~~in~~ his weariness a place of rest
~~A place~~
336 *Within his Fathers Gates. —Whence*
came He? —clothed
337 In tatter'd garb from Hovels where abides
338 Necessity the stationary Host
339 Of vagrant poverty; from rifted barns
340 Where no one dwells but the wide-staring
{P Owl
341 And the owl's {prey, none permanently house
342 But many harbour, from these Haunts
to which
343 He had descended from the proud Saloon
344 He came the Ghost of beauty and of health
345 The Wreck of gaiety. But soon revived
346 In strength, in power refitted, he renewd
{F
347 His suit to {fortune [?&] —and she smile again
348 Upon a faithless Ingrate! Thrice he rose
349 Thrice sunk as willingly. For He
whose Heart
350 Was used to thrill with pleasure
while his Voice

[57v]

VI, 351 Softly accompanied the tuneful Harp
352 By the nice finger of fair Ladies touchd
{Halls
353 In glittering {[?] was able to derive
354 Not less enjoyment from an abject
choic[?e].
355 Who happier for the moment?—who
more blithe
{ [?Ange]
356 Than this fallen {Spirit in those
dreary Holds
357 His talents lending to exalt the freaks
358 Of merry-making Beggars,—now provoked
359 To laughter multiplied in louder peals
360 By his malicious wit, then all enchained
amazement
361 With mute ~~astonishment~~ themselve
to see
362 In their own art outdone, their fame eclips'd
{F
363 As by the very Presence of the {fiend

---

339 Possibly a cap "P" is intended in "poverty."
347 Del by eras.
350 Possibly a lowercase "v" is intended in "Voice."

364 Who dictates & inspires illusive feats
365 For knavish purposes. The City, too,
366 With shame I speak it to her guilty Bowers
367 Allured him sunk so low in self respect

[58r]

{As
VI, 368 {[?] there to linger there to eat his bread
369 Hired Minstrel of volupt[?ou]s blandishm
ent
370 Charming the air with skill of Hand or
Voice
371 Listen who would be wrought upon who
might
372 Sincerely wretched Hearts or falsely gay.
s { u
373 Truths I record to many know, for^ {[?i]ch
374 The not unfrequent tenor of his boast
375 In ears that relished the report, but
all
376 Was from his Parents happily concealed
blame & pitying
377 Who saw enough for pity & for love.
{i
378 They also were permitted to rece{ ve
379 His last repentant breath & clos'd
his eyes
{at {x
380 No more to open on th{e ve{[?]ing world
381 Where he had long existed in the state
F }
382 Of a young [?T]}owl beneath one Mother
hatched
{ Though
383 {[?From] from another sprung—of different
race;
384 Where he had lived & could not
cease to live

[58v]

VI, 385 Distracted in properity—content
386 With neither element of good or ill
[?ei]
387 And yet in both rejoicing—Man
unblest
[?t]}
388 Of cons}radictions infinite the Slave
389 Till his deliverance when Mercy
made Him
390 One with himself, and one with
those who sleep.

---

377 A letter may be eras before "blame."

Strange, said the Solitary not [?unmoved],
it seems
391 Tis strange—observed the Solitary—strange
392 It seems & scarcely less than pitiful
393 That in a land where Charity provides
394 For all who can no longer feed themselves
395 A Man like this should chuse to
bring his shame
pat & with his sighs
396 To the [?par]}ernal door; ~~& to infect~~
397 Infect the air which he had freely breathd
398 In happy infancy. He could not [?~~lack~~]
pine

[59^{r}]

~~de[?ser]ted~~ ~~how~~
VI, 399 ~~Howsoeer dishonoured soeer forlorn~~
[399] (Whence e'er rejected howsoe'er forlorn)
400 Through lack of converse—no—he
must have found
thought &
401 Abundant exercise for speech ~~& thought~~
402 In his dividual Being—self-reproved
ca
403 Self-[?cha]}techized self-punished!—
S
[?F]}ome there are
404 Who, drawing near their final Home, & much
lon same
405 And daily [?]}ging that the {[?] were
reached
than
406 Would rather shun {[?] seek the
fellowship
407 Of kindred mold. —Such haply
here are laid?
408 Yes, said the Priest—the Genius
of our Hill[?s]
409 Who might appear, by these stern
barriers cast
410 Round his domain—desirous not alone
411 To keep his own but also to exclude

[59^{v}]

VI, 412 All other progeny doth sometimes
lure

390/391 Rev, in pencil, was not incorporated in *1814*.

---

399 Alt for "de[?ser]ted" is "dejected."
405 Overwritings "lon" and "same" may be reinforcements.

studied
413 Even by this ~~very~~ de[?e]pth of privacy
[?]
~~alien [?either~~] wishing to obtain
414 The unhappy ~~stranger hoping here~~
~~to find~~
with
415 Needful concealment or [?~~in~~] hope
416 In place from outward molestation free
417 Helps to internal ease. Of many such
as their stay was brief
~~b~~
418 Could I discourse, ~~but~~ [?st]}~~rief was~~
their sojourn
419 So their departure only left behind
~~And it would ill become me to repeat~~
But [?there yet]
co
420 Fancies & loose [?gu]}njectures. —Yet this
Vale
~~Survive~~
~~Exists no~~
Survives no
421 ~~Retains of~~ no faint remembrance of a
pair
from the pressure of their several fate
422 ~~Who driven at separate times~~ by
diverse fates
423 ~~Here~~ met as Stranger & remained as
Friends
in sign at once ~~at once~~ ~~at once~~
Content; and finally ^did leave in sign^
^
general to th[?em]
426 Of friendship & of^gratitude ~~their~~ bone
[426] For hospitable kindness left their bones
427, 428 In this green spot, unscutcheon[?e]d, & [?~~remot~~]
remote

[60r]

~~From the domestic Vault~~
VI, 427 To this green cemetery—here to rest
428 With unescutcheoned privacy interred
{C
429 Far from the family Vault.—A {chieftain—
One
430 By right of birth, within whose spotless
breast
431 The fire of antient Caledonia burned.
432 He, with the foremost whose impatience
hailed

Ll. 423–427 rev on 60r (ll. 420–427 further rev on 60v); ll. 427–428 probably rev on 60r at page foot, possibly before entries above rule on 60r.

421 Word "of" del by eras.

423/426 Extra caret before "did" probably added because insertion of "general" obscured first caret.

433 The Stuart—landing to resume, by force
{,
434 Of arms{ —the Crown which Bigotry had
{, lost,
435 Arouzed his clan; &{ fighting at their head,
436 With his brave sword endeavoured to prevent
{E
437 Culloden's fatal overthrow—{escaped
438 With life from that disastrous rout he
fled
439 To foreign ~~la~~ shores, and when the
power of time
440 Those troubles had appeased he sought
and gained
441 For his obscure condition an obscure
nook
442 Retreat withi this [?~~nook~~] of english Ground
both remained
423, 425 Who meeting here as Strangers ~~And remained as~~ Friends
426 True to their choice, and as a last effect
And evidence of friendship & in sign
Of a participated gratitude
[426] For local recollections left their bones
[427] To this green cemetery here to rest

[60v]

VI, 443 The Other, born in Britains southern
fix d tract,
444 Had ~~learned to fix~~ his milder loyalty & place
~~his [?love]~~
{~~ed~~
444, 445 ~~And plac{e, dislike, and hatred~~, (all
could
445 ~~Such as his gentler Nature would~~
support ~~allow~~)
[445] His gentler sentiments of love & hate
446 There, wh[?ere] they placed them who in
prized
conscience ~~set~~
~~Their strength against the adopted line~~,
447 The new Succession as their best defen[?ce]
and prized
~~The House of Brunswick as their~~
~~country shield~~
449 Against the dire assaults of papacy

423–[427] Rev of 59v, these lines below rule on 60r (seemingly later than ll. [426]–428 on bottom of 59v) were probably entered before ll. 427–442 on 60r. Ll. 420–427 are rev on 60v; l. 428 is recopied on 61r as part of the sequence beginning with l. 420 on 60v.

423, 425 WW initially wrote the second half of the line; he then wrote the first half and finally rev the second half.

Rev of 60r, 59v.

450 And arbitrary Rule. But launch thy
Bark
Other trace
420 Fancies and loose conjectures. ~~Such are~~ not
[421] Survives, for worthy mention,
421, 422 The traces ~~still surviving~~ of a Pair
422 Who, from the pressure of their several fates,
M
423 [?He]}eeting, as Strangers, in a petty Town
424 Whose blue roofs ornament a distant
Reach
425 Of this far winding Vale—remained as Friends,
{choice;
426 True to their {[?] : and, as a last
effect
And evidence of friendship, and in sign
Of a participated gratitude
[?] gave
[426] X For local recollections, ~~left~~ their bones
427 X To this loved Cemetery—here to rest

[61^{r}]

VI, 428 With unescutcheoned privacy interred
first [?]
429 Far from the family vault.—A chieftain, One
450 Arbitrary Rule. But launch thy bark
stream
451 On the distempered flood of public life
452 And cause for most rare triumph will be thine
~~And, to thy~~ peril Thou shal[?t] surely find
453 That spite of watchful eye & steadiest
hand
454, 455 The flood will be its master. He, who oft
456 Under the battlements & stately trees
457 That round his Mansion shed a sober
gloom
457 Had moralized on this and other truths
soothed & satisfied
459 Of kindred import,~~—with a sigh~~
~~was forced~~
vent his wisdom
460 Was forced to ~~give this~~ utterance with
{a s}
{[?si]g}igh
462 When he had served his Country—to ~~the~~
loss

---

[426]–427 Left-margin symbols at foot of 60^{v} indicate intended rev and replacement, possibly by the version entered on 59^{v} and rev on 60^{r}. The possible order of entry may be 60^{v}, 59^{v}, 60^{r}.

428–429 Material continues from what is below the rules on 60^{r} and 60^{v}. WW's "first [?]" may be a copying instruction related to ll. 430–449, which are entered on 60^{r}–60^{v}.

The unnumbered passage at page foot (to follow l. [462]) is rev on 61^{v}–62^{r}, 65^{r}–65^{v}. In the second line of the passage here on 61^{r}, the X indicates rev; the word "[?Sweet]" between the third and fourth lines is in pencil.

[462] Of a most plentiful & fair Estate
His old inheritance.—Imagine not
struggle [?proud strife]
That I deride the Patriots ~~worthy~~ [?cause]
~~and [?civic]~~
[?~~this~~]
[?~~Vi~~r] ~~needful~~ efforts in a generous cause
[?Mock] [?stern] [?Sweet]
And
Virtue forbid [?] Liberty reject
A sneer so senseless with thy prouder
sc
[?sn] orn

[61ᵛ]

But
VI, 450 The launch thy Bark
flood
451 On the distempered ~~Fl~~ ~~Stream~~ of public Life
452 And cause for most rare triumph will be thine
h
453 If, spite of watcful Eye & steadiest hand
prove not, soon
454 The Stream that bears thee forward, soon or late,
or late,
455 ~~Prove not~~ a dangerous Master. He who oft
456 Under the battlements & stately trees
457 That round his Mansion shed a sober gloom
458 Had moralized on this & other truths
459 Of kindred import, soothed & satisfied
vent his wisdom
460 Was forced to ~~give it utterance~~ with a sigh
462 When he had served his Country—to the loss
[462] Of a most plentiful & fair Estate,
His old Inheritance. Imagine not
[?ose]
th [?ese] light words were uttered to derid[?e]
That I deride the strife of civic zeal
The zeal that [?suffers]
~~And needful efforts~~ in a generous cause,
Virtue forbid—sweet Liberty rejec
A sneer so senseless with thy prouder Scorn.
I but repeat the censure which tis said
would pass upon himself
The mild good Man recovered from his heat
~~Would freely [?press up] upon himself~~
Most freely when recovered from his heat
Of blood and giddiness of brain, he hear

---

[462] See final note on facing page.

450–462 Rev and expansion of 61ʳ.
450–455 Rev on 62ʳ; variant of 462ff. rev on 62ʳ, 65ʳ–65ᵛ.
456–462 Rev on 62ᵛ.
459 A mark following "import" may reinforce the comma.

[62^r]

~~he~~ in [?fancy]
[?~~He in] the quietn~~ess of [?fancy]
far more distinctly than his living ear
[?e] | so
~~Had~~ [?h|~~ver~~] ~~heard~~ the intelligible [?]|unds
staunch
Of ~~his devoted followe~~r
In the [?rememb~~r duproar~~] uproar of that time
When his staunch followers [?voting returns]
{[?in} slaked their thirs
And [?smiling] {[?his] his [?service],
[?would]
~~Drank up his [?houses deeds] & [?land~~]
{is
By [?drink up h{ouse ~~houses~~]
[~~?~~]} [?woods]
And} [?~~boasted] Title~~, ~~&~~ his wide spread
[?fiel]
[?Among] [?allayed]
Most sparingling when ~~all that~~ heat of blood
[?~~Allays~~], ~~that~~ giddiness of brain recovered,
he heard
Far more distinctly than his living ear
Had ever [?done], and could discriminate
And understand ~~the [?promises] & the hope~~
he look back in peace
With a discriminating & heard
~~In fa[? ?] only, [?what his~~]
In [?fancy] only

But launch thy Bark
On the distempered flood of public life
And cause for most rare triumph will be thine
keenest
If, spite of ~~wateful~~ eye & steadiest Hand,
{S
The {stream that bears thee forward, prove not,
soon
Or late, a perilous Master. He, who oft,

[62^v]

Under the battlements and stately trees
That round his mansion cast a sober gloom
Had moralized on this and other truths
Of kindred import—pleased and satisfied
Was forced to vent his wisdom with a sigh
When he had served his Country—to the loss
Of a most plentiful and fair estate

Unnumbered lines (an attempt to detail the despoliation of the Whig's estate in the election) rev of 61^v, 61^r; rev on 62^v, 65^r–65^v.

450–455 Rev of 61^v; continued on 62^v.

456ff. Continued from 62^r; ll. 456–462 rev of 61^v, 61^r; ll. 465–479 rev and drafted on 65^v (with ll. 467–473 also rev on 63^v).

An honoured birthright fruitlessly
464 ~~His old inheritance:—in vain~~ dispersed{!,
when
For ~~ere~~ the Contest closed, he might have seen
His {T tory Rival, bowing thanks, [?~~o~~] and smiles
Of triumph shedding from the uplifted Chair
Throne dearly bought
~~A dear-bought Throne~~, by mutual ruin gained.
e din of that protracted strife,
465 Forthwith, th~~at din yet rizing in~~
ears
his {ear[?s], [?eye]
466 Not ceasing yet to hang upon his ear
Vex'd, beggard, & discomfited, the Whig
470, 467 Slunk to the shade, beneath a borrowed name
*
468 The very sound & echo of his own
469, 473 So much disgusted him. And here they met

[63r]

VI, 474 Like adverse Planets—flaming Jacobite
I have heard
475, 479 And sullen Hanoverian. ~~In the peace~~
480 My grey haired [?Sire] relate that in the peace
[?Town]
481 ~~Of that small encountering [?un~~awares]
Of this small Town encountering [?thus] they filld
482 ~~Tis said they filled the bo~~wling green with strife
~~The bowl~~{ing [?n]g
483, 484 And church & market suffered from the feuds
Which they excited.
[479] I have heard
[480] My greyhaired Sire relate that, in the Peace
[481] Of that small town encountering thus—they filld
[482] Daily, the bowl{ng- g green with harmless strife
483 And church & market suffered from the feuds
484 Which th{ey y excited. But within the breast
485 Of these {O opponents gradually was wroght

464/465 Rev on 65r–65v.
470, 467 Asterisk indicates rev on 63v.

474–490 Rev on 63v.
474–479 Rev and drafted on 65v.

general
486 With lit[?l]e change of sentiment
487 Such change towards each other, that they
bare
488 The yoke of fellowship from morn to night
Companions friends inseparably dear
{~~clos~~
490 Their very bickering kn[?o]tting them more {[?de]
clos

[63v]

VI, 467 * a[?] borrowed name
468 The sound & echo of his own in him
[?Pro] Producing
469 ~~Exciting~~^ such sensations of disgust
470 As he was glad to lose. The Scottish Laird
{Mid
471, 472 {In these untravelled wilds had long
possess'd
473 An undisturbed Abode. Here then they
met
474 Two doughty Champions—flaming Jacobite
475, 479 And sullen Hanoveriann. I have heard
{e
480 My grey-haired Sire relate that in th{eir
calm
~~peace~~
481 Of that small Town encountering thus they
filled
482 Daily its bowling green with harmless strife
483, 484 And church and market from the feuds
484 By them excited. But within the breast
wrought
485 Of these Opponents gradually was ~~raised~~
486 With little change of general sentiment
[?~~they~~]
~~They~~
487 Such change towards each other that, ~~bore~~
their days
~~The yoke of fellowhip from morn to night~~
{[?nt]
488 By choice were spen{[?t] in constant fellowship
489 ~~Companions friends inseparably dear~~
And if at times they fretted with the yoke
490 Their ~~very bickerings kn[?o]tting them~~
~~more close.~~
Those very bickerings
made them love it more

467–479 Rev on 65v; line 475, 479 expanded on 65v.
467 Asterisk indicates rev of lines on 62v.
474–490 Rev of 63r; ll. 467–473 rev of 62v.

[64r]

VI, 491 A favorite boundary to their lengthened
walks
492 This Churchyard was. And whether they
T} had come
493 [?t]}reading their path in cordial neighbor
hood
494 And sympathizing converse or at [?times]
495 ~~Or wisely~~ parted to preserve the peace
Discreetly ^
496 One Spirit seldom failed to extend its
{, sway
497 Over both minds{. when they had awhile
marked
had [?~~breathd~~],
ground
[498] The visible quiet of this holy ~~place~~,
[?~~rested~~]
498 ~~Together seated in this holy~~ place,
[498] The visible quiet of this place ~~& breathed~~
{,
499 Its tranquillizing air{: the spirit of hope
And breathed its soothing air
That
500 And saintly magnanimity, ~~which, [?lighting~~]
spurning
g} field
501 The f}~~round~~ of selfish difference & dispute
502 And every care which transtory Things,
503 Earth, & the kingdoms of the earth,
create,
504 Doth by a rapture of forgetfulness
505 Preclude forgiveness from the praise
V} debarred
[?R]}irtue
506 Which else the Christian ^ might
{There have claimed.
507 {[?A l] live who yet remember
here to have seen
[493] Treading their path in symathy & linked
[494] ~~By~~ In social converse, or by some short space

[64v]

i
VI, 508 Their courtly Fgures seated on the stump
{!
509 Of an old Yew, their favorite resting place{.
510 But, as the Remnant of the long lived Tree
511 Was disappearing by a swift decay,
c} {re
512 They, with joint }[?a{t], determine'd to erect

499 The comma appears to overwrite the colon, but possibly the rev is the other way around or meant to form a semicolon.

~~yon~~ Dial which might stand
a
513 Upon its site ~~a little work of Art~~
and
514 For public use, ~~which~~ also might
survive
{ir {at
515 As the{r own private monument—for th{[?is]
wished
516 Was the particular sport in which they
517 And Heaven was pleasd to accomplish their desire
~~wished~~
518 That undivided Their Remains should lie
519 So, where the moulder'd Tree had stood, was
raised
~~So where the Tree had~~
structure
520 Yon ~~Dial~~, framing with the ascent of steps
Pillar
521 That to the decorated ~~Column~~ lead
522 Work of art too sumptuous, as might seem
~~m~~}
522, 523 ~~A sup}ptuous Structure~~, built in no
proud scorn
523 To suit this Place yet
524 ~~Of homely rustic taste~~ but thus they hope
{[?ess]}
of rustic homline{ss [?of]}, they only hope
525 To ensure for it respect[?ed] guardianship
526 Around the margin of the plate whereon
527 The Shadow falls to note the stealthy
hours

[65r]

VI, 528 Winds an Inscriptive Legend"—As ~~he~~
at these words
~~spake~~
529 Thither we turned, and gathered as we read,
530 The appropriate sense—in Latin
numbers couchd.
531 "Time flies; it is his melancholy task
532 "To bring & bear away delusive hopes
533 "And reproduce the trouble[?s] he [?escapes]
534 "But, while his blindness thus is occupied,
535 "Do Thou, discerning Mortal, serve the
will
536 Of Time's eternal Master, and [?T]hat
W} peace,
537 Which the w}orld wants, shall be for Thee
confirmed.

516 For "sport," *1814* reads "spot."
524 Reinforcement of "homliness" may be to obscure the "[?of]."

An honoured birthright—in his own
despite
Consumed by an insatiable crowd
{— bawling
Of Partizan{, [?t] good wishes ~~shouting~~ forth
For all the precious right of Church & State
{[?D]
And [?Him] their staunch {defender. But
{c at length
The Contest {Close, & then he might have
seen
His Tory Rival bowing thanks; & smiles

[65v]

Of triumph shedding from the uplifted
chair
{ t
Throne dearly bought by mu{[?ut]ual
ruin gained.
VI, 465 Forthwith the uproar of that desperate
strife
{ ar
466 Not ceasing yet to vibrate on his e{[?y]
467 The vanquished Whig beneath a
borrow d name
468 For the mere sound & echo of his own
469 Haunted him with sensations of disgust
470 Which he was glad to lose slunk from the
world
471 To the deep shade of these untravelled
wilds
472 In which the Scottish Laird had long
possess d
473 An undisturbed Abode.—Here then they
met
474 Two doughty Chappions, flaming Jacobite
475 And sullen Hanoverian. You might think
476 That losses & vexations less severe
477 Than those which they had severally sustaind
478 Would have inclind each to abate his zeal
N }
479 For his ungrateful cause; [?]}o—I have heard

Unnumbered passage is rev of 62v; related to drafts of l. 462 variant on 61r–62r.

First two lines on page are rev of 62v; related to drafts of l. 462 variant on 61r–62r.
465–479 Rev of 63v, 63r, 62v.

[95v]

R—
[?~~bosom~~]

IX, 400/410 As from the virtues of a petty seed
Which in his thievish bill the flying Crow
evolved
Transports without encumbrance are ~~evolvd~~
T
[?L]runk, limbs, and umbrage of the
mighty oak
F
Darkening the noontide, as from humblest fount
Which the victorious Traveller bestrides
In sportive ease of proud complacency
Proceeds the state of Ganges or of Nile

River
along the level Turf
gliding
d
Now sli gi[?g] sheen and sheer as Angel's cut
Their way with steady wings, from rock
to rock
leaping [?bent]
Now bounding like a desperate [?hunter bound]

Leaf 66 is now a closely cut stub, and leaves 67–94r are blank and uncut.
Rev on 23v–24r. Probably entered between the time of drafting 22r–22v and 23r–24r.
WW inverted the notebook before entering the lines.
There is a six-line space above the word "River." The following draft seems to be a rejected description of the river.

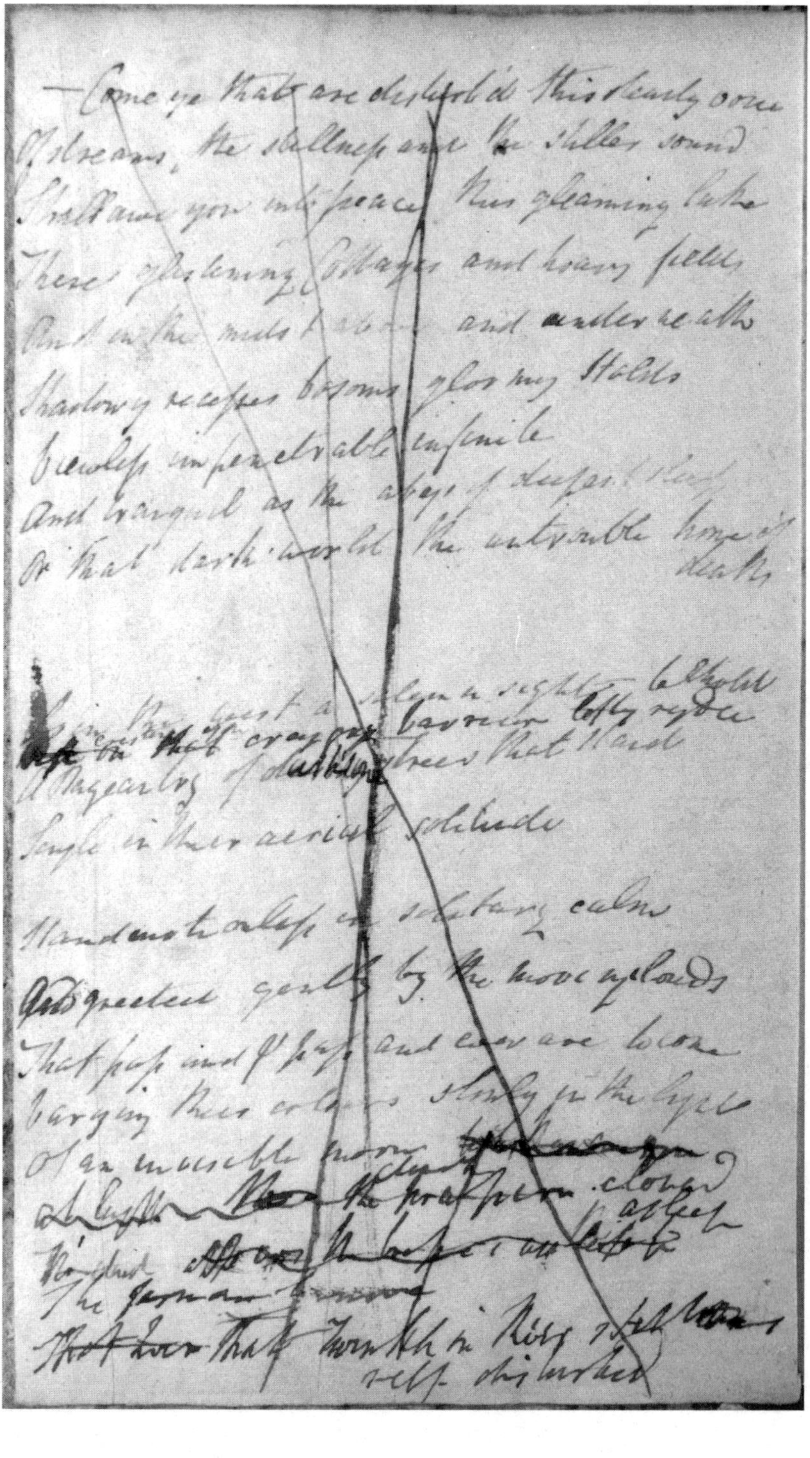
Come ye that are disturb'd at this steady voice
Of streams, the stillness and the stiller sound
Shall awe you into peace. This gleaming lake
These glistening cottages and hoary fields
And on the mists above and underneath
Shadowy recesses bosoms glooming holds
Bottomless impenetrable infinite
And tranquil as the abyss of deepest sleep
Or that dark world the untroubled home of
death

[illegible] in the west a solemn sight to behold
[illegible] craggy barrier lofty ridge
Of [illegible] of dark trees that stand
Single in their aerial solitude

Stand motionless in solitary calm
And greeted gently by the moving clouds
That pass and [illegible] and ever are borne
Varying their colours slowly in the lapse
Of an invisible motion [illegible]
At length [illegible] the prospect closed
[illegible] asleep
The [illegible]
That [illegible] that breathe in [illegible]
self disturbed

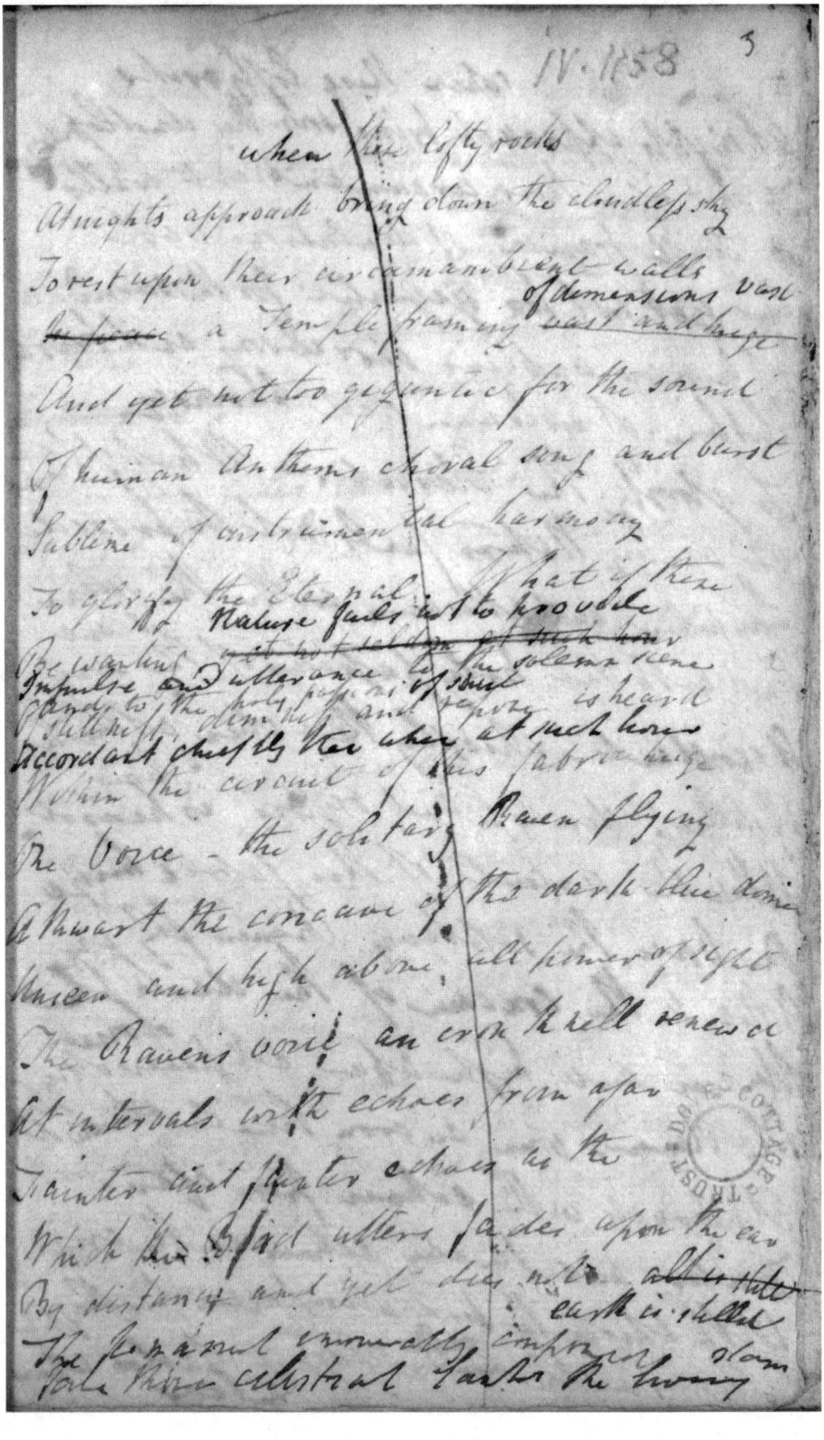

IV. 1158 3

when these lofty rocks
At night's approach bring down the cloudless sky
To rest upon their circumambient walls
~~he forms~~ a Temple framing ~~vast and huge~~ of dimensions vast
And yet not too gigantic for the sound
Of human Anthems choral song and burst
Sublime of instrumental harmony
To glorify the Eternal What if these
Be wanting ~~yet not seldom of such hour~~ Nature fails not to provide
Impulse and utterance to the solemn scene
Accordant to the holy passion of soul
Stillness dimness and repose is heard
Accordant chiefly then when at such hours
Within the circuit of this fabric huge
One Voice – the solitary Raven flying
Athwart the concave of the dark blue dome
Unseen and high above all power of sight
The Ravens voice an iron knell renewed
At intervals with echoes from afar
Fainter and fainter echoes as the
Which the Bird utters fades upon the ear
By distance and yet dies not ~~all is still~~
earth is stilled
The permanent unwearably composes
To the three celestial Sisters the living slam

IV 1158

when these lofty rocks
At nights approach bring down the unclouded sky
To rest upon their circumambient walls
A Temple framing of dimensions vast
But yet not too gigantic for the sound
Of human anthems choral song and burst
Sublime of instrumental harmony
To glorify the Eternal. — What if these
Be wanting Nature fails not to provide
Impulse and utterance, with the solemn scene
And with the holy passions of the soul
Accordant — chiefly then when all the hush
Of stillness deepness and repose is heard
Within the circuit of this fabric huge
One voice the solitary Raven flying
Athwart the concave of the dark blue dome
Unseen and high above all power of sight
The Raven, voice an iron knell renewed
At intervals with echoes from afar
Fainter and fainter echoes as the cry
With which the bird accompanies his flight
Through the calm region fades upon the ear

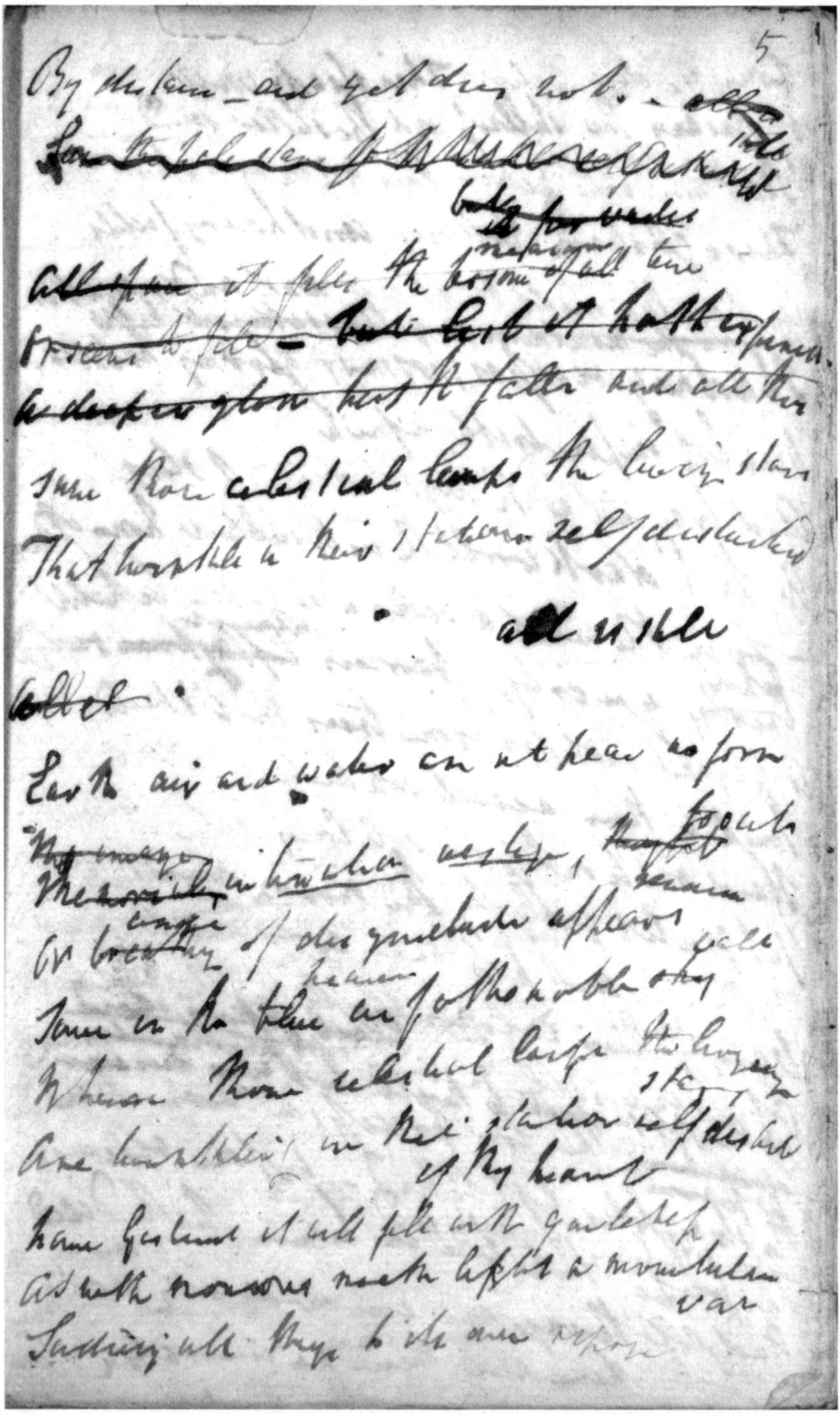

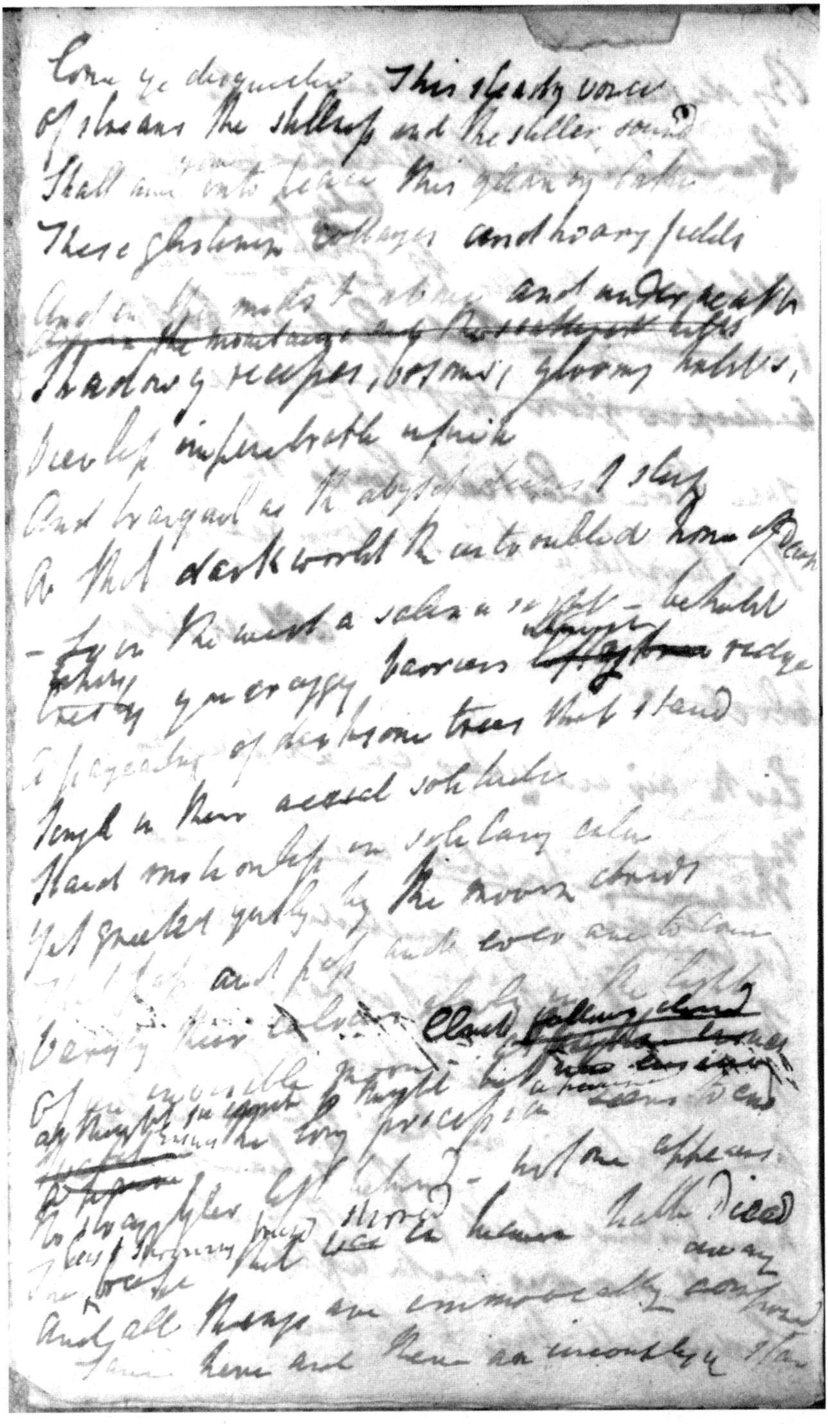

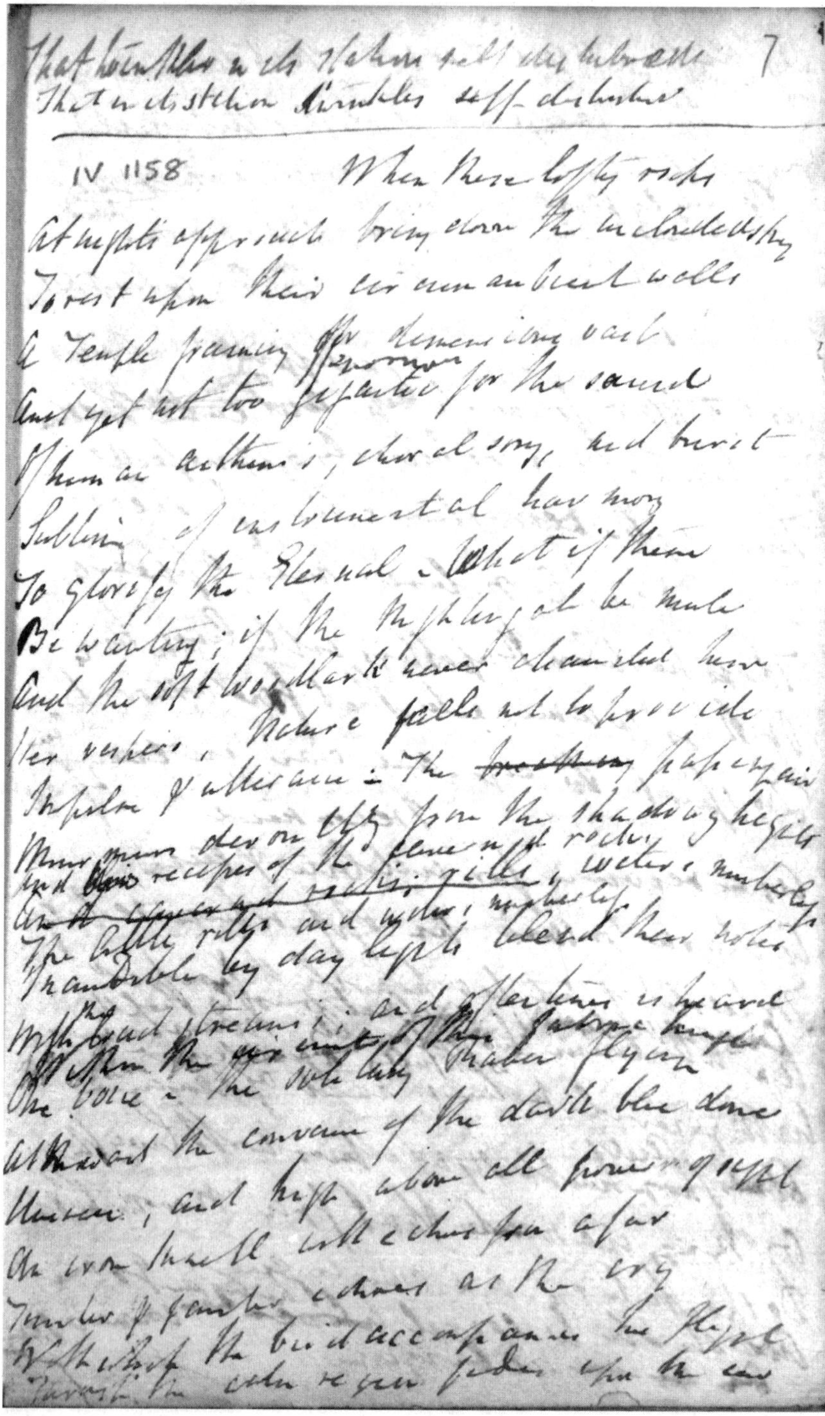
[illegible] 7
[illegible]

IV 1158 When these lofty rocks
At night's approach bring down the unclouded sky
To rest upon their circumambient walls
A Temple framing of dimensions vast
And yet not too enormous for the sound
Of human anthems, choral song, and burst
Sublime of instrumental harmony
To glorify the Eternal. What if these
Be wanting; if the Nightingale be mute
And the soft woodlark never chaunted here
Her vespers, Nature fails not to provide
Impulse & utterance. The ~~[illegible]~~ [illegible]
Murmurs descending from the shadowy heights
[illegible]
[illegible]
The little rills and waters numberless
Inaudible by daylight blend their notes
With the loud streams; and oftentimes is heard
[illegible]
One voice, the solitary Raven flying
Athwart the concave of the dark blue dome
Unseen, and high above all power of sight
An iron knell with echoes from afar
[illegible]
With which the bird accompanies her flight
Through the calm region fades upon the ear

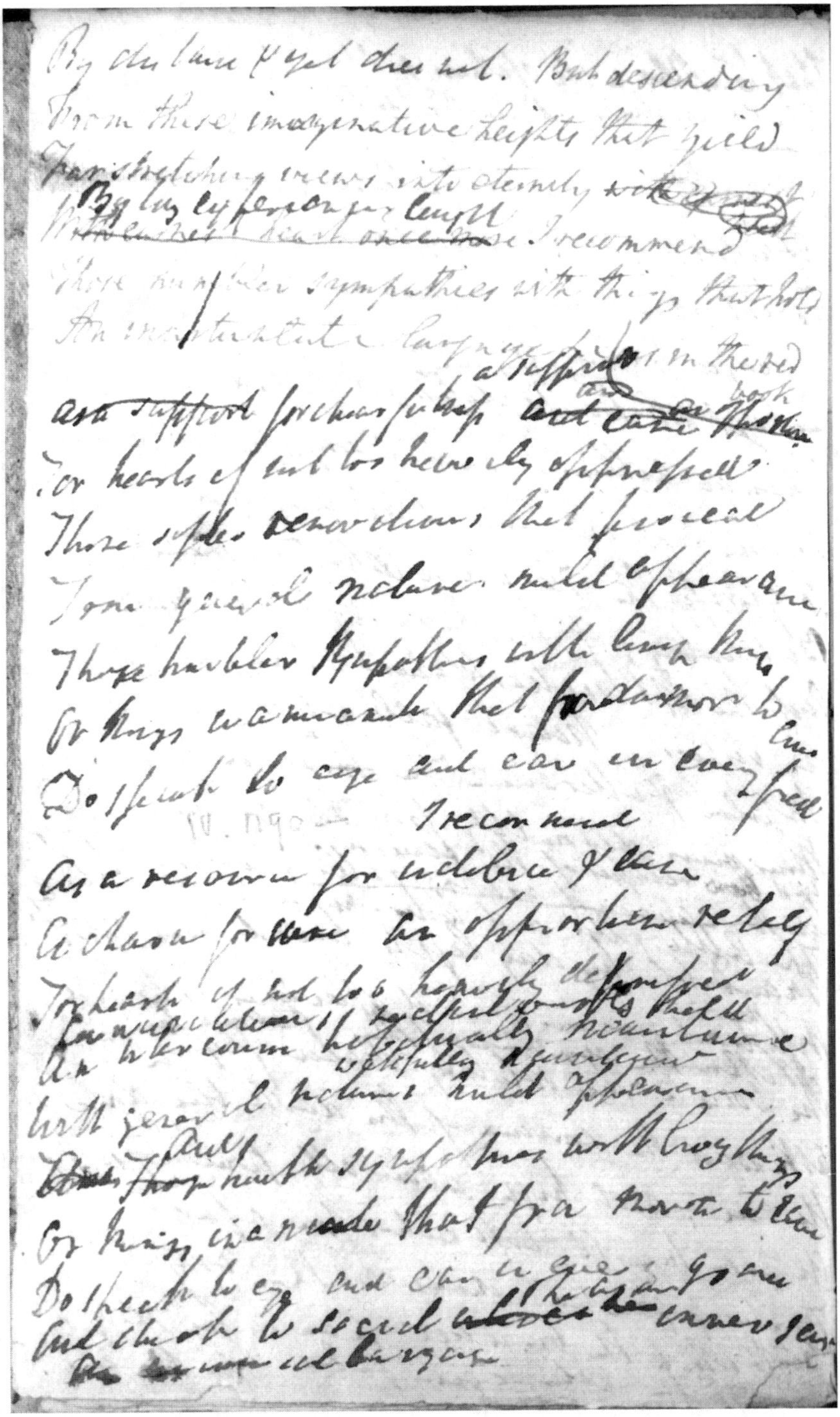
By distance & yet dies not. But descending
From these imaginative heights that yield
Far stretching views into eternity with
By long experience taught
With ... once more. I recommend
Those humbler sympathies with things that hold
An inarticulate language ... in the reed
a support
As a support for those who ... and ... book
For hearts of not too heavily oppressed
Those softer renovations that proceed
From general nature's mild appearance
Those humbler sympathies with living things
Or things inanimate that found no voice
Do speak to eye and ear in every sense
I recommend
As a resource for indolence & ease
A charm for ... an opportune relief
For hearts of not too heavily depressed
An intercourse habitually maintained
With general nature's mild appearance
And those humble sympathies with living things
Or things inanimate that from mouth to ear
Do speak to eye and ear in ...
And through the social ... inner sense
... language

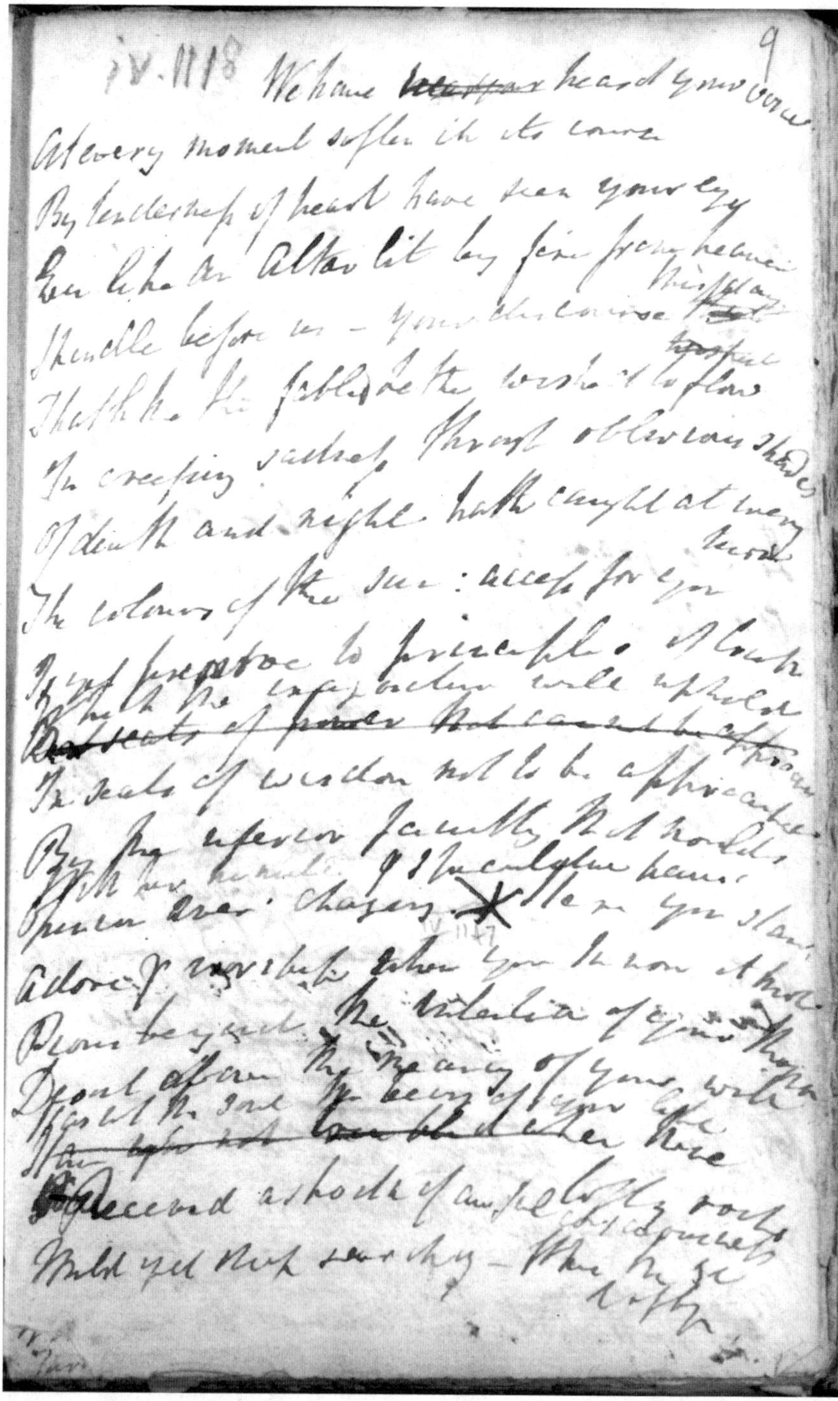
iv. 1118

9

We have ~~[illegible]~~ heard your voice
At every moment soften in its course
By tenderness of heart have seen your eye
Even like an Altar lit by fire from heaven
Kindle before us — Your discourse ~~[illegible]~~ this day
That like the fabled Lethe wished to flow
In creeping sadness through oblivious shades
Of death and night hath caught at every turn
The colours of the sun: access for you
Is yet preserved to principles of truth
Which the imaginative Will upholds
~~In seats of power that cannot be approach~~
The seats of wisdom not to be approached
By the inferior faculty that moulds
With her minute & speculative pains
Opinion ever changing. * [illegible]
[illegible]
[illegible]
[illegible]
[illegible]
[illegible]
[illegible]

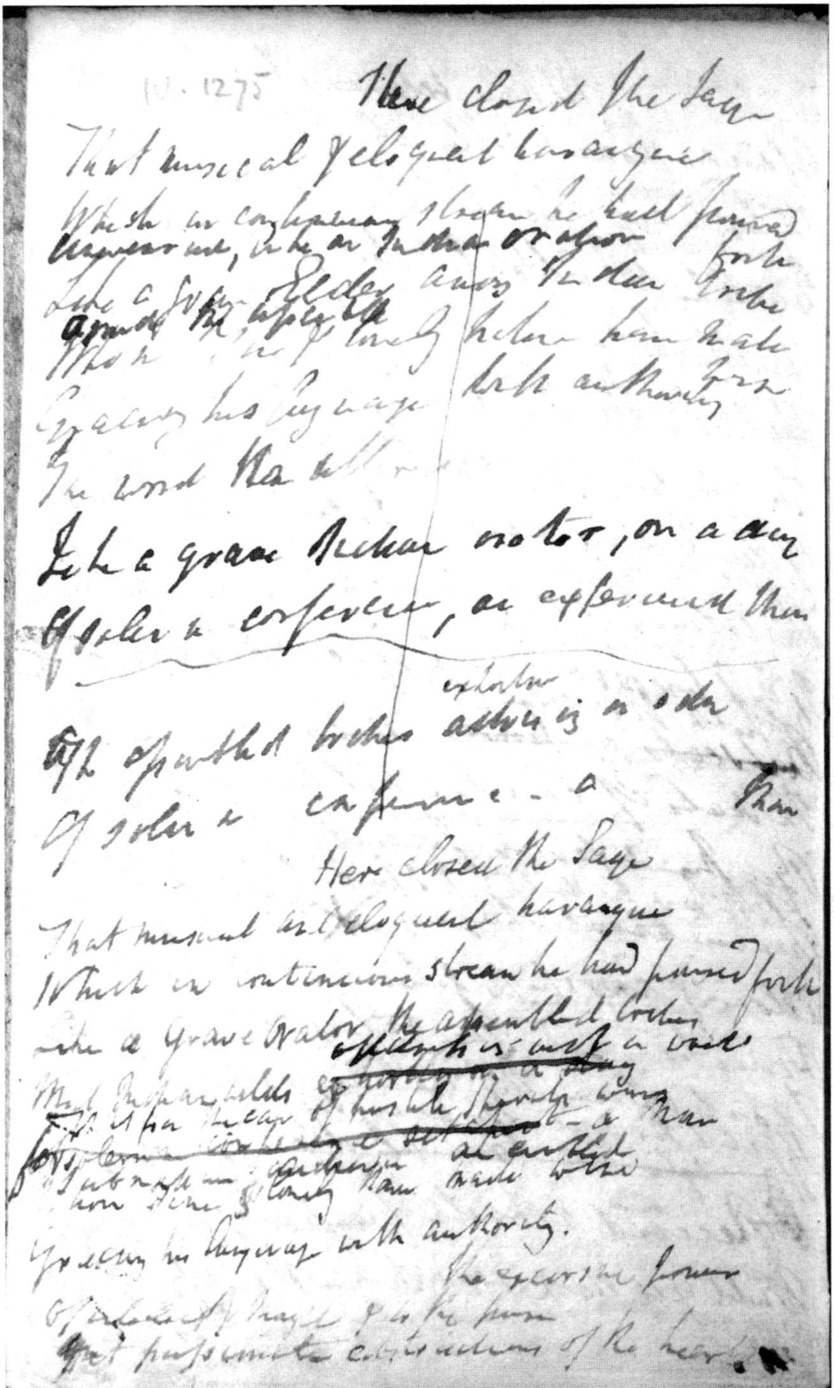
Here closed the Sage
That musical & eloquent harangue
Which in continuous stream he had poured forth
Like a grave Indian orator, on a day
Of solemn conference, an assembled throng
Here closed the Sage
That musical and eloquent harangue
Which in continuous stream he had poured forth
Gracing his language with authority.
passionate contractions of the heart.

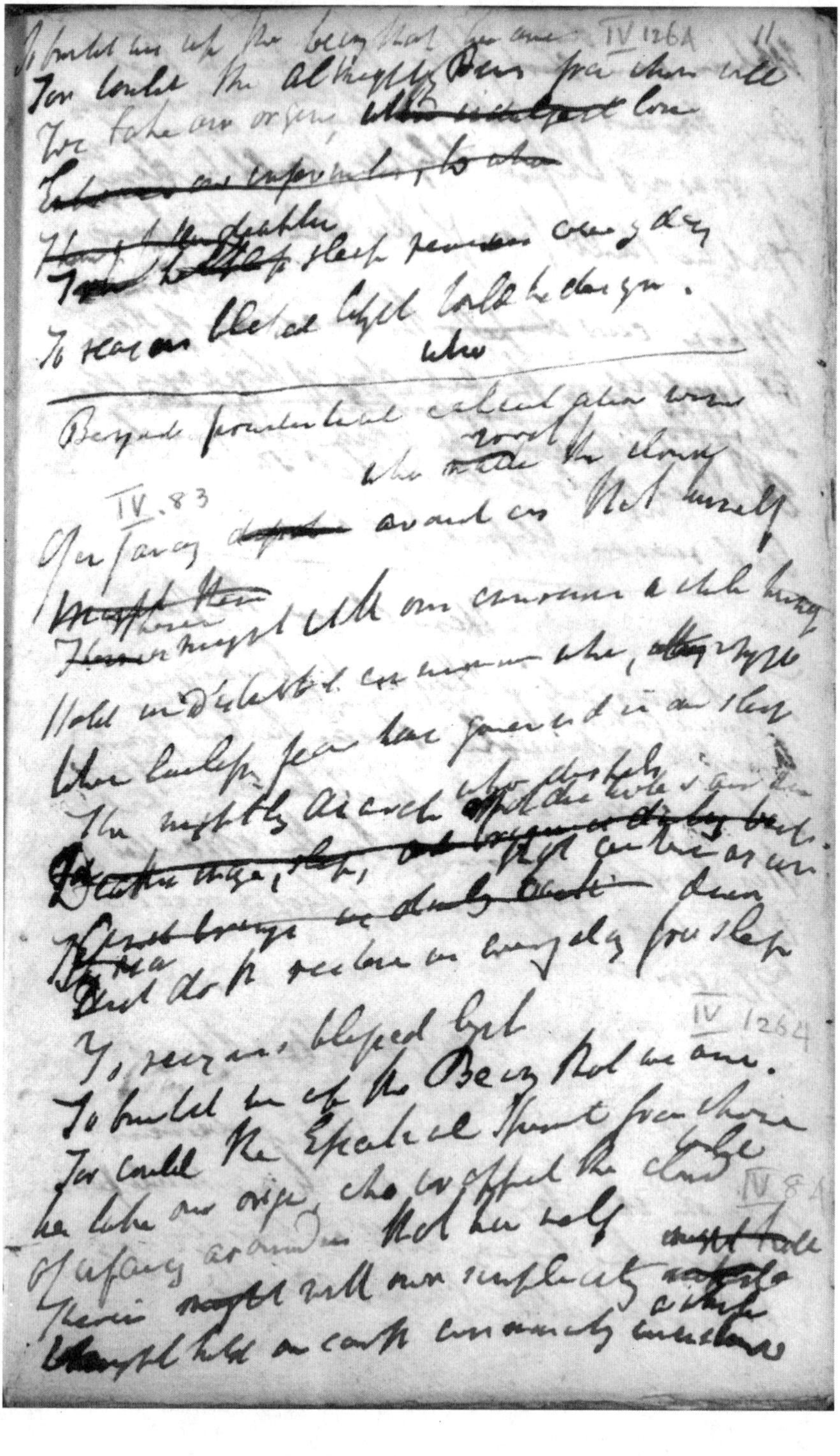

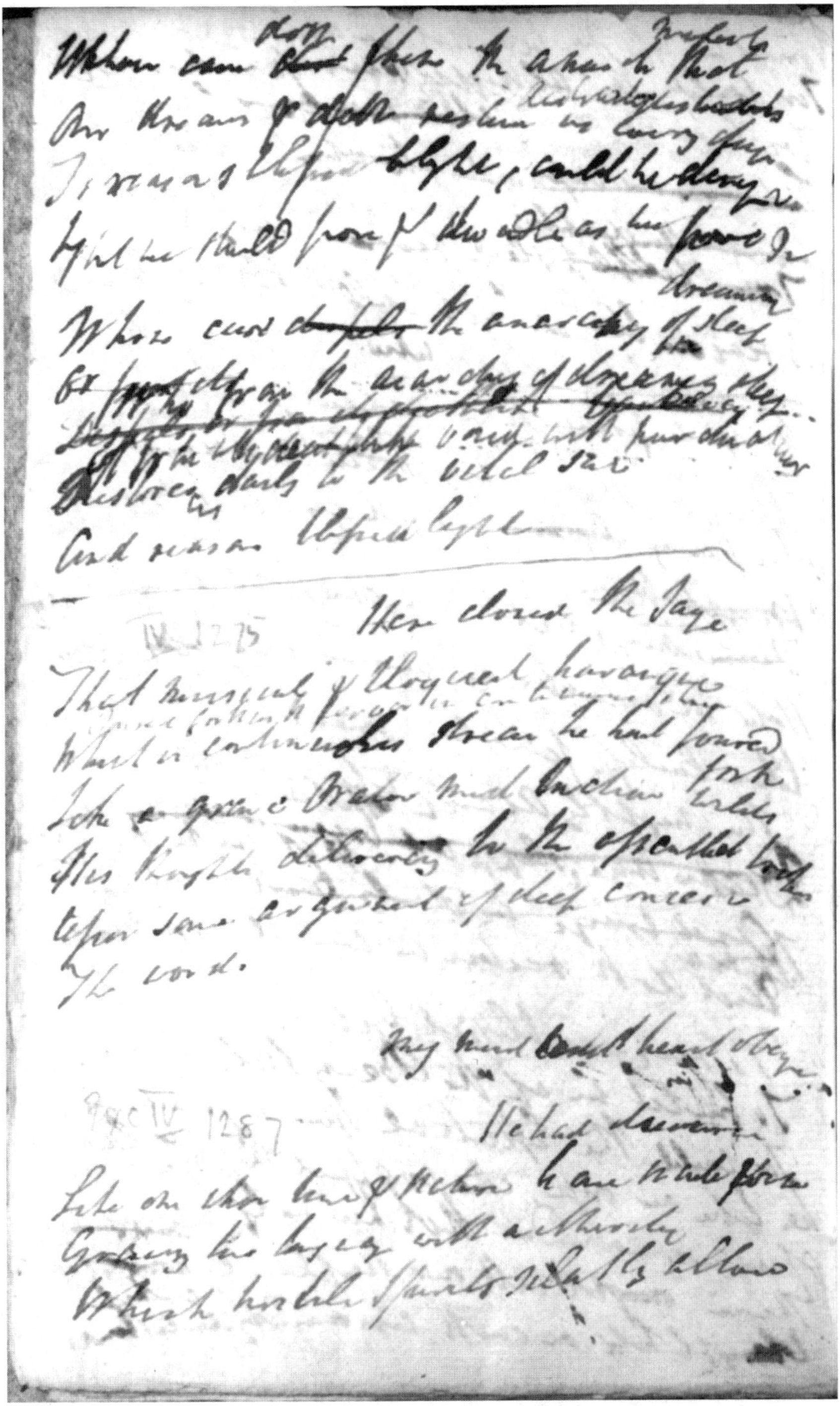

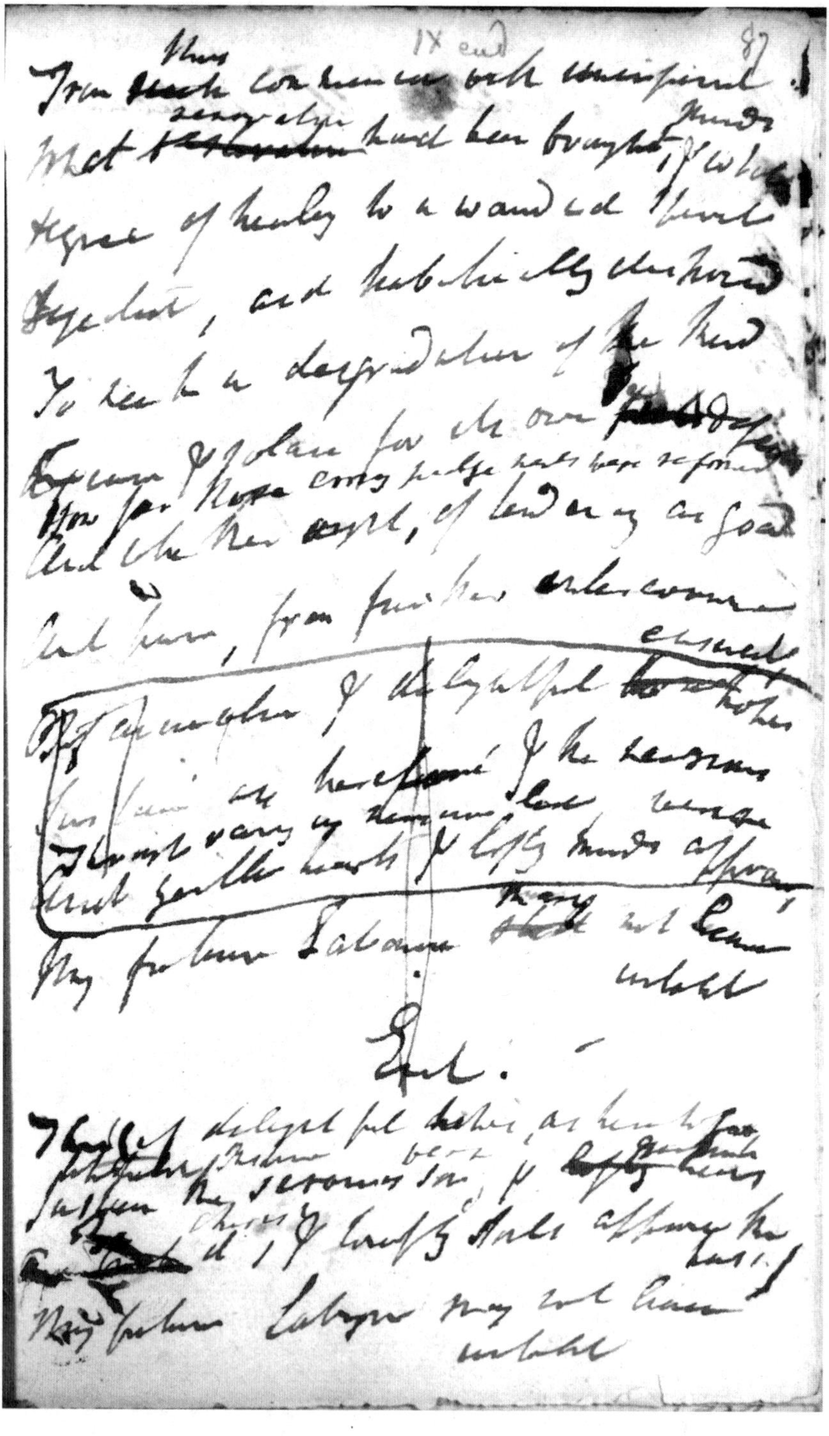

DC MS. 74

DC MS. 74—in use at the fourth, sixth, seventh, and eighth stages of *Excursion* composition for work on Books V, VI, VII, and IX—is described in the Manuscript Census, pp. xxiv–xxv, above. For a discussion of this manuscript and its role in the composition of *The Excursion*, see pp. 446–448, 455–465, 468–477, above.

Left-hand margin line numbers on the transcriptions of DC MS. 74 provide cross-references to the line count in the 1814 reading text in this edition. Right-hand margin numbers in italic type fall into two categories: (1) numbers preceded by *SBC* refer to what we have called *The Shepherd of Bield Crag*, which was once part of *The Excursion*; (2) numbers preceded by *TPL* refer to what we have called *The Peasant's Life*, also once part of *The Excursion*. For more on *The Shepherd of Bield Crag* and *The Peasant's Life*, see pp. 468–473, above, and Appendix II (which also includes reading texts), below.

On pp. 1100–1104, below, we present sample photographs of these leaves of DC MS. 74:

DC MS. 74, 30r
DC MS. 74, 34r
DC MS. 74, 42v
DC MS. 74, 76v
DC MS. 74, 77v

The image size of the photographs of DC MS. 74 is 84 percent of actual size.

[inside front cover]

V, 257 this Cottage Nurseling *TPL, 90*
259 Learned in that tedious time to gain such *91*
strengt,
260 Though yet irrational [?and] of soul to grasp *92*
261 With tiny fingers to let fall a tear *93*
evening the cloud
262 And when the heavy cloud of sleep dissolve *94*
263 To stretch his limbs, bemocking as might seem *95*
264 The outward functions of intelligent Man. *96*

265 A grave profic[?ie]t in a various round *97*
266 Of Puppetry *98*

VIII, 137 Hence that sum
lodge spatious
138 Of Keels that ~~lie~~ ~~rest~~ within her ~~crowded~~
strands
139 And ride at anchor in her sounds & bays

140 That animating spectacle of sails
308 behold him!—in the school
309 Of his attainments?—no; but with the
air
310 Fanning his temples under heaven's blue
arch.

[1r]

V, 419, 420 ~~The simple race of Mountaineers~~
419 the simple race
420 Of Mountaineers by Natures' self removed
had it chanced that any
VII, 900 And ~~verily if any~~ wandering there,
901 From some commanding eminence had look d
[?~~this mountain~~] to him it [?seen]
902 Down on this spot ~~he~~ would have [?showd]
903 A glittering spectacle; but every face
904, 905 Was pallid—all eyes wept; nor wer the
few
905, 906 ~~The few~~ who from their dwellings came not forth
to
In join
907 ~~To~~ this sad service less disturb'd than we

90–98 Late rev of *TPL*, probably after separated from Book V. Rev of 12r, 13r, 33v, 34r. Book V, ll. 257–266, probably rev on 13r in a form close to that of Book V in MS. 74A on 7r–7v.
137–140 Rev of 14v, rev on 15r.
308–310 Rev of 20r, 19v.

419, 420–420 These lines are incorporated on MS. 74A, 11r. Cf. 28v (V, 414). In the first line on the page, "race of Mountaineers," in pencil, partially del by eras. "The simple race" also del in ink.
These draft lines for Book VII lead into ll. 913ff. on 1v, then copied on 2r. Book VII is continued from 119r, VII, 720.

908 They started at the tributary peal
909 Of instantanteous thunder that announc[?]
910 Through the still air the closing of the grave
ech[?oe]
911 And distant Mountains answered with a
sound
912 Of lamentation never heard before

[1ᵛ]

ing
VII, 916 Listen{[?] as if another voice yet spake
917 In confirmation, or in still response
Such as the echoes utter'd render d back
quiet
That funeral tribute from their {[?peac] cells
Listening as to another voice from far
918 Yea to the antient soul
This [?best]
913 The Pastor ceased—my venerable Friend
914 Victoriously uprais d his clear bright eye
915 And when that eulogy was ended stood
as if the [?internal]
[?~~eye~~]
[916] Enrapt in thought and his inward {[?] sense
As if he listened to a voice that spake
to another voice that spake
~~There li~~[?t]en[?i]g^ could hear
response
[917] Fr far in confirmation, or ~~reply~~,
[918] Yea to the antient soul of this wide
land

921 to that Deity
~~heart~~
922 Des[?en]ding, and supporting his pure ~~soul~~
923 With patriotic confidence & joy

[2ʳ]

VII, 913 *The Pastor ceased. My venerable Friend*
914 *Victoriously upraised his clear bright eye*
915 *And when that eulogy was ended stood*
916 *Enrapt as if his inward sense perceived*

---

909 Word "announced" partially obscured by inkblot.

Rev on 2ʳ.
913 "This [?best]" above the line may be WW's reminder, at one stage, indicating which version he preferred.
915 Rev below possibly obscures a comma after "ended."

Rev of 1ᵛ.
913–932 Base text is in DW's hand.

917 *The prolongation of some still response*
918 *Sent by the ancient soul of this wide Land*
{S
919 *The spirit of its mountains & its {seas*
920 *Its cities, Temples, fields its awful power*
921 *Its rights & virtues by that Deity*
mind
922 *Descending;—and supporting his pure heart*
923 *With patriotic confidence & joy.*
924 *And at the last of those memorial words*
925 *The pining Solitary turned aside*
926 *Whether through manly instinct to conceal*
927 X *~~Nature's involuntary workings felt~~*
928 *On his worn cheek or with uneasy shame*
929 *For those cold humours of habitual spleen*
930 *Which fondly seeking in dispraise of man*
931 *Solace & self excuse had sometimes urged*
932 [?~~In~~] ~~*self*~~ – *To self-abuse a not ineloquent*
tongue

[927] X Tender emotions spreading from the heart
[928] To the worn cheek

[2^v]

VII, 933 *Right tow'ards the sacred Edifice his steps*
934 *Had been directed; & we saw him now*
935 *Intent upon a monumental stone,*
Whose
936 *~~Of~~ uncouth frame was grafted on the wall*
into the
937 *Or rather seemed to have grown ~~out of~~*
the side
938 *Of the rude Pile,* as oft times Trunks of
Trees
939 Where Nature works in wild & craggy spots
940 Are seen incorporate with the living Rock
taking note
941 *To endure for aye—The Vicar ~~with a smile~~*
courteous
942 *Of his employment, with a* ^*smile*
{A
943 *Exclaimed, the Sagest {antiquarians eye*
944 *That task would fail; & with these added*
words
945 *He towards the spot advanced. "Tradition*
tells
946 *That in Eliza's golden days a Knight*
Came,
947 ^ *~~Upon~~ a War Horse sumptuously attired,*
948 *And fixed his home in this sequestered*
Vale."

---

927 The X in left margin signals rev at page foot.

---

933 MW's hand begins here and continues for base text lines through l. 997 on 4^v.
947–948 Lines are apparently added as rev of l. 948 on 3^r.

[3r]

VII, 948 ~~Came to this Valley here to make abode~~

untold

949 *Tis left*^ *if here he first drew breath* ~~*or as*~~

{S

950 *Or as a* {*stranger reached this deep recess*

951 *Unknowing & unknown. A pleasing thought*

952 *I sometimes entertain—that haply bound*

953 *To Scotland's court in service of his Queen*

[?~~english~~] ~~Seat~~

954 *Or sent on mission to some nothern Chief*

Eng} this Vale he might have seen

955 *Of* [?*his*]} *land's realm*—~~*he might passed*~~ *this way*

[956] With transient observation, & thence caught

956 ~~*And from this Valley caught with transient g*~~*lance*

957 *An image fair, that, brightening in his soul*

958 *When years admonished him of failing strength*

delights

959 *And he no more rejoiced in War's* ~~*pursuits*~~

from the world,

960 *Had power to draw him* ~~*to this Vale*~~ *resolved*

961 *To make that lovely spot his chosed home*

962 *To which his peaceful fancy oft had turned*

~~*But*~~ .

963 *Vague thoughts are these but if belief may*

rest

[3v]

VII, 963, 964 ~~*But if belief may rest upon unwritten*~~

964 *Upon unwritten story fondly* ~~*told*~~ *trace*

965 From sire to son, in this obscure recess

{s

964, 965 ~~*On story traceable from Son to*~~ {[?*S*] ~~*on*~~

966 *The Knight arrived with pomp of Spear & Shield,*

967 *And borne upon a Charger covered oer*

{,

968 *With gilded housings* {[?:] *& the lofty Steed*

969 *His sole Companion & his faithful friend*

970 *Whom he in gratitude let loose to range*

{was

971 *In fertile pastures* {[?*he*] *beheld with eyes*

972 *Of admiration & delightful awe*

o}

973 *By the*}*se untravelled Dalesmen. With*

less pride

974 *Yet free from touch of envious discontent*

975 *They saw a Mansion at his bidding rise*

---

948 Cf. rev at bottom of 2v.

962/963 Line del at top of 3v begins with "But," suggesting some rev of these lines in process rather than a miscopying. WW is quite possibly dictating and making changes as he does so. The second line on 3v follows the last line on 3r.

See note to l. 962/963 on 3r.

976 *Like a bright Star amid the lowly band*
Homesteads
977 *Of their rude ~~Dwellings~~. Here the Warrior*
dwelt

[4^r]

{C
VII, 977, 978 *~~Dwelt~~, & in that Mansion* {*children of his own*
~~Were~~ *~~High & low~~*
a a Tree {^
979, 980 *Or Kindred gathered round him*{. *~~It is gone~~*
That falls & disappears *H* }
980 *The ~~waves of fortune beat~~ the* [?*l*]} *ouse is gone*
981 *And thro' improvidence or want of love*
For }
982 [?*Or*]} *ancient worth & honorable things*
983 *The spear & shield are vanished which*
the Knight
984 *Hung in his rustic Hall One ivied arch*
{G
985 *Myself have seen, a* {*gateway, last remains*
986 *Of that foundation in domestic care*
~~trac[?e]s left~~
987 *Raised by his hand*[?*s*]. *~~But all~~* [?*~~that now survives~~*]
And now no trace is left
~~Of th~~ [?*~~is~~*]
the
988 *Of ~~that~~ mild hearted-Champion save this stone*
989 *Faithless memorial, & his family name*
990 *Borne by yon clustering Cottages that sprang*
Lodge
991 *From out the ruins of his stately ~~House~~*
992 *These & the name & title at full length*

[4^v]

{w with appropriate words
VII, 993 *Sir Alfred In*{*thin ~~with appropriate words~~*
Accompanied *~~still~~*
994 *~~Accompanied~~*∧ *extant like a wreath*
d}
995 *Or poesy girt*}*ing round the several*
fronts
clear sounding &
996 *Of these*∧ *harmonious bells*
997 *That in the Steeple hang his pious gift*

---

977 WW's "dwelt" apparently corrects a copying error in the first line on 4^r, strongly suggesting dictation.

Again, the evidence at the top of the page suggests WW's dictating and revising. MW's "Were" is del but was probably her false start on the second line. Her "High & low" is possibly the first attempt to alter the del sequence beginning "It is gone."

979, 980 First "a" in WW's rev intended to be "as"; *1814* reads "As a Tree."

---

997 MW's copying, probably through dictation, was apparently interrupted so that WW could work on a difficult passage. She then resumed at l. 1017 on 5^v by copying ll. [1017]–1021a (the last line on 5^r and the first line on 5^v) and ll. 1021b–1025 (from the top of 5^r).

998 So fails so languishe, grows dim & dies

pensively

999 ~~So [?fails~~], the greyhaired Wanderer ^exclaimed

{at w}

1000 All th{[?is] this [?]}orld is proud of. From their

{spheres [?stars]}

1001 The Stars of human Glory are cast down;

{R

1002 Perish the {roses & the flowers of kings

1003 Princes and Emperors and the crowns & palms

withered & consumed

1004 Of all the mighty ~~w[?] blasted or decayed~~.

{iest

1005 Nor is power given to lowl{y Innocence

1006 Long to protect her own. The Man himself

1007 Departs, and soon is spent the line of those

[5r]

VII, 1008 Who in the bodily image, in the mind

1009 In heart or soul in station or pursuit

1010 Did most resemble him. Degrees & Ranks

1011 Classes and orders all are swept away

W}

1012, 1013 [?H]}ealth heaped on weath & privilege confirm'd

And reconfirmed are

1018 Their virtue, service happiness and state

1021 Their monuments and their memory. The vast Frame

1022 Of social nature changes ever more

1023 Her organs and her members with decay

1024 Restless and restless generation, powers

1025 And functions dying and produced at need.

we}

[1012, 1013] Wea[?lt] heap d on [?]}alth & privilege confirmed

proved to be the toil

1014 And reconfirmed are shattered & dispersed

{D

of vanity {[?d]istr[?uct]

1017 As with a breath ~~and Ruin~~ overwhelms

finally [?sweet] [?her vernal]

1019 And ~~the~~ green grass [?~~sweets~~] Nature robe

Humanitys appointed

1020 And certa Ambition certain shroud, enwraps

vain

[1021] Their monuments & their memory

[1010] ~~degrees and Rank~~

{O

Fraternities & {order heaping [?~~upon~~] high

[1011] ~~Classes and Orders~~ with ~~new wealth upheaped~~

---

998 What we read as a comma following "languishe" may be intended as an "s."

1000 Another possible conjecture for "stars" is "state."

1011 The "o" in orders may be intended as a cap as in l. [1011] below.

1017 Conjectured "Distruct" may be "Distrust."

1012 New wealth upon the burthen of the old
1013 ~~On the old store~~—& privilege confirmed
And placing trust in
[1014] And reconfirmed are scoffed at with a smile
1015 Of greedy foretaste from the secret stand
{D {aim'd {: {T
1016 Of {desolation {[?]{, {to slow decline
[1017] ~~All must give way or suddden overthrow~~

[5v]

VII, 1018 Their virtue service happiness & state
1019 Expire, and natures pleasant robe of green
Humanity
1020 ~~Mortality~~ appointed shroud enwraps
1021 Their monuments & their memory
1017 *These yield & these to sudden overthrow*
[1018] *Their virtue service happiness & state*
[1019] *Expire, & Natures pleasant robe of green*
[1020] *Humanity's appointed shroud enwraps*
[1021] *Their monuments & their memory. The vast frame*
1022 *Of social nature changes evermore*
with
1023 *Her organs & her members ~~by~~ decay*
1024 *Restless, & restless generation Powers*
1025 *And functions dying & produced at need*
1026 And thus ever thus the mighty whole subsists
1027 With an ascent & progress in the main X
{e
1030 *Th{is courteous Knight whose bones are here*
interred
1031 Lived in an age conspicous as our own
1032 For strife & ferment in the minds of [–?–] men
1031, 1035 ~~*Lived at a time when twas his pensive lot*~~
on
1033 Whence alterati[?]{in the forms of things
1036 ~~*To linger mid the last of those bright clouds*~~
1034 Various & vast a memorable age
1035 Which did to him assign a pensive lot;
[1036] —To linger mid the last of those bright clouds

1028 Yet or how disproportion'd to the hopes
minds
{[?&]
1029 {T Expectations [?&] self flattering hearts.

[6r]

VII, 1037 *That on the steady breeze of honour sailed*
1038 *In long procession calm & beautiful*
1039 *He who had seen his own bright order fade*
1040 *And its devotion gradually decline*

1016 Overwriting "aim'd" may be a reinforcement of the same word.

1017 Base text is in MW's hand (through first line on 7r). See note to l. 997 on 4v.
1027 The X in the right margin probably signals the rev entered vertically in the right margin.
1032 The "inds" of "minds" is reinforced in pencil, probably by WW. Illeg word del by eras.

1041 (While war compelled to assume a different shape
bow
1042 X Her temper changed & [?]ed to other laws)
1043 *Had also witnessed in his morn of Youth*
1044 *That violent commotion which oe'rthrew*
1045 *In Town in City & sequestered glen*
1046 *Altar & Cross & Church of solemn roof*
1047 *And old religious House pile after pile*
1048 *And sneek the Tenants out into the fields*
T
1049 *Like wild beasts without home their hour*
was come
1050 *But why no softening thought of gratitude*
1051 *No just remembrance scruple or wise doubt*
1052 *Benevolence is mild nor borrows help*
1053 *Save at worst need from bold impetuous force*
1054 *Fitliest allied with anger & revenge*
[1041] X While war relinquishing the lance & shied
[1042] Her temper changed & bow'd to other laws

[6^v]

exalts
~~congratulates the approach~~
VII, 1055 *But human kind* ~~*rejoices in the might*~~ in
~~rejoice~~
1056 *Of mutability & airey hopes* [-?-]
[1057] Dancing around her hinder & disturb
1057 ~~*Prevent, around her dancing giddily*~~
1058 *Those meditations of the soul which feed*
1059 *The retrospective Virtues Festive songs*
at the sight
1060 *Break from the madden'd nations,* ~~*to hail*~~
1061 *Of sudden overthrow: & cold neglect*
1062 *Is the sure consequence of slow decay.*
courteous
1063 *Even said the Wanderer as that* ~~*gentle*~~ *Knight*
1064 Bound by his vow to labour for redress relief
~~*Who unattended came to wear out here*~~
1065 Of all who suffer d wrong & to enact
~~*The last & better portion of life's day*~~
1066 By sword and lance the law of gentleness
€
~~*As in a*~~ ~~*convents hallowed privacy*~~
1067 *If I may venture of myself to speak*
~~Hoping~~ Trusting
1068 [—?—] that not incongruously I blend
1069 *Low things with lofty I too shall be doomed*
1070 *To outlive the kindly use & fair esteem*
1071 Of the poor calling which my youth embraced
1072 With no unworthy prospect. But enough

1041 Pencil X and angle brace signal rev at page foot, where the X is also in pencil.
[1041] For the last word, *1814* reads "shield."

1055 *1814* reverts to the base text reading.
1056 Del by eras, possibly of a "P" (as in "Prevent" in the next line of base text).

[7r]

VII,
1071, 1072 *Of my own humble calling*—But enough—
1073 —Thoughts crowd upon me—and 'twere seemlier
now
1074 XTo stop; and to our gracious Teacher yield
1074, 1075 Thanks ~~for the moving lessons~~ which his Voice
1076 Hath here deliver'd—words of heartfelt
Truth
1077 Tending to patience when Affliction strikes
1078 To hope and love; to ~~and~~ confident repose
{;
1079 In god{, and reverence for the dust of
{—
Man.{
End
[1074] X To stop, and yield our Gracious teacher Thanks
Records
1075 For the pathetic lessons which his voice
Life
VIII, 10 ~~Fame~~ death Eternity momentous themes
11 Are these, and might demand a Seraphs
tongue
12 Were they not equal to their own support
13 And therefore no incompetence of mine
14 Could do them wrong.—The universal
{Of Forms
15 {[?And] human nature in a spot like this
16 present themselves at once to all mens
view

[7v]

VIII, 1 The Pensive Sceptic of the lonely vale
2 To those acknowledgements subscribed his
{: own
3 With a sedate compliance{. ~~And the P~~riest
Which the Priest
4 Fail'd not to notice, inly pleased, and said,
5 If ye, by whom invited I commenced
o{
6 The{se Narrative of calm & humble life
7 Be satisfied, tis well, the end is gained.
8 And in return for sympathy bestow[?e]

1074 Pencil X signals rev below, where the matching X is also in pencil.
1074, 1075 Del in pencil.
1076 Pencil mark after "deliver'd" may possibly be intended as a comma.
1079 Line, possibly accidental, after "Man" has been added in pencil. "End" signals the conclusion of Book VII.
10–16 Rev of 7v.
10 Del and rev in pencil.

3–4 Line spacing suggests that rev to l. 3 preceded the writing of l. 4.

accept
9 And patient listening thanks are due from me.
Time E | momentous
10 ~~Life~~, death [?t]|ternity ~~thus far the~~ themes
{ey,
11 th{[?ese]—& might require a seraphs tongue
12 Are ~~grand~~ & ~~equal to their own support~~,
{Were
[12] {B[?ut] they not equal to their own support
~~A[?r]~~
14 ~~But~~ the main outline & the general form
man's
15 Of [?~~mans~~] condition in a spot like this
16 Presents itself at onc to all men view
wished for act
{ e ~~act~~ deed
17 Y{[?ou] asked for ~~place~~ & circumstance that [?mak]
18 The individual known & understood
19 And such as my best judgement could select
20 From what this place afforded have been
given

[8[r]]

VIII, 19, 20 And such as were afforded have been given.
[?many]|
[?]|
Yet there were ^times I frankly will confess
~~Yet [?be] it frankly [?uttered] times there were~~
21 When apprehension cross d me in the course
22 Of this self pleasing exercise that Ye
23 My zeal to his would liken who possessed
24 Of some rare gems or pictures finely wrought
dr |
25 Unlocks his Cabinet & [?lo]|aws them forth
{ing
26 One after one solicit{[?n]g regard
[26] ~~One after one soliciting regard~~
27 To this—and this—as worthier than the last
~~at first~~
awhile
28 Till the Spectator who, was pleased ~~at first~~
29 More than the Exhibitor himself becomes
30 Weary & faint & longs to be released.
31 But let us hence my Dwelling is in sight.
32 And there—"
At this the Solitary shrank
{ing
33 With backward [?~~thoughts~~] will—but, want{[?ed] not address

---

10–16 Rev on 7[r].
19–20 Rev of 8[r].

19, 20 Rev at bottom of 7[v].
28 A mark after "who" probably signals the rev above.

[?vit]
in [?t] ation to suspend
That motion
34 [?In] inward [?picture] to disguise, he said
[?~~Here stands~~]
smiling as he spake [?~~ere~~]
35 To his Compatriot ~~turning—We have h~~ [?eard]
36 The peaceable remains of this good Knight
37 Would be disturbed, I fear with
wrathful scorn

[8^v]

e [?i]
~~Rich~~ [?s]c ~~ho~~[?c] ~~e of~~
~~To guard us from the slowly veering Sun~~
Abundant choice of hospitable shade
when
Which we may turn to, ~~as~~ the [?veering] Sun
a
Makes change of [?seat] des[?c]irl ble, awhile
Here
[?] let us then remain while you [?impart]
active
Those thoughts which pressed upon your [?]
mind
[?]
VIII, 36 This good Knight
stir
37 Maugre his gentleness I fear would [?~~purse~~]
~~His brow in scorn, or stir[?s] his bones in wrath~~
[?~~to scorn~~]
[36] peaceable remains in
[37] His ~~bones in~~ wrathful scorn
38 If consciousness could reach them where ~~they~~ he lies
That one, albeit of these
That
39 [?In] ~~even a~~ man of these degenerate times
Deploring changes past or dreading change
[?~~private~~]
41 ~~Had dared to couple in the~~ [?]
[~~?~~]
even in [?this]
[41] ~~Foreseen had dared to couple, [?in one~~] breath
Of ~~his [?regret~~] nay [?move] in open words
[41] Foreseen, had dared to couple, even in thought,
42 The fine vocation of the sword & lance
aims
43 With the gross ~~ends~~ & body bending toil
my Friend is
yoke
yoke
To which your ~~servile~~ brotherhood ^are [?]
44 Of a poor Brotherhood who walk the earth

35–37 Rev of ll. 35–37 on 8^r are rev of draft on 8^v and are followed by l. 38 on 8^v.

Ll. 35–37 rev on 8^r.
36 In the line above l. 36, overwriting of "mind" may be a reinforcement.

What [?matter], might his [?indignation cry]
{ ~~Pitied~~
{[?Pit] Pitied & where they are not known
despised
45 Where such offensive drudgery [?expired]
by
46 Yet ~~with~~ the good Knights leave, [?~~though~~]
The two Estates

[9r]

VIII, 47 Are graced with some resemblance—Errant
{ose
Th{ey
48 Exiles & wanderers & the like are ye—
~~carrying~~ hill & dale
traverse
49 Who with your burthen among lonely wilds
Carrying for
50 Pass for relief ~~of~~ natures simple wants
~~Cheered by good fortune—to mishap expo~~sed.
they seek
51 What though no higher recompense ~~he sought~~
[?~~tire~~]~~some~~
52 Than honest maintenance by irksome toil
yet such may claim respect
53 Full oft procured ~~content meanwhile to live~~
54 Among the intelligent for [?what ~~they]~~ ~~[?]~~
45 ~~Pitied & where ye are not known despised~~
this course
55 Enables them to be & to perform
[?]
67 ~~Yet such have been & are in their degree~~
so }
69 Apts instruments to [?re]}ften & refine
{[?soul]
[?And gradual raise] the s{[?tate]
[69] Rude minds ~~a[?]~~ ~~and~~ [?spirites] ~~grovelling~~
~~& inert~~
{[?~~Of~~]
{From ~~out their [?mist] and raise the grovellin~~
~~soul~~
71 and sava torpor to ~~expel~~
{looked depose
70 By importation of un{[?] for arts
And By the awakening beams of her deisres.
in breast
76 The pure affection ~~of~~ the mothers ~~heart~~

---

45 The base text line is first entered as part of the sequence continuing on 9r. Ll. 56–63 at the foot of 9v are meant to follow "despised" at one early stage of rev. Vertical lines in the left margin on 8v are matched by one beside the last two lines on 9v, although lines may signal only intended rev or del.

---

52 Another possibility for "tiresome" may be "irksome."
55/67 Ll. 56–63 are entered on 9v and ll. 64–72 on 10v; the passages were probably originally intended to follow l. 45 on 8v. Cf. note to l. 45 on 8v.
69–75 Recopied by DW and rev on 9v.
[69]/71 Other possible readings for "mist" are "dust" or "dark."

77 And in the Lovers fancy, by the stars
[?~~mazines~~]
74 Draws from their moveing magazine
75 Are and quickened alientated minds
Are in their presence tempted to unite

[9v]

VIII, 69, 72 Apt intruments for raising savage life
73 To rustic & the rustic to urbane.
~~And seal the treaty of returning love~~
~~With interchange of gifts parting friends~~
69 ~~*Apt instruments to soften and refine*~~
71 ~~*Rude winds & savage torpor*~~ *to dispel*
70 ~~*By importation of unlook'd for arts*~~
~~*And penetrating force of her desires.*~~
74 *Within their moving magazines is lodged*
75 *Power that comes forth to quicken & exalt*
seated
76 *The ~~pure~~ affections in the Mother's breast*
77 *And in the Lover's fancy, & to feed*
78 *The sober sympathies of long-tried Friends*
[?~~human Beings~~]
79 [?*Fri*] *By these Itinerants, as experienced men*
~~speech~~
~~*That intimately mingle with their*~~ [~~?*counsel*~~]
80 *Counsel is given, contention they appease*
With
81 ~~*By*~~ *healing words & in remotest wilds*
82 *Tears wipe away & pleasant tidings bring*
proud quest
83 ~~*What*~~ *could the ~~pride~~ ^ of Chivalry do more.*
45 despised
Their tardy
56 ~~Yet your slow~~ steps give leisure to observe
57 While solitude permits the mind to feel
58 And doth intru[?s]ct her to supply defects
59 By the division of her inward self
60 For grateful converse, and to these poor
men
61 As I have heard you boast with honest pride
[?e]
62 Nature is bountiful wheree[?r]r they go;
63 Kind Natures various wealth is all their own.
For them if not for others more at ease
Birds warble, rivers run, and fragrant
smel[?ls]

69–77 These lines are rev of 9r. The top two lines on the page offer WW's further rev; work on this passage is continued on 10v.

69–83 Base text is in DW's hand.

83 Copy of Book VIII continues on 11v.

45, 56–63 See note to l. 45 on 8v. Ll. 64–72 on 10v continue the copy from the bottom of 9v. In the final rev, l. 72 on 10v led to l. 73 at the top of 9v.

Vertical line in left margin of the last two lines probably indicates intention to cancel.

[10r]

~~I know no more~~
Than doth the Sod that roofs it. Yet methinks
Than doth the grass [?grown] sod that covers it
If mere Imagination might presume
Yet If
To touch a theme that wants the steadier light
Of your experience—might I step before
V, 413 And with no better guide than chance regards
414 Or notice forc'd upon incurious ears
Attempt an honest sample to set forth
Natures rustic offspring
Of ~~those by doom of nature~~ hither brought
From their sequestered Cottages—a race
Thrice favored, uncorrupted men, who share
The elevation of a Christian land
A land of peace and liberty and truth
Thus would I paint him—thus from morn to eve
dim [?dimmer] close
From lifes ~~first~~ opening to its ~~last decay~~
re}
Would I }trace his history.—At these words
A sudden influx of enlivening thought
Brightened the sick man's faded countenance
My expectation shaped for him a path
On the plain ground inscrib'd—but his discourse
Mounted aloft and under many a cloud
And crossing many a streak of ether blue
Saild high or low; upon the inconstant wind
Part wheeling—blown about in part—with bold
And not ungraceful struggles. —Let the
house

[10v]

Rise from the bosom of the stedfast earth
on
Or pass, [?&] or meets them wafted ~~by~~ the breeze
In characters & [?humanity] versed
VIII, 64 Versed in the character of men, and bound
By tie of daily interest
65 ~~And bound daily bound~~ by interest to maintain

This page is part of a sequence of *TPL* passages, some continuous and some rev, entered on 10r, 11r, 10v—and on 12r, 13r, and inside front cover—as rev of work on 27r–27v, 28v, 29v, 30v, 31v–34r. Vertical line in the right margin here on 10r probably marks the passage for rev or del. Vertical lines are also on 11r and 12r.

20–44 Rev of 27v, 28v, 32v, 33r.

20 Half-line del here is reincorporated on 33r.

V, 413–V, 414 Cf. MS. 74A, 11r.

43 Rev of 37r.

64–72 Continued from 9v, rev of 9r, 9v. Line in the left margin indicates intention to cancel the first two lines.

tory
66 Concialo[?try] manners & smooth speech
67 Such have been & still are in their degree
Ex
68 [?]amples efficacious to refine
69 Rude intercourse apt instrument to expel
70 By importation of unlooked for arts
&
[?] Penetratin[?g] force of her desires
71 Barbarian torpor & blind prejudice
72 Raising through just gradation savage life.
[?n]
~~From this [?calm]~~ [?]ight whe[?re] Natur [?] hath fix'd *TPL, 60*
A throne of [?power] for infant innocence
Stooping as needs she must let fancy tell *61*
But how *62*

But who, though versed in sciences occult *[62]*
As far as skill can go [?i]n earth or heaven *64*

As far as skill can go [?i]n earth or sky *[64]*

[?~~lore~~]
May trace this [?] through all its curious maze *66*
Of hope or fear, what industry [?suffice]
~~note~~
To [?~~count~~] the spells *67*

[11[r]]

(Thus buyountly did that discourse ascend) *TPL, 45*
Where first he breathes the vital air be glad *46*
w
For a Manchild is born. See Weakness now, *47*
Impersonated here in human form *48*
h
Assert her rights, and Helplessness ensure *49*
From eager tendance all that it requires. *50*
naked
Beneath the ~~lowly~~ rafters of the roof *51*
supine
That shelters, him, [?] the Infant lies *52*
[?~~supine~~]
Senseless and powerless—yet a King of state *53*
Of high observance and of prime concern *54*

Some of the *TPL* lines on 10[v] are probably meant to replace lines del on 11[r], but WW's specific intent is not clear.

60–67 Rev of 11[r], 29[v], 32[v].

45–69 Rev of 28[v], 29[v], 32[v], 33[r]; *TPL*, ll. *60–67*, rev on facing 10[v].

47 Possibly cap "W" overwrites lowercase "w."

49 Possibly cap "H" overwrites lowercase "h."

[*]
And every eye that enters turns to him [?]} [?out] 55
{[?~~now~~]
~~That star unseen before that~~ {[?] ~~hath risen~~ 56
~~Such welcome nature[?s] care for him provides~~ 57
[?embrace] as
Not less ~~than~~ if he were the destined Lord 58
Of large domains exultin[?g]ly announced 59
With churchtower music rung in clamorous 60
peal
~~Stooping as needs she must, let Fancy tell~~ 61
why?
But ~~how~~? though vers d in sciences occult 62
{ary
Prognostics, tokens,—planet{y sway 63
And fireside omens, far as skill can go. 64
What tongue, for this occasion competent 65
May trace th[?e] lore through all its curious maze 66
or note
~~Re[?count~~] the spells the forms that must be kept 67
Strictly, or not less scrupulously shunned 68
As each sage Gossip dictates to protect 69

[11v]

{[?~~for~~]
~~Smiles of [?good fortune~~], {[?on] ~~his future years~~
~~A length of days by fortun[?es sunshine cheered~~] *TPL, 73*
VIII, 84 "Happy, rejoinned the Wander, he who gains
85 A Panegyric from your generous tonge
to
86 But, if these Wayfarers once pertained
{Aught
87 {[?] of romantic interest—tis gone
88 Their purer service in this realm at least
89 Is past forever. An inventive Age
90 Has wrought, if not with speed of magic—yet
91 To most strange issues. I have lived to mark
92 A new and unforeseen creation rise
93 From out the labours of a peaceful land
94 Wielding her potent Enginry to frame
95 And to produce with appetites as keen
~~not resting~~
o}
96 As that of War whi{~~ch~~ rests not night or
W} day
97 Industrious to destroy. *w}ith fruitless search*
should
98, 106 *Now might I look for many a rugged path*
107, 108 *And horse track wild & formidable lane*

First two del lines on 11v are rejected rev of *TPL* on 12r.
84ff. Continued from 9v; continued on 12v.
97b Lines at page foot are rev and recopied on 13v. MW's hand begins at l. 97b and continues on 12v.

[12^r]

For the uncons ious object of their care TPL, 70
And regent of their busy services 71
{or
Body {and mind from evil and ensure 72
Health and long life
A length of days by fortunes sunshine cheered 73
{mix
Nor fail their garrulous tongues to inter{pose 74
Brief words of ready preayer for honest ways 75
And Gods good grace to aid & crown the whole 76
Meanwhile how pure or exquisite the bliss 77
That from the touch or sensible approach 78
{A
Of her new {acquisition shall pervade 79
{M
The languid {mothers heart, what yearning 80
love
What tender awe or pious gratitude 81
To the still spirit may convey delight 82
r }
And lift it in this sabbath of her [?l] }est 83
Above the level of lifes daily ~~tasks~~ [?~~work~~] 84
cares
This is a mystery—a saintly lamp 85
Burns here within its own peculiar shrine 86
Forbid to blend its light with common day. 87
Due honour will the ensuing months obtain 88
If we record that like his Brother Babes 89
V, 257 Cradled in palaces this Cottage nursling 90
259 Learn d in that tedious time to yawn 91
smile sneeze
260 Though yet irrational of soul to grasp 92

[12^v]

VIII, 99 *Which not unthankfully in youth I trod*
100 *A lone Pedestrian with a scanty frieght*
101 *Wished for or welcome wheres[?eer] I came*
109 *These prized when other avenue was none*
110 *Or easier link connecting place with place*
ample
111 *Have vanished giving way to ~~stately~~ roads*

Continued from 11^r; continued on 13^r.

257–260 Rev of 33^v, 34^r, inside front cover, 13^r; expanded on 13^r after inside front cover rev. On marginal vertical line, see note on 10^r. Cf. MS. 74A, 7^r–7^v.

70–75 Rev of 32^v, 30^v.

78–92 Rev of 33^v, 34^r.

85–87 Draft toward these lines on 27^r–27^v is incorporated on 34^r.

Continued from 11^v.

99–117 MW continues copy from 11^v; WW picks up the copy at midpage; MW resumes copy in the last two lines but quickly breaks off to allow the entire sequence of lines beginning with l. 97 on 11^v to be rev by WW on 13^v–14^r.

112 *Stately & bold that penetrate the gloom*
113 *Of England's farthest glens. The earth hath*
lent
114 *Her waters Air her breezes & the sail ~~of traffic~~*
Of traffic
115 *Glides with endless intercharge ~~glistening~~*
116 *Glistening along the low & woody dale*
117 *Or on the naked mountain's lofty side*
What growth in memory of men whose hairs
{unbl[?an]ch'd
Are yet {[?~~un~~][?][?~~blanch~~] what growth of mighty
Towns
~~outspread~~
petty produced
119, 120 From germ of ~~little~~ Villages ~~or spr[?u]~~
Or sprung, as from the bosom of the earth
123 Where not a habitation stood before.
tell
The new born Hamlets who shall ^the kinds
Of Houses scattered with a hasty hand
The Hamlets scattered with a speedy hand
Who shall ennumerate the fair

[13[r]]

V, 261 With tiny finger to let fall a tear *TPL, 93*
262 And as the heavy cloud of sleep dissolves *94*
263 To stretch his limbs—bemocking as might seem *95*
264 The outward functions of intelligent Man *96*
265 A grav proficient in amusive feats *97*
266 Of puppetry that from the lap declare *98*
267 His expectations and announce his claims *99*
268 On that inheritance which Millions rue *100*
born
269 That they were ever [?~~b~~][?] to.—~~But the~~ day *101*
257 Behold a Babe
259 One that hath barely learn d to shape a smile
260 Though yet irrati *92*

[269] See for him
comes
270 A day of solemn ceremonial ~~comes~~ *102*
271 When they who for this minor *103*
hold in trust

The Travellers eye wheresoeer turn[?s]
VIII, 129 Meanwhile wheer the eye is turned—behold
The unproductiv
130 ~~Behold the barren~~ wilderness erased

Continued from 12[r]. Ll. 257–260 and 269–271 (although fragmentary) are closer to the drafting of Book V proper than other *TPL* rev of these lines on 12[r], inside front cover, 33[v], 34[r]. Cf. MS. 74A, 7[r]–7[v].

129–133 These lines, below the *TPL* material entered earlier, appear to be a continuation of WW's drafting on 12[v]. A version very close to *1814* is on 14[r]. Alternatively, but less likely, these lines on 13[r] are a rejected rev of the material on 14[r].

Beholds
131 Or disappearing triumphs that proclaim
132 How much the mild Directress of the plough
{A
133 Owes to alliance with these novel {arts

[13v]

VIII, 97 Industrious to destroy.—With fruitless pains
98 Might one like me now visit many a tract
99 Which in his youth he trod & trod again
100 Alone Pedestrian with a scanty frieght
101 Wished for or welcome wheresoeer he came
102 Amond the tenantry of Thorp and Vill
Or
103 ~~And~~ straggling Bourg of antient Charter
by proud
104 And dignified ~~with~~ battlement & towers
105 Of some stern Castle mouldering on the brow
106 Of a green hill or bank of rugged stream.
107 The foot path faintly trac d—the horsestrack
wild
{eng }th of plashy Lane
108 And formidable L{ane} ~~by waters [?]~~],
109 (Prise avenues when others were unshaped
{)
110 Or easier link connecting place with place{,
111 Have vanished swallow'd up by stately Roads
112 Easy and bold that penetrate the gloom
{E
113 Of Englands farthest glens. The {earth has
{W {A lent
114 Her {waters {air her breezes, and the Sail

[14r]

VIII, 115 Of Traffic glides with ceaseless interchange
116 Glistening along the low & woody dale
117 Or on the naked Mountains lofty side.
{[?As] While
{[?] those communications stretch their line
From shore to shore from to [?stream extend]
What growth in memory of men whose hairs
What growth meanwhile appears of street & roof
roof
~~Are yet unblanch d what growth of street & [?house~~]
118 ~~Among the seats of social industry~~
[118] Meanwhile at social Industrys demand

Lines on 13v are rev of 11v, 12v.

Rev of 12v–13r.

117/118 Vertical line in right margin signals rev or del. In the line immediately above l. 118, another possibility for conjectured "house" is "town."

119 How quick how vast an encrease. From the germ
120 Of some poor hamlet radidly produc d
121 Here a huge Town continuous & compact
122 Hiding the face of earth for leagues—and there
123 Where not a Habitation stood before
124 The Abodes of Men irregularly massed
125 Like trees in forests spread through spatious
tracts
126 Oer which the smoke of unremitting fires
127 Hangs permanent, and plentiful as wreaths
128 Of vapour glittering in the morning sun.
t}
129 And whereesoeeer [?h]}he Traveller turns his
steps
130 He sees the barren wilderness erased
131 Or disappearing triumph that proclaims
132 How much the mild Directress of the plough
133 Owes to alliance with these newborn
Arts.

[14[v]]

Hence are the shores of Britain sought by ships
VIII, 134 Hence is the wide sea peopled: and the Shores
135 Of Britain hence are sought by gallant Ships
136 Freighted from every climate of the world
~~A proud sum~~
choicest Hence that sum
137 With the worlds richest produce. In her
P}
[?]}orts
Of maritime grandeur & internal wealth
138 The keels that rest within her ~~crowde~~d ports
139 ~~They rest or lie at anchor in her~~ bays
{[?at] [?shalows]
[139] And ride {[?] in her sounds and bays
That
141 2 ~~Or with~~ through her inland regions to & fro
140 1 An animating spectacle [?the] sails.
142 Pass with the respirations of the Tide
143 Perpetual multitudinous: Finally
floating {V
144 Hence a dread arm of ~~nat[?ur~~] power a {voice
{ing
145 Of Thunder daunt {[?] those who would approach
146 With hostile purpose the blessed ~~H~~ Isle
147 Truths consecreated Residence—the seat

129–133 A draft of these lines (or, less likely, a rejected rev of them) appears on 13[r].

---

134 *1814* retains the base text rather than the rev.

137–141 An early attempt at rev occurs at page foot; another is on the inside front cover. A late rev close to *1814* appears at the foot of facing 15[r].

141,140 Numbers in the left margin reverse the line order, as in *1814*.

143 A mark between the first two words is possibly intended as a comma.

144 Possibly, WW intended "native" for "nat[?ur]."

146 Del by eras.

{P
148 Impregnable of Liberty & {Peace

149 —And yet o happy Pastor of a flock
150 Faithfully watched, and, by that loving care
151 And Heaven's good prov[?iend]ence, preserv d
from taint
152 With you I grieve when on the darker side
153 Of this great change I look & there behold
whence proceeds
[137] But from the [?ingenuity] that sum
Of maritime grandeur & internal wealt
The [?valor] that [?is]

[15r]

novel gainful
VIII, 154 (Through strong temptation of these self same Arts)
155 Such outrag done to Nature as compels
156 The indignant Power to justify herself
157 Yea to avenge her violated rights
158 For Englands Banes.—When soothing Darkness
spreads
159, 160 Oer hill & valley and the Punctual Stars
161 (While all things else are gathering to their homes)
162 Advance and in the firmament of heaven
163 Glitter but undisturbing undisturbd
164 As if their silent Company were charged
165 With peaceful admonitions for the heart
166 Of all-beholding Man earth's thoughtful Lord
Now that another of his toilsome day
Is past and Time has left another step
To be recorded in his noiseless march
Towards Eternity, and sweet Repose
Scatters her weary blessing & by thanks
And Prayer preceded holy sleep descends

{at
137 Hence th{e ~~Keels~~ sum
138 Of Keels that rest within her crowded ports
139 Or ride at anchor in her sounds & bays
140 That animating spectacle of sails
141 That through her inland regions to & fro

[15v]

VIII, [168] 2 The assured Domain of calm simplicit[?ies]
167 1 Then, in full many a Region, once like this [?l]

---

[137] Among other possible readings for the last line of rev are (1) "sailor" or "sales" for "valor," and (2) "in" for "is."

159, 160 Cap in "Stars" may be intended as lowercase.
137–141 Rev of 14v, inside front cover.
137 Cap in "Keels" may be lowercase.

---

[168], 167 Numbers in the left margin reverse the line order, as in *1814*.

~~Endeared to Nature & the assur'd domain~~
168 ~~The assured domain of calm s~~implicity
169 ~~The [?home] of~~ quiet an unnatural light
The as|
[168] [? ?]|sured domain of calm simplicity
171, 170 ~~Breaks forth for never resting Labours eyes~~
[169] And pensive [?&] quiet an unnatural light
172 ~~Duly prepared and at the appointed hour~~
171 Rings from the many windowed fabric huge
~~Blazing as if on a fire~~
[170] Prepared for never resting Labours eyes
[171] Breaks from a many window'd Fabric huge,
170 ~~Prepared for never resting Labours eyes~~.
[172] And at the appointed hour a Bell is heard
173 Of harsher import than the curfews knoll
stern
174 That spake the norman Conquerers behest,
175 A local sumons to unceasing Toil.
Behold
176 Disgorged are now the ministe[?s] of day
[?ese] issue from
177 And a[?s] th{[?ey] ~~portal[?s] of~~ the Illumined Pile
door
at the crowded ~~Gate~~
178 A Fresh Band meets them ^~~where the rumbling~~
And in the courts and where the rumbling
stream
180 That turns the multitude of dizzy [?~~glaring~~]
wheels
181 Glares like a troubled Spirit in its bed
182 Among the rocks below.—Men maidens youth
183 Mother and little Children, Boys and girls
The[?se] not alone [?in ~~why why~~ did] [? ?]
~~Ev[?en] at th[?at]~~
~~That yield [?reli~~]
[?Still]
[?Passes by Still lost] still to bend to natures
[?subdu d] [?kindly ~~seemly~~] laws

[16r]

[?~~stationry tasks~~]
~~To their accustomed services repair~~
VIII, 184 Enter and each his wonted task resumes
185 Within this Temple where is offered up
186 To gain the Master Idol of the Realm
187 Perpetual sacrifice. Even thus of old
188 Our ancesters within the still Domai
C
189 Of vast Cathedral or {conventual Church

---

[169] Queried ampersand is blotted over.
171, 170–[170] Vertical line probably marks for rev.
177 Possibly "a[?s]" is intended as "at," and either "they" or "these" is intended as "the."
180 Another possible reading for "glaring" is "spinning."
183 Draft lines at page foot are perhaps intended to describe the occupation of the laboring poor.

In the first line of rev on this leaf, "stationry" may be "stations," and "tasks" may be "servic."

day & night
190 Their vigils kept where tapers ~~night & day~~
191 On the [?~~stil~~] dim altar burn'd continually
192 In token that the House was ever more
193 Watching to God. ~~Their Thoughts beyond~~
above this world
Religious
~~For pious~~ men were they
~~Were [?r] raised~~
194 ~~And their minds~~
reason
Nor would their ~~spirits~~ tutored to aspire
above
195 ~~Beyond~~ this tra[?n]tory world ~~for[?bade~~]
at allow
196 Th[?] ere there should pass a moment of the year
197 When in their land the Almightys service ceased.
198 Triumph who will in these profaner rites
199 Which we a generation self-extolled
200 As zealously perform I too will share
201 Thus far his proud complacency—
With him,

[16v]

do exalt
VIII, 202 Casting reserve away, ~~will~~ I ~~rejo~~ice
203 To see an intellectual [?law] imposed
204 On the blind Elements—a purpose given
ance
205 A perser[?ver] [?] [?e] fed; almost a soul
206 Imparted to brute matter—I rejoice
ose
207 Measuring the force of th[?eir] gigantic Power
208 Which by the the thinking Mind have been compelled
will
209 To serve the needs of feeble bodied man
Yet should I ~~think~~ deem this grant too dearly bought
[?must] [?will]
210, 211 For we will dare to hope that time may come
Unless I dared yet
212 When strengthened [?an] not dazzled by the might
213 Of this dominion over nature gained
214 Men of all lands that exercise the same
215 In due proportion to their Countrys need
216 Learning thought late that all true glory rests

---

203 Another possibility for "law" is "Aim," as indicated in *PW*, V, 271.
210, 211 The two rev "[?must]" and "[?will]" are overwritten by the line above. At page foot is additional rev (not included in *1814*).
216 *1814* reads "though."

217 All praise all safety and all happiness
                                    Th
218 Upon the moral Law. Egyptian th[?e] ebes
219 Tyre by the margin of the sounding
                                    waves
    Thus far do I rejoice & yet shall deem
    This trust [?purchased at]

[17ʳ]

VIII, 220 Palmyra, Central in the desart fell
221 And the Arts died by which they had
                                    been rais [?d]
222 Call [?a] Archimedes from his buried Tomb
223 Upon the plains of vanished Syracuse
                        S
224 And feelingly the sage shall make report
225 How insecure how baseless in itself
                              [~~? ?~~]
                                    sway is
                        hose   [?~~Laws~~]
226 Is that Philosophy w[?]   [?] ~~are~~ framd
                        ~~that only [?deals~~]
227 ~~For mere material things~~
    ~~With gross~~
[227] For mere material instruments how weak
228 Those arts and high inventions if unproppd
                        with sighs of pensive grief
229 By virtue—He~~—abstracted spirit—~~
                              [?~~would] own~~
230 Amid his calm abstractions would admit
231 That not the slender privilege is theirs
232 To save themselves from blank forgetfulness
235 —And were these otherwise could we escape
    C
    continued thus the tender hearted [?Sage]
    ~~Meanwhile shall we give way to empty joy~~
[236] Regret & painful sadness
236 ~~And inconsiderate boasting~~ who revere
237 And would preserve as thing above all price
238 The old domestic morals of the Land

[17ᵛ]

VIII, 239 And simple manners yet are doomed to see
The objects of our reverential love
Perish as [?g] Victims, & oblations brought
To an insatiate Idol whom the State
Worships with sanction for that worship drawn
241 From treacherous Thievery. O where is now
    worth, the stable
239, 240 The ~~stable~~ worth that dignified ~~& cheared~~

226 Partial overwriting of "whose" may be a reinforcement.

240, 241 A low estate the character of peace
242 Sobriety and order & chaste love
{t
243 And hones{[?ty] dealing & untainted speech
~~B[?enevolent]~~ & hospitable cheer
244 And pure goodwill country
245 That made they very thought of ~~rural~~ life
246 A thought of refuge for a mind detained
Reluctantly
247 ~~Amid the turmoil of a vexing world~~.
[247] ~~Against its will~~ amid the bustling crowd
~~The ornament of beauty of that life~~
248 ~~Where [?is it now] the sabbaths holy grace~~
{kept
[248] Where now the beauty of the sabbat—{[?]
249 With conscientious reverence as a day
250 By the Almighty Lawgiver pronounced

[18r]

VIII, 251 Holy and blessed, and when the winning grace
252 Of all the lighte ornaments attached
{'d
253 To time and season as the year roll{s round
[255] Fled utterly or only to be traced

O sad reverse
Rill
When every crystal that from its fount
Flows with a vigourous current nay [?become]
A guide to introduce disease & want
264 And dire depravity. Domestic bliss
265 Or call it comfort by a humbler name
{C
Wherever their {communities take root
{~~poor~~
266 How art thou blighted for the {[?]
poor mans
heart
255 ~~Fled utterly (with sorrow I repeat~~)
traced
[255] ~~From their old haunts or onl~~y to be ~~found~~
256 In few fortunate retreats like this
257 Which I behold with trembling when I think
ye }
258 What lamentable change—a [?mo]}ar—a month—
259 May bring—that brook converting as it runs
{ bane
260 Into an Instrument of deadly {[?harm]
261 For those, who, yet untempted to forsake

L. 255, rev at midpage, is also rev above the crossed-out passage (in a space left between l. 253 and "O sad reverse").

265–266 Rev of 18r.

left them by
262 The simple occupations ~~of~~ their sires
water
263 Drink the pure of its innocent stream
[264] With lip almost as pure. Domestic
Bliss

[18v]

VIII, 265 Or call it Comfort by a humbler name
thou
266 How art ~~ye~~ blighted for the poor Mans
heart.
such neighbourhood from morn to eve
~~Ha~~ }
267 Lo in ~~the fields and~~ [?vi]} ~~mlets all~~ day long
268 The Habitations empty or perchance
{hand
269 The Mother left alone no helping {[?]
her
270 To rock the cradle of ~~the~~ peevish Babe
271 No Daughters round her busy at the wheel
272 Or in dispatch of each days little growth
273 Of household occupation no nice arts
274 Of needle work no bustl at the fire
275 Where once the dinner was prepared with
pride
~~cheer the mind~~
276 Nothing to speed the day, or cheer the mind,
277 Nothing to praise to teach or to command.
~~Meanwhile the Father if retains [?he] still~~
278 The father if [?~~he~~] perchance he still retain
e }
279 His old employments go[?o]}s to field or
wood
280 No longer led or followed by his Sons
281 Idler perchance they were but in <u>his</u> sight

[19r]

green { ea
VIII, 282 Breathing fresh air & tread[?n]g the [~~?~~] {[?]rth
283 Till their short holiday of childhood ceased
[?w]} of of ~~th[?eir] natural~~ right
No[?r]} of their birthright robbed
284 [?~~Ne'er] to return. [?But hard] they toil they~~
spin
[? ?] they now are doomed to toil &
285, 286 The State their ~~false~~ unnatural Mother
thrives

---

269 Overwriting "hand" may be a reinforcement: the pen was running dry.
278 Conjectured and del "he" is blotted over.

284–285, 286 Ink blot obscures opening words. Another version of l. 284 is entered at page foot.

hard unfeeling
289 For them a premature necessity
290 Blocks out the forms of nature preconsumes
291 The reason famishes the heart shuts up
292 The infant being in itself and makes
season
293 Its very spring a [?] of decay.
The lot is wretched the
294 O ~~miserable lot~~ condition sad
297 They are d[?epr]essed dejected even to love
298 Of their dull tasks & close captivity
296 Habitual thraldom has so far prevailed
That joy is uncongenial, to the soul
295 Whether a pining discontent survive
[?or]
[296] ~~Or [?by] habitual~~
[296] And thirst for change or habit has subdued
[297] The soul depressed dejected even to love
[298] Of those dull tasks and close captivity
Now of their birthright robbd
[284] Stripped of their [?privilege] they toil they
spin

[19v]

banish far such
VIII, 299 O ~~guard us from such~~ wisdom as condemns
native Briton to these inward chains
300 A ~~Briton born to these internal chains~~
in
301 Fixed ~~on~~ his soul so early & so deep
[?s]
304 ~~For~~ whereer[?r] oer he turns his steps, the Boy
But
305 [?His] still a prisoner when the wind is up
306 Among the clouds & in the antient woods
h
307 Or when the sun is rising in the [?] eavens
~~Behold in the school~~
in the
308 Quiet and calm.— Behold him ~~as he~~
moves
On path or public Road his raiment soiled
311 His raiment sullied oer with ~~cotton flakes~~
And whitened oer with cotton flakes [?remains]
312 Or locks of woold announces when he comes
313 Creeping his gait, & cowering, is lip pale
quick &
314 His respiration audible
315 And scar[?c]ly could you fancy that a gleam

293 Overwriting "season" may be a reinforcement: the pen was running dry.
297 Ink blot obscures the questioned letters.

299–305 Passage is rev and expanded at page foot below the rule.
305 "[?His]" in l. 305 at the top, is probably a miswriting for "Is" – the reading of *1814*.
308–311 Rev and expansion of these lines appear at foot of 20r and on the inside front cover.
313 *1814* reads "his" for the obvious miswriting "is."

316 From out those eyes could ever break or blush
h
317 Mantle upon ~~that~~ c is cheek. I this form
[299] O banish far such wisdom as condemns
[300] A native Briton to these inward chains
[301] Fixed in his soul so early so deep,
own
302 Without his wish, consent, or knowledge,—fixed
~~For hi[?m] release is not & cannot be~~
303 He is slave to whom release comes not
The Boy whereer [?turn]
[304] And cannot come. ~~Whereer The Boy~~, whereer
he turn his steps
305 Is still a prisoner

[20r]

at
VIII, 318 Is thi~~s~~ the Countenance & such the port
319 Of no mean Being one who should be clothed
With
320 [?In] dignity befitting his proud hopes
321 Who in his very childhood should appear,
322 Sublime from present purity & joy
323 The limbs increase but liberty of mind
324 Is gone for ever & the avenues
[324] Of sense impeded this organic frame
gladsome in its m
326 So joy~~ful~~ [?on his p] otions soon becomes
327 Dull, to the joy of its own motions dead
328 And even the touch so exquisitely
poured
329 Through the whole body with a languid will
[?rar] hardly competent
330 Performs its functions ~~as~~ he sits or [?moves]
T
331 [?I] o impress a faint perception on the brain
332 Of what there is deligtful in the breeze
333, 334 The sunshine, & the changeful elements.
308 Behold him!—in the School
309 Of his attainments?—no! but the air
under heavens blue arch
310 Fanning his temples under heavens
[? ? ?]
blue [?Arch]
[?] [?]
311 His raiment whitened oer ~~with~~ cotton [?flax]

---

317 *1814* reads "Is this the form."
303 Rev del in pencil.
[304] Rev is in pencil.

---

320 At end of line, marks may be punct, possibly a dash or period.
326 An alternative conjecture for "on" is "as."
330 Possibly the conjectured "rar" was intended as "rarely" as in *1814*.
308–311 Rev and expansion of 19v; rev on inside front cover. Vertical del slashes are in pencil.
310 Illeg words below line are partly eras and entered before the half-line of rev above l. 310 and the overwriting below. The overwriting "blue" may be a reinforcement.

[20^{v}]

VIII, 336 Can hope look forward to a manhood raised
~~What hope ye for the manhood of this Child~~
337 On such foundations.
~~Yet is he one of Thousands.~~"— ×
"Hope is none for him
"~~I believe~~,
exclaim
338 The pale Recluse indignantly ~~observ~~ed,
And
339 "~~That~~ tens of thousands suffer wrong as deep
340 Yet be it asked in justice to our age
341 If there were not before th[?e]se arts
appeared
342 These Structures rose commingling old & young
343 And unripe sex with sex for mutual taint
344 If there were not ~~ye a~~ and are not
at this day
hd
345 Multitudes who from infancy had breat{ed
lived
346 Air unimprisoned & have ~~walked~~ at large
347 Yet walk beneath the sun in human
shape
From the door
365 ~~Such are [?found]~~
348 As abject as degraded. ~~Who [?would]~~
~~think~~
[365] Upon the breast of many a hungry heath
372 Or forest purl[?es] and in sheltered lanes
lane
377 Among the pride of cultivated fi[?e]ds

[21^{r}]

VIII, 395 That they were born [?and] reared within
~~the pale~~
349 crazy hovel
[350] of many a [?clay] [?] ~~who~~ issues forth
396 Of ~~civil polity the ragged brood~~
[350] ~~From many a [?clabuilt] by highway side)~~
Who to besiege the Traveller, issue forth
351 A ragged Offspring

---

337 The X in the right margin and del of "I believe" are in pencil.

348 The del half-line "Who [?would] think" was directly followed by the first line on 21^{r}. The first rev "Such are [?found]"—followed by ll. 348, [365], 372, and 377—is rev and expanded on 21^{v}, 22^{r}–22^{v}.

[365]–377 See rev on 21^{v}–22^{v}.

377 *1814* reads "fields."

Interlineations at top may be related to rev "From the door," above l. 348 on 20^{v}.

395–396 These lines at the top, slightly rev, are used for a later sequence on 22^{r}.

[350] In the third line from the top, queried letters following "[?clay]" may be "bu" for "built" or "hu" for "hut."

~~From many~~
From own [?ed]
350, 351 Or clay built hovels, with their blanch{d
hair
352 Crowned, like the image of phantastic fear,
shall we say in that white growth
353 Or wearying, (should you better like that
thought)
{t
354 An ill-ajusted {Turban, for defence
355 Or fierceness, wreathed around their
una} sunburnt brows
356 By savage natures [?]}ssisted care.
and coloured
357 Naked ~~the feet [?on w~~] like the soil, the feet
358 On which they stand as if thereby they drew
by
359 Some nourishment as Trees do ~~from~~ their
roots
360 From earth the common mother of us all.
361 Figure and mien complection & attire
362 Are framed to strike dismay but the out
stretchd
dv } hand
as they a[?]}ance to [?grasp]
363 ~~And w~~hining voice denote them supplicants
~~To grasp~~ The traveller[?s]
364 For the least boon that Pity
shall bestow

[21v]

The [?like]
VIII, 365 ~~On heath or commons edge are found~~
Such on the breast of hungry heaths are found
[365] ~~Such may be found on many a hungry~~ heath
In
372 ~~And~~ forest purlie[?u] And in sheltered
lanes
377 Among the pride of cultiv[?at] fields
And such The like may be passed
379 ~~The like~~ do I remember to have ~~seen~~
Mid
380 ~~On~~ Buxtons dreary heights. Upon the
wat[?c]h
381 Till the swift vehicle approach
ing They stand
382 Then follow closely with the cloud of dust
386 Fix on the freight of merry Passengers
387 A steady eye, and [?clipping] at full
[?step]

---

356 The overwriting "una" may be a reinforcement.

365–379 Rev and expansion of 20v; rev and expanded on 22r–22v.
377 *1814* reads "cultivated."
380 *1814* reads "watch."

383 An uncouth feat exhibit, and are gone
384 Heels over head like Tumblers on a
stage
385 Up from the ground they snatch the
copper
[?dole]
[386] And on the freight of merry Passengers
388 ~~And spin & pant & overhead again~~
[387] Fixing a steady eye maintain their speed
[388] And spin & pant and overhead again,

[22r]

untill their breath
VIII, 389 Wild pursuivants ~~till they~~ have lost their
breath
face {smiled
390 Of bounty tires & every eye that {[?gave]
391 Encouragement hath ceased to look that
But way.
392 ~~These~~ like the vagrants of the gypsy tribe
These
{,
393 ~~Are~~{ bred to lit[?l]e pleasure in themselves
394 And profitless to other turn we then
those born ~~reared~~
395 To such as fairly ~~bread~~ within the pale
396 Of civil polity are early trained
by
{~~by~~
397 To earn {[?th] wholesome labour in the field
ea}
398 The bread they ge}t.
365 Such on the breast of darksome heaths are found
366 And with their parents dwell upon the skirts
367 Of furze-clad commons —and are born & reared
beneath
368 At the mine's mouth, [?~~beneath~~] impending rocks [~~?~~]
{ in
369 Or {[?at] the chambers of some natural cave,
370 And where their Ancestors erected huts
371 For the convenience of unlawful gain.
372 In forest purlieus and the like
are bred
[367] ~~[?] furze-clad commons~~
[?eer] {and
373 All England through, where nooks {or slips
{ ound
~~o of gr~~{[?nd]
of ground

395–396 These lines are related to lines first drafted at the top of 21r.
398 Continued on 23r.
365–373 Continued on 22v; rev and expansion of 21v, 20v.

[22v]

VIII, 374 Purloined in times less jealous than our
own
375 From the green margin of the public way
A Residence afford them
{A
376 {[?] resi[?n]dence affords them mid the bloom
377 And gaiety of cultivated fields.
{(
378 Such{, we will hope the lowest in the scale
379 Do I remember oftimes to have seen

[23r]

give
VIII, 398 The bread they eat. A sample should I ~~take~~
c}
399 Of what this stock produces to enri[?]}h
400 And beautify the tender age of life
401 A sample fairly called—ye would exclaim
402 "Is this the whistling Ploughboy whose shrill
notes
403 Impart new gladness to the morning air
if I venture to suspect
404 Forgive me!—~~but I [?] I am not without~~
[?~~dread~~]
405 That many sweet to hear of in soft verse
406 Are of no finer frame. His joints are stiff:
407 Beneath the cumbrous frock that to the
thriving knees
408 Invests the ~~sturdy~~ churl—his legs appear
409 Fellows to those which lustily upheld
410 The wooden stools for everlasting use
411 On which our fathers sate. And mark
his brow
412 Under whose shaggy canopy are set
{o
413 Tw{[?i] eyes, not dim but of a healthy
stare
414 Wide sluggish blank & ignorant & strange

[23v]

VIII, 415 Proclaiming boldly that they never drew
416 A look or motion of intelligence
417 From infant conning of the Christ-cross
row
418 Or puzzling through a Primer line by line

Leaf 22v is continued from 22r; rev and expansion of 21v, 20v.

Leaf 23r is continued from 22r.
404 "I [?]" may have been del first, followed by del of half-line.

419 Till perfect mastery crown the pains
at last
[?~~lov~~]
420 What kindly warmth from touch of [?~~fostring~~]
~~hand~~
fostering hand
421 What penetrating power of sun or breeze
422 Shall eer dissolve the crust wherein his soul
423 Sleeps like a Caterpillar sheathed in ice
pitiable
424 This torpor is no ~~lamentable~~ work
425 Of modern ingenuity—nor town
426 Or crowded City may be taxed with aught
427 Of sottish vice or desperate breach of law
428 To which in after years he may be rouzed
{~~is~~ produce
429 This boy {of ~~of~~ the fields his spade & Hoes
Hoes

[24r]

VIII, 430 The Carters whip which on his shoulder[?'s] rests
{ - {ing
431 In air high{[?t] tower{g with a boorish pomp
432 The sceptre of his sway. His Countrys name
[433] Her equal rights her churches & her schools
433 ~~Her boasted honours & her equal rights~~
[433] ~~Her charity & charitable schools~~
434 What have they done for him & let me ask
435 For tens of thousands uninformed as he
436 In brief what liberty of mind is here?

437 This chearful sally pleased the mild
good Man
438 To whom the Appeal couch'd in those final
words
th}
439 Was pointedly addressed; and to the [?]}oughts
440 Which in assent or opposition rose
441 Within his mind he seemed prepared to give
442 Prompt utterance; but rising from our seat
Beneath the umbrage of those churchyard
trees
443 The hospitable Vicar interposed
e}
e[?r]}arnestly
444 With invitation ~~courteously~~ renew'd

[24v]

VIII, 445 We followed, taking as he led a Path
446 Along a Hedge of stately Hollies framed

---

428 Ink blot at the end of line may obscure a period.

447 Whose flexile Boughs descending with a weight
448 Of leafy spray, concealed the stems & roots
449 That gave them nourishment. How
sweet methought
450 When the fierce Wind comes howling from
the north
451 How grateful this impenetrable screen.
452 Not shaped by simple wearing of the foot
453 On rural business passing to & fro
(
454 Was this commodious walk,) that wound along
e)
As though a pleasure-ground, from field to fi ld ,
For
[454] But here a careful Hand had been employed
mark
455 To ~~shape~~ the line & strew the surface oer
456, 457 With purest gravel from the mountain brook
[454] a careful hamd
[455] Had marked the line—& strewn—

[25r]

VIII, 458 The stately Fence accompanied our steps
459 And thus the Pathway by perennial green
460 Guarded & graced, seemed fashioned to unite
461 As by a beautiful yet solemn chain
462 The Pastors Mansion with the House of pra
prayer.
463 Like Image of solemnity conjoined
464 With feminine allurement soft & fair
en
465 The Mansions self displayed, a rever[?]d
Pile
466 With bold projections & recsses deep
467 Shadowy, yet gay & lightsome as it stood
468 Fronting the noontide Sun. We paused
to admire
469 The Pillar d Porch elaborately embossd
u
470 The low wide Windows with their millions
old
471 The cornice, richly fretted, of grey stone
472 And that smooth slope from which
the Dwelling
rose
473 By beds & banks Arcadian of gay flower[?s]

Cf. Berg MS., recto.
462 Lack of space and ink running out forced WW to rewrite "prayer."
466 *1814* reads "recesses."

[25v]

VIII, 474 And flowering shrubs protected & adorned
476 A more than natural vividness of Hue
475, 477 The bright flowers took from contrast
[?leave]
with the ~~gloom~~
478 Of sober cypress & the darker foil
479 Of eugh in which survived some traces,
here
480 Not unbecoming of grotesque device
uncouth
481 And antique fancy. From the behind
R
the [?]oof
482 Rose the slim ash & Massy sycamore
483 Blending their diverse foliage with the green
484 Of ivy flourishing and thick that clasped
485 The huge round chimneys harbour of delight
486 For wren & Redrebreast where they sit & sing
ditties when the neighbouring trees
487 Their slender ditties when the trees are
bare.
488 Nor must I pass unnoticed, leaving else
489 The picture incomplete, as it appeared
490 Before our eyes, a relique of old times
491 Happily spared, a little gothic nich[?e]

[26r]

A
VIII, 602 [?E]bruptly broken off. The ruddy Boys
603 Did now withdraw to take their
[?~~well~~]
[?] [?~~earned~~]
well-earn'd meal,
604 And He (to whom all tongues resignd
n
their rights
605 With willing[?]ess, to whom the general ear
606 Listened with readier patience than
o
to strain
607 Of music, lute [?a]r harp, a long delight
608 That ceased not when his voice had ceased) as
One
609 Who from an Eminence serenely views
610 The Compass of his Argument began
611 Mildly, and with a clear & steady tone.

For 25v, cf. Berg MS., recto and verso.

A number of pages (perhaps eight in four conjugate leaves) are missing between 25v and 26r; those leaves almost certainly contained a version of VIII, 492–601, continuing from 25v and leading into 26r. See *Chronology: MY*, p. 679 (and p. 463, above).

IX, 3 There is an active principle alive
in the stars
5 In all things, in all nature, ~~from the stars~~
Of highest heave[?n]
6, 7 Of ~~highest heav[?e] to flower & shrub & tree~~
~~In every~~
7 In flower & tree & every pebbly stone
8 That paves the brooks the stationary
rocks
9 The moving waters and the invisible air

[26[v]]

IX, 10 Whateer exists hath properties that spread
in ever form of being
11 Beyond itself ~~all being[?s] have a power~~
11, 12 for evil or for good
d for evil or for good
Is lo[?n]ged a Power ~~by which it make~~
By
[11, 12] [?Some] which it make for evil or for good
Some other being conscious of its place
[11, 12] Beyond itself for evil or for good,
13 Spirit that knows no insulated spot
14 No chasm no solitude from link to link
15 It circulates—the soul of all the worlds
16 This is the freedom of the Universe
17 Unfolded still the more, more visible
18 The more we know & yet is reverenc'd least
19 And least respected in the human mind
20 Its most conspicuous home. The food of
hope
21 Is meditated action—robbed of this
22 Her sole support she languishes and dies
23 We perish also for we live by hope
24 And by desire—we see by the glad light
25 And breathe the sweet air of futurity:

[27[r]]

IX, 26 And so we live, or else we have no life
27 Tomorrow—nay perchance this very hour
28 For every moment has its own tomorrow
29 Those blooming Boys whose hearts
are almost sick
30 With present triumph, will be sure to
find

3ff. This passage (continuing through l. 26 on 27[r]) was composed in Germany in 1798 or 1799; see *Poems, 1797–1800*, pp. 309–310, 472–473, 721, 728.

See note to 26[r]. The left-margin line connects l. 10 to the final rev of l. [11, 12].

For 27[r], see note to 26[r].

A
~~The~~ field before them freshen'd with the dew
Of other expectations—in which course
Their happy year spins round.—The Youth
obeys
The like glad impulse—and so moves
the Man
Mid all his apprehensions cares & fears
so he
Or, ought to ~~be so~~ moved. Ah why in age
Do we revert so fondly to the walks
Of Childhood but that there the
Soul discerns
The dear memorial footmarks
unimpaired
See Mark ℋ
From
~~By impulses~~ &
V, 318 By impulse from the illusive power
~~From~~
Of [?mans imagination] that [?transcends]
So far, the [?moral] competence of [?man]
a mystery—a saintly lamp *TPL*, *85*

Burns here within its own peculiar shrine *86*
Forbid to blend its light with common *87*
That [?fails] & [?]

[27ᵛ]

V, 486/487 ~~As from the~~
For as by passion only we
For as by passion only we can act,
~~F[?our]~~ Left otherwise inert and powerless even
~~Through all relations in the [?moral world]~~

---

36 The mark after "or" signals the insertion of "so he."

39 WW's instruction "See Mark" refers to leaf 46ᵛ where there is a similar mark and the copy of Book IX continues.

V, 318 Cf. MS. 74A, 8ᵛ. This draft, perhaps related to passages on 35ᵛ and 36ʳ, appears to have been entered last on the page between WW's copying instruction ("See Mark") and *TPL*, ll. *85–87*.

85–87 Rev of 27ᵛ, 33ᵛ, 34ʳ; incorporated in rev (between lines of base text) on 34ʳ; rev and recopied on 12ʳ. The last line may be an attempt to write an alternate transition to "But turn we from the parent to the child" on 27ᵛ (after l. 87), and a variant rev of 27ᵛ on 34ʳ.

Sequence of composition here is probably as follows: (1) V, 486/487ff., as rev of facing 28ʳ, entered from one-third of the way down the page to a few lines from page foot (these entries partially eras and overwritten by the third sequence below); (2) *TPL*, ll. *85–87*, entered at page foot; (3) *TPL*, ll. *27–35*, with many rev, entered from the top of the page (over first sequence) and jumping over the second sequence to include l. *75*, perhaps once intended to follow l. *35*.

486/487ff. Cf. MS. 74A, 13ʳ–13ᵛ. The canceled line, "Through all relations in the [?moral world]," on 27ᵛ may have been intended as a replacement for the del and asterisked line on 28ʳ, "In all the intimate concerns of life." The symbol in the left margin probably indicates that this passage ("For as ...") replaces the one above it. The same mark appears in the left margin of l. 491 on 28ʳ, possibly indicating that this rev on 27ᵛ was to replace the boxed lines on 28ʳ and follow l. 490 rather than l. 486 as in the first copy; see also note to 28ʳ. Neither these added lines nor the ones they replace are included in the line count on 32ʳ.

As
To climb the hill of holiest [?purposes]
As from the affections only we can act
{through
{[?]
ℋ For as ~~by~~ passion only we can act
So by the affections is opinion ruled
{C
And gravest {censors see but as they feel
V, 494, 495 ~~Judging but never with indifferent mind~~

From their sequesterd Cottages, a race *TPL,* [29]
~~Thrice~~ *30*
~~Britain [?s]~~
Of natures rustic offspring ~~here interred~~ *28*
[?born]
A pattern might I venture to describ[?e] *27*
~~Earth's [?favoured]~~ [*30*]
by doom of nature higher brought [*28*]
Of this sequester d peasantry a race *29*
Thrice favored uncorrupted men who share [*30*]
Thrice favoured uncorrupted men who share [*30*]
The elevation of a christian land *31*
truth {peace
A land of ~~light~~ & liberty and {[?fame] *32*
{its
Thus from life opening to {[?his] last decay *34*
from their sequestered [*29*]
Britain,
Thus would I paint him, thus from morn to *33*
eve
From
From lifes first opening to its last decay [*34*]
Would I retrace his history. *35*

a saintly light *85*
Burns here
Apart within its won peculiar shrine *86*
That burn ~~apart in~~ natures inmost shrine *86*
Forbid to
~~And may not~~ mingle with the common day *87*
But turn we from the parent to the child

Brief words of ready prayer *75*

494, 495 A version of this line, but closer to the original on 28[r], appears in MS. 74A, 13[v]. Possibly its del here on 27[v] is part of working toward the MS. 74A text.

27–35 Rev and expansion of 28[v], 32[v], 33[r]; rev on 10[r]. The two entries of "Britain" in this passage may be related to attempts to describe the "christian land"; see l. *31*).

85–87 Rev of 33[v], 34[r]; rev on 27[r] (incorporated in rev of 34[r], between base text lines), 12[r].

75 This last line on the page, in the same ink as l. *35* above, is related to draft on 30[v] and rev on 12[r].

[28^{r}]

V, 480 Our Nature, said the Priest in mild reply
481 Angels may weigh and fathom: and perceive
482 With undistempered and unclouded {[?s] / [?S]}pirit
483 The object as it is; but for our selves
484 That speculative height we may not reach
485 The good and evil are our own, and we
486 Are that which we would contemplate from far.

For, {since / [?as]} by passion only we can act
The almighty wisdom hath ordained that Man
In all the intimate concerns of life
It joys and pains should see but as he feels
494, 495 Judging, yet never an indifferent judge

* ~~In all the intimate concerns of life~~
487 Knowledge for us is difficult to gain
488 Is difficult to gain and hard to keep
489 As ~~truth and~~ virtue's self like virtue is beset
490 With snares; tried, tempted subject to decay.
491 ℋ Love, admiration, fear, desire, and hate
492 Blind were we without these; though these alone
493 Are capable to notice or discern
494, 495 Or to record, yea spite of proudest boast
496 Reason, best Reason is to imperfect Man
497 An effort {only a / [? ?]}nd a noble aim
498 A crown and attribute of sovereign power
499 Still to be courted never to be won.

[28^{v}]

This truth has often flashed upon my mind
natural harmony
[?] In powerful correction with a [?~~a voice~~]
{spot / [?plac]}
[?Seen] on the [?very] [?plac] where now we stand
observed

Here begins the sequence of lines, drafted on successive rectos and with rev entered on versos, that leads into *TPL*. Multiline del of Book V material are probably late and represent their exclusion from *TPL* and/or their separate inclusion in Book V. Cf. rectos of 29, 30, 31, 32, and 36, where large crosses are marked on the page.V, 480–558, 904–928 are followed closely in MS. 74A, 13^{r}–14^{v}, 23^{r}–24^{v}.

Boxed enclosure signals WW's successive attempts at rev on facing verso. Asterisk in margin below the box, next to a line that is a recopy of the third line within the box, suggests that at one point copy was to continue directly from that asterisked line. Possibly later, this del line was replaced by rev on 27^{v} of the boxed lines. Still later, the symbol in the margin of l. 491 on 28^{r} indicates that the last rev on 27^{v} was to precede l. 491.

494, 495 Rev and del on 27^{v}, this line (in a form close to its first state) appears in MS. 74A, 13^{v}, beginning as the half-line 494.

497 Overwriting may be a reinforcement.

Three lines of rev at top of page (apparently entered after *TPL*, ll. *21ff.*, below) may be intended as rev of lines on facing 29^{r}, possibly ll. 509ff. Possibly the lines are meant as a transition connecting some part of Book V and perhaps VI, 615, on 32^{r}.

than does [?if words]
Than does the sod that roofs it—yet methinks *TPL,* *21*
of mere Imagination might presume
~~Might I from mere imagination treat~~ *22*
To to touch a theme
[?theme]
An [?imagin]ed that wants the steadier light *23*
Of your experience: might I step before; *24*
And, with no better guide than chance regards *25*
V, 414 Or notice forced upon incurious ears, *26*
Attempt an honest sample to set forth *27*
Of Nature's rustic offspring here interred *28*
That from life's opening to its last decay *34*
Would I retrace his history.—At these words *35*
A sudden influx of enliv[?i]ng thought *36*
B
[?br] righten'd the sick man's faded countenance *37*
My expectation shaped for him a path, *38*
On the plain ground inscribed; but his discourse *39*
Mounted aloft and under many a cloud *40*
And crossing many a streak of ether blue *41*
[?Moved]; high or low; upon the inconstant wind *42*
with
Part wheeling, blown about in part, [?in] bold *43*
And not ungraceful struggles.—
H
"Let the [?h]ouse *44*
[? ?]
Thus buoyantly did that discourse ascend. *45*

[29r]

V, 500 Look forth or each Man dive into himself
C
501 What sees he but a creature too perturbed
transported
502 That is exalted to excess, that yearns
503 Regrets or trembles wrongly or too much
504 Hopes rashly, in disgust as rash recoils
505 Battens on spleen or moulders in despair;
506 Thus truth is miss'd and comprehension fails
507 And darkness and delusion round our path
injuries
508 Spread from disease whose subtle spirit^ lurk[?s]

21–28, 34–45 Continued on 29v. Rev and expansion of 31v, 32v, 33r; rev and expanded (including ll. *29–33*) on 27v, 10r, 11r.
21 Rev "[?if words]" may be part of the rev to l. 22.
414 Cf. MS. 74A, 11r.
43 Taken from later passage on 37r.
44/45 Illeg words are partially eras.

500–511/521–533 Cf. MS. 74A, 13v–14r, which adds ll. 512–520 as rev.

509 Within the very faculty of sight
510 Yet for the general purposes of faith
511 In providence of solace and support
And for those hopes without whose blessed aid
{se
Duty would be a burthen; for the{[?] ends
521 We safely may affirm that human life
522 Is either fair and tempting, a soft scene
523 grateful to sight refreshing to the soul
~~By sight of which the Spirit is refreshed~~
524 Or a forbidding tract of chearless view
525 Even as the same is looked at or approached
[529] In aprils changeful month when [?]
[?showers of]
h}
529, 530 Winter as he is wont [?]}ath reassumed
529 —In changeful April, when with frost or snow
[530] Winter, as he is wont, hath reassumed
530 ~~Departed winter hath resumed his sway~~
[530] A short liv'd sway
~~As he is wont~~ returning unawares
Then
532 If from the sullen region of the north
{[?a] hallow'd
533 If Tow'{ rds the circuit of this ~~holy~~ ground

A short liv'd sway and whiten'd hill and dale

530, 531

[29v]

V, [541] X On the same circuit of this churchyard ground
[541] before you will appear
537 ~~This selfsame~~
~~A cold & [?and]~~
545 B The same enclosure from its southern bound
~~snow~~
538 A dreary [~~?~~] plain of unullumined [?snow]
539 a spot with more than wintry chearlessness
a}
542 ~~Look} from the~~
[541] ~~Upon the self-same~~
upon the lap he
540 Saddening the
So diverse are the
541 That through the ~~limits~~ circuit of this churchyard ground

530, 531 Line entered vertically in the left margin is closer to *1814* text than is the MS. 74A reading on 14r (which follows the interlinear rev of l. 530 at bottom of MS. 74, 29r).

Cf. MS. 74A, 14r–14v. Rev of ll. 537–545 on 30r is probably entered first on the page in a complex interaction with rev on 30r. The "B" in the left margin corresponds to the same mark on 30r, probably signaling the inclusion of ll. 537–540 to replace the rev on 30r. The X (at the top of the page and in the left margin of l. [541]) probably signals inclusion of this rev after so many attempts at the line. Rev to 30r are shown in small type to distinguish them from *TPL*, ll. 46–68, below.

This
draws
~~brea~~
Where first he [?] ~~thes~~ the vital air be glad TPL, *46*
For a Man-child is born—see weakness now *47*
Impersonated here in human frame *48*
Assert her rights and helplessness ensure *49*
From eager tendance all that it requires *50*
doth need
requires [*50*]
Beneath the lowly rafters of the roof *51*
breathing
That shelter him the dozing Infant lies *52*
Senseless K
~~Helpless~~ & power[?less] yet a king of state *53*
Of high observance and of prime concern *54*
And every eye that enters turns to him *55*
The star unseen before that now hath risen *56*
Stooping as needs she must let fancy tell *61*
sciences occult
But how? though versed in ~~planetary sway~~ *62*
Prognostics, tokens, planerary sway *63*
skill an
And fire-side omens far as ~~tongue~~ c [?] go *64*
competent
What tongue for this occasion may suffice *65*
May [?~~Lore] to trac[?k~~]
[?ce]
~~And [?trac~~k] that lore through all its curious *66*
[?maze]
Recall the spells—the forms that must be kept *67*
Strictly *68*

[30[r]]

V, 534 Your walk conducts you ere the vigorous [?sun]
th
535 High climbing, has attained his noontide height
transver[?e] ly lying side by side
536 These mounds as side by side transverse
they lie
before you will ~~presen~~t appear
537 From eas to west will ~~everywhere~~ display
~~p~~ level
A [?~~snowlad~~] [?] ~~rospect desolate & cold~~
539 B ~~A [?snowhite] wintry su~~rface cold and dreary
538, 539 ~~A snow clad plain~~ a surface cold & dreary
then
540 Saddening the heart—go forward—~~&~~ look back.

46–68 Continued from 28[v]; rev and expansion of 32[v], 31[v], 33[r]; rev on 32[v] (below the rule), 11[r], 10[v].

52 An alt for "the dozing infant lies" ("upon the lap he lies") appears on 31[v].

534–558 MS. 74A, 14[r]–14[v], closely follow rev here.
534 The last word is blotted.
539 "B" in left margin signals rev on facing 29[v].

{~~On the~~}
[541] {Upon the} same circuit of this churcyard ground
542 Look from the quarter whence the Lord of light
543 Of life of love and gladness doth dispense
544 His beams which unexcluded in their
fall
545 Have reach d the turf clad slope of every grave
{And
546 {Have gently exercised a melting power
547 Then will a vernal prospect greet your eyes
541 ~~the circuit of this churchyard ground~~
~~And all [?the]~~
{[?T] [?throughout]
548 {~~All~~ fresh & beautiful and green & bright
[?] [?]} ~~all trace~~
549 Hopeful & chearful—vanished is} the snow
~~Of winter [?barren] desolate and cold~~
550 Vanished or hidden and the whole domain
nded,
551 To some, too lightly mi ght might appear
552 A meadow carpet for the dancing hours
~~Strange difference~~ contrast capable methinks
Of ~~novel application~~—
suitable to human life
[?~~fit~~] ~~to~~ [?~~be~~]
not unsuitable to life
553 This Contrast ~~which to life may be applied~~,
554 Is to that other state more apposite,
555 Death, and its two-fold aspect, wintry one
hope
556 Cold sullen ~~and~~ blank from ~~love~~ and joy shut out
{[?touch]'d
the ray divine hath {[?]
[?~~b~~]}
557 The other which [?~~hath~~] [?~~felt~~]—~~the~~ [?d]} [?~~eam~~] ~~divine~~
558 Replete with vivid promise, brigh
[~~?~~] as spring
bright as spring

[30ᵛ]

V, 904 A not ungrateful task ye have imposed
And to your memories my voice will trust
A few brief records
Whose calm of earthly sleep shall such discourse
Disturb, though utter'd in parental tone
Then to the more remote, on either hand

[541] Rev is first entered following l. 547, below, and on facing 29ᵛ.

552/553 Composition seems to have broken off for a time after "application—." Vertical slashes cancel this line and a half, and copy resumes in an ink of a different color.

553 *1814* reads "This Contrast, not unsuitable to Life."

558 End of base text line is smudged, perhaps causing its double rewriting. Illeg letter del by eras.

Book V rev of 31ʳ are here recorded in small type to distinguish them from *TPL*, ll. 72–76, even though the Book V rev may have been entered first. The fourth and fifth lines from the top ("Whose calm…tone") and ll. 911–913, below, appear to be in the same pen and ink as 31ʳ. For ll. 904–913, cf. MS. 74A, 24ʳ–24ᵛ. For ll. 660–662, cf. MS. 74A, 17ᵛ.

and ensure *TPL*, *72*
Health, and long life by fortunes sunshine cheared, *73*
intermix
Nor fail their garrulous tongue to interpose *74*
Ejaculations brief for honest ways *75*
aid
And god's good grace to [?~~crown] & [?ai~~] *76*
and crown the whole
by [?rite,]
Brief words of prayer, for honest ways [*75*]

660 the priest replie
[660] The priest replied—this office to perform
661 Though some peculiar requisites are mine
[?n]
662 Many, I feel, are wa[?t]ing—Yet the task
Is not [?ungrately be]
911 This place is hallowed—to death [?and] life
[?infernal]
From that ~~most awful~~ union doom'd to last
vanish
913 Till time shall ~~perish~~—consecrate to faith

[31^r]

ye
V, 660 The employment which on me ~~you~~ have
imposed
663, 904 Is not ungrateful—whence shall I begin
~~mortal~~ such [?theme]
~~Whose hallowed sleep shall~~ ^ ~~[?unusual] voice~~
~~Disturb: though speaking in parental tone~~
905 Who shall be first selected of from my flock
eir
906 Gathered together in this peaceful fold
Th[?i]s said the Reve[?ren]d Pastor silent
stood
In thoughtful hesitation; on the ground
Looking; upon the graves that nearest
lay
on
to [?he] grassy heaps [?]
Then on ~~the mounds that rose~~ on either hand
Whereat the Wanderer ing
~~This noticing the Itinerant~~ interpos[?e] [?]
& said
~~I wonder not the~~
I wonder not
~~Said gently~~ that a meditative awe
here to uplift the [?scale]
Hath seized you doubting on ~~this sacred~~
spot
ground
[?]

72–[75] Rev on 12^r. For l. 75, cf. 27^v.

662/911 Conjectured "ungrately" may be an attempt at "ungrateful" or "ungratefully." The line is continued by l. 904b on facing 31^r. Cf. MS. 69, stub 238^r, 237^v.

Rev on 30^v (see note to ll. 662/911 there). Cf. MS. 74A, 17^v.

904–918 MS. 74A, 24^r–24^v, includes rev not present in MS. 74 (but close to *1814*), indicating that the entire passage was rev elsewhere for inclusion in MS. 74A.

to
~~stand~~ [?~~to~~]
To [?sit] ~~in judgement~~ [?and] uplift the scale
And weigh albeit in a spirit of Love.
[?consorted]
910 To a mysteriously consorted pair
place
911 This spot is consecrate, to Death, and life
~~To that mysteriously consorted pair~~
912 And to the best affection: ~~that~~ proceed
which
C
913 From their conjunction; [?to] onsecrate to faith
s sublime
916 To reasons mandate [?tes] and the hopes divine
917 Of pure imagination—above all
peace
918 To charity and love that have provided

[31v]

E Modest
V, 923 [?As] ven as the multitude of kindred brooks
[924] And streams, whose murmurs fill this hollow
vale
924 Whose murmurs fill this hollow val
Whose [?spoken]
[924] That murmur in this hollow vale, whose [?foam]
[?Whitens] these words
at this *TPL, 35*
enlivening
A sudden influx of [?] thought[?s] *36*
Brighten d the sick Mans faded countenance *37*
My expectation shaped for him a path *38*
On the plain ground inscribed, but his discourse *39*
under
Mounted aloft and ~~crossing~~ many a cloud *40*
And crossing many a streak of ether blue *41*
Listening we both shall gather our reward
high or low upon
Moved ~~in the regions of~~ the inconstant wind *42*
Part wheeling blown about in part, with bold *43*
Listening we both shall
gather
our reward
And not ungraceful struggles *44*
Upon a chosen vantage ground—tis well 2

923–[924] Rev of 32r, uncanceled reading adopted on 32r and written between lines of base text; cf. MS. 74A, 24v. These Book V rev to 32r are shown in small type to distinguish them from *TPL*, ll. *35–52*, even though the Book V rev may be earlier. Rev to V, 923–924 and *TPL*, ll. *2*, *10*, were entered first, followed by the pencil entry between *TPL*, ll. 43 and 44, and last the sequence *TPL*, ll. *35–52*. Perhaps the word "Modest" was written at the top of the page to test the pen.

35–52 Rev on 28v, 29v, 10r, 11r; ll. *44–52* rev of 32v–33r.

36 A small tear in the page follows the final "t" in "thought[?s]."

43 Taken from later passage on 37r.

43/44 Entered in pencil, partly overwritten by ll. *43* and *44*, and then copied in ink above ll. *41/42*. The pencil may be an early tentative rev of *TPL*, ll. *4–7*.

2, *10* Rev of 32r.

Let the House [44]
Thus buoyantly did that discourse ascend 45
In which he draws the [?vi] 46
in the presence of
Even ~~here, within~~ this privileged spot 10
{rame
Impersonated her in human f{[?orm] require 48
From watcful tendance all that it doth need 50
{Beneath
{Upon the lowly rafters of the roof 51
That shelter him upon the lap he lies 52

[32r]

V, 919 Within these precincts a capacious bed
920 And receptable open to the good
921 And evil to the just and the unjust
922 In which they find an equal resting-place
{e kindred brooks
923 Even as th{[?at] multitude of brooks ~~& streams~~
924 And streams whose murmurs fill this hollow vale
925 Whether their course be turbulent or smooth
926 Their waters clear or sullied, all are
{the lost
927 Within {[?] bosom of yon crystal lake
928 And end their journey in the same repose
~~A~~ {oppo[?s] yo[?u]
"~~My Venerable~~ [?]{~~dversa~~ry stands
[?I fear] that here my Adversary stands
{S
Thus with a smile the {solitary spake TPL, 1
100 Upon a place of vantag—I [?complain not] 2
An eloquent voice [?is] grateful [?to] my Soul 3
Speak as it may and wheresoeer inspired 4
Within this }
VI, 607 If in this court} court let judgement be pronouncd 5
seemly is the course
~~tis a seemly~~ course
{[?~~tis a seem~~] [?]
609 In mercy, {[?I object not] [?]—[?~~n~~]ay perchance 6
May be deem'd [?wis] but if the thing we seek 7
{shall
Be what the [?understanding] {[?may] respect 8
genuine {nd
610 [?As] truth a{[?] knowledge bear we then in 9
Even here mind

46 The ink has run dry at the queried word before copy resumes at l. *48* below.

919–928 Cf. MS. 74A, 24v.
923–924 Rev on facing 31v; rev incorporated on 32r (written between base text lines).
928/607 WW's line count in left margin apparently includes copy on the preceding rectos, beginning with 28r. Cf. 34r, l. [267].
1ff. The Solitary's narrative (here given the editorial title of *The Peasant's Life*) was originally written for inclusion in Books V or VI. Some of the material did appear in those books in *1814*, but much of the Peasant's story was excluded (see pp. 470–473, above, and pp. 1160–1162, below).
607–614 Inserted on 89v as rev of continuous copy of Book VI.

{How
611 (That from his lofty seat the sun can paint 10
risen
612 Coulours as bright as exhalations ~~sent~~ 11
weedy pool [?while] noisome
613 From ~~pestilential~~ bog or [?~~rotten~~] swamp 12
614 As from the Rivulet sparkling while it 13
runs
615 Or the pellucid lake. While here I 14
stand

[32^v]

and personated here *TPL, 48*
In human frame [*48*]

X him
So call for humanity to him *18*
the rest to me are mute
No parent was, ~~a desolate location, here~~ *19*
~~Well lodged in last quiet~~
some outward help from
If with ~~no better guide than~~ chance 25
regards
in
Or notice forced upon ~~no~~ curious ear *26*
[?presume]
If from Imagination might ~~describe~~ 22
bring forth
A pattern or a sample to describe 27
Of nature's rustic offspring here interred *28*
Thus from lifes opening to his last decay *34*
Would I retrace his history *35*
from eager tendance all that it *50*
requires

[?] Descending, as she must, let Fancy tell, *61*
But how?—Though vers d in sciences occult *62*
Tokens and signs and planetary sway *63*
And fireside omens far as skill can go *64*
count the rite
{ount
What tongue may venture to rec{[?ord] the ~~spells~~ *65, 66*
course that must be held
~~sp[?ells]~~ [?i] }
The rites, the forms;—the process [?a]}s maintained *67*
strictly or
~~With care~~, ~~and~~ not less scrupulously shunned *68*

Lines above rule rev of 33^r; lines below rule rev of 29^v. Lines above rule rev on 31^v, 29^v, 28^v, 27^v, 11^r, 10^r. Lines below rule are rev on 30^v, 11^r, 12^r, 10^v.

18 The X in the left margin signals rev of ll. *17/20* on facing 33^r, which is then incorporated on 33^r (between the lines of the base text).

61 Ink blot at beginning of line may obscure or cancel a letter. Symbol in right margin corresponds to one in left margin of 33^r, l. *56*, signaling that these lines on 32^v were once to follow directly from l. *56*.

each
As ~~the~~ sage gossip dictates;—to protect 69
For the unconscious object of their care 70
And Regent of their busy services 71
[?~~preserve~~]
ensure
Body and mind from evil, and ~~forestall~~ 72
{[?his] {[?uture]
[?Smiles] of good [?for] {[?] f{[?] days 73

[33r]

round these narrow mansions cast my eyes
And ~~cast my eyes around these still abod[?es]~~ TPL, 15
abodes
One I behold which hath today been filled 16
V, 892 By a poor friendless Man an aged orphan X 17
893 So call him for humanity to him 18
~~Well lodged in lasting quiet—for the rest~~
894 No parent was, the rest to me are mute 19
no more
I know ~~not who~~ what Tenant each 20
contains.
T}
D}han doth the grass that roofs it. Yet, 21
methinks,
Guided by what I have observ'd, or learn'd:
{Might {me
{[?Pres] I presu{[?] from out the mult[?u]de 22
Of Natures rustic children here interr'd 28
One to select who might have many peers
Thus would I trace his history. Let the 33, 44
House
Where first he breathes the vital air be glad 46
S}
For a Manchild is born. [?]}ee weakness 47
~~Assert her rights [?as here] in human [?frame]~~
{here in
Impersonated, {[?] human frame 48
Assert her rights and helplessness ensure 49
From tendance ever on the watch or near 50
~~By~~∧ ~~proud and ever watchful ministry~~
All that it needs—Upon the lap he lies [50], 51
Senseless and powerless yet a King of state 53
Of high observance and of prime concern. 54
And every eye that enters turns to him 55
The star unseen before that now 56
hath risen.

---

73 Overwriting may be reinforcement.

Partly drafted on 32v; partly rev and expanded on 32v, 31v, 29v, 28v, 27v, 10r–11r.

17–19 The X in the right margin signals rev first entered on facing 32v and then incorporated on 33r.

47 Ink blot below "weakness" obscures a word, possibly "now" as in later readings.

48, 50 Rev is drafted on facing 32v.

56 See note to l. *61* on 32v.

[33^v]

[?More than we know, as man of woman born]
{That
{[?From] from the touch or sensible approach — *TPL, 78*
her
Of ~~this~~ new acq[?u]sition may pervade — *79*
The languid Mothers heart what yearning love — *80*
What tender awe or pious gratitude — *81*
Though with a [?loving] and imperfect glimps
not to be revealed
holy is the light
~~Yet~~ light
{. [?grovelling]
This is a mystery{, ~~but~~ a holy ~~gleam~~ — *85*
Shines
[?~~Comes~~] from that quarter—and we feel its power
As man—of woman born—But turn we thence
[?who]
~~To [?] objects by no [?sanctity removed]~~
~~From common sight and with our tale proceed~~
That with
Due — *88*
Turn we thence
~~To objects [?removed] from common sight~~
{n dim
V, 260 — [?A{l]though yet irrational & blank of soul — [92]
that tedious time [?~~sneeze~~] sneeze
259 — Learned in ~~their [?course]~~ to yawn [?~~smile~~] smile ^~~& [?sne]~~ — *91*
~~T~~} [?~~us~~]
[260] — W{~~h~~{o ~~though irrational and blank of soul~~ — *TPL, 92*
263, 264 — Mocking the functions of intelligent man — *95, 96*
grave
265 — An ~~apt~~ proficient in amusive feats — *97*
266 — Of puppetry that from the lap declare — *98*
267 — His expectations and announce his claims — *99*
[?On]
268 — ~~To~~^ that Inheritance which millions — *100*
rue
269 — That they were ever born to. — *101*

[Right margin, vertical: *TPL, 91, 92 93*]
[Right margin, vertical: to yawn smile snees—to grasp / With tiny fingers to let fall a tear — V, 259 261]

[34^r]

{ine
Meanwhile how f{[?air] or exquisite the bliss — *TPL, 77*
Which may pervade the languid Mothers — *79, 80*
hear

Rev of 34^r; rev on 27^v, 27^r, 12^r, 13^r, inside front cover. For V, 260–269, cf. MS. 74A, 7^r–7^v.
The top line on 33^v is a variant of a line (beginning "As man") in the passage below l. *85*.
85/88 "That with" is possibly an aborted rev to 34^r.
259, 261 Rev of 34^r, entered vertically in the right margin; rev continued in left margin of 34^r. Rev on 34^v.

Rev on 33^v, 27^v, 27^r, 12^r, 13^r, inside front cover. For V, 257ff., cf. MS. 74A, 7^r–7^v.
79, 80 Last word is intended as "heart."

What pious gratitude what yearning love *81, 80*
To the still spirit may convey Delight *82*
And lift it in this sabbath of her rest *83*

TPL, 94 [95]

tasks
Above the level of Lives daily [?cares] *84*
This is a mystery:—a saintly lamp *85*
Burns here within its own peculiar shrine *86*
This is to her a mystery. Turn we [?thence]
Forbid to blend its light with common day *87*
But from the Parent turn we to the Child
n obtain
Due honour will the ensuing mo[?th] ths [?~~receive~~] *88*
If we record that like his Brother Babe[?s] *89*
~~If we record that in their tedious [?lapse~~]
Cradled in ~~gilded~~ [?Palaces], this Cottage *90*
nursling
~~This nursling like his Brother~~
Babe
[?]
T[?]
~~Cradled in gilded [?p] [?]~~

dissolves
And as the [?heavy] cloud of sleep dispers d
To stretch his limbs bemocking as might seem

at time
V, 259 Learn'd in th [?eir] tedious [?~~lapse~~], to yawn
smile sneeze *91*
Thus [?dim]
260 And though irrational & blank of soul *92*
outwardly outward *95*
[?ing]
V, 262 263 [?~~To~~] mock intelligent
264 ~~Ape outwardly~~ the ^ function of a man *96*
[?musive] feats
265 A grave proficient in ~~a vari~~ous round *97*
~~And by this~~
266 ~~And by this puppetry, from the lap~~ declare. *98*
Of puppetry that from the lap declares
267 ~~His expectations and assert his cla[?im~~,] *99*
announce [?the]
[267] 150 His expectations and ~~asserts hi~~s claim[?s] *[99]*
On
268 [?] that inheritance which millions rue *100*
269 That they were ever born to. But the day *101*
now
270 Of solemn ceremonial ~~is~~ arrived *102*
Minor
271 When they who for this ~~Infant~~ hold in *103*
trust

85–87 Rev between base text lines incorporates rev on 27ʳ, 27ᵛ, 33ᵛ, and is incorporated on 12ʳ.

99 The "150" is WW's line count of an indeterminate stage of composition. Cf. 32ʳ, note to l. 928/607. Ink blot obscures last word.

Lines entered vertically in left margin are continued from right margin of 33ᵛ; see the note there to ll. 259, 261.

[34v]

From [?this] this time forward from this fluttering hour
desires
V, 282 Corrupt affections covetous ~~are all renounced~~ *TPL, 114*
[283] Are all renounced—high as the thought of man [*115*]
[284] Can carry virtue virtue is profess'd [*116*]
[285] A dedication made a surety give [*117*]
[288] ~~That good shall be promoted and all truth~~ [*120*]
[?~~h~~] adva[?nc]
[288] ~~And~~ [?] [?~~oli~~]~~ness~~ [*120*]

From this time forward from this fluttering hour

286 For due provision to promote all good *118*
[288] And holiness [*120*]
[283] high as the thought of Man [*115*]
[284] Can carry virtue, virtue is profess d [*116*]
285 A dedication made a [?surety given] *117*
288 ~~All~~ good shall be promoted and all truth *120*
That
[288] And holiness {[?~~to~~] [*120*]
283 ~~and~~ {[?the] ~~the [?utmost height~~] *115*
284 Of ~~mans conception virtue is prof~~ess *116*
grasp
{clasp
259 Learned in that time to yawn smile, sneeze—to {[?grasp] *91*
261 With tiny fingers to let fall a tear, *93*
262 And when the heavy cloud of sleep with[?r]aws, *94*
263 To stretch his limbs bemocking as might *95*
{[?L] L} seem
{[?] [?]}ike all that is most beautiful or [?seems]
calm
Most fixd in man's inconstant [?state]
[259] Learned in that tedious time to yawn smile [*91*]
sneeze
260 Though yet irrational of soul, to grasp *92*
[261] With tiny finger to let fall a tear [*93*]
[262] And as the heavy cloud of sleep dissolves [*94*]
[263] To stretch his limbs [*95*]

[35r]

V, 272 Rights that trancend the unbless'd heritage *TPL, 104*
{[?their]
273 Of mere humanity: present their {[?] charge *105*
274 For that occasion daintily adorn'd, *106*
A} {pure
275 T}t the baptismal font—and when the {[?] *107*
pure
276 And consecrated element hath cleansed *108*

For Book V lines, cf. MS. 74A, 7v–8r.
In the first line, "[?this]" is obscured by an ink blot. The line is not included in the rev on 35v.
Between ll. 6 and 7 of rev at top of page, "adva[?nc]" is possibly an alt for "promote" in l. 286.
282–288 Rev and expansion of 35r; rev on 35v.
259–263 Rev of 33v, 34r; rev on 12r, 13r.
263/[259] Rev of 35r.

272–283 Cf. MS. 74A, 7v.

ir
277 The original stain behold him th[?eir] [?]} [?recievd] *109*
second Christ's church [?with]
278 Into the arck of Christ church ~~to float~~ *110*
[?trust]
{T shall
279 {[?F]hat he from wrath redeemed therein may float *111*
{[?waters]
280 Over the {[?billows] of this troubsome [?some] *112*
world

fair { life
281 To the ~~bright~~ land of everlasting {[?hope] *113*
282 Corruption affection & covetous desire *114*
283 Are all renounc[?ed].—Did ere the
~~advancing~~
~~impatient~~ sun *115*
impatient
A yet invisible traveller on his path *123*
Behind the easter hills [?shed] brighter *124*
[?gleams]
Among the leaden [?clouds], and yet ~~are brush~~ *[124]*
how soon
The radiant prospect shall be brush'd *125*
Or shattered, tis dependent on a breath *126*
away
Even whil we gaze a dimness or decay *127*
Hath reach'd it. *128*
Like al that is most beautiful or [?seems]
sphere
Most fix'd in mans inconstant [?state] *[124]*
how soon
The radiant prospect shall be *[125]*
brushed away
Or shatter'd tis dependant on a b[?re] *[126]*
breath

[35v]

V, 282 Corrupt affections covetous desires *TPL; 114*
283 Are all renounc'd; high as the thought of Man *115*
284 Can carry virtue virtue is professed *116*
285 A dedication made a promise given *117*
286 For due provision to controul & guide *118*
287 And unremitting progress to ensure *119*
288 Holiness and truth. No brighter gleams *120*
Kindled at dawn among the leaden clouds *121*
In summers stillest hour precede the Sun *122*
A yet invisible Traveller on his path *123*

114–128 Rev and expanded on 34v, 35v. Ll. *127ff.* are continued on 36r.
128/[124] Rev on 34v but not included in rev on 36r.

282–288 Rev and expansion of 34v, 35r.
282–319 Cf. MS. 74A, 7v–8v.

Behind the eastern hill and yet how soon 124
The radiant prospect shall be brushd 125
away
Or shatter'd, tis dependant on a breath 126
Even while we gaze a dimness or decay 127
[288] Hath reach'd it. Deem not Sir that I condemn 128

~~by~~ through pains and
302 May be, ~~through~~ [?~~through~~] ~~strength~~ of persevering hope, 143
303 Recovered, or if hitherto unknown 144
316 So, on this earth no fear [?and in my heart] 156
317 Better not move at all 157
a}
319 That finds [?f]}nd cannot fasten down, that 159
grasps
And is rejoiced and loses while it grasps 160
So [?]
Thus [?in these mountain climes] the life of
[?Is spent] & purest intelectual [?life]
[?]
[?Melt into] [?] [?bodily] [?] that at [?last]
is the
[?] [?fatal] [?] This [?be] one destiny of
[?man]
[?Such] the [?completion] of his [?hours]—[?etc]

[36r]

Even while we gaze a dimness or decay *TPL*, 127
V, 288 Hath reach'd it. Deem not Sir that I condemn 128
290 The rites by which your ministry attests 129
Echoing the assurance of the inmost heart 130
[290] That unregenerate Man by Nature lies 131
291 Bedded, for good and evil, in a gulph 132
292 Fearfully low—or that my judgement 133
e} scorns
293 Th[?i]}s services whereby attempt is made 134
294 To lift the Creature towards that Eminence 135
now fallen, erewhile in majes
295 On which ~~erewhile~~ in majesty ~~he stood~~, 136
~~Erewhile~~ He stood
296 ~~Now fallen~~, or if not so, whose top serene 137
297 At least, he feels, tis given him to descry 138
298 Not without aspiration ever more 139
299 Returning, and injunctions from within 140
[?~~To~~] doubt to cast off trust
300 ~~To cast~~ of weariness ~~and~~ [?~~fear~~], in faith 141

127–128 This reading on 35v incorporates reading on 36r; *127ff.* continued on 36r.
143–144 This rev of 36r is then incorporated on 36r between the base text lines.
316ff. Cf. MS. 69, stub 248v–248r.
156–160 Rev and expansion of 36r; rev on 36v.

127–128 Incorporated in rev on 35v.

301 That what the soul perceives if glory lost, *142*
302 May be through pains & persevering hope *143*
~~May be recovered, or if yet unknown~~
303 Recover'd: or if hitherto unknown *144*
304 Lies within reach and one day shall *145*
314 If to be weak is be gained. *154*
317 Ah better not to move at all than move *157*
illusive
318 By impulse sent from such ~~a treacherous~~ power *158*
321 That tempts, emboldens, doth a while sustain *161*
and call on conscience [?to]
322 [?And then] betrays, accuses, and inflicts *162*
323 Remorseless punishmen, ~~this done~~ *163*
and so
retreads
inevitable happier
324 The ~~never ending~~ circle—~~better~~ far *164*
325 Than this to graze the herb in thought *165*
calm
less ~~peace~~

[36^v]

{[?with]
V, 306, 307 The Forms {[?in] which commnities of men *TPL, 146, 147*
307, 308 Invest these feelings and the [?~~solemn v~~] aspiring vows *147, 148*
310 Are both *150*
the visible forms
[306] The outward ritual & establish d forms *146*
[?To] Establish d [?]
{C
[307] ~~With~~ which {communities of men invest *[148]*
To invest ~~Inwards~~ aspiri
aspir }
[308] [?Invest] these feelings and the [?]}ing vows *[148]*
lip gives
309 To which the public utterance ~~is given~~ *149*
{ shall
310, 311 Are both a natural process, and {[?by me] pass *150*
311 By me uncensured though the issue prove, *151*
312 Bringing from age to age its own reproach, *152*
313 Incongruous, impotent & blank, but oh *153*
314 If to be weak is to be wretched—miserable *154*
315 As The lost Angel by a human voice *155*
mourn
[?mourn]} {n
316 Hath [?fear]}fully pronounced the{ in my mind *156*

For lines on 36^r, cf. MS. 74A, 8^r–8^v and MS. 69, stub 248^v–248^r.
143–144 Rev on 35^v, rev incorporated on 36^r.
145/161 Rev and expanded on 36^v.
157–161 Rev, and l. 156 added, on 35^v; rev on 36^v.
165 *TPL* continues on 37^r.

Another attempt to begin passage on this page appears at page foot (ll. [306–307]–[309]).
146–161 Rev and expansion of 35^v, 36^r; *TPL*, l. 162, continues on 36^r.
306ff. Cf. MS. 69, stub 248^v–248^r; MS. 74A, 8^r–8^v.
[148] In the penultimate base text line, another conjecture for "Humiliation" is "Ministration."

317 Far better not to move at all than move *157*
illusive power
318 By impulse sent from such a ~~treacherous~~ *158*
power
319 That find and cannot fasten down, that grasp *159*
320 And is rejoiced and loses while it grasps *160*
321 That tempts emboldens [?ec] *161*
Which neither thrilled by exctasy nor [?dashd]
By fear, perform life's work in steady peace
that [?serve]
[306, 307] The forms ~~by which~~ communities of men *[146, 147]*
To in
[308] [?Express] this fe ward feeling, the [?profered] *[148]*
[309] [?Humiliation] & the aspiring vows *[148]*
[309] To which the lip gives public utterance *[149]*
607 be hailed *179*
608 With honour which encasing by the power *180*
609 Of long companionship the Artists *181*
hand

[37ʳ]

V, 326 By foresight undisturbed and vain regret *TPL, 166*
Yet if the upright form & countenance reard *167*
Aloft, as if {to} the heavens it would present *168*
A [?m{ore / as}] magnificent impress than their own *169*
Forbid that discontent should stoop {~~thus~~ / [?] [?lo]} *170*
thus lo
Then welcome reasons least ambitious course *171*
And envied be without reproof their lot *172*
600 Who to and fro, from morn to evening pace *173*
601 The narrow avenue of daily toil *174*
602/603 For daily bread. Praise to the sturdy plough *175*
604 And patient spade & shepherds simple crook *176*
encas[?ing]
607 Nor be the light ~~tool~~ mechanic tool ungraced *179*
~~And let the~~ {~~tool~~ / [?]} ~~be praised which [?converts~~]
608 With honour, which encasing by the power *180*
609 Through long companionship the artists hand *181*
With indurated substance like its
~~Into a substance~~ {[?Like] / [?as] itself} *182*
Cuts off that hand
610 ~~Hath cut~~ it off with all its world of nerves *183*

---

161 This phrase gives the opening words of l. 161 as it appears on 36ʳ.
161/[146–147] Draft is related to rev entered on 37ʳ, possibly once meant to follow l. *184* there.
607–609 Continued from bottom of 37ʳ. Cf. MS. 74A, 16ʳ.

---

326 Cf. MS. 74A, 8ᵛ.
604/611 Cf. MS. 74A,16ʳ.
179, 180 Rev again below and at page foot on 36ᵛ.

611 From a too busy commerce with the heart 184
Unthrilled by exctasy [?undash'd] by fear
But like a hawk upon the inconstant wind
And free to aid lifes work in steady peace
I move, part wheeling, blown about in part 43
I who profess'd to tread an onward path 38
On the plain ground inscribed. I undertook 39
To treat of one born to the plough & spade
605 And pondrous loom resounding while it holds 177
606 Body and mind in one captivity 178
607 And ~~let~~ may the light mechanic tool be [?haild] [179]

[37v]

V, 984 *But whence this tribute wherefor these regards*
The sentiments and opinions ~~here~~
here uttered *in unison*
~~uttered that follow~~ are ~~so much in~~
~~the same spirit~~ with those expressed
in the following essay upon epitaphs
which was furnished by the Author
to Mr C's periodical work the
as *~~tend to illustrate~~*
Friend & they ~~have so direct a~~
succeding
~~bearing upon the 2 following books~~
~~of the Poem that the Reader who~~
Here [?musing]
~~in justice to the subject to the~~
~~subject they are here reprinted~~
are
as they are [*?wi*] *dictated by a*
c *to that*
spirit w ongenial which pervades
the 2 succeeding books the
sympathising [?~~*d*~~] *read will not*
be displeased that it is here
reprinted

---

184 *TPL* continues with l. *185* on 38r.
184/43 The interlinear lines of rev ("Unthrilled...peace") appear to be rev of similar lines (*161*/[*146–147*]) on 36v.
43, 38, 39 After rejection here, partially included in rev on 31v, 28v, 10r.
177–[*179*] These lines of late rev are continued at the bottom of 36v and are meant to follow l. *176* on 37r. Cf. MS. 69, stub 247v.

This draft of the introductory sentence (keyed to V, 984) of WW's note for *1814* introducing an "Essay on Epitaphs" (*Prose*, II, 49n) is evidence that MS. 74 was employed in making final copy of *Exc* for printer. WW probably dictated the passage to the copyist, MW. This passage suggests that WW already planned this note before the completion of MS. 74A, since l. 984 represents an intermediate state between what is on 123r and the final rev of MS. 74A, 28v.

[38^r]

V, 327 Philosophy and thou more vaunted name *TPL, 185*
328 Religion with thy statelier retinue *186*
329 Faith Hope and Charity—from the visible world *187*
330 Chuse for your emblem whatsoeer ye find *188*
331 Of safest guidance and of firmest trust *189*
nor except
332 The torch the star the anchor ~~and the~~ *190*
[?~~cro~~]
333 The cross its at whose unconscious feet *191*
334 The generations of mankind have knelt *192*
335 Ruefully seized and shedding bitter tears *193*
rest
336 And through that conflict seeking, of you *194*
337 High titled Powers am I constrained to ask, *195*
338 Here standing with the unvoyageable sky *196*
339 In faint reflection of infinitude *197*
n
340 Stretch'd overhead, at|d at my pensive feet *198*
341 A subterraneous magazine of bones *199*
soon
342 In whose dark vault my own shall be laid *200*
343 Where are your triumphs your dominion *201*
where
344 And in what age admitted and confirm'd *202*
[?host]
345 Not for a happy ~~land~~ do I inquire *203*
346 Island or grove that hides a blessed few *204*
willing & sincere
[?~~sincere~~]
347 Who with obedience [?~~fearful~~] ~~&~~ [?] *205*
348 To your serene authority conform *206*

[39^r]

V, 349 But whom, I ask, of individual souls *TPL, 207*
350 Have ye withdrawn from Passion's crooked *208*
ways
351 Inspired and thorough[?t]ly fortified—if the heart *209*
352 Could be inspected to its [?~~last~~] inmost fold *210*
353 By sight undazzled with external fame, *211*
354 Who shall be named, in the resplendent line *212*
355 Of sages martyrs confessors—the man *213*
Whom
356 [?~~H~~] ~~[?~~] the best might of Conscience faith & hope *214*

TPL continues from 37^r.
327ff. Cf. MS. 69, stub 247^r; MS. 74A, 8^v–9^v.
333 MS. 74A and *1814* read "Cross itself, at."

Leaf 38^v is blank, except for a small ink X; see note to l. 361, below.
349ff. Cf. MS. 69, stubs 247^r, 246^v; MS. 74A, 9^v.

day's compass hath
357 For one [?~~better~~] little space sufficed to gain *215*
[?to save] [?little]
Sufficed {[?for on] for one days scanty space *216*
358 From painful & discreditable shocks *217*
some false
359 Of contradiction & from [?base] desires *218*
361 Or some unsanctioned fear. The hail once more *219*
bodily
612 The inglorious implements of ~~rustic~~ toil *220*
613 Both these that shape & build & those that force *221*
earth to yield
614 By slow solicitation, ~~from the earth~~ *222*
[?orth]
615 Her annual bounty sparingly dealt f[?~~ort~~] *223*
617 Not less for grosser good which they produce *225*
618 Than for the vanities and baffl[?ing] thoughts *226*
619 Which they preclud *227*
616 With wise reluctance, these do I extol *224*
[617] Not for gross goo[?o]d alone which
[?those]
they produce [*225*]
[?procure]

[39^v]

V, 618 [?B fort]th impertinent or baffling [?th] *TPL, 226*
~~Vain~~[?t] [?] & perplexing [?hope] [*226*]

jocund *231*
No } Behold the Peasant Boy *242*
[?]} longer now in leading strings detained [*242*]
{G {C
And from the {go-{carts moving prison escaped *243*

no better help
Awaits his opening reason—such the [?minds]
That must restrain him fashion or inure *241*
But [?see him]
~~such help he [?find~~]

---

358 Added line is in different ink from base text.

361 An X on facing 38^v may be intended to signal a rev, probably addition of l. 360 as in MS. 74A. "The hail once more" probably should begin "Then"; the phrase is probably related to rev of l. 607 on 37^r and 36^v.

612–617 Cf. MS. 74A, 16^r; MS. 74A includes rev not in MS. 74.

612/617 Lines appear to be added in two stages. Ll. 613–614 appear to be in different pen and ink than the base text lines on the page.

616–[617] These lines may have been entered in space left after the del lines above. They continue on 40^r, and an attempt in pencil to alter them is found at the top of 39^v.

Top two lines, in pencil, are partial rev of 40^r and 39^r. Cf. MS. 69, stub 239; MS. 74A, 16^r.

231 Word "jocund" is rev of 40^r, where the word is entered in pencil.

Draft for ll. 241–243 is attempted rev of 40^r; related pencil draft is on 125^v.

light
no better {[?help]
[?~~him~~]
[?~~Awaits] such society~~
Awaits his opening ~~reason~~—[?~~these m~~]
[?sense] that is to judge
[?guest]
Of right and wrong, with such domestic [?~~gues~~]
[?~~T check~~] [?hi]
And guides [?to check] foster and inure [*241*]

[40^r]

baffling
B [?dreams]
V, 618 [?F]}ut for the impertinence & ~~vexing~~ *TPL, 226*
619 Which they preculde, in that contented *227*
race
620 Who to their dull society are born. *228*
child
So let our Rustic Ba[?be]—a freight in arms *229*
Go forth, besprinkled with their flattering *230*
[?~~dew~~]
[?dews]
{e jocund{. [?Be nor]
Nor be th{ { [?~~nor] be~~ they harsly judged *231*
~~To which they~~
If that abode to which they turn; whose hearth *232*
Glows like a furnace with the festal fire *233*
do here
Ere this days light be wasted, shall resound *234*
With boisterous merriment & jests impure *235*
Which
{~~which~~
~~To~~ {[?whom] even the Mother whom her natur *236*
al [?strains]
~~Erewhile~~
Did lately fling upon a stiller shore *237*
w}
Is not} not unprepared to greet with *238*
smiles
Of arch complaiscenc or at least receive *239*
Without [?an] altered [?cheek]. With these to *240*
teach
Restrain him, fashion, foster, and inure *241*
The Peasant Boy from leading strings is freed *242*
And from the Go-cart's moving Prison escapes *243*
Running and struggling wheresoer his feet *244*
Can totter with him, on the perilous edge *245*

618ff. Rev of 39^r, attempted pencil rev is on 39^v. Cf. MS. 69, stub 239; MS. 74A, 16^r.
229 Rev is in pencil.
231 Addition "e jocund" is in pencil; word "jocund" is also on 39^v.
234 Alt is in pencil.
236 Another conjecture for "strains" is "stren."
240–243 Attempted rev is on 39^v; pencil draft is on 125^v.

[40v]

~~Parent's Mothers~~ creed
~~Confirmation~~
[?T]
I~~n confirmation of his~~ *TPL*, 249
His Mother honest and confiding creed [249]
The event confirms, for stray wh[?e]ereer he 248
will
Heaven [?wat] tender care protects him from 251
through all risks
him
And harms not. ~~Confiding in the creed~~ 248
For stray where er [?hell] will
~~Heavens tender care protects through all~~ [251]
Approving by the event the Mothers creed [249]
Confidingly received from age to [?~~to~~] age [250]
Heavens tender care protects him through all [251]
risks
And hence through [?lack] of th[?eir cont] 262
to give or purch
[?doom]
Or purchase, twas his ~~lot~~ to lag behind 266
[?lovliness]
In thriving infant ~~beauty far~~ surpassed [267]

to give or purchase, this less favoured child
In thriving infant beauty [?was] surpassed 267
By his coevals of more high decree 268

If skill were mine 274
Thus would I represent him to your view 275
Such and so fair a child as on[?ce] I marked 276

[41r]

steep rock or sullen
Of tempting fire, ~~or deep and silent~~ pool *TPL*, 246
roars
[?]
Or rain-swoln flood that near the Cottage [?~~roars~~] 247
~~Yet~~ Heavens good care protects him through all risks 251
watchful in
Risen with the sun's first ~~coming~~ [?to] the east 252
rising
~~Dismissed to sleep of [?t]~~
And to his aeery loft & couch of straw 253
Dismiss'd not seldom ere the sun retires 254
day
A ~~length~~ of many-weatherd hour he sees, 255
and
Neglected humoured scolded [?or] caress d 256

Rev and expansion of 41r; rev on 41v–42r (page foot).
267 Another conjecture for "was" is "far."

Rev and expanded on 40v, 41v–42r; related pencil draft is on 125v.

But health of body, strength, and prosperous 257
growth
Thanks to fresh air and hardy liberty 258
He for himself provides: and though, ~~erewhile~~, 259
so late
Deprived deprived
~~T~~
T[?]}~~hrough lack~~ of tendance due and those nice 262
so late [?aids]
Which ease and opulence are free to give
Or purchase, he a firmer aspect showed
of more high
Than his Coevals ~~higher in~~ degree 268
Y
[?T]}et mark the recompen[?s]e, no longer now 269
By teazing incapacities detained 270
how soon
{ness,
And burthensom through helpless{ ~~infancy~~ 271
~~He far~~ {ose
Matched with th{e ornaments of wealthier flower 272
Hath he
~~He far out~~strips them all. robust of limb 273
~~Brighteyed~~
~~And ro[?ss] chee[?ek]ed~~ {such
[?th{us]
Bright eyed and rosy cheeked. ~~To~~ my minds eye 274
I represent him such as once I marked 275, 276
In spring-time sporting on the threshold step[?s] 277
weedless
And where the plot of [~~ ?] [?les~~] pavement 278
fronted

[41^v]

~~a~~ perilous edge TPL, 245
~~Calling to mind the wan uncoloured face~~ 280
Of tempting fire, steep rock, or sullen pool 246
Or rain-swoln flood that near the Cottage roars 247
stray where he will, Heaven[?s care]
And harms him not; ~~for, stray whereer he will~~, 248
t} {e
Approving by the event }[?h{is] Mother's creed 249
Confidingly received from age to age
th}
Heavn's tender care protects him fr}rough all risks 251
Ris n with the suns first rising in the east 252
ft }
And to his aery lo[?ss]} and couch of straw 253
Dismiss'd not seldom ere the sun retires 254
A day of many-weather'd hours he sees 255
Neglected humoured scolded and caress'd 256
But health of body strength & prosperous growth 257

Leaf 41^v is rev of 40^v, 40^r, 41^r, continued below rule on 42^r; related pencil draft is on 125^v.
280 Entered first as rev of 42^r and then incorporated on 42^r.

[?confidence]
Thanks to fresh air and hardy liberty 258
~~full soon~~
[?fu]
he [?~~course~~]
[?In course]
Left to himself
He for himself provides, ~~and though the course~~ 259
The
{[?P]
{[?p]} by each days [?~~bread~~ intails]
[?need]
Of [?]}ressing tasks ~~which scanty means enjoin~~ 260
Upon the Inmate of a poor [?mans house] 261
~~Full soo~~n deprived him of that tendance strict 262
~~Deprived~~
Which on his first consignment to the world 263
Nature exacted for him, with some help 264
v }
By [?]}ain officious novelty supplied 265
from month to month he lags
And hence his lot ha[?s] been to lag behind 266
In thriving infant loveliness surpass'd 267
{C
By his {coevals of more high degree 268
Yet mark the recompense—no longer now 269
Mid teazing incapacities detained 270
And burthensome through helplessness, how soon 271
[?In faulted] Boast
Match d with those ornaments of wealthier flower, 272
Hath he outs ripped them all, robust of limb 273

[42r]

The door not often closed, and as I passed TPL, 279
Calling to mind a wan uncoloured face 280
~~With recollection of the pa~~llid face,
Remembering that pale face, and nothing more 281
i }
Which, in the mother's arms m[?y]}ne eyes 282
~~had [?there~~]
W } had there
[?]}ith some slight touch of pitiful regard 283
Encountered while dark winte chilled the plains 284
now play[?ed] before [?me]
The florid Youngling which ~~I now beheld~~ 285
With the warm light of april on his cheek 286
Or basking on his hair exposed like leaves 287
to my thoughts
Or clustering blossoms ~~did to me~~ appear 288

266 Possibly the "s" is a "t" in "ha[?s]" with the word then intended as "hath."

279ff. Continued from 41r.
280 Rev drafted on 41v.

t|
Less like a Creature heref|ofore oppressed 289
Whose state had undergone a balmy 290
change
Than one created on that sunny day [?X] 291
robust of limb 273
Bright eyed and rosy cheeked—if skill were mine 274
[?Here]
~~Thus~~ would I represent him to you view 275
Such and so fair a Child as once I marked 276
In sprin time, sporting on the threshold step 277
And where the plot of weedless pavement fronts 278
The door not often clos'd—and as I pass d [279]
Calling to mind &c see above [280]
The years proceed 292
~~And what~~

[42v]

S|
X [?]|uch would I paint him—What *TPL,* [292]
if yon
Such he—so fair and to the passing eye
As rich in promise what if yon low pile 292
~~Yon antient edifice [?within] fern-clad roof~~
Within whose walls methinks I see him sit 293
Where now upon his form through half the day
{the
In durance seated, he {[?] primmer cons 295
{e
With poring ey{es or thumbs a holier book, 296
~~So nature favours him; as [?g]~~ [292]
So is he favoured— [292]
By glaring ~~allured~~
~~With the~~ first heat of vernal days ~~he strips~~
[?Importund] {~~id~~
~~And g[?ambols] naked in the gel~~{[?y] pool
{~~A~~
~~Tha~~{t [?]|~~dventurer stripps off his his homely tweed~~,
Allured and by urged
~~And by~~ his elder comrades ~~led & cheer d~~
Th Adventurer strips off his homely [?tweed]
~~to some croft or plot of orchard ground~~ 302

---

291 An ink blot obscures the possible X.

274–[280] Continued from 41v; rev of 41r, 42r. From l. [*280*] at page foot, the text goes to l. *280* at the top of the page, as "see above" at page foot indicates.

292 The last lines, beginning "The years proceed," probably indicate the final sequence of rev on 42v–43r (see second note to 42v).

Rev of 43r.

At the top, line beginning "Such would I paint him" is probably the earliest of several attempts on this page to provide a new transition. The left-margin X probably indicates the rev is to follow l. *291* on 42r. Entry of l. *292* (beginning "The years proceed") at the bottom of 42r probably signals the last sequence intended (see l. [*292*] near page foot on 42v).

302 Rev entered opposite l. *302* on 43r.

l}
And g[?ambols] naked in the gelid po[?n]d}
and what
~~Even such~~ ~~[?so years]~~
Such he [292]
{ methink
Within whose walls {[?] I see him sit [293]
Conducting seemlingly eyes
[?Transferringing], to and fro, deliberate ~~looks~~ *294*
Of close regard along the primmers page [295]
O }
[?T]}r thumbing earnestly a holier book [296]
~~do [?of] his progress~~
{ Of
{[?Do] his advancement make no proud report *297*
So Nature favours him as years proceed [292]
Such He, so fair, and to the passing eye
p }
The years [?]}roceed
~~As rich in pro~~mise; what if yon low pile [292]
e }
Within whose walls methinks I [?se] [?]} him sit [293]
Conducting, to and fro, deliberate eyes [294]
Of close regard along the Primmers page [295]
Or thumbing earnestly a holier book [296]
Of his advancement make no proud report [297]

[43[r]]

~~So fair, and to the passing eye as rich~~
~~In promise he whose journey I retrace~~
~~Not sparing devious notice far and wide~~
What if yon Pile beneath whose fern clad roof *TPL, 292*
He now in durance seated, half the day *295*
His primmer cons or thumbs a holier book, *296*
Of his advancement make no proud report *297*
Yet in the glad hours when restraint hath ceased *298*
The fields accept him as their genuine growth *299*
Sauntering he plays upon his sycamore pipe *300*
Or with his Mates, at the earlier seasons call *301*
~~croft or plot of orchard~~
~~Hies to some well [?known] plot of household~~ ground *302*
Hies to some orchard ground or household croft
Where blow the splendid daffodils of March *303*
And from that bed his rusty hat entwines *304*
With golden wreath—the plunderer ye may *305*
track
{ir are [?condemned]
Each to his home—the{ garland ~~is~~ dispersed *306*

Leaf 43 is the first of four (43–46) once removed from the notebook and now restored to it. The leaves may have been removed because *SBC* on 43[v]–46[r] was not to be a part of *Exc*; possibly the removal was to preserve (or make a subsequent copy of) *SBC*. For more on *SBC*, see pp. 468–470, 1212–1213, as well as note to 44[r], below.

Lines del at top of page are rev on 42[v].

gay
Almost as soon as woven—the ~~bright~~ spoil 307
{bunches
So late, in {[?] proudly grasp'd is now 308
Slighted as burthensome, or only prized 309
As matter for detruction—leaves & stalks 310
F } {ng
[?S]}lu{g here and there bestrew the path[?s] & road. 311
~~To [?musingl] Traveller as he walk~~ 313
To the brisk traveller or to him who walks 312
notice
Musing with down cast eye a [?~~notice~~] ~~gay~~ bright [313]
Yet pensive, that the flowering spring is come. 314
Nor will the musing Traveller & 315

[43v]

Were long to tell—Suffice that he who lies SBC, 14
Reposing near his [?breathren] of the vale
Beneath this

The man who here is laid
Venturing along the edge of yon blue steep [14]
That perilous descent of shivery stone 15
To prosecute his well known way in quest 17
Of some endangered straggler of his floc 18
Slippe in the turmoil of a winters 19

The man who here is laid
Venturing to take his well known way in quest [17]
Of some endangered straggler of his flock [18]

Of yon huge Heigt the Man who here is laid [17]
~~Along the brink of that~~ edge
Venturing along the brink of that [?huge] height [17]
To take his well known way in eager quest [17]
To thy sad mishap 3
A word shall be devoted for the sake
Of a dumb Friend and servant who though 11
weak
To save [?] [?was] marvellously true 12

[44r]

Yet Thee I will not pass
~~Nor~~ unregarded ~~may I pass thee~~ by, SBC, 1
Thee, poor ill fated Shepherd of Bield Crag 2

[313] Apparently accidental blotting of "[?notice]" caused the overwriting.
315 Phrase signals first line of 94r, where *TPL* continues.

Loose leaf; see notes to 43r, 44r. Rev of 44r; rev on 46r.
12 Mark after "save" may be intended as a comma.

Loose leaf; see note to 43r. Rev on 43v, 46r.

To thy sad mishap
Who next dost meet me/—Thou wert longer used
trackless Hills
To range the Coves and Heights with different aim,
Far different thoughts, and Thou didst perish there.
he his
—There was {t/h}{ou/e} doomed to breathe {t/~~h~~}{y/is} latest breath:—
than the Old Man whom we this day
More hapless [?~~t~~]~~end than his whom we this day~~
Have given to earth!—But Arthur did not
want
House of his own, and lands, and numerous flock,
And wife and children to bewail his loss,
And a dumb Friend and Servant, in its kind
Loving as they, and marvellously true.
The Tale with all its moving incidents
Were long to tell.—Behold that smooth
blue steep
e
Th~~at~~ perilous descent of shivery stone
Behold that smooth blue steep of shivery
That sinks abruptly from the grassless Crown
{brink
high Mountains; he along that {[?Height]
brink
Of yon ~~huge Height.—He, roaming there~~,
in quest
Venturing to take his well-known way,
Of some endanger'd Stragglers from his Flock
Slipp'd in the turmoil of a winter storm,
And, far beneath, by next day's light, was
found
A wounded Corse, with face towards the snow
And raiment by that long precipitous fall
Torn from his back: and there was found his
Dog
In mournful posture, oer the naked part

---

7 Queried "t" is del by eras.

10 The words "wife" and "children" may be capitalized.

Sequence of composition for *SBC* is complex: (1) Original copy (ll. *1–52*) runs from 44^{r} to 45^{r} to 46^{r} (above the rule). (2) WW altered the opening by omitting ll. *1–14a* and beginning the tale at l. *14b* on 44^{r} or at "The man who here is laid" on 43^{v}. (3) On 45^{v} he started a new copy, writing ll. *1–3a*, copying ll. *31b–47* from 45^{r} and ll. *48–49* from 46^{r}. This third-stage revised text continues on 46^{r} below the rule with ll. [*50*]–[*52*] as rev of the same lines above the rule. Then on 46^{r} below the rule he rev and expanded ll. *14–17* from 43^{v}. It is probable that these lines about the faithful dog were repositioned to follow l. [*52*] on 46^{r} as a restructuring of the tale, linking back to earlier copy on 45^{r}. In that case, the first half-line of l. *31* (or its rev, "Beneath this heap of undistinguished turf") on 45^{r} may have been intended as the last line of *SBC*. (4) On 44^{v}, WW altered his text of l. *31* (possibly as a new opening for the poem) and rev and expanded ll. *41–45*; in his rev of ll. *41–45*, the poet worked not from the third-stage-copy on 45^{v} but from the first-stage text on 45^{r}. WW's intent for the final state of *SBC*—if, indeed, the text reached such a state—is difficult to determine. See pp. 468–470, above, and 1212–1213, below.

[44v]

The undistinguished Sod
Doth tempt said I my fancy here to place
Suitable Record. Often are we stopped *SBC, 31*
But [?fi] But fixing now his eye
Upon a heap of turf that near him rose
The Priest resumed. Not seldom [31]

this
Beneath this turf—[?an] undistinguish d Heap [31]
a brief tablet of memorial words
Which ~~some memorial words [?are put] upon~~
~~For~~ In for
~~Of~~ warning and ~~of~~ pity well would grace
[?~~it befalls~~]
Not seldom doth it chance that [31]
we are stopp'd
Which
this undistinguished heap
Oer which my fancy oftentimes hath laid 44
Not otherwise than I before described
A prostrate group of rudely-sculptured forms 45
And which a tablet of memorial words
In
~~For~~^ warning or for pity well might grace

In open air in view of sun stars *SBC, 44/45*
dews ex
And to the ~~rain~~ [?a]posed and battering storms
To rain and dew exposed and battering storm

[45r]

Couching, as if to shield it from the cold! *SBC, 25*
Thither, with sorrowful and decent care
A Bier was brought, and underneath that bier 26
The afflicted Creature from the fatal spot 27
would quit
Walk'd with his Masters Body, nor withdrew 28
would forsake [?dear master]
Nor quitted the forlorn society 29
[?D] The dear
~~Of those~~ remains, till weeping Friends had laid them 30
heap of undistinguished turf
Beneath this turf.———~~Not seldom are we stopp'd~~ 31

Loose leaf; see notes to 43r, 44r. Rev of 45r; these rev are not incorporated in the copy on 45v. At middle of page, "[?it befalls]" del by eras.

Loose leaf; see notes to 43r, 44r. Continued from 44r, rev on 44v, 45v.

{ through
Wandering, {[?mid an] antient churches 32
~~Not seldom doth it chance that we are stoppd~~
among tombs,
By scuptur'd image of the buried Man 33
Recumbent, Knight or Squire, with Sword & Shield, 34
And, at his feet, armorial Figure couch d, 35
Lion, or Greyhound, Lamb, or gentle Fawn, 36
The bold or timid Creature each alike 37
{ Resting stillness
{[?Couch] in duteous quiet, without fear 38
Of the sword's point and unoffending spurs, 39
That deck the Warrior in his last repose. 40
So, to assist Tradition, ~~that will long~~ 41
~~Preserve in our unvarying solitude~~ 42
a
~~No weak remembrance of that~~^~~sad event~~, 43
~~So have I some=times wished that~~ oer this grave 44
~~In open air in view of sun & stars~~
{l laid
Like Scu{ pture might be ~~placed~~, albeit 45
rude
And by some rustic hand uncouthly wrought 46
A Shepherd imaged in his mountain 47
garb

[45v]

[?leapt]
Nor unregarded may I pass thee by *SBC, 1*
Thee poor ill-fated Shepherd of Bield-crag 2
Who next dost meet me. —Oftimes [?we] 3, 31
we are stopped
Wandering through antient Churches among tombs 32
By scultured of image of some buried Man 33
Recumbent—Knight or Squire—with 34
Sword & Shield
And at his feet armorial Figure couch'd 35
Lion or Greyhound—Lamb—or gentle—fawn 36
The bold or timid creature—each alike 37
Resting in duteous quiet without fear 38
Of the sword's point and unoffending spurs 39
That deck the Warrior in his last repose. 40
So to assist Tradition that will long 41
Preserve in our unvarying solitude 42
No weak remembrance of a sad event 43
So have I sometimes wished that oer this grave 44
Like Sculputre might be placed, albeit 45
rude,

Loose leaf; see notes to 43r, 44r. Rev of 44r, 45r; rev and continued on 46r. Rev of 44v is not incorporated on 45v.

—A Shepherd imaged in his mountain garb 47
And at his side the serviceable staff 48
[?bounds] across the brook & leaps
With which he ~~lightly bounds oer brook &~~ 49
crag
~~With [?hectic~~ speed]
From crag to crag

[46^{r}]

And at his side the serviceable Staff *SBC, 48*
With which he lightly bounds oer brook and crag *49*
And/ couchant, ~~like a pillow~~ at the soles *50*
Of his unarmed feet, the faithful Dog *51*
That loved his Lord and clung to him in *52*
death.

And couchant at the soles [*50*]
Of his unarmed feet the faithful dog [*51*]
L
That loved his {[?l]ord & clung to him in Death. [*52*]
The Tale with all its moving Incidents *13*
Were long to tell. Behold that smooth blue steep *14*
That sinks abruptly from the grassless Crown *16*
Of yon huge height—The Man who here is *17*
laid
steep height
Venturing along the brink of that [?sharp] ~~edge~~ [*17*]
To take his wellknown way in eager quest [*17*]
Of some endangered straggler from his flock *18*
[?on]
Slipped, ~~in~~ the turmoil of a winters storm *19*
And far beneath by next days light was *20*
found,
snow
A wounded Corse with face toward[?s] the {[?] *21*
long
And Raiment by that {[?] precipitous fall *22*
Torn from his back—and there was found his *23*
Dog
In mournful Posture oer the naked part *24*

[46^{v}]

ℋ

IX, 38 discerns
39 The dear Memorial footmarks unimpaired

Loose leaf; see notes to 43^{r}, 44^{r}. Rev and continuation of 45^{v}, 43^{v}, 44^{r}.
50 Comma after "And" del by eras.
Inserted at the bottom, with the page reversed, are measurements ("3–8 long," "1–7 wide," "[?3–4]" and "16 inches"), in pencil and possibly in hand of WW.

Loose leaf; see notes to 43^{r}.
Symbol at top of page signals continuation of copy from 27^{r}; see note to l. 39 on 27^{r}.

Of her own native vigour but for this
That it is given her thence in age to hear
Reverberations, and a choral song
Commingling with the incense that ascends
Undaunted tow'rds the everlasting heaven
From her own lonely altar— —Do not think
That good and wise will ever be
allowed
Though Strength decay to breathe in such
estate
As shall divide them wholly from the stir
Of hopeful nature. Rightly is it said
That man descends into the vale of years
Yet I have thought that we might also
speak
And not presumptuously I trust of age
bare
As of a final eminence—though [?bla]
In aspect & forbidding yet a point
On which tis not impossible to sit

[47r]

In awful sovereignty—a place of power—
h}
—A Tr}rone which may be likened unto his
[?loo]
Who, on some gentle day of summer, looks
Down from a mountain top—~~say[?s]~~ say one of
those
High Peaks that bound the vale where
now we are.
~~H~~} ~~ng~~}
[?Fi]}~~ill dale fields woodlands to the gaz~~ [?eye]} ~~eye~~
~~Of one [?s]~~
Faint and diminished to the gazing eye
a}
Of one so stationed hill & dale [?s]}ppear
shapes
Will all the ~~forms~~ upon their surface spread
But while the gross and visibl frame
of things
Relinquishes its hold upon the sense
Yea almost on the mind itself & seems
All unsubstantialized, how loud the voice
Of waters, ~~from the~~ with invigorated peal

---

45 First dash is possibly intended as a period.

Cf. MS. 75, C2r.
60/61 Possibly, the overwriting in "gazing" is reinforcement of poorly formed letters.

B
69 [?F] from [?Ri]}rook & River in the vale below
who gains that lofty point
70, 73 Ascending—for ~~he stands above the~~
host
72, 73 Is privileged he stand above the [?Hos]
74 Of ever-humming insects mid thin air

[47v]

IX, 75 That suits not them—the murmur of the leaves
76 Many and idle touches not his ear
is ~~every sound~~
77 Th{[?] he freed from & from ~~thousand note~~
these
78 Not less unceasing not less vain than [?]
79 By which the finer passages of sense
~~Are~~
Is o}~~ccupied~~
80 Are occupied; & the soul that would
incline
81 To listen is prevented or disturbed.
82 —And may it not be hoped that
placed by age
83 In like removal tranquil though severe
[?]
84 We are not so removed for utter loss
85 But for some favour suited to our need
86 What more than this that we thereby
should
gain
87 Fresh power to commune with the invisible
world
88 And hear the mighty stream of tendency
t te
89, 90 U[?n] [?]}ring a clear sonorous voice
unknown
is
91 Unto the multitude whose doom it {[?]
92 To run the giddy round of vain delight

70, 73 Pencil del and rev above and below the line.

Rev of MS. 75, C2r

82–93 This passage is loosely related to lines in the Alfoxden Notebook, and l. 88 is drawn directly from that source (see *RC & Pedlar*, pp. 114–115).

83/84 Queried reading is blotted by offset from 48r (del of "And" in l. 99 there).

[48ʳ]

Or [?~~toil~~]} a} d} labour
IX, 93 [? ?]} fret [?]}n[?]} ~~murmur~~ on the plain
below.—

Or fret and labour on the plain below
[?reservd]
But such/ old/age/is not ~~ordained~~ for [?them]
Oh never never/can be theirs whose minds
94 But if to such sublime ascent the hopes
welcome close
95 Of man may rise as to a ~~natural~~ [?~~fount~~]
{ course
96 And termination of his mortal {[?end]
That hope can only comfort ~~those~~
97 They only such ascent can reach whose
minds
98 Have not been starved by absolute neglect
Nor
99 ~~And~~ b[?ol]dies crushed by unremitting [?~~toid~~]
toil

a
100 To whom kind Nature therefore my [?be]
[?true]
102 Whose birth right reason therefore
[?se]{[?ss]
may ~~a~~ {[?ffure].
103, 105 For me ~~I boast~~ I cannot but believe
that far
106, 107 That far as these predominate, even so
far
108 Country society and time itself
saps
109 (That ~~lays~~ the individuals bodily flame
110 And lays the generations low in dust),
~~Partakes~~
111 Do, by the almighty Rulers grace,
partake

[48ᵛ]

IX, 112 Of one maternal spirit bringing forth
ever constant
113 And cherishing with ~~never wearied love~~e,

Cf. MS. 75, C2ʳ, D1ʳ.

95–131 These lines, continued on 48ᵛ and 49ʳ, are also entered in a different sequence on 49ʳ, 49ᵛ, 50ʳ. See note on 49ʳ.

99 For the second word, *1814* reads "bodies."

102 The "[?se]" above "may a" is perhaps the start of a rev of "assure" (such as "secure").

Cf. MS. 75, D1ʳ.

112–129 Text continues from l. 111 at bottom of 48r.

114 That tires not, nor betrays. Our life is
turned
115 Out of its course wherever man is made
116 An offering or a sacrifice—a tool
117 Or implement—a passive thing employed
118 As a brute mean without acknoledgement
119 Of common right—or interest in the end,
120 Used or abused as selfishness may prompt
121 Say what can follow for a rational Soul
122 Perverted thus but weakness in all good
123 And strength in evil; hence an after
~~–call~~
call
124 For chastisement & custody, & bonds
125 And oftimes Death avenger of the past
126 And the sole Guardian in whose
hands we dare
127, 128 Entrust the future.—But the
genuine law
Tis one that prompts & urges & impels
129 A law of life & action—for tis known

[49r]

IX, 130 Tha when we stand upon our native
distort
131 Unelbowed by such objects as ~~constrain~~
~~he continued I believe that men~~
Yes I believe that Men exist for whom
~~Do, by the almightys grace exist for whom~~
108 Country, society, and time itself
109 That saps [?a] th Indiviuals bodily frame
110 And lays the generations low in dust
participate
111 Do, by the almightys grace ~~partake~~
[?~~Have~~]
112 Of one maternal spirit bringing forth
113 And cherishing with ever constant love
114, 95 That tires not nor betrays— —But such
{With a close
96 {And termination of their mortal course

---

119 The last word, "end," is reinforced. Possibly, what we read as a comma is an accidental mark.

Cf. MS. 75, D1r.

Rev and restructuring of ll. 95–131 (48r, 48v, 49r) on leaves 49r, 49v, 50r seems to take place in this order on 49r: (1) drafting of a new line to introduce ll. 108–114, probably intended to come after l. 93 on 48r; following of the half-line of l. 114 with the half-line of l. 95 through l. 100 (ll. 100–101 are added in rev); (3) including of a variant of l. 114 through l. 131 at the top of the page, incorporating rev of the earlier entries on leaves 48r, 48v, 49r; (4) continuing of composition with l. 132 on 50r.

111 The "a" in "almightys" may be a cap.

114, 95 First dash may be intended as a period.

{see
97 They never can [?expect] to {[?] whose
{ minds
{[?spir]
From ~~infancy neglect his [?starve~~]
~~Whose bodie~~ toil
Neglect has [?starved] whose bodies [?told]
[?hath crush]
~~Oh who shall count the mighty host to whom~~
to whom
Oh who shall count that mighty host
of Men
100 ~~To who[?m] kind Nature therefore~~ cannot shew
~~Her love~~
has not power to give
[100] Impartial Nature ~~cannot shew~~
101 Proof of that sacred love she feels for all

[49^v]

IX, [100] To whom kind Nature therefore cannot give
101 Proof of that sacred love she feels for all
100 ~~To whom kind Nature cannot shew her love~~.
This truth is obvious
114 ~~What truth more plain~~ than that our
[?^] life is turnd
is made
115 Out of its course—wherever man [?~~becomes~~]
116 An offering or a sacrifice—a tool
{ng
117 Or implement—a passive thi{g employed
118 As a brute mean without acknowledgement
119 Of common right or interest in the end
120 Used or abused as selfishness may
for} prompt
121 Say what can follow [?]} a rational soul
122 perverted thus but weakness in all
good
123 And strength in evil—hence an
after call
124 For chastisement & custody & bonds
125 And oftimes Death Avenger of the past
126 And the sole Guardian in whose
hands we dare

97/100 Although the rough drafting here would initially seem to suggest that this passage is earlier than the copy on 48^r, all the other evidence (including the rev of ll. [100]–101 at page foot) indicates that lines on 49^r, and the following two pages, are redrafting.

[100]–101 Rev at top of 49^v.

Cf. MS. 75, D1^r.

[100]–101 Rev of 49^r.

100–129 See first note to 49^r.

114/115 Queried caret probably indicates insertion of rev above l. 114. Less likely, it is a rev (perhaps "or") to l. 115.

121 Overwriting may be a reinforcement.

127 Entrust the future—not for these sad
issues
128 Was man created but to obey the law
And
129 Of life and hope & action. ~~Yet~~ tis known

[50r]

IX, 130 That when we stand upon our native [?~~sold~~]
soil
131 Unelbowed by such objects as oppress
132 Our active powers those powers themselves
become
133 Subversive[?] of our noxious qualities
135 And by the substitution of delght
136 And by new inf[?luence] of strength suppress
whence
[136] All evil—~~the[?r]~~ the Being spreads abroad
137 His branches to the wind & all who see
138 Bless him rejoicing in his neighbourhood.
There is one only liberty tis his:
Who by beneficen[?e] is circumscribed
Tis his to whom the power of doing good
Is law & statute penalty & bond
His prison & his warder his who finds
His freedom in the joy of virtuous thoughts

141 Then sorrow for the many they in whom
142 We look for hea[?lt] from seeds which
have been
[?~~sowd~~]
sown

[50v]

IX, 143 In sickness and for encrease in a power
144 That works but by extinction. On themselves
145 They cannot lean or turn to their own
hearts
146 To know what they must do their wisdom is
147 To look into the eyes of others, thence
148 To be instructed what they must avoid

Cf. MS. 75, D1r.
130–131 Rev of 49r; see first note to 49r.
133 Letters after "Subversive" are perhaps "rs," written in a mistaken attempt to repeat "rsive."
136 What we read as conjectured "influence" may be "influxes."
138/141 Angle bracket probably marks this passage for rev or del.
141 There is possibly a comma after "many."
142 For the fourth word, *1814* reads "health."

Cf. MS. 75, D1v, D2r.

149 Or let us rather say how least observd
150 How with most quiet & most silent
death
151 With the least taint & injury to the air
152 The rich man breathes, their human
form divine
153 And their eternal soul may waste away

~~Imagine not~~
Then do not [?deem] & with those
calmer words
The old Man to the Solitary turned
In all his natural gentleness of [?love]
157 That heretofore when I was urged to
point

[51r]

IX, 158 A most familiar object of our days
159 A little one subjected to the arts
160 Of modern ingenuity & made
161 The senseless member of a vast Machine
162 Serving as doth a spindle or a wheel
163 Think not that pitying him I could
forget
164 The Rustic Boy who walks the field[?s]
untaught
165 The slave of ignorance; but bear in mind
~~at~~
184 ~~Th~~[?is]} That no one takes delight
185 In this oppression none are proud of it
186 It bears no sounding name nor ever bore
187 ~~For~~ A standing grievance an indigenous
vice
188 Of every age, & country under heaven.
spoke cherished
189 I [?~~mourned~~] of evils new & chosen,
[?a blight,]
190 A Bondage lurking under shape of good
191 Arts in themselves beneficent & kind

[51v]

IX, 192 But all too fondly followed & too far
193 Of victims which the merciful can
see

For 51r, cf. MS. 75, D1v, D2r, D2v.
165–184 Ll. 164–184 are entered on 52r–52v.
186 Mark after "name" may be intended as a comma.

194 Nor thin that they are victims; sp[?a]ke
of wrongs
195 Which Women who have children of
their own
196 Regard without compassion yea with praise
197 I spake of mischief which the wise
diffuse
~~wisest~~ spread
more
198 With gladness, thinking that the [~~?~~]
it spreads
199 The healthier the securer we become
More potent to annoy or to defend
A water rising without risk of fall
[?In invincible], true magnificence:
200 Delusion which a moment may destroy
201 Lastly [?mo] I mourned for those
whom I had
202 Corrupted & cast down in favoured [?~~spots~~]
spots
203 Where circumstance & nature had
combined

[52ʳ]

IX, 204 To shelter innocence & cherish love,
205 Who but for this Intrusion would
have lived
206 Possessed of healt & strength &
peace of mind
And all their old hereditary rights
207 Thus would have liv'd or never have
been born
who walks the field [?untaug]
164 The rustic boy [?~~unstudied] & untaught~~
untutored & untaught
Whose [?~~tasks~~]
Sl ve t of
165 ~~The~~ [?] a [?] of ignorance and of [?th] want
166 And miserable hunger. Much too much
On dreary moor beneath the Scottish plain
[?~~have~~]
167 ~~We both~~ of ~~seen of this most wretched lot~~
You in your native country might have seen
168, 169 ~~Which I myself in early childhood shared~~

---

194 For the second word, *1814* reads "think."
197 Base text entry may be "wisest, " then del and rev to "wise."
201 *1814* reads "had seen" at end of line.

Cf. MS. 75, D1ᵛ, D2ʳ, D2ᵛ.
204 An "s" instead of a comma may possibly follow "love."
164–184 Rev and expansion, continuing on 52ᵛ, of 51ʳ.
166/167 Possibly, the line beginning "On dreary moor" has been added as part of the general rev of this section. If so, WW left space for its insertion between ll. 166 and 167.

~~Shared though~~
T{
169 B{~~hough but in mild & merciful degree~~
[168] Of this most wretched lot which I myself
[169] Shared though in mild & merciful de[?]
170 Yet was my mind to hindrances exposed
171 Through which I struggled not without distress
172 And sometimes injury like a sheep enthralled
{Mid
173 {[?In] thorns & brambles, or a bird that breaks
174 Through a strong net & mounts upon the wind
175 Though with her plumes impaired. If they whose Souls
176 Should open while they range the richer fields

[52ᵛ]

how
H[?er] own disgrace & easily re[?moved]

IX, 177 Of merry England are obstructed less
~~a [?cloud]~~]
178 By indigence their ignorance is not less.
· [?Yes oftime to] England [?or her]
[?]
T{
[?]{~~hat overhangs the[?m~~]
{[?Nr]
179 {[?I] less to be deplored. For who can doubt
180 That tens of thousands at this day exist
181 Such as the Boy you painted lineal heirs
182 Of those who once were vassals of the soil
183 Following its fortunes like the beast or trees
184 Which it sustained. But no one takes delight

[53ʳ]

alas!
IX, 208 What differs more ~~alas~~! than Man from
And
209 Whence that difference whence but from himself
Man
210 ~~Yet see~~ the universal Race endowed
for
211 With the same upright form!—the sun is fixed

For 52ᵛ, cf. MS. 75, D2ᵛ.
Rev of 51ʳ, continued from 52ʳ. Another possibility for "removed" is "renounced."

Passage continues from the top of 52ʳ.

212 And the infinite magnificence of heaven
human
213 Within the reach of every^eye
214 The sleepless ocean murmurs for all ears
215 The vernal field infuses fresh delight
216 Into all hearts. Throughout the world of sense
217 Even as an object is sublime or fair
the view
218 That object is laid open to ~~Mans~~
219 Without reserve or veil; and as a power
220 Is salutary or an influence sweet
221 Are each and all enabled to perceive
~~an equal~~
222 That power and influence by impart
ial law
223 Gifts nobler are voutchsafed alike to all
224 Reason, and with that reason smiles
and tears

[53v]

IX, 225 Imagination, freedom in the will
226 Conscience to guide and check; and
death to be
227 Foretasted, immortality presumed.
228 Strange, then, nor less than monstr
ous might be deemd
229 The failure, if the Almighty, to this point
hide
should [?~~hide had~~]
230 Liberal and undistinguishing should [?~~left~~]
~~leave~~
231 ~~The saving charities and moral~~
The excellence of moral qualities
[?~~perception~~]
understanding
232 From common ~~observation~~, leaving truth
~~ordinary~~ [?~~virtue~~]
d
233 And virtue [?&]}ifficult abtruse & dark
234 Hard to be won & only by a few
[?s] ~~here~~
235 ~~Strange he deal~~[?]} ~~this~~ [?]} ~~in with nice~~
~~respect~~
[?nice]
[235] Strange should he deal herein with {[?res]
nice respects

---

218 Del in pencil but rev in ink.
222 Rev in ink but del in pencil.

229/230 Del of "[?hide had]" is in pencil as is the undeleted "hide."The conjectured "had" may be "hid" or "hide."
231 Possibly "qualities" was part of the base text line.
231/232, 232, 233 Del in pencil; rev "ordinary [?virtue]" is also in pencil. Another possibility for "virtue" is "nature."

236 And frustrate all the rest. Believe
it not
237 The primal duties shine aloft like stars
[?~~many~~]
[?~~bountiful~~] save
[?noblest] {~~heal~~ & heal & bless
238 The charities that {[?] ~~soothe & heal~~
s }
239 And [?]}cattered at the feet of man like flowers.

[54^r]

IX, 240 The generous inclination the just rule
241 Kind wishes & good actions & pure thoughts.
242 No mystery is here no special boon
not for
{~~low~~ {low
243 For high &^{[?in] {[?], for proudly graced
244 And not for meek of heart. The smoke
ascends
245 To heaven as lightly from the Cottage hearth
haughty
246 As from the ~~proudest~~ palace. He
whose soul
247 Ponders this true equality may walk
248 The fields of earth with gratitude & hope
249 Yet in that meditation will he find
250 Motive to sadder grief as we have
found
251 Lamenting antient virtues overthrown. X
gladdened [?gladsome]
[?~~A~~]} [?choice]
[?B]} [?~~nd th~~]
254 But let us rather fix our happy thoughts
brighter sene
255 Upon the ~~fairer side~~. How blessed
that pair
256 Of blooming boys whom we beheld even now
{eir
257 Blessed in th{e several & their common
[?by] grievings lot
X sorrows
252 And ~~griefing~~ for the injustice that hath
made
[?division]
253 So wide a difference betwixt Man
& man

---

239 Period may be an additional "s" reinforcing the partially formed "s" in "flowers."

241 Mark at end of line is possibly intended as a dash.
243 Possibly the undeleted "low" is a reinforcement.
251 The X on the right signals the inclusion of ll. 252–253 below, also marked with an X.
251/254 Queried interlinear rev at left may be a first attempt at added ll. 252–253 below; "gladdened" is in pencil.
257/252 Phrase "[?by] grievings" is in pencil.

[54v]

IX, 258 A few short hours of each returning day
259 The thriving Prisoners of their village school
[?to]
260, 261 And then let loose to range the grassy lawn[?s]
In vacancy {[?to] [?for] seek their chearfu
262 To breathe & to be happy

pleasant
~~chearful~~
260 And thence let loose to seek their ~~several~~ homes
261 Or range the grassy lawns in vacancy
[262] To breathe & to be happy, run & shout
263 Idle but no delay no harm no loss
all the genial power heaven & earth
To Through
265 ~~For~~ every season of the changeful year
266 Obsequiously doth take upon itself
turn
em {in turn
267 To labour for th{[?eir] bringing each {in [?~~turn~~]
knowledge health
268 Its tribute of enjoyment ~~health or str~~ength
health
269 Beauty or strength, such privilege is theirs
270 Granted alike to both. And when they part
[?Courts]
~~One haply summoned to the groves of law~~
[?~~or is in~~]
272 I grieve not (to the Pastor here he turned)
273 Much as I glory in that of yours
274 Repine not for the fair faced peasant lad
His lowly [?C]

[55r]

in this begining [?~~their~~] of their
IX, 270 Granted ~~alike~~ in this ~~present~~ course
alike in the outset of their race
271 To both, & if hereafter they must part

Rev on 55r.
259/260, 261 First stroke of a letter, possibly an "s," follows "[?to]."
265 Del and rev ("To Through') are in pencil.
267–268 Overwriting "in turn" is in pencil, probably clarifying the phrase, which is surrounded by messy rev.
270–274 Rev on 55r.
270/272 Rev above "groves" may be "bars." Rev below "haply" may be false start of a line. First word appears to overwrite the curl of the "I" in l. 272.

Rev of 54v.

272 I grieve not to the Pastor here he turn)
273 Much as I glory in that Child of yours
274 Repine not for the fair faced
Boy
{C peasant lad
275 His lowly {comrade—destined here
perhaps
calm obscurity
277, 278 To live & die in humble innocence

---

269 such ~~privilege [?] is~~ their[?s]
[270] Granted, ~~in this beginning of their~~ course,
[271] To ~~Both [?in] equal [?measure~~] dealt
with eaqual ~~dea~~lt
privilege
~~In this beginning of lifes [?Cours~~]
[270] Granted in the [?beggin] of their Course
[271] To both
calm obscurity
[277, 278] To live and and die in humble innocence

[55v]

IX, 292 Oh for that happy period, [?] ages past
Not unforseen or unprepared, though Heaven
Royal Youth
A ~~Youthful Prince~~ removing from his Throne
Before his Souls dear purpose was fulfilled
Did to this Land's unworthiness refuse
P
The [?pr]}retious boon!—oh that the ~~this~~
T [?time] were [?come]
294 [?S]}oo long deferred—when this Enlighten d
Shall Realm
298 [?T]o all} bind herself by statute to accord
299 To all the Children of her soil—at least
Shall place within the easy reach of all
{[?L]
300, 302 The Rudiments of {learning so that none
303 However needy poor or destitute
{dge the
305, 306 Shall be compelled to dru{ge without aid
n
307 Of i[?ll]}tellectual implements and tools,
~~[?] to [?]~~ ~~are born~~
~~As tens of thousands now are forced to~~ do,

---

269 Query after "privilege" may be a copying error, perhaps an extra "ege."
[271] Conjectured "in" may be "an."
Ll. 277–292 are entered on 56v, 57r, 119v.

Rev on 56r–56v, 119v–120r.
292 Single vertical stroke before "ages" is del.

308 A savage horde among the civilized
309 A servile Band among the lordly free.
310 This right as sacred almost as the
live right
311 To breathe & be supplied with sustenance

[56r]

IX, 312 The Infant lisping on the [?knee asserts]
313, 314 To be Invested in his innocence
{y
315, 317 And the rude Lad who knits his angr{[?ed]
brow
318 And lifts his untaught hand on mis
chief bent
declares his due
320, 321 By process indirect ~~makes known~~ his
[?~~dues~~]
~~Pref~~ers Prefers
321 [?~~Asserts~~] his claim while he makes
known his
331 ~~Grant [?it]~~ - need.

O} ages
292 oh} for that happy period—centuries past
n}
Not unforeseen [?or] }or unprepared—but Heaven
~~T~~} A Prince
[?S]}~~he~~ saintly Youth removing from his Throne
the
Before [?~~the~~]}
[?Did to] [?]} [?his]} cherished purpose was
fulfilled
Did to this Land's unworthiness refuse
[292] The pretious boon—o that the time were
Oh for the ~~time~~ day come
294 ~~Too long deferred~~ when this enlighten'd
Realm
295 While she exacts allegiance shall admit
296 An obligation on her part to teach
her
297 Them who are born to serve and obey
secure
298 Binding herself by statute to ~~accord~~
a}
299 To all—[?f]}t least place within reach
of all
300, 302 The Rudiments of Learning [?s]o that none
303 ~~Howev~~

312–321 Rev on 56v, 120r–120v.
321 A lighter vertical stroke may be intended to form an exclam above the period.
292–303 Rev of 55v; rev on 119v, 120r.

[56^v]

labour
IX, 306 Shall be compelled to drudge without
the aid
307 Of intellectual implements & tools
308 A savage Horde among the civilized
309 A servile Band among the lordly free.
310 This right as sacred almost as the right
[?~~breathe~~] exist
311 To live & be supplied with susten[?a]nce
312 And means of life. the lisping Babe [?announce]
313, 314 To be invested in his innocence
315, 317 And the Rude Lad who knits his angry
check'd brow
318 And lifts his untaught hand on mischief
bent
320, 321 By process indirect declares his due
321 His claim prefers while he makes
known his need.

destined here perchance
277, 278 To live & and die in calm obscurity
At least whatever
280 ~~Th[?is], whatsoever~~ fate the noon of life
Both
281 Reserves for either this is sure that ~~they~~
282 have been permitted to enjoy the dawn
jocund
283 Whether regarded as a ~~careless~~ time

[57^r]

IX, 284 That in itself may terminate, or lead
285 In course of nature to a sober eve.
Bo
286 [?For]th have been fairly dealt with—
ng
looki g back
287 They will allow that justice has to them
288 Been shown alike to body & to [?mind]

[?haply] not
Distant ~~& not [?perhaps~~] to be [?attained]
Without [?] unthought of [?now]
And [?intervention] of tempestuous [?hours].

306–321 Rev of 56^r, 55^v; rev on 120^r–120^v.
277–283 Rev of 55^r; rev on 119^v.

Rev on 119^v.

Draft below rule may have been intended as a possibility following l. 283 on 56^v or, less likely, as part of rev of VI, 828, on 58^v.

In the penultimate line, queried word after "Without" may be "vicissitudes" but possibly miswritten "vicissut[?i]es." Other possibilities are "necessities" and "occupation." In the last line, another possible reading for "intervention" is "interaction" and for "hours" is "times."

[57[v]]

sacred
VI, 807 That little flower clad mound ~~of holy~~ earth
808 Lies guarded by its neighbour
[?]
[807] Even so—said he, that little mound of earth

[825] in grove or field
[825] Or by some chearful brook a spot of earth
sent
[825, 826] However [?present] could that spot pre [?]
[826] An~~d~~ image to his fancy of the pangs
Wh[?ich] since ~~the birth of man it hath~~ been
doomed
[827] ~~To witness could it render back~~ an echo
825 ~~could earth present~~
828 Of the sad steps by which hath been trod

in grove or field
some
or ~~by~~ by ~~the~~ chearful brook
[825] 1 [?a] spot of earth
825, 826 However [?pre easant] and could the same present
826 An image to his fancy of the pangs
since the birth of man it hath been
doomed
827 Which ~~it hath witness d~~
[?]
[827] To witness could it render back [?and] [?]

[58[r]]

sunny bank
VI, 805 *As on a ~~green hill slope~~ a tender lamb*
806 *Lurks in safe shelter from the winds of March*
so, methinks
807 *Screen'd by its nursing parent;—in such sort*
Even in ~~such sort~~ that little mound of earth
Even so, methinks that little hillock lies
Lies guarded [?of] [?flower clad] of holy earth
808 *Protected by its neighbour:—the small heap*
809 *Speaks for itself—an Infant there doth rest*

Rev of 58[r], 59[r]. Cf. MS. 75, B1[r]–B1[v].

[807] Two indecipherable marks above "said" may be random or entered earlier than the line.

Drafts related to ll. 825–828 appear to have begun with l. 825 ("could earth present"), del and partly overwritten by l. [827]), followed by copy at page foot (ll. [825]–[827]), and concluding at upper part of page (ll. [825]–828). Another attempt at rev of ll. 828ff. is entered on 58[v].

[825, 826] In the line beginning "However," queried "present" is possibly a miscopy for "pleasant"; cf. l. 825, 826, below, and l. 825 on 58[r].

In the last line, what we read as "and" may be "or" followed by a "d."

Continued from 105[v]; rev on 57[v]. Base text is in hand of DW. Cf. MS. 75, B1[r]–B1[v].

808 The "[?of]" above the line may have been entered first, possibly intended to begin the phrase "of holy earth" entered to the right.

810 The sheltering Hillock is the Mothers grave
~~The Mother at its side in fearless peace~~
If m[?a] discourse and manners that conferr'd
811 *~~If natural manners & discourse that gave~~*
natural [-?-] on
812 *A ~~genuine~~ dignity ~~to~~ ^ lowest rank*
813 *If gladsome spirits & benignant looks*
814 *That for a face not beautiful did more*
815 *Than beauty for the fairest face can do,*
816 *And if religious tenderness of heart,*
817 *Grieving for sin, & penitential tears*
818 *Shed when the clouds had gather'd*
ain
& dist[?urb]} 'd
819 *The spotless Ether of a maiden life*
820 *If these may make a hallow'd spot of earth*
821 *More holy in the sight of God or Man*
[?hum]
822 *~~Then on this grave humble grave upon~~*
Then on that mold *~~that pair~~*
[822] *~~Of humble graves~~, a sanctity shall brood*
823 *Till the stars sicken at the day of doom*
824 *Ah what a warning for a thoughtless*
man
Where'er he might be found could earth present
825 *Could any pleasant field or grove of earth*

[58v]

bright [?honour]
whose [?triumph has]
[?and often times]
[?Here recently its circuit]
in war or peace
[?its circuit hath]
Through {[?~~we~~]
[?As time flows on] {[?] [?like it not]
Through all the various cruelties of man
VI, 828 By night or day its [?circuits] hath been
[?trod]

[828] it hath been trod
In time's long course producing war, or peace,
Sorrows of nature and the pangs of guilt
men [?men]
~~And all the cruelties of man to~~ Man

Probable sequence of entry on 58v is as follows: (1) ll. 829, 833–834, 851–855, and 849–850 were entered in scattered groups down most of the page; (2) unnumbered lines shown at the top of the page and l. 828, all in pencil, were entered from the top to the middle of the page in spaces left by entry of the first sequence; (3) l. [828] and following unnumbered lines were entered at the top of the page in spaces left between penciled lines of the second sequence. For clearer presentation, we have grouped related lines of these three sequences in our transcriptions.

Another attempt at rev of ll. 825–828 is on 57v; possibly lines drafted on 57r are related.

And all the strange [?vicissitudes] of things.

men to me
829 There by her innocent

833 the thickening sward reports
834 Of the fresh shower

851 An oak distinguished by that festive use
852 Time out of mind since first our Peasant met
{M
853 At sunrise and gave welcome to the {may
854 By dances round its [?trunk]—and if the sky
855 Permit

a spreading Oak
849 ~~In single~~e state
~~An antient flourishing, [?unbrageous] oak~~
850 Stands in

[59[r]]

VI, 826 *Shew to his eye an image of the pangs*
827 *Which it hath witnessed render back in echo*
{th
828 *Of the sad steps by which it ha{s been trod*
There said the Priest & pointed as he spake
ie}
829 *There by her innocent baby}s precious grave*
830 *Yea doubtless on the turf that roofs her own*
831 *The Mother oft was seen to stand, or kneel*
g}
832 *In the broad day a weeping Mad}alene*
833 *Now she is not the* <u>*swelling*</u> *turf reports*
834 *Of the fresh shower but of poor Emma's tears*
i}
835 *Is silent nor is any vesta}ge left*
836 *Upon the pathways of her mournful tread*
837 *Nor of that pace with which she once had moved*
838 *In virgin fearlessness a step that seem'd*
839 *Caught from the pressure of elastic turf*
840 *Upon the* mountains wet with morning dew
841 In the prime hour of sweetest scents and airs.
842 Serious and thoughtful was her mind, and yet,
843 By reconcilement exquisite and rare,
of this Cottage Girl
{The t} t} {~~of~~
844 {[?Her] form, }~~her~~ port, }~~her~~ motions, {all ~~were such~~

851–855 Rev of 59[v]; rev on 59[v].

Continues from 58[r]; rev on 60[v], 58[v], 59[v].

828/829, 829 A faint mark below "e" in "grave" (l. 829) may be intended as a comma, possibly intended after rev "spake" in l. 828/829.

833 Underlining is in different ink, one similar to that used for rev on 58[v].

might
845 Were such as would have quicken'd and inspired
846 A Titians hand address'd to picture forth
847 Oread or Dryad glancing through the shade
en first
848 What ~~time~~ the Hunters startling Horn is heard
849 Upon the golden Hills . .—A
called
850 Stands in our Valley, ~~named~~ The joyful
Tree

[59v]

gloomy depth
beneath its ~~ample~~ gloom [?profound]
VI, 856 Of leafless boughs twinkling with frosty star
[?i] acceptable light
Oer, l ver d it oer with ~~cold & [?piercing] lig~~ht
857 From the clear moon

punctual
In ~~annual~~ celebration too [?converge]
dawn and
853 At ~~sunrise~~ [?~~and] give~~ welcome to the May
854 With danc[?es] round

beneath its gloomy depth
[856] Of leafless boughs twinkling with frosty stars
Or silver d oer with acceptable light
[857] From the clear moon. The Queen &c

~~Or when the ground is chequer d by~~
on
Or [?] the chequered [?what] ground what time
the tree
Is silver d oer with acceptable light
[857] From the clear moon.

Or on the shadowy checkered [?mossy] [?g]round
is
Th[?at] revelry proceed what time the tree

beneath its gloomy depth
[856] of leafless boughs twinking with frosty stars
Or on shadow moss [?is]
[?] the ~~shadow-~~^chequered floor of moss[?y] turf [?or]

Leaf 59v is rev of 59r, 60r, 58v, 60v.

The grouping of lines at the top of the page (ll. 856–857) is in pencil; those lines are partially overwritten by the next grouping, in ink.

856/857 Second word seems clearly to be intended as "silver'd"; possibly what appears to be a comma after "O'er" may have been meant to serve as an "s."

[856]/[857] In the base text line eleven lines from page foot, overwriting "Or on" may be a reinforcement.

The revelry proceeds, what time the tree
Is siver d oer with aceptable light
~~By~~ From
[857] ~~From~~ the clear moon ⊗

851 Time out of mind distinguished by that name
of
852 From festive usage—[?fo] our shepherd[?s] [?meet]
At sunrise & give
{ ~~At~~
[853] {[?On] ~~sunrise and give~~ welcome to the May
[851] An oak distinguished by that festive [?]
[852] From dateless usage which our Peasan[?s] hold
In annual celebration met to give,
[853] At sunrise, welcome to

[60r]

⊗ oak
VI, 851 An ~~Elm~~ distinguished by that festive name
dateless
852 From ~~antient~~ usage which our Peasants hold
{ing
Assembl{ed there greet the
853 ~~Of giving welcome~~ to the first of May
Of giving welcome
854 By dances round its trunk:—and if the sky
855 Permits, like honours, dance and song, are paid
856 To the twefth night ~~beneath the frosty stars~~
857 Or the clear Moon. The Queen of these gay sports
858 If not in beauty yet in spritely air
Ellen A[?]
859 Was ~~Emma~~ Dalton; no one touchd the ground
860 So deftly, and the nicest Maiden's locks
861 Less gracefully were braided; but this praise
862 Methinks would better suit another place.
863 She lov'd, and fondly deem'd herself belov'd.
864 The rooad is dim; the current unperceived
865 The weakness painful and most pitiful
{W
866 By which a vurtuous {woman in pure youth
867 May be delivered to distress and shame.
868 Such fate was hers: the last time Emma danc'd
{J
869 Among her equals round the {joyful Tree
870 She bore a secret burthen, and full soon
871 Was left to tremble for a breaking vow
872 Then to bewail a sternly-broken vow

851ff. Mark in the upper-right margin signals inclusion of rev and is also entered at top of 60r. Another rev is on 58v. Rev on 60r is adopted in *1814*.

[851] Queried mark following "festive" may be a dash.

Rev on 60v, 58v, 59v.

856 Reading "beneath the frosty stars" is restored in *1814*.

859 Change in name may be to "Arland" or "Arbant" or "Arbunt" or "Arbout."

873 Alone, within her widow'd Mother's house.
874 It was the season sweet of budding leaves
875 Of days advancing tow'rds their utmost length
{M
876 And small birds singing to their happy {mates.

[60v]

VI, 849 a spreading Oak
850 Stands in our valley—called the <u>Joyful</u> <u>Tree</u>
851 Time out of mind distinguished by that name

---

879 [?and I speak] is } {n
For, from each nook of th[?at]} sequester'd gle{[?~~ns~~]
Maiden and Youth, by annual custom, meet
853 At sunrise, and give welcome to the May
854 By dances round its trunk: and if the sky
855 Permit, like honours, dance & song are paid
856 To the <u>Twelfth</u> <u>Night</u>, beneath its gloomy depth
[856] Of leafless boughs twinkling with frosty stars
Or on the shadow-chequered floor of moss
887 voiceless in the
The revelry proceeds what time the Tree
{Is
{The silver'd oer with acceptable light
857 From the clear Moon.
852 Our Peasantry

humble {Cr
899 hear him hunbly gifted {[?g]eature
900 One of Gods simple children that yet know not
901 The universal parent—how aloft
i}{ g[?s] {[?adily]
[901] On the bare tw }{[?ig] perch d [?ste{d ?], he sings

[?~~branch boug~~]
[?bough]
Openly perched upon the [?~~boughs~~] bare twig

[61r]

VI, 877 Wild is the music of the Autumnal wind
878 Among the faded woods; but these blithe notes
879 Strike the deserted to the heart; I speak
880 Of what I know and what we feel within.

Rev of 59r, 60r, 61r; rev on 58v, 59v.
849–857 This passage, in ink similar to that of copy on rectos, may have been first rev of 59r and 60r, and subsequently rev on 58v, 59v.
851 Conjectured rev below the rule may have been entered first as an attempted rev to 61r, l. 879.
852 "Our Peasantry" appears to be written with different ink and pen than the line above.

Rev on 60v.
880 Punct may be a colon instead of a period.

881 Beside the Cottage in which Emma dwelt
882 Stands a tall ashtree, to whose topmost twig
chaunts
883 A Thrush resorts and annually ~~sings~~,
884 At morn or evening, from that naked perch
885 While all the undergrove is thick with leaves
886 A time-beguiling ditty for delight
887 Of his fond partner, silent in the nest.
888 Ah why, said Emma, sighing to herself,
889 Why do not words, and kiss, and solemn pledge
ever which is
890 And Nature ~~which [?is~~] kind in woman's breast
891 And reason that in man is wise and good
892 And fear of him who is a righteous judge
893 Why do not these prevail for human life
894 To keep two hearts together that began
895 Their spring-time with one love, and that have
need
896 Of mutual pity, and forgiveness, sweet
{,
897 To grant or to receive{?—while that poor Bird
who
898 O come and hear him Thou ~~that~~ hast to me
899 Been faithless, hear him though a lowly Creature
900 One of Gods simple Children that yet know
not
901 The universal Parent, how he sings 100
902 As if he wishd, the firmament of heaven

[61v]

VI, 916 How thankful for the warmth of summer days

[917] ♓ And their long twilight friendly to that stealth
[918] With which she slipp'd into the Cottage barn
919 And found a secret oratory there
garden
{garden
[920] Or in the {orchard pored upon her book
917 ~~And thus protracted twilight to that Stealth~~
918 ~~Friendly, when from the dwelling house she slipp'd~~
920 ~~And in the orchard pored upon her book~~

[918] ~~With which she to the Cottage-barn retired~~
[920] ~~Or in the orchard pored upon her book~~

---

881 "Beside" may be "Besides."
896 Punct after "forgiveness" may be a semicolon or colon.
897 Possibly the question mark overwrites the comma.
901 Line count at right includes the base text recto copy beginning on 58r.

Rev of 62r. Passage begins one-third of the way down the page.
917 Symbol signals rev to be inserted on facing 62r at l. 917/920.

[62[r]]

VI, 903 Should listen, and give back to him the voice
904 Of his triumphant constancy and love,
905 The proclamation {that / [?which]} he makes, how far
906 His darkness doth trascend our fickle light.
907 Such was the tender passage, not by me
908 Repeated without loss of simple phrase
909 Which I perus'd even as the words had been
910 Committed by forsaken Emma's hand
911 To the blank margin of a valentine
912 Bedropp'd with tears.—Twill please you to be told
913 That studiously withdrawing from the eye
914 Of all conpanionship, the Sufferer yet
915 In lonely reading found a meek resource
916 And she was thankful for the summer days
917 And their long twilight friendly to that stealth
~~And that employment follow'd out of doors~~
920 ~~Or in the~~ {[?~~garden~~] / orchard} ~~pored upon her b~~
921 By the last lingering help of open sky
922 Till the dark night dismiss'd her to her bed.
923 Thus did ~~her~~ ^a waking Fancy sometimes lose
924 The unconquerable pang of despised love.
925 A kindlier passion opened on her soul
926 When that poor child was born. Upon its face
927 She looked {as / [?up]}on a pure & spotless gift
928 Of unexpected promise where a grief
929 Or ~~fear~~ dread was all that had been thought of;—joy

[63[r]]

VI, 930 Far sweeter than bewildered Traveller feels
931 Upon a perilous waste where all night long
932 Through darkness he hath toild and fearful storm
933 When he beholds the first pale speck serene
934 Of day-spring in the gloomy east revealed
935 And greets it with thanksgiving.— "Till this hour
936 Thus in her Mothers hearing Emma spake
937 There was a stony region in my heart
938 But he at whose command the parched barren rock

Leaf 62[r] is rev on 61[v].
917/920 Symbol in left margin signals insertion of rev on 61[v].

Leaf 62[v] is blank.

939 Was smitten and pour'd forth a quenching stream
940 Hath soften'd that obduracy and made
941 Unlooked for gladness in the desart place
942 To save the perishing, and henceforth I look
943 Upon the light in chearfulness, for thee
Infant
944 My Baby, and for that good Mother dear
945 Who bore me & hath pray'd for me in vain,
n ,
946 Yet not in vail, it shall not be in vain."—
Then follow'd other workings; self-reproach
Grief for a human being born to shame
And fatherless and friendless in the world.
949 What need of more? The blameless Infant grew
950 The Child which Emma and her Mother loved
951 They soon were proud of; tended it and nursed
952 A soothing Comforter although forlorn
953 Like a poor Singing-bird from distant lands
954 Or a choice shrub, which he who passes by
vacant
955 With^mind ~~at [?ease~~] not seldom may observe[?d]
956 Fair-flowering in a thinly-peopled House

[63v]

VI, 964 The scanty sum of their united hours.
~~With this regard she shrank not from an~~
[?an act] ~~act~~
She shrank not from a painful sacrifice
And [?trusting]
[964] Of ~~sacrifice~~ but to her mothers care
her
965 Trusting the child for that occasion weaned
From her own breast she chearfully became
[964] Their slender means. By this regard endured
[?The]
~~She shrank n~~ot [?from]

Peculiar to the frame of social life
968 Existing in these simple vales that here
969 The natural feeling of equality
970 Is by domestic service unimpaired
assumes
The Master on his privelege ~~doth build~~
law
No haughtiness the Servant to a ~~tie bond~~
doth
Of [?~~du~~] strict obedience tied, ~~yet~~ in his mind
~~Admits~~ of no abasement.
Acknowledge
The eye is quickened and the mind prepared

Leaf 63v is rev of 64r.

For future cares when they themselves shall rule
In their own houses process not

[64r]

VI, 957 Whose window somewhat sadly adorns.
Throu gh four
958 For ∧ ~~three~~ month's space the Infant drew its food
959 From the maternal breast; then scruples rose
960 Thoughts, which the rich are free from, came &
cross d
961 The sweet affection. She no more can bear
962 By her offense to lay a twofold weight
963 On a kind parent willing to forget
Their slender means. [?And now]
964 How slender are their means. With this regard
She shrunk not from a painful sacrifice
965 And trusting to her Mother's care the Child
For that occasion weaned from her own breast
965, 966 She left her home and chearfully became
966 A Foster-parent in a neighbouring farm.
967 Perchance Ye may not know, for tis I think
968 Peculiar to these simple vales that here
takes not from the mind
970 Domestic service ~~is a state from which~~
969 The natural feeling of equality:
No haughtiness the Master thence derives
The servant no abasement.—Youth and Maid
with
Go forth, constrained or ~~of~~ free choice, and take
The hire of strangers or of nearest kin,
glen
Within their native or some neighbouring ~~Vale~~
Even as may chance. Meanwhile they see and learn
Their eyes are quickend and their minds prepared
For future duties—process not unlike
[?is]
To that of old (if th [?e] rude common wealth
~~Established in the bosom of these vales Hills~~
And its inglorious arts may be compared
To the proud world) when Youths of gentle blood
Nay of the noblest stock were duly sent

Rev on 63v.
960 Commas are heavily reinforced and thus may have been added.
967 Mark above last letter of "Perchance" may be intended as a comma.
969 The account of rural independence (even in domestic service), continued on 65r and rev on 63v, does not appear in *1814*. In the fifth line of this unnumbered passage, the "V" in "Vale" may be intended as lowercase.

[65r]

To undertake the office of a Page
In house of Prelate or exalted Peer
There to be disciplined in goodly thewes.
VI, 971 —Yet though this service be with us removed
972 From sense of degradation, not the less
973 The ungentle Mind can easily find means
974 To impose severe restraints and laws unjust,
975 Which hapless Emma now was doom'd to feel.
976 —In selfish blindness, for I will not say
977 In naked and deliberate cruelty
bound
978 The Pair whose Infant she was ~~doomd~~ to nurse
979 Forbad her all communion with her own.
980 They argued that such meeting would disturb
981 The Mothers mind distract her thoughts, and thus
d
982 Unfit her for her office—in which [?f]read
week
{Week {week {e {enforcd
983 {Day after {day the {[?at] mandate was {renew'd. 200
984 So near!—yet not allowed, upon that sight
{ard
985 To fix her eyes—alas! twas h{[?] to bear
986 But worse affliction must be borne—far worse
is
987 For ~~twas~~ heav'ns will that after a disease
988 Begun and ended within three days space
{Her
989 {The child should die—as Emma now exclaimed
990 Her own deserted Child! Once, only once,
991 She saw it in that mortal malady
burial
992 And on the ~~funeral~~ day could scarcely gain
993 Permission to attend its obsequies.
{H
994 She reach'd the {house, last of the funeral
train

[66r]

VI, 995 And some one, as she entered, having chanced
996 To urge unthinkingly their prompt departure,
997 "Nay," said she with commanding look, a spirit
998 Of anger never seen in her before,
999 "Nay ye must wait my time"!—and down
she sate
1000 And by the unclosed Coffin kept her seat

Leaf 64v is blank.
983 Line count ("200") is continued from 61r, l. 901.

Leaf 65v is blank.

1001 Weeping and looking looking on & weeping
1002 Upon the last sweet slumber of her ~~babe~~ child
1003 Untill at length her soul was satisfied.
1004 —You see the infant's grave—and to this spot
1005 The Mother, oft as she was sent abroad
1006 And whatsoeer the errand, urged her steps:
or
1007 Hither she came, and here she stood, ~~and~~ knelt
g
1008 In the broad day a rueful Mad dalene.
1009 So call her for not only she bewailed
1010 A Mother's loss but mourn'd in bitterness
1011 Her own transgression, penitent sincere
1012 As ever raised to heaven a streaming eye.
1013 —At length the Parents of the Foster Child
1014 Noting that in despite of their commands
1015 She still renew'd and could not but renew
1016 Those visitations, ceased to send her forth
And she remained a prisoner: to the house
1017 Or to the gardens narrow bounds confined.
1018 When this was known by me I did not fail
[1018] To admonish and remind them that
that erred

[66v]

A
~~The~~ anxious hope
The binding duty and the tender care
The confidential life sustaining love
Thus to a Mother slighted and betray'd
The innocent uncons[?c]ous babe had brought,
[?~~From~~]
And ~~fa[?r]~~
Unask'd, and with the giver they were gone

That dear abiding place of tranquil thought
tender
Of binding duties and of ~~anxious~~ cares
VI, 1042, 1043 A hasty summer flood had swept away
1043 And thus [?~~forl~~] deprived her homeless spirit

1002 Inserted line may have been added during the initial stages of composition and included in line count; cf. note to 69r, l. 1073.

Rev of 67r. These lines appear to rev ll. 1039ff., with the lines in the lower grouping having probably been drafted first. The first set of lines appears more than halfway down the page, opposite l. 1032 on 67r. The second passage is opposite l. 1041 on 67r.

[67r]

For   cross d
VI, 1019 ~~That~~ holy Nature might not thus be ~~wrong'd~~
{~~Thus~~
{In wo~~mans~~
1020 Thus wrong'd in Womans breast—in vain I pleaded
1021 But the green stalk of Emma's life was snapp'd
1022 And the flower droop'd; as every eye could see
1023 It hung its head in mortal languishment.
Aided   at length
1024 ^ By this appearance ~~aided~~ I ^ ~~prevailed~~ at length
Prevaild, and from those bonds releas'd she went
1025 ~~And from those bonds releasd the Sufferer went~~
1026 Home to her Mothers House.—The Youth was
~~f[?le]~~
fled
{B
1027 The rash {betrayer could not face the shame
1028 Or sorrow which his senseless guilt had caused,
1029 And little would his presence, or proof given
1030 Of a relenting Soul have now availed
{[?S]
1031 For like a {shadow he was pass'd away
1032 From Emma's thoughts had perished to her mind
1033 For all concerns of fear, or hope, or love,
1034 Save only those which to their common shame
1035 And to his moral being appertained:
1036 Hope from that quarter, would, I know, have brought
th}
1037 A heavenly comfort, [?]}ere she recognized
1038 An unrelaxing bond, a mutual need,
Her fond
1039 There, and as seemed, there only.—~~She had~~
Heart
raised
1040 Her fond maternal Heart had built a nest
{the
1041 In blindness all too near {[?] Rivers edge
sw}
1042 That work a summer flood with hasty [?]}ell
{her
1043 Had swept away, and now {[?br] Spirit longd
1044 For its last flight to heavens security.
1045 The bodily frame was wasted day by day

[68r]

VI, 1046 Meanwhile relinquishing all other cares
1047 Her mind she strictly tutored to find a peace

Rev on 66v.

1020, 1025, 1043 What we read as caps in "Womans," "Sufferer," and "Spirit" may be lowercase.

1036 Comma after "quarter" appears to be eras.

Leaf 67v is blank.

And pleasure in endurance. Much she thought
And much she read; and brooded feelingly
Upon her own unworthiness. To me
As to a spiritual Comforter and Friend
spared no pains
Her heart she opened; and ~~I did not fail~~
no pains were spared
To mitigate as gently as I could
The sting of self-reproach, with healing words.
Meek Saint! through patience glorified
on earth
In whom, as by her lonely hearth she sate,
The ghastly face of cold decay put on
A sun-like beauty, and appeared divine!
May I not mention that within these walls
~~May I not mention that at her desire~~,
At ~~her desire~~
~~Her pious wish, within these holy wa~~lls
In due observance of her pious wish
The Congregation joined with me in prayer
?
For her soul's good ; nor was that office vain.
F
—Much did she suffer: but if any friend
Beholding her condition, at the sight
Gave way to words of pity or complaint,
She stilled them with a prompt reproof, & said
He who afflicts me knows what I can bear
And when I fail and can endure no more
Will mercifully take me to himself.
So through the cloud of death her spirit
passed

[68v]

The pensive silence saying, Blest are the[?y]
Whose sorrow rather is to suffer wrong
Than to do wrong, although themselves have
err'd
[~~?~~]
This tale gives proof that heaven most gently
With such in their affliction. Emma's fate,
Her ~~broken~~ tender spirit and her contrite heart
Bring to my mind dark hi[?nts]

Leaves 68–71 were once separate and loose but, after restoration, are now joined in pairs (68 and 71, 69 and 70). See pp. xxiv–xxv, above.

1062 Possibly the semicolon may be a colon; it may also overwrite the question mark.

Leaf 68v is rev of 69r; rev on 69v. Loose sheet; see note, above, to 68r.

Sequence of composition seems to be the following: (1) ll. 1078, 1079–1080 and ll. 1095ff.; (2) ll. 1090–1094; (3) ll. [1090] ("they are blest")–1093; (4) ll. [1090] ("The pensive silence...")–1096.

1092 Possibly, the queried word below the line began "tran," intended perhaps for "transgressed."

1096 Pen ran dry at the last three letters.

1078, 1079 ~~Two days before when sitting in the shade~~
~~Of those~~
t
1079 Beneath those shady elm[?s] {rees, whe[?n] I heard
1080 The story that retraced the slow decline

they are blest
[1090]
[1091] Whose sorrow rather is to suffer wrong
[1092, 1093] Than to do wrong the tale which we have heard
1093, 1094 Gives proof [?that] heaven deals with such
[1094] In their distress. This hapless Womans fate
we have heard
1093 A tale that proves how gently they are dealt with

blest are they
1090
1091 Whose sorrow rather is to suffer wrong
1092, 1093 Than to do wrong, heaven gently deals with them
;
1094 In ther [?ir] distress{. this hapless Womans fate

1095 Her broken and her contrite nor less
That blisfull~~ness~~ stillness of her patient soul

[69^{r}]

VI, 1071 Into that pure and unknown world of love
;
1072 Where injury cannot come{, and here is laid
I
1073 The mortal Body by her {infants side 29[?2]

1074 The Vicar paused; nor did his Audience fail
To
[1074] {The shew by silence and by ~~downcast looks~~
inmost heart
1075 That each had listened with his ~~downcast looks~~
1076 For me the emotion scarcely was less deep
1077 Or less benign than that which I had felt

1078, 1079 Phrase "two days" on 68^{v} and "Three" in l. 1079 on 69^{r} both conflict with the time scheme established in Book II by MSS. 47 and 71 and present in *1814*, where the Vicar's tale takes place on the fifth day, four days after the Poet met the Wanderer and heard Margaret's tale. Possibly, WW here in MS. 74 had in mind shortening the time span and cutting two days of wandering, described at the start of Book III (before the journey to the Solitary's valley on the fourth day). Such an alteration would give the meeting with Margaret on day one, the meeting with the Solitary on day two, and the meeting with the Pastor on day three; thus, the line "two days before" on 68^{v} would be correct.

1093, 1094 Conjectured "that" is partly blotted.

Rev on 68^{v}, 69^{v}. Loose sheet; see note to 68^{r}.

1073 Line count is continued from 65^{r}, l. 983. If the last numeral is a "2" (less likely, it may be a "1"), the count seemingly includes the added l. 1002 on 66^{r}. Composition appears to have stopped here for a time, at least while the line count was made, before being resumed with a different or a sharpened pen.

~~Within the noontide~~ [?s]
1079 [?T] ~~Three days before, within the noontide shade~~
Beneath the noontide shade,
Then when the grey-haired Pedlar, step by step,
While
Had led} ~~me to re~~
1078, 1079 ~~While we were seated in the noontide shade~~
led me tracing back
1080 Had ~~faithfully retraced~~ the slow decline
1081 Of Margaret sinking on the lonely Heath
1082 With the deserted House in which she dwelt.
{S
1083 I noted that the {solitary's cheek
1084 Confess'd the power of Nature.—Pleas'd
pleas'd though sad
1085 More ~~sad~~ than ~~pl~~ sad the Grey hair'd Pedlar sate;
1086 Thanks to his pure Imaginative mind
1087 Capacious and serene, his blameless life
1088 His knowledge, wisdom, love of truth, and love
1089 Of human kind.—He was it who first broke
1090, 1094 The pensive silence, saying; "Emma's Fate,
1095 Poor erring Maid!—her pain and self-reproach
tender
[1095] Her ~~broken~~ Spirit and her contrite heart
1096 Call to my mind dark hints which I have
heard

[69v]

VI, 1074 The Vicar ceased; nor did his Audience fail
[1074] To shew by silence and by downcast looks
1075 That each had listened with his inmost heart
1076 For me the emotion scarcely was less strong
1077 Or less benign than that which I had felt
near
When seated ~~with~~ my venerable Friend
1078 ~~Two days before, when seated with my Friend~~
1079 Beneath those shady elms from him I heard
1080 The story that retrac'd the slow decline
1081 Of Margaret sinking on the lonely Heath
{H
1082 With the neglected {house in which she dwelt.
1083 I noted that the Solitary's cheek
1084 Confess'd the power of Nature.—Pleas'd, though
sad

1079 Queried "T" may be part of blotted eras or, alternately, a mark signaling insertion of rev on 68v. See note to 68v, l. 1078, 1079.

1079/1078, 1079, 1085 The Wanderer is still called the Pedlar here, possibly indicating that the story of Emma (Ellen) dates from an earlier period than rev of MS. 71 in 1813, where the Pedlar is changed to the Wanderer. This use of "Pedlar" supports the idea that this story was one of the first entered in MS. 74. (Rev on 69v in MS. 74 has Pedlar in l. 1085, but the word is later altered to Wanderer.) See also note to l. 1078, 1079 on 68v for conflict with chronology of MSS. 47 and 71.

Rev of 68v–69r. Loose sheet; see note to 68r.

Wanderer
1085 More pleased than sad the grey-haired ~~Pedlar~~
sate
1086 Thanks to his pure imaginative soul
1087 Capacious and serene, his blameless life
1088 His knowledge, wisdom, love of truth, and love
1089 Of human kind. He was it who first broke
1090 The pensive silence, saying, "Blest are they
1091 Whose sorrow rather is to suffer wrong
1092 Than to do wrong ~~tho~~ although themselves have
erred.
1093 This Tale gives proof that Heaven most gently
deals
1094 With such in their affliction.—Emma's Fate
1095 Her tender spirit and her contrite heart
1096 Call to my mind dark hints which I have heard

[70^r]

VI, 1097 Of one who died within this Vale, by doom
1098 Heavier, as his offense was heavier far.
1099 [?~~Which], Sir, I pray you is the last [?retreat~~]
Where, Sir, I pray you, where ar laid the bones
1100 Of Wilfred Armathwaite.—The Vicar answe[?red]
{that Priest replied
1101 In {[?gre] green nook close by the churchward wall
{yon
1102 Beneath {[?that] hawthorn planted by myself
1103 In memory and for warning, and in sign
[?~~worst~~] dire
1104 Of sweetness where ~~much~~ anguish had been known
1105 Of reconcilement after deep offence
1106 ~~There doth [?la] [?] he lie. [?That Man in this~~]
~~our vale~~
~~valley was his~~
[?~~native~~]
[?~~la~~]
In this his native
[1106] There doth he lie. ~~This was~~ his native vale
~~Was~~
He ownd & tilled land
1107 ~~And~~ here he ownd a little plot of ~~land~~ ~~gr[?o]~~

1085 See last note to 69^r.
1088–1092 Right margin line may be random or a mark for rev; *1814* reads as here.

Loose sheet; see note to 68^r.
1100 Conjectured letters are blotted.
1101–1154 The tale of Wilfred Armathwaite, continuing on 70^v–71^r, draws on *Home at Grasmere* MS. B, ll. 469–532. Some of the rev to this story in MS. B, leaves 22^r–24^r (especially on 21^v and 22^v), possibly dates from about the same time as MS. 74 (see *H at G*, pp. 323–333) and shows in MS. B rev toward including the tale in *Exc.*
1106 Party del by eras; "[?la] [?]" was first del in ink.
[1106]/1107 Single word "Was," beginning the line meant to follow l. 1106, is partly del by eras. Other del and rev here are in pencil.

A man of grave deportment and discourse
Placid in countenance, studious and reserved
on[?e]
Yet know beyond his neighbourhood as ~~a Friend~~
To whom the need and distress'd might turn
Nor fear repulse. A Tiller of the soil
And Shepherd, healthy in his bodily frame
And
1108 He with his Consort and his Children saw
1109 Days that were seldom crossed by petty strife
1110 Years safe from large misfortune; long maintaind
1111 That course which men the wisest & most pure
entire
1112 Might look on with [?~~entire~~] complacency. ~~And yet~~
Yet in
1113 ~~Within~~ ^ himself and near him there were faults
y state
1114 At work to undermine his happ~~iness~~
1115 By little and by little. Active, prompt

[70v]

VI, 1116 And lively was the Housewife; in the vale
1117 None more industrious, but her industry
1118 Ill judg'd full oft and specious tended more
1119 To splendid neatness, to a shewy, trim,
1120 And overlaboured purity of House
1121 Than to substantial thrift. He, on his part,
1122 Generous and easy-minded was not free
{ lapse
1123 From carelessness, and thus, in {[?course] of time
1124 These joint infirmities induced decay
1125 Of worldly substance and distress of mind
That
1126 ~~Which~~ to a thoughtful Man was hard to shun
1127 And which he could not cure. A blooming Girl
house.
[?~~and~~] } {D
in their [?house} he] {[?d]isquieted in mind,
1128 Serv'd ~~them; an Inmate of the House —Alas~~!
And poor in tranquil now
1130 ~~Poor now in tranquil pleas~~ure, ~~he~~ gave way
Poor now in tranquil pleasure
1131 To thoughts of troubled pleasure; he became
1132 A lawless Suitor to the Maid and she
1133 Yielded unworthily. Unhappy Man
1134 That which he had been weak enough to do

1107/1108 Del in pencil; the ink line in margin signals intended rev or del of passage.
1112 Pencil rev; the last two words are del in pencil.
1113 Del, caret, and rev are in pencil.
1114 Pencil del; rev "y," which is in pencil, appears to be overwritten in ink.

Loose sheet; see note to 68r.
1126 Pencil del and rev.

1135 Was misery in remembrance; he was stung
1136 Stung by his inward thoughts and by the smiles
1137 Of Wife and Children stung to agony.
His temper urg'd him not to seek relief
Amid the noise of Revellers nor from draughts
Of lonely stupefaction, he himself
ir a blooming Girl
[1128] Serv'd in the{ House a Favourite whom he oft
[?~~mien~~]
~~Both for her [?Com]liness & modest grace~~
[?blush]
Had noticed heretofore with innocent pride
And commendation undisguised but now
[1130] Made poor in tr

[71^{r}]

A rational ~~and~~ suffering Man, himself
Was his ~~own~~ world without a resting place
VI, 1138 Wretched at home he gained no peace abroad
1139 Ranged through the mountains, slept upon the earth
1140 Ask'd comfort of the open air, and found
1141 No quiet in the darkness of the night
1142 No pleasure in the beauty of the day.
1143 His flock he slighted: his paternal fields
1144 Became a clog to him whose spirit wished
1145 To fly, but whither?—And this gracious Church
wears
1146 That ~~has~~ a look so full of peace and hope
1147 And love, benignant Mother of the Vale,
1148 How fair amid her brood of Cottages!
1149 She was to him a sickness and reproach.
1150 Much to the last remained unknown—but this
1151 Is sure, that through remorse and grief he died
1152 Though pitied among men, absolved by God,
1153 He could not find forgiveness in himself;
1154 He could not bear the weight of his own shame.

1155 There rests a Mother; but from her I turn
1156 And from her grave.—Look yonder! halfway up

1137/[1128] Line in the right margin probably indicates intended rev or del of these lines, which are continued on 71^{r} before the later decision to cut them is confirmed by cancellation lines.

[1128] Line below, including rev "[?mien]," is del in pencil; conjectured "blush," below, is also in pencil.

Rev on 85^{v}. Loose sheet; see note to 68^{r}.

Angle brace at top in left margin indicates intended rev or del of these lines before the decision to cancel is confirmed by the cross-out.

1152 First comma is either reinforced or a false start of a letter, possibly an "s," which is superseded by a comma. Second comma, possibly an accidental mark, is in pencil.

1155–1232 The story of The Widower with Six Daughters, continuing on 71^{v}–73^{r}, draws on *Home at Grasmere* MS. B, ll. 533–606. Some of the rev to this story in MS. B, leaves 23^{v}–27^{r} (especially on 23^{v}, 24^{v}, and 26^{v}), possibly dates from about the same time as MS. 74 (see *H at G*, pp. 330–343) and shows in MS. B rev toward including the tale in *Exc.*

1156, 1157 That ridge, which elbowing from the mountain side
1158, 1159 Carries into the plain its rocks & woods
[?hither] she was brought
stands { [?rein]
1159 ~~Behold~~ the Cottage^whe{[?re] ~~she dwelt, where~~ now
1160 ~~Her Husband dwells in widowhood, whom she left~~
1161 Eight winters past and where he now abides
[1161] Who then was left the solitary prop

[71ᵛ]

VI, 1161 ~~Full eight years past, the solitary prop~~
{in
1162 Of many helpless children. I beg{an
1163 With words which might be prelude to tale
heart-depressing sorrow
1164 Of ~~sorrow and dejection~~, but I feel,
Though in the midst of sadness as might seem
{,
1165 No sadness{ when I think of what mine eyes
1166 See daily in that happy family
the pensive
1167 Bright garland form they for ~~their Fathers~~ brow,
[?u] respected
1168 Of their [?~~delighted~~] Father's widowhood
undrooping
1169 Those six fair Daughters, budding yet, not one,
{f
1170 Not one of all the band a full-blown {Flower.
Conspicuous evidence this Household yields
~~Go to the Dwelling: their she shall have proof~~
1174 That He who takes away yet takes not half
1175 Of what he seems to take, or gives it back
1176 Not to our prayer, but far beyond our prayer;
1177 He gives it the boon produce of a soil
1178, 1179 Which our endeavours have not tilled, and Hope
{H
1179 ~~Which Hope~~ {hath never watered:—Ye will see
shall
1179, 1181 A House, which, at small distance ~~will~~ appear
risen above
1182 In no distinction to have passed beyond

1161–[1161] Rev of 71ᵛ.

Rev on 85ᵛ–86ᵛ. Loose sheet; see note to 68ʳ.

1161 Rev at page foot on 71ʳ; *1814* restores the original reading.

1167/1168 Rev "respected" is in pencil; the conjectured "u" may have been the first attempt to write "undrooping," since it is in similar ink.

1176 Possibly only a comma is intended at the end, and the point of what we read as a semicolon is a random mark.

1178, 1179, 1179 Rev may be meant to be followed by rev to 72ʳ, l. 1204 ("verily Tis a spot"). Rev to line below l. 1204 on 72ʳ may be toward the *1814* reading of l. 1179.

1179–1188 Three-line draft at page foot probably was meant at one stage to replace the end of l. 1179, "Ye will see," and possibly is an attempt to replace the entire canceled passage with the rev on 72ʳ, ll. 1204ff. The passage is restored and rev on 86ʳ and 86ᵛ. Original lines on 72ʳ, l. 1204, "thither go [?turn]," are later used on 86ʳ toward new draft of ll. 1179–1182.

1179, 1181 In this line (beginning "A House"), del and rev are in pencil.

1184 Its fellows, will appear like them to have grown
1185 Out of the native Rock but nearer view
Will shew it not so grave in outward [?mien]
And soberly array'd, as for the most
Are these rude Mountain-dwellings, Nature's care
1186, 1187 Mere friendless Nature's, but a studious work
~~guiding~~ prompting
1188 Of many fancies ~~and of~~ ^ many hands
[?Go]

I believe
The sight [?of the Recess would]
[?please]

[72^r]

A Plaything and a pride, for such the air
And aspect which the little spot maintains
Even in the midst of winter's nakedness.
They have their woodbine resting on the porch
VI, 1192 Their rose-trees strong in health that will be soon
wild pink crowns the garden wall
1193 Roof-high; the garden wall is crown topped
1194 With intermingled stones a shewy pile
Curious for shape or hue, some round like balls
Worn smooth and round by fretting of the brook
1195 From which they have been gather'd, others bright
[1195] And sparry, the rough scatterings of the Hills.
[?lasting] that fade not with the year
1196 These ~~latter~~ ornaments ~~the Cottage owes~~
1197 A Hardy Girl continues to provide
1197, 1198 ~~To one a hardy Girl, who mounts the rocks~~
Who mounting fearlessly the rocky heights
1198 ~~Such is her choice; she fears not the bleak wind~~
[?prompt]
Her Fathers [?~~glad~~] attendant
1199 Companion of her father; does for him
Whereer he wanders in his pastoral course
All that a Boy could do
1200 The service of a Boy, and with delight
1201 More keen, and prouder daring; yet hath she
1202 Within the garden like the rest, a bed
1203 For her own flowers, or favorite Herbs, a space
I believe
verily Tis a spot [?turn]
1204 Holden by sacred charter—thither ~~go~~

1188 "[?Go]" below the line may be an attempt to restore the canceled l. 1170/1174, above, or may be related to l. 1204 on 72^r, "thither go." Remaining draft below is in pencil.

Rev on 86^v, 87^r, 88^v.

1193 Rev "topped" is in pencil.

1204ff. Rev is ultimately rejected in favor of later rev on 87^r. The first copy ("thither go [?turn]") forms the basis for ll. 1179–1182 as rev on 86^r. At one point, as the pencil draft at the bottom of 71^v suggests, rev beginning with "I believe" was probably meant to follow l. 1179 on 71^v. Because of its position, rev "verily Tis a spot" is perhaps later; base text, whether or not later, is possibly meant to follow the rev l. 1178, 1179 on 71^v. Rev "[?abode]" may be toward the *1814* reading of the last words of l. 1179, or possibly it is "work" and part of the rev "choicest" two lines

[?a] this [?fine nook]
The sight of which methinks would please you more
~~And the trim outside of this low abode~~
[?abode.]
[?~~pomp~~] ~~stateliest~~
~~Will please you more than sight of lordliest~~ dome
choicest sight mid
Or ~~any natural~~ work of nature [?in] these hills
Embosomed, lake or headlong waterfall,
Whose fame attracts the traveller from afar
~~By such expressive language it declares~~
~~The happyness of state of th[?ose] who dwell~~
~~within~~

[72[v]]

Whose fame attracts the Traveller from a-far
For tis a Volume of Arcadian [?peace]
~~In quest of which the traveller comes from far~~
And unreproved enjoyment to all eyes
~~For tis a little volume to all eyes~~ the sun
. A
Laid open a fair picture [?~~wh~~] [?] mong trees
[?~~The~~] [?e]
VI, 1211 ~~And by a sparkling stream th [?at tunes] its voice~~
The Cottage stands And by a plenteous stream
~~And by a running stream~~ of human peace
[1211] ~~That sparkles [?through] the shade, and~~
1212 To the pure course of human life, which there,
~~And leisure [?comfort] industry and love~~.
1213 Flows on in solitude from year to year
[?~~thr~~] through
1214 But in the darkness of the night—then most
. C
1215 This Dwelling charms me, cover d by the gloom
1216 Then in my walks I often-times stop short
(Who
1217 And could refrain?) and feed by stealth my sight
1218 With prospect of the company within
1219 Laid open through the blazing window,—there
1220 I see the eldest Daughter at her wheel
1221 Spinning amain, as if to overtake
[1222] The never-halting Time or in turn
1222 She knows not what, or teaching in her turn
Teaching
1223 Some ^ ~~little~~ Novice of the Sisterhood

---

below. The last two lines appear to be the first part of a set of rev related to 72[v], possibly intended to lead into the third base text line on 72[r], "Laid open…." The last line is a foot too long; its closing phrase and concept, pointing to those "within" the dwelling, are used later in l. 1218 on 72[v]. Rev "Whose fame" is also entered at the top of 72[v]; possibly, though, this rev is part of the later rev on 88[v].

Rev on 72[r], 86[v]–88[v].

First rev at top of page is also entered as rev to lines at bottom of 72[r]. First two base text lines on 72[v] ("In quest…all eyes") were probably meant to be replaced by rev at page foot; that page foot rev was then canceled and the interlinear revs entered as ll. 1211, [1211], 1212–1213. The opening phrase of the third base text line ("Laid open") is used later in l. 1219.

1211 Vertical mark in right margin probably signals rev at page foot.

t
1224 That skill in this or or|her household work
1225 Which from her Father's honor'd hand, herself
1226 While she was yet a Little-one, had learn'd,
1227 Mild man! he is not gay but they are gay
1228 And the whole House seems filled with gaiety.
~~—Now have ye not received good recompense~~
and by a plenteous stream
in
[1211] That sparkles ~~through~~ the shade, and tunes its voice
[1215, 1211] [?~~That dashes~~] That sparkling [?~~thrids~~] thrids the rocks
and tunes its voice
[?]

[73r]

For that distressful tale which last I told.
These fruits, (so God the poor Man's Friend ordains)
Shall deck the board of Innocence and love.
Where oeconomic wisdom doth not fail
Within doors or without, such the reward
Of conjugal fidelity through life
And partnership when Death has interfered
ha
VI, 1229 Thrice [?then]|ppy then the Mother may be deemed
W
1230 The w|ife who rests beneath that turf, from which
1231 I turn'd, that Ye in mind might witness, where
1232 And how her Spirit yet survives on earth.

left
1233 The next three Ridges—those upon the ~~right~~;
By close
1234 ~~Do, in~~ connection with our present thoughts,
in praise of
me add {in praise
1235 Tempt^ to ~~give~~ {[?as briefly as] I may of humble worth
unobtrusive
1236 Their brief and ~~uneventful~~ history.
~~grassy~~ e may note
1237 One Hillock, ~~you observe~~, is ~~low~~ small & low
down
1238 Sunk almost to [?] a level with the ~~earth~~ plain
undepress'd
{s
1239 By weight of time, the other{ ~~Ridges~~ both
{.
1240 Are bold and swelling{,—There a Husband sleeps,

The queried and blotted mark at page foot may indicate rev on 87v–88r.

Rev on 87v. Ll. [1246]–1247 at page foot are probably rev of drafts on 73v.

Angle brace at top in left margin probably signals exclusion of these lines prior to the more extensive vertical cancellation mark, which seems related to recopying the passage on 87v.

1235 What we read as a caret may be a comma, del.

De
1241 [?As] posited in pious confidence
1242 Of glorious resurection with the just,
1243 Near the loved partner of his earlier days
1245 And in the bosom of that family mold
1246 A second Wife is gathered to his side
[1246] The approved Associate of an arduous course
[?H]
1247 From h is mid noon of manhood to old age.

[73v]

VI, 1247, 1248 ~~in manhoods prime was left sole prop~~
For he, too, had
1248 ~~—He too was left the solitary prop~~
He also had been left, in manhoods prime
[?] sole prop
1249 Of many ~~helpless~~ Children, one a Babe
S ~~lifes~~
1250 Orphan'd as soon as born.—His ~~souls~~ [?dear] life's dear help
[1250] Is taken from him: and alas! tis not
1251 In course of Nature that a Father's wing
1252 Should warm these little ones: And can he feed?
1253 That was a thought of agony more keen.
1254 For, hand in hand with Death, by strange mishap
1255 And chance-encounter on their diverse road,
~~ghastlier~~
~~The~~ that
1257 ~~Into his House~~
[?i]
[?y]
1256 The ghastl[?e] er shape of poverty had entered
at
[1257] Into th[?is] house, unfeared and unforeseen,
1258 His generous mind had urg'd him to stand forth
I fear
1259 In surety for a Brother; who, ~~tis said~~,
[1259] Ill merited such ~~love~~ proof of love; and now
1260 The widow'd Father found that all his rights
1261 In his paternal fields were undermined.
1262 Landless he was & pennyless—These hills
sides
1263 The dews of night and morn that wet their ~~turf~~
1264 The solitary stars upon their tops
Were conscious of his anguish ~~when driven fo~~rth
for he left
1265 ~~Were conscious of that anguish~~
Wer conscious of that pain
[?that by]
~~pain~~ ~~drove him forth~~
[1265] ~~Witnessd [?these gusts] of anguish which impelled him~~

1247, 1248–1249 Lines at top of page are rev at bottom of page and bottom of 73r. A mark to the left of l. 1249 perhaps signals one of those rev.

1264/1265 Mark partly overwriting the "h" of "anguish" in l. 1265 may be a comma following "anguish" in l. 1264/1265.

1266 His hopeless door
~~To l~~
[1266] From his own door to [?ranged] he knew not whe[?re]
brain
1267 He knew not when; distracted was his ~~head~~
For in mid
1247 ~~In the~~ mid noon of Manhood had he too
{B
[1248] {been left the sad and solitary prop
[1249] Of many helpless children

[74^r]

VI, 1268 His heart was cloven and full oft he pray'd
{ bl[?ank]
1269 In {[?his] despair that God would take them all.
suddenly, as if in one kind moment
1270 But ~~with a sudden burst, as if at once~~
To encourage & reprove
encourage
1271 To ~~[?] chear and to reprove~~, a gleam of light
~~Came~~
1272 ~~Broke~~ from the very bosom of that cloud
1273 Which darken'd the whol prospect of his days.
1274 For He—who now possess'd the joyless right
1275 To force the Bondsman from his house & lands,
1276 In pity, and by admiration stirred
muring
1277 Of that unmu~~ring~~ and considerate mind
1278 With which the Sufferer shewed himself prepard
1279 For prompt obedience to the voice of law,
Remitted, in free grace, a weighty sum
fift total
The ~~sixth~~ part of the^penalty—. ~~Forthwith~~
{A
~~Forthwith~~ {[?a]t this forebearance shewn this kindness done
~~At once encouraged and reproved~~
~~Forthwith~~ The desolate
1280 ~~The desolate~~^father raised his head, and lookd
bring
1281 On the wide word in hope.—~~Few words may serve~~
~~This mercy shewn~~
~~To [?tell] the rest~~
~~To tell the rest~~
~~The story to its close~~
~~This kindness done~~
The ~~sixt~~ fifth part of the total penalty.
At this forebearance shewn this kindness done
and looked
[1280] The desolate Father raised his head ~~in hope~~
[1281] On the wide world in hope. Few words may serve
serve

1266/[1266] The "l" in the partially entered line is possibly the initial letter of "leave," since rev of interlinear l. 1264/1265 is "for he left."

Rev on 74^v.

To tell the rest. With calm prudential choice

[74[v]]

With
To tell the rest. [?*In*] calm prudential choice
one
~~*He made his suit to her who in his house*~~
[?one]
To [?wh]
Had served & tended now his new-born Babe
he made his suit
VI, 1283 *A Matron of grave years.* ~~*To her he sued*~~
1281, 1282 *Within these walls were solemnized the rites*
By
1283, 1284 *With which the virtuous Woman undertook*
1285 *The sacred office of a Wife to him*
1286 *Of Mother to his helpless Family*
1287 *Nor did she fail: in nothing did she fail*
~~more than~~
1288 *Through ~~various~~ exercise of twenty years*
1289 *Save in some partial fondness to that Child*
1290 *Which at the birth she had received, the Babe*
1291 *Whose heart had known no Mother but herself*
1292 *By mutual efforts, by united hopes*
ever
1293 By daily-growing help of boy & girl
1294 Train'd early to participate that zeal
Of
1295 [?*By*] *industry that runs before the day*
of
1296 *And linger'd after it by strong restraint*[?*s*]
1297 *Of prudence which however did not check*
motions
motions
1298 *The heart's more generous* [~~?~~] *towards themselves*
and by
1299 *Or to their neighbours & by* [?~~*force*~~] *trust in God.*
1300 [?P] This pair insensibly sudued the fears
1301 And troubles that beset their life, and thus
1302 ~~Did Gawain Loveredge and his second Mate~~
1303 Redeem at length their plot of smiling field [?s]

Recall to me those [?hours] VII,3, 4
When in some dell 5

Hand of DW on 74[v] and 75[r]. Rev and continuation of 74[r]; ll. 1300–1303 are rev of 75[r].

These entries are in pencil: word "one" between first and second base text lines; del of second base text line; phrase (and rev to it) between second and third base text lines; del and rev of l. 1283; rev of l. 1283, 1284; del of l. 1302; and vertical entry in right margin. The vertical entries are part of the rev on 75[r].

1288 Rev "more than" del by eras.

1295 Curved line and "of" below l. 1295 clarify its intended opening.

[75r]

VI, 1300, 1301 ~~*The Pair beat off the fear of want—and thus*~~
1302 ~~Did Gawain Loveredge and his second mate~~
1303 *~~Did they redeem at length~~ their smiling fields*
~~Redeem by slow degree their~~
1304 *These at this day the eldest-Son retains*
1305, 1306 *The ~~oth~~ younger Children ~~have been~~ all are scatter'd wide*
1306 ~~*The rest are scatterd wide by various fates*~~
1305 *Throughout the busy world*
1307 *But each departed from their native Vale*
1308 *In Beauty flourishing, in health & worth—.*
[1305] *The Younger Children through the busy world*
Have all been
~~ave all~~
[1306] *~~H~~ [?is] younger ~~been~~ scatter'd wide by various fates—*
[1307] *But each departed from their native Vale*
and moral
[1308] *In beauty flourishing, ~~in health~~, & worth.*
~~Once more did looks of~~
by
Once more ~~did~~ looks of pleasure and of praise
or speach of no un[?meaning] courtesy
To him from whose pure lips these truths had flowd
~~We all~~ 'd
~~Or words~~, express our thanks. And for myself
I said, "Your promise, Sir, so kindly given
~~in truth~~ ~~touchingly~~ The word[?s]
~~truth~~,
Hath been, ~~ind~~ ee[?d] most movingly fulfill'd.
VII, 2 The words which you have uttered and the scene
~~our eye~~
3, 4 ~~Before~~ [?us] ~~to my mind recall~~ those hours
3 Before our eyes bring back to me
13 —~~Oft in the~~ stillness of a green recess
quiet
[13] ~~When in the quiet of a green recess~~
7 ~~Lonesome and deep, beneath the craggy top~~
When in some dell beneath the craggy top
8 Of Cader Idris, or huge Penmanmaur
9 My very soul hath listened with delight
10 To pastoral melody or warlike air
Britains antient
11 Drawn from the chords of the antient british harp
[2] Which you have uttered and the scene ~~that l[?pay]~~
[3] Before our eyes, awaken in my mind
[?sweet] long past
rs
[4] A ~~grateful~~ recollection of those hou[?]e
[5] [?When in ?]

In grateful memory of long past hours

VII, 4

Rev on 82v. Ll. 3–5 rev in pencil in right margin on 74v.

Since Books VI and VII run together here, their separation was a later rev. Both books bear the same title. These entries are in pencil: del and rev in l. [1308]; del of rev to base text above VII, 2 ("in truth" and "touchingly"); phrase "The word[?s]" two lines above VII, 2; del of ll. [13] and 7; rev entered below l. 7 (beginning "When"); ll. [2]–[5] at page foot, which are partly rev (again in pencil) vertically in right margin of 74v and left margin of 75r.

[75^{v}]

VII, [13] Within the quiet
12 By some accomplish d Master, while he sate
13 And in the quiet of the green recess
14, 15 Dispensing an unwearied interchange
[14, 15] Dispens'd, with interchange unwearied, tunes
15 Of soft or solemn tunes, severe or grave
[?Solem] or soft
16 Tender or blithe, now as the varying mood
17 Of his own Spirit urg'd, now as a voice
18 From youth or Maiden, or some honoured chief
that
19 Of his Compatriot Villagers, ~~who~~ hung
Around him flood
20 ~~In circle~~ drinking in the festal ~~stream~~
the
21 Of ~~that~~ time-hallow'd minstrels[?e]y, required
22 For their heart's ease or pleasure.—Sweet those strains
But yours are sweeter far; for while they move
25, 26 They teach; and when that overflowing stream
26, 27 Is past away I feel that it hath left
28 Deposited upon the silent shore
precious
29 Of memory, images ~~of life~~, and^thoughts
cannot
T} m[?ay] will {[?~~cannot~~]
30 [?O}hat ~~can~~not die, and {may not be destroy'd.
Did you not say that three contiguous vales
Do each possess within this hallow'd ground
Its own compartment, yet from side to side
Save in the vacant quarter of the north
Entrusted safely to
73 Whose motion rocked them as he paced along
74 Two rosy children hung, a well poised freight
pa}
75 Each from his several [?ba]}nnier peeping forth

[76^{r}]

VII, 31 The grassy heaps rise amicably close.
32 Like surges heaving in a gentle wind
O}
33 [?L]}er the small surface of a mountain pool
34 Whence comes it then that yonder I behold
and only five that lie apart
35 Five graves ~~divided from all neighbour~~
e} hood
36 Unsociably} company and sad

Rev of 76^{v}–77^{r}; rev on 83^{r}, 84^{r}. Cf. MS. 75, F1^{r}.

These entries are in pencil: all rev to first four base text lines; del and rev in l. 19; del and rev in l. 21.

Rev on 83^{r}–83^{v}. Cf. MS. 75, F1^{r}–F1^{v}.

34 Possibly a comma, overwritten by rev "that" below, follows "then."

37 And furthermore appearing to encroach
38 On the smooth playground of the village school.
39 The Vicar Answered. "No disdainful pride
rest beneath
[?~~repose~~]
40 In them who ~~there are laid~~, nor any course
41 Of strange or tragic accident hath help'd
42 To place those hillocks in that lonely guise.
{follow
43 Once more look forth and {see with your eyes
44 That length of road which from yon mountain's base
stretches
45 Through bare enclosures ~~mounts climbs~~ till its ~~grey~~ line
46 Is lost amid a little tuft of trees
~~You see it reappear~~
47, 48 Then reappearing quits the cultured fields
~~as you see [?wind] through the heathy [?w]~~
48, 49 And through the heath empurpled waste ascends
In the broad light with mazes serpentine
Up,
50 Towards ~~yon~~ an easy outlet of the vale.

47 Then, reappearing in a moment, quits
up the
[?up] slope
48 The cultured fields, and through the heathy ~~was~~
~~In the broad light with~~
49 Mounts as you see in mazes serpentine
[50] ~~Mounts~~ towrds an easy outlet of the vale

[76v]

VII, 51 That little shady spot that sylvan tuft
52 By which the road is hidden also hides
view
53 The body of a Cottage from our ~~sight~~
we ~~sea[?e]ly can~~
{And {cern
54 {[?Whi] ~~scarcely~~ as ~~we sit can we~~ di{[?]
And seated here we scarcely can discern
55 The smokeless chimney top. All unembowerd
{P
56 And naked stood that lowly {parsonage-House
{in
57 (For such {[?] truth it is and appertains
{the
58 To a small chapel in {[?a] vale beyond)
59 When hither came its last Inhabitant.
60 {Rough and forbidding were the choicest Roads
{[?Through all] [? ? ? ? ? ?]

Leaf 76v is rev of 77r; rev on 77r, 75v, 83v–84r. Cf. MS. 75, F1v.

By {which our northern [?wastes] could then
64 ~~The~~ {~~Priest at his [?abiding-] place arrived~~
be crossd

62 And into most of these secluded Vales
~~T~~}
W}~~he ways where wheels might pass were~~
~~few & rare~~

63 Was no access for heavy wain, or light
~~With~~ 2 1
[64] So at his Dwelling-place the Priest arrived
in
65 With store of Household goods ~~on~~ panniers
On sturdy ~~P[?on]~~ slung
66 ~~Upon [?rough]~~ Horses grac'd with gingling Bells
cross
67 And on the back of more ignoble beast
T} of effects most priz'd
68 W}hat with like burthen ~~closed the motley train~~
69 Or easiest carried, clos'd the motley train.
70 Young was I then a School-boy of ~~six~~ years—
{~~I~~ eight
71 ~~But~~ {[?tis] ~~have clear rememembrance of that~~
~~sight~~

[71] But still methinks I see them as they pass'd.
Delighted
72 ~~Well pleased, now d~~rawing towards their wish'd for home.
a basket well-poised freight {b
75, 74 Each in ~~his~~ several pannier—on the {[?p]ack
For a blooming ruddy
73, 74 ~~Of a~~ stout ass two ~~rosy~~ children hung
76 Their bonnets, I remember, wreathed with flowers
the [?time,]
77 Which told that 'twas the pleasant month of June
[77] That blow & wither in the month of ^

[77r]

{~~Within~~ {~~ier~~
VII, 74 {[?Upon] ~~one pann~~ {[?er] hung ~~a ruddy~~
~~blooming~~
close behind child
78 And ~~by its side~~ the comely Mother rode
79 A Woman of soft speach & gracious smile
80 And with a Lady's mien.—From far they came
81 Even from Northumbrian Hills, yet theirs had
been

---

64 Line is first del in ink, then eras. The line under " be crossd" connects it to the rest of the line above, the one that overwrites the eras.

62/63 Del by eras.

63 Transposition line and numerals reverse word order of "heavy' and "wain"; "light" overwrites eras "few &" of l. 62/63.

71 Rev may have been entered before the first line of 77r, which in turn seems to precede rev of ll. 72–77 at page foot.

75, 74 Del and rev of "his" are in pencil.

[77] Line-ending caret points to "June" in line above.

Rev on 76v, 75v, 77v, 84r–85r.

rich in pastime, cheered
82 A merry journey, ~~wanting no delight~~
By music
83 ~~Of gamesome~~, prank, or laughter-stirring jest—
or arch
84 Or freak put on, or dark word dropped, [?to swell]
~~to raise~~
[85] The cloud of Fancy and uncouth surmise
85 ~~Uncouth surmises in the curious mind~~
86 That gathered round them as the train move on
{B ~~moved~~
98 Of {boor or Burgher as th~~ey pass d~~ along.
87 Whence do they come? upon what errand
88 Do they tell their fortunes? bent
And of what calling? drugs have they
to vend
91 Or will they act the Children of the Wood
at
94 ~~In~~ their next village?—Hearing this
you }
[?y]} guess
That in their sage migration all the
band
Priest wife and servant smiled with
or laugh'd with joy
~~inward joy~~
109, 110 Of which adventures of the pair would tell
111 With undiminished glee in hoary age

r }
73 [?Be}ock] by the motion of a pannier
Entrusted safely [?to] a [?humble] [?]
~~A band of~~
[?whose fortune] [?troop]
[?skilled]
[88] Belong they to the [?cuning] gypsey ~~tribe~~
{[?In all]
[74] {Two rosy Children hung a well poised freight
[?fr]} [?om]
75 Each [?on]} his several pannier peeping forth

[77ᵛ]

What erran {[?here]
errand draws the {[?I] the [?whisper ran]
Belong the
VII, 87 "Whence do they come, upon what errand bent
88 Belong they to the fortune telling tribe
te }
Do they [?]}ll fortunes? drugs have they to vend—
~~are they Strollers furnished to enact~~
90 ~~Or with their scenes and puppets will they act~~

---

98 Missing apos in "pass d" may be obscured by rev and del above.
94 The "ir" in "their" may be added.
[88], [74] Conjectured rev "skilled" and "In all" are in pencil, as is del of "tribe."

Rev of 77ʳ; rev on 84ᵛ–85ʳ.
These entries are in pencil: rev "Belong the" in l. 87; all of l. 88; transposition mark in l. [90]; ll. 94–[95] as rev (between ink ll. 92 and 93).

|S
[90] Or |strollers are they furnished to enact
F| t|
91 [?R]|air Rosamond, or [?c]|he Children of the wood
|T
92 Or by that whiskered |tabby's aid set forth
94 When the next village hears the show announcd
[95] By blast of trumpet |W
93 The lucky venture of sage |whittington
For| ~~by blast of Trumpet gather'd round~~
[?To]| ~~Friends together brought by beat of drum~~
[?had]| announc[?d] the show
95 When blast of trumpet [?that| ~~awaked] their friends~~
plenteous was the growth
94, 96 In the next Village? ~~Such enquiries bold~~
of such conjectures, overheard, or seen,
Depicted
97 [?~~In picture~~,] upon many a staring face
96 ~~Were put to them and such conjectures~~ they
And oftimes earnest questions of like drift
~~Did oftener~~
106 [?~~were] boldy [?put to th~~]
107 By traveller halting in his own despite
[96] ~~Mo[?re] often overheard~~—whereat ye guess
|e
Were bodly put to them. Whereat y|[?ou] guess
110 That in their grave migration all the band
Priest wife and Servant, smiled, or
laugh'd with joy
109, 110 Of which adventures oft the Pair would tell
111 With undimished glee in hoary age.
112 —A Priest he was by function; but his course
113 From his youth up, and high as manhoods noon
114 The hour of life to which he then was brought
|&
115 Had been irrregular, |[?] I might say, wild,
116 By Books unsteadied, by his pastoral care
[95] plenteous was the growth
~~such conjectures they~~
[96] Of such conjectures, overheard, or seen
[97] Read in the staring and inquisitive looks
|e
98 Of boor or burgher as th|~~eir~~ train pass d on
earnest sober [?sifting]
|[?sifting] drift
And many a |[?ques] question of like [?~~kind~~] aim
[107] —By traveller halting in his own
despite
[106] ~~Was bodly put to them~~
was boldy put to them

[78r]

~~rather say~~
Too little check'd.—An active ardent mind
VII, 117 ~~A more than active a most ardent mind~~
118 A fancy pregnant with resourse and scheme
119 To cheat the sadness of a rainy day
120 Hands apt for all in[?e]genious arts and games
121 A generous spirit and a body strong

122 To cope with stoutest Champions of the bowl
123 Had earnd from him sure welcome and the rights
124 Of a priz'd visitant in the jolly hall
~~Of C~~
123, 124 [?Had} ~~won him] easy entrance to the hall~~
125 Of Country Squire or at the statelier Board
126 of Duke or Earl from senate and from court
125, 126 ~~Of country Squire,—or board of lofty Duke~~
{to pass
127 With-drawn, {[?] [?spend] the vacant summer hour[?s]
126, 127 ~~Or Baron [?] in their leisure summer~~ hours
In} from scenes of courtly pomp
128 Of} condescention among rural guests.
129 With these high Comrades he had revell'd
long
{C
130 Had frolic'd many a year, a simple {clerk
131 By hopes of coming Patronage beguild
132 And vex d, [?~~till~~] untill the weary heart
grew sick.
133 And so abandoning all higher aims
134 And all his shewy Frieds at lengh he turnd
135 For an assured though scanty livelihood
136 To this remote and humble Chapelry
137 Which had been offered to his doubtful choice
earn'd for him
[123] Had ~~given him the [?glad a~~] sure welcome and the rights
[124] Of a priz'd visitant, in the jolly hall
[125] Of Country Squire and at the ~~board of Duke~~
statelier board
from senate [?and] from court
[126] Of Duke or Earl ~~in vacant summer hour[?s~~]
Withdrawn }
[127] [?Baron] [?]} to while away the summer hours

[78v]

Patron
VII, 138 From an unthought of quarter. Bleek and bare
139 They found the Cottage their allotted home
140 Naked without and rude within, a spot
{C
141 With which the scantily-provided {cure
142 Not long had been endowed; and far remote
stood} divided from that House
143 The Chapel lay}, ~~three miles of moss and moor~~.
144 By an unpeopled tract of mountain waste.
145 Yet cause was none whateer regret might hang
146 On his own mind to quarrel with the choice
147 Which fix'd him in this homely solitude,
148 Apart from old temptations and constrained
If not to arduous labour yet at least

---

127 Overwriting "to" may be a reinforcement.

126, 127 Queried mark after "Baron" appears to be a colon, perhaps partly overwritten by a comma or caret.

126, 127/128 Rev "from scenes of courtly pomp" is in pencil.

149 To punctual labour in his sacred charge.
150 See him a constant preacher to the Poor

154 And by as salutary change compelled
155 Month after month in this obscure abode
156 To rise from timely sleep and meet the day
157 With no engagement in his thoughts more proud
158 Or splendid than his garden could afford

[79r]

To an industrious and a lonely spade, [?2]
VII, 159 His fields, or mountains by the heath-cock ranged,
160 Or these wild Brooks from which he now return[?ed]
and contented
161 Contentedly to take a temperate meal
{ ate Mate
162 At his own board where s{[?its] a gentle ~~Wife~~
163 And three fair Children plentifully fed,
164 Though simple, from their little household farm
treat
{ change
165 With acceptable {[?] of fish or fowl
166 By Nature yielded to his practised hand
In hours of eager sport—~~and~~ by these supplid
167
{ ut
To help the small b{[?y] certain comings-in
And other small though
not the less
168 Of that spare benefice. Yet ~~sure it is~~
169 Theirs was a hospitable board, and theirs
pass d on
170 A charitable door. So days and years
And years
171 Pass'd on: the inside of that rugged H[?]ouse
172 Was trimm'd and brightened by the Matrons care
173 And gradually enrichd with things of price
174 Which might be lack'd for use or ornament.
175 What though no soft and costly sofa there
176 Insidiously stretch'd out its lazy length

[79v]

VII, 177 And no vain mirror glitter'd on the walls
178 ~~Yet [?Shutter] did the low Abode in this surpass~~
[178] Yet were the windows of the low abode
which at once
179, 180 By shutters weather fended, ~~that repelled~~
[180] Repelled the storm, and deaden'd its loud roar

What appears to be a "2" in the right margin of the first line on 79r may perhaps be a question mark or a "Q" for "Query." In any case, the mark probably indicates WW's intent to alter or cancel the line.

171 Queried letter (perhaps an "h") is blotted over; cap "H' may thus be rev.

[181] There snow white curtains hung in plenteous folds
180 ~~The tempest and subdued its deafening roar~~
181 ~~And [?there] white curtains hung in folds.~~
182 Tough moss, and long-enduring mountain-plants
That creep } with
184, [183] [?Braided] [?]} along the ground [~~—?—~~] {[?] sinuous trail
[184] ~~Were braided with nice hand and framed a work~~
[184] Were nicely braided and composed a work
185, 182 ~~Mats curiously constructed of tough moss~~
[185] Like Indian Mats that with appropriate grace
182, 183 ~~And long enduring mountain-plants that creep~~
183 ~~Close to the ground with thick and sinuous~~ [?trail]
~~trail~~
186 Lay at the threshold or ~~in~~ the inner doors.
185 ~~In sign of neatness, with appropriate grace~~
187 And a fresh carpet woven of homespun wool
i}
188 And tinctured dainty}ly with florid hues,
{ on
189 For seemliness and warmth ~~of~~ {[?fo] festive days
190 Cover'd the ~~plain sl[?im~~] smooth blue slabs of mountain stone
191 With which the parlour floor, in simplest guise
Homesteads had been long inlaid
192 Of these old pastoral Homesteads, was inlaid
Mothers and her Daughters
193 These were the ~~gentle~~ Housewifes pleasing [?care;]
and served
Betimes, to[?discipline] her eldest girl[?s],
For a [?strict] course of houshold Industry

[80r]

VII, 194 Meanwhile the unsedentary Master's hand
195 Was busier with <u>his</u> task—to <u>rid</u>—to plant,
{r
196 To real{[?], for food, for shelter, and delight,
humble [?~~thoughts~~] heavens wish
{ [?~~favor~~]
197 A thriving covert! and when {[?] ~~of [?time~~]
And hopes ~~with~~ which with heavens blessing have not failed
199 Restored me to my native valley, here
200 To spend my days well pleas'd was I to see
bare { on
201 The once ~~rude~~ Cottage {[?f] the mountain side
202 Screend from assault of every bitter blast
203 While the dark shadows of the summer leaves
204 Danced in the breeze upon its mossy roof
205 Time which had thus afforded willing help

---

193 Another possibility for "care" is "cure." What we conjecture as a semicolon may be a period.

Rev at page foot may have been intended to follow l. 193, after del of "gentle."

Cf. MS. 75, F2r.

194 Indentation may signal start of a para.

~~my fellow pastor's home~~
with nature's fairest growths
206, 207 To beautify ~~his [?home] had gently shed~~
~~With nature's fairest wealth had gently~~ shed
208 Upon his bodily frame a wintry grace
209 The comeliness of unenfeebled age.
~~But littl obvious change had rea[?cd] his mind~~
X
210 But how could I say gently? for he still
211 Retain'd a flashing eye, a burning palm
a stirring
212 ~~Still the same restless~~ foot, and head that beat[?s]
its at night
213 Upon ~~his~~ ^ pillow with a thousand schemes
207 X This rustic tenement had gently shed
[208] Upon his Masters frame a wintry grace
[209] The comeliness of unenfeebled age

[80v]

VII, 214 Few likings had he dropp'd few pleasures lost
and charitable,
215 Generous and prompt to serve|as heretofore
216 And still his harsher passions kept their hold
he talk'd
217 * Anger and indignation, sill his tonge
[218] Of titled names and old exalted Friends
220 And, from these genial fits of vain delight
218 ~~Talked of those old exalted friends with glee~~
221 Uproused by recollected injury, talked
[222] Of their false ways disdainfully and too oft
222 ~~And railed with pride at their deceitful way~~
[?W]
222, 223 And all too oft in words of bitter scorn
From which no [?] time could shield them
X ^ nor the grave
225 Thes transports, with staid looks of pure good
will
{[?Or] C}onsort {.
226 {[?And] with soft smile, his l}~~ady~~ would reprove{,
227 She far behind him in the race of years,
228 Yet keeping her first mildness, was advanc'd
229 Far nearer in the habits of her soul
230 To that still region whither all are bound.
231 Him might we liken to the setting sun
232 As I have seen it on some gusty day
233 Struggling and bold; and shining from the
unquiet west
234 With an inconstant and unmellow'd light
a
235 She was ~~the~~ soft attendant cloud, that hung

Leaf 80v is rev on 81r. Cf. MS. 75, F2r–F2v.
215 Marking at end of line indicates an intended del.
217, 225 Marks at these lines signal rev at page foot.

[218] still he talked
[?of] long-past banquettings
219 Of ~~those old~~ banquets with his titled friends
[?T] still did he love to [?harp] upon their names
{[?such]
[220] And from {[?those] genial fit of vain delight
[221] Uprouz'd by recollected injury rail'd
[222] At their false ways disdainfully—and too oft
223 In bitterness and with a threatening eye
224 [?of fire] incensed beneath a hoary brow

[81[r]]

VII, 236 ~~As if it wished to veil the res~~tless orb
237 ~~From which it did itself imbibe a~~ ray
238 ~~Of pleasing lustre—~~ loved
217 Anger and indignation;—still he ~~loved~~ ~~talked~~
218 The sound of titled names and talked in glee
~~exalted~~
high born
219 Of long-past banquettings with ~~titled~~ Friends
~~exalted~~
217, 218 ~~Still did he love the sound of titled names~~
Then lulling
220 ~~And~~, from those genial fits of vain delight
,
221 Uprouz'd by recollected injury, rail[?e] }d
oft
222 At their false ways disdainfully, and ~~full~~ too oft
[?Too of in b] [?in]
223 In bitterness and with a threatening eye
224 Of fire, incensed beneath its hoary brow.
225 These transports, by staid looks of pure good
{his will
226 And by soft smiles {[?] consort &c

---

235 r } that hung
236 As if with wish to veil the [?h]}estless orb
237 From which it did itself imbibe a ray
of this
238 Of pleasing lustre. But ~~enough~~—I wish
239 For I would rather sprinkle on the [?earth]
239, 241 To sprinkl[?ier] [?~~holier] praises upon~~ their [?grave]
240 That now divides them
241 ~~Unsullied~~ praise pure as the dews of
heaven
242 Without ditinction falling upon both

---

[220] Possibly "[?those]" overwrites "[?such]."
[221] A colon may follow "injury."

Rev of 80[v]; rev on 81[v]. Cf. MS. 75, F2[r]–F2[v].
222–223 Rev in pencil ("full" is del in ink).
239 Another possible reading for "earth" is "sod."

the
240 That now divides pair or rather say
[241] That still unites them praises like heavens
[?dew]
[241] Unites them, ~~praises like the dews of heaven~~
[242] Without distinction falling upon both
~~Unsullied [?generous~~]

[81v]

~~enough~~
VII, 238 Of pleasing lustre—~~but too much~~ of this
but no more of this
~~Better it [?were~~]
239 For I would ~~rather~~ sprinkle on the sod
I better love to
240 Which now divides the pair, or rather say
241 Which still unites them praises like heavens
dew
242 Without distinction falling for them both.
243 Yoke fellows were they, long and well-approved
244 To endure & to perform. With frugal pains
245 Yet in a course of generous discipline
246 Did this poor Churchman & his consort rear
[?in]
247 Their progeny [?~~yet] when of~~ three went forth to
{the
{[?] world
{his
249, 251 A Son remain'd to till {[?] fathers glebe
252 Nor was the youngest daughter loth to make
adventurous
A sacrifice of all ambitious hope,
253 ~~And lighten her decl[?ing] mothers cares~~

{[?ing]
To bend{ adventurous hope to humble duties
[253] ~~And lighten~~
A }
[?]} son of hea[?lt] impaired by close pursuit
mid
Of earnest trade ~~in~~ uncongenial air
251 Withdrew and came to till his Fathers
glebe
[252] X Nor was the youngest Daughter loth to bend
And in the house where she was born remain'd
[253] To lighten her declining Mother's cares
Youth's flattering hopes to unambit
ious duties

Leaf 81v is rev of 81r; rev on 82r.

[82^{r}]

This said, abruptly from his seat he rose
Nor, at that moment, were his audience free
from some uneasy feeling of regret
kind
That he in ~~fond~~ compliance with their wish
A Task had undertaken which must needs
Excite some painful and disturbing thoughts
Unfit for Strangers to participate
But this regret was speedily dispersd
his wonted
For with recover d quietness of mien
The Vicar thus resumed

[?Deep tha]

VII, 247 [?] [?s], of three that left their home
{[?&]
To earn [?an honest] maintenance, {or try

~~And of~~
248 To try the path[?s] of fortune, one [?acquire]
The paths of fortun, [?to a] foreign clime[?s]
Till by untimely death, the eldest [?chose]
quiet
A [?scholars ~~safer~~] industry and lived
Not undistinguished by [?poetic power]

[82^{v}]

VII, [5] ~~When in a [?hollow] vale whose [?]~~
[5] When, in a Vale whose depth the Sun had ceasd
farewell
To shine upon though yet his beam in sight
[?some]
[5] When, in a vale, whose depth the setting Sun
6 Had ceasd to shine upon though yet his beam
Once more by looks of pleasure and of praise
And speech of no unmeaning Courtesy
To him from whose pure lips those truths had
flowed
Did we express our thanks. And for myself
I said your promise Sir so kindly given
Hath been most movingly fulfilled. The words

Canceled passage may possibly be a conclusion to the continuation of the tale as found in *Tuft* (see pp. 27, 43–45, 151, 214–225) or perhaps a rejected ending of Book VI or opening of Book VII. Uncanceled lines on the bottom half of the page are alt or rev of 81^{v}. Last three lines are probably a description of the elder son of the family (see p. 1222, below, and IF [Curtis], p. 191). The first queried word in the penultimate line may be "scholar's" or "studious."

Rev of 75^{r}–75^{v}.
In the first base text line, the "O" in "Once" is four lines high, as if it marks a section break.

have
2 Which we^heard you utter and the scene
3 Before our eyes awaken in my mind
Most ~~vivid~~
4 ~~A lively recollection of those hours~~
[?beams]
[?hollow Vale]
[?shadow dept]
Vivid remembrance of those long-past hours
Vale whose shadowy depth
5 When, in a lonesome ~~Valley, while the beams~~
farewell
{ farewell
The Sun had left though yet his {[?closing] beams
6, 7 Of sunset lay upon the craggy top
[?on snow]
7 Lay beautiful upon the craggy top
8 Of Cader Idris or huge Penmanmaur,
On
A} A
9 My} wandering Youth I listened with delight
10 To pastoral melody or warlike air
11 Drawn from the chords of the antient
British harp
12 By some accomplish'd Master while he
sate
{depths the setting Sun }
5, 6 When, in a vale whose {[?whose shadowy depth]}
{Had ceased to illuminate though yet his beams }
{The Sun had left though yet [?his farewell beams]}
[7] Lay beautiful on Snowdons craggy top

[83^r]

VII, 13 Within the quiet of the green recess
14 And inexhaustibly as bird that sings
{[?ey]
15, 14 In leaf{y bower an interchange dispensed
15 Of soft or solemn tunes, severe or grave,
16 Tender or blithe, now as the varying mood
17 Of his own Spirit urged, now as a Voice,
18 From Youth or Maiden, or some honoured Chief
19 Of his Compatriot Villagers, that hung
20 Around him—drinking in the potent flood

4–8 The following sequence of rev appears to be the most likely: (1) pencil rev at page foot (the underwritings in ll. 5, 6 and the following line); (2) pencil and ink interlinear rev in midpage at ll. 4/5 and 5/6, 7; (3) ink overwriting and addition at page foot (ll. 5, 6 to [7]); (4) five lines of ink rev at top of page.

4/5 These phrases and words are in pencil: "[?shadow dept]," "[?hollow Vale]," and "[?beams]." The phrase "Vale whose shadowy depth" is in pencil, overwritten in ink.

5/6, 7 Rev is in pencil, overwritten in ink; the pencil word "[?closing]" is still visible under ink "farewell"; the upper "farewell" is a pencil rev earlier than the ink overwriting.

7 "Lay beautiful" is in pencil overwritten in ink.

Rev of 75^v–76^r. Cf. MS. 75, F1^r.

15, 14 Possibly the "y" overwrites the queried "ey."

19 Del by eras.

21 Of the time hallowed minstrelsy, required
22 For their hearts ease or pleasure.
Sweet those Strains
But yours are sweeter far for while they move
25, 26 They teach; and when the overflowing Stream
26, 27 Is passed away I feel that it has left
28 Deposited upon the silent shore
29 Of memory images and pretious thoughts
30 That will not die and cannot be destroyed.
you
Did not say that three Contiguous Vales
Do each possess within this hallowed ground
Its own compartment; yet from side to side
Save in the vacant Quarter of the North
31 The grassy heaps rise amicably close
32 Like surges heaving in a gentle wind
Ov
33 O}er the small surface of a mountain
pool

[83^v]

VII, 34 Whence comes it, then, that yonder I behold
35 Five graves and only five that lie apart
36 Unsociable company and sad
37 And furthermore appearing to encroach
38 On the smooth playground of the Village School
39 The Vicar answered. No disdainful pride
e
40 In them who rest bneath nor any course
41 Of strange or tragic accident hath helped
42 To place those Hillocks in that lonely guise.
43 —Once more look forth and follow with your eye
44 The length of Road that from yon mountain's base
{E
45 Through bare {enclosures stretches till its line
46 Is lost amid a little Tuft of Trees,
47 Then, reappearing in a moment, quits
48 The cultured fields & up the heathy waste
49 Mounts, as you see in mazes serpentine
50 Towards an easy outlet of the Vale.
51 That little shady Spot that sylvan Tuft
52 By which the Road is hidden also hides
53 The Body of a Cottage from our view
54 And seated here we scarcely can
discern
55 The smokeless chimney top. All unembowerd

Leaf 83^v is rev of 76^r–76^v. Cf. MS. 75, F1^r–F1^v.
52 Rev "also hides" is in pencil overwritten in ink.

[84r]

o
VII, 56 And naked stod that lowly Parsonage House
{F
57 ({for such in truth it is and appertains
{C
58 To a small {chapel in the vale beyond)
59 When hither came its last Inhabitant.
60 Rough and forbidding were the choicest Roads,
61 By which our northern wilds could then be crossed
62 And into most of these secluded Vales
Was no access
63 Access was rare for wain heavy or light.
64 So at his Dwelling Place the Priest arrived
65 With store of Household Goods in panniers slung
66 On sturdy Horses graced with gingling Bells
67 And on the back of more ignoble Beast.
68 That with like burthen of effects most prized
69 Or easiest carried, closed the motley train.
70 Young was I then a School boy of eight years
71 But still methinks I see them as they pass d
~~In order~~,
{In order,
{[?Before me]
72 ~~Delighted~~ drawing toward their wished for home.
73 Rock'd by the motion of a trusty ass
74 Two ruddy children Hung, a well-pois'd, freight,
~~his[?s]~~]
75 ~~Each from their several pann baskets peeping forth~~
{in
[75] Each {by his basket nodding drowsily,
76 Their bonnets, I remember, wreathed with flowers
Wh}
77 Th}ich told that 'twas the pleasant month of June.

[84v]

comely
VII, 78 And close behind the [?lonely] mother rode
79 A woman of soft speech and gracious smile
80 And with a Lady's mien. From far they came
81 Even from Northumbrian Hills yet theirs had been
82 A merry journey, rich in pastime, cheared
83 By music, prank, or laughter stirring jest

Rev of 76v–77r, 75v. Cf. MS. 75, F1v.
63 Rev in pencil.
72 "[?Before me]" is in pencil but rev in ink; the upper "In order" is in pencil but del in ink.
[75] Rev "in" is in pencil.

Rev of 77r–77v, 85r.
78 Rev, in pencil, corrects miscopying (cf. 77r).

{And
84 {Or freak put on & arch word dropp'd to
The swell
{ose
85 The{e clouds of fancy & uncouth surmise
86 That gather'd round them as the train moved
{— ?} on
Whence come they{, on what errand— }whither bound
87 ~~What errand draws them? thus the whisper ran~~
88 Belong they to the fortune-telling tribe
{pitch
89 Who {fix their tents beneath the green wood tree
90 Or are they Strollers furnished to enact
and
{and
91 Fair Rosamond {or the Children of the Wood
And by
{And
92 {Or that whisker d Tabby's aid set forth
h}
93 The lucky venture of sage W[?i]}ittington
94 When the next Village hears the show
announc'd
95 By blast of trumpet. Plenteous was the
growt
96 Of such conjectures overheard, or [?read] seen
97 On many a staring Countenance pourtrayed
{B marched
98 Of {[?b]oor or Burger as the ~~pa[?ce]d~~ along
waits
That like the dust which upon the speed
Of some impatient traveller gathered round
And followed with [?them as the] train moved on

[85[r]]

VII, 97 Depicted upon many a staring Face
marched
98 Of ~~Bo~~ Boor or Burger as they ~~paced~~ along.
99 And oftentimes their steadiness of face
109, 110 Of which adventures oft the Pair would
{like tell
100 Were put to proof by questions of {[?]like drif
111 With undiminished glee in hoary age
109 Of which Adventures that beguiled & cheared
110 Their grave migration oft the Pair would
tell
[111] With undiminished glee, in hoary age
[99] And oftentimes their steadiness of face
[100] Was put to proof by questions of like drift

89, 92 Rev "pitch" and overwriting "And" are in pencil.

97ff. Symbol in right margin may indicate that ll. 97–98 replace related lines on 85[r]. Canceled lines below rule appear to have been intended to follow l. 86.

Loose leaf. Rev of 77[r]–77[v]; rev on 84[v]. For more of Book VII, see leaves 108[v]–119[r], below.

107 From Tra^v^ller halting in his own despite
[109] Of which adventures—that beguiled & cheared
[110] Their grave migration, oft the Pair would
tell
[111] With undiminished glee, in hoary age.
And oft
[99] Sometimes their steadiness of face was tried
101, 100 Or their inventive humour exercis'd
102 By questions, in authoritative tone
~~To their veracity address d~~
~~To their veracity address d~~
From
By }
{From} { staid {G
103 {[?] some {[?grave] {guardian of the Public
peace;
In his w } as they [?met]
105 ~~With a~~^suspicious [?]}isdom, ~~for [?this] end~~,
104 Checking the sober steed on which he rode
[107] Or traveller halting in his own despite
108 A simple curiosity to ease.

[85^v]

~~from that abode~~
VI, 1155 Here rests a Mother. But from her I turn
[?~~Look on~~] [?But uplift]
1156 ~~And from~~ her grave—Look!—halfway up that
Look up & midway on that Ridge behold Ridge
1157 (That Ridge which elbowing from the Mountain-side
centre
1158 Carries into the middle of the vale
T } where She dwelt
1159 It rocks and woods) a}he cottage may be seen
~~dwelt~~ lived & died, & where
{ ~~yet~~
~~In which the Matron & where~~ {[?] ~~dwells~~
~~Mate who there~~
And where yet dwells Partner
{H
1160 ~~Yet dwells~~ {~~her faithful Husband~~ who was left
her Partner
1161 (Full eight years past) the solitary prop
1162 Of many helpless Children. I begin
1163 With words which might be Prelude to a Tale
1164 Of heart-depressing sorrow, but I feel,
(~~Though in the midst of sadness, as might seem~~)
1165 No sadness, when I think of what mine eyes

Leaf 85^v is a loose leaf. Rev of 71^r–71^v, 86^r.

1155–1157 Pencil rev and del.

1158/1159 Pencil rev to "where She dwelt."

1159/1160 Base text line from "&" is del in ink; entire line is del in pencil.

1160 "And where yet dwells" above and "her Partner" below are in pencil; "Yet dwells Her faithful" is canceled in pencil. A pencil mark connects "And where yet dwells" to the base text line above, possibly indicating the shift of the canceled words ("& where yet dwells") to begin a new verse line.

1164/1165 Del in pencil.

1166 See daily in that happy Family.
Bright garland form they, for the pensive brow
1167 ~~Bright Garland form they for the pensive~~
Brow
Of their undrooping Father's widowhood
1168 ~~Of their undrooping Fathers widowhood~~
1169 Those six fair Daughters budding yet—not one
1170 Not one of all the band a full blown Flower.
[1171] Depressed and desolate of soul as once
[1167] ~~Form a bright Garland for the pens~~ive brow
[1172] That father was & filled with anxious fear
[1168] ~~Of their undrooping Fathers widowhood~~
1173 Now by experience taught he stands assured
1171 Who [?once] was desolate of soul & filled
1172 With ~~anxious~~ [?burdens] but now stands
assured [?&]

[86r]

VI, 1173 ~~And, by experience, long hath known & fel[?l]t~~
~~Conspicuous evidence this Houshold yields~~
God
1174 That ~~He~~ who takes away yet takes not half
1175 Of what he seems to take, or gives it back
1176 Not to our prayer but far beyond our prayer
1177 He gives it the boon produce of a soil
1178 Which our endeavours have refused to till
1179 And Hope hath never watered.— —As the
spot
Chosen for the Raven[?s] nest—the nest itself
And all the unsightly spoil around it spread
Proclaim the savage Naure of the Bird
e humble Lodge
Which there inhabits, so that ~~Dwelling-place~~
~~happy~~
In which That Family abide
rustic
Leaves not uncertain to a transient glance
That tis a covert of content & peace
And unreproved enjoyment.—Thither turn!
such this
The antient Cottage (~~at this~~ distance seen)
distance
[1179] ~~Seen at this the Abode appears~~
Appears surpass ~~passed beyond~~
1182 In no distinction to ~~have risen above~~
rudest ye might think
1183 [?Our] humblest habitation, ~~seems like them, to~~
~~have grown~~
1184 That it had sprung self raised from earth, or grown

Leaf 86r is rev of 71v; rev on 85v.

1179/[1179] Rev between fourth and fifth unnumbered base text lines had left a space before "Family." The two adjectives ("happy" and "rustic") are entered in lighter, more reddish ink than what was used for the base text.

1183–1184 Rev in l. 1183 precedes writing of l. 1184.

[86v]

{ng
livi{g
{[?~~livin~~]
VI, 1185 Out of the {native Rock—to be adorned
1186 By nature only—but, on nearer view,
a
1187 Will be discovered there ~~the~~ studious work
{ies
1188 Of many fan{cy[?s] prompting many hands.—
1189 Brought from the woods the honeysuckle twines
A } trim
1190 Around the porch—[?b]}nd seems in that ~~neat~~
place
{Plant
1191 A {Flower no longer wild—the cultured rose
1192 There blossoms, strong in hea[?t]h, & will be soon
1193 Roof-high—the wild Pink crowns the garden
wall
And with the flowers { ers {Stones
1194 ~~And with the~~ flow{[?] are intermingled {stones
In comely order set
~~Curious for shape or hue~~, some round, like Balls,
Worn smooth and round by fretting of the Brook
1195 From which they have been gathered, others bright
[1195] And sparry—the rough scatterings of the Hills.
1196 These ornaments that fade not with the year
1197 A hardy Girl continues to provide
1198 Who, mounting fearlessly the rocky heights
1199 Her Fathers prompt Attendant does for him

[87r]

VI, 1200 All that a boy could do—but with delight
1201 More keen and prouder daring—yet hath She
1202 Within the Garden, like the rest, a Bed
1203 Of her own Flowers and favorite Herbs—a space
en}
1204 By sacred charter hold f} for her use. X
1205 These &c
at the closing in of night
1214 O—But ~~in the darkness of the night~~—then most
1215 This Dwelling charms me—covered by the gloom
1216 Then, in my walks I oftentimes stop short
1217 (Who could refrain?) and feed by stealth my
sight
1218 With prospect of the company within
1219 Laid open through the blazing window—there
1220 I see the eldest Daughter at her wheel

Rev of 71v–72r.

Rev of 72r–72v; rev on 87v–88v.

1205 Rev "These &c" is in pencil. Additional lines on 88v are signaled by the X in the right margin (and the O in the left margin of l. 1214); see also 87v–88r.

1221 Spinning amain as if to over-take
{t
1222 The never-halting {Time; or, in her turn
1223 Teaching some Novice of the Sisterhood
1224 That skill in this or other Household work
1225 Which from her Father's honor'd hand herself

[87^v]

VI, 1226 While she was yet a Little-one—had learned.
1227 Mild Man—he is not gay but they are gay
1228 And the whole House seems filled with gaiety. *
1229 —Thrice happy then the Mother may be deemed
[?hillock where]
1230 The Wife who rests beneath this turf, ~~from~~ which
1231 I turned that ye in mind might witness where
1232 And how her Spirit yet survives on Earth.
85
1208 A not unfrequent pleasure tis for me
to lift the lac[?h] to
~~To~~ turning aside & enter that domain
and gather fruit or
{. {or flow
1206 Leave asked or not{, and {[?] in the shade [?sit dow]
[?at work]
1209 And watch ~~the industrious~~ bees, ~~among~~ the flower
And listen to the industrious [?bee]
while
~~or listen to~~ the bees
[1209] Are murmuring [?roun] their hives & I sit
[?industrious]
At noontide listening to the [?~~mur~~] ~~busy~~ [?bees]
1210 Or to the murmur of the mountain Rill
1211 That sparkling thrids the rocks & tunes his
voice
1212 To the pure course of human life which there
1213 Flows on in solitude from year to year

Within this [?s]
a row
Of shelter d [?beehives] the [?common stock]
{[?e]
Of the industrious sist{[?hor]hood, I love
To watch the humming laborers at their work

1222 Mark after "turn" may be intended as a comma.

Rev of 72^v–73^r; rev on 88^r–88^v.

1228 The right-margin asterisk may indicate an intention to include transition drafted on 72^v–73^r, although this draft lacks a similar asterisk.

1230 Del and rev in pencil. Another possibility for the second word of queried rev is "which."

1232 The number "85" appears to be a line count from 85^v.

[88r]

Nor is the luxury of other wealth
Wanting in that enclosure; for there stand
VI, 1209 ~~A shelter~~ row of [?beehives];
W } also
[?I w]}ithin that [?trim] enclosure {[?] stands
[1209] ~~A shelter'd~~ row of [?beehives],
~~That gardens growt my hands are free [?I~~]
[?ever else]
1205 ~~Yet~~ these & whatsoer the garden [?shows]
I gather enter[?d]
1206 Of fruit & flower ~~my hands~~ are free
to [?cut]
stand
and [?there] I sit & watch
permission I [?enter there]
[1206] ~~Leave~~ asked or not, as inclination prompts
I [?entered] there [?& and there] I sit & watch
I enter, there, ~~sit~~ and
work
[1209] The Bees at [?~~work at~~] around their sheltering
[?h]
[?and] watch the bees
B}
[1209] T b}usily round the shelter

Lulled or sit
1210 Sooth'd by the [?tinkling] of the mountain [?r]
Nor do I [?scruple] to sit down & watch
[1210] While the leaves rustle & the mountain
rill
1211 That sparkling thrids the rocks attunes
his V
~~and there~~ I
1206 Leave asked or not, ~~if inclination~~ prompts
~~there~~ [?~~rest~~]
I enter ~~as I pass, & watch d the~~ bees
~~ere I [?w~~]
That plot of garden ground I seldom
pass
1208 Without a conscious pleasure, and [?am moved]
To lift the latch permission asked or not

[88v]

What choice work of nature or of [?ar] art
Whose fame attracts the traveller from afar

Rev of 87v, 72v; rev on 88v.
In the fourth base text line, conjectured "trim" may be related to the rejected line following l. 1204 on 72r.
In the sixth base text line, the conjectured "growt" (for "growth") may be "ground."

Rev of 88r, 87v, 72r–72v, 89v; rev on 87r.

X enclosure (struck through)

VI, 1205 These and whatever else the garden bears ~~enclosure~~
1206 Of fruit or flower, permission asked
2 1 or not
1207 I freely gather & my leisure draws
A pastime
1208 [?N] not unfrequent ~~pleasure~~ from the sight
[?round]
1209 Of the Bees murmuring [?sounds] their sheltered
hives
1210 In that Enclosure while the mountain rill
1211 That sparkling thrids the rocks attunes
his voice
1212 To the pure course of human life which
there
And in the fields & in the neighbouring
[?vale]
1213 ~~Flows on in solitude from year to year~~
O

606 laws of charity
607 Let judgement here in mercy be pronounced
608 This self-respecting nature prompts, & this
609 Wisdom enjoins—but if the thing we seek
610 Be genuine knowledge bear we then in mind
throne
611 Now from his lofty [?seat] the sun can paint
612 Colours as bright on exhalations risen
613 From weedy pool or pestilential swamp
614 As from the Rivulet sparkling where it runs
615 Or the pellucid Lake.
Small risk said I
616 Of such illusion ~~her~~ do we here incur.
617 Temptaton here is more to exceed the truth

[89r]

ye
Whom shall we turn to next?— we ask'd for
ye truth
And unadu[?le]rate truth shall [?] receive
VI, 590 But vice depravity & low desires
These will creep in where[?ver] man is found
591 And out of such materials might be framed
[?~~ra~~]
592 Harsh Portratiture in which a vulgar
face

1205, 1213 The X and O signal the insertion of these lines on 87r, following l. 1204.
1206/1207 The numerals probably represent WW's intention to transpose "fruit or flower" or possibly "freely gather."
606ff. Lines are continued from 89r.

Continued on 88v.

[?perverted]
And a coarse outside of ~~repulsive~~ life
And unattractive manners may at once
Be recognized by all.—
~~Imagine not~~
Ah—do not think,
(The Wanderer ~~said~~ somewhat eagerly exclaimd,
Wish could be ours that you for such poor gain
Gain shall I call it—gain of what—for
word } whom?
Should breathe a [?]} tending to violate
Your own pure spirit not a step we look for
forbearance & reser
In slight of that ~~reserve~~
Which common human heartedness inspires
And mortal ignorance, & frailty claim
Upon this sacred ground if no where else.
True, said the pensive Sceptic—be it far
From us to infring the laws of charity

[89^v]

Far be it (the Recluse observ d, from us
I interfere not ~~said (the Recluse~~ observed)
To infring the laws of
ju }
~~With the~~ [?cl]} ~~st claims of ch~~arity, I wish
Let judgement here in mercy be pronounced
~~That judgement shall in mercy be~~ pronounced,
~~Th[?is course] at least is seemly and perchance~~
[?]
But if the thing we seek
~~May be [?deemed] wise~~ So wisdom bids
r }
Be what the understanding may [?be]}espect
{[?B]
{[?As] genuine knowledg bear we then in mind
How from his lofty throne the Sun can paint
Colours as bright as exhalations risen
~~out the~~ & pestilential swamp
~~From weedy pool or noisome swamp~~
From noisome swamps, from the sparkling Rill
~~As from the Rivulet sparkling where it~~ runs
or
~~And~~ from the Rivulet sparkling where it runs
Or the pellucid Lake. — — —
at least tis plain
~~At least s~~ At least
~~No proof appears~~

---

593 Del and rev in pencil.
599 Possibly "word" is a reinforcement.
605–606 Rev of 89^v; rev on 88^v.

Rev on 89^r, 88^v, 90^r.
In the first line, comma after "observ d" may be paren.
607/608 Mark after "seemly" may be a comma.
610 Conjectured "B" overwriting probably intends to form "Be."

615, 618, 619 Said I—that they who rest within this
grave
[?Covet]
619 [?Covet] Desire to leave behin to leave
behind them
false report

621 Green is the churchyard beautiful & green—
hath made
622 Ridge rising by the side of Ridge ~~like~~
~~waves~~
623 A heaving surface almost wholly free
[608] This self respecting nature prompts & this
[609] Wisdom enjoins—but if the

[90r]

VI, 624 From interruption of sepulcral stones

626 These dalesmen trust
627 The lingering gleam of their departed lifes
628 To oral Records and the silent heart
629 Depository faitthful & more kind
630 Than fondest Epitaphs—for if it fail
631 What boots the sculptured Tomb.—~~I do not~~
b
[?f] ~~lame~~
And who can blame
~~This mutual confidence, that fears not [?time~~]
~~That disregards~~
~~And fears not [?time] if such it be~~
615 small risk said I
said I
~~at least [?allow~~]
616 of such illusion here do we incur
617 Temptation here is none to exceed the truth
618 No evidence appears that they who
rest
619 Within ~~with~~ this ground were covetous
of praise
620 Or of remembrance even;—deserved or not
621 Green is the churchyard beautiful & green
[?like waves]
g [?ve]
622 Ridge rising by the side of ri de ha [?th]
heaving ~~made~~
billowing
623 An ~~undulating~~ surface almost wholly free
[624] From interruption of sepulcral stones
[615] at least said I
[617] Temptation here is none to exceed the truth

Leaf 90r is rev of 89v; rev on 90v.

[90v]

VI, 625 And mantled oer with aboriginal turf
These
626 And everlasting flowers—~~Yon~~ Dales
men trust
&

631 What boots the sculptured stone & who
can blame
Men [?~~em~~] } [?hold]
632 Who rather would not envy, [?~~th~~ose] } ~~who~~ feel
that
633 This mutual confidence if from ~~such~~
source ~~flow~~
634 The practice flows, if thence, or from a
deep
635 And general humility in death
636 Nor should I much condemn it if it
[?rise]
~~spring~~
637 From disregarding of Times con
suming power
{ to prey on
638 As only capable { [?] [?~~mendacity] for~~ things
mortal
639 Of earth & human Natures earthly part
640 Yet in less simple districts where we see
641 Stone lift its forehead emulous of stone
~~Upon the front of each memorial stone~~
642 In courting notice & the ground all paved
~~Conspicous attestation, in a str[?ain~~]
643 With commendations of departed [?~~word~~] worth;
644 Reading, whereer we turn of Innocent lives
645 ~~Of each domestic~~

[91r]

~~Unvaried, of integrity & worth~~,
~~Religious duties zealously performed~~
of
VI, 645 ~~And~~ each domestic charity fulfill[?ed]
646 And sufferings meekly borne, I for my part
647 Though with the silence pleased which here
prevails,
648 Among those fair recitals also range
649 Soothed by the natural spirit which
they breathe.
651 ~~Nor do I blush to say that compass~~ed round

Rev of 90r, 91r.
633 Possibly, rev "that" applies to "hold" in l. 632, above.

Rev on 90v.

times
652 ~~by such memorials I have~~ some felt
whose soil
650 That in the centre of [?~~an unkin~~] world
Is }
[651] [?If]} rank with all unkindness [?twas]
[650] And in the centre of a world whose soil
compass d round
[651] Is rank with all unkindness, [?~~tis~~]
[?~~no brief~~]
[?]
[652] With such memorial I have sometime[?s] felt
652, 653 ~~No As I felt a happiness to [?have~~]
653 That twas no momentary happiness
~~safe~~
654 ~~One small~~ enclosure where the voice
To have one that speaks
655 In envy or detraction is not heard
656 Which malice may not enter, where
the traces
657 Of evil inclinations are unknown

[91v]

VI, 658 Where love & pity tenderly unite
659 With resignation, and no jarring tone
660 Intrudes the peaceful concert
to disturb
661 Of amity & gratitude. Thus sanctioned
662 The Pastor said, I willingly confine
663 My narratives to subjects that excite
664 Feelings with these accordant, love, esteem
665 And admiration—lifting up a veil
666 A sunbeam introducing among a hearts
667 Retired & covert so that ye shall have
C} a}
668 c}lear img}ges before your gladdened
eyes
669 Of natures unambitious underwood
670 And flowers that prosper in the shade.
And when
671 I speak of such among my flock as swerv'd
672 Or fell those only will I single out

[92r]

{ng
VI, 673 Upon whose lapse or error somethi{g more
674 Than brotherly forgiveness may attend
675 To such will we restrict our notice
else

[652] The last word ("felt") is reinforced—or overwrites the last letters of the queried word above.

676 Better my tongue were mute. And
yet there are
677 I feel good reasons why we should not leave
678 Wh[?ole] untraced a more forbidding way.
For pasionate regards of love & hate
Magnanimous disdain & courage high
{An[?d]
679 {For strength to persevere & to support
{to
680 And energy {& conquer & repel
~~exalts~~ [?finds]
~~Ambition that [?confirms] & hope that [?spurs]~~]
~~The [?enthusiastic] purpose, firm disdain~~
~~fearless~~
~~And dreadless cou~~
~~Magnanimous disdain & courage high~~
~~And in the~~
681 These elements of virtue that declare
682 The native grandeur of the human soul
~~shown~~
683 Are ofttime not unprofitably ~~seen~~
684 In the perversness of a selfish course
[?true]
Enthusiastic hopes and [?in] the [?~~frame~~ frame]
[?In all]
Of the the affections passions & desires
[681] That vigourous constitution that declares
For regards
~~And~~ passionate [?~~extremes~~] of love & hate
Magnanimous disdain & courage

[92v]

VI, 685 Truth every day exemplified no less
686 In the grey Cottage by the murmuring stream
687 That in fantastic conquerers roving [?camp]
[?~~amid~~] the
688 Or ~~in~~ the factious Senate, unappalled
689 While merciless pro cription ebbs & flows.
690 There—said the Priest, and pointed
as he spake
in peace surpass d by none
691 A woman rests ~~distinguished above all~~
Of her estate whom I have chanced to know
In power
692 ~~For power~~ful mind & eloquent discourse
T}
693 [?C]}all was her stature—her complexion dark
p}
694 And saturnine, ~~erect~~ her [?m]}ort erect, her
mien
695 Not absolutely rais[?e] as if to hold

---

693 The "s" in "stature" and the "c" in "complexion" may be caps.

[?~~nor~~]
696 Converse with heaven, [?towa~~rd~~] nor yet depress d, ~~but the~~
~~Save only that the head, the Citadel~~ head
nor downcast but the head
[?towrd]
~~And watchtower of the meditative mind~~
[697] In firm projection carried as she walked
697 ~~Stooped & projected firmly as she walked~~
~~along~~
698 For ever musing—Sunken were her eyes
forehead
700, 699 Her ample [?~~thought &~~] by habitual thought
[?owed]
699, 700 Was furr[?ow]d & wrinkled like the brow of one
her head
[695] Not absolutely raised as if to hold
towards earth
[696] Conversed with heaven not yet depress d
~~towr'd~~
[697] But in projection carried as she walked
[698] For ever musing

[93r]

VI, 701 Whose visual nerve shrinks from a painful
ov glare
702 Of [?]erpowering light— —While yet a
The Child

She
703 [?So] mid the humble flowerests of the vale
Tower'd like the
704 [?~~Rose~~] [?] imperial thistle not unfurnishd
705 With its appropriate grace, yet rather
framed
706 [?~~F~~]~~o~~ to be admired & than coveted & loved
S
707 Even at that age she ruled as sovereign
Queen
708 Among her Playmates yet she was hersel
710 ~~Yet was herself subjected~~ to controul
[710] In turn subjected to a strong
711 Of studious application se[?l]-imposed.
712 Books were her Creditors—to them she paid
713 With pleasing anxious eagerness the hours
T
713, 714 [?H]he hours which they exacted, whether time
714 Which they exacted whether time allowd
~~for recreation~~
715 ~~Allowed, or stolen~~, or seized by stealth, or
Or seized upon by steal fairly won
716 By strectch of industry from other tasks
717 Oh pang of sorrowful regret for them

---

712 Cap in "Creditors" may be lowercase.

718 Whom in their youth sweet study has
[?enslaved]
harsher
719 That they have lived for other servitude
720 Whether in soul in body or her estate
721 Such doom was hers yet nothing could [?~~efface~~]
abate
722 Her keen desire of knowledge or efface
by
723 Those brigther images which ~~Youth~~
Books had fixed
impressed

[93^v]

him
And now methinks I see on the edge
Standing of yon sharp slope from which his pains *TPL, 334, 335*
Unsettling *[336]*

~~from those prying eyes~~
~~Shrouded in vain within her hopeful nest~~
thi{ le {
[?Stu]diously shrouded among [?]{ckening [?]{aves X *320*

{[?]}
per{[?ple }xing] law
of the soul-perverting *[325]*
the melancholy law *325*
sin-producing law *[325]*

Methinks I see him standing on the brink
sharp
{ [?~~sharp~~]
Of yon {[?steep] ~~mountain~~ slope from which his pains *[335]*
at length
Unsettling in its ant[?e]nt seat a mass *[336]*
Of Rock

---

723 Book VI continues on 94^v.

Rev of 94^r.

320 The right-margin X signals the line's insertion on 94^r. This line, the next group of lines related to l. *325*, and ll. *333–338*, below, are in black ink similar to the rev of ll. *335* and *337–338* on 94^r. Two attempted (and partial) rev of ll. *333–338* at the top and middle of 93^v are in ink different from that black ink; those rev appear to be entered in space left on the page and are not clearly indicated as superseding the rev reading on 94^r.

325, [*325*] It is difficult to determine which of these rev was entered first. Both "the melancholy law" and "sin-producing law" are entered opposite the line on 94^r. Although "sin -producing" is closer to the reading on 94^r, its appearance and spacing below "the melancholy law" suggest it is later.

~~down the rugged way~~ 333
steep {ng
~~Of the ~~sharp~~ mountains lo{[?g] declivity~~ 334
~~Wheeling on f[?reel]ly bounding—and aloft~~ [334]
~~Mark the triumphant hero of my Tale~~ 335
~~Whose pains unsettled in its antient seat~~ 336
~~The mass & sent it headlong from the brink~~ 337

Down the steep mountains long declivity 338

[94[r]]

Nor will the Musing Traveller reprove TPL, 315
on } [?havoc]
The wa[?n]t[?ing]} ~~mischief~~ or deplore the waste 316
Of inoffensive beauty from such source 317
h}
Proceeding;—and, hereafter, if the Tr}rush 318
Or
~~And~~ Mother Linnet in her hopeful nest 319
^ ~~Unable to escape th[?ose preyers] eyes~~
Be subject to worse injury, for the Bird 321
He grieves, regrets her loss, but spares meanwhile 322
That overnice humanity which would brand 323
Their enterprize and pleasure-seeking ways 324
Who ignorant of the law that calls forth [?sin to] 325
In pure activity of rustic childhood 326
T} the
D}o range about rejoicing while ~~that~~ joy 327
the
[?~~e~~]}
{[?at]}
Is yet allow'd them in ~~th~~{[?is] law's despite. 328
Hark what an uproar from the hills—and see, 329
th}
(Nay do not smile—[?ti}s] Fancy that must see 330
By virtue of her own creative eye 331
And Fancys ear must listen to the sound) 332
Behold a fragment down the rugged breast 333
and aloft
Of the steep mountain bounding; ~~for delight~~ 334
Mark
~~To~~}~~See~~
Of} ~~the~~ bold hero of my Tale, whose pains 335
At }
[?Un]} length unsettling in its antient seat 336

TPL continues on 94[r] from 43[r]; rev on 93[v].

316 What we read as "waste" may be "wasting."

319/321 Left-margin caret signals the rev, l. *320*, on 93[v].

329ff. Ink and pen change here.

333–338 See rev on 93[v] and the note there to l. *320*. Rev entered on 94[r] appears to be later than the rejected alt at bottom of 93[v]; on 94[r], black ink similar to rev on 93[v] is used for rev "Mark" in l. *335*, for "the brink" and "that brink" in l. *337*, and for l. *338*.

ve| ~~the brink~~
The mass hath} sent it headlong from on high 337
sharp that brink
Of the the ~~steep~~ mountains dizzy eminence 338

[94^v]

VI, 724 Upon her memory faithfully as stars
725 That occupy their places & though oft
and of
726 ~~Which [?though~~] conceled by clouds & dimmed
by haze
[?en]|
[726] Hidden by clouds & oft be} dimmed by ha[?z]
727 Are not to be extinguished or impaired
728 Two passions, both degenerate, for they both
729 Began in honor, ~~mastered~~ gradually obtained
730 Rule over her, & vex d her daily life,
731 An unrelenting avaricious thrift
~~passion~~ thraldom
732 And a strange ~~bondage~~ of Maternal Love
733 That held her spirit in its own despite
734 Bound by forgiveness & by tender thoughts
[734] Mortification & regret & scorn
736 And tears in pride suppress d in shame concealed
737 To a poor dissolute Son—her only Child.—
738 ~~Her~~—Her wedded days had open'd with
mishap
~~On the green Mountain[?s] by the rocky streams~~,
739 Whence dire dependance. What could she
perform
740 To shake the burthen off—ah there was felt
741 Indignantly the weakness of her sex
742 The injustice of her low estate—she mused
743 Resolved adhered to her resolved, her
heart
744 Closed by degrees to charity nor thence
g |
745 Expecting [?go]}ods good blessing placed her
trust
746 In ceaseless pains & parsimonious care
747 That got & sternly hoarded each
days gain.

[95^r]

Thundering and smoking ploughing the gree turf *TPL, 339*

Leaf 94^v is continued from 93^r; continues on 97^v.
742 A mark after "mused" may be intended as a period.

Continued from 94^r.

d
Shattering and shatter'd. With [?t] elight subl[?me] 340
dr[?iv'n]
By apprehension, the Boy surveys 341
The ungovernable motion; with the speed 342
~~and [?shapes]~~ [?s]
guesses [?~~ir~~ect]
course
Of Thought he calculates, ~~d~~ [?ivine] its [?] 343
~~Foretells~~
[?Assigns] [?while]
Inquires its period—[?for] the timid sheep 344
All unendanger'd,, far and near, disperse 345
~~W~~
with
[?With]
[?In] trepidation innocent & wild 346
Not pacified though in the pool below 347
Arleady the huge block hath found repose 348
Echo is hushed and silence hath return'd 349

Thus undepraved by labour, in excess 350
Imposed
~~Grievous~~, or premature, and unappalled 351
By ghastly Poverty the Peasant Lad 352
[?it] hourly acts
Thrives, and exhibits in his ~~daily life~~ 353
A flattering miniature of native man 354
Unruly daring active indolent 355
B[?ent] sometimes, nor without a shortlived 356
Zeal
To useful services but happiest then 357
When danger tempts him—nay with serpent 358
eye
Enthralls and fascinates; or when Mischief 359
a pleads
Restless Ambitions [?A] dvocate & Guide 360

[95v]

~~faith~~
~~y[?ie]d not to that dream~~ *TPL, 361*
~~A [?current] dream of languid poesy~~
~~It springs~~
yield not to that fait [361]
A current dream of lanquid Poesy
Self soothed in pure forgetfulnes no days [361]
yield not to that thought [361]
Tis one of pure forgetfulnes—no days [361]

340/341 Another possible reading for "driv'n" is "dread."
343 Overwriting "course" may be a reinforcement.
356 Another possible reading for "Bent" is "Bad."

---

361 Several attempts to rev and expand this line (here and on 96r) do not clearly indicate which one, if any, is final.

Of human life & B *362*
More than sensations more intense delight *363*
To this new service bound his fervent zeal *384*
~~Outwatching every star in middle heaven~~ *385*
The liveliest star outwarches, in mid heaven [*385*]
~~Or [?slo~~]
Fix d, or slow travelling on the horizons [?brink] *386*
{[~~?~~]
~~Happy~~ {[?if] ~~in his native~~ [?d]} ~~ale detained~~ v *387, 388*
~~And not less~~ [?move] *390*
Happy if call be none that he should [?~~pass~~] [*387*]
Beyond the limits of his native Vale *388*
But not less [*390*]
Happy if she for whom he wakes abide [*387*]
Within the limits of his native vale [*388*]
{the Youth
And not less happy if need be {[?he post] [*390*]
Posts *391*

[96^r]

H
[?D]}is days are happy—think not so—no days *TPL, 361*
Of human life with happiness are blest *362*
But his are fraught with pleasures manifold *363*
native {ra
Nor destitute of ~~Nature's~~ g{[?o]ce a wild *364*
B more keen delight
And generous dignity. But livelier joy *365*
Awaits his ripen'd Station; the fresh [?brand] *366*
Of Independence eagerly assumed *367*
The first pure relish of life's personal *368*
cares
And the free earnings of his sinewy arms *369*
To his own use for purposes appli'd. *370*
glittering ~~happ[?y~~ polishd]
By his own will the[?re] ~~thoughtful~~ novelties *371*
With store of self applause for shrewdness, *372*
[?put fort] pain[?s]
Or steadness applied before their time *373*
mightier
And [?~~dearer~~] far than these, love rushing in *374*
With perturbation. To the yoke he bends *375*

---

362 "B" in the right margin is connected by a diagonal line to "B" on 96^r, indicating intended rev. Possibly, the rev reading on 96^r, "more keen delight," is the result. The line entered on 95^v could not be inserted in the place marked on 96^r without further rev of the passage on 96^r.

386–391 Rev of 96^v–97^r; rev on 98^r. See also drafts in MS. 80, 32^v–33^r, and note to ll. *375–465* on 96^r, below.

361–362 See rev on 95^v and note there to l. *361*.

365 "B" and a diagonal line signal rev on 95^v.

375–465 These *TPL* lines appear in rev form in MS. 80, 32^v–35^r. See *PW*, V, 432, where there is speculation that WW may have considered this passage for publication in *PW*, 1815. For ll. *378–390* and *435–438*, cf. Morgan MS., recto.

Conquer[?ng]
Receives the Chain from Nature[?s] sovereign hand 376
Not loth nor sad but inwardly rejo[?icd] 377
Even like the whistling Blackbird in the 378
lordly the grove
Or ~~lonesome~~ Egle in ~~his~~ rocky wild 379
{y
[?Sudued]—His da{ys shew little, by that light 380
You cannot read him; into the hours of rest 381
{w
His spirit and course of action overflo{[?d] 382
No ghost familiar with the night 383
like him.

[96^{v}]

~~The Stripling~~ strip
[?enamoured] str ~~in [?his]~~ fervent
The ~~subjugated~~ Stripling's ~~fervent~~ zeal TPL, 384
[—?—?—]
Outwactches, ~~and [?enamoured]~~, and [?if need] 385
stat[?ionary] zeal
and [?enamoured], over moss
And moor & mountain top, if need should be 391
His fervent zeal [?to] to this new service [384]
{[?Her]
{[?]
The enamoured stripling happily [?detain]
Within the [?limits] of his native vale 388
Outwatches, nor less happy if need be 390
Post over moss & moor & mountain top [391]
His fervent zeal, to this new service [?vowd], [384]
Outwatches
~~To [?this new] service vow'd his fervent~~ zeal [384]

~~vivifying~~
[?~~Fitful], yet noiseless [?beautyfing light~~] 404
[?~~A~~]}
[?I]}~~nd her still glow~~ oh happy hours [404]
His zeal vow[?s] his fervent [384]
^ To this new service dedicate, his zeal [384]
thereby
Outwatches, happy if detained ~~thereby~~ ⊗ [385]
Within the limits of his native vale [388]
And not less happy if need be the Youth [390]
Posts over ~~plain~~ moor & plain & mountain top [391]

Or from beneath the cottage eves ascends 398

Leaf 96^{v} is rev of 97^{r}, partly recopied on 95^{v} and recopied on 98^{r}. See note to ll. *375–465* on 96^{r}.

[*384*]–[*391*] This passage, beginning eight base text lines from page foot ("To this new service"), is in different ink. The circled X in the right margin corresponds to the mark in the top left margin of 97^{r} and indicates that this passage on 96^{v} supplies the reading there before subsequent rev entered on 95^{v} and 97^{r} (and later incorporated in MS. 80).

A his
~~The~~ stifled cough warning [?the] chosen maid 399
That now when sleep has hushed the world he comes 400

[97[r]]

The liveliest star in middle firmament *TPL, 385*
Fix'd, or slow travellng on the horizon's brink *386*
To this new service vowed his fervent zeal *384*
~~His zeal~~ outwatched, and if need should be
⊗ Outwatches happy if thereby detained &c
Within the *388*
[?~~Then] over moss and moor and mountain top~~ *391*
And not less happy if need be the youth *390*
[?~~dale~~]
Posts over moor & [?] & mountain top *[391]*
Through wood and brook across, by shortest line *392*
chiding oft
Hasting and [?blames] oft the darksome clouds *393*
That the sky breeds to blind his eager steps *394*
sundry
What ~~various~~ shapes of hazard paths obscure, *395*
ati
And leng[?h]th of undef[?g]gable march *396*
~~For a brief taste of stea[?t]hy intercourse~~ *401*
door ~~gentle~~ soft low
Ere at the [?wind~~ow~~] the ~~fearful~~ tap be giv[?'n] *397*
Or stifled cough[?t] beneath the window heard *399*
ing Maid
Warn [?g] the chosen [?lover] that he is come *[399]*
For a brief taste of stealthy intercourse *[401]*

Ten thousand sparks do from this covert fire *402*
[?M]ount up t
Spring up at each inci[?n]ement of the breeze *403*
[?issful]
bl essed
Vivid though noiseless; [?~~beautifying~~]
~~happy~~ hours, if doubt *404*
Be not nor jealousy but hours they are *405*
T
And time has wings & pleasure is [?it]ime's slave. *406*
by
begone ~~ere~~ blush of morning light
H :
[?P]e must depart; with th[?e] far wandering *407*
[?ing] fox fox
With the far wander[?d] [?blush of] slink to his h[?ouse] *408*
Slink to his h[?ouse] by^morning light *408*

Leaf 97[r] is rev on 96[v], 95[v], 98[r]. See note to ll. *375–465* on 96[r].

388 The circled X in the left margin, and "&c" in the right, indicate the reading on 96[v] (see the note there).

~~Remeasure [?ba~~]
For short repose or haply to commence 409
A long days labour with the sun new 410
risen

[97v]

VI, 748 Thus all was reeestablished & a pile
[?] Constructed
749 Raised that suffi[?ced] for every end
750 Save the contentment of the Builders mind.
[?~~T~~]} A {by aught
751 [?] } ~~that~~ mind {[?] nature undispose to [?~~augh~~]
placid
752 So ~~meek~~ so inactive as content
A } {[?eace,]
753 [?S]} mind intolerant of lasting p{[?]
which
754 And cherishing the pang ~~that~~ it deplored.
[?its]
And in ~~the~~ [?] [?silence it must chear]
Proud of the ~~pangs~~ enduring pangs which {[?live]
Thus in her humble station [?did she] {[?]
it deplored
755 A Life of confit—which I oft compared
756 To the agitation ~~of~~ a brook that runs
757 Down rocky mountains buried now & lost
758 In silent pools unfathomably deep
759 Now in a moment starting forth again
glad pleased
760 With violence, & proud of its escape
761 Untill it sink once more by slow degrees
{Or instantly
762 {A[?nd] ~~suddenly~~ into as deep repose.— —
strength
763 A sudden illness seized her in the strength
L}
764 Of l}ifes autumnal season—shall I tell
765 How on her bed of death the Matron lay
766 To Providence submissive—so she thought
{—
767 But fretted vex d & wrought upon{, almost
i}
768 to Anger by the malady that gra}ped

Leaf 97v is continued from 94v, continues on 104v.
749 Another possible reading for "sufficed" is "sufficient."
755 For the fourth word, *1814* reads "conflict."
762 Overwriting is in pencil; possibly the word overwritten is "As."
768 The cap in "Anger" may be lowercase.

[98ʳ]

To this new service bound his fervent zeal *TPL, 384*
The liveliest star outwatches in mid heaven *385*
Fix'd, or slow-travelling on the horizon's brink. *386*
Happy if She for whom he wakes abide *387*
Within the limits of his native vale, *388*
T }
[?]}he native vale of both or common home *389*
And not less happy if need be the Youth *390*
Post over moss & dale & mountain top *391*
Through wood & brook across by shortest line *392*
[?~~watr~~] watry
Hasting and chiding oft the ~~darksome~~ *393*
clouds
That the sky breeds to blind his eager steps. *394*
p }
What sundry sha[?d]}es of hazard, paths obscure *395*
And length of indefatigable march *396*
Ere at the door the soft low tap be given *397*
be } a
Or from [?the]}neath the Cottge[?s] eaves ascend *398*
The stifled cough warning his chosen Maid *399*
[?w] }
That now [?]}hen sleep has hushed the world *400*
he comes
For a brief taste of stealthy intercourse *401*
see last
Ten thousand sparks &c [?~~see la~~] *402*

[98ᵛ]

no shower
[?Sh] to stain the long d for dawn
When open[?ed]ly

When openly claims the dear reward
his assiduous care {[?~~and~~] secret
Of ~~all his~~ patience {[?~~watchfulness~~] and pain
Contrivance disappointment

sky
No weeping ~~shower~~ shall stain the long for day

Thus far then shall our Lovers [?meet] their wish *TPL, 424*
the sky shall shun to stain [?his] day *[425]*
Fullfilled, ~~nor weeping sky shall stain the day~~ *425*

Rev of 95ᵛ, 96ᵛ–97ʳ. See note to ll. *375–465* on 96ʳ.
386 Period may be an accidental mark.
387 The cap in "She" may be lowercase.
402 WW's instruction, "see last," refers to continuation of passage on 97ʳ.

Rev of first draft on 99ʳ, partly incorporated into second draft on 99ʳ. See note to ll. *375–465* on 96ʳ.
424 The "et" in conjectured "meet" is partly blotted, perhaps as a result of an attempt to rev to "have."

That gives [?him]
~~When~~ openly ~~he claims~~ [?his] dear reward
With the discouragement of weeping shower[?s]
And on that morning shall the unclouded sun *427*
[?Dart] gladsome radian[?ce] *428*
~~till~~
So fares this ~~youthful passion, and, at length~~
Each
~~The~~ current stemm'd of adverse circumstance *411*
The rocks of absence either shunned or touchd *412*
Without a fatal shock, the insidious shoals *413*
Of dire mistrust triumphantly escaped *414*
And fancy's cross winds and her peevish squalls *415*
All stoutly weather'd the trim vessel [?hold] *416*
the day
it dawns the day { it dawns
Her port in open view. ~~At length~~ {[?is come] *417*
The wish for day, that [?brgt] the recompense *418*
of [?solid] recompense
By frugal preparation in *419, 420*

[99^r]

Merry the Bride on whom the Sun doth shine *TPL, 422*
~~But happy, so th attendant [?adage runs]~~
Happy the dead on who the rain doth fall *423*
Thus far then [?L] { have
[?Thus] shall our { l}overs {[?find] their wis, the sky *424*
{eir {[?morn]
Forbid its shower to stain th{e nuptial {day
And from his [?throne] the unclouded sun
dale
[?Dart] gladsom radiance so that hill & ~~plain~~. *428*
[?~~attend~~] troop
Partake [?]
~~Shall share~~ the pleasure of the gay ~~dress d~~ train *429*
As they advance or from the church~~yard~~ *430*
[?returned]
[?Marri d] with the [?pair] of life remaining day[?s] *432*
~~Indissolubly bound~~ *433*
~~For lifes [?remain day span throug] good & evil~~ *[432]*
~~Indissolubly bound~~ *[433]*
Each gives to each indissolubly bound *433*
Blithe company of
~~The train attendant~~, elders, Maid & youth *431*
And the bless d pair for Life remaining *[432]*
course
Each gives to each indissolubly bound. *[433]*

428/ Passage beginning "So fares" and continuing at top of 99^v is added as transition between *TPL*, ll. *410* and *422* (see 99^r). That transition is incorporated into MS. 80 on 33^v–34^r. Unnumbered lines at the top of 98^v seem to be attempts to fashion a new beginning for ll. *422ff.* on 99^r.

Continues from 97^r. Rev on 98^v, 99^v (which also have a draft of a transition between *TPL*, ll. *410* and *422*). See note to ll. *375–465* on 96^r.

422–424 Lines are not included in MS. 80. In l. *424* "wish" is miswritten as "wis."

429 Conjectured rev "attend" may be "attired" or rev to "attire" by the queried letters below.

Merry the Bride on whom the Sun doth shine [422]
Happy the dead on whom the Rain doth fall [423]
our betrothed shall see w
Thus far then ~~shall our Lovers~~^ ~~find~~ their f/ish [424]
Fullfill'd—the orb that animates the earth 425
And chears the frame fill the spirit of man 426
at day shall shine
With genial thoughts upon the/ ~~long for day~~ 427
~~That gives him openly the dear reward~~

[99v]

The important day of lasting recompense *TPL*, 418
[?throng]
Not unpreceeded by a frugal s/tore 419
Of household preparations, intermixd 420
~~gayly mixd~~
With inoffensive vanity and show 421

And laughs to see the laughin chi[?d], at once 444
d
[?gi]/izzy height
Pleased, and half frightend at the [?boisterous] din 445
Th[?us] he [?dismisses him]
From the first hour but to the Father then 436
dear
~~proud~~
Became a ~~dear~~ possession 437
to
when the Father then [436]
heart
To the father [?then]
Became a dear possession when the Babe [437]
~~Has gather d strength~~ 438
Strengthend by time, [?~~endure~~] uninjured may endure [438]
loves
~~A~~ t
[?His] boisterous assaul/ts ~~of love [?a] happy Man~~ 439, 440
The [?Man is]
~~[?A least] of happy feeling when he quits~~ 440
~~His ho[?me]~~ 441
[?~~rough~~]
At his [?strong] ~~hands~~ loves boisterous assaul [439, 440]
love boisterously
Rough fondness and the gaiety of love [439]
In boisterous assaults. Then, ere he quits [440]
His ho[?me] [441]
Pleas'd, yet half frightend by [445]
the giddy din

---

427 Rev "day shall shine" is the result of del at the top of 100r, where the passage continues.

Continuation from 98v of a draft intended as transitional between *TPL*, ll. 410 and 422. Remainder of page is rev of 100r, in turn rev on 100v–101r. See note to ll. 375–465 on 96r.

[100[r]]

~~Of his assiduous cares & pains, shall shine~~ *TPL, 427*
{ & reflect
In splendour, so that hill {[?] dale ~~partake~~ *428*
c}
[?In] ~~The eng}ouragement, reflecting the delight~~
{And
{The satisfaction of the festive troop *429*
As they advance or from the church return, *430*
~~Maiden & youth and elders~~
{Gay {, M}
{Blithe company of elders{ &} aids & youths *431*
And the blest pair for lif[?s] remaining *432*
course
Each gives to each indissolubly bound. *433*

Fair fruit this natural wedlocck doth *434, 435*
presen
a gift of pride and joy
In season due, ~~right acceptable gift~~ *435*
To either parent—ere he quits his home *436, 440*
{ on
Nor less {[?at] entiering from the fields or hills *441*
this} Peasant
Lightly the} Father on a vigorous arm *442*
Tosses his lusty Boy a loft in air *443*
{[?d]
Hal~~f pleas~~[?ed] half frightend by the {[?] [?izzy] heig
Pleas[?ing if]
A momentary plaything, and [?delight] *447*
Occasional for six successive days *448*
Of work, and at more frequent intervals *449, 450*
And [?thus], too
Sweetening the day of leisure and repose *451*
proceed
With innocent pastime—so the years ~~pass~~ on *452, 456*
claim
{ claim
Discord shall {[?place] no place by this fire side *463*
dread
Nor shall the ~~fear~~ of poverty oppress *464*
n}
Their waking thoughts }or guilt disturb *465*
their dreams

[100[v]]

brings
This natural wedlock bears in season due *TPL, 434*
Fair fruit, a welcome gift of joy and pride *435*

Continues from 99[r], where l. 427 also appears. Rev on 98[v], 99[v], 100[v]–101[v]. See note to ll. *375–465* on 96[r].

Rev of 99[v], 100[r], rev on 101[r]. See note to ll. *375–465* on 96[r].

From the first hour, but to the Father heart 436
Doubly endeared soon as the tender Babe 437
~~Became a dear possession when the Babe~~
By creeping [?Time] is strength to endur 438
Strengthened by time uninjured [?can] endure
Rough fondness and the gaiety of love [?withstand] 439
In boist[?e]rous assault. Then, ere he quits 440
~~and [?as he~~] nor less
{[?~~or~~]
{[?on]}
His home, [?at]} entering from the field {~~and~~
{[?or] ~~hills~~ 441
~~The [?cottage door] or enters from the fields~~
Lightly the Peasant of a vigorous arm 442
vigorous peasant at arm's length
Tosses his lusty boy aloft in air 443
And laughs to see the laughing child, at onc[?e] 444
and daunted
Pleased ~~yet~~ half ~~fright~~[?e] d by the dizzy heig[?t] 445
Gained in an instant in an instant lost 446
~~still within his reach~~
~~Thus ever within reach— the Father find~~
[?~~The~~]
This momentary plaything his delght 447
Occasional and ever within reach 448
l}
[?pleasur] re[?f }i]f
A solace and occasional delight [447]
[?Brif solace]
Or
To in[?s]tersperse through six labor [448]
Enlivening six days ious days [448]
{e
seasonable gladnes reli{ ff
A momentary solace a ~~delght~~ [447]
Occasional for six laborious days [448]
at hand
Is here provided, a resource is here 449
[?a]}
[?~~Briefer~~] [?]}~~nd, which at more frequent intervals~~ 450
{by more
Which, {oft[?ener], frequ {t
and by more con{[?f]inous [?fits] [450]
lei}
Sweetens the day of [?day]}sure and repose[?s] 451
With innocent 452

[101r]

{rings
This natural wedlock b{ears in season due TPL, 434
A welcome gift
~~Fair fruit~~, a ~~welcome~~ gift of joy and pride 435

In the passage del by vertical strokes (and just below that passage), "A solace and occasional delight/Enlivening six days" may have been entered earlier than "To in[?s]tersperse through six laborious days/A momentary solace a delght."

Rev of 100v, 99v, 100r; rev and continued on 101v. See note to ll. 375–465 on 96r.

{a g}
Fair fruit, {[?in] [?w]}ift wit joy and pride rec[?i]ved
~~From the first hour~~; but to the Fathers heart 436
e
By [?h]}ither parent,—to
Doubly endeared soon as the tender Babe 437
Strengthen d by Time is able
By creeping Time is strengthend to endure 438
Rough fondness and the gaiety of love 439
In boisterous assault. Then, ere he quits 440
{H
{[?h]is home, or as he enters from the fields 441
Lightly the vigorous Peasant at arm's length 442
Tosses his lusty Boy aloft in air 443
And laughs to see the laughing child—at once 444
Pleased and half-daunted by the dizzy height 445
Gained in an instant in an instant lost. 446
{relief
A seasonable gladness a {delight 447
Occasional, for six laborious days 448
prepared and oftener This resource
{[?is here]
{e {[?at hand]
Is her{es ~~provided, a resourse at hand~~ 449
More often in
Which ~~by~~ oftener and ~~by~~ more continu[?o]s [?fits] 450
Sweetens the day of leisure and repose 451
[?time]
With innocent pastime. So the years proceed 452, 456
{all
Discord th{at claim no place by this fire side 463
oppress
Nor shall the dread of poverty ~~disturb~~ 464
Their waking thoghts nor guilt disturb their dreams. 465
Their strength immoderate Labour shall [?not not waste] 461
Ungratefully
Nor sickness overturn their plans or cross 462

[101v]

along the path of wedded life TPL, 457
~~so this wedded Pair~~ 456
~~Proceed in smooth and favorable course~~ [456]
Th
[?Imm]}eir strength immoderate Labour shall not waste 461
Nor sickness overturn their plans, or thwart, 462
{is
Discord shall claim no place by th{eir fire-side 463
Nor shall the dread of Poverty oppress 464
Their waking thoughts nor guilt disturb their dreams 465
{Safe
{[?Far] from the [?open] world[?s indecent air] [453]
In a sheltered spot 452

---

463 The first "t" in base text "that" stands for an "s" in the rev to form "shall."

Expansion and rev of 101r, 100r. See note to ll. *375–465* on 96r.

worlds contagious intercours
Far from the ^ gross contagion of the worl 453
Thus are the earlier years of wedded life 454
Adornd, as Spring with flowers: and more to uphold 455
they advance
The Pair and favor them, as Time Proceeds, [456]
{e
In later time [?avoid] along th{eir humble path [457]
~~They shall [?]scape the pitfalls of mistake~~ 458
The Pitfalls of mistake they shall avoid [458]
By Prudence guarded, whose sure hand shall heal 459
The hurts of unavoidable mischance 460
Immoderate Labour shall not sap their strength 461
plans
Nor sickness overturn their schemes or thwart 462
{find
Discord shall {claim no place by their fire side [463]
Nor shall the dread of poverty oppress [464]
Their waking thoughts nor guilt disturb their [465]
dreams.
t
The [?pair and] favour [?oer]}hrogh after years [456]
{[?~~on~~] time
~~The Pair advancing~~ {[?in] ~~the[?ir]~~ 456, 457
The pitfalls of mist [?k] 458
that spring is there 470
Not loth to put her vigor to the proof 471
Of many a rough untoward blast that shakes 472
with [?fear] {B
And sends her back into her holds—{bright 473
Spring
Whe[?nce] laughing she comes forth again—Bright 474

[102[r]]

V, 387 Ah what avails it?—in the life of Man— TPL, 466
{of
388 If to the Poetry {?or] common speech 467
389 Faith may be given, we see as in a glass 468
A}
390 T} true reflection of the circling year 469
390/391 ~~The seasons of the circling year set forth~~
With all its seasons—
{ ~~By~~
391 {[?In ~~true~~] reflection—Grant that spring 470
is there
~~In spite of many a rough untoward blast~~
Hopeful and promising with buds & flowers
394 Yet where is glowing Summers long rich day 483

455–[457] Diagonal slash canceling these lines appears to be related to rev in MS. 80, 34[v]. MS. 80 (which starts at *TPL*, l. *375*) stops at *TPL*, l. *465*.
470–474 Rev of 102[r], rev on 125[v], inside back cover, 102[v], 103[r].

Rev and expanded on 101[v], 125[v], inside back cover, 102[v]–103[r]. Cf. MS. 74A, 10[v].

That
395 ~~Which~~ ought to follow faithfully express d 484
[?crown]
396 And mellow Autumn charged with 485
bounteous fruits
397 Where is she imaged in what favored ~~clime~~ 486
v| soil
398 Her laf|ish pomp & ripe magnificence 487
399 Yet while the better part is miss'd, the 488
worse
mans autumnal season set forth
400 ~~In what we call our Autumn~~—is ~~expressd~~ 489
401 With a resemblance not to be denied 490
{ him
402 And that contents {[?us]—bowers that hear 491
no more
403 The voice of gladness—less and less supply 492
404 Of outward sunshine and internal warmth 493
[?sharp air a]
405 And, with this change, their [?~~blasts~~], & falling leaves 494
406 Fore running total winter, bl[?an]k & cold 495

[102^v]
V, 389 we see as in a glass *TPL*, 468
390 A true reflection of the circling year 469
391 With all its seasons—grant that spring is there 470
Not loth to tempt encounter hazardous 471
392 Of froward blasts that exercise and shake 472
And send her back with fear into her holds 473
Whence she returns in hasty confidence 474
And interweave[?s] new buds & fresher blooms 475
With those that yet are lingering undismiss d 476
that
~~From her torn wreath—Grant th[?ese] restless~~ 477
their hours
With all gleams and shifting promises
Springs natural portion and her dear delight 481
Are in our Youth familiarly displayed 482
Her gleams and shifting promises, and strife 479
Of hope & fear 480
394 Yet where 483
restless
admit that strife of fear [477]
~~With hope, & hope trumphant in the main~~ [480]
Peril a|
~~Trial~~ and strif[?d] and trembling eg|gerness
shif fitful
And ~~fitful~~ gleams & shifting promises
Springs natural portion & her dear light [481]
That these are all familiar to our Youth [482]
And hope, blithe hope triumphant in the main [480]

Leaf 102^v is expansion and rev of 125^v, inside back cover, 101^v, 102^r; rev on 103^r, which continues from *TPL*, l. *476* on 102^v ("undismiss d"), incorporating rev at lower half of page. Cf. MS. 74A, 10^v.

[103^{r}]

undismissd *TPL, 476*
From her torn wreath—Admit that restless hours *477*
Peril and strif and trembling eagerness *478*
shiftin
l } {shifting }
And fitful g[?r]}eams, and {[?fitful]} promises *479*
And hope, blithe hope triumphant in the main *480*
d}
Springs natural [?portion] and her dear l}elight *481*
That these are all familiar to our youth *482*
V, 394 Yet where is glowing Autumns long rich day *483*
o }
395 That [?u]}ught to follow faithfully expressed *484*
canker } admit that perilous [?hour] [*477*]
Of blight, that [?]} lodged invisibly *478*
And restless interchange of hope and fear [*479*]
With hope blithe hope triumphant in the main [*480*]
Springs natural portion and her dear delight [*481*]
That these are all familiar to our [*482*]

[103^{v}]

{[?~~co~~] choice
{[?ch] [?] Look low or high
What change doth haughty ~~man~~hood bring to prove *TPL, 510*
[?That or choice proves] the [?w]
{[?~~was~~]
Is faded or {[?th] flung scornfully away
[?sole crown]
In hopes to gain a ~~wreath~~ of sparkling gems

V, 433 And all the coming novelties at best *515*
434 Imperfect substitutes whose very power *516*
435 Acknowledges the weakness whence they spring *517*
{ And
{[?Or] whose acknowledge d use evince that want [*516*]
{[?whence] }
Or weakness {[?] [?for]} they spring. [*517*]

432 Old things repeated with diminishd grace [?a] *514*
[433] And all the slow paced novelties to come [*515*]
[434] Fallacious substititutions, signs of want [*516*]
Failure and weakness rather than of powe [*517*]

The toiling engine for the gushing fount *519, 518*
The sail, that sought the help of every wind *521*
The sail abandoned for the creeping oar *522*

Rev of 102^{v}, 101^{v}, 125^{v}, inside back cover, 102^{r}. Cf. MS. 74A, 10^{v}.

WW's intention seems to be to rev first draft of *TPL*, ll. *477–482*, as signified by the vertical line in left margin, by entering the rev (ll. [*477*]–[*482*]) below and by continuing with *TPL*, l. *483*, above and as on 102^{r}. "Autumns" in l. *483* is probably an error for "Summers"; cf. 102^{r}, l. *483*.

478 Possibly, "canker" is merely a reinforcement.

This rev and expansion of 104^{r} substantially differs from another rev on 105^{r}. Cf. MS. 74A, 11^{v}.

And on the basis of some goodly pile 523
Insensibly decay[?e] or with harsh hand 524
D
[?Ar/e]molished, and sub[?s]erv[?e]ted utterly, 525
structure
Unsightly reared with needless pains. 526

---

seek
~~look~~ low or high
What cho[?ce] what change doth mankind bring to prove [510]
[?counselor] sup
That [?rea guides] that reason is [?]/reme
That [?pleasure]
What [?gain] what [?praise] brings [?to choice or chance] [510]
And life [?hath] reach[?e] its grand maturity 512

[104r]

[?At]
Spare then regret, misplace not your contempt *TPL*, 496
If with no happier fate than others, born 497
To Fortunes pure advantages, and reared 498
With Learnings boasted aid,—this Shepherd Swain 499
Albeit in Christian precepts not unschooled 500
And with an ear not ignorant of the threat 501
Denounc'd, the promise and the high com 502
his mand,
Do in ~~this~~/ noiseless solitude partake 503
V, 423 Mans general lot; and lead a life whose 504
course
ducted
428 Is fashioned like an ill-constructed Tale 505
on
429 That in the outset wastes its gay desire 506
enlivening
430 Its fair adventures, ~~all~~ its lively hopes 507
431 And pleasant interests; leaving for the rest 508
432 Things old repeated with diminished 514
grace
433 And all the laboured novelties to come 515
No better than unsightly structures reared 525
On the foundation of some goodly Pile 523
Insensibly decay'd, or with harsh hand 524
Demolish'd, and subverted utterly. [525]

Leaf 104r is rev on 103v, 105r; see note to 103v. Cf. MS. 74A, 11r–11v.

Ink of conjectured "At" at the top differs from that on rest of page; the word may be unrelated to other copy.

499 Dash may be eras.

503 Vertical mark after "this" signals insertion.

[104v]

VI, 768 that griped
wi
769 Her prostrate frame [?un]}th unrelaxing Power
770 As the fierce E[?a]gle fastens on the Lamb
771 She prayed—she moaned—her Husbands sister watch'd
772 Her dreary Pillow—waited on her needs
773 And yet the very sound of that kind foot
774 Was anguish in her ears—& must she rule
775 This wa[?y] the dying woman heard to say
{In
776 {[?A] bitterness and must she rule & reign
777 Sole mistres of this house when I am gone
778 Sit by my fire possess what I possessed
779 Tend what I tended—calling it her own
780 —Enough—I fear too much—[?~~of work~~]
~~In scanty measure dealt or cistern's hoard~~ *TPL, 520*
[?~~That~~] ~~fear[?s] the sun, of life and motion~~ [?~~void~~] [520]
of nobler feeling
781 Take this example—one autumnal evening
782 While she was yet in prime of health & strength
783 I well remember—while I passed her door
Musing step
784 [?~~Musing~~] with loitering ^ and upward eye
785 Fixed on the planet Jupiter that hung
786 Above the centre of the Vale—a voice
787 [?Rouz'd] me—her voice— —it said that glorious star
788 In its untroubled Element will shine
789 As now it shines when we are laid in earth
790 And safe from all our sorrows—She is safe

[105r]

V, 431 And pleasant interests. Thus far step by step *TPL, 508*
{we
That life {[?I] have retraced—and what remains *509*
What proof doth Manhood bring that now a scheme *510*
Is rounded and complete, a promise kept *511*
A height attained a noble growth matured. *512*
Day follows day and year succeeds to year *513*
432 Old things repeating with diminish[?e]d grace, *514*
high priz'd
433 And all the ~~freight of~~ laboured novelties, at best *515*
434 Imperfect substitutes whose use and power *516*
435 Evince the want or weakness whence they spring *517*

Continued from 97v; continues on 105v.

Rev of 103v–104r. Cf. MS. 74A, 11v. The drafting on the verso of the Morgan MS. may be another attempt at recounting the peasant's last days.

See for the gushing founts continous stream 518
The toiling engines interrupted gifts, 519
Ci
Or joyless [?]sterns' hoard, that fears the sun, 520
caught
The sail that ~~sought~~ the help of every wind 521
The sail abandoned for the creeping oar. 522
And on the basis of some goodly pile 523
th
Insensibly decay or wis{[?h] [?harrs ha] hand 524
Demolish'd and subverted utterly 525
Unsightly structure reared with needless pains. 526

[105ᵛ]

VI, 791 And her uncharitable acts I trust
[?ar]
is
792 And all her harsh unkindness ~~are~~ forgiven
793 Though in this vale remembered with deep awe.
794 The Vicar ceased & towr'ds a seat advanced
795 A long-stone seat framed in the Church yard wall
796 Part under shadow sycamore & part
797 Offering a place of rest in pleasant sunshine
798 Even as may suit the Comers old or young
799 Who reach the house of worship while the Bells
800 Yet ring with all their voices, or before
ceased
801 The last hath [?~~closed~~] its solitary knoll
802 To this commodious resting place he led,
[?~~readily~~] by his side
803 Where, ~~by his side~~ we all sate down & ther
804 His office uninvited he resumed.
805 As on a sunny bank &c—
[?Confined] in [?swamps] to multiply their kind
Swarming abroad

[?Soreness] of heart forbids & keeps the brain
that swarm
[?Free] from the fly [?blown tomb] of busy thougt
~~[?] [?forth a] [?]~~
~~And~~ ^ th[?at] miracle a [?heart] of [?human] pride
Thus [?~~far th~~] gain is his, but he is [?man]
Thus far doth his humility obtain
ier
The happy{ worthier state—but he is [?man]

Leaf 105ᵛ is continued from 104ᵛ; continues on 58ʳ.

Passage below l. 805 was probably entered first. It seems to be drafting toward *TPL*, possibly related to copy on 106ʳ and possibly meant to follow the last line there.

[106r]

Why look with nearer view—? enough that he *TPL*, *527*
Who when a Child among the flowery fields *528*
Convers'd, not lacking either eye or soul *529*
With Natures beauty—on the dizzy height *530*
Who stood in [?loneliness] a Shepherd Lad *531*
{And
{Who nurs d the daring appetite of power *532*
Who skimm'd the hills and dales as if *533*
on wings
A Youthful Lover and who, lastly, gained, *534*
Following as no unworthy passion led *535*
A Husbands calm assurances, and reaped *536*
The tender first fruits of a Fathers love, *537*
for all that to himself pertains
That he ~~ere life's mid stage be fairly reached~~ *538*
{true
Of {happier enjoyment dignity or power, *539*
{the
Already ere {lifes middle stage of life *540*
Be pass d nay fairly reache doth walk the *541*
[?M]} earth
In degradation. [?H}an] has breathed too long *542*
{O
Ask of thyself thou proud {one of the world *543*
If this be not thy doom no less than his *544*
[?Yours]}
{ [?Thine]} Toil—daily toil
{[?To have], and in worse degree—His daily toil *545*
Secure his vigorous hea[?lt] and tranquil *546*
sleep
But time & custom overpower his soul *547*
| Upon the tablet the bright colour[?s] fade *548*
[?Image]
| The [?~~fair~~] form steal insensbl[?i]ly away *549*
[?lineaments] behind
And leaves unsightly ~~structure in its~~ place *550*
a meagre outline in its plac
The ~~ghost[?s] of van~~ished beauty— *551*
[~~— ? —~~][?ing]
A ghost a [?shadow]

[107v]

lie
{ere original bed
V, 1010 Th{is the chanel [?~~formed~~] And ~~capacious~~
{rom
1011 F{[?or] the beginning hollow d out & shaped

Leaves 106 and 107 are uncut at the top, thus leaving 106v and 107r blank. *TPL* ends here, with the exception of draft on the bottom half of 105v and rev of *TPL* on 125v and the inside back cover. See the note to 105r about possible rev on the verso of the Morgan MS.

The ink is different from what is on preceding leaves; the passage on 107v may have been written later than those leaves. Rev and expansion of 108r; cf. MS. 74A, 29v.

else betray d & lost
best e |
1012 For mans affections [?th]|lse forlorn, [?dreading]
bewild else
1013 ~~In the blank de~~sert—
i |
[1013] And swallo[?wup] in desarts [?d]|nfinite
the law & rule
1014 This is the aim & end the hope & hope
1015 Of Prescient reason

[108^r]

V, 1008 That life is love and immortality
1009 The Being one and one the Element
1014 This is the genuine Course the aim & end
1015 Of Prescient reason, all conclusions else
1016 Are abject vain presumptuous & perverse
1018 Life I repeat is energy of love
1019 Divine or human, exercised in pain
1020 In strife and tribulation and ordained
1021 If so approved and sanctified, to pass
1022 Through shades and silent rest to endless
joy

[108^v]

VII, 321 The Hermit, lodged
322 [?St] in the untrodden desart, tells his beads
323 With each repeating its allotted prayer
324 And thus divides & thus relieves the time
325 Smooth talk &c

[327] Of keen domestic anguish, and beguile
328 A solitude unchosen unprofessed
ge |
329 Till [?]|ntle death releas d him. Who shall pry

say
327 Of keen domestic anguish. Who shall ~~pry~~
~~Into the heart and confidently say~~
[?~~if to the fountain head~~]
but the blind result—
[?~~N~~]|
331 How much of this is ~~merely~~ n|~~ature's praise~~

Leaf 108^r is rev and expanded on 107^v (see the note there); cf. MS. 74A, 29^r–29^v.

Cf. 81^v–82^r (previous Book VII work in MS. 74 ends on 85^r). Ll. 254–321a of Book VII (originally written for *Tuft of Primroses*) are not present in MS. 74, but revisionary work in MS. 65 (converting this passage for its place in *Exc*) may date from the same time as MS. 74; see *Tuft*, pp. 214–225.

[?~~praise~~] ~~results~~
331, 332 ~~The blind effect of~~ vital temperament
Of cordial spirits &
333 And what to higher Powers is justly due.
334 But in the compass of these pastoral Vales
335 A Priest abides before whose life such
doubts
336 Fall to the ground whose gifts of nature
lie
337 Retired from notic lost in attributes

[109r]

VII, 327 Of keen domest
338 Of Reason, honourably effaced by debts
339 Which her poor treasure House is content
to owe
340 And conquests over her dominion gained
341 To which her frowardness must needs submit
342 In this one man is shown a temperance proof
343 Against all trials industry severe
344 And constant as the motion of the day;
with
345 Stern self denial round him spread ~~like shades~~
shade
346 That might be deem'd forbidding did not there
347 All generous feelings flourish & rejoice
deed &
348 Forbearance charity in every thought
349 And resolution competent to take
350 Out of the bosom simplicity
351 All that her holy customs recommend
352 And the best ages of the world prescribe
i work
353 —Preaching, adminsterg}ng in every ~~thought~~
354 Of his sublime vocation in the ~~ways~~ walks
an
355 Of worldly intercourse 'twixt man & & m{[?aid]
in
356 And {[?his] his humble mansion he appears
357 A Labourer with moral virtue girt,
358 With spiritual graces, like a glory,
crowned

[109v]

VII, 359 Doubt can be none the Pastor said for whom
360 This Portraiture is sketch'd.—The Great the Good
361 The Well-beloved the Fortunate, the Wise

---

327 Partly overwritten by l. 338 and reentered on 108v.

Chiefs
362 These titles Emperors and ~~Kings~~ have borne
363 Honour assumed or given: and Him the Wonder
ful
364 Our Simple Shepherds speaking from the heart
{styled
365 Deservedly have {named.—From his Abode
366 In a dependant Chapelry that lies
wild
367 Behind yon Hill a poor and rugged spot
368 Which in his soul he lovingly embraced
369 And having once espoused would never quit
370 Hither erelong that lowly great good Man
371 Will be conveyed. An unelaborate Stone
372 May cover him and by its help perchance
373 A century shall hear his name pronounc'd
374 With images attendant on the sound
375 Then shall the slowly-gathering twilight close
376 In utter night, and of his course ~~be found~~ remain
391 Ah who, (and with such rapture as befits
392 The hallowed theme will rise & celebrate
393 The good Man's deeds & purposes retrace

[110r]

VII, 377 No cognizable vestiges no more
378 Than of this breath which frames itself in words
379 To speak of him and instantly dissolves.
resumed
[380] Noise is their not the Pastor [?thus] ~~exclaimed~~
After short pause exclaiming with a sigh
380 —Noise is there not enough in doleful War
T}
[?]}he Pastor thus continued his discourse
After short pause resuming with a sigh
381 But that the heaven born Poet must stand
forth
382 And lend the echoes of this sacred Shell
T}
383 [?A]}o multiply and aggravate the din?
[?ain] is
384 Pangs are there not enough in hopeless love
385 And in requite passion all too much
386 Of turbulence anxiety and fear
387 But that the Minstrel of the rural shade
388 Must tune his pipe insidiously to nurse
389 The perturbation in the suffering breast
390 And propagate its kind whereer he
may.

---

364 Cap "S' in "Simple" may be lowercase.
391–393 Rev of 110r.

rehearse
— {them trace
391, 393 ~~Oh~~{! who will take upon {him to record
{[?honour]
~~Praise~~ {[?lif]
393 The Good Man's ~~praise~~ in lyric strain
or hymn
396 That Virtue like the fumes & vapoury
clouds
397 Through fancy's heat redounding in the brain
such
391 Who not without rapture that befits
392 The hallowed Theme will rise & celebrate
394 His struggle his discomfiture deplore
395 His triumphs hail & glorify his end

[110v]

VII, 398 And like the soft infections of the heart
charm of measured
399 By ~~the [?sweet] power~~ of words may spread
through fields
400 And Cottages and piety survive
401 Upon the lips of men in hall or bower
402 Not for reproof but high & warm delight
{.
403 And grave encouragement, by song inspired?{

~~Digressing only to resume his way~~
~~With mind refreshed—The Pastor said—"~~
~~As if the Pastor~~ ~~speaker had been drawn~~
~~aside~~
~~Even like an [?untired] Traveller~~
~~And carried forward only to return~~
~~Upon the appointed way~~
~~Upon his way with~~ ~~mind refresh d—~~~~tis well~~
~~The pastor fe[?v]ently exclaim'd tis well~~
405 * The memory of the just survives in heav[?en]
406 And without sorr[?y] sorrow will this ground
c } me } receive
407 That venerable [?cl]}lay [?and]}anwhile the best
{ olds d }
408 Of what it h{[?as] confines to [?g]}egrees
409 In excellence less difficult to reach
milder
410 And ~~humbler~~ worth nor need we
travel far
404 Vain thought—but wherefore murmur or repine
[405] The memory of the just survive in heaven

391ff. Rev at bottom of 109v.

405 Asterisk probably signals rev (ll. 404–[405]) at page foot.

[111[r]]

VII, 411 From those to whom our last regards were
paid
412 For such example. Almost at the root
bare
413 Of that tall Pine the shadow of whose [?~~bare~~]
414 And slender stem while here I sit at even
415 Oft stretches tow'rds me like a long strait
path
416 Traced faintly in the green sward—There
beneath
417 A Plain blue stone a gentle Dalesman
lies.
&c

{L
499 Soul-cheering {light! most bountiful of Thing
500 Guide of our way mysterious Comforter
501 Whose sacred influence spread through
all } earth and Heave
502 Too thanklessly we [?will]} participate
{H
503 Thy gifts were utterly withheld from {him
504 Whose place of rest is near yon ivied
Porch
505 Yet of the wild Brooks ask if he Complained
506 Ask of the channeled Rivers if they
held

[111[v]]

{[?r]
VII, 507 A safe{[?er] easier more determined course
{( )}
{ ~~Than that wherein he mov'd from morn to even~~ }
With them he oftimes walked from morn to even
To ~~them his ways were known with them he wal~~ked
Nor other company required, the sport
Following in darkness which their streams supplied.
515, 516 No floweret blooms throughout the lofty range
top
~~On mountain height in wood or shady dell~~
[?or] [?~~wood~~]
516, 517 Of these rough hill in ~~open field or~~ wood
or open
sunless [?lawn]
517 ~~Flowers have we none~~ that could from him

417/499 The "&c" suggests that some version of VII, 418–498, was entered elsewhere and not in need of rev. This passage is copied into the Beaumont Commonplace Book (see p. xxii, above, and *Chronology: MY*, pp. 675–676) and is quoted by WW at the end of the text of his third *Essay upon Epitaphs*; see the Manuscript Census and the transcription for MS. 67 on pp. xxii, 815, above.
502 *1814* follows the transposition indicated.

516, 517 Rev "[?wood]" del by eras.
517 Rev "sunless" above line is probably of "shady" below line.
Ll. 524ff. appear on 112[r]–113[r].

Or ~~shady~~ dell conceal
518 Its birthplace none whose figure did not live
519 Upon his touch, nay further (to such height
The grateful wonder mounts) he could peruse
The dappled skin of each familiar beast
f}
That serves in House or [?]}ield, and every spot
Could tell by nature painted on the coat
Of all the little Creatures slim & sleek
~~clefts~~
{[?~~clefts~~] under earth
Who hide in {[?] clefts or burrow ~~in~~
~~the ground~~
Shy as the guilty: and the featherd Bird
Adorned for sight with variegated hues
Brought to his tutored hand appeared to
yield

[112[r]]

Those subtle colours to some inward sense
VII, 539 Such conquest heaven permits; and not alone
540 That the bereft may win their recompence
541 But for remoter purposes of love
nor last or least
542 And charity, ~~and not the least~~ for this
543 That to the Im gination might be given
544 A type and shadow of an awful truth
545 How, likewise, under sufferance divine
is banished
546 Darkness ^ from the realms of Death
Being
547 By man's imperishable ~~spirit~~, quelld.

524 —Methinks I see him how his eyeballs rolled
ample
525 Beneath a ~~spatious~~ brow in darkness pair d
nay with thought
526 But each instict with spirit, while
the Voice
528 Fancy & understanding while
{or
529 Discoursed of natural {& moral truth
Fancy
530 With eloquence & such authentic power
531 That in his presence humbler knowledge
Abashed stood ~~abashd~~
532 And tender pity over awed

Leaf 112[r] is rev on 112[v]–113[r]. Cf. MS. 75, E2[v].

and the frame
[526] Instinct with spirit, of its own
Of
527 And the while Countenance alive with thought
[528] Fancy and understanding while the Voice

[112v]

VII, 536 Yes, said the Wanderer faculties that seem
537 Extinguished have not therefore ceased to be.
be taught
From such example Reason may ~~correc~~t
Her pride to check her foolishness to warn
Her foolishness, ~~Affections that are prone~~
~~To grovel & descend may be up~~raised
539 ~~From power to [?power] such transfers are~~
[?allow]
Affections prone to grovel & descen
{Among
538 May be upraised. {[?the] the powers of sense
This
[539] ~~Such~~ transfer is permitted—not alone
[?haired]
534 Hence said the grey [?~~haired~~] Wanderer
not [?unmoved]
[536] This ~~truth is clear~~ that faculties which seem
[537] Extinguished have therefore ceased to be
Unto
548 [?~~Thence~~] to the Men who see not as we see
549 Futurity was thought in antient times
550 To be laid open & they prophesied
551 And know we not that from the blind have
r} [?come]
552 ~~And [?hence] the~~ holiest [?l]}aptures of the
The highest lyre
553 And wisdom married to immortal vers.
e
533 A noble & to unrflecting Minds
a
534 A marvellous ~~and~~ surprising spectacle
535 Beings like these present—but proof abounds
534, 536 The Wanderer said that faculties which
seem

[113r]

VII, 524 Methinks I see him how his eyeballs rolled
525 Beneath his ample brow, in darkness paired,

Leaf 112v is rev of 112r, 113r; rev on 113r–113v. Cf. MS. 75, E2v.

539 Pen had run dry at "[?allow]."

533–536 Passage at page foot is rev of 113r and is drafting toward 113r–113v. This passage on 112v is written with the same ink and pen as rev at bottom of 113r.

Rev of 112v, 112r; cf. MS. 75, E2v.

526 But each instinct with spirit, and the frame
527 Of the whole countenance alive with thought
528 Fancy and understanding while the voice
529 Discoursed of natural and moral truth
530 With eloquence & such authentic power
531 That in his presence humbler knowledge stood
532 Abash'd and tender pity overawed.

534 —Yes said the grey haired Wanderer not
unmoved
535, 536 Like proof abounds that Faculties which
seem
537 Extinguish d do not <u>therefore</u> cease to be:
538 And to the Mind among her Powers of sense
{This
539 {[?Such] transfer is permitted; not alone
540 That the bereft may win their recompence
541 But for remoter purposes of love
542 And charity not last or least for this
543 That to the Imagination might be given
[543] Yes the grey haired Wanderer not unmoved
{A
533 {[?] noble, and to unreflecting Minds
~~marvellous~~
[534] ~~A spectacle [?is] [?]~~ is her!
[534] A spectacle with [?wonder fraught] is here
[535, 536] But proof abounds that faculties
which seem

[113^v]

A }
VII, 544 [?I] [?]} Type and shadow of an awful truth
545 How, likewise, under sufferance divine
546 Darkness is banish d from the realms of death
547 By mans imperishable spirit, quelled.
548 Unto the Men who see not as we see
549 Futurity was thought in antient times
550 To be laid open; & they prophesied
551 And know we not that from the blind have
come
552 The highest holiest raptures of the lyre
553 And wisdom married to immortal verse".
556, 557 ~~Whose lineanements would next have been pourtray~~
554 Among the humbler Worthies at our feet
555 Lying insensible to human praise
~~I guess not, but it chanced~~
556 Love or regret, ~~whose lineaments would next~~
whose lineaments would next
557 Have been pourtray'd, I guess not, but it chanced
Ŧ } S}
560 [?H]}~~hat at this moment down the rugged~~ l}~~lope~~

Rev at page foot (ll. 533–536) is in turn rev, in the same ink and pen, at the bottom of 112^v.

Rev of 112^r–112^v. Cf. Houghton MS.; MS. 75, E2^v.

That our attention now was drawn aside
For near C{
558 ~~Bordering~~ the quiet g{hurchyard where we sate
559 A Team of horse slackened & confused
559, 562 ~~A lusty Team came ringing noisily~~
560, 559 By the rough slope down which their ponderous
ow freight
562 Was folling them, came ringing noisily
[558] That^near the quiet Churchyard where we sate
[559] A Team of Horses with a ponderous Freight
[560] Pressing behind adown a rugged slope

[114r]

VII, 561 Whose sharp descent confounded their array
562 Came, at that moment, ringing noisily
563 Here said the Pastor do we muse, & mourn
564 The waste of death and lo the giant Oak
massy
565 Stretch d on his Bier that ~~ponderous~~ timber-
wain,
[566] Nor fail to note the Man who guides the Team
note
566 ~~And mark the Man who guides the jolly~~ team.
lowest
567 "He was a Peasant of the ~~humblest~~ class;
568 Grey locks profusely round his Temples hung
569 In clustering curls like ivy which the bite
570 Of winter cannot thin[?k] the fresh air lodged
571 Within his cheek as light within a cloud
{ng
572 And he returned our greeti{g with a smile.
{P {pake
573 When he had {[?P]assed the Solitary s{aid
{A Man }
574 {He seems} ~~a Man~~ he seems of chearful yesterdays
575 And confident tomorrows, with a face
576 Not worldly minded for it bears too much
577 Of nature's Impress gaiety & health
568 Freedom & hope but keen withal & shrewd.
579 His gestures note & hark his tones of voice
580 Are all vivacious as his mien & looks

---

[558]–[560] Rev at page foot is continued on the top of 114r, and is in pen and ink different from the other rev on 114r.

Cf. Houghton MS.
561–562 Continued from rev at bottom of 113v.
565 Possibly, the comma may be a period.
566 A mark above the period may be single quot or exclam.
570 The conjectured "k" may be an added "n"; *1814* reads "thin."
572 This line appears to be added in a one-line space left between ll. 571 and 573.

[114v]

VII, 581 The Pastor Answered you have read him well
582 Year after year is added to his store
583 With silent encrease summers winters past
584 Past or to come, yea boldly might I say
585 Ten summers & ten winters of the space
586 That lies beyond life's ordinary bounds
587 Upon his spriteful vigor cannot fix
588 The obligation of an anxious mind
589 A pride in having or a fear to lose
590 Possess d like outskirts or some large domain
591 By any one more thought of than by him
592 Who holds the land in fee its careless Lord.
endowed
593 Yet is the Creature rational—a Man
[?from] every
[594] With foresight, [?~~and] he~~ hears ~~on~~ Sabbath days
too,
594 ~~Endowed with sacred reason & he hears~~
with attentive ear
595 The Christian promises ~~on sabbath days~~
596 Nor disbelieves the tidings which he hears.

[115r]

VII, 597 Meanwhile the incense offered up by him
598 Is of the kind which Birds & Beasts present
599 In grove & pasture chearfulness of soul
F
600 [?I]rom trepidation & repining free
601 How many scrupulous worshippers fall
down
602 Upon their knees and daily homage pay
603 Less worthy less religious even than ~~this~~ his.
P the Old Mans due
604 This qualified respect ~~which he deserves~~
605 Is paid without reluctance but in truth
606 Said the good Vicar with a fond half
smile
607 I feel at times a motion of despite
O
608 Tow'rds onne whose bold Contrivances & skill
609 As you have seen, bear such conspicuous
part
610 In works of havoc; taking from these vales

Cf. Houghton MS.
595 Eras was probably of a roughly formed attempt at "days" followed by a comma.

Cf. Houghton MS.; MS. 75, B2v.
603/604 The "P," probably signaling a para (as in *1814*), may be partially del by eras.

~~Year after year~~
One after one
611 ~~And the steep crags~~ their prodest ornaments.
612 Full oft his doings leave me to deplore
{[?tree]
613 Tall as{[?tree] sown by winds by
vapours nursed

[115ᵛ]

VII, 614 In the dry crannies of the pendant rocks
615 Light Birch aloft upon the horizon's edge
[?~~Rooted,]~~ ~~as if in air & spreading~~ forth
{[?~~Spreading~~] } slender
616 {A [?texture} her] ~~texture thin of leaves~~^ ~~& twi~~gs
~~A texture thin of leaves & twigs that make~~
617 A veil of glory for the ascending moon
~~In the pure confines of the eastern sky~~
618 And Oak whose roots by noontide dew
were damp
619 And on whose forehead in[?ac]cessible
620 The Raven lodged in safety. Many a Ship
hath owed to him
to him
621 Launch d into Morecamb Bay from him receives
622 Her strong knee Timbers and the Mast that
bears
623 The loftiest of her Pendants. Help he gives
624 To lordly Mansion rising ~~far &~~ near or far
625 The enormous wheel that turns ten thousand
spindles,
626 And the [?] vast Engine labouring in the Mine,
627 Content with meaner prowess must have lacked
marvellous
628 The very trunk and Body of thier strength
629 I his undaunted Enterprise had failed
Or coves & woods
630 ~~And [?their~~] his keen search among the ~~groves & fields~~
In forest, park, or chase ~~spreading fir~~
631 ~~And the wide Plains: The sheltering h~~oushold
[?fir]
The fir that [?shields]
[?~~northern]~~ ~~blast~~
632 His neighbour Cottage from the [?~~keen~~] cutting [?wind]
642 Would fall if he were master of its doom

Leaf 115ᵛ is rev on 116ʳ–116ᵛ, 117ʳ–117ᵛ. Cf. MS. 75, B2ᵛ.
627–628 Lines may be added in space left.
629 *1814* begins "If."
631 Conjectured "fir" in the base text line is partially obscured by rev "blast" below.
632 Conjectured "wind" may be "blast" (if it is "blast," the "l" is missing).
632/642 Attempts leading to the *1814* version of intervening lines appear at the bottom of the next four pages, probably entered before major copy on those pages.

[116^r]

broad
VII, 635 [?~~If our] domestic sycamore [?is ripe~~]
cool shad
635, 636 The thick leaved sycamore [?] [?in] whose cool
[?silver] [?~~shad~~]
639 Year after year the ~~bleating~~ floc[?ks] are shorn
639, 640 The Elm round which the lasses dance in
May
641, 643 And the Lords Oak—not one would he reprieve
644 For kind accommodant pleasant use
or
645 For dignity ~~for~~ old acquaintance sake
646 For antient custom or distinguished name,
647 His sentence to the axe would doom them all
648 But green in age and lusty as he is
649 And promising to stand a hundred years
650 Less as might seem in rivalship with [?Men]
651 Than with the forest more enduring growth
652, 654 ~~His hour will come &~~ he must fall at
last
The fatal hour will come & he must fall
[639] The joyful Elm
640 Around whose trunk the lasses dance in May

~~The broad [?le~~]
642, 641 In vain the/broad lea/ved /Sycamore might plead
That with i/mpenetra/ble /[?roof] [?] [?it hides]
A

[116^v]

VII, 627 Content with meaner prowess must have lack'd
marvellous
628 The ~~very~~ trunk and body of their strength
629 If his undaunted Enterprize had failed
~~Or keen resear~~
630 [?~~Or] his keen search among the mountain~~
coves
Among the mountain coves or keen research
[?]⎫ [?or]
631 In⎭ forest park or chase. The Household
Fir
stationed
[632] ~~Planted to screen~~ A guardian ~~planted~~ to fend off the blast
sc⎫
632 That [?]⎭reens the Cottage from the northern
Blast

Rev of 115^v; rev on 116^v–117^v. Cf. Houghton MS.; MS. 75, B2^v.
635–639 Ink blot obscures words in second half of these lines.
644 *1814* reads "accommodation."
[639]–642 See note to l. 632/642 on 115^v.
In the second half of the last line at page foot, an ink blot obscures words.

Rev of 115^v–116^r; rev on 117^r–117^v. Cf. MS. 75, B2^v.
630 Rev appears to be del by eras.

636 The umbrageous Planetree like a stately Tent
637 On all sides open to the fanning breeze
shady depth
~~The Plane-tree spreading as its roof-like~~
shade
And for its roof impervious to the shower {[?S]
~~Impervious covert in the heats of~~ {[?~~sum~~]
635 And the hot sunshine annually chosen
{By
638 {For the grave Company who sit & shear
639 The fleece encumber d flock—the joyful
Elm
640 Around whose trunk the lasses dance in may
would
641 And the Lords Oak ~~mig[?h~~] plead their several
rights
642 In vain, if He were Master of their fate.
643 Not one would have his pitiful regard
644 For priz d accommodation, pleasant
use
645 For dignity for old acquaintance sake
646 For antient custom or distinguished name
633 ~~But [?risen] to loftiness mature as if~~
634 ~~That humble~~ destination were forgot
[632] A guardian ~~planted~~ to fend off the blast
humble thatch
[633] But towering high above the ~~Cottage roof~~
[634] As if that destination were forgot

[117r]

VII, 647 His sentence to the axe would doom them
all,
g}
648 But [?t}r]reen in age and lusty as he is
from year to year
649 And promising to stand a hundred years
650 Less, as might seem, in rivalship with men
651 Than with the Forest's more enduring growth
[652] His own appointed hour will come at last
652 ~~His fatal hour will [?he] come & he must~~
fall
653 And like the haughty spoilers of the world
654 This keen Destroyer in his turn must fall
{ pass
655 ~~But~~ from the living {[?turn] we once again
Now
Now,
657 From age that often unlamented droops
658 Turn to that daisied Hillock
three spans long.
659 Seven lusty Sons sate daily round the Board

646 The "c" in "custom" may be a cap.
633–[634] For draft at page foot, see note to l. 632/642 on 115v.

Rev of 115v–116v; rev on 117v. Cf. Houghton MS.; MS. 75, B2r, B2v.

660 Of Gold ril side and when the hope had
ceased
661 Of other progeny a Daughter then
662 Was given the crown & glory of the whole.
663 Welcomed with joy whose penetrating power
amid
664 Was not unfelt^ [?~~even in~~] that heavenly
calm

636 The Umbrageous planetree like a stately Tent
[?fanning]
637 ~~Wide, and~~ on all sides open to the breeze
635 Such And for protection annually chosen
638 By the grave company who sit & shear

[117v]

VII, 665 With which by Nature every Mothers Soul
666 Is stricken, in the moment when her throes
r} th}
667 Are ended, and her ears} have} heard the
cry
~~told~~ tells
~~old~~ }
668 Which tells} her that a living child is born
{blissful
669 And she lies conscious in a {[?] rest
{That
670 {And the dread storm is weather d by them
both.
[?~~'s~~]}
671 The Father } [?him] Him at this unlooked
for gift
672 A bolder transport seizes. From the side
673 Of his bright hearth and from his open door
674 And from the laurel shaded seat thereby
675 Day after day the gladness is diffused
676 To all that come & almost all that
pass
~~Called to the festal board & [?summ]~~
677 ~~Invited to partake the festal chear~~
[677] Invited summoned to partake the Chear
{[?&]
678 Spread on the never empty board, {[?dr] and drink
Girl
678, 679 ~~And drink~~ good wishes to his new born ~~Babe~~
Health & girl
680 From cups replenished by his joyous hand
635 The sycamore that annually holds
636 Within its shade as in a stately Tent
637 On all sides open to the fanning breeze
638 A grave assemblage seated while they
shear

635–638 For draft at page foot, see note to l. 632/642 on 115v.
636 Cap "U" in "Umbrageous" may be lowercase.

Rev of 117r, 116v, 116r, 115v. Cf. MS. 75, B2v.
638–638 For draft at page foot, see note to l. 632/642 on 115v.

[118r]

x ~~tha[?n]ful~~ ~~thank~~ful
VII, 681 Those six fair Brothers variously were moved
{years
682 Each by the thoughts best suited to his {[?age]
thankful
and with most ~~const~~ant [?~~thank~~]
mind
683 But most of all ~~the Grandsire~~, ~~Him that~~
~~Birth~~
684 The hoary Grandsire felt himself enriched;
o
684, 685 ~~Enrich'd with happiness if not~~ in sh[?e]}w
685 ~~With~~ happiness that ebb d not but remained
A
~~Most lowly yet most constant & assured~~.
686 To fill the total measure of his Soul
687 From the low Tenement his own Abode
688 Whither{, as to a little private Cell{,
689 He had withdrawn from bustle care & noise
690 To spend the sabbath of old age in peace
691 Once every day he duteously repaired
in
692 To rock the cradle of the slumberg Babe
693 For in that female Infants name he heard
694 The silent Name of his departed Wife
Heart
695 ~~Soul~~-stirring music hourly heard that name
696 Full blest he was; Another Margaret
{did Green
697 Of {[?this] he say was come to Goldril
side.

[118v]

unmeasured boon
VII, 698 Oh pang unthought of as the precious ~~g[?r]~~
699 Itself had been unlooked for oh dire Stroke
700 Of desolating anguish for them all
701 Just as the Child could totter on the floor
702 And by some friendly fingers help upsta[?y]y d
low, ground
[?lo]
703 Range round the garden walk whose ~~winter~~ flowers
704 Were peeping forth shy messengers of spring,
705 Even at that hopeful time the winds of March
706 One sunny day smiting insidiously
707 Raised in the tender passage of the throat
708 Viewless obstruction—whence—all
unforewarned

---

681 Both words above the line are related to rev of l. 683, below.
682/683 Rev "thankful" is in pencil, as is the partial del of "constant."

p
709 The Household lost their ho{me & Soul's
delight.
710 But Providence that gives & takes
711 By its own law, is merciful & just
712 Time wants not power to soften all regrets

[119r]

bring to distress
VII, 713 And prayer and thought can ~~soften~~ worst ^
~~regrets~~
714 Due resignation. Therefore though some tears
715 Fail not to spring from either Parent's eyes
716 Oft as they hear of sorrow like their own
717 Yet this departed little one too long
718 ~~The innocent Troubler~~

[717] , too long
[718] The innocent troubler of their quiet, sleeps
719 In what may now be called a peaceful
grave
720 On a bright day the brightest of the year &c

[119v]

To [?]
IX, 277, 278 To live & die in calm obscurity—
280 But this what fate soe'er the noon of life
at least
[280] This, whatsoever fate^
281 Reserves for either this is sure that both
ve} its
282 Hath} been permitted to enjoy ~~the~~ dawn
And [?mid] such service with their Liberty
As best shall occupy the [~~?~~] the fleeting hours
283 Whether regarded as a careless time
—
284 That in itself may terminate{, or lead,
285 In course of nature, to a sober eve
286 Both have been fairly dealt with—looking
back
287 The will allow that Justice hath [?to] them
shewn
288 Be done alike to body & to mind.

292 O for that happy period ages past

---

717 Last three words are blotted, possibly obscuring a comma after "one."
720 Book VII continues with ll. 900ff. on MS. 74, 1r. Ll. 721–899 are not present in MS. 74.

Rev of 55r–57r.
In first line on page, illeg letter following "To" is del by eras.
282/283 Another possible reading for "mid" is "mix."

Not unforeseen nor unprepared—though Heaven
A saintly Youth removing from his throne
Before the cherished purpose was fulfilled
Did to this land's unworthiness refuse
The pretious boon. that [?e] era I invoke
294 Too long deferred when the Imperial
Realm

[120r]

IX, 293 On Knowledge resting as her surest prop
295 While she exacts allegiance shall admit
296 An obligation on her part to teach
297 Them who are born to serve her & obey
298 Binding herself by statute to secure
299 To all ~~the~~ the Children whom her Soil
[?~~Pl~~] maintains
forever within
[299] Or place ~~at least well within~~ the reach
of all
300, 302 The rudiments of Learning—so that none
303 As they grow up—however destitute
~~languish~~
to [?languish] help
~~d~~
305, 306 Shall be compelled ~~to dru~~ gge without
the aid
Of discipline or drudge without
307 Of Intellectual implements & tools
age
308 A sav ^ horde among the civilized
309 A servile band among the Lordly free
ri
310 This sa ght as sacred almost as the
right
311 To exist & be supplied with sustenance
fe proclaim
312 And means of li [?ves] the lisping Babe
announces
313, 314 To be invested in his innocence
315 And the rude Boy who having over steppd
316 The sinless age by cons ience is enrolled
& [?knows]
~~Who~~ knows & feels himself [?accountable]

[120v]

knits
IX, 317 Yet mutinously ~~lifts~~ his sullen brow

Leaf 120r is rev of 55v–57r.
299 What we read as a cap in "Children" may be lowercase.

Rev of 56v, 56r; rev on 121r.

318 And lifts his wilful hand on mischief
bent
320, 321 ~~By process indirect declares~~ his due
321 ~~His plan propos while he makes~~ known
his need
319 Or turn the sacred faculty of speech
320 To impious use—by process indirect
[321] Declares his due while he makes known
his need
322, 323 This plea of nature is in vain address[?]
324 To eyes & ears of parents who themselves
325 Did in the time of their necessity
326 Urge it in vain and therefore [?~~hath~~]
[?~~acquir~~]
A
[326] ~~Beyond [?their narrow limi~~ts] like
a prayer
{ floor
327 That from the humbles { [?t born] ascends to heaven
[?~~Hath] it [?acquire a~~]
~~Hath gained [?a] privilege to [?spread] &~~
mount
328 It mounts to reach the states parental
ear

[121^r]

IX, 329 Who if indeed she own a Mothers heart
England
Must } [?give] [?~~Britain~~—]
331, 332 [?Will]} ~~grant~~ what ~~England happily~~
secur
consciously { &
{ [?of] }
333 From all external shocks [?I]} long end[?owed]
With liberty is [?competetent] to give.
352 The dicipline of slavery is unknown
353 To England hence the more doth she
require
354 The Discipline of virtue how can else
354, 355 Order exist security or peace.

323 The plea is universal—the demand
A just deman of human Nature, yet
322, 323 It is & must be fruitless ad[?d]ressd
[323] The plea is universal—the demand
A just demand of human nature, yet
[322, 323] It is & must be fruitlessly address'd
324 To eyes and ears of Parents who themselves

Leaf 121^r is rev of 120^v, 56^v, 56^r; rev on 121^v, 122^v.

325 Did in the time of their necessity
326 Urge it in vain, & therefore like
a prayer
floor
327 That from the humblest ascends to [?~~asceen~~]
heaven
328 It mounts to reach the
State's parental
ear

[121ᵛ]

e
IX, 329 Who if indeed she own a Mothers hart
~~Will [?give~~] to
331, 332 Must grant what ~~Eng~~land Consciously secure
333 From interference of external force
at
334 May grant {[?what] leisure, without risk
incurred
335 That what in Wisdom for herself she doth
u o
336 Others shall eer be able to [?]}[?nd]{[?er]—
sunburnt cliffs
337 Look & behold from Calpes ~~southern cli~~
338 To the flat margin of the Baltic sea
The Conqueror sword extends its bloody
sway
A [?reversing]
{The Tyrants will [?decide on] right & wrong
And thus [?continue to] continues to confound
the world
~~While Mercy [?with~~ its]
~~While Mercy~~
~~Not for a day but length of doleful years~~
For length of doleful years.
While Mercy wetting with her tears the ground
[?spreads]
On which she ~~pleads~~ weeps kneels & sues in
vain
And justice forced, among mankind to see
ic
Her [?heaven] controuling d[?]tates laughed
to scorn
Turns from the accurs d [?continents]
in [?despair]
Wh[?eneer] Truth in silence finds his [?~~sole~~]
[?only] Friend

Leaf 121ᵛ is rev of 121ʳ; rev on 122ʳ (see second note there).

[122ʳ]

Foundations old
& remain consent
Rest ~~on their [?b~~ases] if her ~~permits~~ else
[?See] not
[?~~So~~] at the [~~?~~] choice of one fantastic [?mind]
[~~?~~] long
IX, 339 ~~Long~~ reverenced titles thrown aside like
weeds
[?~~Customs annulled], society [?disturb~~ed]
340 Laws overturned & territory split
[?ren] ~~severed~~
by
341 Like field of ice ~~rent~~ [?t] the polar wind
342 And forced to join in less obnoxious shapes
343 Which ere they gain consistence, by a
gust
344 Of the same breath are shattered & dest[?roy]
[345] Meantime the sovereignty of these fair Isles
[346] Remains entire & indivisible
~~And~~ thus continued to confound the [?worl]
dole
For length of [?mourn] ful years, heroic deed
Receive the [?recompens] of foules crimes
[?resist]
And they who [?wanted] virtue to offend

M
[?T] time —[?expiate]
345 [?B] eanw~~hile~~ the sovereignty of these
fair Isles
346 Remains entire & indivisible
~~Through all~~
351 ~~Like~~ heavenly bodies shining in their
[?] sphere
[?A] [?a]
Appear [?to]

[122ᵛ]

~~A~~
IX, 347 [?T] ~~nd if [?there were] no cause~~
348 ~~Of~~ And [?~~if~~] [?if which in] the [?circumference]

Rev of 121ᵛ.

Possibly, "Foundations old" at the top was intended to follow the rev two-thirds of the way down on 121ᵛ: "For length of doleful years." Drafting from the middle of 122ʳ, especially the first four lines following l. [346], may have been entered earlier than the passage above it on 122ʳ and in conjunction with rev on 121ᵛ.

339/340 Other possible readings for "annulled" are "assaulted" or "disturbed"; other possibilities for "disturbed" are "degraded" or "disgraced."

345 The conjectured rev "expiate," possibly "exhibits," may be related to drafting toward ll. 347ff. on 122ᵛ.

The conjectured letters in the penultimate line may be partly eras.

Rev of 122ʳ, 121ʳ; rev on 124ᵛ.

348 Another possible reading for the first "if" is "of"; "which in" may possibly be "within"; "circumference" may possibly be "circumstance."

[?h]
And if [?when] within the [?~~belt~~ of sore],
349 Of trouble or commotion, side by side
~~They [?meet~~]
[347] And did there not exist

[?] which
[347] And if ~~the~~ cause were remov d that acts
[348] Within the limits of their several shores
commotion
d } or
[349] To breed [?]}isturbance ~~&~~ disquietude
350 Each might preserve the beautiful repose
351 Of heavenly bodies shining in their
spheres.
352 The discipline of slavery is unknown
353 In England hence the more doth she
require
order
354 The discipline of virtue ~~how~~ can else
[?ord] confidence or
354, 355 ~~Order~~ exist ~~secur~~ity & peace
nor pea
Cannot ~~exist~~ cannot subsist nor confidence
Nor thoughtless of those darkened Realms
~~attempt~~
Such high distinctions bind you ~~to [?become~~]
Y } [?ence]
356 T}~~our grat[?ud]titude to Provide—[?awake~~]
m } to reflect
Upon the [?fo]}eans whereby ye [?best may prove]
gratit to heavenly Providen
[?These ~~do both~~] gratitude to heaven
[?]
For high distinct[?ions] for good [?dispensd]
[? ? ?]
357 And prudent caution needful to [?avoid]
[?to avoid]
obv obviously require
358 Impendent evils, [?~~both enjoin~~] [?]

[123r]

V, 984, 989 And wherefor, said the philosophic Priest
do these regards proceed
984 This tribute? whence are these regards
derived
985 Not from &c
Touched by these words the Wanderer
exclaimed

For 123r, cf. 107v–108r; MS. 74A, 28v. These lines on 123r seem to envisage a concluding response by the Wanderer, never developed. These Book V lines are entered below WW's poem "Upon the Sight of a Beautiful Picture" (here not transcribed; see *Poems, 1807–1820*, pp. 76–77, 514).

[124v]

IX, 356 Thus gratitude to Heaven for good [?vouchsafd]
357 And prudent caution needful to avert
358 Impendent evils obviously [?~~enjo~~] require
[?Your one exception—]
360 [?~~So th~~] That the whole people should be taught & traind
361 So that [?~~ferocity~~] & black resolve
licentiousness
habits
362 May [?e] disappear, and virtuous [?~~habits~~]
[?~~sh~~] take strike
deep roots & [?thrive]
363 Form root, & piety descend
364 Like an inheritance from age to age
364, 365 Too thoughtless Rulers of [?these] favour[?e]
[?d]
~~If ye were faithful to your sacred~~
~~trust~~
386 Change wide & deep & silently perform,
[?would]
{L [?lan] nor this land alone
387 This {land witness & ~~the earth~~ shall
But universal earth feel
388 And for her benefit shall feel theffect
Throughout her peopled continents
and [?Isles]
Even to the smallest habitable Rock
O }
Which [?th]}cean lulls with solitary
voice
[387] This land should witness nor this land
alone
For Britain is the whole Earth[?'s vital heart]
[388] Whose universal frame would feel
theffect
359 That permanent provision should be ma[?d]
[360] For the whole to be taught & trained

On 123v and 124r is WW's copy of his poem "—That vast eugh-tree," later titled *Yew-Trees* (not transcribed here; see *Poems, 1800–1807*, pp. 605, 664–667 [photographs and transcriptions of MS. 74, 123v–124r]).

Copy on 124v is a continuation and partial rev of 122v.

386/387 Possibly, the conjectured rev "would" is intended as "world."

388ff. Parts of the right section of the page are heavily blotted, obscuring some of the readings.

[125r]

If then in a creature endowed with the
faculties of foresight & reason the social
affections could not have unfolded themselves
uncountenanced by the faith that Man
and consequently
is an immortal Being, ~~it is true, as~~
hath been assumed that neither
could the Individual dying have
had a desire to survive in the
remembrance of his fellows nor, on
their side, could they have felt
a wish to preserve for future
times vestiges of the departed;
~~that these several desires however~~
~~[? ?placed] in the human mind it~~
still further,
follows [?] that without the
wherein
belief in immortality whence these
several originate
^ desires take their rise, neither
{in
monuments nor epitaphs {[?]
affectionate or laudatory commemoration
of the deceased, could have existed
in the world.

[125v]

Ah
[?O] would that thousands whom the reckless world
Hath hardened to like guilt would melt & feel
Some portion of his penitence and shame

Peas is freed
The Cottage Boy from leading [?~~set~~] escapes *TPL, 242*
[?g]}
~~And~~ [?]} [?lad]
[?~~And] to some~~

[?gathered]

Neglected humoured [?scolde] *256*

This passage (included in a note to *Exc*; see p. 305, above) is an addition to WW's *Essay upon Epitaphs*, I, as it was published in 1810 in STC's *The Friend* (see *Prose*, I, 52, ll. 102–112). Cf. MS. 74, 37v.
An ink blot obscures readings in the fourteenth and fifteenth lines.

The first three lines of base text may be related to the tale of Wilfred Armathwaite (*Exc*, VI, 1100–1154); perhaps this moral comment on 125v was once intended to follow VI, 1154.
242–256 This draft, in pencil, is related to *TPL* work on 39v, 41r–41v.

Not loth to tempt encounter hazardous 471
and [?sway]:
With rough untoward blasts that [?twis] 472
that [?twist] and shake
[?~~And~~ to] blasts that exercize & shake
froward
And send her back with fear into her hold 473
hasty
Whence she returns in confidence bright Spring 474
Hopeful & [?promising] [?]
To [?reopen] her wreath of buds 475

~~Repairs~~ w
And her torn [?r] reath repairs of buds & flower[?s] 477, 475

[?e]
Grant that th[?i] s 477
And interweave new buds & [?fresher] [475]
With th[?o]se that yet are lingr g undismiss d 476
w
From he torn [?re] reath. Grant that th[?os] restless [477]
hours
Springs natural portion & her dear light 481
o
Are in [?our] [?] ur youth [?unquestioned &c] 482

[inside back cover]

The hours the natural portion of the spring *TPL*, 477, 481
As doth the races of human kind
[?this]
Of [?~~man's~~] Imagination that involves
The [?hu] race

and [?sustain]
The [?in dividual]
Such is the [?divi nity] of [?Man] the race
[?Involved]

Out of myself I speak—nor nearly touch
[?I]
[?Them] for the contradictions that beset
The [?speaker]
[?re]
[?To speak]
[?Can] restrict
Such the [?condition] of mankind, yet once
Out of myself I speak & [?nearly touched]

471–482 Draft is related to *TPL* work on inside back cover. Rev of 101^{v}; rev on 102^{v}, 103^{r}.

Text on inside back cover appears to be in the same pen and ink throughout. Possibly, WW's drafts are an aborted attempt at an introduction to *TPL* that makes clear the Solitary's uneasy role as narrator of a universalized tale.

In the fourth line from page foot, conjectured "re" overwriting "speak" may be an attempt to form "restrict."

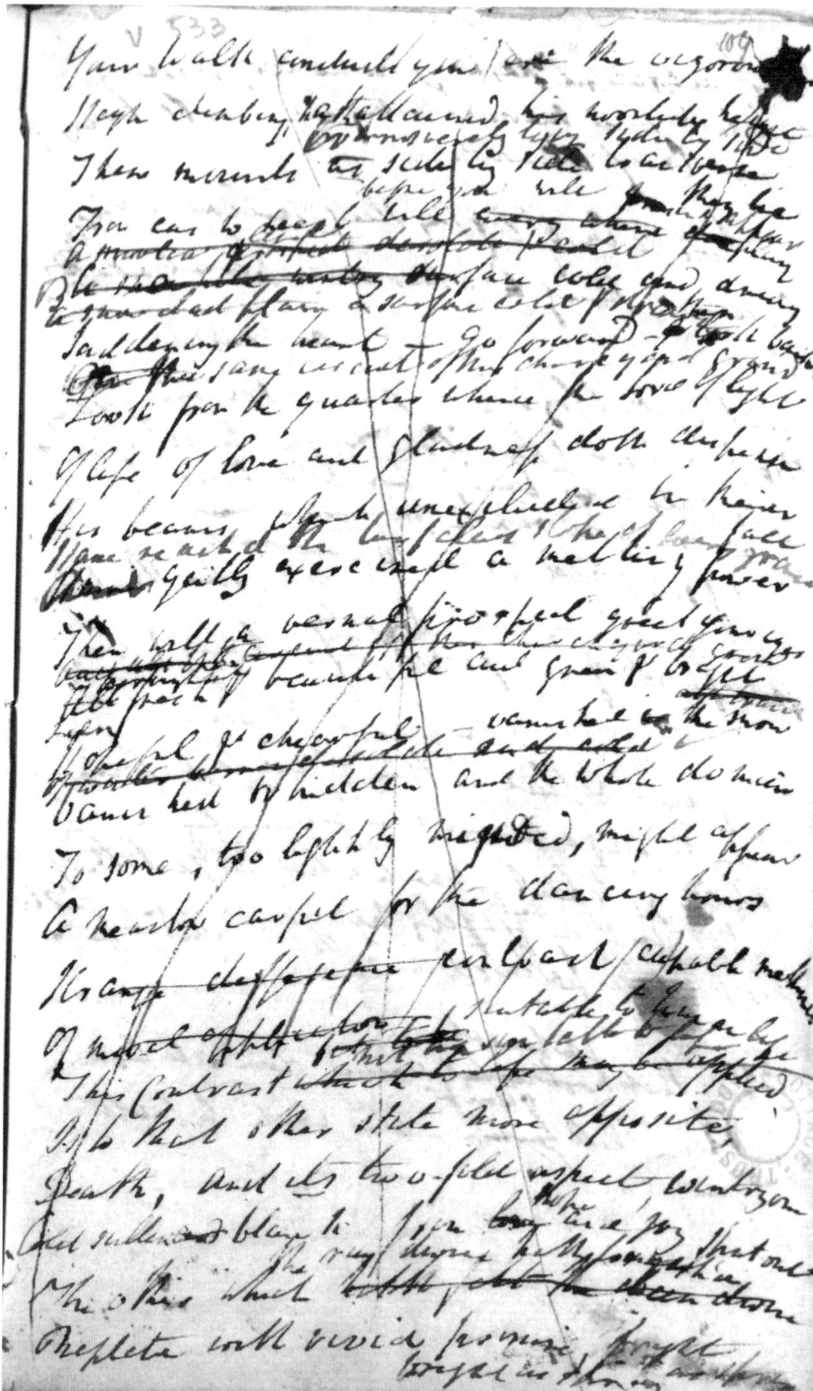

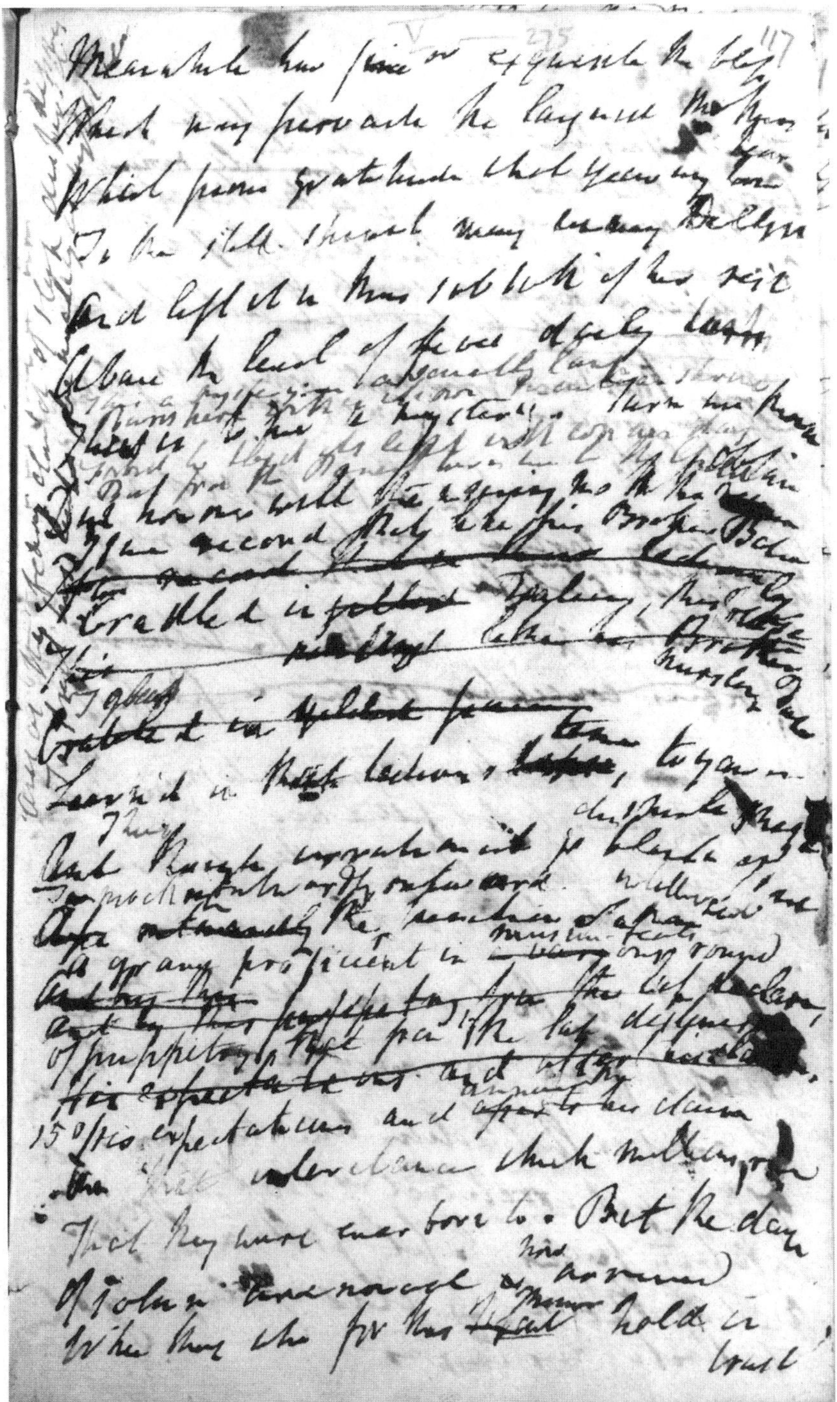

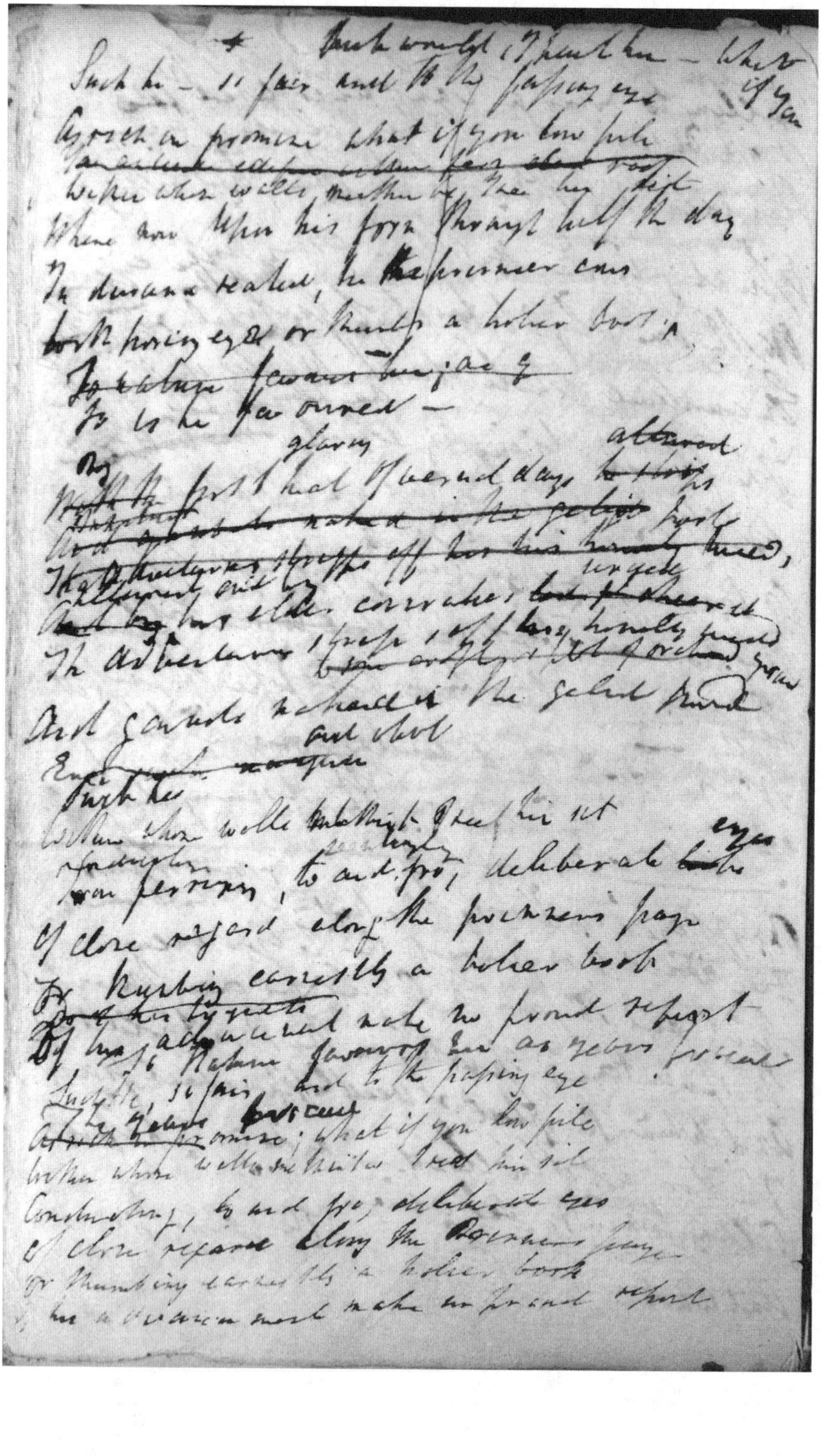

Such lie — so fair and to the passing eye
Afford a promise what if you there spie
[illegible]
Within whose walls [illegible]
Where one upon his form through half the day
In durance seated, to the breviary cons
With poring eyes or thumbs a holier book,
[illegible]
To be favored —
glory
[illegible] first heat of vernal days
[illegible]
[illegible]
[illegible] his elder comrades, [illegible]
The adventurous [illegible]
And [illegible] the [illegible]
and Stool
[illegible]
Such lie
Within whose walls [illegible] his set
[illegible] to and fro, deliberate eyes
Of close regard along the breviary page
Or thumbing earnestly a holier book
[illegible] advancement make no proud report
[illegible] favour [illegible] as years [illegible]
Such lie so fair and to the passing eye
[illegible] promise; what if you there spie
Within whose walls [illegible] his set
Conducting, to and fro, deliberate eyes
Of close regard along the Breviary page
Or thumbing earnestly a holier book
[illegible] his advancement make no proud report

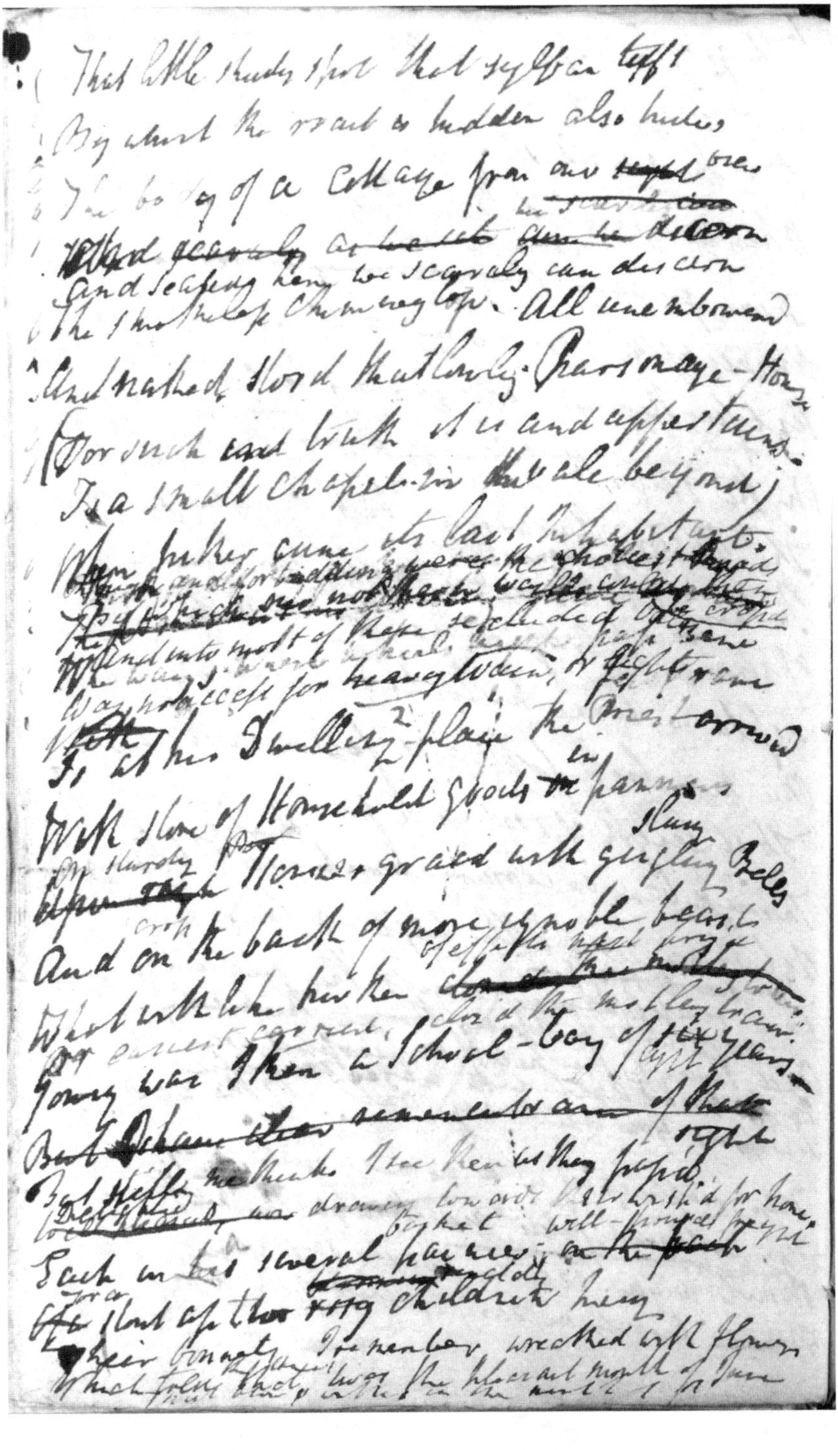
That little shady spot that sylvan tuft
By which the road is hidden also hides
The body of a cottage from our view
And scarcely here we scarcely can discern
The smoke of chimney top.– All unembowered
And naked stood that lowly Parsonage-House
For such in truth it is and appertains
To a small Chapel in the vale beyond
When hither came its last Inhabitant.
To this Dwelling-place the Priest arrived
With store of Household goods in panniers slung
On sturdy Horses graced with jingling bells
And on the back of more ignoble beasts
Young was I then a School-boy of eight years
But still methinks I see them as they passed
Each in his several pannier
Of the last of those young children hung
Their bonnets I remember wreathed with flowers
Which the pleasant month of June

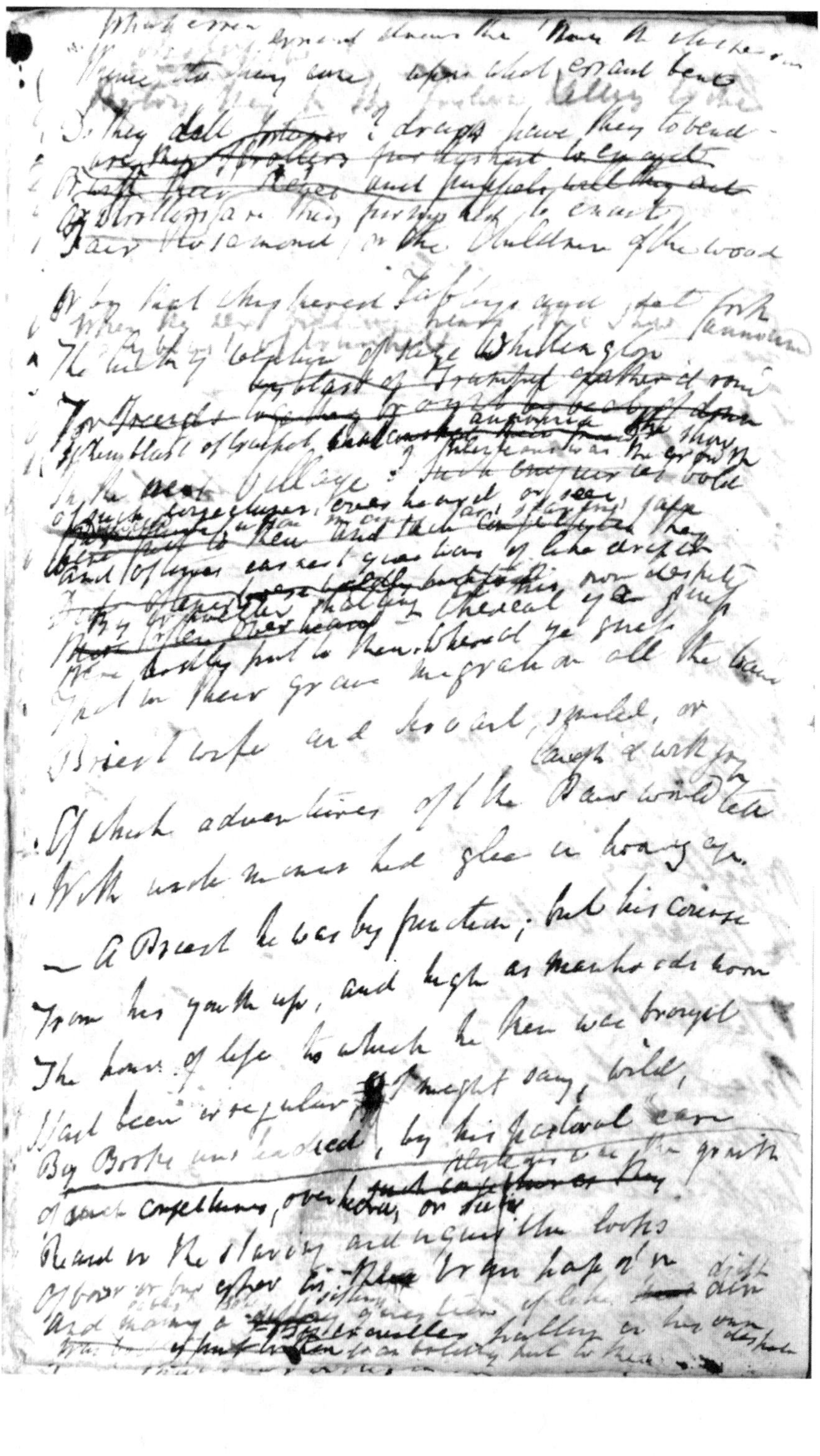
Whate'er around them the [illegible]
Whence [illegible] they come, upon what errand bent
Do they deal [illegible] drugs have they to vend
[illegible]
Of Strollers are they purposing to enact
Fair Rosamond, or the Children of the Wood
Or by that [illegible] eyes agape set forth
The birth of [illegible] Whittington
[illegible]
In the next Village: Such conjectures bold
[illegible]
Priest [illegible] and devout, smiled, or
laugh & wink [illegible]
Of which adventures of the Pair would tell
With [illegible] glee in hoary eyes.
— A Priest he was by function, but his course
From his youth up, and high as manhood's noon
The hour of life to which he then was brought
Had been irregular, I might say, wild,
By Books unsteadied, by his pastoral care
Of such conjectures, overheard, or seen
Read in the [illegible] the looks
[illegible]
And many a [illegible] falling in his own [illegible]
[illegible]

Wordsworth to Lord Lonsdale

Wordsworth to Lord Lonsdale—in use at the fifth stage of *Excursion* composition for work on III, 582–607—is described in the Manuscript Census, p. xxvii, above. For a discussion of this manuscript and its role in the composition of *The Excursion,* see p. 450, above. This draft on the back of a copy of Wordsworth's letter to Lord Lonsdale, January 8, 1813, was composed after the text on DC MS. 71, 86^r (which does not include the passage transcribed below) and before the expanded version on inserted leaves 87^r–87^v in DC MS. 71 (which does include the passage).

Left-hand margin line numbers on the transcriptions of Wordsworth to Lord Lonsdale provide cross-references to the line count in the 1814 reading text in this edition.

[WW to Lord Lonsdale]

we dwelt
III, 592 ~~We dwelt~~ in privacy—a wedded pair
593 Companions daily often all day long
594 Not placed by fortune within easy reach
craving
595 Of various intercourse nor wishing aught
596 Beyond the allowance of our own fireside
597 The Twan within our happy Cottage born
598 Inmates, & Heirs of our united love;
599 Grac'd mutually by difference in sex
600 By the endearing names of nature join'd
~~And also joined by sympathy in age~~
601 And with no wider interval of time
that did [?suffer] fro
[?m]
602 Between their several birth than servd for one
603 ~~For~~ To establish something of a Leaders sway
604 Yet left join d by sympathy in age
605 Equals in pleasure fellows in pursuit
{On
606 {[?] these two pillars rested as in air
607a Our solitude. Within a wiry [?grate]
The nun encaged can to a Captive Bird
Yield her affections to that [?Centre] drawn
{[~~—?—~~]
[?her] life {[?cells]
Amid the quiet of ~~the~~ Cloister's ~~gloom~~
As Moths at evening to a shining light
[?]
Then her thoughts [?hurry thither] doth she
[?pray]

---

597 MS. 71, 87[r], and *1814* read "The Twain."
In the penultimate line, "Moths" is clearly intended, but WW seems to have miswritten it as "Mothers."

DC MS. 75

DC MS. 75—seven sets (here designated "A" through "G") of octavo double sheets in use at the sixth stage of *Excursion* composition for work on Books V, VI, VII, VIII, and IX—is described in the Manuscript Census, p. xxvi, above. For a discussion of this manuscript and its role in the composition of *The Excursion*, see pp. 457–464, above.

Left-hand margin line numbers on the transcriptions of DC MS. 75 provide cross-references to the line count in the 1814 reading text in this edition.

On pp. 1128–1132, below, we present sample photographs of these leaves of DC MS. 75:

DC MS. 75, A1^{r}
DC MS. 75, A2^{v}
DC MS. 75, B1^{r}
DC MS. 75, C2^{r}
DC MS. 75, E2^{v}

The image size of the photographs of DC MS. 75 is 84 percent of actual size.

[A1r]

VII, 804 Oft have I mark'd him on the high way side
805, 806 Beneath some shady tree with map in hand
See
806, 810 Discoursing to his Fellows; '~~there~~ the Rhine
{D
811, 816 Here flows the {danube, there along the tract
818, 819 His finger moved where War was at that time
g}
819, 820 Ragin[?d]} and where the last fields had been
fought
{A
To {austerliz that ignominious word
[820] He [?He pointed], pointed to the fatal field
~~and [?there] the field~~
820 Of Austerliz and that more fatal field
upon which
~~And plain~~ of Jena ~~where~~ oh shame o pride
For where no Country is there man is not.
A battle lost an empire

This honourd Youth and once it was my lot
[805, 806] To note him seated near the public way
[805, 806] Beneath a tree, with map in hand, and so
As I could overhear myself [?an] see
{R
[806, 810] Discoursing with his Fellows. Here the {rhine
811 There, eastward, said he, towards that inland sea
812 [?a] [?] pool it [?seems] from realm to realm
Dan }
811, 813 The [?wind]}ube winds like an enormous serpent
813 And in the sunshine shews h[?is] glittering back
814 Bespotted with innumerable Isles
815 The Russia here bears sway and there the Turk
Mankind
842 Power [?th] to the Oppressors of ~~the World~~ is given
843 A Power of which they dream not—O the curse
To sally forth in
~~Forth sallying in~~ a blind distemper'd rage
[?] their good [?heart] only
To be in good mens hearts a scorn that shakes
{[~~—?—~~]
~~That [?strife]~~ {[?] ~~& [?wastes] but scatters seeds~~
And nourishes and strengthen while it shakes
A spark that gives existence to a flame,
Which else had never kindled, I might say
844 To be the father of divinest thoughts
847 Author & [?creator] of capacities
848 [~~ ?] Author of heroic~~ powers, nor yet

Composition probably began midway on the page at l. 842 ("Power [?th] to the Oppressors"), a passage that continues at the top of A1v. Then WW seems to have written the draft at the top of A1r (ll. 804–820); that passage is recopied and rev on A1v below the rule. The passage continues to l. 838 on A2r, with rev at bottom of A2r (ll. [830]–[829]) in the same ink, and at the middle of A2r (ll. 828–[831]) in different ink. Squeezed between preexisting drafts on A1r is rev of ll. 805–815; this rev is the last written version of these lines in this bifolium. On A2v, WW drafted a passage (unnumbered lines in the middle of the page) as a continuation of ll. 842–852 on A1r–A1v. Judging from the incomplete sentence at page foot on A2v, other pages—no longer extant—once followed.

815/842 "Mankind" is overwritten by "sway and" in the line above; hence ll. 842ff. seem to have been entered before rev to ll. 805–815.

Nor yet [? ?] [?yet heroic]
849 Have sense of one connatural wish nor yet
[?In]
850 ~~Have title to the~~ thanks of God or Man

[A1^v]

hate
VII, 851 Winning there by no recompense but ~~shame~~
852 Astonishment & pity and disdain,
Such is the Tyrants doom.
804 Oft have I mark d him seated on the wall
{ with
806 Of that rude bridge—{[?and] map in hand, and so
806, 810 Discoursing with his Fellows.—There the Rhine
816 the[?n] along a tract,
811, 816 [?~~Here~~] ~~Here flows the Danube; then along the tract~~
817 Of livelier interest to his hopes and fears
[?in] m }
818, 819 ~~His finger moved where at that~~ [?w]}~~oment war~~
[818, 819] The Striplings fingers moved ~~where at that~~ time
war was the[?n]
819, 820 ~~Was raging, and the last fields had been fought~~
[819, 820] ~~War rag[?ed~~] And where the last fields had been fought
820 & where the last fields had be[?e]
[?~~Raging~~] Ragin &
To Austerli[?t]z he pointed to the plain
Of Jena, ~~wh[?e~~] upon which o shame o pride
For where no Country is there man is not.
A battle lost an Empire.—Here behold
823 Southward the Switzers land a nobler race
Vales deeper far
824 ~~Far de~~ep vales than these of ours huge woods
825 And mountains white with everlasting snows
826 And surely he that spake and he whose brow
Had crimsoned like a Rock on side
When from the west the sun through stormy cloud
{brow
kindling {[?]
Hath smitten it with gleam sudden & deep
true ful
827 ~~He~~ was a patriot hope as the best ~~of~~
828 Of that young Peasantry which to the side

[A2^r]

VII, 832 Of Tell came trooping from a thousand huts
833 When he had risen alone. No more braver Youth

See note to A1^r.
851–852 Text continues from A1^r.
804–828 Rev of A1^r; rev on A1^v, A2^r.

See note to A1^r.
832–838 Text continues from A1^r–A1^v.

The Pastor with majestic air resumed
None more inclined to good and glorious acts
834 Decended from Judean heights to march
vengeful
835 With Joshua or appeared in arms that hour
836 Then, after grove and altar wer cast down
837 When Gideon blew the trumpet soul enflamed
838 And strong in hatred of Idolatry.

828 of that young Peasantry who in our days
by thousand
829 Have perished for Helvetias ~~antient~~ rights
830 Ah not [?~~not~~] in vain, or those who in old time
831 For work of happier issue, to the side
the scatter d [?homes]
[832] Of Tell came troopin[?g] from ~~a [?thousand] huts~~
had risen
[833] When he ~~was~~ left alone.
[828] Of that young Peasantry who in our days
[829] Have perished for Helvetias antient rights
in old time
[830] Ah not in vain,—of those who ~~to this~~ side
for work
{happier
[831] ~~Will~~ {[?turn] issue to the side

Helve[?tas antient]
[830] Of those who in [?] our age and not in vain
[?their accustom]
[829] Have perish[?er] d ~~on their [?] [?stands~~]
[?for] their venerable right
ose} {~~s~~
Have swoln th[?eir]} headlong ~~brooks~~ {streams with Gallic blood
The Pastor [?then assum d]

[A2^v]

VII, 869 But here doth lie
Here at our feet so Heav[?n] hath will'd is laid
870 An unknown champion of the better cause
871 A Peasant in whose face deportment air
872, 873 And gait, our countrry look d most beautiful
876 England the antient and the free appear d
877 In him to stan before my swimming eyes
878 Invincible in virtue and in rights
{this
[?Flower was] {[?] youth
~~A youth~~ the flower and pride of all that [?land]

828–[831] This passage in the middle of the page is in an ink differing from work above and below; ll. 828–[831] were probably entered last, since the text is closer to *1814*.

See note to A1^r.
Unnumbered lines are a continuation of ll. 842–852 on A1^r–A1^v.

And yet I trust he had a thousand peers
[?–]
~~When the abusers of the world had~~ [?r]
When in our Realm the abusers of the world
Had rouz d and sanctified, he [?thence has, slept]
[?s]
~~How many noble thoug[?ts to]~~ ~~to [?them] he [?cared]~~
who might else have slept
How they had strr[?ide] him ~~on the pastoral~~
~~through his long day~~
Upon the pastoral hill ~~in idle peace~~.
Long [?lonely], [?strove]
How many noble thoughts for them he [?cared]
~~His life~~
And nightly daily with a grateful soul
In this [?his humble statio ~~hundred~~] st[?irrs] hundreds
862 He thirsted for their overthrow who yet
[? ?] ever
865 ~~Are suffered~~ with ~~daily~~ spreading boughs to stand
866 Like Cedars on the top of Lebanon
867 Darkening the sun.—Be still my heart be still
864 In spite of vice and misery and disease
Which manifold Labour in the arts of [?Trade]
Work in its benefic[?ent] and good
Yet all too fondly followed and too far
Have
~~Had~~ spread through every corner of the land
O sad regret the innocent streams & rills
[?Converting] into [?guides] for [?bane] of those

[B1^{r}]

in power
VII Entering by force our sheltered valley strikes
antient
This ~~moss grown~~ steeple which it cannot shake
At len[?gth] when he had stood a hundred years
Church [?Tower]
[?Fir] [ ] [?as] this moss grown [?tower] , rather say
Fir [ ] as the noblest patriarch

VI, 809, 810 There—to the left, a mother & her Babe
Res [?~~by~~] side by side in everlasting peace

For B1^{r}, cf. MS. 74, 58^{r}, 59^{r}.

The present center fold on Sheet B seems to have been reversed when drafting was entered (the initial letters of B2^{r} are entered to the left of the present fold). The original order of these pages, as once folded, may thus have been B2^{r}, B2^{v} facing B1^{r}, B1^{v}. Possibly composition started on B2^{v} and continued through VII, 646. Drafting for Book VII seems to have continued on B2^{r}, followed by work at the bottom of B2^{v} (below l. 646, and perhaps introductory to the B2^{r} passage), which continues at the top of B1^{r} as the first block of lines there. The second block of lines on B1^{r} seems to have been entered next, perhaps as a continuation of what is on B2^{r}. The third block of lines on B1^{r} (ll. [805]–819), continuing on B1^{v}, is rev and expansion of the second block of lines on B1^{r}.

Near the top left, a hole torn in the page and an ink blot prevent full readings.

Cf. *Tuft of Primroses*, ll. 169–171 (*Tuft*, p. 44) and *1814*, VII, 261, for indication that Joseph Sympson, described here and on B2^{r}, is "the oldest in the vale" (l. 810/813).

805 As on a green hill slope a tender lamb
Li[?es]
806 ~~Rests~~ in safe shelter from the winds of march
807 Screend by its nursing parent, so to me
[807] The larger hillock seems to guard the
less

[805] As on a green hills slope a tender lamb
[?Rest]
[806] ~~Lies~~ in safe shelter from the winds of march
[807] Screen'd by its tender parent,—in such sort
807, 808 Even so methinks that little hillock lies
~~That~~ {T
808 Protected by its neighb[?ours]. {the small heap
809 Speaks for itself; an infant there is laid
810 The mother by its side in fearless peace.
bright decay,
Such was the ~~happy and~~ the sudden fate,
Of that old Man the oldest in the vale
Now let us leave and turn our eyes elswhere
813 If gladsome spirits, and benignant looks
814 That for a face not beautiful did more
815 Than beauty for the fairest face can do
818 If when the clouds had gathe[?r] and distained
819 The spotless ether of a maide[?ens] life

[B1v]

That oer the [?inner world] of [?conscience spread]
Th' universal canopy, [?if therein,]
[?To] that [?innocence hence] a [?light upon]
[?and love] [ ]
VI, 816 ~~Religious tenderness~~
B[?roke] forth
[?nor]
[816] Patience, religious tenderness of [?] [ ] [?art]
And [?lovely spirits]
~~Grieves~~
817 ~~Sorrow for sin~~ & pen[?iten]tial tears
Yet [?not as leading clearly for human]
[?hopes]
And [?constatn penitence], if these [?virtues hav]
~~And these affections~~
If a [?n]atural

If there are natural [?manner]

838 and a step that [?seemd]
839 Caught from the pressure of elastic

815/818 Ll. 816–817 are drafted on B1v.

See note to B1r.

A tear obscures some words in lines near the top of the page. In the fourth base text line, the word following "tenderness of" is probably "heart" as in *1814*.

If natural [?m]
And these affections displayd
[?~~Was] sanctified~~
820, 822 Have power to sanctify then be that spi[?r]
For ever [?lovely]
[?] [?sad change]
[816] But if religious tender[?ne]
[?tenderness]
In that [~~? ?~~] [?how]

[B2^r]

At length when he had stood a hundred years
Firm as the finest Patriarch of the woods
VII, 648 Lusty and green in age yet with dry top
Hoarey an[?d] somewhat shrunken in the limbs
Yet b[?y] m[?i]shap unscath'd from weakness free
And all unsightlly withering or decay
Himself without a moments warning, fell
Such and not ~~rare sel~~dom is the kindly end
Of spriteful temperate and industrious men
o
After l[?i]ng life among these healthy hills.
So have I seen on some mild day of March
high
When the bright sun was ~~up~~ in heaven, refreshed
[?pristine] [?]
With growth of vernal power, a [?splending] Pile
Of ice & icles which lingering frost
Against the surface of an upright rock
tall
In monumental shape serene and high
Had reared and more than monumental lustre
Meanwhile, faint tricklings as I gaz'd, were heard
t ng
A voice of mel[?o]i [?g] that in whispers sang
Of easy dissolution and decay
~~Insensibly and ever going on~~
[?s] soft air
In presen[?]nce & by influence of ~~the sun~~
at once,
And flattering [?~~fr~~] sunshine, when with [?instant] touch
Insensibly the total fabric fell
And spread a confused ruin at the feet
Of the bare rocks whose wall[?s] it had adorn d
So proudly [?] giving back the days bright beams
But soon, while on the [?pensive] ground it lies
Soon to dissolve, and wholly disappear.

For B2^r, cf. Houghton MS. See note to B1^r.
Text continues from B2^v.
Ink blots and tears obscure readings in fourth and fifth base text lines.
In third line from page foot, illeg letter after "proudly" is del by eras.

[B2^{v}]

~~With all [?its]~~ [?~~boughs~~]
And the [?wiide] plains for far and wide he sought
VII, 630, 631 Through mountain cove through forest park & chase
for [?bulk renow]
Wherever tree might ~~stand~~ grow of name or note.
stately [?sound]
608 He bought he chaffered, and with words [?of s]kill
e
Suited to various tempers and [?his]}states
Plied the reluctant Owner till he gained
631 Full oft, his purpos[?es]. The tall household Fir
A not unfrequent [?or]nament & guard
old
Of our [?~~rude~~] Homestands, providently placed
632 To break the onset of the firce north-wind
635, 636 The honied sycamore in whose cool shade
638, 639 Year after year the bleating flock are shorn
639, 640 The elm round which the lasses dan[?e] in may
641 And the Lords oak—not one would he have spar'd
645 For dignity for long acquaintance sake
{[?custom],
646 For antient {[?] or distinguish'd name.

Him as I said the seasons difference
Distress d not, and the noisy worlds report
Of tumult, war; and victories & defeats
~~Of war and pea~~
~~Pass'd by [?them] like an [?unregarded] blast~~
as
Or reach d him not or pass d him like the wind
Entering by force
~~Intruding [?upon]~~ our sheltered valley strikes
This antient steeple which it cannot shake
At length when he had stood a hundred years
Of tumults wars and victories and defeats
From his first dawn of youth to latest age
[?breath]
spent its blustering force
Had reach d him not or ~~passed him [?as] the~~
wind
as the wind
Against his heedless spirit

[C1^{r}]

VIII, 564 Triumphant moment this for him!—he bear[?s]
Proudly between

Cf. Houghton MS. and MS. 74, 115^{r}–116^{v}. See note to B1^{r}.

Rev of C2^{v}; rev on C1^{v}. WW may have drafted C1^{r} and C2^{v} before the sheet was folded; if so, the leaves would then be facing ones, making it easier to rev C2^{v} on C1^{r}.

First line begins about six lines from top of page.

565 between his hands he bears a
smooth blue s[?la]
~~A broad blue slate on~~
~~Upon On~~ capacious
566 ~~A slate~~ on whose flat surface are outspread
A store
567 ~~A pile~~ of gleaming crimson spotted trouts
~~R~~ Ranged array
568 L~~aid~~ side by side in regular ascent
~~First~~ then less & and
~~From those of lordliest size to tiny dwarf~~
The[?r] lordliest first and then of smalle[?r] size
569 ~~From base to lesser~~ lessening by [?r]egrees
One after one & lessening by degrees
From [?base]
571 Upon the bord he lays the sky blue stone
572 With its rich spoil their numbers he proclaim[?s]
had been
573 ~~An~~ Tells in what pools the luckiest ~~were~~ caught
574 And where the very Monarch of the Brook
575 After long struggle had escaped at last
at
576 ~~And~~ stealing alternately and them or us
577 Nor doth his comrade less a look of pride
578 And verily the silent creatures made
579 A splendid sight, together thus exposed
580 Dead, but not sullied or deformed by death
581 That seemed to pity what he could not
spare.

[C1^{v}]

But now when we had ended our repast
[?~~b~~]
And one was looking leisurely [?~~ap~~] abroad
Upon the living scene, hills, woods, and lake
Bright in the sun and one perhaps content
ir
To scan the ~~comli~~ internal comliness & grace
Of that antique apartment where we sate
Its shining furniture and portraits old
And landscapes by the shading pencil drawn
VIII, 552 Till suddenly our willing eyes were calld
m
[552] To other entertaine[?r]ent for the door
553 Opening with eager haste two lusty Boys
554 Appeared, confusion checking their delight
555 Not Brothers they in feature or attire
556 But fond comp[?onis], so I guess, in field
557 And by the River side[?s] from which they come
558 A pair of Anglers laden with their spoil.
559 One bears a willow pann[?e]er on his back

571 Continues from C1^{v}.

Rev of C1^{r}, C2^{v}.

560 The Boy of plainer garb and more abash'd
shy and more
dis
561 In look at least more [?shy] tant & retired
562 The Other might be twin to that fair Girl
563 Who bounded towards us from the garden mount
to see
564 Triumphant entry this ~~for~~ him—for look
He
565 B bears between his hands a smooth blue slate
566 On whose capacious surface are outspread
567 Large store of gleaming crimson-spotted Trouts
568 Ranged side by side in regular ascent
The lordliest first and then of smaller size
569 One after one still lessening by degrees
tops
570 ~~From base to lesser~~ Up to that dwarf that [?pin]
the pinnacle

[C2^r]

a throne of [?state]
IX, 57, 58 That may be like unto his who looks
59 Down from a mountain top ~~like~~ on[?e] of those
[?say]
the say
What time [?] air is undisturbed & [?sound]
60 High peaks that bound the vale where [?now] now we are
[?there]
~~Woods~~ by [?hi]
l [?town] roads [?~~these~~]
62 Fields moor [?s,] and ~~mead~~ows houses roads are seen
baffled
61 Faintly distinguished to the gazing eye
frame of things
64 But wh[?il] there the gross and visible ~~world obeys~~
to him appear[?s]
~~The law of distance and doth thus become~~
es
65 Relinquish ing its power upon the sense
[?Nay] ~~even~~ on
66 ~~Say too upon~~ ^ the very heart its [?~~soul~~] itself & seems
67 All unsubstantialize, ~~how~~ how loud the voice
68, 69 Of waters from the River far below
host
70, 73 Ascending; for he stands above the ~~h[?ive~~]
ng insects
Of ever humm [?and] [?]
74 ~~Of summer [?myriad~~ insect] in thin air
75 That suits not them, the murmur of the leaves
76 Many and idle touches not his ear

57 That may be liken'd unto his
58 Who, on some gentle day of summer, looks
59 Down from a mountain top

---

570 Continues on C1^r.

Cf. MS. 74, 47^r–48^r. The canceling slash on C2^v has bled through to C2^r.

59/60 Line beginning "What time" appears to be related to the lines at page foot; all three of these lines of rev are possibly connected with the thought expressed by the onlooker in IX, 57–58.

from
77 These he freed from and ~~a~~ thousand [?~~thous~~] sounds
2 { these
78 Nor less unceasing and less vain than {[?]
1 [?Which] } occupy
80 [?That] } ~~occupy~~ molest and interfere

{ it
82 And shall {[?] not be hoped that Placed by age
like quiet though severe
83 In ~~such~~ removal quiet ~~and [?seveve~~]
84 We are not so removed for utter loss
suited to our need,
85 But for some favour that we attain
{ What
86 ~~More~~ {[?from] more than this that we thereby should gain
87 ~~A~~ power to commune with the invisible world
Fresh
88 And hear the mighty stream of tendency
89, 90 Uttering a clear sonorous voice unknown
94 To them so busy on the plain below?
sky [?or] earth
When [?~~nature] air~~ vale [?are in their] [?] [?place]
Some day when nature is in gentle [?mood]

[C2ᵛ]

[?And now] partakes
VIII, 565 Between his hands upon a sky blue stone
566 He bears the spoil triumphantly outspread
567 A pile of gleaming crimpsoned spotted trouts
568 Laid side by side in regu[?]lar ascent
[?tiny] to those are
From dwarf to spoil that is of lordly size
571 Upon the bord[?d] he lays the sky blue stone
572 With its rich spoil from brook & [?lordly lake]
To [?open praising] a bright [?monarch]
576 And steals alternately at them and us
~~A silent Company~~
look
~~A look~~ [?anxious] smile
577 A ~~sheep~~ish smile of vainity and joy
~~Stealing a~~
578 And verily the silent Creatures ~~lay~~ [?made]
579 A splend[?ig] sight before us as they lay
580 Dead but not sullied or deform by Death
~~That [?s~~]
581 Seeming to Pity what it might not spare.

77/78, 78/80 Left-margin numbers possibly indicate rev on another sheet or perhaps a reversal of ll. 78 and 80.

82–94 Rev on MS. 74, 47ᵛ–48ʳ. These lines are drawn from 1798 draft toward the character of the Pedlar in MS. 14, the Alfoxden Notebook (see *RC & Pedlar*, pp. 114–115).

Rev on C1ʳ and C1ᵛ. Unnumbered rough draft passage following l. 581 appears to contain the argument on old age advanced at opening of Book IX (cf. C2ʳ).

"Dorothy" is hand printed, with the page inverted, at page foot.

the[?n] if ~~so exalted~~ so favored
[?~~their~~]
But [?this] ~~old~~ age so ~~gifted~~ is the [?age]
Of those alone who have [?not been opress d]
[?~~or~~]
~~Of [?wise~~ and] ~~good of [?those alone] to whom~~
but in some degree
From life first opening [?~~justice hath been dealt~~]
~~Soothe~~ Cheared, and sustained, & aided in their growth
Who further more have to themselves been true
acting
Observing th[?is nay ~~acting~~] to the end ~~that they~~
[?even]
May be [?~~prese~~ preserved] from [?stain], and [?~~in their~~ faith]
[?~~Mature~~]
[?~~More firm~~] and [?absolute]
~~May [?be] the crown of reason, and the [?will~~]
A [?~~blameless sceptre], acting to the~~ end
That they may know & serve the one supreme.

[D1^{r}]

Yet tis set forth in colours of the sun
IX, 106, 107 That far as these predominate even so far
108 Country, society, and time itself
109 That saps the individuals bodily frame
110 And lays the generations low in dust
112 Have one maternal spirit, bringing forth
113 And cherishing, with never wearied love
O
114 That faints not nor betrays. our life is turnd
its
115 Out of [?her] course wherever man is made
116 An offering or a sacrifice, a tool
117 Or implement, a passive thing employ'd
118 As a brute mean without acknowledgement
119 Of common right or interest in the end
120 Used or abused as selfishness may prompt
121 Say what can follow for a rational soul
122 Perverted thus but weakness in all good
c
123 And strength for evil: hence an after fall
124 For chastisement and custody, and bonds
oftimes
125 And deat the avenger of the past
in
126 And the sole guardian ~~to~~ whose hands we dare
[?to tr]
~~E~~
127, 128 [?T] ~~n~~ trust the future. But the genuine law
Is that which is an impulse, yea a soul
Akin for
Allied to our own nature: [?as] we know

For D1^{r}, cf. MS. 74, 48^{r}–50^{r}.
Bottom left corner of page was torn before copy was entered.

130 That when we stand upon our native soil
If not assiduously [?mannered] at least
Not wholly wanting culture and
meanwhile
131 Unelbow'd by such
[?obje]

[D1^v]

In the close prison-house of human pride.
Then, do not deem, and while he spake these words
The old man to the Solitary turnd
[?was] charged to paint
IX, 157 That heretofore when I described the estate
158 An object most familiar to us all [?e]
159 Of the poor Child subjected to the arts [?scheme]
Even as it is, I mean a hapless child
160 Of modern ingenuity, and made
[159] A little one {wheel
162 In manner of a spindle or a {tool
161 The senseless member of a vast machine
y}
And s}et a living, drooping, human Creature.
{T
163 ~~Ah~~ {think not that pitying him I overlookd
164 ~~The [?entrusted] peasant~~ Boy, ~~no les untaught~~ [?uncheer]
~~Not less a~~ slave who walks the field
[164] The boy who walks the fields untaught [?uncheer]
A}
E}nd therefore by a necessary law
181 Entrusted she[?peherd] the lineal heir
Of vassals i}
[181] ~~In~~ No better than the lineal he[?e]}r
182 Of those who once were to the soil attachd
{hrubs
183 Following its fortune like the s{[?] & trees
That grew upon it or the birds & beast[?s]
That it support, [?~~a poor~~ unenfranchis d slav]
w}
165 Of ignorance or worse perhaps of [?hu]}ant
166 An miserable hunger.

[D2^r]

Then do not deem and with these calmer words
The old Man to the Solitary turnd
In wonted
With all his natural gentleness of look
IX, 157 That when I represented heretofore
158 A most familiar object of our days

Leaf D1^v is rev on D2^r. Cf. MS. 74, 50^v–51^r.

Rev of D1^v. Cf. MS. 74, 50^v–51^r.
Lower half of this page (and of its verso) was torn away before copy was entered.

Even as it is, I mean a hapless Child
[?schemes]
159 A little One subjected to the arts
160 Of modern ingenuity and made
162 To serve, as doth a spindle or a wheel
senseless
161 The ~~lifeless~~ member of a vast machine
And yet a living drooping human Creature
overlookd
163 Think not that pitying him I could forget
164 The boy who walks the fields uncheered untaught
[?Entrusted] therefore and debas[?ed,] the slave
~~T~~
165 A ~~he slav The slave of ignorance, or worse of want~~
166 ~~And miserable hunger~~.

[D2ᵛ]

IX, [165] The slave [?o]f ignorance or worse of want
165 Of ignorance, and oftimes worse of w[?an]t
[?~~We have~~] ~~seen~~
Much too much
166 And miserable hunger. ~~Much, too much~~,
167 2 We in our native country both have seen
moors
1 On dreary ~~heaths~~ beneath th scottish plain
Of [?this most rueful]
168 ~~Too much of this~~ lot which I myself ~~shared~~
169 ~~Though~~ Shared, though in mild and merciful degree
y
170 Yet was my Youth to hindrances exposed
171 Through which I struggled not without distress
172 And sometimes injury, like a sheep [?~~th~~] enthralled
173 In thorns or brambles, or a bird that breaks
174 Through a strong net and mounts upon the wind
175 Though with her plume impaird. If they whose
souls
176 Should open while the range the the richer fields
177 Of merry England, are obstructed less
178 By indigence, their ignorance is not less
Less general culture is on them bestowed
180 I grant, that tens of thousands may
be found

For D2ᵛ, cf. MS. 74, 51ʳ. See note to D2ʳ.
[165] Ink blot obscures "o" in "[?o]f]."
165 Line probably continues directly from rev above l. 165 on D2ʳ. Ink blot obscures "an" in "want."
167 The left-margin numbers "2" and "1" probably reverse the sequence of lines.
176 *1814* reads "while they range."

[E1^r]

{[?se]
are they who{[?s] sleep
V, 929 *And blest ~~the holy Man continued blest~~*
[929] *~~Our Brethren are that sleep~~, & we that know*
930 *While in a spot like this we breathe & walk*
beneath
931 *That all ~~around~~ us by the wings are covered*
932 *Of motherly humanity outspread*
within
933 *And gathering all ~~beneath~~ their tender shade*
934 *Though loth and slow to come. A battle field*
935 *To stillness left when slaughter is no more*
936 *With this compared is a strange spectacle*
937 *—A rueful sight the wild shore strewn with wrecks*
938 *And trod by people in afflicted quest*
939 *Of friends or kindred whom the angry Sea*
940 *Restores not to their prayer. This Contrast yet*
A little longer may our thoughts pursue.
~~Behold and where? where but in polished realms~~
~~For arts & arms & luxury renouned~~
{*~~is~~*
~~That to our minds present th~~{[*?at*] *~~sight of truth~~*
~~A man~~ Mark him
~~Mark him~~ ^*who shuts & opens his sad eyes*
{*c*
In some sepulchral dungeons tri{ *kling vault*
Buried where scarcely he can note or feel
The several qualities of night & day
947 *To lull a Tyrant's fear or please his will*
And in the end & quietness of all

[E1^v]

~~polished realms~~
The bones remaining when the breath expired.
~~Christian~~
From this dire truth which ~~polishd lands~~ afford
{Realms
polishd {[?land] afford
Turn to the region of the East & see
Where sandy desarts to the walls extend
{*C*
Of some proud {*city, which the Turbaned chief*

Cf. MS. 74A, 24^v, 26^r–27^v.

MW wrote the base text on E1^r and E1^v.

Unnumbered passage on E1^r–E2^r is a further expansion—not used in the poem—of the Pastor's speech in Book V concerning tyranny and oppression (see l. 947).

At page foot, and inverted, are two lines in continuation from E2^v of WW's prose draft of his letter to Lord Lonsdale (see note to E2^v).

937 Possibly a colon, eras, followed "sight."

See note to E1^r.

Cf. MS. 74A, 26^v–27^r.

a fainting wretch
~~inting~~
Rules with his scymetar, ~~*see a fa*~~ *mished* ~~*tribe*~~
Yea more, a Company of either sex
[?u]
Crawled forth & thankf o lly set down to take
The gaunt Hyena's leavings they themselves
Destined perhaps ere mornings light return
~~in this our land~~
~~home~~
To be the wild Beast's prey: ~~*and nearer*~~ [*?turn*]
splendid streets
~~*Look we on those who from the*~~ [*?sheltered hold*]
~~In this our land see many driven by want~~
~~*By nakedness & want & hunger driven*~~
See those who driven from splendid streets by want
es
Retire like birds to hol [*?ds*] *& corners chased*
i
By pity less winter—miserable Men
Making that place their home where they
can die!
course
Track where you may the [*?track*] *of those*
n
who be[*?n*] *t*
On strange adventures or desiring gain
Or urged by thirst of knowledge wander on
with
Restless encountering in their own free choice
laced
All shapes of danger & unso [*?cial*] *death*

[E2^r]

behold & this
~~keener~~ keener wretchedness
Thus though a sight of [?] ~~wretched~~
[?perhaps]
~~Which though [?unknowingly] our bodily eyes~~
~~Which though without the knowledge of~~
~~the [?mind]~~]
e
Perhaps our bodily h yes have often seen
from
One of the many who by splendid streets
driven
own
our ^ christian land
ury
pen [?ry]
by
~~In this our [?land] by want~~ & ~~hunger~~ driven

Right-margin X at middle of page is in the center fold to the left of corresponding rev on E2^r. Part of cancellation line of "and nearer home" on E1^v extends to rev on E2^r.

A diagonal line (not shown on the transcriptions) connects last line on E1^v to its continuation on E2^r (the four lines below the rule there).

See note to E1^r.
Rev of E1^v (see the notes there). Cf. MS. 74A, 26^v–27^v.

Hopeless of all relief & unrelieved
Retire like birds to holes & corners chased
By pitiless winte, miserable men
Making that place their home where
they die.

{B
To be the wild {beast's prey. — Behold, {(& this
This though a sight of keener wretchedness

{)
Perhaps our bodily eyes have often seen{
One of the many who from splendid streets
In our own christian land by penury driven
Hopeless of all relief and unrelieved
Retire, like Birds to holes & corners
~~driven~~
chased
By pitiless winter miserable men &c

{o
Wherever f{[?i]ot can go. From these dispersed
And lonely to a field of battle turn
see
Once more, but ere the fight begin—and [?~~hear~~]
A mighty number taught

[E2ᵛ]

Such conquest heaven permits & here [?methin]
VII, 544 ~~Affor~~ Is seen a shadow of that awful truth
[?S ,] [?], under ~~of [?God]~~ divine
545 That [?under] sufferance ~~of almighty power~~
~~And [?thrgh rediscovery~~]
~~The dark[?nes~~]
546 Darkness is banished from th[?is] realm of
Deat
547 By [?~~th] imperishable~~
[?~~man~~] [?~~his~~]
[?~~An~~]
[?facult]
536 ~~So~~ [?~~po~~wer]—that seem[?s] to be extinct & lost
[?exists]
and in some other [?their]
[?the]{
[?Retiring] ~~into each other~~ lodge [?its} power]
[?On]
[?Ar] To other
A Philosoph[?ic teacher] might have [?been]
And [?the harmony]

For E2ᵛ, cf. MS. 74, 112ʳ–113ᵛ.

On the lower half of the leaf, and inverted, is draft for the first para of WW's letter to Lord Lonsdale, 6 March 1813 (see *MY*, II, 83). The draft continues at the bottom of E1ʳ. This draft letter is later than the poetry on E1ʳ and E2ᵛ (as overwritings of the poetry by the prose on E2ᵛ show), but entry of the poetry is almost certainly close in date to 6 March 1813. Another possibility is that WW had earlier MSS. out to work on preparing MS. 74A; conceivably, then, WW's poetic drafts on E2ʳ and E2ᵛ (and his prose drafts for the letter) could be significantly later than MW's fair copy on E1ʳ and E1ᵛ.

[?arm d with ~~with~~]
Of [?almost]
[?D]
[?T]isturbance] the [? ?]

[F1^r]

VII, 30 *That shall not die & cannot be destroyed*
re
Did not you say that th[?os]e contiguous Vales
Do each possess within this hallowed ground
Its own Compartment; yet from side to side
Save in the vacant quarter of the North
31 *The grassy heaps lie amicably close*
32 *Like surges heaving in a gentle wind*
Upon
e
33 *~~Ov~~ ~~er~~ the ~~small~~ surface of a mountain pool*
We
34 *Whence comes it then that yonder ~~I~~ ^ behold*
35 *Five graves & only five that lie apart*
le
36 *Unsociab Company and sad—*
37 *And furthermore appearing to encroach*
38 *On the smooth play-ground of the Village School*
39 *The Vicar answered. "No disdainful pride*
40 *In them who rest beneath nor any course*
c
41 *Of strange or tragi[?t] accident hath helped*
42 *To place those hillocks in that lonely guize*

[F1^v]

VII, 43 *—Once more look forth & follow with your eye*
44 *The length of road which from yon mountain's*
base
45 *Through bare enclosures stretches till its line*
46 *Is lost among a little Tuft of Trees*
47 *Then, reappearing in a moment, quits*
48 *The cultured fields & up the heathy waste*
49 *Mounts as you see in mazes serpentine*
50 *Towards an easy outlet of the Vale.*
51 *That little shady Spot that sylvan Tuft*
52 *By which the road is hidden also hides*
53 *The Body of a Cottage from our view*
cern
53, 54 *And seated here we scarcely can dis[?ern]*

For F1^r, cf. MS. 74, 75^v–76^r.
MW wrote the base text on Sheet F. See note to F1^v, l. 59.

Cf. MS. 74, 76^r–76^v.

55 *The smokeless chimney top. All unembowered*
56 *And naked stood that lowly Parsonage House*
57 *(For such in truth it is & appertains*
58 *To a small Chapel in the Vale beyond)*
59 *When hither came its last Inhabitant*

[F2^{r}]

VII, 202 *Screened from assault of every bitter blast*
203 *While the dark shadows of the summer leaves*
204 *Danced in the breeze upon its mossy roof*
205 *Time which had thus afforded willing help*
206 *To beautify with Nature's fairest growth*
207 *This rustic tenement had gently shed*
208 *Upon its Master's frame a wintry grace*
209 *The comeliness of unenfeebled age*
210 *But how could I say gently for he still*
211 *Retained a flashing eye a burning palm*
212 *A stirring foot & head that beat by night*
213 *Upon its pillow with a thousand schemes*
~~*Though like old Men comparing present*~~
~~*powers*~~
~~*With past he sometimes yielded to complaint*~~
214 *Few likings had he dropped few pleasures*
lost
~~*Of those that speed the day or chear the mind*~~
215 *Generous & charitable prompt to serve*
s
216 *And still his harsher pas[?t]ions kept their hold*
217 *Anger & indignation still he loved*
218 *The sound of titled names & talked in glee*

[F2^{v}]

VII, 219 *Of long past banquettings with high-born friends*
220 *Then from those lulling fits of vain delight*
z
221 *Uprou[?s]ed by recollected injury railed*
222 *At their false ways disdainfully & oft*
223 *In bitterness & with a threatening eye* ~~*of fire*~~
224 *Of fire incensed beneath its hoary brow*

---

59 Since Sheet F preserves a fair copy of this section of Book VII, it is possible that leaves intervening between F1^{v} and F2^{r} may have contained the missing 143 lines. If there once intervened two folded sheets (eight sides), they could contain about 144 lines at MW's approximate rate of copying here (18 lines per page). If an additional folded sheet (four sides) once enclosed the extant leaves of Sheet F, the first two pages of that added sheet could hold the 29 lines leading into F1^{r}, and the last two pages could hold the 34 lines between F2^{v} and G1^{r}.

Cf. MS. 74, 80^{r}–80^{v}. See note to F1^{v}, l. 59.

Cf. MS. 74, 80^{v}–81^{r}. See note to F1^{v}, l. 59.

225 *These transports with staid looks of pure good*
will
226 *And with soft smile his Consort would reprove*
227 *She far behind him in the race of years*
228 *Yet keeping her first mildness was advanced*
229 *Far nearer in the habits of her soul*
230 *To that still region whither all are bound*
231 *Him might we liken to the setting Sun*
I have seen it on
232 *As it appears upon some gusty day*
g
233 *Strugling and bold and shining from the West*
234 *With an inconstant & unmellowed light*
235 *She was a soft attendant cloud that hung*
236 *As if with wish to veil the restless orb*
237 *From which it did itself imbibe a ray*

[G1^r]

VII, 271 *As by a plague yet no rapacious plague*
272 *Had been among them all was gentle death*
273 *One after one with intervals of peace*
274 *A happy consummation, an accord,*
{*~~harp~~*
~~Though framed of s~~ {[?] *~~& melancholy notes~~*,
275 *Sweet, perfect, to be wished for; save that here*
might
276 *Was something which to mortal sense ~~did~~* ^ *sound*
{*S*
277 *Like harshness that the old grey-headed* {*sire*
278 *The oldest, he was taken last, survived*
prime, his Son
279 *When the dear Partner of his ~~Manhood's prime~~*
280 His Daughter, and her Husband, and their Child
{*S*
~~His~~ {*~~son~~ ~~[?&] Daughter~~* on
280, 281 *~~Daughter and~~ smiling Grandc~~hild~~* ^ *were no more.*
His little
282 *All gone all vanished he deprived & bare*
283 *How will he face the remnant of his life*
284 *What will become of him we said & mused*
{sad
285 *In* {*vain conjectures shall we meet him now*
286 *Haunting with rod & line the craggy brooks*

MW wrote the base text on Sheet G. See note to F1^v, l. 59.

271ff. *Tuft of Primroses,* ll. 148–199 (see *Tuft,* pp. 43–45) contributes to VII, 261–310. MS. 65, the final *Tuft* MS., contains rev that adapts this passage for *Exc;* see *Tuft,* pp. 214–225. No drafting for VII, 261–270, 305–310, is preserved in any *Exc* MS.; but, given that Sheet G is fair copy, missing preceding and following leaves probably contained the complete text.

pools
287 ~~*And mountain torrents or shall we as we*~~
~~*pass*~~

[G1v]

VII, 287 *Or shall we overhear him as we pass*
288 *Striving to entertain the lonely hours*
289 *With music for he had not ceased to touch*
framed
290 *The harp or viol which himself had* {*made*
291 *For their sweet purposes with perfect skill*
292 *What titles will he keep, will he remain*
c
293 musit|ian gardener builder mechanist
~~*A mechanist within doors, & without*~~*,*
294 *A Planter & a rearer from the seed*
295 *A Man of hope & forward looking mind*
?
296 *Even to the last*{ *—such was he unsubdued*
297 *But heaven was gracious; yet a little while*
298 *And this Survivor with his cheerful throng*
299 *Of open schemes, and all his inward hoard*
300 *Of unsunned griefs, too many & too keen*
301 *Was overcome by unexpected sleep*
302 *In one blest moment. Like a Shadow thrown*
303 *Softly & lightly from a passing Cloud*
304 *Death fell upon him while reclined he lay*

G2r and G2v are blank.

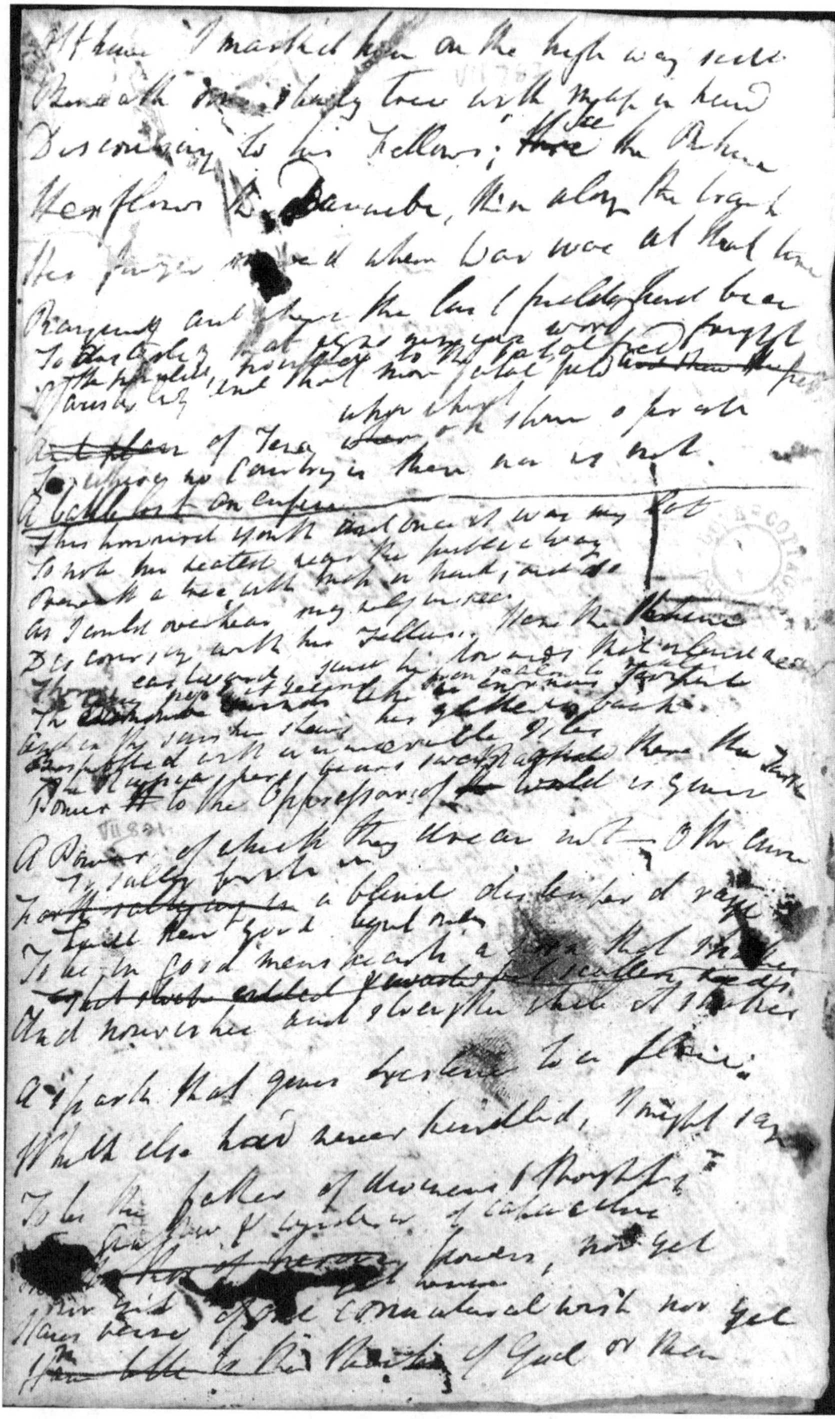

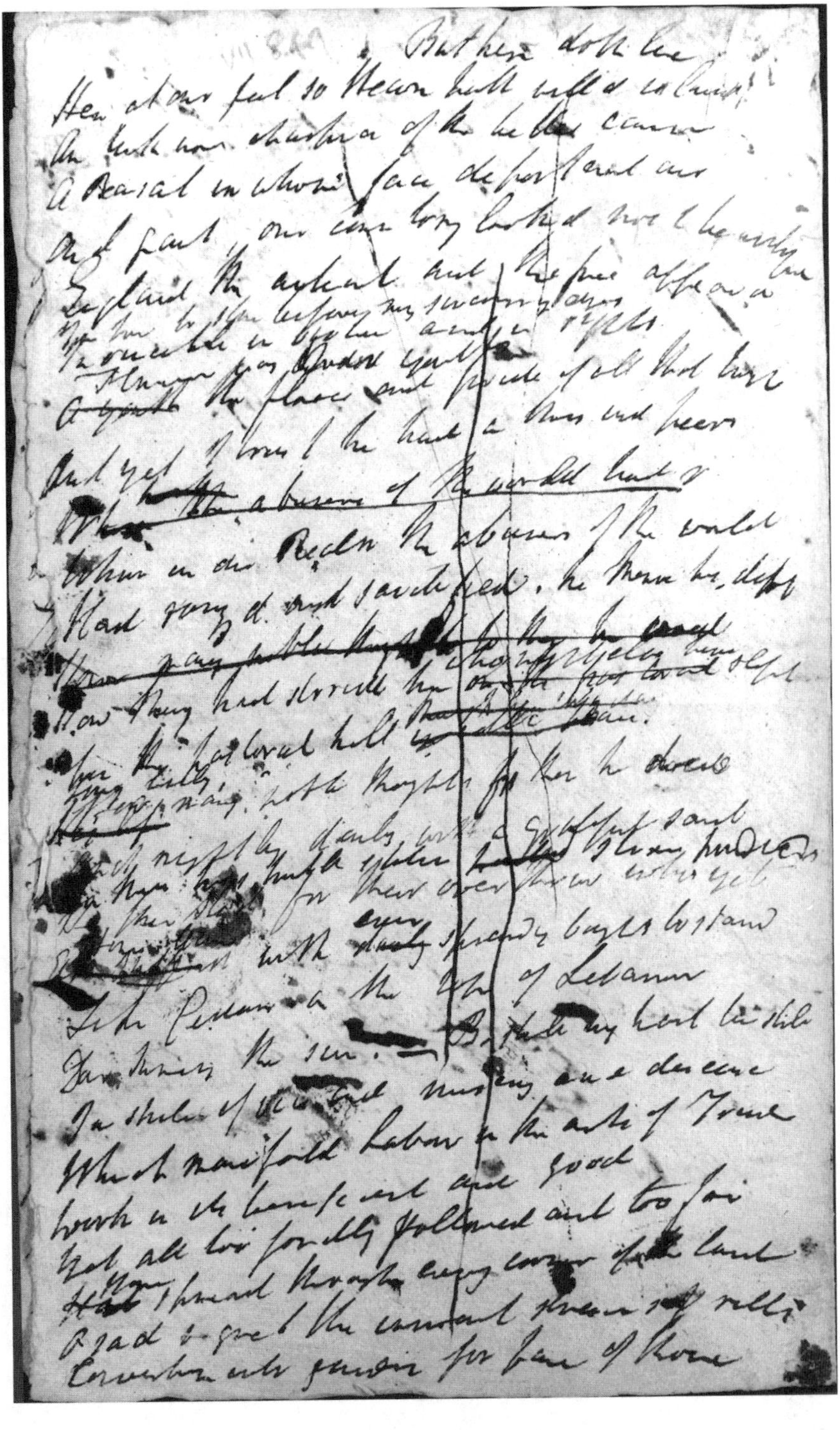

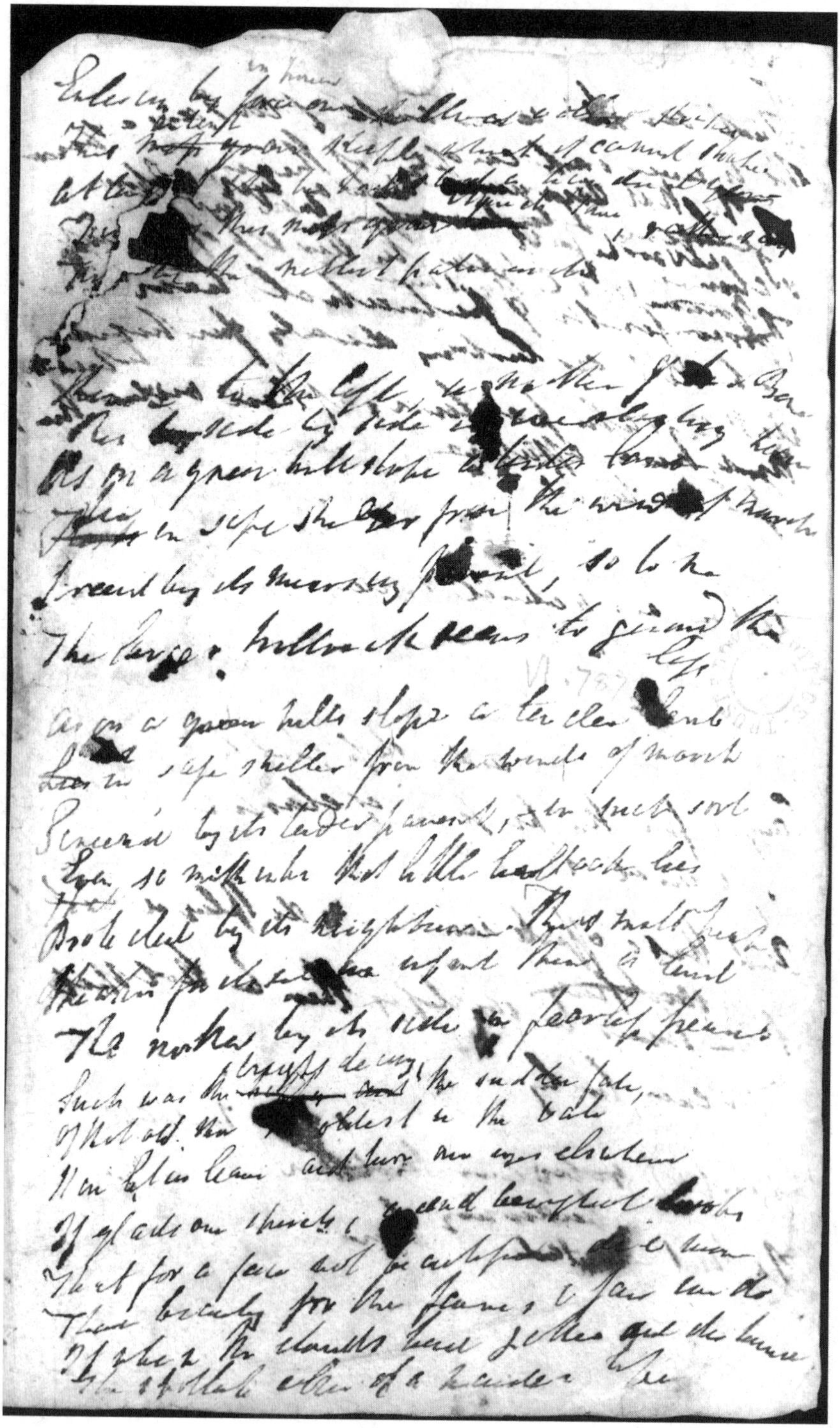

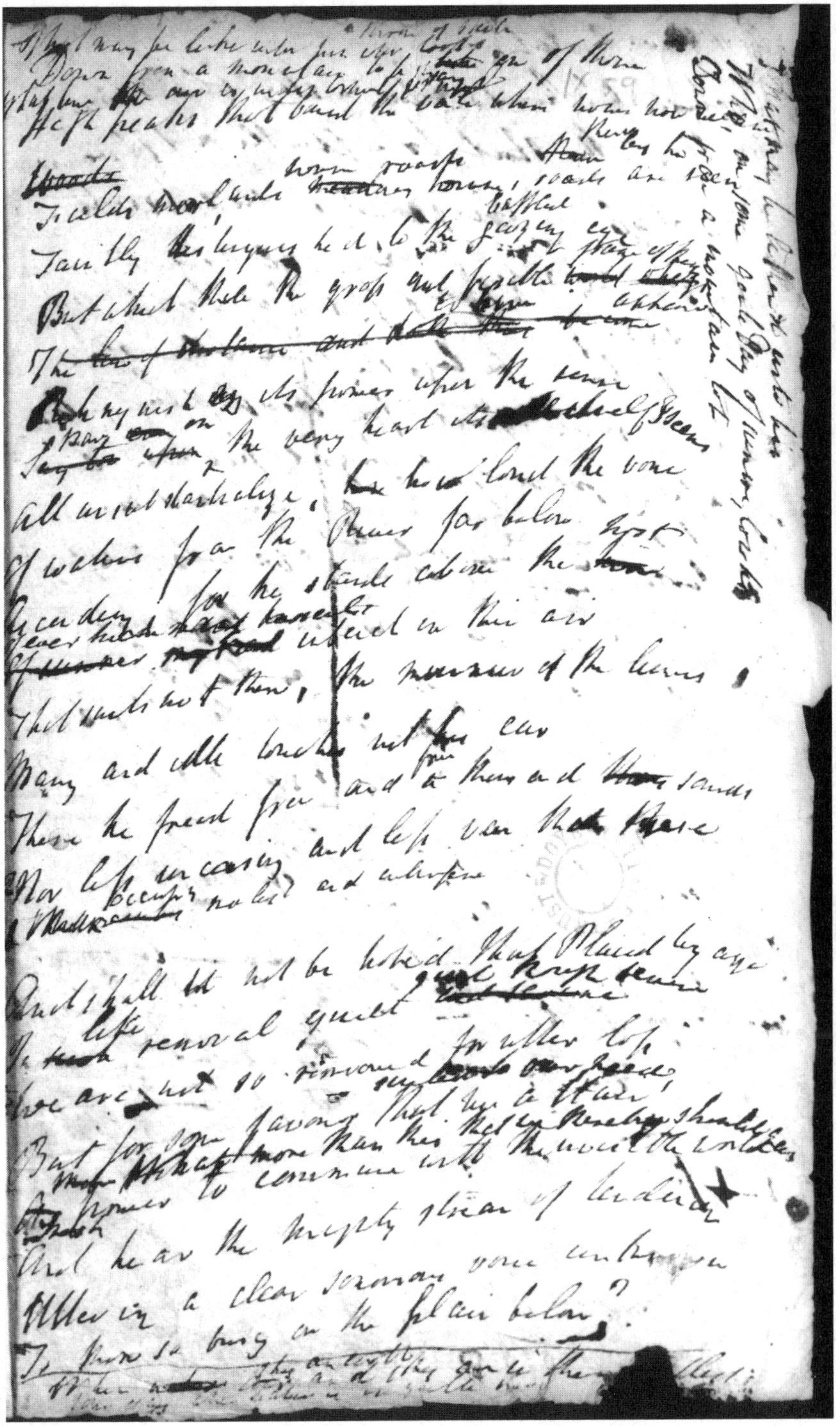

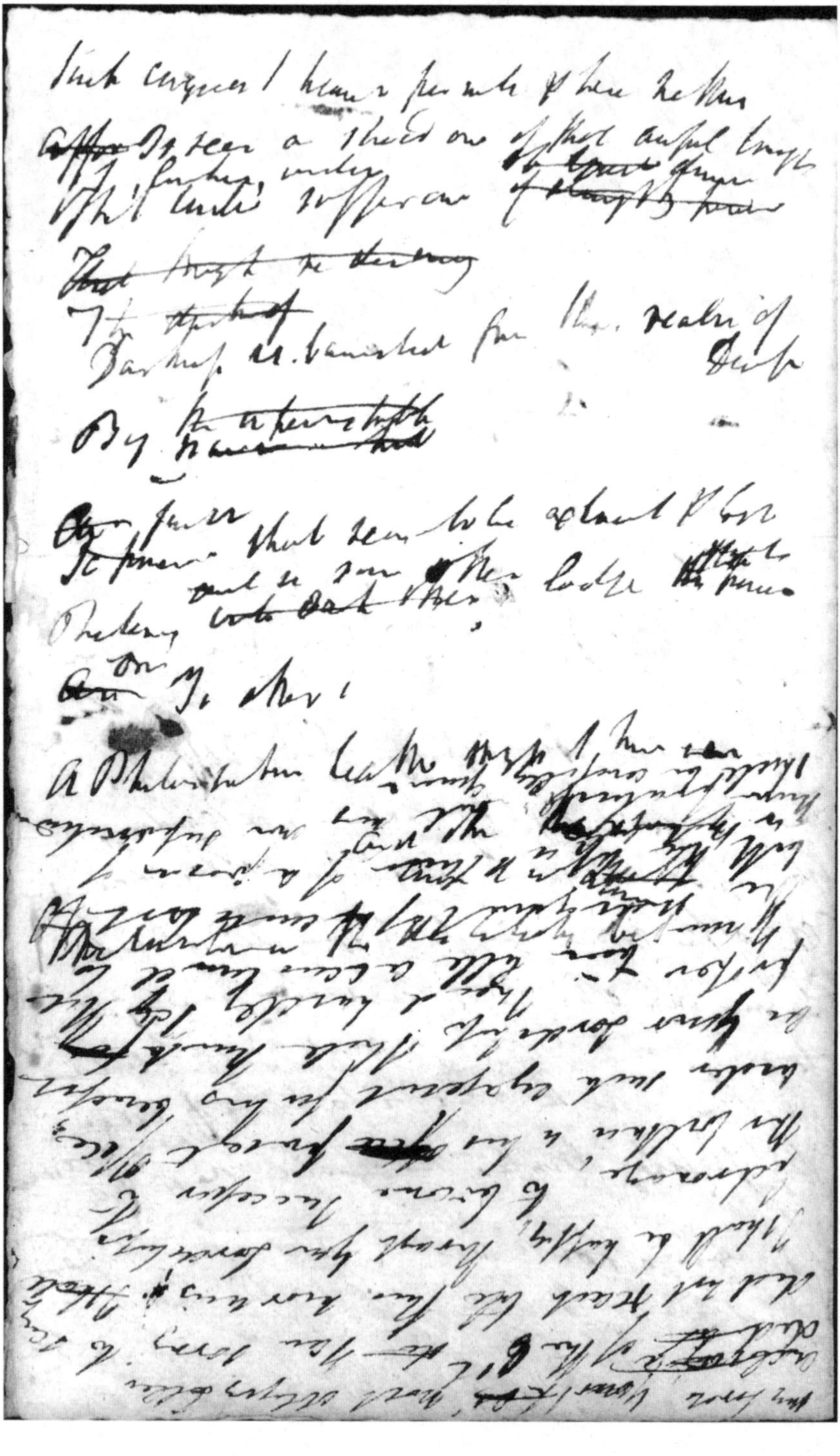

Berg MS.

The Berg MS.—in use at the sixth stage of *Excursion* composition for work on Book VIII—is described in the Manuscript Census, pp. xxi–xxii, above. For a discussion of this manuscript and its role in the composition of *The Excursion,* see pp. 458, 462–463, above.

Left-hand margin line numbers on the transcriptions provide cross-references to the line count in the 1814 reading text in this edition.

[recto]

VIII, 463 Like Image of solemnity conjoin'd
464 With lady-like allurement, soft and fair
as we turned
465 The Mansion's self display d ~~when northward turning~~
our ~~the [?] appeared~~
~~Abruptly with the pathway we beheld some [?]~~
Abruptly with our pathway it appeared
us noontide
468 Before as it fronts the ~~morning~~ sun.
Instinctively we halted to admire
469 Its venerable grace; the pillard porch
With modest pomp of heraldry embossed
470 The long wide windows with their mullions old
471 And cornice richly-sculptured of grey stone
472 And that smooth slope from which the Dwelling rose
A
473 By beds and banks a[rcadian of gay flowers
474 And flowering shrubs protected and adorned.
[?] by the [?stream] [?been check d but [? ?]
479 Eugh trees, not free from vestige that the [?stream]
[?on ? ?] [? ?]
Had check'd their early growth but ~~which were~~
~~now~~
as they long had [?been] to spread
[?stood—]
Permitted to throw out loose branches, ~~stood [?sprea~~]
Their branches [?loomed] stood in [?dusky] line
[?Spread]
In line, oer either side, like wings outstretch'd
On each side of the house like wings [?outstretch]
481 High above [?these] [?] [?or] behind the roof
482 The massy Sycamore and lightsome ash
Blending
483 Their diverse foliage ~~blending~~ with the green
484 Of ivy flourishing and thick that clasp'd
[?These]
485 The huge round Chimneys harbour of delig[ ]
485/486 For wren or redbreast when the trees ar[ ]
ba[ ]
486 To sing their song in darkness [?but in warm]

A right-margin tear at page foot results in some loss of text.

[verso]

[?]
VIII, 496 But Lo! when from the rocky garden [?mount]
497 Crowned by its antient summer House descends
G
498 Light as the silver fawn a radiant g}irl
[~~?~~]
499 For She hath recogniz d her antient friend
500 The wanderer ever welcome. A prompt [?kiss]
The gladsome Child
501 ~~Of greeting she~~ bestows at his request
502 And up the flowery lawn as we advance
~~gladsome~~
503 Hangs on the old Man with a happy look
504 And with a pretty, restless hand of love
paint [?~~graceful~~]
[?]
505 ~~The door~~ we entered: need I ~~tell~~ the guise
506 In what the Lady of the place receiv d
little band with
507 Our ~~company~~ a [?salution] nice
[?graceful] was her mien
508, 513 Of each accorded. When a stately
Her [?stature] [?] the prettiest of her [?] ~~c~~
514 Thro~~ugh [?gall weather] sails along the~~ s}~~oast~~
[? ?] the placid
[514] Sails in smooth weather by [~~? ?~~] soast
Who [? ?] sails the placid seas
515 In homeward voyage what if wind and wave
[?course] [?]
On long [~~? ? ?~~] various seas
course her [?]
517 Have caused her to abate the virgin pride
518 And that [?full trim] of inexperienced hope
519 [?] With which she left her house, not the less
520 When the sun strike her and the [?impartial breeze]
521 Play on her [?streamers] doth she then appear
522 Brightness and touching beauty of her own
bright [?]
So
523 With which all eyes are pleased. [?] ~~fair~~ so [?]

Houghton MS.

The Houghton MS.—in use at the sixth stage of *Excursion* composition for work on VII, 554–603, 648–654—is described in the Manuscript Census, pp. xxvi–xxvii, above. For a discussion of this manuscript and its role in the composition of *The Excursion*, see p. 459, above. We have assigned the designation "recto" to the side of this single sheet that contains the address panel (see Manuscript Census). Since the entries in the Houghton MS. are often written at right angles to each other (or with the sheet inverted), we have inserted horizontal rules to demarcate the various stages of composition. These drafts are related to DC MS. 74, 113^v–115^r, 116^r, 117^r; see DC MS. 75, $B2^r$–$B2^v$, for draft related to VII, 630–648.

Left-hand margin line numbers on the transcriptions of the Houghton MS. provide cross-references to the line count in the 1814 reading text in this edition.

[recto]

VII, 581 The Pastor answer d answered you have read him well
[?Once I inquired]
{I
{~~[?A] asked him~~
[?once] the [?number] of his [?years]
[?~~Their season~~]
Again th[?ese] [?] the [?] your &
590 Were but like outskirts of some large domain
{ of
591 By any one more thought {[?] than by him
592 Who holds the land in fee its careless lord
where he
[?~~Exists] in [?his] [?~~]
Or in entail no anxiousness of mind
No pride in having & no fear to lose
in age
648 But green & lusty as he is [~~?~~]
649 And promising to stand a hundred years
hour
652 His [?~~turn~~] will come & he will fall at last

Three years [?or less]
Or near that [?number] [? ?]
The [?first] [?] [?correctly] he exclaims
[?seve]
[?And] ~~eigh~~ to seventy years, [?ye have my age]
[?Free] as [? ?] & his voice [?serene]
He left [?us]

---

582 Year after year is added to [?his] store
summers winters past
583 With silent encrease ~~from [?the earth~~ then note]
585 Ten summers & ten winters of the space
586 That lies beyond lifes ordinary Bound
587 ~~Upon his~~
597 The incense which he offers up to heaven
598 Is of the kind which Bird & beast present
599 To the great father chearfulness of soul
In grove & pasture
600 In which repining find no place
From ~~dread~~ &
grief & [?horror] & [?re] & repining [?free]
A [?worthier] offering [?perchance than fr]
[?Then may] the

581–652 Entered across the top of the page. Expanded below and on verso.
581/590 Draft related to the axeman's age is found inverted below and on the verso, ll. 578/597. These indicate his age as 77, but in *1814*, ll. 585–586, the Pastor generalizes his age.
The lines beginning "Three years" and concluding "[?Then may] the" are inverted and entered across the sheet below the address.

[verso]

W
VII, 554 Among the humbler Worthies at our feet
555 Lying, insensible to human praise
556 Love or regret whose lineaments would next [?P]
557 Have been pourtrayd I guess not, but it chancd
sloping
That at this [?moment down ~~the~~] ~~narrow~~ road
~~While~~ [?Into a] the rugged [?slope]
final
558 ~~Bordering~~ the ~~chur~~ yard where lie
T
559 A lusty [?]eam came ringing noisily
[?~~Here~~] ~~[?]~~]
~~Here sa the~~
w
563 Here said the Pastor do [?]e muse & mourn
A
564 The waste of death— [?]nd lo the giant oak
S
565 [?Ly]trecthed on his bier that [?ponderous timber]
wain
And see [?an] object [?] of wh
566 The man who guides & guards the jolly team
A d[?] [?] by the [? ?]
[?~~He~~]
[?Had turned that way]
upon a [~~?~~] [?locks]
568 ~~He look d but slack~~ [?a] man whose hair was grey
[568] But round his temples pridefully hung
569 In climbing curls like ivy which the bite
570 Of winter cannot thin the fresh air lodged
571 Within his cheek as light within a cloud

In him to whom our [?notice] thus was turned
567 We saw a Peasant of the hublsst Class
P
[567] He was a peasant of the humblest class
[568] Grey locks profusely round his temples hung
[569] In clustering curls like ivy which the bite
[570] Of winter cannot thin the fresh air lodged
[?had] as
[571] Within his cheek ~~like~~ light within a cloud
573 [?Who] as [?he] pass d the [?solit said]
he
574 A man seemd of chearful yesterdays
[?]
575 And confident tomorrows, with a face
576 Not worldly minded for it bore too much
577 Of natures ~~better~~ impress, gaiety & & healt

554–578ff. These blocks of lines are entered in two columns. Ll. 554–571 form the first column, and ll. 567–578ff. (continuing on our next page, passage above the rule) form the second.

578 Freedom & life but keen withal & shrewd
The pastor hailed him & ~~his~~
turned & stopped
Obedient [?to answer ~~happy to have talk~~] a child
[? ?] note & hark
Of [?~~prattling fond] gesture~~. His [?tones] [?] of voice
r
[?~~Were~~] [?Was] all vivacious as his [?step] & mien.
He
[?Add seven to that] & ye will [?have my age]
[?] as the [?Register] and with kind words
{H
{We left [?us standing]

In work of [?humblest taking forward]
And these rocks their fondest [?severance]

---

597 The incense which he offerd up to Heaven
598 Is of the kind which Birds & beast present
599 In grove or pasture chearfulness of heart
600 ~~Five years [?] [?sorrow~~] & repin
[600] From [?trepidation] & repining free
[?scrupulous]
601 The [?more thoughtful] worshipper [?approach]
grace
The throne of ~~with offering~~ [?then]
~~With offering let~~
603 ~~Less worthy~~ less religious
with offering le
Than The [?almighty throne of] [?]

578/597 Other draft related to the axeman's age is found on the recto, ll. 581/590 and in the middle band of composition there.

597–603ff. These lines are inverted on the sheet.

DC MS. 74A

DC MS. 74A—in use at the eighth stage of *Excursion* composition for work on Book V—is described in the Manuscript Census, pp. xxv-xxvi, above. For a discussion of the role of this manuscript in the composition of *The Excursion*, see pp. 473–475, above.

The opening loose bifolium of DC MS. 74 provides a fair copy of *Excursion*, V, 1–65, based on revisions to leaves 1^r–2^r; the loose bifoilum was once loosely attached at the front of the four gatherings of the main manuscript, and we have so placed it in our transcriptions.

Left-hand margin line numbers on the transcriptions of DC MS. 74A provide cross-references to the line count in the 1814 reading text in this edition.

[loose bifolium, 1ʳ]

V, 1 *Farewell deep Valley with thy lonesom*
2 *And its small lot of life-sustaining fie*
3, 9 *And guardian rocks! farewell attract*
11 *By Nature destined at the birth of thin*
12 *For quietness profound!*
{reen Upon the side
13 *Of that g{[?ra] [?] slope the Outlet of the*
14 *Lingering behind my Comrades thus I breathed*
In a hushed voice and with reverted eyes
15 *A parting tribute to a spot that seemed*
troubled
16 *Like the fixed centre of a ~~breathing~~ world*
17 *Thence, the smooth bank ascending with slow step*
{by change
18 *How vain it is, thought I, {chan of place*
19 *To seek that comfort which the mind denies*
20 *Yet trial and temptation oft are shunned*
21 *Wisely, and by such tenor do we hold*
22 *Frail life's possessions that even some whose*
fate
23 *Yields no peculiar reason of complaint*
24 *Might by the promise that is here be won*
25 *To steal from active duties and embrace*
26 *Obscurity and calm forgetfulness.*
20

[loose bifolium, 1ᵛ]

[ ] *more I stopped to cast a backward look*
[ ] *at profound recess: and while I gazed*
[ ] *~~elier~~*
[ ] [?~~el~~] *~~er strain of feeling thus broke forth~~*
[ ] [?*in*] *my full heart a livelier strain broke forth*
[ ] *sition such as animates the grove*
[ ] *spring-time, when a Bird, that for a while*
[ ] *soothed himself with notes subdued and low,*
[ ] *to a lofty pitch mount suddenly.*
[ ] *happy Britain! heaven protected Isle,*
From that immense Metropolis through all

This bifolium, now separately preserved with MS. 74A, was once stitched at the front of that MS. to form its first gathering; the text of the bifolium incorporates rev of original 1ʳ–2ʳ, ll. 1–65 (see below). Base text is in MW's hand. Her numbering (see "20" at page foot) continues by twenties throughout the loose bifolium and then onto the original leaves (see note to l. 78 on original 2ʳ, below).

The top third of the outer margin of leaf 1 of the loose bifolium is torn, thus removing any signs of pagination, possibly "1" and "2."

1ff. Rev of original 1ʳ (see below). Cf. MS. 70, 6ʳ.

See note to loose bifolium, 1ʳ, (above) for description of tear in margin; the missing letters can be supplied from original 1ʳ–1ᵛ (see below), which are here rev. This passage, continuing onto loose bifolium, 2ʳ, may have been omitted in *1814* because of its similarity to the opening of Book VI. Cf. MS. 70, 4ᵛ, 6ʳ.

Her
{~~Her~~ {C {ies
{*Thy humbler* {*cit*{[?*es*] *Towns and Villages*
her
To the bare rock upon ~~thy~~ sounding shores
her {[?P]
And ~~thy~~ remotest Dwelling-{*places—blest*
Oh my beloved Country, favoured, blest
{ *Above*
{[?*Far*] *all Countries, enviably blest*
her haughty
When with thy ^ *neighbour, haughty France, compared*
her
For justice rules thy wide domain—the voice
her
Of Liberty is heard throughout thy bounds.
{is
Dells deep as th{~~*ese*~~ *the Mountains of Auvergne*
Include, and gay Burgundia's vine clad Hills
Hold many a green and habitable nook

[loose bifolium, 2[r]]

3

Of Beauty more luxuriant nor less safe
Perchance from notice and intrusive feet
But what avails allurement in a Land
Where none are free to chuse? Whose sons if
crossed
By aught which they would fly from may not flee?
Predestined all to works of violence
Born to be Slaves and ripened for the Sword
V, 27 *Knowledge methinks in these disordered times*
28 *Should be allowed a privilege to have*
29 *Her Anchorites like Piety of Old;*
a }
30 *Men, who from Faction s*[?*t*]}*cred and unstained*
31 *By war might if so minded turn aside*
In age in manhood or in ardent youth
32 *Unthwarted, and subsist, a scattered few*
33 *Living to God and Nature, and content*
34 *With that communion. Consecrated be*
35 *The Spots where such abide! But happier still*
attends
36 *The Man whom futhermore a hope ~~inspires~~*
{guide
37 *That meditation and research may* {*lea*
privacy
38 *His ~~loneliness~~ to principles and powers*

In the lines near page foot beginning "When," "For," and "Of," rev—including underlining—is in pencil.

The first seven lines, as well as ll. 27ff., are rev of original 1[v], 2[r] (see below).

38 Rev to this line and to l. 61 on loose bifolium, 2[v], are in fainter ink than other rev to the loose bifolium and may represent a separate stage of rev.

Discovered or invented: or set forth
Through his acquaintance with the ways of
truth

[loose bifolium, 2^v]

3
In lucid order so that when his course ~~is~~
Is run some faithful Eulogist may say
He sought not praise and praise did overlook
His inobtrusive merit but his life ~~s~~
Sweet to himself was exercised in good
That shall survive his name and memory.
{Nor would I, as a Patriot and a Man,
{Acknowledgments of gratitude sincere
~~Quit the~~
Accompan} ~~secluded harbour that inspired~~
The harbour quit whose stillness had inspired
These farewell musings without fervent thanks
For my own peaceful lot and happy choice,
A choice that from the passions of the world
Withdrew and fixed me in a safe retreat
Sheltered but not to social duties lost
Secluded but not buried: and with song
Cheering my days and with industrious thought.
With
^ *The ever-welcome company of books*
And virtuous friendship's soul-sustaining aid
And with the blessings of domestic love *80*
Thus occupied in mind I paced along
{[?and]
Following a rugged road by sledge {*or* *wheel*
Worn in the moorland, till I overtook
My two Associates in the morning sunshine
Halting together on a rocky knoll
From which the road descended rapidly
To the green meadows of another Vale
Here did our pensive Host put forth his
hand

[1^r]

Once more I stopped to cast a backward look *I*
On that profound Recess: and while I gazed

41–43, 47–65 Rev of original 2^r, 1^v (see below).
41, 44 Del by eras.
44–46 These lines do not appear elsewhere in MS. 74A nor in any other extant MS. WW perhaps used a stray sheet, no longer extant, to continue his drafting on original 2^r (see below).
47–48 *1814* does not adopt the rev but follows the readings on original 1^v (see below).
59 Conjectured "and" is in pencil.
61 MW failed to complete the line, as on original 1^v (see below and the note to loose bifolium, 2^r, l. 38).

MS. 74A originally began here (its opening was then rev on the loose bifolium preserved with the MS. and presented first in this transcription).

A livelier strain of feeling thus broke forth
Transition such as animates the Grove
In springtime, when a Bird that for a time
Hath sooth'd himself with notes subdued & low
Doth to a lofty pitch mounts suddenly

V, 1 *Farewell deep Valley with thy lonesome House*
2 *And its small lot of life-sustaining fields*
3, 4 *And guardian rocks! farewell attractive seat*
{*N*
11 *By* {*nature destined at the birth of things*
12 *For quietness profound!*
Upon the side
13 *Of that green slope the Outlet of the Vale*
14 *Lingering behind my Comrades thus I breathed*
hushed
In a ~~low~~ voice and with reverted eyes
15 *A parting tribute to a spot that seemed*
16 *Like the fixed centre of a troubled world.*
Thence, the smooth bank ascending with slow step
17 ~~*And now pursuing leisurely my way*~~
{*thought*
18 *How vain it is,* {*by* *I, by change of place*
19 *To seek that comfort which the mind denies*
20 *Yet trial and temptation oft are shunned*
21 *Wisely and by such tenor do we hold*
some
22 *Frail life's possessions that even ~~those~~ whose fate*
23 *Yields no peculiar reason of complaint*
24 *Might by the promise that is here be won*
25 *To steal from active duties and embrace*
26 *Obscurity and calm forgetfulness.* {[?d]
Once more I stopp'd to cast a backward look' {[?es]
On that Recess: and like a Bird of Song
That from a low key passes suddenly
Thus with livelier impulse I exclaimed
{H
"O happy Britain! {heaven-protected Isle
From [?that immense]

[1v]

through all
From that immense Metropolis ~~of thine~~
{T humbler {V
~~Through all~~ {thy ^ Cities Towns & {villages
2 bare
To the ~~bleak~~ rock upon thy sounding shores

Base text is in MW's hand. She numbers each page consecutively, except as noted. MS. 69, stub 248v, begins at V, c. 300, but other missing leaves in MS. 69 may once have contained a version of V, 1–299.

1–4, 11–65 Rev on loose bifolium, 1r, 2r–2v. Cf. MS. 70, 4v, 6r.

WW's rev at page foot is then rev at the top of the page, continuing onto the top of 1v (where space had been left for rev); the passage is next rev on loose bifolium, 1v.

19–23 A diagonal rust-colored mark runs across these lines and through to the verso, caused by contact with some object after composition.

A space of approximately five base text lines was left at the top of the page and was subsequently used for rev.

Rev at top and bottom of page is rev of 1r; passage is then rev on loose bifolium, 1v.

And thy remotest Dwelling-places—blest!
O my beloved Country, favored blest
Above all Countries, enviably blest!
n
When with thy h|eighbour haughty France, compared,
For [?~~equal~~] Justice rules thy wide domain—the voice X
Dells deep as this the Mountains of Auvergne
Include, and gay Burgundias vine-clad Hills
Hold many a green and habitable nook
Of Beauty more luxuriant nor less safe
Perchance, from notice and obtrusive feet.
But what avails allurement in a Land

XOf Liberty is heard throughtout thy bounds

Born to be slave and ripened for the sword

V, 47 X *Acknowledgments of gratitude sincere*
48 *Accompanied these musings fervent thanks*
49 *For my own peaceful lot and happy choice*
50 *A choice that from the passions of the world*
51 *Withdrew and fixed me in a safe retreat*
52 *Sheltered but not to social duties lost*
53 *Secluded but not buried and with song*
54 *Chearing my days and with industrious thought*
55 *The ever welcome company of books*
56 *And virtuous friendship's soul-sustaining aid*
57 *And with the blessings of domestic love*
58 *Thus occupied in mind I paced along*
59 *Following a rugged road by sledge and wheel*
60 *Worn in the moorland, till I overtook*
61 *My two Associates*
62 *Halting together on a rocky knoll*
63 *From which the road descended rapidly*
64 *To the green meadows of another Vale.*
65 *Here did our pensive Host put forth his hand*

are
* Where none |[?is] free to chuse;? Whose Sons, if cross'd
By aught which they would fly from, may not flee?
Predestined all to work of violence
27 X Knowlege, methinks, in these disordered times
28 Should be allowed a privilege to have
29 Her Anchorites like Piety of old;
30 Men who from Faction sacred, and unstained
31 By war, might if so minded turn aside

In the eighth line, cross in the right margin signals the insertion of the line of verse entered vertically in the right margin.

47 Cross in the left margin above line probably signals the continuation of rev at page foot.

47–65 Rev on loose bifolium, 2^{v}.

27–31 Rev on loose bifolium, 2^{r}.

Line of verse written vertically in the right margin corresponds to line near page foot on loose bifolium, 1^{v}; the cross signals its insertion after the matching cross in the eighth line of rev here on original 1^{v}. The line of verse entered vertically in the left margin corresponds to the seventh line on loose bifolium, 2^{r}, the conclusion of the passage.

Cross in the left margin immediately below the rule probably signals continuation of the passage of rev at the top of the page.

27 Cross in the left margin probably signals the insertion of the line of verse entered vertically in the left margin as in loose bifolium, 2^{r}, the seventh line.

31 Rev continued on top of 2^{r}.

[2r]

3

In age in manhood, or in ardent youth
V, 32 Unthwarted, and subsist a scattered few
33 Living to God and Nature, and content
34 With that communion. Consecrated be
35 The spots where such abide. But happier still
66 *In sign of farewell. Nay the Old Man said*
dewy freshness {still
67 *The air its ~~morning~~ ^ freshness {yet retains*
Pleasant and cool You must not leave us yet
71 *To this injunction earnestly expressed*
72 *He yielded, though reluctant; for his mind*
73 *Instinctively disposed him to retire*
74 *To his own covert as a billow heaved*
75 *Upon the beach rolls back into the sea*
76 *So we descend; and at the bottom gain*
A jutting crag and winding round its base
{*We* {*point*
77 {*[?And] reach a* {*[?base] that shewed the Valley stretched*
78 *In length before us and not distant far* 100
79 *Upon a rising ground a grey Church Tower*
80 *Whose battlements were screened by peaceful Trees*
81 *And towards a chrystal mere that lay beyond*
82 *Among steep hills and woods embosomed flowed*
83 *A copious stream with boldly-winding course*
84 *Here traceable there hidden there again*
85 *To sight restored and glittering in the sun*
86 *On the streams bank and every where appeared*
87 *Fair Dwellings single or in social knotts*
88 *Some scattered oer the level others perched*
36 The Man whom furthermore a hope inspires
[41] in lucid order
{ds
37 That meditation and research may lea{[?]
{&
38 His loneliness to principles {or powers
39 Discovered or invented or [?~~exposed~~] [?] or set forth
40 By his acquaintance with the ways of truth
[?prospect,] so that when [?co] course
41 In clearer ~~view~~, [?~~to] [?] [?main~~tained]
[?Is run]
42 ~~So that~~ some faithful Eulogist may say
43 He sought not Praise an[?d P]raise did overlook

32–43 Rev continued from 1v; rev on loose bifolium, 2r–2v, which provide ll. 44–46.

78 MW's line count ("100") in the right margin seems to follow from "80" on loose bifolium, 2v. Throughout the MS., she continues to number by twenties, except where noted.

[41] Phrase "in lucid order" (which begins l. 41 on loose bifolium, 2v) is probably further work on rev to l. 41, below.

40/41 Word preceding "course" in loose bifolium, 2v, l. 41, is "his."

43 Ink blot obscures the queried letters.

[2^v]

4 et
V, 89 *On the hill sides, a chearful qui* {[?*l*] *scene*
90 Now in its morning purity arrayed
mid
91 *As* {*in some happy Valley of the Alps*
92 *Said I, once happy ere tyrannic Power*
93 *Wantonly breaking in upon the Swiss*
94 *Destroyed their unoffending Commonwealth*
95 *A popular equality doth seem*
96 *Here to prevail and yet a House of State*
97 *Stands yonder one beneath whose roof methinks*
98 *A rural Lord might dwell. "No feudal pomp"*
99 *Replied our Friend a Chronicler who stood* *120*
100 *Whereer he moved upon familiar ground*
101 *"Nor feudal power is there, but there abides*
102 *In his allotted home a genuine Priest*
103 *The Shepherd of his Flock or as a King*
104 *Is stiled whien most affectionately praised*
: Such was he
105 *The Father of his People—* {~~*gathered round him*~~
106 And rich and poor & young & old
~~*In this sequestered realm they*~~ *rejoice*
107 *Under his spiritual sway collected round him*
108 *In this sequestered realm. He hath vouchsafed*
109 *To me some portion of his kind regard*
110 *And something also of his hidden mind*
111 *Hath he imparted—but I speak of him*
112 *As he is known to all. The tranquil joys*

[3^r]

piety 5
V, 113 *Of unambitious* {[?*life*] *he chose*
114 *And learnings solid dignity, though born*
115 *Of Knightly race nor wanting powerful friends*
116 *This good to reap these pleasures to secure*
117 *Hither in prime of manhood he withdrew*
118 *From academic bowers he loved the spot*
119 *Who does not love his native soil—he prized*
120 *The ancient rural character composed*
2 *1.* *140*
121 *Of manners simple feelings unsuppressed*
122 *And undisguised, and strong and serious thought*
123 *And these are all reflected in himself*
124 *With such embellishments as well beseems*
125 *His rank and sacred function. This deep Vale*
126 *Is lengthened out by many a winding reach*
127 *Not visible to us and one of these*

96–108 Cf. MS. 70, 7^r–8^r.

105–106 There are two stages of rev: (1) cancellation through "realm" with a wavy deletion stroke to form one line of verse; (2) cancellation of "they" and addition of interlinear rev.

---

121 Numbers "2" and "1" alter text to what is in *1814*: "simple manners."

128 *A turretted Manorial Hall adorns*
129 *In which the good Man's Ancestors have dwelt*
130 *From age to age the Patrons of this Cure*
131 *To them and more to his adorning hand*
132 *The Vicar's Dwelling and the whole Domain*
ch
133 *Owes that presiding aspect whi{ch / [?gh]} might well*
e
134 *Attract your notice—stat{e} lier than could else*
135 *Have been bestowed in course of common chance*
136 *On an unweathy mountain Benifice*

[3ᵛ]

~~While he was speaking slowly we advanced~~
V, 137 *Thus said oft halting we pursued our way*
~~And slowly still pursued our pleasant way~~
6 *till*
138 *Nor reached the village-church yard {till / ere} the sun*
had risen
139 *Travelling at steadier pace than ours*
136 *~~On an unwealthy mountain Benefice.~~* X
A
140 *~~Had risen~~ {A} above the summits of the highest hills*
~~This said [?—] proceeding on our pleasant way~~
141 *And round our path darted oppressive heat*
~~We reached the Village Church Yard. At that time~~
Pile
142 *As chanced the Portals of the sacred {Pile / House}*
143 *Stood open and we entered. On my frame* *160*
fervid air
144 *At such transition from the ~~sunny~~ air*
145 *A grateful coolness fell that seemed to strike*
concert
146 *The heart, in ~~union~~ with that temperate awe*
147 *And natural reverence which the place inspired*
148 *Not framed to nice proportions was the Pile*
149 *But large and massy; for durtaion built,*
150 *With pillars crowded and the roof upheld*
naked
151 *By rafters intricately crossed*
152 *Like leafless underboughs in some thick grove*
153 *All withered by the depth of shade above*
154 *Admonitory texts inscribed the walls*
155 *Each in its ornamental scroll enclosed*
156 *Each also crowned with winged heads—a pair*
157 *Of rudely painted Cherubim.—The floor*
158 *Of Nave and Aisle in unpretending guise*

---

136 Rev is the result of drafting and expansion of this passage above canceled l. 136 on 3ᵛ.

---

136 Cross in right margin signals rev above, which includes recopying of l. 136 at bottom of 3ʳ.
137 There may be a comma or colon after "said."
143 MW's line count does not include rev to ll. 136–141.
146 Word "concert" is in pencil, then overwritten in ink.
151 Rev, perhaps correction of a miscopy, supplies missing foot in the line.

Was
Were occupied by Oaken benches, ranged
In seemly rows; the Chancel only shewed
Some inoffensive marks of earthly state

[5^r]

7
And vain distinction[?s]. *A capacious Pew*
Of sculptured Oak stood here with drapery lined
And marble monuments were here displayed 180
Upon the Walls, and on the floor beneath
epulcral {*n*
Sc~~ulptural~~ stones appeared with emblems grave
And footworn epitaphs and some with small
{*ies*
And shining effig [?*ys*] *of brass inlaid.*
The tribute by these various records claimed
Without reluctance did we pay, and read
The ordinary chronicle of birth[?s]
Office, alliance, and promotion—all
Ending in dust; or upright Magistrates
Grave Doctors strenuous for the Mother Church
And uncorrupted Senators alike
To King and People true. A brazen plate
Not easily decyphered told of one
{*r*
Whose course of earthly honou rs was begun
In quality of page among the train
Of the eight Henry when he crossed the Seas
royal
His ^ *state to shew and prove his strength*
In tournament upon the fields of France

[5^v]

8
Another tablet registered the death 200
And praised the gallant bearing of a Knight

---

159 Rev, in pencil, adopted in *1814*.

Leaf 4, which originally followed leaf 6 (see Manuscript Census, above) has been removed from the MS., leaving a stub. On stub 4^r, the remaining initial letters, in the hand of MW, probably draw upon MS. 74 (cf. 12^r, 13^r, inside front cover, 34^r, 34^v), and correspond to V, 257–266: A / [?M] / O / Th / W / A / [?To] / [?A] / [?O]. The initial "A" may correspond to V, 246, leading directly into V, 256. Stub 4^v, whose one-time contents are rev and entered on leaf 7, probably draws upon MS. 74, 34^v, 35^r, 35^v; terminal letters in the hand of MW correspond to V, 277–286: ceived / trust / float / - / - / - / - / Man / - / - / de / - / [?e].

Page numbering in MS. 74A continues consecutively from 3^v ("6") to 5^r ("7"), and the line count on 5^r, l. 164, does not include the contents of stub 4^r and 4^v; instead, those contents appear as part of consecutive draft on 7^r–7^v.

162 Del by eras.

166–182 Cf. MS. 70, 8^v–9^r.

171 Del by eras.

181 Rev, perhaps correction of a miscopy, supplies missing foot in the line.

183–204 Cf. MS. 70, 9^r–9^v.

185 *Tried in the Sea-fights of the second Charles*
186 *Near this brave Knight his Father lay entombed*
187 *And to the silent language giving voice*
{in
188 *I read,—how {by his youth and earlier day*
189 *He, mid the afflictions of intestine War*
190 *And rightful government subverted found*
191 *This only solace that a gentle Dame*
192 *He had espoused a Lady most beloved*
193 *For her benign perfections, and for this*
196 *That she with numerous issue filled his House*
197 *Who throve like plants uninjured by the storm*
198 *That laid their country waste. No need to speak*
199 *Of less particular notices assigned*
200 *To youth or maiden gone before their time*
201 *And Matrons and unwedded Sisters old*
202 *Whose Charity and goodness were rehearsed*
203 *In modest panegyric. These dim lines*
204 *What would they tell said I—but from the task*

[6^r]

9
V, 205 *Of puzzling out that faded narrative* 220
206 *With whisper soft by venerable Friend*
{looking down the darksome Aisle
207 *Called me and {[?turning] round my head I saw*
{I saw the
208 *{The [?pensive] Tenant of that lonely vale*
209 *Our Comrade, standing with his arm reclined*
210 *On the baptismal font; his palid face*
211 *Upturned, as if his mind were rapt or lost*
212 *In some abstraction; gracefully he stood*
213 *The semblance bearing of a sculptured form*
214 *That leans upon a monumental Urn*
215 *In peace, from morn to night from year to year*
216   *Him from that posture did the Sexton rouze*
217 *Who entered humming carelessly a tune*
218 *Continuation haply of the notes*
219 *That had beguiled the work from which he came*
220 *With spade and mattock on his shoulder hung*
221 *To be deposited for further need*
ointed
222 *In their ap~~propriate~~ place. The pale Recluse*
223 *Withdrew, and strait we followed,—to a spot*
224 *Where sun and shade were intermixt for*
there
225 *A broad oak, stretching forth its leafy arms*
240

205–225 Cf. MS. 70, 9^v–10^r.
208 Del by eras. Intended rev is from "that" to "the"; *1814* reads "the."
210 MS. 70, 9^v, reads "pallid" as does *1814*, perhaps indicating the use of an intervening MS.
225 Line count includes l. 208.

[6[v]]

10

V, 226 *From an adjoining pasture, overhung*
227 *Small space of that green church yard with a*
                                    .}{*O*   *light*
228 *And pleasant awning* }{*on the moss-grown wall*
229 *My ancient Friend and I together took*
230 *Our Seats and thus the Solitary spake,*
On the smooth plat-form of this church yard ground
231 *Standing before us. "Did you note the mien*
232 *Of that self-solaced easy-hearted churl*
233 *Death's minister who digs his neighbour's grave*
234 *Or wraps an old acquaintance up in clay*
235 *As unconcerned as when he plants a tree?*
236 *I was abruptly summoned by his voice*
237 *From some affecting images and thoughts*
238 *And from the company of serious words.*
239 *Much, yesterday, was said in glowing phrase*
240 *Of our sublime dependancies, and hopes*
241 *For future states of being; and the wings*
242 *Of speculation, joyfully outspread,*
243 *Hovered above our destiny on earth;*
I soared along with you but now am forced
But what ~~more differ than~~ the ~~human soul~~,
of Things most different in kind   *260*
244 *The powers and prospect in the human Soul,*
[244] To stoop and place the brilliant views in
contrast
[244] The power it boast the prospects of [?the soul]
Even I, though used to level ground, was tempted
To soar along with you, [?b] compeled [?him soon]

[7[r]]

V, 244 *But stoop & soberly compare*
More differ than the prospects   *11*
246 *And Man's substantial life. If this mute earth*
247 *Of what it holds could speak, and every grave*
248 *Were as a Volume, shut, yet capable*
249 *Of yielding its contents to eye and ear,*
250 *We should recoil striken with sorrow and shame*
251 *To see disclosed by such dread proof how far*
252 *That which is done falls short of what is known*
253 *To reason, and by conscience is enjoined,*
254 *How idly, how perversly, lifes whole course*

226–227 Cf. MS. 70, 10[r].
234 The "a" in "acquaintance" may be intended as a cap as in *1814*.
[244] "The power . . . . [?the soul]" is in pencil and earlier than other rev on the page.
Last two lines, rev of lines between 243 and 244, are continued on the top and bottom of facing 7[r].

This leaf originally followed leaf 4 (now a stub); see note to 5[r], above.
Rev at top of page, continued from 6[v], is continued at page foot.

255 *To this conclusion deviates from the line,*
256 *Or of the end stops short, proposed to all*
257 *At its aspiring outset. Mark the Babe,*
258 *Not long accustomed to this breathing world,*
259 *One that hath barely learned to shape a smile,*
260 *Though yet irrational of Soul to grasp*
261 *With tiny fingers, to let fall a tear,*
262 *And, as the heavy cloud of sleep dissolves,*
263 *To stretch his linbs, bemocking as might seem*
264 *The outward functions of intelligent Man,*
265 *A grave proficient in amusive feats* *280*
[244] *But stoop & place the prospects of the soul*
{*In*
245 {*And sober contrast with reality*
o}
[244] To stop}p and place the brilliant views
in contr

[7^v]

1[?]
V, 266 *Of puppetry that from the lap decleare*
267 *His expectations and announce his claims*
268 *To that inheritance which millions rue*
269 *That they were ever born to. In due time*
270 *A day of solemn ceremonial comes*
271 *When they who for this minor hold in trust*
272 *Rights that transcend the unblest heritage*
273 *Of mere humanity present their charge*
274 *For that occasion daintily adorned*
275 *At the baptismal font and when the pure*
276 *And consecrating element hath cleansed*
{ *re*
277 *The original stain the Child is the*{[?*ir*] *received*
278 *Into the second ark Christ's Church with trust*
279 *That he from wrath redeemed therein shall float*
280 *Over the billows of this troublesome world*
281 *To the fair land of everlasting life.*
282 *Corrupt affections covetous desires*
283 *Are all renounced high as the thought of Man*
284 *Can carry Virtue Virtue is professed* *300*
285 *A dedication made a promise given*
286 *For due provision to controul and guide*

257ff. Cf. MS. 74, 12^r, 13^r, inside front cover, 33^v–34^v.
265 Line count does not include the rev at l. 243/244 (see last note to 6^v, above).

Ink blot obscures part of page number.
266ff. Cf. MS. 74, inside front cover, 13^r, 33^v–35^v.

[8^r^]

1[?]

V, 287 *And unremitting progress to ensue*
288 *In holiness and truth.” “You cannot blame”*
289 *Here interposing fervently I said*
{*ites*
290 *“R*{*ights which attest that Man by Nature lies*
291 *Bedded for good and evil in a gulph*
292 *Fearfully low nor will your judgment scorn*
293 *Those services whereby attempt is made*
294 *To lift the Creature towards that Eminence*
295 *On which now fallen erewhile in majesty*
296 *He stood, or if not so, whose top serene*
297 *At least he feels ‘tis given him to descry*
298 *Not without aspirations evermore* { *in*
299 *Returning, and injunctions from with*{ [?*out*]
300 *Doubt to cast off and weariness, in trust*
301 *That what the soul perceives if glory lost,*
{*and persevering hope*
302 *May be through pains* {*cast off and* [? ?]
303 *Recovered, or if hitherto unknown*
304 *Lies within reach and one day shall be gained”*
t} {*e* 2 1 *320*
305 *“I blame* }*h*{*im not” he answered calmly— “no*
established
306 *The outward ritual and ~~accustomed~~ Forms*

[8^v^]

1[?*4*]

V, 307 *With which communities of Men invest*
308 *These inward feelings and the aspiring Vows*
309 *To which the lips gives public utterance*
310 *Are both a natural process and by me*
311 *Shall pass uncensured; though the issue prove*
312 *Bringing from age to age its own reproach*
313 *Incongruous impotent and blank . but oh*
314 *If to be weak is to be wretched—miserable*
315 *As the lost Angel by a human Voice*
316 *Hath mournfully pronounced, then in my mind*
317 *Far better not to move at all than move*
318 *By impulse sent from such illusive power*

Ink blot obscures part of page number.
287ff. Cf. MS. 74, 34^v^, 35^v^–36^v^.
287 The reading in MS. 74, 35^v^, is clearly “to ensure” as in *1814*.
290 Rev possibly corrects a dictation error as the reading in MS. 74, 36^r^, is clear.
300ff. Cf. MS. 69, stub 248^v^.
302 The underlying reading is not found in any other MS.; possibly, eras and rev reflect work in progress (i.e., rev of this line in MS. 74, 36^r^–36^v^).
305 Transposition signaled by the numbers above is adopted in *1814*.

Ink blot obscures part of page number.
307ff. Cf. MS. 69, stubs 248^v^–248^r^, 247^r^; MS. 74, 35^v^–36^v^, 38^r^.
313 The centered period may indicate indecision on MW’s part as to punct, perhaps as a result of the rush of dictation or uncertainty in MS. 69. MS. 74, 36^v^, has a comma, *1814* a period followed by a dash.

That finds and cannot fasten down that grasps
And is rejoiced, and loses while it grasps
That tempts emboldens doth a while sustain
And then betrays accuses and inflicts
Remorseless punishment and so retreads
The inevitable circle better far 340
ze
Than this to gra{[?sp]} the herb in thoughtless peace
By foresight or remembrance undisturbed
Phylosophy! and thou more vaunted name
Religion with thy statlier retinue

[9r]

Faith 15
{[?Tr] [?] *hope and Charity—from the visible world*
us or
Ch[?*oos*]} *e* {*rom your emblems whatsoeer ye find*
a
Of s[?*o*]} *fest guidance and of firmest trust*
The Torch, the Star, the Anchor, nor except
The Cross itself, at whose unconscious feet
The Generations of Mankind have knelt
Ruefully seized and shedding bitter tears
And through that conflict seeking rest—of You
High-titled Powers am I constrained to ask,
Here standing, with the unvoyageble sky
In faint reflection of infinitude
Stretched overhead, and at my pensive feet
ra b
A subter[?*an*]} *aneous magazine of* [?*s*]} *ones*
In whose dark Vaults my own shall soon be laid
s
Where are your triumph{ *your dominion where*
And in what age admitted and confirmed? 360
L
Not for a happy {*land do I enquire*
Island or grove that hides a blessed Few
incere
Who with obedience willing and s{[?*evere*]

[9v]

16
To your serene Authority conform
But whom I ask of individual Souls
Have ye withdrawn from Passion's crooked ways

---

320 Added line is included in MW's line count at l. 324; that added line is present in MS. 74, 36v and presumably (but not certainly) in MS. 69, stub 248r.

329ff. Cf. MS. 69, stub 247r; MS. 74, 38r, 39r.
343 Rev is in pencil.

348ff. Cf. MS. 69, stubs 246v, 246r; MS. 74, 38r, 39r.

Inspired and thoroughly fortified?—if the Heart
m
Could be inspected to its in[?*f*]|*ost folds ~~light~~*
{*with*
By sight undazzled {*of the the glare of praise*
Who shall be named, in the resplendent line
Of Sages, Martyrs, Confessors, the Man
Whom the best might of Conscience, Faith and Hope
{*or*
F{*rom one days little compass have preserved*
From painful, and discreditable shocks
vague
Of contradiction from some false desire
Culpably {*ed or*
~~*Sinfully*~~ *cherish*{*ished corrupt relapse*
[?~~Langour &~~] ~~disappointment & despair~~
To some unsanctioned fear?"
Or *If this be so*
And Man" said I "be in his noblest shape
Thus pitiably infirm then he who made
sha| *380*
And who wi|*ll judge the Creature will forgiv*[?*e*]
Yet in its general tenor your Complaint
Is all too true, and surely not misplaced

[10r]

17
For from this pregnant spot of ground such thoughts
Rise to the notice of a serious mind
By natural exhalations—With the dead
In their repose the living in their mirth
Who can reflect unmoved upon the ground
Of smooth and solemnized complaciencies
By which on Christian lands from age to age
Profession mocks performance. Earth is sick
And heaven is weary of the hollow words
Which states and kingdoms utter when they
talk
Of truth and justice. Turn to private life
And social neighbourhood look we to ourselves
A light of duty shines on every day
For all, and yet how few are warmed or cheered
How few who mingle with their fellow men
And still remain self-governed and apart

---

352 Del by eras.
360/361 Rev in pencil; line does not appear to be present in MS. 69, stub 246v; it is included in MW's line count at l. 363.
361/362 "Or" is in pencil.
364 Queried "e" is obscured by center fold.

367ff. Cf. MS. 69, stubs 246r, 245v.
369 Del in pencil.
371 Del by eras.

383 *Like this our honoured Friend and thence acquire*
{*s* *400*
384 *Right*{ *to expect his vigorous decline*
{*That promises to*
385 {[?*His*] *blest old age the end a bless'd old age"*

[10^v]

18

V, 386 *"Yet" with a smile of triumph thus exclaimed*
387 *The Solitary "In the life of Man*
388 *If to the Poetry of common speech*
389 *Faith may be given we see as in a glass*
390 *A true reflection of the circling year*
391 *With all its seasons. Grant that Spring is there*
392 *In spite of many a rough untoward blast*
393 *Hopeful and promising with buds and flowers*
394 *Yet where is glowing Summer's long rich day*
395 *That ought to follow faithfully expressed*
396 *And mellow Autumn charged with bounteous fruits*
397 *Where is she imaged, in what favoured clime*
398 *Her lavish pomp and ripe magnificence?*
399 *Yet while the better past is missed the worse*
400 *In Man's autumnal season is set forth*
401 *With a resemblance not to be denied*
402 *And that contents him; flowers that hear no more*
403 *The voice of gladness less and less supply* *420*
404 *Of outward sunshine and internal warmth*
405 *And with this change sharp air and falling leaves*
406 *Forewarning total winter blank and cold*

[11^r]

19

V, 407 *How gay the habitations that adorn*
408 *This fertile Valley not a house but seems*
409 *To give assurance of content within*
410 *Embosomed happiness and placid love*
411 *As if the sunshine of the day were met*
412 *With answering brightness in the hearts of all*
413 *Who walk this favoured ground but chance regards*
414 *And notice forced upon incurious ears*
415 *These if these only acting in despite*
416 *Of those encomiums by my friend pronounced*
{*d*
417 *On humble life forbid the judging min*{[?*g*]
418 *To trust the smiling aspect of this fair*

---

384 Rev in pencil.

386ff. Cf. MS. 69, stubs 245^v, 245^r.

407ff. Cf. MS. 69, stubs 245^r, 244^v.
414, 419–420 Cf. MS. 74, 1^r, and copy in that MS. related to *TPL* on 10^r and 27^v.

T R
419 *And noiseless commonwealth {the simple {race*
420 *Of Mountaineers by Nature's self removed*
421 *From foul temptation, and by constant care*
422 *Of a good Shepherd tended—as themselves*
Flocks
423 *Do tend their {[?Sheep] these share Mans*
general lot
424 *With little mitigation they escape* 440
425 *Perchance guilts heavier woes and do not feel*
426 *The tedium of fantastic idleness*

[11ᵛ]

20
V, 427 *Yet life, as with the multitude, with them*
428 *Is fashioned like an ill constructed tale*
et
429 *That on the outs{ide wastes its gay desires*
e ure
430 *Its fair adva}ntage}s its enlivening hopes*
431 *And pleasant interests—for the sequel leaving*
432 *Old things repeated with diminished grace*
433 *And all the laboured novelties at best*
434 *Imperfect substitutes whose use and power*
435 *Evince the want and weakness whence they spring*
Here see no less than in the wider world
gushing
See for the {[?jutting] fount's continuous stream
The toiling engines interrupted gifts
Or joyless Cisterns hoard that fears the sun
wind
The sail that caught the help of every {breeze
The sail abandoned for the creeping oar!
This barter these exchanges manhood brings
Proud of his charge and thus we prove a scheme
Well rounded and compleat a promise kept 460
[?th]
A heig{[?ht] attained a noble growth matured.

[12ʳ]

21
V, 436 *While in this pensive way we held discourse*
437 *The reverend Pastor towards the Church yard gate*
438 *Approached, and with a mild respectful air*
439 *Of native cordiallity our Friend*
mien
440 *Advanced to greet him. With a gracious {smile*

427ff. Cf. MS. 69, stubs 244ᵛ, 244ʳ.
431–435ff. Cf. MS. 74, 105ʳ, where the passage omitted from *1814* was originally part of *TPL*.

436ff. Cf. MS. 69, stubs 244ʳ, 243ᵛ.

ei
Was he recie|ved and mutual joy prevailed.
A while they stood in conferrence and I guess
That he who now upon the mossy wall
Sate by my side had vanished if a wish
Could have transferred him to his lonely House
Rocks
Within the circuit of those guardian [?*Hills*]
For me I looked upon the pair well pleased
Like and unlike by nature framed and
marked
By circumstance with intermixture fine
Of contrast and resemblance. To an Oak
Hardy and grand a weather beaten Oak
age
age
Fresh in the strength and majsety of time
One might be likened. flourishing appeared
Though somewhat past the fulness of his prime

[12^v]

22

The Other, like a stately Sycamore
That spreads in gentler pomp its honied shade
A general greeting was exchanged and soon
~~*That his approach had given*~~
The Pastor learned that his approach had given
A welcome interruption to discourse
Grave and in truth full often sad.— "Is Man
A Child of Hope? Do generations press
On generations without progress made?
Halts the Individual ere his hairs be grey
Perforce? Are we a Creature in whom good
Preponderates, or evil? Doth the Will
: A
Acknowledge Reason's law ? a *living Power*
Is Virtue, or no better than a name
Fleeting as health or beauty and unsound
which
So that the only substance that *remains*
ha
(For thus the tenor of complaint do|th run)
Among so many shadows are the pains
And penalties of miserable life

455ff. Cf. MS. 69, stubs 243^v, 243^r.

457/458 Del by wavy strokes; the copy error may have been caused by rev in MS. 69, stub 243^v.

[13^{r}]

23

V, 473 *Doomed to decay, and then expire in dust?*

{*500*
{*480*

474 *Our cogitations this way have been drawn*
475 *These are the points" the Pedlar said "on*
which
476 *Our Inquest turns; accord good Sir! the light*
477 *Of your experience to dispel this gloom*
478 *By your persuasive wisdom shall the heart*
479 *That frets or languishes be stilled and cheered"*
480 *"Our Nature" said the Priest in mild reply*
{*: they*}
481 *"Angels may weigh and fathom{ and} perceive*
482 *With undistempered and unclouded spirit*
483 *The object as it is; but for ourselves*
484 *That speculative height we may not reach*
485 *The good and evil are our own, and we*
486 *Are that which we would contemplate from far.*
487 *Knowledge for us is difficult to gain*
488 *Is difficult to gain and hard to keep*
489 *As Virtues self like Virtue is beset*
490 *With snares; tired, tempted, subject to decay*
491 *Love, admiration, fear, desire and hate*
492 *Blind were we without these; through these*
alone

[13^{v}]

24

V, 493 *Are capable to notice or discern* 520
494 *Or to record, we judge but cannot be*
495 *Indifferent judges: spite of proudest boast*
496 *Reason, best reason is to imperfect Man*
497 *An effort only and a noble aim*
498 *A crown and attribute of sovereign power*
499 *Still to be courted never to be won.*
500 *Look forth, or each Man dive into himself*
e
501 *What sees he but a Creature too p[?u]}rturbed*
502 *That is transported to excess, that yearns*
503 *Regrets, or troubles wrongly or two much*
504 *Hopes rashly, in disgust as rash, recoils*

473ff. Cf. MS. 69, stubs 243^{r}, 242^{v}.

475 "Wanderer" replaces "Pedlar" in *1814*. Copy on MS. 69, 243^{r} (on which this passage is probably based) may have been composed before the decision to change the name was taken (cf. 14^{v}, l. 559, below).

482–492 Cf. MS. 74, 28^{r}. MS. 69, stubs 243^{r}, 242^{v}, may omit ll. 480–490. MW closely follows revised MS. 74, excepting a few changes in punct.

493–*c.* 512 Cf. MS. 69, stubs 242^{v}, 242^{r}, 241^{v}, which appear to omit V, c. 512–c. 526.

493–511 Cf. MS. 74, 28^{r}, 29^{r}.

503 Word "two," a copy or dictation error, reads "too" in *1814*.

505 *Battens on spleen, or moulders in despair.*
506 *Thus truth is missed and comprehension fails*
507 *And darkness and delusion round our path*
injury [?lu]
508 *Spread from disease whose subtile* ^ ~~*spirit*~~ *lurks*
509 *Within the very faculty of sight*
510 *Yet for the general purposes of faith*
511 *In providence, of solace and support*
And for those hopes without whose blessed aid
Duty would be a burthen; for these ends
512 We may not doubt that who can best subject
and [?l] str[?ic]liest live
513 The will to Reason's law ~~he shall obtain~~
514 And act in that obedience, he shall gain
515 The clearest apprehension even in things
[?search] {. B}
516, 517 Which Reason cannot <u>teach</u> {b}ut waiving that
[?] [?fathom]

[14ʳ]

V, 518 And our regards confining within bounds
519 Of less exalted consciousness through which 25
520 The very multitude are free to range
f
521 *We sa[?v]ely may affirm that human life*
522 *Is either fair or tempting a soft scene*
523 *Grateful to sight refreshing to the soul*
524 *Or a forbidding tract of cheerless view*
525 *Even as the same is looked at or approached"*
526 *—The Priest continued "I am tempted here*
527 *To use an illustration of my thoughts*
528 *Drawn from the very spot on which we stand*
529 *—In changeful April when with frost and snow*
530 *Winter, as he is wont, has reassumed*
531 *A short-lived sway returning unawares*
532 *If from the sullen region of the North*
533 *Towards the circuit of this holy ground*
534 *Your walk conducts you ere the vigorous sun*
535 *High climbing hath attained his noon-tide height*
536 *These mounds transversly lying side by side*
537 *From east to west before you will appear*
538 *A dreary plain of unillumined snow*

512–517 Rev is continued at top of facing 14ʳ, but it is not included in MW's line count at l. 540.

512/513, 514 Rev, from "and" through "shall gain," is added in a second stage of rev.

516, 517 Underlining of "teach" apparently signals WW's intention to revise.

518–520 Rev, continued from bottom of 13ᵛ, is not included in MW's line count at l. 540.

521–525, 529ff. Cf. MS. 74, 29ʳ, 30ʳ–30ᵛ.

527ff. Cf. MS. 69, stub 241ᵛ, which appears to omit V, 518–526.

530–531 MS. 69, stub 241ᵛ, appears to follow MS. 74, 29ʳ, except for the vertical rev in MS. 74, 29ʳ, l. 530–531, "A short liv'd sway and whiten'd hill and dale," which is closer than MS. 74A to the reading in *1814*: "Winter has reassumed a short lived sway / And whitened all the surface of the fields."

With more than wintry cheerlessness and gloom
Saddening the heart—go forward and look back
560

[14v]

26
On the same circuit of this Church yard ground
L
Look from the quarter whence the {*L* / *lord of light*
of
Of life and love and gladness doth dispence
His beams which, unexcluded in their fall,
2 *Have gently excercised a melting power*
1 *Upon the southern side of every grave*
Then will a vernal prospect greet your eye
All fresh and beautiful and green and bright
Hopeful and cheerful vanished is the snow
Vanished or hidden and the whole domain
To some too lightly minded might appear
A meadow carpet for the dancing hours.
This contrast not unsuitable to life
Is to that other state more apposite
Death and its two fold aspect wintry one
Cold, sullen, blank, from hope and joy shut out
hath
The other which the ray divine {*hath* / [?*th*] *touched*
as spring
Replete with vivid promise bright {*as spring* / *and* [?*fair*]
"*We see then as we feel*" *the Pedlar thus*
With a complaisant animation spake *580*
"*And in your judgment, Sir! the minds repose*

[15r]

27
On evidence is not to be ensured
By act of naked reason. Moral truth
Is no mechanic structure built by rule
And which once built retains a stedfast
shape
And undisturbed proportions; but a thing
Subject you deem, to vital accidents
ly *ives*
And like the water-li{*ly* / *y l*} {*ives* / [?*eaves*] *and thrives*
Whose root is fixed in the stable earth
whose head

541ff. Cf. MS. 69, stubs 241v, 241r.
541–558 MS. 74, 29v–30r.
546/545 MW's numbers in the left margin reorder the sequence of lines, possibly as the result of rev in MS. 69, stub 241r, continuing the rev in MS. 74, 29v.
559 "Wanderer" replaces "Pedlar" in *1814*; see note to 13r, l. 475 (above).

562ff. Cf. MS. 69, stubs 241r, 240v.

tossing
Floats on the ~~restless~~ {waves. With joy
sincere
I re salute these sentiments confirmed
By your authority but how acquire
The inward principle that gives effect
To outward argument? the passive will
Meet to admit the active energy
Strong and unbounded to embrace and firm [?~~unite~~]
To keep and cherish how shall Man unite
{A self *{tenderness*
{A [?] *forgetting {dignity of heart*
And earth despising dignity of soul
Wise in that union and without it blind"
"The way" said I, "to court if not obtain

[15^v]

28
The ingenuous mind apt to be set aright.
This while we conversed in the lonely dell
You shewed at large and by what exercise
From visible nature or the inner self
Power may be trained, and renovation brought
To those who need the gift: but after all
Is aught so certain as that Man is doomed
within
To breathe ~~beneath~~ a Vault of Ignorance
{House
The natural roof of that dark {roof in which
His soul is pent. How little can be known
This is the wise man's sigh, how far we err
This is the good man's not unfrequent pang
{err *{wly*
And they perhaps {[?*are*] *least the lo{l*[?*e*] *class*
Whom a benign necessity compels
To follow Reason's least ambitious course
Such do I mean who unperplexed by doubt
And unincited by a wish to look
Into high objects farther than they may
Pace to and fro from morn to even-tide
The narrow avenue of daily toil

---

571 *1814* reads "re-salute."
575 "Meet" is a copy error; MS. 69, stub 240^v, as *1814*, clearly reads "Meek."
576 Del by eras.

582ff. Cf. MS. 69, stub 240^r.
589 *1814* restores "beneath."

[16^r]

V, 602 *For daily bread"* 29
"Yes!" buoyantly exclaimed
603 *The pale Recluse— "Praise to the sturdy plough*
604 *And patient spade and Shepherd's simple crook*
g
605 *And ponderous loom, resoundind while it*
holds
606 *Body and mind in one captivity*
607 *And let the light mechanic tool be hailed*
608 *With honour, which encasing by the power*
609 *Of long companionship the Artist's hand*
610 *Cuts off that hand with all its world of nerves*
heart
611 *From a too busy commerce with the world*
612 *Inglorious implements of craft and toil*
613 *Both ye that shape and build and ye that force*
614 *By slow solicitation earth to yield*
615 *Her annual bounty sparingly dealt forth*
Y
616 *With wise reluctance you would I extol*
617 *Not for gross good alone which ye produce*
618 *But for the impertinent and ceaseless strife*
619 *Of proofs and reasons ye preclude in those*
620 *Who to your dull society are born* 640

[16^v]

30
V, 621 *And with that humble birth-right rest content*
622 *Would I had neer renounced it!"*
A slight flush
623 *Of moral anger previously had tinged*
624 *The Old Man's cheek but at this closing turn*
625 *Of self-reproach it passed away. Said he*
626 *"That which we feel we utter, as we think*
627 *So have we argued, reaping by our pains*
628 *No visible recompence. For our relief*
629 *You" (to the Pastor turning thus he spake)*
630 *"Have kindly interposed. May I entreat*
631 *Your further help. The mine of real life*
632 *Dig for us and present us in the shape*
633 *Of virgin ore that gold which we by pains*
634 *Fruitless as those of aeiry Alchemists*
635 *Seek from the torturing crucible. There lies*
636 *Around us a domain where you have long*
637 *Held spiritual sway have guided and consoled*
638 *And watched the outward course and inner heart*

605ff. Cf. MS. 69, stub 247^v, possibly stub 239.
607–620 Cf. MS. 74, 36^v–37^r, 39^v–40^r.

629ff. Cf. MS. 69, stub 238^r.

[17r]

31

V, 639 *Give us for our abstractions solid facts*
640 *For our disputes, plain pictures. Say what*
Man 660
641 *He is who cultivates yon hanging field*
642 *What qualities of mind she bears who comes*
643 *For morn and evening service with her pail*
644 *To that green pasture, place before our sight*
{*The*
645 {*Who family who dwell within yon house*
Fenc'd round with
646 ~~*Embowered in*~~ ^*glittering laurel or in that*
curling moke
{c
647 *Below from which the* {~~*peering*~~ ~~*shrubs*~~ *ascends*
648 *Or, rather as we stand on holy earth*
649 *And have the Dead around us take from*
them
650 *Your instances for they are both best known*
{ *Man*
651 *And by frail* {[?*Nature*] *most equitably judged*
652 *Epitomize the life, pronounce, you can,*
653 *Authentic epitaphs on some of these*
w}
654 *Who from their lol*}*ly mansions hither brought*
655 *Beneath this turf lie mouldering at our feet*
656 *So by your records may our doubts be solved*
n
o}
657 *And so, b*^*u*}*t searching higher we may learn*
658 *To prize the breath we share with human*
kind

[17v]

32 {*upon*
V, 659 *And look* {*look the dust of Man with awe"*
Yo} u
660 *The Priest replied. An office ye*} ^*impose* 680
661 *For which peculiar requisites are mine*
662 *Yet much I feel is wanting, else the task*
indeed
663 *Would be most grateful. True*^*it is,* ~~*most tru*~~[?*e*]
664 *That they whom Death has hidden from our*
sight
665 *Are worthiest of the minds regard*~~*s*~~ *with these*
666 *The future cannot contradict the past*

639ff. Cf. MS. 69, stubs 238v, 238r.
657 Rev forms "not."

659–676 Cf. MS. 69, stubs 238r, 237v, 236v, 236r.
660–663 Cf. MS. 74, 30v–31r.
663 Conjectured "e" in "true" is partly obscured by center fold.
665 Del by eras.

Mortalitys last exercise and proof
Is undergone the transit made that shews
The very soul revealed as it departs
Yet on your first suggestion will I give
Ere we descend into these silent Vaults
One Picture from the living. You behold
High on the breast of yon dark mountain dark
With stony barrenness, a shining speck
Bright as a sunbeam sleeping till a shower
Brush it away or cloud pass over it{.
And such it might be deemed—a sleeping sunbeam
But tis a ~~s~~pot of cultivated ground [l inserted above]
Cut off, an~~d~~ {i/Island in the barren waste,
And that attractive brightness is its own.
7/6 *oo*

[18r]

33
The lofty site by nature framed to tempt
Amid a wilderness of rocks and stones
The {*T*/*tiller's hand as Hermit might have chosen*
For opportunity presented thence
Far forth to send his wandering eye oer land
And ocean and look down upon the works
The habitations and the ways of men
Himself unseen. But no tradition tells
That hermit ever dipped his maple dish
In the sweet spring that lurks mid yon green fields
And no such visionary views belong
To those who occupy and till the ground
And on the bosom of the mountain dwell
A wedded pair in childless solitude
♓ House of stones collected on the spot
A ~~hut~~, of rough materials rudely built
~~Shielding by rock~~
By rude hands built with rocky knolls in front
And in a vegetable garb disguised *720*

---

676 Period added at end of line is in same ink as WW's copy, beginning at l. 677.

677–680 WW's brief copy may be a sign that he was still drafting these lines in another MS. or dissatisfied with the copy available. Possibly, MW allowed space for the later insertion of these lines. It is a further sign of WW's direct involvement, and perhaps dictation, in much of the copying. MW's line count includes these lines.

679 Del by eras.

---

695 The symbol may indicate indentation of the line as in *1814*, as well as the inclusion of the rev at page foot.

696 MW's line count appears to include the lines drafted at page foot, as well as the line below l. 696 ("And in a vegetable . . ."), and—perhaps by mistake—the line at 695/696 ("A hut, of rough . . .").

     O
[?A]}*f ferns self planted on the roof and walls*
                      an Abode
699 ℋ *In shape in size and colour ~~such a Hut~~*
[695] *A House, of stones collected on the spot,*
[696] *By rude hands built with rocky knolls in front*
697 *Backed also by a ledge of rock whose crest*
698 *Of birch trees waves above the chimney top*
[?and] in a &c

[18v]

34
Such as in unsafe time
V, 700 *~~As in the unsettled time~~ of Border War*
701 *Might have been wished for and contrived*
to illude
Plunderer
702 *The eye of roving ~~Traveller~~ for their need*
703 *~~Suffices and protects them from the assault~~*
unshaken bears
[703] *Suffices, and ~~unharmed withstands~~ the assault*
704 *Of their most dreaded foe, the strong south west,*
705 *In anger blowing from the distant sea.*
{~~House~~,
706 *Alone within her solitary* {*hut* Hut
707 *There, or within the compass of her fields,*
708 *At any moment may the Dame be found,*
709 *True as the Stockdove to her shallow nest*
710 *And to the grove that holds it. She beguiles*
711 *~~With~~ By intermingled work of house and field*
712 *The Summer's day and winter's, with success*
713 *Not equal, but sufficient to maintain,*
714 *Even at the worst, a smooth stream of Content,*
715 *Untill the expected hour at which her Mate*
716 *From the far distant Quarry's Vault returns;*
717 *And by his converse crowns a silent day*
740
718 *With evening chearfulness. In powers of mind*
719 *In scale of culture few among my Flock*

[19r]

35
V, 720 *Hold lower rank than this sequestered Pair*
721 *But humbleness of heart descends from heaven*
{ *on*
722 *And that best gift of heaven hath fallen* {*f[?r]* *them*

---

698 The partial line below, "[?and] in a &c" signals the resumption of the text at the line below l. 696.

---

701 Word "illude" is a copy or dictation error; *1814* reads "elude."
712 The "w" in "winter's" may have been intended as a cap.
719ff. Cf. MS. 69, stub 237r, for possible draft related to these lines.

720ff. Cf. MS. 69, stub 237r, for possible draft related to these lines.

723 *Abundant recompence for every want*
724 *Stoop from your height ye proud and copy these*
725 *Who in their noiseless dwelling-place can hear*
726 *The voice of wisdom whispering Scripture texts*
727 *For the mind's government or temper's peace*
728 *And recommending for their mutual need*
729 *Forgiveness patience hope and charity*
730 *Much was I pleased they grey-haired Wanderer said*
shining
731 *When to those ~~lonely~~ fields our notice first*
732 *You turned, and yet more pleased have from your*
{em *lips*
733 *Gathered this fair report of th{ose who dwell*
734 *In that retirement whither by such course*
735 *Of evil hap and good as oft awaits*
736 *A lone way-faring Man I once was brought* *760*
738 2 *While I was traversing yon mountain pass*
737 1 *Dark on my road the autumnal evening fell*
739 *And night succeeded with unusual gloom*
740 *So that my feet & hands at length became*
741 *Guides better than mine eyes untill a light*

[19ᵛ]

36
V, 742 *High in the gloom appeared too high methought*
743 *For human habitation but I longed*
744 *To reach it destitute of other hope*
745 *I looked with steadiness as Sailor's look*
746 *On the north star or watch-towers distant lamp*
747 *And saw the light now fixed & shifting now*
748 *Not like a dancing meteor but in line*
749 *Of never varying motion to & fro*
750 *It is no night-fire of the naked hills*
751 *Said I some friendly Covert must be near*
752 *With this persuasion thitherward*[?s] *my steps*
at last
reach the guiding light ~~at last~~
753 *I turned ~~& floundering over pathless wastes~~*
~~Attained the object of that toil at last,~~

---

730 Word "they" is an uncorrected copy error for "the."
732 The final "r" in "your" is over the fold at edge of page.
738/737 WW's marginal numbers signal transposition of these lines.

---

750 A mark after "hills" may be intended as a comma as in *1814*.

753–768 These lines undergo complex rev both here and on facing 20ʳ. It is, however, possible to conjecture the sequence of rev. MW's fair copy through l. 769a on 20ʳ was entered first, and WW then continued copy from l. 769b. MW's rev of l. 755, altering and transferring the line to precede l. 757, appears to be the next stage. WW then rev, probably in the order cited, ll. 753, 753/754, 758/759, 756, [756], 761 on 19ᵛ; l. 761–762 on 20ʳ; ll. 763, 762 on 19ᵛ; l. 765/766 on 20ʳ; ll. 759, 761, 765 on 19ᵛ; l. 766 on 20ʳ. At some point MW intervened and consolidated WW's rev with her copy at the bottom of 19ᵛ (ll. 762–[764]), marked by crosses at ll. 761 and 762, and possibly l. 767 on 20ʳ. WW's l. 765 appears to overwrite MW's l. 762 below on 19ᵛ. If so, MW's ll. 762–[764] at the bottom of the page preceded WW's ll. 761, 765. These rev were probably then followed by WW's remaining rev on 20ʳ, l. 765.

the
754 *Joy to myself but to ~~a female's~~ heart,* *of her*
{~~eight~~
[755] *Who there was standing on the open h{ill* hill
[756] The same kind Matron whom your tongue has praisd,
757 *Alarm and disappointment. The alarm* *780*
{*l* {*n'd*
758 *Ceased when she {Lear{[?nt] through what mishap I*
came
~~*And to the spot how guided words addressed*~~
gained
759 And by what help had ~~reached~~ those distant fields.
756 ~~*Even to the Matron whom your tongue has praised*~~
761 There with a lantern in her hand she stood
755 ~~*There was she standing on the open hill*~~ X
~~*in discharge*~~
lonely to perform
{*C*
760 *Drawn from her ~~neighbouring~~ {cottage* ^ ~~*by an act*~~
~~A careful~~ an anxious {*S*
764 ~~*Of anxious*~~ *duty which the lofty {site*
765 Far from all public road or beaten way
762 X *Or paced the ground to guide her H. home*
763 *By that unwear[?e]d signal kenned afar*
[764] *An anxious duty which the lofty site*

[20r]

37

V, 765 Far from — & —
~~*By nothing led to but a few faint paths*~~
766 And travers d only by a few faint paths
~~stood~~ &
767 ,} *whensoeer untoward chance*
767, 761 *Imposes.*} ~~*With a lantern in her hand*~~
~~That night~~ to guide
or ~~that night~~
761, 762 ~~*Alone she stood, and paced, as she is wont*~~
763 ~~*By this unwearied signal kenned af*~~*ar*
~~Her husband home home; [?as]; she is wont if chance~~
762 ~~*To guide her husband home if any chance*~~
Such
{Such
768 *({The chance is rare) detains him till the*
black *night*
769 *Falls dark upon the Hills.* But come, she said
770 Come let me lead you to our poor Abode.
771 Behind these rocks it stands as if it shunn'd
772 In churlishness the eye of all mankind
773 But the few guests who seek the door receive

---

757 MW's line count does not include l. [756]. Since the other rev constitutes the same number of lines as the original copy, it is not possible to determine whether that rev is included in the line count.

765–768 See note to 19v, ll. 753–768.
761, 762 Commas appear to be in darker ink and may have been added by WW in an early stage of rev.

Most
774 [?A] hearty welcome.—Entering I beheld
775 A blazing fire—upon the cleanly hearth
776 Sate down and to her office, with leave ask'd
777 The Dame return'd.—Before that glowing
800 Pile
B
778 Of mountain turf required the [?H]uilders hand
n
779 Its wasted spled dors to repair the Door
780 Opened and with she reenter'd with glad
looks
781 Her Helpmate following. Hospitable fare
782 Frank conversation made the evening's treat
783 Need a bewilder'd Traveller wish for more
Escaped from darkness & uncertain toil.

[20^v]

V, 784 *But more was given the eye the mind the heart*
785 *Found exercise in noting as we sate*
786 *By the bright fire the good Man's face, compo*
sed
an open brow
787 *Of features elegant ~~the countenance~~ mild*
788 Of undisturb'd humanity a cheek
~~*The expression slowly varying*~~
789 Suffused with something of a feminine hue
~~*A brow of undisturbed humanity*~~
790 Eyes beaming courtesy and mild regard
~~*And as the course of conversation changed*~~
791 But in the quicker turns of the discourse
that evinced
792 *Expression slowly varying. From a fount*
793 A tardy apprehension. From a fount
794 *Lost thought I in the obscurities of time*
may
795, 796 *But honoured once these features might descend*
797 *In such a Man so gently and subdued*
raceful in
798 *Withall so gentle [?] his gentleness*
799, 800 ~~*A race of noble Heroes may expire*~~
dis
799 A race [?gr]tinguished for heroic deeds,
800 Humbled but not degraded, may expire.
801, 802 This pleasing fancy streng th[?en]d by such fall
803 From high to low, ascent from low to high
801 This pleasing fancy whether vain or not

---

777 MW's line count includes the complete rev on 19^v and 20^r.

This leaf, canceled and left unpaginated, is recopied on 21^r–21^v.

799–[803] Rev on 21^r–21^v, through an intervening MS. no longer extant or through dictation.

802 By recollection strengthened of such fall
[803] From high to low, ascent from low to high

[21r]

36

V, 784 *But more was given the eye the mind the heart*
785 *Found exercise in noting as we sate*
786 *By the bright fire the good Man's face composed*
787 *Of features elegant an open brow*
788 *Of undisturbed humanity a cheek*
in
789 *Suffused with something of a femal}ine hue*
790 *Eyes beaming courtesy and mild regard*
791 *But in the quicker turns of the discourse*
792 *Expression slowly varying that evinced*
793 *A tardy apprehension. From a fount*
794 *Lost thought I in the obscurities of time*
and that mien
795 *But honoured once these features ~~may descend~~* *820*
796 May have descended though I see them here.
797 *In such a Man so gentle and subdued*
r
798 *Withal so ge}aceful in his gentleness*
799 *A race illustrious for heroic deeds*
e *aded*
800 *Humbld but not dis}gr}aced, may expire.*
~~*This*~~ ✕ ~~maintained its~~ hold
801 *This J} pleasing fancy ^ ~~that derived support~~*
By
802 ~~*From*~~ *sundry recollections of such fall*
✕cherished & upheld

[21v]

37
l
V, 803 *From high to low ascent from h}ow to high*
804 *As Books record, & even the careless mind*
805 *Cannot but notice among Men and things*
806 *Went with me to the place of my repose*
uz
807 *Ro[?ws]}ed by the crowing Cock at dawn*
risen *Of day*
808 *I yet had {h[?] too late to interchange*
809 *A morning salutation with my Host*
810 *Gone forth already to the far off seat*
811 *Of his day's work. Three dark mid-winter*
months

784–802 Rev of 20v; see note to 20v.
795 MW's line count continues from 20r but either includes the added l. 796 or miscounts by one.
799–802 See note to 20v, ll. 799–[803].
801 The X signals inclusion of rev at page foot.

803 Rev of 20v continued from 21r; see note to 20v.

812 *Pass, said the Matron and I never see*
{brings
813 *Save, when the Sabbath-{day its kind*
release
:} {H
814 *My Helpmates face by light of day;} {he*
quits
815 *His door in darkness, nor till dusk returns*
816 *And through Heaven's blessing thus we gain*
840 the bread
817 *For which we pray; and for the wants provide*
818 *Of sickness, accident, and helpless age.*
819 *Companions have I many, many Friends*
820 *Dependants Comforters—my wheel my Fire*

[22^r]

l} *38*
V, 821 *All day the House Ch}ock ticking in mine*
ear
822 *The cackling Hen the tender Chicken brood*
823 *And the wild Birds that gather round*
my porch
824 *This honest Sheep-dogs countenance I read*
nor seldom
825 *With him can talk ~~and often~~ waste a word*
826 *On Creatures less intelligent and shrewd*
827 *And if the blustering Wind that drives the*
Clouds
828 *Care not for me he lingers round my door*
829 *And makes me pastime when our tempers*
suit
830 *But above all my thoughts are my support*
832 *"Oh happy"! said I yielding to the Law*
833 *Of these privations richer in the main*
{ankless
834 *While th{ought[?ful] thousands are oppressed*
and cloyed
835 *By ease and leisure by the very wealth*
836 *And pride of opportunity made poor*
837 *While tens of thousands falter in their path*
838 *And sink, through utter want of cheering light* *860*
839 *For you the hours of labour do not flag*

[22^v]

39
V, 840 *For you each evening hath its shining star*
841 *And every Sabbath-day its golden Sun"*
842 *"Yes" said the Solitary—with a smile*
g}
843 *That seemed to break from an expandind} heart*

---

814 What appears to be a random mark following "Helpmates" may be intended as an apos.

844 The untutord Bird can found and so construct
~~*"The little Bird by happy instinct taught*~~
{And er}
845 {*Can with such soft materials line his} nest*
Fix'd
{~~Fixed~~
846 {*Built in the centre of a prickly brake*
847 *That the thorns wound her not they only guard.*
~~What in this instance of the little~~ Bird
X { ~~Up~~ { ~~doth~~
850, 851 *—W{[?hat] ~~on the Species Nature~~ {[?here] ~~confer~~[?s]*
~~*Is sometimes to the Individual given*~~
851 Upon the individual doth confer
852 *Among the higher Creatures born & trained*
853 *To use of reason. And I own that tired*
world
854 *Of the ostentatious ^ a swelling stage*
855 *With empty actions* & vain passions stuff'd
856 *And from the private struggles of mankind*
857 *Hoping for less then I could wish to hope 880*
858 *Far less than once I trusted and believed*
859 *I love to hear of those who not contending*
860 *Nor summoned not to contend for Virtues* ~~*880*~~
prize
848 X Powers not unjustly likened to these gifts
849 Of happy instinct which the woodland Bird
850 Shares with her species Nature's grace sometimes

[23r]

40
V, 861 *Miss not the humbler good at which they*
aim
862 *Blest with a kindly faculty to blunt*
863 *The edge of adverse circumstance and*
turn
864 *Into their contraries the petty plagues*
865 *And hinderances with which they stand*
beset
~~*Though this is rather Nature's praise than*~~
~~*theirs*~~
849 ~~*As the small Bird by happy instinct taught*~~
~~*Can with such soft materials line her nest*~~
866 *In early youth among my native hills*
867 *I knew a Scottish Peasant who possessed*
868 *A few small crofts of stone encumbered ground*
869 *Masses of every shape & size that lay*

---

847 The cross in the left margin below this line signals inclusion of rev at page foot.

858, 860 MW's first line count at l. 860 does not include rev at page foot; her second line count at l. 858 does include the rev, suggesting an intervention by WW during copying.

Rev at page foot alters ll. 865/849, 849, 849/866 on facing 23r; the cross signals its inclusion following l. 847 at midpage on 22v.

865/849, 849, 849/866 Canceled lines are rev on the bottom of 22v.

870 *Scattered about beneath the mouldering*
walls
rough
871 *Of a ~~huge~~ precipice and some apart*
872 *In quarters unobnoxious to such chance*
873 *As if the moon had showered them down in*
spite
{. {T {ere
874 *But he repined not{ {though the plough w{as*
scared
875 *By these obstructions, round the shady stones*
877 *Gather said he the dews: and feeding dews*

[23ᵛ]

41
V, 878 *And damps through all the droughty summers day* *900*
879 *From out their substance issuing maintain*
880 *Herbage that never fails no grass springs up*
{*so*
881 *So green, so fresh, and { plentiful as mine*
{T
882 *See in this well-conditioned Soul a {third*
883 *To match with your good Couple that put forth*
884 *Their homely graces on the Mountain side*
885 *But thinly sown these Natures—rare at least*
e}
886 *Thr}~~ough~~ mutual aptitude of seed & soil*
That yields
887 *Such kindly product. He whose Bed ~~perhaps~~*
Perhaps
888 ^*Yon loose sods cover the poor Pensioner*
889 *Brought yesterday from our sequestered*
dell
890 *Here to lie down in lasting quiet he*
891 *If living now, could otherwise report*
loneliness
{~~loneliness~~ {*grey haired*
892 *Of rustic {solitude that {[?aged] Orp*
Orphan
893 *So call him for humanity to him ~~no~~*
894 *No Parent was could feelingly have told*
{S
895 *In life in death what {solitude can breed*

[24ʳ]

42
V, 896 *Of selfishness & cruelty & vice*
897 *Or if it breeds not hath not power to cure*
898 *But your compliance Sir! with our request*

---

874 *1814* retains "was."

---

878 MW's line count appears to proceed from her first count ("880") at l. 860 and includes the canceled lines on 23ʳ.

886, 893 Del by eras.

My words too long have hindered" 920
Undeterred
Perhaps incited rather by these shocks
In no ungracious opposition given
To the confiding Spirit of his own
{F {*r*
Experienced {*faith the* [?*s*] {*everend Pastor said*
Looking around him "Where shall I begin
3 1 2
Who shall be first selected from my flock
Gathered together in their peaceful fold"
He paused and having lifted up his eyes
To the pure Heaven he cast them down again
{pake
Upon the Earth beneath his feet & s{*aid*
"To a mysteriously-consorted Pair
This Place is consecrate to Death & Life
And to the best affections that proceed
From their conjunction. Consecrate to Faith

[24v]

43
In Him who bled for Man upon the Cross
Hallowed to revelation & no less
To reason's mandates & the hopes divine
Of pure imagination above all
To Charity and Love that have provided
Within these precincts a capacious bed 940
And receptacle open to the good ~~*& e*~~
And evil to the just & ~~*to*~~ *the unjust*
In which they find an equal resting-place
Even as the multitude of kindred brooks
And streams whose murmur fills this
hollow Vale
{or
Whether their course be turbulent {*and smooth*
Their Waters clear or sullied all are lost
Within the bosom of yon chrystal lake
And end their journey in the same repose.
The holy Man continued, blest
X {,
And blest { ~~*are they who sleep & we that know*~~
Our bretheron are that sleep & we that know
While in a spot like this we breathe & walk

904–913 Cf. MS. 74, 30v–31r.
904 *1814* reorders the first three words as indicated by the numbers below the line: "Around him looking."

916–928 Cf. MS. 74, 31r–32r.
920 Del by eras.
928/929 The left-margin X probably signals insertion of rev as indicated by the added lines at ll. 928/929, 929/930, possibly continued on the recto of missing leaf 25 or on MS. 75, E1r–E2r. The rev, related to rev of MS. 75, E1r, is not adopted, and 26r begins its copy with l. 929.

[26^{r}]

V, 929 *And blest are they who sleep & we that know*
930 *While in a spot like this we breathe & walk*
931 *That all beneath us by the wings are covered*
932 *Of motherly humanity outspread*
933 *And gathering all within their tender shade*
934 *Though loth & slow to come. A battle field*
935 *In stillness left when slaughter is no more*
936 *With this compared is a strange spectacle*
937 *—A rueful sight the wild shore strewn*
with wrecks
938 *And trod by people in afflicted quest* 960
939 *Of friends & kindred whom the angry sea*
B
940 *Restores not to their prayer. This Contrast*
yet
A little longer may our thoughts pursue
—Mark him who shuts & opens his sad eyes
In some sepulchral dungeon's trickling vault
Buried where scarcely he can note or feel

[26^{v}]

The several qualities of night & day
V, 947 *To lull a Tyrant's fears or please his will*
And in the end & quietness of all
The bones remaining where the breath expired
Fr } om
[? *To*]} ^*this dire truth which polished realms afford*
Turn to the region of the East & see
Where sandy desarts to the walls extend
Of some proud City which the Turbaned chief
Rules with his scymetar—a fainting wretch
Yea more, a Company of either sex

Leaf 25 has been removed; the recto of the stub has no writing visible except two crosses probably meant to signify insertions. The contents of the missing leaf probably drew on rev of draft following l. 940 found in MS. 75, $E1^{r}$–$E2^{r}$ (or some rev of MS. 75, E, in a MS. no longer extant) and probably represented an intermediate state of the copy found on inserted leaves 26^{r}–27^{v}, before being removed, recopied, and rev again on 26^{r}–27^{v}. The verso of the stub contains terminal letters corresponding to lines one (possibly), five, 940, eight, 941, and 943 on 27^{v}: [?t] / - / - / - / - / bough / [?think] / - / [?d] / [?] / - / ose / - / - / - / ved / ed / - /- /[?d] / [?]. This work may represent rev of MS. 75, $E1^{r}$–$E2^{r}$, before being used on 27^{v} as part of an unpublished passage. In MS. 74, 32^{r}, line V, 928, leads into the Solitary's narrative of *TPL.*

Leaves 26–27 are inserted and replace leaf 25 ; they are unpaginated.

929–940ff. This passage is probably rev of copy once existing on stub 25. See the first note to 26^{r}, the notes to 27^{v}, and MS. 75, $E1^{r}$–$E2^{r}$. Ll. 929–930 are copied from lines on 24^{v}, omitting rev there.

938 MW's line count follows directly from 24^{v}, l. 919, suggesting that, as in other rev in this MS. for which there are no ancillary MSS., WW's supervision and intercession were direct and swift.

940 The "B" here and on 27^{v}, l. 940, marks the passage for use elsewhere, probably before the cancellation lines were entered.

This passage is probably rev of copy once existing on stub 25. Cf. MS. 75, $E1^{r}$–$E1^{v}$. See notes to 26^{r}, 27^{r}–27^{v}.

Crawled forth & thankfully set down to
take
The gaunt Hyena's leavings, they themselves
Destined perhaps ere morning light return
To be the wild beasts prey. Behold (and
This

[27r]

uproar
effect
This though ~~a sig~~ht of keener wretchedness
often
Perhaps our bodily eyes have [?*never*] *seen)*
While the heart knew not what they looked upon)
~~*One of the many who from splendid streets*~~
~~born to fate as hard~~
One out of many, who ~~through some gay street~~
~~Who through the [?hurry] of~~ some splendid street
~~*In our own Christian land by penury*~~ *driven*
One out of many in our Christian land
Who hop[?elss] of relief &
~~*Hopeless of all relief &*~~ *unrelieved,*
~~*Retire, like Birds to Holes & corners*~~
Is marching forward through the crowded street[?s]
chased
[?]
[?~~a~~]
~~*By pitiless Winter miserable M*~~[?*e*]~~*n*~~
In some unh[?ee]ded corner to lie down
[~~?~~] his
~~*Making*~~ *that place* ~~*their*~~ *home where* he
~~*they*~~ *can die!*
Track where you may the course of those who
bent
On strange adventures or desiring gain
Or urged by thirst of knowledge wander
on
Restless encountering with their own free
choice
All shapes of danger & unsolaced death
Before the mind once [?more]
Wherever foot can go. ~~*From these* [?*dispersed*~~]
Place if you can a City to the flames
And lonely to the field of battle turn
Once more, but ere the fight begin & see
Of war delivered & the [?]less [?sword]
Turn to
Or to a field of battle turn once more
But ere the Fight begin & there behold

"This" below the last line on 26v probably cues the first line on 27r.

Cf. MS. 75, E1v, E2r. See notes to 26r–26v, 27v.

The word "uproar" at the top of the page is probably related to the description of battle in rev at page foot.

At bottom of MS. 75, E2r, is rev related to last two lines here on 27r and first line on 27v.

[27v]

A mighty number taught by pride of heart
And martial dicipline to stand or move
Firm & compact as with one soul inspired
Till irresistibly the storm break in 100
And sever them, like green-leaves from
their boughs
V, 940 *By summer whirlwinds torn!—Ah who would*
B *think*
That they who issue the destroying word
And they who thus consent to be destroyed
What Man, or Angel looking from the height
Of tranquil pity, in his heart could deem
941 *That all the scattered subjects which compose*
Earths
942, 943 *~~This~~ melancholy vision wretched some*
943 *Some careless desperate these & these depraved*
947 *Tyrants &*
948 *And Slaves who will consent*
949 *Were of one species with the sheltered few*
950 *Who with a dutiful & tender hand*
951 *Did lodge in an appropriated spot*
952 *This file of Infants, some that never*
breathed

[28r]

46
V, 953 *The vital air & others who allowed*
954 *That privilege did yet expire too soon*
955 *Or with too brief a warning to admit*
956 *Administration of the holy rite*
957 *That lovingly consigns the Babe to the arms*
958 *Of Jesus & his everlasting care*
959 *These that in trembling hope are laid apart*
1020 unrequired
960 *And the besprinkled nursling ~~spared by~~*
~~1000~~ ~~death~~
961 *Till be begins to smile upon the breast*

See last note to 27r, above.

In the fourth line, MW's line count should read "1000"; it does not include rev on 27r.

940 The "B" here and on 26r (l. 940) probably marks the passage for use elsewhere and signals the continuation of l. 940b from l. 940a on 26r.

940/947 Cf. MS. 75, E2r. See notes to 26r, 27r.

947 Cf. 26v, l. 947.

Copy once continued here directly from removed leaf 25, before the insertion of leaves 26–27. The pagination in the MS. assumes the two pages of leaf 25 and does not assume the inserted four pages of leaves 26–27.

959 The corrected line count, following from the fourth line on 27v, does not include the rev on 27v.

960 The unrevised (and now del) line count follows from that on 24v, l. 918, and assumes the lines on the removed leaf 25; according to this line count, there were forty lines (probably including rev that raised the average of sixteen to seventeen base text lines per page in this MS) on the two pages of leaf 25.

[?]
962 *That feeds him & the tottering little one*
963 *Taken from air & sun-shine when the*
rose
964 *Of Infancy first blooms upon his cheek*
965 *The thinking thoughtless School Boy the*
bold Youth
966 Of soul impetuous and the basful Maid
~~*The bold Youth*~~ [?*ex*]
[966] ~~*Exulting & impetuous & the Maid*~~
967 *Smitten while all the promises of life*
ose of middle age
968 *Are opening round her th* [?*ese* ~~*of*~~] ~~*the mature*~~
ast in
969 *C ut down while confident* ~~*of*~~ *strength they*
stand
fixd more firmly as might seem
970 Like Pillars, ~~and~~ like Pillars do appear
970, 971 ~~More firmly fix'd~~ by very weight of all
971 And more secure

[28v]

V, [972] *46* That, for support, rests on them; the decayed
970, 971 ~~*As if more firmly fixed by very weight*~~
972 ~~*Of those that rest upon them*~~ *the decayed*
And bur
973 *And la thensome & lastly that poor few*
age
974 *Whose light of Reason is with life extinct*
975 ~~all, the~~ hopeful & the hopeless first, & last
The The
[?Those]
[?*Ye*] & the
976 [?*The*] *earliest summoned* ^ ~~*& the*~~ *longest spared*
977 *Are here deposited & with tribute paid*
each
978 *Various but unto* ~~*all*~~ *some tribute paid*
979 *As if amid these peaceful hills & groves*
980 *Society were touched with kind concern* *1040*
981 *And gentle Nature grieved that one should*
1 *die*
[?*8*] *020*
o
~~*when*~~ *if the change demanded no t*
[?~~*loved*~~]
982 *Or* ~~*if*~~ ^ ~~*un*~~ [?*touch*] ~~*with sorrowful*~~ *regret*

970, 971 Rev of 28v.

The page is apparently misnumbered, as 28r is "46"; the text follows directly from 28r to 28v.

970, 971 Rev on bottom of 28r.

980 The corrected line count follows from 28r, l. 959; see the note there.

981 The unrevised line count follows from 28r, l. 960; see the note there. MW here and in the next two line counts on 29r (l. 1004) and 29v (l. 1022) seems to have entered a mistaken 8,000 count for 1,000 before correcting all three.

e

983 *Observed the lib* }*rating stroke, & blest*

~~*And*~~ ~~*And wherefore these regards*~~

at

984 *And whence this*} *tribute wherefore these regards*

~~Oh think not said the philo[?pher]~~

985 *Not from the naked heart alone of Man*

986 *Though framed to high distinction upon earth*

987 *As the sole spring & fountain-head of tears*

988 *His own peculiar utterance for distress* ~~*or*~~

no *soul*

989, 992, 993 *Or gladness*—{[?*And*] *but from the* ~~*eye*~~ *sublime*

[29ʳ]

ministers 47

V, 993 *With her two* ~~*faculties*~~ *of eye & ear*

994 *The one by which a Creature whom his sins*

995 *Have rendered prone can upwards look to heaven*

996 *The other that empowers him to perceive*

997 *The voice of Deity on height & plain*

998 *Whispering those truths in stillness which*

{W

the {*word*

999 *To the four quarters of the winds proclaims*

1000 *Not without such assistance could the use*

1001 *Of these benign observances prevail*

Thus are they born [?thus forster &]

1002 *Proceeding thence thereby they are maintaind*

1003 *And by the care prospective of our wise*

10

F} *60*

1004 *Forefathers who to guard against the*

~~*1*~~ *shocks*

[?*8*]} ~~*040*~~

1005 *The fluctuation & decay of things*

1006 *Embodied & established these high truths*

983/984 The first "And" is del by eras.

984ff. Cf. MS. 74, 37ᵛ, 123ʳ; On 37ᵛ in MS. 74, a prose draft for an introduction to *Essay on Epitaphs* refers to l. 984. On 123ʳ there, WW attempts a rev of ll. 984ff. and drafts a line that seems to suggest a concluding response by the Wanderer that was never developed.

984/985 The line, in pencil, is also del in pencil.

988 Del by eras.

989, 992, 993 Draft in MS. 74, 123ʳ, conflates l. 984a with l. 989b (as found in *1814*): "And wherefor, said the philosophic Priest."

1002–1008 Cf. MS. 74, 108ʳ.

1002 Rev in pencil.

1003 MW's corrected line count, following from that of 28ᵛ, l. 980, overwrites the miscopied "F" of "Forefathers" in the next line and includes material from inserted leaves 26–27; that count does not include rev on 29ʳ. See notes to ll. 959 and 960 on 28ʳ.

1004 MW corrects her unrevised line count (this original count precedes the inserted leaves 26–27) as a result of a miscopy on 28ᵛ, l. 981 (see the note there),

1007 *In solemn Institutions. Men believing*
1008 *That life is Love & Immortality*

[29v]

48
V, 1009 *The Being one, & one the Element.*
1010 *There lies the channel & original bed*
1011 *From the beginning hollowed out & scooped*
1012 *For Man's affections else betrayed & lost*
1013 *And swallowed up mid Desarts infinite*
1014 *—This is the genuine course the aim & end*
1015 *Of prescient Reason all conclusions else*
b
1016 *Are a*[?*p*]*ject, vain, presumptious & perverse*
1018 *Life I repeat is energy of Love ~~div~~*
1019 *Divine or Human exercised in pain*
1020 *In strife & tribulation & ordained*
1021 *If so approved & sanctified to pass*
1022 *Through shades & silent rest to endless*
1078 *1* *Joy.*
[?*8*]*~~057~~*

1009–1022 Cf. MS. 74, 107v–108r.

1016/1018 MS. 74A follows MS. 74, which does not include l. 1017.

1022 MW corrects her unrevised line count, "1057," which preceded the inserted leaves 26–27, as a result of a miscopy on 28v, l. 981 (see the note there); this count follows from l. 1004 on 29r. Her corrected line count, "1078," does not include rev on 29r; this count follows from l. 1003 on 29r. See notes to ll. 1003 and 1004 on 29r.

Leaf 30 is blank.

DC MS. 80

DC MS. 80—in use at the eighth stage of *Excursion* composition to recopy a shortened version of what we have called *The Peasant's Life* after the passages had been excluded from Book V of *The Excursion*—is described in the Manuscript Census, p. xxvi, above. For a discussion of this manuscript and its role in the composition of *The Peasant's Life*, see pp. 468–476, above, and Appendix II (which also includes a reading text based on DC MS. 80), below.

Right-hand margin numbers in italic type refer to *The Peasant's Life*, using the same numbers we have assigned to the long version that was once part of *The Excursion* in DC MS. 74. Left-hand margin numbers, by fives, correspond to the line numbers of the reading text of *The Peasant's Life* presented in Appendix II, below.

The inside front cover and 1^r–2^r of DC MS. 80 contain drafting (further developed on the verso of the Morgan MS.) that may be related to *The Peasant's Life*, perhaps as an attempt at a concluding passage about the end of that life.

On pp. 1189–1198, below, we present photographs of all ten leaves of DC MS. 80 that are here transcribed. The image size of the photographs of DC MS. 80 is 98 percent of actual size.

[inside front cover]

Come to their hearts the fullness of content
And pious gratitude and sober joy
[?higher]
With every passing year come firmer
faith
And firmer faith nor shall life re
fuse

[?]
Come [?or the Poet else] might find
[?a theme]
With—
{theme might else be
Come or a {[? ? ?]} found
[?more rich]
With golden contemplation mid the
[?fanes]
That fancy paints in pagan Arcady
bliss
Come pious gratitude & sober joy
{year [?higher ?hope]
With every passing {[?] come firmer
{they
And firmer faith—{[?] cannot
chuse but
come
These ills averted nor shall Life withold
The most authentic she can give

[1r]

[?come]
Come joy come happiness ~~with~~ [?higher ?worth]
And firmer faith they cannot chuse but
come
These ills averted with assurance given
[?Strong] as the uncertainty of life allows
{partnership
Of {~~fellowship~~ in scarcely felt decay
but call it not decay
~~If truth reject not such~~ injurious name,
For seasonable ripeness — that requires
Not even the handling of the gentlest
breeze
To lay the fruit within the lap of earth
All hopes complete & not without the
joy

The passage drafted here continues on 1r–2r and is rev on the Morgan MS., verso; this material may be work toward a new conclusion for *TPL*. Cf. phrasing in *Tuft*, pp. 49–51, 52 (ll. 358–363; 429–438).

See note to inside front cover.

Of conscious Heaven all purposes fulfill'd
For which the blossom first adorned
the [?bound]
Come pious fervent [?saintly] gratitude
Forbearance meekness patience strength
in love
[?Justice] & soul sustaining charity
Come higher [?warmth/?worth] with every passing
year
And firmer faith

[1v]

This compass'd may a further wish obtain
cep
Amid an imper[?tib]tible decay
If uninjuriously that name attach
To seasonable ripeness that invites
d
Death's kin[?g]ly gather for a glorious
change
[?wish obtain]
This ~~granted~~ need the Poet for their
sakes
Or for his own, contemplating the [?~~close~~]
[?~~close~~]
a ~~theme~~ ~~a life~~ [?~~course~~]
lot
Tha The [?~~close~~]
[?~~That~~]
[?] ~~runs on~~
times
Throw back his wishes to fictitious [?]
[?]
Pregnant with interest more high & pure
Than [?] yet the [?fanes] of pagan Arcady
Could furnish pictures for the
faithful pair
Companionship in scarcely felt decay [?~~de~~]
[?Bounties] of delight
and should nature hold
Her rightful course for [?her] [?] to assure
Companionship in scarcely felt decay
If truth reject not such injurious name
For seasonable ripeness that requires
Not even the of the
~~No harsher~~ handling ~~than~~ the gentlest [? breeze]
To
[?] lay the fruit [?~~age~~] within the lap of earth
All hopes complete and not without the
joy

Queried "bound" in the line beginning "For which" is probably a miswriting of "bough."

See note to inside front cover.

Of conscious heavn all purposes fulfilled
For which the blossom first adornd the bough

[2^r]

[?companionship]
higher hope
Come ~~Come~~ Come joy come happiness
come constant hope
And
[?] constant faith they cannot chuse
but come
And constant faith [?] come constant hope

These ills averted and without a wish
Attends a natural [?course a course] [?]
spontaneously [?ornate]
Attends a a natural course
There comes a

and if nature [?hold]
higher worth
And [?purer] [? ?]

[32^v]

by his [?aereal]
[?note]
shy bird
Like the [?~~first~~] Black [? ?] *TPL, 378*
Loud
[?]
[?] whistled in ~~the ye~~ unfoliaged grove
Or lordly
Outw[?h]watches all the company of lights
[?shine in]
That continuously [?~~spangle~~] heavens blue Vault
happy Youth
Happiest of men
~~Outwatches every~~

For leaf 2^r, see note to inside front cover.

This leaf's main text (not here transcribed) is of WW's poem *Laodamia* (cf. *Poems, 1807–1820*, pp. 360–361); later drafting, possibly for *TPL*, was added at the top and interlineally.

TPL passage is entered below copy of WW's poem *Artegal and Elidure* (see *Poems, 1807–1820*, pp. 386–387). Rev of 33^r, 34^r. Cf. MS. 74, 95^v–97^r, 99^v, 100^v–101^r; Morgan MS., recto.

385, 390 These two lines are in pencil.

Like the first blackbird by his [378]
[?distant Mate]
Heard whistling in the yet unfoliaged grove

But if the less fortunate th enamoured Youth 384

[?whose] power

Fair fruit most precious to the Mothers heart 435
the
From the first hour—the father ~~in the [?s] a~~ pride 436
Of spirit [?jealous] to maintain unlowerd
The [?approach] carriage of the sterner sex
[?~~Towards] the helpless [?] stranger [?of~~]
[?]
in
Exhibits [?honor d] the ~~stranger~~ helpless his house
A dignified indifference scarcely felt

[33r]

To the Yoke he bends *TPL*, 375
Receives the chain from Natures conquering hand 376
t
Nor loth, nor sad; but inwardly rejoiced 377
E'en ~~proud~~ [?]
Like the Blackbird whistling in the grove 378
Or lordly Eagle in the rocky wild 379
By ~~march~~ of all commanding time subdued
force
~~Subdued. His day~~ shews little, by that light 380
The Striplings day
You cannot read him; into the hours of rest 381
[?wildly] s
His ~~Spirit and~~ course of action ^ overflow 382
G
No ghost familiar with the night like Him. 383
vowed
To this new service ~~bound~~ his fervent Zeal 384
blest if she
The liveliest star outwatches, ~~in mid hea~~ven 385
~~Fix d or slow-travelling on the horizons bound~~ 386
how blest if she abide
~~Happy if s~~he for whom he wakes ~~abide~~ 387
the val abide
Within the limits of his native Vale 388
The native vale of both, or common Home; 389
But if less fortunate the
~~And not less happy if need be~~, the Youth 390
moss [?moor]
Posts over ~~Hill~~ & dale & mountain top 391

436ff. Text continues at bottom of 33r.

Rev on 32v. Cf. MS. 74, 95v–97r, 98r; Morgan MS., recto.

Through wood, and brook across, by shortest
line 392
Hasting, and chiding oft the watry clouds 393
Which the sky breeds to blind his eager steps. 394
What sundry shapes of hazard, paths obscure 395
But how endeared the tender Babe 437
as soon
As creeping Age hath strengthen d him to 438
bear

[33v]

And length of indefatigable march TPL, 396
Ere at the door the soft low tap be ~~heard~~ givn 397
Or from beneath the cottage eves ascend 398
M
The stifled Cough—warning his chosen [?]}aid 399
That now when sleep has hushed the world
he comes 400
For a brief taste of stealthy intercourse. 401
~~Mute Rapture[?s noisless]~~ ~~exctas[?y] enjo[?y]~~
Ten thousand sparks do from this covert fire 402
[?that]
Spring up at each incitement of the breeze 403
~~Vivid though noiseless blessed hours if do~~ubt 404
[?nor conscious dread]
{~~n~~
Be ~~not~~ { ~~or jealousy but hours they [?be]~~ ~~are~~ 405
Of [?] [?dread]
~~And~~ Time has wings & Pleasure is Time's slave 406
He must depart—ere blush of mornings
light 407
With the far wandering Fox slink to his home 408
For short repose or haply to commence 409
{ new
A long days labour with the sun {[?] risen. 410
Each current stem[?m]d of adverse circumstance 411
The rock of absence either shunned or touch 412
o
Without a fatal shock the insidious sh^als 413
[?O] jealousy triumphantly escaped 414
And fancy's cross winds & her peevish squalls 415
glad
All stoutly weather'd the trim vessel holds 416
p
Her port in o[?]}en view.—It dawns the
day 417
~~Now dawns the day of lasting recompe~~ 418

437–438 Text continued from 32v, rev of 34r. Cf. MS. 74, 99v, 100v–101r.

Cf. MS. 74, 96v–97r, 98r–98v, 99v.
401/402 Rev del in pencil.
404/405 Queried rev is in pencil.
405/406 Rev is in pencil.

[34^r]

The important day of lasting recompense *TPL, 418*
un
Not pr proceeded by a throng of cares *419*
Of frugal preparations intermix d *420*
With inoffensive vanity & show. *421*
And see the orb that animates the earth *425*
And cheers the frame & fills the Spirit of man *426*
With genial thoughts upon that morning shine *427*
In splendour so that Hill & dale reflect *428*
The satisfaction of the festive troop *429*
As they advance or from the Church return *430*
Blithe company of Elders Maids & Youths *431*
And the blest pair for life's remaining *432*
course
Each gives to each indissolubly bound. *433*
~~This nature wedlock~~ [~~?fails not~~]
Fair fruit this natural wedlock doth *434*
produce
by
In season due, a ~~gift of pride & joy~~ *435*
To either parent
wedl
This natural [?wel] ock yiels in season due *[434]*
F [?more welcome] to natural [?~~love~~]
A air fruit ~~a gift by either Parent pri~~zed *[435]*
[~~?~~]
[?trusting]
F and [?Mind]
Sa rom the first hour—~~but~~ to the father's ~~heart~~ *[436]*
Doubly endeared soon as the tender Babe *437*
By creeping Time is strengthen d to endure *438*
y
Rough fondness and the gaiet [?l] of love *439*

[34^v]

In boisterous assault. Then ere he quits *TPL, 440*
His home, or as he enters from the fields *441*
Lightly the vigorous Peasant at *442*
arms length
Tosses his lusty Boy aloft in air *443*
And laughs to see the laughing Child *444*
at once
Pleased & half da[?n]ted by the dizzy hight *445*
instant in an instant
n
Gain d in a moment in a moment lost *446*

Rev on 32^v, 33^r. Cf. MS. 74, 98^v–99^v, 100^r–101^r; Morgan MS., recto.
[*435*]/[*436*] Queried "trusting" may be meant to follow "natural [?love]" above l. [*435*].

Cf. MS. 74, 99^v–101^v.

A seasonable gladness a relief 447
Occasional for six laborious days 448
Is here prepared and duly this resource 449
Sweeten the day of l[?ie]sure & repose 451
blameless [?shelter d] vale [?Remain]
With innocent pastime. ~~In a~~ sheltered 452
~~vale~~
o
Far from the gr[?]}ss contagion of the world 453
An decorated thus as spring with flowers
~~Thus are the earlier years of wedded~~ life 454
Adornd as spring with flowers, and to uphold 455
The Pair and favor them as they 456
proceed
~~advance~~
In later time along their humble path 457
Oh [?th Po~~ets] wish~~
~~And~~ could a wish of mine avail, This Pair
In later time along their humble path
Should [?prove] as blest as some [?whom] ~~Nature~~
[?~~favours~~]
[?of] [?]
he hath [?wished]

[35r]

should
The pitfalls of mistake they shall avoid *TPL*, 458
should
By prudence guarded whose sure shall 459
heal
The hurts of unavoidable mischance 460
{should
{[?]
Immoderate labour, shall not sap their 461
strength
Nor sickness overturn their plans, or thwart. 462
should
Discord shall find no place by their 463
fire side
ould
Nor shall the dread of Poverty oppress 464
Their waking thoughts nor guilt 465
disturb their dreams

---

457 Conjectured reading below the line ("Poets") perhaps suggests that, in this separate state of *TPL*, WW was considering replacing the Solitary as narrator with the Poet; that change may be related to WW's thinking of *TPL* as a piece to be published on its own.

Cf. MS. 74, 100r, 101r–101v, 100r.

459 WW failed to copy "hand" after "sure" (cf. MS. 74, 101v). Below *TPL* on 35r, WW copied the beginning of *Extract from the conclusion of a Poem, composed upon leaving School,* which was published in *PW*, 1815 (see *Poems, 1807–1820*, pp. 141–142; *Poems, 1785–1797*, p. 452n.).

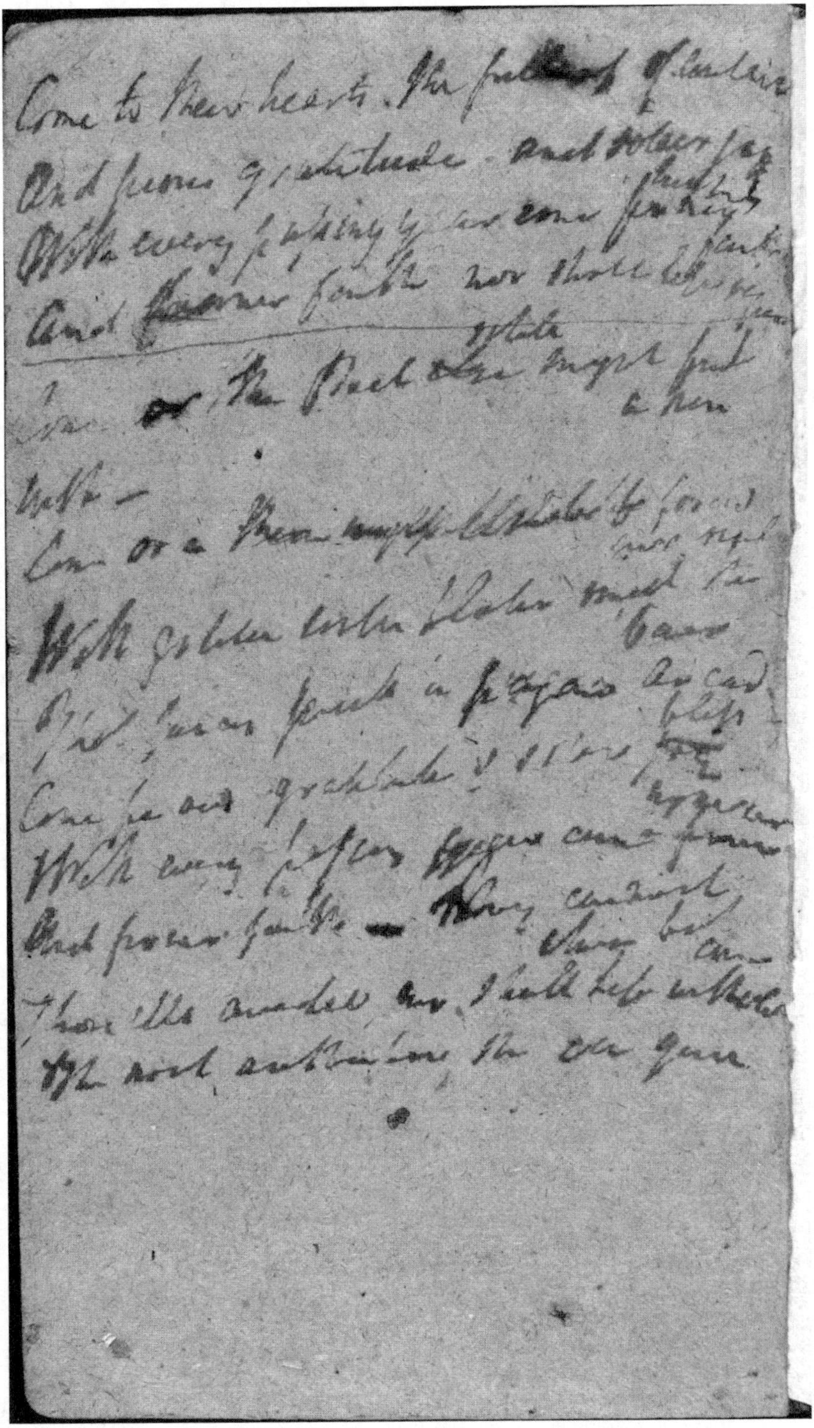

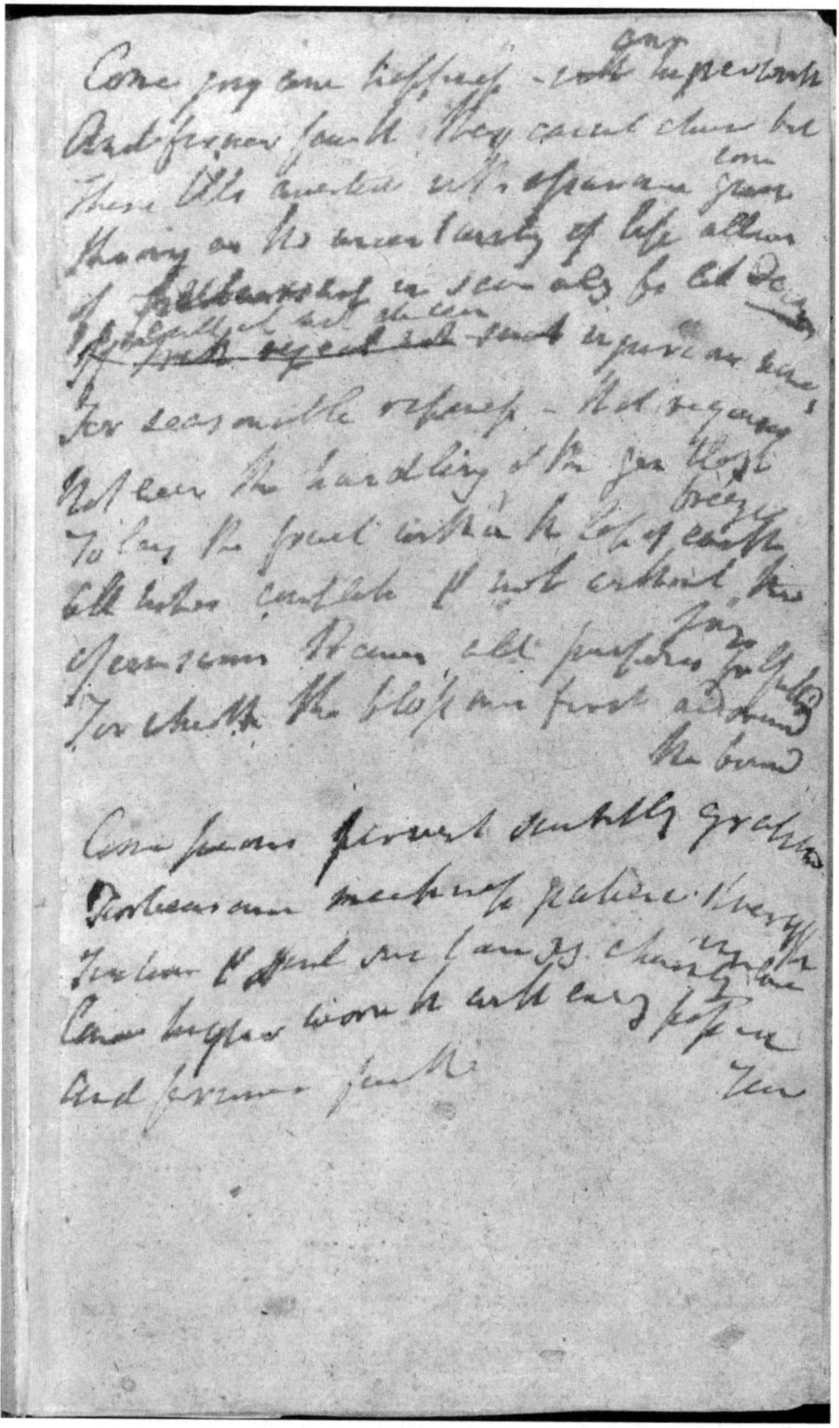

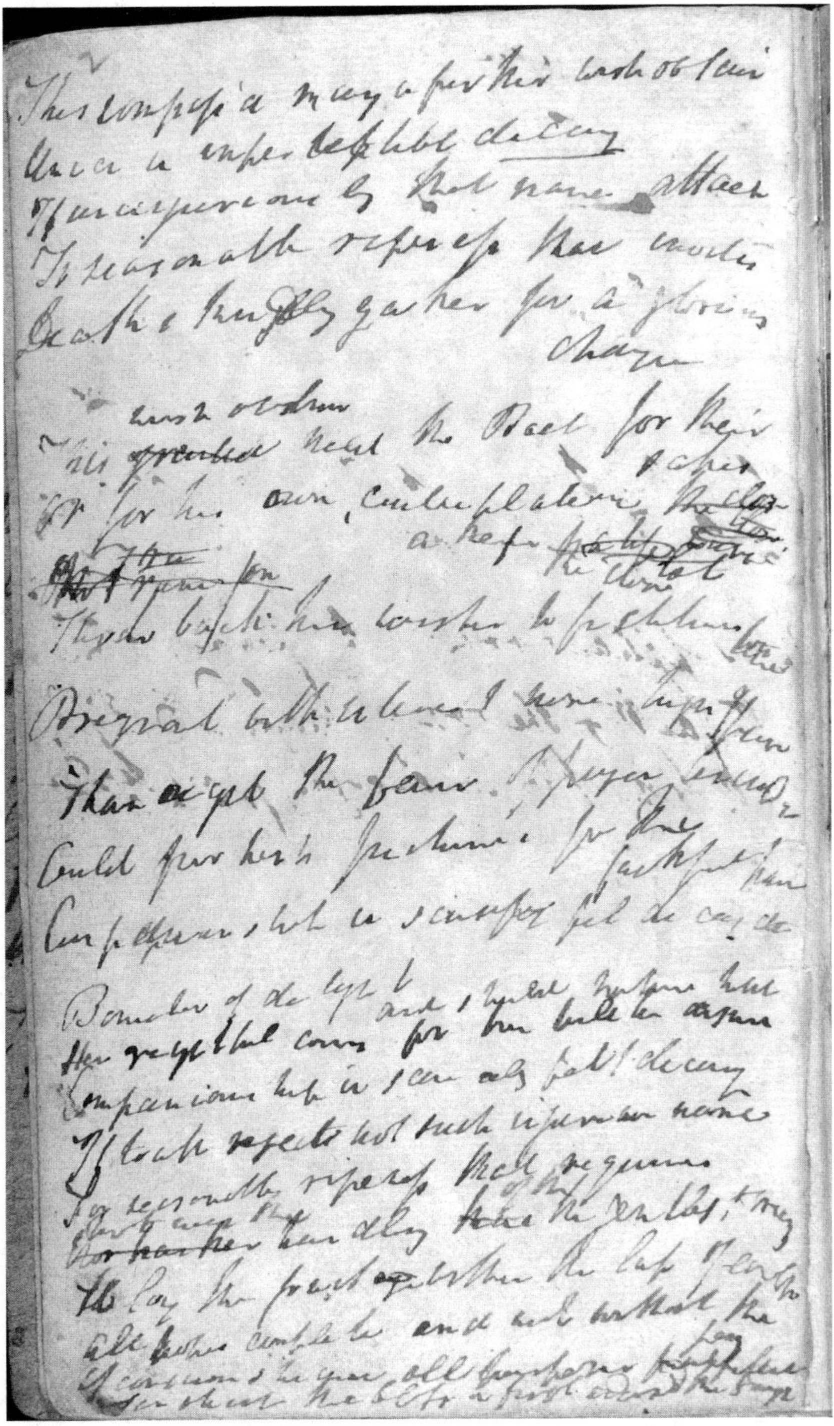

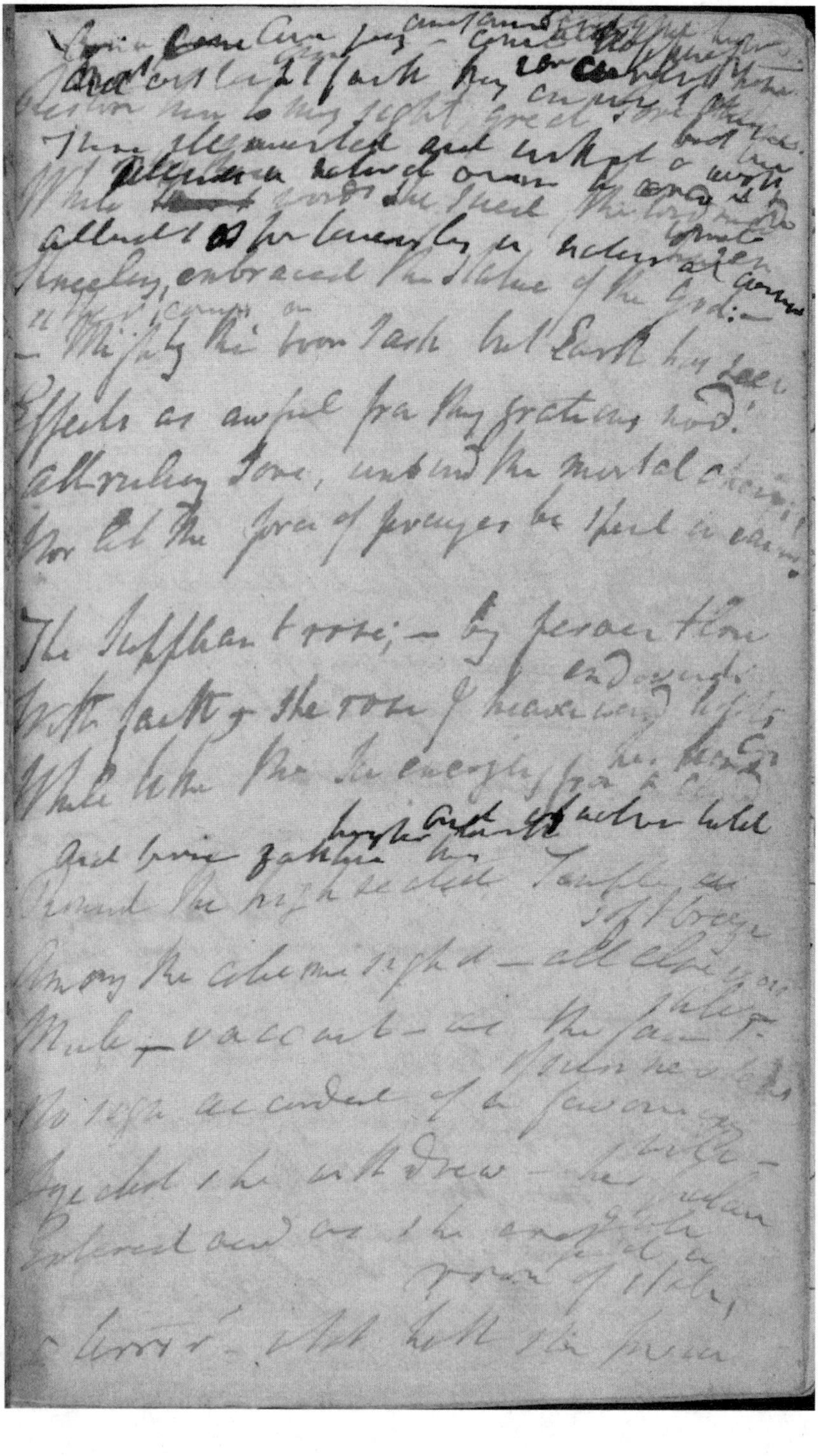

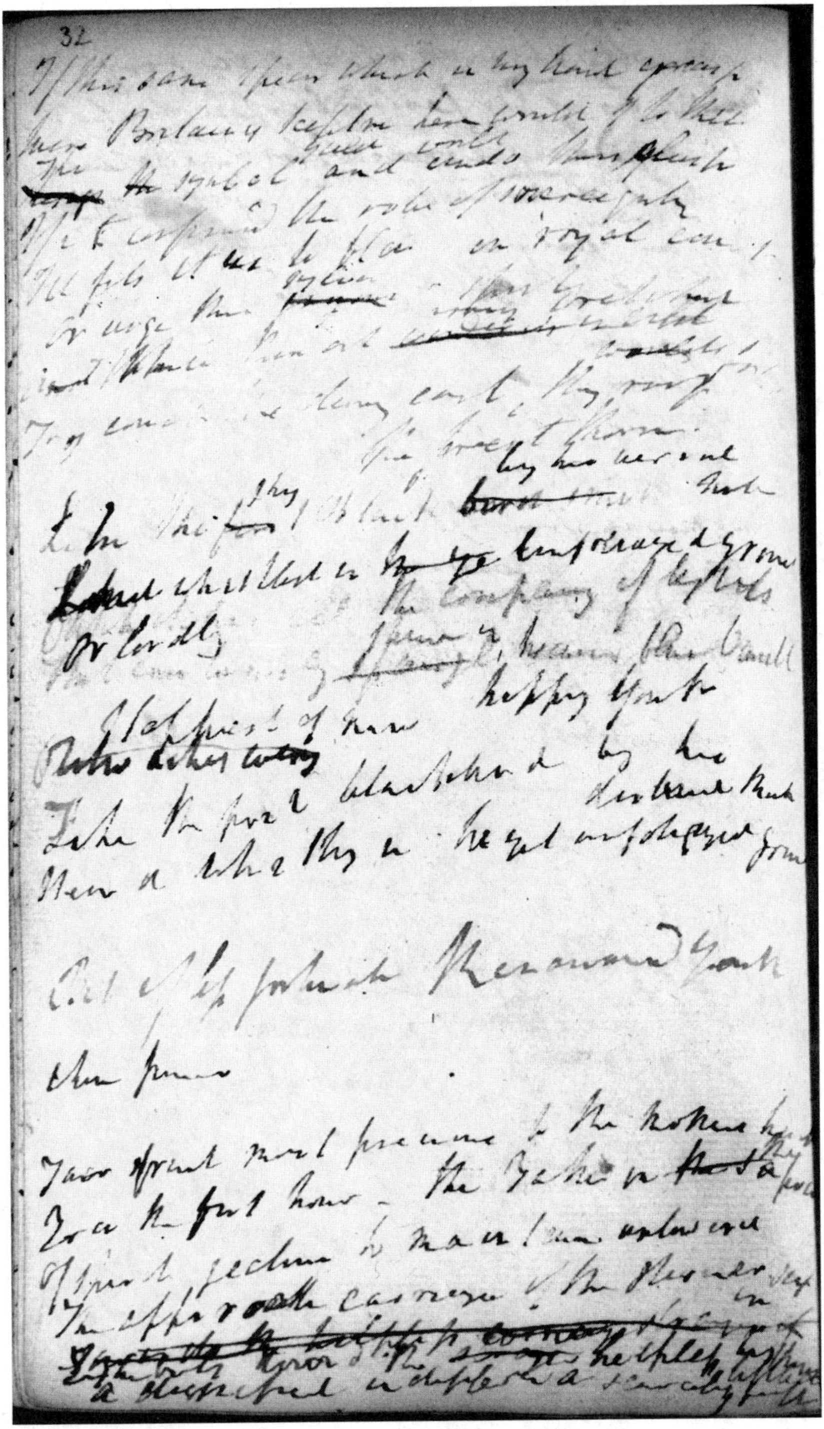

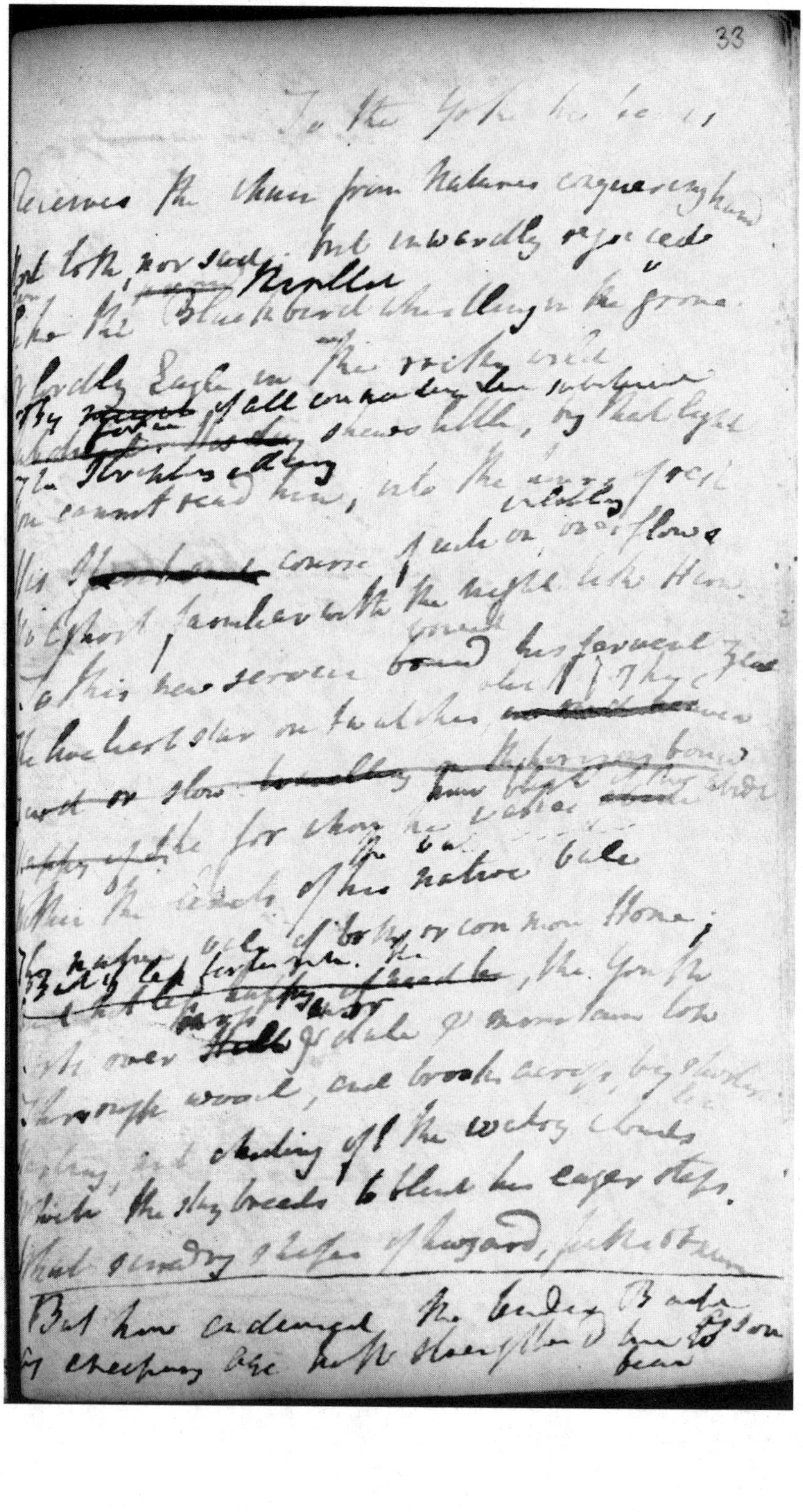

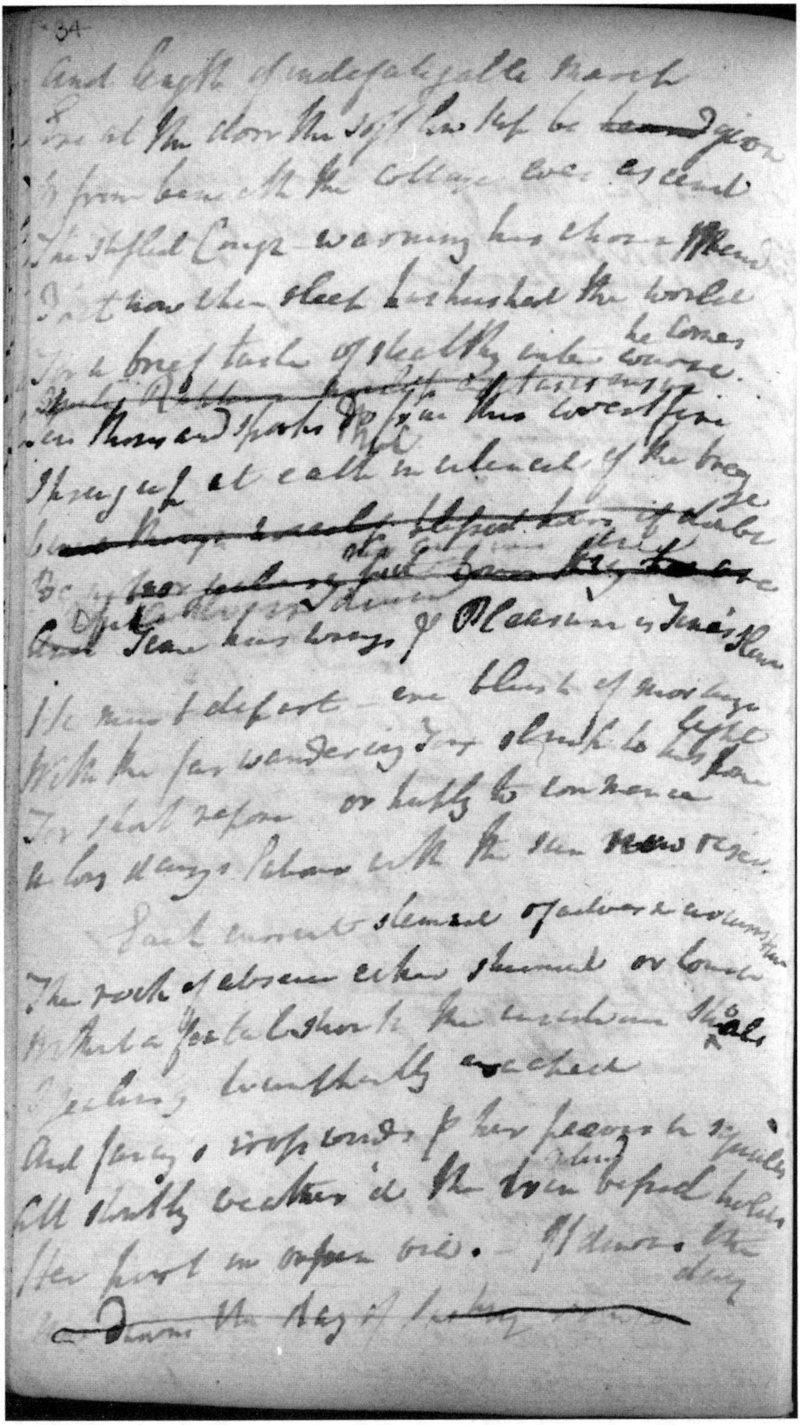

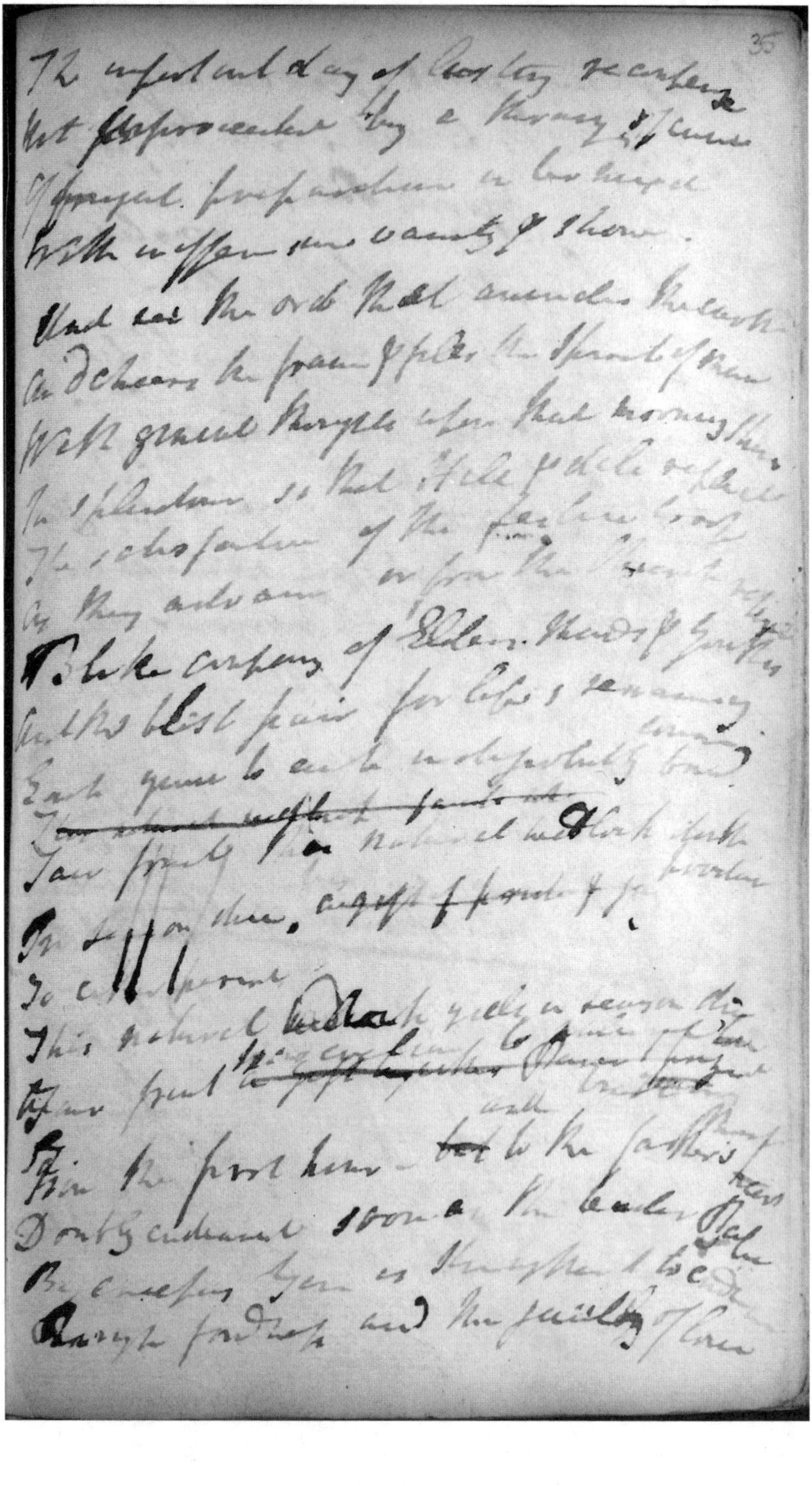

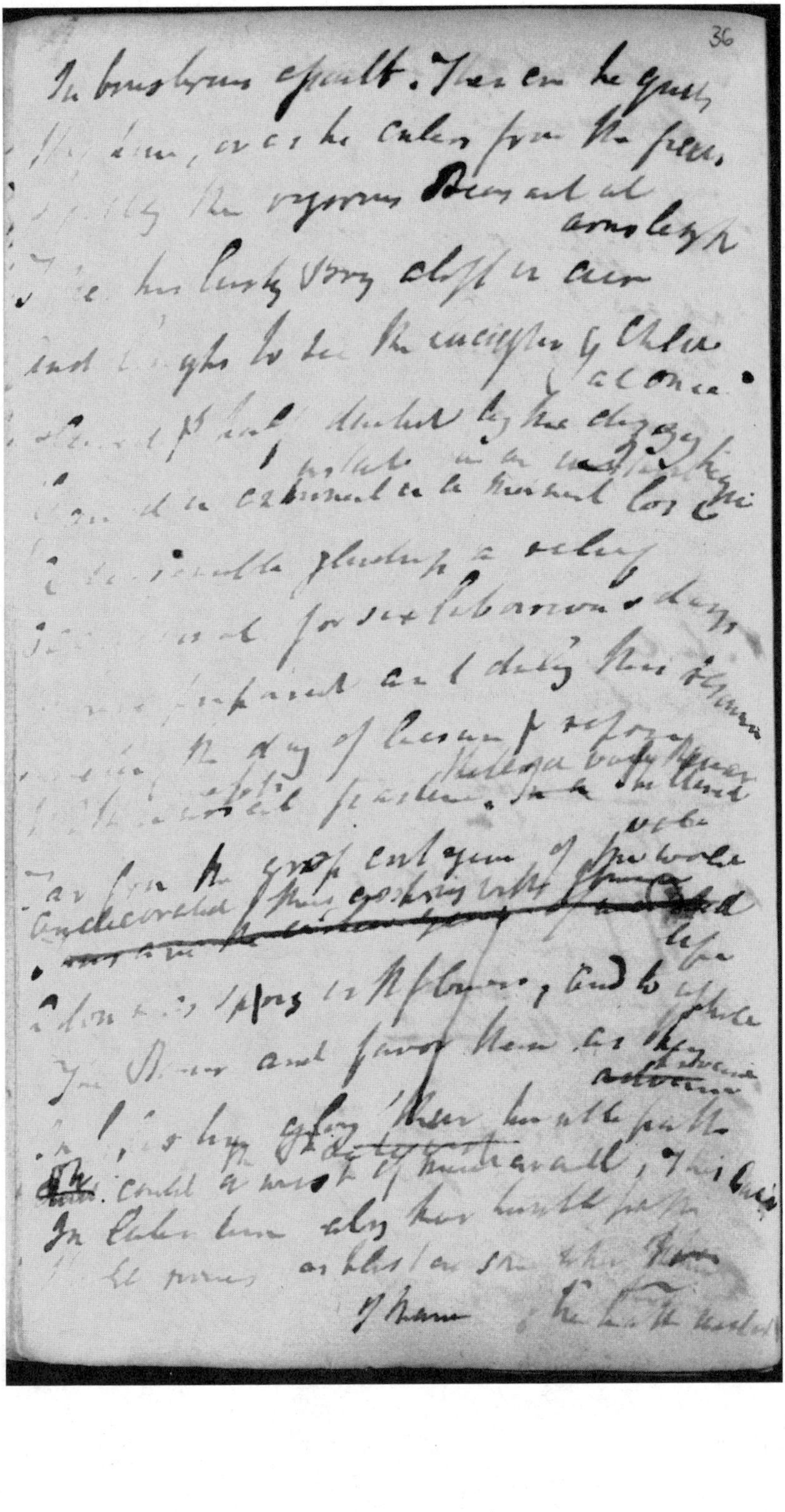

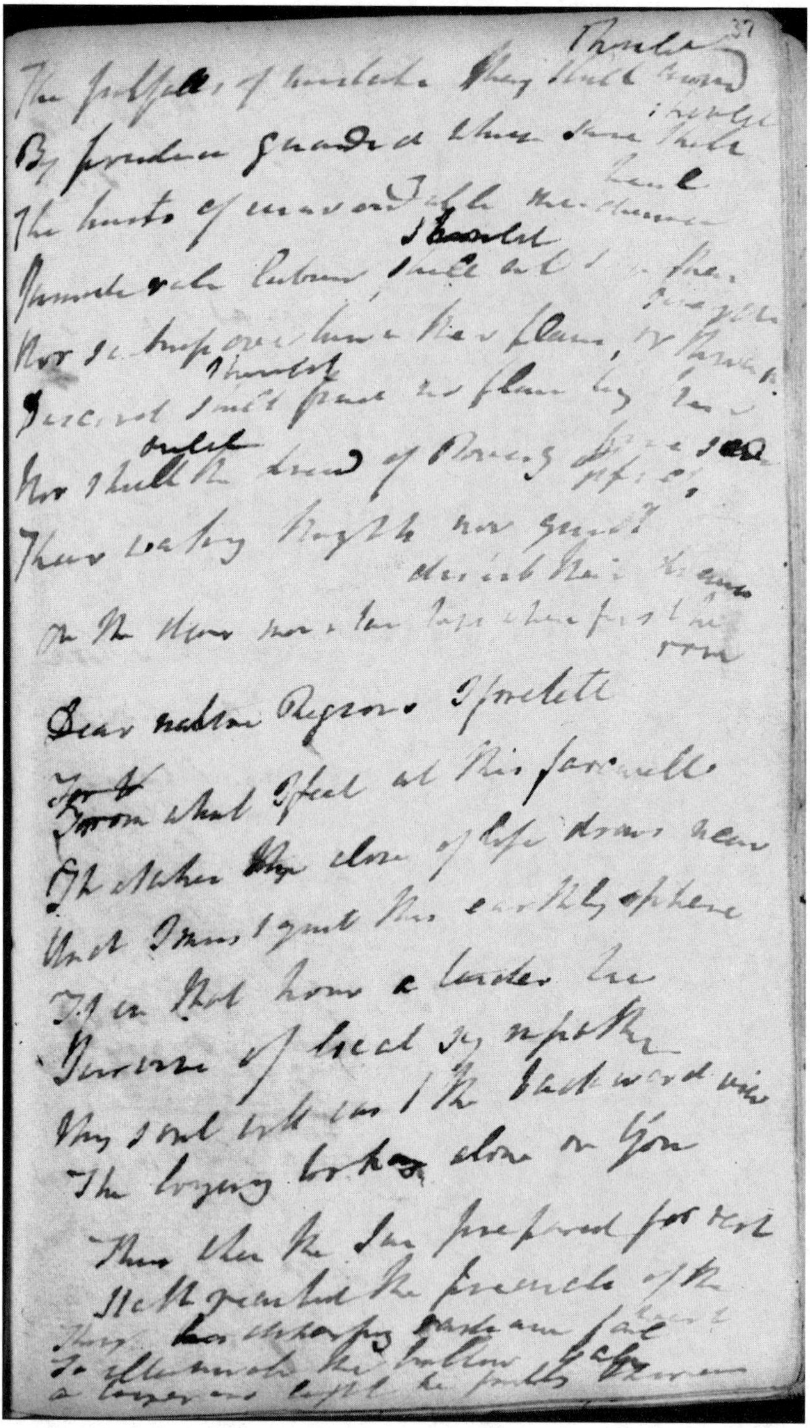

Morgan MS.

The Morgan MS.—its recto in use at the eighth stage of *Excursion* composition (or later) to revise passages of *The Peasant's Life* in DC MS. 80, 32^v–33^r, 34^r—is described in the Manuscript Census, p. xxvii, above. For a discussion of this manuscript and its role in the composition of *The Peasant's Life*, see pp. 469–471, 476, above, and Appendix II (which also includes a reading text based on DC MS. 80), below. Right-hand margin numbers in italic type refer to *The Peasant's Life*, using the same numbering sequence assigned to the long version that was once part of *The Excursion* in DC MS. 74 (that numbering is also employed as cross-references in the shorter text of *The Peasant's Life* in DC MS. 80).

The passage on the verso of the Morgan MS. is a further development of drafting on the inside front cover and on 1^r–2^r of DC MS. 80. This blank verse material about the end of life may be an attempt at a concluding passage for *The Peasant's Life* after its separation from *The Excursion.*

[recto]

Like the shy black bird whom his distant mate *TPL, 378*
Hears whistling in the yet unfoliaged grove
Or lordly eagle in the rocky wild

blest if she
For whom he wakes within the vale abide *387, 388*
The native Vale of both or common home. *389*
But, if less fortunate, the enamoured [?Youth] *390*
Fair fruit Most precious to the mother s heart *435*
From the first hour—he jealous to maintain *436*
Unlowerd the bearing of the sterner sex
Exhibits tow'rds the helpless [?child~~ren~~]
A dignified indifference [?scarcely felt]
tender Babe
But how endear'd the ~~helpless~~ as soon *437*
As creeping months have strengthened him to endure *438*

May [?move] together—not less perhaps
Nor favoured less than some whom I have known

[verso]

Come—or a theme might else be found more rich .
b }
In golden contemplations mid the [?]}owers
That fancy built in pagan Arcady
Come pious gratitude, of time and tide
Observant, and inviting unawares
To sober transport the instructed heart,

Come meek forbearance
~~Forbearance, meekness~~ absolute content
[?Justice] and soul-sustaining charity
W }
[?]}ith every passing year ~~come~~ come firmer faith
And higher worth—they cannot chuse but come
Those ills averted nor shall life refuse
The most authentic promise she can give
Of partnership in scarcely felt decay
call
But ~~name~~ it not decay, injurious name
For seasonable ripeness—that requires
Not even the handling of the gentlest breeze
To lodge the fruit within the lap of earth
All hopes complete & not without the joy
Of conscious heaven all purposes fulfilled
For which the blossom first adorned the bough.

Appendixes

Appendix I

Key to Manuscript Transcriptions

The Key to Manuscript Transcriptions makes it possible to locate all of this volume's transcriptions for a particular set of lines. Two listings are provided, one for *The Excursion* and one for *The Peasant's Life*. For *The Excursion*, the left-hand line numbers for each book in the following key refer to the reading text (1814) in this volume; for *The Peasant's Life*, those numbers refer to the italicized ones in the right-hand margins of the transcriptions of the Morgan MS. and DC MSS. 74 and 80. A separate listing is not provided for the line numbers assigned to the shorter reading text of *The Peasant's Life* as published in Appendix II because that text includes cross-references to the italicized numbers. The key includes both leaves and stubs, provided that the stubs have enough identifiable letters to suggest what passage was once entered there. For each manuscript, leaves and stubs are listed in the order in which they appear. In the case of DC MS. 69, however, entries run from both ends toward the middle of the notebook, thus producing a sequence of leaf and stub numbers that is in reverse numerical order when working forward from the back of the notebook.

I. *The Excursion*

BOOK I

1–99	MS. 69: 114^{v}, 120^{r}, stubs 115^{r} and 119^{v} (possibly)
	MS. 71: 2^{v}–6^{r}
100–199	MS. 69: 120^{r}, stubs 115^{r}–119^{v} (possibly)
	MS. 71: 6^{r}–8^{v}
200–299	MS. 71: 8^{v}–11^{v}
300–399	MS. 71: 11^{v}–14^{r}
400–499	MS. 71: 2^{r}, 14^{r}–16^{v}, 112^{v}–113^{r}
500–599	MS. 71: 16^{v}–19^{v}
600–699	MS. 71: 1^{r}, 19^{v}–22^{v}
700–799	MS. 71: 1^{r}, 22^{v}–25^{v}
800–899	MS. 71: 25^{v}–28^{v}
900–998	MS. 71: 28^{v}–31^{v}

BOOK II

1–99	MS. 47: 33^{r}–33^{v}
	MS. 71: 34^{r}–36^{v}, 64^{v}–65^{r}, 112^{v}–113^{r}
100–199	MS. 47: 38^{r}–38^{v}
	MS. 70: 58^{v}–60^{v}
	MS. 71: 35^{v}, 36^{v}–39^{v}
200–299	MS. 47: 38^{v}–39^{v}, 40^{v}
	MS. 70: 57^{v}, 59^{v}–62^{v}
	MS. 71: 39^{v}–44^{v}
300–399	MS. 47: 32^{v}, 34^{r}–35^{r}, 40^{r}
	MS. 70: 62^{v}, inside back cover
	MS. 71: 44^{v}–48^{r}
400–499	MS. 47: 32^{v}, 35^{r}–37^{v}
	MS. 71: 1^{r}, 48^{r}–51^{r}
500–599	MS. 47: 37^{v}–38^{r}, 41^{r}–42^{v}, 45^{r}–45^{v}
	MS. 71: 32^{r}, 33^{v}, 51^{r}–54^{r}, 113^{v}
600–699	MS. 47: 42^{v}, 44^{r}–46^{v}
	MS. 71: inside front cover, 33^{v}, 53^{v}–56^{v}, 61^{v}, 113^{v}
700–799	MS. 47: 12^{v}, 46^{v}–49^{v}
	MS. 71: 56^{v}–59^{v}
800–899	MS. 71: 59^{v}–63^{r}
900–938	MS. 47: stub 51^{v} (possibly; see note to transcription of 49^{v})
	MS. 71: 63^{r}–64^{r}

BOOK III

1–99	MS. 69: 72^{r}–72^{v}; stubs 71^{r}–71^{v}, 73^{r}, 74^{r}, 75^{r}, 76^{r}
	MS. 71: 64^{v}–68^{v}
100–199	MS. 69: 7^{r}–7^{v}; stubs 6^{r}, 76^{r}, 77^{r}, 78^{r}, 79^{r}
	MS. 71: 32^{v}–33^{r}, 68^{v}–71^{r}
200–299	MS. 69: 84^{r}; stubs 79^{r}, 80^{r}, 81^{r}, 82^{r}, 83^{r}
	MS. 71: 32^{v}–33^{r}, 68^{v}–69^{r}, 70^{v}–73^{v}
300–399	MS. 69: 84^{r}; stub 83^{r}
	MS. 70: 6^{r}–6^{v}
	MS. 71: 64^{v}, 73^{v}–77^{r}
400–499	MS. 71: 76^{r}–79^{v}
500–599	MS. 71: 79^{v}–86^{r}, 87^{r}
	WW to Lord Lonsdale
600–699	MS. 71: 86^{r}–91^{r}, 92^{r}, 96^{r}–98^{r}, 113^{v}
	WW to Lord Lonsdale
700–799	MS. 71: 98^{r}–101^{v}
800–899	MS. 71: 101^{v}–104^{v}, 106^{r}–107^{v} (stubs), 108^{r}
900–998	MS. 71: 104^{v}–105^{v}, 108^{v}–110^{r}
	MS. 73: 8^{r}–9^{r}

BOOK IV

1–99	MS. 69 (all stubs): 235^{v}, 235^{r}, 234^{v}, 69^{r}, 68^{v}, 68^{r}, 67^{v}

	MS. 73: 7^{r}–7^{v}
100–199	MS. 69 (all stubs): 234^{r}, 233^{v} and 233^{r} (possibly), 232^{v}, 232^{r}, 231^{v}, 231^{r}, 230^{v}, 230^{r}, 69^{v}, 67^{v}, 67^{r} (possibly), 66^{v}, 66^{r} (possibly)
200–299	MS. 69 (all stubs): 230^{r}, 229^{v}, 229^{r}, 228^{v}, 228^{r}, 227^{v}, 227^{r}, 226^{v}, 226^{r}, 226^{v}, 226^{r}, 225^{v}, 66^{r} (possibly), 67^{v}, 65^{r}, 64^{v}, 64^{r} (possibly)
	MS. 70: 45^{r}
300–399	MS. 69 (all stubs): 225^{r}, 224^{v}
	MS. 70: 16^{r}, 17^{r}–18^{r}, 19^{r}–20^{v}
400–499	MS. 70: 13^{r}–15^{v}, 18^{v}–19^{v}, 20^{v}–23^{r}
500–599	MS. 70: 13^{v}–14^{r}, 22^{r}, 23^{r}–26^{r}, 27^{v}–28^{r}, 55^{r}
600–699	MS. 69 (all stubs): 224^{v}, 224^{r}, 223^{v}, 223^{r}
	MS. 70: 1^{v}, 12^{v}–13^{r}, 26^{v}–27^{v}, 28^{v}–33^{r}, 34^{v}–35^{r}
700–799	MS. 69: 220^{v}; stubs 223^{r}, 222^{v}, 222^{r}, 221^{v}, 221^{r}
	MS. 70: 1^{v}–4^{r}, 31^{v}–32^{r}, 33^{r}–38^{v}
800–899	MS. 70: 2^{v}–4^{v}, 49^{v}–51^{r}, 52^{v}–54^{r}
900–999	MS. 70: 39^{v}–40^{v}, 51^{r}–52^{r}
1000–1099	MS. 70: inside front cover, 40^{v}–43^{v}, 44^{v}–45^{r}, 55^{v}–57^{r}, 58^{r}
1100–1199	MS. 70: 16^{v}, 21^{r}–22^{v}, 44^{r}
	MS. 73: 3^{r}–3^{v}, 5^{r}–6^{r}
1200–1299	MS. 73: 5^{v}, 6^{v}–7^{v}
1300–1319	MS. 70: 6^{v}–7^{r}

BOOK V

1–99	MS. 70: 4^{v}, 6^{r}, 7^{r}–7^{v}
	MS. 74A: 1^{r}–2^{v}
	MS. 74A, loose bifolium: 1^{r}, 2^{r}–2^{v}
100–199	MS. 70: 7^{r}–9^{r}
	MS. 74A: 2^{v}–5^{v}
200–299	MS. 70: 9^{r}–10^{r}
	MS. 74: inside front cover, 12^{r}, 13^{r}, 33^{v}–36^{r}
	MS. 74A: 5^{v}–8^{r}
300–399	MS. 69 (all stubs): 248^{v}, 248^{r}, 247^{r} (possibly), 246^{v}, 246^{r}, 245^{v}, 245^{r}
	MS. 74: 27^{r}, 35^{v}–37^{r}, 38^{r}, 39^{r}, 102^{r}–103^{r}
	MS. 74A: 8^{r}–10^{v}
400–499	MS. 69 (all stubs): 245^{r}, 244^{v}, 244^{r}, 243^{v}, 243^{r}, 242^{v}
	MS. 74: 1^{r}, 10^{r}, 27^{v}–28^{v}, 102^{r}, 103^{v}–104^{r}, 105^{r}
	MS. 74A: 10^{v}–13^{v}
500–599	MS. 69 (all stubs): 242^{r}, 241^{v}, 241^{r}, 240^{v}, 240^{r}
	MS. 74: 29^{r}–30^{r},
	MS. 74A: 13^{v}–15^{v}
600–699	MS. 69 (all stubs): 247^{v} (possibly), 240^{r}, 239^{v} and 239^{r} (possibly), 238^{v}, 238^{r}, 237^{v}, 236^{v} (possibly), 236^{r}
	MS. 74: 30^{v}–31^{r}, 36^{v}–37^{r}, 39^{r}–40^{r}
	MS. 74A: 15^{v}–18^{r}

700–799	MS. 69: stub 237^{r} (possibly)
	MS. 74A: 18^{v}–21^{r}
800–899	MS. 74: 33^{r}
	MS. 74A: 20^{v}–24^{r}
900–999	MS. 69: stub 237^{r} (possibly)
	MS. 74: 30^{v}–32^{r}, 37^{v}, 123^{r}
	MS. 74A: 24^{r}–29^{r}
	MS. 75: $E1^{r}$–$E2^{r}$
1000–1022	MS. 74: 107^{v}, 108^{r}
	MS. 74A: 29^{r}–29^{v}

BOOK VI

1–99	MS. 73: 46^{v}–49^{v}
100–199	MS. 73: 50^{r}–53^{v}
200–299	MS. 73: 52^{v}–56^{r}
300–399	MS. 73: 56^{r}–59^{r}
400–499	MS. 73: 59^{r}–64^{r}, 65^{v}
500–599	MS. 73: 64^{r}–65^{r}
	MS. 74: 89^{r}
600–699	MS. 74: 32^{r}, 88^{v}–92^{v}
700–799	MS. 74: 92^{v}–93^{r}, 94^{v}, 97^{v}, 104^{v}, 105^{v}
800–899	MS. 74: 57^{v}–61^{r}, 105^{v}
	MS. 75: $B1^{r}$–$B1^{v}$
900–999	MS. 74: 60^{v}–66^{r}
1000–1099	MS. 74: 66^{r}–70^{r}
1100–1199	MS. 74: 70^{r}–72^{r}, 85^{v}–86^{v}
1200–1299	MS. 74: 72^{r}–74^{v}, 87^{r}–88^{v}
1300–1308	MS. 74: 74^{v}–75^{r}

BOOK VII

1–99	MS. 74: 75^{r}–77^{v}, 82^{v}–85^{r}
	MS. 75: $F1^{r}$–$F1^{v}$
100–199	MS. 74: 77^{r}–80^{r}, 85^{r}
200–299	MS. 74: 80^{r}–82^{r}
	MS. 75: $F2^{r}$–$F2^{v}$, $G1^{r}$–$G1^{v}$
300–399	MS. 74: 108^{v}–110^{v}
	MS. 75: $G1^{v}$
400–499	MS. 67: 6^{r}–6^{v}
	MS. 74: 110^{v}–111^{r}
500–599	MS. 74: 111^{r}–115^{r}
	Houghton MS.: recto, verso
	MS. 75: $E2^{v}$
600–699	MS. 74: 115^{r}–118^{v}
	MS. 75: $B2^{r}$–$B2^{v}$
	Houghton MS.: recto
700–799	MS. 74: 118^{v}–119^{r}

800–899	MS. 75: A1^{r}–A2^{v}
900–999	MS. 74: 1^{r}–4^{v}
1000–1079	MS. 74: 4^{v}–7^{r}

BOOK VIII

1–99	MS. 74: 7^{r}–9^{v}, 10^{v}, 11^{v}, 12^{v}, 13^{v}
100–199	MS. 74: inside front cover, 12^{v}–16^{r}, 11^{v}
200–299	MS. 74: 16^{r}–19^{v}
300–399	MS. 74: 19^{v}–23^{r}
400–499	Berg MS.: recto, verso
	MS. 74: 23^{r}–25^{v}
500–599	MS. 75: C1^{r}–C1^{v}, C2^{v}
	Berg MS.: verso
600–611	MS. 74: 26^{r}

BOOK IX

1–99	MS. 74: 26^{r}–27^{r}, 47^{r}–48^{r}, 49^{r}
	MS. 75: C2^{r}
100–199	MS. 74: 48^{r}–52^{v}
	MS. 75: D1^{r}–D2^{v}
200–299	MS. 73: 18^{v}–19^{r}
	MS. 74: 51^{v}–52^{r}, 53^{r}–57^{r}, 119^{v}–120^{r}
300–399	MS. 73: 19^{r}–22^{r}, 23^{r}–23^{v}
	MS. 74: 55^{v}–56^{v}, 120^{r}–122^{v}, 124^{v}
400–499	MS. 73: 9^{r}–9^{v}, 18^{v}, 22^{v}, 23^{v}–28^{r}, 30^{v}, 95^{v}
500–599	MS. 73: 28^{r}–34^{r}, 35^{v}–36^{v}
600–699	MS. 73: 14^{v}–15^{r}, 33^{v}–42^{v}
700–795	MS. 73: 15^{r}–18^{r}, 42^{v}–46^{r}

II. *The Peasant's Life*

1–99	MS. 74: inside front cover, 10^{r}–12^{r}, 13^{r}, 27^{r}–27^{v}, 28^{v}, 29^{v}, 30^{v}, 31^{v}–34^{v}
100–199	MS. 74: 13^{v}, 33^{v}–37^{r}, 38^{r}
200–299	MS. 74: 38^{r}–43^{r}, 125^{v}
300–399	MS. 74: 43^{r}, 93^{v}–94^{r}, 95^{r}–97^{r}, 98^{r}
	MS. 80: 32^{v}–33^{v}
	Morgan MS.: recto
400–499	MS. 74: 96^{v}–97^{r}, 98^{r}–103^{r}, 104^{r}, 125^{v}, inside back cover
	MS. 80: 32^{v}–35^{r}
	Morgan MS.: recto
500–551	MS 74: 103^{v}, 104^{r}–105^{r}, 106^{r}

Appendix II

Fragments Related to *The Excursion*

I. "As when, upon the smooth pacific deep"

Wordsworth wrote the ten-line extended simile of "As when, upon the smooth pacific deep" on DC MS. 69, 198r, which is preceded by 156 blank sides and followed by 31 more; the notebook contains work toward Books I, III, IV, and V of *The Excursion* (see the Manuscript Census, above). The Solitary's voyage to America, as recounted in Book III, might be one occasion for using such maritime imagery. Since, however, this blank verse fragment stands by itself in the notebook and independent of any obvious *Excursion* context, it seems impossible to say how—or if—the lines might have fit into the poem.

The reading text presents the revised version of the text on DC MS. 69, 198r. The punctuation in the reading text is Wordsworth's (with the exception of the editorial comma in l. 5); the capitalization and spelling are also the poet's. Line numbers are editorial. The *Oxford English Dictionary* defines "Emprize" (see l. 3; also spelled "Emprise") as "An undertaking, enterprise; *esp.* one of an adventurous or chivalrous nature."

["As when, upon the smooth pacific deep"]

As when, upon the smooth pacific deep,
Dense fogs, to sight impervious, have withheld
A gallant vessel from some bold Emprize
Day after day deferred, till anxious hope
Yields to despair, if chance a sudden breeze
Spring up and dissipate the Veil all hearts
Throb at the change, and every sail is spread
To speed her course along the dazzling waves
For recompense of glorious conquest soon
To be atchieved upon the astonish'd foe.

II. *The Peasant's Life*

Wordsworth's account of the life of the typical peasant, part of *The Excursion* in DC MS. 74 but for the most part excluded from the published poem, is given in two texts within this edition.

Drafting for this passage when it was part of *The Excursion*, and when its 551 lines included work subsequently used in Books V and VI, is designated *TPL* and numbered in italics in the right-hand margins of the transcriptions of DC MS. 74. Thus, the italic numbers and the transcription notes enable the reader to follow the text from *TPL, 1,* on 32^{r}, to *TPL, 551,* on 106^{r} (additional drafting toward the conclusion of the text may be on the verso of the Morgan MS.). Numbers in roman type in the left-hand margins of the transcriptions of DC MS. 74 identify the lines of the peasant's story that ultimately were used in Books V and VI. While uncertainties remain about whether various revisions to the account of the peasant in DC MS. 74 precede or follow the decision to omit most of it from *The Excursion,* the italic and roman line numbers do facilitate study of Wordsworth's many attempts to develop this material.

The editorial title *The Peasant's Life* is more appropriately used after Wordsworth separated most of the narrative material about the peasant from *The Excursion.* (For discussion of *The Peasant's Life* and for the possible reasons for excluding most of it from *The Excursion,* see pp. 470–473, above.) After excluding the material, Wordsworth copied eighty-six of his discarded lines about the peasant into DC MS. 80, a notebook in which he was collecting work for possible publication in *Poems,* 1815. The poet, however, never did publish these lines about the peasant's "stealthy" lovemaking and early married life.

The reading text of *The Peasant's Life,* below, is the base text on DC MS. 80, 33^{r}–35^{r}. It is impossible to date the stage or stages when Wordsworth returned to revise *The Peasant's Life* in DC MS. 80 on 33^{r}–35^{r} (and on 32^{v}) and in the Morgan MS. Some of this revision is incompletely carried out, and—in any case—the base text of DC MS. 80 provides a version closer to *The Excursion* itself and thus to the origins of *The Peasant's Life.* Similarly, it is not possible to know for sure how—or, indeed, whether—drafting in DC MS. 80 (on the inside front cover and on 1^{r}–2^{r}) and in the Morgan MS. (verso) was intended as part of *The Peasant's Life.*

Our reading text preserves Wordsworth's spelling and capitalization (with the exception of our expansion of ampersands, and of our changes from "eves" to "eaves" in l. 24 and from "hight" to "height" in l. 68); punctuation in the manuscript has been preserved (except for Wordsworth's comma after "labour" in l. 83) but supplemented. At ll. 44 and 57–58, Wordsworth wrote incomplete base text lines and seems to have revised them immediately; these revisions have been included in the reading text. In l. 81, the omitted word ("hand") has been supplied from text on DC MS. 74, 101^{v}; lines on leaves 96^{r} and 97^{r} in the same manuscript provide evidence for treating changes to the base text in ll. 3, 4, 23, and 31 as corrections of miswritings. Line numbers are editorial, and the bracketed left-hand margin numbers provide cross-references to the transcription line numbers in DC MSS. 74 and 80, and in the Morgan MS.

[*The Peasant's Life*]

To the Yoke he bends,
Receives the chain from Nature's conquering hand,
Not loth, nor sad; but inwardly rejoiced
E'en like the Blackbird whistling in the grove
Or lordly Eagle in the rocky wild
Subdued. His day shews little, by that light
You cannot read him; into the hours of rest
His Spirit and course of action overflow.
No ghost familiar with the night like Him.
To this new service bound, his fervent Zeal
The liveliest star outwatches, in mid heaven
Fix'd or slow travelling on the horizon's bound.
Happy if she for whom he wakes abide
Within the limits of his native Vale,
The native vale of both, or common Home;
And not less happy if need be, the Youth
Posts over Hill and dale and mountain top
Through wood, and brook across, by shortest line
Hasting, and chiding oft the wat'ry clouds
Which the sky breeds to blind his eager steps.
What sundry shapes of hazard, paths obscure
And length of indefatigable march,
Ere at the door the soft low tap be giv'n
Or from beneath the cottage eaves ascend
The stifled Cough—warning his chosen Maid
That now when sleep has hushed the world he comes
For a brief taste of stealthy intercourse.
Ten thousand sparks do from this covert fire
Spring up at each incitement of the breeze
Vivid, though noiseless, blessed hours if doubt
Be not nor jealousy; but hours they are
And Time has wings and Pleasure is Time's slave.
He must depart—ere blush of morning's light—
With the far wandering Fox slink to his home,
For short repose or haply to commence
A long day's labour with the sun new risen.
Each current stemm'd of adverse circumstance,
The rock of absence either shunned or touch[ed]
Without a fatal shock, the insidious shoals
[?Of] jealousy triumphantly escaped,
And fancy's cross-winds and her peevish squalls
All stoutly weather'd, the trim vessel holds
Her port in open view.— It dawns; the day,
The important day of lasting recompense,
Not unproceeded by a throng of cares
Of frugal preparations intermix'd

With inoffensive vanity and show.
[425] And see the orb, that animates the earth
And cheers the frame and fills the Spirit of man
With genial thoughts upon that morning shine
In splendour, so that Hill and dale reflect
The satisfaction of the festive troop
[430] As they advance, or from the Church return
Blithe company of Elders, Maids and Youths
And the blest pair for life's remaining course
Each gives to each indissolubly bound.
This natural wedlock yields in season due
[435] Fair fruit, a gift by either Parent prized
From the first hour—but to the father's heart
Doubly endeared, soon as the tender Babe
By creeping Time is strengthen'd to endure
Rough fondness and the gaiety of love
[440] In boisterous assault. Then, ere he quits
His home, or as he enters from the fields,
Lightly the vigorous Peasant at arm's length
Tosses his lusty Boy aloft in air
And laughs to see the laughing Child at once
[445] Pleased and half daunted by the dizzy height
Gain'd in a moment, in a moment lost.
A seasonable gladness, a relief
Occasional for six laborious days
Is here prepared, and duly this resource
[451] Sweeten[s] the day of leisure and repose
With innocent pastime. In a sheltered vale,
Far from the gross contagion of the world,
Thus are the earlier years of wedded life
[455] Adorn'd as spring with flowers, and to uphold
The Pair, and favor them as they advance
In later time along their humble path,
The pitfalls of mistake they shall avoid
By prudence guarded whose sure [hand] shall heal
[460] The hurts of unavoidable mischance.
Immoderate labour shall not sap their strength,
Nor sickness overturn their plans, or thwart.
Discord shall find no place by their fire side,
Nor shall the dread of Poverty oppress
[465] Their waking thoughts, nor guilt disturb their dreams.

III. *The Shepherd of Bield Crag*

The lines editorially titled *The Shepherd of Bield Crag* appear in DC MS. 74 on leaves 43v–46r; those four leaves, once removed from the notebook, are now inserted as loose sheets within it. The tale's subject matter and revisions indicate that Wordsworth at one time planned that this narrative be included in the epitaphic books of *The Excursion.* In revision on 44v, for example, Wordsworth assigns the story to the priest, as he fixes "his eye / Upon a heap of turf that near him rose." For discussion of *The Shepherd of Bield Crag,* of its potential positioning within *The Excursion,* and of the possible reasons for its exclusion from the final text, see pp. 469–470, above.

The reading text provided below is the base text of the earliest state of *The Shepherd of Bield Crag* as it appears in DC MS. 74 on leaves 44r, 45r, and 46r. Spelling and capitalization have been preserved, with the exception of our expanding of ampersands; Wordsworth's punctuation has also been preserved but supplemented. Line numbers are editorial.

As is explained in notes to the transcriptions of leaves 43v–46r of DC MS. 74 (see pp. 980–984, above), there are complex revisions to the earliest state of *The Shepherd of Bield Crag,* including a much-altered opening and a probable repositioning of two major passages. Wordsworth's final choice for the text of his revised narrative is unclear, but the various changes in DC MS. 74 show his detailed reworking of the tale.

[*The Shepherd of Bield Crag*]

Nor unregarded may I pass thee by,
Thee, poor ill fated Shepherd of BIELD CRAG
Who next dost meet me.— Thou wert longer used
To range the Coves and Heights with different aim,
Far different thoughts, and Thou didst perish there.
—There was he doomed to breathe his latest breath:—
More hapless end than his whom we this day
Have given to earth!— But Arthur did not want
House of his own, and lands, and numerous flock,
And wife and children to bewail his loss,
And a dumb Friend and Servant, in its kind
Loving as they, and marvellously true.
The Tale with all its moving incidents
Were long to tell.— Behold that smooth blue steep
That perilous descent of shivery stone
That sinks abruptly from the grassless Crown
Of yon huge Height.— He, roaming there, in quest
Of some endanger'd Stragglers from his Flock
Slipp'd in the turmoil of a winter storm,
And, far beneath, by next day's light, was found
A wounded Corse, with face towards the snow

And raiment by that long precipitous fall
Torn from his back: and there was found his Dog
In mournful posture, o'er the naked part
Couching as if to shield it from the cold!
A Bier was brought, and underneath that bier
The afflicted Creature from the fatal spot
Walk'd with his Master's Body, nor withdrew
Nor quitted the forlorn society
Of those remains, till weeping Friends had laid them
Beneath this turf.—— Not seldom are we stopp'd
Wandering, through antient churches among tombs,
By sculptur'd image of the buried Man
Recumbent, Knight or Squire, with Sword and Shield,
And, at his feet, armorial Figure couch'd,
Lion, or Greyhound, Lamb, or gentle Fawn,
The bold or timid Creature each alike
Resting in duteous quiet, without fear
Of the sword's point and unoffending spurs,
That deck the Warrior in his last repose.
So, to assist Tradition, that will long
Preserve in our unvarying solitude
No weak remembrance of that sad event,
So have I sometimes wished that o'er this grave
Like Sculpture might be placed, albeit rude
And by some rustic hand uncouthly wrought
A Shepherd imaged in his mountain garb
And at his side the serviceable Staff
With which he lightly bounds o'er brook and crag
And couchant, like a pillow at the soles
Of his unarmed feet, the faithful Dog
That loved his Lord and clung to him in death.

Appendix III

Fenwick Note to *The Excursion*

That part of the Fenwick Notes pertaining to *The Excursion* is given here. The only surviving manuscript, DC MS. 153, is a copy of Isabella Fenwick's lost original made by Wordsworth's daughter and son-in-law, Dora and Edward Quillinan, which concludes: "To dearest Miss Fenwick are we obliged for these notes, every word of which was taken down by her kind pen from my Father's dictations. The former portion was transcribed at Rydal by M^r^. Quillinan, the latter by me & finished at the Vicarage Brigham *this Twenty fifth day of Aug^st^*. 1843, *D. Q.*" Internal evidence in which Wordsworth refers to the date of Robert Southey's death suggests late April 1843 for the beginning of Wordsworth's comments on *The Excursion.* His dictation of the note to *The Excursion* was completed on June 24, 1843, the date Dora copied from the now-lost original manuscript.

The base text of the note covering *The Excursion* is in Dora's hand, in ink; Edward Quillinan, Mary Wordsworth, and Gordon Graham Wordsworth (the poet's grandson) made later pencil annotations. The most developed version of Dora's ink copy provides the main reading text below. Readings in square brackets and in the notes record ink revisions toward that main text or later pencil annotations of it. Unless otherwise indicated, revisions are in ink, and the pencil entries are in the hand of Edward Quillinan. Dora's spelling and punctuation have been retained, including her occasional practice of omitting terminal periods and beginning a sentence with a lowercase letter. Words underlined in ink are presented in italic type. In order to help the reader locate notes related to specific passages in *The Excursion,* we provide in the text bracketed, boldface line references.

As anyone must be who works with DC MS. 153, we are indebted to *The Fenwick Notes of William Wordsworth,* ed. Jared Curtis (London, 1993).

Wordsworth's references to *The Excursion* in Fenwick Notes to other poems are not reproduced below. They are instead quoted in our Editors' Notes, above. The following list provides the poem to which each such Fenwick Note refers, the cross-reference to our Editors' Notes, and the page number to the full note in the edition by Jared Curtis.

Poem	**Editors' Note, Above**	**Curtis Edition**
Matthew	I, 337–340	IF, p. 38
Maternal Grief	III, 647–658	IF, p. 67
To Joanna	IV, 404–414	IF, p. 18
Composed by the Sea-shore	IV, 1125–1134	IF, p. 74
Evening Voluntaries	IV, 1172	IF, p. 55
"The fairest, brightest, hues of ether fade"	V, 763	IF, p. 19
Epistle to Sir George Howland Beaumont. Bart.	V, 763; VI, 623–624	IF, pp. 64–66

The Excursion.

Something must now be said of this Poem but chiefly, as has been done through the whole of these notes, with reference to my personal friends, & especially to Her who has perseveringly taken them down from my dictation.[1] Towards the close of the first book, stand the lines that were first written beginning "Nine Tedious years" & ending Last human tenant of these ruined walls." **[I, 906–951]** These were composed in /95. at Race Down & for several passages describing the employment & demeanour of Margaret during her affliction I was indebted to observations made in Dorsetshire & afterwards at Alfoxden in Somersetshire where I resided in 97. & 98. The lines towards the conclusion of the 4th. book, "Despondency corrected," beginning, "For the Man who in this Spirit" to the words "intellectual soul" **[IV, 1201–1271]** were in order of time composed the next either at Race Down or Allfoxden, I do not remember which. The rest of the Poem was written in the Vale of Grasmere chiefly during our residence at Allan Bank. The long Poem on my own education was, together with many minor Poems, composed while we lived at the Cottage at Town End. Perhaps my purpose of giving an additional interest to these my Poems in the eyes of my nearest & dearest Friends may be promoted by saying a few words upon the character of the Wanderer, the Solitary, & the Pastor, & some other of the persons introduced—and first of the principal one the Wanderer.—My lamented friend Southey (for this is written a month after his decease)[2] used to say that had he been born a Papist, [that *del*] the course of life which would in all probability have been his, was the one for which he was most fitted & most to his mind, that of a Benedictine Monk in a Convent furnished, as many once were & some still are, with an inexhaustable Library. *Books,*—[were in fact, *del; dash added*] as appears from many passages in his writings & was evident to those who had opportunities of observing his daily life—were in fact [*rev from* life, were] *his passion,* & *wandering,* I can with truth affirm, was mine, but this propensity in me was happily counteracted by inability from want of fortune to fulfil my wishes. But had I been born in a class which would have deprived me of what is called a liberal education, it is not unlikely that being strong in body, I should have taken to a way of [*rev from* in] life such as that in which my Pedlar passed the greater part of his days. At all events I am here called upon freely to acknowledge that the character I have represented in his

[1]A penciled note on the opposite page reads "Miss Fenwick—."
[2]RS died on March 21, 1843.

person is chiefly an idea of what I fancied my own character might have become in his [*rev from* become his] circumstances. Nevertheless much of what he says & does had an external existence that fell under my own youthful & subsequent observation. An Individual named Patrick, by birth & education a Scotchman, followed this humble occupation for many years & afterwards settled in the Town of Kendal. He married a kinswoman of my wife's, & her Sister Sarah was brought up from her early Childhood [*alt by MW in pencil* her ninth year] under this good man's eye [*rev by MW in pencil to* roof].[3] My own imaginations I was happy to find clothed in reality & fresh ones suggested by what she reported of this man's tenderness of heart, his strong & pure imagination, & his solid attainments in literature chiefly religious whether in prose or verse. At Hawkeshead also, while I was a school boy, there occasionally resided a Packman (the name then generally given to this calling) with whom I had frequent conversations upon what had befallen him & what he had observed during his wandering life, &, as was natural, we took much to each other; & upon the subject of *Pedlarism* in general, as *then* followed, & its favorableness to an intimate knowledge of human concerns, not merely among the humbler classes of society. I need say nothing here in addition to what is to be found in The Excursion & a note attached to it. **[I, 370n]**

Now for the *Solitary*. Of Him I have much less to say. Not long after we took up our abode at Grasmere, [came *del*] came to reside there, from [*rev from* for] what motive I either never knew or have forgotten, [*rev from* forgotten—] a Scotchman a little past the middle of life who had for many years been Chaplain to a Highland Regim[t]. he was in this [this *rev by MW in pencil to* no][4] respect, as far as I know, an interesting character, tho' in his appearance there was a good deal that attracted attention as if he had been shattered in fortune & not happy in mind. Of his quondam position I availed myself to connect with the Wanderer, also a Scotchman, a character suitable to my purpose the elements of which I drew from several persons with whom I had been connected & who fell under my observation during frequent residences in London at the beginning of the French Revolution. The chief of these was, one may *now* say, *a* Mr. Fawcett, a preacher at a dissenting meeting-House at the Old Jewry. It happened to me several times to be one of his congregation thro' my connection with M[r]. Nicholson of Cat S[t]. [*rev in pencil to* Catherine S[t]. *rev in pencil to* Cateaton S[t]., Strand],[5] who, at a time when I had not many acquaintances in London, used often to invite me to dine with him on Sundays, & I took that opportunity (M[r]. N. being a Dissenter) of going to hear Fawcett who was an able & eloquent man. He published a Poem on War,[6] w[h] had a good deal of merit & made me think more [more *rev from* a] now about him than I should otherwise have done. But [*rev from* but] his Xtianity was probably never very deeply rooted; &, like many others in those times of like shewy talents, he had not strength of character to withstand the effects of the French Revolution & of the wild & lax opinions which had done so much towards producing it & far more in carrying it forward in its extremes. Poor Fawcett, I have been [have been *rev from* was] told, became pretty much such a person as I have described; early [*rev in pencil to* & early] disappeared from the Stage, having fallen into habits of intemperance, which I have heard (tho' I will not answer for the fact) hastened his death. Of him I need say no more: there were many like him at that time which the world will never be without

[3]On the facing page MW wrote in pencil: "Sarah went to Kendal on our Mother's death but M[r]. P died in the course of a year or two." The preceding note overwrites another pencil note, also by MW, partially erased: "Sarah went to Kendal within 2 years after our Mother's death but M[r]. P. died [?when she was 10 years old]." WW's grandson, Gordon Graham Wordsworth, added another pencil note: "M[rs]. Hutchinson d. March 31. 1783. James Patrick March 2 1787."

[4]EQ's query "X" on the facing page probably produced MW's correction.

[5]The original incomplete entry of "Cat St." is noted on the facing page by a pencil mark and then by the pencil entry, subsequently partially erased, of "Cateaton ST."

[6]Fawcett's book was *The Art of War, A Poem* (1798); for more on him and on Nicholson, see IF (Curtis), p. 188.

but w[h]. were more numerous then for reasons too obvious to be dwelt upon.[7]

The Pastor. To what is said of the Pastor in the Poem I have little to add but what may be deemed superfluous It has ever appeared to me highly favorable to the beneficial influence of the Church of England upon all gradations & Classes of Society that the patronage of its benefices is in numerous instances attached to the estates of noble families of ancient Gentry, & accordingly I am gratified by the opportunity afforded me in the Excursion to pourtray the character of a country clergyman of more than ordinary talents, born & bred in the upper ranks of society so as to partake of their refinements, & at the same time brought by his pastoral office & his love of rural life into intimate connection with the peasantry of his native district. To illustrate the relation which in my mind this Pastor bore to the Wanderer & the resemblances between them, or rather the points of community in their nature, I likened one to an Oak & the other to a Sycamore, **[V, 450–456]** &, having here referr'd to this comparison, I need only add I had no one individual in my mind, wishing rather to embody this idea than to break in upon the simplicity of it by traits of individual character or any [*rev in pencil to* or of any] peculiarity of opinion.

And now for a few words upon the scene where these interviews & conversations are supposed to occur. The scene of the first book of the Poem is, I must own, laid in a tract of country not sufficiently near to that which soon comes into view in the second book to agree with the fact. All that relates to Margaret & the ruined cottage &c was taken from observations made in the South West of England & certainly it would require more than seven leagued boots [*emended from* books] to stretch in one morning from a common in Somersetshire or Dorsetshire, to the heights of Furness Fells & the deep vallies they embosom. For thus dealing with space I need make, I trust, no apology; but my friends may be amused by the truth.

In the Poem I suppose that the Pedlar & I ascended from a plain country up the vale of Langdale & struck off a good way above the Chapel to the Western side of the Vale we ascended the hill & thence looked down upon the circular recess in which lies Blea Tarn chosen by the Solitary for his retreat. After we quit his cottage, passing over a low ridge, we descend into another Vale that of Little Langdale towards the head of which stands embowered or partly shaded by Yews & other Trees something between a Cottage & a Mansion or Gentleman's house such as they once were in this country. This I convert into the Parsonage, & at the same time & as by the waving of a magic wand, I turn the comparatively confined Vale of Langdale, its Tarn, & the rude Chapel[8] which once adorned the Valley, into the stately & comparatively spacious Vale of Grasmere & its ancient Parish Church,[9] & upon the side of Loughrigg-fell at the foot of the Lake & looking down upon it & the whole Vale & its encompassing mountains, the Pastor is supposed by me to stand, when at Sunset he addresses his companions in words [*emended from* wwords] which I hope my readers will remember **[IX, 614–752]** or I should[10] not have taken the trouble of giving so much in detail the materials on which my mind actually worked.

Now for a few particulars of, *fact* respecting the persons whose stories are told or characters described by the different speakers. To Margaret I have already alluded. I will add here that the lines beginning "She was a woman of a steady mind" "—live on earth a life of happiness" **[I, 544–550]** faithfully delineate as far as they go, the character possessed in common by many women whom it has been my happiness to know in humble life, & that several of the most touching things which she is represented as saying & doing are

[7]Underlined in pencil are "many," "time," "which," and "w[h]."; on the facing page is a question mark, in pencil.

[8]In the right margin by the lines containing "the rude Chapel" is a vertical pencil line; on the facing page is an "X" in pencil.

[9]Underlined in pencil are "Grasmere" and "Parish Church"; on the facing page are "XX" and a dash.

[10]Above "or I should" EQ writes "last book—end" in pencil; on the facing page, he adds in pencil "last book—at the end."

taken from actual observation of the distresses & trials under which different persons were suffering, some of them Strangers to me, & others daily under my notice.

I was born too late to have a distinct remembrance of the origin of the American war, but the state in w^h^. I represent Robert's mind to be [in *del*] I had frequent opportunities of observing at the commencement of our rupture with France in 93. opportunities of which I availed myself in the Story of the Female Vagrant as told in the Poem on Guilt & Sorrow. The account given by the Solitary towards the close of the 2^d^. Book in all that belongs to the character of the Old Man **[II, 755–929]** was taken from a Grasmere Pauper who was boarded in the last house quitting the Vale on the road to Ambleside; the character of his hostess, & all that befell the poor man upon the mountain, belongs to Paterdale. The woman I knew well; her name was Ruth Jackson, & she was exactly such a person as I describe. The Ruins of the old Chapel, among which the old man was found lying, may yet be traced, & stood upon the ridge that divides Paterdale from Boardale & Martindale, having been placed there for the convenience of both districts. The glorious appearance disclosed above & among the mountains was described partly from what my friend M^r^. Luff who then lived in Paterdale witnessed upon this melancholy occasion & partly from what Mary & I had seen in company with Sir G. & Lady Beaumont above Hartshope Hall in our way from Paterdale to Ambleside.

And now for a few words upon the Church, its Monuments, & of the Deceased who are spoken of as lying [*rev from* laying] in the surrounding Churchyard. But first for the one picture given by the Wanderer of the Living. **[V, 672–841]** In this nothing is introduced but what was taken from Nature & real life. The Cottage was called Hackett & stands as described on [on *rev from* at] at the Southern extremity of the ridge which separates the two Langdales; the Pair who inhabited it were called Jonathan & Betty Yewdale. Once when our children were ill,[11] of whooping cough I think, we took them for change of air to this cottage & were in the habit of going there to drink tea upon fine summer afternoons so that we became intimately acquainted with the characters, habits & lives of these good, & let me say, in the main, wise, [*last five words rev from* say ?wise] people. The Matron had in her early youth been a servant in a house at Hawkeshead where several boys boarded while I was a school boy there. I did not remember her as having served in that capacity; but we had many little anecdotes to tell to each other of remarkable boys, incidents, & adventures which had made a noise in their day in that small town. These two persons were afterwards induced to settle [*rev in pencil to* persons afterwards settled] at Rydal where they both died.

Church & Churchyard. The Church, as already noticed, is that of Grasmere. The interior of it has been improved lately—made warmer by underdrawing the roof & raising the floor, but the rude & antique majesty of its former appearance has been impaired by painting the rafters. And the oak benches with a simple rail at the back dividing them from each other have given way to seats that have more the appearance of Pews. It is remarkable that excepting only the Pew belonging to Rydal Hall, that to Rydal Mount, the one to the Parsonage & I believe another, the Men & Women still continue, as used to be the Custom in Wales, to sit separate from each other Is this practice as old as the Reformation? and when & how did it originate? in the Jewish synagogues & in Lady Huntingdon's Chapels[12] the sexes are divided in the same way. In the adjoining church yard greater changes have taken place. it is now not a little crowded with Tomb stones and near the school house which stands in the Church yard is an ugly structure built to [to *over eras*] receive the Hearse which is recently come into use. It would not be worth while to allude to this building or the Hearse Vehicle it contains, but that the latter has

---

[11]On the facing page, in pencil, EQ writes a question mark and "Dora."

[12]On the founding of Methodist chapels by Selena Hastings, Countess of Huntingdon (1707–1791), see IF (Curtis), p. 189.

been the means of introducing a change much to be lamented in the mode of conducting funerals among the Mountains. Now the Coffin is lodged in the Hearse at the door of the house of the Deceased & the Corpse is so convey'd to the Church yard gate; all the solemnity which formerly attended its progress, as described in this Poem is put an end to, so much do I regret this, that I beg to be excused for giving utterance here to a wish that should it befall me to die at Rydal Mount, [that *del*] my own body may be carried to Grasmere Church after the manner in which, till lately, that of every one was borne to that place of Sepulture [*rev from* Sepulchre], namely on the shoulders of neighbours no house being passed without some words of a funeral Psalm being sung at the time by the attendants bearing it. When I put into the mouth of the Wanderer, "Many precious rites & customs [*rev from* rights & manners] of our rural ancestry are gone or stealing from us," "this I hope will last for ever," & what follows, **[II, 577–619]** little did I foresee that the observance & mode of proceeding w[h]. had often affected me so much would so soon be superceded. Having said much of the injury done to this Church-yard let me add that one is at liberty to look forward to a time when by the growth of the Yew Trees, thriving there, a solemnity will be spread over the place that will in some degree make amends for the old simple character which has already been so much encroached upon & will be still more every year. I will here set down by way of memorial that my Friend Sir G. Beaumont having long ago purchased the beautiful piece of Water called Loughrigg Tarn on the banks of which he intended to build, I told him that a person in Kendal who was attached to the place wished to purchase it. Sir George finding the possession of no use to him consented to part with it & placed the purchase money £20. at my disposal for any local use which I thought proper. Accordingly I resolved to plant Yew Trees in the Church Yard & had four pretty strong large oak enclosures made, in each of w[h]. was planted, under my own eye & principaly if not entirely by my own hand, two young trees, with the intention of leaving the one that throve best to stand. Many years after M[r]. Barker, who will long be remembered in Grasmere, M[r]. Greenwood, the [*rev in pencil to* Greenwood (the] chief landed proprietor, [*rev in pencil to* proprietor)] & myself had four other enclosures made in the church-yard at our own expence in each of w[h]. was planted a tree taken from its neighbour & they all stand thriving admirably, the fences having been removed as no longer necessary. May the trees be taken care of hereafter when we are all gone & some of them will perhaps at some far distant time rival in majesty the Yew of Lorton & those which I have described as growing in Borrowdale where they are still to be seen in grand assemblage.[13]

And now for the persons that are selected as lying in the Church yard. But first for the Individual whose grave is prepared to receive him. **[VI, 96–218]**

His story is here truly related he was a school-fellow of mine for some years. he came to us when he was at least 17. years of age very tall, robust & full grown. This prevented him from falling into the amusements & games of the school consequently he gave more time to books. He was not remarkably bright or quick but by industry he made a progress more than respectable. His parents not being wealthy enough to send him to college when he left Hawkeshead he became a school-master with a view to preparing himself for holy orders. About this time he fell in love as related in the Poem & every thing followed as there described except that I do not know exactly when & where he died. The number of youths that came to Hawkeshead School from the families of the humble yeomanry to be educated to a certain degree of Scholarship as a preparation for the Church was considerable, & the fortunes of these persons in after life various of course, & of some not a little remarkable. I have now one of this class in my eye who became an Usher in a preparatory school & ended in making a large fortune. His manners when he came to Hawkeshead were as uncouth as well could be; but he had good abilities with skill to turn them to account & when the Master of the School to w[h]. he was Usher died he stept into

[13]WW wrote of the Borrowdale yews in *Yew-trees*; see also IF (Curtis), pp. 108, 189.

his place & became Proprietor of the Establishment—he contrived to manage it with such address & so much to the taste of what is called High Society & the fashionable world that no school of the kind, even till he retired, was in such high request—Ministers of State, the wealthiest gentry, & nobility of the first rank vied with each other in bespeaking a place for their sons in the Seminary of this fortunate Teacher.[14]

In the solitude of Grasmere while living as a married man, in a Cottage of £8 p^{r}. annum rent I often used to smile at the tales which reached me of the brilliant career of this quondam clown, for such in reality he was in manners & appearance before he was polished a little by attrition with *gentlemen's* sons trained at Hawkeshead, rough & rude as many of our juveniles were. Not 200. yards from the Cottage in Grasmere just mentioned to which I retired, this gentleman, who many years afterwards purchased a small estate in the neighbourhood, is now erecting a boat-house[15] with an upper story to be resorted to as an entertaining-room when he & his associates may feel inclined to take their pastime on the Lake. Every Passenger will be disgusted with the sight of this Edifice not merely as a tasteless thing in itself, but as utterly out of place & peculiarly fitted as far as it is observed (& it obtrudes itself on notice at every point of view) to mar the beauty & destroy the pastoral simplicity of the Vale. For my own part & that of my household it is our utter detestation standing by a shore to which, before the high road was made to pass that way, we used daily & hourly to repair for seclusion & for the shelter of a grove under which I composed many of my Poems, The Brothers [*underlined in pencil*] especially, & for this reason we gave the grove that name. "That which each man loved & prized in his peculiar Nook of Earth dies with him or is changed" **[I, 503–505]** So much for my old School fellow & his exploits. I will only add that as the foundation has twice failed from the Lake no doubt being intolerant of the intrusion there is some ground for hoping that the impertinent structure will not stand.[16] The Miner next described **[VI, 219–264]** as having found his treasure after twice ten years of labour, lived in Paterdale & the story is true to the letter. It seems to me however rather remarkable that the strength of mind which had supported him through this long unrewarded labour did not enable him to bear its successful issue. Several times in the course of my life I have heard of sudden influxes of great wealth being followed by derangement [*rev in pencil to* derangement,] & in one instance the shock of good fortune was so great as to produce absolute Idiotcy. But these all happened where there had been little or no previous effort to acquire the riches & therefore such a consequence might the more naturaly be expected than in the case of the Solitary Miner.[17] In reviewing his story[18] one cannot but regret that such perseverance was not sustained by a worthier object. Archimedes leapt out of his bath & ran about the streets proclaiming his discovery in a transport of joy, but we are not told that he lost either his life or his senses in consequence.

The next character **[VI, 285–390]** to whom the Priest is led by contrast with the resoluteness displayed by the foregoing is taken from a person born & bred in Grasmere by name Dawson, & whose talents, dispositions & way of life were such as are here delineated

---

[14]On the facing page EQ wrote, "M^{r}. Pearson" in pencil; see IF (Curtis), p. 190, for more information about him.

[15]EQ writes, in pencil over an illegible erasure, on the facing page: This boat house, badly built, gave way & was rebuilt. It again tumbled, & was a third time reconstructed but in a better fashion than before. It is not now, per se, an ugly building, however obtrusive it may be." As is pointed out in IF (Curtis), p. 190, the building still stands; "W.P. 1843" is inscribed above the door.

[16]EQ writes in pencil after "stand": "It has been rebuilt in somewhat better taste, & much as one wishes it away it [*continues on facing page*] is not now so very unsightly.—The structure is an emblem of the man—perseverance has conquered difficulties, and given something of form and polish to rudeness."

[17]Beneath "Solitary" EQ entered an "X," referring to a note in pencil on the facing page: "as an epithet interfering?"; apparently he is questioning whether use of the phrase "the Solitary Miner" causes confusion with "the Solitary."

[18]EQ also entered "In reviewing his story" in pencil on the facing verso.

[*rev from* deleniated]. I did not know him, but all was fresh in memory when we settled at Grasmere in the beginning of the Century. From this point the conversation leads to the mention of two Individuals **[VI, 420–537]** who by their several fortunes were at different times driven to take refuge at the small and obscure town of Hawkeshead on the skirt of these Mountains Their stories I had from the dear old Dame with whom, as a school-boy, & afterwards, I lodged for nearly the space of ten years.[19] The elder, the Jacobite, was named Drummond & was of a high family in Scotland; the Hanoverian Whig bore the name of Vandepat, & might perhaps be a descendant of some Dutchman who had come over in the train of King William.[20] At all events his zeal was such that he ruined himself by a contest for the representation of London or Westminister undertaken to support his party & retired to this corner of the world, selected as it had been by Drummond, for that obscurity which since visiting the Lakes became fashionable it has no longer retained. So much was this region considered out of the way till a late period, that persons who had fled from justice used often to resort hither for concealment & some were so bold as to not unfrequently make excursions from the place of their retreat for the purpose of committing fresh offences. Such was particularly the case with two brothers of the name of Weston who took up their abode at Old Brathay [*rev from* Brathey], I think about 70 years ago. They were High-way-Men & lived there some time without being discovered tho' it was known that they often disappeared in a way [a way *rev from* ?hours] and upon errands which could not be accounted for. Their horses were noticed as being of a choice breed & I have heard from the Relf [*rev in pencil to* Relpf] family, one of whom was a Saddler in the town of Kendal, that they were curious in their Saddles & housings & accoutrements of their horses They as I have heard, & as was universaly believed, were in the end both taken & hanged.

"Tall was her stature, her complexion dark and saturnine. This person **[VI, 693–793]** lived at Town End & was almost our next neighbour. I have little to notice concerning her beyond what is said in the Poem. She was a most striking instance how far a woman may surpass in talent, in knowledge & culture of mind those with & among [& among *inserted*] whom she lives & yet fall below them in Xtian virtues of the heart & spirit. It seemed almost, & I say it with grief, that in proportion as she excelled in the one she failed in the other. How frequently has one to observe in both sexes the same thing. & how mortifying is the reflection!

As on a sunny bank the tender Lamb. The story that follows **[VI, 805–1073]** was told to [told to *rev from* told] M^rs^. Wordsworth & my Sister by the Sister of this unhappy young woman, every particular was exactly as I have related. The party was not known to me tho' she lived at Hawkeshead, but it was after I left school. The Clergyman who administered comfort to her in her distress I knew well. Her Sister who told the story was the wife of a leading Yeoman in the Vale of Grasmere & they were an affectionate Pair & greatly respected by every one who knew them. Neither lived to be old, & their Estate which was perhaps the most considerable then in the Vale & was endeared to them by many remembrances of a salutory character not easily understood or sympathised with by those who are born to great affluence, past to their eldest Son according to the practice of these Vales, who died soon after he came into possession. He [*rev from* possession, he] was an amiable & promising youth, but was succeeded by an only brother a good natured man, who fell into habits of drinking by which he gradualy reduced his property & the other day the last acre of it was sold, & his wife & children, & he himself still surviving, have very little left to live upon, which it would not perhaps have been worthwhile to record here but that through all trials this woman has proved a model of patience, meekness, affect^te^. forebearance, &

[19]The "dear old Dame" is Ann Tyson (1713–1796).

[20]EQ marks an "X" under "Vandepat" and enters "Sir George Vandeput" in pencil on the facing verso. For more information on Vandeput and Drummond, see IF (Curtis), p. 190.

forgiveness. Their eldest Son, who thro' the vices of his Father has thus been robbed of an ancient family inheritance, was never heard to murmur or complain against the cause of their distress & is now deservedly the chief prop of his Mother's hopes.

Book VII. The Clergyman & his family described at the beginning of this book **[VII, 31–309]** were during many years our principal associates in the Vale of Grasmere unless I was to except our very nearest neighbours. I have entered so particularly into the main points of their history that I will barely testify in prose that with [*rev in pencil to* (with] the single exception of the particulars of their journey to Grasmere, which however was exactly copied from [*rev in pencil to* from,] in[21] another instance, [*rev in pencil to* instance)] the whole that I have said of them is as faithful to the truth as words can make it. There was much talent in the family & the eldest son was distinguished for poetical talent [talent *underlined in pencil*] of which a specimen is given in my notes to the Sonnets on the Duddon.[22] Once when in our Cottage at Town-End I was talking with him about Poetry, in [*rev from* Poetry, &] the course of conversation I presumed to find fault with the versification of Pope of whom he was an enthusiastic Admirer; he defended him with a warmth that indicated much irritation, nevertheless I would not abandon my point & said, "in compass & variety of sound your own versification surpasses his." Never shall I forget the change in his countenance & tone of voice, the storm was laid in a moment, he no longer disputed my judgment & I passed immediately in his mind, no doubt, for as great a critic as ever lived. I ought to add he was a Clergyman & a well educated man, & his verbal memory was the most remarkable of any Individual I have known except a M^r^. Archer [*rev in pencil to* Archer,] an Irishman who lived several years in this neighbourhood [*rev in pencil to* neighbourhood,] & who in this faculty was a prodigy: he afterwards became deranged & I believe [*alt in pencil* fear] continues so if alive.

Then [*rev from* The] follows the character of Robert Walker **[VII, 334–412]** for which see notes to the Duddon—[23]

—That of the *Deaf Man* **[VII, 412–498]** whose Epitaph may be seen in the Church yard at the Head of Hawes water, & whose qualities of mind & heart & their benign influence in conjuction with his privation [privation *over eras*] I had from his relatives on the spot.

The *blind Man* next commemorated **[VII, 499–553]** was John Gough of Kendal a man known far beyond his neighbourhood for his talents & attainments in Natural History and Science

Of the *Infants* Grave next noticed **[VII, 655–719]** I will only say it is an exact picture of what fell under my own observation; & all persons who are intimately acquainted with Cottage Life must often have observed like instances of the working of the domestic affections.

"*A Volley thrice* [rev from *twice*] *repeated.*"[24] This young Volunteer **[VII, 720–912]** bore the name of Dawson & was younger brother if I am not mistaken to the Prodigal of whose character & fortunes an account is given towards the beginning of the preceding book. The Father of the family I knew well: he was a man of literary education, & [ ][25] experience in society much beyond what was common among the inhabitants of the Vale. He had lived a good while in the Highlands of Scotland as a Manager of Iron Works at Bunaw & had acted as clerk to one of my predecessors in the office of Distributor of Stamps, when he used to travel round the country collecting & bringing home the money due to Government in gold, which, it may be worth while to mention for the sake [*underlined in pencil*]

---

[21]Beneath "in" is a penciled cross; on the facing page is a penciled question mark.

[22]For the poem by the clergyman's son, Joseph Sympson, see *Sonnet Series*, p. 83.

[23]For the *Memoir* of Walker, see *Sonnet Series*, pp. 86–98.

[24]The reading in *Exc*, VII, 722, is "thrice."

[25]EQ penciled a cross and a question mark on the facing page, probably drawing attention to the omitted word.

of my Friends, was deposited in the cell or Iron-closet under the west window which still[26] exists with the Iron doors that guarded the property. This of course was before the time of bills & notes. The two sons of this person had no doubt been led by the knowledge of their Father to take more delight in Scholar ship & had been accustomed in their own minds to take a wider view of social interests than was usual among their associates The premature death of this gallant young man was much lamented & as an attendant upon the funeral I myself witnessed the ceremony & the effect of it as described in the Poem

"Tradition tells that in Eliza's golden days", "A knight came on a Warhorse" "The House is gone." **[VII, 945–980]** The Pillars of the Gate way in front of the Mansion remained when we first took up our abode at Grasmere. Two or three cottages still remain which are called Nott Houses from the name of the Gentleman (I have called him a knight) concerning whom these Traditions survive. He was the Ancestor of the Knott family formerly considerable proprietors in the district. What follows in the discourse of the Wanderer **[VIII, 89–197]** upon the changes he had witnessed in Rural Life by the introduction of Machinery, is truly described from what I myself saw during my boy-hood and early youth & from what was often told me by persons of this humble calling. Happily [*rev in pencil to* Happily,] most happily, for these Mountains, the mischief was diverted from the banks of their beautiful streams & transferred to open & flat Countries abounding in coal where the agency of Steam was found much more effectual for carrying on those demoralizing works. Had it not been for this invention, long before the present time, every torrent & river in this district would have had its factory large & populous in proportion to the power of the water that could there be commanded. Parliament has interfered to prevent the night work which was once carried on in these Mills as actively as during the day time, & by necessity still more perniciously—a sad disgrace to the proprietors & to the nation which could so long tolerate such unnatural proceedings. Reviewing at this late period, *1843*, what I put into the mouths of my Interlocutors a few years after the commencement of the Century, I grieve that so little progress has been made in diminishing the evils deplored, or promoting the benefits of education which the Wanderer anticipates. The results of Lord Ashley's labours to defer the time when Children might legally be allowed to work in factories & his endeavours to still further limit [*alt in pencil* limit still further] the hours of permitted labour have fallen far short of his own humane wishes & those of every benevolent and right-minded man who has carefully attended to this subject & in the present Session of Parliament (1843) Sir James Graham's[27] attempt to establish a course of religious education among the children employed in factories has been abandoned in consequence of what might easily be foreseen, the vehement & turbulent opposition of the Dissenters; so that for many years to come it may be thought expedient to leave the religious instruction of Children entirely in the hands of the several denominations of Christians in the Island, each body to work according to its own means and in its own way. Such is my own confidence, a confidence I share with many others of my most valued friends, in the superior advantages both religious & social w^{h}. attend a course of instruction presided over, & guided by, the Clergy of the Church of England, that I have no doubt that if but once its Members, Lay & clerical, were duly sensible of those benefits, their Church would daily gain ground, & rapidly, upon every shape & fashion of Dissent: & in that case a great majority in Parliament being sensible of these benefits, the Ministers of the Country might be emboldened, were it necessary, to apply funds of the State to the support of Education on Church Principles. Before I conclude I cannot

---

[26]EQ entered a dash in pencil after "still"; an apparently matching penciled dash is on the facing page. EQ also marked, in pencil, this sentence as "not clear." The note as published in *PW*, 1857, makes it obvious that the "Iron-closet" was a built-in safe at Rydal Mount, which was once owned by one of WW's predecessors as Distributor of Stamps; see IF (Curtis), p. 192.

[27]For the reform activities of Anthony Ashley, seventh earl of Shaftesbury (1801–1885), and James Robert Graham (1792–1861), see IF (Curtis), pp. 192–193.

forbear noticing the strenuous efforts made at this time in Parliament by so many persons to extend manufactoring & commercial industry at the expence of agricultural, tho' we have recently had abundant proofs that the apprehensions expressed by the Wanderer were not groundless

"I spake of mischief by the Wise diffused
With gladness, thinking that the more it spreads
The healthier, the securer we become;
Delusion which a moment may destroy! **[IX, 197–200]**

The Chartists are well aware of this possibility & cling to it with an ardor & perseverance which [*rev from* ?when/?where] nothing but wiser and more brotherly dealing towards the many on the part of the wealthy few can moderate or remove.

Book IX. towards conclusion. "While from the grassy mountains open side
"We gazed"— **[IX, 609–610]**

The point here fixed upon in my imagination is half way up the northern side of Loughrigg fell from which the Pastor & his companions are supposed to look upwards to the sky & mountain tops, & round the Vale with the Lake lying immediately beneath them.

"But turned not without welcome promise given
"That he would share the pleasures & pursuits
"Of yet another summer's day, consumed
"In wandering with us." [*rev in pencil to* us.——] **[IX, 773–777]**

When I reported this promise of the Solitary, & long after, it was my wish, & I might say intention, that we should resume our wanderings & pass the borders into his native country where as I hoped he might witness in the Society of the Wanderer some religious ceremony—a sacrament say, in the open fields, or a preaching among the Mountains, which by recalling to his mind the days of his early Childhood, when he had been present on such occasions in company with his Parents & nearest Kindred, might have dissolv'd his heart into tenderness & so done more towards restoring the Christian Faith in which he had been educated, & with that, contentedness & even cheerfulness of mind, than [than *rev from* &] all that the Wanderer & Pastor by their several effusions & addresses had been unable [*alt* able] to effect—an issue like this was in my intentions—But alas!

—Mid the Wreck of is & was
Things incomplete & purposes betrayed
Make sudden transits o'er thoughts optic glass
Than noblest objects utterly decayed.[28]

[28]The passage is from WW's sonnet *Malham Cove*, ll. 11–14.

Appendix IV

The Excursion and *The Christian's Miscellany*

On July 11, 1842, Wordsworth wrote to Samuel Wilkinson, Church of England clergyman and editor of the periodical *The Christian's Miscellany.* Wilkinson had sent to the poet a copy of his "Contributions of S. T. Coleridge to the Revival of Catholic Truths" and asked whether he could publish a similar work containing excerpts from Wordsworth's works.[1] With the proviso that he be permitted to look over the material before publication, the poet gave his permission. Wordsworth next wrote to Wilkinson on September 21, 1842, telling the editor that his selection of excerpts from his poetry, including seven from *The Excursion,* "judiciously fulfilled" the purpose of his article (*LY,* IV, 370). Publication of "Contributions of Wm. Wordsworth to the Revival of Catholic Truths" followed in the October issue of *The Christian's Miscellany*; and a twenty-four-page pamphlet version appeared in 1842 (Leeds: T. W. Green; London: J. G. F. and J. Rivington, and Houlston and Stoneman).

Whether Wordsworth fully appreciated it or not when he granted Wilkinson's request, the poet's works now became part of the debate about the Oxford Movement. John Newman's *Tract No. 90, Remarks on Certain Passages in the Thirty-Nine Articles* (February 1841) had argued that those Articles of the Church of England were consistent with the core beliefs of Roman Catholicism. Some members of the Church of England suspected—a suspicion later confirmed—that their co-religionist Newman was leaning toward Roman Catholicism. The title phrase "Catholic Truths" in Wilkinson's pamphlet echoed Tractarian usage of "Catholic" as meaning the one true church of Christ rather than the Roman Catholic Church. Nevertheless, Wilkinson's phrasing was contentious, and his article appeared at a particularly volatile time: in May 1842 the Bishop of Oxford had censured *Tract No. 90* and banned publication of additional *Tracts.* Wordsworth wrote to Wilkinson that he was somewhat removed from these disputes; "happily," he wrote, "little

[1] *LY,* IV, 353. The article containing excerpts from STC's works appeared in *The Christian's Miscellany* in the issue of July 1842; the article was also published that year as a pamphlet by T. W. Green of Leeds.

of it reached my ears among these mountains" (*LY*, IV, 371). The only one of the Tractarians that Wordsworth knew personally was John Keble.[2]

When Wilkinson sent his article to Wordsworth for approval, the poet in his response asked that Book VIII, ll. 187b–197 of *The Excursion* be added, and Wilkinson complied. Wordsworth also suggested substituting for *The Old Cumberland Beggar* "the beginning of the 6th Book of the Excursion or an Ex: from the close of the preceding one" (*LY*, IV, 370); this change was not implemented. Wilkinson headed each of the seven excerpts from *The Excursion* with his own title; we provide those titles in the listing, below, preserving the capital letters used in the article and the pamphlet. The line numbers given below refer to our reading text of *The Excursion* (1814). Wilkinson's excerpts include revisions first appearing in Wordsworth's *Poetical Works* 1836 (for these lines, there are no changes to the edition of 1836 in *Poetical Works* 1840 or 1841).

THE SCIENCES.
IV, 953–975a, 981–991.

UTILITARIAN KNOWLEDGE.
IV, 608–626.

THE DIFFICULTIES OF REASON.
V, 487–497, 500–509 (in l. 509, just the word "Yet"), 512–517a.

THE DIFFICULTY OF VIRTUE.
IV, 130–139.

THE AIDS.
IV, 215b–228.

BAPTISM.
V, 275b–288a.

ANCIENT TIMES.
VIII, 187b–197.

---

[2]A fuller account of WW, Wilkinson, and the Oxford Movement is in Stephen Gill, *Wordsworth and The Victorians* (Oxford, 1998), pp. 63–66; we draw extensively from Gill's presentation. See also Gill's "Wordsworth and 'Catholic Truth': The Role of Frederick William Faber," *Review of English Studies* 45 (1994): 204–220, and his "England's Samuel: Wordsworth in the 'Hungry-Forties,'" *Studies in English Literature, 1500–1900* 4 (1993): 841–858.